This text supports GREAT TEACHING!

Sociology, Thirteenth Edition, does more than ever before to help students excel in their first sociology course. And the text goes the extra mile for the instructors, too.

Here are some recent e-mails sent to John Macionis by sociology faculty who have used this text:

To: macionis@kenyon.edu

I've decided to go with one of the Macionis texts this fall. John is so engaged with teaching intro that I . . . trust his judgment about what today's college students want in a text. Further, if he does the supplements, I have confidence that they will be good.

To: macionis@kenyon.edu

I began using your intro text my first semester of teaching seventeen years ago, and I continue to use your intro text today. I am thrilled with the style, the content, the updated nature of the examples used, and the impressive photo layouts. I have enjoyed it for years and look forward to continued success with your new editions.

To: macionis@kenyon.edu

[You] have definitely written this textbook with the student in mind. Other texts talk over the student, yet *Sociology* has always been excellent reading for all levels of student ability. I have had hundreds of students who would not have done as well in my introductory course had I not used this textbook. [You] do a terrific job of explaining difficult topics in a down-to-earth manner.

To: macionis@kenyon.edu

I teach sociology at [Florida college] issuing associate degrees, and I use your text. Let me say how much I enjoy teaching from this book, which is also enjoyable for students. . . . I marvel at your travels and the manner in which the material is presented. All my best to you and your family!

To: macionis@kenyon.edu

Now that I have decided to retire, I want you to know that I count you among my colleagues and friends. I have used the . . . Macionis text from its inception . . . and it remains the best on the market. . . . Thanks for making my job easier and certainly more interesting. As a result, I have been able to "turn more students on" to the fascinating study of human society. . . .

To: macionis@kenyon.edu

I have been adopting this text for my introductory classes for many years, and my students consistently find it to be both rewarding and entertaining. And over the years, these teaching assignments have run the gamut—both day and evening classes, both traditional and adult learners, both community colleges and universities. I have been loyal to this text because I can find no better teaching tool and because students say they could not meet high academic standards and expectations without it.

To: macionis@kenyon.edu

I'm sure you heard this before, but the following must be said: I use your sociology book and it is great. I appreciate the fact that you understand the importance of using examples that actually relate to the everyday lives of those we teach. Your book is miles ahead of other Intro books.

...and ensures STUDENT SUCCESS

Drawing on John Macionis's almost forty years as a classroom teacher, this text provides many features that help all students succeed.

Theory throughout, with clarity and balance

This text presents sociology as a theoretical discipline and, just as important, it also makes theory easy. The discipline's major theoretical approaches are introduced in Chapter 1 and are carried through later chapters. The text highlights the social-conflict, structural-functional, and symbolic-interaction approaches and also introduces social-exchange analysis, ethnomethodology, cultural ecology, and sociobiology.

This text offers **Applying Theory** tables that provide quick and easy summaries of the key insights of each theoretical approach as it is applied to the topic at hand. All theoretical sections also conclude with a **Critical Review** discussion that highlights the approach's strengths and limitations followed by a **Check Your Learning** question.

socioeconomic status (SES) a composite ranking based on various dimensions of social inequality

○ MAKING THE GRADE
Marx viewed social stratification in terms of classes. Weber viewed inequality in terms of a socioeconomic status hierarchy with multiple dimensions. Individuals stand higher on some dimensions and lower on others, so there are no clear-cut classes.

APPLYING THEORY

Social Stratification

	Structural-Functional Approach	Social-Conflict Approach	Symbolic-Interaction Approach
What is the level of analysis?	Macro-level	Macro-level	Micro-level
What is social stratification?	Stratification is a system of unequal rewards that benefits society as a whole.	Stratification is a division of a society's resources that benefits some people and harms others.	Stratification is a factor that guides people's interactions in every-day life.
What is the reason for our social position?	Social position reflects personal talents and abilities in a competitive economy.	Social position reflects the way society divides resources.	The products we consume all say something about social position.
Are unequal rewards fair?	Yes. Unequal rewards boost economic production by encouraging people to work harder and try new ideas. Linking greater rewards to more important work is widely accepted.	No. Unequal rewards only serve to divide society, creating "haves" and "have-nots." There is widespread opposition to social inequality.	Maybe. People may or may not define inequality as fair. People may view their social position as a measure of self-worth, justifying inequality in terms of personal differences.

CRITICAL REVIEW Gilligan's work sharpens our understanding of both human development and gender issues in research. Yet the question remains, does nature or nurture account for the differences between females and males? In Gilligan's view, cultural conditioning is at work, a view that finds support in other research. For example, Nancy Chodorow (1994) claims that children grow up in homes in which, typically, mothers do much nurturing than fathers. As girls learn to identify with moth become more concerned with care and responsibility to c contrast, boys become more like fathers, who are often the home, and they may develop more detached perso a greater concern for abstract rules. Perhaps the mor of females and males will become more similar as r organize their lives around the workplace.

CHECK YOUR LEARNING According t do boys and girls differ in their approach to und and wrong?

CRITICAL REVIEW Weber's multidimensional view of social stratification influenced sociologists enormously and made the concept of socioeconomic status hierarchy popular. But critics (particularly those who favor Marx's ideas) argue that although social class boundaries may have blurred, industrial and postindustrial nations still show striking patterns of social inequality.

As will be explained shortly, economic inequality has increased recently in the United States. Although some people favor Weber's multidimensional hierarchy, others think, in light of this trend, that Marx's view of the rich versus the poor is closer to the truth.

CHECK YOUR LEARNING What are Weber's three dimensions of social inequality? According to Weber, which of them would you expect to be most important in the United States? Why?

Emphasis on critical thinking

Critical-thinking skills include the ability to challenge common assumptions by formulating questions, to identify and weigh appropriate evidence, and to reach reasoned conclusions. By teaching all these skills, this text empowers students to learn on their own.

NEW! Making the Grade student annotations

Because students want to do well in their course, **Making the Grade** annotations in the top margins make sure students correctly understand the material—especially in areas where they might otherwise get off track.

○ MAKING THE GRADE

Because multiculturalism supports greater social equality for people of various cultural backgrounds, this theory falls within sociology's social-conflict approach.

Clear and accessible key terms and definitons

Key concepts and their definitions are reprinted at the top of the page, often linked together in ways that help students master their meaning and importance.

Freud's Model of Personality

id Freud's term for the human being's basic drives ← **ego** Freud's term for a person's conscious efforts to balance innate pleasure-seeking drives with the demands of society → **superego** Freud's term for the cultural values and norms internalized by an individual

Based on classroom experience

One reason that this text works so well is that it is based on the author's many decades of experience in the classroom, both at two-year and four-year colleges. John Macionis, who received the American Sociological Association's Award for Distinguished Contributions to Teaching, also carries on e-mail conversations with faculty and students, constantly refining the text based on feedback and suggestions.

Based on focus-group research

Before this revision was underway, the publisher assembled separate focus groups of students and instructors and asked them all what they liked and didn't like in our text or in some other book. Just as important, we asked them to imagine their ideal book.

What did we learn? First, we found good reason to feel confident that we have been doing many things right. Students told us that Macionis texts were the most exciting and easiest to use of any textbooks they had used, regardless of discipline. They told us that they wanted textbooks that were relevant and would help them do well in their courses. This led us to add a number of new features mentioned earlier, including the student annotations and the end-of-chapter photo essays. In short, this revision is based on research in which students and faculty have helped us understand the most effective ways to increase classroom learning.

Recent research and the latest data

Instructors can rely on *Sociology* to include all the latest research and statistical data. While some texts ignore new work reported in sociology journals, *Sociology* reflects recent research found in a dozen of the discipline's top publications. More than 1,000 research citations support this revision, and most are publications of the past ten years. In addition, this revision includes the very latest statistical data available—in most cases, for 2006, 2007, and even 2008.

The only author-written annotated instructor's edition

Available to instructors, the annotated instructor's edition is a complete text that has been annotated by the author on every page. These annotations provide additional data, notable quotations, comments about maps, and pop culture observations. The full listing of supplements for this textbook is found in the preface.

Author-written Test Item File

You can count on the quality of the testing material included in *Sociology*. John Macionis writes all of the end-of-chapter testing material used by students and he also authors the Test Item File that is available to instructors.

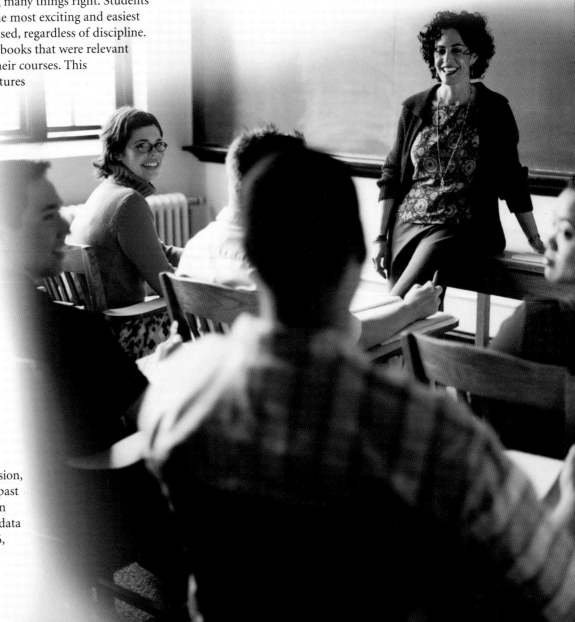

A focus on everyday life

As feedback from students and faculty alike makes clear, this text shows students how society is at work in their everyday lives. This "vision" is the key to personal transformation—a life-changing way to understand the opportunities and challenges we all face. Once "turned on" to the importance of society, students gain the power to change the world—and their own lives—for the better.

Seeing Sociology in Everyday Life boxes

One of the four types of feature boxes in this text, Seeing Sociology in Everyday Life boxes focus on experiences familiar to all of us, such as feeling society's pressure to be thin or wondering when we'll be regarded as truly "adult"; examine the everyday life of certain categories of people, such as minimum-wage workers in the United States or people living in poverty in India; and assess social patterns, such as the campus practice of "hooking up" or the role of the economy in people's decisions about when to retire.

NEW! Seeing Sociology in Everyday Life photo essays

A new and really fun feature of this new edition—one that comes out of John Macionis's own classroom teaching—is found at the end of every chapter. Seeing Sociology in Everyday Life photo essays offer an interactive, sociological take on familiar, real-life issues. For example, the photo essay at the end of Chapter 1 carries forward the idea that society guides people's selection of marriage partners and then asks students to look for ways society is at work in the romantic choices made by several popular celebrities. Chapter 3's photo essay rounds out the "Culture" chapter with a look at Superman and other popular "superheroes" and helps students to see surprising patterns in how and why our culture creates these larger-than-life characters.

There are twenty-four photo essays in all, and every one is as much fun as it is a great, new way to learn. Accompanying each are three Applying Sociology in Everyday Life exercises that extend the learning, giving students additional activities they can do on their own.

NEW! Seeing Sociology in the News real-life articles

What better way to connect sociology to our everyday lives than to provide students with brief, well-written news articles that apply sociology to today's world! In this edition, every chapter includes an article about some dimension of U.S. society that recently appeared in a wide range of news media, including *The New York Times, Newsweek, The Christian Science Monitor*, CNN.com, *Rolling Stone*, WIRED, and *USA Today*. These articles have been carefully selected by John Macionis to present important and current issues that are sure to engage student readers, and to do so in sociological terms.

Chapter-by-Chapter Changes

What's new to the Thirteenth Edition?

- **Seeing Sociology in Everyday Life** photo essays—in every chapter

- **Seeing Sociology in the News features**—in every chapter; twenty-one articles are new to this edition

- **More effective pedagogy**—new Making the Grade annotations and all student annotations substantially rewritten

- **Reflecting the world around us**—descriptions and analyses of events such as the economic recession, the presidential election, and the changes sought by the new Obama administration

- **Most current data available**—More than 25 percent of reference citations are new to this edition, and almost half are 2005 or later

Chapter 1 The Sociological Perspective

- Updated data on the number of high-, middle-, and low-income countries
- Seeing Sociology in the News—"Interest in Military on the Rise"
- Seeing Sociology in Everyday Life photo essay—Society and marriage
- Updated suggestions for sociological activities
- Updated "Making the Grade" summary

Chapter 2 Sociological Investigation

- Discussion on research orientations in sociology has been expanded to better explain positivist, interpretive, and critical research
- Seeing Sociology in the News—"If You Want to Observe 'Em, Join 'Em"
- Seeing Sociology in Everyday Life box—Is What We Read in the Popular Press True? The Case of Extramarital Sex
- Seeing Sociology in Everyday Life photo essay—Research studies highlight importance of friendships

Chapter 3 Culture

- New research on global cultural values, including updated Figure 2-2
- Updated statistics on number of states enacting laws making English the official language
- Updated statistics on the increasing number of people who speak a first language other than English and the share of the U.S. population born abroad
- Updated research on goals and priorities of today's youth culture
- Seeing Sociology in the News—"Now Hip Hop, Too, Is Made in China"
- Seeing Sociology in Everyday Life photo essay—Superheroes and popular culture

Chapter 4 Society

- Research on the pattern of self-destructive living among rock stars
- Seeing Sociology in the News—"Nomadic Herders Go High-Tech"
- Seeing Sociology in Everyday Life photo essay—Advantages and disadvantages of modern technology

Chapter 5 Socialization

- Expanded discussion of George Herbert Mead and his theory of how "self" develops
- Gender research of Nancy Chodorow has been added to the discussion of the role of gender in human development
- "Critical Thinking" and "Check Your Learning" material has been added to the section on "Agents of Socialization"
- Seeing Sociology in the News—"As Kids Get Savvy, Marketers Move Down the Age Scale"
- Seeing Sociology in Everyday Life photo essay—How societies mark young people's coming of age as adults

Chapter 6 Social Interaction in Everyday Life

- Seeing Sociology in the News—"Putting Your Best Cyberface Forward"
- Seeing Sociology in Everyday Life photo essay—Constructing social identity on Facebook

Chapter 7 Groups and Organizations

- New data showing how race, gender, and ethnicity shape management of private industry in the United States
- Discussion of the McDonaldization of society has been expanded
- Seeing Sociology in the News—"FEMA's Toxic Bureaucracy"
- Seeing Sociology in Everyday Life photo essay—McDonaldization in familiar settings

> *"Allows the reader to appreciate the relevance of sociology in everyday life."*
>
> —Boyejo Adefuye,
> Collin County Community College

Chapter 8 Sexuality and Society

- Latest data tracking attitudes on premarital sex, extramarital sex, sexual orientation, teen pregnancy, pornography, prostitution, and abortion
- Updated and expanded discussion of premarital sex
- Updated and expanded section on prostitution
- Latest data on the incidence of rape
- Seeing Sociology in the News—"Campus Sexperts"
- Seeing Sociology in Everyday Life photo essay—Feminine and masculine sexuality in the mass media

Chapter 9 Deviance

- Update on the distinctive social norms found across the United States and around the world
- Expanded discussion of primary and secondary deviance
- Statistical updates on hate crimes, categories of violent and property crime, and statistical data from the FBI for all serious crimes
- Updated and expanded discussion of gun control
- Latest data on the use of the death penalty
- Major new discussion of the death penalty
- Seeing Sociology in the News—"More Than 1 in 100 Adults Are Now in Prison in United States"
- Seeing Sociology in Everyday Life photo essay—How communities use heroes and villains to reflect and strengthen social norms

Chapter 10 Social Stratification

- Thinking Globally box updated—Racial caste in South Africa
- Updated and expanded discussion of social stratification in China
- Updated discussion of the functions of stratification to include CEO salaries
- Updated chapter maps
- Discussion of income polarization has been expanded to note efforts by the Obama administration to raise taxes on high-income individuals
- Seeing Sociology in the News—"Languishing at the Bottom of Yemen's Ladder"
- Seeing Sociology in Everyday Life photo essay—Elements of caste and meritocracy in U.S. society

Chapter 11 Social Class in the United States

- All the data on social standing for the U.S. population have been updated, with the latest on income, wealth, schooling, and occupational prestige, as well as the latest trends in inequality including race, class, and gender
- Social Diversity: Race, Class, & Gender box—How social class differences affect experiences of low-income college students
- Discussion of social mobility presents new research that shows mobility patterns for both women and men
- Discussion of the "myth versus reality" of social mobility has been reorganized for greater clarity
- New data on the extent of poverty and homelessness
- Effects of the recent economic recession are included in a number of discussions
- Seeing Sociology in the News—"The End of Upward Mobility?"
- Seeing Sociology in Everyday Life photo essay—Differences between affluent black and white families

Chapter 12 Global Stratification

- Updated listing of high-, middle-, and low-income nations
- New figure estimating global wealth inequality
- Revisions have been made based on several new studies of global economic inequality
- Greater discussion of the impacts of economic development in India and China on global inequality
- Seeing Sociology in the News—"Bottom of the Barrel"
- Seeing Sociology in Everyday Life photo essay—Extremes of wealth and poverty in Dubai

Chapter 13 Gender Stratification

- International comparisons on the extent of gender inequality have been updated, showing that the United States has slipped to 16th in the world
- Latest data are included for the share of women and men in the labor force, as well as what types of work they do, what they earn, and inequality in income and wealth
- New data on schooling for men and women as well as the majors the two sexes select
- The 2008 election data are included in the profile of women's political power in the United States
- Latest estimates for the extent of female genital mutilation around the world
- New survey data on the extent of sexual harassment
- New major section on symbolic-interaction analysis of gender in everyday life
- Seeing Sociology in the News—"Don't Judge Me by My Tights"
- Seeing Sociology in Everyday Life photo essay—Gender messages in mass-media advertising

Chapter 14 Race and Ethnicity

- Updated data on the size of all racial and ethnic categories
- Expanded discussion of genocide
- New data on the increasing minority share of the U.S. population as well as the social standing of the major racial and ethnic categories
- Seeing Sociology in the News—"Beyond Just Black and White"
- Seeing Sociology in Everyday Life photo essay—Race and ethnicity in mass media advertising

Chapter 15 Aging and the Elderly

- New chapter-opening story
- Updated data on income, employment, and poverty among seniors
- Discussion of retirement has been revised to reflect the recent economic downturn
- Updated discussion of physician-assisted suicide
- Seeing Sociology in the News—"Grandparents Raising Grandkids: 'Everybody Understands'"
- Seeing Sociology in Everyday Life photo essay—Baby boomers rewrite rules about growing old

Chapter 16 The Economy and Work

- Expanded discussion of the spread of socialist economies in South America
- Thinking Globally box—Examines how Denmark combines economic prosperity with political freedom
- New economic data reflects the latest in employment patterns for race, ethnicity, and gender
- National Map 16-1 has been updated to show where jobs are likely to be plentiful a decade from now
- Seeing Sociology in the News—"College Students Look to Future with Worry, Hope"
- Seeing Sociology in Everyday Life photo essay—Material possessions differ in low-, middle-, and high-income nations

> *"Crisp writing, excellent examples, and visually interesting."*
>
> —J. Beth Mabry,
> Indiana University of Penn

Chapter 17 Politics and Government

- Chapter-opening story highlighting the election of Barack Obama as the first African American president of the United States
- Updates on the extent of political freedom in the world
- All the results of the 2008 U.S. elections
- New county-by-county map showing the voting outcome in the 2008 presidential election
- Level of global terrorism as well as the state of global war and peace has been updated
- Seeing Sociology in Everyday Life photo essay—Young people as a political force in 2008 election

Chapter 18 Families

- Updates on all the trends, including family size, preferred number of children, the cost of raising children, the divorce rate, single-parenting, and infidelity
- Latest changes in same-sex marriage laws
- Seeing Sociology in the News—"American Dating—Muslim Style"
- Seeing Sociology in Everyday Life photo essay—Hollywood's changing picture of family life

Chapter 19 Religion

- New data on the share of U.S. clergy that are women as well as the latest on all religious attitudes and behaviors
- Expanded discussion of both spiritual "seekers" and religious fundamentalists
- Updated discussion of "prime-time preachers"
- Seeing Sociology in Everyday Life photo essay—Everyday life as examples of civil religion

Chapter 20 Education

- Updates on the level of schooling in the United States and around the world
- Grades of public schools, dropping out, the school choice debate, grade inflation, and adult education
- Seeing Sociology in Everyday Life photo essay—Inequality of schooling in the United States

Chapter 21 Health and Medicine

- Updates on the problems of obesity and cigarette smoking in the United States
- Latest statistics for the AIDS epidemic
- Latest information on who pays for medical care and the share of the population without any medical coverage plan
- New section describing religious health collectives
- Seeing Sociology in the News—"How Fat Went Global"
- Seeing Sociology in Everyday Life photo essay—Deadly jobs

Chapter 22 Population, Urbanization, and Environment

- Updated data on fertility, mortality, migration, and population increase
- Expanded discussion of the demographic divide between rich and poor nations
- Thinking About Diversity box—China's one-child policy
- Latest urbanization statistics, including the notable fact that, in 2008, the world population became mostly urban for the first time
- Recent research showing that improving U.S. air quality has added almost half a year to longevity
- Seeing Sociology in the News—"Boyz under the Hood"
- Seeing Sociology in Everyday life photo essay—Why the state of the natural environment is a social issue

Chapter 23 Collective Behavior and Social Movements

- Updates on all public opinion issues
- Updated examples of various types of collective behavior and social movements
- Seeing Sociology in the News—"Cairo Activists Use Facebook to Rattle Regime"
- Seeing Sociology in Everyday Life photo essay—Students support local, national, and international social movements

Chapter 24 Social Change: Traditional, Modern, and Postmodern Societies

- Updated discussions of how life is better or worse today compared to several decades ago
- Seeing Sociology in the News—"The Refugees Who Saved Lewiston"
- Seeing Sociology in Everyday Life photo essay—How traditional and modern social patterns are often combined

SOCIOLOGY

*This book is offered to teachers of sociology in the hope
that it will help our students understand their place
in today's society and in tomorrow's world.*

John J. Macionis

Thirteenth Edition

SOCIOLOGY

John J. Macionis

KENYON COLLEGE

Prentice Hall

Boston   Columbus   Indianapolis   New York   San Francisco   Upper Saddle River
Amsterdam   Cape Town   Dubai   London   Madrid   Milan   Munich   Paris   Montreal   Toronto
Delhi   Mexico City   Sao Paulo   Sydney   Hong Kong   Seoul   Singapore   Taipei   Tokyo

Editorial Director: Leah Jewell
Editor in Chief: Dickson Musslewhite
Editorial Assistants: Nart Varoqua, Kate Fernandes
Director of Marketing: Brandy Dawson
Executive Marketing Manager: Kelly May
Marketing Assistant: Elaine Almquist
Managing Editor: Maureen Richardson
Production Editor: Barbara Reilly
Copy Editor: Bruce Emmer
Proofreaders: Donna Mulder, Louise Rothman
Text Permissions Research: Margaret Gorenstein
Senior Operations Specialist: Sherry Lewis
Operations Specialist: Christina Amato
Manager of Design Development: John Christiana

Art Director: Kathryn Foot
Manager, Visual Research: Beth Brenzel
Photo Researcher: Rachel Lucas
Manager, Rights and Permissions: Zina Arabia
Image Permission Coordinator: Debra Hewitson
Manager, Cover Visual Research & Permissions: Karen Sanatar
Cover Art: Radius Images /Jupiter Images
Media Director: Karen Scott
Senior Media Editor: Melanie MacFarlane
Lead Media Project Manager: Diane Lombardo
Composition: Nesbitt Graphics, Inc.
Printer/Binder: Courier Companies, Inc.
Cover Printer: Phoenix Color Corp.
Text Font: 10/12 Minion

Credits and acknowledgments borrowed from other sources and reproduced, with permission, in this textbook appear on appropriate page within text (or on pages 696–98).

Microsoft® and Windows® are registered trademarks of the Microsoft Corporation in the U.S.A. and other countries. Screen shots and icons reprinted with permission from the Microsoft Corporation. This book is not sponsored or endorsed by or affiliated with the Microsoft Corporation.

10 9 8 7 6 5 4 3 2 1

Prentice Hall
is an imprint of

PEARSON

www.pearsonhighered.com

Mixed Sources
Product group from well-managed
forests, controlled sources and
recycled wood or fibre
www.fsc.org Cert no. SW-COC-002985
© 1996 Forest Stewardship Council
FSC

Student edition (hardback) ISBN 10:   0-205-73574-6
ISBN 13: 978-0-205-73574-7
Student edition (paperback) ISBN 10:   0-205-78616-2
ISBN 13: 978-0-205-78616-9
AIE ISBN 10:   0-205-74949-6
AIE ISBN 13: 978-0-205-74949-2

Brief Contents

Contents

9 Deviance   215

PART III SOCIAL INEQUALITY

10 Social Stratification   247

11 Social Class in the United States   273

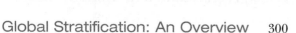

12 Global Stratification 299

13 Gender Stratification 327

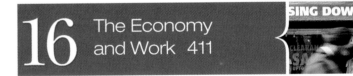

17 Politics and Government   435

18 Families   461

24 Social Change: Traditional, Modern, and Postmodern Societies   625

Boxes

CONTROVERSY & DEBATE

Seeing SOCIOLOGY in the NEWS

Maps

Preface

The world needs more sociology. We live in an age when—to read the polls—most people are anxious about their economic future, unhappy with government, and worried about the future of the planet. Perhaps it is not too far from the truth to say that many of us feel overwhelmed, as if we were up against forces we can barely grasp.

That's where sociology comes in. For the last 150 years, sociologists have been working to better understand how society operates. We sociologists may not have all the answers, but we have learned a lot. A beginning course in sociology is your introduction to the fascinating and very useful study of the world around you, the world we all have a stake in understanding and, as best we can, improving. *Sociology, Thirteenth Edition*, provides you with all the basics about how this world works. You will find the book to be informative and even entertaining. Sociology is fun. It is also a field of study that can change the way you see the world and open the door to many new opportunities. What could be more exciting than that?

A Word about Language

This text's commitment to describing the social diversity of the United States and the world carries with it the responsibility to use language thoughtfully. In most cases, this text uses the terms "African American" and "person of color" rather than the word "black." Similarly, we use the terms "Latino," "Latina," and "Hispanic" to refer to people of Spanish descent. Most tables and figures refer to "Hispanics" because this is the term the Census Bureau uses when collecting statistical data about our population.

Students should realize, however, that many individuals do not describe themselves using these terms. Although the word "Hispanic" is commonly used in the eastern part of the United States and "Latino" and the feminine form "Latina" are widely heard in the West, across the United States people of Spanish descent identify with a particular ancestral nation, whether it be Argentina, Mexico, some other Latin American country, or Spain or Portugal in Europe.

The same holds for Asian Americans. Although this term is a useful shorthand in sociological analysis, most people of Asian descent think of themselves in terms of a specific country of origin, say, Japan, the Philippines, Taiwan, or Vietnam.

In this text, the term "Native American" refers to all the inhabitants of the Americas (including Alaska and the Hawaiian Islands) whose ancestors lived here prior to the arrival of Europeans. Here again, however, most people in this broad category identify with their historical society, such as Cherokee, Hopi, Seneca, or Zuni. The term "American Indian" refers to only those Native Americans who live in the continental United States, not including Native peoples living in Alaska or Hawaii.

On a global level, this text avoids the word "American"—which literally designates two continents—to refer to just the United States. For example, referring to this country, the term "the U.S. economy" is more precise than "the American economy." This convention may seem a small point, but it implies the significant recognition that we in this country represent only one society (albeit a very important one) in the Americas.

Supplements

Sociology, Thirteenth Edition, is the heart of an unprecedented multimedia learning package that includes a wide range of proven instructional aids as well as several new ones. As the author of the text, I maintain a keen interest in all the supplements to ensure their quality and integration with the text. The supplements for this revision have been thoroughly revised and updated.

For the Instructor

Annotated Instructor's Edition. (0-205-74949-6) The AIE is a complete student text with author annotations on every page. These annotations, which have been thoroughly revised for this edition, have won consistent praise from instructors for enriching class presentations. The annotations are especially useful to new instructors, but they are written to be helpful to even the most seasoned teachers. Margin notes include summaries of research findings, statistics from the United States and other nations, insightful quotations, information highlighting patterns of social diversity in the United States, and high-quality survey data from the General Social Survey conducted by the National Opinion Research Center (NORC) and from World Values Survey data from the Inter-University Consortium for Political and Social Research (ICPSR).

Instructor's Manual. (0-205-7495-0) This text offers an instructor's manual that will be of interest even to those who have never chosen to use one before. The manual—now revised by the author—provides the expected detailed chapter outlines and discussion questions and much more, including statistical profiles of the United States and other nations, summaries of important developments, recent articles from *Teaching Sociology* that are relevant to classroom discussions, suggestions for classroom activities, and supplemental lecture material for every chapter of the text.

Test Item File. (0-205-749518) This key author-created supplement reflects the material in the textbook—both in content and in language—far better than the testing file available with any other introductory sociology textbook. The file contains over 2,000 items—more than 100 per chapter—in multiple-choice, true-false, and essay formats. All of the questions are identified by level of difficulty.

MyTest. (0-205-74961-5) This online, computerized software allows instructors to create their own personalized exams, to edit any or all of the existing test questions, and to add new questions. Other special features of this program include random generation of test questions, creation of alternative versions of the same test, scrambling question sequence, and test preview before printing.

Prentice Hall Introductory Sociology PowerPoint® Slides. These PowerPoint slides combine graphics and text in a colorful format to help you convey sociological principles in a new and exciting way. Each chapter of the textbook has approximately fifteen to twenty-five slides that communicate the key concepts in that chapter. For easy access, they are available in the instructor portion of MySocLab for *Sociology, Thirteenth Edition*.

Media Supplements

MySocLab™ is an engaging student and faculty learning system for introductory sociology courses. MySocLab is a state-of-the-art, interactive and instructive online solution for introductory sociology. Designed to be used as a supplement to a traditional lecture course or to completely administer an online course, MySocLab combines multimedia, tutorials, video, audio, tests, and quizzes to make teaching and learning fun. Here's how MySocLab can help you save time and improve results:

- **Writing tutorials** and a searchable **research database are at your fingertips.**
- **Practice tests** and **flash cards** help you prepare for quizzes and exams.
- **Video clips, animations, maps,** and **sociology blogs bring concepts to life.**
- **Social Explorer®** provides easy access to rich demographic data about the United States.
- **MySocLibrary** is your virtual bookshelf of classic and contemporary readings.
- **And much more!**
- **MySearchLab.** Pearson's MySearchLab™ is the easiest way for students to start a research assignment or paper. Complete with extensive help on the research process and four databases of credible and reliable source material, MySearchLab™ helps students quickly and efficiently make the most of their research time.
- **Telecourse.** The Macionis texts *Sociology* and *Society: The Basics* have been selected for use in the new telecourse "The Way We Live," available on DVD from INTELECOM. To find out more about this truly outstanding course, go to http://www.intelecom.org, and under the Alphabetical Listing of Courses, click on "The Way We Live," or call (800) 576–2988.

For the Student

Study Guide. (0-205-74952-6) This complete guide helps students review and reflect on the material presented in *Sociology, Thirteenth Edition*. Each of the twenty-four chapters in the Study Guide provides an overview of the corresponding chapter in the student text, summarizes its major topics and concepts, offers applied exercises, and features end-of-chapter tests with answers.

VangoNotes. These chapter reviews from *Sociology, Thirteenth Edition*, in downloadable mp3 format allow students to study on the go. Students can listen to the following selections for each chapter of the textbook:

- **Big Ideas:** The "need to know" for each chapter
- **Practice Test:** A gut check for the Big Ideas—tells students if they need to keep studying
- **Key Terms:** Audio "flash cards" to help students review key concepts and terms
- **Rapid Review:** A quick drill session to be used right before the test

Sociological Classics: A Prentice Hall Pocket Reader. (0-13-191806-0) Compiled by the sociologist David Kauzlarich, this edited volume features fourteen selections from classical sociological theorists. Contact your local Prentice Hall sales representative for more information.

"10 Ways to Fight Hate." (0-13-028146-8) Produced by the Southern Poverty Law Center, the leading hate crime and crime watch organization in the United States, this free supplemental brochure walks students through ten steps they can take on their own campus or in their own neighborhood to fight hate every day.

In Appreciation

The usual practice of crediting a book to a single author hides the efforts of dozens of women and men who have helped create *Sociology: Thirteenth Edition*. I offer my deep and sincere thanks to the Pearson editorial team, including Yolanda de Rooy, division president; Leah Jewell, editorial director; and Dickson Musslewhite, editor-in-chief, for their steady enthusiasm in the pursuit of both innovation and excellence.

Day-to-day work on the book is shared by the author and the production team. Barbara Reilly, Pearson production editor, is a key member of the group who is responsible for the attractive page layout of the book; indeed, if anyone "sweats the details" as much as I do, it is Barbara! Kimberlee Klesner is a new member of the team, a highly talented social science researcher who works with John to provide much of the very latest data that keeps the book accurate and current. Kimberlee has brought a level of enthusiasm that matches her considerable abilities, and I thank her for both.

I also want to thank the members of the Pearson sales staff, the men and women who have given this text such remarkable support over the years. My hat goes off especially to Brandy Dawson and Kelly May, who share responsibility for our marketing campaign.

Thanks, too, to Kathie Foot for providing both the interior and cover design of the book. Developmental and copy editing of the manuscript was skillfully done by Bruce Emmer.

It goes without saying that every colleague knows more about a number of topics covered in this book than the author does. For that reason, I am grateful to the hundreds of faculty and the many students who have written to me to offer comments and suggestions. More formally, I am grateful to the following people who have reviewed some or all of this manuscript:

Rebecca Riehm, Jefferson Community College
William Wood, California State University Fullerton
Rudy Harris, Des Moines Area Community College
Judi Kessler, Monmouth College
Dale Howard, NorthWest Arkansas Community College
Robert Atkins, North Seattle Community College
Richard Sweeney, Modesto Junior College
Dave Conz, Arizona State University
Robert Brainerd, Highland Community College

I also wish to thank the following colleagues for sharing their wisdom in ways that have improved this book:

Doug Adams (Ohio State University), Kip Armstrong (Bloomsburg University), Rose Arnault (Fort Hays State University), William Beaver (Robert Morris University), Scott Beck (Eastern Tennessee State University), Lois Benjamin (Hampton University), Philip Berg (University of Wisconsin, La Crosse), Kimberly H. Boyd (Germanna Community College), John R. Brouillette (Colorado State University), Cathryn Brubaker (DeKalb College), Brent Bruton (Iowa State University), Richard Bucher (Baltimore City Community College), Evandro Camara (Emporia State University), Bill Camp (Lucerne County Community College), Karen Campbell (Vanderbilt University), Francis N. Catano (Saint Anselm College), Harold Conway (Blinn College), Allison Cotton (Prairie View A&M University), Gerry Cox (Fort Hays State University), Lovberta Cross (Shelby State Community College), James A. Davis (Harvard University), Sumati Devadutt (Monroe Community College), Keith Doubt (Northeast Missouri State University), Thomas Dowdy (Oklahoma Baptist University), William Dowell (Heartland Community College), Doug Downey (Ohio State University), Denny Dubbs (Harrisburg Area Community College), Travis Eaton (Northeast Louisiana State University), Helen Rose Fuchs Ebaugh (University of Houston), John Ehle (Northern Virginia Community College), Roger Eich (Hawkeye Community College), Heather FitzGibbon (College of Wooster), Kevin Fitzpatrick (University of Alabama, Birmingham), Dona C. Fletcher (Sinclair Community College), Charles Frazier (University of Florida), Karen Lynch Frederick (Saint Anselm College), Patricia Gagné (University of Kentucky, Louisville), Pam Gaiter (Collin County Community College), Jarvis Gamble (Owens Technical College), Patricia L. Gibbs (Foothill College), Steven Goldberg (City College, City University of New York), Charlotte Gotwald (York College of Pennsylvania), Norma B. Gray (Bishop State Community College), Rhoda Greenstone (DeVry Institute), Jeffrey Hahn (Mount Union College), Harry Hale (Northeast Louisiana State University), Dean Haledjian (Northern Virginia Community College), Dick Haltin (Jefferson Community College), Marvin Hannah (Milwaukee Area Technical College), Chad Hanson (Casper College), Charles Harper (Creighton University), Michael Hart (Broward Community College), Gary Hodge (Collin County Community College), Elizabeth A. Hoisington (Heartland Community College), Sara Horsfall (Stephen F. Austin State University), Peter Hruschka (Ohio Northern University), Glenna Huls (Camden County College), Jeanne Humble (Lexington Community College), Cynthia Imanaka (Seattle Central Community College), Craig Jenkins (Ohio State University), Patricia Johnson (Houston Community College), Sam Joseph (Lucerne County Community College), Ed Kain (Southwestern University), Audra Kallimanis (Mount Olive College), Paul Kamolnick (Eastern Tennessee State University), Irwin Kantor (Middlesex County College), Thomas Korllos (Kent State University), Rita Krasnow (Virginia Western Community College), Donald Kraybill (Elizabethtown College), Howard Kurtz (Oklahoma City University), Michael Lacy (Colorado State University), George Lowe (Texas Tech University), Don Luidens (Hope College), Larry Lyon (Baylor University), Li-Chen Ma (Lamar University), Setma Maddox (Texas Wesleyan University), Errol Magidson (Richard J. Daley College), Kooros Mahmoudi (Northern Arizona University), Mehrdad Mashayekhi (Georgetown University), Allan Mazur (Syracuse University), Karen E. B. McCue (University of New Mexico, Albuquerque), Rodney A. McDanel (Benedictine University), Doug McDowell (Rider University), Ronald McGriff, (College of the Sequoias), Meredith McGuire (Trinity College), Lisa McMinn (Wheaton College), Jack Melhorn (Emporia State University), Will Melick (Kenyon College), Ken Miller (Drake University), Linda Miller (Queens University of Charlotte), Richard Miller (Navarro College), Joe Morolla (Virginia Commonwealth University), Peter B. Morrill (Bronx Community College), Craig Nauman (Madison Area Technical College), Dina B. Neal (Vernon College), Therese Nemec (Fox Valley Technical College), Joong-Hwan Oh (Hunter College), Richard Perkins (Houghton College), Marla A. Perry (Iowa State University), Anne Peterson (Columbus State Community College), Marvin Pippert (Roanoke College), Lauren Pivnik (Monroe Community College), Nevel Razak (Fort Hays State College), Jim Rebstock (Broward Community College), George Reim (Cheltenham High School), Virginia Reynolds (Indiana University of Pennsylvania), Laurel Richardson (Ohio State University), Keith Roberts (Hanover College), Ellen Rosengarten (Sinclair Community College), Frederick Roth (Marshall University), Mark Rubinfeld (Westminster College, Salt Lake City), Paulina Ruf (University of Tampa), Michael Ryan (Dodge City Community College), Marvin Scott (Butler University), Ray Scupin (Linderwood College), Steve Severin (Kellogg Community College), Harry Sherer (Irvine Valley College), Walt Shirley (Sinclair Community College), Anson Shupe (Indiana University–Purdue University at Fort Wayne), Brenda Silverman (Onondaga Community College), Ree Simpkins (Missouri Southern State University), Scott Simpson (Arkansas Northeastern College), Glen Sims (Glendale Community College), Toni Sims (University of Louisiana, Lafayette), Sylvia Kenig Snyder (Coastal Carolina University), Thomas Soltis (Westmoreland Community College), Nancy Sonleitner (University of Oklahoma), Larry Stern (Collin County Community College), Randy Ston (Oakland Community College), Vickie H. Taylor (Danville Community College), Don Thomas (Ohio State University), Mark J. Thomas (Madison Area Technical College), Len Tompos (Lorain County Community College), Christopher Vanderpool (Michigan State University), Phyllis Watts (Tiffin University), Murray Webster (University of North Carolina, Charlotte), Debbie White (Collin County Community College), Marilyn Wilmeth (Iowa University), Stuart Wright (Lamar University), William Yoels (University of Alabama, Birmingham), Dan Yutze (Taylor University), Wayne Zapatek (Tarrant County Community College), Jin-kun Wei (Brevard Community College), Amy Wong (San Diego State University), and Frank Zulke (Harold Washington College).

Finally, I would like to dedicate this thirteenth edition of the book to my wife Amy. We have traveled a long way together on our life journey. Amy, my greatest thanks for simply by being the magnificent woman you are. Keep getting better!

With best wishes to my colleagues and love to all,

John J. Macionis

The sociological perspective shows us that the society around us influences how we act and even what we think and how we feel. Learning to see the world sociologically is useful in many ways—and it is also fun!

CHAPTER 1

DISCUSS: Observe male-female couples holding hands. In almost every case the male will hold hands with his wrist to the front, and the female will do so with hers to the rear. What is "the general" (power of society) in this "particular" (personal behavior) situation?

DISCUSS: Confronting the strange gives us a new sense of the familiar. The anthropologist Clifford Geertz once commented that nothing made him aware of home as much as being in the world's most remote places. Have students had similar experiences?

sociology the systematic study of human society

sociological perspective the special point of view of sociology that sees general patterns of society in the lives of particular people

● SEEING SOCIOLOGY in Everyday Life

What effect did your social class background have on your decision to go to college? How do you think your background shapes the kind of job you expect to have after you graduate?

We can easily see the power of society over the individual by imagining how different our lives would be had we been born in place of any of these children from, respectively, Bolivia, Ethiopia, Thailand, Mali, South Korea, and India.

Seeing the Strange in the Familiar

At first, using the sociological perspective may seem like *seeing the strange in the familiar.* Consider how you might react if someone were to say to you, "You fit all the right categories, which means you would make a wonderful spouse!" We are used to thinking that people fall in love and decide to marry based on personal feelings. But the sociological perspective reveals the initially strange idea that society shapes what we think and do.

Because we live in an individualistic society, learning to see how society affects us may take a bit of practice. If someone asked you why you "chose" to enroll at your particular college, you might offer one of the following reasons:

"I wanted to stay close to home."

"I got a basketball scholarship."

"With a journalism degree from this university, I can get a good job."

"My girlfriend goes to school here."

"I didn't get into the school I *really* wanted to attend."

Any of these responses may well be true. But do they tell the whole story?

Thinking sociologically about going to college, it's important to realize that only about 5 out of every 100 people in the world earn a college degree, with the enrollment rate much higher in high-income nations than in poor countries (Organization for Economic Cooperation and Development, 2008; World Bank, 2008). Even in the United States a century ago, going to college was not an option for most people. Today, going to college is within the reach of far more people. But a look around the classroom shows that social forces still have much to do with who goes to college. For instance, most U.S. college students are young, generally between eighteen and about thirty. Why? Because in our society, attending college is linked to this period of life. But more than age is involved, because fewer than half of all young men and women actually end up on campus.

Another factor is cost. Because higher education is so expensive, college students tend to come from families with above-average incomes. As Chapter 20 ("Education") explains, if you are lucky enough to belong to a family earning more than $75,000 a year, you are almost three times as likely to go to college as someone whose family earns less than $20,000. Is it reasonable, in light of these facts, to say that attending college is simply a matter of personal choice?

NOTE: Suicide rates are relatively high among college students, probably due to lower social integration.

GLOBAL: About 22% of the world's people live in high-income countries, 58% live in middle-income nations, and just 19% live in low-income countries. (See Chapter 12, "Global Stratification.)

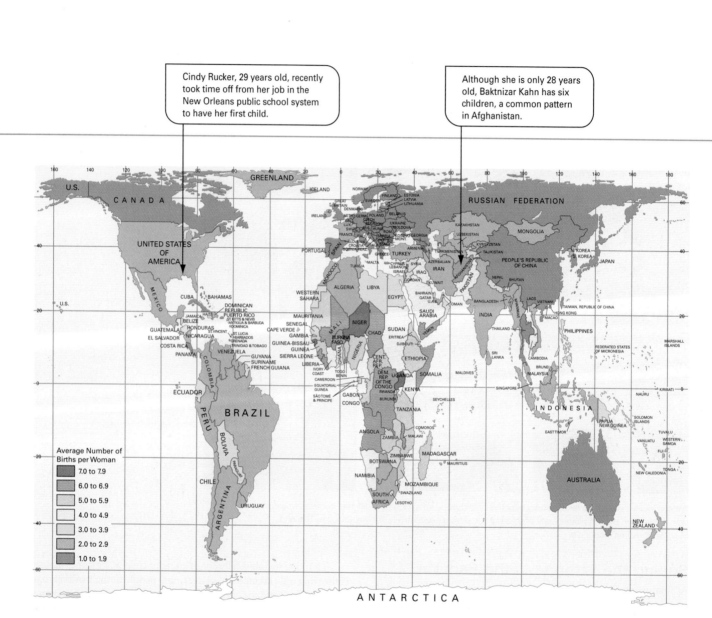

Cindy Rucker, 29 years old, recently took time off from her job in the New Orleans public school system to have her first child.

Although she is only 28 years old, Baktnizar Kahn has six children, a common pattern in Afghanistan.

Average Number of Births per Woman
- 7.0 to 7.9
- 6.0 to 6.9
- 5.0 to 5.9
- 4.0 to 4.9
- 3.0 to 3.9
- 2.0 to 2.9
- 1.0 to 1.9

Window on the World

GLOBAL MAP 1–1   Women's Childbearing in Global Perspective

Is childbearing simply a matter of personal choice? A look around the world shows that it is not. In general, women living in poor countries have many more children than women in rich nations. Can you point to some of the reasons for this global disparity? In simple terms, such differences mean that if you had been born into another society (whether you are female or male), your life might be quite different from what it is now.

Sources: Data from Martin et al. (2007), Population Reference Bureau (2007), United Nations Development Programme (2007), and Central Intelligence Agency (2008). Map projection from *Peters Atlas of the World* (1990).

Seeing Society in Our Everyday Lives

To see how society shapes personal choices, consider the number of children women have. As shown in Global Map 1–1, the average woman in the United States has about two children during her lifetime. In India, however, the average is about three; in Guatemala,

about four; in Ethiopia, about five; in Yemen, about six; and in Niger, the average woman has seven children (United Nations Development Programme, 2007).

What accounts for these striking differences? Because poor countries provide women with less schooling and fewer economic opportunities, women's lives are centered in the home, and they are less

SUPPLEMENTS: The *Instructor's Manual* contains a chapter outline, discussion topics, and additional lecture material for this chapter. Interactive material for review, discussion, and further research is available at the Macionis Web site, http://www.prenhall.com/macionis

GLOBAL: Support for Durkheim's thesis comes from rising suicide rates (especially among the young) in Hong Kong, Singapore, and other Asian countries experiencing rising affluence. Moreover, after the breakup of the former Soviet Union, Latvia, Lithuania, and Russia had the world's highest suicide rates.

● SEEING SOCIOLOGY
in Everyday Life

Single people are at higher risk of suicide than married people. Can you explain why?

likely to use contraception. Clearly, society has much to do with the decisions women and men make about childbearing.

Another illustration of the power of society to shape even our most private choices comes from the study of suicide. What could be a more personal choice than the decision to end your own life? But Emile Durkheim (1858–1917), one of sociology's pioneers, showed that even here, social forces are at work.

Examining official records in France, his own country, Durkheim found that some categories of people were more likely than others to take their own lives. Men, Protestants, wealthy people, and the unmarried had much higher suicide rates than women, Catholics and Jews, the poor, and married people. Durkheim explained the differences in terms of *social integration:* Categories of people with strong social ties had low suicide rates, and more individualistic categories of people had high suicide rates.

In Durkheim's time, men had much more freedom than women. But despite its advantages, freedom weakens social ties and thus increases the risk of suicide. Likewise, more individualistic Protestants were more likely to commit suicide than more tradition-bound Catholics and Jews, whose rituals encourage stronger social ties. The wealthy have much more freedom than the poor, but once again, at the cost of a higher suicide rate.

A century later, Durkheim's analysis still holds true. Figure 1–1 shows suicide rates for various categories of people in the United States. Keep in mind that suicide is very rare—a rate of 10 suicides for every 100,000 people is about the same as 6 inches in a mile. Even so, we can see some interesting patterns. In 2005, there were 12.3 recorded suicides for every 100,000 white people, more than twice the rate for African Americans (5.1). For both races, suicide was more common among men than among women. White men (19.7) were more than four times as likely as white women (5.0) to take their own lives. Among African Americans, the rate for men (8.7) was about five times higher than for women (1.8) (Kung et al., 2008). Applying Durkheim's logic, the higher suicide rate among white people and men reflects their greater wealth and freedom, just as the lower rate among women and African Americans reflects their limited social choices. As Durkheim did a century ago, we can see general patterns in the personal actions of particular individuals.

Seeing Sociologically: Marginality and Crisis

Anyone can learn to see the world using the sociological perspective. But two situations help people see clearly how society shapes individual lives: living on the margins of society and living through a social crisis.

From time to time, everyone feels like an outsider. For some categories of people, however, being an outsider—not part of the

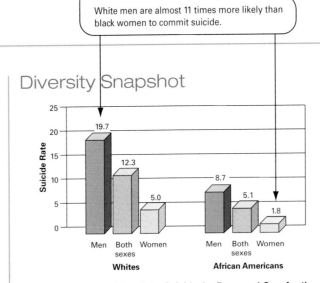

White men are almost 11 times more likely than black women to commit suicide.

Diversity Snapshot

FIGURE 1–1 **Rate of Death by Suicide, by Race and Sex, for the United States**

Suicide rates are higher for white people than for black people and higher for men than for women. Rates indicate the number of deaths by suicide for every 100,000 people in each category for 2005.

Source: Kung et al. (2008).

dominant group—is an everyday experience. The greater people's social marginality, the better they are able to use the sociological perspective.

For example, no African American grows up in the United States without understanding the importance of race in shaping people's lives. Rap lyrics by groups such as Three 6 Mafia, who say that they "Done seen people killed, done seen people deal, done seen people live in poverty with no meals," show that some people of color—especially African Americans living in the inner city—feel like their hopes and dreams are crushed by society. But white people, as the dominant majority, think less often about race and the privileges it provides, believing that race affects only people of color and not themselves as well. People at the margins of social life, including women, gay people, people with disabilities, and the very old, are aware of social patterns that others rarely think about. To become better at using the sociological perspective, we must step back from our familiar routines and look at our lives with a new curiosity.

Periods of change or crisis make everyone feel a little off balance, encouraging us to use the sociological perspective. The sociologist C. Wright Mills (1959) illustrated this idea using the Great Depression of the 1930s. As the unemployment rate soared to 25 percent, people who were out of work could not help but see general social forces at work in their particular lives. Rather than saying,

DISCUSS: Consider that only 5% of humans alive today have a college degree. Of *all* people who ever lived, just a small fraction of 1% ever enrolled at a college. Ask students to explain this rare opportunity.

EXERCISE: To help students see the power of society, suggest that students speak to grandparents about their lives as children.

Q: "The farther one travels, the less one knows." George Harrison

Q: "One can be an excellent physicist without ever stepping outside of one's society; I know this is not so for a sociologist." Peter Berger (1992)

global perspective the study of the larger world and our society's place in it

high-income countries the nations with the highest overall standards of living

middle-income countries nations with a standard of living about average for the world as a whole

low-income countries nations with a low standard of living in which most people are poor

The Importance of a Global Perspective

December 10, Fez, Morocco. This medieval city—a web of narrow streets and alleyways—is alive with the laughter of playing children, the silence of veiled women, and the steady gaze of men leading donkeys loaded with goods. Fez seems to have changed little over the centuries. Here, in northwestern Africa, we are just a few hundred miles from the more familiar rhythms of Europe. Yet this place seems a thousand years away. Never have we had such an adventure! Never have we thought so much about home!

As new information technology draws even the farthest reaches of the planet closer together, many academic disciplines are taking a **global perspective,** *the study of the larger world and our society's place in it.* What is the importance of a global perspective for sociology?

First, global awareness is a logical extension of the sociological perspective. Sociology shows us that our place in society shapes our life experiences. It stands to reason, then, that the position of our society in the larger world system affects everyone in the United States. The Thinking Globally box on page 8 describes a "global village" to show the social shape of the world and the place of the United States within it.

The world's 194 nations can be divided into three broad categories according to their level of economic development (see Global Map 12–1 on page 303). **High-income countries** are the *nations with the highest overall standards of living.* The sixty-six countries in this category include the United States and Canada, Argentina, the nations of Western Europe, South Africa, Israel, Saudi Arabia, Japan, and Australia. Taken together, these nations produce most of the world's goods and services, and the people who live there own most of the planet's wealth. Economically speaking, people in these countries are very well off, not because they are smarter or work harder than anyone else but because they were lucky enough to be born in a rich region of the world.

A second category is **middle-income countries,** *nations with a standard of living about average for the world as a whole.* People in any of these seventy-two nations—many of the countries of Eastern Europe, some of Africa, and almost all of Latin America and Asia—are as likely to live in rural villages as in cities and to walk or ride tractors, scooters, bicycles, or animals as to drive automobiles. On average, they receive eight to ten years of schooling. Most middle-income countries also have considerable social inequality within their own borders, so that some people are extremely rich (members of the business elite in nations across North Africa, for example), but many more lack safe housing and adequate nutrition (people living in the shanty settlements that surround Lima, Peru, or Mumbai, India).

People with the greatest privileges tend to see individuals as responsible for their own lives. Those at the margins of society, by contrast, are quick to see how race, class, and gender can create disadvantages. The rap artist Kanye West has given voice to the frustration felt by many African Americans living in this country's inner cities.

"Something must be wrong with me; I can't find a job," they took a sociological approach and realized, "The economy has collapsed; there are no jobs to be found!" Mills believed that using what he called the "sociological imagination" in this way helps people understand not only their society but also their own lives, because the two are closely related. The Seeing Sociology in Everyday Life box takes a closer look.

Just as social change encourages sociological thinking, sociological thinking can bring about social change. The more we learn about how "the system" operates, the more we may want to change it in some way. Becoming aware of the power of gender, for example, has caused many women and men to try to reduce gender inequality in our society.

Q: "The first fruit of [the sociological] imagination is that the individual can understand [personal] experience only by becoming aware of those of all individuals in [similar] circumstances. In many ways this is a terrible lesson; in many ways a magnificent one." C. Wright Mills

Q: "The world is a book, and those who study just their own society read only a single page." Old saying

Q: C. Wright Mills compares using the sociological perspective to "waking up in a stranger's house."

SEEING SOCIOLOGY IN EVERYDAY LIFE

The Sociological Imagination: Turning Personal Problems into Public Issues

As Mike opened the envelope, he felt the tightness in his chest. The letter he dreaded was in his hands—his job was finished at the end of the day. After eleven years! Years in which he had worked hard, sure that he would move up in the company. All those hopes and dreams were now suddenly gone. Mike felt like a failure. Anger at himself—for not having worked even harder, for having wasted eleven years of his life in what had turned out to be a dead-end job—grew inside him.

But as he returned to his work station to pack his things, Mike soon realized that he was not alone. Almost all his colleagues in the tech support group had received the same letter. Their jobs were moving to India, where the company was able to provide telephone tech support for less than half the cost of keeping workers in California.

By the end of the weekend, Mike was sitting in the living room with a dozen other ex-employees. Comparing notes and sharing ideas, they now realized that they were simply a few of the victims of a massive outsourcing of jobs that is part of what analysts call the "globalization of the economy."

In good times and bad, the power of the sociological perspective lies in making sense of our individual lives. We see that many of our particular problems (and our successes, as well) are not unique to us, but are the result of larger social trends. Half a century ago, sociologist C. Wright Mills pointed to the power of what he called the sociological imagination to help us understand everyday events. As he saw it, society—not people's personal failings—is the main cause of poverty and other social problems. By turning *personal problems* into *public issues*, the sociological imagination also is the key to bringing people together to create needed change.

In this excerpt, Mills (1959:3–5) explains the need for a sociological imagination:*

When society becomes industrialized, a peasant becomes a worker; a feudal lord is liquidated or becomes a businessman. When classes rise or fall, a man is employed or unemployed; when the rate of investment goes up or down, a man takes new heart or goes broke. When wars happen, an insurance salesman becomes a rocket launcher; a store clerk, a radar man; a wife lives alone; a child grows up without a father. Neither the life of an individual nor the history of a society can be understood without understanding both.

Yet men do not usually define the troubles they endure in terms of historical change. . . .

The well-being they enjoy, they do not usually impute to the big ups and downs of the society in which they live. Seldom aware of the intricate connection between the patterns of their own lives and the course of world history, ordinary men do not usually know what this connection means for the kind of men they are becoming and for the kinds of history-making in which they might take part. They do not possess the quality of mind essential to grasp the interplay of men and society, of biography and history, of self and world. . . .

What they need . . . is a quality of mind that will help them [see] what is going on in the world and . . . what may be happening within themselves. It is this quality . . . [that] may be called the sociological imagination.

WHAT DO YOU THINK?

1. As Mills sees it, how are personal troubles different from public issues? Explain this difference in terms of what happened to Mike in the story above.

2. Living in the United States, why do we often blame ourselves for the personal problems we face?

3. By using the sociological imagination, how do we gain the power to change the world?

*In this excerpt, Mills uses "man" and male pronouns to apply to all people. As far as gender was concerned, even this outspoken critic of society reflected the conventional writing practices of his time.

The remaining fifty-six nations of the world are **low-income countries,** *nations with a low standard of living in which most people are poor.* Most of the poorest countries in the world are in Africa, and a few are in Asia. Here again, a few people are very rich, but the majority struggle to get by with poor housing, unsafe water, too little food, and perhaps most serious of all, little chance to improve their lives.

Chapter 12 ("Global Stratification") explains the causes and consequences of global wealth and poverty. But every chapter of this text makes comparisons between the United States and other nations for four reasons:

1. **Where we live shapes the lives we lead.** As we saw in Global Map 1–1 on page 4, women living in rich and poor countries have very different lives, as suggested by the number of children they have. To understand ourselves and appreciate how others live, we must understand something about how countries differ, which is one good reason to pay attention to the global maps found throughout this text.

2. **Societies throughout the world are increasingly interconnected.** Historically, people in the United States took only passing note of the countries beyond our own borders. In recent decades, however, the United States and the rest of the world have become linked as never before. Electronic technology now transmits sounds, pictures, and written documents around the globe in seconds.

NOTE: Travel is hard work: Note the common root of "travel" and "travail," or "work." "Tour," by contrast, refers simply to "going in a circle." Thus for cross-cultural experiences to involve learning rather than simply fun, we need to work at it!

GLOBAL: Evidence of cultural and economic ties linking the U.S. and the rest of the world: Many rock stars sell more records abroad than in the U.S. Conversely, salsa has replaced ketchup as this nation's best-selling condiment.

Q: "The world belongs to me because I understand it." Honoré de Balzac

GLOBAL: The incorporation of global material into U.S. sociology texts has been common for less than 20 years. This text introduced the first global map in 1991.

MAKING THE GRADE

Think of the global perspective as an extension of the sociological perspective. Here at home, where we are "placed" within society affects how we act, think, and feel. Expanding our vision shows that our nation's place in the world affects the lives of all who live in this country.

SEEING SOCIOLOGY
in Everyday Life

How would your life be different if you had been born into a family in a poor farming village in Asia? What might you be doing right now instead of reading this textbook?

THINKING GLOBALLY   The Global Village: A Social Snapshot of Our World

Earth is currently home to 6.7 billion people who live in the cities and villages of 194 nations. To grasp the social shape of the world on a smaller scale, imagine shrinking the planet's population to a "global village" of just 1,000 people. In this village, more than half (604) of the inhabitants would be Asian, including 198 citizens of the People's Republic of China. Next, in terms of numbers, we would find 145 Africans, 109 Europeans, 86 people from Latin America and the Caribbean, 5 people from Australia and the South Pacific, and just 50 North Americans, including 45 people from the United States.

A close look at this settlement would reveal some startling facts: The village is a rich place, with a spectacular range of goods and services for sale. Yet most of the villagers can only dream about such treasures, because they are so poor: 75 percent of the village's total income is earned by just 200 people.

For most, the greatest problem is getting enough food. Every year, village workers produce more than enough to feed everyone; even so, about 150 people in the village do not get enough to eat, and many go to sleep hungry every night. These 150 residents (who together have less money than the single richest person in the village) lack both clean drinking water and safe shelter. Weak and often unable to work, they are at risk of contracting deadly diseases and dying.

The village has many schools, including a fine university. About 50 inhabitants have completed a college degree, but about one-fifth of the village's adults are not even able to read or write.

We in the United States, on average, would be among the village's richest people. Although we may like to think that our comfortable lives are the result of our individual talent and hard work, the sociological perspective reminds us that our achievements also result from our nation's privileged position in the worldwide social system.

WHAT DO YOU THINK?

1. Do any of the statistics presented in this box surprise you? Which ones? Why?

2. How do you think the lives of poor people in a lower-income country differ from those typical of people in the United States?

3. Is your "choice" to attend college affected by the country in which you live? How?

Sources: Calculations by the author based on international data from the United Nations Development Programme (2007) and the U.S. Census Bureau (2008).

One effect of new technology is that people the world over now share many tastes in food, clothing, and music. Rich countries such as the United States influence other nations, whose people are ever more likely to gobble up our Big Macs and Whoppers, dance to the latest hip-hop music, and speak English.

But the larger world also has an impact on us. We all know the contributions of famous immigrants such as Arnold Schwarzenegger (who came to the United States from Austria) and Gloria Estefan (who came from Cuba). About 1.5 million immigrants enter the United States each year, bringing their skills and talents, along with their fashions and foods, greatly increasing the racial and cultural diversity of this country (U.S. Department of Homeland Security, 2008b).

Trade across national boundaries has also created a global economy. Large corporations make and market goods worldwide. Stock traders in New York pay close attention to the financial markets in Tokyo and Hong Kong even as wheat farmers in Kansas watch the price of grain in the former Soviet republic of Georgia. Because most new U.S. jobs involve international trade, global understanding has never been more important.

3. **Many social problems that we face in the United States are far more serious elsewhere.** Poverty is a serious problem in the United States, but as Chapter 12 ("Global Stratification") explains, poverty in Latin America, Africa, and Asia is both more common and more serious. In the same way, although women have lower social standing than men in the United States, gender inequality is even greater in the world's poor countries.

4. **Thinking globally helps us learn more about ourselves.** We cannot walk the streets of a distant city without thinking about what it means to live in the United States. Comparing life in various settings also leads to unexpected lessons. For instance, in Chapter 12, we visit a squatter settlement in Chennai, India. There, despite desperate poverty, people thrive in the love and support of family members. Why, then, are so many poor people in our own country angry and alone? Are material things—so central to our definition of a "rich" life—the best way to measure human well-being?

In sum, in an increasingly interconnected world, we can understand ourselves only to the extent that we understand others. Sociology is an invitation to learn a new way of looking at the world around us. But is this invitation worth accepting? What are the benefits of applying the sociological perspective?

DIVERSITY: Other examples of research driving public policy include Kenneth Clark's study of the self-image of African American children, research that helped convince the U.S. Supreme Court to outlaw intentional school segregation.

APPLIED: Henry Ford set up what he called his Sociological Department to monitor the behavior of his workers in order to discourage them from spending wages on vices such as alcohol and tobacco.

NOTE: The gap in pay between high school graduates and college graduates has roughly doubled in the last 30 years, meaning that a college degree has never been more valuable in terms of earnings.

DISCUSS: In assessing the value of sociology for careers, ask students to identify jobs that do not demand some understanding of human social behavior.

◉ SEEING SOCIOLOGY
in Everyday Life

This discussion shows you that using the sociological perspective is valuable for changing society by shaping public policy, for your personal enrichment, and for advancing your career.

Applying the Sociological Perspective

Applying the sociological perspective is useful in many ways. First, sociology is at work guiding many of the laws and policies that shape our lives. Second, on an individual level, making use of the sociological perspective leads to important personal growth and expanded awareness. Third, studying sociology is excellent preparation for the world of work.

Sociology and Public Policy

Sociologists have helped shape public policy—the laws and regulations that guide how people in communities live and work—in countless ways, from racial desegregation and school busing to laws regulating divorce. For example, in her study of how divorce affects people's income, the sociologist Lenore Weitzman (1985, 1996) discovered that women who leave marriages typically experience a dramatic loss of income. Recognizing this fact, many states passed laws that have increased women's claims to marital property and enforced fathers' obligations to provide support for women raising their children.

Sociology and Personal Growth

By applying the sociological perspective, we are likely to become more active and aware and to think more critically in our daily lives. Using sociology benefits us in four ways:

1. **The sociological perspective helps us assess the truth of "common sense."** We all take many things for granted, but that does not make them true. One good example is the idea that we are free individuals who are personally responsible for our own lives. If we think we decide our own fate, we may be quick to praise very successful people as superior and consider others with fewer achievements personally deficient. A sociological approach, by contrast, encourages us to ask whether such common beliefs are actually true and, to the extent that they are not, why they are so widely held. The Seeing Sociology in Everyday Life box on page 10 gives an example of how the sociological perspective sometimes makes us rethink commonsense ideas about other people.

2. **The sociological perspective helps us see the opportunities and constraints in our lives.** Sociological thinking leads us to see that in the game of life, we have a say in how to play our cards, but it is society that deals us the hand. The more we understand the game, the better

players we will be. Sociology helps us learn more about the world so that we can pursue our goals more effectively.

3. **The sociological perspective empowers us to be active participants in our society.** The more we understand how society works, the more active citizens we become. As C. Wright Mills (1959) explained in the box on page 7, it is the sociological perspective that turns a personal problem (such as being out of work) into a public issue (a lack of good jobs). As we come to see how society affects us, we may support society as it is, or we may set out with others to change it.

4. **The sociological perspective helps us live in a diverse world.** North Americans represent just 5 percent of the world's people, and as the remaining chapters of this book explain, many of the other 95 percent live very differently than we do. Still, like people everywhere, we tend to define our own way of life as "right," "natural," and "better." The sociological perspective encourages us to think critically about the relative strengths and weaknesses of all ways of life, including our own.

Careers: The "Sociology Advantage"

Most students at colleges and universities today are very interested in getting a good job. A background in sociology is excellent preparation for the working world. Of course, completing a bachelor's degree in sociology is the right choice for people who decide they would like to go

Just about every job in today's economy involves working with people. For this reason, studying sociology is good preparation for your future career. In what ways does having "people skills" help police officers perform their job?

DISCUSS: Ask the class to assess the common belief that anyone in the U.S. can truly become president. Of 44 presidents: men = 44; whites = 43; Jews = 0; Catholics = 1 (JFK); divorced = 1 (Ronald Reagan); born in a log cabin = 1 (Millard Fillmore). Note, too, that only 16 were clearly in the upper class of their day.

DISCUSS: Ask the questions in the box below to members of the class.
DISCUSS: How does Ehrenreich's research show the power of society to shape people's lives?

● SEEING SOCIOLOGY
in Everyday Life

Write down five jobs that appeal to you. Then identify ways in which sociological thinking would increase your chances for success in each one.

SEEING SOCIOLOGY IN EVERYDAY LIFE

Nickel and Dimed: On (Not) Getting By in America

All of us know people who work at low-wage jobs as waitresses at diners, clerks at drive-throughs, or sales associates at discount stores such as Wal-Mart. We see such people just about every day. Many of us actually *are* such people. In the United States, "common sense" tells us that the jobs people have and the amount of money they make reflect their personal abilities as well as their willingness to work hard.

Barbara Ehrenreich (2001) had her doubts. To find out what the world of low-wage work is really like, the successful journalist and author decided to leave her comfortable middle-class life to live and work in the world of low-wage jobs. She began in Key West, Florida, taking a job as a waitress for $2.43 an hour plus tips. Right away, she found out that she had to work much harder than she ever imagined. By the end of a shift, she was exhausted, but after sharing tips with the kitchen staff, she averaged less than $6.00 an hour. This was barely above the minimum wage at the time and provided just enough income to pay the rent on her tiny apartment, buy food, and cover other basic expenses. She had to hope that she didn't get sick, because the job did not provide health insurance and she

couldn't afford to pay for a visit to a doctor's office.

After working for more than a year at a number of other low-wage jobs, including cleaning motels in Maine and working on the floor of a Walmart in Minnesota, she had rejected quite a bit of "common sense." First, she now knew that tens of millions of people with low-wage jobs work very hard every day. If you don't think so, Ehrenreich says, try one of these jobs yourself. Second, these jobs require not just hard work (imagine thoroughly cleaning three motel rooms per hour all day long) but also special skills and real intelligence (try waiting on ten tables in a restaurant at the same time and keeping everybody happy). She found that the people she worked with were, on average, just as

smart, clever, and funny as those she knew who wrote books for a living or taught at a college.

Why, then, do we think of low-wage workers as lazy or as having less ability? It surprised Ehrenreich to learn that many low-wage workers felt this way about themselves. In a society that teaches us to believe personal ability is everything, we learn to size people up by their jobs. Subject to the constant supervision, random drug tests, and other rigid rules that usually come along with low-wage jobs, Ehrenreich imagined that many people end up feeling unworthy, even to the point of not trying for anything better. Such beliefs, she concludes, help support a society of extreme inequality in which some people live very well thanks to the low wages paid to the rest.

WHAT DO YOU THINK?

1. Have you ever held a low-wage job? If so, would you say you worked hard? What was your pay? Were there any benefits?

2. Ehrenreich claims that most well-off people in the United States are dependent on low-wage workers. What do you think she means by this?

3. Do you think most people with jobs at Wendy's or Wal-Mart have a real chance to enroll in college and to work toward a different career? Why or why not?

---

on to graduate work and eventually become a professor or researcher in this field. Throughout the United States, tens of thousands of men and women teach sociology in universities, colleges, and high schools. But just as many professional sociologists work as researchers for government agencies or private foundations and businesses, gathering important information on social behavior and carrying out evaluation research. In today's cost-conscious world, agencies and companies want to be sure that the programs and policies they set in place get the job done at the lowest cost. Sociologists, especially those with advanced research skills, are in high demand for this kind of work (Deutscher, 1999).

In addition, a smaller but increasing number of professional sociologists work as clinical sociologists. These women and men work, much as clinical psychologists do, with the goal of improving the lives of troubled clients. A basic difference is that sociologists

focus on difficulties not in the personality but in the individual's web of social relationships.

But sociology is not just for people who want to be sociologists. People who work in criminal justice—in police departments, probation offices, and corrections facilities—gain the "sociology advantage" by learning which categories of people are most at risk of becoming criminals as well as victims, how effective various policies and programs are at preventing crime, and why people turn to crime in the first place. Similarly, people who work in health care—including doctors, nurses, and technicans—also gain a sociology advantage by learning about patterns of health and illness within the population, as well as how factors such as race, gender, and social class affect human health.

The American Sociological Association (2002) reports that sociology is also excellent preparation for jobs in dozens of additional fields,

Q: O, when degree is shak'd, Which is the ladder of all high designs, The enterprise is sick! . . . Take but degree away, untune that string, And hark what discord follows!

Shakespeare (*Troilus and Cressida*) links the loss of the traditional feudal hierarchy to greater awareness of society.

DISCUSS: How did changes in society spark the development of sociology?

Comte's Three Stages of Society

Theological Stage	Metaphysical Stage	Scientific Stage
(the Church in the Middle Ages)	(the Enlightenment and the ideas of Hobbes, Locke, and Rousseau)	(physics, chemistry, sociology)

MAKING THE GRADE

Sociology developed when and where social change was greatest.

positivism (p. 13) a scientific approach to knowledge based on "positive" facts as opposed to mere speculation

including advertising, banking, business, education, government, journalism, law, public relations, and social work. In almost any type of work, success depends on understanding how various categories of people differ in beliefs, family patterns, and other ways of life. Unless you plan to have a job that never involves dealing with people, you should consider the workplace benefits of learning more about sociology.

The Origins of Sociology

Like the "choices" made by individuals, major historical events rarely just happen. The birth of sociology was itself the result of powerful social forces.

Social Change and Sociology

Striking changes took place in Europe during the eighteenth and nineteenth centuries. Three kinds of change were especially important in the development of sociology: the rise of a factory-based industrial economy, the explosive growth of cities, and new ideas about democracy and political rights.

A New Industrial Economy

During the Middle Ages in Europe, most people plowed fields near their homes or worked in small-scale *manufacturing* (a term derived from Latin words meaning "to make by hand"). By the end of the eighteenth century, inventors used new sources of energy—the power of moving water and then steam—to operate large machines in mills and factories. Instead of laboring at home or in small groups, workers became part of a large and anonymous labor force, under the control of strangers who owned the factories. This change in the system of production took people out of their homes, weakening the traditions that had guided community life for centuries.

The Growth of Cities

Across Europe, landowners took part in what historians call the *enclosure movement*—they fenced off more and more farmland to create grazing areas for sheep, the source of wool for the thriving textile mills. Without land, countless tenant farmers had little choice but to head to the cities in search of work in the new factories.

As cities grew larger, these urban migrants faced many social problems, including pollution, crime, and homelessness. Moving through streets crowded with strangers, they faced a new and impersonal social world.

Political Change

Europeans in the Middle Ages viewed society as an expression of God's will: From the royalty to the serfs, each person up and down the social ladder played a part in the holy plan. This theological view of

What we see depends on our point of view. When gazing at the stars, lovers see romance, but scientists see thermal reactions.

society is captured in lines from the old Anglican hymn "All Things Bright and Beautiful":

> The rich man in his castle,
> The poor man at his gate,
> God made them high and lowly
> And ordered their estate.

But as cities grew, tradition came under attack. In the writings of Thomas Hobbes (1588–1679), John Locke (1632–1704), and Adam Smith (1723–1790), we see a shift in focus from a moral obligation to God and king to the pursuit of self-interest. In the new political climate, philosophers spoke of *personal liberty* and *individual rights.* Echoing these sentiments, our own Declaration of Independence states that every person has "certain unalienable rights," including "life, liberty, and the pursuit of happiness."

The French Revolution, which began in 1789, was an even greater break with political and social tradition. The French social analyst Alexis de Tocqueville (1805–1859) thought the changes in society brought about by the French Revolution were so great that they amounted to "nothing short of the regeneration of the whole human race" (1955:13, orig. 1856).

A New Awareness of Society

Huge factories, exploding cities, a new spirit of individualism—these changes combined to make people more aware of their surroundings. The new discipline of sociology was born in England, France, and Germany—precisely where the changes were greatest.

NOTE: Comte first called his new discipline "social physics." Thinking the term stolen by Adolphe Quetelet, Comte renamed the fledgling field "sociology."

GLOBAL: Brazil, a country that has long embraced ambitious social planning (consider the building of the capital, Brasilia, deep in the interior), was guided by Comte's ideas. In fact, the Brazilians adopted for their national flag Comte's slogan, "Order and Progress."

Seeing SOCIOLOGY in the NEWS

Rocky Mountain News

Interest in Military on the Rise

By DAVID MONTERO
February 2, 2009

Across the street from the U.S. Navy recruiting station in Aurora [Colorado] is a restaurant that has gone out of business. Less than a mile away, bankrupt Circuit City is unloading its merchandise at deep discounts.

Inside the narrow office, four recruiters and two freshly minted recruits are talking about what seems like the topic on most Americans' minds: jobs and the economy.

Troy Torreyson, wearing a blue Navy hat and a white T-shirt that reads, "Property of the U.S. Navy," can't wait to start basic training in May. The 30-year-old is scheduled to go to the Great Lakes naval facility in Illinois for nine weeks and after that will train to be a Navy corpsman.

He wants to be in nursing care, but the economy sidelined those plans for awhile.

"It's a huge issue," he said. "I have a culinary arts degree and I work at Burger King right now. I can't find a job."

Chief Petty Officer Mario Laracuente has heard similar tales before. He's been hearing it for months actually, ever since the economy went south. People getting laid off. People having trouble finding work and making ends meet. People looking for a [bit] of stability.

Laracuente believes the military is well-positioned in this environment to meet and exceed recruiting goals—even as the United States continues to fight in Iraq and Afghanistan.

"You can sense that as the economy appears more unstable, people are looking at the military more," Laracuente said. . . .

Stable jobs attractive

All branches of the military are showing strong recruiting numbers with the flagging economy.

The last reporting period for December showed the Army and Marine Corps exceeding recruitment goals, reaching 115 percent and 113 percent of their goals, respectively.

The Air Force and Navy met their targets as well.

Those results came as private employers made sweeping rounds of layoffs. In December, the U.S.

Department of Labor reported that unemployment rates increased from 6.8 percent to 7.2 percent. . . .

Finding refuge in the military during tough economic times isn't unusual. Safe harbors can often be found in government and the military, which accounts for about a fifth of the nation's budget and is set at $515 billion for fiscal year 2009.

Gordon Von Stroh, professor of management at the University of Denver, said the lure of incentive-laden deals offered by the military coupled with staggering job losses make for plum pickings among military recruiters.

"They get a larger pool of people and can be more selective," he said. "For the applicants, they see an opportunity to train in some fairly advanced fields while having the job stability provided by the military."

Job dries up

Mark Sabatino got laid off last week from his job as a commercial sign installer. . . . The 22-year-old from Arvada had thought about the

Science and Sociology

And so it was that the French social thinker Auguste Comte (1798–1857) coined the term *sociology* in 1838 to describe a new way of looking at society. This makes sociology one of the youngest academic disciplines—far newer than history, physics, or economics, for example.

Of course, Comte was not the first person to think about the nature of society. Such questions fascinated many of the brilliant thinkers of ancient civilizations, including the Chinese philosopher K'ung Fu-tzu, or Confucius (551–479 B.C.E.), and the Greek philosophers Plato (c. 427–347 B.C.E.) and Aristotle (384–322 B.C.E.).[1] Over the next several centuries, the Roman emperor Marcus Aurelius (121–180), the medieval thinkers Saint Thomas Aquinas (c. 1225–1274) and Christine de Pisan (c. 1363–1431), and the English playwright William Shakespeare (1564–1616) wrote about the workings of society.

Yet these thinkers were more interested in imagining the ideal society than in studying society as it really was. Comte and other pioneers of sociology all cared about how society could be improved,

but their major objective was to understand how society actually operates.

Comte (1975, orig. 1851–54) saw sociology as the product of a three-stage historical development. During the earliest, the *theological stage,* from the beginning of human history to the end of the European Middle Ages about 1350 C.E., people took a religious view that society expressed God's will.

With the dawn of the Renaissance in the fifteenth century, the theological approach gave way to a *metaphysical stage* of history in which people saw society as a natural rather than a supernatural system. Thomas Hobbes (1588–1679), for example, suggested that society reflected not the perfection of God so much as the failings of a selfish human nature.

What Comte called the *scientific stage* of history began with the work of early scientists such as the Polish astronomer Copernicus (1473–1543), the Italian astronomer and physicist Galileo (1564–1642), and the English physicist and mathematician Isaac Newton (1642–1727). Comte's contribution came in applying the scientific approach—first used to study the physical world—to the study of society.[2]

---

[1] The abbreviation B.C.E. means "before the common era." We use this throughout the text instead of the traditional B.C. ("before Christ") to reflect the religious diversity of our society. Similarly, in place of the traditional A.D. (*anno Domini,* or "in the year of our Lord"), we use the abbreviation C.E. ("common era").

[2] Illustrating Comte's stages, the ancient Greeks and Romans viewed the planets as gods; Renaissance metaphysical thinkers saw them as astral influences (giving rise to astrology); by the time of Galileo, scientists understood planets as natural objects moving according to natural laws.

NOTE: Comte called sociology the "Queen of the Sciences," an assertion that inspired sociologists at Brown University to suggest that their entire college be reorganized under the sociology department.

NOTE: A positive function is also termed a *eufunction* (*eu-* is the Greek prefix for "good"), which contrasts with *dysfunction* (*dys-* means "ill" or "bad").

military before, but decided after high school to see if he could make a go of it in the private sector first.

Things went pretty well. The work was steady, the money was good and Sabatino figured his ambitions of working with airplanes could wait awhile.

Then it all slowed down.

He said when things were going well, he'd have five jobs a week installing signs on businesses as well as doing some side jobs with smaller signs. But as businesses constricted, the jobs dried up to about one per week.

It wasn't enough.

"I had bills," he said. "They weren't going away."

So on Thursday, Sabatino found himself sitting in an overheated U.S. Marine Corps recruiting station in Thornton answering questions about his education and job history and explaining why he wanted to join.

Staff Sgt. Chris Tari dutifully filled out the paperwork, told Sabatino that he'd have to pass some tests and that, if all went according to plan,

he could ship out to recruit training as early as August—though September was more likely.

In the meantime, his plan is to learn aviation electronics and eventually cycle back into the private sector and work with planes.

"I'll probably get out when the going is good again," he said.

For love of country

Sgt. 1st Class Brett Scarcelli is pure U.S. Army. Standing in the recruiting station at Metropolitan State College in Denver, he clutches a tennis ball in one hand and never lowers his gaze when talking to someone. For him, the Army is about service to country. Period.

But that approach doesn't necessarily work on potential recruits. So, Scarcelli is armed with the things that might matter to college students wandering around the Tivoli Student Union on the Auraria campus. There are increasing tuition costs, budget cuts at state universities, and difficulties in getting hired right now straight out of college, for instance.

The message seems to work.

"I talked to a guy who just got his degree and has six months before he has to start paying. And he can't find a job," Scarcelli said. "The Army is willing to pay off the loans, and he can wait four years to see what the economy does."

WHAT DO YOU THINK?

1. How does the surge in military recruiting reflect not just personal choices by individuals but also larger changes in society?

2. Can you point to other personal choices people are making that may be linked to the weaker economy? What are they?

3. Did the weakening economy affect your life in terms of work? What about your decision to attend college? Explain.

Adapted from the original article, "Interest in Military on the Rise," by David Montero, *Rocky Mountain News*, February 2, 2009. Reprinted with the permission of the E.W. Scripps Company.

Comte's approach is called **positivism,** *a way of understanding based on science.* As a positivist, Comte believed that society operates according to its own laws, much as the physical world operates according to gravity and other laws of nature.

By the beginning of the twentieth century, sociology had spread to the United States and showed the influence of Comte's ideas. Today, most sociologists still consider science a crucial part of sociology. But as Chapter 2 ("Sociological Investigation") explains, we now realize that human behavior is far more complex than the movement of planets or even the actions of other living things. We are creatures of imagination and spontaneity, so human behavior can never be fully explained by any rigid "laws of society." In addition, early sociologists such as Karl Marx (1818–1883), whose ideas are discussed in Chapter 4 ("Society"), were troubled by the striking inequalities of industrial society. They hoped that the new discipline of sociology would not just help us understand society but also lead to change toward greater social justice.

Sociological Theory

The desire to translate observations into understanding brings us to the important aspect of sociology known as *theory*. A **theory** is *a statement of how and why specific facts are related.* The job of sociological theory is to explain social behavior in the real world. For example,

recall Emile Durkheim's theory that categories of people with low social integration (men, Protestants, the wealthy, and the unmarried) are at higher risk of suicide. Seeing Sociology in the News explains one consequence of the recent economic recession.

As the next chapter ("Sociological Investigation") explains, sociologists test their theories by gathering evidence using various research methods. Durkheim did exactly this, finding out which categories of people were more likely to commit suicide and which were less likely and then devising a theory that best squared with all available evidence. National Map 1–1 on page 14 displays the suicide rate for each of the fifty states.

In building theory, sociologists face two basic questions: What issues should we study? And how should we connect the facts? In the process of answering these questions, sociologists look to one or more theoretical approaches as "road maps." Think of a **theoretical approach** as *a basic image of society that guides thinking and research.* Sociologists make use of three major theoretical approaches: the structural-functional approach, the social-conflict approach, and the symbolic-interaction approach.

The Structural-Functional Approach

The **structural-functional approach** is *a framework for building theory that sees society as a complex system whose parts work together to promote solidarity and stability.* As its name suggests, this approach points to **social structure,** *any relatively stable pattern of*

NOTE: Herbert Spencer was influenced by Thomas Robert Malthus (whose thesis on population is covered in Chapter 22). Spencer, a friend of the industrialist Andrew Carnegie, wrote the first textbook on sociology, *Principles of Sociology*, in 1879.

THE MAP: The highest suicide rates are found in states with low population density such as Wyoming and Alaska. By contrast, densely populated places, including New York and the District of Columbia, have low suicide rates.

theory (p. 13) a statement of how and why specific facts are related

theoretical approach (p. 13) a basic image of society that guides thinking and research

structural-functional approach (p. 13) a framework for building theory that sees society as a complex system whose parts work together to promote solidarity and stability

social structure (p. 13) any relatively stable pattern of social behavior

In the Plains and Mountain regions of the country, where population density is very low, people are more isolated and have a higher rate of suicide.

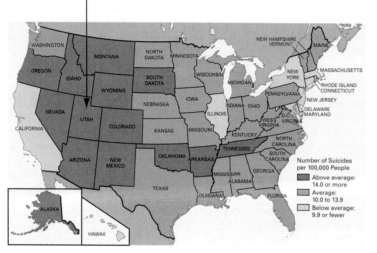

Seeing Ourselves

NATIONAL MAP 1–1

Suicide Rates across the United States

This map shows which states have high, average, and low suicide rates. Look for patterns. By and large, high suicide rates occur where people live far apart from one another. More densely populated states have low suicide rates. Do these data support or contradict Durkheim's theory of suicide? Why?

Source: Kung et al. (2008).

Number of Suicides per 100,000 People

Above average: 14.0 or more
Average: 10.0 to 13.9
Below average: 9.9 or fewer

social behavior. Social structure gives our lives shape—in families, the workplace, the classroom, and the community. This approach also looks for a structure's **social functions,** *the consequences of any social pattern for the operation of society as a whole.* All social structures, from a simple handshake to complex religious rituals, function to keep society going, at least in its present form.

The structural-functional approach owes much to Auguste Comte, who pointed out the need to keep society unified at a time when many traditions were breaking down. Emile Durkheim, who helped establish the study of sociology in French universities, also based his work on this approach. A third structural-functional pioneer was the English sociologist Herbert Spencer (1820–1903). Spencer compared society to the human body. Just as the structural parts of the human body—the skeleton, muscles, and various internal organs—function interdependently to help the entire organism survive, social structures work together to preserve society. The structural-functional approach, then, leads sociologists to identify various structures of society and investigate their functions.

Robert K. Merton (1910–2003) expanded our understanding of the concept of social function by pointing out that any social structure probably has many functions, some more obvious than others. He distinguished between **manifest functions,** *the recognized and intended consequences of any social pattern,* and **latent functions,** *the unrecognized and unintended consequences of any social pattern.* For example, the manifest function of the U.S. system of higher education is to provide young people with the information and skills they need to perform jobs after graduation. Perhaps just as important, although less often acknowledged, is college's latent function as a "marriage broker," bringing together

young people of similar social backgrounds. Another latent function of higher education is to limit unemployment by keeping millions of young people out of the labor market, where many of them might not easily find jobs.

But Merton also recognized that not all the effects of social structure are good. Thus a **social dysfunction** is *any social pattern that may disrupt the operation of society.* People often disagree about what is helpful and what is harmful to society as a whole. In addition, what is functional for one category of people (say, high profits for Wall Street bank executives) may well be dysfunctional for other categories of people (workers who lose pension funds invested in banks that fail, people who cannot pay their mortgages and end up losing their homes).

CRITICAL REVIEW The main idea of the structural-functional approach is its vision of society as stable and orderly. The main goal of the sociologists who use this approach, then, is to figure out "what makes society tick."

In the mid-1900s, most sociologists favored the structural-functional approach. In recent decades, however, its influence has declined. By focusing on social stability and unity, critics point out, structural-functionalism ignores inequalities of social class, race, and gender, which cause tension and conflict. In general, its focus on stability at the expense of conflict makes this approach somewhat conservative. As a critical response, sociologists developed the social-conflict approach.

CHECK YOUR LEARNING How do manifest functions differ from latent functions? Give an example of a manifest function and a latent function of automobiles in the United States.

RESOURCE: For a closer look at the larger role women played in the development of sociology, see Patricia Madoo Lengermann and Jill Niebrugge-Brantley, "Women and the Birth of Sociology," in the reader *Seeing Ourselves*, 8th ed.

NOTE: Harriet Martineau's lifelong activism was guided by a Comtean view of the world as comprehensible and changeable. Her achievements are all the more impressive in light of her almost total deafness from about the age of twelve.

Q: "Liberals have devised whole disciplines like sociology and women's studies to prove that nothing is anybody's fault." P. J. O'Rourke

social functions the consequences of a social pattern for the operation of society as a whole

manifest functions the recognized and intended consequences of any social pattern

latent functions the unrecognized and unintended consequences of any social pattern

social dysfunction any social pattern that may disrupt the operation of society

social-conflict approach a framework for building theory that sees society as an arena of inequality that generates conflict and change

gender-conflict approach a point of view that focuses on inequality and conflict between women and men

feminism support of social equality for women and men

race-conflict approach (p. 16) a point of view that focuses on inequality and conflict between people of different racial and ethnic categories

The Social-Conflict Approach

The **social-conflict approach** is *a framework for building theory that sees society as an arena of inequality that generates conflict and change.* Unlike the structural-functional emphasis on solidarity and stability, this approach highlights inequality and change. Guided by this approach, which includes the gender-conflict and race-conflict approaches, sociologists investigate how factors such as social class, race, ethnicity, gender, sexual orientation, and age are linked to a society's unequal distribution of money, power, education, and social prestige. A conflict analysis rejects the idea that social structure promotes the operation of society as a whole, focusing instead on how social patterns benefit some people while harming others.

Sociologists using the social-conflict approach look at ongoing conflict between dominant and disadvantaged categories of people—the rich in relation to the poor, white people in relation to people of color, and men in relation to women. Typically, people on top try to protect their privileges while the disadvantaged try to gain more for themselves.

A conflict analysis of our educational system shows how schooling carries class inequality from one generation to the next. For example, secondary schools assign students to either college preparatory or vocational training programs. From a structural-functional point of view, such "tracking" benefits everyone by providing schooling that fits students' abilities. But conflict analysis argues that tracking often has less to do with talent than with social background, with the result that well-to-do students are placed in higher tracks while poor children end up in the lower tracks.

Thus young people from privileged families get the best schooling, which leads them to college and later to high-income careers. The children of poor families, by contrast, are not prepared for college and, like their parents before them, typically get stuck in low-paying jobs. In both cases, the social standing of one generation is passed on to the next, with schools justifying the practice in terms of individual merit (Bowles & Gintis, 1976; Oakes, 1982, 1985).

Many sociologists use the social-conflict approach not just to understand society but also to bring about societal change that would reduce inequality. Karl Marx, whose ideas are discussed at length in Chapter 4 ("Society"), championed the cause of the workers in what he saw as their battle against factory owners. In a well-known statement (inscribed on his monument in London's Highgate Cemetery), Marx asserted, "The philosophers have only interpreted the world, in various ways; the point, however, is to change it."

The social-conflict approach points out patterns of inequality in everyday life. In the TV show *Gossip Girl*, Jenny Humphrey, a girl from a modest background, often feels awkward in the presence of her more affluent classmates. Do you see similar patterns of social inequality on your campus?

Feminism and the Gender-Conflict Approach

One important type of social-conflict analysis is the **gender-conflict approach,** *a point of view that focuses on inequality and conflict between women and men.* The gender-conflict approach is closely linked to **feminism,** *support of social equality for women and men.*

The importance of the gender-conflict approach lies in making us aware of the many ways in which our way of life places men in positions of power over women: in the home (where men are usually considered "head of the household"), in the workplace (where men earn more income and hold most positions of power), and in the mass media (how many hip-hop stars are women?).

Another contribution of the gender-conflict approach is making us aware of the importance of women to the development of sociology. Harriet Martineau (1802–1876) is regarded as the first woman sociologist. Born to a wealthy English family, Martineau made her mark in 1853 by translating the writings of Auguste Comte from French into English. In her own published writings, she documented the evils of slavery and argued for laws to protect factory workers, defending workers' right to unionize. She was particularly concerned

NOTE: Each approach's key thinkers: *functional*, Comte, Durkheim, and Spencer; *conflict*, Marx, Weber, Martineau, Addams, and Du Bois; *interaction*, Weber, G. H. Mead, Blumer, Garfinkel.

Q: "It has historically been the case with white people, in their regard for black people, that even though we might be with them, we weren't considered of them." Malcolm X

Q: "My life had its significance and its only deep significance because it was part of a problem; but the problem was, I continue to think, the central problem of the greatest of the world's democracies and so the problem of the future world." W. E. B. Du Bois

Q: "The Negro is a sort of seventh son . . . gifted with second sight . . . the sense of always looking at oneself through the eyes of others." W. E. B. Du Bois

● MAKING THE GRADE

The feminist and gender-conflict approaches and the race-conflict approach are all examples of social-conflict theory.

We can use the sociological perspective to look at sociology itself. All of the most widely recognized pioneers of the discipline were men. This is because in the nineteenth century, it was all but unheard of for women to be college professors, and few women took a central role in public life. But Jane Addams was an early sociologist in the United States, who founded Hull House, a Chicago settlement house where she spent many hours helping young people.

about the position of women in society and fought for changes in education policy so that women could have more options in life than marriage and raising children.

In the United States, Jane Addams (1860–1935) was a sociological pioneer whose contributions began in 1889 when she helped found Hull House, a Chicago settlement house that provided assistance to immigrant families. Although widely published (she wrote eleven books and hundreds of articles), Addams chose the life of a public activist over that of a university sociologist, speaking out on issues involving immigration and the pursuit of peace. Despite the controversy caused by her pacifism during World War I, she was awarded the Nobel Peace Prize in 1931.

All chapters of this book consider the importance of gender and gender inequality. For an in-depth look at feminism and the social standing of women and men, see Chapter 13 ("Gender Stratification").

The Race-Conflict Approach

Another important type of social-conflict analysis is the **race-conflict approach,** *a point of view that focuses on inequality and conflict between people of different racial and ethnic categories.* Just as men have power over women, white people have numerous social advantages over people of color, including, on average, higher incomes, more schooling, better health, and longer life expectancy.

The race-conflict approach also points out the contributions made by people of color to the development of sociology. Ida Wells Barnett (1862–1931) was born to slave parents but rose to become a teacher and then a journalist and newspaper publisher. She campaigned tirelessly for racial equality and, especially, to put an end to the lynching of black people. She wrote and lectured about racial inequality throughout her life (Lengerman & Niebrugge-Brantley, 1998).

An important contribution to understanding race in the United States was made by William Edward Burghardt Du Bois (1868–1963). Born to a poor Massachusetts family, Du Bois (pronounced doo-boyss) enrolled at Fisk University in Nashville, Tennessee, and then at Harvard University, where he earned the first doctorate awarded by that university to a person of color. Like most people who follow the social-conflict approach (whether focusing on class, gender, or race), Du Bois believed that sociologists should try to solve society's problems. He therefore studied the black community (1967, orig. 1899), spoke out against racial inequality, and served as a founding member of the National Association for the Advancement of Colored People (NAACP). The Thinking About Diversity box takes a closer look at the ideas of W. E. B. Du Bois.

○ **CRITICAL REVIEW** The various social-conflict approaches have gained a large following in recent decades, but like other approaches, they have met with criticism. Because any conflict analysis focuses on inequality, it largely ignores how shared values and interdependence unify members of a society. In addition, say critics, to the extent that the conflict approaches pursue political goals, they cannot claim scientific objectivity. Supporters of social-conflict approaches respond that *all* theoretical approaches have political consequences.

A final criticism of both the structural-functional and the social-conflict approaches is that they paint society in broad strokes—in terms of "family," "social class," "race," and so on. A third type of theoretical analysis—the symbolic-interaction approach—views society less in general terms and more as the everyday experiences of individual people.

○ **CHECK YOUR LEARNING** Why do you think sociologists characterize the social-conflict approach as "activist"? What is it actively trying to achieve?

NOTE: An interesting illustration of "the human process of attaching meaning to our surroundings": The first act of Adam and Eve in Genesis is to name the elements around them.

NOTE: Herbert Blumer first used the term "symbolic interactionism" in 1937.

EXERCISE: Motivated students can learn to appreciate the power of social structures by reading John Howard Griffin's classic, *Black Like Me* (Houghton Mifflin, 1960).

DISCUSS: Use the three questions in the box below to develop class dicussion.

macro-level orientation a broad focus on social structures that shape society as a whole

structural-functional approach (p. 13)
social-conflict approach (p. 15)

micro-level orientation a close-up focus on social interaction in specific situations

symbolic-interaction approach a framework for building theory that sees society as the product of the everyday interactions of individuals

THINKING ABOUT DIVERSITY: RACE, CLASS, & GENDER

An Important Pioneer: W. E. B. Du Bois on Race

One of sociology's pioneers in the United States, William Edward Burghardt Du Bois saw sociology as the key to solving society's problems, especially racial inequality.

Du Bois spoke out against racial separation and was a founding member of the National Association for the Advancement of Colored People (NAACP). He made his colleagues in sociology—and people everywhere—aware of the deep racial divisions in the United States. White people can simply be "Americans," Du Bois pointed out; African Americans, however, have a "double consciousness," reflecting their status as people who are never able to escape identification based on the color of their skin.

In his sociological classic *The Philadelphia Negro: A Social Study* (1899), Du Bois explored Philadelphia's African American community, identifying both the strengths and the weaknesses of people who were dealing with overwhelming social problems on a day-to-day basis. He

challenged the belief—widespread at that time—that blacks were inferior to whites, and he blamed white prejudice for creating the problems that African Americans faced. He also criticized successful people of color for being so eager to win white acceptance that they gave up all ties with the black community, which needed their help.

Du Bois described race as the major problem facing the United States in the twentieth century. Early in his career, he was hopeful about overcoming racial divisions. By the end of his life, however, he had grown bitter, believing that little had changed. At the age of ninety-three, Du Bois left the United States for Ghana, where he died two years later.

WHAT DO YOU THINK?

1. If he were alive today, what do you think Du Bois would say about racial inequality in the twenty-first century?

2. How much do you think African Americans today experience a "double consciousness"?

3. In what ways can sociology help us understand and reduce racial conflict?

Sources: Based in part on Baltzell (1967) and Du Bois (1967, orig. 1899).

The Symbolic-Interaction Approach

The structural-functional and social-conflict approaches share a **macro-level orientation,** *a broad focus on social structures that shape society as a whole.* Macro-level sociology takes in the big picture, rather like observing a city from high above in a helicopter and seeing how highways help people move from place to place or how housing differs from rich to poor neighborhoods. Sociology also uses a **micro-level orientation,** *a close-up focus on social interaction in specific situations.* Exploring urban life in this way occurs at street level, where you might watch how children invent games on a school playground or how pedestrians respond to homeless people they pass on the street. The **symbolic-interaction approach,** then, is *a framework for building theory that sees society as the product of the everyday interactions of individuals.*

How does "society" result from the ongoing experiences of tens of millions of people? One answer, explained in Chapter 6 ("Social Interaction in Everyday Life"), is that society is nothing more than the shared reality that people construct as they interact. Human beings live in a world of symbols, attaching *meaning* to virtually everything, from the words on this page to the wink of an eye. "Reality," therefore, is simply how we define our surroundings, our obligations toward others, and even our own identities.

The symbolic-interaction approach has roots in the thinking of Max Weber (1864–1920), a German sociologist who emphasized the need to understand a setting from the point of view of the people in it. Weber's approach is discussed in detail in Chapter 4 ("Society").

Since Weber's time, sociologists have taken micro-level sociology in a number of directions. Chapter 5 ("Socialization")

DISCUSS: Use the Applying theory tables in this text to assess student understanding of each theoretical approach.

NOTE: Encourage students to respond to all the "Check Your Learning" questions in the text, or use these questions to develop class discussion.

MAKING THE GRADE

The Applying Theory table summarizes the three major theoretical approaches in sociology. Study the table to be sure you understand each one.

APPLYING THEORY

Major Theoretical Approaches

	Structural-Functional Approach	Social-Conflict Approach	Symbolic-Interaction Approach
What is the level of analysis?	Macro-level	Macro-level	Micro-level
What image of society does the approach have?	Society is a system of interrelated parts that is relatively stable. Each part works to keep society operating in an orderly way. Members generally agree about what is morally right and morally wrong.	Society is a system of social inequalities based on class (Marx), gender (feminism and gender-conflict approach), and race (race-conflict approach). Society operates to benefit some categories of people and harm others. Social inequality causes conflict that leads to social change.	Society is an ongoing process. People interact in countless settings using symbolic communications. The reality people experience is variable and changing.
What core questions does the approach ask?	How is society held together? What are the major parts of society? How are these parts linked? What does each part do to help society work?	How does society divide a population? How do advantaged people protect their privileges? How do disadvantaged people challenge the system seeking change?	How do people experience society? How do people shape the reality they experience? How do behavior and meaning change from person to person and from one situation to another?

discusses the ideas of George Herbert Mead (1863–1931), who explored how our personalities develop as a result of social experience. Chapter 6 ("Social Interaction in Everyday Life") presents the work of Erving Goffman (1922–1982), whose *dramaturgical analysis* describes how we resemble actors on a stage as we play our various roles. Other contemporary sociologists, including George Homans and Peter Blau, have developed *social-exchange analysis.* In their view, social interaction is guided by what each person stands to gain or lose from the interaction. In the ritual of courtship, for example, people seek mates who offer at least as much—in terms of physical attractiveness, intelligence, and wealth—as they offer in return.

CRITICAL REVIEW Without denying the existence of macro-level social structures such as the family and social class, the symbolic-interaction approach reminds us that society basically amounts to *people interacting.* That is, micro-level sociology tries to show how individuals actually experience society.

But on the other side of the coin, by focusing on what is unique in each social scene, this approach risks overlooking the widespread influence of culture, as well as factors such as class, gender, and race.

CHECK YOUR LEARNING How does a micro-level analysis differ from a macro-level analysis? Provide an illustration of a micro-level social pattern and another of a social pattern that operates at a macro level.

The Applying Theory table summarizes the main characteristics of sociology's three major theoretical approaches: the structural-functional approaches, the social-conflict approach, and the symbolic-interaction approach. Each of these approaches is helpful in answering particular kinds of questions about society. However, the fullest understanding of our social world comes from using all three, as you can see in the following analysis of sports in the United States.

● SEEING SOCIOLOGY
in Everyday Life

Apply the three theoretical approaches to the issues that opened this chapter—love and marriage. Consider questions such as these: What categories of people are you most likely to date? Why? Why are today's younger college students likely to wait many more years to marry than students did fifty years ago?

Applying the Approaches: The Sociology of Sports

Who among us doesn't enjoy sports? Children as young as six or seven take part in organized sports, and many teens become skilled at three or more. Weekend television is filled with sporting events for viewers of all ages, and whole sections of our newspapers are devoted to teams, players, and scores. In the United States, top players such as Mark McGwire (baseball), Tiger Woods (golf), and Serena Williams (tennis) are among our most famous celebrities. Sports in the United States are also a multibillion-dollar industry. What can we learn by applying sociology's three theoretical approaches to this familiar part of everyday life?

The Functions of Sports

A structural-functional approach directs our attention to the ways in which sports help society operate. The manifest functions of sports include providing recreation as well as offering a means of getting in physical shape and a relatively harmless way to let off steam. Sports have important latent functions as well, from building social relationships to creating tens of thousands of jobs across the country. Sports encourage competition and the pursuit of success, both of which are values that are central to our society's way of life.

Sports also have dysfunctional consequences. For example, colleges and universities that try to field winning teams sometimes recruit students for their athletic skill rather than their academic ability. This practice not only lowers the academic standards of a school but also shortchanges athletes, who spend little time doing the academic work that will prepare them for later careers (Upthegrove, Roscigno, & Charles, 1999).

Sports and Conflict

A social-conflict analysis of sports points out that the games people play reflect their social standing. Some sports—including tennis, swimming, golf, sailing, and skiing—are expensive, so taking part is largely limited to the well-to-do. Football, baseball, and basketball, however, are accessible to people at almost all income levels.

Throughout history, sports have been oriented mostly toward males. For example, the first modern Olympic Games, held in 1896, barred women from competition; in the United States, Little League

teams in most parts of the country have only recently let girls play. Traditional ideas that girls and women lack the strength to play sports have now been widely rejected. But our society still encourages men to become athletes while expecting women to be attentive observers and cheerleaders. At the college level, men's athletics attracts a greater amount of attention and resources compared to women's athletics, and men greatly outnumber women as coaches, even in women's sports (Welch & Sigelman, 2007). At the professional level, women also take a back seat to men, particularly in the sports with the most earnings and social prestige.

For decades, big league sports excluded people of color, who were forced to form leagues of their own. Only in 1947 did Major League Baseball admit the first African American player when Jackie Robinson joined the Brooklyn Dodgers. More than fifty years later, professional baseball honored Robinson's amazing career by retiring his number 42 on *all* of the teams in the league. In 2007, African Americans (13 percent of the U.S. population) accounted for 8 percent of Major League Baseball players, 66 percent of National Football League (NFL) players, and 76 percent of National Basketball Association (NBA) players (Lapchick, 2008).

One reason for the high number of African Americans in many professional sports is that athletic performance—in terms of batting average or number of points scored per game—can be precisely measured and is not influenced by racial prejudice. It is also

As the television show *Friday Night Lights* makes clear, sports are an important element of social life in countless communities across the United States. Sociology's three theoretical approaches all contribute to our understanding of the role of sports in society.

DISCUSS: Ask the class to explain the pattern shown in Figure 1–2. Can individual traits such as talent and motivation account for stacking? How can society itself create this pattern?

DISCUSS: Ask the class to identify specific questions about sports that reflect each of sociology's three major theoretical approaches.

MAKING THE GRADE

Figures are useful because they contain a lot of information in a small space. In Figure 1.2, look first at the title to see what the figure shows. Then read the caption, which should summarize a pattern. Then look at the art to see the pattern for yourself.

76% of quarterbacks but only 2% of cornerbacks are white.

Diversity Snapshot

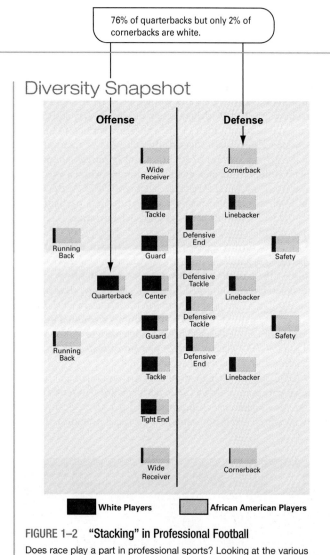

White Players   **African American Players**

FIGURE 1–2   **"Stacking" in Professional Football**

Does race play a part in professional sports? Looking at the various positions in professional football, we see that white players are more likely to play the central and offensive positions. What do you make of this pattern?

Source: Lapchick (2008).

But racial discrimination still exists in professional sports. For one thing, race is linked to the *positions* athletes play on the field, in a pattern called "stacking." Figure 1–2 shows the results of a study of race in football. Notice that white athletes are much more likely than African American athletes to play offense and to take the central positions on both sides of the line. More broadly, African Americans have a large share of players in only five sports: baseball, basketball, football, boxing, and track. In all professional sports, the vast majority of managers, head coaches, and owners of sports teams are white (Lapchick, 2008).

Although many individual players get supersized salaries and millions of fans enjoy following their teams, sports are a big business that provides big profits for a small number of people (predominantly white men). In sum, sports in the United States are bound up with inequalities based on gender, race, and economic power.

Sports as Interaction

At the micro-level, a sporting event is a complex, face-to-face interaction. In part, play is guided by the players' assigned positions and the rules of the game. But players are also spontaneous and unpredictable. Following the symbolic-interaction approach, we see sports less as a system than as an ongoing process.

From this point of view, too, we expect each player to understand the game a little differently. Some players enjoy a setting of stiff competition; for others, love of the game may be greater than the need to win.

In addition, the behavior of any single player may change over time. A rookie in professional baseball, for example, may feel self-conscious during the first few games in the big leagues but go on to develop a comfortable sense of fitting in with the team. Coming to feel at home on the field was slow and painful for Jackie Robinson, who knew that many white players, and millions of white fans, resented his presence. In time, however, his outstanding ability and his confident and cooperative manner won him the respect of the entire nation.

The three theoretical approaches—the structural-functional approach, the social-conflict approach, and the symbolic-interaction approach—provide different insights into sports, and none is more correct than the others. Applied to any issue, each approach generates its own interpretations. To appreciate fully the power of the sociological perspective, you should become familiar with all three.

The Controversy & Debate box discusses the use of the sociological perspective and reviews many of the ideas presented in this chapter. This box raises a number of questions that will help you understand how sociological generalizations differ from the common stereotypes we encounter every day.

true that some people of color make a particular effort to excel in athletics, where they see greater opportunity than in other careers (S. Steele, 1990; Edwards, 2000; Harrison, 2000). In recent years, in fact, African American athletes have earned higher salaries, on average, than white players.

SEEING SOCIOLOGY
in Everyday Life

Can you recall hearing someone use a stereotype about some category of students on your campus? How valid do you think the stereotype is?

stereotype a simplified description applied to every person in some category

CONTROVERSY & DEBATE

Is Sociology Nothing More than Stereotypes?

JENA: (*raising her eyes from her notebook*) Today in sociology class, we talked about stereotypes.

MARCIA: (*trying to focus on her science lab*) OK, here's one: Roommates don't like to be disturbed when they're studying.

JENA: Seriously, my studious friend, we all have stereotypes, even professors.

MARCIA: (*becoming faintly interested*) Like what?

JENA: Professor Chandler said today in class that if you're a Protestant, you're likely to kill yourself. And then Yannina—this girl from, I think, Ecuador—says something like, "You Americans are rich, you marry, and you love to divorce!"

MARCIA: My brother said to me last week that "everybody knows you have to be black to play professional basketball." Now there's a stereotype!

College students, like everyone else, are quick to make generalizations about people. And as this chapter has explained, sociologists, too, love to generalize by looking for social patterns. However, beginning students of sociology may wonder if generalizations aren't really the same thing as stereotypes. For example, are the statements reported by Jena and Marcia true generalizations or false stereotypes?

Let's first be clear that a **stereotype** is *a simplified description applied to every person in some category*. Each of the statements made at the beginning of this box is a stereotype that is false for three reasons. First, rather than describing averages, each statement describes every person in some category in exactly the same way; second, even though many stereotypes often contain an element of truth, each statement ignores facts and distorts reality; and third, each statement seems to be motivated by bias,

sounding more like a "put-down" than a fair-minded observation.

What about sociology? If our discipline looks for social patterns and makes generalizations, does it express stereotypes? The answer is no, for three reasons. First, *sociologists do not carelessly apply any generalization to everyone in a category*. Second, *sociologists make sure that a generalization squares with the available facts*. And third, *sociologists offer generalizations fair-mindedly, with an interest in getting at the truth*.

Jena remembered her professor saying (although not in quite the same words) that the suicide rate among Protestants is higher than among Catholics or Jews. Based on information presented earlier in this chapter, that is a true statement. However, the way Jena incorrectly reported the classroom remark—"If you're a Protestant, you're likely to kill yourself"—is not good sociology. It is not a true generalization because the vast majority of Protestants do no such thing. It would be just as wrong to jump to the conclusion that a particular friend, because he is a Protestant male,

is about to end his own life. (Imagine refusing to lend money to a roommate who happens to be a Baptist, explaining, "Well, given the way people like you commit suicide, I might never get paid back!")

Second, sociologists shape their generalizations to the available facts. A more factual version of the statement Yannina made in class is that on average, the U.S. population does have a high standard of living, almost everyone in our society does marry at some point in life, and although few people take pleasure in divorcing, our divorce rate is also among the world's highest.

Third, sociologists try to be fair-minded and want to get at the truth. The statement made by Marcia's brother, about African Americans and basketball, is an unfair stereotype rather than good sociology for two reasons. First, it is simply not true, and second, it seems motivated by bias rather than truth-seeking.

The bottom line is that good sociological generalizations are *not* the same as harmful stereotyping. A college sociology course is an excellent setting for getting at the truth behind common stereotypes. The classroom encourages discussion and offers the factual information you need to decide whether a particular statement is a valid sociological generalization or just a stereotype.

WHAT DO YOU THINK?

1. Can you think of a common stereotype of sociologists? What is it? After reading this box, do you still think it is valid?

2. Do you think taking a sociology course can help correct people's stereotypes? Why or why not?

3. Can you think of a stereotype of your own that might be challenged by sociological analysis?

A sociology classroom is a good place to get at the truth behind common stereotypes.

Seeing Sociology in Everyday Life

"Why do couples marry?"

We asked this question at the beginning of this chapter. The commonsense answer is that people marry because they are in love. But as this chapter has explained, society guides our everyday lives, affecting what we do, think, and feel. Look at the three photographs, each showing a couple who, we can assume, is "in love." In each case, can you provide some of the rest of the story? By looking at the categories that the people involved represent, explain how society is at work in bringing the two people together.

> **HINT** Society is at work on many levels. Consider (1) rules about same-sex and other-sex marriage, (2) laws defining the number of people who may marry, (3) the importance of race and ethnicity, (4) the importance of social class, (5) the importance of age, and (6) the importance of social exchange (what each partner offers the other). All societies enforce various rules that state who should or should not marry whom.

Jada Pinkett met Will Smith in 1995 when she auditioned for a part on his hit show, *The Fresh Prince of Bel Air*. Two years later, they married. What social patterns do you see?

In 1997, during the fourth season of her hit TV show, *Ellen*, Ellen DeGeneres "came out" as a lesbian, which put her on the cover of *Time* magazine. Since then, she has been an activist on behalf of gay and lesbian issues. Following California's brief legalization of same-sex marriage in 2008, she married her longtime girlfriend, Australian actress Portia de Rossi.

In 2000, at the age of fifty-six, Michael Douglas ended a twenty-three-year marriage in order to marry actress Catherine Zeta-Jones, who was then thirty-one. How likely is it that a fifty-six-year-old woman would marry a thirty-one-year-old man?

Applying SOCIOLOGY in Everyday Life

1. Analyze the marriages of your parents, other family members, and friends in terms of class, race, age, and other factors. What evidence can you find that society guides the feeling we call "love"?

2. Figure 18–2 on page 476 shows the U.S. divorce rate over the past century. Using the sociological perspective, and with an eye to the timeline inside the back cover of this book, try to identify societal factors that caused the divorce rate to rise or fall.

3. Explore your local area, and draw a sociological map of the community. Include the types of buildings (for example, "big, single-family homes," "rundown business district," "new office buildings," "student apartments") found in various places, and guess at the categories of people who live or work there. What patterns do you see?

MAKING THE GRADE

CHAPTER 1 The Sociological Perspective

What Is the Sociological Perspective?

The **SOCIOLOGICAL PERSPECTIVE** reveals the power of society to shape individual lives.

- What we commonly think of as personal choice—whether or not to go to college, how many children we will have, even the decision to end our own life—is affected by social forces.
- Peter Berger described the sociological perspective as "seeing the general in the particular."
- C. Wright Mills called this point of view the "sociological imagination," claiming it transforms personal troubles into public issues.
- The experience of being an outsider or of living through a social crisis can encourage people to use the sociological perspective.

`pp. 2–6`

sociology (p. 2) the systematic study of human society

sociological perspective (p. 2) the special point of view of sociology that sees general patterns of society in the lives of particular people

The Importance of a Global Perspective

Where we live—in a **high-income country** like the United States, a **middle-income country** such as Brazil, or a **low-income country** such as Mali—shapes the lives we lead.

`pp. 6–7`

Many social problems that we face in the United States are far more serious in other countries.

`p. 8`

Learning about life in other societies helps us learn more about ourselves.

`p. 8`

Societies throughout the world are increasingly interconnected.

- New technology allows people around the world to share popular trends.
- Immigration from around the world increases the racial and ethnic diversity of the United States.
- Trade across national boundaries has created a global economy.

`pp. 7–8`

global perspective (p. 6) the study of the larger world and our society's place in it

high-income countries (p. 6) nations with the highest overall standards of living

middle-income countries (p. 6) nations with a standard of living about average for the world as a whole

low-income countries (p. 7) nations with a low standard of living in which most people are poor

Applying the Sociological Perspective

Research by sociologists plays an important role in shaping **public policy**.

`p. 8`

A background in sociology is excellent preparation for success in many different **careers**.

`pp. 9–11`

On a **personal level**, using the sociological perspective helps us see the opportunities and limits in our lives and empowers us to be active citizens.

`p. 9`

Origins of Sociology

RAPID SOCIAL CHANGE in the eighteenth and nineteenth centuries made people more aware of their surroundings and helped trigger the development of sociology:

- The **rise of an industrial economy** moved work from homes to factories, weakening the traditions that had guided community life for centuries.
- The **explosive growth of cities** created many social problems, such as crime and homelessness.
- **Political change** based on ideas of individual liberty and individual rights encouraged people to question the structure of society.

`p. 11`

AUGUSTE COMTE named sociology in 1838 to describe a new way of looking at society.

- Early philosophers had tried to describe the ideal society.
- Comte wanted to understand society as it really is by using **positivism**, a way of understanding based on science.
- Karl Marx and many later sociologists used sociology to try to make society better.

`pp. 12–13`

positivism (p. 13) a way of understanding based on science

✓ The countries that experienced the most rapid social change were those in which sociology developed first (p. 11).

Sociological Theory

A **THEORY** states how facts are related, weaving observations into insight and understanding. Sociologists use three major **THEORETICAL APPROACHES** to describe the operation of society.

p. 13

macro-level

The **STRUCTURAL-FUNCTIONAL APPROACH** explores how **social structures**—patterns of behavior, such as religious rituals or family life—work together to help society operate.
- Auguste Comte, Emile Durkheim, and Herbert Spencer helped develop the structural-functional approach.
- Thomas Merton pointed out that social structures have both **manifest functions** and **latent functions**; he also identified **social dysfunctions** as patterns that may disrupt the operation of society.

pp. 13–14

The **SOCIAL-CONFLICT APPROACH** shows how inequality creates conflict and causes change.
- Karl Marx helped develop the social-conflict approach.
- The **gender-conflict approach**, linked to **feminism**, focuses on ways in which society places men in positions of power over women. Harriet Martineau is regarded as the first woman sociologist.
- The **race-conflict approach** focuses on the advantages—including higher income, more schooling, and better health—that society gives to white people over people of color.
- W. E. B. Du Bois identified the "double consciousness" of African Americans.

pp. 14–16

 micro-level

The **SYMBOLIC-INTERACTION APPROACH** studies how people, in everyday interaction, construct reality.
- Max Weber's claim that people's beliefs and values shape society is the basis of the social-interaction approach.
- Social-exchange analysis states that social life is guided by what each person stands to gain or lose from the interaction.

pp. 17–18

See the Applying Theory table on page 18.

✓ To get the full benefit of the sociological perspective, apply all three approaches.

theory (p. 13) a statement of how and why specific facts are related

theoretical approach (p. 13) a basic image of society that guides thinking and research

structural-functional approach (p. 13) a framework for building theory that sees society as a complex system whose parts work together to promote solidarity and stability

social structure (p. 13) any relatively stable pattern of social behavior

social functions (p. 14) the consequences of any social pattern for the operation of society as a whole

manifest functions (p. 14) the recognized and intended consequences of any social pattern

latent functions (p. 14) the unrecognized and unintended consequences of any social pattern

social dysfunction (p. 14) any social pattern that may disrupt the operation of society

social-conflict approach (p. 15) a framework for building theory that sees society as an arena of inequality that generates conflict and change

gender-conflict approach (p. 15) a point of view that focuses on inequality and conflict between women and men

feminism (p. 15) support of social equality for women and men

race-conflict approach (p. 16) a point of view that focuses on inequality and conflict between people of different racial and ethnic categories

macro-level orientation (p. 17) a broad focus on social structures that shape society as a whole

micro-level orientation (p. 17) a close-up focus on social interaction in specific situations

symbolic-interaction approach (p. 17) a framework for building theory that sees society as the product of the everyday interactions of individuals

Applying the Approaches: The Sociology of Sports

The Functions of Sports

The structural-functional approach looks at how sports help society function smoothly.
- Manifest functions of sports include providing recreation, a means of getting in physical shape, and a relatively harmless way to let off steam.
- Latent functions of sports include building social relationships and creating thousands of jobs.

p. 19

stereotype (p. 21) a simplified description applied to every person in some category

Sports and Conflict

The social-conflict approach looks at the links between sports and social inequality.
- Historically, sports have benefited men more than women.
- Some sports are accessible mainly to affluent people.
- Racial discrimination exists in professional sports.

pp. 19–20

Sports as Interaction

The social-interaction approach looks at the different meanings and understandings people have of sports.
- Within a team, players affect each other's understanding of the sport.
- The reaction of the public can affect how players perceive their sport.

p. 20

✓ Sociology helps us understand the difference between well-grounded generalizations and unfair stereotypes (p. 21).

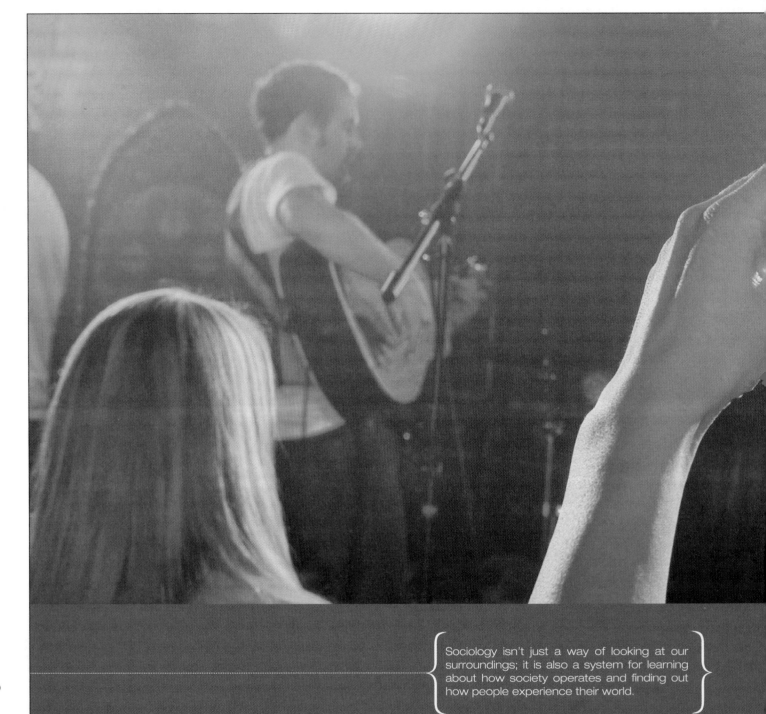

{ Sociology isn't just a way of looking at our surroundings; it is also a system for learning about how society operates and finding out how people experience their world. }

CHAPTER 2

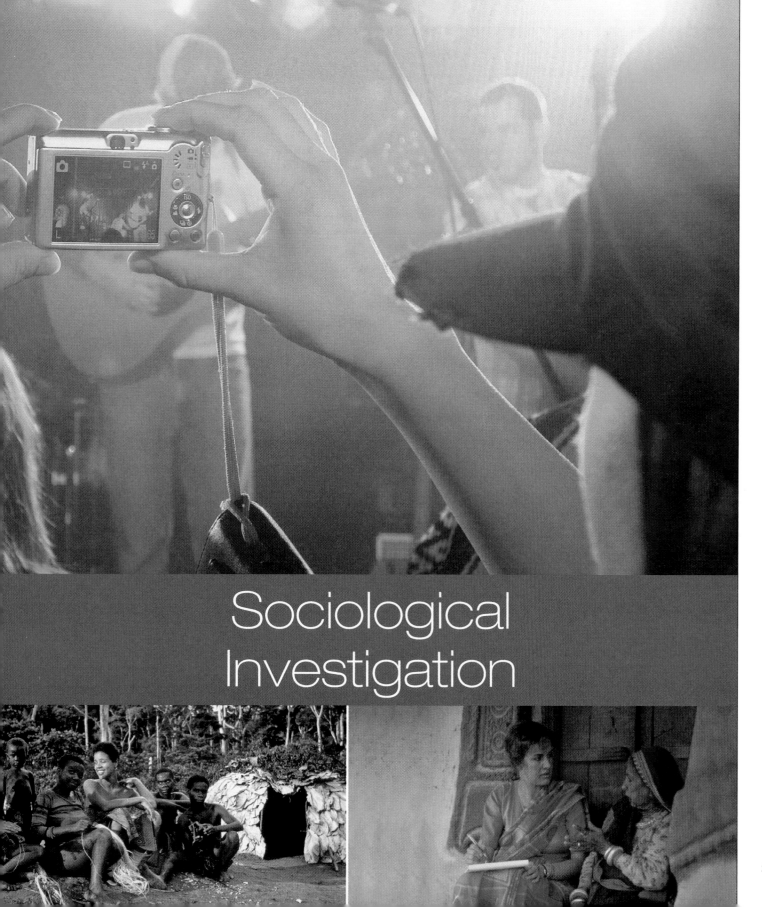

Sociological Investigation

SUPPLEMENTS: The *Instructor's Manual* contains an annotated outline of Chapter 2, supplemental lecture material, and suggestions for class discussion.

Q: "Everything should be made as simple as possible, but not one bit simpler." Albert Einstein

NOTE: Science and religion do not conflict but complement one another. Scientific truths involve proximate causes of events; religious truths deal with ultimate causes.

Q: "Plato is dear to me, but dearer still is truth." Aristotle

CHAPTER OVERVIEW

This chapter explains how sociologists "do" sociology. First, it looks at science as a way of knowing and then discusses two limitations to scientific sociology that are addressed by two other approaches to knowing—interpretive sociology and critical sociology. Finally, it explains four methods of data collection.

While on a visit to Atlanta during the winter holiday season, the sociologist Lois Benjamin (1991) called up the mother of an old college friend. Benjamin was eager to learn about Sheba; both women had dreamed about earning a graduate degree, landing a teaching job, and writing books. Now a successful university professor, Benjamin had seen her dream come true. But as she soon found out, this was not the case with Sheba.

Benjamin recalled early signs of trouble. After college, Sheba had begun graduate work at a Canadian university. But in letters to Benjamin, Sheba became more and more critical of the world and seemed to be cutting herself off from others. Some classmates wondered if she was suffering from a personality disorder. But as Sheba saw it, the problem was racism. As an African American woman, she felt she was the target of racial hostility. Before long, she flunked out of school, blaming the failure on her white professors. At this point, she left North America, earning a Ph.D. in England and then settling in Nigeria. Benjamin had not heard from her friend in the years since.

Benjamin was happy to hear that Sheba had returned to Atlanta. But her delight dissolved into shock when she saw Sheba and realized that her friend had suffered a mental breakdown and was barely responsive to anyone.

For months, Sheba's emotional collapse troubled Benjamin. Obviously, Sheba was suffering from serious psychological problems. Having felt the sting of racism herself, Benjamin wondered if this might have played a part in Sheba's story. Partly as a tribute to her old friend, Benjamin set out to explore the effects of race in the lives of bright, well-educated African Americans in the United States.

Benjamin knew she was calling into question the common belief that race is less of a barrier than it used to be, especially to talented African Americans (W. J. Wilson, 1978). But her own experiences—and Sheba's too, she believed—seemed to contradict such thinking.

To test her ideas, Benjamin spent the next two years asking 100 successful African Americans across the country how race affected their lives. In the words of these "Talented One Hundred"[1] men and women, she found evidence that even among privileged African Americans, racism remains a heavy burden.

Later in this chapter, we will take a closer look at Lois Benjamin's research. For now, notice how the sociological perspective helped her spot broad social patterns in the lives of individuals. Just as important, Benjamin's work shows us the *doing* of sociology, the process of *sociological investigation*.

Many people think that scientists work only in laboratories, carefully taking measurements using complex equipment. But as this chapter explains, although some sociologists do conduct scientific research in laboratories, most work on neighborhood streets, in homes and workplaces, in schools and hospitals, in bars and prisons—in short, wherever people can be found.

This chapter examines the methods that sociologists use to conduct research. Along the way, we shall see that research involves not just ways of gathering information but controversies about values: Should researchers strive to be objective? Or should they point to the need for change? Certainly Lois Benjamin did not begin her study just to show that racism exists; she wanted to bring racism out in the open as a way to challenge it. We shall tackle questions of values after presenting the basics of sociological investigation.

---

[1] W. E. B. Du Bois used "The Talented Tenth" to refer to African American leaders.

Q: "There are other avenues to knowledge besides the objective experience of our senses." Ralf Dahrendorf

NOTE: Empiricism (the Greek root means "experience") is the philosophical doctrine that only the senses support claims of truth. The closely linked concept of positivism defines truth as "positive" facts based on sensory experience and dismisses as speculation metaphysical or theological claims about ultimate causes of events.

science a logical system that develops knowledge from direct, systematic observation

empirical evidence information we can verify with our senses

Basics of Sociological Investigation

Sociological investigation starts with two simple requirements. The first was the focus of Chapter 1: *Apply the sociological perspective.* This point of view reveals curious patterns of behavior all around us that call for further study. It was Lois Benjamin's sociological imagination that prompted her to wonder how race affects the lives of talented African Americans.

This brings us to the second requirement: *Be curious and ask questions.* Benjamin wanted to learn more about how race affects people who are high achievers. She began by asking questions: Who are the leaders of this nation's black community? What effect does being part of a racial minority have on their view of themselves? On the way white people perceive them and their work?

Seeing the world sociologically and asking questions are basic to sociological investigation. As we look for answers, we need to realize that there are various kinds of "truth."

Science as One Form of Truth

Saying that we "know" something can mean many things. Most people in the United States, for instance, say they believe in God. Few claim to have direct contact with God, but they say they believe all the same. We call this kind of knowing "belief" or "faith."

A second kind of truth comes from recognized experts. Students with a health problem, for example, may consult a campus physician or search the Internet for articles written by experts in the field.

A third type of truth is based on simple agreement among ordinary people. Most of us in the United States would probably say we "know" that sexual intercourse among ten-year-old children is wrong. But why? Mostly because just about everyone says it is.

People's "truths" differ the world over, and we often encounter "facts" at odds with our own. Imagine yourself a Peace Corps volunteer just arrived in a small, traditional village in Latin America. Your job is to help local people grow more crops. On your first day in the fields, you observe a strange practice: After planting seeds, the farmers lay a dead fish on top of the soil. When you ask about this, they explain that the fish is a gift to the god of the harvest. A village elder adds sternly that the harvest was poor one year when no fish were offered.

From that society's point of view, using fish as gifts to the harvest god makes sense. The people believe in it, their experts endorse it, and everyone seems to agree that the system works. But with scientific training in agriculture, you have to shake your head and wonder. The scientific "truth" in this situation is something entirely different: The decomposing fish fertilize the ground, producing a better crop.

Science represents a fourth way of knowing. **Science** is *a logical system that bases knowledge on direct, systematic observation.* Stand-

In a complex and ever-changing world, there are many different "truths." This Peace Corps volunteer on a small island in the South Pacific learned a crucial lesson—that other people often see things in a different way. There is great value in our own scientific approach to truth, but there are also important truths in the ancient traditions of people living around the world.

ing apart from faith, the wisdom of "experts," and general agreement, scientific knowledge rests on **empirical evidence,** that is, *information we can verify with our senses.*

Our Peace Corps example does not mean that people in traditional villages ignore what their senses tell them or that members of technologically advanced societies use only science to know things. A medical researcher using science to develop a new drug for treating cancer, for example, may still practice her religion as a matter of faith, turn to financial experts when making decisions about money, and pay attention to the political opinions of her family and friends. In short, we all hold various kinds of truths at the same time.

Common Sense versus Scientific Evidence

Like the sociological perspective, scientific evidence sometimes challenges our common sense. Here are six statements that many North Americans assume are true:

1. **"Poor people are far more likely than rich people to break the law."** Not true. If you regularly watch television shows like *COPS,* you might think that police arrest only people from "bad" neighborhoods. Chapter 9 ("Deviance") explains that poor people do stand out in the official arrest statistics. But research also shows that police and prosecutors are more likely to treat well-to-do people more leniently, as when a Hollywood celebrity is accused

Q: "The truth is rarely pure and never simple." Oscar Wilde

NOTE: Many traditional people (especially today) have a good sense of science. There is an old joke about a tribal shaman using his power to make rain, which always comes soon after. A visitor asks him, "I can't help but notice that you only do your rain ritual when dark clouds gather in the sky." "Of course," he responds, "I would be a fool to hope for rain when there are no clouds!"

GLOBAL: People in other times and places recognize different "truths." Regarding childhood sexuality, the Melanesians of New Guinea typically shrug off as harmless sexual intercourse among children too young to reproduce.

NOTE: Two examples of misleading common sense: The birth rate of "welfare mothers" is actually below that of all women; remarriages are more prone to divorce than first marriages.

SEEING SOCIOLOGY IN EVERYDAY LIFE

Is What We Read in the Popular Press True? The Case of Extramarital Sex

Every day, we see stories in newspapers and magazines that tell us what people think and how they behave. But a lot of what we read turns out to be misleading or even untrue.

Take the issue of extramarital sex, which refers to a married person having sex with someone other than his or her spouse. A look at the cover of many of the so-called women's magazines you find in the checkout aisle at the supermarket or a quick reading of the advice column in your local newspaper might lead you to think that extramarital sex is a major issue facing married couples. The popular media seem full of stories about how to keep your spouse from "cheating" or pointing out clues to tip you off that your spouse is having an affair. Most of the studies reported in the popular press and on Internet Web sites suggest that more than half of married people—women as well as men—cheat on their spouses.

But is extramarital sex really that widespread? No. Researchers who conduct sound sociological investigation have found that in a given year, only about 3 or 4 percent of married people have an extramarital relationship and no more than 15 to 20 percent of married people have *ever* done so. Why, then, do surveys in the popular media report rates of extramarital sex that are so much higher? We can answer this question by taking a look at who fills out "pop" surveys.

First, it is people with a personal interest in some topic who are most likely to respond to an offer to complete a survey on that topic. For this reason, people who have had personal experience with extramarital sex (either their own behavior or their partner's) are more likely to show up in these studies. In contrast, studies correctly done by skilled researchers involve carefully selected subjects so that the results are representative of the entire population.

Second, because the readership of the magazines and online sources that conduct these surveys is, on average, young, their surveys end up attracting a high proportion of young respondents. And one thing we know about young people—married or unmarried—is that they are more likely to have sex. For example, the typical married person who is thirty years of age is more than twice as likely to have had an extramarital relationship than the typical married person over age sixty.

Third, women are much more likely than men to read the popular magazines that feature sex surveys. Therefore, women are more likely to fill out the surveys. In recent decades, the share of women (especially younger women) who have had extramarital sex has gone up. Why are today's younger women more likely than women a generation or two earlier to have had extramarital sex? Probably because women today are working outside of the home and many are traveling as part of their job. This lifestyle gives today's women a wider social network that brings them into contact with more men.

Chapter 8 ("Sexuality and Society") takes a close look at sexual patterns, including extramarital relationships. For now, just remember that a lot of what you read in the popular media and online may not be as true as some people think.

WHAT DO YOU THINK?

1. Can you think of other issues in which pop media surveys may give misleading information? What are they?

2. Explain why we should have more trust in the results of sound research carried out by skilled sociologists than in the surveys conducted by the popular media.

3. Do you think companies are likely to sell more magazines or newspapers if they publish "research" results that distort the truth? Explain.

Sources: T. W. Smith (2006), Black (2007), and Parker-Pope (2008).

of shoplifting or drunk driving. Some laws are even written in a way that criminalizes poor people and affluent people less.

2. **"The United States is a middle-class society in which most people are more or less equal."** False. Data presented in Chapter 11 ("Social Class in the United States") show that the richest 5 percent of U.S. families control 60 percent of the nation's total wealth, but almost half of all families have scarcely any wealth at all (Mishel, Bernstein, & Allegretto, 2009).

3. **"Most poor people don't want to work."** Wrong. Research described in Chapter 11 indicates that this statement is true of some but not most poor people. In fact, about half of poor individuals in the United States are children and elderly people who are not expected to work.

4. **"Differences in the behavior of females and males are just 'human nature.'"** Wrong again. Much of what we call "human nature" is constructed by the society in which we live, as Chapter 3 ("Culture") explains. Further, as Chapter 13 ("Gender Stratification") argues, some societies define "feminine" and "masculine" very differently from the way we do.

5. **"People change as they grow old, losing many interests as they focus on their health."** Not really. Chapter 15 ("Aging and the Elderly") reports that aging changes our personalities

NOTE: Facts, standing alone, do not constitute compelling truth. Myth (from the Greek *mythos*, meaning "story" or "word") is a means of conveying broad cultural truths without factual details. The success of the film *E.T.—The Extra-Terrestrial* resulted partly from its mythic elements: a main character who was born elsewhere, came to Earth, underwent a great testing, and finally returned to his origins. The same four elements underlie the lives of Moses, Jesus, and Superman.

Q: "Social science is part of the social world as well as a conception of it. . . . Utilitarian culture . . . fostered acute sentiments of detachment. Positivism transformed this detachment into an ideology and morality." Alvin Gouldner

Q: "The facts we see depend on where we are placed and the habits of our eyes." Walter Lippmann

positivist sociology the study of society based on scientific observation of social behavior

concept a mental construct that represents some aspect of the world in a simplified form

variable a concept whose value changes from case to case

very little. Problems of health increase in old age, but by and large, elderly people keep the distinctive personalities they have had throughout their adult lives.

6. **"Most people marry because they are in love."** Not always. To members of our society, few statements are so obvious. Surprisingly, however, in many societies, marriage has little to do with love. Chapter 18 ("Families") explains why.

These examples confirm the old saying that "it's not what we *don't* know that gets us into trouble as much as the things we *do* know that *just aren't so.*" The Seeing Sociology in Everyday Life box explains why we also need to think critically about "facts" we find in the popular media and on the Internet.

We have all been brought up hearing many widely accepted truths, being bombarded by "expert" advice in the popular media, and feeling pressure to accept the opinions of people around us. As adults, we need to evaluate more critically what we see, read, and hear. Sociology can help us do that.

Three Ways to Do Sociology

"Doing" sociology means learning more about the social world. There is more than one way to do this. Just as sociologists can use one or more theoretical approaches (described in Chapter 1, "The Sociological Perspective"), they may also use different research orientations. The following sections describe three ways to do research: positivist sociology, interpretive sociology, and critical sociology.

Positivist Sociology

Chapter 1 explained how early sociologists such as Auguste Comte and Emile Durkheim applied science to the study of society just as natural scientists investigate the physical world. **Positivist sociology,** then, is *the study of society based on systematic observation of social behavior.* A positivist approach to the world assumes that an objective reality exists "out there." The job of the scientist is to discover this reality by gathering empirical evidence, facts we can verify with our senses, say, by seeing, hearing, or touching.

Concepts, Variables, and Measurement

Let's take a closer look at how science works. A basic element of science is the **concept,** *a mental construct that represents some part of the world in a simplified form.* Sociologists use concepts to label aspects of social life, including "the family" and "the economy," and to categorize people in terms of their "gender" or "social class."

A **variable** is *a concept whose value changes from case to case.* The familiar variable "price," for example, has a value that changes from item to item in a supermarket. Similarly, we use the concept "social

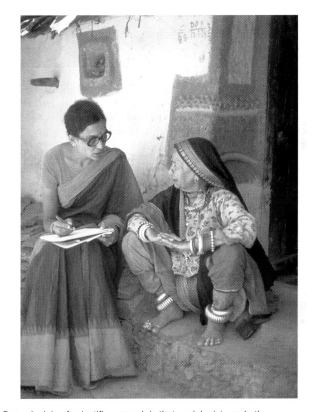

One principle of scientific research is that sociologists and other investigators should try to be objective in their work, so that their personal values and beliefs do not distort their findings. But such a detached attitude may discourage the connection needed for people to open up and share information. Thus sociologists have to decide how much to pursue objectivity and how much to show their own feelings.

class" to describe people's social standing as "upper-class," "middle-class," "working-class," or "lower-class."

The use of variables depends on **measurement,** *a procedure for determining the value of a variable in a specific case.* Some variables are easy to measure, as when you step on a scale to see how much you weigh. But measuring sociological variables can be far more difficult. For example, how would you measure a person's social class? You might start by evaluating the person's clothing, patterns of speech, or home and neighborhood. Or trying to be more precise, you might seek details about the person's income, occupation, and education.

Because most variables can be measured in more than one way, sociologists often have to decide which factors to consider. For example, having a very high income might qualify a person as "upper-class." But what if the income comes from selling automobiles, an

NOTE: Awards in medical malpractice cases illustrate wild variations in statistical measures. One study noted that the modal settlement was zero (the most common award); the median award was around $20,000 because most awards are small; yet the mean award was about $100,000 because the average is skewed upward by a few high awards.

NOTE: U.S. family income (mean of $78,845; median of $61,355) provides another example of a mean pulled up by extreme scores.

measurement (p.31) a procedure for determining the value of a variable in a specific case

operationalize a variable specifying exactly what is to be measured before assigning a value to a variable

reliability consistency in measurement

validity actually measuring exactly what you intend to measure

SEEING SOCIOLOGY in Everyday Life

Write three questions you might ask to measure people's social class. Why would you have to ask more than one question?

SEEING SOCIOLOGY IN EVERYDAY LIFE

Three Useful (and Simple) Descriptive Statistics

The admissions office at your school is preparing a new brochure, and as part of your work-study job in that office, your supervisor asks you to determine the average salary received by last year's graduating class. To keep matters simple, assume that you talk to only seven members of the class (a real study would require contacting many more) and gather the following data on their present incomes:

$30,000	$42,000	$22,000
$165,000	$22,000	$35,000
$34,000		

Sociologists use three different descriptive statistics to report averages. The simplest statistic is the *mode,* the value that occurs *most often* in a series of numbers. In this example, the mode is $22,000, since that value occurs two times and each of the others occurs only once. If all the values were to occur only once, there would be no mode; if two different values each occurred two or three times, there would be two modes.

Although it is easy to identify, sociologists rarely use the mode because it reflects only some of the numbers and is therefore a crude measure of the "average."

A more common statistic, the *mean,* refers to the *arithmetic average* of a series of numbers, calculated by adding all the values together and dividing by the number of cases. The sum of the seven incomes is $350,000. Dividing by 7 yields a mean income of $50,000. But notice that the mean in this case is not a very good "average" because it is higher than six of the seven incomes and is not particularly close to any of the actual numbers. Because the mean is "pulled" up or down by an especially high or low value (in this case, the $165,000 paid to one graduate, an athlete who signed as a rookie with the Cincinnati Reds farm team), it can give a distorted picture of data that include one or more extreme scores.

The *median* is the *middle case,* the value that occurs midway in a series of numbers arranged from lowest to highest. Here the median income for the seven graduates is $34,000, because when the numbers are placed in order from lowest to highest, this value occurs exactly in the middle, with three incomes higher and three lower. (With an even number of cases, the median is halfway between the two middle cases.) The median (unlike the mean) is not affected by any extreme scores. In such cases, the median gives a better picture of what is "average" than the mean.

WHAT DO YOU THINK?

1. Your grade point average (GPA) is an example of an average. Is it a mode, a median, or a mean? Explain.

2. Sociologists generally use the median instead of the mean when they study people's incomes. Can you see why?

3. Do a quick calculation of the mean, median, and mode for these simple numbers: 1, 2, 5, 6, 6.

Answers: mode = 6, median = 5, mean = 4.

---

occupation most people think of as "middle-class"? Would having only an eighth-grade education make the person "lower-class"? In a case like this, sociologists usually combine these three measures—income, occupation, and education—to determine social class, as described in Chapter 10 ("Social Stratification") and Chapter 11 ("Social Class in the United States").

Sociologists also face the problem of dealing with huge numbers of people. For example, how do you report income for thousands or even millions of U.S. families? Listing streams of numbers would carry little meaning and tells us nothing about the people as a whole. To solve this problem, sociologists use *descriptive statistics* to state what is "average" for a large number of people. The Seeing Sociology in Everyday Life box explains how.

Defining Concepts   Measurement is always somewhat arbitrary because the value of any variable in part depends on how it is defined. In addition, it is easy to see that there is more than one way to measure abstract concepts such as "love," "family," or "intelligence."

Good research therefore requires that sociologists **operationalize a variable** by *specifying exactly what is to be measured before assign-*

ing a value to a variable. Before measuring the concept of "social class," for example, you would have to decide exactly what you were going to measure—say, income level, years of schooling, or occupational prestige. Sometimes sociologists measure several of these things; in such cases, they need to specify exactly how they plan to combine these variables into one overall score. The next time you read the results of a study, notice the way the researchers operationalize each variable. How they define terms can greatly affect the results.

When deciding how to operationalize variables, sociologists often take into account the opinions of the people they study. Starting in 1977, for example, researchers at the U.S. Census Bureau defined race and ethnicity in terms of making a choice from this list: white, black, Hispanic, Asian or Pacific Islander, and American Indian or Alaska Native. One problem with this system is that someone can be both Hispanic *and* white or black; similarly, people of Arab ancestry might not identify with any of these choices. Just as important, an increasing number of people in the United States are *multiracial.* Because of the changing face of the U.S. population, the 2000 census was the first one to allow people to describe their race and ethnicity by selecting more than one category and almost 7 million people did

NOTE: An independent variable in one situation may be a dependent variable in another; the designation is arbitrary and determined by the specific experiment in question.

Q: "The most incomprehensible thing about the world is the fact that it is comprehensible." Albert Einstein

Q: "Knowledge is the antidote of fear." Ralph Waldo Emerson

NOTE: Precision and accuracy have an inverse relationship: The more precise our statement, the more likely it is to be wrong. When weather forecasters predict a high of, say, 73, a week ahead, they are almost always wrong.

cause and effect a relationship in which change in one variable (the independent variable) causes change in another (the dependent variable)

Independent variable the variable that causes the change

dependent variable the variable that changes

so. The multiracial option has resulted in a more accurate description of the true diversity of the population.

Reliability and Validity For a measurement to be useful, it must be both reliable and valid. **Reliability** refers to *consistency in measurement.* A measurement is reliable if repeated measurements give the same result time after time. But consistency does not guarantee **validity,** which means *actually measuring exactly what you intend to measure.*

Getting a valid measurement is sometimes tricky. Say you want to know just how religious the students at your college are. You might ask students how often they attend religious services. But is going to a church, temple, or mosque really the same thing as being religious? People may attend religious services because of deep personal beliefs, but they may also do so out of habit or because others pressure them to go. And what about spiritual people who avoid organized religion altogether? Even when a measurement yields consistent results (making it reliable), it may not measure what we want it to (and therefore lack validity). Chapter 19 ("Religion") suggests that measuring religiosity should take account of not only participation in prayer services but also a person's beliefs and the degree to which a person lives by religious convictions. Good sociological research depends on careful measurement, which is always a challenge to researchers.

Relationships among Variables Once measurements are made, investigators can pursue the real payoff: seeing how variables are related. The scientific ideal is **cause and effect,** *a relationship in which change in one variable causes change in another.* Cause-and-effect relationships occur around us every day, as when studying hard for an exam results in a high grade. *The variable that causes the change* (in this case, how much you study) is called the **independent variable.** *The variable that changes* (the exam grade) is called the **dependent variable.** The value of one variable depends on the value of another. Linking variables in terms of cause and effect is important because it allows us to *predict* the outcome of future events—if we know one thing, we can accurately predict another. For example, knowing that studying hard results in a better exam grade, we can predict with confidence that if you do study hard for the next exam, you will receive a higher grade, and if you do not study hard, your grade will suffer.

But just because two variables change together does not mean that they are linked by a cause-and-effect relationship. For example, sociologists have long recognized that juvenile delinquency is more common among young people who live in crowded housing. Say we operationalize the variable "juvenile delinquency" as the number of times a person under the age of eighteen has been arrested, and we define "crowded housing" by a home's number of square feet of living space per person. It turns out that these variables are related: Delinquency rates are high in densely populated neighborhoods. But should we conclude that crowding in the home (in this case, the independent variable) is what causes delinquency (the dependent variable)?

FIGURE 2–1 Correlation and Cause: An Example

Correlation is not the same as cause. Here's why.

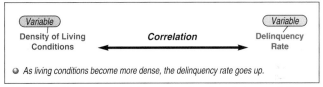

(a) If two variables increase and decrease together, they display correlation.

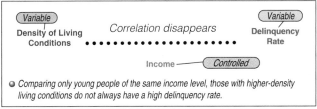

(b) Here we consider the effect of a third variable: income. Low income may cause *both* high-density living conditions *and* a high delinquency rate.

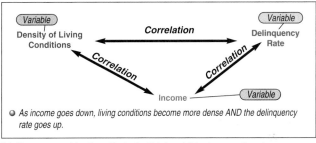

(c) When we control for income—that is, examine only young people of the same income level—we find that density of living conditions and delinquency rate no longer increase and decrease together.

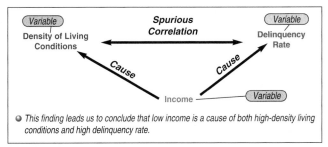

(d) Density of living conditions and delinquency rate are correlated, but their correlation is *spurious* because neither one causes the other.

NOTE: Earl Babbie suggests that we think of bad measurement as bullet holes scattered all around a target, of reliable but not valid measurement as holes clustered together on a target but not on the bull's-eye, and of reliable and valid measurement as holes clustered on the bull's-eye. Note that validity implies reliability, but not vice versa.

SOCIAL SURVEY: Members of our "scientific" society still cling to some meta-physics: 97% of General Social Survey respondents claim to know their astrological sign.

Q: "One unerring mark of the love of truth is not entertaining any proposition with greater assurance than the proofs it is built on will warrant." John Locke (1690)

correlation a relationship in which two (or more) variables change together

spurious correlation an apparent but false relationship between two (or more) variables that is caused by some other variable

control holding constant all variables except one in order to see clearly the effects of that variable

Not necessarily. **Correlation** is *a relationship in which two (or more) variables change together*. We know that density and delinquency are correlated because they change together, as shown in part (a) of Figure 2–1 on page 33. This relationship *may* mean that crowding causes more arrests, but it could also mean that some third factor is causing change in *both* of the variables under observation. To identify a third variable, think what kinds of people live in crowded housing: people with less money and few choices—the poor. Poor children are also more likely to end up with police records. In reality, crowded housing and juvenile delinquency are found together because *both* are caused by a third factor—poverty—as shown in part (b) of Figure 2–1. In short, the apparent connection between crowding and delinquency is "explained away" by a third variable—low income—that causes them both to change. So our original connection turns out to be a **spurious correlation,** *an apparent but false relationship between two (or more) variables that is caused by some other variable.*

Exposing a correlation as spurious requires a bit of detective work, assisted by a technique called **control,** *holding constant all variables except one in order to see clearly the effect of that variable.* In our example, we suspect that income level may be causing a spurious link between housing density and delinquency. To check whether the correlation between delinquency and crowding is spurious, we control for income—that is, we hold income constant by looking at only young people of one income level. If the correlation between density and delinquency remains, that is, if young people of the same income level living in more crowded housing show higher rates of arrest than young people in less crowded housing, we have more reason to think that crowding does, in fact, cause delinquency. But if the relationship disappears when we control for income, as shown in part (c) of Figure 2–1, then we know we were dealing with a spurious correlation. In fact, research shows that the correlation between crowding and delinquency just about disappears if income is controlled (Fischer, 1984). So we have now sorted out the relationship among the three variables, as illustrated in part (d) of the figure. Housing density and juvenile delinquency have a spurious correlation; evidence shows that both variables rise or fall according to income.

To sum up, correlation means only that two (or more) variables change together. To establish cause and effect, three requirements must be met: (1) a demonstrated correlation, (2) an independent (causal) variable that occurs before the dependent variable, and (3) no evidence that a third variable could be causing a spurious correlation between the two.

Natural scientists usually have an easier time than social scientists in identifying cause-and-effect relationships because most natural scientists work in laboratories, where they can control other variables. Carrying out research in a workplace or on the streets, however, makes control very difficult, so sociologists often have to settle for demonstrating only correlation. Also, human behavior is highly complex, involving dozens of causal variables at any one time, so establishing all the cause-and-effect relationships in any situation is extremely difficult.

The Ideal of Objectivity

Ten students are sitting around a dorm lounge discussing the dream vacation spot for the upcoming spring break. Do you think one place will end up being everyone's clear favorite? That hardly seems likely.

In scientific terms, each of the ten people probably operationalizes the concept "dream vacation" differently. For one, it might be a deserted, sunny beach in Mexico; for another, the choice might be New Orleans, a lively city with a very active social scene; for still another, hiking the Rocky Mountains below snow-capped peaks may be the choice. Like so many other "bests" in life, the best vacations turn out to be mostly a matter of individual taste.

Personal values are fine when it comes to choosing travel destinations, but they pose a challenge to scientific research. Remember, science assumes that reality is "out there." Scientists need to study this reality without changing it in any way, and so they strive for **objectivity,** *personal neutrality in conducting research.* Objectivity means that researchers carefully hold to scientific procedures and do not let their own attitudes and beliefs influence the results.

Scientific objectivity is an ideal rather than a reality, of course, because no one can be completely neutral. Even the topic someone chooses to study reflects a personal interest of one sort or another, as Lois Benjamin showed us in the reasons for her decision to investigate race. But the scientific ideal is to keep a professional distance or sense of detachment from the results, however they turn out. With this ideal in mind, you should do your best when conducting research to see that conscious or unconscious biases do not distort your findings. As an extra precaution, many researchers openly state their personal leanings in their research reports so that readers can interpret the conclusions with those considerations in mind.

The German sociologist Max Weber expected that people would select their research topics according to their personal beliefs and interests. Why else, after all, would one person study world hunger, another investigate the effects of racism, and still another examine how children manage in one-parent families? Knowing that people select topics that are *value-relevant,* Weber urged researchers to be *value-free* in their investigations. Only by controlling their personal feelings and opinions (as we expect any professionals to do) can researchers study the world *as it is* rather than tell us *how they think it should be.* This detachment, for Weber, is a crucial element of science that sets it apart from politics. Politicians are committed to particular outcomes; scientists try to maintain an open mind about the results of their investigations, whatever they may turn out to be.

RESOURCE: Max Weber's statement on value-free research is among the classics in the Macionis and Benokraitis reader, *Seeing Ourselves*, 8th ed.

Q: "Instructors who feel called upon to intervene in the struggles of world views and party opinions . . . may do so outside, in the marketplace, in the press, in meetings. . . . But after all it is somewhat too convenient to demonstrate one's courage in taking a stand where the audience and possible opponents are con-

demned to silence." Max Weber, "Science as a Vocation"

NOTE: Only a small proportion of social science research is actually subjected to replication (far less than in the natural sciences).

Q: "Every social theory is a tacit theory of politics [and] also a personal theory inevitably representing . . . the personal experience of the individuals who author it." Alvin Gouldner (1970)

SEEING SOCIOLOGY
in Everyday Life

Why do you think many doctors, teachers, and police officers avoid working professionally with their own children?

objectivity personal neutrality in conducting research

replication repetition of research by other researchers

A basic lesson of social research is that being observed affects how people behave. Researchers can never be certain precisely how this will occur; some people resent public attention, but others become highly animated when they think they have an audience.

Weber's argument still carries much weight, although most sociologists admit that we can never be completely value-free or even aware of all our biases. Keep in mind, however, that sociologists are not "average" people: Most are white, highly educated, and more politically liberal than the population as a whole (Klein & Stern, 2004). Remember that sociologists, like everyone else, are influenced by their social backgrounds.

One way to limit distortion caused by personal values is **replication,** *repetition of research by other investigators.* If other researchers repeat a study using the same procedures and obtain the same results, we gain confidence that the results are accurate (both reliable and valid). The need for replication in scientific investigation probably explains why the search for knowledge is called "*re*-search" in the first place.

Keep in mind that the logic of science does not guarantee objective, absolute truth. What science offers is an approach to knowledge that is *self-correcting* so that in the long run, researchers stand a good chance of limiting their biases. Objectivity and truth lie, then, not in any one study but in the scientific process itself as it continues over time.

Some Limitations of Scientific Sociology

Science is one important way of knowing. Yet, applied to social life, science has several important limitations.

1. **Human behavior is too complex for sociologists to predict any individual's actions precisely**. Astronomers calculate the movement of objects in the skies with remarkable precision, but comets and planets are unthinking objects. Humans, by contrast,

have minds of their own, so no two people react to any event (whether it be a sports victory or a natural disaster) in exactly the same way. Sociologists must therefore be satisfied with showing that *categories* of people *typically* act in one way or another. This is not a failing of sociology. It simply reflects the fact that we study creative, spontaneous people.

2. **Because humans respond to their surroundings, the presence of a researcher may affect the behavior being studied**. An astronomer's gaze has no effect on a distant comet. But most people react to being observed. Try staring at someone for a few minutes and see for yourself. People being watched may become anxious, angry, or defensive; others may be especially friendly or helpful. The act of studying people can cause their behavior to change.

3. **Social patterns vary; what is true in one time or place may not hold true in another**. The same laws of physics will apply tomorrow as today, and they hold true all around the world. But human behavior is so variable that there are no universal sociological laws.

4. **Because sociologists are part of the social world they study, they can never be 100 percent value-free when conducting social research**. Barring a laboratory mishap, chemists are rarely personally affected by what goes on in their test tubes. But sociologists live in their "test tube," the society they study. Therefore, social scientists may find it difficult to control—or even to recognize—personal values that may distort their work.

35

Q: "Truth is what serves the German people." Joseph Goebbels (who had a Ph.D.)

NOTE: In principle, the contrast between positivistic and critical sociology can be cast as a choice between "scientific correctness" (based on empirical data) and "political correctness" (based on political priorities).

NOTE: The increasing popularity of critical sociology means that more sociologists are defining "truth" not so much in terms of "what is" but in terms of "what ought to be."

Q: "Until recently, only Nazis and Stalinists spoke of 'political correctness.' It is indeed a purely totalitarian concept. It asserts the right of those in power to suppress all but the party line's official lies." Peter F. Drucker

research orientations

positivist sociology (p. 31)
the study of society based on systematic observation of social behavior

interpretive sociology
the study of society that focuses on discovering the meanings people attach to their social world

critical sociology
the study of society that focuses on the need for social change

SUMMING UP

Three Research Orientations in Sociology

	Positivist Sociology	Interpretive Sociology	Critical Sociology
What is reality?	Society is an orderly system. There is an objective reality "out there."	Society is ongoing interaction. People construct reality as they attach meanings to their behavior.	Society is patterns of inequality. Reality is that some categories of people dominate others.
How do we conduct research?	Using a scientific orientation, the researcher carefully observes behavior, gathering empirical, ideally quantitative, data. Researcher tries to be a neutral observer.	Seeking to look "deeper" than outward behavior, the researcher focuses on subjective meaning. The researcher gathers qualitative data, discovering the subjective sense people make of their world. Researcher is a participant.	Seeking to go beyond positivism's focus on studying the world as it is, the researcher is guided by politics and uses research as a strategy to bring about desired social change. Researcher is an activist.
Corresponding theoretical approach	Structural-functional approach	Symbolic-interaction approach	Social-conflict approach

Interpretive Sociology

Not all sociologists agree that science is the only way—or even the best way—to study human society. This is because, unlike planets or other elements of the natural world, humans do not simply move around as objects in ways that can be measured. Even more important, people are active creatures who attach meaning to their behavior, meaning that cannot be directly observed.

Therefore, sociologists have developed a second research orientation, known as **interpretive sociology,** *the study of society that focuses on the meanings people attach to their social world.* Max Weber, the pioneer of this framework, argued that the proper focus of sociology is *interpretation,* or understanding the meaning that people create in their everyday lives.

The Importance of Meaning

Interpretive sociology does not reject science completely, but it does change the focus of research. Interpretive sociology differs from positivist sociology in four ways. First, positivist sociology focuses on actions—on what people do—because that is what we can observe directly. Interpretive sociology, by contrast, focuses on people's understanding of their actions and their surroundings. Second, positivist sociology claims that objective reality exists "out there," but interpretive sociology counters that reality is subjective, constructed by people in the course of their everyday lives. Third, positivist sociology tends to favor *quantitative* data—numerical measurements of people's behavior—while interpretive sociology favors *qualitative* data, or researchers' perceptions of how people understand their world.

Fourth, the positivist orientation is best suited to research in a laboratory, where investigators stand back and take careful measurements. On the other hand, the interpretive orientation claims that we learn more by interacting with people, focusing on subjective meaning, and learning how they make sense of their everyday lives. This type of research is best carried out in a natural or everyday setting.

Weber's Concept of *Verstehen*

Max Weber believed the key to interpretive sociology lay in *Verstehen* (pronounced "fair-SHTAY-in"), the German word for "understanding." The interpretive sociologist does not just observe *what* people do but also tries to understand *why* they do it. The thoughts and feelings of subjects, which scientists tend to dismiss because they are difficult to measure, are the focus of the interpretive sociologist's attention.

Critical Sociology

Like the interpretive orientation, critical sociology developed in reaction to the limitations of positivist sociology. In this case, however, the problem involves the central principle of scientific research: objectivity.

Positivist sociology holds that reality is "out there" and the researcher's task is to study and document how society works. But Karl Marx, who founded the critical orientation, rejected the idea that society exists as a "natural" system with a fixed order. To assume that society is somehow "fixed," he claimed, is the same as saying that society cannot be changed. Positivist sociology, from this point of view, ends up supporting the status quo. **Critical sociology,** by contrast, is *the study of society that focuses on the need for social change.*

Q: "For the most part we do not first see and then define; we define and then see."
Walter Lippmann

Q: "Don't make the mistake of thinking human beings can't change the world. They're the only ones who ever have." Margaret Mead

NOTE: The gender issues Eichler noted are both threats to sound research and barriers to gender equality.

NOTE: Subtle gender biases are evident even in our tendency to speak of "males and females," despite the alphabetical convention that would reverse them.

MAKING THE GRADE

Imagine that you are a positivist sociologist. How might you criticize critical sociology? Now imagine that you are a critical sociologist. How might you criticize positivist sociology?

gender the personal traits and social positions that members of a society attach to being female or male

The Importance of Change

Rather than asking the scientific question "How does society work?" critical sociologists ask moral and political questions, such as "Should society exist in its present form?" Their answer to this question, typically, is that it should not. Critical sociology does not reject science completely—Marx (like critical sociologists today) used scientific method to learn about inequality. But critical sociology does reject the positivist claim that researchers should try to be "objective" and limit their work to studying the status quo.

One recent account of this orientation, echoing Marx, claims that the point of sociology is "not just to research the social world but to change it in the direction of democracy and social justice" (Feagin & Hernán, 2001:1). In making value judgments about how society should be improved, critical sociology rejects Weber's goal that researchers be value-free and emphasizes instead that they should be social activists in pursuit of greater social equality.

Sociologists using the critical orientation seek to change not just society but the character of research itself. They often identify personally with their research subjects and encourage them to help decide what to study and how to do the work. Typically, researchers and subjects use their findings to provide a voice for less powerful people and to advance the political goal of a more equal society (Hess, 1999; Feagin & Hernán, 2001; Perrucci, 2001).

Sociology as Politics

Positivist sociologists object to taking sides in this way, charging that critical sociology (whether feminist, Marxist, or of some other critical orientation) becomes political, lacks objectivity, and cannot correct for its own biases. Critical sociologists reply that *all* research is political or biased—either it calls for change or it does not; sociologists thus have no choice about their work being political, but they can choose *which* positions to support.

Critical sociology is an activist approach that ties knowledge to action and seeks not just to understand the world as it exists but also to improve it. Generally speaking, positivist sociology appeals to researchers with nonpolitical or more conservative political views; critical sociology appeals to those whose politics range from liberal to radical left.

Research Orientations and Theory

Is there a link between research orientations and sociological theory? There is no precise connection, but each of the three research orientations—positivist, interpretive, and critical—does stand closer to one of the theoretical approaches presented in Chapter 1 ("The Sociological Perspective"). The positivist orientation is linked to the structural-functional approach (because both are concerned with

If you ask only male subjects about their attitudes or actions, you may be able to support conclusions about "men" but not more generally about "people." What would a researcher have to do to ensure that research data support conclusions about all of society?

understanding society as it is), interpretive sociology to the symbolic-interaction approach (because both focus on the meanings people attach to their social world), and critical sociology to the social-conflict approach (because both seek to reduce social inequality). The Summing Up table provides a quick review of the differences among the three research orientations. Many sociologists favor one orientation over another; however, because each provides useful insights, it is a good idea to become familiar with all three (Gamson, 1999).

Gender and Research

Sociologists also know that research is affected by **gender,** *the personal traits and social positions that members of a society attach to being female or male.* Margrit Eichler (1988) identifies five ways in which gender can shape research:

1. **Androcentricity.** Androcentricity (literally, "focus on the male") refers to approaching an issue from a male perspective.

DISCUSS: In the past, investigators (especially psychologists) readily employed deception in research; a well-known example is Solomon Asch's experiment (see Chapter 7). If the research depends on deception, is it ethical? When does deception move from benign to dangerous?

Q: "All human errors are impatience, a premature breaking off of methodological procedure, an apparent fencing in of what is apparently at issue." Franz Kafka

NOTE: Point out to students that the methods here can be arranged from "hard" science (experiment) through "soft" research (participant observation). Surveys fall in the middle.

NOTE: The word "experiment" contains the Latin root *peri*, "try, attempt." This is also the root of the word "peril," a link demonstrated by the Zimbardo research.

SEEING SOCIOLOGY
in Everyday Life

Think of three research topics about U.S. society that might be affected by the gender of the researcher. In each case, explain why.

research method a systematic plan for doing research

experiment a research method for investigating cause and effect under highly controlled conditions

Sometimes researchers act as if only men's activities are important, ignoring what women do. For years, researchers studying occupations focused on the paid work of men and overlooked the housework and child care traditionally performed by women. Research that seeks to understand human behavior cannot ignore half of humanity.

Gynocentricity—seeing the world from a female perspective—can also limit good sociological investigation. However, in our male-dominated society, this problem arises less often.

2. **Overgeneralizing.** This problem occurs when researchers use data drawn from people of only one sex to support conclusions about "humanity" or "society." Gathering information by talking to only male students and then drawing conclusions about an entire campus would be an example of overgeneralizing.

3. **Gender blindness.** Failing to consider gender at all is known as gender blindness. As is evident throughout this book, the lives of men and women differ in countless ways. A study of growing old in the United States might suffer from gender blindness if it overlooked the fact that most elderly men live with their wives but elderly women typically live alone.

4. **Double standards.** Researchers must be careful not to distort what they study by judging men and women differently. For example, a family researcher who labels a couple as "man and wife" may define the man as the "head of the household" and treat him as important while assuming that the woman simply plays a supporting role.

5. **Interference.** Another way gender can distort a study is if a subject reacts to the sex of the researcher, interfering with the research operation. While studying a small community in Sicily, for instance, Maureen Giovannini (1992) found that many men treated her as a woman rather than as a researcher. Some thought it was wrong for an unmarried woman to speak privately with a man. Others denied Giovannini access to places they considered off-limits to women.

There is nothing wrong with focusing research on people of one sex or the other. But all sociologists, as well as people who read their work, should be mindful of how gender can affect an investigation.

Research Ethics

Like all researchers, sociologists must be aware that research can harm as well as help subjects or communities. For this reason, the American Sociological Association (ASA)—the major professional association of sociologists in North America—has established formal guidelines for conducting research (1997).

Sociologists must try to be skillful and fair-minded in their work. They must disclose all research findings without omitting signifi-

cant data. They should make their results available to other sociologists who may want to conduct a similar study.

Sociologists must also make sure that the subjects taking part in a research project are not harmed, and they must stop their work right away if they suspect that any subject is at risk of harm. Researchers are also required to protect the privacy of anyone involved in a research project, even if they come under pressure from authorities, such as the police or the courts, to release confidential information. Researchers must also get the *informed consent* of participants, which means that the subjects must understand the responsibilities and risks that the research involves before agreeing to take part.

Another guideline concerns funding. Sociologists must reveal in their published results the sources of all financial support. They must avoid accepting money from a source if there is any possibility of a conflict of interest. For example, researchers must never accept funding from any organization that seeks to influence the research results for its own purposes.

The federal government also plays a part in research ethics. Colleges and universities that seek federal funding for research involving human subjects must have an *institutional review board* (IRB) to review grant applications and ensure that research will not violate ethical standards.

Finally, there are global dimensions to research ethics. Before beginning research in another country, an investigator must become familiar enough with that society to understand what people *there* are likely to regard as a violation of privacy or a source of personal danger. In a diverse society such as the United States, the same rule applies to studying people whose cultural background differs from your own. The Thinking About Diversity box offers some tips on the sensitivity outsiders should apply when studying Hispanic communities.

Methods of Sociological Research

A **research method** is *a systematic plan for doing research.* Four commonly used methods of sociological investigation are experiments, surveys, participant observation, and the use of existing data. None is better or worse than any other. Rather, just as a carpenter selects a particular tool for a specific task, researchers select a method—or mix several methods—according to whom they want to study and what they wish to learn.

Testing a Hypothesis: The Experiment

The **experiment** is *a research method for investigating cause and effect under highly controlled conditions.* Experiments closely follow the logic of science, and experimental research is typically *explanatory,* asking not just what happens but also why. In most cases, researchers create

GLOBAL: Cultural differences, at home or abroad, may significantly impede research in unfamiliar settings. Language problems, for example, may slow interviewing as well as generate errors of understanding. A researcher abroad may also unintentionally "steer" subjects, perhaps even coercing agreement to participate in the study in the first place.

Q: "Truth must have one face, the same and universal." Michel de Montaigne

NOTE: Diagram of experiment: measure → treatment → measure (Δ_1)
measure → placebo → measure (Δ_2)
$\Delta_1 - \Delta_2$ = treatment effect

hypothesis a statement of possible relationship between two (or more) variables

THINKING ABOUT DIVERSITY: RACE, CLASS, & GENDER

Studying the Lives of Hispanics

JORGE: If you are going to include Latinos in your research, you need to learn a little about their culture.

MARK: I'm interviewing lots of different families. What's special about interviewing Latinos?

JORGE: Sit down and I'll tell you a few things. . . .

Because U.S. society is racially, ethnically, and religiously diverse, all of us have to work with people who differ from ourselves. The same is true of sociologists. Learning, in advance, the ways of life of any category of people can ease the research process and ensure that there will be no hard feelings when the work is finished.

Gerardo Marín and Barbara Van Oss Marín (1991) have identified five areas of concern in conducting research with Hispanic people:

1. **Be careful with terms**. The Maríns point out that the term "Hispanic" is a label of convenience used by the U.S. Census Bureau. Few people of Spanish descent think of themselves as "Hispanic" or "Latino"; most identify with a particular country (generally, with a Latin American nation, such as Mexico or Argentina, or with Spain).

2. **Be aware of cultural differences**. By and large, the United States is individualistic and competitive. Many Hispanics, by contrast, place more value on cooperation and community. An outsider may judge the behavior of a Hispanic subject

as conformist or overly trusting when in fact the person is simply trying to be helpful. Researchers should also realize that Hispanic respondents might agree with a particular statement merely out of politeness.

3. **Anticipate family dynamics**. Generally speaking, Hispanic cultures have strong family loyalties. Asking subjects to reveal information about another family member may make them uncomfortable or even angry. The Maríns add that in the home, a researcher's request to speak privately with a Hispanic woman may provoke suspicion or outright disapproval from her husband or father.

4. **Take your time**. Spanish cultures, the Maríns explain, tend to place the quality of relationships above simply getting a job done. A non-Hispanic researcher who tries to hurry an interview with a Hispanic family out of a

desire not to delay the family's dinner may be considered rude for not proceeding at a more sociable and relaxed pace.

5. **Think about personal space**. Finally, Hispanics typically maintain closer physical contact than many non-Hispanics. Thus researchers who seat themselves across the room from their subjects may seem standoffish. Researchers might also wrongly label Hispanics as "pushy" if they move closer than non-Hispanic people find comfortable.

Of course, Hispanics differ among themselves just as people in any category do, and these generalizations apply to some more than to others. But investigators should be aware of cultural dynamics when carrying out any research, especially in the United States, where hundreds of distinctive categories of people make up our multicultural society.

WHAT DO YOU THINK?

1. Give a specific example of damage to a study that might take place if researchers are not sensitive to the culture of their subjects.

2. What do researchers need to do to avoid the kinds of problems noted in this box?

3. Discuss the research process with classmates from various cultural backgrounds. In what ways are the concerns raised by people of different cultural backgrounds similar? In what ways do they differ?

an experiment to test a **hypothesis,** *a statement of a possible relationship between two (or more) variables.* A hypothesis typically takes the form of an *if-then* statement: *If* this particular thing were to happen, *then* that particular thing will result.

An experiment gathers the evidence needed to reject or not to reject the hypothesis in four steps: (1) State which variable is the *independent variable* (the "cause" of the change) and which is the *dependent variable* (the "effect," the thing that is changed). (2) Mea-

sure the initial value of the dependent variable. (3) Expose the dependent variable to the independent variable (the "cause" or "treatment"). (4) Measure the dependent variable again to see what change, if any, took place. If the expected change took place, the experiment supports the hypothesis; if not, the hypothesis must be modified.

But a change in the dependent variable could be due to something other than the supposed cause. (Think back to our discussion of spurious correlations.) To be certain that they identify the correct

POP CULTURE: Films including *One Flew over the Cuckoo's Nest, Brubaker,* and *The Shawshank Redemption* support the conclusion of the Zimbardo experiment that prisons generate conflict, a view also supported by cases of prisoner abuse at Iraq's Abu Ghraib facility as well as at Guantanamo Bay, Cuba.

DISCUSS: Ask students to assess the Zimbardo research in light of the discussion of ethics on page 38.

NOTE: A slide show of the Zimbardo research is online at http://www.prisonexp.org/.

SEEING SOCIOLOGY
in Everyday Life

Hawthorne effect a change in a subject's behavior caused simply by the awareness of being studied

How might Zimbardo's findings help explain the abuse of Iraqi prisoners by U.S. soldiers in the Abu Ghraib prison?

cause, researchers carefully control other factors that might affect the outcome of the experiment. Such control is easiest in a laboratory, a setting specially constructed to neutralize outside influences.

Another strategy to gain control is dividing subjects into an *experimental group* and a *control group.* Early in the study, the researcher measures the dependent variable for subjects in both groups but later exposes only the experimental group to the independent variable or treatment. (The control group typically gets a *placebo,* a treatment that the members of the group think is the same but really has no effect on the experiment.) Then the investigator measures the subjects in both groups again. Any factor occurring during the course of the research that influences people in the experimental group (say, a news event) would do the same to those in the control group, thus controlling or "washing out" the factor. By comparing the before and after measurements of the two groups, a researcher can learn how much of the change is due to the independent variable.

The Hawthorne Effect

Researchers need to be aware that subjects' behavior may change simply because they are getting special attention, as one classic experiment revealed. In the late 1930s, the Western Electric Company hired researchers to investigate worker productivity in its Hawthorne factory near Chicago (Roethlisberger & Dickson, 1939). One experiment tested the hypothesis that increasing the available lighting would raise worker output. First, researchers measured worker productivity or output (the dependent variable). Then they increased the lighting (the independent variable) and measured output a second time. Productivity had gone up, a result that supported the hypothesis. But when the research team later turned the lighting back down, productivity increased again. What was going on? In time, the researchers realized that the employees were working harder (even if they could not see as well) simply because people were paying attention to them and measuring their output. From this research, social scientists coined the term **Hawthorne effect** to refer to *a change in a subject's behavior caused simply by the awareness of being studied.*

Illustration of an Experiment: The "Stanford County Prison"

Prisons can be violent settings, but is this due simply to the "bad" people who end up there? Or as Philip Zimbardo suspected, does the prison itself somehow generate violent behavior? This question led Zimbardo to devise a fascinating experiment, which he called the "Stanford County Prison" (Zimbardo, 1972; Haney, Banks, & Zimbardo, 1973).

Zimbardo thought that once inside a prison, even emotionally healthy people are likely to engage in violence. Thus Zimbardo treated the *prison setting* as the independent variable capable of causing *violence,* the dependent variable.

To test this hypothesis, Zimbardo's research team constructed a realistic-looking "prison" in the basement of the psychology building on the campus of California's Stanford University. Then they placed an ad in the local newspaper, offering to pay young men to help with a two-week research project. To each of the seventy who responded they administered a series of physical and psychological tests and then selected the healthiest twenty-four.

The next step was to randomly assign half the men to be "prisoners" and half to be "guards." The plan called for the guards and prisoners to spend the next two weeks in the mock prison. The prisoners began their part of the experiment soon afterward when the city police "arrested" them at their homes. After searching and handcuffing the men, the police drove them to the local police station, where they were fingerprinted. Then police transported their captives to the Stanford prison, where the guards locked them up. Zimbardo started his video camera rolling and watched to see what would happen next.

The experiment turned into more than anyone had bargained for. Both guards and prisoners soon became embittered and hostile toward one another. Guards humiliated the prisoners by assigning them tasks such as cleaning out toilets with their bare hands. The prisoners resisted and insulted the guards. Within four days, the researchers removed five prisoners who displayed "extreme emotional depression, crying, rage and acute anxiety" (Haney, Banks, & Zimbardo, 1973:81). Before the end of the first week, the situation had become so bad that the researchers had to cancel the experiment. Zimbardo explains:

> The ugliest, most base, pathological side of human nature surfaced. We were horrified because we saw some boys (guards) treat others as if they were despicable animals, taking pleasure in cruelty, while other boys (prisoners) became servile, dehumanized robots who thought only of escape, of their own individual survival and of their mounting hatred for the guards. (Zimbardo, 1972:4)

The events that unfolded at the "Stanford County Prison" supported Zimbardo's hypothesis that prison violence is rooted in the social character of jails themselves, not in the personalities of guards and prisoners. This finding raises questions about our society's prisons, suggesting the need for basic reform. Notice, too, that this experiment shows the potential of research to threaten the physical and mental well-being of subjects. Such dangers are not always as obvious as they were in this case. Therefore, researchers must carefully consider the potential harm to subjects at all stages of their work and halt any study, as Zimbardo did, if subjects suffer harm of any kind.

CRITICAL REVIEW In carrying out the "Stanford County Prison" study, the researchers chose to do an experiment because they were interested in testing a hypothesis. In this case, Zimbardo and his colleagues wanted to find out if the prison setting itself (rather than the personalities of individual guards and

NOTE: *Literary Digest* began political polling in 1916; in 1932, the publication correctly predicted Franklin Delano Roosevelt's victory over Herbert Hoover. Three months before the 1936 election, however, George Gallup disputed the *Digest* poll foretelling Alf Landon's victory. The *Digest* predicted the Landon margin at 57%, although he actually received only 37% of the vote. The *Digest* sent out 20 million postcards based on telephone listings and automobile registrations, of which only 3 million came back. Gallup's prophecy made him the national pollster, although he subsequently erred when he wrongly predicted the victory of Thomas Dewey over Harry Truman in the presidential race of 1948 (Reeves, 1983).

NOTE: Sometimes samples produce better results than populations do, considering that the tedious work of contacting a whole population can lead to all sorts of errors unrelated to sampling.

population the people who are the focus of research

sample a part of a population that represents the whole

SEEING SOCIOLOGY
in Everyday Life

Suggest a research topic that might lead a researcher to use a questionnaire. What about a topic that would call for interviews?

prisoners) is the cause of prison violence. The fact that the "prison" erupted in violence—even using "healthy" people—supports their hypothesis.

CHECK YOUR LEARNING What was Zimbardo's conclusion? How might Zimbardo's findings help explain the abuse of Iraqi prisoners by U.S. soliders in the Abu Ghraib prison in Iraq?

Asking Questions: Survey Research

A **survey** is *a research method in which subjects respond to a series of statements or questions on a questionnaire or in an interview.* The most widely used of all research methods, surveys are especially good for studying what cannot be observed directly, such as political attitudes or religious beliefs. Sometimes surveys provide clues about cause and effect, but typically they yield *descriptive* findings, painting a picture of people's views on some issue.

Population and Sample

A survey targets some **population,** *the people who are the focus of research.* Lois Benjamin, in her study of racism described at the beginning of this chapter, studied a select population—talented African Americans. Other surveys, such as political polls that predict election results, treat every adult in the country as the population.

Obviously, contacting millions of people is impossible for even the best-funded and most patient researcher. Fortunately, there is an easier way that yields accurate results: Researchers collect data from a **sample,** *a part of a population that represents the whole.* Benjamin chose 100 talented African Americans as her sample. National political polls typically survey a sample of about 1,000 people.

Everyone uses the logic of sampling all the time. If you look at students sitting near you and notice five or six heads nodding off, you might conclude that the class finds the day's lecture dull. In reaching this conclusion, you are making a judgment about *all* the people in the class (the population) from observing *some* of your classmates (the sample).

But how can researchers be sure that a sample really represents the entire population? One way is through *random sampling,* in which researchers draw a sample from the population at random so that every person in the population has an equal chance of being selected. The mathematical laws of probability dictate that a random sample is likely to represent the population as a whole. Selecting a random sample usually involves listing everyone in the population and using a computer to make random selections to make up the sample.

Beginning researchers sometimes make the mistake of assuming that "randomly" walking up to people on the street or in a mall produces a sample that is representative of the entire city. But this technique does *not* produce a random sample because it does not give every person an equal chance to be included in the study. For one thing, any street or mall, whether in a rich neighborhood or near a college campus, contains more of some kinds of people than others. The fact that some people are more approachable than others is another source of bias.

Although constructing a good sample is no simple task, it offers a considerable savings in time and expense. We are spared the tedious work of contacting everyone in a population, yet we can obtain essentially the same results.

Using Questionnaires

Selecting subjects is just the first step in carrying out a survey. Also needed is a plan for asking questions and recording answers. Most surveys use a questionnaire for this purpose.

A **questionnaire** is *a series of written questions a researcher presents to subjects.* One type of questionnaire provides not only the questions but also a selection of fixed responses (similar to a multiple-choice examination). This *closed-ended format* makes it fairly easy to analyze the results, but by narrowing the range of responses, it can also distort the findings. For example, Frederick Lorenz and Brent Bruton (1996) found that the number of hours per week students say they study for a college course depends on the options offered to them on

Philip Zimbardo's research helps explain why violence is a common element in our society's prisons. At the same time, his work demonstrates the dangers that sociological investigation poses for subjects and the need for investigators to observe ethical standards that protect the welfare of people who participate in research.

NOTE: Some questions elicit "expected" answers. For example, one Harris poll found that 64% of U.S. adults "expect to go to heaven," but just 2% say they "expect to go to hell."

NOTE: Survey organizations have found that enclosing a small amount of money with a questionnaire (say, a dollar bill) greatly improves the response rate. Even with follow-up mailings, however, response rates rarely exceed 75%.

Q: "From my earliest years, I have accepted many false opinions as true." René Descartes

NOTE: Although widely used in survey research, snowball sampling is crude and unlikely to represent a population accurately.

● MAKING THE GRADE

A *population* is all the people we want to learn about; you can collect data from an entire population if it is small enough (say, campus sociology majors). If the population is too large, select a *sample*, which will give good results as long as it is representative of the entire population.

survey (p. 41) a research method in which subjects respond to a series of statements or questions on a questionnaire or in an interview

questionnaire (p. 41) a series of written questions a researcher presents to her subjects

interview a series of questions a researcher asks respondents in person

the questionnaire. When the researchers presented students with options ranging from one hour or less to nine hours or more, 75 percent said that they studied four hours or less per week. But when subjects in a comparable group were given choices ranging from four hours or less to twelve hours or longer (a higher figure that suggests students should study more), they suddenly became more studious; only 34 percent reported that they studied four hours or less each week.

A second type of questionnaire, using an *open-ended format,* allows subjects to respond freely, expressing various shades of opinion. The drawback of this approach is that the researcher has to make sense out of what can be a very wide range of answers.

The researcher must also decide how to present questions to subjects. Most often, researchers use a *self-administered survey,* mailing or e-mailing questionnaires to respondents and asking them to complete the form and send it back. Since no researcher is present when subjects read the questionnaire, it must be both inviting and clearly written. *Pretesting* a self-administered questionnaire with a small number of people before sending it to the entire sample can prevent the costly problem of finding out—too late—that instructions or questions were confusing.

Using the mail or e-mail allows a researcher to contact a large number of people over a wide geographic area at minimal expense. But many people treat such questionnaires as junk mail, so typically no more than half are completed and returned (in 2000, just two-thirds of people returned U.S. Census Bureau forms). Researchers must send follow-up mailings (or, as the Census Bureau does, visit people's homes) to urge reluctant subjects to respond.

Finally, keep in mind that many people are not capable of completing a questionnaire on their own. Young children obviously cannot, nor can many hospital patients or a surprising number of adults who simply lack the required reading and writing skills.

Conducting Interviews

An **interview** is *a series of questions a researcher asks respondents in person.* In a closed-format design, researchers read a question or statement and then ask the subject to select a response from several that are presented. More commonly, however, interviews are open-ended so that subjects can respond as they choose and researchers can probe with follow-up questions. In either case, the researcher must guard against influencing a subject, which can be as easy as raising an eyebrow when a person begins to answer.

Although subjects are more likely to complete a survey if contacted personally by the researcher, interviews have some disadvantages: Tracking people down is costly and takes time, especially if subjects do not live in the same area. Telephone interviews allow far greater "reach," but the impersonality of cold calls by telephone (and reaching answering machines) can lower the response rate.

In both questionnaires and interviews, how a question is worded greatly affects how people answer. For example, when asked during the last presidential campaign if Barack Obama's race would make them less likely to vote for him, only 3 or 4 percent of people said yes. Yet if the question was changed to ask if the United States is ready to elect a black president, then almost 20 percent expressed some doubt. Similarly, if researchers asked U.S. adults if they support our military, a large majority of people said yes. Yet when researchers asked people if they supported what the military was trying to do in Iraq, most said no.

When it comes to survey questions, the exact wording will always affect responses. This is especially true if emotionally loaded language is used. Any words that trigger an emotional response in subjects will sway the results. For instance, using the expression "welfare mothers" rather than "women who receive public assistance" adds an emotional element to a question that encourages people to express a negative attitude.

Another problem is that researchers may confuse respondents by asking a double question, such as "Do you think that the government should reduce the deficit by cutting spending and raising taxes?" The issue here is that a subject could very well agree with one part of the question but not the other, so that forcing a subject to say yes or no distorts the opinion the researcher is trying to measure.

Conducting a good interview means standardizing the technique—treating all subjects in the same way. But this, too, can be problematic. Drawing people out requires establishing rapport, which in turn depends on responding naturally to the particular person

Focus groups are a type of survey in which a small number of people representing a target population are asked for their opinions about some issue or product. Here a sociology professor asks students to evaluate textbooks for use in her introductory class.

NOTE: Conducting interviews, as Lois Benjamin did, is something like traveling abroad. We have some idea of our direction and destination, but the unexpected always arises along the way. Imaginative improvisation is needed to make the most of an interview opportunity and sometimes even to save a situation.

NOTE: Lois Benjamin did not clearly operationalize "talented African Americans," so the population her sample represents remains only vaguely defined.

NOTE: Among the first systematic participant observers of U.S. society was Alexis de Tocqueville, who, along with his companion, Gustave Beaumont, traveled some 7,000 miles across the U.S. and Canada between May 11, 1831, and February 20, 1832, before writing *Democracy in America*.

MAKING THE GRADE

In general, questionnaires allow a researcher to collect lots of easily reported information—age, sex, voter participation—from lots of people. Interviews allow researchers to explore in-depth attitudes on a particular topic from a few people.

being interviewed, as you would in a normal conversation. In the end, researchers have to decide where to strike the balance between uniformity and rapport (Lavin & Maynard, 2001).

Illustration of Survey Research: Studying the African American Elite

This chapter began by explaining how Lois Benjamin came to investigate the effects of racism on talented African American men and women. Benjamin suspected that personal achievement did not prevent hostility based on skin color. She believed this because of her own experiences after becoming the first black professor at the University of Tampa. But was she the exception or the rule? To answer this question, Benjamin set out to discover whether—and if so, how—racism affected other successful African Americans.

Benjamin decided to interview subjects rather than distribute a questionnaire because she wanted to talk with her subjects, ask follow-up questions, and pursue topics that she could not anticipate. A second reason Benjamin favored interviews over questionnaires is that racism is a sensitive topic. A supportive investigator can make it easier for subjects to respond to painful questions more freely (Bergen, 1993).

Choosing to conduct interviews made it necessary to limit the number of people in the study. Benjamin settled for a sample of 100 men and women. Even this small number kept Benjamin busy for more than two years as she scheduled interviews, traveled all over the country, and met with her respondents. She spent two more years analyzing the tapes of her interviews, deciding what the hours of talk told her about racism, and writing up her results.

In selecting her sample, Benjamin first considered using all the people listed in *Who's Who in Black America*. But she rejected this idea in favor of starting out with people she knew and asking them to suggest others. This strategy is called *snowball sampling* because the number of individuals included grows rapidly over time.

Snowball sampling is an easy way to do research—we begin with familiar people who introduce us to their friends and colleagues. But snowball sampling rarely produces a sample that is representative of the larger population. Benjamin's sample probably contained many like-minded individuals, and it was certainly biased toward people willing to talk openly about race and prejudice. She understood these problems, and she did what she could to make her sample diverse in terms of sex, age, and region of the country. The Thinking About Diversity box on page 44 presents a statistical profile of Benjamin's respondents and some tips on how to read tables.

Benjamin based all her interviews on a series of questions with an open-ended format so that her subjects could say whatever they wished. As usually happens, the interviews took place in a wide range of settings. She met subjects in offices (hers or theirs), in hotel rooms,

and in cars. In each case, Benjamin tape-recorded the conversation, which lasted from two-and-one-half to three hours, so that she would not be distracted by taking notes.

As research ethics demand, Benjamin offered full anonymity to participants. Even so, many—including notables such as Vernon E. Jordan Jr. (former president of the National Urban League) and Yvonne Walker-Taylor (first woman president of Wilberforce University)—were used to being in the public eye and allowed Benjamin to use their names.

What surprised Benjamin most about her research was how eager many people were to be interviewed. These normally busy men and women seemed to go out of their way to contribute to her project. Benjamin reports, too, that once the interviews were under way, many became very emotional—at some point in the conversation, about 40 of her 100 subjects cried. For them, apparently, the research provided a chance to release feelings long kept inside. How did Benjamin respond? She reports that she cried right along with them.

Of the research orientations described earlier in the chapter, you will see that Benjamin's study fits best under interpretive sociology (she explored what race meant to her subjects) and critical sociology (she undertook the study partly to document that racial prejudice still exists). Many of her subjects reported fearing that race might someday undermine their success, and others spoke of a race-based "glass ceiling" preventing them from reaching the highest positions in our society. Benjamin concluded that despite the improving social standing of African Americans, black people in the United States still feel the sting of racial hostility.

CRITICAL REVIEW Professor Benjamin chose the survey as her method because she wanted to ask a lot of questions and gather information from her subjects. Certainly, some of the information she collected could have been done using a questionnaire. But she decided to carry out interviews because she was dealing with a complex and sensitive topic. Interacting with her subjects, one on one, for several hours, she could put them at ease, discuss personal matters, and ask them follow-up questions.

CHECK YOUR LEARNING Do you think this research could have been carried out by a white or Asian American sociologist? Why or why not?

In the Field: Participant Observation

Lois Benjamin's research demonstrates that sociological investigation takes place not only in laboratories but also "in the field," that is, where people carry on their everyday lives. The most widely used strategy for field study is **participant observation,** *a research method in which*

NOTE: Other classic examples of participant-observer studies include Robert and Helen Lynd's *Middletown* and *Middletown in Transition* (Muncie, Ind.), W. Lloyd Warner's *Yankee City* series (Newburyport, Mass.), Herbert Gans's *Levittowners* (Willingboro, N.J.), Elliot Liebow's *Tally's Corner* (Washington, D.C.), and Elijah Anderson's *Code of the Street* (Philadelphia, Penn.).

RESOURCE: In the methodological appendix to *Street Corner Society* (1981, orig. 1943), William Foote Whyte candidly assesses how his own values influenced his work.

EXERCISE: Motivated students can learn a great deal from reading research reports. For example, Elliot Liebow's classic *Tally's Corner* (1967) and his last book, *Tell Them Who I Am: The Lives of Homeless Women* (1993), both detail the research experience.

● MAKING THE GRADE

In her study of the African American elite, Lois Benjamin made great effort to explain who her subjects were. Always consider this question when reading anyone's research results.

THINKING ABOUT DIVERSITY: RACE, CLASS, & GENDER

Using Tables in Research: Analyzing Benjamin's African American Elite

Say you want to present a lot of information about a diverse population. How do you do it quickly and easily? The answer is by using a *table*. A table provides a lot of information in a small amount of space, so learning to read tables can increase your reading efficiency. When you spot a table, look first at the title to see what information it contains. The title of the table presented here provides a profile of the 100 subjects participating in Lois Benjamin's research. Across the top of the table, you will see eight variables that describe these men and women. Reading down each column, note the categories within each variable; the percentages in each column add up to 100.

Starting at the top left, we see that Benjamin's sample was mostly men (63 percent, versus 37 percent women). In terms of age, most of the respondents (68 percent) were in the middle stage of life, and most grew up in a predominantly black community in the South or in the North or Midwest region of the United States.

These individuals are indeed a professional elite. Notice that half have earned either a doctorate (32 percent) or a medical or law degree (17 percent). Given their extensive education (and Benjamin's own position as a professor), we should not be surprised that the largest share (35 percent) work in academic institutions. In terms of income, these are wealthy individuals, with most (64 percent) earning more than $50,000 annually back in 1990 (a salary that only 37 percent of full-time workers make even today).

Finally, we see that these 100 individuals are generally left-of-center in their political views. In part, this reflects their extensive schooling (which encourages progressive thinking) and the tendency of academics to fall on the liberal side of the political spectrum.

WHAT DO YOU THINK?

1. Why are statistical data, such as those in this table, an efficient way to convey a lot of information?

2. Looking at the table, can you determine how long it took most people to become part of this elite? Explain your answer.

3. Do you see any ways in which this African American elite might differ from a comparable white elite? If so, what are they?

The Talented One Hundred: Lois Benjamin's African American Elite

Sex	Age	Childhood Racial Setting	Childhood Region	Highest Educational Degree	Job Sector	Income	Political Orientation
Male 63%	35 or younger 6%	Mostly black 71%	West 6%	Doctorate 32%	College or university 35%	More than $50,000 64%	Radical left 13%
Female 37%	36 to 54 68%	Mostly white 15%	North or Midwest 32%	Medical or law 17%	Private, for-profit 17%	$35,000 to $50,000 18%	Liberal 38%
	55 or older 26%	Racially mixed 14%	South 38%	Master's 27%	Private, nonprofit 9%	$20,000 to $34,999 12%	Moderate 28%
			Northeast 12%	Bachelor's 13%	Government 22%	Less than $20,000 6%	Conservative 5%
			Other 12%	Less 11%	Self-employed 14%		Depends on issue 14%
					Retired 3%		Unknown 2%
100%	100%	100%	100%	100%	100%	100%	100%

Source: Adapted from Lois Benjamin, *The Black Elite: Facing the Color Line in the Twilight of the Twentieth Century* (Chicago: Nelson-Hall, 1991), p. 276.

---

investigators systematically observe people while joining them in their routine activities.

This method allows researchers an inside look at social life in any natural setting, from a nightclub to a religious seminary. Sociol-ogists call their account of social life in some setting a *case study*. Cultural anthropologists use participant observation to study other societies, calling this method *fieldwork* and their research results an *ethnography*.

Q: "Theories and concepts emerge in sociology like popcorn, puffed up by their own steam." Joseph Gusfield, explaining why no "social-scientific Newton" is likely to emerge from sociology.

NOTE: A recent example of participant observation is the Seeing Sociology in the News feature on pages 46–47.

NOTE: Walk students through the four research methods diagramed below: The first three flow from "hard" (explanatory) to "soft" (exploratory and descriptive).

research method (p. 38) a systematic plan for doing research

experiment (p. 38)
a research method for investigating cause and effect under highly controlled conditions

survey (p. 41)
a research method in which subjects respond to a series of statements or questions on a questionnaire or in an interview

participant observation (p. 43)
a research method in which investigators systematically observe people while joining them in their routine activities

use of existing sources (p. 47)

At the beginning of a field study, most investigators do not have a specific hypothesis in mind. In fact, they may not yet realize what the important questions will turn out to be. Thus most field research is *exploratory* and *descriptive*.

As its name suggests, participant observation has two sides. On one hand, getting an insider's look depends on becoming a participant in the setting—"hanging out" with the research subjects and trying to act, think, and even feel the way they do. Compared to experiments and survey research, participant observation has fewer hard-and-fast rules. But it is precisely this flexibility that allows investigators to explore the unfamiliar and adapt to the unexpected.

Unlike other research methods, participant observation may require that the researcher enter the setting not just for a week or two but for months or even years. At the same time, however, the researcher must maintain some distance as an observer, mentally stepping back to record field notes and later to interpret them. Because the investigator must both "play the participant" to win acceptance and gain access to people's lives and "play the observer" to maintain the distance needed for thoughtful analysis, there is an inherent tension in this method. Carrying out the twin roles of insider participant and outsider observer often comes down to a series of careful compromises.

Most sociologists perform participant observation alone, so they—and readers, too—must remember that the results depend on the work of a single person. Participant observation usually falls within interpretive sociology, yielding mostly qualitative data—the researcher's accounts of people's lives and what they think of themselves and the world around them—although researchers sometimes collect some quantitative (numerical) data. From a scientific point of view, participant observation is a "soft" method that relies heavily on personal judgment and lacks scientific rigor. Yet its personal approach is also a strength: Where a high-profile team of sociologists administering formal surveys might disrupt many social settings, a sensitive participant observer can often gain important insight into people's behavior.

The Seeing Sociology in the News article on pages 46–47 provides a recent example of a sociologist using participant observation to study gang behavior in one of Chicago's toughest housing projects. Next we turn to a classic sociological study using participant observation that took place in Boston many decades earlier.

Illustration of Participant Observation: *Street Corner Society*

Did you ever wonder what everyday life was like in an unfamiliar neighborhood? In the late 1930s, a young graduate student at Harvard University named William Foote Whyte (1914–2000) was fascinated by the lively street life of a nearby,

rather rundown section of Boston. His curiosity led him to carry out four years of participant observation in this neighborhood, which he called "Cornerville," and in the process to produce a sociological classic.

At the time, Cornerville was home to first- and second-generation Italian immigrants. Many were poor, and many people living in the rest of Boston considered Cornerville a place to avoid: a poor slum that was home to racketeers. Unwilling to accept easy stereotypes, Whyte set out to discover for himself exactly what kind of life went on in this community. His celebrated book, *Street Corner Society* (1981, orig. 1943), describes Cornerville as a complex community with its own code of values, complex social patterns, and particular social conflicts.

In beginning his investigation, Whyte considered a range of research methods. Should he take questionnaires to one of Cornerville's community centers and ask local people to fill them out? Should he invite members of the community to come to his Harvard office for interviews? It is easy to see that such a formal approach would have gained little cooperation from the local people. Whyte decided, therefore, to set out on his own, working his way into Cornerville life in the hope of coming to understand this rather mysterious place.

Right away, Whyte discovered the challenges of even getting started in field research. After all, an upper-middle-class WASP graduate student from Harvard did not exactly fit into Cornerville life. Even a friendly overture from an outsider could seem pushy and

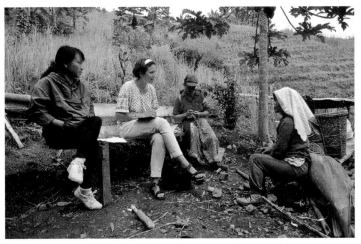

Participant observation is a method of sociological research that allows a researcher to investigate people as they go about their everyday lives in some "natural" setting. At its best, participant observation makes you a star in your own reality show; but living in what may be a strange setting far from home for months at a time is always challenging.

45

DISCUSS: Sweden's National Bureau of Economic Research found that couples who cohabit before marriage are more likely to divorce than those who do not cohabit. Researcher Neil Bennett claims cohabiters are less religious and less committed a partner to begin with; this "weak ties" pattern persists among cohabiters who marry. David Popenoe's research, noted in Chapter 18 ("Families"), supports Bennett's conclusion, arguing that cohabiting fosters a culture of low commitment.

Q: "Prediction is very difficult. Especially of the future." Niels Bohr

Seeing SOCIOLOGY in the NEWS

The New York Times

If You Want to Observe 'Em, Join 'Em

By WILLIAM GRIMES
January 16, 2008

On a hot summer day in 1989, Sudhir Venkatesh, a callow sociology student with a ponytail and tie-dyed T-shirt, walked into one of Chicago's toughest housing projects, clipboard in hand, ready to ask residents about their lives. Sample question: "How does it feel to be black and poor?" Suggested answers: "very bad, somewhat bad, neither bad nor good, somewhat good, very good." Actual answers: unprintable.

Mr. Venkatesh got rid of the clipboard and the questionnaire, but not his fascination with life in the Chicago housing projects. He stuck around, befriended a gang leader and for the next decade lived a curious insider-outsider life at the notorious Robert Taylor Homes on the city's South Side, an eye-opening experience he documented in the high-octane *Gang Leader for a Day*. In a bit of bravado Mr. Venkatesh, who now teaches at Columbia, styles himself a "rogue sociologist."

Dissatisfied with opinion surveys and statistical analysis as ways to describe the life of the poor, he reverted to the methods of his predecessors at the University of Chicago, who took an ethnographic approach to the study of hobos, hustlers and politicians. Much like a journalist, he observed, asked questions and drew conclusions as he accumulated raw data. . . .

Mr. Venkatesh, reared in the comfortable suburbs of Southern California by Indian parents, crossed the line from observer to participant on more than one occasion as he penetrated deeper into the life of the Black Kings and its local captain, the ruthless, charismatic J. T.

When a rival gang swept by, guns blazing, he dodged bullets and helped drag a gang lieutenant to safety. When local squatters meted out street justice to a crackhead who had beaten a woman in the projects, he got a boot in.

One glorious day J. T. let Mr. Venkatesh get a taste of power and the problems that come with it. He allowed him to make the daily rounds of the platoons under his command—six-man crews that deal in crack cocaine—and try to sort out the petty squabbles and mistakes endemic in a criminal enterprise comprising 250 underpaid, uneducated and violent soldiers.

All this is much better than toting a clipboard. "It was pretty thrilling to have a gang boss calling me up to go hang out with him," wrote Mr. Venkatesh, who ridiculed his own naïveté. . . .

Without question, Mr. Venkatesh was dazzled by J. T. and seduced by the gang life. He maintained enough distance, however, to appraise the information he was given and to build up, through careful observation, a detailed picture of life at the project. He writes what might be called tabloid sociology, but it rests on a solid foundation of data, like records of the gang's finances turned over to him by T-Bone, its treasurer. . . .

The Black Kings, which Mr. Venkatesh observed throughout the 1990s, operated a hugely

rude. One night, Whyte dropped in at a local bar, hoping to buy a woman a drink and encourage her to talk about Cornerville. Looking around the room, he could find no woman alone. But then he saw a man sitting down with two women. He walked up to them and asked, "Pardon me. Would you mind if I joined you?" Instantly, he realized his mistake:

> There was a moment of silence while the man stared at me. Then he offered to throw me down the stairs. I assured him that this would not be necessary, and demonstrated as much by walking right out of there without any assistance. (1981:289)

As this incident suggests, gaining entry to a community is the difficult (and sometimes hazardous) first step in field research. "Breaking in" requires patience, quick thinking, and a little luck. Whyte's big break came when he met a young man named "Doc" at a local social service agency. Whyte explained to Doc how hard it was to make friends in Cornerville. Doc responded by taking Whyte under his wing and introducing him to others in the community. With Doc's help, Whyte soon became a neighborhood regular.

Whyte's friendship with Doc illustrates the importance of a *key informant* in field research. Such people not only introduce a researcher to a community but often remain a source of information and help. But using a key informant also has its risks. Because any person has a particular circle of friends, a key informant's guidance is certain to "spin" or bias the study in one way or another. In addition, in the eyes of others, the reputation of the key informant, good or bad, usually rubs off on the investigator. So although a key informant is helpful early on, a participant observer must soon seek a broader range of contacts.

Having entered the Cornerville world, Whyte quickly learned another lesson: A field researcher needs to know when to speak up and when to shut up. One evening, he joined a group discussing neighborhood gambling. Wanting to get the facts straight, Whyte asked innocently, "I suppose the cops were all paid off?"

> The gambler's jaw dropped. He glared at me. Then he denied vehemently that any policeman had been paid off and immediately switched the conversation to another subject. For the rest of that evening I felt very uncomfortable.

The next day, Doc offered some sound advice:

> "Go easy on that 'who,' 'what,' 'why,' 'when,' 'where' stuff, Bill. You ask those questions and people will clam up on you. If people accept you, you can just hang around, and you'll learn the answers in the long run without even having to ask the questions." (1981:303)

In the months and years that followed, Whyte became familiar with life in Cornerville and even married a local woman with whom he would spend the rest of his life. In the process, he learned that the common stereotypes were wrong. In Cornerville, most people worked hard, many were quite successful, and some even boasted of sending children to college. Even today, Whyte's book is a fascinating story of the deeds, dreams, and disappointments of immigrants and their children living in one ethnic community, and it contains the rich detail that can come only from years of participant observation.

NOTE: The U.S. Census Bureau was formed in 1902, more than a century after the first census was taken (1790).

Q: "[Community studies are] the poor sociologist's substitute for the novel." Ruth Glass

profitable drug ring, often selling crack in building lobbies, and extorted protection money from every project resident engaged in economic activity, no matter how trivial: prostitutes, street-corner car mechanics, squatters, home beauticians and even old women selling candy from their apartments to earn an extra $20 a week.

Mr. Venkatesh failed to gauge the feelings of project residents about the Black Kings, probably because he was perceived as part of them and therefore someone to steer clear of. Most residents avoided him . . . or limited their conversation to "a quick hello." . . .

On the other hand, Mr. Venkatesh, through sheer persistence, unraveled a complex, intertwined system of political and economic relationships that made the housing project run in the near-total absence of city services. The police and ambulance crews, in particular, regarded Robert Taylor as a no-go area. . . . Local warlords like J. T. and quasi-political figures like the fearsome

Ms. Bailey, a building president who manipulated her connections to the Chicago Housing Authority, held sway. They exacted tribute and dispensed favors. . . .

No one got rich. Mr. Venkatesh was shocked to discover that foot soldiers in the drug operation barely made minimum wage. . . .

Violent, paranoid and manipulative, [J. T.] offered a fascinating study in leadership, and Mr. Venkatesh made the most of his opportunity, trying desperately to maintain some saving skepticism. Smitten, he never quite got over his initial attraction, even when J. T. double-crossed him, ingeniously, by encouraging him to carry out a detailed study of the housing project's economy, whose results he used to tighten his hold on the residents.

Overnight Mr. Venkatesh became a pariah. A sympathetic prostitute told him . . ., "Just don't take the stairs when you leave, 'cause if you get caught there, they may never find your body." . . .

. . . The City of Chicago began demolishing the Robert Taylor Homes soon after [Mr. Venkatesh] completed his research.

WHAT DO YOU THINK?

1. Why do you think Sudhir Venkatesh chose to use participant observation to do this research? What advantages and disadvantages can you see in his choice?
2. What special dangers did this research pose to the researcher?
3. From this article, did you learn anything about gang life that surprised you? If so, what?

CRITICAL REVIEW To study the community he called "Cornerville," William Whyte chose participant observation. This was a good choice because he did not have a specific hypothesis to test, nor did he know at the outset exactly what the questions were. By moving into this community and living there for several years, Whyte was able to come to know the place and to paint a complex picture of social life there.

CHECK YOUR LEARNING Give an example of a topic for sociological research that would be best studied using (1) an experiment, (2) a survey, and (3) participant observation.

Using Available Data: Existing Sources

Not all research requires investigators to collect their own data. Sometimes sociologists analyze existing sources, data already collected by others.

The most widely used statistics in social science are gathered by government agencies. The U.S. Census Bureau continuously updates a wide range of data about the U.S. population. Comparable data on Canada are available from Statistics Canada, a branch of that nation's government. For international data, there are various publications of the United Nations and the World Bank. In short, data about the whole world are as close as your library or the Internet.

Using available data, whether government statistics or the findings of individual researchers, saves time and money. This approach has special appeal to sociologists with low budgets. For anyone, however, government data are generally more extensive and more accurate than what most researchers could obtain on their own.

But using existing data has problems of its own. For one thing, available data may not exist in the exact form needed. For example, you may be able to find the average salary paid to professors at your school but not separate figures for the amounts paid to women and to men. Further, there are always questions about the meaning and accuracy of work done by others. For example, in his classic study of suicide, Emile Durkheim soon discovered that there was no way to know whether a death classified as a suicide was really an accident or vice versa. In addition, various agencies use different procedures and categories in collecting data, so comparisons may be difficult. In the end, then, using existing data is a little like shopping for a used car: There are plenty of bargains out there, but you have to shop carefully.

Illustration of the Use of Existing Sources: A Tale of Two Cities

Why might one city have been home to many famous people and another's history show hardly any famous people at all? To those of us living in the present, historical data offer a key to unlocking secrets of the past. The award-winning study *Puritan Boston and Quaker Philadelphia*, by E. Digby Baltzell (1979), is a good example of how a researcher can use available data to do historical research.

This story begins with Baltzell making a chance visit to Bowdoin College in Maine. As he walked into the college library, he saw up

RESOURCE: Two good U.S. data sites are http://www.census.gov (U.S. Census Bureau) and http://www.prb.org/Countries/UnitedStates.aspx (Population Reference Bureau).

NOTE: In conducting historical research, sociologists can discern the contours and impacts of most significant social developments (such as industrialization or deindustrialization), which come to light only over long periods.

EXERCISE: You can have your sociological imagination working even when watching television. For example, national surveys suggest that television sitcom watchers tend to be young, single, and politically liberal, whereas network news watchers tend to be older, married, and more conservative. Watch both kinds of television and, based on the commercial advertising, see whether your perceptions confirm this pattern. What exactly would you look for in each case? Sketch out a research plan.

MAKING THE GRADE

Using existing sources—especially in clever and creative ways, as Baltzell did—is the key to conducting historical research in sociology.

on the wall three large portraits—of the celebrated author Nathaniel Hawthorne, the famous poet Henry Wadsworth Longfellow, and Franklin Pierce, the fourteenth president of the United States. He soon learned that all three men were members of the same class at Bowdoin, graduating in 1825. How could it be, Baltzell wondered, that this small college had graduated more famous people in a single year than his own, much bigger University of Pennsylvania had graduated in its entire history? To answer this question, Baltzell was soon paging through historical documents to see whether New England had really produced more famous people than his native Pennsylvania.

What were Baltzell's data? He turned to the *Dictionary of American Biography,* twenty volumes profiling more than 13,000 outstanding men and women in fields such as politics, law, and the arts. The dictionary told Baltzell *who* was great, and he realized that the longer the biography, the more important the person is thought to be.

By the time Baltzell had identified the seventy-five individuals with the longest biographies, he saw a striking pattern. Massachusetts had the most by far, with twenty-one of the seventy-five top achievers. The New England states, combined, claimed thirty-one of the entries. By contrast, Pennsylvania could boast of only two, and all the states in the Middle Atlantic region had just twelve. Looking more closely, Baltzell discovered that most of New England's great achievers had grown up in and around the city of Boston. Again, in stark contrast, almost no one of comparable standing came from his own Philadelphia, a city with many more people than Boston.

What could explain this remarkable pattern? Baltzell drew inspiration from the German sociologist Max Weber (1958, orig. 1904–05), who argued that a region's record of achievement was influenced by its major religious beliefs (see Chapter 4, "Society"). In the religious differences between Boston and Philadelphia, Baltzell found the answer to his puzzle. Boston was originally a Puritan settlement, founded by people who highly valued the pursuit of excellence and public achievement. Philadelphia, by contrast, was settled by Quakers, who believed in equality and avoided public notice.

Both the Puritans and the Quakers were fleeing religious persecution in England, but the two religions produced quite different cultural patterns. Boston's Puritans saw humans as innately sinful, so they built a rigid society in which family, church, and school regulated people's behavior. The Puritans celebrated hard work as a means of glorifying God and viewed public success as a reassuring sign of God's blessing. In short, Puritanism fostered a disciplined life in which people both sought and respected achievement.

Philadelphia's Quakers, by contrast, built their way of life on the belief that all human beings are basically good. They saw little need for strong social institutions to "save" people from sinfulness. They

believed in equality, so that even those who became rich considered themselves no better than anyone else. Thus rich and poor alike lived modestly and discouraged one another from standing out by seeking fame or running for public office.

In Baltzell's sociological imagination, Boston and Philadelphia took the form of two social "test tubes": Puritanism was poured into one, Quakerism into the other. Centuries later, we can see that different "chemical reactions" occurred in each case. The two belief systems led to different attitudes toward personal achievement, which in turn shaped the history of each region. Today, we can see that Boston's Kennedys (despite being Catholic) are only one of that city's many families who exemplify the Puritan pursuit of recognition and leadership. By contrast, there has never been even one family with such public stature in the entire history of Philadelphia.

Baltzell's study uses scientific logic, but it also illustrates the interpretive approach by showing how people understood their world. His research reminds us that sociological investigation often involves mixing research orientations to fit a particular problem.

CRITICAL REVIEW The main reason Baltzell chose to use existing sources is that this is a good way to learn about history. The *Dictionary of American Biography* offers a great deal of information about people who lived long ago and obviously are not available for an interview. At the same time, existing sources were not created with the purpose of answering a modern-day sociologist's questions. For this reason, using such documents requires a critical eye and a good deal of creative thinking.

CHECK YOUR LEARNING What other questions about life in the past might you wish to answer using existing sources? What sources might you use to find the answers?

The Summing Up table provides a quick review of the four major methods of sociological investigation. We now turn to our final consideration: the link between research results and sociological theory.

The Interplay of Theory and Method

No matter how sociologists collect their data, they have to turn facts into meaning by building theory. They do this in two ways: inductive logical thought and deductive logical thought.

Inductive logical thought is *reasoning that transforms specific observations into general theory.* In this mode, a researcher's thinking runs from the specific to the general and goes something like this: "I have some interesting data here; I wonder what they mean." Baltzell's research illustrates the inductive logical model. His data

inductive logical thought (p. 48) reasoning that transforms specific observations into general theory

deductive logical thought reasoning that transforms general theory into specific hypotheses suitable for testing

SUMMING UP

Four Research Methods

	Experiment	Survey	Participant Observation	Existing Sources
Application	For explanatory research that specifies relationships between variables Generates quantitative data	For gathering information about issues that cannot be directly observed, such as attitudes and values Useful for descriptive and explanatory research Generates quantitative or qualitative data	For exploratory and descriptive study of people in a "natural" setting Generates qualitative data	For exploratory, descriptive, or explanatory research whenever suitable data are available
Advantages	Provides the greatest opportunity to specify cause-and-effect relationships Replication of research is relatively easy	Sampling, using questionnaires, allows surveys of large populations Interviews provide in-depth responses	Allows study of "natural" behavior Usually inexpensive	Saves time and expense of data collection Makes historical research possible
Limitations	Laboratory settings have an artificial quality Unless the research environment is carefully controlled, results may be biased	Questionnaires must be carefully prepared and may yield a low return rate Interviews are expensive and time-consuming	Time-consuming Replication of research is difficult Researcher must balance roles of participant and observer	Researcher has no control over possible biases in data Data may only partially fit current research needs

showed that one region of the country (the Boston area) had produced many more high achievers than another (the Philadelphia region). He worked "upward" from ground-level observations to the high-flying theory that religious values were a key factor in shaping people's attitudes toward achievement.

A second type of logical thought moves "downward," in the opposite direction: **Deductive logical thought** is *reasoning that transforms general theory into specific hypotheses suitable for testing.* The researcher's thinking runs from the general to the specific: "I have this hunch about human behavior; let's collect some data and put it to the test." Working deductively, the researcher first states the theory in the form of a hypothesis and then selects a method by which to test it. To the extent that the data support the hypothesis, a researcher concludes that the theory is correct; on the other hand, data that refute the hypothesis suggest that the theory needs to be revised or perhaps rejected entirely.

Philip Zimbardo's "Stanford County Prison" experiment illustrates deductive logic. Zimbardo began with the general theory that a social environment can change human behavior. He then devel-

oped a specific, testable hypothesis: Placed in a prison setting, even emotionally well-balanced young men will behave violently. The violence that erupted soon after his experiment began supported Zimbardo's hypothesis. Had his experiment produced friendly behavior between prisoners and guards, his hypothesis clearly would have been wrong.

Just as researchers often employ several methods over the course of one study, they typically use *both* kinds of logical thought. Figure 2–2 on page 50 illustrates both types of reasoning: inductively building theory from observations and deductively making observations to test a theory.

Finally, turning facts into meaning usually involves organizing and presenting statistical data. Precisely how sociologists arrange their numbers affects the conclusions they reach. In short, preparing your results amounts to spinning reality in one way or another.

Often we conclude that an argument must be true simply because there are statistics to back it up. However, we must look at statistics with a cautious eye. After all, researchers choose what data to present, they interpret their statistics, and they may use tables and

DISCUSS: Inductive logical thought amounts to saying, "If this is what happens, then what is true?" Deductive logical thought runs the other way: "If this is true, then what ought to happen?"

NOTE: The ten steps are all important but need not necessarily follow the order suggested here.

EXERCISE: Students come across research reports in the media all the time. Ask them to bring one to class and offer some critical comment about how well the research was carried out.

Q: "Science is meaningless because it gives no answer to the question, the only question of importance for us: 'What shall we do and how shall we live?'" Leo Tolstoy

● MAKING THE GRADE

The ten steps listed below are a summary of what is needed to conduct good sociological research.

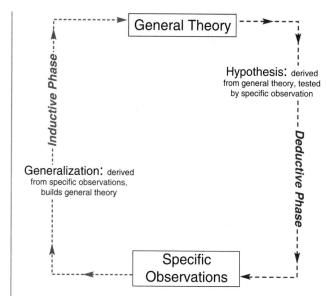

FIGURE 2–2   Deductive and Inductive Logical Thought
Sociologists link theory and method through both inductive and deductive logic.

graphs to steer readers toward particular conclusions. The Controversy & Debate box takes a closer look at this important issue.

Putting It All Together: Ten Steps in Sociological Investigation

We can summarize this chapter by outlining ten steps in the process of carrying out sociological investigation. Each step takes the form of an important question.

1. **What is your topic?** Being curious and applying the sociological perspective can generate ideas for social research at any time and in any place. Pick a topic that you find interesting and important to study.

2. **What have others already learned?** You are probably not the first person with an interest in the issue you have selected. Visit the library to see what theories and methods other researchers have applied to your topic. In reviewing the existing research, note problems that have come up to avoid repeating past mistakes.

3. **What, exactly, are your questions?** Are you seeking to explore an unfamiliar social setting? To describe some category of peo-

ple? To investigate cause and effect among variables? If your study is exploratory or descriptive, identify *whom* you wish to study, *where* the research will take place, and *what* kinds of issues you want to explore. If it is explanatory, you must also formulate the hypothesis to be tested and operationalize each variable.

4. **What will you need to carry out research?** How much time and money are available to you? Is special equipment or training necessary? Will you be able to complete the work yourself? You should answer all these questions as you plan the research project.

5. **Are there ethical concerns?** Not all research raises serious ethical questions, but you must be sensitive to this possibility. Can the research cause harm or threaten anyone's privacy? How might you design the study to minimize the chances for injury? Will you promise anonymity to the subjects? If so, how will you ensure that anonymity will be maintained?

6. **What method will you use?** Consider all major research strategies, as well as combinations of approaches. Keep in mind that the best method depends on the kinds of questions you are asking as well as the resources available to you.

7. **How will you record the data?** Your research method is a plan for data collection. Record all information accurately and in a way that will make sense later (it may be some time before you actually write up the results of your work). Watch out for any bias that may creep into the research.

8. **What do the data tell you?** Study the data in terms of your initial questions, and decide how to interpret the data you have collected. If your study involves a specific hypothesis, you must decide whether to confirm, reject, or modify the hypothesis. Keep in mind that there may be several ways to look at your data, depending on which theoretical approach you use, and you should consider them all.

9. **What are your conclusions?** Prepare a final report stating your conclusions. How does your work advance sociological theory? Does it suggest ways to improve research methods? Does your study have policy implications? What would the general public find interesting in your work? Finally, evaluate your own work. What problems arose during the research process? What questions were left unanswered?

10. **How can you share what you've learned?** Consider sending your research paper to a campus newspaper or magazine or making a presentation to a class, a campus gathering, or perhaps a meeting of professional sociologists. The point is to share what you have learned with others and to let them respond to your work.

NOTE: Why is there not more fraud in research? Probably because the gains of dishonesty are significant only in situations in which the odds of detection are very high.

NOTE: "Facts" rarely speak for themselves. Surveys show that among people over the age of 80, men are much more sexually active than women. Does this suggest a biological difference allowing older men to continue to be sexually active? Or is it the fact that given the difference in longevity, most older men live with wives, whereas older women live alone?

CONTROVERSY & DEBATE

Can People Lie with Statistics?

Josh: (*discussing job prospects after graduation*) Well, you know, college students today just aren't as smart as they were fifty years ago.

Sam: Come on, that's not true at all.

Josh: (*smugly*) Sorry, pal. I happen to have the data to prove it.

We have all been in arguments when someone has presented us with "data" as if that were "proof." But are numbers the same as "truth"? It is worth remembering the words of the nineteenth-century English politician Benjamin Disraeli, who once remarked, "There are three kinds of lies: lies, damned lies, and statistics!"

In a world that bombards us with numbers—often described as "scientific data" or "official figures"—it is important to realize that "statistical evidence" is not necessarily the same as truth. For one thing, any researcher can make mistakes. More important, because data do not speak for themselves, someone has to decide what they mean. Sometimes people (even sociologists) "dress up" their data almost the way politicians deliver campaign speeches—with an eye more to winning you over than to getting at the truth.

The best way to avoid being fooled is to understand how people can mislead with statistics.

1. **People select their data**. Many times, the data presented are not wrong, but they do not tell the whole story. Let's say someone who thinks that television is ruining our way of life presents statistics indicating that we watch more TV today than people did a generation ago. It also turns out that during the same period, SAT scores have fallen. Both sets of data may be correct, but the suggestion that there is a cause-and-effect link here—that television viewing is lowering test scores—is not proved. A person more favorable to television might counter with the additional "fact" that the U.S. population spends much more money buying books today than it did a generation ago, suggesting that television creates new intellectual interests. It is possible to find statistics that seem to support just about any argument.

2. **People interpret their data**. People can also "package" their data with a ready-made interpretation, as if the numbers can mean only one thing. The pie chart shows the results of one study of U.S. children living in poverty (National Center for Children in Poverty, cited in *Population Today*, 1995). The researchers reported that 43 percent of these children lived in a household with no working parent, 39 percent lived in a household with one or two parents employed part time, and 18 percent lived in a household with one or two parents working full time. The researchers labeled this figure "Majority of Children in Poverty Live with Parents Who Work." Do you think this interpretation is accurate or misleading? Why or why not?

3. **People use graphs to spin the truth**. Graphs, which often show an upward or downward trend over time, are a good way to present data. But using graphs also gives people the opportunity to spin data in various ways. The trend depends in part on the time frame used. During the past ten years, for instance, the U.S. crime rate has fallen. But if we were to look at the past fifty years, we would see an opposite trend: The crime rate rose sharply.

The scale used to draw a graph is also important because it lets a researcher "inflate" or "deflate" a trend. Both graphs shown here present identical data for SAT critical reading scores between 1967 and 2008. But the left-hand graph stretches the scale to show a downward trend; the right-hand graph compresses the scale, making the trend seem steady. So understanding what statistics mean—or don't mean—depends on being a careful reader!

Poor children living in household with no parent working
43%

Poor children living in household with one or two parents working full time
18%

Poor children living in household with one or two parents working part time
39%

WHAT DO YOU THINK?

1. Why do you think people are so quick to accept "statistics" as true?

2. From a scientific point of view, is spinning the truth acceptable? Is this practice OK from a critical approach, in which someone is trying to advance social change?

3. Find a news story on some social issue that you think presents biased data or conclusions. What are the biases?

SAT SCORES DIP!

SAT SCORES HOLD STEADY!

Seeing Sociology in Everyday Life

Chapter 2   Sociological Investigation

What are friends for?

Sociological research is the key to a deeper understanding of our everyday social world and also to knowing more about ourselves. Take friendship, for example. Everyone knows that it is fun to be surrounded by friends. But did you know that friendship has real benefits for human health? What do you think these benefits might be? Take a look at the photos below and learn more about what research has taught us about the positive effects of having friends.

> **HINT** In the first case, researchers defined having friends as the independent variable, and they defined longevity and health as the dependent variables. On average, those with friends (the experimental group) actually lived longer and were healthier than those without friends (the control group). In the second case, researchers found that women with many friends were several times more likely to survive their illness than those without friends. The third case reminds us that correlation does not demonstrate cause and effect. This study looked at more than 700 men, some with many friends (the experimental group) and also other men of comparable health (the control group) and few friends, over six years. Finding those with friends had better heart health tells us that friendship is the independent variable. In the fourth case, researchers did indeed find that the longer the people had been friends, the more positive the subject's attitude about making the climb turned out to be. Long live friendship!

One ten-year study of older people found that those women and men who had many friends were significantly less likely to die over the course of the research than those with few or no friends. Other long-term research confirms that people with friends not only live longer but live healthier lives than those without friends. In basic terms, how would such a study be conducted?

Another study looked at 3,000 women diagnosed with breast cancer and compared the rate of survival for women with many friends with that for women with few or no friends. What do you think they concluded about the effect of friendship on surviving a serious illness?

Perhaps the reason that friendship improves health is that friends raise our spirits and give us a more positive attitude about our lives. A final study placed young college students carrying heavy backpacks at the base of a steep hill and asked them how tough it would be to climb to the top. Subjects in the company of a friend were much more optimistic that they could make the climb than those standing there alone. Would you expect that the better the friend, the more positive the person's attitude?

The "friendship effect" improves the health of men, too. A study of older men found that those with many friends had lower rates of heart disease than those without friends. How would you be sure of the causal direction linking these variables? That is, how can we be sure that friendship is improving health rather than good health encouraging friendship?

Applying SOCIOLOGY in Everyday Life

1. The research studies discussed above demonstrate that friendship means more to people than we might think. Recall Emile Durkheim's study of suicide in Chapter 1. How did he use sociological research to uncover more about the importance of relationships?

2. Observe your instructor in class one day to grade his or her teaching skills. Operationalize the concept "good teaching" in terms of specific traits you can measure. How easy is it to measure "good teaching"?

3. Visit three sociology instructors (or other social science instructors) during their office hours. Ask each whether they think sociology is an objective science. Do they agree? Why or why not?

MAKING THE GRADE

CHAPTER 2 Sociological Investigation

Basics of Sociological Investigation

Two basic requirements for **SOCIOLOGICAL INVESTIGATION** are
- Know how to apply the sociological perspective.
- Be curious and ready to ask questions about the world around you.

p. 29

What people accept as "truth" differs around the world.
- **SCIENCE**—a logical system that bases knowledge on direct, systematic observation—is one form of truth.
- Scientific evidence gained from sociological research often challenges common sense.

pp. 29–31

Research Orientations: Three Ways to Do Sociology

POSITIVIST SOCIOLOGY studies society by systematically observing social behavior.
Positivist sociology
- requires carefully operationalizing variables and ensuring that measurement is both reliable and valid
- observes how variables are related and tries to establish cause and effect
- sees an objective reality "out there"
- favors quantitative data
- is well suited to research in a laboratory
- demands that researchers be objective and suspend their personal values and biases as they conduct research

pp. 31–35

✓ *Positivist sociology is also called* scientific sociology.

INTERPRETIVE SOCIOLOGY focuses on the meanings that people attach to behavior.
Interpretive sociology
- sees reality as constructed by people in the course of their everyday lives
- favors qualitative data
- is well suited to research in a natural setting

p. 36

✓ *Weber's concept of* Verstehen *refers to learning how people understand their world.*

CRITICAL SOCIOLOGY uses research to bring about social change.
Critical sociology
- asks moral and political questions
- focuses on inequality
- rejects the principle of objectivity, claiming that all research is political

pp. 36–37

✓ *Marx, who founded the critical orientation, criticized scientific sociology as supporting the status quo.*

Research Orientations and Theory

- Positivist sociology is loosely linked to the structural-functional approach.
- Interpretive sociology is related to the symbolic-interaction approach.
- Critical sociology corresponds to the social-conflict approach.

p. 37

📖 See the Summing Up table on page 36.

---

science (p. 29) a logical system that bases knowledge on direct, systematic observation

empirical evidence (p. 29) information we can verify with our senses

positivist sociology (p. 31) the study of society based on systematic observation of social behavior

concept (p. 31) a mental construct that represents some part of the world in a simplified form

variable (p. 31) a concept whose value changes from case to case

measurement (p. 31) a procedure for determining the value of a variable in a specific case

operationalize a variable (p. 32) specifying exactly what is to be measured before assigning a value to a variable

reliability (p. 33) consistency in measurement

validity (p. 33) actually measuring exactly what you intend to measure

cause and effect (p. 33) a relationship in which change in one variable causes change in another

independent variable (p. 33) the variable that causes the change

dependent variable (p. 33) the variable that changes

correlation (p. 34) a relationship in which two (or more) variables change together

spurious correlation (p. 34) an apparent but false relationship between two (or more) variables that is caused by some other variable

control (p. 34) holding constant all variables except one in order to see clearly the effect of that variable

objectivity (p. 34) personal neutrality in conducting research

replication (p. 35) repetition of research by other investigators

interpretive sociology (p. 36) the study of society that focuses on the meanings people attach to their social world

critical sociology (p. 36) the study of society that focuses on the need for social change

Gender and Research

Gender, involving both researcher and subjects, can affect research in five ways:
- androcentricity
- overgeneralizing
- gender blindness
- double standards
- interference

`pp. 37–38`

Research Ethics

Researchers must
- protect the privacy of subjects
- obtain the informed consent of subjects
- indicate all sources of funding
- submit research to an institutional review board (IRB) to ensure it doesn't violate ethical standards

`p. 38`

Methods: Strategies for Doing Research

The **EXPERIMENT** allows researchers to study cause and effect between two or more variables in a controlled setting.
- Researchers conduct an experiment to test a **hypothesis**, a statement of a possible relationship between two (or more) variables.
- ✓ Example of an experiment: Zimbardo's "Stanford County Prison"

`pp. 38–41`

SURVEY research uses questionnaires or interviews to gather subjects' responses to a series of questions.
- Surveys typically yield descriptive findings, painting a picture of people's views on some issue.
- ✓ Example of a survey: Benjamin's "Talented One Hundred"

`pp. 41–43`

Through **PARTICIPANT OBSERVATION**, researchers join with people in a social setting for an extended period of time.
- Participant observation, also called *fieldwork*, allows researchers an "inside look" at a social setting. Because researchers are not attempting to test a specific hypothesis, their research is exploratory and descriptive.
- ✓ Example of participant observation: Whyte's *Street Corner Society*

`pp. 43–47`

Sometimes researchers analyze **EXISTING SOURCES**, data collected by others.
- Using existing sources, especially the widely available data collected by government agencies, can save researchers time and money.
- Existing sources are the basis of historical research.
- ✓ Example of using existing sources: Baltzell's *Puritan Boston and Quaker Philadelphia*

`pp. 47–48`

See the Summing Up table on page 49.

✓ Researchers combine these methods, depending on the specific goals of their study.

✓ Which method the researcher uses depends on the question being asked.

---

gender (p. 37) the personal traits and social positions that members of a society attach to being female or male

research method (p. 38) a systematic plan for doing research

experiment (p. 38) a research method for investigating cause and effect under highly controlled conditions

hypothesis (p. 39) a statement of a possible relationship between two (or more) variables

Hawthorne effect (p. 40) a change in a subject's behavior caused simply by the awareness of being studied

survey (p. 41) a research method in which subjects respond to a series of statements or questions on a questionnaire or in an interview

population (p. 41) the people who are the focus of research

sample (p. 41) a part of a population that represents the whole

questionnaire (p. 41) a series of written questions a researcher presents to subjects

interview (p. 42) a series of questions a researcher asks respondents in person

participant observation (p. 43) a research method in which investigators systematically observe people while joining them in their routine activities

inductive logical thought (p. 48) reasoning that transforms specific observations into general theory

deductive logical thought (p. 49) reasoning that transforms general theory into specific hypotheses suitable for testing

Culture refers to a way of life, which includes what people do (such as forms of dance) and what people have (such as clothing). But culture is not only about what we see on the outside; it also includes what's inside— our thoughts and feelings.

CHAPTER 3

Culture

SUPPLEMENTS: Chapter 3 of the *Instructor's Manual* includes a detailed chapter outline, supplementary lecture material, and discussion questions.

Q: "Culture … is that complex whole which includes knowledge, belief, art, morals, laws, customs, and any other capabilities and habits acquired by man as a member of society." Edward B. Tylor, who offered perhaps the first formal definition of culture

Q: "Natives who beat drums to drive off evil spirits are objects of scorn to smart Americans who blow horns to break up traffic jams." Mary Ellen Kelly

CHAPTER OVERVIEW

This chapter focuses on the concept of "culture," which refers to a society's entire way of life. Notice that the root of the word "culture" is the same as that of the word "cultivate," suggesting that people living together actually "grow" their way of life over time.

It's late on a Tuesday night, but Fang Lin gazes intently at her computer screen. Dong Wang, her husband, walks up behind the chair.

"I'm trying to finish organizing our investments," Fang explains, speaking in Chinese.

"I didn't realize that we could do that online in our own language," Dong says, reading the screen. "I like that a lot."

Fang and Dong are not alone in feeling this way. Back in 1990, executives of Charles Schwab & Co., a large investment brokerage corporation, gathered in a conference room at the company's headquarters in San Francisco to discuss ways they could expand their business. They came up with the idea that the company would profit by giving greater attention to the increasing cultural diversity of the United States. Pointing to data collected by researchers at the U.S. Census Bureau, they saw that the number of Asian Americans was rising rapidly, not just in San Francisco but all over the country. The data also showed that Asian Americans, on average, are doing pretty well, with more than half of households earning more than $75,000 a year (U.S. Census Bureau, 2008).

This meeting led Schwab to launch a diversity initiative, assigning three executives to work on building awareness of the company among Asian Americans. The program has taken off, and Schwab now employs more than 300 people who speak Chinese, Japanese, Korean, Vietnamese, or some other Asian language. Having account executives who speak languages other than English is smart because research shows that most immigrants who come to the United States prefer to communicate in their first language, especially when dealing with important matters such as investing their money. In addition, the company has launched Web sites using Chinese, Korean, and other Asian languages. Fang Lin and Dong Wang are just two of the millions of people who have opened accounts with companies that reach out to them in a language other than English.

Schwab now manages a significant share of the investments made by Asian Americans, who are expected to spend more than $500 billion a year by 2009. So any company would do well to follow the lead Schwab has taken. Other ethnic and racial categories that represent even larger markets in the United States are Hispanics and African Americans (each spending some $700 billion) (Fattah, 2002; Karrfalt, 2003; U.S. Department of Labor, 2007).

Businesses like Schwab are taking note of the fact that the United States is the most *multicultural* of all the world's nations. This cultural diversity reflects the country's long history of receiving immigrants from all over the world. The ways of life found around the world differ, not only in language and forms of dress but also in preferred foods, musical tastes, family patterns, and beliefs about right and wrong. Some of the world's people have many children, while others have few; some honor the elderly, while others seem to glorify youth. Some societies are peaceful, while others are warlike; and societies around the world embrace a thousand different religious beliefs as well as particular ideas about what is polite and rude, beautiful and ugly, pleasant and repulsive. This amazing human capacity for so many different ways of life is a matter of human culture.

What Is Culture?

Culture is *the ways of thinking, the ways of acting, and the material objects that together form a people's way of life.* Culture includes what we think, how we act, and what we own. Culture is both our link to the past and our guide to the future.

NOTE: The Latin root of "culture," *cultura*, means "a tilling." Note that "cultivate" and "agriculture" have the same root. In this sense, culture is the means by which humans cultivate the world.

Q: What we have loved,
   Others will love,
   And we will teach them how.
Wordsworth

culture the ways of thinking, the ways of acting, and the material objects that together from a people's way of life

nonmaterial culture (p.60) the ideas created by members of a society

material culture (p.60) the physical things created by members of a society

Human beings around the globe create diverse ways of life. Such differences begin with outward appearance: Contrast the women shown here from Brazil, Kenya, New Guinea, South Yemen, and the United States and the men from Taiwan (Republic of China), India, Canada, and New Guinea. Less obvious but of even greater importance are internal differences, since culture also shapes our goals in life, our sense of justice, and even our innermost personal feelings.

Q: "Man has no nature; what he has is history." José Ortega y Gassett

DISCUSS: Culture shock happens even in our own communities as we confront people of other colors, cultures, and class positions. Can students provide examples from their own lives?

Q: "I was a student in the department of anthropology. They taught me that nobody was ridiculous or bad or disgusting." Kurt Vonnegut

NOTE: Note that sociologists use "culture" in an all-inclusive way, not with highbrow connotations ("cul-chah").

NOTE: The early human ancestor known as Lucy, who lived about 3 million years ago, stood about 3 ft. 6 in. tall and weighed 65 lbs.; at that time, men might have reached 5 ft. and 100 lbs. Today's global averages are 5 ft. 6 in. tall and 150 lbs. for men, 5 ft. 2 in. and 125 lbs. for women.

culture shock personal disorientation when experiencing an unfamiliar way of life

SEEING SOCIOLOGY
in Everyday Life

Can you describe specific practices or patterns familiar to us in the United States that would shock people living in some other part of the world? Explain your response.

To understand all that culture is, we must consider both thoughts and things. **Nonmaterial culture** is *the ideas created by members of a society,* ideas that range from art to Zen. **Material culture,** by contrast, is *the physical things created by members of a society,* everything from armchairs to zippers.

Culture shapes not only what we do but also what we think and how we feel—elements of what we commonly, but wrongly, describe as "human nature." The warlike Yąnomamö of the Brazilian rain forest think aggression is natural, but halfway around the world, the Semai of Malaysia live quite peacefully. The cultures of the United States and Japan both stress achievement and hard work, but members of our society value individualism more than the Japanese, who value collective harmony.

Given the extent of cultural differences in the world and people's tendency to view their own way of life as "natural," it is no wonder that travelers often find themselves feeling uneasy as they enter an unfamiliar culture. This uneasiness is **culture shock,** *personal disorientation when experiencing an unfamiliar way of life.* People can experience culture shock right here in the United States when, say, African Americans explore an Iranian neighborhood in Los Angeles, college students venture into the Amish countryside in Ohio, or New Yorkers travel through small towns in the Deep South. But culture shock is most intense when we travel abroad: The Thinking Globally box

tells the story of a researcher from the United States making his first visit to the home of the Yąnomamö living in the Amazon region of South America.

> **January 2, high in the Andes Mountains of Peru.** In the rural highlands, people are poor and depend on one another. The culture is built on cooperation among family members and neighbors who have lived nearby for generations. Today, we spent an hour watching a new house being built. A young couple had invited their families and friends, who arrived at about 6:30 in the morning, and right away they began building. By midafternoon, most of the work was finished, and the couple then provided a large meal, drinks, and music that continued for the rest of the day.

No way of life is "natural" to humanity, even though most people around the world view their own behavior that way. The cooperative spirit that comes naturally to people in the Andes Mountains of Peru is very different from the competitive living that comes naturally to many people in, say, Chicago or New York City. Such variations come from the fact that as human beings, we join together to create our own way of life. Every other animal, from ants to zebras, behaves very much the same all around the world because behavior is guided by *instincts,* biological programming over which the species has no control. A few animals—notably chimpanzees and related primates—have the capacity for limited culture, as researchers have noted by observing them using tools and teaching simple skills to their offspring. But the creative power of humans is far greater than that of any other form of life and has resulted in countless ways of "being human." In short, *only humans rely on culture rather than instinct to create a way of life and ensure our survival* (Harris, 1987; Morell, 2008). To understand how human culture came to be, we need to look back at the history of our species.

Culture and Human Intelligence

Scientists tell us that our planet is 4.5 billion years old (see the timeline inside the front cover of this text). Life appeared about 1 billion years later. Fast-forward another 2 to 3 billion years, and we find dinosaurs ruling Earth. It was after these giant creatures disappeared, some 65 million years ago, that our history took a crucial turn with the appearance of the animals we call primates.

The importance of primates is that they have the largest brains relative to body size of all living creatures. About 12 million years ago, primates began to evolve along two different

All societies contain cultural differences that can provoke a mild case of culture shock. This woman traveling on a British subway is not sure what to make of the woman sitting next to her, who is wearing the Muslim full-face veil known as the *niqab*.

○ MAKING THE GRADE

Humans are not the only creatures who have culture, but we are the only creatures who *depend on* culture to survive.

THINKING GLOBALLY	Confronting the Yąnomamö: The Experience of Culture Shock

A small aluminum motorboat chugged steadily along the muddy Orinoco River, deep within South America's vast tropical rain forest. The anthropologist Napoleon Chagnon was nearing the end of a three-day journey to the home territory of the Yąnomamö, one of the most technologically simple societies on Earth.

Some 12,000 Yąnomamö live in villages scattered along the border of Venezuela and Brazil. Their way of life could not be more different from our own. The Yąnomamö wear little clothing and live without electricity, automobiles, or other familiar conveniences. Their traditional weapon, used for hunting and warfare, is the bow and arrow. Most of the Yąnomamö knew little about the outside world, so Chagnon would be as strange to them as they would be to him.

By 2:00 in the afternoon, Chagnon had almost reached his destination. The heat and humidity were almost unbearable. He was soaked with perspiration, and his face and hands swelled from the bites of gnats swarming around him. But he hardly noticed, so excited was he that in just a few moments, he would be face to face with people unlike any he had ever known.

Chagnon's heart pounded as the boat slid onto the riverbank. He and his guide climbed from the boat and headed toward the sounds of a nearby village, pushing their way through the dense undergrowth. Chagnon describes what happened next:

I looked up and gasped when I saw a dozen burly, naked, sweaty, hideous men staring at us down the shafts of their drawn arrows! Immense wads of green tobacco were stuck between their lower teeth and lips, making them look even more hideous, and strands of dark green slime dripped or hung from their nostrils—strands so long that they clung to their [chests] or drizzled down their chins.

My next discovery was that there were a dozen or so vicious, underfed dogs snapping at my legs, circling me as if I were to be

their next meal. I just stood there holding my notebook, helpless and pathetic. Then the stench of the decaying vegetation and filth hit me and I almost got sick. I was horrified. What kind of welcome was this for the person who came here to live with you and learn your way of life, to become friends with you? (1992:11–12)

Fortunately for Chagnon, the Yąnomamö villagers recognized his guide and lowered their weapons. Though reassured that he would survive the afternoon, Chagnon was still shaken by his inability to make any sense of the people surrounding him. And this was going to be his home for the next year and a half! He wondered why he had given up physics to study human culture in the first place.

WHAT DO YOU THINK?

1. As they came to know Chagnon, might the Yąnomamö, too, have experienced culture shock? Why?

2. Can you think of an experience you had that is similar to the one described here?

3. How can studying sociology help reduce the experience of culture shock?

lines, setting humans apart from the great apes, our closest relatives. Some 3 million years ago, our distant human ancestors climbed down from the trees of Central Africa to move about in the tall grasses. There, walking upright, they learned the advantages of hunting in groups and made use of fire, tools, and weapons; built simple shelters; and fashioned basic clothing. These Stone Age achievements may seem modest, but they mark the point at which our ancestors set off on a distinct evolutionary course, making culture their primary strategy for survival. By about 250,000 years ago, our own species, *Homo sapiens* (Latin for "intelligent person"), finally emerged. Humans

continued to evolve so that by about 40,000 years ago, people who looked more or less like ourselves roamed the planet. With larger brains, these "modern" *Homo sapiens* developed culture rapidly, as the wide range of tools and cave art from this period suggests.

About 12,000 years ago, the founding of permanent settlements and the creation of specialized occupations in the Middle East (today's Iraq and Egypt) marked the "birth of civilization." About this point, the biological forces we call instincts had mostly disappeared, replaced by a more efficient survival scheme: *fashioning the natural environment for ourselves.* Ever since, humans have made and

MAKING THE GRADE

The United States is culturally diverse, reflecting our historically high level of immigration.

symbol anything that carries a particular meaning recognized by people who share a culture

remade their world in countless ways, resulting in today's fascinating cultural diversity.

Culture, Nation, and Society

The term "culture" calls to mind other similar terms, such as "nation" and "society," although each has a slightly different meaning. *Culture* refers to a shared way of life. A *nation* is a political entity, a territory with designated borders, such as the United States, Canada, Peru, or Zimbabwe. *Society,* the topic of Chapter 4, is the organized interaction of people who typically live in a nation or some other specific territory.

The United States, then, is both a nation and a society. But many nations, including the United States, are *multicultural;* that is, their people follow various ways of life that blend (and sometimes clash).

How Many Cultures?

In the United States, how many cultures are there? One indicator of culture is language; the Census Bureau lists more than 300 languages spoken in this country—about half of them are native languages, and half were brought by immigrants from nations around the world (NVTC, 2007).

Globally, experts document almost 7,000 languages, suggesting the existence of as many distinct cultures. Yet the number of languages spoken around the world is declining, and roughly half now are spoken by fewer than 10,000 people (Gordon, 2005). Experts expect that the coming decades may see the disappearance of hundreds of these languages, from Gullah, Pennsylvania German, and Pawnee (all spoken in the United States) to Han (spoken in northwestern Canada), Oro (spoken in the Amazon region of Brazil), Sardinian (spoken on the European island of Sardinia), Aramaic (the language of Jesus of Nazareth, still spoken in the Middle East), Nu Shu (a language spoken in southern China that is the only one known to be used exclusively by women), and Wakka Wakka and several other Aboriginal tongues spoken in Australia. What accounts for the decline? Likely causes include high-technology communication, increasing international migration, and an expanding global economy (UNESCO, 2001; Barovick, 2002; Hayden, 2003).

The Elements of Culture

Although cultures vary greatly, they all have common elements, including symbols, language, values, and norms. We begin our discussion with the one that is the basis for all the others: symbols.

Symbols

Like all creatures, humans use their senses to experience the surrounding world, but unlike others, we also try to give the world *meaning.* Humans transform elements of the world into *symbols.* A **symbol** is *anything that carries a particular meaning recognized by people who share a culture.* A word, a whistle, a wall covered with graffiti, a flashing red light, a raised fist—all serve as symbols. We can see the human capacity to create and manipulate symbols reflected in the very different meanings associated with the simple act of winking an eye, which can convey interest, understanding, or insult.

Societies create new symbols all the time. The Seeing Sociology in Everyday Life box describes some of the "cyber-symbols" that have developed along with our increasing use of computers for communication.

We are so dependent on our culture's symbols that we take them for granted. However, we become keenly aware of the importance of a symbol when someone uses it in an unconventional way, as when a person burns a U.S. flag during a political demonstration. Entering an unfamiliar culture also reminds us of the power of symbols; culture shock is really the inability to "read" meaning in strange surroundings. Not understanding the symbols of a culture leaves a person feeling lost and isolated, unsure of how to act, and sometimes frightened.

Culture shock is a two-way process. On one hand, travelers *experience* culture shock when encountering people whose way of life

People throughout the world communicate not just with spoken words but also with bodily gestures. Because gestures vary from culture to culture, they can occasionally be the cause of misunderstandings. For instance, the commonplace "thumbs up" gesture we use to express "Good job!" can get a person from the United States into trouble in Greece, Iran, and a number of other countries, where people take it to mean "Up yours!"

GLOBAL: Societies show significant cultural variation in their favorite sports. Canada: ice hockey; Brazil: soccer; Jamaica: cricket; China: tai chi chuan; Thailand: kite flying.

NOTE: In the Bible, the first thing Adam and Eve do as human beings is name things.

GLOBAL: Sanskrit is the oldest living language.

NOTE: For decades, a "nurture vs. nature" debate has surrounded language. Nurture advocates argue that language systems are distinctive and that language is learned along with other cultural elements. Nature advocates counter that all linguistic systems have similar internal structures, suggesting that language construction is "wired" into the human brain. Noam Chomsky, probably the best-known researcher in this area, subscribes to the latter view.

MAKING THE GRADE

Anything can serve as a symbol; what makes something a symbol is simply that humans attach meaning to it.

SEEING SOCIOLOGY IN EVERYDAY LIFE

New Symbols in the World of Instant Messaging

MOLLY: gr8 to c u!

GREG: u 2

MOLLY: jw about next time

GREG: idk, lotta work!

MOLLY: no prb, xoxoxo

GREG: thanx, bcnu

The world of symbols changes all the time. One reason that people create new symbols is that we develop new ways to communicate. Today, almost 100 million people in the United States (most of them young and many of them students) communicate using an instant messaging (IM) program. All you need to have is a computer connected to the Internet or a cell phone. The exchange featured above shows how everyday social interaction can take place quickly and easily using IM symbols. The symbols people use change all the time, so the IM language used a year from now will differ, just as IM symbols differ from place to place. Here are some common IM symbols:

b   be
bc   because
b4   before
b4n   'bye for now
bbl   be back later
bcnu   be seeing you
brb   be right back
cu   see you
def   definitely
g2g   got to go

gal   get a life
gmta   great minds think alike
gr8   great
hagn   have a good night
h&k   hugs and kisses
idc   I don't care
Idt   I don't think
idk   I don't know
imbl   it must be love
jk   just kidding
jw   just wondering
j4f   just for fun
kc   keep cool
l8r   later
lmao   laugh my ass off
ltnc   long time no see
myob   mind your own business
no prb   no problem
omg   oh my gosh

pcm   please call me
plz   please
prbly   probably
qpsa   ¿Que pasa?
rt   right
thanx   thanks
u   you
ur   you are
w/   with
w/e   whatever
w/o   without
wan2   want to
wtf   what the freak
y   why
2l8   too late
?   question
2   to, two
4   for, four

WHAT DO YOU THINK?

1. What does the creation of symbols such as these suggest about culture?

2. Do you think that using such symbols is a good way to communicate? Does it lead to confusion or misunderstanding? Why or why not?

3. What other kinds of symbols can you think of that are new to your generation?

Sources: J. Rubin (2003) and Berteau (2005); updated by Megan Bacher, 2009.

is different. For example, North Americans who consider dogs beloved household pets might be put off by the Masai of eastern Africa, who ignore dogs and never feed them. The same travelers might be horrified to find that in parts of Indonesia and the People's Republic of China, people roast dogs for dinner.

On the other hand, a traveler may *inflict* culture shock on local people by acting in ways that offend them. A North American who asks for a steak in an Indian restaurant may unknowingly offend Hindus, who consider cows sacred and never to be eaten. Global travel provides almost endless opportunities for this kind of misunderstanding.

Symbolic meanings also vary within a single society. To some people in the United States, a fur coat represents a prized symbol of success, but to others, it represents the inhumane treatment of animals. In the debate about flying the Confederate flag over the South Carolina statehouse a few years ago, some people saw the flag as a symbol of regional pride, but others saw it as a symbol of racial oppression.

POP CULTURE: The oral tradition is evident in U.S. society in the passing of cultural experience through hip-hop music. Initially focusing on the oppression of African Americans, hip-hop became mainstream with messages that echoed the widespread cultural values of individualism, materialism, and male power.

DISCUSS: Does the Sapir-Whorf thesis imply that people have the power to change reality by changing their symbols? What happened, for example, when people in the

U.S. started using words like "African American" rather than "Negro"? How does the meaning of "colored person" differ from "person of color"?

NOTE: In societies with the oral tradition, people display what we would consider amazing powers of memorization. Ancient Romans recited Virgil's *Aeneid*, the mythic tale of the founding of Rome, from memory, although it is some 400 pages long.

language a system of symbols that allows people to communicate with one another

cultural transmission the process by which one generation passes culture to the next

Sapir-Whorf thesis the idea that people see and understand the world through the cultural lens of language

Language

An illness in infancy left Helen Keller (1880–1968) blind and deaf. Without these two senses, she was cut off from the symbolic world, and her social development was greatly limited. Only when her teacher, Anne Mansfield Sullivan, broke through Keller's isolation using sign language did Helen Keller begin to realize her human potential. This remarkable woman, who later became a famous educator herself, recalls the moment she first understood the concept of language:

> We walked down the path to the well-house, attracted by the smell of honeysuckle with which it was covered. Someone was drawing water, and my teacher placed my hand under the spout. As the cool stream gushed over one hand, she spelled into the other the word *water,* first slowly, then rapidly. I stood still, my whole attention fixed upon the motions of her fingers. Suddenly I felt a misty consciousness as of something forgotten—a thrill of returning thought; and somehow the mystery of language was revealed to me. I knew then that "w-a-t-e-r" meant the wonderful cool something that was flowing over my hand. That living word awakened my soul; gave it light, hope, joy, set it free! (1903:24)

Language, the key to the world of culture, is *a system of symbols that allows people to communicate with one another.* Humans have created many alphabets to express the hundreds of languages we speak. Several examples are shown in Figure 3–1. Even rules for writing differ: Most people in Western societies write from left to right, but people in northern Africa and western Asia write from right to left, and people in eastern Asia write from top to bottom. Global Map 3–1 shows where we find the three most widely spoken languages, English, Chinese, and Spanish.

FIGURE 3–1 **Human Languages: A Variety of Symbols**
Here the English word "read" is written in twelve of the hundreds of languages humans use to communicate with one another.

Language not only allows communication but is also the key to **cultural transmission,** *the process by which one generation passes culture to the next.* Just as our bodies contain the genes of our ancestors, our culture contains countless symbols of those who came before us. Language is the key that unlocks centuries of accumulated wisdom.

Throughout human history, every society has transmitted culture using speech, a process sociologists call the "oral cultural tradition." Some 5,000 years ago, humans invented writing, although at that time only a privileged few learned to read and write. Not until the twentieth century did high-income nations boast of nearly universal literacy. Still, at least 10 percent of U.S. adults (more than 30 million people) are functionally illiterate, unable to read and write in a society that increasingly demands such skills. In low-income countries of the world, 15 percent of men and 24 percent of women are illiterate (U.S. Department of Education, 2008; Population Reference Bureau, 2009).

Language skills may link us with the past, but they also spark the human imagination to connect symbols in new ways, creating an almost limitless range of future possibilities. Language sets humans apart as the only creatures who are self-conscious, aware of our limitations and ultimate mortality, yet able to dream and to hope for a future better than the present.

Does Language Shape Reality?

Does someone who speaks Cherokee, an American Indian language, experience the world differently from other North Americans who think in, say, English or Spanish? Edward Sapir and Benjamin Whorf claimed that the answer is yes, since each language has its own distinctive symbols that serve as the building blocks of reality (Sapir, 1929, 1949; Whorf, 1956, orig. 1941). Further, they noted that each language has words or expressions not found in any other symbolic system. Finally, all languages fuse symbols with distinctive emotions so that, as multilingual people know, a single idea may "feel" different when spoken in Spanish rather than in English or Chinese.

Formally, the **Sapir-Whorf thesis** states that *people see and understand the world through the cultural lens of language.* In the decades since Sapir and Whorf published their work, however, scholars have taken issue with this thesis. Current thinking is that although we do fashion reality from our symbols, evidence does not support the notion that language *determines* reality the way Sapir and Whorf claimed. For example, we know that children understand the idea of "family" long before they learn that word; similarly, adults can imagine new ideas or things before inventing a name for them (Kay & Kempton, 1984; Pinker, 1994).

Values and Beliefs

What accounts for the popularity of Hollywood film characters such as James Bond, Neo, Erin Brockovich, Lara Croft, and Rocky Balboa? Each is ruggedly individualistic, going it alone and relying on personal skill and savvy to challenge "the system." We are led to admire

Chinese is spoken as a native language by twice as many people in the world as English, but English is a widely spoken second language almost everywhere in the world.

Window on the World

GLOBAL MAP 3–1 Language in Global Perspective

Chinese (including Mandarin, Cantonese, and dozens of other dialects) is the native tongue of one-fifth of the world's people, almost all of whom live in Asia. Although all Chinese people read and write with the same characters, they use several dozen dialects. The "official" dialect, taught in schools throughout the People's Republic of China and the Republic of Taiwan, is Mandarin (the dialect of Beijing, China's capital). Cantonese, the language of Canton, is the second most common Chinese dialect; it differs in sound from Mandarin roughly the way French differs from Spanish.

English is the native tongue or official language in several world regions (spoken by one-tenth of humanity) and has become the preferred second language in most of the world.

The largest concentration of Spanish speakers is in Latin America and, of course, Spain. Spanish is also the second most widely spoken language in the United States.

Sources: R.G. Gordon (2005) and National Virtual Translation Center (2007).

DISCUSS: What cultural value is expressed in Benjamin Franklin's belief that "God helps those who help themselves"?

GLOBAL: Regarding Williams's ten points for traditional societies: (1 and 2) Traditional societies generally embrace fate as a key value. (3) Spiritual comfort and well-being. (4) Greater reflectiveness (especially Eastern cultures). (5) Implies a rational worldview; this value also suggests why we devalue academics as "eggheads." (6) Members of most traditional societies are not optimistic (even the Japanese are less so). (7) Religion plays much more of a role than science. (8) Collective sentiment is higher, as is compliance to official authority; for example, Moroccans accept high-handed police direction with little evident complaint. (9) Most of the world is less individualistic than we are. (10) Most of the traditional world is much more group-oriented than we are.

values culturally defined standards that people use to decide what is desirable, good, and beautiful and that serve as broad guidelines for social living

beliefs specific ideas that people hold to be true

SEEING SOCIOLOGY
in Everyday Life

Think about the games you played when you were growing up, like Tag or Capture the Flag, or board games, like Monopoly or Chutes and Ladders. What cultural values do they teach? What about video games like Grand Theft Auto, God of War, or Rainbow Six Vegas?

The Australian artist and feminist Sally Swain alters famous artists' paintings to make fun of our culture's tendency to ignore the everyday lives of women. This spoof is titled *Mrs. Warhol Is of Two Minds About What to Cook for Dinner.*

Mrs. Warhol Is of Two Minds About What to Cook for Dinner, from *Great Housewives of Art* by Sally Swain, copyright © 1988, 1989 by Sally Swain. Used by permission of Viking Penguin, a division of Penguin Group (USA) Inc.

such characters by certain **values,** *culturally defined standards that people use to decide what is desirable, good, and beautiful and that serve as broad guidelines for social living.* Values are what people who share a culture use to make choices about how to live.

Values are broad principles that support **beliefs,** *specific thoughts or ideas that people hold to be true.* In other words, values are abstract standards of goodness, and beliefs are particular matters that individuals consider true or false. For example, because most U.S. adults share the *value* of providing equal opportunities for all, they believe that a qualified woman could serve as president of the United States, as the 2008 campaign of Hillary Clinton demonstrated (NORC, 2008:285).

Key Values of U.S. Culture

Because U.S. culture is a mix of ways of life from other countries all around the world, it is highly diverse. Even so, the sociologist Robin Williams (1970) has identified ten values that are widespread in the United States and viewed by many people as central to our way of life:

1. **Equal opportunity.** Most people in the United States favor not *equality of condition* but *equality of opportunity.* We believe that our society should provide everyone with the chance to get ahead according to individual talents and efforts.

2. **Achievement and success.** Our way of life encourages competition so that each person's rewards should reflect personal merit. A successful person is given the respect due a "winner."

3. **Material comfort.** Success in the United States generally means making money and enjoying what it will buy. Although we sometimes say that "money won't buy happiness," most of us pursue wealth all the same.

4. **Activity and work.** Popular U.S. heroes, from golf champion Tiger Woods to the winners of television's *American Idol,* are "doers" who get the job done. Our culture values action over reflection and taking control of events over passively accepting fate.

5. **Practicality and efficiency.** We value the practical over the theoretical, "doing" over "dreaming." Activity has value to the extent that it earns money. "Major in something that will help you get a job!" parents tell their college-age children.

6. **Progress.** We are an optimistic people who, despite waves of nostalgia, believe that the present is better than the past. We celebrate progress, viewing the "very latest" as the "very best."

7. **Science.** We expect scientists to solve problems and improve the quality of our lives. We believe we are rational, logical people, which probably explains our cultural tendency (especially among men) to look down on emotion and intuition as sources of knowledge.

8. **Democracy and free enterprise.** Members of our society believe that individuals have rights that governments should not take away. We believe that a just political system is based on free elections in which adults select government leaders and on an economy that responds to the choices of individual consumers.

9. **Freedom.** We favor individual initiative over collective conformity. While we know that everyone has responsibilities to others, we believe that people should be free to pursue their personal goals.

10. **Racism and group superiority.** Despite strong ideas about equal opportunity and freedom, most people in the United States judge

SEEING SOCIOLOGY
in Everyday Life

Would you say that physical fitness is an emerging cultural value? Why or why not?

social control (p.68) attempts by society to regulate people's thoughts and behavior

norms rules and expectations by which a society guides the behavior of its members

mores (p.68) norms that are widely observed and have great moral significance

folkways (p.68) norms for routine or casual interaction

individuals according to gender, race, ethnicity, and social class. In general, U.S. culture values males above females, whites above people of color, rich above poor, and people with northwestern European backgrounds above those whose ancestors came from other parts of the world. Although we like to describe ourselves as a nation of equals, there is little doubt that some of us are "more equal" than others.

Values: Often in Harmony, Sometimes in Conflict

In many ways, cultural values go together. Williams's list includes examples of *value clusters* that are part of our way of life. For instance, we value activity and hard work because we expect effort to lead to achievement and success and result in greater material comfort.

Sometimes, however, one key cultural value contradicts another. Take the first and last items on Williams's list, for example: People in the United States believe in equality of opportunity, yet they may also look down on others because of their sex or race. Value conflict causes strain and often leads to awkward balancing acts in our beliefs. Sometimes people might say they support equal opportunity while at the same time opposing the acceptance of homosexual people in the U.S. military. In such cases, people simply learn to live with the contradictions.

Emerging Values

Like all elements of culture, values change over time. People in the United States have always valued hard work. In recent decades, however, we have placed increasing importance on leisure—having time off from work to do things such as reading, travel, or community service that provide enjoyment and satisfaction. Similarly, although the importance of material comfort remains strong, more people are seeking personal growth through meditation and other spiritual activity.

Values: A Global Perspective

Values vary from culture to culture around the world. In general, the values that are important in higher-income countries differ somewhat from those common in lower-income countries.

Lower-income nations develop cultures that value survival. This means that people place a great deal of importance on physical safety and economic security. They worry about having enough to eat and a safe place to sleep at night. In addition, lower-income nations tend to be traditional, with values that celebrate the past and emphasize

How does the popularity of the television show *American Idol* illustrate many of the key values of U.S. culture listed here?

the importance of family and religious beliefs. These nations, in which men have most of the power, typically discourage or forbid practices such as divorce and abortion.

People in higher-income countries develop cultures that value individualism and self-expression. These countries are rich enough that most of their people take survival for granted, focusing their attention instead on which "lifestyle" they prefer and how to achieve the greatest personal happiness. In addition, these countries tend to be secular-rational, placing less emphasis on family ties and religious beliefs and more on people thinking for themselves and being tolerant of others who differ from them. In higher-income countries, women have social standing more equal to men, and there is widespread support for practices such as divorce and abortion (World Values Survey, 2008). Figure 3–2 on page 68 shows how selected countries of the world compare in terms of their cultural values.

Norms

Most people in the United States are eager to gossip about "who's hot" and "who's not." Members of American Indian societies, however, typically condemn such behavior as rude and divisive. Both patterns illustrate the operation of **norms**, *rules and expectations by which a society guides the behavior of its members.* In everyday life, people respond to each other with *sanctions,* rewards or punishments that encourage conformity to cultural norms.

Q: "Cultures are dramatic conversations about things that matter to their participants." Robert Bellah

NOTE: Not all norms are neatly characterized as mores or folkways; these concepts are most effectively used as endpoints of a continuum.

NOTE: The number of motor vehicles on U.S. roads has increased more than 50% since 1980.

DISCUSS: Ideal culture is often revealed in "legend," derived from Latin meaning "things to be read." The Greeks celebrated Homer; the Romans, Virgil; the Christians, saints and Joan of Arc; medieval nobles, King Arthur; and moderns, a list of rugged individualists, from Davy Crockett to James Bond, Rambo, and Erin Brockovich. Ask the class to characterize these figures.

SEEING SOCIOLOGY
in Everyday Life

Figure 3–2 shows that as a rich nation, the United States ranks high in terms of self-expression but is more traditional than many other high-income nations, such as those in Europe. Can you point to specific beliefs or practices that set us apart from Europeans as more traditional?

SEEING SOCIOLOGY
in Everyday Life

Give two examples of campus folkways and two examples of campus mores. What are the likely consequences of violating each type of norm?

Global Snapshot

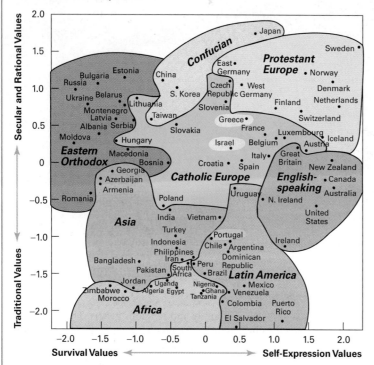

FIGURE 3–2 **Cultural Values of Selected Countries**

A general global pattern is that higher-income countries tend to be secular and rational and favor self-expression. By contrast, the cultures of lower-income countries tend to be more traditional and concerned with economic survival. Each region of the world, however, has distinctive cultural patterns, including religious traditions, that affect values. Looking at the figure, what patterns can you see?

Sources: Inglehart and Weizel (2005) and Inglehart (2009).

Mores and Folkways

William Graham Sumner (1959, orig. 1906), an early U.S. sociologist, recognized that some norms are more important to our lives than others. Sumner coined the term **mores** (pronounced "more-ayz") to refer to *norms that are widely observed and have great moral significance.* Mores, or *taboos,* include our society's insistence that adults not engage in sexual relations with children.

People are more flexible about **folkways,** *norms for routine or casual interaction.* Examples include ideas about appropriate greetings and proper dress. In short, mores distinguish between right and wrong,

and folkways draw a line between right and *rude.* A man who does not wear a tie to a formal dinner party may raise eyebrows for violating folkways. If, however, he were to arrive at the party wearing *only* a tie, he would violate cultural mores and invite a more serious response.

Social Control

Mores and folkways are the basic rules of everyday life. Although we sometimes resist pressure to conform, we can see that norms make our dealings with others more orderly and predictable. Observing or breaking the rules of social life prompts a response from others, in the form of either reward or punishment. Sanctions—whether an approving smile or a raised eyebrow—operate as a system of **social control,** *attempts by society to regulate people's thoughts and behavior.*

As we learn cultural norms, we gain the capacity to evaluate our own behavior. Doing wrong (say, downloading a term paper from the Internet) can cause both *shame* (the painful sense that others disapprove of our actions) and *guilt* (a negative judgment we make of ourselves). Of all living things, only cultural creatures can experience shame and guilt. This is probably what Mark Twain had in mind when he remarked that people "are the only animals that blush—or need to."

Ideal and Real Culture

Values and norms do not describe actual behavior so much as they suggest how we *should* behave. We must remember that *ideal* culture always differs from *real* culture, which is what actually occurs in everyday life. For example, most women and men agree on the importance of sexual faithfulness in marriage, and most say they live up to that standard. Even so, about 20 percent of married people report having been sexually unfaithful to their spouses at some point in their marriage (NORC, 2008:1877). But a culture's moral standards are important even if they are sometimes broken, calling to mind the old saying "Do as I say, not as I do."

Material Culture and Technology

In addition to symbolic elements such as values and norms, every culture includes a wide range of physical human creations called *artifacts.* The Chinese eat with chopsticks rather than forks, the Japanese put mats rather than rugs on the floor, and many men and women in India prefer flowing robes to the close-fitting clothing common in

NOTE: For a detailed discussion of how technology has shaped human society throughout history, see Chapter 4 ("Society").

NOTE: More complex technology empowers humans to manipulate the natural world; members of industrial societies therefore risk losing sensitivity to the natural environment and the requirements of living in an ecological system. Look ahead to Chapter 22 ("Population, Urbanization, and Environment").

DISCUSS: Why do Amish children attend school only through eighth grade? Why do the Amish refuse to be part of the Social Security system? Tension between the Amish and the rest of society has increased with more modern technology.

POP CULTURE: Consider the importance to popular culture of instant messaging to today's young people, as well as the popularity of new "smart phones."

SEEING SOCIOLOGY
in Everyday Life

If archaeologists dig up our civilization 50,000 years from now, based on the artifacts they find, what kind of people will they think we were? Point to specific artifacts (such as SUVs, cell phones, and credit cards) and what they say about us.

technology knowledge that people use to make a way of life in their surroundings

the United States. The material culture of a people may seem as strange to outsiders as their language, values, and norms.

A society's artifacts partly reflect underlying cultural values. The warlike Yąnomamö carefully craft their weapons and prize the poison tips on their arrows. By contrast, our society's emphasis on individualism and independence goes a long way toward explaining our high regard for the automobile: We own almost 250 million motor vehicles—more than one for every licensed driver—indicating the importance we place both on material things and the ability to move about independently.

In addition to reflecting values, material culture also reflects a society's **technology**, *knowledge that people use to make a way of life in their surroundings.* The more complex a society's technology is, the more its members are able (for better or worse) to shape the world for themselves. Advancements in technology have allowed us to crisscross the country with superhighways and to fill them with automobiles. At the same time, the internal-combustion engines in those cars release carbon dioxide into the atmosphere, which contributes to air pollution and global warming.

Because we attach great importance to science and praise sophisticated technology, people in our society tend to judge cultures with simpler technology as less advanced than our own. Some facts support such an assessment. For example, life expectancy for children born in the United States is more than seventy-seven years; the life span of the Yąnomamö is only about forty years.

However, we must be careful not to make self-serving judgments about other cultures. Although many Yąnomamö are eager to acquire modern technology (such as steel tools and shotguns), they are generally well fed by world standards, and most are very satisfied with their lives (Chagnon, 1992). Remember too that while our powerful and complex technology has produced work-reducing devices and seemingly miraculous medical treatments, it has also contributed to unhealthy levels of stress in the population and created weapons capable of destroying in a blinding flash everything that humankind has achieved.

Finally, technology is not equally distributed within our population. Although many of us cannot imagine life without a personal computer, television, and iPhone, many members of U.S. society cannot afford these luxuries. Others reject them on principle. The Amish, who live in small farming communities in Pennsylvania, Ohio, and Indiana, reject most modern conveniences on religious grounds. With

Standards of beauty—including the color and design of everyday surroundings—vary significantly from one culture to another. These two Ndebele women in South Africa dress in the same bright colors with which they decorate their homes. Members of North American and European societies, by contrast, make far less use of bright colors and intricate detail, so their housing appears much more subdued.

their traditional black clothing and horse-drawn buggies, the Amish may seem like a curious relic of the past. Yet their communities flourish, grounded in strong families that give everyone a sense of identity and purpose. Some researchers who have studied the Amish have concluded that these communities are "islands of sanity in a culture gripped by commercialism and technology run wild" (Hostetler, 1980:4; Kraybill, 1994).

New Information Technology and Culture

Many rich nations, including the United States, have entered a postindustrial phase based on computers and new information technology. Industrial production is centered on factories and machinery that generate material goods. By contrast, postindustrial production is based on computers and other electronic devices that create, process, store, and apply information.

In this new information economy, workers need symbolic skills in place of the mechanical skills of the industrial age. Symbolic skills include the ability to speak, write, compute, design, and create images in fields such as art, advertising, and entertainment. In today's computer-based economy, people with creative jobs are generating new cultural ideas, images, and products all the time.

high culture cultural patterns that distinguish a society's elite

popular culture cultural patterns that are widespread among a society's population

subculture cultural patterns that set apart some segment of a society's population

counterculture (p. 72) cultural patterns that strongly oppose those widely accepted within a society

Cultural Diversity: Many Ways of Life in One World

In the United States, we are aware of our cultural diversity when we hear the distinctive accents of people from New England, the Midwest, or the Deep South. Ours is also a nation of religious pluralism, a land of class differences, and a home to individualists who try to be like no one else. Compared to a country like Japan, whose historic isolation has made it the most *monocultural* of all high-income nations, centuries of immigration have made the United States the most *multicultural* of all high-income countries.

Between 1820 (when the government began keeping track of immigration) and 2008, more than 75 million people came to our shores. Our cultural mix continues to increase as more than 1 million people arrive each year. A century ago, almost all immigrants came from Europe; today, most newcomers arrive from Latin America and Asia (U.S. Department of Homeland Security, 2008). To understand the reality of life in the United States, we must move beyond broad cultural patterns and shared values to consider cultural diversity.

High Culture and Popular Culture

Cultural diversity involves not just immigration but also social class. In fact, in everyday talk, we usually use the term "culture" to mean art forms such as classical literature, music, dance, and painting. We describe people who regularly go to the opera or the theater as "cultured," because we think they appreciate the "finer things in life."

We speak less kindly of ordinary people, assuming that everyday culture is somehow less worthy. We are tempted to judge the music of Haydn as "more cultured" than hip-hop, couscous as better than cornbread, and polo as more polished than Ping-Pong.

These differences arise because many cultural patterns are readily available to only some members of a society. Sociologists use the term **high culture** to refer to *cultural patterns that distinguish a society's elite* and **popular culture** to designate *cultural patterns that are widespread among a society's population.*

Common sense may suggest that high culture is superior to popular culture, but sociologists are uneasy with such judgments, for two reasons. First, neither elites nor ordinary people share all the same tastes and interests; people in both categories differ in many ways. Second, do we praise high culture because it is inherently better than popular culture or simply because its supporters have more money, power, and prestige? For example, there is no difference between a violin and a fiddle; however, we name the instrument a violin when it is used to produce classical music typically enjoyed by a person of higher position and a fiddle when the musician plays country tunes appreciated by people with lower social standing.

Subculture

The term **subculture** refers to *cultural patterns that set apart some segment of a society's population.* People who ride "chopper" motorcycles, traditional Korean Americans, New England "Yankees," Ohio State football fans, the southern California "beach crowd," Elvis impersonators, and wilderness campers all display subcultural patterns.

It is easy but often inaccurate to place people in some subcultural category because almost everyone participates in many subcultures without necessarily having much commitment to any of them. In some cases, however, cultural differences can set people apart from one another with tragic results. Consider the former nation of Yugoslavia in southeastern Europe. The 1990s' civil war there was fueled by extreme cultural diversity. This *one* small country used *two* alphabets, embraced *three* religions, spoke *four* languages, was home to *five* major nationalities, was divided into *six* political republics, and absorbed the cultural influences of *seven* surrounding countries. The cultural conflict that plunged this nation into civil war shows that subcultures are a source not only of pleasing variety but also of tension and even violence.

Many people view the United States as a "melting pot" where many nationalities blend into a single "American" cul-

Sometimes the distinction between high culture and popular is not so clear. Bonham's Auction House in England recently featured spray-painted works by the graffiti artist Banksy. This particular one was expected to be sold for more than $250,000.

DISCUSS: Should immigrant youngsters be taught in their native language or English? Or both?

NOTE: Chemists tell us that only 92 elements occur naturally on Earth, but sociologists know that the world is home to countless variations of human culture.

GLOBAL: Music's roots throughout the world can be seen in the invention of instruments, such as the banjo (Africa), harmonica (Germany), saxophone (France), and guitar (Afghanistan, with guitar moving west and sitar moving east).

NOTE: The term "ethnocentrism" was introduced by William Graham Sumner in *Folkways* (1906:13).

RESOURCE: Discuss ethnocentrism and cultural relativism using Horace Miner's "Body Ritual among the Nacirema" and Alejandro Portes's article, "The English Only Debate," in the companion reader, *Seeing Ourselves*, 8th ed.

multiculturalism a perspective recognizing the cultural diversity of the United States and promoting equal standing for all cultural traditions

Eurocentrism the dominance of European (especially English) cultural patterns

Afrocentrism emphasizing and promoting African cultural patterns

A generation ago, most people regarded tattoos as a mark of low social status. Today, this cultural pattern is gaining popularity among people at all social class levels. Kat Von D is a tattoo artist on the nationwide television show *L.A. Ink.*

ture (Gardyn, 2002). But given so much cultural diversity, how accurate is the "melting pot" image? For one thing, subcultures involve not just *difference* but also *hierarchy*. Too often what we view as "dominant" or "mainstream" culture are patterns favored by powerful segments of the population, and we view the lives of disadvantaged people as "subculture." But are the cultural patterns of rich skiers in Aspen, Colorado, any less a subculture than the cultural patterns of skateboarders in Los Angeles? Some sociologists therefore prefer to level the playing field of society by emphasizing multiculturalism.

Multiculturalism

Multiculturalism is *a perspective recognizing the cultural diversity of the United States and promoting equal standing for all cultural traditions.* Multiculturalism represents a sharp change from the past, when our society downplayed cultural diversity and defined itself primarily in terms of well-off European and especially English immigrants. Today there is a spirited debate about whether we should continue to focus on historical traditions or highlight contemporary diversity.

E pluribus unum, the Latin phrase that appears on all U.S. coins, means "out of many, one." This motto symbolizes not only our national political union but also the idea that immigrants from around the world have come together to form a new way of life.

But from the outset, the many cultures did not melt together as much as harden into a hierarchy. At the top were the English, who formed a majority early in U.S. history and established English as the nation's dominant language. Further down, people of other backgrounds were advised to model themselves after "their betters." In practice, then, "melting" was really a process of Anglicization—adoption of English ways. As multiculturalists see it, early in our history, this society set up the English way of life as an ideal that everyone else should imitate and by which everyone should be judged.

Ever since, historians have reported events from the point of view of the English and other people of European ancestry, paying little attention to the perspectives and accomplishments of Native Americans and people of African and Asian descent. Multiculturalists criticize this as **Eurocentrism,** *the dominance of European (especially English) cultural patterns.* Molefi Kete Asante, a supporter of multiculturalism, argues that "like the fifteenth-century Europeans who could not cease believing that the Earth was the center of the universe, many today find it difficult to cease viewing European culture as the center of the social universe" (1988:7).

One controversial issue involves language. Some people believe that English should be the official language of the United States; by 2009, legislatures in thirty states had enacted laws making it the official language (ProEnglish, 2009). But some 55 million men and women—nearly one in five—speak a language other than English at home. Spanish is the second most commonly spoken language, and across the country we hear several hundred other tongues, including Italian, German, French, Filipino, Japanese, Korean, and Vietnamese, as well as many Native American languages. National Map 3–1 on page 72 shows where in the United States large numbers of people speak a language other than English at home.

Supporters of multiculturalism say it is a way of coming to terms with our country's increasing social diversity. With the Asian and Hispanic populations of this country increasing rapidly, some analysts predict that today's children will live to see people of African, Asian, and Hispanic ancestry become a *majority* of this country's population.

Supporters also claim that multiculturalism is a good way to strengthen the academic achievement of African American children. To counter Eurocentrism, some multicultural educators call for **Afrocentrism,** *emphasizing and promoting African cultural patterns,* which they see as necessary after centuries of minimizing or ignoring the cultural achievements of African societies and African Americans.

Although multiculturalism has found favor in recent years, it has drawn its share of criticism as well. Opponents say it encourages divisiveness rather than unity because it urges people to identify with their own category rather than with the nation as a whole. Instead of recognizing any common standards of truth, say critics, multiculturalism maintains that we should evaluate ideas according to the race (and sex) of those who present them. Our common humanity thus breaks down into an "African experience," an "Asian experience," and so on. In addition, critics say, multiculturalism actually harms minorities themselves. Multicultural policies (from African American studies to all-black dorms) seem to support the same racial segregation that our nation has struggled so long to overcome. Furthermore,

Elvira Martinez lives in Zapata County, Texas, where about three-quarters of the people in her community speak Spanish at home.

Jeffrey Steen lives in Adams County, Ohio, where almost none of his neighbors speaks a language other than English.

cultural integration the close relationships among various elements of a cultural system

cultural lag the fact that some cultural elements change more quickly than others, disrupting a cultural system

Seeing Ourselves

NATIONAL MAP 3–1
Language Diversity across the United States

Of more than 281 million people age five or older in the United States, the Census Bureau reports that more than 55 million (20 percent) speak a language other than English at home. Of these, 62 percent speak Spanish and 15 percent use an Asian language (the Census Bureau lists a total of 39 languages and language categories, each of which is favored by more than 100,000 people). The map shows that non–English speakers are concentrated in certain regions of the country. Which ones? What do you think accounts for this pattern?

Sources: U.S. Census Bureau (2008).

Percentage of Population That Speaks a Language Other than English at Home
- 60.0% or more
- 35.0% to 59.9%
- 17.9% to 34.9%
- 4.6% to 17.8%
- 0.4% to 4.5%
U.S. average = 19.7%

in the early grades, an Afrocentric curriculum may deny children a wide range of important knowledge and skills by forcing them to study only certain topics from a single point of view.

Finally, the global war on terror has drawn the issue of multiculturalism into the spotlight. In 2005, British Prime Minister Tony Blair responded to a terrorist attack in London, stating, "It is important that the terrorists realize [that] our determination to defend our values and our way of life is greater than their determination to . . . impose their extremism on the world." He went on to warn that the British government would expel Muslim clerics who encouraged hatred and terrorism (Barone, 2005; Carle, 2008). In a world of cultural difference and conflict, we have much to learn about tolerance and peacemaking.

Counterculture

Cultural diversity also includes outright rejection of conventional ideas or behavior. **Counterculture** refers to *cultural patterns that strongly oppose those widely accepted within a society.*

During the 1960s, for example, a youth-oriented counterculture rejected mainstream culture as overly competitive, self-centered, and materialistic. Instead, hippies and other counterculturalists favored a cooperative lifestyle in which "being" was more important than "doing" and the capacity for personal growth—or "expanded consciousness"—was prized over material possessions like homes and cars. Such differences led some people to "drop out" of the larger society.

Countercultures are still flourishing. At the extreme, small militaristic communities (made up of people born in this country) or bands of religious militants (from other countries) exist in the United States, some of them engaging in violence intended to threaten our way of life.

Cultural Change

Perhaps the most basic human truth of this world is that "all things shall pass." Even the dinosaurs, which thrived on this planet for 160 million years, exist today only as fossils. Will humanity survive for millions of years to come? All we can say with certainty is that given our reliance on culture, for as long as we survive, the human record will show continuous change.

Figure 3–3 shows changes in attitudes among first-year college students between 1969 (the height of the 1960s' counterculture) and 2008. Some attitudes have changed only slightly: Today, as a generation ago, most men and women look forward to raising a family. But today's students are less concerned with developing a philosophy of life and much more interested in making money.

Change in one part of a culture usually sparks changes in others. For example, today's college women are much more interested in making money because women are now far more likely to be in the labor force than their mothers or grandmothers were. Working for income may not change their interest in raising a family, but it does increase both the age at first marriage and the divorce rate. Such connections illustrate the principle of **cultural integration**, *the close relationships among various elements of a cultural system.*

Cultural Lag

Some elements of culture change faster than others. William Ogburn (1964) observed that technology moves quickly, generating new elements of material culture (things) faster than nonmaterial culture (ideas) can keep up with them. Ogburn called this inconsistency **cultural lag,** *the fact that some cultural elements change more quickly*

NOTE: William Ogburn (1964) called nonmaterial culture "adaptive culture" because it helps us adapt to technological change.

GLOBAL: Remember that change involving globalization means not only a rise in emigration by poor people to rich nations but also global tourism by rich people in poor nations.

DISCUSS: Refer to Figure 3–3 below and ask students to describe their own life objectives.

DISCUSS: Is child labor, a common practice in poor nations, morally wrong or a useful support to family income?

◖● MAKING THE GRADE

Three sources of social change are mentioned here. *Invention* refers to creating new cultural elements, *discovery* refers to recognizing existing cultural elements, and *diffusion* is the spread of cultural elements from one place to another.

than others, disrupting a cultural system. For example, in a world in which a woman can give birth to a child by using another woman's egg, which has been fertilized in a laboratory with the sperm of a total stranger, how are we to apply traditional ideas about motherhood and fatherhood?

Causes of Cultural Change

Cultural changes are set in motion in three ways. The first is *invention,* the process of creating new cultural elements. Invention has given us the telephone (1876), the airplane (1903), and the computer (late 1940s); each of these elements of material culture has had a tremendous impact on our way of life. The same is true of the minimum wage (1938), school desegregation (1954), and women's shelters (1975), each an important element of nonmaterial culture. The process of invention goes on constantly. The timeline on the inside cover of this text shows other inventions that have helped change our way of life.

Discovery, a second cause of cultural change, involves recognizing and understanding more fully something already in existence—perhaps a distant star or the foods of another culture or women's political leadership skills. Some discoveries result from painstaking scientific research, and some result from political struggle. Some even result from luck, as in 1898, when Marie Curie left a rock on a piece of photographic paper, noticed that emissions from the rock had exposed the paper, and thus discovered radium.

The third cause of cultural change is *diffusion,* the spread of cultural traits from one society to another. Because new information technology sends information around the globe in seconds, cultural diffusion has never been greater than it is today.

Certainly our own society has contributed many significant cultural elements to the world, ranging from computers to jazz. Of course, diffusion works the other way, too, so that much of what we assume to be "American" actually comes from elsewhere. Most of the clothing we wear and the furniture we use, as well as the watch we carry and the money we spend, all had their origin in other cultures (Linton, 1937a).

It is certainly correct to talk about "American culture," especially when we are comparing our way of life to the culture of some other society. But this discussion of cultural change shows us that culture is always complex and always changing. The Thinking About Diversity box on pages 74–75 offers a good example of the diverse and dynamic character of culture with a brief look at the history of rock-and-roll music.

Ethnocentrism and Cultural Relativism

December 10, a small village in Morocco. Watching many of our fellow travelers browsing through a tiny ceramics factory, we have little doubt that North

Compared to college students 40 years ago, today's students are less interested in developing a philosophy of life and more interested in making money.

Student Snapshot

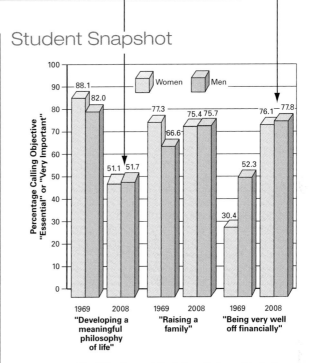

FIGURE 3–3 **Life Objectives of First-Year College Students, 1969 and 2008**

Researchers have surveyed first-year college students every year since 1969. While attitudes about some things such as the importance of family have stayed about the same, attitudes about other life goals have changed dramatically.

Sources: Astin et al. (2002) and Pryor et al. (2008).

Americans are among the world's greatest shoppers. We delight in surveying hand-woven carpets in China or India, inspecting finely crafted metals in Turkey, or collecting the beautifully colored porcelain tiles we find here in Morocco. Of course, all these items are wonderful bargains. But one major reason for the low prices is unsettling: Many products from the world's low- and middle-income countries are produced by children—some as young as five or six—who work long days for pennies per hour.

We think of childhood as a time of innocence and freedom from adult burdens like regular work. In poor countries throughout the world, however, families depend on income earned by children. So what people in one society think of as right and natural, people elsewhere find puzzling and even immoral. Perhaps the Chinese philosopher

NOTE: The history of rock and roll shows the dynamic character of human culture. The idea of "cultural transmission" is valid, but what we pass along is never exactly what we received.

DISCUSS: Ask students to describe changes in the music scene from about 1970 to the present. The timeline inside the front cover of the book provides some important points in this history.

DISCUSS: Is there a class dimension to various types of music? (Link this question to the discussion of high culture and popular culture on page 70.)

MAKING THE GRADE

Youth cultures tend to develop as societies industrialize because young people gain more independence from parents and have more money to spend on their own interests.

ethnocentrism the practice of judging another culture by the standards of one's own culture

cultural relativism the practice of judging a culture by its own standards

THINKING ABOUT DIVERSITY: RACE, CLASS, & GENDER

Early Rock-and-Roll: Race, Class, and Cultural Change

In the 1950s, rock-and-roll emerged as a major part of U.S. popular culture. In the decades that followed, rock grew to become a cultural tide that swept away musical tastes and traditions and changed the country in ways we still experience today.

Early in the 1950s, mainstream "pop" music was largely aimed at white adults. Songs were written by professional composers, recorded by long-established record labels, and performed by well-known artists such as Perry Como, Eddie Fisher, Doris Day, and Patti Page. Just about every big-name performer was white.

The country at that time was also rigidly segregated racially, which meant that the cultures of white people and black people were different. In the subcultural world of African Americans, music had different sounds and rhythms, reflecting jazz, gospel singing, and rhythm and blues. All of these musical styles were the creations of African

American composers and performers working with black-owned record companies broadcast on radio to an almost entirely black audience.

Class, too, divided the musical world of the 1950s, even among whites. A second musical subculture was country and western, a musical style popular among poorer whites, especially people living in the South. Like rhythm and blues, country and western music had its own composers and performers, its own record labels, and its own radio stations.

In the early 1950s, there were separate musical worlds in U.S. society, separated by the walls of race and class. "Crossover" music was rare, meaning that very few performers or songs moved from one world to gain popularity in another.

This musical segregation began to break down about 1955 with the birth of rock-and-roll. Rock was a new mix of many existing musical patterns, drawing on mainstream pop but

including country and western and, especially, rhythm and blues.

The new rock-and-roll music drew together musical traditions, but it soon divided society in a new way—by age. Rock-and-roll was the first music clearly linked to the emergence of a youth culture—rock was all the rage among teenagers but was little appreciated or even understood by their parents. One reason for this age split was that in the prosperous 1950s, young people had more money to spend, and record companies quickly realized that they could make a fortune selling products to the new "youth market." Young performers and groups began springing up in suburban garages and on inner-city street corners, and many were signed by new record labels and their music played on new teen-targeted radio stations.

The new youth culture gave birth to musical stars who looked and acted nothing like their parents. The rock-and-roll performers were men

Elvis Presley (*center*) drew together the music of rhythm and blues singers, such as Big Mama Thornton (*left*), and country and western stars, including Carl Perkins (*right*). The development of rock-and-roll illustrates the ever-changing character of U.S. culture.

Confucius had it right when he noted that "all people are the same; it's only their habits that are different."

Just about every imaginable idea or behavior is commonplace somewhere in the world, and this cultural variation causes travelers both excitement and distress. The Australians flip light switches down to turn them on; North Americans flip them up. The Japanese name city blocks; North Americans name streets. Egyptians stand very close to others in conversation; North Americans are used to maintaining several feet

of "personal space." Bathrooms lack toilet paper in much of rural Morocco, causing considerable discomfort for North Americans, who recoil at the thought of using the left hand for bathroom hygiene, as the locals do.

Given that a particular culture is the basis for each person's reality, it is no wonder that people everywhere exhibit **ethnocentrism,** *the practice of judging another culture by the standards of one's own culture.* Some degree of ethnocentrism is necessary for people to be

DISCUSS: Ask the class to develop a sociological analysis of rap music along the same lines as the box below.

Q: "Let's have a drink. It's five o'clock somewhere." J.J.M.

● MAKING THE GRADE

During the 1950s, rock-and-roll helped bring together black and white musical styles, but because this music was popular among the young, it also divided people by age.

● SEEING SOCIOLOGY
in Everyday Life

Just for fun, go to http://www.TheSociologyPage. com, where you can hear one of the author's "cover" performances of oldies rock-and-roll.

(and a few women) who took a rebellious stand against "adult" culture. The typical rocker was a young man who looked like what parents might have called a "juvenile delinquent" and who claimed to be "cool," an idea that most parents did not even understand.

The first band to make it big in rock-and-roll was Bill Haley and His Comets. These men (Haley lowered his stated age to gain greater acceptance) came out of the country and western tradition. Haley's first hits in 1954—"Shake, Rattle, and Roll" and "Rock around the Clock"—were recordings of earlier rhythm and blues songs.

Very quickly, however, young people began to lose interest in older performers such as Bill Haley and turned their attention to younger performers who had a stronger juvenile delinquent image—musicians sporting sideburns, turned-up collars, and black leather jackets. By the end of 1955, the unquestioned star of rock-and-roll was a poor white southern boy from Tupelo, Mississippi, named Elvis Aron Presley. From his rural roots, Elvis Presley knew country and western music, and after he moved to his adopted hometown of Memphis, Tennessee, he learned all about black gospel and rhythm and blues.

Before the 1950s ended, Presley had become the first superstar of rock-and-roll—not only because he had talent but also because he had great crossover power. With early hits including "Hound Dog" (a rhythm and blues song originally recorded by Big Mama Thornton) and "Blue Suede Shoes" (written by country and western star Carl Perkins), Presley broke down many of the walls of race and class in the music of the United States.

Elvis went on to a twenty-year career as "the King." But during that time, illustrating the expanding and dynamic character of culture, popular music developed in many new and different directions. By the end of the 1950s, popular musical styles included soft rock (Ricky Nelson, Pat Boone), rockabilly (Johnny Cash), and dozens of doo-wop groups, both black and white (often named for birds—the Falcons, the Penguins, the Flamingos—or cars—the Imperials, the Impalas, the Fleetwoods).

During the 1960s, the diversity of rock music was even greater, including folk music (the Kingston Trio; Peter, Paul, and Mary; Bob Dylan), surf music (the Beach Boys, Jan and Dean), and the "British invasion" led by the Beatles.

The Beatles were at first very close to the clean-cut, pop side of rock, but they soon shared the spotlight with another British band who was proud of its "delinquent" clothing and street fighter looks—the Rolling Stones. During the 1960s, music became a huge business, including not just the hard rock of the Beatles and Stones but softer "folk rock" performed by the Byrds, the Mamas and the Papas, Simon and Garfunkel, and Crosby, Stills, and Nash. Mainstream rock continued with bands like the Who, but rhythm and blues gave birth to "Motown" (named after the "motor city," Detroit, the automobile-building capital of the United States at the time), and "soul" music, launching the careers of dozens of African American stars, including James Brown, Aretha Franklin, the Four Tops, the Temptations, and Diana Ross and the Supremes.

On the West Coast, San Francisco developed a more political rock music performed by Jefferson Airplane, the Grateful Dead, and Janis Joplin. West Coast spin-off musical styles included "acid rock," influenced by drug use, performed by the Doors and Jimi Hendrix. The jazz influence also returned to the world of rock, creating such "jazz rock" groups as Chicago and Blood, Sweat, and Tears.

What does this brief look at the early decades of rock-and-roll tell us about culture? It shows the power of race and class to divide and separate people, shaping different subcultural patterns. It also shows us that the production of culture—in terms of music as well as movies and music videos—has become a megabusiness. Most of all, it shows us that culture is not a rigid system that stands still but rather a living process, changing, adapting, and reinventing itself over time.

WHAT DO YOU THINK?

1. Many dimensions of our way of life shaped rock-and-roll. In what ways do you think the emergence of rock-and-roll changed U.S. culture?

2. Throughout this period of musical change, most musical performers were men. What does this tell us about our way of life? Do you think today's popular music is still dominated by men?

3. Can you carry on the story of musical change in the United States to the present? (Think of disco, heavy metal, punk rock, rap, and hip-hop.)

Source: Based on Stuessy & Lipscomb (2008).

emotionally attached to their way of life. But ethnocentrism also generates misunderstanding and sometimes conflict.

Even language is culturally biased. Centuries ago, people in Europe and North America referred to China as the "Far East." But this term, unknown to the Chinese, is an ethnocentric expression for a region that is far to the east *of us.* The Chinese name for their country translates as "Central Kingdom," suggesting that they, like us, see their own society as the center of the world.

The logical alternative to ethnocentrism is **cultural relativism,** *the practice of judging a culture by its own standards.* Cultural relativism can be difficult for travelers to adopt: It requires not only openness to unfamiliar values and norms but also the ability to put aside cultural standards we have known all our lives. Even so, as people of the world come into increasing contact with one another, the importance of understanding other cultures becomes ever greater.

● MAKING THE GRADE

One good piece of evidence supporting the claim that a global culture is emerging is the widespread use of English as a second language almost everywhere in the world (see Global Map 3–1 on page 65).

In the world's low-income countries, most children must work to provide their families with needed income. This seven-year-old boy in eastern Ilam, Nepal, works long hours in a tea field. Is it ethnocentric for people living in high-income nations to condemn the practice of child labor because we think youngsters belong in school? Why or why not?

As the opening to this chapter explained, businesses in the United States are learning the value of marketing to a culturally diverse population. Similarly, businesses are learning that success in the global economy depends on awareness of cultural patterns around the world. IBM, for example, now provides technical support for its products using Web sites in more than thirty languages (IBM, 2008).

This trend is a change from the past, when many corporations used marketing strategies that lacked sensitivity to cultural diversity. Coors's phrase "Turn It Loose" startled Spanish-speaking customers by proclaiming that the beer would cause diarrhea. Braniff Airlines translated its slogan "Fly in Leather" so carelessly into Spanish that it read "Fly Naked." Similarly, Eastern Airlines' slogan "We Earn Our Wings Every Day" became "We Fly Daily to Heaven." Even poultry giant Frank Perdue fell victim to poor marketing when his pitch "It Takes a Tough Man to Make a Tender Chicken" was transformed into the Spanish words reading "A Sexually Excited Man Will Make a Chicken Affectionate" (Helin, 1992).

But cultural relativism introduces problems of its own. If almost any kind of behavior is the norm *somewhere* in the world, does that mean everything is equally right? Does the fact that some Indian and Moroccan families benefit from having their children work long hours justify child labor? Since we are all members of a single species, surely there must be some universal standards of proper conduct. But what are they? And in trying to develop them, how can we avoid imposing our own standards on others? There are no simple answers. But when confronting an unfamiliar cultural practice, it is best to resist making judgments before grasping what people in that culture think of the issue. Remember also to think about your own way of life as others might see it. After all, what we gain most from studying others is better insight into ourselves.

A Global Culture?

Today more than ever, we can observe many of the same cultural practices the world over. Walking the streets of Seoul, South Korea; Kuala Lumpur, Malaysia; Chennai, India; Cairo, Egypt; or Casablanca, Morocco, we see people wearing jeans, hear familiar music, and read ads for many of the same products we use at home. Seeing Sociology in the News on pages 78–79 takes a look at how U.S. rap music is taking root in China. Recall, too, from Global Map 3–1 on page 65 that English is rapidly emerging as the preferred second language around the world. Are we witnessing the birth of a single global culture?

Societies now have more contact with one another than ever before, thanks to the flow of goods, information, and people:

1. **The global economy: The flow of goods.** International trade has never been greater. The global economy has spread many of the same consumer goods—from cars and TV shows to music and fashions—throughout the world.

2. **Global communications: The flow of information.** The Internet and satellite-assisted communications enable people to experience the sights and sounds of events taking place thousands of miles away, often as they happen. In addition, because most of the world's Web pages are written in English, the spread of computer technology has helped spread the English language around the world. Recall from Global Map 3–1 that English is now the preferred second language in most parts of the world.

3. **Global migration: The flow of people.** Knowing about the rest of the world motivates people to move to where they imagine life will be better. In addition, today's transportation technology, especially air travel, makes relocating easier than ever before. As a result, in most countries, significant numbers of people were born elsewhere, including some 38 million people in the United States, which is 13 percent of the total population (U.S. Census Bureau, 2008).

DISCUSS: An interesting way to launch a functional analysis of culture is to analyze cultural heroes. What makes an act heroic? See the photo essay on page 82.

Q: "The function of any recurrent activity, such as the punishment of a crime, or a funeral ceremony, is the part it plays in the social life as a whole and therefore the contribution it makes to the maintenance of the structural continuity." Radcliffe-Brown (1935:395–96)

NOTE: Ralph Linton (1937) first used the term "cultural universals" to refer to cultural traits found throughout a *single* society. The term has come to be used to designate a surprising number of cultural traits common to *all* societies.

NOTE: More detailed analysis of the social-conflict approach to society is found in the section of Chapter 4 ("Society") dealing with the work of Karl Marx.

MAKING THE GRADE

The concept "cultural universal" is an older concept linked to the structural-functional approach. It is based on the idea that if some cultural trait is found everywhere, it must be very useful for society.

cultural universals traits that are part of every known culture

sociobiology (p. 78) a theoretical approach that explores ways in which human biology affects how we create culture

These global links help make the cultures of the world more similar. Even so, there are three important limitations to the global culture thesis. First, the global flow of goods, information, and people is uneven in different parts of the world. Generally speaking, urban areas (centers of commerce, communication, and people) have stronger ties to one another, while many rural villages remain isolated. In addition, the greater economic and military power of North America and Western Europe means that these regions influence the rest of the world more than the rest of the world influences them.

Second, the global culture thesis assumes that people everywhere are able to *afford* various new goods and services. As Chapter 12 ("Global Stratification") explains, desperate poverty in much of the world deprives people of even the basic necessities of a safe and secure life.

Third, although many cultural practices are now found in countries throughout the world, people everywhere do not attach the same meanings to them. Do children in Tokyo draw the same lessons from reading the Harry Potter books as their counterparts in New York or London? Similarly, we enjoy foods from around the world while knowing little about the lives of the people who created them. In short, people everywhere still see the world through their own cultural lenses.

Theoretical Analysis of Culture

Sociologists have the special task of understanding how culture helps us make sense of ourselves and the surrounding world. Here we will examine several macro-level theoretical approaches to understanding culture; a micro-level approach to the personal experience of culture is the focus of Chapter 6 ("Social Interaction in Everyday Life").

The Functions of Culture: Structural-Functional Analysis

The structural-functional approach explains culture as a complex strategy for meeting human needs. Borrowing from the philosophical doctrine of *idealism,* this approach considers values the core of a culture (Parsons, 1966; R. M. Williams, 1970). In other words, cultural values direct our lives, give meaning to what we do, and bind people together. Countless other cultural traits have various functions that support the operation of society.

Thinking functionally helps us understand an unfamiliar way of life. Consider the Amish farmer plowing hundreds of acres on an Ohio farm with a team of horses. His farming methods may violate our cultural value of efficiency, but from the Amish point of view,

hard work functions to develop the discipline necessary for a highly religious way of life. Long days of working together not only make the Amish self-sufficient but also strengthen family ties and unify local communities.

Of course, Amish practices have dysfunctions as well. The hard work and strict religious discipline are too demanding for some, who end up leaving the community. Then, too, strong religious beliefs sometimes prevent compromise; slight differences in religious practices have caused the Amish to divide into different communities (Kraybill, 1989; Kraybill & Olshan, 1994).

If cultures are strategies for meeting human needs, we would expect to find many common patterns around the world. **Cultural universals** are *traits that are part of every known culture.* Comparing hundreds of cultures, George Murdock (1945) identified dozens of cultural universals. One common element is the family, which functions everywhere to control sexual reproduction and to oversee the care of children. Funeral rites, too, are found everywhere, because all human communities cope with the reality of death. Jokes are another cultural universal, serving as a safe means of releasing social tensions.

CRITICAL REVIEW The strength of the structural-functional approach is that it shows how culture operates to meet human needs. Yet by emphasizing a society's dominant cultural patterns, this approach largely ignores the cultural diversity that exists in many societies, including our own. Also, because this approach emphasizes cultural stability, it downplays the importance of change. In short, cultural systems are not as stable or a matter of as much agreement as structural functionalism leads us to believe.

CHECK YOUR LEARNING In the United States, what are some of the functions of sports, July Fourth celebrations, and Black History Month?

Inequality and Culture: Social-Conflict Analysis

The social-conflict approach stresses the link between culture and inequality. Any cultural trait, from this point of view, benefits some members of society at the expense of others.

Why do certain values dominate a society in the first place? Many conflict theorists, especially Marxists, argue that culture is shaped by a society's system of economic production. "It is not the consciousness of men that determines their being," Karl Marx proclaimed; "it is their social being that determines their consciousness" (Marx & Engels, 1978:4, orig. 1859). Social-conflict theory, then, is rooted in the philosophical doctrine of *materialism,* which holds that a society's system of material production (such as our own capitalist economy) has a

DISCUSS: Will the long-run consequences of the Industrial Revolution be the emergence of a global culture? (See Chapter 12, "Global Stratification" and Chapter 24, "Social Change".)

Q: "Although the genes have given away most of their sovereignty, they maintain a certain amount of influence in at least the behavioral qualities that underlie the variations between cultures." Edward O. Wilson

Seeing SOCIOLOGY in the NEWS

The New York Times

Now Hip-Hop, Too, Is Made in China

By JIMMY WANG
January 24, 2009

BEIJING—A week before Americans tune in to the Super Bowl, another televised mega-event will kick off on the other side of the globe. On Sunday more than half a billion people here are expected to watch the annual Chinese Lunar New Year gala. Organized by the state-owned China Central Television, the marathon event showcases the country's musical diversity with an extensive lineup of Chinese pop stars performing hit songs. But one genre audiences are unlikely to see is Chinese hip-hop, despite its growing popularity among the country's urban youth.

Over the last decade many students and working-class Chinese have been writing rap as a form of self-expression. Rougher and more rebellious than the well-scrubbed pop that floods the airwaves here, this kind of hip-hop is not sanctioned by broadcast media producers or state censors but has managed to attract a grass-roots fan base.

"Hip-hop is free, like rock 'n' roll—we can talk about our lives, what we're thinking about, what we feel," said Wang Liang, 25, a popular hip-hop D.J. known as Wordy. "The Chinese education system doesn't encourage you to express your own character. They feed you stale rules developed from books passed down over thousands of years. There's not much opportunity for personal expression or thought; difference is discouraged."

While American rappers like Eminem and Q-Tip have been popular in China since the 1990s, home-grown rap didn't start gaining momentum until a decade later. The group Yin Ts'ang (its name means "hidden"), one of the pioneers of Chinese rap, is made up of global nomads: a Beijinger, a Chinese-Canadian and two Americans.

"The big change was when rappers started writing verse in Chinese, so people could understand," said Zhong Cheng, 27, a member of the group who was raised in Canada but born in Beijing, where he returned in 1997. "Before that, kids listened to hip-hop in English but maybe less than 1 percent could actually understand."

Yin Ts'ang's first hit was "In Beijing," from the band's 2003 debut album, "Serve the People" (Scream Records); the title is a twist on an old political slogan. It sets a melody played on a thousand-year-old Chinese fiddle called the Erhu against a hip-hop beat that brings Run D.M.C. to mind. The song, an insider's look at Beijing's sights and sounds, took the underground music scene by storm, finding its way into karaoke parlors, the Internet and even the playlist of a radio station in Beijing. . . .

Since "In Beijing," the Chinese hip-hop scene has quickly grown. Hiphop.cn, a Web site listing events and links to songs, started with just a few hundred members in 2007; in 2008 it received millions of views, according to one of the site's directors.

Dozens of hip-hop clubs have opened up in cities across the country, and thousands of raps and music videos by Chinese M.C.'s are spreading over the Internet. But making Chinese hip-hop is

---

powerful effect on the rest of a culture. This materialist approach contrasts with the idealist leanings of structural functionalism.

Social-conflict analysis ties our cultural values of competitiveness and material success to our country's capitalist economy, which serves the interests of the nation's wealthy elite. The culture of capitalism further teaches us to think that rich and powerful people work harder or longer than others and therefore deserve their wealth and privileges. It also encourages us to view capitalism as somehow "natural," discouraging us from trying to reduce economic inequality.

Eventually, however, the strains of inequality erupt into movements for social change. Two examples in the United States are the civil rights movement and the women's movement. Both have sought greater equality, and both have encountered opposition from defenders of the status quo.

> **CRITICAL REVIEW** The social-conflict approach suggests that cultural systems do not address human needs equally, allowing some people to dominate others. This inequity in turn generates pressure toward change. Yet by stressing the divisiveness of culture, this approach understates the ways that cultural patterns integrate members of society. We should therefore consider both social-conflict and structural-functional insights for a fuller understanding of culture.

> **CHECK YOUR LEARNING** How might a social-conflict analysis of college fraternities and sororities differ from a structural-functional analysis?

Evolution and Culture: Sociobiology

We know that culture is a human creation, but does human biology influence how this process unfolds? A third theoretical approach, standing with one leg in biology and one in sociology, is **sociobiology,** *a theoretical approach that explores ways in which human biology affects how we create culture.*

Sociobiology rests on the theory of evolution proposed by Charles Darwin in *On the Origin of Species* (1859). Darwin asserted that living organisms change over long periods of time as a result of *natural selection,* a matter of four simple principles. First, all living things live to reproduce themselves. Second, the blueprint for reproduction is in the genes, the basic units of life that carry traits of one generation into the next. Third, some random variation in genes allows a species to "try out" new life patterns in a particular environment. This variation allows some organisms to survive better than others and pass on their advantageous genes to their offspring. Fourth and finally, over thousands of generations, the genetic patterns that promote reproduction survive and become dominant. In this way, as biologists say, a species *adapts* to its environment, and dominant traits emerge as the "nature" of the organism.

Sociobiologists claim that the large number of cultural universals reflects the fact that all humans are members of a single biological species. It is our common biology that underlies, for example, the apparently universal "double standard" of sexual behavior. As the sex researcher Alfred Kinsey put it, "Among all people everywhere in the world, the male is more likely than the

Q: "What the U.S. does best is understand itself. What it does worst is understand others." Carlos Fuentes, Mexican writer

Q: "The problem with other cultures is that other people don't behave the way we expect them to, that is, like us." Craig Storti

still a relatively profitless—and often subversive—activity. Some Chinese rappers address what they see as the country's most glaring injustices. As Wang Li, a 24-year-old from Dongbei, says in one of his freestyle raps:

If you don't have a nice car or cash
You won't get no honeys
Don't you know China is only a heaven for rich old men
You know this world is full of corruption
Babies die from drinking milk.

. . . Mr. Wang, who became interested in hip-hop when he heard Public Enemy in the mid-'90s. [He] said rapping helps him deal with bitterness that comes with realizing he is one of the millions left out of China's economic boom.

"All people care about is money," he said. "If you don't have money, you're treated like garbage.". . .

In the recent hit "Hello Teacher," Yin Tsar, one of the hip-hop scene's biggest acts (its name means "The Three Shadows"), rails against the authority of unfair teachers: "You're supposed to be a role model, but I've seen you spit in public.". . .

While Beijing's underground music scene is generally under the authorities' radar—hip-hop, indie rock and reggae groups perform regularly at nightclubs here—the producers representing broadcast media in China avoid musicians perceived as threatening.

"There are pockets of freedom here," said Wang Miao, 24, the director of Acupuncture Records. . . . "Anyone can play what they want in clubs, and as long as you aren't insulting the party, generally you'll be left alone. But if you want to take the next step to becoming mainstream, you hit a wall. If you aren't singing their type of stuff or aren't incredibly rich, they won't sign you.". . .

After seven years together, Mr. Zhong and Mr. Johnston of Yin Ts'ang still struggle to pay the bills, but they haven't stopped making hip-hop. . . .

In a nondescript apartment on the west side of Beijing, Mr. Johnston nodded his head to a song playing on his computer while Mr. Zhong explained how the group started:

"When I got here and met Jeremy, we were both so inspired by these people, we were like, 'Let's drop some Chinese rhymes for the locals,' and our Chinese friends were like, 'There are no Chinese rhymes!,' and we were like, 'That's crazy!' From that day, we haven't stopped rhyming."

WHAT DO YOU THINK?

1. Explain how and why hip-hop in China is an example of cultural diffusion.

2. Do you think rap music is encouraging the development of counterculture in China? Why or why not?

3. Can you think of Chinese cultural patterns that have changed U.S. society? If so, give examples.

female to desire sex with a variety of partners" (quoted in Barash, 1981:49). Why is this so?

We all know that children result from joining a woman's egg with a man's sperm. But the biological importance of a single sperm and of a single egg is quite different. For healthy men, sperm represent a "renewable resource" produced by the testes throughout most of the life course. A man releases hundreds of millions of sperm in a single ejaculation—technically, enough to fertilize every woman in North America (Barash, 1981:47). A newborn female's ovaries, however, contain her entire lifetime supply of eggs. A woman generally releases a single egg cell from her ovaries each month. So although a man is biologically capable of fathering thousands of offspring, a woman is able to bear only a relatively small number of children.

Given this biological difference, men reproduce their genes most efficiently by being promiscuous—readily engaging in sex with any willing partner. This scheme, however, opposes the reproductive interests of women. Each of a woman's relatively few pregnancies demands that she carry the child for nine months, give birth, and provide care for years afterward. Thus efficient reproduction on the part of the woman depends on carefully selecting a mate whose qualities (beginning with the likelihood that he will simply stay around) will contribute to her child's survival and, later, successful reproduction.

The double standard certainly involves more than biology and is tangled up with the historical domination of women by men.

But sociobiology suggests that this cultural pattern, like many others, has an underlying "bio-logic." Simply put, the double standard exists around the world because biological differences lead women and men everywhere to favor distinctive reproductive strategies.

CRITICAL REVIEW Sociobiology has generated intriguing theories about the biological roots of some cultural patterns. But the approach remains controversial for two main reasons.

First, some critics fear that sociobiology may revive biological arguments, from over a century ago, that claimed the superiority of one race or sex. But defenders counter that sociobiology rejects the past pseudoscience of racial and gender superiority. In fact, they say, sociobiology unites all of humanity because all people share a single evolutionary history. Sociobiology does assert that men and women differ biologically in some ways that culture cannot easily overcome. But far from claiming that males are somehow more important than females, sociobiology emphasizes that both sexes are vital to human reproduction and survival.

Second, say the critics, sociobiologists have little evidence to support their theories. Research to date suggests that biological forces do not *determine* human behavior in any rigid sense. Rather, humans *learn* behavior within a cultural system. The contribution of sociobiology, then, lies in explaining why some cultural patterns seem easier to learn than others (Barash, 1981).

NOTE: From the point of view of sociobiology, genes use bodies (and societies) to create more genes. Thus the chicken and egg dilemma is solved in the following way: Eggs come first; eggs use chickens to create more eggs.

DISCUSS: Use the Applying Theory table below as the basis of a review of the theoretical approaches to culture.

MAKING THE GRADE

Because multiculturalism supports greater social equality for people of various cultural backgrounds, this theory falls within sociology's social-conflict approach.

MAKING THE GRADE

Theories dealing with how biology affects human behavior do not have wide support in sociology. Sociobiology is a theory—supported by some sociologists, not by others—that has one foot in biology and the other in sociology.

APPLYING THEORY

Culture

	Structural-Functional Approach	Social-Conflict Approach	Sociobiology Approach
What is the level of analysis?	Macro-level	Macro-level	Macro-level
What is culture?	Culture is a system of behavior by which members of societies cooperate to meet their needs.	Culture is a system that benefits some people and disadvantages others.	Culture is a system of behavior that is partly shaped by human biology.
What is the foundation of culture?	Cultural patterns are rooted in a society's core values and beliefs.	Cultural patterns are rooted in a society's system of economic production.	Cultural patterns are rooted in humanity's biological evolution.
What core questions does the approach ask?	How does a cultural pattern help society operate?	How does a cultural pattern benefit some people and harm others?	How does a cultural pattern help a species adapt to its environment?
	What cultural patterns are found in all societies?	How does a cultural pattern support social inequality?	

CHECK YOUR LEARNING Using the sociobiology approach, explain why some cultural patterns such as sibling rivalry are widespread.

Because any analysis of culture requires a broad focus on the workings of society, the three approaches discussed in this chapter, and summarized in the Applying Theory table, are all macro-level in scope. The symbolic-interaction approach, with its micro-level focus on behavior in everyday situations, will be explored in Chapter 6 ("Social Interaction in Everyday Life").

Culture and Human Freedom

This chapter leads us to ask an important question: To what extent are human beings, as cultural creatures, free? Does culture bind us to each other and to the past? Or does culture enhance our capacity for individual thought and independent choice?

Culture as Constraint

As symbolic creatures, humans cannot live without culture. But the capacity for culture does have some drawbacks. We may be the only animal to name ourselves, but living in a symbolic world means that we are also the only creature that experiences alienation. In addition, culture is largely a matter of habit, which limits our choices and drives us to repeat troubling patterns, such as racial prejudice and sex discrimination, in each new generation.

Our society's emphasis on competitive achievement urges us toward excellence, yet this same pattern also isolates us from one another. Material things comfort us in some ways but divert us from the security and satisfaction that come from close relationships and spiritual strength.

Culture as Freedom

For better or worse, human beings are cultural creatures, just as ants and bees are prisoners of their biology. But there is a crucial difference. Biological instincts create a ready-made world; culture forces us to choose as we make and remake a world for ourselves. No better evidence of this freedom exists than the cultural diversity of our own society and the even greater human diversity around the world.

Learning more about this cultural diversity is one goal shared by sociologists. The Thinking Globally box offers some contrasts between the cultures of the United States and Canada. Wherever we may live, the better we understand the workings of the surrounding culture, the better prepared we are to use the freedom it offers us.

GLOBAL: Canada has a population of 33 million people (versus 300 million for the U.S.); Canada has lower per-person income ($31,000 vs. $37,000) but a broader system of social services, reflected in its higher life expectancy (80.0 years vs. 77.5).

NOTE: Illustrating the distinction between nation and society, French-speaking Canada (Quebec) is largely a separate society from the remainder of English-speaking Canada.

Q: "To most people a savage nation is one that wears comfortable clothes."
Finley Peter Dunne

SEEING SOCIOLOGY
in Everyday Life

Our tendency to pay little attention to countries with which we share borders is one example of ethnocentrism.

THINKING GLOBALLY

The United States and Canada: Two National Cultures or One?

The United States and Canada are two of the largest high-income countries in the world, and they share a common border of about 4,000 miles. But do the United States and Canada share the same culture?

One important point to make right away is that both nations are *multicultural*. Not only do the two countries have hundreds of Native American societies, but immigration has brought people from all over the world to both the United States and Canada. Most early immigrants to both countries came from Europe, but in recent decades, most have come from Asia and Latin America. The Canadian city of Vancouver, for example, has a Chinese community of about the same size as the Latino community in Los Angeles.

Canada and the United States differ in one important respect: Historically, Canada has had *two* dominant cultures: French (about 25 percent of the population) and British (roughly 40 percent). People of French ancestry are a large majority in the province of Quebec (where French is the official language) and represent almost half of the population of New Brunswick (which is officially bilingual).

Are the dominant values of Canada much the same as those we have described for the United States? Seymour Martin Lipset (1985) finds that they differ to some degree. The United States declared its independence from Great Britain in 1776, but Canada did not formally separate from Great Britain until 1982, and the British monarch is still Canada's official head of state. Thus, Lipset continues, the dominant culture of Canada lies somewhere between the culture of the United States and that of Great Britain.

The culture of the United States is more individualistic, and Canada's is more collective. In the United States, individualism is seen in the historical importance of the cowboy, a self-sufficient loner, and even outlaws such as Jesse James and Billy the Kid are regarded as heroes because they challenged authority. In Canada,

by contrast, it is the Mountie—Canada's well-known police officer on horseback—who is looked on with great respect. Canada's greater emphasis on collective life is also evident in stronger unions: Canadian workers are three times more likely to be members of a union as workers in the United States (Steyn, 2008).

Politically, people in the United States tend to think individuals ought to do things for themselves. In Canada, however, much as in Great Britain, there is a strong sense that government should look after the interests of everyone. The U.S. Constitution emphasizes the importance of "life, liberty, and the pursuit of happiness" (words that place importance on the individual), while Canadian society is based on "peace, order, and good government" (words that place importance on the government) (Steyn, 2008). One clear result of this difference is that Canada has a much broader social welfare system (including universal health care) than the United

States (the only high-income nation without such a program). It also helps explain the fact that about one-third of all U.S. households own a gun, and the idea that individuals are entitled to own a gun, although controversial, is widespread. In Canada, by contrast, the government restricts gun ownership, as in Great Britain.

WHAT DO YOU THINK?

1. Why do you think some Canadians feel that their way of life is overshadowed by that of the United States?

2. Ask your friends to name the capital city of Canada. (The correct answer is Ottawa, in the province of Ontario.) Are you surprised by how many know the answer? Why or why not?

3. Why do many people in the United States not know very much about either Canada or Mexico, countries with which we share long borders?

The individuals that a society celebrates as heroic are a good indication of that society's cultural values. In the United States, outlaws such as Jesse James (and later, Bonnie and Clyde) were regarded as heroes because they represented the individual standing strong against authority. In Canada, by contrast, people have always looked up to the Mountie, who symbolizes society's authority over the individual.

Seeing Sociology in Everyday Life

Chapter 3   Culture

What clues do we have to a society's cultural values?

The values of any society—that is, what that society thinks is important—are reflected in various aspects of everyday life, including the things people have and the ways they behave. An interesting way to "read" our own culture's values is to look at the "superheroes" that we celebrate. Take a look at the characters in the three photos shown here and, in each case, describe what makes the character special and what each character represents in cultural terms.

Superman first appeared in an *Action Comic* book in 1938, as the United States struggled to climb out of economic depression and faced the rising danger of war. Since then, Superman has been featured in a television show as well as in a string of Hollywood films. One trait of most superheroes is that they have a secret identity; in this case, Superman's everyday identity is "mild-mannered news reporter" Clark Kent.

Buffy the Vampire Slayer, a more recent star of television, film, comic books, and video games, is a rare example of a woman playing a superhero character.

Another longtime superhero important to our culture is Spiderman. In all three *Spiderman* movies, Peter Parker (who transforms into Spiderman when he confronts evil) is secretly in love with Mary Jane Watson, but—in true superhero style—he does not allow himself to follow his heart.

Applying SOCIOLOGY in Everyday Life

1. What traits define popular culture "heroes" such as Clint Eastwood's film character "Dirty Harry," Sylvester Stallone's film characters "Rocky" as well as "Rambo," and Arnold Schwarzenegger's character "the Terminator"?

2. Find someone on campus who has lived in another country, and ask how the culture of that society differs from the way of life here. Look for ways in which the other person sees U.S. culture differently from people who have lived here all their lives.

3. Watch an animated Disney film such as *Finding Nemo, The Lion King, The Little Mermaid, Aladdin,* or *Pocahontas.* One reason for the popularity of these films is that they all share cultural themes. Using the list of key values of U.S. culture on pages 66–67 as a guide, what makes the film you selected especially "American"?

MAKING THE GRADE

CHAPTER 3 Culture

What Is Culture?

Culture is a **WAY OF LIFE**.
- Culture is shared by members of a society.
- Culture shapes how we act, think, and feel.

p. 58

Culture is a **HUMAN TRAIT**.
- Although several species display a limited capacity for culture, only human beings rely on culture for survival.

p. 60

Culture is a **PRODUCT OF EVOLUTION**.
- As the human brain evolved, culture replaced biological instincts as our species' primary strategy for survival.

pp. 60–62

- We experience **CULTURE SHOCK** when we enter an unfamiliar culture and are not able to "read" meaning in our new surroundings.
- We create culture shock for others when we act in ways they do not understand.

pp. 60–61

✓ Approximately 300 different cultures exist in the United States. Worldwide, there are roughly 7,000 different cultures (p. 62).

culture (p. 58) the ways of thinking, the ways of acting, and the material objects that together form a people's way of life

nonmaterial culture (p. 60) the ideas created by members of a society

material culture (p. 60) the physical things created by members of a society

culture shock (p. 60) personal disorientation when experiencing an unfamiliar way of life

The Elements of Culture

Culture relies on **SYMBOLS** in the form of words, gestures, and actions to express meaning.
- The fact that different meanings can come to be associated with the same symbol (for example, a wink of an eye) shows the human capacity to create and manipulate symbols.
- Societies create new symbols all the time (for example, new computer technology has sparked the creation of new cyber-symbols).

p. 62-63

LANGUAGE is the symbolic system by which people in a culture communicate with one another.
- People use language—both spoken and written—to transmit culture from one generation to the next.
- Because every culture is different, each language has words or expressions not found in any other language.

p. 64

VALUES are abstract standards of what *ought to be* (for example, equality of opportunity).
- Values can sometimes be in conflict with one another.
- Lower-income countries have cultures that value survival; higher-income countries have cultures that value individualism and self-expression.

BELIEFS are specific statements that people who share a culture hold to be true (for example, "A qualified woman could be elected president").

pp. 64–67

NORMS, rules that guide human behavior, are of two types:
- **mores** (for example, sexual taboos), which have great moral significance
- **folkways** (for example, greetings or dining etiquette), which are matters of everyday politeness

pp. 67–68

✓ Values and norms (standards for how we should behave) reflect **ideal culture**, which differs from **real culture** (what actually occurs in everyday life) (p. 68).

▭ See pages 66–67 for ten key values of U.S. culture.

symbol (p. 62) anything that carries a particular meaning recognized by people who share a culture

language (p. 64) a system of symbols that allows people to communicate with one another

cultural transmission (p. 64) the process by which one generation passes culture to the next

Sapir-Whorf thesis (p. 64) the idea that people see and understand the world through the cultural lens of language

values (p. 66) culturally defined standards that people use to decide what is desirable, good, and beautiful and that serve as broad guidelines for social living

beliefs (p. 66) specific thoughts or ideas that people hold to be true

norms (p. 67) rules and expectations by which a society guides the behavior of its members

mores (p. 68) norms that are widely observed and have great moral significance

folkways (p. 68) norms for routine or casual interaction

social control (p. 68) attempts by society to regulate people's thoughts and behavior

technology (p. 69) knowledge that people use to make a way of life in their surroundings

Technology and Culture

- A society's **artifacts**—the wide range of physical human creations that together make up a society's material culture—reflect underlying cultural values and technology.
- The more complex a society's technology, the more its members are able to shape the world as they wish.

pp. 68–69

✓ *Members of societies that possess sophisticated technology should be careful not to judge cultures with simpler technology as inferior (p. 69).*

Cultural Diversity

We live in a **CULTURALLY DIVERSE SOCIETY**.
- This diversity is due to our country's history of immigration.
- Diversity reflects regional differences.
- Diversity reflects differences in social class that set off **high culture** (available only to elites) from **popular culture** (available to average people).

p. 70

A number of values are central to our way of life. But **CULTURAL PATTERNS** are not the same throughout our society.
Subculture is based on differences in interests and life experiences.
- Hip-hop fans and jocks are two examples of youth subcultures in the United States.
Multiculturalism is an effort to enhance appreciation of cultural diversity.
- Multiculturalism developed as a reaction to the earlier "melting pot" idea, which was thought to result in minorities' losing their identity as they adopted mainstream cultural patterns.
Counterculture is strongly at odds with conventional ways of life.
- Militant religious fundamentalist groups in the United States who plot to destroy Western society are examples of a counterculture.

pp. 70–72

CULTURAL CHANGE results from
- **invention** (examples include the telephone and the computer)
- **discovery** (for example, the recognition that women are capable of political leadership)
- **diffusion** (for example, the growing popularity of various ethnic foods and musical styles).
CULTURAL LAG results when some parts of a cultural system change faster than others.

pp. 72–73

How do we understand cultural differences?
- **ETHNOCENTRISM** links people to their society but can cause misunderstanding and conflict between societies.
- **CULTURAL RELATIVISM** is increasingly important as people of the world come into more and more contact with each other.

pp. 73–76

✓ *Global cultural patterns result from the worldwide flow of goods, information, and people (pp. 76–77).*

high culture (p. 70) cultural patterns that distinguish a society's elite

popular culture (p. 70) cultural patterns that are widespread among a society's population

subculture (p. 70) cultural patterns that set apart some segment of a society's population

multiculturalism (p. 71) a perspective recognizing the cultural diversity of the United States and promoting equal standing for all cultural traditions

Eurocentrism (p. 71) the dominance of European (especially English) cultural patterns

Afrocentrism (p. 71) emphasizing and promoting African cultural patterns

counterculture (p. 72) cultural patterns that strongly oppose those widely accepted within a society

cultural integration (p. 72) the close relationships among various elements of a cultural system

cultural lag (p. 72) the fact that some cultural elements change more quickly than others, disrupting a cultural system

ethnocentrism (p. 74) the practice of judging another culture by the standards of one's own culture

cultural relativism (p. 75) the practice of judging a culture by its own standards

Theoretical Analysis of Culture

The **STRUCTURAL-FUNCTIONAL APPROACH** views culture as a relatively stable system built on core values. All cultural patterns play some part in the ongoing operation of society.

p. 77

The **SOCIAL-CONFLICT APPROACH** sees culture as a dynamic arena of inequality and conflict. Cultural patterns benefit some categories of people more than others.

pp. 77–78

SOCIOBIOLOGY explores how the long history of evolution has shaped patterns of culture in today's world.

pp. 78–80

cultural universals (p. 77) traits that are part of every known culture

sociobiology (p. 78) a theoretical approach that explores ways in which human biology affects how we create culture

See the Applying Theory table on page 80.

Culture and Human Freedom

- Culture can limit the choices we make.
- As cultural creatures, we have the capacity to shape and reshape our world to meet our needs and pursue our dreams.

pp. 80

All human beings live in societies. But societies around the world differ from one another in many ways, just as each society changes over time. This chapter presents classic theories that explain what "society" is all about.

CHAPTER 4

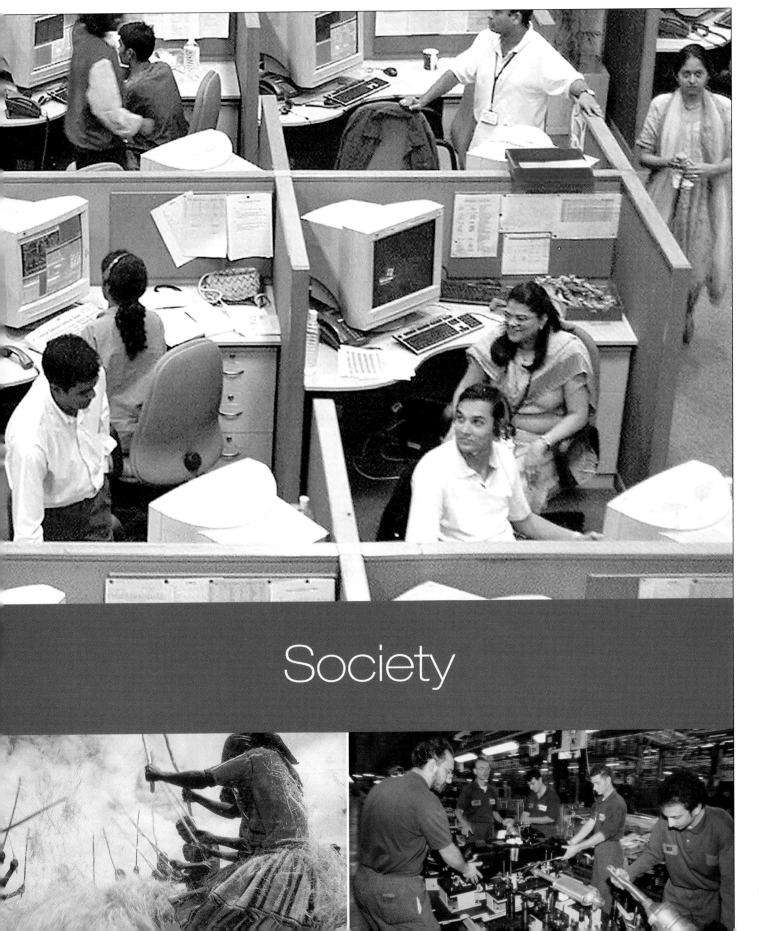

Society

NOTE: Use this chapter in any number of ways. Assign all of it to give students a detailed introduction to important historical material and key theorists whose ideas inform later chapters. Or assign sections separately along with later chapters: Use the Weber section to preface the discussion of bureaucracy in Chapter 7, the Durkheim section before the structural-functional analysis of deviance in Chapter 9, and the Marx section before discussion of social inequality in Chapter 10. Instruc-

tors may also omit the chapter entirely without breaking the flow of the text.
SUPPLEMENTS: The *Instructor's Manual* provides an outline of Chapter 4 along with discussion questions and supplementary lecture material.

NOTE: Chapter 24 ("Social Change: Traditional, Modern, and Postmodern Societies") is a logical extension of this chapter. In teaching this chapter, you may wish to have students read through Chapter 24.

CHAPTER OVERVIEW { This chapter examines the concept of "society" through the work of one of today's leading sociologists, Gerhard Lenski, and three of sociology's founders, Karl Marx, Max Weber, and Emile Durkheim.

Sididi Ag Inaka has never used instant messaging, logged on to the Internet, or spoken on a cell phone. Does such a person really exist in today's high-technology world? Well, how about this: Neither Inaka nor anyone in his family has ever been to a movie, watched television, or even read a newspaper.

Are these people visitors from another planet? Prisoners on some remote island? Not at all. They are Tuareg nomads who wander over the vast Sahara in the western African nations of Mali and Niger. Known as the "blue men of the desert" for the flowing blue robes worn by both men and women, the Tuareg herd camels, goats, and sheep and live in camps where the sand blows and the daytime temperature often reaches 120 degrees Fahrenheit. Life is hard, but most Tuareg try to hold on to traditional ways. With a stern look, Inaka says, "My father was a nomad. His father was a nomad. I am a nomad. My children will be nomads."

The Tuareg are among the world's poorest people. When the rains fail to come, they and their animals are at risk of losing their lives. Some are hopeful that the Tuareg people can gain some of the wealth that comes from mining uranium below the desert across which they have traveled for centuries. But whatever their economic fate, Inaka and his people are a society set apart, with little knowledge of the larger world and none of its advanced technology. But Inaka does not complain: "This is the life of my ancestors. This is the life that we know" (Buckley, 1996; Matloff, 1997; Lovgren, 1998; McConnell, 2007).

Society refers to *people who interact in a defined territory and share a culture.* In this chapter, you will learn more about human societies with the help of four important sociologists. We begin with the approach of **Gerhard Lenski,** who describes how societies have changed over the past 10,000 years. Lenski points to the importance of *technology* in shaping any society. Then we turn to three of sociology's founders. **Karl Marx,** like Lenski, took a long historical view of societies. But Marx's story of society is all about *social conflict* that arises as people work within an economic system to produce material goods. **Max Weber** tells a different tale, showing that the power of *ideas* shapes society. Weber contrasted the traditional thinking of simple societies with the rational thought that dominates complex societies today. Finally, **Emile Durkheim** helps us see the different ways that traditional and modern societies hang together.

All four visions of society answer a number of important questions: What makes the way of life of people such as the Tuareg of the Sahara so different from your life as a college student in the United States? How and why do all societies change? What forces divide a society? What forces hold a society together? This chapter will provide answers to all of these questions as we look at the work of important sociologists.

Gerhard Lenski: Society and Technology

Members of our society, who take instant messaging and television, as well as schools and hospitals, for granted, must wonder at the nomads of the Sahara, who live the same simple life their ancestors did centuries ago. The work of Gerhard Lenski (Nolan & Lenski, 2007) helps us understand the great differences among societies that have existed throughout human history.

Lenski uses the term **sociocultural evolution** to mean *changes that occur as a society gains new technology.* With only simple technology, societies such as the Tuareg have little control over nature, so they can support just a small number of people. Societies with complex technology such as cars and cell phones, while not necessarily "better," support hundreds of millions of people in far more affluent ways of life.

Inventing or adopting new technology sends ripples of change throughout a society. When our ancestors first discovered how to make a sail so that wind power could move a boat, they created a new form of transportation that would take them to new lands, greatly expand their economy, and increase their military power. In addition,

Q: "How is society possible?" Georg Simmel

NOTE: Simple societies have yielded information about the medicinal properties of plants and also a general model for living in balance with nature (see Chapter 22, "Population, Urbanization, and Environment").

NOTE: Given the greater productivity of gathering relative to hunting, should the term be "gathering and hunting"?

NOTE: Lenski explains that hunters and gatherers limited property rights to personal tools and weapons. Natural resources, including fields and forests, were available to all, but ownership was claimed by a group. Thus members of such societies expected outsiders to seek permission before entering an area. Horticulturalists, by contrast, typically (but not always) define land as private property.

society people who interact in a defined territory and share a culture

| **Gerhard Lenski** (society is defined by level of technology) | **Karl Marx** (society is defined by type of social conflict) | **Max Weber** (society is defined by ideas/mode of thinking) | **Emile Durkheim** (society is defined by its type of solidarity) |

the more technology a society has, the faster it changes. Technologically simple societies change very slowly; Sididi Ag Inaka says he lives "the life of my ancestors." How many people in U.S. society can say that they live the way their grandparents or great-grandparents did? Modern, high-technology societies such as our own change so fast that people usually experience major social changes during a single lifetime. Imagine how surprised your great-grandmother would be to hear about "Googling" and instant messaging, artificial intelligence and iPods, replacement hearts and test-tube babies, space shuttles and screamo music.

Drawing on Lenski's work, we will examine five types of societies, defined by their technology: hunting and gathering societies, horticultural and pastoral societies, agrarian societies, industrial societies, and postindustrial societies.

Hunting and Gathering Societies

In the simplest of all societies, people live by **hunting and gathering,** *making use of simple tools to hunt animals and gather vegetation for food.* From the time that our species appeared 3 million years ago until about 12,000 years ago, *all* humans were hunters and gatherers. Even in 1800, many hunting and gathering societies could be found around the world. But today just a few remain, including the Aka and Pygmies of Central Africa, the Bushmen of southwestern Africa, the Aborigines of Australia, the Kaska Indians of northwestern Canada, and the Batek and Semai of Malaysia.

With little ability to control their environment, hunters and gatherers spend most of their time looking for game and collecting plants to eat. Only in lush areas with lots of food do hunters and gatherers have much chance for leisure. Because it takes a large amount of land to support even a few people, hunting and gathering societies have just a few dozen members. They must also be nomadic, moving on to find new sources of vegetation or to follow migrating animals. Although they may return to favored sites, they rarely form permanent settlements.

Hunting and gathering societies depend on the family to do many things. The family must get and distribute food, protect its members, and teach the children. Everyone's life is much the same; people spend most of their time getting their next meal. Age and gender have some effect on what individuals do. Healthy adults do most of the work, leaving the very young and the very old to help out as they can. Women gather vegetation—which provides most of the food—while men take on the less certain job of hunting. Although men and women perform different tasks, most hunters and gatherers probably see the sexes as having about the same social importance (Leacock, 1978).

After a nearby forest was burned, these Aboriginal women in Australia spent the day collecting roots, which they will use to make dye for their clothing. Members of such societies live closely linked to nature.

Hunting and gathering societies usually have a *shaman,* or spiritual leader, who enjoys high prestige but has to work to find food like everyone else. In short, people in hunting and gathering societies come close to being socially equal.

Hunters and gatherers use simple weapons—the spear, bow and arrow, and stone knife—but rarely to wage war. Their real enemy is the forces of nature: Storms and droughts can kill off their food supply, and there is little they can do for someone who has a serious accident or illness. Being at risk in this way encourages people to cooperate and share, a strategy that raises everyone's chances of survival. But the truth is that many die in childhood, and no more than half reach the age of twenty (Lenski, Nolan, & Lenski, 1995).

During the past century, societies with more powerful technology have closed in on the few remaining hunters and gatherers, reducing their food supply. As a result, hunting and gathering societies are disappearing. Fortunately, study of this way of life has given us valuable information about human history and our basic ties to the natural world.

Horticultural and Pastoral Societies

Some 10,000 to 12,000 years ago, as the timeline inside the back cover shows, a new technology began to change the lives of human beings. People developed **horticulture,** *the use of hand tools to raise crops.* Using a hoe to work the soil and a digging stick to punch holes in the

NOTE: You might express the transition from hunting and gathering to pastoralism and horticulture as moving from seeking food to growing your own.

NOTE: The reason that warfare is more common among horticulturalists and rare among hunting and gathering people probably involves increasing population density that limits both available land and game.

Q: "We have too many men of science, too few of God. We have grasped the mystery of the atom and rejected the Sermon on the Mount. . . . Ours is a world of nuclear giants and ethical infants. We know more about war than we do about peace, more about killing than about living." General Omar N. Bradley

Seeing SOCIOLOGY in the NEWS

Nomadic Herders Go High-Tech

By MARSHA WALTON
December 4, 2006

Satellites, cell phones and spectrometers: Probably not the first things you think of when you picture sheep and goat herders in Afghanistan. But those modern tools may soon make the lives of nomadic families a little more stable.

Afghanistan is the latest location for projects coordinated by the University of California-Davis and Texas A&M University, to provide early warning systems about animal health and to help pinpoint the location of the healthiest grazing areas.

A $4.4 million grant from the U.S. Agency for International Development's Mission to Afghanistan will fund the effort for four years.

"Agriculture is so fundamental to helping people become economically self-sufficient," said Elsa Murano, dean of Agriculture and Life Sciences at Texas A&M University in College Station, Texas.

"And the economic stability that comes from being able to sell your goods, produce your goods,

and get an income from that is a stabilizing force like no other," she said.

Texas A&M research scientist Jay Angerer, who worked with herders in Mongolia, says there is a mixed reaction when he first explains the tools and how they might help.

"I think that they're welcoming in the sense that they're glad that someone is concerned about their issues and problems, and I think they're very curious and interested," said Angerer.

But he says it is also important to respect the understanding they have gained from generations of tending sheep, goats, cattle, and horses. In addition to the natural disasters of drought and dust storms, herding families in east Africa and Afghanistan have also had to survive civil wars and unstable governments.

"I always tell people that I train that this shouldn't be the only tool that you use to make a decision. There's lots of information out there," said Angerer.

The U.S. researchers are often joined by scientists and college students from the region to col-

lect and analyze plant samples. That data about forage is added to information about climate and precipitation, some from satellite information, and some from ground reporting stations.

Computer models then predict how those plants will grow, based on soil conditions and rainfall. The researchers can then forecast where the richest vegetation will be, especially if drought or other crisis conditions exist.

"By giving that information you could provide the herder the information to know whether they need to sell animals, buy supplements or to make a decision that, 'I'm going to cope with this drought by hanging on just a little bit longer,'" said Angerer.

The livestock experts also gain important clues about animal health from the herds' manure.

"We're using a very convenient product, manure, to determine what the animals were consuming, what their diet was, which tells us, are they healthy? Are they going to gain weight? Are they going to meet their reproductive demands?"

ground to plant seeds may not seem like something that would change the world, but these inventions allowed people to give up gathering in favor of growing their own food. The first humans to plant gardens lived in fertile regions of the Middle East. Cultural diffusion spread this knowledge to Latin America and Asia and eventually all over the world.

Not all societies were quick to give up hunting and gathering for horticulture. Hunters and gatherers living where food was plentiful probably saw little reason to change their ways. People living in dry regions (such as the deserts of Africa or the Middle East) or mountainous areas found little use for horticulture because they could not grow much anyway. Such people (including the Tuareg) were more likely to adopt **pastoralism,** *the domestication of animals.* Today, societies that mix horticulture and pastoralism can be found throughout South America, Africa, and Asia. Seeing Sociology in the News describes how some nomadic herders in Afghanistan are benefiting from high technology supplied by scientists in the United States.

Growing plants and raising animals greatly increased food production, so populations expanded from dozens to hundreds of people. Pastoralists remained nomadic, leading their herds to fresh grazing lands. But horticulturalists formed settlements, moving only when the soil gave out. Joined by trade, these settlements formed societies with populations reaching into the thousands.

Once a society is capable of producing a *material surplus*—more resources than are needed to support the population—not everyone has to work at providing food. Greater specialization results: Some

make crafts, while others engage in trade, cut hair, apply tattoos, or serve as priests. Compared to hunting and gathering societies, horticultural and pastoral societies are more socially diverse.

But being more productive does not make a society "better" in every sense. As some families produce more than others, they become richer and more powerful. Horticultural and pastoral societies have greater inequality, with elites using government power—and military force—to serve their own interests. But leaders do not have the ability to communicate or to travel over large distances, so they can control only a small number of people, rather than vast empires.

Religion also differs among types of societies. Hunters and gatherers believe that many spirits inhabit the world. Horticulturalists, however, are more likely to think of one God as the creator of the world. Pastoral societies carry this belief further, seeing God as directly involved in the well-being of the entire world. The pastoral roots of Judaism and Christianity are evident in the term "pastor" and the common view of God as a shepherd ("The Lord is my shepherd," says Psalm 23) who stands watch over us all.

Agrarian Societies

About 5,000 years ago, another revolution in technology was taking place in the Middle East, one that would end up changing life on Earth. This was the emergence of **agriculture,** *large-scale cultivation using plows harnessed to animals or more powerful energy sources.* So important was the invention of the animal-drawn plow, along with other breakthroughs of the period—including irrigation, the wheel,

NOTE: More complex technology empowers humanity to manipulate the natural world; members of industrial societies, therefore, risk losing sensitivity to the natural environment and the requirements of living in an ecological system. Look ahead to Chapter 22.

NOTE: *Hort* is a Latin root meaning "garden." Latin *horti cultura* thus means "cultivation of a garden"; *agri cultura* means "cultivation of a field." "Pastoral" is

derived from the Latin meaning "shepherd" or, literally, "feeder."

NOTE: Marion Levy suggests that a good index of modernization is the ratio of inanimate to animate sources of energy (that is, fuel to muscle power).

NOTE: Chapter 16 ("The Economy and Work") details the facets of the Industrial Revolution: new forms of energy, factories, mass production, productive specialization, and wage labor.

said Kris Banik, lab manager at the Grazingland Animal Nutrition Lab at Texas A&M.

At that Texas lab, samples from farms and ranches are carefully dried and pulverized before they are analyzed with a Near Infrared Reflectance Spectroscopy machine, or NIRS. The device provides a biochemical snapshot of the organic material, indicating how much protein and other digestible organic matter the animals have consumed.

But shepherds and herders, often on the move in mountains or deserts, do not have the luxury of a nearby lab. So researchers developed a tool to take to their turf.

A portable spectroscopy unit can accomplish the same thing, with almost instant results that can provide early warning to herders of their animals' health.

"If we can go out in the pasture in real time and be able to take a scan of that sample, and then be able to give an answer right then, we'll cut five days off that decision-making process," said Doug Tolleson, director of the Grazingland

Animal Nutrition Lab. "If you had a rapid onset of a drought, that could make a lot of difference." . . .

[Professor Robert Kaitho, an animal nutritionist] says technology now goes beyond just keeping animals healthier. It can help families get a better price for their animals, through a cell phone, or any Internet connection. Sending a text message to a cell phone number will get within a couple of minutes the current market prices for livestock.

"They are able to get information otherwise that was only limited to middlemen, and those who had connections in the cities," he said. "Now, the common people have access to that same information." . . .

So how do the herders feel about scientists from other countries bringing in their new tools to a very established lifestyle?

Michael J. Jacobs . . . visited Policharkhe, an area where Kuchi tribespeople spend a few months between their summer and winter grazing lands.

Through a translator, Jacobs talked to one sheep and goat herder. At one point the translator started to chuckle. Jacobs asked him what the herder had said.

The translator said: "He is asking what took you so long to help them."

WHAT DO YOU THINK?

1. What specific benefits can nomadic herders in Afghanistan gain from cooperation with scientists using high technology?

2. What unexpected and possibly undesirable consequences might develop from this cooperation?

3. Do you think there are lessons high-technology societies can learn from these nomadic herders in Afghanistan? If so, what are they?

Excerpted by permission from "Nomadic Herders Go High-Tech" by Marsha Walton, December 4, 2006, from cnn.com <http://cnn.com>

---

writing, numbers, and the use of various metals—that this moment in history is often called the "dawn of civilization."

Using animal-drawn plows, farmers could cultivate fields far bigger than the garden-sized plots planted by horticulturalists. Plows have the added advantage of turning and aerating the soil, making it more fertile. As a result, farmers could work the same land for generations, encouraging the development of permanent settlements. With the ability to grow a surplus of food and to transport goods using animal-powered wagons, agrarian societies greatly expanded in size and population. About 100 C.E., for example, the agrarian Roman Empire contained some 70 million people spread over 2 million square miles (Nolan & Lenski, 2007).

Greater production meant even more specialization. Now there were dozens of distinct occupations, from farmers to builders to metalworkers. With so many people producing so many different things, people invented money as a common standard of exchange, and the old barter system—in which people traded one thing for another—was abandoned.

Agrarian societies have extreme social inequality, typically more than modern societies such as our own. In most cases, a large number of the people are peasants or slaves, who do most of the work. Elites therefore have time for more "refined" activities, including the study of philosophy, art, and literature. This explains the historical link between "high culture" and social privilege noted in Chapter 3 ("Culture").

Among hunters and gatherers and also among horticulturalists, women provide most of the food, which gives them social importance. Agriculture, however, raises men to a position of social dominance. Using heavy metal plows pulled by large animals, men take charge of food production in agrarian societies. Women are left with the support tasks, such as weeding and carrying water to the fields (Boulding, 1976; Fisher, 1979).

In agrarian societies, religion reinforces the power of elites by defining both loyalty and hard work as moral obligations. Many of the "Wonders of the Ancient World," such as the Great Wall of China and the Great Pyramids of Egypt, were possible only because emperors and pharaohs had almost absolute power and were able to control a large political system and order their people to work for a lifetime without pay.

Of the societies described so far, agrarian societies have the most social inequality. Agrarian technology also gives people a greater range of life choices, which is the reason that agrarian societies differ more from one another than horticultural and pastoral societies do.

Industrial Societies

Industrialism, which first took hold in the rich nations of today's world, is *the production of goods using advanced sources of energy to drive large machinery.* Until the industrial era began, the major source of energy had been the muscles of humans and the animals they tended. Around the year 1750, people turned to water power and then steam boilers to operate mills and factories filled with larger and larger machines.

NOTE: Chapter 10 ("Social Stratification") examines the relative degree of social inequality in the types of societies described by Lenski. See especially Figure 10–2, the Kuznets curve.

NOTE: Worth repeating is the link between agrarian "cultivation" and the flowering of human "culture"—these words share a single root.

NOTE: Peter Berger (1986:99) points out that even average people today live better than agrarian elites. As late as World War I, for example, Schoenbrunn, the fabulous summer palace of the Habsburgs (monarchs of Austria), had not a single indoor toilet.

sociocultural evolution (p. 88) changes that occur as a society gains new technology

hunting and gathering (p. 89) the use of simple tools to hunt animals and gather vegetation for food → **horticulture** (p. 89) the use of hand tools to raise crops / **pastoralism** (p. 90) the domestication of animals → **agriculture** (p. 90) large scale cultivation using plows harnessed to animals or more powerful energy sources → **industialism** (p. 91) the production of goods using advanced sources of energy to drive large machinery → **postindustrialism** the production of information using computer technology

Industrial technology gave people such power to alter their environment that change took place faster than ever before. It is probably correct to say that the new industrial societies changed more in one century than they had over the course of the previous thousand years. As explained in Chapter 1 ("The Sociological Perspective"), change was so rapid that it sparked the birth of sociology itself. By 1900, railroads crossed the land, steamships traveled the seas, and steel-framed skyscrapers reached far higher than any of the old cathedrals that symbolized the agrarian age.

But that was only the beginning. Soon automobiles allowed people to move quickly almost anywhere, and electricity powered homes full of modern "conveniences" such as refrigerators, washing machines, air conditioners, and entertainment centers. Electronic communication, beginning with the telegraph and the telephone and followed by radio, television, and computers, gave people the ability to reach others instantly, all over the world.

Work also changed. In agrarian communities, most men and women worked in the home or in the fields nearby. Industrialization drew people away from home to factories situated near energy sources (such as coalfields) that powered their machinery. The result was a weakening of close working relationships, strong family ties, and many of the traditional values, beliefs, and customs that guide agrarian life.

> December 28, Moray, in the Andes highlands of Peru. We are high in the mountains in a small community of several dozen families, miles from the nearest electric line or paved road. At about 12,000 feet, breathing is hard for people not used to the thin air, so we walk slowly. But hard work is no problem for the man and his son tilling a field near their home with a horse and plow. Too poor to buy a tractor, these people till the land in the same way that their ancestors did 500 years ago.

With industrialization, occupational specialization became greater than ever. Today, the kind of work you do has a lot to do with your standard of living, so people now often size up one another in terms of their jobs rather than according to their family ties, as agrarian people do. Rapid change and people's tendency to move from place to place also make social life more anonymous, increase cultural diversity, and promote subcultures and countercultures, as described in Chapter 3 ("Culture").

Industrial technology changes the family, too, reducing its traditional importance as the center of social life. No longer does the family serve as the main setting for work, learning, and religious worship. As Chapter 18 ("Families") explains, technological change also plays a part in making families more diverse, with a greater share of single people, divorced people, single-parent families, and stepfamilies.

Perhaps the greatest effect of industrialization has been to raise living standards, which increased fivefold in the United States over the past century. Although at first it only benefits the elite few, industrial technology is so productive that incomes rise over time and people have longer and more comfortable lives. Even social inequality decreases slightly, as explained in Chapter 10 ("Social Stratification"), because industrial societies provide extended schooling and greater political rights. Around the world, industrialization has had the effect of increasing the demand for a greater political voice, a pattern evident in South Korea, Taiwan, the People's Republic of China, and the nations of Eastern Europe and the former Soviet Union.

Postindustrial Societies

Many industrial societies, including the United States, have now entered a new phase of technological development, and we can extend Lenski's analysis to take account of recent trends. A gen-

What would it be like to live in a society with simple technology? That's the premise of the television show *Survivor*. What advantages do societies with simple technology afford their members? What disadvantages do you see?

NOTE: The industrial era moved goods, first by ship, then by rail, and more recently by truck on interstate highways. The postindustrial equivalent is information moving at the speed of light along the information "superhighway."

GLOBAL: Marvin Harris (1987) describes the power of expanding technology, estimating that hunters and gatherers had to expend 1 calorie of human energy to produce 3 calories of food value. For horticultural societies, the ratio is 1:15; for agrarian societies, 1:50; and for industrial societies, 1:5000.

DISCUSS: Consider how modern communication and information technology mass produces culture and directs it at people, rather than the earlier pattern by which culture emerged organically from our own lives.

MAKING THE GRADE

The beginning of "modernity" is linked to the development of industrial production, first in Europe and soon after in the United States. The concept of modernity is discussed in more depth in Chapter 24. As explained in Chapter 1, the industrial era also sparked the development of sociology.

SEEING SOCIOLOGY
in Everyday Life

How do the *Jurassic Park* movies portray the advantages and disadvantages of modern technology?

Does advancing technology make society better? In some ways, perhaps. However, many films—as far back as *Frankenstein* (left) in 1931 and as recently as the 2009 film *Terminator Salvation* (right)—have expressed the concern that new technology not only solves old problems but also creates new ones. All the sociological theorists discussed in this chapter shared this ambivalent view of the modern world.

eration ago, the sociologist Daniel Bell (1973) coined the term **postindustrialism** to refer to *the production of information using computer technology.* Production in industrial societies centers on factories and machinery generating material goods; postindustrial production relies on computers and other electronic devices that create, process, store, and apply information. Just as people in industrial societies learn mechanical skills, people in postindustrial societies such as ours develop information-based skills and carry out their work using computers and other forms of high-technology communication.

As Chapter 16 ("The Economy and Work") explains, a postindustrial society uses less and less of its labor force for industrial production. At the same time, more jobs become available for clerical workers, teachers, writers, sales managers, and marketing representatives, all of whom process information.

The Information Revolution, which is at the heart of postindustrial society, is most evident in rich nations, yet new information technology affects people in all countires around the world. As discussed in Chapter 3 ("Culture"), a worldwide flow of products, people, and information now links societies and has advanced a global culture. In this sense, the postindustrial society is at the heart of globalization.

The Summing Up table on pages 94–95 provides a review of how technology shapes life in societies at different stages of sociocultural evolution.

The Limits of Technology

More complex technology has made life better by raising productivity, reducing infectious disease, and sometimes just relieving boredom. But technology provides no quick fix for social problems. Poverty, for example, remains a reality for some 38 million women and men in the United States (detailed in Chapter 11, "Social Class in the United States") and 1.4 billion people worldwide (U.S. Census Bureau, 2008; see Chapter 12, "Global Stratification").

Technology also creates new problems that our ancestors (and people like Sididi Ag Inaka today) could hardly imagine. Industrial and postindustrial societies give us more personal freedom, but they often lack the sense of community that was part of preindustrial life. Most seriously, an increasing number of the world's nations with nuclear technology have stockpiles of weapons that could send the world back to the Stone Age—if we survive at all.

Advancing technology has also threatened the physical environment. Each stage in sociocultural evolution has introduced more powerful sources of energy and increased our appetite for Earth's resources. Ask yourself whether we can continue to pursue material prosperity without permanently damaging our planet (see Chapter 22, "Population, Urbanization, and Environment").

Technological advances have improved life and brought the world's people closer. But establishing peace, ensuring justice, and protecting the environment are problems that technology alone cannot solve.

NOTE: Roughly 5% to 10% of all people who have ever lived are alive now. However, about 90% of all scientists who have ever lived are living today.

NOTE: Marx was born in Trier, Germany, earned a doctorate in 1841, and went to work as a newspaper editor. He became controversial and moved to Paris; he soon resettled in London. Marxism played a very minor role in sociology until the 1960s.

RESOURCE: The *Manifesto of the Communist Party* is included in the companion reader, *Seeing Ourselves*, 8th ed.

Q: "The truth is that we are all caught in a great economic system which is heartless." Woodrow Wilson

social conflict the struggle between segments of society over valued resources

capitalists people who own and operate factories and other businesses in pursuit of profits

proletarians people who sell their labor for wages

SEEING SOCIOLOGY in Everyday Life

How might Marx view the advertising of products that promise to make our lives more meaningful as an example of false consciousness in a capitalist society?

SUMMING UP

Sociocultural Evolution

Type of Society	Historical Period	Productive Technology	Population Size
Hunting and Gathering Societies	Only type of society until about 12,000 years ago; still common several centuries ago; the few examples remaining today are threatened with extinction	Primitive weapons	25–40 people
Horticultural and Pastoral Societies	From about 12,000 years ago, with decreasing numbers after about 3000 B.C.E.	Horticultural societies use hand tools for cultivating plants; pastoral societies are based on the domestication of animals	Settlements of several hundred people, connected through trading ties to form societies of several thousand people
Agrarian Societies	From about 5,000 years ago, with large but decreasing numbers today	Animal-drawn plow	Millions of people
Industrial Societies	From about 1750 to the present	Advanced sources of energy; mechanized production	Millions of people
Postindustrial Societies	Emerging in recent decades	Computers that support an information-based economy	Millions of people

Karl Marx: Society and Conflict

The first of our classic visions of society comes from Karl Marx (1818–1883), an early giant in the field of sociology whose influence continues today. Keenly aware of how the Industrial Revolution had changed Europe, Marx spent most of his adult life in London, the capital of what was then the vast British Empire. He was awed by the size and productive power of the new factories going up all over Britain. Along with other industrial nations, Britain was producing more goods than ever before, drawing resources from around the world and churning out products at a dizzying rate.

What astounded Marx even more was that the riches produced by this new technology ended up in the hands of only a few people. As he walked around the city of London, he could see for himself that a handful of aristocrats and industrialists lived in fabulous mansions staffed by servants, where they enjoyed both luxury and privilege. At the same time, most people labored long hours for low wages and lived in slums. Some even slept in the streets, where they were likely to die young from diseases brought on by cold and poor nutrition.

Marx saw his society in terms of a basic contradiction: In a country so rich, how could so many people be so poor? Just as important, he asked, how can this situation be changed? Many people think Marx set out to tear societies apart. But he was motivated by compassion and wanted to help a badly divided society create a new and more just social order.

At the heart of Marx's thinking is the idea of **social conflict,** *the struggle between segments of society over valued resources.* Social conflict can, of course, take many forms: Individuals quarrel, colleges have longstanding sports rivalries, and nations go to war. For Marx, however, the most important type of social conflict was *class conflict* arising from the way a society produces material goods.

Society and Production

Living in the nineteenth century, Marx observed the early decades of industrial capitalism in Europe. This economic system, Marx explained, turned a small part of the population into **capitalists,** *people who own and operate factories and other businesses in pursuit of profits.* A capitalist tries to make a profit by selling a product for more

Q: "The bourgeoisie, during its rule of scarcely one hundred years, has created more massive and more colossal productive forces than have all preceding generations together." Marx and Engels

NOTE: "Capitalism" is derived from the Latin word *caput*, meaning "head." The term was first used in 12th-century Europe at a time of expanding commerce. "Conflict" is derived from the Latin meaning "a striking together."

POP CULTURE: One example of what Marx might call "false consciousness" is playing the lottery. Games such as Powerball can be found in most states. Such games encourage people to think that anyone can get rich.

social institutions the major spheres of social life, or societal subsystems, organized to meet human needs

false consciousness explaining social problems as the shortcomings of individuals rather than as the flaws of society

MAKING THE GRADE

Marx's analysis of society uses the social-conflict approach. In his eyes, class conflict (rather than gender conflict or racial conflict) is most important.

Settlement Pattern	Social Organization	Examples
Nomadic	Family-centered; specialization limited to age and sex; little social inequality	Pygmies of Central Africa, Bushmen of southwestern Africa, Aborigines of Australia, Semai of Malaysia, Kaska Indians of Canada
Horticulturalists form small permanent settlements; pastoralists are nomadic	Family-centered; religious system begins to develop; moderate specialization; increased social inequality	Middle Eastern societies about 5000 B.C.E., various societies today in New Guinea and other Pacific islands, Yąnomamö today in South America
Cities become common, but they generally contain only a small proportion of the population	Family loses significance as distinct religious, political, and economic systems emerge; extensive specialization; increased social inequality	Egypt during construction of the Great Pyramids, medieval Europe, numerous predominantly agrarian societies of the world today
Cities contain most of the population	Distinct religious, political, economic, educational, and family systems; highly specialized; marked social inequality persists, lessening somewhat over time	Most societies today in Europe and North America, Australia, and Japan, which generate most of the world's industrial production
Population remains concentrated in cities	Similar to industrial societies, with information processing and other service work gradually replacing industrial production	Industrial societies are now entering the postindustrial stage

than it costs to produce. Capitalism turns most of the population into industrial workers, whom Marx called **proletarians,** *people who sell their labor for wages.* To Marx, a system of capitalist production always ends up creating conflict between capitalists and workers. To keep profits high, capitalists keep wages low. But workers want higher wages. Since profits and wages come from the same pool of funds, the result is conflict. As Marx saw it, this conflict could end only with the end of capitalism itself.

All societies are composed of **social institutions,** *the major spheres of social life, or societal subsystems, organized to meet human needs.* Examples of social institutions include the economy, the political system, the family, religion, and education. In his analysis of society, Marx argued that one institution—the economy—dominates all the others and defines the true nature of a society. Drawing on the philosophical approach called *materialism,* which says that how humans produce material goods shapes their experiences, Marx believed that the other social institutions all operate in a way that supports a society's economy. Lenski focused on how technology molds a society, but Marx argued that the economy is a society's "real foundation" (1959:43, orig. 1859).

Marx viewed the economic system as society's *infrastructure* (*infra* is Latin, meaning "below"). Other social institutions, including the family, the political system, and religion, are built on this foundation; they form society's *superstructure* and support the economy. Marx's theory is illustrated in Figure 4–1 on page 96. For example, under capitalism, the legal system protects capitalists' wealth, and the family allows capitalists to pass their property from one generation to the next.

Marx was well aware that most people living in industrial-capitalist societies do not recognize how capitalism shapes the entire operation of their society. Most people, in fact, regard the right to own private property or pass it on to their children as "natural." In the same way, many of us tend to see rich people as having "earned" their money through long years of schooling and hard work; we see the poor, on the other hand, as lacking skills and the personal drive to make more of themselves. Marx rejected this type of thinking, calling it **false consciousness,** *explaining social problems as the shortcomings of individuals rather than as the flaws of society.* Marx was saying, in effect, that it is not "people" who make society so unequal but rather the system of capitalist production. False consciousness, he believed, hurts people by hiding the real cause of their problems.

Q: "The economic structure of society always furnishes the real basis, starting from which we can alone work out the ultimate explanation of the whole super-structure of judicial and political institutions as well as of the religious, philo-sophical, and other ideas of a given historical period." Friedrich Engels

NOTE: In opposing capitalism, Marx encouraged workers to cease to be merely a social class in themselves and become a social class acting for themselves.

Q: "The needs of the poor must take priority over the desires of the rich; and the rights of workers over the maximization of profits." Pope John Paul II

Q: "I am not a Marxist." Karl Marx

MAKING THE GRADE

Take a careful look at Figure 4–1, which shows Marx's belief that the economy is the foundation of society (the "infrastructure") that affects the operation of the other social institutions as well as cultural ideas and values (the "superstructure"). This approach is called *materialism* because how a society produces material goods is seen as defining the whole social system.

class conflict conflict between entire classes over the distribution of a society's wealth and power

class consciousness workers' recognition of themselves as a class unified in opposition to capitalists and ultimately to capitalism itself

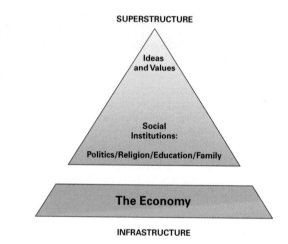

FIGURE 4–1 **Karl Marx's Model of Society**

This diagram illustrates Marx's materialist view that the system of eco-nomic production shapes the entire society. Economic production involves both technology (industry, in the case of capitalism) and social relationships (for capitalism, the relationship between the capitalists, who own the factories and businesses, and the workers). On this infrastruc-ture, or foundation, rests society's superstructure, which includes its major social institutions as well as core cultural values and ideas. Marx maintained that every part of a society supports the economic system.

Conflict and History

For Marx, conflict is the engine that drives social change. Sometimes societies change at a slow, *evolutionary* rate. But they may erupt in rapid, *revolutionary* change.

To Marx, early hunters and gatherers formed primitive commu-nist societies. *Communism* is a system in which people commonly own and equally share the food and other things they produce. Peo-ple in hunting and gathering societies do not have much, but they share what they have. In addition, because everyone does the same kind of work, there is little chance of social conflict.

With technological advance comes social inequality. Among hor-ticultural, pastoral, and early agrarian societies—which Marx lumped together as the "ancient world"—warfare was frequent, and the vic-tors made their captives slaves.

Agriculture brings still more wealth to a society's elite but does little for most other people, who labor as serfs and are barely better off than slaves. As Marx saw it, the state supported the feudal system (in which the elite or nobility had all the power), assisted by the church, which claimed that this arrangement was God's will. This is why Marx thought that feudalism was simply "exploitation, veiled by religious and political illusions" (Marx & Engels, 1972:337, orig. 1848).

Gradually, new productive forces started to break down the feu-dal order. As trade steadily increased, cities grew, and merchants and skilled craftsworkers formed the new capitalist class or *bourgeoisie* (a French word meaning "people of the town"). After 1800, the bour-geoisie also controlled factories, becoming richer and richer so that they soon rivaled the ancient landowning nobility. For their part, the nobles looked down their noses at this upstart "commercial" class, but in time, these capitalists took control of European societies. To Marx's way of thinking, then, new technology was only part of the Industrial Revolution; it also served as a class revolution in which capitalists overthrew the old agrarian elite.

Industrialization also led to the growth of the proletariat. English landowners converted fields once plowed by serfs into grazing land for sheep to produce wool for the textile mills. Forced from the land, millions of people migrated to cities to work in factories. Marx envi-sioned these workers one day joining together to form a revolution-ary class that would overthrow the capitalist system.

Capitalism and Class Conflict

"The history of all hitherto existing society is the history of class strug-gles." With these words, Marx and his collaborator, Friedrich Engels, began their best-known statement, the *Manifesto of the Communist Party* (1972:335, orig. 1848). Industrial capitalism, like earlier types of society, contains two major social classes: the ruling class, whose mem-bers (capitalists or bourgeoisie) own productive property, and the oppressed (proletarians), who sell their labor, reflecting the two basic positions in the productive system. Like masters and slaves in the ancient world and like nobles and serfs in feudal systems, capitalists and proletarians are engaged in class conflict today. Currently, as in the past, one class controls the other as productive property. Marx used the term **class conflict** (and sometimes *class struggle*) to refer to *conflict between entire classes over the distribution of a society's wealth and power.*

Class conflict is nothing new. What distinguishes the conflict in capitalist society, Marx pointed out, is how out in the open it is. Agrar-ian nobles and serfs, for all their differences, were bound together by traditions and mutual obligations. Industrial capitalism dissolved those ties so that loyalty and honor were replaced by "naked self-interest." Because the proletarians had no personal ties to the capital-ists, Marx saw no reason for them to put up with their oppression.

Marx knew that revolution would not come easily. First, work-ers must *become aware* of their oppression and see capitalism as its true cause. Second, they must *organize and act* to address their prob-lems. This means that false consciousness must be replaced with **class consciousness,** *workers' recognition of themselves as a class unified in opposition to capitalists and ultimately to capitalism itself.* Because the inhumanity of early capitalism was plain for him to see, Marx con-

NOTE: Marx used the term "species being" to imply that humans are social beings. Thus, he maintained, humans are neither individualistic nor self-serving but derive satisfactions from social pursuits. In this view, Marx opposed the utilitarian thought of James Mill, John Stuart Mill, and Jeremy Bentham.

RESOURCE: The *Seeing Ourselves* reader includes Marx's selection "Alienated Labor."

NOTE: According to Anthony Campolo (1985), Marx rejected capitalism, despite its obvious productivity, because it was a system that turns us from people who use things and love people into people who love things and use people.

alienation the experience of isolation and misery resulting from powerlessness

cluded that industrial workers would soon rise up to destroy this economic system.

How would the capitalists react? Their wealth made them strong. But Marx saw a weakness in the capitalist armor. Motivated by a desire for personal gain, capitalists feared competition with other capitalists. Marx predicted, therefore, that capitalists would be slow to band together despite their common interests. In addition, he reasoned, capitalists kept employees' wages low in order to maximize profits, which made the workers' misery ever greater. In the long run, Marx believed, capitalists would bring about their own undoing.

Capitalism and Alienation

Marx also condemned capitalist society for producing **alienation,** *the experience of isolation and misery resulting from powerlessness.* To the capitalists, workers are nothing more than a source of labor, to be hired and fired at will. Dehumanized by their jobs (repetitive factory work in the past and processing orders on a computer today), workers find little satisfaction and feel unable to improve their situation. Here we see another contradiction of capitalist society: As people develop technology to gain power over the world, the capitalist economy gains more control over people.

Marx noted four ways in which capitalism alienates workers:

1. **Alienation from the act of working.** Ideally, people work to meet their needs and to develop their personal potential. Capitalism, however, denies workers a say in what they make or how they make it. Further, much of the work is a repetition of routine tasks. The fact that today we replace workers with machines whenever possible would not have surprised Marx. As far as he was concerned, capitalism had turned human beings into machines long ago.

2. **Alienation from the products of work.** The product of work belongs not to workers but to capitalists, who sell it for profit. Thus, Marx reasoned, the more of themselves workers invest in their work, the more they lose.

3. **Alienation from other workers.** Through work, Marx claimed, people build bonds of community. Industrial capitalism, however, makes work competitive rather than cooperative, setting each person apart from everyone else and offering little chance for companionship.

4. **Alienation from human potential.** Industrial capitalism alienates workers from their human potential. Marx argued that a worker "does not fulfill himself in his work but denies himself, has a feeling of misery rather than well-being, does not freely develop his physical and mental energies, but is physically exhausted and mentally debased. The worker, therefore, feels himself to be at home only during his leisure time, whereas at work he feels

homeless" (1964:124–25, orig. 1848). In short, industrial capitalism turns an activity that should express the best qualities in human beings into a dull and dehumanizing experience.

Marx viewed alienation, in its various forms, as a barrier to social change. But he hoped that industrial workers would overcome their alienation by uniting into a true social class, aware of the cause of their problems and ready to change society.

Revolution

The only way out of the trap of capitalism, Marx argued, is to remake society. He imagined a system of production that could provide for the social needs of all. He called this system *socialism.* Although Marx knew that such a dramatic change would not come easily, he must have been disappointed that he did not live to see workers in England rise up. Still, convinced that capitalism was a social evil, he believed that in time the working majority would realize they held the key to a better future. This change would certainly be revolutionary and perhaps even violent. Marx believed that a socialist society would bring class conflict to an end.

Chapter 10 ("Social Stratification") explains more about changes in industrial-capitalist societies since Marx's time and why the revolution he wanted never took place. In addition, as Chapter 17 ("Politics and Government") explains, Marx failed to foresee that the

A common fear among thinkers in the early industrial era was that people, now slaves to the new machines, would be stripped of their humanity. No one captured this idea better than the comic actor Charlie Chaplin, who wrote and starred in the 1936 film *Modern Times.*

NOTE: Weber was born to a rich family. His father was a major politician (giving Weber his interest in politics), and his mother was a devout Calvinist (sparking his interest in religion). His wife, Marianne, was a leading feminist. For much of his life, mental problems limited his productivity.

NOTE: In times of trouble, traditional people consult religious leaders (as the Irish people did during the 19th-century potato famines). Today, troubled people consult physicians (and other scientific specialists) and, of course, lawyers.

NOTE: Notice how we characterize a mentally healthy person as "rational." In a rational society, to lack rationality is to court the label of mental illness.

NOTE: Chapter 7 ("Groups and Organizations") presents additional material on Max Weber and the rise of a rational society. Before teaching this chapter, it may be useful to look ahead to that chapter, especially pages 176–79.

ideal type an abstract statement of the essential characteristics of any social phenomenon

rationalization of society the historical change from tradition to rationality as the main type of human thought

tradition values and beliefs passed from generation to generation

rationality a way of thinking that emphasizes deliberate, matter-of-fact calculation of the most efficient way to accomplish a particular task

revolution he imagined could take the form of repressive regimes, such as Stalin's government in the Soviet Union, that would end up killing tens of millions of people (R. F. Hamilton, 2001). But in his own time, Marx looked toward the future with hope: "The proletarians have nothing to lose but their chains. They have a world to win" (Marx & Engels, 1972:362, orig. 1848).

Max Weber: The Rationalization of Society

With a wide knowledge of law, economics, religion, and history, Max Weber (1864–1920) produced what many experts regard as the greatest individual contribution to sociology. This scholar, born to a prosperous family in Germany, had much to say about how modern society differs from earlier types of social organization.

Weber understood the power of technology, and he shared many of Marx's ideas about social conflict. But he disagreed with Marx's philosophy of materialism. Weber's philosophical approach, called *idealism,* emphasized how human ideas—especially beliefs and values—shape society. He argued that societies differ not in terms of how people produce things but in how people think about the world. In Weber's view, modern society was the product of a new way of thinking.

Weber compared societies in different times and places. To make the comparisons, he relied on the **ideal type,** *an abstract statement of the essential characteristics of any social phenomenon.* Following Weber's approach, for example, we might speak of "preindustrial" and "industrial" societies as ideal types. The use of the word "ideal" does not mean that one or the other is "good" or "best." Nor does an ideal type refer to any actual society. Rather, think of an ideal type as a way of defining a type of society in its pure form. We have already used ideal types in comparing "hunting and gathering societies" with "industrial societies" and "capitalism" with "socialism."

Two Worldviews: Tradition and Rationality

Rather than categorizing societies according to their technology or productive systems, Weber focused on ways people think about their world. Members of preindustrial societies are bound by *tradition,* and people in industrial-capitalist societies are guided by *rationality.*

By **tradition,** Weber meant *values and beliefs passed from generation to generation.* In other words, traditional people are guided by the past. They consider particular actions right and proper mostly because they have been accepted for so long.

People in modern societies, however, favor **rationality,** *a way of thinking that emphasizes deliberate, matter-of-fact calculation of the most efficient way to accomplish a particular task.* Sentimental ties to the past have no place in a rational worldview, and tradition becomes simply one kind of information. Typically, modern people think and act on the basis of what they see as the present and future consequences of their choices. They evaluate jobs, schooling, and even relationships in terms of what they put into them and what they expect to receive in return.

Weber viewed both the Industrial Revolution and the development of capitalism as evidence of modern rationality. Such changes are all part of the **rationalization of society,** *the historical change from tradition to rationality as the main type of human thought.* Weber went on to describe modern society as "disenchanted" because scientific thinking has swept away most of people's sentimental ties to the past.

The willingness to adopt the latest technology is one strong indicator of how rationalized a society is. To illustrate the global pattern of rationalization, Global Map 4–1 shows where in the world personal computers are found. In general, the high-income countries of North America and Europe use personal computers the most, but they are rare in low-income nations.

Why are some societies more eager than others to adopt new technology? Those with a more rational worldview might consider new computer or medical technol-

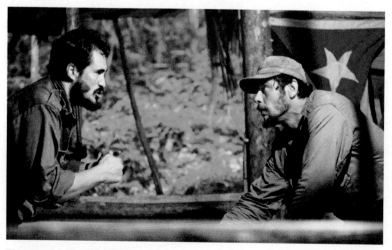
The 2008 film *Che* tells the story of Ernesto "Che" Guevara, who put Marxist theory into action by encouraging revolutionary movements throughout Latin America. Che played an important role as an advisor to Fidel Castro during the Cuban revolution, after which he went on to organize an unsuccessful revolution in Bolivia.

THE MAP: Another indicator of the uneven pace of rationalization in the world is that half the world's scientific output is generated by six nations: U.S., U.K., Japan, Russia, France, and Germany.

Q: "Marxist social scientists typically ask questions about matters on which they already believe to have the answers, at least in broad outline. This is a useful methodology for prophets; it decisively flaws the work of social scientists." Peter Berger

NOTE: The German word *Weltanschauung* (*Welt* = world, *Anschauung* = perception), designating the distinctive ideas with which people embrace the world, has no English equivalent, although *worldview* comes close. For Weber, early Protestantism was more than a religion, as capitalism was more than an economic system: Both represented a distinctive *Weltanschauung*.

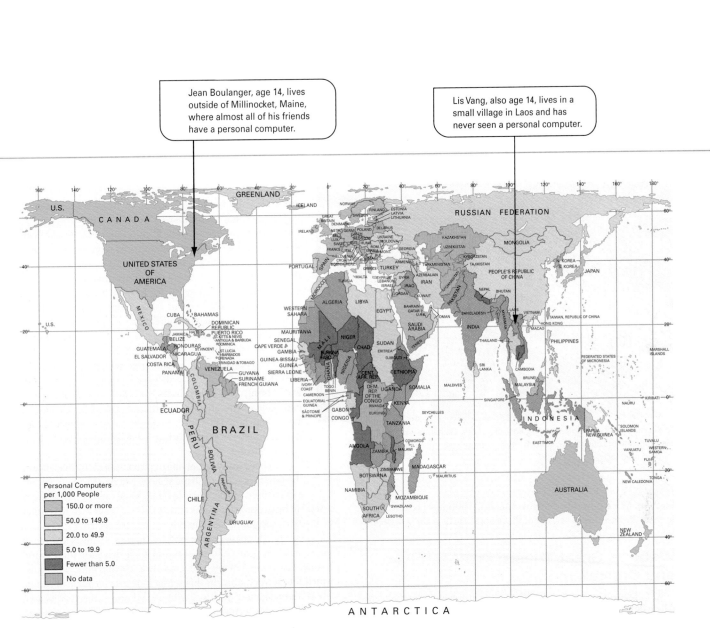

Jean Boulanger, age 14, lives outside of Millinocket, Maine, where almost all of his friends have a personal computer.

Lis Vang, also age 14, lives in a small village in Laos and has never seen a personal computer.

Personal Computers per 1,000 People
- 150.0 or more
- 50.0 to 149.9
- 20.0 to 49.9
- 5.0 to 19.9
- Fewer than 5.0
- No data

Window on the World

GLOBAL MAP 4–1 **High Technology in Global Perspective**

Countries with traditional cultures cannot afford, choose to ignore, or even intentionally resist new technology that nations with highly rationalized ways of life quickly embrace. Personal computers, central to today's high technology, are commonplace in high-income countries such as the United States. In low-income nations, by contrast, they are unknown to most people.

Source: International Telecommunication Union (2006, 2007).

ogy a breakthrough, but those with a very traditional culture might reject such devices as a threat to their way of life. The Tuareg nomads of northern Mali, described at the beginning of this chapter, shrug off the idea of using telephones: Why would anyone in the desert want a cell phone? Similarly, in the United States, the Amish refuse to have telephones in their homes because it is not part of their traditional way of life.

In Weber's view, the amount of technological innovation depends on how a society's people understand their world. Many people throughout history have had the opportunity to adopt new technology, but only in the rational cultural climate of Western Europe did people exploit scientific discoveries to spark the Industrial Revolution (Weber, 1958, orig. 1904–05).

Is Capitalism Rational?

Is industrial capitalism a rational economic system? Here again, Weber and Marx were on different sides. Weber considered industrial capitalism highly rational because capitalists try to make money in any way

NOTE: The Protestant ethic and the spirit of capitalism are not synonymous. Weber explained that the former becomes the latter only as it is disenchanted. The disenchanted spirit of Calvinism then creates three modern "types," all highly disciplined but devoid of piety: the capitalist (devotion to profits), the scientist (devotion to knowledge), and the bureaucrat (devotion to duty).

GLOBAL: The Portuguese founded the colony of Macau in 1557 and introduced a Catholic culture; the British founded Hong Kong almost three centuries later in 1840 with a Protestant culture. Economically speaking, the latter greatly surpassed the former. (Hong Kong reverted to China in 1997 and Macau in 1999.)

GLOBAL: Peter Berger (1986:155) notes that certain ethnic groups everywhere stand out as more productive: the Chinese in Southeast Asia, Buddhists in Thailand and Sri Lanka, Sikh peasants in the Punjab of India, and the Ibos in Nigeria.

◗ MAKING THE GRADE

Weber's approach, *idealism,* is opposite to Marx's materialism. Weber tries to show that the way people think about their world affects all of society, including production. Weber agreed with Marx that economic production can shape ideas, but he claimed that the process also works the other way around.

◗ MAKING THE GRADE

It is probably fair to say that Weber viewed modern capitalism as Calvinism minus Christianity: a *religious* ethic evolving into a *work* ethic.

To the outside observer, the trading floor of a stock exchange may look like complete craziness. But in such activity Weber saw the essence of modern rationality.

they can. Marx, however, thought capitalism irrational because it fails to meet the basic needs of most of the people (Gerth & Mills, 1946:49).

Weber's Great Thesis: Protestantism and Capitalism

Weber spent many years considering how and why industrial capitalism developed in the first place. Why did it emerge in parts of Western Europe during the eighteenth and nineteenth centuries?

Weber claimed that the key to the birth of industrial capitalism lay in the Protestant Reformation. Specifically, he saw industrial capitalism as the major outcome of Calvinism, a Christian religious movement founded by John Calvin (1509–1564). Calvinists approached life in a highly disciplined and rational way. One of Calvin's most important ideas was *predestination,* the belief that an all-knowing and all-powerful God had predestined some people for salvation and others for damnation. Believing that everyone's fate was set before birth, early Calvinists thought that people did not know what their destiny was and could do nothing to change it. So Calvinists swung between hopeful visions of spiritual salvation and anxious fears of eternal damnation.

Frustrated at not knowing their fate, Calvinists gradually came to a resolution of sorts. Wouldn't those chosen for glory in the next world, they reasoned, see signs of divine favor in *this* world? In this way, Calvinists came to see worldly prosperity as a sign of God's grace. Eager to gain this reassurance, Calvinists threw themselves into a quest for success, applying rationality, discipline, and hard work to their tasks. They did not pursue wealth for its own sake, because spending money on themselves would be self-indulgent and sinful. Neither were Calvinists likely to share their wealth with the poor, because they viewed poverty as a sign of God's rejection. Calvinists' duty was pressing forward in what they saw as their personal *calling* from God, reinvesting profits for still greater success. It is easy to see how such activity—saving money, using wealth to create more wealth, and adopting new technology—became the foundation of capitalism.

Other world religions did not encourage the rational pursuit of wealth the way Calvinism did. Catholicism, the traditional religion in most of Europe, taught a passive, "otherworldly" view: Good deeds performed humbly on Earth would bring rewards in heaven. For Catholics, making money had none of the spiritual significance it had for Calvinists. Weber concluded that this was the reason that industrial capitalism developed primarily in areas of Europe where Calvinism was strong.

Weber's study of Calvinism provides striking evidence of the power of ideas to shape society. Not one to accept simple explanations, Weber knew that industrial capitalism had many causes. But by stressing the importance of ideas, Weber tried to counter Marx's strictly economic explanation of modern society.

As the decades passed, later generations of Calvinists lost much of their early religious enthusiasm. But their drive for success and personal discipline remained, and slowly a *religious* ethic was transformed into a *work* ethic. In this sense, industrial capitalism can be seen as "disenchanted" religion, with wealth now valued for its own sake. This trend is seen in the fact that the practice of "accounting," which to early Calvinists meant keeping a daily record of moral deeds, before long came to mean simply keeping track of money.

Rational Social Organization

According to Weber, rationality is the basis of modern society, giving rise to both the Industrial Revolution and capitalism. He went on to identify seven characteristics of rational social organization:

1. **Distinctive social institutions.** In hunting and gathering societies, the family is the center of all activity. Gradually, however, religious, political, and economic systems develop as separate social institutions. In modern societies, new institutions—including education and health care—also appear. Specialized social institutions are a rational strategy to meet human needs efficiently.

2. **Large-scale organizations.** Modern rationality can be seen in the spread of large-scale organizations. As early as the horticultural era, small groups of political officials made decisions con-

cerning religious observances, public works, and warfare. By the time Europe developed agrarian societies, the Catholic church had grown into a much larger organization with thousands of officials. In today's modern, rational society, almost everyone works for large formal organizations, and federal and state gov-ernments employ tens of millions of workers.

3. **Specialized tasks.** Unlike members of traditional societies, peo-ple in modern societies are likely to have very specialized jobs. The Yellow Pages of any city's telephone directory suggest just how many thousands of different occupations there are today.

4. **Personal discipline.** Modern societies put a premium on self-discipline. Most business and government organizations expect their workers to be disciplined, and discipline is also encouraged by our cultural values of achievement and success.

5. **Awareness of time.** In traditional societies, people measure time according to the rhythm of sun and seasons. Modern people, by contrast, schedule events precisely by the hour and even the minute. Clocks began appearing in European cities some 500 years ago, about the same time commerce began to expand. Soon people began to think (to borrow Benjamin Franklin's phrase) that "time is money."

6. **Technical competence.** Members of traditional societies size up one another on the basis of *who* they are—their family ties. Modern rationality leads us to judge people according to *what* they are, with an eye toward their education, skills, and abilities. Most workers have to keep up with the latest skills and knowledge in their field in order to be successful.

7. **Impersonality.** In a rational society, technical competence is the basis for hiring, so the world becomes impersonal. People interact as specialists concerned with particular tasks rather than as individuals concerned with one another as people. Because showing your feelings can threaten personal discipline, modern people tend to devalue emotion.

All these characteristics can be found in one important expres-sion of modern rationality: bureaucracy.

Rationality, Bureaucracy, and Science

Weber considered the growth of large, rational organizations one of the defining traits of modern societies. Another term for this type of organization is *bureaucracy*. Weber believed that bureaucracy has much in common with capitalism—another key factor in modern social life:

> Today, it is primarily the capitalist market economy which demands that the official business of public administration be discharged precisely, unambiguously, continuously, and with as much speed as possible. Nor-mally, the very large capitalist enterprises are themselves unequaled models of strict bureaucratic organization. (1978:974, orig. 1921)

Max Weber agreed with Karl Marx that modern society is alienating to the individual, but they identified different causes of this problem. For Marx, economic inequality is the reason; for Weber, the problem is isolating and dehumanizing bureaucracy. George Tooker's painting *Landscape with Figures* echoes Weber's sentiments.

George Tooker, *Landscape with Figures*, 1963, egg tempera on gesso panel, 26 X 30 in. Private collection. Reproduction courtesy D. C. Moore Gallery, New York.

As Chapter 7 ("Groups and Organizations") explains, we find aspects of bureaucracy in today's businesses, government agencies, labor unions, and universities. Weber considered bureaucracy highly rational because its elements—offices, duties, and policies—help achieve specific goals as efficiently as possible. Weber saw that capitalism, bureaucracy, and also science—the highly disciplined pursuit of knowl-edge—are all expressions of the same underlying factor: rationality.

Rationality and Alienation

Weber agreed with Marx that industrial capitalism was highly produc-tive. Weber also agreed with Marx that modern society generates wide-spread alienation, although his reasons were different. Marx thought alienation was caused by economic inequality. Weber blamed alien-ation on bureaucracy's countless rules and regulations. Bureaucra-cies, Weber warned, treat a human being as a "number" or a "case" rather than as a unique individual. In addition, working for large organizations demands highly specialized and often tedious routines. In the end, Weber saw modern society as a vast and growing system of rules trying to regulate everything, and he feared that modern soci-ety would end up crushing the human spirit.

MAKING THE GRADE

Durkheim's view of society most clearly follows the structural-functional approach.

SEEING SOCIOLOGY
in Everyday Life

Self-destructive behavior among people who experience sudden wealth is not limited to musicians. Can you think of comedians who have met a similar fate?

Durkheim's observation that people with weak social bonds are prone to self-destructive behavior stands as stark evidence of the power of society to shape individual lives. When rock-and-roll singers become famous, they are wrenched out of familiar life patterns and existing relationships, sometimes with deadly results. The history of rock-and-roll contains many tragic stories of this kind, including (from left) Janis Joplin's and Jimi Hendrix's deaths by drug overdose (both 1970) and Jim Morrison's (1971) and Kurt Cobain's (1994) suicides.

Like Marx, Weber found it ironic that modern society, meant to serve humanity, turns on its creators and enslaves them. Just as Marx described the dehumanizing effects of industrial capitalism, Weber portrayed the modern individual as "only a small cog in a ceaselessly moving mechanism that prescribes to him an endlessly fixed routine of march" (1978:988, orig. 1921). Although Weber could see the advantages of modern society, he was deeply pessimistic about the future. He feared that in the end, the rationalization of society would reduce human beings to robots.

Emile Durkheim: Society and Function

"To love society is to love something beyond us and something in ourselves." These are the words (1974:55, orig. 1924) of the French sociologist Emile Durkheim (1858–1917), another of the discipline's founders. In Durkeim's ideas we find another important vision of human society.

Structure: Society beyond Ourselves

Emile Durkheim's great insight was recognizing that society exists beyond ourselves. Society is more than the individuals who compose it. Society was here long before we were born, it shapes us while we live, and it will remain long after we are gone. Patterns of human behavior—cultural norms, values, and beliefs—exist as established structures, or *social facts,* that have an objective reality beyond the lives of individuals.

Because society is bigger than any one of us, it has the power to guide our thoughts and actions. This is why studying individuals alone (as psychologists or biologists do) can never capture the heart of the social experience. A classroom of college students taking a math exam, a family gathered around a table sharing a meal, people quietly waiting their turn in a doctor's office—all are examples of the countless situations that have a familiar organization apart from any particular individual who has ever been part of them.

Once created by people, Durkheim claimed, society takes on a life of its own and demands a measure of obedience from its creators. We experience the power of society when we see our lives falling into common patterns or when we feel the tug of morality during a moment of temptation.

Function: Society as System

Having established that society has structure, Durkheim turned to the concept of *function.* The significance of any social fact, he explained, is more than what individuals see in their immediate lives; social facts help society operate.

Consider crime. As victims of crime, individuals experience pain and loss. But taking a broader view, Durkheim saw that crime is vital to the ongoing life of society itself. As Chapter 9 ("Deviance") explains, only by defining acts as wrong do people construct and defend morality, which gives direction and meaning to our collective

NOTE: It may help students if you explain that Durkheim's anomie results from the fact that modern society gives individuals too much freedom; for Marx and Weber, alienation resulted from modern society giving individuals too little freedom.

Q: "The nail that stands up gets hit down." Japanese proverb that might describe social control in a traditional society

Q: The term "tyranny of the tribe" suggests the power of the collective conscience in traditional societies.

RESOURCE: An example of a small society that approximates Durkheim's concept of mechanical solidarity is the Amish, described in John Hostetler's article in the companion reader, *Seeing Ourselves*, 8th ed. The Amish practice of shunning illustrates the operation of collective conscience in today's U.S. society.

anomie a condition in which society provides little moral guidance to individuals

mechanical solidarity social bonds, based on common sentiments and shared moral values, that are strong among members of preindustrial societies

organic solidarity social bonds, based on specialization and interdependence, that are stong among members of industrial societies

division of labor specialized economic activity

life. For this reason, Durkheim rejected the common view of crime as abnormal. On the contrary, he concluded, crime is "normal" for the most basic of reasons: A society could not exist without it (1964a, orig. 1893; 1964b, orig. 1895).

Personality: Society in Ourselves

Durkheim said that society is not only "beyond ourselves" but also "in ourselves," helping form our personalities. How we act, think, and feel is drawn from the society that nurtures us. Society shapes us in another way as well—by providing the moral discipline that guides our behavior and controls our desires. Durkheim believed that human beings need the restraint of society because as creatures who can want more and more, we are in constant danger of being overpowered by our own desires. As he put it, "The more one has, the more one wants, since satisfactions received only stimulate instead of filling needs" (1966:248, orig. 1897).

Nowhere is the need for societal regulation better illustrated than in Durkheim's study of suicide (1966, orig. 1897), which was described in Chapter 1 ("The Sociological Perspective"). Why is it that rock stars—from Del Shannon, Elvis Presley, Janis Joplin, and Jim Morrison to Jimi Hendrix, Keith Moon, John Bonham, and Kurt Cobain—seem so prone to self-destruction? Durkheim had the answer long before the invention of the electric guitar: Now as back then, the *highest* suicide rates are found among categories of people with the *lowest* level of societal integration. In short, the enormous freedom of the young, rich, and famous carries a high price in terms of the risk of suicide.

Modernity and Anomie

Compared to traditional societies, modern societies impose fewer restrictions on everyone. Durkheim acknowledged the advantages of modern-day freedom, but he warned of increased **anomie,** *a condition in which society provides little moral guidance to individuals.* The pattern by which many celebrities are "destroyed by fame" well illustrates the destructive effects of anomie. Sudden fame tears people from their families and familiar routines, disrupts established values and norms, and breaks down society's support and regulation of the individual—sometimes with fatal results. Therefore, Durkheim explained, an individual's desires must be balanced by the claims and guidance of society—a balance that is sometimes difficult to achieve in the modern world. Durkheim would not have been surprised to see a rising suicide rate in modern societies such as the United States.

Evolving Societies: The Division of Labor

Like Marx and Weber, Durkheim lived through rapid social change in Europe during the nineteenth century. But Durkheim offered different reasons for this change.

In preindustrial societies, he explained, tradition operates as the social cement that binds people together. In fact, what he termed the *collective conscience* is so strong that the community moves quickly to punish anyone who dares to challenge conventional ways of life. Durkheim used the term **mechanical solidarity** to refer to *social bonds, based on common sentiments and shared moral values, that are strong among members of preindustrial societies.* In practice, mechanical solidarity is based on *similarity.* Durkheim called these bonds "mechanical" because people are linked together in lockstep, with a more or less automatic sense of belonging together and acting alike.

With industrialization, Durkheim continued, mechanical solidarity becomes weaker and weaker, and people are much less bound by tradition. But this does not mean that society dissolves. Modern life creates a new type of solidarity. Durkheim called this new social integration **organic solidarity,** defined as *social bonds, based on specialization and interdependence, that are strong among members of industrial societies.* The solidarity that was once rooted in likeness is now based on *differences* among people who find that their specialized work—as plumbers, college students, midwives, or sociology instructors—makes them rely on other people for most of their daily needs.

For Durkheim, then, the key to change in a society is an expanding **division of labor,** or *specialized economic activity.* Weber said that modern societies specialize in order to become more efficient, and

In traditional societies, everyone does much the same work. These societies are held together by strong moral beliefs. Modern societies, illustrated by urban areas in this country, are held together by a system of production in which people perform specialized work and rely on one another for all the things they cannot do for themselves.

NOTE: By arguing that society has an objective existence, Durkheim (like Comte) may have been attempting to establish a natural social order as a moral authority to replace declining tradition.

GLOBAL: As Edward A. Tiryakian (1994) points out, neither Durkheim nor other social theorists predicted the reemergence of mechanical solidarity in the form of religious, ethnic, racial, and gender conflict around the world and on the U.S. campus.

RESOURCE: Ferdinand Tönnies's "Gemeinschaft and Gesellschaft" is one classic included in the Seeing Ourselves reader. Also find four selections by Weber: "The Case for Value-Free Sociology," "The Characteristics of Bureaucracy," "The Protestant Ethic and the Spirit of Capitalism," and "The Disenchantment of Modern Life."

Q: "We must discover the rational substitutes for those religious notions that for a long time have served as . . . essential moral ideas." Emile Durkheim

MAKING THE GRADE

Both Marx and Weber criticized modern society for producing alienation, but in different ways. Durkheim, too, was critical, claiming that modern society created anomie. Be sure that you are able to clearly define these terms.

MAKING THE GRADE

All the sociologists discussed in this chapter have good and bad things to say about modern society. Weber was the most pessimistic, and Durkheim was the most optimistic.

Durkheim filled out the picture by showing that members of modern societies count on tens of thousands of others—most of them strangers—for the goods and services needed every day. As members of modern societies, we depend more and more on people we trust less and less. Why do we look to people we hardly know and whose beliefs may well differ from our own? Durkheim's answer was "because we can't live without them."

So modern society rests far less on *moral consensus* and far more on *functional interdependence.* Herein lies what we might call "Durkheim's dilemma": The technological power and greater personal freedom of modern society come at the cost of declining morality and the rising risk of anomie.

Like Marx and Weber, Durkheim worried about the direction society was taking. But of the three, Durkheim was the most optimistic. He saw that large, anonymous societies gave people more freedom and privacy than small towns. Anomie remains a danger, but Durkheim hoped we would be able to create laws and other norms to regulate our behavior.

How can we apply Durkheim's views to the Information Revolution? The Seeing Sociology in Everyday Life box suggests that Durkheim, as well as two of the other theorists we have considered in this chapter, would have had much to say about today's new computer technology.

How do we understand something as complex as human society? Each of the thinkers profiled in this chapter offers insights about the meaning and importance of modern society. Each has a somewhat different view and provides a partial answer to a very complex issue.

Critical Review: Four Visions of Society

This chapter opened with several important questions about society. We will conclude by summarizing how each of the four visions of society answers these questions.

What Holds Societies Together?

How is something as complex as society possible? Lenski claims that members of a society are united by a shared culture, although cultural patterns become more diverse as a society gains more complex technology. He also points out that as technology becomes more complex, inequality divides a society more and more, although industrialization reduces inequality somewhat.

Marx saw in society not unity but social division based on class position. From his point of view, elites may force an uneasy peace, but true social unity can occur only if production becomes a cooperative process. To Weber, the members of a society share a worldview. Just as tradition joined people together in the past, so modern societies have created rational, large-scale organizations that connect people's lives. Finally, Durkheim made solidarity the focus of his work. He contrasted the mechanical solidarity of preindustrial societies, which is based on shared morality, with modern society's organic solidarity, which is based on specialization.

How Have Societies Changed?

According to Lenski's model of sociocultural evolution, societies differ mostly in terms of changing technology. Modern society stands out from past societies in terms of its enormous productive power. Marx, too, noted historical differences in productivity yet pointed to continuing social conflict (except perhaps among simple hunters and gatherers). For Marx, modern society is distinctive mostly because it brings that conflict out into the open. Weber considered the question of change from the perspective of how people look at the world. Members of preindustrial societies have a traditional outlook; modern people take a rational worldview. Finally, for Durkheim, traditional societies are characterized by mechanical solidarity based on moral likeness. In industrial societies, mechanical solidarity gives way to organic solidarity based on productive specialization.

Why Do Societies Change?

As Lenski sees it, social change comes about through technological innovation that over time transforms an entire society. Marx's materialist approach highlights the struggle between classes as the engine of change, pushing societies toward revolution. Weber, by contrast, pointed out that ideas contribute to social change. He demonstrated

SEEING SOCIOLOGY
in Everyday Life

To understand how technology has changed our world, make a list of terms (e.g., e-mail, text message, Twitter, etc.) that your grandparents probably don't understand.

SEEING SOCIOLOGY IN EVERYDAY LIFE

Today's Information Revolution: What Would Durkheim, Weber, and Marx Have Thought?

COLLEEN: Didn't Marx predict there'd be a class revolution?

MASAKO: Well, yes, but in the information age, what are the classes that are supposed to be in conflict?

New technology is changing our society at a dizzying pace. Were they alive today, the founding sociologists discussed in this chapter would be eager observers of the current scene. Imagine for a moment the kinds of questions Emile Durkheim, Max Weber, and Karl Marx might ask about the effects of computer technology on our everyday lives.

Durkheim, who emphasized the increasing division of labor in modern society, would probably wonder if new information technology is pushing work specialization even further. There is good reason to think that it is. Because electronic communication (say, a Web site) gives anyone a vast market (already, about 1.2 billion people access the Internet), people can specialize far more than if they were trying to make a living in a small geographic area. For example, while most small-town lawyers have a general practice, an information age attorney, living anywhere, can provide specialized guidance on, say, prenuptial agreements or electronic copyright law. As we move into the electronic age, the number of highly specialized small businesses (some of which end up becoming very large) in all fields is increasing rapidly.

Durkheim might also point out that the Internet threatens to increase our experience of anomie. Using computers has a tendency to isolate people from personal relationships with others.

In addition, although the Internet offers a flood of information, it provides little in the way of moral guidance about what is wise or good or worth knowing.

Weber believed that modern societies are distinctive because their members share a rational worldview, and nothing illustrates this worldview better than bureaucracy. But will bureaucracy be as important during the twenty-first century? Here is one reason to think it may not: Although organizations will probably continue to regulate workers performing the kinds of routine tasks that were common in the industrial era, much work in the postindustrial era involves imagination. Consider such "new age" work as designing homes, composing music, and writing software. This kind of creative work cannot be regulated in the same way as putting together automobiles as they move down an assembly line. Perhaps this is the reason many high-technology companies have done away with worker

dress codes and having employees punch in and out on a time clock.

Finally, what might Marx make of the Information Revolution? Since Marx considered the earlier Industrial Revolution a *class* revolution that allowed the owners of industry to dominate society, he would probably be concerned about the emergence of a new symbolic elite. Some analysts point out that film and television writers, producers, and performers now enjoy vast wealth, international prestige, and enormous power. Just as people without industrial skills stayed at the bottom of the class system in past decades, so people without symbolic skills may well become the "underclass" of the twenty-first century. Globally, there is a "digital divide" by which most people in rich countries, but few people in poor countries, are part of the Information Revolution (United Nations Development Programme, 2008).

Durkheim, Weber, and Marx greatly improved our understanding of industrial societies. As we continue into the postindustrial age, there is plenty of room for new generations of sociologists to carry on.

WHAT DO YOU THINK?

1. Is computer technology likely to continue to increase specialization? Why or why not?

2. Can you think of examples of "creative" businesses that are less bureaucratic than industrial companies used to be? Why would you expect this to be the case?

3. What effect will the increased importance of symbolic skills have on the "earning power" of a college degree?

---

how a particular worldview—Calvinism—set in motion the Industrial Revolution, which ended up reshaping all of society. Finally, Durkheim pointed to an expanding division of labor as the key dimension of social change.

The fact that these four approaches are so different does not mean that any one of them is right or wrong in an absolute sense. Society is exceedingly complex, and our understanding of society benefits from applying all four visions.

Seeing Sociology in Everyday Life

Does having advanced technology make a society better?

The four thinkers discussed in this chapter all had their doubts. Here's a chance for you to do some thinking about the pros and cons of computer technology in terms of its effect on our everyday lives. For each of the three photos shown here, answer these questions: What do you see as the advantages of this technology for our everyday lives? What are the disadvantages?

HINT In the first case, being linked to the Internet allows us to stay in touch with the office, and this may help our careers. At the same time, being "connected" in this way blurs the line between work and play, just as it may allow work to come into our lives at home. In addition, employers may expect us to be on call 24-7.

In the second case, cell phones allow us to talk with others or to send and receive messages. Of course, we all know that cell phone and cars don't add up to safe driving. In addition, doesn't using cell phone in public end up reducing our privacy? And what about the other people around us? How do you feel about having to listen to the personal conversations of people sitting nearby?

In the third case, computer gaming can certainly be fun and it may develop various sensory-motor skills. At the same time, the rise of computer gaming discourages physical play and plays a part in the alarming increase of obesity, which now affects more than one in five children. Also, computers (including iPods) have the effect of isolating individuals, not only from the natural world but also from other people.

Mark has recently started a new job and he decided to carry a laptop with him on vacation to a resort with Wi-Fi coverage that allows him to access the Internet even out on the lake. What advantages and disadvantages do you think this technology provides to Mark?

Kanene likes to stay in touch with her friends when she's in the car, waiting for a flight at the airport, having dinner in a restaurant, or even while she is catching an afternoon movie in a theater. What advantages and disadvantages do you see in cell phone technology?

Like children all across the United States, Andy and Trish like to play computer games and they own all the latest devices. Assess the use of computer technology as a form of recreation.

Applying SOCIOLOGY in Everyday Life

1. Spend a few minutes walking around your apartment, dorm room, or home trying to identify every device that has a computer chip in it. How many did you find? Were you surprised by the number?

2. Hunting and gathering people gazed at the stars and named the constellations in terms that reflected their way of life—mostly after animals and hunters. As a way of revealing what is important to everyday life *today*, write a short paper imagining

the meanings we would give clusters of stars if people in postindustrial societies were naming them and starting frrom scratch.

3. Over the next few days, be alert for everyday evidence of these concepts: Marx's alienation, Weber's alienation, and Durkheim's anomie. What type of behavior or social pattern qualifies as an example of each in action? How are they different?

MAKING THE GRADE

CHAPTER 4 Society

SOCIETY refers to people who interact in a defined territory and share a culture.
- What forces hold a society together?
- What makes societies different?
- How and why do societies change over time?

p. 88

society (p. 88) people who interact in a defined territory and share a culture

Four Visions of Society

Gerhard Lenski: Society and Technology

Gerhard Lenski points to the importance of **TECHNOLOGY** in shaping any society. He uses the term **SOCIOCULTURAL EVOLUTION** to mean changes that occur as a society gains new technology.

In **HUNTING AND GATHERING SOCIETIES**, men use simple tools to hunt animals and women gather vegetation.

Hunting and gathering societies
- are the simplest of all societies and were the earliest type of society on Earth;
- are nomadic;
- have only a few dozen members;
- are built around the family;
- consider men and women roughly equal in social importance.

p. 89

HORTICULTURAL AND PASTORAL SOCIETIES developed some 12,000 years ago as people began to use hand tools to raise crops and as they shifted to raising animals for food instead of hunting them. Horticultural and pastoral societies
- are able to produce more food, so populations expand to hundreds;
- show greater specialization of work;
- show increasing levels of social inequality.

pp. 89–90

sociocultural evolution (p. 88) Lenski's term for the changes that occur as a society gains new technology

hunting and gathering (p. 89) making use of simple tools to hunt animals and gather vegetation for food

horticulture (p. 89) the use of hand tools to raise crops

pastoralism (p. 90) the domestication of animals

agriculture (p. 90) large-scale cultivation using plows harnessed to animals or more powerful energy sources

industrialism (p. 91) the production of goods using advanced sources of energy to drive large machinery

postindustrialism (p. 93) the production of information using computer technology

AGRARIAN SOCIETIES developed 5,000 years ago as the use of plows harnessed to animals or more powerful energy sources enabled large-scale cultivation.

Agrarian societies
- may expand into vast empires;
- show even greater specialization, with dozens of distinct occupations;
- have extreme social inequality;
- reduce the importance of women.

pp. 90–91

INDUSTRIAL SOCIETIES, which developed first in Europe 250 years ago, use advanced sources of energy to drive large machinery.
Industrialization
- provides many modern conveniences and advanced forms of transportation and communication;
- moves work from the home to the factory;
- reduces the traditional importance of the family;
- raises living standards.

pp. 91–92

POSTINDUSTRIAL SOCIETIES represent the most recent stage of technological development, namely, technology that supports an information-based economy.
Postindustrialization
- shifts production from heavy machinery making material things to computers and related technology processing information;
- requires a population with information-based skills;
- is the driving force behind the Information Revolution, a worldwide flow of information that now links societies with an emerging global culture.

pp. 92–93

See the Summing Up table on pages 94–95.

Karl Marx: Society and Conflict

Karl Marx's **MATERIALIST APPROACH** claims that societies are defined by their economic systems: How humans produce material goods shapes their experiences.

CONFLICT AND HISTORY

CLASS CONFLICT is the conflict between entire classes over the distribution of a society's wealth and power.

Marx traced conflict between social classes in societies as the source of social change throughout history:

- In "ancient" societies, masters dominated slaves.
- In agrarian societies, nobles dominated serfs.
- In industrial-capitalist societies, capitalists dominate proletarians.

pp. 96–97

CAPITALISM

Marx focused on the role of **CAPITALISM** in creating inequality and class conflict in modern societies.

- Under capitalism, the ruling class (capitalists, who own the means of production) oppresses the working class (proletarians, who sell their labor).
- Capitalism alienates workers from the act of working, from the products of work, from other workers, and from their own potential.
- Marx predicted that a workers' revolution would eventually overthrow capitalism and replace it with socialism, a system of production that would provide for the social needs of all.

pp. 97–98

social conflict (p. 94) the struggle between segments of society over valued resources

capitalists (p. 94) people who own and operate factories and other businesses in pursuit of profits

proletarians (p. 95) people who sell their labor for wages

social institutions (p. 95) the major spheres of social life, or societal subsystems, organized to meet human needs

false consciousness (p. 95) Marx's term for explanations of social problems as the shortcomings of individuals rather than as the flaws of society

class conflict (p. 96) conflict between entire classes over the distribution of a society's wealth and power

class consciousness (p. 96) Marx's term for workers' recognition of themselves as a class unified in opposition to capitalists and ultimately to capitalism itself

alienation (p. 97) the experience of isolation and misery resulting from powerlessness

Max Weber: The Rationalization of Society

Max Weber's **IDEALIST APPROACH** emphasizes the power of ideas to shape society.

IDEAS AND HISTORY

Weber traced the ideas—especially beliefs and values—that have shaped societies throughout history.

- Members of preindustrial societies are bound by **TRADITION**, the beliefs and values passed from generation to generation.
- Members of industrial-capitalist societies are guided by **RATIONALITY**, a way of thinking that emphasizes deliberate, matter-of-fact calculation of the most efficient way to accomplish a particular task.

pp. 98–99

RATIONALISM

Weber focused on the growth of large, rational organizations as the defining characteristic of modern societies.

- Rationality gave rise to both the Industrial Revolution and capitalism.
- Protestantism (specifically, Calvinism) encouraged the rational pursuit of wealth, laying the groundwork for the rise of industrial-capitalism.
- Weber defined six characteristics of rational social organization, or **BUREAUCRACY** (see page 171), and feared that excessive rationality would stifle human creativity.

pp. 99–102

ideal type (p. 98) an abstract statement of the essential characteristics of any social phenomenon

tradition (p. 98) values and beliefs passed from generation to generation

rationality (p. 98) a way of thinking that emphasizes deliberate, matter-of-fact calculation of the most efficient way to accomplish a particular task

rationalization of society (p. 98) Weber's term for the historical change from tradition to rationality as the main type of human thought

Emile Durkheim: Society and Function

Emile Durkheim claimed that society has an objective existence apart from its individual members.

STRUCTURE AND FUNCTION

Durkheim believed that because society is bigger than any one of us, it dictates how we are expected to act in any given social situation.

- He pointed out that social elements (such as crime) have functions that help society operate.
- Society also shapes our personalities and provides the moral discipline that guides our behavior and controls our desires.

pp. 102–3

EVOLVING SOCIETIES

Durkheim traced the evolution of social change by describing the different ways societies throughout history have guided the lives of their members.

- In preindustrial societies, **MECHANICAL SOLIDARITY**, or social bonds based on common sentiments and shared moral values, guides the social life of individuals.
- Industrialization and the **DIVISION OF LABOR** weaken traditional bonds, so that social life in modern societies is characterized by **ORGANIC SOLIDARITY**, social bonds based on specialization and interdependence.
- Durkheim warned of increased **ANOMIE** in modern societies, as society provides little moral guidance to individuals.

pp. 103–4

anomie (p. 103) Durkheim's term for a condition in which society provides little moral guidance to individuals

mechanical solidarity (p. 103) Durkheim's term for social bonds, based on common sentiments and shared moral values, that are strong among members of preindustrial societies

organic solidarity (p. 103) Durkheim's term for social bonds, based on specialization and interdependence, that are strong among members of industrial societies

division of labor (p. 103) specialized economic activity

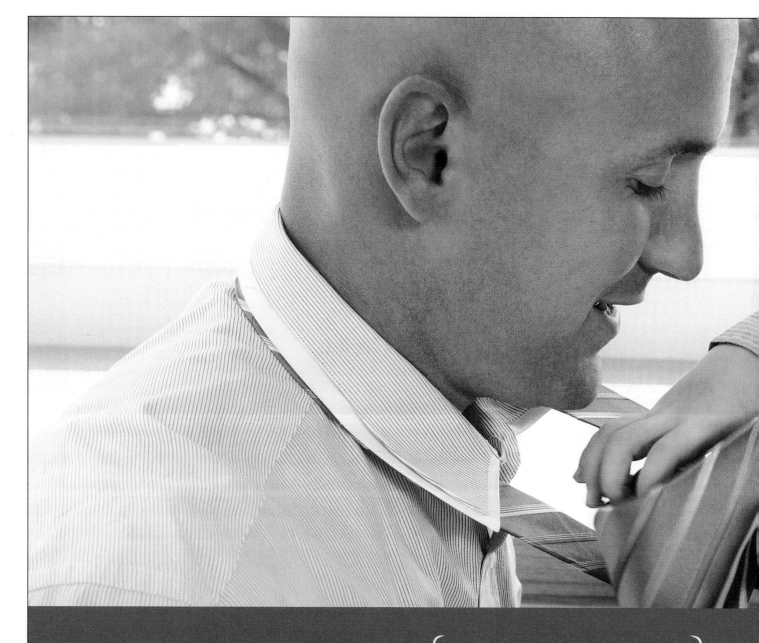

Socialization is the process by which older members of a society teach their way of life to the young. From the point of view of a young girl or boy, socialization is also the process of developing a personality.

CHAPTER 5

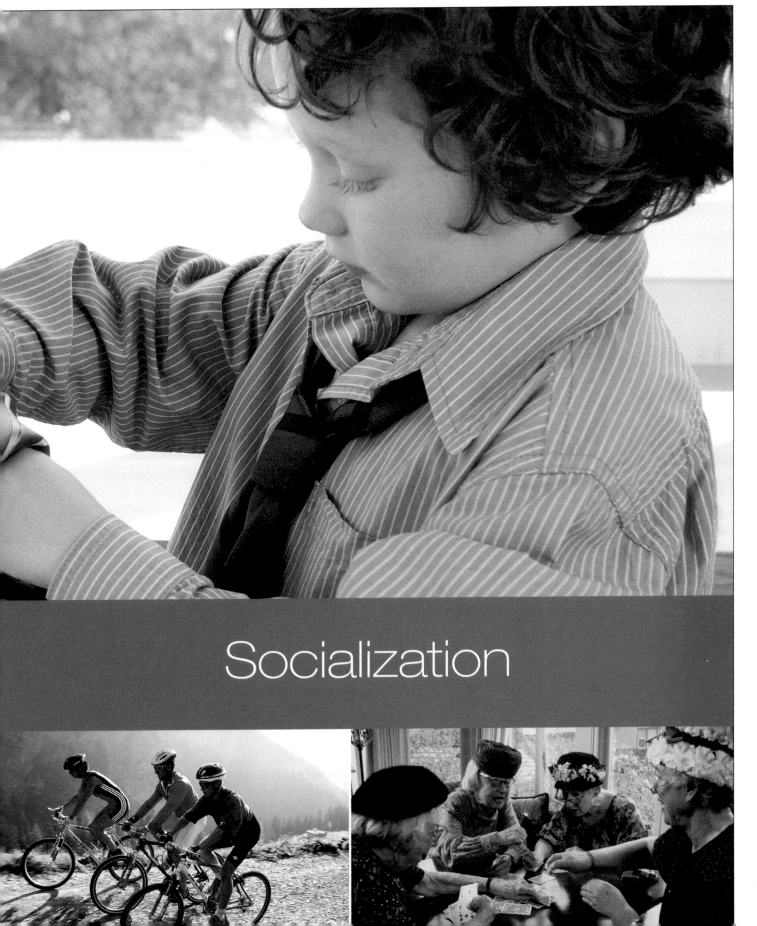

Socialization

SUPPLEMENTS: An outline of Chapter 5, along with supplementary lecture material and discussion questions, is found in the *Instructor's Manual*.

NOTE: The term *tabula rasa* (Latin, meaning "clean slate") was introduced by the English philosopher John Locke (1632–1704). An empiricist, Locke believed that human personalities were "written on" by experience.

NOTE: "Nature" is from the Latin root meaning "born"; "nurture" is from the Latin root meaning "nourished."

Q: "Thought makes the whole dignity of man." Blaise Pascal, French mathematician and philosopher (1623–1662)

CHAPTER OVERVIEW

Having completed macro-level Chapters 3 ("Culture") and 4 ("Society"), we turn now to a micro-level look at how individuals become members of society through the process of socialization.

On a cold winter day in 1938, a social worker walked quickly to the door of a rural Pennsylvania farmhouse. Investigating a case of possible child abuse, the social worker entered the home and soon discovered a five-year-old girl hidden in a second-floor storage room. The child, whose name was Anna, was wedged into an old chair with her arms tied above her head so that she couldn't move. She was wearing filthy clothes, and her arms and legs were as thin as matchsticks (K. Davis, 1940).

Anna's situation can only be described as tragic. She had been born in 1932 to an unmarried and mentally impaired woman of twenty-six who lived with her strict father. Angry about his daughter's "illegitimate" motherhood, the grandfather did not even want the child in his house, so for the first six months of her life, Anna was passed among several welfare agencies. But her mother could not afford to pay for her care, and Anna was returned to the hostile home of her grandfather.

To lessen the grandfather's anger, Anna's mother kept Anna in the storage room and gave her just enough milk to keep her alive. There she stayed—day after day, month after month, with almost no human contact—for five long years.

Learning of Anna's rescue, the sociologist Kingsley Davis immediately went to see the child. He found her with local officials at a county home. Davis was stunned by the emaciated girl, who could not laugh, speak, or even smile. Anna was completely unresponsive, as if alone in an empty world.

Social Experience: The Key to Our Humanity

Socialization is so basic to human development that we sometimes overlook its importance. But here, in the terrible case of an isolated child, we can see what humans would be like without social contact. Although physically alive, Anna hardly seems to have been human. We can see that without social experience, a child is not able to act or communicate in a meaningful way and seems to be as much an object as a person.

Sociologists use the term **socialization** to refer to *the lifelong social experience by which people develop their human potential and learn culture.* Unlike other living species, whose behavior is mostly or entirely set by biology, humans need social experience to learn their culture and to survive. Social experience is also the foundation of **personality,** *a person's fairly consistent patterns of acting, thinking, and feeling.* We build a personality by internalizing—taking in—our surroundings. But without social experience, as Anna's case shows, personality hardly develops at all.

Human Development: Nature and Nurture

Anna's case makes clear that humans depend on others to provide the care and nurture needed not only for physical growth but also for personality to develop. A century ago, however, people mistakenly believed that humans were born with instincts that determined their personality and behavior.

The Biological Sciences: The Role of Nature

Charles Darwin's groundbreaking 1859 study of evolution, described in Chapter 3 ("Culture"), led people to think that human behavior was instinctive, simply our "nature." Such ideas led to claims that the U.S. economic system reflects "instinctive human competitiveness," that some people are "born criminals," or that women are "naturally" emotional while men are "naturally" rational.

People trying to understand cultural diversity also misunderstood Darwin's thinking. Centuries of world exploration had taught Western Europeans that people behaved quite differently from one society to another. But Europeans linked these differences to biology

Q: "The differences between individuals who are members of different cultures, like the differences between individuals within a culture, are almost entirely to be laid to differences in conditioning, especially during early childhood, and this conditioning is culturally determined." Margaret Mead (1963:280, orig. 1935)

NOTE: An interesting twist on the nature-nurture debate: Throughout history, naturalists believed that an untaught child would speak but wondered what language. The Holy Roman Emperor Frederick II thought it would be Latin or Greek; King James I of Scotland opined it would be Hebrew.

socialization the lifelong social experience by which people develop their human potential and learn culture

personality a person's fairly consistent patterns of acting, thinking, and feeling

MAKING THE GRADE

Sociologists and others have long debated the relative importance of biology (nature) and social environment (nurture). Cases of isolated children show that nurture is crucial to human development. But the text ends up avoiding a "nature versus nurture" argument in favor of linking the two concepts: It is human nature to nurture.

Human infants display various *reflexes*—biologically based behavior patterns that enhance survival. The sucking reflex, which actually begins before birth, enables the infant to obtain nourishment. The grasping reflex, triggered by placing a finger on the infant's palm, causing the hand to close, helps the infant maintain contact with a parent and, later on, grasp objects. The Moro reflex, activated by startling the infant, has the infant swinging both arms outward and then bringing them together across the chest. This action, which disappears after several months of life, probably developed among our evolutionary ancestors so that a falling infant could grasp the body hair of a parent.

rather than culture. It was an easy, although incorrect and very damaging, step to claim that members of technologically simple societies were biologically less evolved and therefore "less human." This ethnocentric view helped justify colonialism: Why not take advantage of others if they seem not to be human in the same sense that you are?

The Social Sciences: The Role of Nurture

In the twentieth century, biological explanations of human behavior came under fire. The psychologist John B. Watson (1878–1958) developed a theory called *behaviorism*, which holds that behavior is not instinctive but learned. Thus people everywhere are equally human, differing only in their cultural patterns. In short, Watson rooted human behavior not in nature but in *nurture.*

Today, social scientists are cautious about describing *any* human behavior as instinctive. This does not mean that biology plays no part in human behavior. Human life, after all, depends on the functioning of the body. We also know that children often share biological traits (like height and hair color) with their parents and that heredity plays a part in intelligence, musical and artistic talent, and personality (such as how you react to frustration). However, whether you develop your inherited potential depends on how you are raised.

For example, unless children use their brain early in life, the brain does not fully develop (Goldsmith, 1983; Begley, 1995).

Without denying the importance of nature, then, we can correctly say that nurture matters more in shaping human behavior. More precisely, *nurture is our nature.*

Social Isolation

As the story of Anna shows, cutting people off from the social world is very harmful. For ethical reasons, researchers can never place human beings in total isolation to study what happens. But in the past, they have studied the effects of social isolation on nonhuman primates.

Research with Monkeys

In a classic study, the psychologists Harry and Margaret Harlow (1962) placed rhesus monkeys—whose behavior is in some ways surprisingly similar to that of humans—in various conditions of social isolation. They found that complete isolation (with adequate nutrition) for even six months seriously disturbed the monkeys' development. When returned to their group, these monkeys were passive, anxious, and fearful.

DISCUSS: Ask the class to imagine the effects of growing up in a violent world, as suggested by the photo below.

NOTE: Emphasize that research by the Harlows with rhesus monkeys and the cases of isolated children point to the same conclusion: Prolonged lack of social experience has devastating and permanent consequences.

SEEING SOCIOLOGY
in Everyday Life

An ad campaign for strengthening families used the tag line "Have you hugged your child today?" What new understanding of this line do you gain from the Harlow research?

MAKING THE GRADE

Both the cases of isolated children and the Harlow studies with rhesus monkeys lead to the same conclusion: Social experience is necessary for healthy human development.

The personalities we develop depend largely on the environment in which we live. When a child's world is shredded by violence, the damage can be profound and lasting. This drawing was made by thirteen-year-old Rahid in the Darfur region of Sudan, where armed militia have killed more than 300,000 people since 2003. What are the likely effects of such experiences on a young person's self-confidence and capacity to form trusting ties with others?

Courtesy of Dr. Annie Sparrow, Human Rights Watch.

The Harlows then placed infant rhesus monkeys in cages with an artificial "mother" made of wire mesh with a wooden head and the nipple of a feeding tube where the breast would be. These monkeys also survived but were unable to interact with others when placed in a group.

But monkeys in a third category, isolated with an artificial wire mesh "mother" covered with soft terry cloth, did better. Each of these monkeys would cling to its mother closely. Because these monkeys showed less developmental damage than earlier groups, the Harlows concluded that the monkeys benefited from this closeness. The experiment confirmed how important it is that adults cradle infants affectionately.

Finally, the Harlows discovered that infant monkeys could recover from about three months of isolation. But by about six months, isolation caused irreversible emotional and behavioral damage.

Studies of Isolated Children

Tragic cases of children isolated by abusive family members show the damage caused by depriving human beings of social experience. We will review three such cases.

Anna: The Rest of the Story   The rest of Anna's story squares with the Harlows' findings. After her discovery, Anna received extensive medical attention and soon showed improvement. When Kingsley Davis visited her after ten days, he found her more alert and even smiling (perhaps for the first time in her life). Over the next year, Anna made slow but steady progress, showing more interest in other people and gradually learning to walk. After a year and a half, she could feed herself and play with toys.

But as the Harlows might have predicted, five long years of social isolation had caused permanent damage. At age eight, her mental development was less than that of a two-year-old. Not until she was almost ten did she begin to use words. Because Anna's mother was mentally retarded, perhaps Anna was also. The riddle was never solved, however, because Anna died at age ten of a blood disorder, possibly related to the years of abuse she suffered (K. Davis, 1940, 1947).

Another Case: Isabelle   A second case involves another girl found at about the same time as Anna and under similar circumstances. After more than six years of virtual isolation, this girl, named Isabelle, displayed the same lack of responsiveness as Anna. But Isabelle had the benefit of an intensive learning program directed by psychologists. Within a week, Isabelle was trying to speak, and a year and a half later, she knew some 2,000 words. The psychologists concluded that intensive effort had pushed Isabelle through six years of normal development in only two years. By the time she was fourteen, Isabelle was attending sixth-grade classes, damaged by her early ordeal but on her way to a relatively normal life (K. Davis, 1947).

A Third Case: Genie   A more recent case of childhood isolation involves a California girl abused by her parents (Curtiss, 1977; Rymer, 1994). From the time she was two, Genie was tied to a potty chair in a dark garage. In 1970, when she was rescued at age thirteen, Genie weighed only fifty-nine pounds and had the mental development of a one-year-old. With intensive treatment, she became physically healthy, but her language ability remains that of a young child. Today, Genie lives in a home for developmentally disabled adults.

SEEING SOCIOLOGY
in Everyday Life

How does the case of Anna confirm that "nurture is our nature"?

Freud's Model of Personality

id Freud's term for the human being's basic drives ← **ego** Freud's term for a person's conscious efforts to balance innate pleasure-seeking drives with the demands of society → **superego** Freud's term for the cultural values and norms internalized by an individual

○ **CRITICAL REVIEW** All evidence points to the crucial importance of social experience in personality development. Human beings can recover from abuse and short-term isolation. But there is a point—precisely when is unclear from the small number of cases studied—at which isolation in childhood causes permanent developmental damage.

○ **CHECK YOUR LEARNING** What do studies of isolated children teach us about the importance of social experience?

Understanding Socialization

Socialization is a complex, lifelong process. The following discussions highlight the work of six researchers who have made lasting contributions to our understanding of human development.

Sigmund Freud's Elements of Personality

Sigmund Freud (1856–1939) lived in Vienna at a time when most Europeans considered human behavior to be biologically fixed. Trained as a physician, Freud gradually turned to the study of personality and mental disorders and eventually developed the celebrated theory of psychoanalysis.

Basic Human Needs

Freud claimed that biology plays a major part in human development, although not in terms of specific instincts, as is the case in other species. Rather, he theorized that humans have two basic needs or drives that are present at birth. First is a need for sexual and emotional bonding, which he called the "life instinct," or *eros* (named after the Greek god of love). Second, we share an aggressive drive he called the "death instinct," or *thanatos* (the Greek word for "death"). These opposing forces, operating at an unconscious level, create deep inner tension.

Freud's Model of Personality

Freud combined basic needs and the influence of society into a model of personality with three parts: id, ego, and superego. The **id** (Latin for "it") represents *the human being's basic drives,* which are unconscious and demand immediate satisfaction. Rooted in biology, the id is present at birth, making a newborn a bundle of demands for attention, touching, and food. But society opposes the self-centered id, which is why one of the first words a child typically learns is "no."

To avoid frustration, a child must learn to approach the world realistically. This is done through the **ego** (Latin for "I"), which is *a person's conscious efforts to balance innate pleasure-seeking drives with the demands of society.* The ego arises as we become aware of our distinct existence and face the fact that we cannot have everything we want.

In the human personality, **superego** (Latin for "above or beyond the ego") is *the cultural values and norms internalized by an individual.* The superego operates as our conscience, telling us *why* we cannot have everything we want. The superego begins to form as a child becomes aware of parental demands and matures as the child comes to understand that everyone's behavior should take account of cultural norms.

Personality Development

To the id-centered child, the world is a bewildering assortment of physical sensations that bring either pleasure or pain. As the superego develops, however, the child learns the moral concepts of right and wrong. Initially, in other words, children can feel good only in a physical way (such as by being held and cuddled), but after three or four years, they feel good or bad according to how they judge their behavior against cultural norms (doing "the right thing").

The id and superego remain in conflict, but in a well-adjusted person, the ego manages these two opposing forces. If conflicts are not resolved during childhood, Freud claimed, they may surface as personality disorders later on.

Culture, in the form of the superego, *represses* selfish demands, forcing people to look beyond their own desires. Often the competing demands of self and society result in a compromise that Freud called *sublimation.* Sublimation redirects selfish drives into socially acceptable behavior. For example, marriage makes the satisfaction of sexual urges socially acceptable, and competitive sports are an outlet for aggression.

○ **CRITICAL REVIEW** In Freud's time, few people were ready to accept sex as a basic human drive. More recent critics have charged that Freud's work presents humans in male terms and devalues women (Donovan & Littenberg, 1982). Freud's theories are also difficult to test scientifically. But Freud influenced everyone who later studied human personality. Of special importance to sociology are his ideas that we internalize social norms and that childhood experiences have a lasting impact on personality.

○ **CHECK YOUR LEARNING** What are the three elements in Freud's model of personality? Explain how each one operates.

Jean Piaget's Theory of Cognitive Development

The Swiss psychologist Jean Piaget (1896–1980) studied human *cognition,* how people think and understand. As Piaget watched his own three children grow, he wondered not just what they knew but how they made sense of the world. Piaget went on to identify four stages of cognitive development.

Q: "Anatomy is destiny." Sigmund Freud

NOTE: Champions of psychoanalysis include Franz Boas, Margaret Mead, and Ruth Benedict, all of whom interpreted this approach as favoring nurture over nature.

NOTE: An example of preoperational thinking: Young children prefer nickels to dimes because nickels are bigger.

Q: "I count him braver who overcomes his desire than him who conquers his enemies; for the hardest victory is the victory over self." Aristotle

NOTE: Stress that Piaget's stages of development are maturational; in this, he stands apart from George Herbert Mead, for whom biology played virtually no role in social development. (Piaget was trained as a biologist.)

Piaget's Stages of Development

sensorimotor stage → **preoperational stage** → **concrete operational stage** → **formal operational stage**

sensorimotor stage	preoperational stage	concrete operational stage	formal operational stage
Piaget's term for the level of human development at which individuals experience the world only through their senses	Piaget's term for the level of human development at which individuals first use language and other symbols	Piaget's term for the level of human development at which individuals first see causal connections in their surroundings	Piaget's term for the level of human development at which individuals think abstractly and critically

Childhood is a time to learn principles of right and wrong. According to Carol Gilligan, however, boys and girls define what is "right" in different ways. After reading about Gilligan's theory, can you suggest what these two children might be arguing about?

The Sensorimotor Stage

Stage one is the **sensorimotor stage,** *the level of human development at which individuals experience the world only through their senses.* For about the first two years of life, the infant knows the world only through the five senses: touching, tasting, smelling, looking, and listening. "Knowing" to young children amounts to what their senses tell them.

The Preoperational Stage

About age two, children enter the **preoperational stage,** *the level of human development at which individuals first use language and other symbols.* Now children begin to think about the world mentally and use imagination. But "pre-op" children between about two and six still attach meaning only to specific experiences and objects. They can identify a toy as their "favorite" but cannot explain what *types* of toys they like.

Lacking abstract concepts, a child also cannot judge size, weight, or volume. In one of his best-known experiments, Piaget placed two identical glasses containing equal amounts of water on a table. He asked several children aged five and six if the amount in each glass was the same. They nodded that it was. The children then watched Piaget take one of the glasses and pour its contents into a taller, narrower glass so that the level of the water in the glass was higher. He asked again if each glass held the same amount. The typical five- or six-year-old now insisted that the taller glass held more water. By about age seven, children are able to think abstractly and realize that the amount of water stays the same.

The Concrete Operational Stage

Next comes the **concrete operational stage,** *the level of human development at which individuals first see causal connections in their surroundings.* Between the ages of seven and eleven, children focus on how and why things happen. In addition, children now attach more than one symbol to a particular event or object. If, for example, you say to a child of five, "Today is Wednesday," she might respond, "No, it's my birthday!"—indicating that she can use just one symbol at a time. But a ten-year-old at the concrete operational stage would be able to respond, "Yes, and it's also my birthday."

The Formal Operational Stage

The last stage in Piaget's model is the **formal operational stage,** *the level of human development at which individuals think abstractly and critically.* At about age twelve, young people begin to reason abstractly rather than thinking only of concrete situations. If, for example, you were to ask a seven-year-old, "What would you like to be when you grow up?" you might receive a concrete response such as "a teacher." But most teenagers can think more abstractly and might reply, "I would like a job that helps others." As they gain the capacity for abstract thought, young people also learn to understand metaphors. Hearing the phrase "A penny for your thoughts" might lead a child to ask for a coin, but a teenager will recognize a gentle invitation to intimacy.

CRITICAL REVIEW Freud saw human beings torn by opposing forces of biology and culture. Piaget saw the mind as active and creative. He saw an ability to engage the world unfolding in stages as the result of both biological maturation and social experience.

But do people in all societies pass through all four of Piaget's stages? Living in a traditional society that changes slowly probably limits a person's capacity for abstract and critical thought. Even in the United States, perhaps 30 percent of people never reach the formal operational stage (Kohlberg & Gilligan, 1971).

CHECK YOUR LEARNING What are Piaget's four stages of cognitive development? What does his theory teach us about socialization?

Q: "If we examine the intellectual development of the individual . . . we shall find that the human spirit goes through a certain number of stages, each different from the other." Jean Piaget

GLOBAL: Kohlberg claims, in essence, that good and evil span a continuum from selflessness at one end to selfishness at the other. This is a virtually universal theme of world religions.

Q: "In Gilligan's studies females moved from an early 'selfish' stage to an overly altruistic stage. The developmental task for the women in Gilligan's study was to achieve a position where they could take their own interests into account. . . . A mature person, according to the ethic of care, recognizes her connection to others . . . and at the same time can articulate her own wants and needs." John R. Hall and Mary Jo Neitz (1993:37)

SEEING SOCIOLOGY
in Everyday Life

Using Piaget's concepts, can you explain why young children will reach for a nickel rather than a dime?

MAKING THE GRADE

Kohlberg's theory is similar to Piaget's theory, but Kohlberg focuses on one aspect of cognition—moral reasoning. Gilligan's theory is similar to Kohlberg's theory, but she focuses on the link between gender and moral reasoning.

THINKING ABOUT DIVERSITY: RACE, CLASS, & GENDER

The Importance of Gender in Research

Carol Gilligan (1990) has shown how gender guides social behavior. Her early work exposed the gender bias in studies by Kohlberg and others who had used only male subjects. But as her research progressed, Gilligan made a major discovery: Boys and girls actually use different standards in making moral decisions. By ignoring gender, we end up with an incomplete view of human behavior.

Gilligan has also looked at the effect of gender on self-esteem. Her research team interviewed more than 2,000 girls, aged six to eighteen, over a five-year period. She found a clear pattern: Young girls start out eager and confident, but their self-esteem slips away as they pass through adolescence.

Why? Gilligan claims that the answer lies in our society's socialization of females. In U.S. society, the ideal woman is calm, controlled, and eager to please. Then too, as girls move from the elementary grades to secondary school, they have fewer women teachers and find that most authority figures are men. As a result, by their late teens, girls struggle to regain the personal strength they had a decade earlier.

When their research was finished, Gilligan and her colleagues returned to a private girls' school where they had interviewed their subjects to share the results of their work. As their conclusions led them to expect, most younger girls who had been interviewed were eager to have their names appear in the forthcoming book. But the older girls were hesitant—many were fearful that they would be talked about.

WHAT DO YOU THINK?

1. How does Gilligan's research show the importance of gender in the socialization process?

2. Do you think boys are subject to some of the same pressures and difficulties as girls? What about the fact that a much smaller share of boys than girls make it to college? Explain your answer.

3. Can you think of ways in which your gender has shaped the development of your personality? Point out three significant ways gender has shaped your own life.

Lawrence Kohlberg's Theory of Moral Development

Lawrence Kohlberg (1981) built on Piaget's work to study *moral reasoning*, how individuals judge situations as right or wrong. Here again, development occurs in stages.

Young children who experience the world in terms of pain and pleasure (Piaget's sensorimotor stage) are at the *preconventional* level of moral development. At this early stage, in other words, "rightness" amounts to "what feels good to me." For example, a young child may simply reach for something on a table that looks shiny, which is the reason parents of young children have to "childproof" their homes.

The *conventional* level, Kohlberg's second stage, appears by the teen years (corresponding to Piaget's final, formal operational stage). At this point, young people lose some of their selfishness as they learn to define right and wrong in terms of what pleases parents and conforms to cultural norms. Individuals at this stage also begin to assess intention in reaching moral judgments instead of simply looking at what people do. For example, they understand that stealing food to feed one's hungry children is not the same as stealing an iPod to sell for pocket change.

In Kohlberg's final stage of moral development, the *postconventional* level, people move beyond their society's norms to consider abstract ethical principles. Now they think about liberty, freedom, or justice, perhaps arguing that what is legal still may not be right. When the

African American activist Rosa Parks refused to give up her seat on a Montgomery, Alabama, bus in 1955, she violated that city's segregation laws in order to call attention to the racial injustice of the law.

CRITICAL REVIEW Like the work of Piaget, Kohlberg's model explains moral development in terms of distinct stages. But whether this model applies to people in all societies remains unclear. Further, many people in the United States apparently never reach the postconventional level of moral reasoning, although exactly why is still an open question.

Another problem with Kohlberg's research is that his subjects were all boys. He committed a common research error, described in Chapter 2 ("Sociological Investigation"), by generalizing the results of male subjects to all people. This problem led a colleague, Carol Gilligan, to investigate how gender affects moral reasoning.

CHECK YOUR LEARNING What are Kohlberg's three stages of moral development? What does his theory teach us about socialization?

Carol Gilligan's Theory of Gender and Moral Development

Carol Gilligan, whose approach is highlighted in the Thinking About Diversity box, compared the moral development of girls and boys and concluded that the two sexes use different standards of rightness.

RESOURCE: Mead's statement "The Self" is among the classics included in the author's companion reader *Seeing Ourselves*, 8th ed.

RESOURCE: Besides believing in the plasticity of human personality, Mead also believed in people's ability to reform society.

Q: "Each to each a looking glass, / Reflects the other that doth pass." Charles Horton Cooley (1964:184, orig. 1902)

POP CULTURE: Illustrating Mead's and Cooley's view of the self, young people are especially sensitive to what others think of them, which is a theme in a number of films such as *Clueless, Mean Girls,* and *American Pie,* which focus on the struggle to be popular.

self George Herbert Mead's term for the part of an individual's personality composed of self-awareness and self-image

looking-glass self Charles Horton Cooley's term for a self-image based on how we think others see us

SEEING SOCIOLOGY
in Everyday Life

Have you ever seen young children put on their parents' shoes, literally putting themselves "in the shoes" of another person? How does this action help children learn to "take the role of the other"?

The self is able simultaneously to take the role of:

| *no one* (no ability to take the role of the other) | *one* other in *one* situation | *many* others in *one* situation | *many* others in *many* situations |

when: engaging in imitation   engaging in play   engaging in games   recognizing the generalized other

FIGURE 5–1   **Building on Social Experience**

George Herbert Mead described the development of the self as a process of gaining social experience. That is, the self develops as we expand our capacity to take the role of the other.

Boys, Gilligan (1982, 1990) claims, have a *justice perspective,* relying on formal rules to define right and wrong. Girls, by contrast, have a *care and responsibility perspective,* judging a situation with an eye toward personal relationships and loyalties. For example, as boys see it, stealing is wrong because it breaks the law. Girls are more likely to wonder why someone would steal and to be sympathetic toward a person who steals, say, to feed her family.

Kohlberg treats rule-based male reasoning as superior to the person-based female approach. Gilligan notes that impersonal rules dominate men's lives in the workplace, but personal relationships are more relevant to women's lives as mothers and caregivers. Why, then, Gilligan asks, should we set up male standards as the norms by which to judge everyone?

CRITICAL REVIEW   Gilligan's work sharpens our understanding of both human development and gender issues in research. Yet the question remains, does nature or nurture account for the differences between females and males? In Gilligan's view, cultural conditioning is at work, a view that finds support in other research. Nancy Chodorow (1994) claims that children grow up in homes in which, typically, mothers do much more nurturing than fathers. As girls identify with mothers, they become more concerned with care and responsibility to others. By contrast, boys become more like fathers, who are often detached from the home, and develop the same formal and detached personalities. Perhaps the moral reasoning of females and males will become more similar as more women organize their lives around the workplace.

CHECK YOUR LEARNING   According to Gilligan, how do boys and girls differ in their approach to understanding right and wrong?

George Herbert Mead's Theory of the Social Self

George Herbert Mead (1863–1931) developed the theory of *social behaviorism* to explain how social experience develops an individual's personality (1962, orig. 1934).

The Self

Mead's central concept is the **self,** *the part of an individual's personality composed of self-awareness and self-image.* Mead's genius was in seeing the self as the product of social experience.

First, said Mead, *the self is not there at birth; it develops.* The self is not part of the body, and it does not exist at birth. Mead rejected the idea that personality is guided by biological drives (as Freud asserted) or biological maturation (as Piaget claimed).

Second, Mead explained, *the self develops only with social experience,* as the individual interacts with others. Without interaction, as we see from cases of isolated children, the body grows, but no self emerges.

Third, Mead continued, *social experience is the exchange of symbols.* Only people use words, a wave of the hand, or a smile to create meaning. We can train a dog using reward and punishment, but the dog attaches no meaning to its actions. Human beings, by contrast, find meaning in almost every action.

Fourth, Mead stated that *seeking meaning leads people to imagine other people's intentions.* In short, we draw conclusions from people's actions, imagining their underlying intentions. A dog responds to *what you do;* a human responds to *what you have in mind* as you do it. You can train a dog to go to the hallway and bring back an umbrella, which is handy on a rainy day. But because the dog doesn't understand intention, if the dog cannot find the umbrella, it is incapable of the *human* response: to look for a raincoat instead.

Fifth, Mead explained that *understanding intention requires imagining the situation from the other's point of view.* Using symbols, we imagine ourselves "in another person's shoes" and see ourselves as that person does. We can therefore anticipate how others will respond to us even before we act. A simple toss of a ball requires stepping outside ourselves to imagine how another will catch our throw. All social interaction involves seeing ourselves as others see us—a process that Mead termed *taking the role of the other.*

The Looking-Glass Self

In effect, others are a mirror (which people used to call a "looking glass") in which we can see ourselves. What we think of ourselves,

significant others people, such as parents, who have special importance for socialization

generalized other Mead's term for widespread cultural norms and values we use as a reference in evaluating ourselves

then, depends on how we think others see us. For example, if we think others see us as clever, we will think of ourselves in the same way. But if we feel they think of us as clumsy, then that is how we will see ourselves. Charles Horton Cooley (1864–1929) used the phrase **looking-glass self** to mean *a self-image based on how we think others see us* (1964, orig. 1902).

The I and the Me

Mead's sixth point is that *by taking the role of the other, we become self-aware.* Another way of saying this is that the self has two parts. One part of the self operates as the subject, being active and spontaneous. Mead called the active side of the self the "I" (the subjective form of the personal pronoun). The other part of the self works as an object, that is, the way we imagine others see us. Mead called the objective side of the self the "me" (the objective form of the personal pronoun). All social experience has both components: We initiate an action (the I-phase, or subject side, of self), and then we continue the action based on how others respond to us (the me-phase, or object side, of self).

Development of the Self

According to Mead, the key to developing the self is learning to take the role of the other. Because of their limited social experience, infants can do this only through *imitation.* They mimic behavior without understanding underlying intentions, and so at this point, they have no self.

As children learn to use language and other symbols, the self emerges in the form of *play.* Play involves assuming roles modeled on **significant others,** *people, such as parents, who have special importance for socialization.* Playing "mommy and daddy" is an important activity that helps young children imagine the world from a parent's point of view.

Gradually, children learn to take the roles of several others at once. This skill lets them move from simple play (say, playing catch) with one other to complex *games* (such as baseball) involving many others. By about age seven, most children have the social experience needed to engage in team sports.

Figure 5–1 charts the progression from imitation to play to games. But there is a final stage in the development of the self. A game involves taking the role of specific people in just one situation. Everyday life demands that we see ourselves in terms of cultural norms as *any* member of our society might. Mead used the term **generalized other** to refer to *widespread cultural norms and values we use as references in evaluating ourselves.*

As life goes on, the self continues to change along with our social experiences. But no matter how much the world shapes us, we always remain creative beings, able to react to the world around us. Thus, Mead concluded, we play a key role in our own socialization.

CRITICAL REVIEW Mead's work explores the character of social experience itself. In the symbolic interaction of human beings, he believed he had found the root of both self and society.

Mead's view is completely social, allowing no biological element at all. This is a problem for critics who stand with Freud (who said our general drives are rooted in the body) and Piaget (whose stages of development are tied to biological maturity).

Be careful not to confuse Mead's concepts of the I and the me with Freud's id and superego. For Freud, the id originates in our biology, but Mead rejected any biological element of the self (although he never clearly spelled out the origin of the I). In addition, the id and the superego are locked in continual combat, but the I and the me work cooperatively together (Meltzer, 1978).

CHECK YOUR LEARNING Explain the meaning and importance of Mead's concepts of the I and the me. What did Mead mean by "taking the role of the other"? Why is this process so important to socialization?

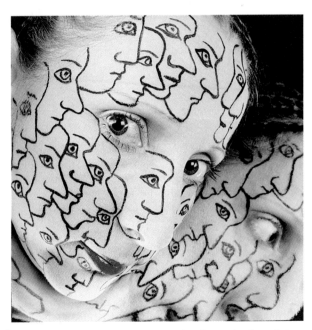

George Herbert Mead wrote, "No hard-and-fast line can be drawn between our own selves and the selves of others." The painting *Manyness* by Rimma Gerlovina and Valeriy Gerlovin conveys this important truth. Although we tend to think of ourselves as unique individuals, each person's characteristics develop in an ongoing process of interaction with others.
Rimma Gerlovina and Valeriy Gerlovin, *Manyness*, 1990. © the artists, New City, N.Y.

EXERCISE: For motivated students, assign a special report on George Herbert Mead's ideas about teaching. Sources include "The Psychology of Social Consciousness Implied in Instruction" (1910) and "The Teaching of Science in College" (1906).

NOTE: Another way to present the theorists is to pose the question "How do we learn?" Freud emphasizes internalization of culture; Piaget underscores internal cognitive development; behaviorists Watson and Skinner highlight environmental stimulation; Mead advances a social behaviorist approach based on gaining the capacity for symbolic interaction.

MAKING THE GRADE

Most theorists discussed in this chapter focus on childhood as the critical time when personality is formed. What sets Erik Erikson apart is the focus on socialization throughout the life course.

Sociological research indicates that wealthy parents tend to encourage creativity in their children while poor parents tend to foster conformity. Although this general difference may be valid, parents at all class levels can and do provide loving support and guidance by simply involving themselves in their children's lives. Henry Ossawa Tanner's painting *The Banjo Lesson* stands as a lasting testament to this process.

Henry Ossawa Tanner, *The Banjo Lesson*, 1893. Oil on canvas. Hampton University Museum, Hampton, Virginia.

Erik H. Erikson's Eight Stages of Development

Although some analysts (including Freud) point to childhood as the crucial time when personality takes shape, Erik H. Erikson (1902–1994) took a broader view of socialization. He explained that we face challenges throughout the life course (1963, orig. 1950).

Stage 1: Infancy—the challenge of trust (versus mistrust). Between birth and about eighteen months, infants face the first of life's challenges: to establish a sense of trust that their world

is a safe place. Family members play a key part in how any infant meets this challenge.

Stage 2: Toddlerhood—the challenge of autonomy (versus doubt and shame). The next challenge, up to age three, is to learn skills to cope with the world in a confident way. Failing to gain self-control leads children to doubt their abilities.

Stage 3: Preschool—the challenge of initiative (versus guilt). Four- and five-year-olds must learn to engage their surroundings—including people outside the family—or experience guilt at failing to meet the expectations of parents and others.

Stage 4: Preadolescence—the challenge of industriousness (versus inferiority). Between ages six and thirteen, children enter school, make friends, and strike out on their own more and more. They either feel proud of their accomplishments or fear that they do not measure up.

Stage 5: Adolescence—the challenge of gaining identity (versus confusion). During the teen years, young people struggle to establish their own identity. In part, teenagers identify with others, but they also want to be unique. Almost all teens experience some confusion as they struggle to establish an identity.

Stage 6: Young adulthood—the challenge of intimacy (versus isolation). The challenge for young adults is to form and maintain intimate relationships with others. Falling in love (as well as making close friends) involves balancing the need to bond with the need to have a separate identity.

Stage 7: Middle adulthood—the challenge of making a difference (versus self-absorption). The challenge of middle age is contributing to the lives of others in the family, at work, and in the larger world. Failing at this, people become self-centered, caught up in their own limited concerns.

Stage 8: Old age—the challenge of integrity (versus despair). As the end of life approaches, people hope to look back on what they have accomplished with a sense of integrity and satisfaction. For those who have been self-absorbed, old age brings only a sense of despair over missed opportunities.

CRITICAL REVIEW Erikson's theory views personality formation as a lifelong process, with success at one stage (say, as an infant gaining trust) preparing us to meet the next challenge. However, not everyone faces these challenges in the exact order presented by Erikson. Nor is it clear that failure to meet the challenge of one stage of life means that a person is doomed to fail later on. A broader question, raised earlier in our discussion of Piaget's ideas, is whether people in other cultures and in other times in history would define a successful life in Erikson's terms.

NOTE: To illustrate the significance of the family: Four of the five most powerful "social readjustment" challenges, rated on a scale topping out at 100, involve family members: death of spouse (100), divorce (73), marital separation (65), death of close family member (63), and jail term (63) (Holmes & Rahe, 1967).

THE MAP: Children in some regions of the country (and, generally, in urban areas) have more social experience with people of different racial or ethnic categories than their counterparts in other (often rural) regions.

DISCUSS: Why is it that a substantial majority of people incarcerated for violent crimes had poor family lives as children?

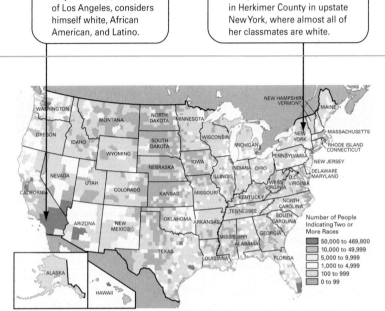

Alejo Gonzalez, a native of Los Angeles, considers himself white, African American, and Latino.

Emily Johnston attends school in Herkimer County in upstate New York, where almost all of her classmates are white.

Number of People Indicating Two or More Races

■	50,000 to 469,800
■	10,000 to 49,999
□	5,000 to 9,999
□	1,000 to 4,999
□	100 to 999
□	0 to 99

Seeing Ourselves

NATIONAL MAP 5–1
Racially Mixed People across the United States

This map shows the county-by-county distribution of people who described themselves as racially mixed in the 2000 census. How do you think growing up in an area with a high level of racially mixed people (such as Los Angeles or Miami) would be different from growing up in an area with few such people (for example, in upstate New York or the Plains States in the middle of the country)?

Source: U.S. Census Bureau (2001).

In sum, Erikson's model points out that many factors, including the family and school, shape our personalities. In the next section, we take a close look at these important agents of socialization.

CHECK YOUR LEARNING In what ways does Erikson take a broader view of socialization than other thinkers presented in this chapter?

Agents of Socialization

Every social experience we have affects us in at least a small way. However, several familiar settings have special importance in the socialization process.

The Family

The family affects socialization in many ways. For most people, in fact, the family may be the most important socialization agent of all.

Nurture in Early Childhood

Infants are totally dependent on others for care. The responsibility for providing a safe and caring environment typically falls on parents and other family members. For several years—at least until children begin school—the family also has the job of teaching children skills, values, and beliefs. Overall, research suggests, nothing is more likely to produce a happy, well-adjusted child than a loving family (Gibbs, 2001).

Not all family learning results from intentional teaching by parents. Children also learn from the type of environment adults create. Whether children learn to see themselves as strong or weak, smart or

stupid, loved or simply tolerated—and as Erik Erikson suggests, whether they see the world as trustworthy or dangerous—depends largely on the quality of the surroundings provided by parents and other caregivers.

Race and Class

Through the family, parents give a social identity to children. In part, social identity involves race. Racial identity can be complex because, as Chapter 14 ("Race and Ethnicity") explains, societies define race in various ways. In addition, in the 2000 census, more than 7 million people (about 2.4 percent) said they consider themselves to be of two or more racial categories. This number is rising, and 3.5 percent of all births in the United States are now recorded as interracial (U.S. Census, 2008). National Map 5–1 shows where people who describe themselves as racially mixed live.

Social class, like race, plays a large part in shaping a child's personality. Whether born into families of high or low social position, children gradually come to realize that their family's social standing affects how others see them and, in time, how they come to see themselves.

In addition, research shows that class position affects not just how much money parents have to spend on their children but also what parents expect of them (Ellison, Bartkowski, & Segal, 1996). When people in the United States were asked to pick from a list of traits that are most desirable in a child, those with lower social standing favored obedience and conformity. Well-to-do people, by contrast, chose good judgment and creativity (NORC, 2008).

What accounts for the difference? Melvin Kohn (1977) explains that people of lower social standing usually have limited education and perform routine jobs under close supervision. Expecting that

Q: "Middle-class parents seem to regard child rearing as more problematic than do working-class parents." Melvin Kohn (1977:6)

NOTE: Schooling emerged only with the declining economic value of children. "School" is derived from the Greek word *schole*, meaning "leisure time devoted to learning."

NOTE: The word "peer" is derived from the Latin *par*, meaning "equal."

Q: "I am always ready to learn, although I do not always like being taught." Winston Churchill

GLOBAL: The mass media (especially television) are most widespread in industrial and postindustrial societies that change quickly; however, the media are a powerful force for change when introduced to traditional societies—see the box about Brazil's Kaiapo Indians in Chapter 24.

SEEING SOCIOLOGY IN EVERYDAY LIFE

Are We Grown Up Yet? Defining Adulthood

SOLLY: *(seeing several friends walking down the dorm hallway, just returned from dinner)* Yo, guys! Jeremy's twenty-one today. We're going down to the Box Car to celebrate.

MATT: *(shaking his head)* Dunno, dude. I got a lab to finish up. It's just another birthday.

SOLLY: Not just any birthday, my friend. He's twenty-one—an *adult*!

MATT: *(sarcastically)* If turning twenty-one would make me an adult, I wouldn't still be clueless about what I want to do with my life!

Are you an adult or still an adolescent? Does turning twenty-one make you a "grown-up"? According to the sociologist Tom Smith (2003), in our society, there is no one factor that announces the onset of adulthood. In fact, the results of his survey—using a representative sample of 1,398 people over the age of eighteen—suggest that many factors play a part in our decision to consider a young person "grown up."

According to the survey, the single most important transition in claiming adult standing in the United States today is the completion of schooling. But other factors are also important: Smith's respondents linked adult standing to taking on a full-time job, gaining the ability to support a family financially, no longer living with parents, and finally, marrying and becoming a parent. In other words, almost everyone in the United States thinks a person who has done *all* of these things is fully "grown up."

At what age are these transitions likely to be completed? On average, the answer is about twenty-six. But such an average masks an important difference based on social class. People who do not attend college (more common among people growing up in lower-income families) typically finish school before age twenty, and a full-time job, independent living, marriage,

and parenthood may follow in a year or two. Those from more privileged backgrounds are likely to attend college and may even go on to graduate or professional school, delaying the process of becoming an adult for as long as ten years, past the age of thirty.

WHAT DO YOU THINK?

1. Do you consider yourself an adult? At what age did your adulthood begin?

2. Consider a woman whose children are grown, who has had a recent divorce, and is now going to college getting a degree so that she can find a job. Is she likely to feel that she is suddenly not quite "grown up," now that she's back in school? Why or why not?

3. How does the research described in this box show that adulthood is a socially defined concept rather than a biological stage of life?

their children will hold similar positions, they encourage obedience and may even use physical punishment like spanking to get it. Because well-off parents have had more schooling, they usually have jobs that demand imagination and creativity, so they try to inspire the same qualities in their children. Consciously or not, all parents act in ways that encourage their children to follow in their footsteps.

Wealthier parents typically provide their children with an extensive program of leisure activities, including sports, travel, and music lessons. These enrichment activities—far less available to children growing up in low-income families—build *cultural capital*, which advances learning and creates a sense of confidence in these children that they will succeed later in life (Lareau, 2002).

Social class also affects how long the process of growing up takes, as the Seeing Sociology in Everyday Life box explains.

The School

Schooling enlarges children's social world to include people with backgrounds different from their own. It is only as they encounter people who differ from themselves that children come to understand the importance of factors such as race and social position. As they do, they are likely to cluster in playgroups made up of one class, race, and gender.

Gender

Schools join with families in socializing children into gender roles. Studies show that at school, boys engage in more physical activities and spend more time outdoors, and girls are more likely to help teachers with various housekeeping chores. Boys also engage in more aggressive behavior in the classroom, while girls are typically quieter and better behaved (Best, 1983; Jordan & Cowan, 1995).

What Children Learn

Schooling is not the same for children living in rich and poor communities. As Chapter 20 ("Education") explains, children from well-off families typically have a far better experience in school than those whose families are poor.

For all children, the lessons learned in school include more than the formal lesson plans. Schools informally teach many things, which together might be called the *hidden curriculum*. Activities such as spelling bees teach children not only how to spell but how society divides the population into "winners" and "losers." Sports help students develop their strength and skills and also teach children important lessons in cooperation and competition.

School is also the first experience with bureaucracy for most children. The school day is based on impersonal rules and a strict

Q: Question: "How many hours do you spend each day watching TV?" Bart Simpson: "Six. Seven if there's something good on."

Q: "Television is democracy at its ugliest." Paddy Chayevsky

Q: "The powerful play goes on and you may contribute a verse." Walt Whitman

DIVERSITY: Women watch more television than men, people over 55 more than those under 25, and African Americans more than whites.

peer group a social group whose members have interests, social position, and age in common

anticipatory socialization learning that helps a person achieve a desired position

In high-income countries such as the United States, television is an important part of socialization.

In low-income countries such as Nigeria, the mass media play a smaller role in socialization.

time schedule. Not surprisingly, these are also the traits of the large organizations that will employ young people later in life.

The Peer Group

By the time they enter school, children have joined a **peer group,** *a social group whose members have interests, social position, and age in common.* Unlike the family and the school, the peer group lets children escape the direct supervision of adults. Among their peers, children learn how to form relationships on their own. Peer groups also offer the chance to discuss interests that adults may not share with their children (such as clothing and popular music) or permit (such as drugs and sex).

It is not surprising, then, that parents express concern about who their children's friends are. In a rapidly changing society, peer groups have great influence, and the attitudes of young and old may differ because of a "generation gap." The importance of peer groups typically peaks during adolescence, when young people begin to break away from their families and think of themselves as adults.

Even during adolescence, however, parental influence on children remains strong. Peers may affect short-term interests such as music or films, but parents have greater influence on long-term goals, such as going to college (Davies & Kandel, 1981).

Finally, any neighborhood or school is made up of many peer groups. As Chapter 7 ("Groups and Organizations") explains, individuals tend to view their own group in positive terms and put down other groups. In addition, people are influenced by peer groups they would like to join, a process sociologists call **anticipatory socialization,** *learning that helps a person achieve a desired position.* In school, for example, young people may copy the styles and slang of a group they hope will accept them. Later in life, a young lawyer who hopes to become a partner in the law firm may conform to the attitudes and behavior of the firm's partners in order to be accepted.

The Mass Media

August 30, Isle of Coll, off the west coast of Scotland.   The last time we visited this remote island, there was no electricity and most of the people spoke the ancient Gaelic language. Now that a power cable comes from the mainland, homes have lights, appliances, television, and the Internet! Almost with the flip of a switch, this tiny place has been thrust into the modern world. It is no surprise that the island's traditions are fast disappearing, with few performances of its historical dancing or music to be found. A rising share of the population now consists of mainlanders who ferry over with their cars to spend time in their vacation homes. And everyone now speaks English.

FIGURE 5–2 **Television Ownership in Global Perspective**

Television is popular in high- and middle-income countries, where almost every household owns at least one TV set.

Sources: U.S. Census Bureau (2008) and International Telecommunication Union (2008).

The **mass media** are *the means for delivering impersonal communications to a vast audience.* The term *media* (plural of *medium*) comes from the Latin word for "middle," suggesting that media connect people. *Mass* media arise as communications technology (first newspapers and then radio, television, films, and the Internet) spreads information on a massive scale.

In the United States today, the mass media have an enormous influence on our attitudes and behavior. Television, introduced in the 1930s, became the dominant medium after World War II, and 98 percent of U.S. households now have at least one set (by comparison, just 95 percent have telephones). Five out of six households also have cable or satellite television. As Figure 5–2 shows, the United States has one of the highest rates of television ownership in the world. In this country, it is people with lower incomes who spend the most time watching TV as well as using their television to watch movies and to play video games (Nielsen Media Research, 2008).

The Extent of Mass Media Exposure

Just how "glued to the tube" are we? Survey data show that the average household has at least one television set turned on for seven hours each day and that people spend almost half their free time watching television about four and a half hours a day. One study, by the Kaiser Family Foundation, found that school-age youngsters typically spend

RESOURCE: Jean Kilbourne's "Socialization and the Power of Advertising" is included in the companion reader *Seeing Ourselves*, 8th ed.

NOTE: Ariès is an art historian; his interest in the changing conceptions of childhood began when he noted that medieval artists portrayed children as miniature adults. This was not a lack of technical sophistication, he concluded, but a different view of childhood.

DISCUSS: This nation's 75 million children under age 18 are affected by political elections but cannot vote. Should they have this right? (Remember that about half of their parents do not vote.)

NOTE: Stephanie Koontz (1992) noted that in 1900, children in many Pennsylvania towns went to work in the mines by age 11; in textile mills in the South, roughly one-fourth of the labor force was children as young as 7.

mass media (p. 123) the means for delivering impersonal communications to a vast audience

Concern with violence and the mass media extends to the world of video games, especially those popular with young boys. Among the most controversial games, which include high levels of violence, is the *Hitman* series. Do you think the current rating codes are sufficient to guide parents and children who buy video games, or would you support greater restrictions on game content?

Americans playing gardeners, or Hispanics playing new immigrants). In recent years, however, minorities have moved closer to center stage on television. There are ten times as many Hispanic actors on prime-time television as there were a decade or two ago, and they play a far larger range of characters (Lichter & Amundson, 1997; Fetto, 2003b).

On the other side of the fence, conservative critics charge that the television and film industries are dominated by a liberal "cultural elite." In recent years, they claim, "politically correct" media have advanced liberal causes, including feminism and gay rights (Rothman, Powers, & Rothman, 1993; B. Goldberg, 2002). But not everyone agrees, with some studies suggesting that the mainstream media are fairly conservative on many issues (Adkins & Washburn, 2007). In addition, some television cable channels (such as MSNBC) have a decidedly liberal point of view, while others (such as Fox Network) are more conservative.

One study of the 2008 presidential election found that the Democratic candidate Barack Obama was endorsed by almost three times as many U.S. newspapers as Republican candidate John McCain ("Ongoing Tally," 2008). At the same time, research suggests that a wide range of political opinion is available in today's mass media and that most of us tend to focus on those media sources, whether more liberal or more conservative, that are closer to our own personal opinions (Morris, 2007).

even more time—about about six and a half hours each day—in front of video screens. Younger children favor watching television and playing video games; as children get older, music videos and Web surfing become a bigger part of the mix. At all ages, boys favor video games and girls lean toward music videos, and African American children spend more time watching television and playing video games than white children do (Rideout, Roberts, & Foehr, 2005; Nielsen Media Research, 2008).

Years before children learn to read, television watching is a regular part of their daily routine. As they grow, children spend as many hours in front of a television as they do in school or interacting with their parents. This is the case despite research suggesting that television makes children more passive and less likely to use their imagination (American Psychological Association, 1993; Fellman, 1995).

Television and Politics

The comedian Fred Allen once quipped that we call television a "medium" because it is "rarely well done." For a number of reasons, television (as well as other mass media) provokes plenty of criticism. Some liberal critics argue that for most of television's history, racial and ethnic minorities have not been visible or have been included only in stereotypical roles (such as African Americans playing butlers, Asian

Television and Violence

In 1996, the American Medical Association issued the startling statement that violence in television and films had reached such a high level that it posed a hazard to our health. More recently, a study found a strong link between aggressive behavior and the amount of time elementary school children spend watching television and playing video games (Robinson et al., 2001). The public is concerned about this issue: Three-fourths of U.S. adults report having walked out of a movie or turned off the television because of too much violence. About two-thirds of parents say that they are "very concerned" that their children are exposed to too much media violence. There may be reason for this concern: Almost two-thirds of television programs contain violence, and in most such scenes, violent characters show no remorse and are not punished (B. J. Wilson, 1998; Rideout, 2007).

Back in 1997, the television industry adopted a rating system. But we are left to wonder whether watching sexual or violent programming harms people as much as critics say. More important, why do the mass media contain so much sex and violence in the first place?

Television and the other mass media enrich our lives with entertaining and educational programming. The media also increase our

Q: "From birth to age 18, a girl needs good parents; from 18 to 35, she needs good looks; from 35 to 55, she needs a good personality; from 55 on she needs cash." Sophie Tucker

Q: "Let me be myself and then I am satisfied. I know that I am a woman with inward strength and plenty of courage." Anne Frank

Q: "Kites fly highest against the wind." Winston Churchill

NOTE: Human Rights Watch reports that some tens of thousands of children under 18 are active participants in armed conflicts worldwide. Children are easy to recruit and often deemed expendable. Girls are sometimes recruited for sex.

MAKING THE GRADE

The chapter now turns to stages of the life course. Although we think of these stages as biological (children are children because they are young and immature), comparing our society past and present and comparing various societies today show that culture shapes all stages of the life course.

SEEING SOCIOLOGY
in Everyday Life

In 2005, a thirteen-year-old soccer player named Freddy Adu was offered a $1 million contract by Nike. Can you see any reasons he or his parents should be concerned about accepting this offer?

exposure to diverse cultures and provoke discussion of current issues. At the same time, the power of the media—especially television—to shape how we think remains highly controversial.

CRITICAL REVIEW This section shows that socialization is complex, with many different factors shaping our personalities as we grow. In addition, these factors do not always work together. For instance, children learn certain things from peer groups and the mass media that may conflict with what they learn at home.

Beyond family, school, peer group, and the media, other spheres of life also play a part in social learning. For most people in the United States, these include the workplace, religious organizations, the military, and social clubs. In the end, socialization proves to be not a simple matter of learning but a complex balancing act as we absorb information from a variety of sources. In the process of sorting and weighing all the information we receive, we form our own distinctive personalities.

CHECK YOUR LEARNING Identify all the major agents of socialization discussed in this section of the chapter. What are some of the unique ways that each helps us develop our individual personalities?

Socialization and the Life Course

Although childhood has special importance in the socialization process, learning continues throughout our lives. An overview of the life course reveals that our society organizes human experience according to age—childhood, adolescence, adulthood, and old age.

Childhood

A few years ago, the Nike Corporation, maker of popular athletic shoes, came under attack. Its shoes are made in Taiwan and Indonesia, in many cases by children who work in factories instead of going to school. As many as 160 million of the world's children work, half of them full time, and almost half of these boys and girls do work that is dangerous to their physical and mental health. For their efforts, they earn very little—typically, about 50 cents an hour (Human Rights Watch, 2006; U.S. Department of Labor, 2008). Global Map 5–1 on page 126 shows that child labor is most common in Africa and Asia.

Criticism of Nike springs from the fact that most North Americans think of *childhood*—roughly the first twelve years of life—as a carefree time for learning and play. Yet as the historian Philippe Ariès (1965) explains, the whole idea of "childhood" is fairly new. During the Middle

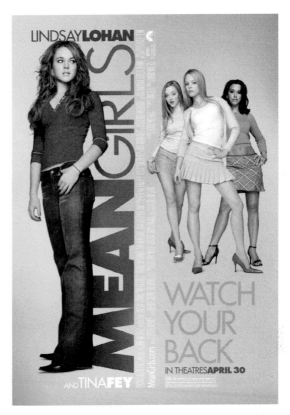

In recent decades, some people have become concerned that U.S. society is shortening childhood, pushing children to grow up faster and faster. Do films such as *Mean Girls,* starring Lindsay Lohan, which show young girls dressing and behaving as if they were much older, encourage a "hurried childhood"? Do you see this as a problem or not?

Ages, children of four or five were treated like adults and expected to fend for themselves.

We defend our idea of childhood because children are biologically immature. But a look back in time and around the world shows that the concept of childhood is grounded not in biology but in culture (LaRossa & Reitzes, 2001). In rich countries, not everyone has to work, so childhood can be extended to allow time for young people to learn the skills they will need in a high-technology workplace.

Because childhood in the United States lasts such a long time, some people worry when children seem to be growing up too fast. In part, this "hurried child" syndrome results from changes in the family—including high divorce rates and both parents in the labor force—that leave children with less supervision. In addition, "adult"

THE MAP: Global maps allow students to compare the United States to countries all over the world. These maps are especially helpful in seeing how social patterns differ in high-income regions (North America and Europe) and lower-income regions (Latin America, Africa, and Asia) of the world. Here we see that in lower-income countries, childhood often means not schooling and carefree play but daily work for income.

Q: "Humanity has survived thanks only to inconsistency." Leszek Kolakowski

Q: "Are you going to let the system eat you up and relieve you of your humanity? Or are you going to use the system to human purposes?" Joseph Campbell

Q: "Idealism is what precedes experience; cynicism is what follows." David Wolf

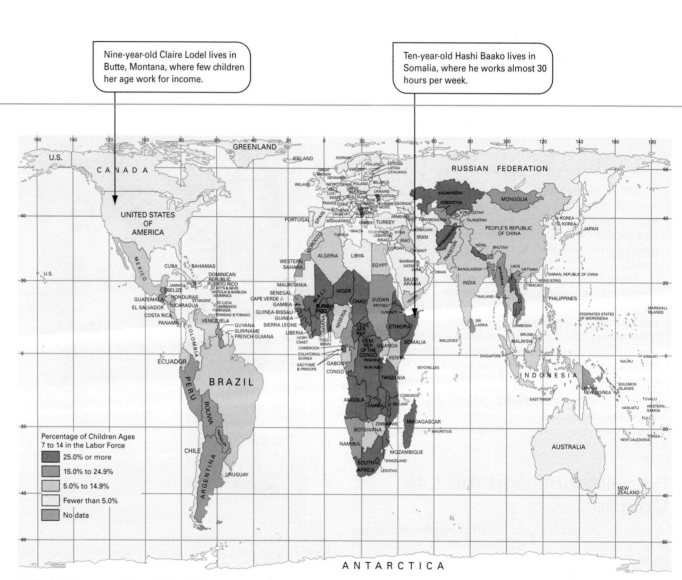

Nine-year-old Claire Lodel lives in Butte, Montana, where few children her age work for income.

Ten-year-old Hashi Baako lives in Somalia, where he works almost 30 hours per week.

Percentage of Children Ages 7 to 14 in the Labor Force
- 25.0% or more
- 15.0% to 24.9%
- 5.0% to 14.9%
- Fewer than 5.0%
- No data

Window on the World

GLOBAL MAP 5–1   **Child Labor in Global Perspective**

Industrialization extends childhood and discourages children from work and other activities considered suitable only for adults. This is why child labor is uncommon in the United States and other high-income countries. In less economically developed nations of the world, however, children are a vital economic asset, and they typically begin working as soon as they are able. How would childhood in, say, the African nation of Chad or Sudan differ from that in the United States or Canada?

Sources: Global March against Child Labor (2008), UNICEF (2008), and World Bank (2008).

programming on television (not to mention in films and on the Internet) carries grown-up concerns such as sex, drugs, and violence into young people's lives. Today's ten- to twelve-year-olds, says one executive of a children's television channel, have about the same interests and experiences typical of twelve- to fourteen-year-olds a generation ago (K. S. Hymowitz, 1998). Perhaps this is why today's children, compared to kids fifty years ago, have higher levels of stress and anxiety (Gorman, 2000). Seeing Sociology in the News on pages 128–29 takes a closer look at how quickly many young children are growing up.

DISCUSS: Is adolescence expanding? Primarily because of economic uncertainty, 60% of 20- to 24-year-olds now live at home with their parents. Ask the class (especially 18- to 22-year-olds) whether they consider themselves adults and why.

NOTE: "Adult" is derived from the Latin word *adultus*, meaning "grown."

Q: "Always go to other people's funerals. Otherwise they won't come to yours." Yogi Berra

Q: "Death, after all, is the only reality that never lets you down." Pico Iyer

SEEING SOCIOLOGY
in Everyday Life

Many of our soldiers in Iraq are still teenagers. Why should we not be surprised to learn that most of these young men and women performing adult jobs are from small-town, working-class families?

SEEING SOCIOLOGY
in Everyday Life

What major events or trends have shaped the personalities of people your age?

THINKING ABOUT DIVERSITY: RACE, CLASS, & GENDER

The Development of Self among High School Students

Adolescence is a time when people ask questions like "Who am I?" and "What do I want to become?" In the end, we all have to answer these questions for ourselves. But race and ethnicity are likely to have an effect on what our answers turn out to be.

Grace Kao (2000) studied the identity and goals of students enrolled in Johnstown High School, a large (3,000-student) school in a Chicago suburb. Johnstown High is considered a good school, with above-average test scores. It is also racially and ethnically diverse: 47 percent of the students are white, 43 percent are African American, 7 percent are Hispanic, and 3 percent are of Asian descent.

Kao interviewed sixty-three Johnstown students, female and male, both individually and in small groups with others of the same race and ethnicity. Talking with them, she learned how important racial and ethnic stereotypes are in young people's developing sense of self.

What are these stereotypes? White students are seen as hardworking in school and concerned about getting high grades. African American students are thought to study less, either because they are not as smart or because they just don't try as hard. In any case, students see African Americans at high risk of failure in school. Because the stereo-

type says that Hispanics are headed for manual occupations—as gardeners or laborers—they are seen as not caring very much about doing well. Finally, Asian American students are seen as hardworking high achievers, either because they are smart or because they spend their time on academics rather than, say, sports.

From her interviews, Kao learned that most students think these stereotypes are true and take them personally. They expect people, including themselves, to perform in school more or less the way the stereotype predicts. In addition, young people—whether white, black, Hispanic, or Asian—mostly hang out with others like themselves, which gives them little chance to find out that their beliefs are wrong.

Students of all racial and ethnic categories say they *want* to do well in school. But not getting to know those who differ from themselves means that they measure success *only in relation to their own category*. To African American students, in other words, "success" means doing as well as other black students and not flunking out. To Hispanics, "success" means avoiding manual labor and ending up with any job in an office. Whites and Asians, by contrast, define "success" as earning high grades and living up to the high-achievement stereotype. For all these young people, then, "self" develops through the lens of how race and ethnicity are defined by our society.

WHAT DO YOU THINK?

1. Were you aware of racial and ethnic stereotypes similar to those described here in your high school? What about your college?

2. Do you think that gender stereotypes affect the performance of women and men in school as much as racial and ethnic stereotypes? Explain.

3. What can be done to reduce the damaging effects of racial and ethnic stereotypes?

Adolescence

At the same time that industrialization created childhood as a distinct stage of life, adolescence emerged as a buffer between childhood and adulthood. We generally link *adolescence,* or the teenage years, with emotional and social turmoil as young people struggle to develop their own identities. Again, we are tempted to attribute teenage rebelliousness and confusion to the biological changes of puberty. But it is in fact the result of cultural inconsistency. For example, the mass media glorify sex and schools hand out condoms, even as parents urge restraint. Consider, too, that an eighteen-year-old may face the adult duty of going to war but lacks the adult right to drink a beer. In

short, adolescence is a time of social contradictions, when people are no longer children but not yet adults.

As is true of all stages of life, adolescence varies according to social background. Most young people from working-class families move directly from high school into the adult world of work and parenting. Wealthier teens, however, have the resources to attend college and perhaps graduate school, stretching their adolescent years into the late twenties and even the thirties (T. W. Smith, 2003). The Thinking About Diversity box provides an example of how race and ethnicity can shape the accedemic performance of high school students.

Q: "One can experience an unconditional affirmation of life only when one has accepted death, not as contrary to life, but as an aspect of it." Joseph Campbell

Q: "When I was fourteen my father was so ignorant I could hardly stand to have the old man around. But when I got to be twenty-one, I was astonished at how much he had learned in seven years." Mark Twain

Q: "For of all sad words, of tongue or pen; / The saddest are these: 'It might have been'!" John Greenleaf Whittier

Seeing SOCIOLOGY in the NEWS

As Kids Get Savvy, Marketers Move Down the Age Scale

By JAYNE O'DONNELL
April 11, 2007

Jill Brown almost cried the day her 9-year-old daughter sold several American Girl dolls at a yard sale so she could buy a Juicy Couture sweat suit.

It was a painful reminder that the emotional and psychological distance between childhood and the teen years is far shorter than ever. . . . .

Chalk it up to "age compression," which many marketers call "kids getting older younger" or KGOY. Retail consultant Ken Nisch says it shouldn't be a surprise or an outrage that kids are tired of toys and kid clothes by 8, considering that they are exposed to outside influences so much earlier. They are in preschool at 3 and on computers at 6.

That's why marketers now target 9-year-olds with apparel and accessories once considered only for teens, says Nisch, chairman of the retail consulting and design firm JGA.

Generation Y, those between about 8 and 26, are considered the most important generation for retailers and marketers because of their spending power and the influence they have over what their parents buy. But just as the 8- to 12-year-old "tweens" are pitched with a dizzying array of music, movie and cellphone choices, the nearly 10 million tween girls also are getting more attention from fashion, skin care and makeup businesses. Last year, NPD Group says 7- to 14-year-old girls spent $11.5 billion on apparel. . . .

With their keen but shifting senses of style, tween girls present some of the biggest rewards and challenges for retailers and brands. What's called for: a delicate marketing dance that tunes in tween girls without turning off their parents, who control both the purse strings and the car. Retailers to tween girls also must stay in close touch with the fashion pulse, because being "out" is even more painful for girls who haven't hit the teen years, say retailers and their consultants. They'll drop a brand faster than you can say Hannah

Montana if the clothes become anything close to dorky. . . .

Some other tween girl traits:

• They're driven by imitation. Tweens want to look like each other but be able to call looks their own, says retail consultant Laura Evans, whose clients include Reebok and Express. Retailers that offer a lot of similar apparel—layers of shirts in a variety of colors—tend to be the most popular. . . .

• They want more of everything. Whether it's lip balm or blue jeans, "More is more," says Nita Rollins, who heads marketing intelligence at the digital marketing agency Resource Interactive. "Nothing succeeds like excess." Tweens aren't aware of "social codes of restraint," says Rollins, so they see no reason why they don't need 10 American Girl dolls or several pairs of jeans or sneakers. The average number of Lip Smacker-brand lip balm and glosses owned by Bonne Bell customers is 10, but, Bell notes, "The girls who have 100 make up for the ones who don't have 10.". . .

Adulthood

If stages of the life course were based on biological changes, it would be easy to define *adulthood*. Regardless of exactly when it begins, adulthood is the time when most of life's accomplishments take place, including pursuing a career and raising a family. Personalities are largely formed by then, although marked changes in a person's environment—such as unemployment, divorce, or serious illness—may cause significant changes to the self.

Early Adulthood

During early adulthood—until about age forty—young adults learn to manage day-to-day affairs for themselves, often juggling conflicting priorities: schooling, job, partner, children, and parents. During this stage of life, many women try to "do it all," a pattern that reflects the fact that our culture gives them the major responsibility for child rearing and housework even if they have demanding jobs outside the home.

Middle Adulthood

In middle adulthood—roughly ages forty to sixty-five—people sense that their life circumstances are pretty well set. They also become more aware of the fragility of health, which the young typically take for granted. Women who have spent many years raising a family find middle adulthood emotionally trying. Children grow up and require less attention, and husbands become absorbed in their

careers, leaving some women with spaces in their lives that are difficult to fill. Many women who divorce also face serious financial problems (Weitzman, 1985, 1996). For all these reasons, an increasing number of women in middle adulthood return to school and seek new careers.

For everyone, growing older means experiencing physical decline, a prospect our culture makes especially painful for women. Because good looks are considered more important for women, the appearance of wrinkles and graying hair can be traumatic. Men have their own particular difficulties as they get older. Some must admit that they are never going to reach earlier career goals. Others realize that the price of career success has been neglect of family or personal health.

Old Age

Old age—the later years of adulthood and the final stage of life itself—begins around the mid-sixties. In the United States, about one in eight people is at least age sixty-five, and the elderly now outnumber teenagers (U.S. Census Bureau, 2008).

Once again, societies attach different meanings to this stage of life. As explained in Chapter 15 ("Aging and the Elderly"), it is older members of traditional societies who typically control most of the land and other wealth. Also, since traditional societies change slowly, older people possess useful wisdom gained over their lifetime, which earns them much respect.

• They are environmentally aware. Tweens start to "feel the pain of everybody. They want to know if animals were hurt in making this," says Nisch. . . . They might even become vegetarians or vegans. Rollins agrees: "They have social consciousness at a very young age. They have great lives, and so they want to give back.". . .

• They like attention, sort of. "Our customer aspires to be like an older girl, so if she's 10 she wants to dress like a 12-year-old, and a 12-year-old wants to dress like a 14-year-old," says Atkinson. But she's also "more self-conscious" and not usually trying to attract boys, he says. . . .

A tween starts to feel more comfortable with fashions when she sees them on her older sister or the babysitter, says Atkinson. Tween Brands' challenge, he says, is to "tastefully interpret them for the younger customer. She's just literally developing into a young woman. She doesn't even want to wear spaghetti straps." The girl "has to want an item because she thinks it's the coolest thing in fashion, but if we don't pass

muster with Mom, that transaction is not going to be completed."

Moms, in fact, are a big influence on tween fashions, experts say. Many tweens may get some fashion cues from celebrities, but they still look first to their moms. "They still want Mom to give them the OK," [Tween Brands spokesman Robert] Atkinson says.

What else would explain all the tweens and teens with quilted and printed cloth backpacks and purses from Vera Bradley, asks Rollins. "You can't say it's because the paisleys are particularly beautiful. It's the exposure to all the brands the parents covet." . . .

Despite the challenges, most brands want to hook kids as early as possible, which explains kid and tween lines from the likes of Lucky Brand Jeans, J. Crew and Juicy Couture. Bell calls her brand's lip balms "a rite of entry into makeup." Tweens are the brand's core customer, but they've developed products that appeal to kids starting at age 4 and then adapt them to teens and beyond. . . .

Lindsey Brown, who turned 13 last month, made almost $1,000 at the yard sale where she sold her American Girl dolls. She banked $800 and spent $200 on the Juicy Couture sweat suit, which included a skirt, pants and a jacket.

Since then, shopping has "become all about clothes," says Jill Brown.

WHAT DO YOU THINK?

1. What factors are encouraging children to grow up faster?

2. Is the fact that children are growing up faster, in your view, helpful or harmful to them? Why?

3. Are boys as well as girls growing up faster? What evidence can you point to that might help answer this question?

Adapted from "As Kids Get Savvy, Marketers Move Down the Age Scale," by Jayne O'Donnell, published in *USA Today*, April 11, 2007. Reprinted by permission.

In industrial societies, however, most younger people work and live apart from their parents, becoming independent of their elders. Rapid change also gives our society a "youth orientation" that defines what is old as unimportant or even obsolete. To younger people, the elderly may seem out of touch with new trends and fashions, and their knowledge and experience may seem of little value.

Perhaps this anti-elderly bias will decline as the share of older people in the United States steadily increases. The percentage of the U.S. population over age sixty-five has more than tripled in the past hundred years. With life expectancy still increasing, most men and women in their mid-sixties today (the "young elderly") can look forward to living decades longer. Analysts predict that by 2030, the number of seniors will double to 72 million, and the "average" person in the United States will be close to forty (U.S. Census Bureau, 2008).

Old age differs in an important way from earlier stages in the life course. Growing up typically means entering new roles and taking on new responsibilities, but growing old is the opposite experience—leaving roles that provided both satisfaction and social identity. For some people, retirement is a period of restful activity, but for others, it can mean losing valued routines and even outright boredom. Like any life transition, retirement demands learning new patterns while at the same time letting go of habits from the past.

Death and Dying

Through most of human history, low living standards and limited medical technology meant that death from accident or disease could come at any stage of life. Today, however, 86 percent of people in the United States die after age fifty-five (Kung et al., 2008).

After observing many dying people, the psychiatrist Elisabeth Kübler-Ross (1969) described death as an orderly transition involving five distinct stages. Typically, a person first faces death with *denial*, perhaps out of fear and perhaps because our culture tends to ignore the reality of death. The second phase is *anger*, when a person facing death sees it as a gross injustice. Third, anger gives way to *negotiation* as the person imagines the possibility of avoiding death by striking a bargain with God. The fourth response, *resignation*, is often accompanied by psychological depression. Finally, a complete adjustment to death requires *acceptance*. At this point, no longer paralyzed by fear and anxiety, the person whose life is ending is able to find peace and makes the most of whatever time remains.

As the share of women and men in old age increases, we can expect our culture to become more comfortable with the idea of death. In recent years, people in the United States have started talking about death more openly, and the trend is to view dying as natural and better than painful or prolonged suffering. More married couples now prepare for death with legal and financial planning.

EXERCISE: Here's a fun exercise to suggest to the class: Rent the video *Trading Places* with Eddie Murphy and Dan Aykroyd, and discuss the plot in terms of John B. Watson's ideas on nurture.

Q: "A basic social arrangement in modern society is that the individual tends to sleep, play, and work in different places, with different co-participants, under different authorities, and without an overall rational plan. The central feature of total institutions can be described as the breakdown of the barriers ordinarily separating these three spheres of life." Erving Goffman (1961:6)

NOTE: The prison population of the U.S. grew 38% over the past 10 years, to 2.2 million currently. Mandatory sentences, especially for drug offenses, are driving the increase.

MAKING THE GRADE

Each stage of life has its own joys and challenges, but in our society, early stages of life typically involve *adding* roles and responsibilities; old age differs in that it typically involves *losing* roles and responsibilities.

cohort a category of people with something in common, usually their age

total institution a setting in which people are isolated from the rest of society and manipulated by an administrative staff

resocialization radically changing an inmate's personality by carefully controlling the environment

This openness may ease somewhat the pain of the surviving spouse, a consideration for women, who, more often than not, outlive their husbands.

The Life Course: Patterns and Variations

This brief look at the life course points to two major conclusions. First, although each stage of life is linked to the biological process of aging, the life course is largely a social construction. For this reason, people in other societies may experience a stage of life quite differently or, for that matter, not at all. Second, in any society, the stages of the life course present certain problems and transitions that involve learning something new and, in many cases, unlearning familiar routines.

Societies organize the life course according to age, but other forces, such as class, race, ethnicity, and gender, also shape people's lives. This means that the general patterns described in this chapter apply somewhat differently to various categories of people within any society.

People's life experiences also vary, depending on when, in the history of the society, they were born. A **cohort** is *a category of people with something in common, usually their age*. Because age cohorts are generally influenced by the same economic and cultural trends, they tend to have similar attitudes and values. Women and men born in the 1940s and 1950s, for example, grew up during a time of economic expansion that gave them a sense of optimism. Today's college students, who have grown up in an age of economic uncertainty, are less confident about the future.

Resocialization: Total Institutions

A final type of socialization, experienced by more than 2.5 million people in the United States, involves being confined—usually against their will—in prisons or mental hospitals (U.S. Department of Justice, 2008). This is the world of the **total institution**, *a setting in which people are isolated from the rest of society and manipulated by an administrative staff*.

According to Erving Goffman (1961), total institutions have three important characteristics. First, staff members supervise all aspects of daily life, including when and where residents (often called "inmates") eat, sleep, and work. Second, life in a total institution is controlled and standardized, with the same food, uniforms, and activities for everyone. Third, formal rules dictate when, where, and how inmates perform their daily routines.

The purpose of such rigid routines is **resocialization**, *radically changing an inmate's personality by carefully controlling the environment*. Prisons and mental hospitals physically isolate inmates behind fences, barred windows, and locked doors and limit their access to the telephone, mail, and visitors. The institution becomes their entire world, making it easier for the staff to bring about personality change—or at least obedience—in the inmate.

Resocialization is a two-part process. First, the staff breaks down the new inmate's existing identity. For example, an inmate must give up personal possessions, including clothing and grooming articles used to maintain a distinctive appearance. Instead, the staff provides standard-issue clothes so that everyone looks alike. The staff subjects new inmates to "mortifications of self," which can include searches, head shaving, medical examinations, fingerprinting, and assignment of a serial number. Once inside the walls, individuals also give up their privacy as guards routinely inspect their living quarters.

In the second part of the resocialization process, the staff tries to build a new self in the inmate through a system of rewards and punishments. Having a book to read, watching television, or making

A cohort is a category of similar-age people who share common life experiences. Just as audiences at Rolling Stones concerts in the 1960s were mainly young people, so most of the group's fans today are over age sixty.

Q: "The principal task of civilization, its actual *raison d'être*, is to defend us against nature." Sigmund Freud

Q: "The beasts have the same senses as ourselves; and very nearly the same appetites." Alexis de Tocqueville

Q: "There is no tyranny so despotic as that of public opinion among a free people." Donn Piat

Q: "And, in the end, the love you take is equal to the love you make." The Beatles

● MAKING THE GRADE

Of the theories of human development we have considered in this chapter, Freud's probably points to the least human freedom, because we are all caught between two powerful forces—biology (id) and culture (superego).

● MAKING THE GRADE

Mead's theory of human development points to the most human freedom, because he saw no biological drives as Freud did and saw humans as spontaneous and creative.

CONTROVERSY & DEBATE

Are We Free within Society?

MIKE: Sociology is an interesting course. Since my professor started telling us how to look at the world with a sociological eye, I'm realizing that a lot of who I am and where I am is because of society.

KIM: *(teasingly)* Oh, so society is responsible for you turning out so smart and witty and good-looking?

MIKE: No, that's all me. But I'm seeing that being at college and playing football is maybe not all me. What do you think? How free are we, really?

This chapter stresses one key theme: Society shapes how we think, feel, and act. If this is so, then in what sense are we free? To answer this important question, consider the Muppets, puppet stars of television and film. Watching the antics of Kermit the Frog, Miss Piggy, and the rest of the troupe, we almost believe they are real rather than objects controlled from backstage or below. As the sociological perspective points out, human beings are like puppets in that we, too, respond to backstage forces. Society, after all, gives us a culture and shapes our lives according to class, race, and gender. If this is so, can we really claim to be free?

Sociologists answer this question with many voices. The politically liberal response is that individuals are *not* free of society—in fact, as social creatures, we never could be. But if we have to live in a society with power over us, it is important to do what we can to make our world as just as possible, by working to lessen class

differences and other barriers to opportunity for minorities, including women. Conservatives agree that society shapes our lives but also point out that we *are* free because society can never dictate our dreams. Our history as a nation, right from the revolutionary acts that led to its founding, is one story after another of people pursuing personal goals despite great odds.

Does understanding more about how society shapes our lives give us greater power to "cut the strings" and choose for ourselves how to live?

Both attitudes are found in George Herbert Mead's analysis of socialization. Mead knew that society makes demands on us, sometimes limiting our options. But he also saw that human beings are spontaneous and creative, capable of continually acting on society and bringing about change. Mead noted the power of society while still affirming the human capacity to evaluate, criticize, and ultimately choose and change.

In the end, then, we may seem like puppets, but only on the surface. A crucial difference is that we can stop, look up at the "strings" that make us move, and even yank on them defiantly (Berger, 1963:176). If our pull is strong enough, we can do more than we might think. As Margaret Mead once remarked, "Never doubt that a small group of thoughtful, committed citizens can change the world. Indeed, it is the only thing that ever has."

WHAT DO YOU THINK?

1. Do you think that our society gives more freedom to males than to females? Why or why not?

2. Do you think that most people in our society feel that they have some control over their lives or not? Why?

3. Has learning about socialization increased or decreased your feeling of freedom? Why?

---

a telephone call may seem like minor pleasures to the outsider, but in the rigid environment of the total institution, gaining such simple privileges as these can be a powerful motivation to conform. The length of confinement typically depends on how well the inmate cooperates with the staff.

Total institutions affect people in different ways. Some inmates may end up "rehabilitated" or "recovered," but others may change

little, and still others may become hostile and bitter. Over a long period of time, living in a rigidly controlled environment can leave some people *institutionalized*, without the capacity for independent living.

But what about the rest of us? Does socialization crush our individuality or empower us to reach our creative potential? The Controversy & Debate box takes a closer look at this question.

Seeing Sociology in Everyday Life

Chapter 5   Socialization

When do we grow up and become adults?

As this chapter explains, many factors come into play in the process of moving from one stage of the life course to another. In global perspective, what makes our society unusual is that there is no one event that clearly tells everyone (and us, too) that the milestone of adulthood has been reached. We have important events that say, for example, when someone completes high school (graduation ceremony) or becomes married (wedding ceremony). Look at the photos shown here. In each case, what do we learn about how the society defines the transition from one stage of life to another?

> **HINT** Societies differ in how they structure the life course, including which stages of life are defined as important, what years of life various stages correspond to, and how clearly movement from one stage to another is marked. Given our cultural emphasis on individual choice and freedom, many people tend to say "You're only as old as you feel" and let people decide these things for themselves. When it comes to reaching adulthood, our society is not very clear—the box on page 122 points out many factors that figure into becoming an adult. So there is no widespread "adult ritual" as we see in these photos. Keep in mind that, for us, class matters a lot in this process, with young people from more affluent families staying in school and delaying full adulthood until well into their twenties or even their thirties. Finally, in these tough economic times, the share of young people in their twenties living with parents goes way up, which can delay adulthood for an entire cohort.

Among the Hamer people in the Omo Valley of Ethiopia, young boys must undergo a test to mark their transition to manhood. Usually the event is triggered by the boy's expressing a desire to marry. In this ritual, witnessed by everyone in his society, the boy must jump over a line of bulls selected by the girl's family. If he succeeds in doing this three times, he is declared a man and the wedding can take place (marking the girl's transition to womanhood). Does our society have any ceremony or event similar to this?

On the San Carlos Reservation in Arizona, young Apache girls perform the Sunrise Dance to mark their transition to adulthood. Carefully painted by an elder according to Apache tradition, each girl holds a special staff, which symbolizes her hope for a long and healthy life and spiritual happiness. Why do many of the world's societies time these coming-of-age rituals to correspond to a girl's first menstrual cycle?

These young men and women in Seoul, South Korea, are participating in a Confucian ceremony to mark their becoming adults. This ritual, which takes place on the twentieth birthday, defines young people as full members of the community and also reminds them of all the responsibilities they are now expected to fulfill. If we had such a ritual in the United States, at what age would it take place?

Applying SOCIOLOGY in Everyday Life

1. Across the United States, many families plan elaborate parties to celebrate a daughter's or son's graduation from high school. In what respects is this a ritual that marks reaching adulthood? How does social class affect whether or not people define this event as the beginning of adulthood?

2. In the United States, when does the stage of life we call "old age" begin? Is there an event that marks the transition to old age? Does social class play a part in this process? If so, how?

3. Watch several hours of prime-time programming on network or cable television. Keep track of every time an act of violence is shown, and calculate the number of violent scenes per hour. On the basis of observing a small and unrepresentative sample of programs, what are your conclusions?

MAKING THE GRADE

CHAPTER 5 Socialization

What Is Socialization?

Socialization is a **LIFELONG PROCESS**.

- Socialization develops our humanity as well as our particular personalities.
- The importance of socialization is seen in the fact that extended periods of social isolation result in permanent damage (cases of Anna, Isabelle, and Genie).

pp. 112–15

Socialization is a matter of **NURTURE** rather than **NATURE**.

- A century ago, most people thought human behavior resulted from biological instinct.
- For us as human beings, it is our nature to nurture.

p. 113

socialization (p. 112) the lifelong social experience by which people develop their human potential and learn culture

personality (p. 112) a person's fairly consistent patterns of acting, thinking, and feeling

Important Contributions to Our Understanding of Socialization

SIGMUND FREUD'S model of the human personality has three parts:

- **id:** innate, pleasure-seeking human drives
- **superego:** the demands of society in the form of internalized values and norms
- **ego:** our efforts to balance innate, pleasure-seeking drives and the demands of society

p. 115

LAWRENCE KOHLBERG applied Piaget's approach to stages of moral development:

- We first judge rightness in **preconventional** terms, according to our individual needs.
- Next, **conventional** moral reasoning takes account of parental attitudes and cultural norms.
- Finally, **postconventional** reasoning allows us to criticize society itself.

p. 117

To **GEORGE HERBERT MEAD**,

- the **self** is part of our personality and includes self-awareness and self-image;
- the self develops only as a result of social experience;
- social experience involves the exchange of symbols;
- social interaction depends on understanding the intention of another, which requires taking the role of the other;
- human action is partly spontaneous (the I) and partly in response to others (the me);
- we gain social experience through imitation, play, games, and understanding the **generalized other.**

pp. 118–19

JEAN PIAGET believed that human development involves both biological maturation and gaining social experience. He identified four stages of cognitive development:

- First, the **sensorimotor stage** involves knowing the world only through the senses.
- Next, the **preoperational stage** involves starting to use language and other symbols.
- Next, the **concrete operational stage** allows individuals to understand causal connections.
- Finally, the **formal operational stage** involves abstract and critical thought.

pp. 115–16

CAROL GILLIGAN found that gender plays an important part in moral development, with males relying more on abstract standards of rightness and females relying more on the effects of actions on relationships.

pp. 117–18

CHARLES HORTON COOLEY used the term **looking-glass self** to explain that we see ourselves as we imagine others see us.

p. 119

ERIK H. ERIKSON identified challenges that individuals face at each stage of life from infancy to old age.

pp. 120–21

id (p. 115) Freud's term for the human being's basic drives

ego (p. 115) Freud's term for a person's conscious efforts to balance innate pleasure-seeking drives with the demands of society

superego (p. 115) Freud's term for the cultural values and norms internalized by an individual

sensorimotor stage (p. 116) Piaget's term for the level of human development at which individuals experience the world only through their senses

preoperational stage (p. 116) Piaget's term for the level of human development at which individuals first use language and other symbols

concrete operational stage (p. 116) Piaget's term for the level of human development at which individuals first see causal connections in their surroundings

formal operational stage (p. 116) Piaget's term for the level of human development at which individuals think abstractly and critically

self (p. 118) George Herbert Mead's term for the part of an individual's personality composed of self-awareness and self-image

looking-glass self (p. 119) Cooley's term for a self-image based on how we think others see us

significant others (p. 119) people, such as parents, who have special importance for socialization

generalized other (p. 119) George Herbert Mead's term for widespread cultural norms and values we use as references in evaluating ourselves

Agents of Socialization

The **FAMILY** is usually the first setting of socialization.
- Family has the greatest impact on attitudes and behavior.
- A family's social position, including race and social class, shapes a child's personality.
- Ideas about gender are learned first in the family.

`pp. 121–22`

SCHOOLS give most children their first experience with bureaucracy and impersonal evaluation.
- Schools teach knowledge and skills needed for later life.
- Schools expose children to greater social diversity.
- Schools reinforce ideas about gender.

`pp. 122–23`

peer group (p. 123) a social group whose members have interests, social position, and age in common

anticipatory socialization (p. 123) learning that helps a person achieve a desired position

mass media (p. 123) the means for delivering impersonal communications to a vast audience

The **PEER GROUP** helps shape attitudes and behavior.
- The peer group takes on great importance during adolescence.
- The peer group frees young people from adult supervision.

`p. 123`

The **MASS MEDIA** have a huge impact on socialization in modern, high-income societies.
- The average U.S. child spends as much time watching television and videos as attending school and interacting with parents.
- The mass media often reinforce stereotypes about gender and race.
- The mass media expose people to a great deal of violence.

`pp. 123–25`

Socialization and the Life Course

The concept of **CHILDHOOD** is grounded not in biology but in culture. In high-income countries, childhood is extended.

`pp. 125–26`

The emotional and social turmoil of **ADOLESCENCE** results from cultural inconsistency in defining people who are not children but not yet adults. Adolescence varies by social class position.

`p. 127`

cohort (p. 130) a category of people with something in common, usually their age

ADULTHOOD is the stage of life when most accomplishments take place. Although personality is now formed, it continues to change with new life experiences.

`p. 128`

OLD AGE is defined as much by culture as biology.
- Traditional societies give power and respect to elders.
- Industrial societies define elders as unimportant and out of touch.

`pp. 128–29`

Acceptance of **DEATH AND DYING** is part of socialization for the elderly. This process typically involves five stages: denial, anger, negotiation, resignation, and acceptance.

`pp. 129–30`

✓ Every stage of life is socially constructed in ways that vary from society to society (p. 130).

Total Institutions

TOTAL INSTITUTIONS include prisons, mental hospitals, and monasteries.
- Staff members supervise all aspects of life.
- Life is standardized, with all inmates following set rules and routines.

`pp. 130–31`

RESOCIALIZATION is a two-part process:
- breaking down inmates' existing identity
- building a new self through a system of rewards and punishments

`pp. 130–31`

total institution (p. 130) a setting in which people are isolated from the rest of society and manipulated by an administrative staff

resocialization (p. 130) radically changing an inmate's personality by carefully controlling the environment

Sociology points to the many rules that guide behavior in everyday situations. The more we learn about the rules of social interaction, the better we can play the game.

CHAPTER 6

Social Interaction in Everyday Life

SUPPLEMENTS: An outline of Chapter 6, as well as supplemental lecture material and topics for class discussion, can be found in the *Instructor's Manual*. Or use the visual summary on pages 158–59 as a set of lecture notes.

NOTE: Statuses sometimes have differing consequences for social identity. Consider introducing the concept of status consistency—the degree of consistency in social ranking—discussed in Chapter 11 ("Social Class in the United States").

CHAPTER OVERVIEW

This chapter takes a "micro-level" look at society, examining patterns of everyday social interaction. First, the chapter identifies important social structures, including status and role. Then it explains how we construct reality in social interaction. Finally, it applies the lessons learned to three everyday experiences: emotion, gender, and humor.

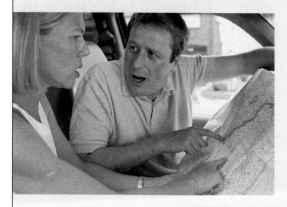

Harold and Sybil are on their way to another couple's home in an unfamiliar area near Fort Lauderdale, Florida. For the last twenty minutes, as Sybil sees it, they have been driving in circles, searching in vain for Coconut Palm Road.

"Look, Harold," says Sybil. "There are some people up ahead. Let's ask for directions."

Harold, gripping the wheel ever more tightly, begins muttering under his breath. "I know where I am. I don't want to waste time talking to strangers. Just let me get us there."

"I'm sure you know where you are, Harold," Sybil responds, looking straight ahead. "But I don't think you know where you're going."

Harold and Sybil are lost in more ways than one: Not only can't they find where their friends live, but they also cannot understand why they are growing angrier with each other with each passing minute.

What's going on? Like most men, Harold cannot stand getting lost. The longer he drives around, the more incompetent he feels. Sybil can't understand why Harold doesn't pull over to ask someone the way to Coconut Palm Road. If she were driving, she thinks to herself, they would already be comfortably settled in with their friends.

Why don't men like to ask for directions? Because men value their independence, they are uncomfortable asking for any type of help and are reluctant to accept it. To ask another person for assistance is the same as saying, "You know something I don't know." If it takes Harold a few more minutes to find Coconut Palm Road on his own—and to keep his sense of being in control—he thinks that's the way to go.

Women are more in tune with others and strive for connectedness. From Sybil's point of view, asking for help is right because sharing information builds social bonds and at the same time gets the job done. Asking for directions seems as natural to her as searching on his own is to Harold. Obviously, getting lost is sure to create conflict for Harold and Sybil as long as neither one understands the other's point of view.

Such everyday social patterns are the focus of this chapter. The central concept is **social interaction,** *the process by which people act and react in relation to others.* We begin by presenting the rules and building blocks of everyday experience and then explore the almost magical way in which face-to-face interaction creates the reality in which we live.

Social Structure: A Guide to Everyday Living

October 21, Ho Chi Minh City, Vietnam. This morning we leave the ship and make our way along the docks toward the center of Ho Chi Minh City, known to an earlier generation as Saigon. The government security officers wave us through the heavy metal gates. Pressed against the fence are dozens of men who operate cyclos (bicycles with small carriages attached to the front), the Vietnamese version of taxicabs. We wave them off and spend the next twenty minutes shaking our heads at several drivers who pedal alongside, pleading for our business. The pressure is uncomfortable. We decide to cross the street but realize suddenly that there are no stop signs or signal lights—and the street is an unbroken stream of bicycles, cyclos, motorbikes, and small trucks. The locals don't bat an eye; they just walk at a steady pace across the street, parting waves of vehicles that immediately close in again behind them. Walk right into traffic? With our small children on our backs? Yup, we did it; that's the way it works in Vietnam.

Q: "It is crucial that responsibilities, resources, and rights be assigned to statuses, not to particular individuals. For only by doing so can societies establish general and uniform rules or norms that will apply to many and diverse individuals who are to occupy the statuses." Melvin Tumin (1985:21)

NOTE: Although some statuses are "ascribed," they are still socially constructed in that a society must define them as relevant.

NOTE: "Status" has two Latin roots that combine to mean, literally, "the use of standing." The term "role" is derived from the French word *rôle*, meaning the page of a scroll that contains an actor's part.

social interaction the process by which people act and react in relation to others

status a social position that a person holds

ascribed status a social position a person receives at birth or takes on involuntarily later in life

achieved status a social position a person takes on voluntarily that reflects personal ability and effort

status set all the statuses a person holds at a given time

master status a status that has special importance for social identity, often shaping a person's entire life

Members of every society rely on social structure to make sense of everyday situations. As our family's introduction to the busy streets of Vietnam suggests, the world can be confusing, even frightening, when society's rules are unclear. Let's take a closer look at the ways in which societies set the rules of everyday life.

Status

In every society, people build their everyday lives using the idea of **status**, *a social position that a person holds*. In everyday use, the word *status* generally means "prestige," as when we say that a college president has more "status" than a newly hired assistant professor. But sociologically speaking, both "president" and "professor" are statuses, or positions, within the collegiate organization.

Status is part of our social identity and helps define our relationship to others. As Georg Simmel (1950:307, orig. 1902), one of the founders of sociology, once pointed out, before we can deal with anyone, we need to know who the person is.

Status Set

Each of us holds many statuses at once. The term **status set** refers to *all the statuses a person holds at a given time*. A teenage girl may be a daughter to her parents, a sister to her brother, a student at her school, and a goalie on her soccer team.

Status sets change over the life course. A child grows up to become a parent, a student graduates to become a lawyer, and a single person marries to become a husband or wife, sometimes becoming single again as a result of death or divorce. Joining an organization or finding a job enlarges our status set; withdrawing from activities makes it smaller. Over a lifetime, people gain and lose dozens of statuses.

Ascribed and Achieved Status

Sociologists classify statuses in terms of how people attain them. An **ascribed status** is *a social position a person receives at birth or takes on involuntarily later in life*. Examples of ascribed statuses include being a daughter, a Cuban, a teenager, or a widower. Ascribed statuses are matters about which we have little or no choice.

By contrast, an **achieved status** refers to *a social position a person takes on voluntarily that reflects personal ability and effort*. Achieved statuses in the United States include honors student, Olympic athlete, nurse, software writer, and thief.

In the real world, of course, most statuses involve a combination of ascription and achievement. That is, people's ascribed statuses influence the statuses they achieve. People who achieve the status of lawyer, for example, are likely to share the ascribed benefit of being born into relatively well-off families. By the same token,

In any rigidly ranked setting, no interaction can proceed until people assess each other's social standing. For this reason, military personnel wear insignia, clear symbols of their level of authority. Don't we size people up in much the same way in routine interactions, noting a person's approximate age, quality of clothing, and manner for clues about social position?

many less desirable statuses, such as criminal, drug addict, or unemployed worker, are more easily achieved by people born into poverty.

Master Status

Some statuses matter more than others. A **master status** is *a status that has special importance for social identity, often shaping a person's entire life*. For most people, a job is a master status because it reveals a great deal about social background, education, and income. In a few cases, name is a master status; being in the Bush or Kennedy family attracts attention and creates opportunities.

A master status can be negative as well as positive. Take, for example, serious illness. Sometimes people, even longtime friends, avoid cancer patients or people with AIDS because of their illnesses. As another example, the fact that all societies limit the opportunities of women makes gender a master status.

Sometimes a physical disability serves as a master status to the point where we dehumanize people by seeing them only in terms of their disability. The Thinking About Diversity box on page 140 shows how.

DISCUSS: Ask students to identify potential role sets linked to the statuses of college student, public school teacher, member of the military, and U.S. senator.

Q: "Status and role serve to reduce the ideal patterns for social life to individual terms." Ralph Linton (1937b:114)

GLOBAL: Typically, members of high-income societies have larger status sets than people in traditional countries for whom kinship represents the core of social organization.

DISCUSS: Can you provide examples from your own life of the process of "becoming an ex"?

SEEING SOCIOLOGY
in Everyday Life

Make a list of ten important statuses in your own life. Indicate whether each one is ascribed or achieved. Is this sometimes difficult to do? Why?

MAKING THE GRADE

Remember that *status* refers to a social position and *role* refers to behavior. We *hold* a status and *perform* a role.

THINKING ABOUT DIVERSITY: RACE, CLASS, & GENDER

Physical Disability as a Master Status

Physical disability works in much the same ways as class, gender, or race in defining people in the eyes of others. In the following interviews, two women explain how a physical disability can become a master status—a trait that overshadows everything else about them. The first voice is that of twenty-nine-year-old Donna Finch, who lives with her husband and son in Muskogee, Oklahoma, and holds a master's degree in social work. She is also blind.

> Most people don't expect handicapped people to grow up; they are always supposed to be children. . . . You aren't supposed to date, you aren't supposed to have a job, somehow you're just supposed to disappear. I'm not saying this is true of anyone else, but in my own case I think I was more intellectually mature than most children, and more emotionally immature. I'd say that not until the last four or five years have I felt really whole.

Rose Helman is an elderly woman who has retired and lives near New York City. She suffers from spinal meningitis and is also blind.

> You ask me if people are really different today than in the '20s and '30s. Not too much. They

Modern technology means that most soldiers who lose limbs in war now survive. How do you think the loss of an arm or a leg affects a person's social identity and sense of self?

are still fearful of the handicapped. I don't know if *fearful* is the right word, but uncomfortable at least. But I can understand it somewhat; it happened to me. I once asked a man to tell me which staircase to use to get from the subway out to the street. He started giving me directions that were confusing, and I said, "Do you mind taking me?" He said, "Not at all." He grabbed me on the side with my dog on it, so I asked him to take my other arm. And he said, "I'm sorry, I have no other arm." And I said, "That's all right, I'll hold onto the jacket." It felt funny hanging onto the sleeve without the arm in it.

WHAT DO YOU THINK?

1. Have you ever had a disease or disability that became a master status? If so, how did others react?

2. How might such a master status affect someone's personality?

3. Can being very fat or very thin serve as a master status? Why or why not?

Source: Based on Orlansky & Heward (1981).

Role

A second important social structure is **role,** *behavior expected of someone who holds a particular status.* A person *holds* a status and *performs* a role (Linton, 1937b). For example, holding the status of student leads you to perform the role of attending classes and completing assignments.

Both statuses and roles vary by culture. In the United States, the status of "uncle" refers to the brother of a mother or a father. In Vietnam, the word for "uncle" is different on the mother's and father's sides of the family, and the two men have different responsibilities. In every society, actual role performance varies with an individual's unique personality, and some societies permit more individual expression of a role than others.

Role Set

Because we hold many statuses at once—a status set—everyday life is a mix of many roles. Robert Merton (1968) introduced the term **role set** to identify *a number of roles attached to a single status.*

Figure 6–1 shows four statuses of one person, each status linked to a different role set. First, as a professor, this woman interacts with students (the teacher role) and with other academics (the colleague role). Second, in her work as a researcher, she gathers and analyzes data (the fieldwork role) that she uses in her publications (the author role). Third, the woman occupies the status of "wife," with a marital role (such as confidante and sexual partner) toward her husband, with whom she shares household duties (domestic role). Fourth, she holds the status of "mother," with routine responsibilities for her children (the maternal role), as well as toward their school and other organizations in her community (the civic role).

A global perspective shows that the roles people use to define their lives differ from society to society. In low-income countries, people spend fewer years as students, and family roles are often very important to social identity. In high-income nations, people spend more years as students, and family roles are typically less important to social identity. Another dimension of difference involves house-

DISCUSS: Would role conflict exist if people had unlimited time, energy, and other resources?

NOTE: Barbara Laslett (1978) points out that role conflict and role strain were probably more pronounced in the Middle Ages than they are today because parents not only raised children but also produced their food, schooled them, guided their worship, and saw to their health.

Q: "For some types of role exit, society has coined a term to denote exiters: divorcé, retiree, recovered alcoholic, widow, alumnus. This is usually the case for exits that are common and have been occurring for a long time. . . . In addition to these institutionalized exits, however, there are numerous exits that are simply referred to with the prefix 'ex': ex-doctor, ex-executive, ex-nun, ex-convict." Helen Rose Fuchs Ebaugh (1988:1)

role behavior expected of someone who holds a particular status

role set a number of roles attached to a single status

role conflict conflict among the roles connected to two or more statuses

role strain tension among the roles connected to a single status

SEEING SOCIOLOGY
in Everyday Life

Give one example of role conflict and one example of role strain in your own life.

work. As Global Map 6–1 on page 142 shows, especially in poor countries, housework falls heavily on women.

Role Conflict and Role Strain

People in modern, high-income nations juggle many responsibilities demanded by their various statuses and roles. As most mothers (and more and more fathers) can testify, the combination of parenting and working outside the home is physically and emotionally draining. Sociologists thus recognize **role conflict** as *conflict among the roles connected to two or more statuses.*

We experience role conflict when we find ourselves pulled in various directions as we try to respond to the many statuses we hold. One response to role conflict is deciding that "something has to go." More than one politician, for example, has decided not to run for office because of the conflicting demands of a hectic campaign schedule and family life. In other cases, people put off having children in order to stay on the "fast track" for career success.

Even roles linked to a single status may make competing demands on us. **Role strain** refers to *tension among the roles connected to a single status.* A college professor may enjoy being friendly with students. At the same time, however, the professor must maintain the personal distance needed to evaluate students fairly. In short, performing the various roles attached to even one status can be something of a balancing act.

One strategy for minimizing role conflict is separating parts of our lives so that we perform roles for one status at one time and place and carry out roles connected to another status in a completely different setting. A familiar example of this idea is deciding to "leave the job at work" before heading home to the family.

Role Exit

After she left the life of a Catholic nun to become a university sociologist, Helen Rose Fuchs Ebaugh began to study her own experience of *role exit,* the process by which people disengage from important social roles. Studying a range of "exes," including ex-nuns, ex-doctors, ex-husbands, and ex-alcoholics, Ebaugh identified elements common to the process of becoming an "ex."

According to Ebaugh (1988), the process begins as people come to doubt their ability to continue in a certain role. As they imagine alternative roles, they ultimately reach a tipping point when they decide to pursue a new life. Even as they are moving on, however, a past role can continue to influence their lives. Exes carry with them a self-image shaped by an earlier role, which can interfere with building a new sense of self. For example, an ex-nun may hesitate to wear stylish clothing and makeup.

Exes must also rebuild relationships with people who knew them in their earlier life. Learning new social skills is another challenge. For

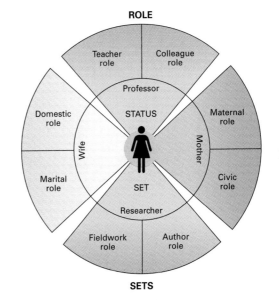

ROLE

STATUS

SET

SETS

FIGURE 6–1 **Status Set and Role Sets**

A status set includes all the statuses a person holds at a given time. The status set defines *who we are* in society. The many roles linked to each status define *what we do*.

example, Ebaugh reports, ex-nuns who enter the dating scene after decades in the church are often surprised to learn that sexual norms are very different from those they knew when they were teenagers.

The Social Construction of Reality

In 1917, the Italian playwright Luigi Pirandello wrote a play called *The Pleasure of Honesty* about a character named Angelo Baldovino, a brilliant man with a checkered past. Baldovino enters the fashionable home of the Renni family and introduces himself in a peculiar way:

> Inevitably we construct ourselves. Let me explain. I enter this house and immediately I become what I have to become, what I can become: I construct myself. That is, I present myself to you in a form suitable to the relationship I wish to achieve with you. And, of course, you do the same with me. (1962:157–58)

Baldovino suggests that although behavior is guided by status and role, we have the ability to shape who we are and to guide what happens from moment to moment. In other words, "reality" is not as fixed as we may think.

DISCUSS: The words we choose are one way we "spin," or construct, reality. Ask the class to consider the ramifications of using two similar phrases, "people of color" and "colored people." Other terms that "spin" reality in different ways: "unemployed" vs. "between jobs"; "sexually active" vs. "promiscuous"; "broken family" vs. "one-parent household"; "ladies" vs. "women"; "handicapped children" vs. "exceptional children."

Q: "When I use a word, it means just what I choose it to mean—nothing more nor less." Humpty-Dumpty

NOTE: Companies spin language to suggest value. With a price of many thousands of dollars, Rolex cannot call its product simply a "watch." Therefore, it sells an "Oyster Perpetual Superlative Chronometer Officially Certified Cosmograph."

Q: "... that depends on what the meaning of 'is' is ..." Bill Clinton

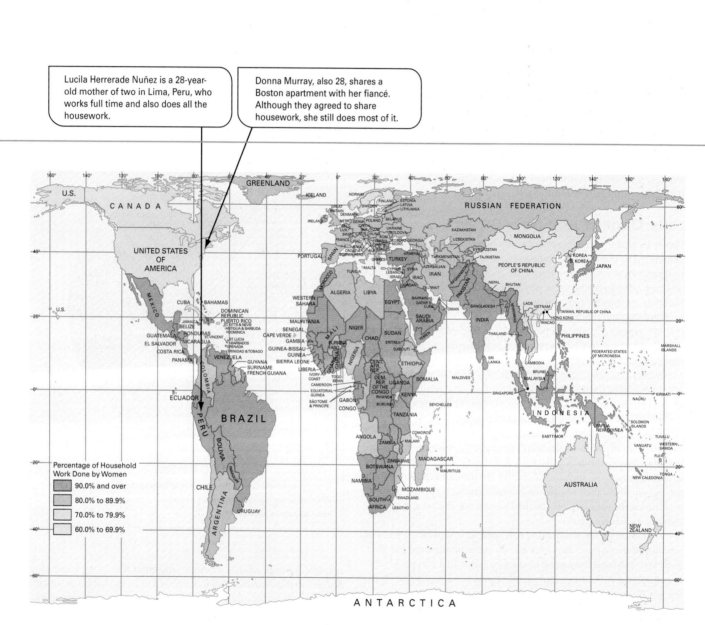

Lucila Herrerade Nuñez is a 28-year-old mother of two in Lima, Peru, who works full time and also does all the housework.

Donna Murray, also 28, shares a Boston apartment with her fiancé. Although they agreed to share housework, she still does most of it.

Percentage of Household Work Done by Women

90.0% and over
80.0% to 89.9%
70.0% to 79.9%
60.0% to 69.9%

Window on the World

GLOBAL MAP 6–1   Housework in Global Perspective

Throughout the world, housework is a major part of women's routines and identities. This is especially true in poor nations of Latin America, Africa, and Asia, where the social position of women is far below that of men. But our society also defines housework and child care as "feminine" activities, even though women and men have the same legal rights and most women work outside the home.

Source: *Peters Atlas of the World* (1990); updated by the author.

142

The **social construction of reality** is *the process by which people creatively shape reality through social interaction.* This idea is the foundation of the symbolic-interaction approach, described in Chapter 1 ("The Sociological Perspective"). As Baldovino's remark suggests, quite a bit of "reality" remains unclear in everyone's mind, especially in unfamiliar situations. So we present ourselves in terms that suit the setting and our purposes, we try to guide what happens next, and as others do the same, reality takes shape. The Seeing Sociology in Everyday Life box on page 144 looks at how this happens on the Internet at the popular Web site "Second Life."

Social interaction, then, is a complex negotiation that builds reality. Most everyday situations involve at least some agreement about what's going on. But how people see events depends on their different backgrounds, interests, and intentions.

NOTE: Another way companies spin language to create value in their ads: Most cars are "bought," but very expensive automobiles are "acquired."

DISCUSS: Read the selection on this page from Piri Thomas's book. Can you think of a personal experience in which you were able to "spin" reality in a clever way? Explain how.

NOTE: Garfinkel's approach runs most directly counter to that of Talcott Parsons.

NOTE: Ethnomethodology has roots not only in symbolic interaction but also in Alfred Schutz's phenomenology. Moreover, it shares with Berger and Luckmann's work an interest in the everyday round of life, not just a society's grand values or political ideologies.

social construction of reality the process by which people creatively shape reality through social interaction

Thomas theorem W. I. Thomas's claim that situations defined as real are real in their consequences

ethnomethodology Harold Garfinkel's term for the study of the way people make sense of their everyday surroundings

 MAKING THE GRADE

"Ethnomethodology" is a long word for an easy idea: To test people's assumptions about everyday life's rules, try breaking them and observe people's reactions.

"Street Smarts"

What people commonly call "street smarts" is actually a form of constructing reality. In his autobiography *Down These Mean Streets,* Piri Thomas recalls moving to an apartment in Spanish Harlem. Returning home one evening, young Piri found himself cut off by Waneko, the leader of the local street gang, who was flanked by a dozen others.

> "Whatta ya say, Mr. Johnny Gringo," drawled Waneko.
> *Think man,* I told myself, *think your way out of a stomping. Make it good.* "I hear you 104th Street coolies are supposed to have heart," I said. "I don't know this for sure. You know there's a lot of streets where a whole 'click' is made out of punks who can't fight one guy unless they all jump him for the stomp." I hoped this would push Waneko into giving me a fair one. His expression didn't change.
> "Maybe we don't look at it that way."
> *Crazy, man,* I cheer inwardly, *the cabron is falling into my setup....* "I wasn't talking to you," I said. "Where I come from, the pres is president 'cause he got heart when it comes to dealing."
> Waneko was starting to look uneasy. He had bit on my worm and felt like a sucker fish. His boys were now light on me. They were no longer so much interested in stomping me as seeing the outcome between Waneko and me. "Yeah," was his reply. . . .
> I knew I'd won. Sure, I'd have to fight; but one guy, not ten or fifteen. If I lost, I might still get stomped, and if I won I might get stomped. I took care of this with my next sentence. "I don't know you or your boys," I said, "but they look cool to me. They don't feature as punks."
> I had left him out purposely when I said "they." Now his boys were in a separate class. I had cut him off. He would have to fight me on his own, to prove his heart to himself, to his boys, and most important, to his turf. He got away from the stoop and asked, "Fair one, Gringo?" (1967:56–57)

This situation reveals the drama—sometimes subtle, sometimes savage—by which human beings creatively build reality. But of course, not everyone enters a situation with equal standing. If a police officer had happened to drive by when Piri and Waneko were fighting, both young men might have ended up in jail.

The Thomas Theorem

By displaying his wits and fighting with Waneko until they both tired, Piri Thomas won acceptance by the gang. What took place that evening in Spanish Harlem is an example of the **Thomas theorem,** named after W. I. Thomas (1966:301, orig. 1931): *Situations that are defined as real are real in their consequences.*

Applied to social interaction, the Thomas theorem means that although reality is initially "soft" as it is being shaped, it can become "hard" in its effects. In the case just described, local gang members saw Piri Thomas act in a worthy way, so in their eyes, he *became* worthy.

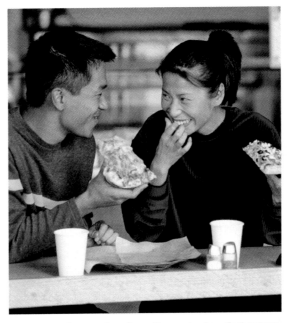

Flirting is an everyday experience in reality construction. Each person offers information to the other and hints at romantic interest. Yet the interaction proceeds with a tentative and often humorous air so that either individual can withdraw at any time without further obligation.

Ethnomethodology

Most of the time, we take social reality for granted. To become more aware of the world we help create, Harold Garfinkel (1967) devised **ethnomethodology,** *the study of the way people make sense of their everyday surroundings.* This approach begins by pointing out that everyday behavior rests on a number of assumptions. When you ask someone the simple question "How are you?" you usually want to know how the person is doing in general, but you might really be wondering how the person is dealing with a specific physical, mental, spiritual, or financial challenge. However, the person being asked probably assumes that you are not really interested in details about any of these things, that you are just "being polite."

One good way to discover the assumptions we make about reality is to break the rules. For example, the next time someone greets you by saying, "How are you?" offer details from your last physical examination or explain all the good and bad things that have happened since you woke up that morning and see how the person reacts.

The results are predictable, because we all have some idea of the "rules" of everyday interaction. The person will most likely become confused or irritated by your unexpected behavior—a reaction that

DIVERSITY: Illustrating the power of language to define reality: The term *homophobe* (Weinberg, 1973) literally means "fear of sameness." The political character of the term lies in the fact that it defines as abnormal not homosexuality but people who condemn it. The term also transforms attitudes toward sexuality from a moral issue (of right and wrong) to a psychological issue of fear (that is, of sickness and health).

NOTE: Erving Goffman avoided being photographed. This allowed him to remain essentially anonymous in public settings.

RESOURCE: Erving Goffman's essay "The Presentation of Self" is among the classic selections included in the companion reader *Seeing Ourselves*, 8th ed.

NOTE: The words "person" and "mask" are derived from a single root, the Latin word *persona*. Perhaps the ancients well understood Goffman's insights.

SEEING SOCIOLOGY
in Everyday Life

Have you used Internet sites such as MySpace, Xanga, Facebook, or YouTube to "present" yourself to others? How "real" are these constructed realities?

SEEING SOCIOLOGY IN EVERYDAY LIFE

Performances Online? Visit "Second Life"!

A small group of young people gathers outside the Straight Talk Café to discuss the Obama administration's economic bailout program. Sophie Yates is explaining her position, "Look, all they're doing is throwing money at the people who caused the problem in the first place." Another young woman, Auryn Karu, reacts quickly. "Well, at least they're doing something. We've got to do something big and do something now to turn this country around."

This event might have played out on any college campus from New York to Los Angeles, but it actually happened nowhere at all—at least nowhere in the real world. This bit of nonreality took place in an outdoor park that is part of Second Life, the virtual world accessed through the Web site http://secondlife.com.

Invented in 2003 by Linden Research, Inc., Second Life has become a popular Web destination that has been visited by as many as 10 million people around the world. If there is anything the visitors to Second Life have in common (other than their speedy connections and very good graphics cards), it is that they tend to be creative people looking for something different from their ordinary lives.

Experiencing something new is exactly the point of Second Life, according to its inventors. Residents of this computer universe can turn loose their imagination and creativity in surroundings "teeming with people, entertainment, experiences, and opportunity."

Second Life allows you to put many of the concepts described in this chapter into action. First, to become a "resident" in the world of Second Life, you need to construct an identity. Your character is called an "avatar," which you create as you decide to be female or male (or both) and design every feature of your "body" from height to hair color, from the contours of your hips to the color of your skin. (That is, assuming you want a "humanoid" appearance at all—anything is possible, and the options are limited only by your imagination.) This virtual world contains people who look rich, poor, attractive, even scary. Whatever you can dream up becomes real in this unreal world.

Having constructed your identity, you can interact with the million or so other avatars who inhabit this virtual world at any given time. Select a setting by looking at events that are going on, and walk, skate, ride, or teleport to whatever activity interests you. There are shopping malls, dance halls, classroom lectures, open-air concerts, quiet beaches for walking, and pulsating clubs for dancing. You can choose to go to a strip club on Saturday night or attend a church service on Sunday morning. Many companies are open for business, and several real-life countries have even set up virtual embassies on the site. Volunteers for both presidential candidates actually set up campaign headquarters in Second Life, and thousands of people spent the election night in this virtual world to await the results of the voting.

Whatever your interest, once you arrive at an event, you walk up to someone (or are prepared to have someone walk up to you). As the avatars interact, "reality" is constructed. As in any society, rules guide behavior (for example, Second Life has recently banned gambling). Also as in real life, you can evaluate your own actions by seeing how others respond to what you say or do. It is not far from the truth to say that Second Life is a laboratory in which you can study many of the elements of social interaction.

Just as in the real world, many of the activities in Second Life cost money. The currency of this virtual society is Linden dollars, which can be purchased for "real" money (have your credit card ready). You can buy and sell property or services, making money or going broke in the process.

Virtual reality sites such as Second Life are gaining in popularity because they allow us to be or do what we have always dreamed about. Put another way, if you don't find everything you need in your real life (RL, for short), try a second life (SL) online. But the experience may not be quite what you would hope. For one thing, researchers who have begun studying Second Life report that the identities and behavior that people create turn out to be not so very different from those of the real world. In addition, some regular visitors to Second Life report that the experience can be lonely, raising questions about how satisfying virtual interaction is compared to the real thing.

WHAT DO YOU THINK?

1. Have you ever visited Second Life? If so, what did you like about the experience? What did you not enjoy?

2. Some analysts claim that Web sites like this one are the future of entertainment because, while television turns people into a passive audience, sites such as Second Life make people active participants. Do you agree or not? Why?

3. If you were to create an online identity, in what ways would it be like your real-life identity? How would it be different? Why?

Sources: Gross (2006), Itzkoff (2007), Lagorio (2007), and Lang (2008).

DIVERSITY: The Chinese American novelist Bette Bao Lord explains that as an Asian American child in Brooklyn, she reconstructed the Pledge of Allegiance in the following way: "I pledge allegiance to the frog of the United States of America. And to the wee puppet for witch's hands. One Asian, in the vestibule, with little tea and just rice for all."

NOTE: Personal interaction usually starts off with "small talk," in which little is at stake. Only once sufficient information has been exchanged to guide more substantial discussion does "big talk" begin.

GLOBAL: Members of modern societies are more attuned to performances because our lives are divided into many spheres, each with different expectations. People in traditional societies, by contrast, have a more coherent identity.

● SEEING SOCIOLOGY
in Everyday Life

Members of every culture have rules about how close people should stand while talking. To see what the rules are in your social world, during a conversation, slowly move closer and closer to the other person and see what happens.

dramaturgical analysis Erving Goffman's term for the study of social interaction in terms of theatrical performance

presentation of self Erving Goffman's term for a person's efforts to create specific impressions in the minds of others

helps us see not only what the rules are but also how important they are to everyday reality.

Reality Building: Class and Culture

People do not build everyday experience out of thin air. In part, how we act or what we see in our surroundings depends on our interests. Gazing at the sky on a starry night, for example, lovers discover romance, and scientists see hydrogen atoms fusing into helium. Social background also affects what we see, which is why residents of Spanish Harlem experience a different world than people living on Manhattan's pricey Upper East Side.

In global perspective, reality construction varies even more. Consider these everyday situations: People waiting for a bus in London typically "queue up" in a straight line; people in New York are rarely so orderly. The law forbids women in Saudi Arabia to drive cars, a ban unthinkable in the United States. In this country, people assume that "a short walk" means a few blocks or a few minutes; in the Andes Mountains of Peru, this same phrase means a few miles.

The point is that people build reality from the surrounding culture. Chapter 3 ("Culture") explains how people the world over find different meanings in specific gestures, so inexperienced travelers can find themselves building an unexpected and unwelcome reality. Similarly, in a study of popular culture, JoEllen Shively (1992) screened western films to men of European descent and to Native American men. The men in both categories claimed to enjoy the films, but for very different reasons. White men interpreted the films as praising rugged people striking out for the West and conquering the forces of nature. Native American men saw in the same films a celebration of land and nature. Given their different cultures, it is as if people in the two categories saw two different films.

Films also have an effect on the reality we all experience. The 2007 film *Away from Her,* for example, about a woman experiencing the devastation of Alzheimer's disease, is one of a series of recent films that have changed people's awareness of the struggle of coping with serious illness for individuals and their family members.

Dramaturgical Analysis: The "Presentation of Self"

Erving Goffman (1922–1982) was another sociologist who analyzed social interaction, explaining that people live their lives much like actors performing on a stage. If we imagine ourselves as directors

People build reality from their surrounding culture. Yet because cultural systems are marked by diversity and even outright conflict, reality construction always involves tensions and choices. Turkey is a nation with a mostly Muslim population, but it has also embraced Western culture. Here, women confront starkly different definitions of what is "feminine." Staton R. Winter, *The New York Times.*

observing what goes on in the theater of everyday life, we are doing what Goffman called **dramaturgical analysis,** *the study of social interaction in terms of theatrical performance.*

Dramaturgical analysis offers a fresh look at the concepts of status and role. A status is like a part in a play, and a role serves as a script, supplying dialogue and action for the characters. Goffman described each individual's "performance" as the **presentation of self,** *a person's efforts to create specific impressions in the minds of others.* This process, sometimes called *impression management,* begins with the idea of personal performance (Goffman, 1959, 1967).

Performances

As we present ourselves in everyday situations, we reveal information to others both consciously and unconsciously. Our performance includes the way we dress (in theatrical terms, our costume), the objects we carry (props), and our tone of voice and gestures (our demeanor). In addition, we vary our performance according to where we are (the set). We may joke loudly in a restaurant, for example, but lower our voice when entering a church or a temple. People design settings, such as homes or offices, to bring about desired reactions in others.

Seeing SOCIOLOGY in the NEWS

The New York Times

Putting Your Best Cyberface Forward

BY STEPHANIE ROSENBLOOM
January 3, 2008

Do you bite your nails? Have you pierced your tongue? Is your tote bag emblazoned with the words "I'm not a plastic bag"?

People look and act the way they do for reasons too numerous to fit into any therapist's notebook. Yet we commonly shape our behavior or tweak our appearance in an attempt to control how others perceive us.

Some call it common sense. Social scientists call it "impression management" and attribute much of their understanding of the process to the sociologist Erving Goffman, who in a 1959 book, *The Presentation of Self in Everyday Life*, likened human interactions to a theatrical performance.

Now that first impressions are often made in cyberspace, not face-to-face, people are not only strategizing about how to virtually convey who they are, but are also grappling with how to craft an e-version of themselves that appeals to multiple audiences—co-workers, fraternity brothers, Mom and Dad.

"Which image do you present?" asked Mark R. Leary, a professor of psychology and neuroscience at Duke, who has been studying impression management in the real world for more than 20 years. . . .

People, of course, have been electronically styling themselves for as long as there has been a Web to surf. But scholars say the mainstreaming of massive social networking and dating sites, which make it easy to publicly share one's likes, dislikes, dreams and losses, . . . is prompting more people to "perform" for one another in increasingly sophisticated ways. . . .

Many of the self-presentation strategies observed by scholars will seem obvious to experienced Internet users: improving one's standing by linking to high status friends; using a screen name like "Batman" or "007" when in reality one is more like Austin Powers; referring to one's gleaming head as "shaved" not "bald"; using cutesy emoticons to charm the demographic that forwards inspirational chain mail; demonstrating leadership by being the first to adopt and turn others onto the latest Facebook applications; listing one's almost-career as a D.J. or model rather than the one that pays the bills; making calculated decisions about what to list as interests or favorite books. . . .

In one study of online dating, professors at Rutgers, Georgetown and Michigan State found that in the absence of visual and oral cues, single people develop their own presentational tactics: monitoring the length of their e-mail messages (too wordy equals too desperate); limiting the times during which they send messages (a male subject learned that writing to women in the wee hours makes them uncomfortable); and noting the day they last logged on (users who visit the site too infrequently may be deemed unavailable or, worse, undesirable).

The scholars found it common for online daters to fudge their age or weight, or to post photographs that were five years old. . . .

In general, scholars do not think of impression management as an intentionally deceptive

Performing for an audience is not limited to face-to-face interaction. Seeing Sociology in the News takes a close look at how people use Web sites such as Facebook.com to construct the "self" they present to others.

An Application: The Doctor's Office

Consider how physicians set up their offices to convey particular information to an audience of patients. The fact that medical doctors enjoy high prestige and power in the United States is clear upon entering a doctor's office. First, the doctor is nowhere to be seen. Instead, in what Goffman describes as the "front region" of the setting, the patient encounters a receptionist, or gatekeeper, who decides whether and when the patient can meet the doctor. A simple glance around the doctor's waiting room, with patients (often impatiently) waiting to be invited into the inner sanctum, leaves little doubt that the doctor and the staff are in charge.

The "back region" is composed of the examination room plus the doctor's private office. Once inside the office, the patient can see a wide range of props, such as medical books and framed degrees, that give the impression that the doctor has the specialized knowledge necessary to call the shots. The doctor is usually seated behind a desk—the larger the desk, the greater the statement of power—and the patient is given only a chair.

The doctor's appearance and manner offer still more information. The white lab coat (costume) may have the practical function of keeping clothes from becoming dirty, but its social function is to let others know at a glance the physician's status. A stethoscope around the neck and a medical chart in hand (more props) have the same purpose. A doctor uses highly technical language that is often mystifying to the patient, again emphasizing that the doctor is in charge.

DISCUSS: Is hypocrisy really such a bad thing, or is some dishonesty necessary to civilized life? What would life be like if everyone agreed to tell the truth in all interactions?

DISCUSS: What techniques do people in public places (airport waiting area, bus station, or café) use to claim a certain space as their own?

or nefarious practice. It is more like social lubrication without a drink in your hand. . . . When people misrepresent themselves, it is often because they are attempting to express an idealized or future version of themselves—someone who is thinner or has actually finished Dante's *Inferno*.

"Everyone felt pretty strongly that they tried to be honest," said Jennifer Gibbs, one of the authors of the online dating study, . . . "They justified slight misrepresentations or distortions as trying to stand out," she said, adding that online and offline, people experience tension between telling the truth and showcasing themselves in the most flattering light. . . .

Scholars do suggest, though, that the photographs people post on the sites are about more than showing what individuals look like. Rather, members carefully choose photos to display aspects of their personalities. . . .

"I use photos that describe me," said Leonard Alonge, 44, a chef and actor in Delray Beach, Fla., who is a member of Facebook. "Photos of me in the kitchen, photos of me with friends. I use it to describe my personality: friendly, outgoing, nothing very explicit. I'm a pretty conservative person. I was raised in a Roman Catholic family."

Clare Richardson, 17, of Los Angeles, is applying to colleges and is therefore mindful of what she posts on Facebook, but she knows teenagers who "want to appear to be the partying type," she said. They post pictures that seem to prove it even if it is not true. "It's clear they're trying to impress everyone out there," Ms. Richardson said.

Keith N. Hampton, an assistant professor at the Annenberg School for Communication at the University of Pennsylvania, said the notion of impressing "everyone out there" is the fundamental problem of networking sites. They are designed so that millions see the same image of a member.

For online impression management to be effective, Mr. Hampton said, the sites should be redesigned to allow people to reveal different aspects of their identity to different users. You should be able to present one face to your boss, and another to your poker buddies. "We have very real reasons for wanting to segment our social network," he said.

WHAT DO YOU THINK?

1. If you have a page on Facebook or a similar Web site, in what ways do you selectively "present" yourself to others?

2. Is presenting ourselves to others in a selective way just "putting our best foot forward," or is it dishonest? Explain.

3. Can you give an example of how you would present a different performance to your boss, your parents, and your friends?

Finally, patients use the title "doctor," but they, in turn, are often addressed by their first names, which further shows the doctor's dominant position. The overall message of a doctor's performance is clear: "I will help you, but you must allow me to take charge."

Nonverbal Communication

The novelist William Sansom describes a fictional Mr. Preedy, an English vacationer on a beach in Spain:

> He took care to avoid catching anyone's eye. First, he had to make it clear to those potential companions of his holiday that they were of no concern to him whatsoever. He stared through them, round them, over them—eyes lost in space. The beach might have been empty. If by chance a ball was thrown his way, he looked surprised; then let a smile of amusement light his face (Kindly Preedy), looked around dazed to see that there were people on the beach, tossed it back with a smile to himself and not a smile *at* the people. . . .
> [He] then gathered together his beach-wrap and bag into a neat sand-resistant pile (Methodical and Sensible Preedy), rose slowly to stretch his huge frame (Big-Cat Preedy), and tossed aside his sandals (Carefree Preedy, after all). (1956:230–31)

Without saying a single word, Mr. Preedy offers a great deal of information about himself to anyone watching him. This is the process of **nonverbal communication,** *communication using body movements, gestures, and facial expressions rather than speech.*

People use many parts of the body to convey information through *body language.* Facial expressions are the most important type of body language. Smiling, for instance, shows pleasure, although we distinguish among the deliberate smile of Kindly Preedy on the beach, a spontaneous smile of joy at seeing a friend, a pained smile of embarrassment after spilling a cup of coffee, and the full, unrestrained smile of self-satisfaction we often associate with winning some important contest.

Eye contact is another key element of nonverbal communication. Generally, we use eye contact to invite social interaction. Someone across the room "catches our eye," sparking a conversation. Avoiding another's eyes, by contrast, discourages communication. Hands, too, speak for us. Common hand gestures in our society convey, among other things, an insult, a request for a ride, an invitation for someone to join us, or a demand that others stop in their tracks. Gestures also supplement spoken words. For example, pointing at someone in a threatening way gives greater emphasis to a word of warning, just as shrugging the shoulders adds an air of indifference to the phrase "I don't know" and rapidly waving the arms adds urgency to the single word "Hurry!"

Body Language and Deception

As any actor knows, it is very difficult to pull off a perfect performance. In everyday interaction, unintended body language can contradict our planned meaning: A teenage boy offers an explanation for getting home late, for example, but his mother begins to doubt his words because he avoids looking her in the eye. The teenage celebrity on a television talk

DISCUSS: In public settings, just as we expect a small amount of personal space, we also expect people to avoid private or personal discussion in the immediate presence of strangers. In recent years, the spread of cellular phones is changing this norm: In airports and on airplanes, for example, people seated right next to you often begin an audible personal conversation on the phone. How do students feel about such experiences?

Q: "If we never tried to seem a little better than we are, how could we improve or 'train ourselves from the outside inward'?" Charles Horton Cooley

DISCUSS: Ask students how faculty idealize their performances.

GLOBAL: Across North Africa, from Cairo to Casablanca, people routinely move to within a foot or two when speaking in public. U.S. travelers may consider such "in your face" behavior provocative.

● SEEING SOCIOLOGY
in Everyday Life

After reading the analysis of doctors' offices (pp. 146–47), try doing a similar analysis of the offices of several faculty members on your campus. What differences do you notice? How can you explain the patterns?

nonverbal communication (p. 147) communication using body movements, gestures, and facial expressions rather than speech

personal space the surrounding area over which a person makes some claim to privacy

show claims that her recent musical flop is "no big deal," but the nervous swing of her leg suggests otherwise. Because nonverbal communication is hard to control, it offers clues to deception, in much the same way that changes in breathing, pulse rate, perspiration, and blood pressure recorded on a lie detector indicate that a person is lying.

Detecting dishonest performances is difficult because no single bodily gesture tells us for sure that someone is lying. But because any performance involves so much body language, few people can lie without some slip-up, raising the suspicions of a careful observer. The key to detecting lies is to view the whole performance with an eye for inconsistencies.

Gender and Performances

Because women are socialized to respond to others, they tend to be more sensitive than men to nonverbal communication. Research suggests that women "read" men better than men "read" women (Farris et al., 2008). Gender is also one of the key elements in the presentation of self, as the following sections explain.

Demeanor

Demeanor—the way we act and carry ourselves—is a clue to social power. Simply put, powerful people enjoy more freedom in how they act. At the office, off-color remarks, swearing, or putting your feet on the desk may be acceptable for the boss but rarely, if ever, for employees. Similarly, powerful people can interrupt others; less powerful people are expected to show respect through silence (Smith-Lovin & Brody, 1989; Henley, Hamilton, & Thorne, 1992; C. Johnson, 1994).

Because women generally occupy positions of lesser power, demeanor is a gender issue as well. As Chapter 13 ("Gender Stratification") explains, 40 percent of all working women in the United States hold clerical or service jobs under the control of supervisors who are usually men. Women, then, learn to craft their personal performances more carefully than men and to defer to men more often in everyday interaction.

Use of Space

How much space does a personal performance require? Power plays a key role here; the more power you have, the more space you use. Men typically command more space than women, whether pacing back and forth before an audience or casually sitting on a bench. Why? Our culture has traditionally measured femininity by how *little* space women occupy—the standard of "daintiness"—and masculinity by how *much* territory a man controls—the standard of "turf" (Henley, Hamilton, & Thorne, 1992).

For both sexes, the concept of **personal space** refers to *the surrounding area over which a person makes some claim to privacy*. In the United States, people typically position themselves several feet apart

when speaking; throughout the Middle East, by contrast, people stand much closer. Just about everywhere, men (with their greater social power) often intrude into women's personal space. If a woman moves into a man's personal space, however, he is likely to take it as a sign of sexual interest.

Staring, Smiling, and Touching

Eye contact encourages interaction. In conversations, women hold eye contact more than men. But men have their own brand of eye contact: staring. When men stare at women, they are claiming social dominance and defining women as sexual objects.

Although it often shows pleasure, smiling can also be a sign of trying to please someone or submission. In a male-dominated world, it is not surprising that women smile more than men (Henley, Hamilton, & Thorne, 1992).

Finally, mutual touching suggests intimacy and caring. Apart from close relationships, touching is generally something men do to women (but less often, in our culture, to other men). A male physician touches the shoulder of his female nurse as they examine a report, a young man touches the back of his woman friend as he guides her across the street, or a male skiing instructor touches young women as he teaches them to ski. In such examples, the intent of touching may be harmless and may bring little response, but it amounts to a subtle ritual by which men claim dominance over women.

Idealization

People behave the way they do for many, often complex reasons. Even so, Goffman suggests, we construct performances to *idealize* our intentions. That is, we try to convince others (and perhaps ourselves) that what we do reflects ideal cultural standards rather than selfish motives.

Idealization is easily illustrated by returning to the world of doctors and patients. In a hospital, doctors engage in a performance commonly described as "making rounds." Entering the room of a patient, the doctor often stops at the foot of the bed and silently reads the patient's chart. Afterward, doctor and patient talk briefly. In ideal terms, this routine involves a doctor making a personal visit to check on a patient's condition.

In reality, the picture is not so perfect. A doctor may see several dozen patients a day and remember little about many of them. Reading the chart is a chance to recall the patient's name and medical problems, but revealing the impersonality of medical care would undermine the cultural ideal of the doctor as deeply concerned about the welfare of others.

Doctors, college professors, and other professionals typically idealize their motives for entering their chosen careers. They describe their work as "making a contribution to science," "helping others,"

NOTE: "Embarrass" is derived from words meaning "to block or obstruct." "Tact" is derived from the Latin *tactus*, meaning "sense of touch."

GLOBAL: Little comparative data exist regarding tact. But logically, one imagines that traditional societies engage in less of it, since reality is more well established.

Q: "There is no crime more infamous than the violation of truth. It is apparent that men can be social beings no longer than they believe each other. When speech is employed only as the vehicle of falsehood, every man must disunite himself from others, inhabit his own cave and seek prey only for himself." Samuel Johnson

● SEEING SOCIOLOGY
in Everyday Life

Watch female-male couples holding hands. Which person has the hand to the front and which has the hand to the rear? Can you see a pattern and offer an explanation?

● SEEING SOCIOLOGY
in Everyday Life

Using Goffman's approach, offer examples of performances, nonverbal communication, idealization, and tact in your own life.

Hand gestures vary widely from one culture to another. Yet people everywhere chuckle, grin, or smirk to indicate that they don't take another person's performance seriously. Therefore, the world over, people who cannot restrain their mirth tactfully cover their faces.

"serving the community," and even "answering a calling from God." Rarely do they admit the more common, less honorable, motives: the income, power, prestige, and leisure time that these occupations provide.

We all use idealization to some degree. When was the last time you smiled and spoke politely to someone you do not like? Have you acted interested in a class that was really boring? Such little lies in our performances help us get through everyday life. Even when we suspect that others are putting on an act, we are unlikely to challenge their performances, for reasons that we shall examine next.

Embarrassment and Tact

The famous speaker giving a campus lecture keeps mispronouncing the college's name; the head coach rises to speak at the team's end-of-season banquet unaware of the napkin still tucked in her dress; the student enters the lecture hall late and soaking wet, attracting the gaze of the hundreds of classmates. As carefully as individuals may try to craft their performances, slip-ups of all kinds occur. The result is *embarrassment*, discomfort following a spoiled performance. Goffman describes embarrassment as "losing face."

Embarrassment is an ever-present danger because idealized performances usually contain some deception. In addition, most performances involve juggling so many elements that one thoughtless moment can shatter the intended impression.

A curious fact is that an audience often overlooks flaws in a performance, allowing the actor to avoid embarrassment. If we do point out a misstep ("Excuse me, but your fly is open"), we do it quietly and only to help someone avoid even greater loss of face. In Hans Christian Andersen's classic fable "The Emperor's New Clothes," the child who blurts out the truth, that the emperor is parading about naked, is scolded for being rude.

Often members of an audience actually help the performer recover from a flawed performance. *Tact* is helping someone "save face." After hearing a supposed expert make an embarrassingly inaccurate remark, for example, people may tactfully ignore the comment, as if it had never been spoken, or with mild laughter treat what was said as a joke. Or they may simply respond, "I'm sure you didn't mean that," hearing the statement but not allowing it to destroy the actor's performance. With such efforts in mind, we can understand Abraham Lincoln's comment that "tact is the ability to describe others the way they see themselves."

Why is tact so common? Because embarrassment creates discomfort not just for the actor but for everyone else as well. Just as a theater audience feels uneasy when an actor forgets a line, people who observe awkward behavior are reminded of how fragile their own performances often are. Socially constructed reality thus functions like a dam holding back a sea of chaos. When one person's performance springs a leak, others tactfully help make repairs. Everyone lends a hand in building reality, and no one wants it suddenly swept away.

In sum, Goffman's research shows that although behavior is spontaneous in some respects, it is more patterned than we like to think. Four centuries ago, William Shakespeare captured this idea in lines that still ring true:

All the world's a stage,
And all the men and women merely players:
They have their exits and their entrances;
And one man in his time plays many parts.

(*As You Like It*, act 2, scene 7)

MAKING THE GRADE

Emotions are complex and reflect both biological and cultural forces. Sociologists are interested in how culture affects our emotional life.

SEEING SOCIOLOGY
in Everyday Life

What emotions are (or are not) expected of a college professor in front of a class?

To most people in the United States, these expressions convey anger, fear, disgust, happiness, surprise, and sadness. But do people elsewhere in the world define them in the same way? Research suggests that all human beings experience the same basic emotions and display them to others in the same basic ways. But culture plays a part by specifying the situations that trigger one emotion or another.

Interaction in Everyday Life: Three Applications

The final sections of this chapter illustrate the major elements of social interaction by focusing on three dimensions of everyday life: emotions, language, and humor.

Emotions: The Social Construction of Feeling

Emotions, more commonly called *feelings,* are an important element of human social life. In truth, what we *do* often matters less than how we *feel* about it. Emotions seem very personal because they are "inside." Even so, just as society guides our behavior, it guides our emotional life.

The Biological Side of Emotions

Studying people all over the world, Paul Ekman (1980a, 1980b, 1998, 2003) reports that people everywhere express six basic emotions: happiness, sadness, anger, fear, disgust, and surprise. In addition, Ekman found that people in every society use much the same facial expressions to show these emotions. Ekman believes that some emotional responses are "wired" into human beings; that is, they are biologically programmed in our facial features, muscles, and central nervous system.

Why might this be so? Over centuries of evolution, emotions developed in the human species because they serve a social purpose: supporting group life. Emotions are powerful forces that allow us to overcome our self-centeredness and build connections with others. Thus the capacity for emotion arose in our ancestors along with the capacity for culture (Turner, 2000).

The Cultural Side of Emotions

But culture does play an important role in guiding human emotions. First, Ekman explains, culture defines *what triggers* an emotion. Whether people define the departure of an old friend as joyous (causing happiness), insulting (arousing anger), a loss (producing sadness), or mystical (provoking surprise and awe) has a lot to do with culture. Second, culture provides rules for the *display* of emotions. For example, most people in the United States express emotions more freely with family members than with colleagues in the workplace. Similarly, we expect children to express emotions freely to parents, but parents tend to hide their emotions from their children. Third, culture guides how we *value* emotions. Some societies encourage the expression of emotion; others expect members to control their feelings and maintain a "stiff upper lip." Gender also plays a part; traditionally, at least, many cultures expect women to show emotions, but they discourage emotional expression by men as a sign of weakness. In some cultures, of course, this pattern is less pronounced or even reversed.

Emotions on the Job

In the United States, most people are freer to express their feelings at home than on the job. The reason, as Arlie Russell Hochschild (1979, 1983) explains, is that the typical company tries to regulate not only the behavior of its employees but also their emotions. Take the case of an airline flight attendant who offers passengers a drink, a bag of pretzels, and a smile. Although this smile may convey real pleasure at serving the customer, Hochschild's study points to a different conclusion: The smile is an emotional script demanded by the airline management as the right way to perform the job. Therefore, we see that the "presentation of self" described by Erving Goffman can involve not just surface acting but also the "deep acting" of emotions.

DISCUSS: Erving Goffman pioneered the idea of "framing" our experiences in his 1974 book *Frame Analysis*. In the box, Keys shows that the antiabortion and pro-choice positions serve as frames that guide the emotional experience of terminating a pregnancy. Ask the class to think of other situations in which social frames guide what people feel.

NOTE: Lesbian couples who undergo artificial insemination in order to bear children refer to the "donor" rather than the "father." This scripting removes any suggestion that the donor is a "father," which allows for two women to be joint "mothers."

SEEING SOCIOLOGY
in Everyday Life

What are the "emotional scripts" that students might apply to college graduation? That is, why might people see this event in positive or negative terms?

CONTROVERSY & DEBATE

Managing Feelings: Women's Abortion Experiences

LIZ: I just *can't* be pregnant! I'm going to see my doctor tomorrow about an abortion. There's no way I can deal with a baby at this point in my life!

JEN: I can't believe you'd do that, Liz! How are you going to feel a few years from now when you think about what that *child* would be doing if you'd let it live?

Few issues today generate as much emotion as abortion. In a study of women's abortion experiences, the sociologist Jennifer Keys (2002) discovered emotional scripts or "feeling rules" that guided how women feel about ending a pregnancy.

Keys explains that emotional scripts arise from the political controversy surrounding abortion. The antiabortion movement defines abortion as a personal tragedy, the "killing of an unborn child." Given this definition, women who terminate a pregnancy through abortion are doing something morally wrong and can expect to feel grief, guilt, and regret. So intense are these feelings, according to supporters of this position, that such women often suffer from "postabortion syndrome."

Those who take the pro-choice position have an opposing view of abortion. From this point of view, the woman's problem is the *unwanted pregnancy*; abortion is an acceptable medical solution. Therefore, the emotion common to women who terminate a pregnancy should be not guilt but relief.

In her research, Keys conducted in-depth interviews with forty women who had recently had abortions and found that all of them used such scripts to "frame" their situation in an antiabortion or pro-choice manner. In part, this construction of reality reflected the women's own attitudes about abortion. In addition, however, the women's partners and friends

typically encouraged specific feelings about the event. Ivy, one young woman in the study, had a close friend who was also pregnant. "Congratulations!" she exclaimed when she learned of Ivy's condition. "We're going to be having babies together!" Such a statement established one "feeling rule"—having a baby is *good*—which sent the message to Ivy that her planned abortion should trigger guilt. Working in the other direction, Jo's partner was horrified by the news that she was pregnant. Doubting his own ability to be a father, he blurted out, "I would rather put a gun to my head than have this baby!" His panic not only defined having the child as a mistake but alarmed Jo as well. Clearly, her partner's reaction made the decision to end the pregnancy a matter of relief from a terrible problem.

Medical personnel also play a part in this process of reality construction by using specific terms. Nurses and doctors who talk about "the

baby" encourage the antiabortion framing of abortion and provoke grief and guilt. On the other hand, those who use language such as "pregnancy tissue," "fetus," or "the contents of the uterus" encourage the pro-choice framing of abortion as a fairly routine medical procedure leading to relief. Olivia began using the phrase "products of conception," which she picked up from her doctor. Denise spoke of her procedure as "taking the extra cells out of my body. Yeah, I did feel some guilt when I thought that this was the beginning of life, but my body is full of life—you have lots of cells in you."

After the procedure, most women reported actively trying to manage their feelings. Explained Ivy, "I never used the word 'baby.' I kept saying to myself that it was not formed yet. There was nothing there. I kept that in my mind." On the other hand, Keys found that all of the women in her study who leaned toward the antiabortion position did use the term "baby." Gina explained, "I do think of it as a baby. The truth is that I ended my baby's life. . . . Thinking that makes me feel guilty. But—considering what I did—maybe I *should* feel guilty." Believing that what she had done was wrong, in other words, Gina actively called out the feeling of guilt—in part, Keys concluded, to punish herself.

WHAT DO YOU THINK?

1. In your own words, what are "emotional scripts" or "feeling rules"?

2. Can you apply the idea of "feeling rules" to the experience of getting married?

3. In light of this discussion, how accurate is it to say that our feelings are not as personal as we may think they are?

The words that doctors and nurses use guide whether a woman having an abortion defines the experience in positive or negative terms.

With these patterns in mind, it is easy to see that we socially construct our emotions as part of our everyday reality, a process sociologists call *emotion management*. The Controversy & Debate box links the emotions displayed by women who decide to have an abortion to their political views and to their personal view of terminating a pregnancy.

● SEEING SOCIOLOGY
in Everyday Life

List words that people use to describe a very sexually active female. How many such terms are there? Are they positive or negative in meaning? Repeat this exercise for a very sexually active male. What differences do you notice?

Many of us think emotions are simply part of our biological makeup. While there is a biological foundation to human emotion, sociologists have demonstrated that what triggers an emotion—as well as when, where, and to whom the emotion is displayed—is shaped by culture. For example, many jobs not only regulate a worker's behavior but also expect workers to display a particular emotion, as in the case of the always-smiling airline flight attendant. Can you think of other jobs that regulate emotions in this way?

Language: The Social Construction of Gender

As Chapter 3 ("Culture") explains, language is the thread that weaves members of a society into the symbolic web we call culture. Language communicates not only a surface reality but also deeper levels of meaning. One such level involves gender. Language defines men and women differently in terms of both power and value (Henley, Hamilton, & Thorne, 1992; Thorne, Kramarae, & Henley, 1983).

Language and Power

A young man proudly rides his new motorcycle up his friend's driveway and boasts, "Isn't she a beauty?" On the surface, the question has little to do with gender. Yet why does he use the pronoun *she* instead of *he* or *it* to refer to his prized possession?

The answer is that men often use language to establish control over their surroundings. A man attaches a female pronoun to a motorcycle

(or car, boat, or other object) because it reflects the power of *ownership*. Perhaps this is also why, in the United States and elsewhere, a woman who marries traditionally takes the last name of her husband. Because many of today's married women value their independence, an increasing share (about 18 percent) now keep their own name or combine the two family names.

Language and Value

Typically, the English language treats as masculine whatever has greater value, force, or significance. For instance, the word *virtuous,* meaning "morally worthy" or "excellent," comes from the Latin word *vir,* meaning "man." On the other hand, the adjective *hysterical,* meaning "emotionally out of control," comes from the Greek word *hystera,* meaning "uterus."

In many familiar ways, language also confers different value on the two sexes. Traditional masculine terms such as *king* and *lord* have a positive meaning, while comparable feminine terms, such as *queen, madam,* and *dame,* can have negative meanings. Similarly, use of the suffixes *-ette* and *-ess* to denote femininity usually devalues the words to which they are added. For example, a *major* has higher standing than a *majorette,* as does a *host* in relation to a *hostess* or a *master* in relation to a *mistress.* Language both mirrors social attitudes and helps perpetuate them.

Given the importance of gender in everyday life, perhaps we should not be surprised that women and men sometimes have trouble communicating with each other. In the Thinking About Diversity box, Harold and Sybil, whose misadventures in trying to find their friends' home opened this chapter, return to illustrate how the two sexes often seem to be speaking different languages.

Reality Play: The Social Construction of Humor

Humor plays an important part in everyday life. Everyone laughs at a joke, but few people stop to think about what makes something funny. We can apply many of the ideas developed in this chapter to explain how, by using humor, we "play with reality" (Macionis, 1987).

The Foundation of Humor

Humor is produced by the social construction of reality; it arises as people create and contrast two different realities. Generally, one reality is *conventional,* that is, what people expect in a specific situation. The other reality is *unconventional,* an unexpected violation of cultural patterns. Humor arises from the contradictions, ambiguities, and double meanings found in differing definitions of the same situation.

There are countless ways to mix realities and generate humor. Contrasting realities are found in statements that contradict them-

GLOBAL: In Japan, reports Ellen Rudolph (1991), women display their greater subservience to men by speaking more quietly, looking down, and employing more deferential language.

DISCUSS: Why are boys—but not girls—designated as Jr., II, III, etc.?

NOTE: The value function of language is also evident in terms such as "lady doctor," which suggests an exceptional case.

NOTE: Laughter also accompanies tickling. This is a disruption of what is conventional in a physical sense. Tickling is also an ambiguous situation in which one does not know if the other's motives are loving or aggressive.

NOTE: Humor can also be generated by leading an audience to expect two incongruent realities, one of which fails to materialize. Groucho Marx once quipped, "I worked myself up from nothing to a state of extreme poverty."

MAKING THE GRADE

The foundation of humor follows from the earlier discussion of the social construction of reality—building and contrasting two different definitions of reality.

THINKING ABOUT DIVERSITY: RACE, CLASS, & GENDER

Gender and Language: "You Just Don't Understand!"

In the story that opened this chapter, Harold and Sybil faced a situation that rings true to many people: When they are lost, men grumble to themselves and perhaps blame their partners but avoid asking for directions. For their part, women can't understand why men refuse help when they need it.

Deborah Tannen (1990) explains that men typically define most everyday encounters as competitive. Therefore, getting lost is bad enough without asking for help, which lets someone else get "one up." By contrast, because women have traditionally had a subordinate position, they find it easy to ask for help. Sometimes, Tannen points out, women ask for assistance even when they don't need it.

A similar gender-linked problem common to couples involves what women consider "trying to be helpful" and men call "nagging." Consider the following exchange (adapted from Adler, 1990:74):

SYBIL: What's wrong, honey?

HAROLD: Nothing.

SYBIL: Something is bothering you. I can tell.

HAROLD: I told you nothing is bothering me. Leave me alone.

SYBIL: But I can see that there is a problem.

HAROLD: OK. Just why do you think there is a problem?

SYBIL: Well, for one thing, you're bleeding all over your shirt.

HAROLD: (now irritated) Yeah, well, it doesn't bother me.

SYBIL: (losing her temper) WELL, IT SURE IS BOTHERING ME!

HAROLD: Fine. I'll go change my shirt.

The problem here is that what one partner *intends* by a comment is not always what the other *hears* in the words. To Sybil, her opening question is an effort at cooperative problem solving. She can see that something is wrong with Harold (who has cut himself while doing

yard work), and she wants to help him. But Harold interprets her pointing out his problem as belittling him, and he tries to close off the discussion. Sybil, believing that Harold would be more positive if he understood that she just wants to be helpful, repeats her question. This reaction sets in motion a vicious circle in which Harold, who feels his wife is thinking that he cannot take care of himself, responds by digging in his heels. This response, in turn, makes Sybil all the more sure that she needs to get through to him. And around it goes until somebody gets really angry.

In the end, Harold agrees to change his shirt but still refuses to discuss the original problem. Defining his wife's concern as "nagging," Harold just wants Sybil to leave him alone. For her part, Sybil fails to understand her husband's view of the situation and walks away convinced that he is a stubborn grouch.

WHAT DO YOU THINK?

1. Have you noticed differences in the way men and women communicate? Explain.

2. In your opinion, what are the reasons for any gender differences in how people use language?

3. Do you think that understanding Tannen's conclusions would help couples communicate better? Why or why not?

---

selves, such as "Nostalgia is not what it used to be"; statements that repeat themselves, such as Yogi Berra's line "It's *déjà vu* all over again"; or statements that mix up words, such as Oscar Wilde's line "Work is the curse of the drinking class." Even switching around syllables does the trick, as in the case of the country song "I'd Rather Have a Bottle in Front of Me than a Frontal Lobotomy."

A comedian can also build a joke the other way around, leading the audience to expect an unconventional answer and then delivering a very ordinary one. When a reporter asked the famous gangster Willy Sutton why he continued to rob banks, for example, he replied dryly, "Because that's where the money is." Regardless of how a joke is constructed, the greater the opposition or difference

is between the two definitions of reality, the greater the humor that is produced.

When telling jokes, the comedian uses various strategies to strengthen this opposition and make the joke funnier. One common technique is to present the first, or conventional, remark in conversation with another actor and then to turn toward the audience (or the camera) to deliver the second, unexpected line. In a Marx Brothers movie, Groucho remarks, "Outside of a dog, a book is a man's best friend." Then, raising his voice and turning to the camera, he adds, "And *inside* of a dog, it's too dark to read!" Such "channel switching" emphasizes the difference between the two realities. Following the same logic, stand-up comedians may "reset" the audience

RESOURCE: Deborah Tannen's article on gender and communication is included in the companion reader *Seeing Ourselves*, 8th ed.

NOTE: Deborah Tannen describes her research as "interactional sociolinguistics."

NOTE: Example of having to "finish a joke" is Woody Allen's line to a guy who backed into his car: "Be fruitful and multiply—but not in those words."

NOTE: Humor's origin in incongruity is evident in Woody Allen's comment:

"More than any time in history, mankind faces a crossroads. One path leads to despair and utter hopelessness, the other to total extinction. Let us pray that we have the wisdom to choose correctly."

Q: "You can pretend to be serious, but you cannot pretend to be witty." Sacha Guitry

Q: "He who laughs, lasts." Dr. Robert Anthony

● SEEING SOCIOLOGY in Everyday Life

Here is a joke about sociologists: How many sociologists does it take to change a light bulb? Answer: None. There is nothing wrong with the light bulb; it's *the system* that needs to be changed! What makes this joke funny? What sort of people are likely to get it? What kind of people probably won't? Why?

---

to conventional expectations by interjecting the phrase, "But seriously, folks, . . ." between jokes. Monty Python comedian John Cleese did this with his trademark line, "And now for something completely different."

Comedians pay careful attention to their performances—the precise words they use and the timing of their delivery. A joke is well told if the comedian creates the sharpest possible opposition between the realities; in a careless performance, the joke falls flat. Because the key to humor lies in the collision of realities, we can see why the climax of a joke is termed the "*punch* line."

The Dynamics of Humor: "Getting It"

After hearing a joke, did you ever say, "I don't get it"? To "get" humor, you must understand both the conventional and the unconventional realities well enough to appreciate their difference. A comedian may make getting a joke harder by leaving out some important information. In such cases, listeners must pay attention to the stated elements of the joke and then fill in the missing pieces on their own. A simple example is the comment of the movie producer Hal Roach on his one hundredth birthday: "If I had known I would live to be one hundred, I would have taken better care of myself!" Here, getting the joke depends on realizing that Roach must have taken pretty good care of himself because he did make it to one hundred. Or take one of W. C. Fields's lines: "Some weasel took the cork out of my lunch." What a lunch! we think to ourselves to "finish" the joke.

Here is an even more complex joke: What do you get if you cross an insomniac, a dyslexic, and an agnostic? Answer: A person who stays up all night wondering if there is a dog. To get this one, you must know that insomnia is an inability to sleep, that dyslexia causes a person to reverse the letters in words, and that an agnostic doubts the existence of God.

Why would a comedian want the audience to make this sort of effort to understand a joke? Our enjoyment of a joke is increased by the pleasure of figuring out all the pieces needed to "get it." In addition, getting the joke makes you an "insider" compared to those who don't get it. We have all experienced the frustration of *not* getting a joke: fear of being judged stupid, along with a sense of being excluded from a pleasure shared by others. Sometimes someone may tactfully explain the joke so that the other person doesn't feel left out. But as the old saying goes, if a joke has to be explained, it isn't very funny.

The Topics of Humor

All over the world, people smile and laugh, making humor a universal element of human culture. But because the world's people live in different cultures, humor rarely travels well.

October 1, Kobe, Japan. Can you share a joke with people who live halfway around the world? At dinner, I ask two Japanese college women to tell me a joke. "You know 'crayon'?" Asako asks. I nod. "How do you ask for a crayon in Japanese?" I respond that I have no idea. She laughs out loud as she says what sounds like "crayon crayon." Her companion Mayumi laughs too. My wife and I sit awkwardly, straight-faced. Asako relieves some of our embarrassment by explaining that the Japanese word for "give me" is kureyo, which sounds like "crayon." I force a smile.

What is humorous to the Japanese may be lost on the Chinese, South Africans, or people in the United States. Even the social diversity of our own country means that different types of people will find humor in different situations. New Englanders, southerners, and westerners have their own brands of humor, as do Latinos and Anglos, fifteen- and fifty-year-olds, construction workers and rodeo riders.

But for everyone, topics that lend themselves to double meanings or controversy generate humor. In the United States, the first jokes many of us learned as children concerned bodily functions kids are not supposed to talk about. The mere mention of "unmentionable acts" or even certain parts of the body can dissolve young faces in laughter.

Are there jokes that do break through the culture barrier? Yes, but they must touch on universal human experiences such as, say, turning on a friend:

I think of a number of jokes, but none seems likely to work. Understanding jokes about the United States is difficult for people who know little of our culture. Is there something more universal? Inspiration: "Two fellows are walking in the woods and come upon a huge bear. One guy leans over and tightens up the laces on his running shoes. 'Jake,' says the other, 'what are you doing? You can't outrun this bear!' 'I don't have to outrun the bear,' responds Jake. 'All I have to do is outrun you!'" Smiles all around.

Humor often walks a fine line between what is funny and what is "sick" or offensive. During the Middle Ages, people used the word *humors* (derived from the Latin *humidus*, meaning "moist") to refer to the various bodily fluids believed to regulate a person's health. Researchers today document the power of humor to reduce stress and improve health. One recent study of cancer patients, for example, found that the greater people's sense of humor, the greater their odds of surviving the disease. Such findings confirm the old saying

SEEING SOCIOLOGY
in Everyday Life

Humor is most common among people with roughly the same
social standing. Why is it risky to joke with people who have
more power than you do? What about joking with people who
have less power?

that "laughter is the best medicine" (Bakalar, 2005; Svebak, cited in
M. Elias, 2007). At the extreme, however, people who always take
conventional reality lightly risk being defined as deviant or even
mentally ill (a common stereotype shows insane people laughing
uncontrollably, and for a long time mental hospitals were known as
"funny farms").

Then, too, every social group considers certain topics too sensitive for humorous treatment, and joking about them risks criticism for having a "sick" sense of humor (and being labeled "sick"
yourself). People's religious beliefs, tragic accidents, or appalling
crimes are some of the topics of sick jokes or no jokes at all. Even
all these years later, no one jokes about the September 11, 2001,
terrorist attacks.

The Functions of Humor

Humor is found everywhere because it works as a safety valve for
potentially disruptive sentiments. Put another way, humor provides an acceptable way to discuss a sensitive topic without appearing to be serious or offending anyone. Having said something
controversial, people can use humor to defuse the situation by simply stating, "I didn't mean anything by what I said—it was just a
joke!"

People also use humor to relieve tension in uncomfortable
situations. One study of medical examinations found that most
patients try to joke with doctors to ease their own nervousness (Baker
et al., 1997).

Because humor involves challenging established conventions, people everywhere make fun of those in power. During the 2008 presidential campaign,
Tina Fey delighted audiences with her impersonations of Sarah Palin.

Humor and Conflict

Humor may be a source of pleasure, but it can also be used to put
down other people. Men who tell jokes about women, for example, are typically expressing some measure of hostility toward them
(Powell & Paton, 1988; Benokraitis & Feagin, 1995). Similarly, jokes
about gay people reveal tensions about sexual orientation. Real conflict can be masked by humor in situations where one or both parties choose not to bring the conflict out into the open (Primeggia
& Varacalli, 1990).

"Put-down" jokes make one category of people feel good at the
expense of another. After collecting and analyzing jokes from many
societies, Christie Davies (1990) confirmed that ethnic conflict is
one driving force behind humor in most of the world. The typical
ethnic joke makes fun of some disadvantaged category of people, at
the same time making the joke teller feel superior. Given the Anglo-
Saxon traditions of U.S. society, Poles and other ethnic and racial
minorities have long been the butt of jokes in the United States, as
have Newfoundlanders in eastern Canada, the Irish in Scotland, Sikhs

in India, Turks in Germany, Hausas in Nigeria, Tasmanians in Australia,
and Kurds in Iraq.

Disadvantaged people also make fun of the powerful, although
usually with some care. Women in the United States joke about men,
just as African Americans find humor in white people's ways and
poor people poke fun at the rich. Throughout the world, people target their leaders with humor, and officials in some countries take
such jokes seriously enough to arrest those who do not show proper
respect (Speier, 1998).

In sum, humor is much more important than we may think. It
is a means of mental escape from a conventional world that is never
entirely to our liking (Flaherty, 1984, 1990; Yoels & Clair, 1995). This
fact helps explain why so many of our nation's comedians are from
the ranks of historically marginalized peoples, including Jews and
African Americans. As long as we maintain a sense of humor, we
assert our freedom and are not prisoners of reality. By putting a smile
on our faces, we can change ourselves and the world just a little and
for the better.

Seeing Sociology in Everyday Life

Chapter 6   Social Interaction in Everyday Life

How do we construct the reality we experience?

This chapter suggests that Shakespeare may have had it right when he said, "All the world's a stage." And if so, then the Internet may be the latest and greatest stage so far. When we use Web sites such as Facebook, as Goffman explains, we present ourselves as we want others to see us. Everything we write about ourselves as well as how we arrange our page creates an impression in the mind of anyone interested in "checking us out." Take a look at the Facebook page below, paying careful attention to all the details. What is the young man explicitly saying about himself? What can you read "between the lines"? That is, what information can you identify that he may be trying to conceal, or at least purposely not be mentioning? How honest do you think his "presentation of self" is? Why? Do a similar analysis of the young woman's Facebook profile shown on the next page.

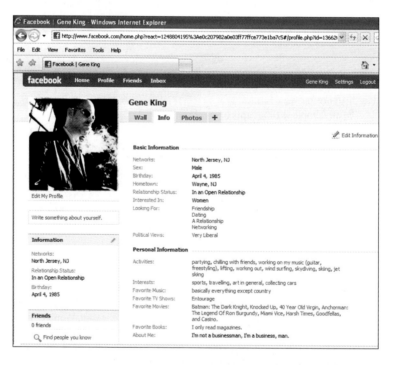

> **HINT**   Just about every element of a presentation conveys information about us to others, so all the information found on a Web site like this one is significant. Some information is intentional—for example, what people write about themselves and the photos they choose to post. Other information may be unintentional but is nevertheless picked up by the careful viewer who may be noting such things as these:
>
> - The length and tone of the person's profile. Is it a long-winded list of talents and accomplishments or humorous and modest?
> - The language used. Poor grammar may be a clue to educational level.
> - What hour of the day or night the person wrote the material. A person creating his profile at 11 P.M. on a Saturday night may not be quite the party person he describes himself to be.

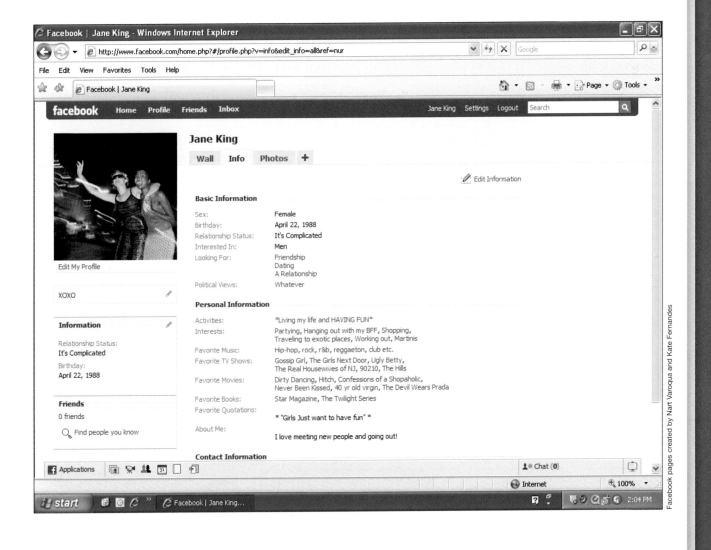

Facebook pages created by Nart Varoqua and Kate Fernandes

Applying SOCIOLOGY in Everyday Life

1. Identify five important ways in which you "present yourself" to others, including, for example, the way you decorate your dorm room, apartment, or house; the way you dress; and the way you behave in the classroom. In each case, think about what you are trying to say about yourself. Have your presentations changed in recent years? If so, how and why?

2. During one full day, every time somebody asks, "How are you?" or "How's it goin'?" stop and actually give a complete, truthful answer. What happens when you respond to a polite question in an honest way? Listen to how people respond, and also watch their body language. What can you conclude?

3. Stroll around downtown or at a local mall. Pay attention to how many women and men you find at each location. From your observations, are there stores that are "gendered" so that there are "female spaces" and "male spaces"? How and why are spaces "gendered"?

MAKING THE GRADE

CHAPTER 6 Social Interaction in Everyday Life

What Is Social Structure?

SOCIAL STRUCTURE refers to social patterns that guide our behavior in everyday life. The building blocks of social structure are

- **STATUS**—a social position that is part of our social identity and that defines our relationships to others
- **ROLE**—the action expected of a person who holds a particular status

pp. 138–40

✓ *A person holds a status and performs a role.*

A status can be either an

- **ASCRIBED STATUS**, which is involuntary (for example, being a teenager, an orphan, or a Mexican American), or an
- **ACHIEVED STATUS**, which is earned (for example, being an honors student, a pilot, or a thief).

A **MASTER STATUS**, which can be either ascribed or achieved, has special importance for a person's identity (for example, being blind, a doctor, or a Kennedy).

p. 139

ROLE CONFLICT results from tension among roles linked to two or more statuses (for example, a woman who juggles her responsibilities as a mother and a corporate CEO).

ROLE STRAIN results from tension among roles linked to a single status (for example, the college professor who enjoys personal interaction with students but at the same time knows that social distance is necessary in order to evaluate students fairly).

p. 141

social interaction (p. 138) the process by which people act and react in relation to others

status (p. 139) a social position that a person holds

status set (p. 139) all the statuses a person holds at a given time

ascribed status (p. 139) a social position a person receives at birth or takes on involuntarily later in life

achieved status (p. 139) a social position a person takes on voluntarily that reflects personal ability and effort

master status (p. 139) a status that has special importance for social identity, often shaping a person's entire life

role (p. 140) behavior expected of someone who holds a particular status

role set (p. 140) a number of roles attached to a single status

role conflict (p. 141) conflict among the roles connected to two or more statuses

role strain (p. 141) tension among the roles connected to a single status

✓ *A person's status set changes over the life course (p. 139).*

✓ *The role sets attached to a single status vary from society to society around the world (pp. 140–41).*

The Social Construction of Reality

Through **SOCIAL INTERACTION**, we construct the reality we experience.

- For example, two people interacting both try to shape the reality of their situation.

pp. 141–42

The **THOMAS THEOREM** says that the reality people construct in their interaction has real consequences for the future.

- For example, a teacher who believes a certain student to be intellectually gifted may well encourage exceptional academic performance.

p. 143

social construction of reality (p. 142) the process by which people creatively shape reality through social interaction

Thomas theorem (p. 143) W. I. Thomas's observation that situations defined as real are real in their consequences

ethnomethodology (p. 143) Harold Garfinkel's term for the study of the way people make sense of their everyday surroundings

ETHNOMETHODOLOGY is a strategy to reveal the assumptions people have about their social world.

- We can expose these assumptions by intentionally breaking the "rules" of social interaction and observing the reactions of other people.

pp. 143–45

Both **CULTURE** and **SOCIAL CLASS** shape the reality people construct.

- For example, a "short walk" for a New Yorker is a few city blocks, but for a peasant in Latin America, it could be a few miles.

p. 145

✓ *Through the social construction of reality, people creatively shape their social world.*

Dramaturgical Analysis: The "Presentation of Self"

DRAMATURGICAL ANALYSIS explores social interaction in terms of theatrical performance: A status operates as a part in a play, and a role is a script.

PERFORMANCES are the way we present ourselves to others.

- Performances are both conscious (intentional action) and unconscious (nonverbal communication).
- Performances include costume (the way we dress), props (objects we carry), and demeanor (tone of voice and the way we carry ourselves).

pp. 145–48

GENDER affects performances because men typically have greater social power than women. Gender differences involve *demeanor, use of space*, and *staring, smiling, and touching*.

- **DEMEANOR**—With greater social power, men have more freedom in how they act.
- **USE OF SPACE**—Men typically command more space than women.
- **STARING** and **TOUCHING** are generally done by men to women.
- **SMILING**, as a way to please another, is more commonly done by women.

p. 148

IDEALIZATION of performances means we try to convince others that our actions reflect ideal culture rather than selfish motives.

pp. 148–49

EMBARRASSMENT is the "loss of face" in a performance. People use **TACT** to help others "save face."

p. 149

dramaturgical analysis (p. 145) Erving Goffman's term for the study of social interaction in terms of theatrical performance

presentation of self (p. 145) Erving Goffman's term for a person's efforts to create specific impressions in the minds of others

nonverbal communication (p. 147) communication using body movements, gestures, and facial expressions rather than speech

personal space (p. 148) the surrounding area over which a person makes some claim to privacy

Interaction in Everyday Life: Three Applications

EMOTIONS: The Social Construction of **FEELING**

The same basic emotions are biologically programmed into all human beings, but culture guides what triggers emotions, how people display emotions, and how people value emotions. In everyday life, the presentation of self involves managing emotions as well as behavior.

pp. 150–51

LANGUAGE: The Social Construction of **GENDER**

Gender is an important element of everyday interaction. Language defines women and men as different types of people, reflecting the fact that society attaches greater power and value to what is viewed as masculine.

p. 152

REALITY PLAY: The Social Construction of **HUMOR**

Humor results from the difference between conventional and unconventional definitions of a situation. Because humor is a part of culture, people around the world find different situations funny.

pp. 152–55

We carry out much of our daily lives as members of small groups, such as sports teams, and large organizations, such as the businesses where we work. Both small groups and large organizations operate according to general rules, which this chapter explains.

CHAPTER 7

Groups and Organizations

RESOURCE: An excerpt of Cooley's analysis of primary groups appears in the companion reader, *Seeing Ourselves*, 8th ed.

NOTE: "Primary" is from the Latin word *prime*, meaning "first"; "secondary" is from the Latin word *secundus*, meaning "following."

Q: "Blood is thicker than water." Old saying

NOTE: Cooley used only the term "primary group"; later, others introduced the term "secondary group" into sociological terminology, inferring the concept from Cooley's writings. Cooley did his first research for the U.S. Census Bureau, collecting statistics on street railways. He became a full-time sociologist at the age of 28.

DISCUSS: Discuss Robert Frost's observation that "good fences make good neighbors." Neighborhood interaction also varies according to class and culture.

CHAPTER OVERVIEW

This chapter analyzes social groups, both small and large, highlighting the differences between them. Then the focus shifts to formal organizations that carry out various tasks in our modern society.

With the workday over, Juan and Jorge pushed through the doors of the local McDonald's restaurant. "Man, am I hungry," announced Juan, heading right into line. "Look at all the meat I'm gonna eat." But Jorge, a recent immigrant from a small village in Guatemala, is surveying the room with a sociological eye. "There is much more than food to see here. This place is all about America!"

And so it is, as we shall see. Back in 1948, people in Pasadena, California, paid little attention to the opening of a new restaurant by brothers Maurice and Richard McDonald. The McDonald brothers' basic concept, which was soon called "fast food," was to serve meals quickly and cheaply to large numbers of people. The brothers trained employees to do specialized jobs: One person grilled hamburgers while others "dressed" them, made French fries, whipped up milkshakes, and presented the food to the customers in assembly-line fashion.

As the years went by, the McDonald brothers prospered, and they opened several more restaurants, including one in San Bernardino. It was there, in 1954, that Ray Kroc, a traveling blender and mixer salesman, paid them a visit.

Kroc was fascinated by the efficiency of the brothers' system and saw the potential for a whole chain of fast-food restaurants. The three launched the plan as partners. In 1961, in the face of rapidly increasing sales, Kroc bought out the McDonalds (who returned to running their original restaurant) and went on to become one of the great success stories of all time. Today, McDonald's is one of the most widely known brand names in the world, with more than 31,500 restaurants serving 52 million people daily throughout the United States and in 118 other countries (McDonald's, 2008).

The success of McDonald's points to more than just the popularity of burgers and fries. The organizational principles that guide this company have come to dominate social life in the United States and elsewhere.

We begin this chapter with an examination of *social groups,* the clusters of people with whom we interact in everyday life. As you will learn, the scope of group life in the United States expanded greatly during the twentieth century. From a world of families, local neighborhoods, and small businesses, our society now turns on the operation of huge corporations and other bureaucracies that sociologists describe as *formal organizations.* Understanding this expanding scale of social life and appreciating what it means for us as individuals are the main objectives of this chapter.

Social Groups

Almost everyone wants a sense of belonging, which is the essence of group life. A **social group** is *two or more people who identify with and interact with one another.* Human beings come together in couples, families, circles of friends, churches, clubs, businesses, neighborhoods, and large organizations. Whatever its form, a group is made up of people with shared experiences, loyalties, and interests. In short, while keeping their individuality, members of social groups also think of themselves as a special "we."

Not every collection of individuals forms a group. People all over the country with a status in common, such as women, homeowners, soldiers, millionaires, college graduates, and Roman Catholics, are not a group but a *category.* Though they know that others hold the same status, most are strangers to one another. Similarly, students sitting in a large stadium interact to a very limited extent. Such a loosely formed collection of people in one place is a *crowd* rather than a group.

However, the right circumstances can quickly turn a crowd into a group. Unexpected events, from power failures to terrorist attacks, can make people bond quickly with strangers.

Primary and Secondary Groups

Friends often greet one another with a smile and the simple phrase "Hi! How are you?" The response is usually "Fine, thanks. How about

NOTE: Primary groups involve bonds of affection but not necessarily bonds of intimacy. Parents generally strive to treat children in an evenhanded and equal—if therefore impersonal—fashion. The adjectival form of "family"—*familiar*—also implies something less than intimacy.

NOTE: Some categories of groups—peer groups, for example—cut across the primary-secondary continuum.

DISCUSS: Under what circumstances does somebody feel used by a friend? What does this feeling tell us about the character of ideal friendship?

NOTE: Emphasizing the expressive dimension while discounting the instrumental element of primary relationships is an example of Goffman's concept of idealization.

social group two or more people who identify with and interact with one another

primary group a small social group whose members share personal and lasting relationships

secondary group a large and impersonal social group whose members pursue a specific goal or activity

SEEING SOCIOLOGY
in Everyday Life

List all the groups in your life that you think of in terms of "we."

you?" This answer is often more scripted than sincere. Explaining how you are *really* doing might make people feel so awkward that they would beat a hasty retreat.

Social groups are of two types, depending on their members' degree of personal concern for one another. According to Charles Horton Cooley (1864–1929), a **primary group** is *a small social group whose members share personal and lasting relationships.* Joined by *primary relationships,* people spend a great deal of time together, engage in a wide range of activities, and feel that they know one another pretty well. In short, they show real concern for one another. The family is every society's most important primary group.

Cooley called personal and tightly integrated groups "primary" because they are among the first groups we experience in life. In addition, family and friends have primary importance in the socialization process, shaping our attitudes, behavior, and social identity.

Members of primary groups help one another in many ways, but they generally think of the group as an end in itself rather than as a means to some goal. In other words, we prefer to think that family and friendship link people who "belong together." Members of a primary group also tend to view each other as unique and irreplaceable. Especially in the family, we are bound to others by emotion and loyalty. Brothers and sisters may not always get along, but they always remain "family."

In contrast to the primary group, the **secondary group** is *a large and impersonal social group whose members pursue a specific goal or activity.* In most respects, secondary groups have characteristics opposite to those of primary groups. *Secondary relationships* involve weak emotional ties and little personal knowledge of one another. Many secondary groups exist for only a short time, beginning and ending without particular significance. Students in a college course, who may or may not see one another again after the semester ends, are one example of a secondary group.

Secondary groups include many more people than primary groups. For example, dozens or even hundreds of people may work together in the same company, yet most of them pay only passing attention to one another. In some cases, time may transform a group from secondary to primary, as with co-workers who share an office for many years and develop closer relationships. But generally, members of a secondary group do not think of themselves as "we." Secondary ties need not be hostile or cold, of course. Interactions among students, co-workers, and business associates are often quite pleasant even if they are impersonal.

Unlike members of primary groups, who display a *personal orientation,* people in secondary groups have a *goal orientation.* Primary group members define each other according to *who* they are in terms of family ties or personal qualities, but people in secondary

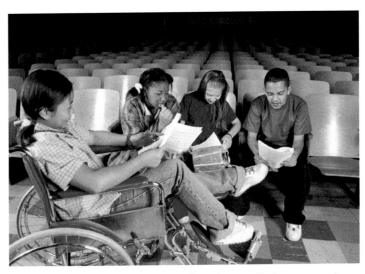

As human beings, we live our lives as members of groups. Such groups may be large or small, temporary or long-lasting, and can be based on kinship, cultural heritage, or some shared interest.

groups look to one another for *what* they are, that is, what they can do for each other. In secondary groups, we tend to "keep score," aware of what we give others and what we receive in return. This goal orientation means that secondary-group members usually remain formal and polite. In a secondary relationship, therefore, we ask the question "How are you?" without expecting a truthful answer.

The Summing Up table on page 164 reviews the characteristics of primary and secondary groups. Keep in mind that these traits define two types of groups in ideal terms; most real groups contain elements of both. For example, a women's group on a university campus may be quite large (and therefore secondary), but its members may identify strongly with one another and provide lots of mutual support (making it seem primary).

Many people think that small towns and rural areas have mostly primary relationships and that large cities are characterized by more secondary ties. This generalization is partly true, but some urban neighborhoods—especially those populated by people of a single ethnic or religious category—are very tightly knit.

Group Leadership

How do groups operate? One important element of group dynamics is leadership. Though a small circle of friends may have no leader at all, most large secondary groups place leaders in a formal chain of command.

163

DISCUSS: Ask students if they have ever experienced group pressure that made them do something they did not want to do. What happened?

Q: "A little doubt came into my mind. . . . Even though you know you are right, you wonder why everybody thinks differently. I was doubting myself and was puzzled." A subject in Solomon Asch's conformity experiment

NOTE: Asch conducted control sessions to test the ability of subjects to make correct comparisons in the absence of group pressure; overall, 99% of such judgments were correct (compared to 66% in the conformity condition).

Q: "It is our nature to conform; it is a force not many can successfully resist." Mark Twain

Q: "I was only following orders." Adolf Eichmann, Nazi death camp officer

● SEEING SOCIOLOGY
in Everyday Life

List five social groups on campus that you belong to. In each case, is the group more primary or more secondary?

instrumental leadership group leadership that focuses on the completion of tasks

expressive leadership group leadership that focuses on the group's well-being

SUMMING UP
Primary Groups and Secondary Groups

	Primary Group ⟵————⟶	Secondary Group
Quality of relationships	Personal orientation	Goal orientation
Duration of relationships	Usually long-term	Variable; often short-term
Breadth of relationships	Broad; usually involving many activities	Narrow; usually involving few activities
Perception of relationships	Ends in themselves	Means to an end
Examples	Families, circles of friends	Co-workers, political organizations

Two Leadership Roles

Groups typically benefit from two kinds of leadership. **Instrumental leadership** refers to *group leadership that focuses on the completion of tasks.* Members look to instrumental leaders to make plans, give orders, and get things done. **Expressive leadership,** by contrast, is *group leadership that focuses on the group's well-being.* Expressive leaders take less interest in achieving goals than in raising group morale and minimizing tension and conflict among members.

Because they concentrate on performance, instrumental leaders usually have formal secondary relationships with other members. These leaders give orders and reward or punish members according to how much the members contribute to the group's efforts. Expressive leaders build more personal primary ties. They offer sympathy to a member going through tough times, keep the group united, and lighten serious moments with humor. Typically, successful instrumental leaders enjoy more *respect* from members, and expressive leaders generally receive more personal *affection.*

Three Leadership Styles

Sociologists also describe leadership in terms of decision-making style. *Authoritarian leadership* focuses on instrumental concerns, takes personal charge of decision making, and demands that group members obey orders. Although this leadership style may win little affection from the group, a fast-acting authoritarian leader is appreciated in a crisis.

Democratic leadership is more expressive and makes a point of including everyone in the decision-making process. Although less successful in a crisis situation, democratic leaders generally draw on the ideas of all members to develop creative solutions to problems.

Laissez-faire leadership allows the group to function more or less on its own (*laissez-faire* in French means "leave it alone"). This style is typically the least effective in promoting group goals (White & Lippitt, 1953; Ridgeway, 1983).

Group Conformity

Groups influence the behavior of their members by promoting conformity. "Fitting in" provides a secure feeling of belonging, but at the extreme, group pressure can be unpleasant and even dangerous. As experiments by Solomon Asch and Stanley Milgram showed, even strangers can encourage conformity.

Asch's Research

Solomon Asch (1952) recruited students for what he told them was a study of visual perception. Before the experiment began, he explained to all but one member in a small group that their real purpose was to put pressure on the remaining person. Arranging six to eight students around a table, Asch showed them a "standard" line, as drawn on Card 1 in Figure 7–1, and asked them to match it to one of three lines on Card 2.

Anyone with normal vision could easily see that the line marked "A" on Card 2 is the correct choice. At the beginning of the experiment, everyone made the matches correctly. But then Asch's secret accomplices began answering incorrectly, leaving the uninformed student (seated at the table so as to answer next to last) bewildered and uncomfortable.

What happened? Asch found that one-third of all subjects chose to conform by answering incorrectly. Apparently, many of us are willing to compromise our own judgment to avoid the discomfort of being seen as different, even by people we do not know.

NOTE: Many studies in social psychology rest on subject deception, a controversial practice included in Chapter 1's discussion of research ethics. The Milgram experiment is troublesome in this regard because it subjected people to high stress.

NOTE: Milgram found that the physical presence of the experimenter generated the highest level of subject compliance. When commands were issued by telephone, compliance dropped by 20%.

NOTE: Ethnocentrism is one expression of valuing one's own in-group while undervaluing those who differ as an out-group.

NOTE: Keep in mind that pressure to conform comes from many sources other than groups, including media presentations, pronouncements of experts, and opinions of significant others.

Q: "Why doth one man's yawning make another yawn?" Robert Burton

SEEING SOCIOLOGY
in Everyday Life

Thinking back to Chapter 2 ("Sociological Investigation"), do you think that sociologists today would consider Milgram's research ethical? Why or why not?

groupthink the tendency of group members to conform, resulting in a narrow view of some issue

Milgram's Research

Stanley Milgram, a former student of Solomon Asch's, conducted conformity experiments of his own. In Milgram's controversial study (1963, 1965; A. G. Miller, 1986), a researcher explained to male recruits that they would be taking part in a study of how punishment affects learning. One by one, he assigned the subjects to the role of teacher and placed another person—actually an accomplice of Milgram's—in a connecting room to pose as a learner.

The teacher watched as the learner was seated in what looked like an electric chair. The researcher applied electrode paste to one of the learner's wrists, explaining that this would "prevent blisters and burns." The researcher then attached an electrode to the wrist and secured the leather straps, explaining that these would "prevent excessive movement while the learner was being shocked." The researcher assured the teacher that although the shocks would be painful, they would cause "no permanent tissue damage."

The researcher then led the teacher back to the next room, explaining that the "electric chair" was connected to a "shock generator," actually a phony but realistic-looking piece of equipment with a label that read "Shock Generator, Type ZLB, Dyson Instrument Company, Waltham, Mass." On the front was a dial that appeared to regulate electric shock from 15 volts (labeled "Slight Shock") to 300 volts (marked "Intense Shock") to 450 volts (marked "Danger: Severe Shock").

Seated in front of the "shock generator," the teacher was told to read aloud pairs of words. Then the teacher was to repeat the first word of each pair and wait for the learner to recall the second word. Whenever the learner failed to answer correctly, the teacher was told to apply an electric shock.

The researcher directed the teacher to begin at the lowest level (15 volts) and to increase the shock by another 15 volts every time the learner made a mistake. And so the teacher did. At 75, 90, and 105 volts, the teacher heard moans from the learner; at 120 volts, shouts of pain; at 270 volts, screams; at 315 volts, pounding on the wall; after that, dead silence. None of forty subjects assigned to the role of teacher during the initial research even questioned the procedure before reaching 300 volts, and twenty-six of the subjects—almost two-thirds—went all the way to 450 volts. Even Milgram was surprised at how readily people obeyed authority figures.

Milgram (1964) then modified his research to see if groups of ordinary people—not authority figures—could pressure people to administer electrical shocks, as Asch's groups had pressured individuals to match lines incorrectly.

This time, Milgram formed a group of three teachers, two of whom were his accomplices. Each of the three teachers was to suggest a shock level when the learner made an error; the rule was that the group would then administer the *lowest* of the three suggested levels. This arrangement gave the person not "in" on the

FIGURE 7–1 Cards Used in Asch's Experiment in Group Conformity

In Asch's experiment, subjects were asked to match the line on Card 1 to one of the lines on Card 2. Many subjects agreed with the wrong answers given by others in their group.

Source: Asch (1952).

experiment the power to deliver a lesser shock regardless of what the others said.

The accomplices suggested increasing the shock level with each error, putting pressure on the third member to do the same. The subjects in these groups applied voltages three to four times higher than the levels applied by subjects acting alone. In this way, Milgram showed that people are likely to follow the lead of not only legitimate authority figures but also groups of ordinary individuals, even when it means harming another person.

Janis's "Groupthink"

Experts also cave in to group pressure, says Irving L. Janis (1972, 1989). Janis argues that a number of U.S. foreign policy errors, including the failure to foresee Japan's attack on Pearl Harbor during World War II and our ill-fated involvement in the Vietnam War, resulted from group conformity among our highest-ranking political leaders.

Common sense tells us that group discussion improves decision making. Janis counters that group members often seek agreement that closes off other points of view. Janis called this process **groupthink,** *the tendency of group members to conform, resulting in a narrow view of some issue.*

A classic example of groupthink led to the failed invasion of Cuba at the Bay of Pigs in 1961. Looking back, Arthur Schlesinger Jr., an adviser to President John F. Kennedy, confessed to feeling guilty for "having kept so quiet during those crucial discussions in the Cabinet Room," adding that the group discouraged anyone from

Q: "Some similarities in status attributes between the individual and the reference group must be perceived or imagined, in order for the comparison to occur at all." Robert K. Merton (1968:296)

NOTE: Regarding reference groups, Durkheim contended that failure to have any reference points invites an intolerable lack of constraints that leaves people at the mercy of their own passions (since humans, unlike animals, do not regulate themselves).

DISCUSS: Expand reference group dynamics with a discussion of relative deprivation (see page 610). A *Times-Mirror* poll found that a growing share of older people in the U.S. have expressed dissatisfaction with their financial situation, while young people are more positive. Actual earnings data, however, show the opposite, with the incomes of the elderly rising in recent decades while incomes of people in their twenties actually fell.

reference group a social group that serves as a point of reference in making evaluations and decisions

in-group a social group toward which a member feels respect and loyalty

out-group a social group toward which a person feels a sense of competition or opposition

The triad, illustrated by Jonathan Green's painting *Friends,* includes three people. A triad is more stable than a dyad because conflict between any two persons can be mediated by the third member. Even so, should the relationship between any two become more intense in a positive sense, those two are likely to exclude the third.

Jonathan Green, *Friends,* 1992. Oil on masonite, 14 in. × 11 in. © Jonathan Green, Naples, Florida. Collection of Patric McCoy.

challenging what, in hindsight, Schlesinger considered "nonsense" (quoted in Janis, 1972:30, 40). Groupthink may also have been a factor in 2003 when U.S. leaders went to war on the assumption that Iraq had stockpiles of weapons of mass destruction.

Reference Groups

How do we assess our own attitudes and behavior? Frequently, we use a **reference group,** *a social group that serves as a point of reference in making evaluations and decisions.*

A young man who imagines his family's response to a woman he is dating is using his family as a reference group. A supervisor who tries to predict her employees' reaction to a new vacation policy is

using them in the same way. As these examples suggest, reference groups can be primary or secondary. In either case, our need to conform shows how others' attitudes affect us.

We also use groups that we do *not* belong to for reference. Being well prepared for a job interview means showing up dressed the way people in that company dress for work. Conforming to groups we do not belong to is a strategy to win acceptance and illustrates the process of *anticipatory socialization,* described in Chapter 5 ("Socialization").

Stouffer's Research

Samuel Stouffer and his colleagues (1949) conducted a classic study of reference group dynamics during World War II. Researchers asked soldiers to rate their own or any competent soldier's chances of promotion in their army unit. You might guess that soldiers serving in outfits with a high promotion rate would be optimistic about advancement. Yet Stouffer's research pointed to the opposite conclusion: Soldiers in army units with low promotion rates were actually more positive about their chances to move ahead.

The key to understanding Stouffer's results lies in the groups against which soldiers measured themselves. Those assigned to units with lower promotion rates looked around them and saw people making no more headway than they were. That is, although they had not been promoted, neither had many others, so they did not feel slighted. However, soldiers in units with a higher promotion rate could easily think of people who had been promoted sooner or more often than they had. With such people in mind, even soldiers who had been promoted were likely to feel shortchanged.

The point is that we do not make judgments about ourselves in isolation, nor do we compare ourselves with just anyone. Regardless of our situation in *absolute* terms, we form a subjective sense of our well-being by looking at ourselves *relative* to specific reference groups.

In-Groups and Out-Groups

Each of us favors some groups over others, based on political outlook, social prestige, or even just manner of dress. On the college campus, for example, left-leaning student activists may look down on fraternity members, whom they consider too conservative; fraternity members, in turn, may snub the "nerds," who they feel work too hard. People in every social setting make positive and negative evaluations of members of other groups.

Such judgments illustrate another important element of group dynamics: the opposition of in-groups and out-groups. An **in-group** is *a social group toward which a member feels respect and loyalty.* An in-group exists in relation to an **out-group,** *a social group toward which a person feels a sense of competition or opposition.* In-groups

NOTE: Because of Simmel's focus on the intricate details of situational social life, Everett Hughes dubbed him "the Freud of sociology."

EXERCISE: Imagine that you are designing a table for classroom use: Students and a professor will sit around the table to hold class. Thinking about the effects of group size on interpersonal dynamics, analyze the difference in patterns of interaction if you build a table big enough for 8 people versus a table big enough for 20.

RESOURCE: Georg Simmel's "The Dyad and the Triad" is one of the classics included in the companion reader, *Seeing Ourselves*, 8th ed.

GLOBAL: Marriage in our society is dyadic; ideally, powerful emotional ties unite husbands and wives. However, marriage in other societies may involve more than two people. In that case, the household is usually more stable, although many of the marital relationships are weaker.

● SEEING SOCIOLOGY
in Everyday Life

In terms of in-groups and out-groups, explain what happens when people who may not like each other discover that they have a common enemy.

dyad a social group with two members

triad a social group with three members

and out-groups are based on the idea that "we" have valued traits that "they" lack.

Tensions between groups sharpen the groups' boundaries and give people a clearer social identity. However, members of in-groups generally hold overly positive views of themselves and unfairly negative views of various out-groups.

Power also plays a part in intergroup relations. A powerful in-group can define others as a lower-status out-group. Historically, in countless U.S. towns and cities, many white people viewed people of color as an out-group and subordinated them socially, politically, and economically. Minorities who internalize these negative attitudes often struggle to overcome negative self-images. In this way, in-groups and out-groups foster loyalty but also generate conflict (Tajfel, 1982; Bobo & Hutchings, 1996).

Group Size

The next time you go to a party, try to arrive first. If you do, you will be able to watch some fascinating group dynamics. Until about six people enter the room, every person who arrives shares a single conversation. As more people arrive, the group divides into two clusters, and it divides again and again as the party grows. Size plays an important role in how group members interact.

To understand why, note the mathematical number of relationships among two to seven people. As shown in Figure 7–2, two people form a single relationship; adding a third person results in three relationships; adding a fourth person yields six. Increasing the number of people one at a time, then, expands the number of relationships much more rapidly since every new individual can interact with everyone already there. Thus by the time seven people join one conversation, twenty-one "channels" connect them. With so many open channels, some people begin to feel left out, and the group usually divides.

The Dyad

The German sociologist Georg Simmel (1858–1918) studied social dynamics in the smallest groups. Simmel (1950, orig. 1902) used the term **dyad** (Greek for "pair") to designate *a social group with two members*. Simmel explained that social interaction in a dyad is usually more intense than in larger groups because neither member shares the other's attention with anyone else. In the United States, love affairs, marriages, and the closest friendships are typically dyadic.

But like a stool with only two legs, dyads are unstable. Both members of a dyad must work to keep the relationship going; if either withdraws, the group collapses. Because the stability of marriages is important to society, the marital dyad is supported by legal, economic, and often religious ties.

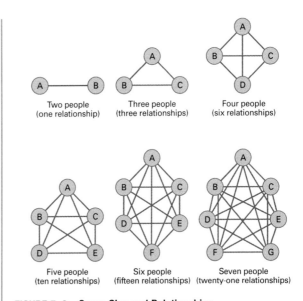

Two people
(one relationship)

Three people
(three relationships)

Four people
(six relationships)

Five people
(ten relationships)

Six people
(fifteen relationships)

Seven people
(twenty-one relationships)

FIGURE 7–2   Group Size and Relationships

As the number of people in a group increases, the number of relationships that link them increases much faster. By the time six or seven people share a conversation, the group usually divides into two. Why are relationships in smaller groups typically more intense?

Source: Created by the author.

The Triad

Simmel also studied the **triad,** *a social group with three members,* which contains three relationships, each uniting two of the three people. A triad is more stable than a dyad because one member can act as a mediator should the relationship between the other two become strained. Such group dynamics help explain why members of a dyad (say, a married couple) often seek out a third person (such as a counselor) to discuss tensions between them.

On the other hand, two of the three can pair up at times to press their views on the third, or two may intensify their relationship, leaving the other feeling left out. For example, when two of the three develop a romantic interest in each other, they will come to understand the meaning of the old saying, "Two's company, three's a crowd."

As groups grow beyond three people, they become more stable and capable of withstanding the loss of one or more members. At the same time, increases in group size reduce the intense personal interaction possible only in the smallest groups. This is why larger groups are based less on personal attachment and more on formal rules and regulations.

DIVERSITY: Illustrating Blau's analysis, members of small racial and ethnic communities are more likely to marry out of their category than are members of larger communities.

NOTE: Networks are a characteristic of modern societies in which social ties are built not on localized kinship and neighborhood but on a wide range of individual experiences and interests.

Q: "In our own life the intimacy of the neighborhood has been broken up by the growth of an intricate mesh of wider contacts which leaves us strangers to people who live in the same house." Charles Horton Cooley (1962:26, orig. 1909)

DISCUSS: Networks are an important resource for newly arrived immigrants (Menjivar, 1997). Ask members of the class who have immigrated (or migrated) to describe their use of networks.

● MAKING THE GRADE

Is a network a group? No, because there is no common identification or frequent interaction among members. But fuzzy or not, networks are a valuable resource, which is probably the best reason to understand a little about how they work.

 network a web of weak social ties

Social Diversity: Race, Class, and Gender

Race, ethnicity, class, and gender each play a part in group dynamics. Peter Blau (1977; Blau, Blum, & Schwartz, 1982; South & Messner, 1986) points out three ways in which social diversity influences intergroup contact:

1. **Large groups turn inward.** Blau explains that the larger a group is, the more likely its members are to have relationships just among themselves. Say a college is trying to enhance social diversity by increasing the number of international students. These students may add a dimension of difference, but as their numbers rise, they become more likely to form their own social group. Thus efforts to promote social diversity may have the unintended effect of promoting separatism.

Today's college campuses value social diversity. One of the challenges of this movement is ensuring that all categories of students are fully integrated into campus life. This is not always easy. Following Blau's theory of group dynamics, as the number of minority students increases, these men and women are able to form a group unto themselves, perhaps interacting less with others.

2. **Heterogeneous groups turn outward.** The more internally diverse a group is, the more likely its members are to interact with outsiders. Members of campus groups that recruit people of both sexes and various social backgrounds typically have more intergroup contact than those with members of one social category.

3. **Physical boundaries create social boundaries.** To the extent that a social group is physically segregated from others (by having its own dorm or dining area, for example), its members are less likely to interact with other people.

Networks

A **network** is *a web of weak social ties.* Think of a network as a "fuzzy" group containing people who come into occasional contact but who lack a sense of boundaries and belonging. If you think of a *group* as a "circle of friends," think of a network as a "social web" expanding outward, often reaching great distances and including large numbers of people.

The largest network of all is the World Wide Web of the Internet. But the Internet has expanded much more in some global regions than in others. Global Map 7–1 shows that Internet use is high in rich countries and far less common in poor nations.

Closer to home, some networks come close to being groups, as is the case with college classmates who stay in touch after graduation through class newsletters and reunions. More commonly, however, a network includes people we know of or who know of us but with whom we interact rarely, if at all. As one woman known as a community organizer explains, "I get calls at home, [and] someone says, 'Are you Roseann Navarro? Somebody told me to call you. I have this problem. . . .'" (quoted in Kaminer, 1984:94).

Network ties often give us the sense that we live in a "small world." In a classic experiment, Stanley Milgram (1967; Watts, 1999) gave letters to subjects in Kansas and Nebraska intended for a few specific people in Boston who were unknown to the original subjects. No addresses were supplied, and the subjects in the study were told to send the letters to others they knew personally who might know the target people. Milgram found that the target people received the letters with, on average, six subjects passing them on. This result led Milgram to conclude that just about everyone is connected to everyone else by "six degrees of separation." Later research, however, has cast doubt on Milgram's conclusions. Examining Milgram's original data, Judith Kleinfeld points out that most of Milgram's letters (240 out of 300) never arrived at their destinations (Wildavsky, 2002). Those that did were typically given to people who were wealthy, a fact that led Kleinfeld to conclude that rich people are far better connected across the country than ordinary women and men.

NOTE: As a network increases in size, its value to members also increases because it offers more social resources. Moreover, key individuals may well be sought out by various networks. The end result is a fusion of numerous small networks into one larger one.

THE MAP: Internet use depends on the availability of personal computers. Much of the Internet's available software demands that users read and write in the Latin alphabet using English. This will change with time, but it is unlikely that the Internet will ever become as multicultural as the world it connects. More than 60% of U.S. households have a personal computer, most connected to an Internet account. Almost half of the U.S. workforce uses the Internet on the job.

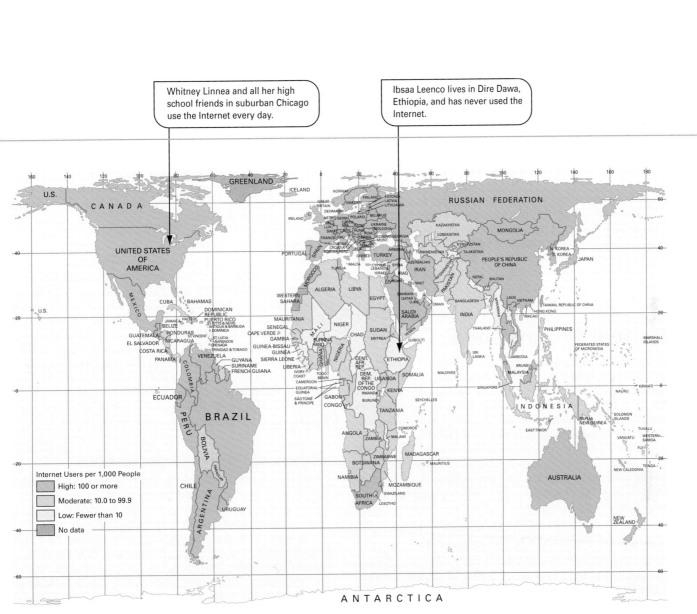

Whitney Linnea and all her high school friends in suburban Chicago use the Internet every day.

Ibsaa Leenco lives in Dire Dawa, Ethiopia, and has never used the Internet.

Internet Users per 1,000 People
High: 100 or more
Moderate: 10.0 to 99.9
Low: Fewer than 10
No data

Window on the World

GLOBAL MAP 7–1   Internet Users in Global Perspective

This map shows how the Information Revolution has affected countries around the world. In most high-income nations, at least one-third of the population uses the Internet. By contrast, only a small share of people in low-income nations does so. What effect does this pattern have on people's access to information? What does this mean for the future in terms of global inequality?

Source: United Nations Statistics Division (2008).

Network ties may be weak, but they can be a powerful resource. For immigrants who are trying to become established in a new community, businesspeople seeking to expand their operations, or new college graduates looking for a job, *whom* you know is often as important as *what* you know (Hagan, 1998; Petersen, Saporta, & Seidel, 2000).

Networks are based on people's colleges, clubs, neighborhoods, political parties, and personal interests. Obviously, some networks contain people with considerably more wealth, power, and prestige than others; that explains the importance of being "well connected." The networks of more privileged categories of people—such as the members of an expensive country club—are a valuable form of "social capital," which is more likely to lead people to higher-paying jobs (Green, Tigges, & Diaz, 1999; Lin, Cook, & Burt, 2001).

Some people also have denser networks than others; that is, they are connected to more people. Typically, the largest social networks

formal organizations large secondary groups organized to achieve their goals efficiently

bureaucracy an organizational model rationally designed to perform tasks efficiently

organizational environment factors outside an organization that affect its operation

SEEING SOCIOLOGY
in Everyday Life

Today's world has so many large organizations that we identify them just by initials: IRS, FBI, IBM, CIA, NATO, CNN, PTA, WWF, and so on. How many more examples can you think of?

include people who are young, well educated, and living in large cities (Fernandez & Weinberg, 1997; Podolny & Baron, 1997).

Gender also shapes networks. Although the networks of men and women are typically the same size, women include more relatives (and more women) in their networks, and men include more co-workers (and more men). Research suggests that women's ties do not carry quite the same clout as typical "old boy" networks. Even so, research suggests that as gender equality increases in the United States, the networks of women and men are becoming more alike (Reskin & McBrier, 2000; Torres & Huffman, 2002).

Formal Organizations

A century ago, most people lived in small groups of family, friends, and neighbors. Today, our lives revolve more and more around **formal organizations,** *large secondary groups organized to achieve their goals efficiently.* Formal organizations, such as business corporations and government agencies, differ from families and neighborhoods in their impersonality and their formally planned atmosphere.

When you think about it, organizing more than 300 million people in this country into a single society is truly remarkable, whether it involves paving roads, collecting taxes, schooling children, or delivering the mail. To carry out most of these tasks, we rely on different types of large formal organizations.

Types of Formal Organizations

Amitai Etzioni (1975) identified three types of formal organizations, distinguished by the reasons people participate in them: utilitarian organizations, normative organizations, and coercive organizations.

Utilitarian Organizations

Just about everyone who works for income belongs to a *utilitarian organization,* one that pays people for their efforts. Large businesses, for example, generate profits for their owners and income for their employees. Becoming part of a utilitarian organization such as a business or government agency is usually a matter of individual choice, although most people must join one or another such organization to make a living.

Normative Organizations

People join *normative organizations* not for income but to pursue some goal they think is morally worthwhile. Sometimes called *voluntary associations,* these include community service groups (such as the PTA, the Lions Club, the League of Women Voters, and the Red Cross), as well as political parties and religious organizations. In global perspective, people living in the United States and other high-income nations with relatively democratic political systems are likely to join voluntary associations. A recent study found that 72 percent of first-year college students in the United States claimed to have participated in some volunteer activity within the past year (Pryor et al., 2008).

Coercive Organizations

Membership in *coercive organizations* is involuntary. People are forced to join these organizations as a form of punishment (prisons) or treatment (some psychiatric hospitals). Coercive organizations have special physical features, such as locked doors and barred windows, and are supervised by security personnel. They isolate people, whom they label "inmates" or "patients," for a period of time in order to radically change their attitudes and behavior. Recall from Chapter 5 ("Socialization") the power of a total institution to change a person's sense of self.

It is possible for a single organization to fall into all three categories. For example, a mental hospital serves as a coercive organization for a patient, a utilitarian organization for a psychiatrist, and a normative organization for a hospital volunteer.

Origins of Formal Organizations

Formal organizations date back thousands of years. Elites who controlled early empires relied on government officials to collect taxes, undertake military campaigns, and build monumental structures, from the Great Wall of China to the pyramids of Egypt.

However, early organizations had two limitations. First, they lacked the technology to let people travel over large distances, to communicate quickly, and to gather and store information. Second, the preindustrial societies they were trying to rule had traditional cultures, so for the most part, ruling organizations tried to preserve cultural systems, not change them. But during the last few centuries, what Max Weber called a "rational worldview" emerged in parts of the world, a process described in Chapter 4 ("Society"). In Europe and North America, the Industrial Revolution ushered in a new structure for formal organizations concerned with efficiency that Weber called "bureaucracy."

Characteristics of Bureaucracy

Bureaucracy is *an organizational model rationally designed to perform tasks efficiently.* Bureaucratic officials regularly create and revise policy to increase efficiency. To appreciate the power and scope of bureaucratic organization, consider that any one of the almost 400 million telephones in the United States can connect you within seconds to any other phone in a home, business, automobile, or even a hiker's backpack on a remote trail in the Rocky Mountains. Such instant communication was beyond the imagination of people who lived in the ancient world.

RESOURCE: An excerpt from Max Weber's analysis of bureaucracy is in the companion reader, *Seeing Ourselves*, 8th ed.

Q: "Hell hath no fury like a bureaucrat scorned." Milton Friedman

NOTE: Following Weber's analysis, the most effective way to destroy a bureaucratic organization would be to eliminate not its officers but its files.

NOTE: Throughout history, people favored "their own kind" (especially kin). A bureaucratic culture erodes ascription in favor of achievement. Favoring kin is transformed into conflict of interest and nepotism.

NOTE: To illustrate the difficulty of disrupting bureaucracy: Early in the 1980s, the IRS issued a statement that even in the event of nuclear war, it expected people to pay their taxes on time.

SEEING SOCIOLOGY
in Everyday Life

Give an example of each of the factors listed here in the operation of your college or university bureaucracy.

MAKING THE GRADE

The six traits listed here defined, for Weber, the *ideal* bureaucracy. This means that in its pure form, bureaucracy has all these traits.

Our telephone system depends on technology such as electricity, fiber optics, and computers. But the system could not exist without the bureaucracy that keeps track of every telephone call—noting which phone calls which other phone, when, and for how long—and then presents the relevant information to more than 250 million telephone users in the form of a monthly bill (CTIA, 2008).

What specific traits promote organizational efficiency? Max Weber (1978, orig. 1921) identified six key elements of the ideal bureaucratic organization:

1. **Specialization.** Our ancestors spent most of their time looking for food and shelter. Bureaucracy, by contrast, assigns people highly specialized jobs.

2. **Hierarchy of positions.** Bureaucracies arrange workers in a vertical ranking. Each person is supervised by someone "higher up" in the organization while in turn supervising others in lower positions. Usually, with few people at the top and many at the bottom, bureaucratic organizations take the form of a pyramid.

3. **Rules and regulations.** Cultural tradition counts for little in a bureaucracy. Instead, rationally enacted rules and regulations guide a bureaucracy's operation. Ideally, a bureaucracy operates in a completely predictable way.

4. **Technical competence.** Bureaucratic officials have the technical competence to carry out their duties. Bureaucracies typically hire new members according to set standards and then monitor their performance. Such impersonal evaluation contrasts with the ancient custom of favoring relatives, whatever their talents, over strangers.

5. **Impersonality.** Bureaucracy puts rules ahead of personal whim so that both clients and workers are treated in the same way. From this impersonal approach comes the image of the "faceless bureaucrat."

6. **Formal, written communications.** It is said that the heart of bureaucracy is not people but paperwork. Instead of the casual, face-to-face talk that characterizes interaction within small groups, bureaucracy relies on formal, written memos and reports, which accumulate in vast files.

Bureaucratic organization promotes efficiency by carefully hiring workers and limiting the unpredictable effects of personal taste and opinion. The Summing Up table on page 172 reviews the differences between small social groups and large bureaucratic organizations.

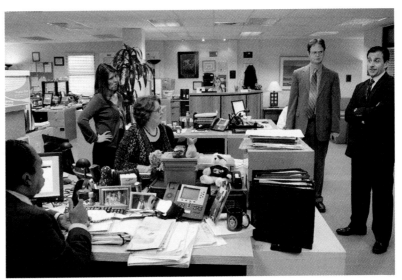

Weber described the operation of the ideal bureaucracy as rational and highly efficient. In real life, actual large organizations often operate very differently from Weber's model, as can be seen on the television show *The Office*.

Organizational Environment

No organization operates in a vacuum. The performance of any organization depends not only on its own goals and policies but also on the **organizational environment,** *factors outside an organization that affect its operation.* These factors include technology, economic and political trends, current events, the available workforce, and other organizations.

Modern organizations are shaped by *technology,* including copiers, fax machines, telephones, and computers. This technology gives employees access to more information and more people than ever before. At the same time, modern technology allows managers to monitor worker activities much more closely than in the past (Markoff, 1991).

Economic and political trends affect organizations. All organizations are helped or hurt by periodic economic growth or recession. Most industries also face competition from abroad as well as changes in laws—such as new environmental standards—at home.

Current events can have significant effects on organizations that are far removed from the location of the events themselves. A regional conflict that sends oil prices spiking upward or the election of a new president affects both government agencies and business organizations.

Population patterns also affect organizations. The average age, typical level of education, social diversity, and size of a local community

NOTE: Earlier editions included (C. Northcote) Parkinson's Law ("Work expands to fill the time available for its completion") and the (Laurence J.) Peter Principle ("Bureaucrats are promoted to their level of incompetence"). Although they are amusing, most empirical evidence fails to support these principles.

DISCUSS: Ask students if they have had any experiences with large, inefficient organizations such as, say, the post office, the military, or your university.

Q: "The Lord's Prayer is 66 words, the Gettysburg Address is 286 words, and there are 1,322 words in the Declaration of Independence. Yet government regulations on the sale of cabbage total 26,911 words." David McIntosh

NOTE: Showing inefficiency in a prebureaucratic world: Two weeks after the U.S. and Great Britain ended the War of 1812, 5,000 British troops, unaware of the peace agreement, attacked U.S. forces at New Orleans, resulting in 2,000 deaths.

● MAKING THE GRADE

Just because an organization is efficient doesn't mean that people enjoy being part of it or that it is actually good for people. Weber feared the opposite: The more rational and bureaucratic society became, the less it would advance human well-being.

SUMMING UP

Small Groups and Formal Organizations

	Small Groups	Formal Organizations
Activities	Much the same for all members	Distinct and highly specialized
Hierarchy	Often informal or nonexistent	Clearly defined according to position
Norms	General norms, informally applied	Clearly defined rules and regulations
Membership criteria	Variable; often based on personal affection or kinship	Technical competence to carry out assigned tasks
Relationships	Variable and typically primary	Typically secondary, with selective primary ties
Communications	Typically casual and face to face	Typically formal and in writing
Focus	Person-oriented	Task-oriented

determine the available workforce and sometimes the market for an organization's products or services.

Other organizations also contribute to the organizational environment. To be competitive, a hospital must be responsive to the insurance industry and to organizations representing doctors, nurses, and other health care workers. It must also be aware of the equipment and procedures available at nearby facilities, as well as their prices.

The Informal Side of Bureaucracy

Weber's ideal bureaucracy deliberately regulates every activity. In actual organizations, however, human beings are creative (and stubborn) enough to resist bureaucratic regulation. Informality may amount to simply cutting corners on your job, but it can also provide the flexibility needed to adapt and prosper.

In part, informality comes from the personalities of organizational leaders. Studies of U.S. corporations document that the qualities and quirks of individuals—including personal charisma, interpersonal skills, and the willingness to recognize problems—can have a great effect on organizational outcomes (Halberstam, 1986; Baron, Hannan, & Burton, 1999).

Authoritarian, democratic, and laissez-faire types of leadership (described earlier in this chapter) reflect individual personality as much as any organizational plan. In the "real world" of organizations, leaders sometimes seek to benefit personally by abusing orga-

nizational power. Many of the corporate leaders of banks and insurance companies that collapsed during the financial meltdown of 2008 walked off with huge "golden parachutes." Throughout the business world, leaders take credit for the efforts of the people who work for them, at least when things go well. In addition, the importance of many secretaries to how well a boss performs is often much greater than most people think (and greater than a secretary's official job title and salary suggest).

Communication offers another example of organizational informality. Memos and other written communications are the formal way to spread information throughout an organization. Typically, however, individuals also create informal networks, or "grapevines," that spread information quickly, if not always accurately. Grapevines, using both word of mouth and e-mail, are particularly important to rank-and-file workers because higher-ups often try to keep important information from them.

The spread of e-mail has "flattened" organizations somewhat, allowing even the lowest-ranking employee to bypass immediate superiors and communicate directly with the organization's leader or with all fellow employees at once. Some organizations object to such "open-channel" communication and limit the use of e-mail. Microsoft Corporation (whose founder, Bill Gates, has an unlisted e-mail address that helps him limit his mail to a few hundred messages a day) pioneered the development of screens that filter out messages from everyone except certain approved people (Gwynne & Dickerson, 1997).

Q: "The only thing that saves us from bureaucracy is its inefficiency." Eugene McCarthy

Q: "Specialists without spirit, sensualists without heart; this nullity imagines that it has attained a level of civilization never before achieved." Max Weber (1958:182, orig. 1904–05)

NOTE: Modern bureaucracy arose at the same time as large, efficient armies; Weber's bureaucratic traits are very militaristic.

Q: "The only thing that saves us from bureaucracy is its inefficiency." Eugene McCarthy

NOTE: Arne L. Kalleberg and Mark E. Van Buren (1996) found that "bigger is better" when it comes to employee rewards, such as salaries and fringe benefits. Yet "small is beautiful" when it comes to giving employees autonomy.

SEEING SOCIOLOGY in Everyday Life

Do you think FEMA or other large government organizations are inherently inefficient, or do you think their leaders sometimes make bad decisions? Explain your answer.

bureaucratic ritualism a focus on rules and regulations to the point of undermining an organization's goals

bureaucratic inertia (p. 174) the tendency of bureaucratic organizations to perpetuate themselves

oligarchy (p. 174) the rule of the many by the few

Using new information technology as well as age-old human ingenuity, members of organizations often try to break free of rigid rules in order to personalize procedures and surroundings. Such efforts suggest that we should take a closer look at some of the problems of bureaucracy.

Problems of Bureaucracy

We rely on bureaucracy to manage everyday life efficiently, but many people are uneasy about large organizations. Bureaucracy can dehumanize and manipulate us, and some say it poses a threat to political democracy. These dangers are discussed in the following sections.

Bureaucratic Alienation

Max Weber held up bureaucracy as a model of productivity. However, Weber was keenly aware of bureaucracy's ability to *dehumanize* the people it is supposed to serve. The same impersonality that fosters efficiency also keeps officials and clients from responding to one another's unique personal needs. Typically, officials at large government and corporate agencies must treat each client impersonally as a standard "case." In 2008, for example, the U.S. Army accidently sent letters to family members of soldiers killed in Iraq and Afghanistan, addressing the recipients as "John Doe" ("Army Apologizes," 2009).

Formal organizations breed *alienation,* according to Weber, by reducing the human being to "a small cog in a ceaselessly moving mechanism" (1978:988, orig. 1921). Although formal organizations are designed to benefit people, Weber feared that people might well end up serving formal organizations.

Bureaucratic Inefficiency and Ritualism

On Labor Day 2005, as people in New Orleans and other coastal areas were battling to survive in the wake of Hurricane Katrina, 600 firefighters from around the country assembled in a hotel meeting room in Atlanta awaiting deployment. Officials of the Federal Emergency Management Agency (FEMA) explained to the crowd that they were first going to be given a lecture on "equal opportunity, sexual harassment, and customer service." Then, the official continued, they would each be given a stack of FEMA pamphlets with the agency's phone number to distribute to people in the devastated areas. A firefighter stood up and shouted, "This is ridiculous! Our fire departments and mayors sent us down here to save lives, and you've got us doing *this*?" The FEMA official thundered back, "You are now employees of FEMA, and you will follow orders and do what you are told!" ("Places," 2005:39)

George Tooker's painting *Government Bureau* is a powerful statement about the human costs of bureaucracy. The artist paints members of the public in a drab sameness—reduced from human beings to mere "cases" to be disposed of as quickly as possible. Set apart from others by their positions, officials are "faceless bureaucrats" concerned more with numbers than with providing genuine assistance (notice that the artist places the fingers of the officials on calculators).

George Tooker, *Government Bureau*, 1956. Egg tempera on gesso panel, 19⅝ × 29⅝ inches. The Metropolitan Museum of Art, George A. Hearn Fund, 1956 (56.78). Photograph © 1984 The Metropolitan Museum of Art.

Criticism of the government response to the hurricane disaster of 2005 was widespread and pointed to the problem of bureaucratic *inefficiency,* the failure of an organization to carry out the work that it exists to perform. Even four years later, as Seeing Sociology in the News on pages 174–75 explains, the complaints continue.

People sometimes describe this inefficiency as too much "red tape," a reference to the ribbon used by slow-working eighteenth-century English administrators to wrap official parcels and records (Shipley, 1985).

To Robert Merton (1968), red tape amounts to a new twist on the already familiar concept of group conformity. He coined the term **bureaucratic ritualism** to describe *a focus on rules and regulations to the point of undermining an organization's goals.* In short, rules and regulations should be a means to an end, not an end in themselves that takes the focus away from the organization's stated goals. After the terrorist attacks of September 11, 2001, for example, the U.S. Postal Service continued to help deliver mail addressed to Osama bin Laden at a post office in Afghanistan, despite the objections of the FBI. It took an act of Congress to change the policy (Bedard, 2002).

Q: "It is organization which gives birth to the dominion of the elected over the electors, of the mandataries over the mandators, of the delegates over the delegators. Who says organization says oligarchy." Robert Michels

DIVERSITY: A growing number of women are trying to resolve role conflicts by leaving organizational jobs ("cashing out") and starting their own small businesses.

NOTE: At Honda's plant at Marysville, Ohio—North America's most productive—assembly line workers (referred to as "associates") have considerable opportunity to shape the production process. All employees, from the president to the maintenance staff, wear similar uniforms to encourage exchange of ideas.

Seeing SOCIOLOGY in the NEWS

CBS News

FEMA's "Toxic Bureaucracy": Are FEMA Managers Holding Up Aid to Hold onto Their Jobs?

By ARMEN KETEYIAN
February 25, 2009

(CBS) FEMA's been under fire from critics who claim the Gulf Coast recovery is moving too slowly. Now FEMA officials said they're investigating allegations of serious misconduct at the New Orleans office. CBS News has learned workers there accuse their bosses of intentionally holding up Katrina aid.

The day Hurricane Katrina hit Slidell, La., in 2005, more than six feet of tidal surge flooded the city's downtown. Today Slidell mayor Ben Morris is still running city hall—out of a trailer.

"When the train goes by, it shakes," Morris said.

All because of endless delays, caused by FEMA, he says, which just last month delayed money for rebuilding yet again, CBS News chief investigative correspondent Armen Keteyian reports exclusively.

"It's been an indescribable nightmare that most people would not believe," Morris explained.

Today, nearly $4 billion intended to rebuild the Gulf Coast remains unspent. That's 68 percent of the $6 billion promised by FEMA.

This is leaving hundreds of projects, like a police station in New Orleans, and the Charity Hospital, waiting.

Now, a CBS News investigation has uncovered what more than a dozen current and former employees say is one key reason help isn't getting to those in need.

They point to a FEMA office in downtown New Orleans, which is responsible for distributing the money. They say the way the office is managed is itself a disaster.

Three senior level staff people—who still work for FEMA—fear they will lose their jobs for speaking out. CBS News agreed to protect their identities.

Keteyian asked one employee to describe the atmosphere in the office.

Keteyian: Cronyism?
FEMA employee: Yes.
Keteyian: Sexual harassment?
FEMA employee: Yes.
Keteyian: Racial discrimination?
FEMA employee: Yes.
Keteyian: Intimidation?
FEMA employee: Yes.
Keteyian: Retaliation?
FEMA employee: Yes.

Bureaucratic Inertia

If bureaucrats sometimes have little reason to work very hard, they have every reason to protect their jobs. Officials typically work to keep an organization going even after its original goal has been realized. As Weber put it, "Once fully established, bureaucracy is among the social structures which are hardest to destroy" (1978:987, orig. 1921).

Bureaucratic inertia refers to *the tendency of bureaucratic organizations to perpetuate themselves.* Formal organizations tend to take on a life of their own beyond their formal objectives. For example, the U.S. Department of Agriculture has offices in nearly every county in all fifty states, even though only one county in seven has any working farms. Usually, an organization stays in business by redefining its goals. For example, the Agriculture Department now performs a broad range of work not directly related to farming, including nutritional and environmental research.

Oligarchy

Early in the twentieth century, Robert Michels (1876–1936) pointed out the link between bureaucracy and political **oligarchy**, *the rule of the many by the few* (1949, orig. 1911). According to what Michels called the "iron law of oligarchy," the pyramid shape of bureaucracy places a few leaders in charge of the resources of the entire organization.

Weber believed that a strict hierarchy of responsibility resulted in high organizational efficiency. But Michels countered that this hierarchical structure also concentrates power and thus threatens democracy because officials can and often do use their access to information, resources, and the media to promote their own personal interests.

Furthermore, bureaucracy helps distance officials from the public, as in the case of the corporate president or public official who is "unavailable for comment" to the local press or the U.S. president who withholds documents from Congress claiming "executive privilege." Oligarchy, then, thrives in the hierarchical structure of bureaucracy and reduces leaders' accountability to the people.

Political competition, term limits, and a legal system that includes various checks and balances prevent the U.S. government from becoming an out-and-out oligarchy. Even so, incumbents, who generally have more visibility, power, and money than their challengers, enjoy a significant advantage in U.S. politics. In recent congressional elections, more than 90 percent of congressional officeholders on the ballot were able to win reelection.

The Evolution of Formal Organizations

The problems of bureaucracy—especially the alienation it produces and its tendency toward oligarchy—stem from two organizational traits: hierarchy and rigidity. To Weber, bureaucracy was a top-down system: Rules and regulations made at the top guide every facet of people's lives down the chain of command. A century ago in the United States, Weber's ideas took hold in an organizational model called *scientific management.* We take a look at this model and then examine three challenges over the course of the twentieth century that gradually led to a new model: the *flexible organization.*

DIVERSITY: An interesting question is whether women need to learn about organizations or organizations need to learn about women.

NOTE: Self-managed work teams are an outgrowth of so-called quality circles in which employees provide critical analyses of operations.

DISCUSS: Do students see any "female advantage" in college instructors? What about a "male advantage"? Explain.

NOTE: Henry Ford, an early fan of scientific management, created a "sociology office" to study (and influence) the lives of his workers.

CBS News has learned that since January 1, nearly 80 employment-related complaints have been filed by staff at the office. . . .

"The harassment, the equal rights—violations that are currently taking place over there, this office is slowing down the recovery in this region," said one former FEMA employee.

And slowing down the recovery—these former employees charge—is exactly what some senior managers at the New Orleans FEMA office want.

Keteyian: But what's in it for them? To slow this process . . .

Former FEMA employee: They're making . . . over $100,000 plus a pension in some cases.

Keteyian: So they've taken a natural disaster and turned it into a huge boondoggle for themselves?

Former FEMA employee: In my opinion, yes.

"Shame on FEMA," said Rep. Joseph Cao of Lousiana. Cao said the New Orleans FEMA office needs to be investigated.

"They're more worried about their own positions in FEMA, their own salaries," Cao said, "than the recovery process down here."

CBS News wanted to speak with Doug Whitmer or Jim Stark, his boss. Stark opened up this morning in Washington. He denied there was any intentional slow down of the recovery process.

"I find that pretty offensive, Armen," said Stark. "I live in New Orleans. I've lived there for six years. I joined FEMA to help my community to recover." . . .

"The word that has been used with us is 'toxic.' That the atmosphere in your office right now is toxic," Keteyian said.

"Then we'll take steps to fix it," Stark said.

Gulf Coast residents shouldn't expect FEMA's recovery work to end here anytime soon.

Employees say they've been told to expect it to go on for as long as 15 years.

WHAT DO YOU THINK?

1. Which of the "problems of bureaucracy" discussed in this section of the chapter do you find in this article?

2. Do the problems described here appear to be the failings of individuals or failings of large organizations? Explain.

3. What might be the solution to the problems described here?

Adapted from the original article, "FEMA's Toxic Bureaucracy," by Armen Keteyian, February 25, 2009, CBS Evening News. Reproduced by permission of CBS News Archives, a division of CBS.

Scientific Management

Frederick Winslow Taylor (1911) had a simple message: Most businesses in the United States were sadly inefficient. Managers had little idea of how to increase their business's output, and workers relied on the same tired skills of earlier generations. To increase efficiency, Taylor explained, business should apply the principles of science. **Scientific management** is thus *the application of scientific principles to the operation of a business or other large organization.*

Scientific management involves three steps. First, managers carefully observe the task performed by each worker, identifying all the operations involved and measuring the time needed for each. Second, managers analyze their data, trying to discover ways for workers to perform each job more efficiently. For example, managers might decide to give the worker different tools or to reposition various work operations within the factory. Third, management provides guidance and incentives for workers to do their jobs more quickly. If a factory worker moves 20 tons of pig iron in one day, for example, management shows the worker how to do the job more efficiently and then provides higher wages as the worker's productivity rises. Taylor concluded that if scientific principles were applied in this way, companies would become more profitable, workers would earn higher wages, and consumers would pay lower prices.

A century ago, the auto pioneer Henry Ford put it this way: "Save ten steps a day for each of 12,000 employees, and you will have saved fifty miles of wasted motion and misspent energy" (Allen & Hyman, 1999:209). In the early 1900s, the Ford Motor Company and many other businesses followed Taylor's lead and made improvements in efficiency.

The principles of scientific management suggested that workplace power should reside with owners and executives, who paid little attention to the ideas of their workers. As the decades passed, formal organizations faced important challenges, involving race and gender, rising competition from abroad, and the changing nature of work. We now take a brief look at each of these challenges.

The First Challenge: Race and Gender

In the 1960s, critics pointed out that big businesses and other organizations engaged in unfair hiring practices. Rather than hiring on the basis of competence as Weber had proposed, organizations had excluded women and other minorities, especially from positions of power. Hiring on the basis of competence is only partly a matter of fairness; it is also a matter of enlarging the talent pool to promote efficiency.

Patterns of Privilege and Exclusion

Even in the early twenty-first century, as shown in Figure 7–3 on page 176, non-Hispanic white men in the United States—33 percent of the working-age population—still held 54 percent of management jobs. Non-Hispanic white women made up 34 percent of the population but held just 29 percent of managerial positions (U.S. Equal Employment Opportunity Commission, 2008). The members of other minorities lagged further behind.

Rosabeth Moss Kanter (1977; Kanter & Stein, 1979) points out that excluding women and minorities from the workplace ignores the talents of more than half the population. Furthermore,

GLOBAL: Ouchi argues that their respective organizational contexts mean that business leaders in the U.S. can make quick decisions but often struggle to achieve implementation. In contrast, Japanese leaders (who involve many others early on) are slow to make decisions, but implementation is subsequently rapid.

NOTE: Worker alienation has been linked to rigid bureaucracy (Weber) and rigid class structure (Marx). Japan has a favorable position in both respects. Japanese workers enjoy greater involvement in a more personalized organizational environment. Additionally, the compensation ratio (management to workers) in Japan is roughly half that in the U.S.

Compared to their percentage of the total population, white men are over-represented in management positions.

scientific management (p. 175) the application of scientific principles to the operation of a business or other large organization

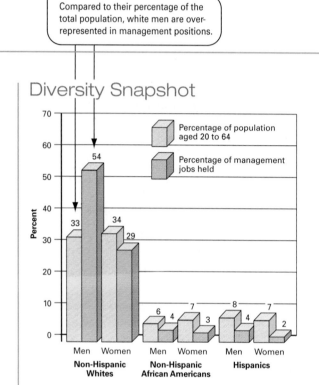

Diversity Snapshot

FIGURE 7–3   **U.S. Managers in Private Industry by Race, Sex, and Ethnicity, 2006**

White men are more likely than their population size suggests to be managers in private industry. The opposite is true for white women and other minorities. What factors do you think may account for this pattern?

Sources: U.S. Census Bureau (2008) and U.S. Equal Employment Opportunity Commission (2008).

more readily ask questions in order to understand an issue. Men, by contrast, have an "image focus" that makes them wonder how asking questions in a particular situation will affect their reputation.

In another study of women executives, Sally Helgesen (1990) found three other gender-linked patterns. First, women place greater value on communication skills than men and share information more than men do. Second, women are more flexible leaders who typically give their employees greater freedom. Third, compared to men, women tend to emphasize the interconnectedness of all organizational operations. These patterns, which Helgesen dubbed the *female advantage*, help make companies more flexible and democratic.

In sum, one challenge to conventional bureaucracy is to become more open and flexible in order to take advantage of the experience, ideas, and creativity of everyone, regardless of race or gender. The result goes right to the bottom line: greater profits.

The Second Challenge: The Japanese Work Organization

In 1980, the U.S. corporate world was shaken to discover that the most popular automobile model sold in this country was not a Chevrolet, Ford, or Plymouth but the Honda Accord, made in Japan. Recently, the Japanese corporation Toyota passed General Motors to become the largest carmaker in the world (Fowler, 2008). This is quite a change. As late as the 1950s, U.S. automakers dominated car production, and the label "Made in Japan" was generally found on products that were cheap and poorly made. The success of the Japanese auto industry, as well as companies making cameras and other products, drew attention to the "Japanese work organization." How was so small a country able to challenge the world's economic powerhouse?

Japanese organizations reflect that nation's strong collective spirit. In contrast to the U.S. emphasis on rugged individualism, the Japanese value cooperation. In effect, formal organizations in Japan are more like large primary groups. A generation ago, William Ouchi (1981) highlighted five differences between formal organizations in Japan and those in the United States. First, Japanese companies hired new workers in groups, giving everyone the same salary and responsibilities. Second, many Japanese companies hired workers for life, fostering a strong sense of loyalty. Third, with the idea that employees would spend their entire careers there, many Japanese companies trained workers in all phases of their operations. Fourth, although Japanese corporate leaders took final responsibility for their organization's performance, they involved workers in "quality circles" to discuss decisions that affected them. Fifth, Japanese companies played a large role in the lives of workers, providing home mortgages, sponsoring recreational activities, and scheduling social events. Together, such policies encourage much more loyalty among members of Japanese organizations than is typically the case in their U.S. counterparts.

underrepresented people in an organization often feel like socially isolated out-groups—uncomfortably visible, taken less seriously, and given fewer chances for promotion. Sometimes what passes for "merit" or good work in an organization is simply being of the right social category (Castilla, 2008).

Opening up an organization so that change and advancement happen more often, Kanter claims, improves everyone's on-the-job performance by motivating employees to become "fast-trackers" who work harder and are more committed to the company. By contrast, an organization with many dead-end jobs turns workers into less productive "zombies" who are never asked for their opinion on anything. An open organization encourages leaders to seek out the input of all employees, which usually improves decision making.

The "Female Advantage"

Some organizational researchers argue that women bring special management skills that strengthen an organization. According to Deborah Tannen (1994), women have a greater "information focus" and

GLOBAL: Some large Japanese corporations have broken with some of these principles, and are now evaluating and advancing employees as individuals.

NOTE: The loose and flat character of the al-Qaeda organization makes it difficult to hunt down its terrorist members.

EXERCISE: Suggest that students who work try to personalize themselves more. The marketing researcher Michael Linn (1996) reports that waiters and waitresses who identified themselves to customers by name boosted their tips by 53%; a casual touch on the shoulder or hand by servers boosted tips 42%.

Q: "Compare what you want with what you have, and you'll be unhappy; compare what you have with what you deserve, and you'll feel better." Evan Esar

● SEEING SOCIOLOGY
in Everyday Life

Have you ever had a "dead-end" job? A job that demanded creativity? Which would you prefer and why?

Not everything has worked well for Japan's corporations. About 1990, the Japanese economy entered a recession that lasted more than a decade, and recent years have seen another wave of economic setbacks. Pressured by the need to cut costs, many Japanese companies have changed their policies, no longer offering workers jobs for life or many of the other benefits noted by Ouchi. But the long-term outlook for Japan's business organizations remains bright.

The Third Challenge: The Changing Nature of Work

Beyond rising global competition and the need to provide equal opportunity for all, pressure to modify conventional organizations is coming from changes in the nature of work itself. Chapter 4 ("Society") described the shift from industrial to postindustrial production. Rather than working in factories using heavy machinery to make *things,* more and more people are using computers and other electronic technology to create or process *information.* The postindustrial society, then, is characterized by information-based organizations.

Frederick Taylor developed his concept of scientific management at a time when jobs involved tasks that, though often backbreaking, were routine and repetitive. Workers shoveled coal, poured liquid iron into molds, welded body panels to automobiles on an assembly line, or shot hot rivets into steel girders to build skyscrapers. In addition, many of the industrial workers in Taylor's day were immigrants, most of whom had little schooling and many of whom knew little English. The routine nature of industrial jobs, coupled with the limited skills of the labor force, led Taylor to treat work as a series of fixed tasks, set down by management and followed by employees.

Many of today's information age jobs are very different: The work of designers, artists, writers, composers, programmers, business owners, and others now demands individual creativity and imagination. Here are several ways in which today's organizations differ from those of a century ago:

1. **Creative freedom.** As one Hewlett-Packard executive put it, "From their first day of work here, people are given important responsibilities and are encouraged to grow" (cited in Brooks, 2000:128). Today's organizations now treat employees with information age skills as a vital resource. Executives can set production goals but cannot dictate how a worker is to accomplish tasks that require imagination and discovery. This gives highly skilled workers *creative freedom,* which means less day-to-day supervision as long as they generate good results in the long run.

2. **Competitive work teams.** Organizations typically give several groups of employees the freedom to work on a problem, offering

During the last fifty years in the United States, women have moved into management positions throughout the corporate world. While some men initially opposed women's presence in the executive office, it is now clear that women bring particular strengths to the job, including leadership flexibility and communication skills. Thus, some analysts speak of women offering a "female advantage."

the greatest rewards to those who come up with the best solution. Competitive work teams, a strategy first used by Japanese organizations, draw out the creative contributions of everyone and at the same time reduce the alienation often found in conventional organizations (Maddox, 1994; Yeatts, 1994).

3. **A flatter organization.** By spreading responsibility for creative problem solving throughout the workforce, organizations take on a flatter shape. That is, the pyramid shape of conventional bureaucracy is replaced by an organizational form with fewer levels in the chain of command, as shown in Figure 7–4 on page 178.

4. **Greater flexibility.** The typical industrial age organization was a rigid structure guided from the top. Such organizations may accomplish a large amount of work, but they are not especially creative or able to respond quickly to changes in the larger environment. The ideal model in the information age is a more open, *flexible* organization that both generates new ideas and, in a rapidly changing global marketplace, adapts quickly.

What does all this mean for formal organizations? As David Brooks puts it, "The machine is no longer held up as the standard that

RESOURCE: A selection by George Ritzer, "McJobs: McDonaldization and the Workplace," is in the companion reader, *Seeing Ourselves*, 8th ed.

DISCUSS: Randall E. Stross (2002) notes the "McPeace dividend" argument: No two countries containing a McDonald's have ever gone to war against each other. Is this fact significant? How?

NOTE: George Ritzer (1998) reports that fast food represents 40% of the more than 6 million U.S. restaurant jobs; 70% of employees are age 20 or younger (for many, it is their first job); about 15% of U.S. workers had their first job at McDonald's; 1 of 8 U.S. adults has worked at McDonald's at some time; the average workweek is 30 hours.

NOTE: McDonald's even varies slightly by region in the U.S.: In the New England states, it sells lobster rolls in the summer.

SEEING SOCIOLOGY
in Everyday Life

Is your college or university a top-down bureaucracy or a flatter, more flexible organization? How might you find out?

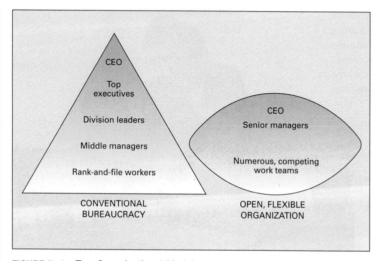

FIGURE 7–4   Two Organizational Models

The conventional model of bureaucratic organizations has a pyramid shape, with a clear chain of command. Orders flow from the top down, and reports of performance flow from the bottom up. Such organizations have extensive rules and regulations, and their workers have highly specialized jobs. More open and flexible organizations have a flatter shape, more like a football. With fewer levels in the hierarchy, responsibility for generating ideas and making decisions is shared throughout the organization. Many workers do their jobs in teams and have a broad knowledge of the entire organization's operation.

Source: Created by the author.

healthy organizations should emulate. Now it's the ecosystem" (2000:128). Today's "smart" companies seek out intelligent, creative people (AOL's main building is called "Creative Center 1") and nurture the growth of their talents.

Keep in mind, however, that many of today's jobs do not involve creative work at all. More correctly, the postindustrial economy has created two very different types of work: high-skill creative work and low-skill service work. Work in the fast-food industry, for example, is routine and highly supervised and thus has much more in common with the factory work of a century ago than with the creative teamwork typical of today's information organizations. Therefore, at the same time that some organizations have taken on a flexible, flatter form, others continue to use the rigid chain of command.

The "McDonaldization" of Society

As noted in the opening to this chapter, McDonald's has enjoyed enormous success, now operating more than 31,000 restaurants in the United States and around the world. Japan has more than 3,700 Golden Arches, and the world's largest McDonald's, which seats more than 1,000 customers, is located in China's capital city of Beijing.

McDonald's is far more than a restaurant chain; it is a symbol of U.S. culture. Not only do people around the world associate McDonald's with the United States, but here at home, one poll found that 98 percent of schoolchildren could identify Ronald McDonald, making him as well known as Santa Claus.

Even more important, the organizational principles that underlie McDonald's are coming to dominate our entire society. Our culture is becoming "McDonaldized," an awkward way of saying that we model many aspects of life on this restaurant chain: Parents buy toys at worldwide chain stores all carrying identical merchandise; we drop in for a ten-minute oil change while running errands; face-to-face communication is being replaced more and more by e-mail, voice mail, and instant messaging; more vacations take the form of resorts and tour packages; television packages the news in the form of ten-second sound bites; college admissions officers size up students they have never met by glancing at their GPA and SAT scores; and professors assign ghost-written textbooks[1] and evaluate students with tests mass-produced for them by publishing companies. The list goes on and on.

Four Principles

What do all these developments have in common? According to George Ritzer (1993), the McDonaldization of society rests on four organizational principles:

1. **Efficiency.** Ray Kroc, the marketing genius behind the expansion of McDonald's back in the 1950s, set out to serve a hamburger, French fries, and a milkshake to a customer in exactly fifty seconds. Today, one of the company's most popular menu items is the Egg McMuffin, an entire breakfast in a single sandwich. In the restaurant, customers dispose of their trash and stack their own trays as they walk out the door or, better still, drive away from the pickup window taking whatever mess they make with them. Such efficiency is now central to our way of life. We tend to think that anything done quickly is, for that reason alone, good.

2. **Predictability.** An efficient organization wants to make everything it does as predictable as possible. McDonald's prepares all food using set formulas. Company policies guide the performance of every job.

[1]A number of popular sociology books were not written by the person whose name appears on the cover. This book is not one of them. Even the test bank that accompanies this text was written by the author.

SEEING SOCIOLOGY
in Everyday Life

Can you point to examples of McDonaldization beyond those noted below? What are they?

The best of today's information age jobs—including working at Google, the popular search engine Web site—allow people lots of personal freedom as long as they produce good ideas. At the same time, many other jobs, such as working the counter at McDonald's, involve the same routines and strict supervision found in factories a century ago.

3. **Uniformity.** The first McDonald's operating manual set the weight of a regular raw hamburger at 1.6 ounces, its size at 3.875 inches across, and its fat content at 19 percent. A slice of cheese weighs exactly half an ounce. Fries are cut precisely 9/32 of an inch thick.

   Think about how many objects around your home, the workplace, and the campus are designed and mass-produced according to a standard plan. Not just our environment but our life experiences—from traveling the nation's interstates to sitting at home viewing television—are more standardized than ever before.

   Almost anywhere in the world, a person can walk into a McDonald's restaurant and purchase the same sandwiches, drinks, and desserts prepared in precisely the same way.[2] Uniformity results from a highly rational system that specifies every action and leaves nothing to chance.

4. **Control.** The most unreliable element in the McDonald's system is the human beings who work there. After all, people have good and bad days, sometimes let their minds wander, or simply decide to try something a different way. To minimize the unpredictable human element, McDonald's has automated its equipment to cook food at a fixed temperature for a set length of time. Even the cash register at McDonald's is keyed to pictures of the items so that ringing up a customer's order is as simple as possible.

Similarly, automatic teller machines are replacing bank tellers, highly automated bakeries now produce bread while people stand back and watch, and chickens and eggs (or is it eggs and chickens?) emerge from automated hatcheries. In supermarkets, laser scanners at self-checkouts are phasing out human checkers. We do most of our shopping in malls, where everything from temperature and humidity to the kinds of stores and products is carefully controlled and supervised (Ide & Cordell, 1994).

Can Rationality Be Irrational?

There is no doubt about the popularity or efficiency of McDonald's. But there is another side to the story.

Max Weber was alarmed at the increasing rationalization of the world, fearing that formal organizations would cage our imaginations and crush the human spirit. As Weber saw it, rational systems were efficient but dehumanizing. McDonaldization bears him out. Each of the four principles just discussed limits human creativity, choice, and freedom. Echoing Weber, Ritzer states that "the ultimate irrationality of McDonaldization is that people could lose control

[2]As McDonald's has "gone global," a few products have been added or changed according to local tastes. For example, in Uruguay, customers enjoy the McHuevo (hamburger with poached egg on top); Norwegians can buy McLaks (grilled salmon sandwiches); the Dutch favor the Groenteburger (vegetable burger); in Thailand, McDonald's serves Samurai pork burgers (pork burgers with teriyaki sauce); the Japanese can purchase a Chicken Tatsuta Sandwich (chicken seasoned with soy and ginger); Filipinos eat McSpaghetti (spaghetti with tomato sauce and bits of hot dog); and in India, where Hindus eat no beef, McDonald's sells a vegetarian Maharaja Mac (B. Sullivan, 1995).

Q: "Mind your own business." Phrase appearing on the first coin minted in the U.S. in 1778

DISCUSS: In 2002, the private Augusta National Golf Club—an all-male club in Georgia—garnered national attention for refusing to admit women as members. The issue pits privacy and the right of free association against equality. Which side do more students support?

DISCUSS: What about implanting computer chips in individuals that contain their identity, medical history, insurance information, and credit card numbers? This might help Alzheimer's patients, but is it a boon or threat to everyone else?

● MAKING THE GRADE

The McDonaldization thesis is that rational organization is coming to define our way of life and this trend is in important ways harmful to our well-being.

CONTROVERSY & DEBATE

Computer Technology, Large Organizations, and the Assault on Privacy

JAKE: I'm doing MySpace. It's really cool.

DUNCAN: Why do you want to put your whole life out there for everyone to see?

JAKE: I'm famous, man!

DUNCAN: Famous? Ha! You're throwing away whatever privacy you have left.

Jake completes a page on MySpace.com, which includes his name and college, e-mail address, photo, biography, and current personal interests. It can be accessed by billions of people around the world.

Late for a meeting with a new client, Sarah drives her car through a yellow light as it turns red at a main intersection. A computer linked to a pair of cameras notes the violation and takes one picture of her license plate and another of her sitting in the driver's seat. In seven days, she receives a summons to appear in traffic court.

Julio looks through his mail and finds a letter from a Washington, D.C., data services company telling

him that he is one of about 145,000 people whose name, address, Social Security number, and credit file have recently been sold to criminals in California posing as businesspeople. With this information, other people can obtain credit cards or take out loans in his name.

These are all cases showing that today's organizations—which know more about us than ever before and more than most of us realize—pose

a growing threat to personal privacy. Large organizations are necessary for today's society to operate. In some cases, organizations using information about us may actually be helpful. But cases of identity theft are on the rise, and personal privacy is on the decline.

In the past, small-town life gave people little privacy. But at least if people knew something about you, you were just as likely to know something about them. Today, unknown people "out there" can access information about each of us all the time without our learning about it.

In part, the loss of privacy is a result of more and more complex computer technology. Are you aware that every e-mail you send and every Web site you visit leaves a record in one or more computers? These records can be retrieved by people you don't know, as well as by employers and other public officials.

Another part of today's loss of privacy reflects the number and size of formal organizations. As explained in this chapter, large organizations tend to treat people impersonally, and they have a huge appetite for information. Mix large organizations with ever more complex computer technology, and it is no wonder that

over the system and it would come to control us" (1993:145). Perhaps even McDonald's understands this—the company has now expanded its more upscale offerings to include premium roasted coffee and salad selections that are more sophisticated, fresh, and healthful (Philadelphia, 2002).

The Future of Organizations: Opposing Trends

Early in the twentieth century, ever-larger organizations arose in the United States, most taking on the bureaucratic form described by Max Weber. In many respects, these organizations resembled armies

led by powerful generals who issued orders to their captains and lieutenants. Foot soldiers, working in the factories, did what they were told.

With the emergence of a postindustrial economy around 1950, as well as rising competition from abroad, many organizations evolved toward a flatter, more flexible model that prizes communication and creativity. Such "intelligent organizations" (Pinchot & Pinchot, 1993; Brooks, 2000) have become more productive than ever. Just as important, for highly skilled people who now enjoy creative freedom, these organizations cause less of the alienation that so worried Weber.

But this is only half the story. Although the postindustrial economy has created many highly skilled jobs over the past half-

SOCIAL SURVEY: "The federal government has a lot of different pieces of information about people that computers can bring together very quickly. Is this a very serious threat to individual privacy, a fairly serious threat, not a serious threat, or not a threat at all to individual privacy?" (GSS 2006, N = 1,518; *Codebook*, 2007:1493)

"Very serious"	26.2%	"Not a threat"	6.9%
"Fairly serious"	39.1%	"Don't know" / No response	1.7%
"Not serious"	26.2%		

● SEEING SOCIOLOGY
in Everyday Life

Have large organizations reduced your privacy in ways you don't like? Explain.

most people in the United States are concerned about who knows what about them and what people are doing with this information.

For decades, the level of personal privacy in the United States has been declining. Early in the twentieth century, when state agencies began issuing driver's licenses, for example, they generated files for every licensed driver. Today, officials can send this information at the touch of a button not only to the police but to all sorts of other organizations. The Internal Revenue Service and the Social Security Administration, as well as government agencies that benefit veterans, students, the unemployed, and the poor, all collect mountains of personal information.

Business organizations now do much the same thing, and many of the choices we make end up in a company's database. Most of us use credit—the U.S. population now has more than 1 billion credit cards, an average of five per adult—but the companies that do "credit checks" collect and distribute information about us to almost anyone who asks, including criminals planning to steal our identity.

Then there are the small cameras found not only at traffic intersections but also in stores, public buildings, and parking garages and across college campuses. The number of surveillance

cameras that monitor our movements is rapidly increasing with each passing year. So-called security cameras may increase public safety in some ways—say, by discouraging a mugger or even a terrorist—at the cost of the little privacy we have left. In the United Kingdom, probably the world leader in the use of security camera, the typical resident of London appears on closed-circuit television about 300 times every day, and all this "tracking" is stored in computer files.

In terms of government monitoring of the population, the United States is not far behind. After the September 11, 2001, terrorist attacks, the federal government took steps (including passage of the USA PATRIOT Act) to strengthen national security. Today, government officials closely monitor not only people entering the country but also the activities of all of us. It is possible that these efforts increase national security, but it is certain that they erode personal privacy.

Some legal protections remain. Each of the fifty states has laws that give citizens the right to examine some records about themselves kept by employers, banks, and credit bureaus. The federal Privacy Act of 1974 also limits the exchange of personal information among government agencies and permits citizens to examine and correct most government files. In response to rising levels

of identity theft, Congress is likely to pass more laws to regulate the sale of credit information. But so many organizations, private as well as public, now have information about us—experts estimate that 90 percent of U.S. households are profiled in databases somewhere—that current laws simply cannot effectively address the privacy problem.

WHAT DO YOU THINK?

1. Do you think that the use of surveillance cameras in public places enhances our personal security? Does it threaten our privacy? Would you limit such surveillance? Why or why not?

2. Do you use Internet sites such as MySpace.com? Why do you think so many young people are eager to spread personal information in this way?

3. Automatic toll payment technology allows traffic to move more quickly through toll gates on our highways but also collects information on which cars are where and when they get there. Do you have any concerns that such technology will be used in ways no one now expects?

Sources: "Online Privacy" (2000), A. Hamilton (2001), Heymann (2002), O'Harrow (2005), Tingwall (2008), and Werth (2008).

century, it has created even more routine service jobs, such as those offered by McDonald's. Fast-food companies now represent the largest pool of low-wage labor, aside from migrant workers, in the United States (Schlosser, 2002). Work of this kind, which Ritzer terms "McJobs," offers few of the benefits that today's highly skilled workers enjoy. On the contrary, the automated routines that define work in the fast-food industry, telemarketing, and similar fields are very much the same as those that Frederick Taylor described a century ago.

Today, organizational flexibility gives better-off workers more freedom but often means the threat of "downsizing" and job loss for many rank-and-file employees. Organizations facing global competition seek out creative employees, but they are also eager to cut

costs by eliminating as many routine jobs as possible. The net result is that some people are better off than ever, while others worry about holding their jobs and struggle to make ends meet—a trend that Chapter 11 ("Social Class in the United States") explores in detail.

U.S. organizations are the envy of the world for their productive efficiency. For example, there are few places on Earth where the mail arrives as quickly and dependably as it does in this country. But we should remember that the future is far brighter for some workers than for others. In addition, as the Controversy & Debate box explains, organizations pose an increasing threat to our privacy—something to keep in mind as we envision our organizational future.

Seeing Sociology in Everyday Life

Chapter 7 Groups and Organizations

What have we learned about the way modern society is organized?

This chapter explains that since the opening of the first McDonald's restaurant in 1948, the principles that underlie the fast food industry—efficiency, predictability, uniformity, and control—have spread to many aspects of our everyday lives. Here is a chance to identify aspects of McDonaldization in several familiar routines. In each of the two photos on the facing page, can you identify specific elements of McDonaldization? That is, in what ways does the organizational pattern or the technology involved increase efficiency, predictability, uniformity, and control? In the photo below, what elements do you see that are clearly not McDonaldization? Why?

> **HINT** This process, which is described as the "McDonaldization of society," has made our lives easier in some ways, but it has also made our society ever more impersonal, gradually diminishing our range of human contact. Also, although this organizational pattern is intended to serve human needs, it may end up doing the opposite by forcing people to live according to the demands of machines. Max Weber feared that our future would be an overly rational world in which we all might lose much of our humanity.

Small, privately owned stores like this one were once the rule in the United States. But the number of "mom and pop" businesses is declining as "big box" discount stores expand. Why are small stores disappearing? What social qualities of these stores are we losing in the process?

Automated teller machines became common in the United States in the early 1970s. A customer with an electronic identification card can complete certain banking operations (such as withdrawing cash) without having to deal with a human bank teller. What makes the ATM one example of McDonaldization? Do you enjoy using an ATM? Why or why not?

At checkout counters in many supermarkets, customers lift each product through a laser scanner linked to a computer in order to identify what the product is and what it costs. The customer then inserts a credit or debit card to pay for the purchases.

Applying SOCIOLOGY in Everyday Life

1. Have colleges and universities been affected by the process called McDonaldization? Do large, anonymous lecture courses qualify as an example? Why? What other examples of McDonaldization can you identify on the college campus?

2. Visit any large public building with an elevator. Observe groups of people as they approach the elevator, and enter the elevator with them. Watch their behavior: What happens to conversations as the elevator doors close? Where do people fix their eyes? Can you explain these patterns?

3. Using campus publications or your school's Web page (and some assistance from an instructor), try to draw an organizational pyramid for your college or university. Show the key offices and how they supervise and report to one another.

MAKING THE GRADE

CHAPTER 7 Groups and Organizations

What Are Social Groups?

SOCIAL GROUPS are two or more people who identify with and interact with one another.

p. 162

A **PRIMARY GROUP** is small, personal, and lasting (examples include family and close friends).

pp. 162–63

A **SECONDARY GROUP** is large, impersonal and goal-oriented, and often of shorter duration (examples include a college class or a corporation).

p. 163

See the Summing Up table on page 164.

Elements of Group Dynamics

GROUP LEADERSHIP

- *Instrumental leadership* focuses on completing tasks.
- *Expressive leadership* focuses on a group's well-being.
- *Authoritarian leadership* is a "take charge" style that demands obedience; *democratic leadership* includes everyone in decision making; *laissez-faire leadership* lets the group function mostly on its own.

pp. 163–64

GROUP CONFORMITY

- The Asch, Milgram, and Janis research shows that group members often seek agreement and may pressure one another toward conformity.
- Individuals use *reference groups*—including both *in-groups* and *out-groups*—to form attitudes and make evaluations.

pp. 164–66

GROUP SIZE and **DIVERSITY**

- Georg Simmel described the *dyad* as intense but unstable; the *triad*, he said, is more stable but can dissolve into a dyad by excluding one member.
- Peter Blau claimed that larger groups turn inward, socially diverse groups turn outward, and physically segregated groups turn inward.

pp. 167–68

NETWORKS are relational webs that link people with little common identity and limited interaction. Being "well connected" in networks is a valuable type of social capital.

pp. 168–70

social group (p. 162) two or more people who identify with and interact with one another

primary group (p. 163) a small social group whose members share personal and lasting relationships

secondary group (p. 163) a large and impersonal social group whose members pursue a specific goal or activity

instrumental leadership (p. 164) group leadership that focuses on the completion of tasks

expressive leadership (p. 164) group leadership that focuses on the group's well-being

groupthink (p. 165) the tendency of group members to conform, resulting in a narrow view of some issue

reference group (p. 166) a social group that serves as a point of reference in making evaluations and decisions

in-group (p. 166) a social group toward which a member feels respect and loyalty

out-group (p. 166) a social group toward which a person feels a sense of competition or opposition

dyad (p. 167) a social group with two members

triad (p. 167) a social group with three members

network (p. 168) a web of weak social ties

What Are Formal Organizations?

FORMAL ORGANIZATIONS are large secondary groups organized to achieve their goals efficiently.

p. 170

UTILITARIAN ORGANIZATIONS pay people for their efforts (examples include a business or government agency).

p. 170

NORMATIVE ORGANIZATIONS have goals people consider worthwhile (examples include voluntary associations such as the PTA).

p. 170

COERCIVE ORGANIZATIONS are organizations people are forced to join (examples include prisons and mental hospitals).

p. 170

formal organization (p. 170) a large secondary group organized to achieve its goals efficiently

What Are Formal Organizations? (continued)

All formal organizations operate in an **ORGANIZATIONAL ENVIRONMENT,** which is influenced by
- technology
- political and economic trends
- current events
- population patterns
- other organizations

pp. 171–72

See the Summing Up table on page 172.

organizational environment (p. 171) factors outside an organization that affect its operation

bureaucracy (p. 170) an organizational model rationally designed to perform tasks efficiently

bureaucratic ritualism (p. 173) a focus on rules and regulations to the point of undermining an organization's goals

bureaucratic inertia (p. 174) the tendency of bureaucratic organizations to perpetuate themselves

oligarchy (p. 174) the rule of the many by the few

scientific management (p. 175) Frederick Taylor's term for the application of scientific principles to the operation of a business or other large organization

Modern Formal Organizations: Bureaucracy

BUREAUCRACY, which Max Weber saw as the dominant type of organization in modern societies, is based on
- specialization
- hierarchy of positions
- rules and regulations
- technical competence
- impersonality
- formal, written communications

pp. 170–71

PROBLEMS OF BUREAUCRACY include
- bureaucratic alienation
- bureaucratic inefficiency and ritualism
- bureaucratic inertia
- oligarchy

pp. 173–74

The Evolution of Formal Organizations

CONVENTIONAL BUREAUCRACY

In the early 1900s, Frederick Taylor's **SCIENTIFIC MANAGEMENT** applied scientific principles to increase productivity.

p. 175

─── MORE OPEN, FLEXIBLE ORGANIZATIONS ───

In the 1960s, Rosabeth Moss Kanter proposed that opening up organizations for all employees, especially women and other minorities, increased organizational efficiency.

pp. 175–76

In the 1980s, global competition drew attention to the Japanese work organization's collective orientation.

pp. 176–77

THE CHANGING NATURE OF WORK

Recently, the rise of a postindustrial economy has created two very different types of work:
- highly skilled and creative work (examples include designers, consultants, programmers, and executives)
- low-skilled service work associated with the "McDonaldization" of society, based on efficiency, uniformity, and control (examples include jobs in fast-food restaurants and telemarketing)

pp. 177–80

{ If you think that sexuality is simply a matter of biology, think again. Sexuality is constructed by society and is an important part of our everyday lives. }

CHAPTER 8

GLOBAL: People accentuate their "gender markers" to give off sexual messages and provoke a response from the other sex. For example, women have longer necks than men. In Burma, women begin stretching their necks with brass rings early in childhood, trying to reach a maximum of 32 rings (a goal rarely achieved). Women also have larger lips than men, and lips also become larger and slightly redder when sexually aroused. Thus women use lipstick (typically red) and enlarge their lips by coloring beyond the lip line. In some African societies, women go to the extreme of inserting plates in their lips. Finally, women have smaller feet than men, so women typically choose smaller (and often uncomfortable) shoes. In China, women went to the extreme of foot binding (beginning in childhood), which was sexually arousing to many men, who caressed (or even sucked on) women's deformed feet.

SEEING SOCIOLOGY
in Everyday Life

Look at the six photos on this page. Do you think that what people in a society consider to be beautiful is more a matter of biology or of culture? Explain your answer.

sex the biological distinction between females and males

We claim that beauty is in the eye of the beholder, which suggests the importance of culture in setting standards of attractiveness. All of the people pictured here—from Morocco, South Africa, Nigeria, Thailand, Japan, and Ecuador—are considered beautiful by members of their own society. At the same time, sociobiologists point out that in every society on Earth, people are attracted to youthfulness. The reason, as sociobiologists see it, is that attractiveness underlies our choices about reproduction, which is most readily accomplished in early adulthood.

industry that includes pornography and prostitution, both of which are multibillion-dollar businesses in this country. The bottom line is that sexuality is an important part of how we think about ourselves as well as how others think about us. For this reason, there are few areas of everyday life in which sexuality does not play some part.

Although sex is a big part of everyday life, U.S. culture has long treated sex as taboo; even today, many people avoid talking about it. As a result, although sex can produce much pleasure, it also causes confusion, anxiety, and sometimes outright fear. Even scientists long considered sex off limits as a topic of research. Not until the middle of the twentieth century did researchers turn their attention to this vital dimension of social life. Since then, as this chapter explains, we have discovered a great deal about human sexuality.

Sex: A Biological Issue

Sex refers to *the biological distinction between females and males.* From a biological point of view, sex is the way the human species reproduces. A female ovum and a male sperm, each containing twenty-three matching chromosomes (biological codes that guide physical development), combine to form an embryo. To one of these pairs of chromosomes—the pair that determines the child's sex—the mother contributes an X chromosome and the father contributes either an X or a Y. Should the father contribute an X chromosome, a female (XX) embryo results; a Y from the father produces a male (XY) embryo. A child's sex is thereby determined biologically at the moment of conception.

NOTE: Transsexuals are also called transgendered people.

DIVERSITY: Cross-dressers differ from transvestites in that the former cross-dress to conform to their self-image and the latter cross-dress with the goal of sexual arousal.

NOTE: Students may confuse transsexuals (people feeling that they are the other sex) with transvestism (wearing clothing appropriate to the other sex). Similarly, bisexuality (attraction to people of either sex) is sometimes confused with androgyny (having physical characteristics of both sexes).

RESOURCE: The companion reader *Seeing Ourselves*, 8th ed., features "Sex in America: How Many Partners Do We Have?" by Robert T. Michael and colleagues.

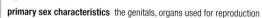

primary sex characteristics the genitals, organs used for reproduction

secondary sex characteristics bodily development, apart from the genitals, that distinguishes biologically mature females and males

intersexual people people whose bodies (including genitals) have both female and male characteristics

transsexuals people who feel they are one sex even though biologically they are the other

SEEING SOCIOLOGY in Everyday Life

In 2001, San Francisco became the first city with a health plan for city employees that includes paying the cost of gender reassignment surgery (which can cost $50,000 or more). Would you support enacting similar policies elsewhere? Why or why not?

The sex of an embryo guides its development. If the embryo is male, the growth of testicular tissue starts to produce large amounts of testosterone, a hormone that triggers the development of male genitals (sex organs). If little testosterone is present, the embryo develops female genitals.

Sex and the Body

Some differences in the body set males and females apart. Right from birth, the two sexes have different **primary sex characteristics,** namely, *the genitals, organs used for reproduction.* At puberty, as people reach sexual maturity, additional sex differentiation takes place. At

this point, people develop **secondary sex characteristics,** *bodily development, apart from the genitals, that distinguishes biologically mature females and males.* Mature females have wider hips for giving birth, milk-producing breasts for nurturing infants, and deposits of soft, fatty tissue that provide a reserve supply of nutrition during pregnancy and breast feeding. Mature males typically develop more muscle in the upper body, more extensive body hair, and deeper voices. Of course, these are general differences; some males are smaller and have less body hair and higher voices than some females.

Keep in mind that sex is not the same thing as gender. *Gender* is an element of culture and refers to the personal traits and patterns of behavior (including responsibilities, opportunities, and privileges) that a culture attaches to being female or male. Chapter 13 ("Gender Stratification") explains that gender is an important dimension of social inequality.

Intersexual People

Sex is not always as clear-cut as has just been described. The term **intersexual people** refers to *people whose bodies (including genitals) have both female and male characteristics.* Another term for intersexual people is *hermaphrodites* (derived from Hermaphroditus, the child of the mythological Greek gods Hermes and Aphrodite, who embodied both sexes). A true hermaphrodite has both a female ovary and a male testis.

However, our culture demands that sex be clear-cut, a fact evident in the requirement that parents record the sex of their new child at birth as either female or male. In the United States, the fact that a small share of people are intersexual can provoke confusion or even disgust. But attitudes in other cultures are quite different: The Pokot of eastern Africa, for example, pay little attention to what they consider a rare biological error, and the Navajo look on intersexual people with awe, seeing in them the full potential of both the female and the male (Geertz, 1975).

Transsexuals

Transsexuals are *people who feel they are one sex even though biologically they are the other.* Tens of thousands of people in the United States have experienced the feeling of being trapped in a body of the wrong sex and a desire to be the other sex. Most become *transgendered,* meaning that they begin to disregard conventional ideas about how females and males should look and behave. Many go one step further and undergo *gender reassignment,* surgical alteration of their genitals and breasts, usually accompanied by hormone treatments. This medical process is complex and takes months or even years, but it helps many people gain a joyful sense of finally becoming on the outside who they feel they are on the inside (Gagné, Tewksbury, & McGaughey, 1997).

We are used to thinking of sex as a clear-cut issue of being female or male. But transgendered people do not fit such simple categories. In 2008, Thomas Beatie, age 34, became pregnant and gave birth to a healthy baby girl. Beatie, who was born a woman, had surgery to remove his breasts and legally changed his sex from female to male, but nonetheless chose to bear a child. What is your response to cases such as this?

THE MAP: There is no simple explanation for the pattern shown here. The interesting fact is that the country is fairly evenly divided on the issue.

NOTE: Regarding incest, we use the term "kissing cousins" in a positive way, and even the evolutionist Charles Darwin married his first cousin. Studies show a slightly elevated risk of genetic disorder among offspring of first cousins (Hobson, 2002).

NOTE: The incest taboo limits kinship confusion. A few years back, Stephen Wyman (then age 32), the son of the Rolling Stones' Bill Wyman (58), announced his intention of marrying the mother (age 45) of his father's ex-wife (age 24). This union would have made Stephen stepfather to his former stepmother and Bill stepgrandfather to his former wife. Bill would also be his son's son-in-law and the father of his father-in-law!

In Montana, marriage between first cousins is against the law.

In Indiana, first cousins Shawn and Delia Dawson were able to marry only because they are both 70 years old.

incest taboo a norm forbidding sexual relations or marriage between certain relatives

Seeing Ourselves

NATIONAL MAP 8–1

First-Cousin Marriage Laws across the United States

There is no single view on first-cousin marriages in the United States: Twenty-four states forbid such unions, twenty allow them, and six allow them with restrictions.* In general, states that permit first-cousin marriages are found in New England, the Southeast, and the Southwest.

*Of the six states that allow first-cousin marriages with restrictions, five states permit them only when couples are past childbearing age.

Source: National Conference of State Legislatures (2008b).

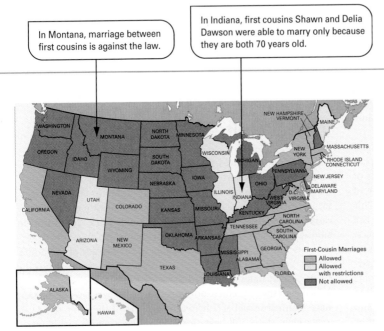

First-Cousin Marriages
- Allowed
- Allowed with restrictions
- Not allowed

Sex: A Cultural Issue

Sexuality has a biological foundation. But like all aspects of human behavior, sexuality is also very much a cultural issue. Biology may explain some animals' mating rituals, but humans have no similar biological program. Although there is a biological "sex drive" in the sense that people find sex pleasurable and may want to engage in sexual activity, our biology does not dictate any specific ways of being sexual any more than our desire to eat dictates any particular foods or table manners.

Cultural Variation

Almost every sexual practice shows considerable variation from one society to another. In his pioneering research study of sexuality in the United States, Alfred Kinsey and his colleagues (1948) found that most heterosexual couples reported having intercourse in a single position—face to face, with the woman on the bottom and the man on top. Halfway around the world, however, on islands in the South Seas, most couples *never* have sex in this way. In fact, when the people of the South Seas learned of this practice from Western missionaries, they poked fun at it as the strange "missionary position."

Even the simple practice of showing affection varies from society to society. Most people in the United States kiss in public, but the Chinese kiss only in private. The French kiss publicly, often twice (once on each cheek), and the Belgians kiss three times (starting on either cheek). The Maoris of New Zealand rub noses, and most people in Nigeria don't kiss at all.

Modesty, too, varies from culture to culture. If a woman stepping into a bath is disturbed, what body parts do you think she would cover? Helen Colton (1983) reports that an Islamic woman covers her face, a Laotian woman covers her breasts, a Samoan woman covers her navel, a Sumatran woman covers her knees, and a European woman covers her breasts with one hand and her genital area with the other.

Around the world, some societies restrict sexuality, and others are more permissive. In China, for example, norms closely regulate sexuality so that few people have sexual intercourse before their wedding day. In the United States, at least over the last few decades, intercourse prior to marriage has become the norm, and some people choose to have sex even without strong commitment to their partner.

The Incest Taboo

When it comes to sex, do all societies agree on anything? The answer is yes. One cultural universal—an element found in every society the world over—is the **incest taboo,** *a norm forbidding sexual relations or marriage between certain relatives.* In the United States, both law and cultural mores prohibit close relatives (including brothers and sisters, parents and children) from having sex or marrying. But in another example of cultural variation, exactly which family members are included in a society's incest taboo varies from state to state. National Map 8–1 shows that about half the states outlaw marriage between first cousins and about half do not; a few permit this practice but with restrictions (National Conference of State Legislatures, 2008b).

Some societies (such as the North American Navajo) apply incest taboos only to the mother and others on her side of the family. There are also societies on record (including ancient Peru and

SOCIAL SURVEY: In a survey of 317,000 people in 41 nations, adults reported having sex, on average, 103 times per year (a bit more often than twice a week). The survey found people in Greece claiming to have sex most often (average: 138 times per year) and people in Japan claiming to have sex least often (45 times per year) (Durex Global Sex Survey, 2005).

GLOBAL: Although many people think of the French as more sexual and the British as less so, survey results indicate that the frequency of sex and also the number of sexual partners is about the same. (Durex Global Sex Suurvey, 2005).

MAKING THE GRADE

Be sure you understand why the incest taboo is more about society than biology.

Egypt) that have approved brother-sister marriages among the nobility as a strategy to keep power within a single family (Murdock, 1965, orig. 1949).

Why does some form of incest taboo exist in every society around the world? Part of the reason is rooted in biology: Reproduction between close relatives of any species raises the odds of producing offspring with mental or physical problems. But why, of all living species, do only humans observe an incest taboo? This fact suggests that controlling sexuality among close relatives is a necessary element of *social* organization. For one thing, the incest taboo limits sexual competition in families by restricting sex to spouses (ruling out, for example, a sexual relationship between parent and child). Second, because family ties define people's rights and obligations toward one another, reproduction between close relatives would hopelessly confuse kinship lines: If a mother and son had a daughter, would the child consider the male a father or a brother? Third, by requiring people to marry outside their immediate families, the incest taboo serves to integrate the larger society as people look beyond their close kin when seeking to form new families.

The incest taboo has long been a sexual norm in the United States and throughout the world. But many other sexual norms have changed over time. In the twentieth century, as the next section explains, our society experienced both a sexual revolution and a sexual counterrevolution.

Sexual Attitudes in the United States

What do people in the United States think about sex? Our cultural attitudes about sexuality have always been somewhat contradictory. Most European immigrants arrived with rigid ideas about "correct" sexuality, typically limiting sex to reproduction within marriage. The early Puritan settlers of New England demanded strict conformity in attitudes and behavior, and they imposed severe penalties for any sexual "misconduct," even if it took place in the privacy of the home. Some regulation of sexuality has continued ever since. As late as the 1960s, several states prohibited the sale of condoms in stores. Until 2003, when the Supreme Court struck them down, laws in thirteen states banned sexual acts between partners of the same sex. Even today, eight states still have "fornication" laws, which forbid intercourse by unmarried couples.

But this is just one side of the story. As Chapter 3 ("Culture") explains, because U.S. culture is individualistic, many of us believe that people should be free to do pretty much as they wish as long as they cause no direct harm to others. The idea that what people do in the privacy of their own home is no one else's business makes sex a matter of individual freedom and personal choice.

When it comes to sexuality, is the United States restrictive or permissive? The answer is both. On one hand, many people in the

Over the course of the past century, social attitudes in the United States have become more accepting of most aspects of human sexuality. What do you see as some of the benefits of this greater openness? What are some of the negative consequences?

Q: "Love is the delusion that one woman [or man] differs from another." H. L. Mencken

DISCUSS: Why was the legalization of abortion in 1973 another important dimension of the sexual revolution?

SOCIAL SURVEY: The Laumann data for a younger cohort born between 1963 and 1972, after the sexual revolution was well along, indicate the gap is smaller still:

62% of men and 51% of women report having five or more sexual partners by age 20 (Laumann et al., 1994:198).

DIVERSITY: A common stereotype is the idea that minorities are more sexual than whites. Data from various surveys show that although African Americans have first intercourse about a year earlier, there are no significant differences among adults in this regard (NORC, 2008).

MAKING THE GRADE

Be sure you understand the differences between the "sexual revolution" and the "sexual counterrevolution" (p. 194).

Nancy Houck, now 73 years old, has lived most of her life in a social world where men have had much more sexual freedom than women.

Sarah Roholt, 47, is a baby boomer who feels that she and her women friends have pretty much the same sexual freedom as men.

United States still view sexual conduct as an important indicator of personal morality. On the other, sex is more and more a part of the mass media—one report concluded that the number of scenes in television shows with sexual content doubled in a mere ten years (Kunkel et al., 2005). Within this complex framework, we now turn to changes in sexual attitudes and behavior that have taken place in the United States over the past century.

The Sexual Revolution

Over the course of the twentieth century, U.S. society underwent major changes in sexual attitudes and practices. The first indications of this change came with industrialization in the 1920s, as millions of women and men migrated from farms and small towns to rapidly growing cities. There, living apart from their families and meeting new people in the workplace, young people enjoyed considerable sexual freedom, one reason that decade became known as the "Roaring Twenties."

In the 1930s and 1940s, the Great Depression and World War II slowed the rate of change. But in the postwar period, after 1945, Alfred Kinsey set the stage for what later came to be known as the *sexual revolution*. In 1948, Kinsey and his colleagues published their first study of sexuality in the United States, and it raised eyebrows everywhere. The national uproar resulted not so much from what he said as from the fact that scientists were actually studying sex, a topic many people were uneasy talking about even in the privacy of their homes.

Kinsey also had some interesting things to say. His two books (Kinsey, Pomeroy, & Martin, 1948; Kinsey et al., 1953) became best-sellers partly because they revealed that people in the United States, on average, were far less conventional in sexual matters than most had thought. These books encouraged a new openness toward sexuality, which helped set the sexual revolution in motion.

The revolution truly came of age in the late 1960s. Youth culture dominated public life, and expressions like "sex, drugs, and rock-and-roll" and "if it feels good, do it" summed up a new, freer attitude toward sex. The baby boom generation, born between 1946 and 1964, became the first cohort in U.S. history to grow up with the idea that sex was part of people's lives, whether they were married or not.

New technology also played a part in the sexual revolution. The birth control pill, introduced in 1960, not only prevented pregnancy but also made sex more convenient. Unlike a condom or a diaphragm, which must be applied at the time of intercourse, the pill could be taken anytime during the day. Now women and men could engage in sex spontaneously without any special preparation.

Because women were historically subject to greater sexual regulation than men, the sexual revolution had special significance for

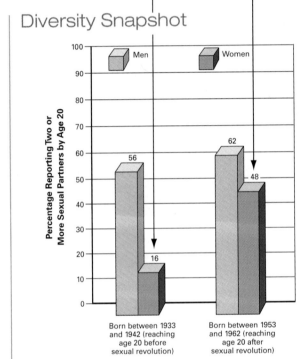

Diversity Snapshot

FIGURE 8–1   The Sexual Revolution: Closing the Double Standard

A larger share of men than women reports having had two or more sexual partners by age twenty. But the sexual revolution greatly reduced this gender difference.

Source: Laumann et al. (1994:198).

them. Society's "double standard" allows (and even encourages) men to be sexually active but expects women to be virgins until marriage and faithful to their husbands afterward. The survey data in Figure 8–1 show the narrowing of the double standard as a result of the sexual revolution. Among people born between 1933 and 1942 (that is, people who are in their sixties and seventies today), 56 percent of men but just 16 percent of women report having had two or more sexual partners by the time they reached age twenty. Compare this wide gap to the pattern among the baby boomers born between 1953 and 1962 (people now in their forties and fifties), who came of age after the sexual revolution. In this category, 62 percent of men and 48 percent of women say they had two or more sexual partners by age twenty (Laumann et al., 1994:198). The sexual revolution increased sexual activity overall, but it changed women's behavior more than men's.

NOTE: Kinsey found that of women born before 1900, only 8% had sexual inter-course before age 20; for women born between 1910 and 1929, the share rose to 22% (K. Davis, 1971:333).

THE MAP: Economic development is positively correlated with contraceptive use.

DIVERSITY: In Laumann's study, 54% of men but only 19% of women claimed to "think about sex daily."

NOTE: Another documented dimension of the sexual revolution is a wider range of sexual practices. Laumann et al. (1994) report that in recent decades, a larger share of adults engaged in oral and anal sex.

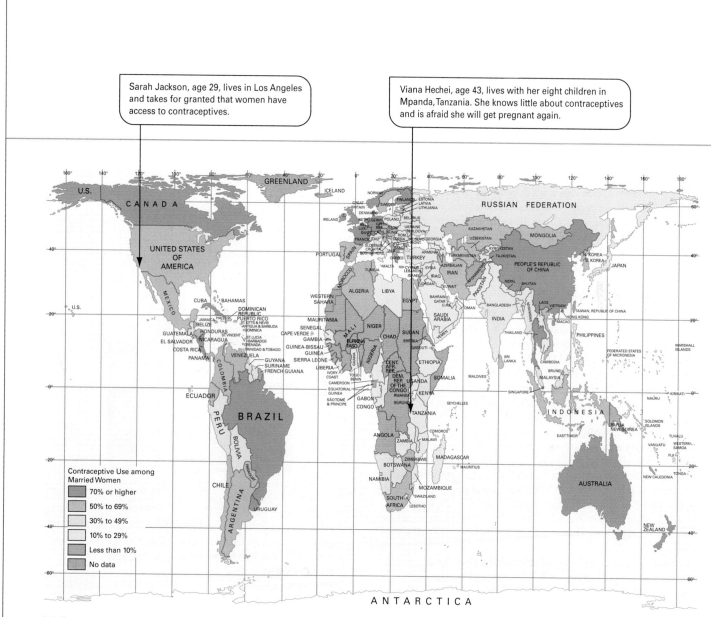

Sarah Jackson, age 29, lives in Los Angeles and takes for granted that women have access to contraceptives.

Viana Hechei, age 43, lives with her eight children in Mpanda, Tanzania. She knows little about contraceptives and is afraid she will get pregnant again.

Window on the World

GLOBAL MAP 8–1 **Contraceptive Use in Global Perspective**

The map shows the percentage of married women using modern contraception methods (such as barrier methods, contraceptive pill, implants, injectables, intrauterine devices, or sterilization). In general, how do high-income nations differ from low-income nations? Can you explain this difference?

Sources: Data from Population Reference Bureau (2008) and United Nations (2008).

Greater openness about sexuality develops as societies become richer and the opportunities for women increase. With these facts in mind, look for a pattern in the global use of birth control shown in Global Map 8–1.

This growing openness to discussion of sexuality is evident on many college and university campuses in the United States. Seeing Sociology in the News on pages 196–97 looks at the recent introduction of campus publications that talk frankly about sex.

The Sexual Counterrevolution

The sexual revolution made sex a topic of everyday discussion and sexual activity more a matter of individual choice. However, by 1980, the climate of sexual freedom that had marked the late 1960s and 1970s began to change as critics voiced the opinion that the sexual revolution was evidence of our country's moral decline. Thus began the *sexual counterrevolution* .

SOCIAL SURVEY: Asked whether their last sexual encounter included oral sex, 27% of men and 19% of women said yes (Laumann et al., 1994).

DISCUSS: The U.S. ambivalence about sex was evident in public response to the Clinton sex scandals. Liberals defended Clinton against what they saw as our tradition of oppressive Puritanism; conservatives, on the other hand, condemned Clinton as embodying 1960s' permissiveness. What do your students think?

SOCIAL SURVEY: "About how often did you have sex during the last 12 months?" (GSS 2006, N = 2,242; NORC, 2008).

"Not at all"	24.6%	"About once a week"	14.2%
"Once or twice"	8.5%	"2 or 3 times a week"	17.8%
"About once a month"	11.0%	"More than 4 times a week"	5.6%
"2 or 3 times a month"	15.0%	"Don't know"/No response	3.3%

● SEEING SOCIOLOGY
in Everyday Life

Can you point to elements of everyday life that are linked to the sexual revolution or the sexual counterrevolution?

● SEEING SOCIOLOGY
in Everyday Life

Why do you think U.S. society has become more accepting of premarital sex but not of extramarital sex?

Politically speaking, the sexual counterrevolution was a conservative call for a return to "family values" and a change from sexual freedom back toward what critics saw as the sexual responsibility valued by earlier generations. Critics of the sexual revolution objected not just to the idea of "free love" but to trends such as cohabitation (living together) and unmarried couples having children.

Looking back, the sexual counterrevolution did not greatly change the idea that people should decide for themselves when and with whom to have a sexual relationship. But whether for moral reasons or concerns about sexually transmitted diseases, more people began limiting their number of sexual partners or choosing not to have sex at all.

Is the sexual revolution over? It is true that many people are making more careful decisions about sexuality. But as the rest of this chapter explains, the ongoing sexual revolution is evident in the fact that there is now greater acceptance of premarital sex as well as increasing tolerance for various sexual orientations.

Premarital Sex

In light of the sexual revolution and the sexual counterrevolution, how much has sexual behavior in the United States really changed? One interesting trend involves premarital sex—sexual intercourse before marriage—among young people.

Consider, first, what U.S. adults *say* about premarital intercourse. Table 8–1 shows that about 34 percent characterize sexual relations before marriage as "always wrong" or "almost always wrong." Another 19 percent consider premarital sex "wrong only sometimes," and about 44 percent say premarital sex is "not wrong at all" (NORC, 2007). Public opinion is much more accepting of premarital sex today than a generation ago, but even so, our society remains divided on this issue.

Now let's look at what young people actually *do*. For women, there has been a marked change over time. The Kinsey studies reported that among people born in the early 1900s, about 50 percent of men but just 6 percent of women had had premarital sexual intercourse before age nineteen. Studies of baby boomers, born after World War II, show a slight increase in premarital intercourse among men and a large increase—to about one-third—among women. The most recent studies show that by the time they are seniors in high school, slightly more than half of young people have had premarital sexual intercourse. In addition, sexual experience among high school students who are sexually active is limited—only 15 percent of students report four or more sexual partners. These statistics have changed little in the last twenty years (Laumann et al., 1994; CDC, 2008; Yabroff, 2008).

A common belief is that an even larger share of young people engage in oral sex. This choice reflects the fact that this practice avoids the risk of pregnancy; in addition, many young people see oral sex

Table 8–1   How We View Premarital and Extramarital Sex

Survey Question: "There's been a lot of discussion about the way morals and attitudes about sex are changing in this country. If a man and a woman have sexual relations before marriage, do you think it is always wrong, almost always wrong, wrong only sometimes, or not wrong at all? What about a married person having sexual relations with someone other than the marriage partner?"

	Premarital Sex	Extramarital Sex
"Always wrong"	25.6%	79.0%
"Almost always wrong"	8.4	11.8
"Wrong only sometimes"	19.0	6.0
"Not wrong at all"	44.3	1.8
"Don't know"/No answer	2.8	1.4

Source: *General Social Surveys, 1972–2006: Cumulative Codebook* (Chicago: National Opinion Research Center, 2007), p. 298.

as something less than "going all the way." Recent research suggests that the share of young people who have had oral sex is greater than that having had intercourse, but only by about 5 percent. Therefore, claims of an "oral sex epidemic" are almost certainly exaggerated.

Finally, a significant minority of young people choose abstinence or not having sexual intercourse. Many also choose not to have oral sex, which, like intercourse, can transmit disease. Even so, research confirms the fact that premarital sex is widely accepted among young people today.

Sex between Adults

Judging from the mass media, people in the United States are very active sexually. But do popular images reflect reality? The Laumann study (1994), the largest study of sexuality since Kinsey's groundbreaking research, found that frequency of sexual activity varies widely in the U.S. population. One-third of adults report having sex with a partner a few times a year or not at all, another one-third have sex once or several times a month, and the remaining one-third have sex with a partner two or more times a week. In short, no single stereotype accurately describes sexual activity in the United States.

Despite the widespread image of "swinging singles" promoted on television shows such as *Sex and the City*, it is married people who have sex with partners the most. Married people also report the highest level of satisfaction—both emotional and physical—with their partners (Laumann et al., 1994).

Extramarital Sex

What about married people having sex outside of marriage? This practice, commonly called "adultery" (sociologists prefer the more neutral term *extramarital sex*), is widely condemned. Table 8–1

DISCUSS: Does homosexuality have a biological basis? If so, some worry that the existence of a gay gene might prompt selective abortion of fetuses thought to be homosexual or even surgery to "correct" the brains of gay men and lesbians.

WEB: For a summary of recent research on sexual orientation, go to http://www.davidmyers.org/Brix?pageID=62

GLOBAL: The share of the homosexual population reported by Laumann and his colleagues corresponds to other recent cross-national research. This seems to support the position that there is a biological foundation to sexual orientation.

NOTE: Same-sex couples (median annual income, $80,610) earn more, on average, than married heterosexual couples ($73,655).

Seeing SOCIOLOGY in the NEWS

Newsweek

Campus Sexperts

By JENNIE YABROFF
February 25, 2008

As the writer of a blog called *Sex and the Ivy*, Harvard student Lena Chen promotes herself as something of an authority on sex. The 20-year-old sociology major is a minor celebrity around campus for her musings on hook-ups, booty calls and friends with benefits. So Chen, as self-appointed poster girl for what could be called a group of brainy girls gone wild, was an obvious choice to document a week's worth of conquests for a national magazine's online sex diary. Except for the tallies at the end of the week: Total acts of intercourse? Zero.

Chen says she's since broken her dry spell, but the episode illustrates a paradox of modern college life: Students are publicly documenting their sex lives more than ever, making it easy to get the impression that elite campuses are an equivalent of the sex club in *Eyes Wide Shut*, with a perfect SAT score as the password. But when it comes to

actual sexual activity, statistics show that coeds are more likely to be virgins when they enter college, and may be having slightly less sex than in previous years. Despite this, blogs such as Chen's, student-paper sex columns, student-run sex magazines like Harvard's *H Bomb*, Yale's *SWAY* (an acronym for Sex Week at Yale) and Boston University's *Boink* have proliferated. As Dr. Jeanne Brooks-Gunn, codirector of the National Center for Children and Families, says, "What's interesting is, why are these journals gaining such popularity even though you're not seeing a big increase in sexual activity among college students?" One answer is that in an era of online exposure, where changing definitions of privacy have shifted sexual mores for the young, enterprising students no longer see a distinction between their bedroom behavior and their publishing activities. . . .

Apparently, when it comes to sex, write what you know doesn't always apply. "Everyone assumes because of the magazine that I'm sleeping with everything that walks," says Alecia Oley-

ourryk, editor of Boston University's *Boink*, [which] . . . claims 40,000 subscribers. . . . "It's not the case. Respective to my girlfriends, I'm the most prudish." Oleyourryk's comments reflect the findings of a new survey by the American College Health Association. When asked to estimate how many sexual partners their peers had had during the past school year, college students guessed three times the number of partners they'd had. . . . The study also found that for male students, the number of sexual partners in the previous year has dropped, from 2.1 in 2000 to 1.6 in 2006. According to a Centers for Disease Control survey, the number of ninth- to 12th-grade students who have had sex dropped almost 10 percent, to fewer than half of respondents, between 1991 and 2005. And a 2001 study found that 39 percent of freshman college women were virgins, and 31 percent of those women still hadn't had sex by senior year. In 2006, nearly half of Harvard undergrads who responded to a survey reported they had never had intercourse.

---

shows that more than 90 percent of U.S. adults consider a married person having sex with someone other than the marital partner "always wrong" or "almost always wrong." The norm of sexual fidelity within marriage has been and remains a strong element of U.S. culture.

But actual behavior falls short of the cultural ideal. The Laumann study reports that about 25 percent of married men and 10 percent of married women have had at least one extramarital sexual experience. Stating this the other way around, 75 percent of men and 90 percent of women remain sexually faithful to their partners throughout their married lives (Laumann et al., 1994:214; NORC, 2007:1877).

Sex over the Life Course

Patterns of sexual activity change with age. In the United States, most young men become sexually active by the time they reach sixteen and women by the age of seventeen. By the time they reach their mid-twenties, about 90 percent of both women and men reported being sexually active with a partner at least once during the past year (Mosher, Chandra, & Jones, 2005).

The picture begins to change by about age fifty, after which advancing age is linked to a decline in the share of people who are sexually active. By age sixty, about 85 percent of men and 60 percent of women say they have been sexually active during the past year. By age seventy, only half of women claim to be sexually active; by age eighty, half of men say the same (Laumann et al., 1994; T. W. Smith,

2006). Contrary to stereotypes popular among young people, these data show that sexual activity is a normal part of life for most older adults.

Sexual Orientation

In recent decades, public opinion about sexual orientation has shown a remarkable change. **Sexual orientation** is *a person's romantic and emotional attraction to another person*. The norm in all human societies is **heterosexuality** (*hetero* is Greek for "the other of two"), meaning *sexual attraction to someone of the other sex*. Yet in every society, a significant share of people experience **homosexuality** (*homo* is Greek for "the same"), *sexual attraction to someone of the same sex*. Keep in mind that people do not necessarily fall into just one of these categories; they may have varying degrees of attraction to both sexes.

The idea that sexual orientation is not always clear-cut is confirmed by the existence of **bisexuality,** *sexual attraction to people of both sexes*. Some bisexual people are equally attracted to males and females; many others are more attracted to one sex than the other. Finally, **asexuality** refers to *a lack of sexual attraction to people of either sex*. Figure 8–2 shows each of these sexual orientations in relation to the others.

It is important to remember that sexual *attraction* is not the same thing as sexual *behavior*. Many people, perhaps even most people, have experienced attraction to someone of the same sex, but far

NOTE: Census data for 2005 report 776,943 same-sex couples in the U.S., about triple the number found in 2000. The likely cause of this dramatic increase is greater willingness to disclose the partnership.

SOCIAL SURVEY: Results of a recent international survey showing the share of adult respondents who claim that homosexuality is wrong: U.S., 42%; Mexico, 41%; U.K., 21%; France, 13%; the Netherlands, 9%; Spain, 5% (cited in Fetto, 2002a:16).

NOTE: Since the "don't ask, don't tell" policy was enacted in 1993, about 12,500 people have been dismissed from the armed forces on grounds of sexual orientation. Estimated cost of replacing them: about $365 million.

The slight decline may be explained by increased awareness of the potential downsides of sex, such as STDs or on-campus abstinence movements such as Harvard's True Love Revolution student group.... Still, students involved in sex publications say there's a need for more conversation about the intricacies and emotions regarding sex, regardless of how much of it they're actually having. Jenna Bromberg, a Cornell senior who writes a sex column for the school paper, says she wants to spur discussion of the pluses and minuses of hooking up. "A lot of the time I put gross stories in there to get people talking," she says. . . .

These publications are not purely academic exercises: their creators hope they lead to professional opportunities after graduation. "People think it's a stigma, but I think we're in changing times, and it can open doors for me," says Oleyourryk. . . . "I continually tell my mom this is a great résumé builder," she says, though she's vague about what she'll use her résumé for. Though the young sexpert's optimism may seem naive, it's not necessarily misguided, says Pepper Schwartz, a sociologist at the University of Washington. "Maybe their generation will take this a lot less seriously than we do," she says. In the age of MySpace and Facebook, sex may be just one more way to network. "To me, talking about sex and one-night stands is superficial. What I keep out of the column is the intimate stuff," says Bromberg, adding that she wouldn't write about a serious relationship.

The students' cavalier attitudes may stem from confidence about their futures fostered by the elite institutions they use as publishing platforms. "A lot of these Ivy League students are bright, self-confident, and they have some extra money to get these things started," says Schwartz. "Whether their class origins are protecting them, or giving them more license, I don't know, but class always has an impact." Certainly, the students behind the publications are earnest and articulate, and may be able to land the jobs of their dreams. If they do experience misgivings about their activities, it may be for personal reasons. "The only times I regret writing the column," says Bromberg, "is when I have to look my dad in the eye."

WHAT DO YOU THINK?

1. Is this article correct in stating that students today are less concerned about keeping their sexual lives private? How do your friends feel about sexuality and privacy?

2. Were you surprised to read that most students think others on campus are much more sexually active than they really are? Can you explain this pattern?

3. Do you agree with the claim that more discussion of sexuality on campus is needed? What particular issues should be more widely discussed?

fewer ever engage in same-sex behavior. This is in large part because our culture discourages such actions.

In the United States and around the world, heterosexuality emerged as the norm because, biologically speaking, heterosexual relations permit human reproduction. Even so, most societies tolerate homosexuality, and some have even celebrated it. Among the ancient Greeks, for example, upper-class men considered homosexuality the highest form of relationship, partly because they looked down on women as intellectually inferior. As men saw it, heterosexuality was necessary only so they could have children, and "real" men preferred homosexual relations (Kluckhohn, 1948; Ford & Beach, 1951; Greenberg, 1988).

What Gives Us a Sexual Orientation?

The question of how people come to have a particular sexual orientation is strongly debated. The arguments cluster into two general positions: sexual orientation as a product of society and sexual orientation as a product of biology.

Sexual Orientation: A Product of Society

This approach argues that people in any society attach meanings to sexual activity, and these meanings differ from place to place and over time. As Michel Foucault (1990, orig. 1978) points out, for example, there was no distinct category of people called "homosexuals" until just over a century ago, when scientists and eventually the public as a whole began defining people that way. Throughout history, many

Diversity Snapshot

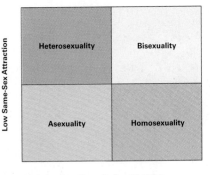

FIGURE 8–2 Four Sexual Orientations

A person's levels of same-sex attraction and opposite-sex attraction are two distinct dimensions that combine in various ways to produce four major sexual orientations.

Source: Adapted from Storms (1980).

RESOURCE: The companion reader *Seeing Ourselves*, 8th ed., features the J. M. Carrier article "Homosexual Behavior in Cross-Cultural Perspective."

RESOURCE: An excerpt titled "Understanding Sexual Orientation" by Alfred Kinsey, Wardell Pomeroy, and Clyde Martin is among the classics in the companion reader.

POP CULTURE: Homosexuality has become a part of pop culture with television shows such as *Will and Grace, Queer as Folk, Queer Eye for the Straight Guy, The L Word,* and *All My Children.*

sexual orientation (p. 196) a person's romantic and emotional attraction to another person

heterosexuality (p. 196) sexual attraction to someone of the other sex

homosexuality (p. 196) sexual attraction to someone of the same sex

bisexuality (p. 196) sexual attraction to people of both sexes

asexuality (p. 196) a lack of sexual attraction to people of either sex

people no doubt had what we would call "homosexual experiences," but neither they nor others saw in this behavior the basis for any special identity.

Anthropological studies show that patterns of homosexuality differ from one society to another. In Siberia, for example, the Chukchee Eskimo have a practice in which one man dresses as a female and does a woman's work. The Sambia, who dwell in the Eastern Highlands of New Guinea, have a ritual in which young boys perform oral sex on older men in the belief that eating semen will make them more masculine. The existence of such diverse patterns in societies around the world seems to indicate that human sexual expression is socially constructed (Murray & Roscoe, 1998; Blackwood & Wieringa, 1999).

Sexual Orientation: A Product of Biology

A growing body of evidence suggests that sexual orientation is innate, or rooted in human biology, in much the same way that people are born right-handed or left-handed. Arguing this position, Simon LeVay (1993) links sexual orientation to the structure of a person's brain. LeVay studied the brains of both homosexual and heterosexual men and found a small but important difference in the size of the hypothalamus, a part of the brain that regulates hormones. Such an anatomical difference, he claims, plays a part in shaping sexual orientation.

Genetics may also influence sexual orientation. One study of forty-four pairs of brothers, all homosexual, found that thirty-three pairs had a distinctive genetic pattern involving the X chromosome. The gay brothers also had an unusually high number of gay male relatives—but only on their mother's side. Such evidence leads some researchers to think there may be a "gay gene" located on the X chromosome (Hamer & Copeland, 1994).

CRITICAL REVIEW Mounting evidence supports the conclusion that sexual orientation is rooted in biology, although the best guess at present is that both nature and nurture play a part. Remember that sexual orientation is not a matter of neat categories. Most people who think of themselves as homosexual have had some heterosexual experiences, just as many people who think of themselves as heterosexual have had some homosexual experiences. Explaining sexual orientation, then, is not easy.

There is also a political issue here with great importance for gay men and lesbians. To the extent that sexual orientation is based in biology, homosexuals have no more choice about their sexual orientation than they do about their skin color. If this is so, shouldn't gay men and lesbians expect the same legal protection from discrimination as African Americans?

CHECK YOUR LEARNING What evidence supports the position that sexual behavior is constructed by society? What evidence supports the position that sexual orientation is rooted in biology?

How Many Gay People Are There?

What share of our population is gay? This is a difficult question to answer because, as noted earlier, sexual orientation is not a matter of neat categories. In addition, not all people are willing to reveal their sexuality to strangers or even to family members. Kinsey estimated that about 4 percent of males and 2 percent of females have an exclusively same-sex orientation, although he pointed out that most people experience same-sex attraction at some point in their lives.

Some social scientists put the gay share of the population at 10 percent. But the Laumann (1994) research shows that how homosexuality is defined makes a big difference in the results. As part (a) of Figure 8–3 shows, about 9 percent of U.S. men and about 4 percent of U.S. women between the ages of eighteen and fifty-nine reported engaging in homosexual activity *at some time in their lives.* The second pair of bars shows that even fewer men and women had a homosexual experience during childhood but not after puberty. And

Homosexuality was all but absent from television until the 1970s, when the first gay and lesbian characters appeared. Today, people with a same-sex orientation are more widely seen on television shows, including *All My Children.* In 2009, this long-time drama featured the first same-sex wedding on daytime television.

DIVERSITY: The Youth Risk Behavior Survey reports these shares of U.S. high school students to be sexually active: non-Hispanic white: 32.9%; Hispanic: 37.4%; non-Hispanic black: 46.0% (CDC, 2008).

NOTE: The concept of homophobia amounts to an effort to socially construct reality in a pro-gay (rather than anti-gay) way.

DISCUSS: Are students surprised to see survey data showing a slight majority of U.S. adults disapproving of homosexuality?

NOTE: The gay rights movement was one part of the sexual revolution.

homophobia discomfort over close personal interaction with people thought to be gay, lesbian, or bisexual

SEEING SOCIOLOGY
in Everyday Life

What changes in laws regarding gay marriage do you expect over the next ten years? Why?

just 2.8 percent of men and 1.4 percent of women defined themselves as "partly" or "entirely" homosexual.

In the Laumann survey, less than 1 percent of adults described themselves as bisexual. But bisexual experiences appear to be fairly common (at least for a time) among younger people, especially on college and university campuses (Laumann et al., 1994; Leland, 1995). Many bisexuals do not think of themselves as either gay or straight, and their behavior reflects aspects of both gay and straight living.

The Gay Rights Movement

The public's attitude toward homosexuality has been moving toward greater acceptance. Back in 1973, as shown in part (b) of Figure 8–3, about three-fourths of adults in the United States claimed that homosexual relations were "always wrong" or "almost always wrong." Although that percentage changed little during the 1970s and 1980s, by 2006 it had dropped to 58 percent (NORC, 2007:299). Among college students, who are generally more tolerant of homosexuality than the general population, we see a similar trend. In 1980, about half of college students supported laws prohibiting homosexual relationships; by 2008, as Figure 8–4 on page 200 shows, roughly one-quarter felt this way (Astin et al., 2002; Pryor et al., 2008).

In large measure, this change was brought about by the gay rights movement, which began in the middle of the twentieth century. Up to that time, most people in this country did not discuss homosexuality, and it was common for employers (including the federal government and the armed forces) to fire anyone who was even *accused* of being gay. Mental health professionals, too, took a hard line, describing homosexuals as "sick" and sometimes placing them in mental hospitals where, it was hoped, they might be "cured." It is no surprise that most lesbians and gay men remained "in the closet," closely guarding the secret of their sexual orientation. But the gay rights movement gained strength during the 1960s. One early milestone occurred in 1973, when the American Psychiatric Association declared that homosexuality was not an illness but simply "a form of sexual behavior."

The gay rights movement also began using the term **homophobia** to describe *discomfort over close personal interaction with people thought to be gay, lesbian, or bisexual* (Weinberg, 1973). The concept of homophobia turns the tables on society: Instead of asking "What's wrong with gay people?" the question becomes "What's wrong with people who can't accept a different sexual orientation?"

In 2004, a number of cities and towns in the United States began to allow gay couples to marry, although these unions were later declared illegal. But gay marriage became legal in Massachusetts in 2004, and is now also legal in Connecticut (2008), Vermont (2009), Iowa (2009), Maine (2009), and New Hampshire (2009). A number of

FIGURE 8–3 **Sexual Orientation in the United States: Survey Data**

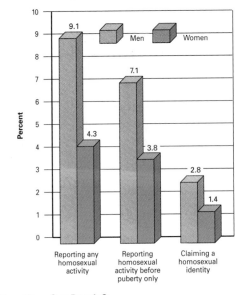

(a) How Many Gay People?

The percentage of people who are classified as having a homosexual orientation depends on how this concept is operationalized. Research suggests that 2.8 percent of adult men and 1.4 percent of adult women claim a homosexual identity.

Source: Adapted from Laumann et al. (1994).

Survey Question: "What about sexual relations between two adults of the same sex—do you think it is always wrong, almost always wrong, wrong only sometimes, or not wrong at all?"

(b) Attitudes toward Homosexual Relations, 1973–2006

Source: NORC (2007).

NOTE: Research by Craig Little and Andrea Rankin (2001) shows that alcohol and marijuana use are significant predictors of sexual activity among eighth graders. Boys, they conclude, initiate sexual activity as a status-seeking effort, and girls do so to gain approval from partners and peers.

NOTE: Although the rate of pregnancy among teenage girls between the ages of 15 and 20 has gone down, the pregnancy rate for younger girls has gone up. The reason is that girls and boys are becoming sexually active at a younger age.

GLOBAL: A clear case of ethnocentrism is that the Japanese child pornography industry—the biggest in the world—almost never uses Japanese girls; they "import" other Asian women.

● SEEING SOCIOLOGY
in Everyday Life

In light of the fact that 80 percent of today's pregnant teens are unmarried, what responsibilities should teen fathers-to-be have toward their children?

Student Snapshot

Since 1980, college students' opposition to homosexual relationships has declined sharply.

FIGURE 8–4 **Opposition to Homosexual Relationships: Attitudes of First-Year College Students, 1980–2008**

The historical trend among college students is toward greater tolerance of homosexual relationships, a view now held by a large majority.

Sources: Astin et al. (2002) and Pryor et al. (2008).

many are not emotionally mature enough to appreciate the consequences of their actions. Surveys show that there are about 750,000 teen pregnancies in the United States each year, most of them unplanned. This country's rate of births to teens is higher than that of all other high-income countries and is twice the rate in Canada (Darroch et al., 2001; Alan Guttmacher Institute, 2006; Ventura et al., 2008).

For young women of all racial and ethnic categories, weak families and low income sharply increase the likelihood of becoming sexually active and having an unplanned child. To make matters worse, having unplanned children raises the risk that young women (as well as young fathers-to-be) will not complete high school and will end up living in poverty (Alan Guttmacher Institute, 2002).

Did the sexual revolution raise the level of teenage pregnancy? Perhaps surprisingly, the answer is no. The rate of pregnancy among U.S. teens in 1950 was higher than it is today, partly because people back then married at a younger age. Because abortion was against the law, many pregnancies led to quick marriages. As a result, there were many pregnant teenagers, but almost 90 percent were married. Today, the number of pregnant teens is lower, but in about 80 percent of cases, the women are unmarried. In a slight majority (57 percent) of such cases, these women keep their babies; in the remainder, they have abortions (29 percent) or miscarriages (14 percent) (Alan Guttmacher Institute, 2006). National Map 8–2 shows the pregnancy rates for women between the ages of fifteen and nineteen throughout the United States.

other states, including California (which briefly legalized gay marriage in 2008), Washington and New Jersey, recognize either "domestic partnerships" or "civil unions," which provide most or all of the benefits of marriage. At the same time, a majority of the states have enacted laws that forbid gay marriage and prohibit recognizing gay marriages performed elsewhere (National Conference of State Legislatures, 2009).

Sexual Issues and Controversies

Sexuality lies at the heart of a number of controversies in the United States today. Here we take a look at four key issues: teen pregnancy, pornography, prostitution, and sexual violence.

Teen Pregnancy

Because it carries the risk of pregnancy, being sexually active—especially having intercourse—demands a high level of responsibility. Teenagers may be biologically mature enough to conceive, but

Pornography

Pornography is *sexually explicit material intended to cause sexual arousal.* But what is or is not pornographic has long been a matter of debate. Recognizing that different people view portrayals of sexuality differently, the U.S. Supreme Court gives local communities the power to decide for themselves what violates "community standards" of decency and lacks "redeeming social value."

Definitions aside, pornography is very popular in the United States: X-rated videos, telephone "sex lines," sexually explicit movies and magazines, and thousands of Internet Web sites make up a thriving industry that takes in at least $5 billion each year. Most pornography in the United States is created in California, and the vast majority of consumers of pornography are men (Steinhauer, 2008).

Traditionally, people have criticized pornography on *moral* grounds. As national surveys confirm, 60 percent of U.S. adults are concerned that "sexual materials lead to a breakdown of morals" (NORC, 2007:300). Today, however, pornography is also seen as a *power* issue because most of it degrades women, portraying them as the sexual playthings of men.

Some critics also claim that pornography is a cause of violence against women. Although it is difficult to prove a scientific cause-

THE MAP: Generally, teen birth rates are higher in states that have lower average incomes. Compare this map and National Maps 11–1 and 11–2.

NOTE: Prostitution was legal throughout the U.S. until 1909. Iowa was first to ban it; by 1920, all states had followed suit.

DISCUSS: What arguments can the class develop in favor of legalizing prostitution? What arguments oppose such a position?

SOCIAL SURVEY: "There is nothing inherently wrong with prostitution, so long as the health risks can be minimized. If consenting adults agree to exchange money for sex, that is their business." (GSS 1996, *N* = 1,444; NORC, 2008)

"Agree strongly"	15.4%	"Disagree strongly"	43.1%
"Agree somewhat"	23.7%	"Don't know"/No response	2.7%
"Disagree somewhat"	15.2%		

In Tucson, Arizona, 18-year-old Ramona Ramirez was just given a baby shower by her high school classmates, many of whom are already married and have children.

In Bangor, Maine, Sandy Johnson, also 18, reports that only "one or two" girls in her high school have become pregnant.

pornography sexually explicit material intended to cause sexual arousal.

prostitution the selling of sexual services

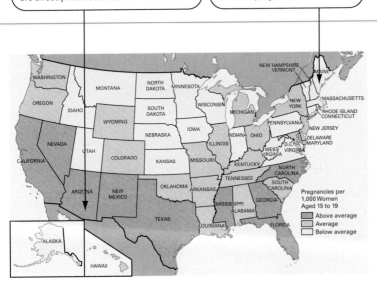

Seeing Ourselves

NATIONAL MAP 8–2

Teenage Pregnancy Rates across the United States

The map shows pregnancy rates for women aged fifteen to nineteen. In what regions of the country are rates high? Where are they low? What explanation can you offer for these patterns?

Source: Alan Guttmacher Institute (2006).

and-effect relationship between what people view and how they act, the public shares a concern about pornography and violence, with almost half of adults holding the opinion that pornography encourages people to commit rape (NORC, 2007:300).

Although people everywhere object to sexual material they find offensive, many also value the principle of free speech and the protection of artistic expression. Nevertheless, pressure to restrict pornography is building from an unlikely coalition of conservatives (who oppose pornography on moral grounds) and liberals (who condemn it for political reasons).

Prostitution

Prostitution is *the selling of sexual services*. Often called "the world's oldest profession," prostitution has been widespread throughout recorded history. In the United States today, about one in six adult men reports having paid for sex at some time (NORC, 2007:1876). Because most people think of sex as an expression of intimacy between two people, they find the idea of sex for money disturbing. As a result, prostitution is against the law everywhere in the United States except for parts of rural Nevada.

Around the world, prostitution is most common in poor countries, where patriarchy is strong and traditional cultural norms limit women's ability to earn a living. Global Map 8–2 on page 202 shows where in the world prostitution is most widespread.

Types of Prostitution

Most prostitutes (many prefer the morally neutral term "sex workers") are women, and they fall into different categories. *Call girls* are elite prostitutes, typically young, attractive, and well-educated women who arrange their own "dates" with clients by telephone. The classified pages of any large city newspaper contain numerous ads for "escort services," by which women (and sometimes men) offer both companionship and sex for a fee.

In the middle category are prostitutes who are employed in "massage parlors" or brothels under the control of managers. These sex workers have less choice about their clients, receive less money for their services, and get to keep no more than half of the money they earn.

At the bottom of the sex worker hierarchy are *streetwalkers*, women and men who "work the streets" of large cities around the country. Some female streetwalkers are under the control of male pimps who take most of their earnings. Many others are addicts who sell sex in order to buy the drugs they need. Both types of people are at high risk of becoming the victims of violence (Davidson, 1998; Estes, 2001).

The lives of sex workers, then, are diverse, with some earning more than others and some at greater risk of violence. But studies of sex workers point to one thing that almost all of these women have in common: They consider their work degrading. As one researcher suggested, one minute, the sex worker is adored as "the most beautiful woman," while the next she is condemned as a "slut" (Barton, 2006).

Most prostitutes offer heterosexual services. However, gay male prostitutes also trade sex for money. Researchers report that many gay prostitutes end up selling sex after having suffered rejection by family and friends because of their sexual orientation (Weisberg, 1985; Boyer, 1989; Kruks, 1991).

DISCUSS: Global prostitution, which often involves rich white males traveling to poor nations, can be understood as a case of class, racial, and gender oppression intersecting.

THE MAP: The global map describes the United States as having a "medium" level of prostitution by global standards. In what regions of the country do peo-ple think prostitution is greater? Consider rural/urban, high-income/low-income, or other factors you think are important.

DISCUSS: Is prostitution (as well as exotic dancing and other sex work) a sign of the oppression of women or an opportunity for some women to make a reasonably good living?

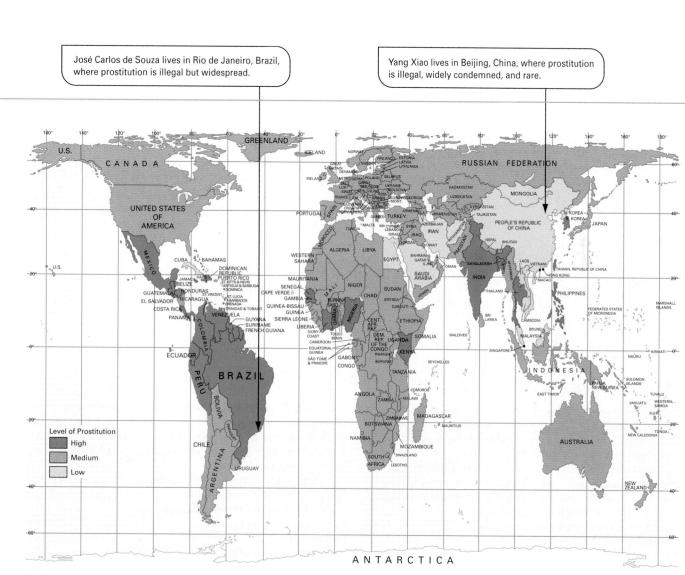

José Carlos de Souza lives in Rio de Janeiro, Brazil, where prostitution is illegal but widespread.

Yang Xiao lives in Beijing, China, where prostitution is illegal, widely condemned, and rare.

Level of Prostitution
- High
- Medium
- Low

Window on the World

GLOBAL MAP 8–2 **Prostitution in Global Perspective**

Generally speaking, prostitution is widespread in societies where women have low standing. Officially, at least, the People's Republic of China boasts of gender equality, including the elimination of "vice" such as prostitution, which oppresses women. By contrast, in much of Latin America, where patriarchy is strong, prostitution is common. In many Islamic societies, patriarchy is also strong, but religion is a counterbalance, so prostitution is limited. Western, high-income nations have a moderate amount of prostitution.

Sources: *Peters Atlas of the World* (1990) and Mackay (2000).

A Victimless Crime?

Prostitution is against the law almost everywhere in the United States, but many people consider it a victimless crime (defined in Chapter 9, "Deviance," as a crime in which there is no obvious victim). As a result, instead of enforcing prostitution laws all the time, police stage only occasional crackdowns. This policy reflects a desire to control prostitution while also recognizing that it is impossible to eliminate it entirely.

Many people take a "live and let live" attitude about prostitution and say that adults ought to be able to do as they please so long as no one is harmed or forced to do anything. But is prostitution really as victimless as these people think? The sex trade subjects many

SOCIAL SURVEY: "Thinking about the time since your 18th birthday, have you ever had sex with a person you paid or who paid you for sex?" (GSS 2006, NORC, 2008).

"Yes" 8.2%   "No" 90.7%   "Don't know"/ No response   1.1%

NOTE: Public support for rape victims has prompted more women to come for

ward, a trend reflected in a steady rise in the number and percentage of forcible rapes reported to police during the 1980s and 1990s.

NOTE: Men also rape men, and there are rare cases of women raping men. Although the federal definition of "forcible rape" focuses on a man raping a woman, other patterns are noted separately by the FBI.

● SEEING SOCIOLOGY
in Everyday Life

Do you consider prostitution a victimless crime or not?
Explain your position.

women to kidnapping, emotional abuse, and outright violence and also plays a part in spreading sexually transmitted diseases, including AIDS. In addition, many poor women—especially in low-income nations—become trapped in a life of selling sex. Thailand, in Southeast Asia, has 2 million prostitutes, representing about 10 percent of all women in the labor force. At least half of these women are teenagers—many begin working before they even reach their teens—and they typically suffer physical and emotional abuse and run a high risk of becoming infected with HIV (Wonders & Michalowski, 2001; Kapstein, 2006).

In the past, the focus of attention has been on the women who earn money as sex workers. But prostitution would not exist at all if it were not for demand on the part of men. For this reason, law enforcement is now more likely to target "Johns" when they attempt to buy sex.

Sexual Violence:
Rape and Date Rape

Ideally, sexual activity occurs within a loving relationship between consenting adults. In reality, however, sex can be twisted by hate and violence. Here we consider two types of sexual violence: rape and date rape.

Rape

Although some people think rape is motivated only by a desire for sex, it is actually an expression of power—a violent act that uses sex to hurt, humiliate, or control another person. According to the U.S. Department of Justice (2008), more than 90,000 women each year report to the police that they have been raped. This reflects only the reported cases; the actual number of rapes is almost certainly several times higher.

The official government definition of rape is "the carnal knowledge of a female forcibly and against her will." Thus official rape statistics include only victims who are women. But men, too, are raped—in perhaps 10 percent of all cases. Most men who rape men are not homosexual; they are heterosexuals who are motivated by a desire not for sex but to dominate another person.

Date Rape

A common myth is that rape involves strangers. In reality, however, only about one-third of rapes fit this pattern. About two-thirds of rapes involve people who know one another—more often than not, pretty well—and these crimes usually take place in familiar surroundings, especially the home and the campus. For this reason, the term "date rape" or "acquaintance rape" is used to refer to forcible sexual

Experts agree that one factor that contributes to the problem of sexual violence on the college campus is the widespread use of alcoholic beverages. What policies are in force on your campus to discourage the kind of drinking that leads to one person imposing sex on another?

violence against women by men they know (Laumann et al., 1994; U.S. Department of Justice, 2008).

A second myth, often linked to date rape, is that the woman must have done something to encourage the man and made him think she wanted to have sex. Perhaps the victim agreed to go out with the offender. Maybe she even invited him into her room. But of course, acting in this way no more justifies rape than it would any other type of physical assault.

Although rape is a physical attack, it often leaves emotional and psychological scars. Beyond the brutality of being physically violated, rape by an acquaintance also undermines a victim's sense of trust. Psychological scars are especially serious among the two-thirds of rape victims who are under eighteen and even more so among the one-third who are under the age of twelve. The home is no refuge from rape: One-third of all victims under the age of eighteen are attacked by their own fathers or stepfathers (Snyder, 2000).

How common is date rape? One study found that about 20 percent of a sample of high school girls in the United States reported being the victim of sexual or physical violence inflicted by boys they were dating. The risk of abuse is especially high among girls who become sexually active before reaching the age of fifteen (Dickinson, 2001; Teenage Research Unlimited, 2008).

DISCUSS: How many words can students think of to characterize a sexually loose female? How many comparable words apply to men? What accounts for the difference?

GLOBAL: Interpol data indicate that the worst nation in the world with regard to rape is South Africa, with about 1.6 million rapes per year (a rate of 116 per 100,000 people versus 33 in the U.S. and 25 in Sweden). (United Nations, 2008).

Q: "Sex is something everyone can do. . . . Love is different. You need to learn about love when you are a baby, and you need lessons until you die. You can't learn love by yourself. You need to grow up with it." Prostitute cited in Sterke (2000).

SEEING SOCIOLOGY
in Everyday Life

Is there much discussion of "hooking up" on your campus? Why or why not?

SEEING SOCIOLOGY IN EVERYDAY LIFE

When Sex Is Only Sex: The Campus Culture of "Hooking Up"

BRYNNE: My mom told me once that she didn't have sex with my dad until after they were engaged.
KATY: I guess times have really changed!

Have you ever been in a sexual situation and not been sure of the right thing to do? Most colleges and universities highlight two important rules. First, sexual activity must take place only when both participants have given clear statements of consent. The consent principle is what makes "having sex" different from date rape. Second, no one should knowingly expose another person to a sexually transmitted disease, especially when the partner is unaware of the danger.

These rules are very important, but they say little about the larger issue of what sex *means*. For example, when is it "right" to have a sexual relationship? How well do you have to know the other person? If you do have sex, are you obligated to see the person again?

Two generations ago, there were informal rules for campus sex. Dating was considered part of the courtship process. That is, "going out" was the way in which women and men evaluated each other as possible marriage partners while they sharpened their own sense of what they wanted in a mate. Because, on average, marriage took place in the early twenties, many college students became engaged and married while they were still in school. In this cultural climate, sex was viewed by college students as part of a relationship that carried a commitment—a serious interest in the other person as a possible marriage partner.

Today, the sexual culture of the campus is very different. Partly because people now marry much later, the culture of courtship has declined dramatically. About three-fourths of women in a national survey point to a relatively new campus pattern, the culture of "hooking up." What exactly is "hooking up"? Most describe it in words like these: "When a girl and a guy get together for a physical encounter—anything from kissing to having sex—and don't necessarily expect anything further."

Student responses to the survey suggest that hookups have three characteristics. First, most couples who hook up know little about each other. Second, a typical hookup involves people who have been drinking alcohol, usually at a campus party. Third, most women are critical of the culture of hooking up and express little satisfaction with these encounters. Certainly,

some women (and men) who hook up simply walk away, happy to have enjoyed a sexual experience free of further obligation. But given the powerful emotions that sex can unleash, hooking up often leaves someone wondering what to expect next: "Will you call me tomorrow?" "Will I see you again?"

The survey asked women who had experienced a recent hookup to report how they felt about the experience a day later. A majority of respondents said they felt "awkward," about half felt "disappointed" and "confused," and one in four felt "exploited." Clearly, for many people, sex is more than a physical encounter. In addition, because today's campus climate is very sensitive to charges of sexual exploitation, there is a need for clearer standards of fair play.

WHAT DO YOU THINK?

1. How extensive is the pattern of hooking up on your campus? Are you aware of differences in these types of encounters between heterosexuals and homosexuals?

2. What do you see as the advantages of sex without commitment? What are the disadvantages of this kind of relationship? Are men and women likely to answer this question differently? Explain.

3. Do you think college students need more guidance about sexual issues? If so, who should provide this guidance?

Source: Based in part on Marquardt & Glenn (2001).

Nowhere has the issue of date rape been more widely discussed in recent years than on college campuses, where the danger of date rape is high. The collegiate environment promotes easy friendships and encourages trust among young people who still have much to learn about relationships and about themselves. As the Seeing Sociology in Everyday Life box explains, the same college environment that encourages communication provides few social norms to help guide young people's sexual experiences. To counter the problem, many schools now actively address myths about rape through on-campus workshops. In addition, greater attention is now focused on the abuse of alcohol, which increases the likelihood of sexual violence.

EXERCISE: Visit a local supermarket, and examine the covers of the magazines displayed at the checkout line. To what extent is sexuality used to sell products? More specifically, are men or women more commonly portrayed in sexual terms?

RESOURCE: A government report on the sexual victimization of college women is available at http://www.ojp.usdoj.gov/bjs/abstract/svcw.htm

NOTE: Kingsley Davis saw prostitution as functional because it provided sexual access for people without committed partners and a sexual outlet that might even keep some marriages together. Generally, however, functionalism views sexually transmitted diseases, teen pregnancy, pornography, prostitution, and sexual violence as dysfunctional patterns that result from the failure of social institutions— notably the family and the church—to operate as they should.

MAKING THE GRADE

Use the Applying Theory table below to review the theoretical approaches to sexuality.

APPLYING THEORY

Sexuality

	Structural-Functional Approach	Symbolic-Interaction Approach	Social-Conflict/Feminist Approach
What is the level of analysis?	Macro-level	Micro-level	Macro-level
What is the importance of sexuality for society?	Society depends on sexuality for reproduction. Society uses the incest taboo and other norms to control sexuality in order to maintain social order.	Sexual practices vary among the many cultures of the world. Some societies allow individuals more freedom than others in matters of sexual behavior.	Sexuality is linked to social inequality. U.S. society regulates women's sexuality more than men's, which is part of the larger pattern of men dominating women.
Has sexuality changed over time? How?	Yes. As advances in birth control technology separate sex from reproduction, societies relax some controls on sexuality.	Yes. The meanings people attach to virginity and other sexual matters are all socially constructed and subject to change.	Yes and no. Some sexual standards have relaxed, but society still defines women in sexual terms, just as homosexual people are harmed by society's heterosexual bias.

Theoretical Analysis of Sexuality

Applying sociology's various theoretical approaches gives us a better understanding of human sexuality. The following sections discuss the three major approaches, and the Applying Theory table highlights the key insights of each approach.

Structural-Functional Analysis

The structural-functional approach highlights the contribution of any social pattern to the overall operation of society. Because sexuality can have such important consequences, society regulates this type of behavior.

The Need to Regulate Sexuality

From a biological point of view, sex allows our species to reproduce. But culture and social institutions regulate *with whom* and *when* people reproduce. For example, most societies condemn a married person for having sex with someone other than his or her spouse. To allow sexual passion to go unchecked would threaten family life, especially the raising of children.

The fact that the incest taboo exists everywhere shows that no society permits completely free choice in sexual partners. Reproduction by family members other than married partners would break down the system of kinship and hopelessly confuse human relationships.

Historically, the social control of sexuality was strong, mostly because sex often led to childbirth. We see these controls at work in the traditional distinction between "legitimate" reproduction (within marriage) and "illegitimate" reproduction (outside marriage). But once a society develops the technology to control births, its sexual norms become more permissive. This occurred in the United States, where over the course of the twentieth century, sex moved beyond its basic reproductive function and became accepted as a form of intimacy and even recreation (Giddens, 1992).

Latent Functions: The Case of Prostitution

It is easy to see that prostitution is harmful because it spreads disease and exploits women. But are there latent functions that help explain why prostitution is so widespread? According to Kingsley Davis (1971), prostitution performs several useful functions. It is one way to meet the sexual needs of a large number of people who may not have ready access to sex, including soldiers, travelers, people who are not physically attractive, or people too poor to attract a marriage

NOTE: Another interaction example involves the meaning attached to AIDS. Various precautions (dentists using gloves and masks, carefully disposing of needles, and so on) began after the AIDS crisis, even though other diseases such as hepatitis are more contagious and have been around far longer. Why?

DISCUSS: In 1920, one analyst offered the following explanation for the pattern of arresting prostitutes more than "johns": "The professional prostitute being a

social outcast may be periodically punished without disturbing the usual course of society.... The man is something more than partner in an immoral act: He discharges important social and business relations, is a father or brother responsible for the maintenance of others.... He cannot be imprisoned without [disrupting] society" (Flexner, 1920:108). How do students react to this analysis?

• SEEING SOCIOLOGY
in Everyday Life

Chastity belts may not be used today, but can you point to other ways in which society controls women's sexuality?

The control of women's sexuality is a common theme in human history. During the Middle Ages, Europeans devised the "chastity belt"—a metal device locked about a woman's groin that prevented sexual intercourse (and probably interfered with other bodily functions as well). While such devices are all but unknown today, the social control of sexuality continues. Can you point to examples?

partner. Some people favor prostitution because they want sex without the "hassle" of a relationship. As a number of analysts have pointed out, "Men don't pay for sex; they pay so they can leave" (Miracle, Miracle, & Baumeister, 2003:421).

○ **CRITICAL REVIEW** The structural-functional approach helps us see the important part sexuality plays in the organization of society. The incest taboo and other cultural norms also suggest that society has always paid attention to who has sex with whom and, especially, who reproduces with whom.

Functionalist analysis sometimes ignores gender; when Kingsley Davis wrote of the benefits of prostitution for society, he was really talking about the benefits *to men*. In addition, the fact that sexual patterns change over time, just as they differ in remarkable ways around the world, is ignored by this perspective. To appreciate the varied and changeable character of sexuality, we now turn to the symbolic-interaction approach.

○ **CHECK YOUR LEARNING** Compared to traditional societies, why do modern societies give people more choice about matters involving sexuality?

Symbolic-Interaction Analysis

The symbolic-interaction approach highlights how, as people interact, they construct everyday reality. As Chapter 6 ("Social Interaction in Everyday Life") explains, people sometimes construct very differ-

ent realities, so the views of one group or society may well differ from those of another. In the same way, our understanding of sexuality can and does change over time.

The Social Construction of Sexuality

Almost all social patterns involving sexuality saw considerable change over the course of the twentieth century. One good illustration is the changing importance of virginity. A century ago, our society's norm—for women, at least—was virginity before marriage. This norm was strong because there was no effective means of birth control, and virginity was the only guarantee a man had that his bride-to-be was not carrying another man's child.

Today, because birth control has separated sex from reproduction, the virginity norm has weakened considerably. In the United States, among people born between 1963 and 1974, just 16.3 percent of men and 20.1 percent of women reported being virgins at first marriage (Laumann et al., 1994:503).

Another example of our society's construction of sexuality involves young people. A century ago, childhood was a time of inno-

The white wedding dress, one of the important symbols of marriage, became popular in the mid-nineteenth century. Only in the last century did people view the white color as symbolizing purity or virginity, reflecting the expectation that a bride (but not a groom) would be a virgin at marriage. Do you think this expectation is still widespread today?

NOTE: In the decades since 1973, new laws and court decisions have restricted—but not eliminated—women's access to abortion. In 1977, Congress (the Hyde Amendment) declared that Medicaid funds could not be used to pay for abortions except to save a mother's life. In 1980, the Supreme Court (*Harris* v. *McRae*) ruled that state and federal governments may decide not to use welfare funds to pay for abortions for poor women. In 1989, the Supreme Court supported a state's law forbidding state doctors and hospitals from performing abortions except to save a mother's life. In 2007, the Court upheld state laws banning so-called partial birth abortion. Most states have enacted laws requiring girls under legal age to obtain parental consent before receiving an abortion.

● SEEING SOCIOLOGY
in Everyday Life

Can you point to other sexual patterns that vary around the world? Explain.

cence in sexual matters. In recent decades, however, thinking has changed. Although few people encourage sexual activity between children, most people believe that children should be educated about sex by the time they are teenagers so that they can make intelligent choices about their behavior as they grow older.

Global Comparisons

Around the world, different societies attach different meanings to sexuality. For example, the anthropologist Ruth Benedict (1938), who spent years learning the ways of life of the Melanesian people of southeastern New Guinea, reported that adults paid little attention when young children engaged in sexual experimentation with one another. Parents in Melanesia shrugged off such activity because, before puberty, sex cannot lead to reproduction. Is it likely that most parents in the United States would respond the same way?

Sexual practices also vary from culture to culture. Male circumcision of infant boys (the practice of removing all or part of the foreskin of the penis) is common in the United States but rare in most other parts of the world. A practice sometimes referred to incorrectly as female circumcision (removal of the clitoris) is rare in the United States and much of the world but common in parts of Africa and the Middle East (Crossette, 1995; Huffman, 2000). (For more about this practice, more accurately called "female genital mutilation," see the Thinking About Diversity box on page 342.)

◌ **CRITICAL REVIEW** The strength of the symbolic-interaction approach lies in revealing the constructed character of familiar social patterns. Understanding that people "construct" sexuality, we can better appreciate the variety of sexual attitudes and practices found over the course of history and around the world.

One limitation of this approach, however, is that not all sexual practices are so variable. Men everywhere have always been more likely to see women in sexual terms than the other way around. Some broader social structure must be at work in a pattern that is this widespread, as we shall see in the following section, on the social-conflict approach.

◌ **CHECK YOUR LEARNING** What evidence can you provide that human sexuality is socially constructed?

Social-Conflict and Feminist Analysis

As you have seen in earlier chapters, the social-conflict approach (particularly the gender-conflict or feminist approach) highlights dimensions of inequality. This approach shows how sexuality both reflects patterns of social inequality and helps perpetuate them. Feminism, a social-conflict approach focusing on gender inequality, links sexuality to the domination of women by men.

From a social-conflict point of view, sexuality is not so much a "natural" part of our humanity as it is a socially constructed pattern of behavior. Sexuality plays an important part in social inequality: By defining women in sexual terms, men devalue them as objects. Would you consider the behavior shown here to be "natural" or socially directed? Why?

Sexuality: Reflecting Social Inequality

Recall our discussion of prostitution, a practice outlawed almost everywhere in the United States. Enforcement of prostitution laws is uneven at best, especially when it comes to who is and is not likely to be arrested. Gender bias is evident here: Although two people are involved, the record shows that police are far more likely to arrest (less powerful) female prostitutes than (more powerful) male clients. Similarly, of all women engaged in prostitution, it is streetwalkers—women with the least income and most likely to be minorities—who face the highest risk of arrest (Saint James & Alexander, 2004). We might also wonder whether so many women would be involved in prostitution in the first place if they had the economic opportunities equal to those of men.

More generally, which categories of people in U.S. society are most likely to be defined in terms of sexuality? The answer, once again, is those with less power: women and people of color. In this way, sexuality—which is a natural part of human life—is used by society to define some categories of people as less worthy.

Q: "If conception occurs in excess . . . have abortion induced before sense and life have begun in the embryo." Aristotle, revealing that the ancient Greeks had developed some ability to control birth

NOTE: The Supreme Court has also ruled that states may require doctors to evaluate if a fetus can survive outside the mother's body before performing an abortion (*Webster* v. *Reproductive Health Services*). Congress has twice passed a law banning "partial birth" abortion, a controversial type of abortion procedure during the third trimester.

queer theory a body of research findings that challenges the heterosexual bias in U.S. society

heterosexism a view that labels anyone who is not heterosexual as "queer"

SEEING SOCIOLOGY
in Everyday Life

Can you think of three social patterns that are examples of heterosexism?

CONTROVERSY & DEBATE

The Abortion Controversy

A black van pulls up in front of the storefront in a busy section of the city. Two women get out of the front seat and cautiously look up and down the street. After a moment, one nods to the other, and they open the rear door to let a third woman out of the van. Standing to the right and left of the woman, the two quickly escort her inside the building.

This scene might describe two federal marshals taking a convict to a police station, but it is actually an account of two clinic workers helping a woman who has decided to have an abortion. Why are they so cautious? Anyone who has read the papers in recent years knows about the angry confrontations at abortion clinics across North America. Some opponents have even targeted and killed doctors who carried out abortions, some 1.2 million of which are performed in the United States each year (Ventura et al., 2008). It is one of the most hotly debated issues of our day.

Abortion has not always been so controversial. In colonial times, midwives and other healers performed abortions with little community opposition and with full approval of the law. But

controversy arose about 1850, when early medical doctors wanted to eliminate the competition they faced from midwives and other traditional health providers, whose income came largely from ending pregnancies. By 1900, medical doctors had succeeded in getting every state to pass a law banning abortion.

Such laws greatly reduced the number of abortions. Those that did occur were performed "underground," as secretly as possible. Many women who wanted abortions—especially those who were poor—had little choice but to seek help from unlicensed "back alley" abortionists, sometimes with tragic results due to unsanitary conditions and the use of medically dangerous techniques.

By the 1960s, opposition to antiabortion laws was rising. In 1973, the U.S. Supreme Court made a landmark decision (in the cases of *Roe* v. *Wade* and *Doe* v. *Bolton*), striking down all state laws banning abortion. In effect, this action established a woman's legal access to abortion nationwide.

Even so, the abortion controversy continues. On one side of the issue are people who

describe themselves as "pro-choice," supporting a woman's right to choose abortion. On the other side are those who call themselves "pro-life," opposing abortion as morally wrong; these people would like to see the Supreme Court reverse its 1973 decision.

How strong is the support for each side of the abortion controversy? A recent national survey asked a sample of adults the question "Should it be possible for a pregnant woman to obtain a legal abortion if the woman wants it for any reason?" In response, 38 percent said yes (placing them in the pro-choice camp) and 59 percent said no (expressing the pro-life position); the remaining 3 percent offered no opinion (NORC, 2007:29).

A closer look shows that circumstances make a big difference in how people see this issue. The figure shows that large majorities of U.S. adults favor legal abortion if a pregnancy seriously threatens a woman's health, if the pregnancy is a result of rape, or if a fetus is likely to have a serious defect. The bottom line is that about 39 percent support access to abortion under *any* circumstances, but nearly

Sexuality: Creating Social Inequality

Social-conflict theorists, especially feminists, point to sexuality as the root of inequality between women and men. Defining women in sexual terms amounts to devaluing them from full human beings into objects of men's interest and attention. Is it any wonder that the word *pornography* comes from the Greek word *porne,* meaning "harlot" or "prostitute"?

If men define women in sexual terms, it is easy to see pornography—almost all of which is consumed by males—as a power issue. Because pornography typically shows women focused on pleasing men, it supports the idea that men have power over women.

Some radical critics doubt that this element of power can ever be removed from heterosexual relations (A. Dworkin, 1987). Most social-conflict theorists do not object to heterosexuality, but they do agree that sexuality can and does degrade women. Our culture often describes sexuality in terms of sport (men "scoring" with women)

and violence ("slamming," "banging," and "hitting on," for example, are verbs used for both fighting and sex).

Queer Theory

Finally, social-conflict theory has taken aim not only at men dominating women but also at heterosexuals dominating homosexuals. In recent years, as lesbians and gay men have sought public acceptance, a gay voice has arisen in sociology. The term **queer theory** refers to *a body of research findings that challenges the heterosexual bias in U.S. society.*

Queer theory begins with the claim that our society is characterized by **heterosexism,** *a view that labels anyone who is not heterosexual as "queer."* Our heterosexual culture victimizes a wide range of people, including gay men, lesbians, bisexuals, intersexuals, transsexuals, and even asexual people. Although most people agree that bias against women (sexism) and people of color (racism) is wrong, heterosexism is widely tolerated and sometimes well within the law.

DISCUSS: Various "isms" can build on one another. Some queer theorists point out that disadvantages are more severe for gay men who are black than for those who are white.

WEB: The Queer Resources Directory looks at a wide range of issues from a queer theory perspective: http://www.qrd.org/qrd

SOCIAL SURVEY: Share of U.S. categories claiming that "abortion should be legal in all cases": all adults, 17%; Republicans, 10%; Democrats, 22%; men, 14%; women, 20%; whites, 17%; blacks, 16%; age 18–29, 18%; age 65 and older, 11%; college grad, 20%; high school or less, 15% (Pew Research Center, 2008).

abortion the deliberate termination of a pregnancy

85 percent support access to abortion under *some* circumstances.

Many of those who take the pro-life position feel strongly that abortion amounts to killing unborn children—more than 45 million since *Roe* v. *Wade* was passed in 1973. To them, people never have the right to end innocent life in this way. But pro-choice advocates are no less committed to the position that women must have control over their own bodies. If pregnancy decides the course of women's lives, women will never be able to compete with men on equal terms, whether it is on campus or in the workplace. Therefore, access to legal, safe abortion is a necessary condition to women's full participation in society.

WHAT DO YOU THINK?

1. The more conservative, pro-life position sees abortion as a moral issue, and the more liberal, pro-choice position views abortion as a power issue. Compare these positions to how conservatives and liberals view the issue of pornography.

2. Surveys show that men and women have almost the same opinions about abortion. Does this surprise you? Why or why not?

3. Why do you think the abortion controversy is often so bitter? Do you think our nation can find a middle ground on this issue?

Survey Question: "It should be possible for a pregnant woman to obtain a *legal abortion . . .*"

Percentage Answering Yes

- 84.5 "... if the woman's own health is seriously endangered by the pregnancy."
- 74.0 "... if she became pregnant as a result of rape."
- 71.1 "... if there is a strong chance of serious defect in the baby."
- 41.0 "... if the family has a very low income and cannot afford any more children."
- 40.8 "... if she is married and does not want any more children."
- 39.1 "... if the woman wants it for any reason."
- 38.8 "... if she is not married and does not want to marry the man."

When Should the Law Allow a Woman to Choose Abortion?

The extent of public support for legal abortion depends on how the issue is presented.

Source: NORC (2008).

For example, U.S. military forces cannot legally discharge a female soldier simply for "acting like a woman" because this would be a clear case of gender discrimination. But the military forces can discharge her for homosexuality if she is a sexually active lesbian.

Heterosexism is also part of everyday culture (Kitzinger, 2005). When we describe something as "sexy," for example, don't we really mean attractive to *heterosexuals?*

○ **CRITICAL REVIEW** The social-conflict approach shows that sexuality is both a cause and an effect of inequality. In particular, it helps us understand men's power over women and heterosexual people's domination of homosexual people.

At the same time, this approach overlooks the fact that many people do not see sexuality as a power issue. On the contrary, many couples enjoy a vital sexual relationship that deepens their commitment to one another. In addition, the social-conflict approach pays little attention to steps U.S. society has taken toward reducing inequality. Today's men are less likely to describe women as sex objects than they were a few decades ago. One of the most important issues in the workplace today is ensuring that all employees remain free from sexual harassment. Rising public concern (see Chapter 13, "Gender Stratification") has reduced the abuse of sexuality in the workplace. Likewise, there is ample evidence that the gay rights movement has secured greater opportunities and social acceptance for gay people.

○ **CHECK YOUR LEARNING** How does sexuality play a part in creating social inequality?

This chapter closes with a look at what is perhaps the most divisive issue involving sexuality: **abortion,** *the deliberate termination of a pregnancy.* There seems to be no middle ground in the debate over this controversial issue. The Controversy & Debate box helps explain why.

Seeing Sociology in Everyday Life

How do the mass media play into our society's views of human sexuality?

Far from it being a "natural" or simply "biological" concept, cultures around the world attach all sorts of meanings to human sexuality. The photos below show how the mass media—in this case, popular magazines—reflect our own culture's ideas about sexuality. In each case, can you "decode" the magazine cover and explain its messages? To what extent do you think the messages are true?

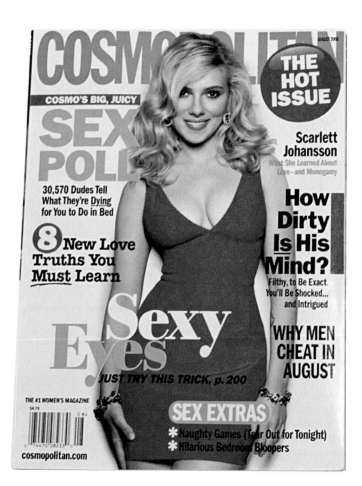

Magazines like this one are found at the checkout lines of just about every supermarket and discount store in the United States. Looking just at the cover, what can you conclude about women's sexuality in our society?

> **HINT**   The messages we get from mass media sources like these not only tell us about sexuality but also tell us what sort of people we ought to be. There is a lot of importance attached to sexuality for women, placing pressure on women to look good to men and to define life success in terms of attracting men with their sexuality. Similarly, being masculine means being successful, sophisticated, in charge, and able to attract desirable women. When the mass media endorse sexuality, it is almost always according to the norm of heterosexuality.

Messages about sexuality are directed to men as well as to women. Here is a recent issue of GQ. What messages about masculinity can you find? Do you see any evidence of heterosexual bias?

Applying SOCIOLOGY in Everyday Life

1. Looking at the *Cosmopolitan* cover, what evidence of heterosexual bias do you see? Explain.

2. Contact your school's student services office, and ask for information about the extent of sexual violence on your campus. Do people typically report such crimes? What policies and procedures does your school have to respond to sexual violence?

3. Use the campus library and Internet sources to learn more about the experiences of women and men involved in prostitution. As you learn more, decide whether you think prostitution should be considered a "victimless crime."

MAKING THE GRADE

CHAPTER 8 Sexuality

What Is Sexuality?

SEX is biological, referring to bodily differences between females and males.

p. 189

GENDER is cultural, referring to behavior, power, and privileges a society attaches to being female or male.

p. 191

sex (p. 189) the biological distinction between females and males

primary sex characteristics (p. 190) the genitals, organs used for reproduction

secondary sex characteristics (p. 190) bodily development, apart from the genitals, that distinguishes biologically mature females and males

intersexual people (p. 190) people whose bodies (including genitals) have both female and male characteristics

transsexuals (p. 190) people who feel they are one sex even though biologically they are the other

incest taboo (p. 191) a norm forbidding sexual relations or marriage between certain relatives

Sexuality is a **BIOLOGICAL ISSUE**.

- Sex is determined at conception as a male sperm joins a female ovum.
- Males and females have different genitals (*primary sex characteristics*) and bodily development (*secondary sex characteristics*).
- *Intersexual people* (*hermaphrodites*) have some combination of male and female genitalia.
- *Transsexual people* feel they are one sex although biologically they are the other.

pp. 189–90

Sexuality is a **CULTURAL ISSUE**.

- For humans, sex is a matter of cultural meaning and personal choice rather than biological programming.
- Sexual practices vary considerably from one society to another (examples include kissing, ideas about modesty, and standards of beauty).
- The *incest taboo* exists in all societies because regulating sexuality, especially reproduction, is a necessary element of social organization. Specific taboos vary from one society to another.

pp. 191–92

✓ *Sexuality is a theme found throughout most areas of social life in the United States (p. 196).*

Sexual Attitudes in the United States

The **SEXUAL REVOLUTION**, which peaked in the 1960s and 1970s, drew sexuality out into the open. Baby boomers were the first generation to grow up with the idea that sex was a normal part of social life.

pp. 193–94

The **SEXUAL COUNTERREVOLUTION**, which began around 1980, aimed criticism at "permissiveness" and urged a return to more traditional "family values."

pp. 194–95

Beginning with the work of Alfred Kinsey, researchers have studied sexual behavior in the United States and reached many interesting conclusions:

- Premarital sexual intercourse became more common during the twentieth century.
- About three-fourths of young men and two-thirds of young women have intercourse by their senior year in high school.
- Among all U.S. adults, sexual activity varies: One-third report having sex with a partner a few times a year or not at all; another one-third have sex once to several times a month; the remaining one-third have sex two or more times a week.
- Extramarital sex is widely condemned, and just 25 percent of married men and 10 percent of married women report being sexually unfaithful to their spouses at some time.

pp. 195–96

Sexual Orientation

SEXUAL ORIENTATION is a person's romantic or emotional attraction to another person. Four sexual orientations are
- heterosexuality
- homosexuality
- bisexuality
- asexuality

`pp. 196–97`

- The share of the U.S. population that is homosexual depends on how you define "homosexuality."
- About 9% of adult men and 4% of adult women report engaging in some homosexual activity; 2.8% of men and 1.4% of women consider themselves homosexual.

`pp. 197–99`

Most research supports the claim that sexual orientation is rooted in biology in much the same way as being right-handed or left-handed.

`p. 198`

Sexual orientation is not a matter of neat categories because many people who think of themselves as heterosexual have homosexual experiences; the reverse is also true.

`pp. 198–99`

The gay rights movement helped change public attitudes toward greater acceptance of homosexuality. Still, a majority of U.S. adults say homosexuality is wrong.

`pp. 199–200`

sexual orientation (p. 196) a person's romantic and emotional attraction to another person

heterosexuality (p. 196) sexual attraction to someone of the other sex

homosexuality (p. 196) sexual attraction to someone of the same sex

bisexuality (p. 196) sexual attraction to people of both sexes

asexuality (p. 196) a lack of sexual attraction to people of either sex

homophobia (p. 199) discomfort over close personal interaction with people thought to be gay, lesbian, or bisexual

Sexual Issues and Controversies

TEEN PREGNANCY About 750,000 U.S. teenagers become pregnant each year. The rate of teenage pregnancy has dropped since 1950, when many teens married and had children. Today, most pregnant teens are not married and are at high risk of dropping out of school and being poor.

`p. 200`

PROSTITUTION The selling of sexual services is illegal almost everywhere in the United States. Many people view prostitution as a victimless crime, but it victimizes women and spreads sexually transmitted diseases.

`pp. 201–3`

PORNOGRAPHY The law allows local communities to set standards of decency. Conservatives condemn pornography on moral grounds; liberals view pornography as a power issue, condemning it as demeaning to women.

`pp. 200–201`

SEXUAL VIOLENCE More than 90,000 rapes are reported each year in the United States, but the actual number is probably several times higher. Rapes are violent crimes in which victims and offenders typically know one another.

`pp. 203–4`

pornography (p. 200) sexually explicit material intended to cause sexual arousal

prostitution (p. 201) the selling of sexual services

abortion (p. 209) the deliberate termination of a pregnancy

ABORTION Laws banned abortion in all states by 1900. Opposition to these laws rose during the 1960s, and in 1973, the U.S. Supreme Court declared these laws unconstitutional. Today, some 1.2 million abortions are performed each year. People who describe themselves as "pro-choice" support a woman's right to choose abortion; people who call themselves "pro-life" oppose abortion on moral grounds.

`pp. 208–9`

Theoretical Analysis of Sexuality

The **STRUCTURAL-FUNCTIONAL APPROACH** highlights society's need to regulate sexual activity and especially reproduction. One universal norm is the incest taboo, which keeps family relations clear.

`pp. 205–6`

The **SYMBOLIC-INTERACTION APPROACH** emphasizes the various meanings people attach to sexuality. The social construction of sexuality can be seen in sexual differences between societies and in changing sexual patterns over time.

`pp. 206–7`

The **SOCIAL-CONFLICT APPROACH** links sexuality to social inequality. Feminist theory claims that men dominate women by devaluing them to the level of sexual objects. Queer theory claims our society has a heterosexual bias, defining anything different as "queer."

`pp. 207–9`

queer theory (p. 208) a body of research findings that challenges the heterosexual bias in U.S. society

heterosexism (p. 208) a view that labels anyone who is not heterosexual as "queer"

We are all familiar with the experience of being "different." Deviance—standing out by not conforming to what is normal or expected—results not just from individual choice but also from the operation and norms of society.

CHAPTER 9

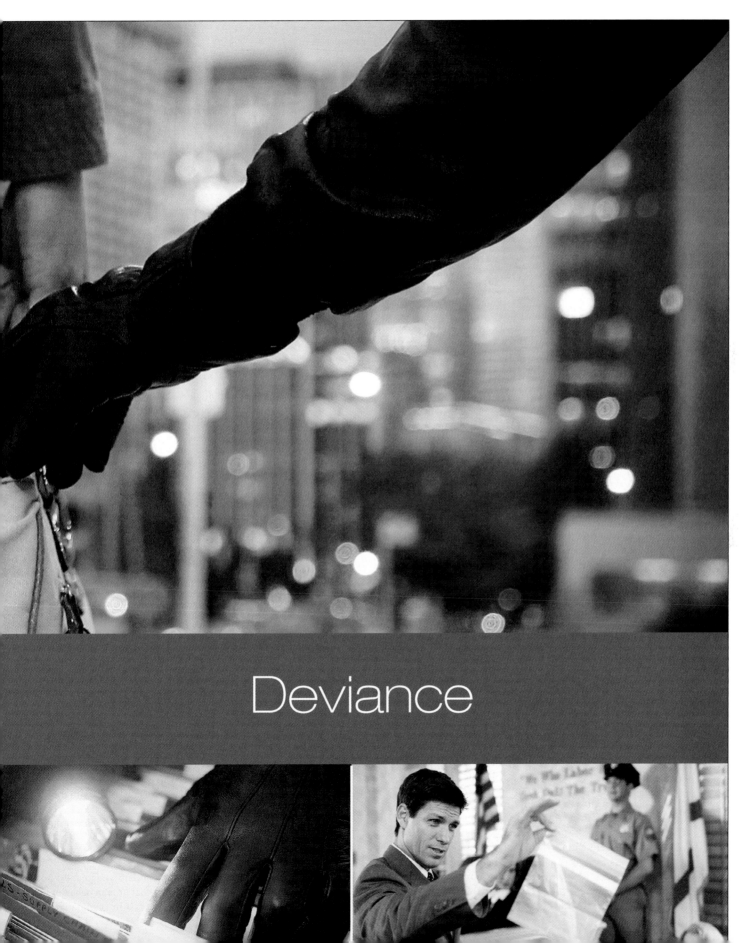

Deviance

RESOURCE: Nathaniel Hawthorne's novel *The Scarlet Letter* is a wonderfully sociological tale of deviance and social control and of the human spirit courageously emerging from a cloak of conformity.

POP CULTURE: Keep the Bruce Glover story (below) in mind as you present various theories of crime.

CHAPTER OVERVIEW } This chapter investigates how society encourages both conformity and deviance and also provides an introduction to crime and the criminal justice system.

"I was like the guy lost in another dimension, a stranger in town, not knowing which way to go." With these words, Bruce Glover recalls the day he returned to his hometown of Detroit, Michigan, after being away for twenty-six years—a long stretch in a state prison. Glover was a young man of thirty when he was arrested for running a call girl ring. Found guilty at trial, he was given a stiff jail sentence.

"My mother passed while I was gone," Glover continues, shaking his head. "I lost everything." On the day he walked out of prison, he realized just how true that statement was. He had nowhere to go and no way to get there. He had no valid identification, which he would need to find a place to live and a job. He had no money to buy the clothes he needed to go out and start looking. He turned to a prison official and asked for help. A state agency finally provided some money and temporary housing to get him started on his journey (C. Jones, 2007).

This chapter explores crime, criminals, and punishment, showing that individuals convicted of wrongdoing do not always fit the common stereotype of the "street criminal." The chapter also tackles the larger question of why societies develop standards of right and wrong in the first place. As you will see, law is simply one part of a complex system of social control: Society teaches us all to conform, at least most of the time, to countless rules. We begin our investigation by defining several basic concepts.

What Is Deviance?

Deviance is *the recognized violation of cultural norms.* Norms guide almost all human activities, so the concept of deviance is quite broad. One category of deviance is **crime**, *the violation of a society's formally enacted criminal law.* Even criminal deviance spans a wide range, from minor traffic violations to prostitution, sexual assault, and murder.

Most familiar examples of nonconformity are negative instances of rule breaking, such as stealing from a campus bookstore, assaulting a fellow student, or driving while intoxicated. But we also define especially righteous people—students who speak up too much in class or people who are overly enthusiastic about new computer technology—as deviant, even if we give them a measure of respect. What deviant actions or attitudes, whether negative or positive, have in common is some element of *difference* that causes us to think of another person as an "outsider" (H. S. Becker, 1966).

Not all deviance involves action or even choice. The very *existence* of some categories of people can be troublesome to others. To the young, elderly people may seem hopelessly "out of it," and to some whites, the mere presence of people of color may cause discomfort. Able-bodied people often view people with disabilities as an out-group, just as rich people may shun the poor for falling short of their standards.

Social Control

All of us are subject to **social control**, *attempts by society to regulate people's thoughts and behavior.* Often this process is informal, as when parents praise or scold their children or when friends make fun of a classmate's choice of music or style of dress. Cases of serious deviance, however, may involve the **criminal justice system**, *the organizations— police, courts, and prison officials—that respond to alleged violations of the law.*

How a society defines deviance, who is branded as deviant, and what people decide to do about deviance all have to do with the way society is organized. Only gradually, however, have people recognized that deviance is much more than a matter of individual choice.

The Biological Context

Chapter 5 ("Socialization") explained that a century ago, most people assumed—incorrectly, as it turns out—that human behavior was the result of biological instincts. Early interest in criminality thus

NOTE: "Glueck" (researchers mentioned below) rhymes with "book."

NOTE: The Gluecks' idea that treating boys as if they were bullies may bring on delinquency nicely illustrates the Thomas theorem: "Situations defined as real become real in their consequences."

NOTE: Psychology's more individualistic orientation is evident in that approach's tendency to speak of personal disorders rather than social deviance.

Q: "There is so much good in the worst of us, and so much bad in the best of us." Anonymous

deviance   the recognized violation of cultural norms

crime   the violation of a society's formally enacted criminal law

social control   attempts by society to regulate people's thoughts and behavior

criminal justice system   the organizations—police, courts, and prison officials—that respond to alleged violations of the law

focused on biological causes. In 1876, Cesare Lombroso (1835–1909), an Italian physician who worked in prisons, theorized that criminals stand out physically, with low foreheads, prominent jaws and cheekbones, hairiness, and unusually long arms. In other words, Lombroso claimed that criminals look like our apelike ancestors.

Had Lombroso looked more carefully, he would have found the physical features he linked to criminality throughout the entire population. We now know that no physical traits distinguish criminals from noncriminals.

In the middle of the twentieth century, William Sheldon took a different approach, suggesting that general body structure might predict criminality (Sheldon, Hartl, & McDermott, 1949). He crosschecked hundreds of young men for body type and criminal history and concluded that criminality was most likely among boys with muscular, athletic builds. Sheldon Glueck and Eleanor Glueck (1950) confirmed Sheldon's conclusion but cautioned that a powerful build does not necessarily *cause* criminality. Parents, they suggested, tend to be somewhat distant from powerfully built sons, who in turn grow up to show less sensitivity toward others. Moreover, in a self-fulfilling prophecy, people who expect muscular boys to be bullies may act in ways that bring about the aggressive behavior they expect.

Today, genetics research seeks possible links between biology and crime. In 2003, scientists at the University of Wisconsin reported results of a twenty-five-year study of crime among 400 boys. The researchers collected DNA samples from each boy and noted any trouble he had had with the law. The researchers concluded that genetic factors (especially defective genes that, say, make too much of an enzyme) together with environmental factors (especially abuse early in life) were strong predictors of adult crime and violence. They noted, too, that these factors together were a better predictor of crime than either one alone (Lemonick, 2003; Pinker, 2003).

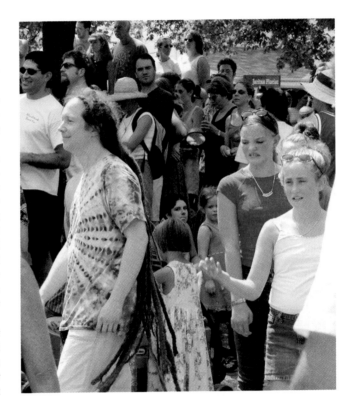

Deviance is always a matter of difference. Deviance emerges in everyday life as we encounter people whose appearance or behavior differs from what we consider "normal." Who is the "deviant" in this photograph? From whose point of view?

CRITICAL REVIEW   Biological theories offer a limited explanation of crime. The best guess at present is that biological traits in combination with environmental factors explain some serious crime. But the biggest problem with this approach is that most of the actions we define as deviant are carried out by people who are biologically quite normal.

In addition, because a biological approach looks at the individual, it offers no insight into how some kinds of behaviors come to be defined as deviant in the first place. Therefore, although there is much to be learned about how human biology may affect behavior, research currently puts far greater emphasis on social influences.

CHECK YOUR LEARNING   What does biological research add to our understanding of crime? What are the limitations of this approach?

Personality Factors

Like biological theories, psychological explanations of deviance focus on abnormality in the individual personality. Some personality traits are inherited, but most psychologists think that personality is shaped primarily by social experience. Deviance, then, is viewed as the result of "unsuccessful" socialization.

Classic research by Walter Reckless and Simon Dinitz (1967) illustrates the psychological approach. Reckless and Dinitz began by asking a number of teachers to categorize twelve-year-old male students as either likely or unlikely to get into trouble with the law. They then interviewed both the boys and their mothers to assess each boy's self-concept and how he related to others. Analyzing their results, Reckless and Dinitz found that the "good boys" displayed a strong conscience (what Freud called superego), could handle frustration, and identified with cultural norms and values. The "bad boys," by

DISCUSS: To illustrate changing conceptions of campus deviance, ask students about the declining rate of traditionally moral offenses concerned with decorum and honesty and the rising rate of offenses concerned with sexual or racial harassment or other "insensitivity."

Q: "The inescapable conclusion is that society secretly wants crime and needs crime." Karl Menninger, *The Crime of Punishment*

DISCUSS: To Polynesians, tattoos are symbols of high social standing. How are tattoos regarded in our society?

DISCUSS: Critics objected to rock-and-roll in the 1950s (Elvis Presley, Little Richard), claiming that it undermined morality. Today, rock-and-roll is mainstream music. Given the increasingly outrageous character of rockers, ask the class whether they find any deviance in it.

─● MAKING THE GRADE

Deviance, the violation of norms, is a broad concept. Crime, the violation of formally enacted law, is one type of deviance.

contrast, had a weaker conscience, displayed little tolerance of frustration, and felt out of step with conventional culture.

As we might expect, the "good boys" went on to have fewer run-ins with the police than the "bad boys." Because all the boys lived in an area where delinquency was widespread, the investigators attributed staying out of trouble to a personality that controlled deviant impulses. Based on this conclusion, Reckless and Dinitz called their analysis *containment theory*.

─○ **CRITICAL REVIEW** Psychologists have shown that personality patterns have some connection to deviance. Some serious criminals are psychopaths who do not feel guilt or shame, have no fear of punishment, and have little or no sympathy for the people they harm (Herpertz & Sass, 2000). However, as noted in the case of the biological approach, most serious crimes are committed by people whose psychological profiles are normal.

Both the biological and psychological approaches view deviance as a trait of individuals. The reason that these approaches have had limited value in explaining deviance is that wrongdoing has more to do with the organization of society. We now turn to a sociological approach, which explores where ideas of right and wrong come from, why people define some rule breakers but not others as deviant, and what role power plays in this process.

─○ **CHECK YOUR LEARNING** Why do biological and psychological analyses not explain deviance very well?

The Social Foundations of Deviance

Although we tend to view deviance as the free choice or personal failings of individuals, all behavior—deviance as well as conformity—is shaped by society. Three social foundations of deviance identified here will be detailed later in this chapter:

1. **Deviance varies according to cultural norms**. No thought or action is inherently deviant; it becomes deviant only in relation to particular norms. Because norms vary from place to place, deviance also varies. State law permits prostitution in rural areas of Nevada, although the practice is outlawed in the rest of the United States. Twelve states have gambling casinos, twenty-nine permit casinos but only on Indian reservations, and four other states have casinos at race tracks. In all other states, casino gambling is illegal. Text messaging while driving is legal in forty-one states but against the law in six others (three other states forbid the practice for young drivers). Until the end of 2008, when a court struck down the law, only Florida legally banned gay men and lesbians from adopting a child (Csere, 2008; National Conference of State Legislatures, 2008c; Ruggeri, 2008; American Gaming Association, 2009).

   Further, most cities and towns have at least one unique law. For example, Mobile, Alabama, outlaws the wearing of stiletto-heeled shoes; Pine Lawn, Missouri, bans saggy, "low-rider" pants; in Juneau, Alaska, it is illegal to bring a flamingo into a barbershop; South Padre Island, Texas, bans the wearing of neckties; Mount Prospect, Illinois, has a law against keeping pigeons or bees; Topeka, Kansas, bans snowball fights; Hoover, South Dakota, does not allow fishing by the light of a kerosene lantern; and Beverly Hills, California, regulates the number of tennis balls allowed on the court at one time (R. Steele, 2000; Wittenauer, 2007).

   Around the world, deviance is even more diverse. Albania outlaws any public display of religious faith, such as crossing oneself; Cuba bans citizens from owning personal computers; Vietnam can prosecute citizens for meeting with foreigners; Malaysia does not allow women to wear tight-fitting jeans; Saudi Arabia bans the sale of red flowers on Valentine's Day; and Iran bans wearing makeup by women and forbids anyone from playing rap music (Chopra, 2008).

2. **People become deviant as others define them that way**. Everyone violates cultural norms at one time or another. Have you ever walked around talking to yourself or "borrowed" a pen from your workplace? Whether such behavior defines us as mentally ill or criminal depends on how others perceive, define, and respond to it.

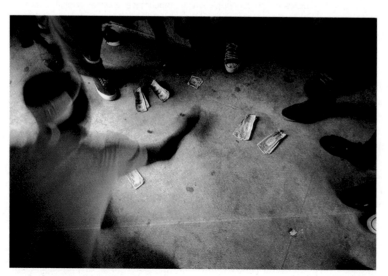

Why is it that street-corner gambling like this is usually against the law but playing the same games in a fancy casino is not?

RESOURCE: A classic selection from Durkheim on crime is included in the companion reader *Seeing Ourselves*, 8th ed.

DISCUSS: Andres Serrano, who created "Piss Christ," a photograph of a crucifix submerged in Serrano's own urine, maintains that art reaches its greatest power when it is most provocative. Is such work art or obscenity?

DISCUSS: Erikson found that 3% to 4% of the Puritans were defined as deviant at any time. What would Durkheim say about the fact that in the U.S. today, about 3% of adults are in prison, on parole, or on probation?

Q: "I don't say we all ought to misbehave; but we ought to look as if we could." Orson Welles

SEEING SOCIOLOGY
in Everyday Life

Keeping in mind Durkheim's claim that society creates deviance to mark moral boundaries, why do we often define people only in terms of their deviance by calling someone an "addict" or a "thief"?

MAKING THE GRADE

Notice that Durkheim considered deviance to be a natural and necessary part of all social organization.

3. **How societies set norms and how they define rule-breaking both involve social power**. The law, declared Karl Marx, is the means by which powerful people protect their interests. A homeless person who stands on a street corner speaking out against the government risks arrest for disturbing the peace; a mayoral candidate during an election campaign who does exactly the same thing gets police protection. In short, norms and how we apply them reflect social inequality.

The Functions of Deviance: Structural-Functional Analysis

The key insight of the structural-functional approach is that deviance is a necessary part of social organization. This point was made a century ago by Emile Durkheim.

Durkheim's Basic Insight

In his pioneering study of deviance, Emile Durkheim (1964a, orig. 1893; 1964b, orig. 1895) made the surprising claim that there is nothing abnormal about deviance. In fact, it performs four essential functions:

1. **Deviance affirms cultural values and norms**. As moral creatures, people must prefer some attitudes and behaviors to others. But any definition of virtue rests on an opposing idea of vice: There can be no good without evil and no justice without crime. Deviance is needed to define and support morality.

2. **Responding to deviance clarifies moral boundaries**. By defining some individuals as deviant, people draw a boundary between right and wrong. For example, a college marks the line between academic honesty and cheating by punishing students who cheat on exams.

3. **Responding to deviance brings people together**. People typically react to serious deviance with shared outrage. In doing so, Durkheim explained, they reaffirm the moral ties that bind them. For example, after the September 11, 2001, terrorist attacks, people across the United States were joined by a common desire to protect the country and bring those responsible to justice.

4. **Deviance encourages social change**. Deviant people push a society's moral boundaries, suggesting alternatives to the status quo and encouraging change. Today's deviance, declared

Durkheim claimed that deviance is a necessary element of social organization, serving several important functions. After a man convicted of killing a child settled in their New Hampshire town, residents came together to affirm their community ties as well as their understanding of right and wrong. Has any event on your campus caused a similar reaction?

Durkheim, can become tomorrow's morality (1964b:71, orig. 1895). For example, rock-and-roll, condemned as immoral in the 1950s, became a multibillion-dollar industry just a few years later; in recent years, hip-hop music has followed the same path.

An Illustration: The Puritans of Massachusetts Bay

Kai Erikson's classic study of the Puritans of Massachusetts Bay brings Durkheim's theory to life. Erikson (2005b, orig. 1966) shows that even the Puritans, a disciplined and highly religious group, created deviance to clarify their moral boundaries. In fact, Durkheim might well have had the Puritans in mind when he wrote this:

> Imagine a society of saints, a perfect cloister of exemplary individuals. Crimes, properly so called, will there be unknown; but faults which appear [insignificant] to the layman will create there the same scandal that the ordinary offense does in ordinary consciousness. . . . For the same reason, the perfect and upright man judges his smallest failings with a severity that the majority reserve for acts more truly in the nature of an offense. (1964b:68–69, orig. 1895)

Deviance is thus not a matter of a few "bad apples" but a necessary condition of "good" social living.

Deviance may be found in every society, but the *kind* of deviance people generate depends on the moral issues they seek to clarify. The Puritans, for example, experienced a number of "crime waves,"

Q: "Conscience is that inner voice that warns us that someone may be watching." H. L. Mencken

Q: "It is the conflict between culturally accepted values and the socially structured difficulties of living up to these values which exerts pressure toward deviant behavior and disruption of the normative system." Robert K. Merton (1968:245)

Q: "Puritanism is the lurking fear that someone, somewhere, may be happy." H. L. Mencken

NOTE: Thomas Szasz (1995) suggests that economically speaking, people fall into one of three categories: producers (Merton's "conformists"), predators ("innovators"), or parasites ("retreatists").

MAKING THE GRADE

Merton's strain theory shows how people's opportunities (or lack of opportunities) to achieve cultural goals can encourage both deviance and conformity. In addition, what sociologists call people's "structure of opportunities" helps explain the type of deviance they engage in.

FIGURE 9–1   Merton's Strain Theory of Deviance

Combining a person's view of cultural goals and the conventional means to obtain them allowed Robert Merton to identify various types of deviance.

Source: Merton (1968).

everyone who wants conventional success has the opportunity to attain it. For example, people raised in poverty may have little hope of becoming successful if they play by the rules. According to Merton, the strain between our culture's emphasis on wealth and the lack of opportunities to get rich may encourage some people, especially the poor, to engage in stealing, drug dealing, or other forms of street crime. Merton called this type of deviance *innovation*—using unconventional means (street crime) rather than conventional means (hard work at a "straight" job) to achieve a culturally approved goal (wealth).

The inability to reach a cultural goal may also prompt another type of deviance that Merton calls *ritualism*. For example, many people may not care much about becoming rich but rigidly stick to the rules (the conventional means) anyway in order to at least feel "respectable."

A third response to the inability to succeed is *retreatism*: rejecting both cultural goals and conventional means so that a person in effect "drops out." Some alcoholics, drug addicts, and street people can be described as retreatists. The deviance of retreatists lies in their unconventional lifestyle and also in what seems to be their willingness to live this way.

The fourth response to failure is *rebellion*. Like retreatists, rebels such as radical "survivalists" reject both the cultural definition of success and the conventional means of achieving it, but they go one step further by forming a counterculture supporting alternatives to the existing social order.

Deviant Subcultures

Richard Cloward and Lloyd Ohlin (1966) extended Merton's theory, proposing that crime results not simply from limited legitimate (legal) opportunity but also from readily accessible illegitimate (illegal) opportunity. In short, deviance or conformity arises from the *relative opportunity structure* that frames a person's life.

The life of Al Capone, a notorious gangster, illustrates Cloward and Ohlin's theory. As the son of poor immigrants, Capone faced barriers of poverty and ethnic prejudice, which lowered his odds of achieving success in conventional terms. Yet as a young man during Prohibition (when alcoholic beverages were banned in the United States between 1920 and 1933), Capone found in his neighborhood people who could teach him how to sell alcohol illegally—a source of illegitimate opportunity. Where the structure of opportunity favors criminal activity, Cloward and Ohlin predict the development of *criminal subcultures,* such as Capone's criminal organization or today's inner-city street gangs.

But what happens when people are unable to find *any* opportunity, legal or illegal? Then deviance may take one of two forms. One is *conflict subcultures,* such as armed street gangs that engage in violence out of frustration and a desire for respect. Another possible

including the well-known outbreak of witchcraft in 1692. With each response, the Puritans answered questions about the range of proper beliefs by celebrating some of their members and condemning others as deviant.

Erikson discovered that even though the offenses changed, the proportion of people the Puritans defined as deviant remained steady over time. This stability, he concluded, confirms Durkheim's claim that society creates deviants to mark its changing moral boundaries. In other words, by constantly defining a small number of people as deviant, the Puritans maintained the moral shape of their society.

Merton's Strain Theory

Some deviance may be necessary for a society to function, but Robert Merton (1938, 1968) argued that society can be set up in a way that encourages too much deviance. In addition, he explained, the type of deviance people engage in depends on whether a society provides them the *means* (such as schooling and job opportunities) to achieve cultural *goals* (such as financial success). Merton's strain theory is illustrated in Figure 9–1.

Conformity lies in pursuing cultural goals through approved means. Thus the U.S. "success story" is someone who gains wealth and prestige through talent, schooling, and hard work. But not

NOTE: A new functional issue is the pattern of "defining deviance upward," the pattern of refocusing a prosecution from a "lesser" issue to a more important one. The "Scooter" Libby case was about lying to a grand jury, but it was "defined up" as an issue of whether the Bush administration broke the law.

NOTE: Although Al Capone had little chance to attend Yale or Harvard, he got his first job working for a gangster who called himself Frankie Yale and who ran a nightclub called the Harvard Inn.

NOTE: Success through illegitimate means explains Capone's preoccupation with being respected and the desire, eventually, to "go legit." He often demanded that others address him as "Anthony Brown" and was delighted to enroll his son at Yale.

outcome is the development of *retreatist subcultures,* in which deviants drop out and abuse alcohol or other drugs.

Albert Cohen (1971, orig. 1955) suggests that delinquency is most common among lower-class youths because they have the least opportunity to achieve conventional success. Neglected by society, they seek self-respect by creating a delinquent subculture that defines as worthy the traits these youths do have. Being feared on the street may not win many points with society as a whole, but it may satisfy a young person's desire to "be somebody" in the local neighborhood.

Walter Miller (1970, orig. 1958) adds that delinquent subcultures are characterized by (1) *trouble,* arising from frequent conflict with teachers and police; (2) *toughness,* the value placed on physical size and strength, especially among males; (3) *smartness,* the ability to succeed on the streets, to outsmart or "con" others, and to avoid being similarly taken advantage of; (4) a *need for excitement,* the search for thrills, risk, or danger; (5) a *belief in fate,* a sense that people lack control over their own lives; and (6) a *desire for freedom,* often expressed as anger toward authority figures.

Finally, Elijah Anderson (1994, 2002; Kubrin, 2005) explains that in poor urban neighborhoods, most people manage to conform to conventional or "decent" values. Yet faced with neighborhood crime and violence, indifference or even hostility from police, and sometimes neglect by their own parents, some young men decide to live by the "street code." To show that they can survive on the street, a young man displays "nerve," a willingness to stand up to any threat. Following this street code, which is also evident in much recent rap music, the young man believes that a violent death is better than being "dissed" (disrespected) by others. Some manage to escape the dangers, but the risk of ending up in jail—or worse—is very high for these young men, who have been pushed to the margins of our society.

Young people cut off from legitimate opportunity often form subcultures that many people view as deviant. Gang subcultures are one way young people gain the sense of belonging and respect denied to them by the larger culture.

○ **CRITICAL REVIEW** Durkheim made an important contribution by pointing out the functions of deviance. However, there is evidence that a community does not always come together in reaction to crime; sometimes fear of crime causes people to withdraw from public life (Liska & Warner, 1991; Warr & Ellison, 2000).

Merton's strain theory has been criticized for explaining some kinds of deviance (stealing, for example) better than others (such as crimes of passion or mental illness). In addition, not everyone seeks success in the conventional terms of wealth, as strain theory suggests.

The general argument of Cloward and Ohlin, Cohen, Miller, and Anderson—that deviance reflects the opportunity structure of society—has been confirmed by subsequent research (Allan

& Steffensmeier, 1989; Uggen, 1999). However, these theories fall short by assuming that everyone shares the same cultural standards for judging right and wrong. In addition, if we define crime to include not only burglary and auto theft but also fraud and other crimes carried out by corporate executives and Wall Street tycoons, then more high-income people will be counted among criminals. There is evidence that people of all social backgrounds are becoming more casual about breaking the rules, as the Seeing Sociology in Everyday Life box on page 222 explains.

Finally, all structural-functional theories suggest that everyone who breaks important rules will be labeled deviant. However, becoming deviant is actually a highly complex process, as the next section explains.

○ **CHECK YOUR LEARNING** Why do you think many of the theories just discussed seem to say that crime is more common among people with lower social standing?

Labeling Deviance: Symbolic-Interaction Analysis

The symbolic-interaction approach explains how people define deviance in everyday situations. From this point of view, definitions of deviance and conformity are surprisingly flexible.

EXERCISE: Students might investigate the rise in cheating on campus, which seems to be linked to use of materials from the Internet. Computer technology is also making it easier to catch cheaters.

Q: "If you steal from one author, it's plagiarism; if you steal from many, it's research." Wilson Mizner

Q: "In this life one frequently finds greater rewards for vice than for virtue." René Descartes (1641)

GLOBAL: The labeling approach casts doubt on the old saying "Sticks and stones can break my bones, but names can never hurt me." Members of our society recognize the power of labels in libel law; some other societies (Islamic nations, for instance) treat labels even more seriously than we do, as suggested by the Salman Rushdie case.

SEEING SOCIOLOGY
in Everyday Life

An old saying goes, "Sticks and stones can break my bones, but names can never hurt me." What might labeling theory have to say about this idea?

MAKING THE GRADE

The development of secondary deviance is one application of the Thomas theorem (see Chapter 6, "Social Interaction in Everyday Life"), which states that situations people define as real become real in their consequences.

SEEING SOCIOLOGY IN EVERYDAY LIFE

Deviant Subculture: Has It Become OK to Break the Rules?

ASTRID: Simon! You're downloading that music illegally. You'll get us both into trouble!

SIMON: Look, everyone cheats. Rich CEOs cheat in business. Ordinary people cheat on their taxes. Politicians lie. What else is new?

ASTRID: So it's OK to steal? Is that what you really believe?

SIMON: I'm not saying it's OK. I'm just saying everyone does it. . . .

It's been a bad couple of years for the idea of playing by the rules. First, we learn that the executives of not just one but many U.S. corporations are guilty of fraud and outright stealing on a scale most of us cannot even imagine. More recently, we realize that the Wall Street leaders running the U.S. economy not only did a pretty bad job of it but paid themselves tens of millions of dollars for doing so. And of course, even the Catholic church, which we hold up as a model of moral behavior, is still trying to recover from the charges that hundreds of priests have sexually abused parishioners (most of them teens and children) for decades while church officials covered up the crimes.

There are plenty of ideas about what is causing this widespread wrongdoing. Some people suggest that the pressure to win—by whatever means necessary—in today's highly competitive world of business and politics can be overwhelming. As one analyst put it, "You can get away with your embezzlements and your lies, but you can never get away with *failing*."

Such thinking helps explain the wrongdoing among many CEOs in the world of business and finance and the conviction of several members of Congress for ethics violations, but it offers little insight into the problem of abusive priests. In some ways at least, wrongdoing seems to have become a way of life for just about everybody.

Do you consider cheating in school wrong? Would you turn in someone you saw cheating? Why or why not?

For example, the Internal Revenue Service reports that many U.S. taxpayers cheat on their taxes, failing to pay an estimated $345 billion each year. The music industry claims that it has lost billions of dollars to illegal piracy of recordings, a practice especially common among young people. Perhaps most disturbing of all, in surveys about half of high school and college students say that they have cheated on a test at least once during the past year (Gallup, 2004).

Emile Durkheim viewed society as a moral system built on a set of rules about what people should and should not do. Years earlier, another French thinker named Blaise Pascal made the contrasting claim that "cheating is the foundation of society." Today, which of the two statements is closer to the truth?

WHAT DO YOU THINK?

1. In your opinion, how widespread is wrongdoing in U.S. society today? Have you downloaded music illegally? What about cheating on your college assignments or tests?

2. Do you think people who break the rules usually think that their actions are wrong? Why or why not?

3. What do you think are the reasons for the apparent increase in dishonesty?

Sources: "Our Cheating Hearts" (2002), Bono (2006), and Lohr (2008).

Labeling Theory

The main contribution of symbolic-interaction analysis is **labeling theory**, *the idea that deviance and conformity result not so much from what people do as from how others respond to those actions.* Labeling theory stresses the relativity of deviance, meaning that people may define the same behavior in any number of ways.

Consider these situations: A college student takes a sweater off the back of a roommate's chair and packs it for a weekend trip, a married woman at a convention in a distant city has sex with an old boyfriend, and a city mayor gives a big contract to a major campaign contributor. We might define the first situation as carelessness, borrowing, or theft. The consequences of the second case depend largely on whether the woman's behavior becomes known back home. In the third situation, is the official choosing the best contractor or paying off a political debt? The social construction of reality is a highly variable process of detection, definition, and response.

Primary and Secondary Deviance

Edwin Lemert (1951, 1972) observed that some norm violations—say, skipping school or underage drinking—provoke slight reaction from

RESOURCE: How important is audience reaction to an episode of deviance in fostering a deviant career? The foundation of the labeling perspective was laid by Frank Tannenbaum in *Crime and the Community* (1938).

NOTE: The term "stigma" is derived from a Greek root meaning "tattoo."

Q: "I can resist everything except temptation." Oscar Wilde

NOTE: In the late 1950s, Thomas Szasz prepared a short article on the myth of mental illness and submitted it to every major U.S. psychiatric journal; every one rejected it. The article finally appeared in *American Psychologist* in 1960.

DISCUSS: As part of the discussion of the medicalization of deviance, do students think being overweight is a personal weakness or an illness?

labeling theory the idea that deviance and conformity result not so much from what people do as from how others respond to those actions

stigma a powerfully negative label that greatly changes a person's self-concept and social identity

medicalization of deviance the transformation of moral and legal deviance into a medical condition

SEEING SOCIOLOGY
in Everyday Life

Explain in your own words sociologist Howard Becker's (1966) statement that deviance is nothing more than behavior that people define as deviant.

others and have little effect on a person's self-concept. Lemert calls such passing episodes *primary deviance.*

But what happens if people take notice of someone's deviance and really make something of it? After an audience has defined some action as primary deviance, the individual may begin to change, taking on a deviant identity by talking, acting, or dressing in a different way, rejecting the people who are critical, and repeatedly breaking the rules. Lemert (1951:77) calls this change of self-concept *secondary deviance.* He explains that "when a person begins to employ . . . deviant behavior as a means of defense, attack, or adjustment to the . . . problems created by societal reaction," deviance becomes secondary. For example, say that people have begun describing a young man as an "alcohol abuser," which establishes primary deviance. These people may then exclude him from their friendship network. His response may be to become bitter toward them, start drinking even more, and seek the company of others who approve of his drinking. These actions mark the beginning of secondary deviance, a deeper deviant identity.

Stigma

Secondary deviance marks the start of what Erving Goffman (1963) calls a *deviant career.* As people develop a stronger commitment to deviant behavior, they typically acquire a **stigma**, *a powerfully negative label that greatly changes a person's self-concept and social identity.*

A stigma operates as a master status (see Chapter 6, "Social Interaction in Everyday Life"), overpowering other aspects of social identity so that a person is discredited in the minds of others and becomes socially isolated. Often a person gains a stigma informally as others begin to see the individual in deviant terms. Sometimes, however, an entire community formally stigmatizes an individual through what Harold Garfinkel (1956) calls a *degradation ceremony.* A criminal trial is one example, operating much like a high school graduation ceremony in reverse: A person stands before the community and is labeled in negative rather than positive terms.

Retrospective and Projective Labeling

Once people stigmatize an individual, they may engage in *retrospective labeling,* interpreting someone's past in light of some present deviance (Scheff, 1984). For example, after discovering that a priest has sexually molested a child, others rethink his past, perhaps musing, "He always did want to be around young children." Retrospective labeling, which distorts a person's biography by being highly selective, typically deepens a deviant identity.

Similarly, people may engage in *projective labeling* of a stigmatized person, using the person's deviant identity to predict future actions. Regarding the priest, people might say, "He's going to keep at it until he gets caught." The more people in someone's social world think such things, the more these definitions affect the individual's self-concept, increasing the chance that they will come true.

Labeling Difference as Deviance

Is a homeless man who refuses to allow police to take him to a city shelter on a cold night simply trying to live independently, or is he "crazy"? People have a tendency to treat behavior that irritates or threatens them not simply as different but as deviance or even mental illness.

The psychiatrist Thomas Szasz (1961, 1970, 2003, 2004) charges that people are too quick to apply the label of mental illness to conditions that simply amount to a difference we don't like. The only way to avoid this troubling practice, Szasz continues, is to abandon the idea of mental illness entirely. The world is full of people who think or act differently in ways that may irritate us, but such differences are not grounds for defining someone as mentally ill. Such labeling, Szasz claims, simply enforces conformity to the standards of people powerful enough to impose their will on others.

Most mental health care professionals reject the idea that mental illness does not exist. But they agree that it is important to think critically about how we define "difference." First, people who are mentally ill are no more to blame for their condition than people who suffer from cancer or some other physical problem. Therefore, having a mental or physical illness is not grounds for being labeled deviant. Second, ordinary people without the medical knowledge to diagnose mental illness should avoid using such labels just to make people conform to their own standards of behavior.

The Medicalization of Deviance

Labeling theory, particularly the ideas of Szasz and Goffman, helps explain an important shift in the way our society understands deviance. Over the past fifty or sixty years, the growing influence of psychiatry and medicine in the United States has led to the **medicalization of deviance**, *the transformation of moral and legal deviance into a medical condition.*

Medicalization amounts to swapping one set of labels for another. In moral terms, we evaluate people or their behavior as "bad" or "good." However, the scientific objectivity of medicine passes no moral judgment, instead using clinical diagnoses such as "sick" or "well."

To illustrate, until the mid-twentieth century, people generally viewed alcoholics as morally weak people easily tempted by the pleasure of drink. Gradually, however, medical specialists redefined alcoholism so that most people now consider it a disease, rendering people "sick" rather than "bad." In the same way, obesity, drug addiction, child abuse, sexual promiscuity, and other behaviors that used to be strictly moral matters are widely defined today as illnesses for which people need help rather than punishment.

The Difference Labels Make

Whether we define deviance as a moral or a medical issue has three consequences. First, it affects *who responds* to deviance. An offense

Q: "An alcoholic is someone you don't like who drinks as much as you do." Dylan Thomas

NOTE: Schools and colleges have expanded their counseling staffs in recent decades. As a result, what people used to describe as student shortcomings now are cast in terms of various disorders. The number of U.S. schoolchildren with "learning disabilities" has more than tripled, from 800,000 in 1970 to 2.7 million in 2007.

NOTE: Illustrate changing labels with the American Psychiatric Association's view of homosexuality. The *Diagnostic and Statistical Manual of Mental Disorders* (DSM) first listed homosexuality as a "personality disorder" in 1952; later, it was a "sexual orientation disorder"; next, unhappy gays were diagnosed with "ego dystonic homosexuality"; in 1987, homosexuality was dropped from the DSM; in 2009 the APA stated that therapy could not change anyone's sexual orientation.

● MAKING THE GRADE

Deviance can be defined as either a moral or a medical issue. Be sure you understand the three key differences between defining deviance one way or the other.

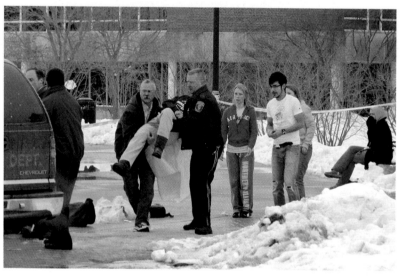

The nation was stunned by the 2008 rampage on the Northern Illinois University campus that left six people dead and eighteen injured. It is easy to imagine that a person who commits such a crime might be "crazy" or "sick." Or might you view the offender as "evil" or just very misguided?

against common morality usually brings about a reaction from members of the community or the police. A medical label, however, places the situation under the control of clinical specialists, including counselors, psychiatrists, and physicians.

A second issue is *how people respond* to deviance. A moral approach defines deviants as offenders subject to punishment. Medically, however, they are patients who need treatment. Punishment is designed to fit the crime, but treatment programs are tailored to the patient and may involve virtually any therapy that a specialist thinks might prevent future deviance.

Third, and most important, the two labels differ on the *personal competence of the deviant person*. From a moral standpoint, whether we are right or wrong, at least we take responsibility for our own behavior. Once we are defined as sick, however, we are seen as unable to control (or if "mentally ill," even to understand) our actions. People who are labeled incompetent are in turn subjected to treatment, often against their will. For this reason alone, attempts to define deviance in medical terms should be made with extreme caution.

Sutherland's Differential Association Theory

Learning any behavioral pattern, whether conventional or deviant, is a process that takes place in groups. According to Edwin Sutherland (1940), a person's tendency toward conformity or deviance depends on the amount of contact with others who encourage or reject conventional behavior. This is Sutherland's theory of *differential association.*

A number of research studies confirm the idea that young people are more likely to engage in delinquency if they believe members of their peer groups encourage such activity (Akers et al., 1979; Miller & Mathews, 2001). One investigation focused on sexual activity among eighth-grade students. Two strong predictors of such behavior for young girls was having a boyfriend who encouraged sexual relations and having girlfriends they believed would approve of such activity. Similarly, boys were encouraged to become sexually active by friends who rewarded them with high status in their peer group (Little & Rankin, 2001).

Hirschi's Control Theory

The sociologist Travis Hirschi (1969; Gottfredson & Hirschi, 1995) developed *control theory,* which states that social control depends on people anticipating the consequences of their behavior. Hirschi assumes that everyone finds at least some deviance tempting. But the thought of a ruined career keeps most people from breaking the rules; for some, just imagining the reactions of family and friends is enough. On the other hand, individuals who feel they have little to lose by deviance are likely to become rule breakers.

Specifically, Hirschi links conformity to four different types of social control:

1. **Attachment**. Strong social attachments encourage conformity. Weak family, peer, and school relationships leave people freer to engage in deviance.

2. **Opportunity**. The greater a person's access to legitimate opportunity, the greater the advantages of conformity. By contrast, someone with little confidence in future success is more likely to drift toward deviance.

3. **Involvement**. Extensive involvement in legitimate activities—such as holding a job, going to school, or playing sports—inhibits deviance (Langbein & Bess, 2002). By contrast, people who simply "hang out" waiting for something to happen have time and energy to engage in deviant activity.

4. **Belief**. Strong belief in conventional morality and respect for authority figures restrain tendencies toward deviance. People who have a weak conscience (and who are left unsupervised) are more open to temptation (Stack, Wasserman, & Kern, 2004).

DISCUSS: People must sometimes contend with deviant labels when they have done nothing at all. What about victims of violent rape—subjected to labeling as deviants based on the misguided assumption that they "led him on"? Or individuals with AIDS, shunned by employers, friends, and even family members?

Q: "Research amply demonstrates that offenders are relatively unable to sustain a course of action directed at some distant goal, whether that goal be education,

friendship, employment, or criminal gain. In fact the defining characteristic of offenders appears to be low self-control." Travis Hirschi

NOTE: Another probable correlate of criminality is intelligence. Gottfredson and Hirschi (1995) state that "research consistently shows that offenders are disadvantaged with regard to intellectual or cognitive skills."

SEEING SOCIOLOGY
in Everyday Life

Why do you think that politicians and other well-known people who get into trouble with the law often claim they have a problem with alcohol or other drugs and check into "rehab"?

Hirschi's analysis combines a number of earlier ideas about the causes of deviant behavior. Note that a person's relative social privilege as well as family and community environment are likely to affect the risk of deviant behavior (Hope, Grasmick, & Pointon, 2003).

○ **CRITICAL REVIEW** The various symbolic-interaction theories all see deviance as a process. Labeling theory links deviance not to action but to the *reaction* of others. Thus some people are defined as deviant but others who think or behave in the same way are not. The concepts of secondary deviance, deviant career, and stigma show how being labeled deviant can become a lasting self-concept.

Yet labeling theory has several limitations. First, because it takes a highly relative view of deviance, labeling theory ignores the fact that some kinds of behavior—such as murder—are condemned just about everywhere. Therefore, labeling theory is most usefully applied to less serious issues, such as sexual promiscuity or mental illness. Second, research on the consequences of deviant labeling does not clearly show whether deviant labeling produces further deviance or discourages it (Smith & Gartin, 1989; Sherman & Smith, 1992). Third, not everyone resists being labeled deviant; some people actively seek it out (Vold & Bernard, 1986). For example, people take part in civil disobedience and willingly subject themselves to arrest in order to call attention to social injustice.

Sociologists consider Sutherland's differential association theory and Hirschi's control theory important contributions to our understanding of deviance. But why do society's norms and laws define certain kinds of activities as deviant in the first place? This question is addressed by social-conflict analysis, the focus of the next section.

○ **CHECK YOUR LEARNING** Clearly define primary deviance, secondary deviance, deviant career, and stigma.

Deviance and Inequality: Social-Conflict Analysis

The social-conflict approach links deviance to social inequality. That is, who or what is labeled deviant depends on which categories of people hold power in a society.

Deviance and Power

Alexander Liazos (1972) points out that the people we tend to define as deviants—the ones we dismiss as "nuts" and "sluts"—are typically not as bad or harmful as they are *powerless*. Bag ladies and unemployed men on street corners, not corporate polluters or international arms dealers, carry the stigma of deviance.

All social groups teach their members skills and attitudes that encourage certain behavior. In recent years, discussion on college campuses has focused on the dangers of binge drinking, which results in several dozen deaths each year among young people in the United States. How much of a problem is binge drinking on your campus?

Social-conflict theory explains this pattern in three ways. First, all norms—especially the laws of any society—generally reflect the interests of the rich and powerful. People who threaten the wealthy are likely to be labeled deviant, either for taking people's property ("common thieves") or for advocating a more egalitarian society ("political radicals"). As noted in Chapter 4 ("Society"), Karl Marx argued that the law and all other social institutions support the interests of the rich. Or as Richard Quinney puts it, "Capitalist justice is by the capitalist class, for the capitalist class, and against the working class" (1977:3).

Second, even if their behavior is called into question, the powerful have the resources to resist deviant labels. The majority of the executives involved in recent corporate scandals have yet to be arrested; only a few have gone to jail.

Third, the widespread belief that norms and laws are natural and good masks their political character. For this reason, although we

NOTE: Power affects how labels are applied. An audience may discredit a privileged person for acting foolishly; observing a less privileged person (say, a woman or person of color) acting foolishly, they are more likely to discredit the individual's entire category.

Q: "To be good is noble. To tell people how to be good is even nobler, and much less trouble." Mark Twain

Q: "Public opinion in regard to picking pockets would not be well organized if most of the information regarding this crime came to the public directly from the pickpockets themselves." Edwin H. Sutherland

Q: "It is no longer unthinkable for white-collar criminals to go to prison." Pronouncement by the judge sentencing 1980s' illegal stock trader Ivan Boesky to 3 years in jail

● SEEING SOCIOLOGY
in Everyday Life

How would a Marxist analysis explain the fact that hundreds of miners have died in coal mines in West Virginia and other states in recent decades without anyone being charged with any crime?

white-collar crime crime committed by people of high social position in the course of their occupations

corporate crime the illegal actions of a corporation or people acting on its behalf

organized crime a business supplying illegal goods or services

---

may condemn the unequal application of the law, we give little thought to whether the laws themselves are really fair or not.

Deviance and Capitalism

In the Marxist tradition, Steven Spitzer (1980) argues that deviant labels are applied to people who interfere with the operation of capitalism. First, because capitalism is based on private control of wealth, people who threaten the property of others—especially the poor who steal from the rich—are prime candidates for being labeled deviant. On the other hand, the rich who take advantage of the poor are less likely to be labeled deviant. For example, landlords who charge poor tenants high rents and evict anyone who cannot pay are not considered criminals; they are simply "doing business."

Second, because capitalism depends on productive labor, people who cannot or will not work risk being labeled deviant. Many members of our society think people who are out of work, even through no fault of their own, are somehow deviant.

Third, capitalism depends on respect for authority figures, causing people who resist authority to be labeled deviant. Examples are children who skip school or talk back to parents and teachers and adults who do not cooperate with employers or police.

Fourth, anyone who directly challenges the capitalist status quo is likely to be defined as deviant. Such has been the case with labor organizers, radical environmentalists, and antiwar activists.

On the other side of the coin, society positively labels whatever supports the operation of capitalism. For example, winning athletes enjoy celebrity status because they express the values of individual achievement and competition, both vital to capitalism. Also, Spitzer notes, we condemn using drugs of escape (marijuana, psychedelics, heroin, and crack) as deviant but encourage drugs (such as alcohol and caffeine) that promote adjustment to the status quo.

The capitalist system also tries to control people who are not economically productive. The elderly, people with mental or physical disabilities, and Robert Merton's retreatists (people addicted to alcohol or other drugs) are a "costly yet relatively harmless burden" on society. Such people, claims Spitzer, are subject to control by social welfare agencies. But people who openly challenge the capitalist system, including the inner-city underclass and revolutionaries—Merton's innovators and rebels—are controlled by the criminal justice system and, in times of crisis, military forces such as the National Guard.

Note that both the social welfare and criminal justice systems blame individuals, not the system, for social problems. Welfare recipients are considered unworthy freeloaders, poor people who express rage at their plight are labeled rioters, anyone who challenges the government is branded a radical or a communist, and those who try to gain illegally what they will never get legally are rounded up as common criminals.

White-Collar Crime

In a sign of things to come, a Wall Street stockbroker named Michael Milken made headlines back in 1987 when he was jailed for business fraud. Milken attracted attention because not since the days of Al Capone had anyone made so much money in one year: $550 million—about $1.5 million a day (Swartz, 1989).

Milken engaged in **white-collar crime**, defined by Edwin Sutherland (1940) as *crime committed by people of high social position in the course of their occupations*. White-collar crimes do not involve violence and rarely attract police to the scene with guns drawn. Rather, white-collar criminals use their powerful offices to illegally enrich themselves and others, often causing significant public harm in the process. For this reason, sociologists sometimes call white-collar offenses that occur in government offices and corporate boardrooms "crime in the suites" as opposed to "crime in the streets."

The most common white-collar crimes are bank embezzlement, business fraud, bribery, and antitrust violations. Sutherland (1940)

Perhaps no one better symbolized the greed that drove the Wall Street meltdown of 2008 than Bernard Madoff, who swindled thousands of people and organizations out of some $50 billion. In 2009, after pleading guilty to eleven felony counts, Madoff was sentenced to 150 years in prison. Do you think white-collar offenders are treated fairly by our criminal justice system? Why or why not?

● SEEING SOCIOLOGY in Everyday Life

Imagine police holding a street gang, but not its individual members, responsible for an outbreak of violence. What does this suggest about the link between crime and power?

─● MAKING THE GRADE

White-collar crime and corporate crime are similar concepts, and there is not always a clear line separating the two. White-collar criminals are *individuals* of high social position who commit crimes while doing their jobs. Corporate crime occurs when a *company* acts in violation of the law.

explains that such white-collar offenses typically end up in a civil hearing rather than a criminal courtroom. *Civil law* regulates business dealings between private parties, and *criminal law* defines the individual's moral responsibilities to society. In practice, then, someone who loses a civil case pays for damage or injury but is not labeled a criminal. Corporate officials are also protected by the fact that most charges of white-collar crime target the organization rather than individuals.

When white-collar criminals are charged and convicted, they usually escape punishment. A government study found that those convicted of fraud and punished with a fine ended up paying less than 10 percent of what they owed; most managed to hide or transfer their assets to avoid paying up. Among white-collar criminals convicted of the more serious crime of embezzlement, only about half ever served a day in jail. One accounting found that just 57 percent of the embezzlers convicted in the U.S. federal courts served prison sentences; the rest were put on probation or issued a fine (U.S. Bureau of Justice Statistics, 2008). As some analysts see it, until courts impose more prison terms, we should expect white-collar crime to remain widespread (Shover & Hochstetler, 2006).

Corporate Crime

Sometimes whole companies, not just individuals, break the law. **Corporate crime** is *the illegal actions of a corporation or people acting on its behalf.*

Corporate crime ranges from knowingly selling faulty or dangerous products to deliberately polluting the environment (Derber, 2004). The collapse of a number of major U.S. corporations in recent years cost tens of thousands of people their jobs and their pensions. Even more seriously, 111 people died in underground coal mines in 2006, 2007, and 2008; hundreds more died from "black lung" disease caused by years of inhaling coal dust. The death toll for all job-related hazards in the United States probably exceeds 50,000 each year (Frank, 2007; Jafari, 2008; U.S. Census Bureau, 2009).

Organized Crime

Organized crime is *a business supplying illegal goods or services.* Sometimes criminal organizations force people to do business with them, as when a gang extorts money from shopkeepers for "protection." In most cases, however, organized crime involves the sale of illegal goods and services—often sex, drugs, and gambling—to willing buyers.

Organized crime has flourished in the United States for more than a century. The scope of its operations expanded among immigrants, who found that this society was not willing to share its opportunities with them. Some ambitious individuals (such as Al Capone, mentioned earlier) made their own success, especially during Prohibition, when the government banned the production and sale of alcohol.

The *Godfather* films offered an inside look at the world of organized crime. How accurately do you think the mass media portray organized crime? Explain.

The Italian Mafia is a well-known example of organized crime. But other criminal organizations involve African Americans, Chinese, Colombians, Cubans, Haitians, Nigerians, and Russians, as well as others of almost every racial and ethnic category. Today, organized crime involves a wide range of activities, from selling illegal drugs to prostitution to credit-card fraud to selling false identification papers to illegal immigrants (Valdez, 1997; Federal Bureau of Investigation, 2008).

─○ **CRITICAL REVIEW** According to social-conflict theory, a capitalist society's inequality in wealth and power shapes its laws and how they are applied. The criminal justice and social welfare systems thus act as political agents, controlling categories of people who are a threat to the capitalist system.

Like other approaches to deviance, social-conflict theory has its critics. First, this approach implies that laws and other cultural norms are created directly by the rich and powerful. At the very least, this is an oversimplification, as laws also protect workers, consumers, and the environment, sometimes opposing the interests of corporations and the rich.

Second, social-conflict analysis argues that criminality springs up only to the extent that a society treats its members unequally. However, as Durkheim noted, deviance exists in all societies, whatever their economic system and their degree of inequality.

Q: "Good laws derive from evil habits." Macrobius

Q: "The fundamental sociological problem is not crime but the law." Peter Berger (1963:37)

Q: "Morality is simply the attitude that we adopt towards people whom we personally dislike." Oscar Wilde

EXERCISE: Study the rapid increase in supermaximum-security ("supermax") prisons: From one 20 years ago, there are now at least 60 in 44 states. These expensive facilities hold the most violent offenders, typically isolating them for 23 hours a day. Critics (and some wardens) claim these prisons cause marked psychological change, which is usually not for the better.

MAKING THE GRADE

The section "Deviance, Race, and Gender" is an extension of the social-conflict approach, which shows how inequality based on race and gender can affect the way we understand deviance.

hate crime a criminal act against a person or a person's property by an offender motivated by racial or other bias

APPLYING THEORY

Deviance

	Structural-Functional Approach	Symbolic-Interaction Approach	Social-Conflict Approach
What is the level of analysis?	Macro-level	Micro-level	Macro-level
What is deviance? What part does it play in society?	Deviance is a basic part of social organization. By defining deviance, society sets its moral boundaries.	Deviance is part of socially constructed reality that emerges in interaction. Deviance comes into being as individuals label something deviant.	Deviance results from social inequality. Norms, including laws, reflect the interests of powerful members of society.
What is important about deviance?	Deviance is universal: It exists in all societies.	Deviance is variable: Any act or person may or may not be labeled deviant.	Deviance is political: People with little power are at high risk of being labeled deviant.

The sociological explanations for crime and other types of deviance that we have discussed are summarized in the Applying Theory table.

CHECK YOUR LEARNING Define white-collar crime, corporate crime, and organized crime.

Deviance, Race, and Gender

What people consider deviant reflects the relative power and privilege of different categories of people. The following sections offer two examples: how racial and ethnic hostility motivates hate crimes and how gender is linked to deviance.

Hate Crimes

A **hate crime** is *a criminal act against a person or a person's property by an offender motivated by racial or other bias.* A hate crime may express hostility toward someone's race, religion, ancestry, sexual orientation, or physical disability. The federal government recorded 7,624 hate crimes in 2007 (U.S. Department of Justice, 2008).

In 1998, people across the country were stunned by the brutal killing of Matthew Shepard, a gay student at the University of Wyoming, by two men filled with hatred toward homosexuals. The National Gay and Lesbian Task Force reported 2,430 hate crimes against gay and lesbian people in 2007 and estimates that one in five

lesbians and gay men will become a victim of physical assault based on sexual orientation (Dang & Vianney, 2007; National Coalition of Anti-Violence Programs, 2007). People who contend with multiple stigmas, such as gay men of color, are especially likely to be victims. Yet it can happen to anyone: In 2007, 18 percent of hate crimes based on race targeted white people (Federal Bureau of Investigation, 2008).

By 2008, forty-five states and the federal government had enacted legislation that increased penalties for crimes motivated by hatred (Anti-Defamation League, 2008). Supporters are gratified, but opponents charge that such laws, which increase penalties based on the attitudes of the offender, punish "politically incorrect" thoughts. The Thinking About Diversity box takes a closer look at the issue of hate crime laws.

The Feminist Perspective: Deviance and Gender

Virtually every society in the world places stricter controls on women than on men. Historically, our own society has centered the lives of women on the home. In the United States even today, women's opportunities in the workplace, in politics, in athletics, and in the military are more limited than men's. Elsewhere in the world, the constraints on women are greater still. In Saudi Arabia, women cannot vote or legally operate motor vehicles; in Iran, women who dare to expose their hair or wear makeup in public can be whipped; and not long

CYBER: The most recent stories and statistics concerning crime and law enforcement are found at the Bureau of Justice Statistics Web site: http://www.ojp.usdoj.gov/bjs

Q: "Between two evils, I always choose the one I've never tried before." Mae West

DIVERSITY: Edwin Schur argues that sociological analysis has long stressed the positive functions of deviance by women (see Kingsley Davis's 1937 analysis of prostitution), with little attention to the structural position of women in relation to men in U.S. society.

Q: "In our society being treated as deviant has been a standard feature of life as a female." Edwin M. Schur

● SEEING SOCIOLOGY
in Everyday Life

Why do you think that women are much less likely than men to be arrested for a serious crime?

THINKING ABOUT DIVERSITY: RACE, CLASS, & GENDER

Hate Crime Laws: Should We Punish Attitudes as Well as Actions?

On a cool October evening, nineteen-year-old Todd Mitchell, an African American, was standing with some friends in front of their apartment complex in Kenosha, Wisconsin. They had just seen the film *Mississippi Burning* and were fuming over a scene that showed a white man beating a young black boy while he knelt in prayer.

"Do you feel hyped up to move on some white people?" asked Mitchell. Minutes later, they saw a young white boy walking toward them on the other side of the street. Mitchell commanded, "There goes a white boy; go get him!" The group swarmed around the youngster, beating him bloody and leaving him on the ground in a coma. The attackers took the boy's tennis shoes as a trophy.

Police soon arrested the teenagers and charged them with the beating. Mitchell went to trial as the ringleader, and the jury found him guilty of aggravated battery *motivated by racial hatred.* Instead of the usual two-year sentence, Mitchell went to jail for four years.

As this case illustrates, hate crime laws punish a crime more severely if the offender is motivated by bias against some category of people. Supporters make three arguments in favor of hate crime legislation. First, as noted in the text discussion of crime, the offender's intentions are always important in weighing criminal responsibility, so considering hatred an intention is nothing new. Second, victims of hate crimes typically suffer greater injury than victims of crimes

with other motives. Third, a crime motivated by racial or other bias is more harmful because it inflames the public mood more than a crime carried out, say, for money.

Critics counter that while some hate crime cases involve hard-core racism, most are impul-

Do you think this example of vandalism should be prosecuted as a hate crime? In other words, should the punishment be more severe than if the spray painting were just "normal" graffiti? Why or why not?

sive acts by young people. Even more important, critics maintain, hate crime laws are a threat to First Amendment guarantees of free speech. Hate crime laws allow courts to sentence offenders not just for their actions but for their attitudes. As the Harvard University law professor Alan Dershowitz cautions, "As much as I hate bigotry, I fear much more the Court attempting to control the minds of its citizens." In short, according to critics, hate crime statutes open the door to punishing beliefs rather than behavior.

In 1993, the U.S. Supreme Court upheld the sentence handed down to Todd Mitchell. In a unanimous decision, the justices stated that the government should not punish an individual's beliefs. But, they reasoned, a belief is no longer protected when it becomes the motive for a crime.

WHAT DO YOU THINK?

1. Do you think crimes motivated by hate are more harmful than those motivated by greed? Why or why not?

2. Do you think minorities such as African Americans should be subject to the same hate crime laws as white people? Why or why not?

3. Do you favor or oppose hate crime laws? Why?

Sources: Terry (1993), A. Sullivan (2002), and Hartocollis (2007).

---

ago, a Nigerian court convicted a divorced woman of bearing a child out of wedlock and sentenced her to death by stoning; her life was later spared out of concern for her child (Eboh, 2002; Jefferson, 2009).

Gender also figures in the theories of deviance you read about earlier in the chapter. Robert Merton's strain theory, for example, defines cultural goals in terms of financial success. Traditionally, at least, this goal has had more to do with the lives of men because women have been taught to define success in terms of relationships, particularly marriage and motherhood (E. B. Leonard, 1982). A more woman-focused theory might recognize the "strain" that results from

the cultural ideal of equality clashing with the reality of gender-based inequality.

According to labeling theory, gender influences how we define deviance because people commonly use different standards to judge the behavior of females and males. Further, because society puts men in positions of power over women, men often escape direct responsibility for actions that victimize women. In the past, at least, men who sexually harassed or assaulted women were labeled only mildly deviant and sometimes escaped punishment entirely.

NOTE: The term "hate crime" was coined in 1985 by John Conyers Jr., a Democratic representative from Michigan. The term's coverage has expanded in the years since so that it now includes bias against 79% of the U.S. population (Grattet, 2000).

POP CULTURE: The HBO movie *The Laramie Project* portrayed the life and death of Matthew Shepard, the victim of one of the most publicized hate crimes in recent years.

THE MAP: Arrest rates are higher for poor, young minority men, who make up a higher share of the population of the "above average" counties.

Q: "A hick town is one where there is no place to go where you shouldn't be." Alexander Woollcott

Q: "The function of vice is to keep virtue within reasonable bounds." Samuel Butler

SEEING SOCIOLOGY in Everyday Life

Do you think a student who downloads music in violation of the law is guilty of theft? Why or why not?

Sam Pearson, who lives in Renville County, North Dakota, rarely locks his doors when he leaves the house.

Serge Shuman, who lives in Mecklenburg County, North Carolina, knows many people who have been victims of crime and avoids going out at night.

Seeing Ourselves

NATIONAL MAP 9–1

The Risk of Violent Crime across the United States

This map shows the risk of becoming a victim of violent crime. In general, the risk is highest in low-income, rural counties that have a large population of men between the ages of fifteen and twenty-four. After reading this section of the text, see whether you can explain this pattern.

Source: CAP Index, Inc., 2009.

Risk of Violent Crime
- Above average
- Average
- Below average

By contrast, women who are victimized may have to convince others—even members of a jury—that they were not to blame for their own sexual harassment or assault. Research confirms an important truth: Whether people define a situation as deviance—and, if so, who the deviant is—depends on the sex of both the audience and the actors (King & Clayson, 1988).

Finally, despite its focus on social inequality, much social-conflict analysis does not address the issue of gender. If economic disadvantage is a primary cause of crime, as conflict theory suggests, why do women (whose economic position is much worse than men's) commit far *fewer* crimes than men?

Crime

Crime is the violation of criminal laws enacted by a locality, a state, or the federal government. All crimes are composed of two elements: the *act* itself (or in some cases, the failure to do what the law requires) and *criminal intent* (in legal terminology, *mens rea*, or "guilty mind"). Intent is a matter of degree, ranging from willful conduct to negligence. Someone who is negligent does not deliberately set out to hurt anyone but acts in a way that results in harm. Prosecutors weigh the degree of intent in deciding whether, for example, to charge someone with first-degree murder, second-degree murder, or negligent manslaughter. Alternatively, they may consider a killing justifiable, as in self-defense.

Types of Crime

In the United States, the Federal Bureau of Investigation (FBI) gathers information on criminal offenses and regularly reports the results in a publication called *Crime in the United States*. Two major types of crime make up the FBI "crime index."

Crimes against the person, also called *violent crimes*, are *crimes that direct violence or the threat of violence against others*. Violent crimes include murder and manslaughter (legally defined as "the willful killing of one human being by another"), aggravated assault ("an unlawful attack by one person upon another for the purpose of inflicting severe or aggravated bodily injury"), forcible rape ("the carnal knowledge of a female forcibly and against her will"), and robbery ("taking or attempting to take anything of value from the care, custody, or control of a person or persons by force or threat of force or violence and/or putting the victim in fear"). National Map 9–1 shows a person's risk of becoming a victim of violent crime in counties all across the United States.

Crimes against property, also called *property crimes*, are *crimes that involve theft of property belonging to others*. Property crimes include burglary ("the unlawful entry of a structure to commit a [serious crime] or a theft"), larceny-theft ("the unlawful taking, carrying, leading, or riding away of property from the possession of another"), auto theft ("the theft or attempted theft of a motor vehicle"), and arson ("any willful or malicious burning or attempt to burn the personal property of another").

A third category of offenses, not included in major crime indexes, is **victimless crimes**, *violations of law in which there are no obvious victims*. Also called *crimes without complaint*, they include illegal drug use, prostitution, and gambling. The term "victimless crime" is misleading, however. How victimless is a crime when young people steal to support a drug habit? What about a young pregnant woman who, by smoking crack, permanently harms her baby? Perhaps it is more correct to say that people who commit such crimes are both offenders and victims.

Because public views of victimless crimes vary greatly, laws differ from place to place. In the United States, although gambling and

NOTE: With 9 on the record for 2007, hate-crime homicides account for only a tiny fraction of the more than 16,929 killings annually in the U.S.

DIVERSITY: Of all hate crimes recorded by the police in 2007, 51% involved race, 18% religion, 17% sexual orientation, 13% ethnicity or national origin, and 1% disability.

GLOBAL: A new form of crime, both high-tech and global in character, is pirating copyrighted software. The Internet now allows anyone with a computer and a modem to send or receive materials globally. Software piracy is especially pronounced in lower-income countries such as Armenia, Bangladesh, Zimbabwe, and Vietnam.

crimes against the person (violent crimes) crimes that direct violence or the threat of violence against others

crimes against property (property crimes) crimes that involve theft of money or property belonging to others

victimless crimes violations of law in which there are no obvious victims

FIGURE 9–2 Crime Rates in the United States, 1960–2006

The graphs show the rates for various violent crimes and property crimes during recent decades. Since about 1990, the trend has been downward.

Source: Federal Bureau of Investigation (2008).

prostitution are legal in only limited areas, both activities are common across the country.

Criminal Statistics

Statistics gathered by the FBI show crime rates rising from 1960 to 1990 and then declining. Even so, police count more than 11 million serious crimes each year. Figure 9–2 shows the trends for various serious crimes.

Always read crime statistics with caution, because they include only crimes known to the police. Almost all homicides are reported, but assaults—especially among people who know one another—often are not. Police records include an even smaller share of the property crimes that occur, especially when the crime involves losses that are small.

Researchers check official crime statistics using *victimization surveys,* in which they ask a representative sample of people if they have had any experience with crime. According to such surveys, the overall crime rate is about three times higher than official reports indicate (Russell, 1995b).

SEEING SOCIOLOGY
in Everyday Life

The 2009 arrest of Harvard professor Henry Louis Gates Jr., an African American, by a white police officer sparked a national debate over racial profiling.

MAKING THE GRADE

Remember that the profile of a criminal depends on the type of crime. Street crime involves a larger share of lower-income people; corporate crime involves mostly high-income people. With regard to race, most street crime is committed by whites.

"You look like this sketch of someone who's thinking about committing a crime."
© The New Yorker Collection 2000, David Sipress from cartoonbank.com. All rights reserved.

The Street Criminal: A Profile

Using government crime reports, we can gain a general description of the categories of people most likely to be arrested for violent and property crimes.

Age

Official crime rates rise sharply during adolescence, peak in the late teens, and then fall as people get older. People between the ages of fifteen and twenty-four represent just 14 percent of the U.S. population, but in 2007, they accounted for 40.9 percent of all arrests for violent crimes and 46.8 percent of arrests for property crimes (Federal Bureau of Investigation, 2008).

Gender

Although each sex makes up roughly half the population, police collared males in 66.6 percent of all property crime arrests in 2007; the other 33.4 percent of arrests involved women. In other words, men are arrested more than twice as often as women for property crimes. In the case of violent crimes, the difference is even greater, with 81.8 percent of arrests involving males and just 18.2 percent females (more than a four-to-one ratio).

It may be that law enforcement officials are reluctant to define women as criminals. In fact, all over the world, the greatest gender differences in crime rates occur in societies that most severely limit the opportunities of women. In the United States, however, the difference in arrest rates for women and men is narrowing, which probably indicates increasing sexual equality in our society. Between 1998 and 2007, there was a 6.6 percent *increase* in arrests of women and a 6.1 percent *drop* in arrests of men (Federal Bureau of Investigation, 2008).

Social Class

The FBI does not assess the social class of arrested persons, so no statistical data of the kind given for age and gender are available. But research has long indicated that street crime is more widespread among people of lower social position (Thornberry & Farnsworth, 1982; Wolfgang, Thornberry, & Figlio, 1987).

Yet the link between class and crime is more complicated than it appears on the surface. For one thing, many people look on the poor as less worthy than the rich, whose wealth and power confer "respectability" (Tittle, Villemez, & Smith, 1978; Elias, 1986). And although crime—especially violent crime—is a serious problem in the poorest inner-city communities, most of these crimes are committed by a few repeat offenders. The majority of the people who live in poor communities have no criminal record at all (Wolfgang, Figlio, & Sellin, 1972; Elliott & Ageton, 1980; Harries, 1990).

The connection between social standing and criminality also depends on the type of crime. If we expand our definition of crime beyond street offenses to include white-collar crime and corporate crime, the "common criminal" suddenly looks much more affluent and may live in a $100 million home.

Race and Ethnicity

Both race and ethnicity are strongly linked to crime rates, although the reasons are many and complex. Official statistics show that 69.7 percent of arrests for FBI index crimes in 2007 involved white people. However, the African American arrest rate was higher than the rate for whites in proportion to their representation in the general population. African Americans make up 12.8 percent of the population but account for 29.8 percent of arrests for property crimes (versus 67.9 percent for whites) and 39.0 percent of arrests for violent crimes (versus 58.9 percent for whites) (Federal Bureau of Investigation, 2008).

There are several reasons for the disproportionate number of arrests among African Americans. First, race in the United States closely relates to social standing, which, as already explained, affects the likelihood of engaging in street crimes. Many poor people living in the midst of wealth come to perceive society as unjust and are therefore more likely to turn to crime to get their share (Blau & Blau, 1982; E. Anderson, 1994; Martinez, 1996).

Second, black and white family patterns differ: More than two-thirds of non-Hispanic black children (compared to one-fourth of

NOTE: The Los Angeles–Long Beach, Calif., metropolitan area reports the highest number of murders in the U.S.: 941 in 2007.

NOTE: Changes in our view of violence are suggested by how common violence between officials was two centuries ago. For example, Vice President Aaron Burr shot and killed Alexander Hamilton (first U.S. secretary of the Treasury) in a duel in 1804.

NOTE: A significant percentage of violent and property crimes are committed by young people. Under 21: 30.3% of arrests for violent crime; 42.2% of arrests for property crime. Under 19: 21.3% of arrests for violent crimes; 32.6% for property crime (Federal Bureau of Investigation, 2008).

Q: "I am as pure as the driven slush." Tallulah Bankhead

MAKING THE GRADE

The profile of the street criminal is based on arrest data and not on convictions in a court of law. This is because the data made available by the FBI are based on arrests.

SEEING SOCIOLOGY
in Everyday Life

Do you think stricter gun control laws would lower the level of deadly violence in the United States? Why or why not?

non-Hispanic white children) are born to single mothers. Single parenting carries two risks: Children receive less supervision and are at greater risk of living in poverty. With more than one-third of African American children growing up poor (compared to one in ten white children), no one should be surprised at the proportionately higher crime rates for African Americans (Hamilton, Martin, & Ventura, 2007; U.S. Census Bureau, 2008).

Third, prejudice prompts white police to arrest black people more readily and leads citizens to report African Americans more willingly, so people of color are overly criminalized (Chiricos, McEntire, & Gertz, 2001; Quillian & Pager, 2001; Demuth & Steffensmeier, 2004).

Fourth, remember that the official crime index does not include arrests for offenses ranging from drunk driving to white-collar violations. This omission contributes to the view of the typical criminal as a person of color. If we broaden our definition of crime to include drunk driving, business fraud, embezzlement, stock swindles, and cheating on income tax returns, the proportion of white criminals rises dramatically.

Keep in mind, too, that categories of people with high arrest rates are also at higher risk of being victims of crime. In the United States, for example, African Americans are six times as likely as white people to die as a result of homicide (Rogers et al., 2001; Kung et al., 2008).

Finally, some categories of the population have unusually low rates of arrest. People of Asian descent, who account for about 4 percent of the population, figure in only 1 percent of all arrests. As Chapter 14 ("Race and Ethnicity") explains, Asian Americans enjoy higher than average educational achievement and income. Also, Asian American culture emphasizes family solidarity and discipline, both of which keep criminality down.

Crime in Global Perspective

By world standards, the crime rate in the United States is high. Although recent crime trends are downward, there were 16,929 murders in the United States in 2007, which amounts to one every half hour around the clock. In large cities such as New York, rarely does a day pass without someone being killed.

The rate of violent crime (but not property crime) in the United States is several times higher than in Europe. The contrast is even greater between our country and the nations of Asia, including India and Japan, where rates of violent and property crime are among the lowest in the world.

Elliott Currie (1985) suggests that crime stems from our culture's emphasis on individual economic success, frequently at the expense of strong families and neighborhoods. The United States also has extraordinary cultural diversity—a result of centuries of immigration—that can lead to conflict. In addition, economic inequality is higher in this country than in most other high-income nations. Thus our society's relatively weak social fabric, combined with considerable frustration among the poor, increases the level of criminal behavior.

Another factor contributing to violence in the United States is extensive private ownership of guns. About two-thirds of murder victims in the United States die from shootings. The U.S. rate of handgun deaths is about six times higher than the rate in Canada, a country that strictly limits handgun ownership (Statistics Canada, 2008).

Surveys suggest that about one-third of U.S. households have at least one gun. In fact, there are more guns (about 285 million) than adults in this country, and 40 percent of these weapons are handguns, commonly used in violent crimes. In large part, gun ownership reflects people's fear of crime, yet the easy availability of guns in this country also makes crime more deadly (NORC, 2007; Brady Campaign, 2008).

Supporters of gun control claim that restricting gun ownership would reduce the number of murders in the United States. For example, the number of murders each year in Canada, where the law prevents most people from owning guns, is about the same as in just the city of New York in this country. But as critics of gun control point out, laws regulating gun ownership do not keep guns out of the hands of criminals, who almost always obtain guns illegally. They also claim that gun control is no magic bullet in the war on crime: The number of people in the United States killed each year by knives alone is three times the number of Canadians killed by weapons of all kinds (Currie, 1985; J. D. Wright, 1995; Munroe, 2007; Federal Bureau of Investigation, 2008).

By the end of 2008, gun sales to private citizens was up sharply, reflecting fears on the part of many gun owners that the Obama administration would act to curtail gun ownership. Changes in law may or may not occur in the next few years, but debate over the consequences of widespread gun ownership will continue (Potter, 2008).

December 24–25, traveling through Peru. In Lima, Peru's capital city, the concern with crime is obvious. Almost every house is fortified with gates, barbed wire, or broken glass embedded in cement at the top of a wall. Private security forces are everywhere in the rich areas along the coast, where we find the embassies, expensive hotels, and the international airport.

The picture is very different as we pass through small villages high in the Andes to the east. The same families have lived in these communities for generations, and people know one another. No gates and fences here. And we've seen only one police car all afternoon.

NOTE: Police reports vs. victimization survey data (2006; cases or victims per 100,000 people aged 12 and older): all violent crime: 474/2,470; murder: 6/6, forcible rape: 31/80; robbery: 149/290; aggravated assault: 288/540; all property crime: 3,335/16,050; burglary: 729/3,020; larceny-theft: 2,207/12,190; motor vehicle theft: 398/840 (Federal Bureau of Investigation, 2008; U.S. Bureau of Justice Statistics, 2008).

DIVERSITY: Our society's readiness to link color to criminality was illustrated by the Susan Smith case, in which a white woman who murdered her children initially convinced investigators and the public that the crime was the work of an African American man.

DIVERSITY: An estimated 10.4% of African American males aged 25–29, 3.6% of Hispanic males, and 1.7% of white males are in prison or jail (FBI, 2008).

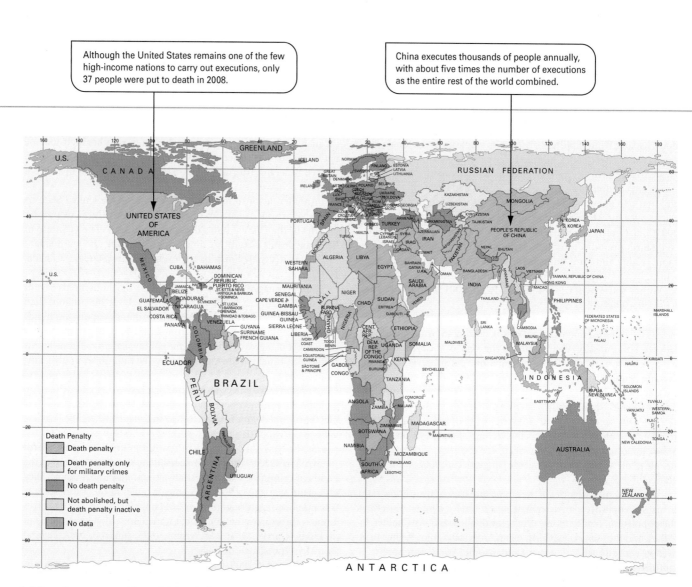

Although the United States remains one of the few high-income nations to carry out executions, only 37 people were put to death in 2008.

China executes thousands of people annually, with about five times the number of executions as the entire rest of the world combined.

Window on the World

GLOBAL MAP 9–1   Capital Punishment in Global Perspective

The map identifies sixty-five countries in which the law allows the death penalty for ordinary crimes; in nine more, the death penalty is reserved for exceptional crimes under military law or during times of war. The death penalty does not exist in ninety-three countries; in thirty-five more, although the death penalty remains in law, no execution has taken place in more than ten years. Compare rich and poor nations: What general pattern do you see? In what way are the United States and Japan exceptions to this pattern?

Source: Amnesty International (2008a).

Crime rates are high in some of the largest cities of the world, including Lima, Peru; São Paulo, Brazil; and Manila, Philippines—all of which have rapid population growth and millions of desperately poor people. Outside of big cities, however, the traditional character of low-income societies and their strong families allow local communities to control crime informally.

Some types of crime have always been multinational, such as terrorism, espionage, and arms dealing (Martin & Romano, 1992).

But today, the globalization we are experiencing on many fronts also extends to crime. A recent case in point is the illegal drug trade. In part, the problem of illegal drugs in the United States is a *demand* issue. That is, the demand for cocaine and other drugs in this country is high, and many people risk arrest or even a violent death for a chance to get rich in the drug trade. But the *supply* side of the issue is just as important. In the South American nation of Colombia, at least 20 percent of the people depend on cocaine production for their

NOTE: The number of licenses in the U.S. to sell guns totaled 54,902 in 2005, down from 284,117 in 1992. The number was only 87,000 in 1969 ("An Analysis of the Decline," 2006).

SOCIAL SURVEY: "Do you happen to have in your home (house or garage) any guns or revolvers?" (GSS 2006, N = 898; NORC, 2008)

"Yes"   33.2%   "No"   65.2%   "Don't know"/No response   1.6%

Q: "The nail that sticks up gets hit down." Japanese proverb

GLOBAL: According to the Foreign Ministry of Japan, Japanese nationals are five times more likely to be victims of homicide while in the U.S. than while in Japan.

Q: "In the severity of its crime rates, the United States more closely resembles the most volatile countries of the Third World than other developed Western societies." Elliott Currie

MAKING THE GRADE

Due process—the idea that the criminal justice system should operate under the rule of law—guides the actions of police, court officials, and corrections officers.

livelihood. Not only is cocaine Colombia's most profitable export, but it outsells all other exports combined—including coffee. Clearly, drug dealing and many other crimes are closely related to social and economic conditions both in the United States and elsewhere.

Different countries have different strategies for dealing with crime. The use of the death penalty provides a case in point. According to Amnesty International (2008b), five nations (China, Iran, Pakistan, Saudi Arabia, and the United States) account for 93 percent of the world's executions carried out by governments. Global Map 9–1 shows which countries currently use capital punishment. The global trend is toward abolishing the death penalty: Amnesty International (2008a) reports that since 1985, sixty-two nations have ended this practice.

The U.S. Criminal Justice System

The criminal justice system is a society's formal system of social control. We shall briefly examine the key elements of the U.S. criminal justice system: police, courts, and the system of punishment and corrections. First, however, we must understand an important principle that underlies the entire system, the idea of due process.

Due Process

Due process is a simple but very important idea: The criminal justice system must operate according to law. This principle is grounded in the first ten amendments to the U.S. Constitution—known as the Bill of Rights—adopted by Congress in 1791. The Constitution offers various protections to any person charged with a crime, including the right to counsel, the right to refuse to testify against oneself, the right to confront all accusers, freedom from being tried twice for the same crime, and freedom from being "deprived of life, liberty, or property without due process of law." Furthermore, the Constitution gives all people the right to a speedy and public trial by jury and freedom from excessive bail and from "cruel and unusual" punishment.

In general terms, the concept of due process means that anyone charged with a crime must receive (1) fair notice of legal proceedings, (2) the opportunity to present a defense during a hearing on the charges, which must be conducted according to law, and (3) a judge or jury that weighs evidence impartially (Inciardi, 2000).

Due process limits the power of government, with an eye toward this nation's cultural support of individual rights and freedoms. Deciding exactly how far government can go is an ongoing process that makes up much of the work of the judicial system, especially the U.S. Supreme Court.

Police

The police generally serve as the primary point of contact between a society's population and the criminal justice system. In principle, the police maintain public order by enforcing the law. Of course, there is only so much that the 699,850 full-time police officers in the United States can do to monitor the activities of 300 million people. As a result, the police use a great deal of personal judgment in deciding which situations warrant their attention and how to handle them.

How do police officers carry out their duties? In a study of police behavior in five cities, Douglas Smith and Christy Visher (1981; D.

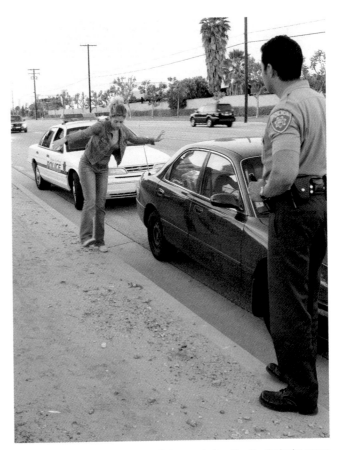

Police must be allowed discretion if they are to handle effectively the many different situations they face every day. At the same time, it is important that the police treat people fairly. Here we see a police officer deciding whether or not to charge a young woman with driving while intoxicated. What factors do you think enter into this decision?

plea bargaining a legal negotiation in which a prosecutor reduces a charge in exchange for a defendant's guilty plea

Television shows like *Law & Order* suggest that the criminal justice system carefully weighs the guilt and innocence of defendants. But as explained below, only 5 percent of criminal cases are actually resolved through a formal trial.

A. Smith, 1987) concluded that because they must act swiftly, police officers quickly size up situations in terms of six factors. First, the more serious they think the situation is, the more likely they are to make an arrest. Second, officers take account of the victim's wishes in deciding whether or not to make an arrest. Third, the odds of arrest go up the more uncooperative a suspect is. Fourth, officers are more likely to take into custody someone they have arrested before, presumably because this suggests guilt. Fifth, the presence of observers increases the chances of arrest. According to Smith and Visher, the presence of observers prompts police to take stronger control of a situation, if only to move the encounter from the street (the suspect's turf) to the police department (where law officers have the edge). Sixth, all else being equal, police officers are more likely to arrest people of color than whites, perceiving suspects of African or Latino descent as either more dangerous or more likely to be guilty.

Courts

After arrest, a court determines a suspect's guilt or innocence. In principle, U.S. courts rely on an adversarial process involving attorneys—one representing the defendant and another the state—in the presence of a judge, who monitors legal procedures.

In practice, however, about 95 percent of criminal cases are resolved prior to court appearance through **plea bargaining**, *a legal negotiation in which a prosecutor reduces a charge in exchange for a defendant's guilty plea.* For example, the state may offer a defendant

charged with burglary a lesser charge, perhaps possession of burglary tools, in exchange for a guilty plea (U.S. Department of Justice, 2008).

Plea bargaining is widespread because it spares the system the time and expense of trials. A trial is usually unnecessary if there is little disagreement over the facts of the case. In addition, because the number of cases entering the system annually has doubled over the past decade, prosecutors could not bring every case to trial even if they wanted to. By quickly resolving most of their work, the courts channel their resources into the most important cases.

But plea bargaining pressures defendants (who are presumed innocent) to plead guilty. A person can exercise the right to a trial, but only at the risk of receiving a more severe sentence if found guilty. Furthermore, low-income defendants enter the process with the guidance of a public defender—typically an overworked and underpaid attorney who may devote little time to even the most serious cases (Novak, 1999). Plea bargaining may be efficient, but it undercuts both the adversarial process and the rights of defendants.

Punishment

In 2008, as he approached the city hall in Kirkwood, Missouri, a man pulled a handgun and shot and killed a police officer. He then entered a city council meeting and killed another police officer and three council members. The city's mayor was critically wounded (C. Leonard, 2008).

Such cases force us to wonder about the reasons for such extreme violence and also to ask how a society should respond to such acts. In the case of the Kirkwood shootings, police shot and killed the man at the crime scene. But typically, of course, a suspect is apprehended and put on trial. If found guilty, the next step is punishment.

What does a society gain through the punishment of wrongdoers? Scholars answer with four basic reasons: retribution, deterrence, rehabilitation, and societal protection.

Retribution

The oldest justification for punishment is to satisfy people's need for **retribution**, *an act of moral vengeance by which society makes the offender suffer as much as the suffering caused by the crime.* Retribution rests on a view of society as a moral balance. When criminality upsets this balance, punishment in equal measure restores the moral order, as suggested in the ancient code calling for "an eye for an eye, a tooth for a tooth."

In the Middle Ages, most Europeans viewed crime as sin—an offense against God as well as society that required a harsh response. Today, although critics point out that retribution does little to reform the offender, many people consider vengeance reason enough for punishment.

DIVERSITY: The U.S. average is 25 police officers per 10,000 people. Washington, D.C., has 73; Louisiana, 38; and New Jersey, 39—the highest averages. The lowest are in Iowa, Minnesota, Oregon, all at 17; Washington, D.C., with the highest police ratio, also has the highest homicide rate, suggesting that police cannot effectively control crime by themselves.

NOTE: Retribution is evident in virtually all ancient codes of law. The Latin concept *lex talionis* refers to the "law of retaliation," prescribing that an offender's punishment fit the crime.

Four Justifications for Punishment

retribution an act of moral vengeance by which society makes the offender suffer as much as the suffering caused by the crime

deterrence the attempt to discourage criminality through the use of punishment

rehabilitation a program for reforming the offender to prevent later offenses

societal protection rendering an offender incapable of further offenses temporarily through imprisonment or permanently by execution

SUMMING UP

Four Justifications for Punishment

Retribution	The oldest justification for punishment. Punishment is society's revenge for a moral wrong. In principle, punishment should be equal in severity to the crime itself.
Deterrence	An early modern approach. Crime is considered social disruption, which society acts to control. People are viewed as rational and self-interested; deterrence works because the pain of punishment outweighs the pleasure of crime.
Rehabilitation	A modern strategy linked to the development of social sciences. Crime and other deviance are viewed as the result of social problems (such as poverty) or personal problems (such as mental illness). Social conditions are improved; treatment is tailored to the offender's condition.
Societal protection	A modern approach easier to carry out than rehabilitation. Even if society is unable or unwilling to rehabilitate offenders or reform social conditions, people are protected by the imprisonment or execution of the offender.

Deterrence

A second justification for punishment is **deterrence**, *the attempt to discourage criminality through the use of punishment*. Deterrence is based on the eighteenth-century Enlightenment idea that humans, as calculating and rational creatures, will not break the law if they think that the pain of punishment will outweigh the pleasure of the crime.

Deterrence emerged as a reform measure in response to the harsh punishments based on retribution. Why put someone to death for stealing if theft can be discouraged with a prison sentence? As the concept of deterrence gained acceptance in industrial nations, the execution and physical mutilation of criminals in most high-income societies were replaced by milder forms of punishment such as imprisonment.

Punishment can deter crime in two ways. *Specific deterrence* is used to convince an individual offender that crime does not pay. Through *general deterrence*, the punishment of one person serves as an example to others.

Rehabilitation

The third justification for punishment is **rehabilitation**, *a program for reforming the offender to prevent later offenses*. Rehabilitation arose along with the social sciences in the nineteenth century. Since then, sociologists have claimed that crime and other deviance spring from a social environment marked by poverty or a lack of parental supervision. Logically, then, if offenders learn to be deviant, they can also learn to obey the rules; the key is controlling their environment. *Reformatories* or *houses of correction* provided controlled settings where people could learn proper behavior (recall the description of total institutions in Chapter 5, "Socialization").

Like deterrence, rehabilitation motivates the offender to conform. In contrast to deterrence and retribution, which simply make the offender suffer, rehabilitation encourages constructive improvement. Unlike retribution, which demands that the punishment fit the crime, rehabilitation tailors treatment to each offender. Thus identical crimes would prompt similar acts of retribution but different rehabilitation programs.

Societal Protection

A final justification for punishment is **societal protection**, *rendering an offender incapable of further offenses temporarily through imprisonment or permanently by execution*. Like deterrence, societal protection is a rational approach to punishment intended to protect society from crime.

Currently, about 2.3 million people are jailed in the United States. Although the crime rate has gone down in recent years, the number of offenders locked up across the country has gone up, tripling since 1980. This rise in the prison population reflects both tougher public attitudes toward crime and punishing offenders and an increasing number of drug-related arrests. As a result, the United States now incarcerates a larger share of its population than any other

NOTE: The last public execution in England took place in 1868.

GLOBAL: China executes more people than the rest of the world combined; the death penalty can be applied for minor offenses such as tax evasion. The current practice is to execute offenders minutes after their convictions and then to harvest their organs before cremating the body (C. S. Smith, 2001).

NOTE: Political pressure to jail offenders leads to prison overcrowding, which in turn tends to produce shorter sentences, generating little or none of the initially expected results (see Clark & Lee, 1996).

DISCUSS: Between 1977 and 2006, 7,433 people were sentenced to death; 1,057 were executed. Is the death penalty an "arbitrary lottery," as opponents claim, or a filter reserving death for only the worst offenders, as supporters claim?

Seeing SOCIOLOGY in the {NEWS}

The New York Times

More Than 1 in 100 Adults Are Now in Prison in United States

By ADAM LIPTAK
February 29, 2008

For the first time in the nation's history, more than one in 100 American adults are behind bars, according to a new report.

Nationwide, the prison population grew by 25,000 last year, bringing it to almost 1.6 million, after three decades of growth that has seen the prison population nearly triple. Another 723,000 people are in local jails.

The number of American adults is about 230 million, meaning that one in every 99.1 adults is behind bars.

Incarceration rates are even higher for some groups. One in 36 adult Hispanic men is behind bars, based on Justice Department figures for 2006. One in 15 adult black men is, too, as is one in nine black men ages 20 to 34.

The report, from the Pew Center on the States, also found that one in 355 white women ages 35 to 39 is behind bars, compared with one in 100 black women. . . .

The increase in the number of prisoners over the last 18 months, the Pew report says, pushed the national adult incarceration rate to just over one in 100.

"We aren't really getting the return in public safety from this level of incarceration," said Susan Urahn, the center's managing director.

But Paul Cassell, a law professor at the University of Utah and a former federal judge, said the Pew report considered only half of the cost-benefit equation and overlooked the "very tangible benefits: lower crime rates."

In the past 20 years, according to the Federal Bureau of Investigation, rates of violent crimes fell by 25 percent, to 464 per 100,000 people in 2007 from 612.5 in 1987.

"While we certainly want to be smart about who we put into prisons," Professor Cassell said, "it would be a mistake to think that we can release any significant number of prisoners without increasing crime rates. One out of every 100 adults is behind bars because one out of every 100 adults has committed a serious criminal offense."

The United States imprisons more people than any other nation in the world. China is second, with 1.5 million people behind bars. The gap is even wider in percentage terms.

Germany imprisons 93 out of every 100,000 people, according to the International Center for Prison Studies at King's College in London. The comparable number for the United States is roughly eight times that, or 750 out of 100,000.

Ms. Urahn said the nation could not afford the incarceration rate documented in the report.

"We tend to be a country in which incarceration is an easy response to crime," she said. "Being tough on crime is an easy position to take, particularly if you have the money. And we did have the money in the '80s and '90s."

Now, with fewer resources available, the report said, "prison costs are blowing a hole in state budgets." On average, states spend almost 7 percent

country in the world (Pew Center on the States, 2008; Sentencing Project, 2008). Seeing Sociology in the News provides details about the rising rate of incarceration in the United States.

CRITICAL REVIEW The Summing Up table on page 237 reviews the four justifications for punishment. However, an accurate assessment of the consequences of punishment is no simple task.

The value of retribution lies in Durkheim's claim that punishing the deviant person increases society's moral awareness. For this reason, punishment was traditionally a public event. Although the last public execution in the United States took place in Kentucky more than seventy years ago, today's mass media ensure public awareness of executions carried out inside prison walls (Kittrie, 1971).

Does punishment deter crime? Despite our extensive use of punishment, our society has a high rate of **criminal recidivism**, *later offenses by people previously convicted of crimes.* About three-fourths of prisoners in state penitentiaries have been jailed before, and about two-thirds of people released from prison are arrested again within three years (DeFina & Arvanites, 2002; U.S. Department of Justice, 2008). So does punishment really deter crime? Only about one-third of all crimes are known to police, and of these, only about one in five results in an arrest. Most crimes, therefore, go unpunished, so the old saying that "crime doesn't pay" rings hollow.

Prisons provide short-term societal protection by keeping offenders off the streets, but they do little to reshape attitudes or behavior in the long term (Carlson, 1976; R. A. Wright, 1994). Perhaps rehabilitation is an unrealistic expectation, because according to Sutherland's theory of differential association, locking up criminals together for years probably strengthens criminal attitudes and skills. Imprisonment also stigmatizes prisoners, making it harder for them to find legitimate employment later on (Pager, 2003). Finally, prison breaks the social ties inmates may have in the outside world, which, following Hirschi's control theory, makes inmates more likely to commit new crimes upon release.

CHECK YOUR LEARNING What are society's four justifications for punishment? Does sending offenders to prison accomplish each of them? Why?

The Death Penalty

Perhaps the most controversial issue involving punishment is the death penalty. Between 1977 and 2009, more than 7,000 people were sentenced to death in U.S. courts; 1,136 executions were carried out.

In thirty-six states, the law allows the state to execute offenders convicted of very serious crimes such as first-degree murder. But while a majority of states do permit capital punishment, only a few states are likely to carry out executions. Across the United States, half of the 3,220 people on death row at the end of 2007 were in just four

GLOBAL: In France, the guillotine was used from 1791 until 1977; in 1981, France abolished the death penalty.

RESOURCE: Good illustrations of how crime functions to reaffirm norms and increase social unity are found in Truman Capote's *In Cold Blood* (Signet, 1965); see especially pp. 279–80.

DISCUSS: Do you think any of the four reasons for punishment are contradictory? For example, does rehabilitation seem to violate the idea of retribution?

Q: "Be careful how you live. You may be the only Bible some person ever reads." William Toms

of their budgets on corrections, trailing only health care, education and transportation.

In 2007, according to the National Association of State Budget Officers, states spent $44 billion in tax dollars on corrections. That is up from $10.6 billion in 1987, a 127 percent increase when adjusted for inflation. . . . By 2011, the Pew report said, states are on track to spend an additional $25 billion.

It cost an average of $23,876 to imprison someone in 2005, the most recent year for which data were available. But state spending varies widely, from $45,000 a year in Rhode Island to $13,000 in Louisiana.

"Getting tough on crime has gotten tough on taxpayers," said Adam Gelb, the director of the public safety performance project at the Pew Center. "They don't want to spend $23,000 on a prison cell for a minor violation any more than they want a bridge to nowhere."

The cost of medical care is growing by 10 percent annually, the report said, and will accelerate as the prison population ages.

About one in nine state government employees works in corrections, and some states are finding it hard to fill those jobs. California spent more than $500 million on overtime alone in 2006.

The number of prisoners in California dropped by 4,000 last year, making Texas's prison system the nation's largest, at about 172,000. But the Texas Legislature last year approved broad changes to the state's corrections system, including expansions of drug treatment programs and drug courts and revisions to parole practices.

"Our violent offenders, we lock them up for a very long time—rapists, murderers, child molesters," said State Senator John Whitmire, Democrat of Houston and the chairman of the Senate's Criminal Justice Committee. "The problem was that we weren't smart about nonviolent offenders. . . ."

The Pew report recommended diverting nonviolent offenders away from prison and using punishments short of reincarceration for minor or technical violations of probation or parole. It also urged states to consider earlier release of some prisoners. . . .

WHAT DO YOU THINK?

1. How does the United States differ from other countries in terms of incarceration rates? Why do you think this country makes such widespread use of prison as a response to crime?

2. In light of the high costs of locking up offenders, what other policies might be implemented to hold down the crime rate?

3. Do you support the idea that prison should be used to protect society from only violent offenders? What about white-collar criminals?

states: California, Texas, Florida, and Pennsylvania (U.S. Bureau of Justice Statistics, 2008).

Opponents of capital punishment point to research suggesting that the death penalty has limited value as a crime deterrent. Countries such as Canada, where the death penalty has been abolished, have not seen a rise in the number of murders. Critics also point out that the United States is the only Western, high-income nation that routinely executes offenders. As public concern about the death penalty has increased, the use of capital punishment has declined, falling from 74 executions in 1997 to 37 in 2008.

Public opinion surveys reveal that the share of U.S. adults who claim to support the death penalty as a punishment for murder remains high (63 percent) and has been fairly stable over time (NORC, 2007:159). College students hold about the same attitudes as everyone else, with about two-thirds of first-year students expressing support for the death penalty (Pryor et al., 2008).

But judges, criminal prosecutors, and members of trial juries are less and less likely to call for the death penalty. One reason is that because the crime rate has come down in recent years, the public now has less fear of crime and is less interested in applying the most severe punishment.

A second reason is public concern that the death penalty may be applied unjustly. The analysis of DNA evidence—a recent advance—from old crime scenes has shown that many people were wrongly convicted of a crime. Across the country, between 1975 and 2008, 131 people who had been sentenced to death were released from death row after new DNA evidence demonstrated their innocence. Such findings were one reason that in 2000, the governor of Illinois stated he could no longer support the death penalty, leading him to commute the death sentences of every person on that state's death row (S. Levine, 2003; Death Penalty Information Center, 2008).

A third reason for the decline in the use of the death penalty is that more states now permit judges and juries to sentence serious offenders to life in prison without the possibility of parole. Such punishment offers to protect society from dangerous criminals who can be "put away" forever without requiring an execution.

Fourth and finally, many states now shy away from capital punishment because of the high cost of prosecuting capital cases. Death penalty cases require more legal work and demand superior defense lawyers, often at public expense. In addition, such cases commonly include testimony by various paid "experts," including physicians and psychiatrists, which also runs up the costs of trial. Then there is the cost of many appeals that almost always follow a conviction leading to the sentence of death. When all these factors are put together, the cost of a death penalty case typically exceeds the cost of sending an offender to prison for life. So it is easy to see why states often choose not to seek the death penalty. One accounting, for example, reveals that the state of New Jersey has been spending more than $10 million a year prosecuting death penalty cases that have yet to result in a single execution (Thomas & Brant, 2007).

Organizations opposed to the death penalty are challenging this punishment in court. In 2008, for example, the U.S. Supreme Court

DISCUSS: One of the most serious criticisms of our system of punishment is the high rate of recidivism. Do you think this high rate of repeat offenses means that punishment has little effect? Or maybe that punishment makes the crime problem worse? Explain.

DISCUSS: Ask the class if making executions public would end this practice or make it more common. Why?

DIVERSITY: Controlling for other factors, David Jacobs and Jason Carmichael (2002) note that states with the death penalty have (a) a higher minority presence, (b) greater economic inequality, and (c) stronger conservative values.

DISCUSS: Is the increasing use of lethal injection the "medicalization of death"? Some oppose this practice because it makes suffering less apparent; others call it humane; still others object to all capital punishment.

criminal recidivism (p. 238) later offenses by people previously convicted of crimes

community-based corrections correctional programs operating within society at large rather than behind prison walls

 MAKING THE GRADE

"Community-based corrections" refers to ways of dealing with offenders without sending them to prison.

To increase the power of punishment to deter crime, capital punishment was long carried out in public. Here is a photograph from the last public execution in the United States, with twenty-two-year-old Rainey Bethea standing on the scaffold moments from death in Owensboro, Kentucky, on August 16, 1937. Children as well as adults were in the crowd. Now that the mass media report the story of executions across the country, states carry out capital punishment behind closed doors.

upheld the use of lethal injection against the charge that this procedure amounts to cruel and unusual punishment, which would be unconstitutional (Greenhouse, 2008). There is no indication at present that the United States will end the use of the death penalty, but the trend is away from this type of punishment.

Community-Based Corrections

Prisons keep convicted criminals off the streets, but the evidence suggests that they do little to rehabilitate most offenders. Furthermore, prisons are expensive, costing more than $25,000 per year to support each inmate, in addition to the initial costs of building the facilities.

One alternative to the traditional prison that has been adopted by cities and states across the country is **community-based corrections**, *correctional programs operating within society at large rather than behind prison walls*. Community-based corrections have three main advantages: They reduce costs, reduce overcrowding in prisons, and allow for supervision of convicts while eliminating the hardships of prison life and the stigma that accompanies going to jail. In general, the idea of community-based corrections is not so much to punish as to reform; such programs are therefore usually offered to individuals who have committed less serious offenses and appear to be good prospects for avoiding future criminal violations (Inciardi, 2000).

Probation

One form of community-based corrections is *probation,* a policy permitting a convicted offender to remain in the community under conditions imposed by a court, including regular supervision. Courts may require that a probationer receive counseling, attend a drug treatment program, hold a job, avoid associating with "known criminals," or anything else a judge thinks is appropriate. Typically, a probationer must check in with an officer of the court (the probation officer) on a regular schedule to make sure the guidelines are being followed. Should the probationer fail to live up to the conditions set by the court or commit a new offense, the court may revoke probation and send the offender to jail.

Shock Probation

A related strategy is *shock probation,* a policy by which a judge orders a convicted offender to prison for a short time but then suspends the remainder of the sentence in favor of probation. Shock probation is thus a mix of prison and probation, used to impress on the offender the seriousness of the situation without resorting to full-scale imprisonment. In some cases, shock probation takes place in a special "boot camp" facility where offenders might spend one to three months in a military-style setting intended to teach discipline and respect for authority (Cole & Smith, 2002).

Parole

Parole is a policy of releasing inmates from prison to serve the remainder of their sentences in the local community under the supervision of a parole officer. Although some sentences specifically deny the possibility of parole, most inmates become eligible for parole after serving a certain portion of their sentences. At that time, a parole board evaluates the risks and benefits of the inmate's early release from prison. If parole is granted, the parole board monitors the offender's conduct until the sentence is completed. Should the offender not comply with the conditions of parole or be arrested for another crime, the board can revoke parole and return the offender to prison to complete the sentence.

CRITICAL REVIEW Evaluations of probation and parole are mixed. There is little question that probation and parole programs are much less expensive than conventional imprisonment; they also free up room in prisons for people who commit more serious crimes. Yet research suggests that although probation and shock probation do seem to work for some people, they do not significantly reduce recidivism. Parole is also useful to prison officials as a means to encourage good behavior among inmates. But levels of crime among those released on parole are so high that a number of states have ended their parole programs entirely (Inciardi, 2000).

NOTE: The 1,004 executions between 1977 and 2005, by method: lethal injection, 836; electrocution, 152; gas chamber, 11; hanging, 3; firing squad, 2.

NOTE: In 2002, the Supreme Court banned the execution of mentally retarded offenders as cruel and unusual, noting that 18 of 38 death penalty states already did so and there was a rising national consensus on the issue. The Court specified as mentally retarded IQs that range from 50 to 70 (Stein, 2002).

NOTE: Of 7.0 million U.S. adults in the criminal justice system, 59% are on probation, 21% are in prison, 11% are on parole, and 9% are in local jails (U.S. Bureau of Justice Statistics, 2008).

NOTE: In 2007, the youngest death row inmate was 20; the oldest, 91.

THEN AND NOW: During 2006, 54 women were under sentence of death, up from 38 in 1993.

CONTROVERSY & DEBATE

Violent Crime Is Down—but Why?

DUANE: I'm a criminal justice major, and I want to be a police officer. Crime is a huge problem in America, and police are what keep the crime rate low.

SANDY: I'm a sociology major. As for the crime rate, I'm not sure it's quite that simple. . . .

During the 1980s, crime rates shot upward. Just about everyone lived in fear of violent crime, and in many large cities, the numbers killed and wounded made whole neighborhoods seem like war zones. There seemed to be no solution to the problem.

Yet in the 1990s, serious crime rates began to fall, until by 2000, they were at levels not seen in more than a generation. Why? Researchers point to several reasons:

1. **A reduction in the youth population.** It was noted earlier that young people (particularly males) are responsible for much violent crime. During the 1990s, the population aged fifteen to twenty-four dropped by 5 percent (in part because of the legalization of abortion in 1973).

2. **Changes in policing.** Much of the drop in crime (as well as the earlier rise in crime) took place in large cities. In New York City, the number of murders fell from 2,245 in 1990 to just 500 in 2007 (the lowest figure since the city began keeping reliable records in 1963). Part of the reason for the decline is that the city has adopted a policy of *community policing,* which means that police are concerned not just with making arrests but with preventing crime before it happens. Officers get to know the areas they patrol and stop young men for jaywalking or other minor infractions so they can check them for concealed weapons (the word has gotten around that you can be arrested for carrying a gun). There are also more police at work in large cities. Los Angeles added more than 2,000 police officers in the 1990s, which contributed to its drop in violent crime during that period. Milwaukee assigned more police officers to foot patrols across the city and saw a sharp decline in deadly violence.

3. **More prisoners.** Between 1985 and 2008, the number of inmates in jails and prisons soared from 750,000 to more than 2.3 million. The main reason for this increase is tough laws that demand prison time for certain crimes, such as drug offenses. Mass incarceration has consequences. As one analyst put it, "When you lock up an extra million people, it's got to have some effect on the crime rate" (Franklin Zimring, quoted in Witkin, 1998:31).

4. **A better economy.** The U.S. economy boomed during the 1990s. Unemployment was down, reducing the likelihood that some people would turn to crime out of economic desperation. The logic here is simple: More jobs equal fewer crimes. By the same token, the recent economic downturn may well send crime rates back upward.

5. **The declining drug trade.** Many analysts agree that the most important factor in reducing rates of violent crime was the decline of crack cocaine. Crack came on the scene about 1985, and violence spread as young people—especially in the inner cities and increasingly armed with guns—became part of a booming drug trade. By the early 1990s, however, the popularity of crack began to fall as people saw the damage it was causing to entire communities. This realization, coupled with steady economic improvement and stiffer sentences for drug offenses, helped bring about the turnaround in violent crime.

The current picture looks better relative to what it was a decade or two ago. But one researcher cautions, "It looks better . . . only because the early 1990s were so bad. So let's not fool ourselves into thinking everything is resolved. It's not."

WHAT DO YOU THINK?

1. Do you support the policy of community policing? Why or why not?

2. What do you see as the pros and cons of building more prisons?

3. Which of the factors mentioned here do you think is the most important in crime control? Which is least important? Why?

One reason that crime has gone down is that there are more than 2 million people incarcerated in this country. This has caused severe overcrowding of facilities such as this Maricopa County, Arizona, prison.

Sources: Winship & Berrien (1999), Donahue & Leavitt (2000), Rosenfeld (2002), Liptak (2008), C. Mitchell (2008), and Antlfinger (2009).

Such evaluations point to a sobering truth: The criminal justice system cannot eliminate crime. As the Controversy & Debate box explains, although police, courts, and prisons do affect crime rates, crime and other forms of deviance are not just the acts of "bad people" but reflect the operation of society itself.

CHECK YOUR LEARNING What are three types of community-based corrections? What are their advantages?

Seeing Sociology in Everyday Life

Chapter 9 Deviance

Why do most of us—at least most of the time— obey the rules?

As this chapter has explained, every society is a system of social control that encourages conformity to certain norms and discourages deviance or norm breaking. One way society does this is through the construction of heroes and villains. Heroes, of course, are people we are supposed to "look up to" and use as role models. Villains are people whom we "look down on" and reject their example. Organizations of all types create heroes that serve as guides to everyday behavior. In each case below, who is being made into a hero? Why? What are the values or behaviors that we are encouraged to copy in our own lives?

HINT A society without heroes and villains would be one in which no one cared what people thought or how they acted. Societies create heroes as role models that should inspire us to be more like them. Societies create heroes by emphasizing one aspect of someone's life and ignoring lots of other things. For example, Babe Ruth was a great ball player, but his private life was sometimes less than inspiring. Perhaps this is why the Catholic church never considers anyone a candidate for sainthood until after—usually long after—the person has died.

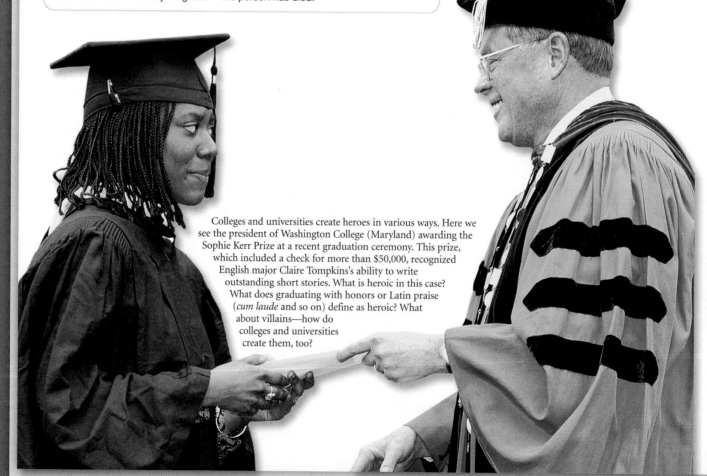

Colleges and universities create heroes in various ways. Here we see the president of Washington College (Maryland) awarding the Sophie Kerr Prize at a recent graduation ceremony. This prize, which included a check for more than $50,000, recognized English major Claire Tompkins's ability to write outstanding short stories. What is heroic in this case? What does graduating with honors or Latin praise (*cum laude* and so on) define as heroic? What about villains—how do colleges and universities create them, too?

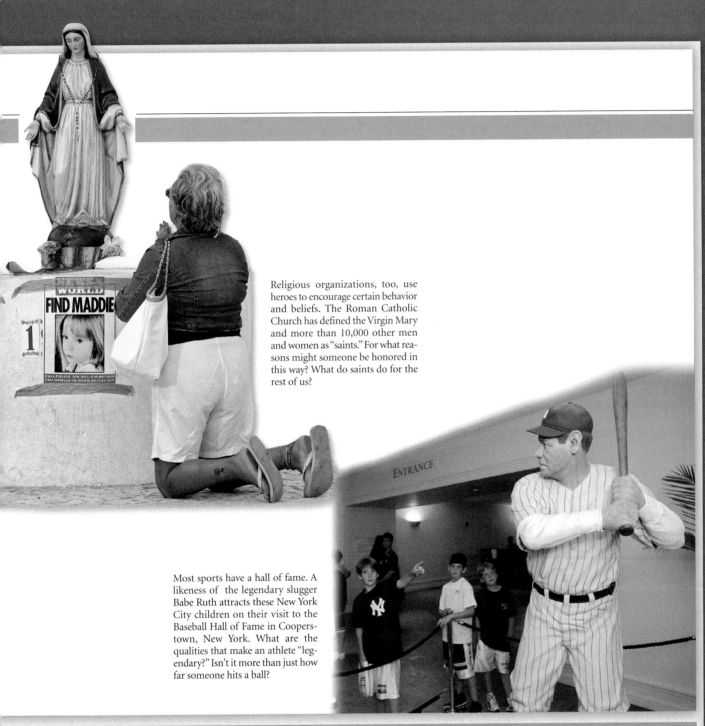

Religious organizations, too, use heroes to encourage certain behavior and beliefs. The Roman Catholic Church has defined the Virgin Mary and more than 10,000 other men and women as "saints." For what reasons might someone be honored in this way? What do saints do for the rest of us?

Most sports have a hall of fame. A likeness of the legendary slugger Babe Ruth attracts these New York City children on their visit to the Baseball Hall of Fame in Cooperstown, New York. What are the qualities that make an athlete "legendary?" Isn't it more than just how far someone hits a ball?

Applying SOCIOLOGY in Everyday Life

1. Do athletic teams, fraternities and sororities, and even people in a college classroom create heroes and villains? Explain how and why.

2. Identity theft is a new type of crime that victimizes as many as 10 million people each year in the United States. Research this phenomenon, and explain how this offense differs from property crime that takes place "on the street." (Consider differences in the crime, the offenders, and the victims.)

3. Watch an episode of any real-action police show such as *Cops*. Based on what you see, how would you profile the people who commit crimes?

MAKING THE GRADE

CHAPTER 9 Deviance

What Is Deviance?

DEVIANCE refers to norm violations ranging from minor infractions, such as bad manners, to major infractions, such as serious violence.

p. 216

deviance (p. 216) the recognized violation of cultural norms

crime (p. 216) the violation of a society's formally enacted criminal law

social control (p. 216) attempts by society to regulate people's thoughts and behavior

criminal justice system (p. 216) the organizations—police, courts, and prison officials—that respond to alleged violations of the law

Theories of Deviance

BIOLOGICAL THEORIES

- focus on individual abnormality
- explain human behavior as the result of biological instincts

Lombroso claimed that criminals have apelike physical traits; later research links criminal behavior to certain body types and genetics.

pp. 216–17

PSYCHOLOGICAL THEORIES

- focus on individual abnormality
- see deviance as the result of "unsuccessful socialization"

Reckless and Dinitz's *containment theory* links delinquency to weak conscience.

pp. 217–18

✓ Biological and psychological theories provide a limited understanding of crime and other deviance because most violations are carried out by people who are normal (p. 218).

SOCIOLOGICAL THEORIES view all behavior—deviance as well as conformity—as products of society. Sociologists point out that

- what is deviant varies from place to place according to cultural norms
- behavior and individuals become deviant as others define them that way
- what and who a society defines as deviant reflect who has and does not have social power

pp. 218–19

Theoretical Analysis of Deviance

The Functions of Deviance: Structural-Functional Analysis

Durkheim claimed that deviance is a normal element of society that

- affirms cultural norms and values
- clarifies moral boundaries
- brings people together
- encourages social change

pp. 219–20

Merton's **strain theory** explains deviance in terms of a society's cultural goals and the means available to achieve them.

Deviant subcultures are discussed by Cloward and Ohlin, Cohen, Miller, and Anderson.

pp. 220–21

labeling theory (p. 222) the idea that deviance and conformity result not so much from what people do as from how others respond to those actions

stigma (p. 223) a powerfully negative label that greatly changes a person's self-concept and social identity

medicalization of deviance (p. 223) the transformation of moral and legal deviance into a medical condition

white-collar crime (p. 226) crime committed by people of high social position in the course of their occupations

corporate crime (p. 227) the illegal actions of a corporation or people acting on its behalf

organized crime (p. 227) a business supplying illegal goods or services

hate crime (p. 228) a criminal act against a person or a person's property by an offender motivated by racial or other bias

Labeling Deviance: Symbolic-Interaction Analysis

Labeling theory claims that deviance depends less on what someone does than on how others react to that behavior. If people respond to primary deviance by stigmatizing a person, secondary deviance and a deviant career may result.

pp. 222–23

The **medicalization of deviance** is the transformation of moral and legal deviance into a medical condition. In practice, this means a change in labels, replacing "good" and "bad" with "sick" and "well."

pp. 223–24

Sutherland's **differential association theory** links deviance to how much others encourage or discourage such behavior.

p. 224

Hirschi's **control theory** states that imagining the possible consequences of deviance often discourages such behavior. People who are well integrated into society are less likely to engage in deviant behavior.

pp. 224–25

See the Applying Theory table on page 228.

Deviance and Inequality: Social-Conflict Analysis

Based on Karl Marx's ideas, social-conflict theory holds that laws and other norms operate to protect the interests of powerful members of any society.

- **White-collar offenses** are committed by people of high social position as part of their jobs. Sutherland claimed that such offenses are rarely prosecuted and are most likely to end up in civil rather than criminal court.
- **Corporate crime** refers to illegal actions by a corporation or people acting on its behalf. Although corporate crimes cause considerable public harm, most cases of corporate crime go unpunished.
- **Organized crime** has a long history in the United States, especially among categories of people with few legitimate opportunities.

pp. 225–28

Deviance, Race, and Gender

- What people consider deviant reflects the relative power and privilege of different categories of people.
- **Hate crimes** are crimes motivated by racial or other bias; they target people with disadvantages based on race, gender, or sexual orientation.
- In the United States and elsewhere, societies control the behavior of women more closely than that of men.

pp. 228–30

What Is Crime?

CRIME is the violation of criminal laws enacted by local, state, or federal governments. There are two major categories of serious crime:

- crimes against the person (violent crime), including murder, aggravated assault, forcible rape, and robbery
- crimes against property (property crime), including burglary, larceny-theft, auto theft, and arson

pp. 230–31

crimes against the person (p. 230) crimes that direct violence or the threat of violence against others; also known as *violent crimes*

crimes against property (p. 230) crimes that involve theft of property belonging to others; also known as *property crimes*

victimless crimes (p. 230) violations of law in which there are no obvious victims

PATTERNS OF CRIME IN THE UNITED STATES

- Official statistics show that arrest rates peak in late adolescence and drop steadily with age.
- About 67% of people arrested for property crimes and 82% of people arrested for violent crimes are male.
- Street crime is more common among people of lower social position. Including white-collar and corporate crime makes class differences in criminality smaller.
- More whites than African Americans are arrested for street crimes. However, African Americans are arrested more often than whites in relation to their population size. Asian Americans have a lower-than-average rate of arrest.
- By world standards, the U.S. crime rate is high.

pp. 231–33

The U.S. Criminal Justice System

Police

The police maintain public order by enforcing the law.

- Police use personal discretion in deciding whether and how to handle a situation.
- Research suggests that police are more likely to make an arrest if the offense is serious, if bystanders are present, or if the suspect is African American or Latino.

pp. 235–36

Courts

Courts rely on an adversarial process in which attorneys—one representing the defendant and one representing the state—present their cases in the presence of a judge who monitors legal procedures.

- In practice, U.S. courts resolve most cases through plea bargaining. Though efficient, this method puts less powerful people at a disadvantage.

p. 236

plea bargaining (p. 236) a legal negotiation in which a prosecutor reduces a charge in exchange for a defendant's guilty plea

retribution (p. 236) an act of moral vengeance by which society makes the offender suffer as much as the suffering caused by the crime

deterrence (p. 237) the attempt to discourage criminality through the use of punishment

rehabilitation (p. 237) a program for reforming the offender to prevent later offenses

societal protection (p. 237) rendering an offender incapable of further offenses temporarily through imprisonment or permanently by execution

criminal recidivism (p. 238) later offenses by people previously convicted of crimes

community-based corrections (p. 240) correctional programs operating within society at large rather than behind prison walls

Punishment

There are four justifications for punishment:

- retribution
- deterrence
- rehabilitation
- societal protection

pp. 236–38

The **death penalty** remains controversial in the United States, the only high-income Western nation that routinely executes serious offenders. The trend is toward fewer executions.

pp. 238–40

Community-based corrections include probation and parole. These programs lower the cost of supervising people convicted of crimes and reduce prison overcrowding but have not been shown to reduce recidivism.

pp. 240–41

See the Summing Up table on page 237.

All societies rank people so that some have far greater opportunities and resources than others. What the specific inequalities are and how great they are vary from place to place and over time.

CHAPTER 10

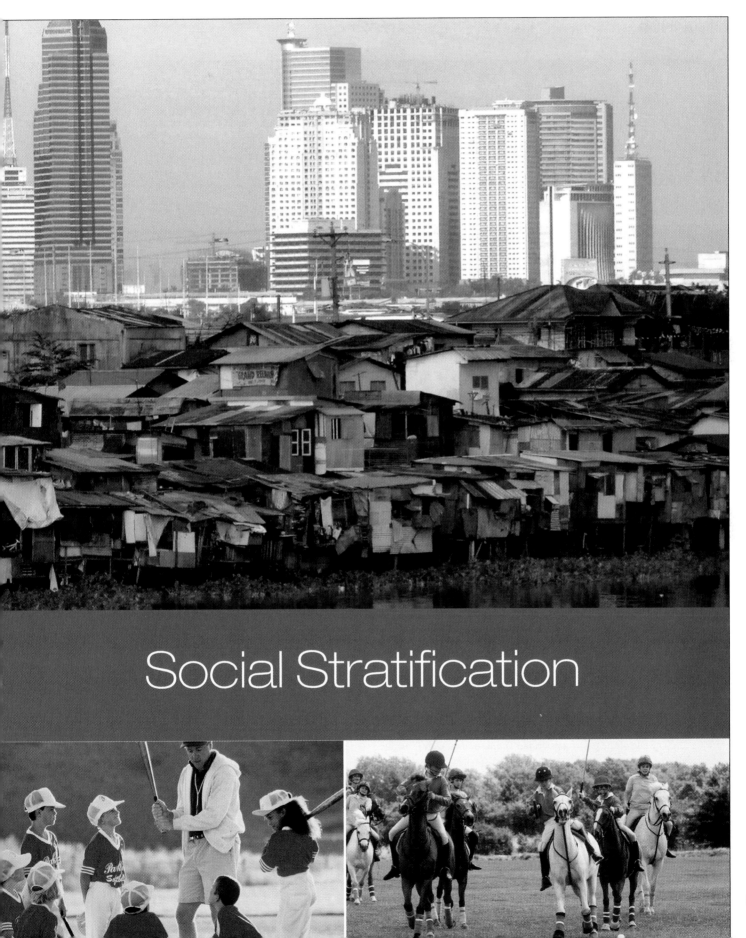

Social Stratification

SUPPLEMENTS: The *Instructor's Manual* contains a detailed outline of Chapter 10, along with supplementary lecture material and additional discussion topics.

Q: "Things are in the saddle, and ride mankind; we do not ride upon the railroad, it rides upon us." Ralph Waldo Emerson

Q: "In this world, a man must be either an anvil or a hammer." Henry Wadsworth Longfellow

DISCUSS: Conforming to the norm "women and children first," 80% of the *Titanic* casualties were men. Perhaps times have changed: In a 1992 *Pittsburgh Post-Gazette* survey, 65% of men said they would not give up their lifeboat seat for a woman or child.

Q: "Every form of social justice tends toward confiscation." Irving Babbitt

CHAPTER OVERVIEW

This chapter introduces the central concept of social stratification, the focus of the next six chapters of the text. Social stratification is important because our social standing affects almost everything about our lives.

On April 10, 1912, the ocean liner *Titanic* slipped away from the docks of Southampton, England, on its maiden voyage across the North Atlantic to New York. A proud symbol of the new industrial age, the towering ship carried 2,300 men, women, and children, some enjoying more luxury than most travelers today could imagine. Poor passengers crowded the lower decks, journeying to what they hoped would be a better life in the United States.

Two days out, the crew received radio warnings of icebergs in the area but paid little notice. Then, near midnight, as the ship steamed swiftly westward, a lookout was stunned to see a massive shape rising out of the dark ocean directly ahead. Moments later, the *Titanic* collided with a huge iceberg, as tall as the ship itself, which split open its side as if the grand vessel were a giant tin can.

Seawater flooded into the ship's lower levels. Within twenty-five minutes of impact, people were rushing for the lifeboats. By 2:00 A.M., the bow was completely submerged, and the stern rose high above the water. Minutes later, all the lights went out. Clinging to the deck, quietly observed by those huddled in lifeboats, hundreds of helpless passengers and crew solemnly passed their final minutes before the ship disappeared into the frigid Atlantic (W. Lord, 1976).

The tragic loss of more than 1,600 lives when the *Titanic* sank made news around the world. Looking back at this terrible accident with a sociological eye, we note that some categories of passengers had much better odds of survival than others. Reflecting that era's traditional ideas about gender, women and children were allowed to board the lifeboats first, with the result that 80 percent of the people who died were men. Class, too, was at work. More than 60 percent of people holding first-class tickets were saved because they were on the upper decks, where warnings were sounded first and lifeboats were accessible. Only 36 percent of the second-class passengers survived, and of the third-class passengers on the lower decks, only 24 percent escaped drowning. On board the *Titanic*, class turned out to mean much more than the quality of accommodations—it was a matter of life or death.

The fate of the passengers on the *Titanic* dramatically illustrates how social inequality affects the way people live and sometimes whether they live at all. This chapter explores the important concept of social stratification. Chapter 11 continues the story by examining social inequality in the United States, and Chapter 12 takes a broader look at how our country fits into a global system of wealth and poverty.

What Is Social Stratification?

For tens of thousands of years, humans lived in small hunting and gathering societies. Although members of these bands might single out one person as swifter, stronger, or more skillful in collecting food, everyone had roughly the same social standing. As societies became more complex—a process detailed in Chapter 4 ("Society")—a major change came about. Societies began to elevate specific categories of people above others, giving some parts of the population more wealth, power, and prestige than others.

Social stratification, *a system by which a society ranks categories of people in a hierarchy,* is based on four important principles:

1. **Social stratification is a trait of society, not simply a reflection of individual differences.** Many of us think of social standing in terms of personal talent and effort, and as a result, we often exaggerate the extent to which we control our own fate. Did a higher percentage of the first-class passengers on the *Titanic* survive because they were better swimmers than second- and third-class passengers? No. They did better because of their privileged position on the ship, which gave them first access to the lifeboats. Similarly, children born into wealthy families are more likely than children born into poverty to enjoy good health, do well in school, succeed in a career, and live a long life. Neither the rich nor the poor created social stratification, yet this system shapes the lives of us all.

2. **Social stratification carries over from generation to generation.** We have only to look at how parents pass their social position

DIVERSITY: Regarding point 4 below, Rytina, Form, and Pease (1970) found that people of higher social position saw the U.S. as a more "open" society. Whites perceived more opportunity than blacks did.

NOTE: The Latin root of "caste," *castus*, means "chaste" or "pure"; its later use (for example, the Portuguese word *casta*) means "race" or "blood."

Q: "Equality of condition is incompatible with civilization." James Fenimore Cooper

GLOBAL: Hope for India's economic development rests on three key elements that should attract foreign investment: widespread use of the English language, a democratic political system, and a legal system suitable for modern business.

Q: "I have used one cake of soap for three months and it is not nearly finished yet." Mahatma Gandhi

Q: "All wealth and power are like clouds passing by." Chinese poet Li Bi

SEEING SOCIOLOGY
in Everyday Life

Are there elements of caste in U.S. society? To what extent do parents pass on their social position to children? What about the idea that there are "women's jobs" and "men's jobs"?

social stratification a system by which a society ranks categories of people in a hierarchy

social mobility a change in position within the social hierarchy

on to their children to see that stratification is a trait of societies rather than individuals. Some individuals, especially in high-income societies, do experience **social mobility**, *a change in position within the social hierarchy.* Social mobility may be upward or downward. We celebrate the achievements of rare individuals such as Christina Aguilera and Michael Jordan, both of whom rose from modest beginnings to fame and fortune. Some people move downward because of business failures, unemployment, or illness. More often people move *horizontally;* they switch from one job to another at about the same social level. The social standing of most people remains much the same over their lifetime.

3. **Social stratification is universal but variable**. Social stratification is found everywhere. Yet *what* is unequal and *how* unequal it is varies from one society to another. In some societies, inequality is mostly a matter of prestige; in others, wealth or power is the key element of difference. In addition, some societies contain more inequality than others.

4. **Social stratification involves not just inequality but beliefs as well**. Any system of inequality not only gives some people more than others but also defines these arrangements as fair. Just as the details of inequality vary, the explanations of *why* people should be unequal differ from society to society.

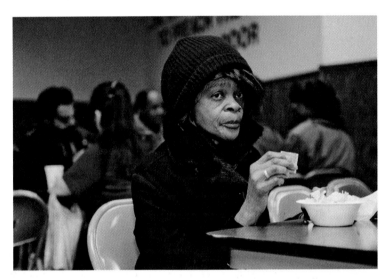

The personal experience of poverty is clear in this photograph of mealtime in a homeless shelter. The main sociological insight is that although we feel the effects of social stratification personally, our social standing is largely the result of the way society (or a world of societies) structures opportunity and reward. To the core of our being, we are all products of social stratification.

Caste and Class Systems

Sociologists distinguish between *closed systems,* which allow for little change in social position, and *open systems,* which permit much more social mobility. Closed systems are called *caste systems,* and more open systems are called *class systems.*

The Caste System

A **caste system** is *social stratification based on ascription, or birth.* A pure caste system is closed because birth alone determines a person's entire future, allowing little or no social mobility based on individual effort. People live out their lives in the rigid categories assigned to them, without the possibility of change for the better or worse.

An Illustration: India

Many of the world's societies, most of them agrarian, are caste systems. In India, for example, much of the population still lives in traditional villages where the caste system persists. The Indian system identifies four major castes (or *varnas,* from a Sanskrit word that means "color"): Brahman, Kshatriya, Vaishya, and Sudra. On the local level, each of these is composed of hundreds of subcaste groups (*jatis*).

From birth, a caste system determines the direction of a person's life. First, with the exception of farming, which is open to everyone, families in each caste perform one type of work, as priests, soldiers, barbers, leather workers, street sweepers, and so on.

Second, a caste system demands that people marry others of the same ranking. If people were to enter into "mixed" marriages with members of other castes, what rank would their children hold? Sociologists call this pattern of marrying within a social category *endogamous* marriage (*endo-* stems from the Greek word for "within"). According to tradition—this practice is now rare today and it is found only in remote rural areas—Indian parents select their children's future marriage partners, often before the children reach their teens.

Third, caste guides everyday life by keeping people in the company of "their own kind." Norms reinforce this practice by teaching, for example, that a "purer" person of a higher caste is "polluted" by contact with someone of lower standing.

Fourth, caste systems rest on powerful cultural beliefs. Indian culture is built on the Hindu tradition that doing the caste's life work and accepting an arranged marriage are moral duties.

SOCIAL SURVEY: "How important for getting ahead in life is ambition?" (GSS 1987, N = 1,285; NORC, 2008)

"Essential"	41.6%	"Not very important"	0.7%
"Very important"	44.9%	"Not important at all"	0.2%
"Fairly important"	10.4%	"Don't know"/No response	2.2%

DISCUSS: Today's class system subjects women to caste: Women should perform traditional tasks as a moral duty, with men more often financially rewarded for their efforts. Is this why most chefs are men who work for income, while most household cooks are women performing a household duty?

Q: "Whether we like to admit it or not, a society which encourages the full flowering of individual liberty is, and can only be, a stratified society." Andrew Hacker

Caste and Class Systems

caste system (p. 249) social stratification based on ascription, or birth

class system social stratification based on both birth and individual achievement

meritocracy social stratification based on personal merit

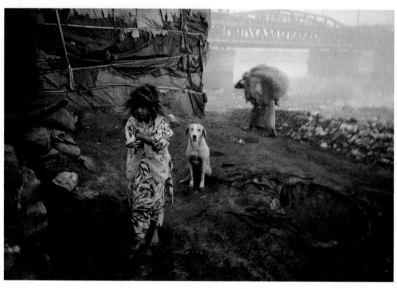

In rural India, the traditional caste system still shapes people's lives. This girl is a member of the "untouchables," a category below the four basic castes. She and her family are clothes washers, people who clean material "polluted" by blood or human waste. Such work is defined as unclean for people of higher caste position.

Caste and Agrarian Life

Caste systems are typical of agrarian societies because agriculture demands a lifelong routine of hard work. By teaching a sense of moral duty, a caste system ensures that people are disciplined for a lifetime of work and are willing to perform the same jobs as their parents. Thus the caste system has hung on in rural areas of India some seventy years after being formally outlawed. Seeing Sociology in the News on pages 252–53 provides another example of caste in the Middle Eastern nation of Yemen.

Another country long dominated by caste is South Africa, although the system of *apartheid,* or separation of the races, is no longer legal and is now in decline. The Thinking Globally box takes a closer look.

The Class System

Because a modern economy must attract people to work in many occupations other than farming, it depends on developing people's talents in diverse fields. This gives rise to a **class system**, *social stratification based on both birth and individual achievement.*

Class systems are more open than caste systems, so people who gain schooling and skills may experience social mobility. As a result, class distinctions become blurred, and even blood relatives may have different social standings. Categorizing people according to their color, sex, or social background comes to be seen as wrong in modern societies as all people gain political rights and, in principle, equal standing before the law. In addition, work is no longer fixed at birth but involves some personal choice. Greater individuality also translates into more freedom in selecting a marriage partner.

Meritocracy

The concept of **meritocracy** refers to *social stratification based on personal merit.* Because industrial societies need to develop a broad range of abilities beyond farming, stratification is based not just on the accident of birth but also on *merit* (from a Latin word meaning "earned"), which includes a person's knowledge, abilities, and effort. A rough measure of merit is a person's job and how well it is done. To increase meritocracy, industrial societies expand equality of opportunity and teach people to expect unequal rewards based on individual performance.

In a pure meritocracy, which has never existed, social position would depend entirely on a person's ability and effort. Such a system would have ongoing social mobility, blurring social categories as individuals continuously move up or down in the system, depending on their latest performance.

Caste societies define merit in terms of loyalty to the system—that is, dutifully performing whatever job comes with a person's birth. Caste systems waste human potential, but they are very orderly. A need for some amount of order is one reason industrial and postindustrial societies keep some elements of caste—such as letting wealth pass from generation to generation—rather than becoming complete meritocracies. A pure meritocracy would weaken families and other social groupings. After all, economic performance is not everything: Would we want to evaluate our family members solely on how successful they are in their jobs outside the home? Probably not. Class systems in industrial societies develop some meritocracy to promote productivity and efficiency, but they keep caste elements, such as family, to maintain order and social unity.

Status Consistency

Status consistency is *the degree of uniformity in a person's social standing across various dimensions of social inequality.* A caste system has limited social mobility and high status consistency, so the typical person has the same relative ranking with regard to wealth, power, and prestige. The greater mobility of class systems produces less status

SEEING SOCIOLOGY
in Everyday Life

How much of your social position is due to merit (personal ability and effort), and how much is due to caste (passed on from your parents)?

status consistency the degree of uniformity in a person's social standing across various dimensions of social inequality

THINKING GLOBALLY

Race as Caste: A Report from South Africa

JEROME: Wow. I've been reading about racial caste in South Africa. I'm glad that's history.

REGGIE: But racial inequality is far from over. . . .

At the southern tip of the African continent lies South Africa, a country about the size of Alaska with a population of more than 48 million. For 300 years, the native Africans who lived there were ruled by white people, first by the Dutch traders and farmers who settled there in the mid-seventeenth century and then by the British, who colonized the area early in the nineteenth century. By the early 1900s, the British had taken over the entire country, naming it the Union of South Africa.

In 1961, the nation declared its independence from Britain, calling itself the Republic of South Africa, but freedom for the black majority was still decades away. To ensure their political control over the black population, whites instituted the policy of *apartheid*, or racial separation. Apartheid, written into law in 1948, denied blacks national citizenship, ownership of land, and any voice in the nation's government. As a lower caste, blacks received little schooling and performed menial, low-paying jobs. White people with even average wealth had at least one black household servant.

The members of the white minority claimed that apartheid protected their cultural traditions from the influence of people they considered inferior. When blacks resisted apartheid, whites used brutal military repression to maintain their power. Even so, steady resistance—especially from younger blacks,

who demanded a political voice and economic opportunity—gradually forced the country to change. Criticism from other industrial nations added to the pressure. By the mid-1980s, the tide began to turn as the South African government granted limited political rights to people of mixed race and Asian ancestry. Next came the right of all people to form labor unions, to enter occupations once limited to whites, and to own property. Officials also repealed apartheid laws that separated the races in public places.

The pace of change increased in 1990 with the release from prison of Nelson Mandela, who led the fight against apartheid. In 1994, the first national election open to all races made Mandela president, ending centuries of white minority rule.

Despite this dramatic political change—and strong economic growth during the last decade—social stratification in South Africa is still based on race. Even with the right to own property, one-fourth of black South Africans

have no work, and half the population lives below the poverty line. The worst off are some 7 million *ukuhleleleka*, which means "marginal people" in the Xhosa language. Soweto-by-the-Sea may sound like a summer getaway, but this cluster of townships is home to thousands of people who live crammed into shacks made of packing crates, corrugated metal, cardboard, and other discarded materials. There is no electricity for lights or refrigeration. Without plumbing, people use buckets to haul sewerage. The community's women line up to take a turn at a single water tap that serves more than 1,000 people. Jobs are hard to come by, and those who do find work are lucky to earn $250 a month.

South Africa's current president, Jacob Zuma, who was elected in 2009, leads a nation still crippled by its history of racial caste. Tourism is up and holds the promise of an economic boom in years to come, but the country can break from the past only by providing real opportunity to all its people.

WHAT DO YOU THINK?

1. How has race been a form of caste in South Africa?

2. Although apartheid is no longer law, why does racial inequality continue to shape South African society?

3. Does race operate as an element of caste in the United States? Explain your answer.

Sources: Mabry & Masland (1999), Murphy (2002), and Perry (2009).

consistency, so people are ranked higher on some dimensions of social standing and lower on others. In the United States, for example, most college professors with advanced academic degrees enjoy high social prestige but earn only modest incomes. Low status consistency means that it is harder to define people's social position. Therefore, *classes* are much harder to define than *castes*.

Caste and Class: The United Kingdom

The mix of caste and meritocracy in class systems is well illustrated by the United Kingdom (Great Britain—consisting of England, Wales, and Scotland—and Northern Ireland), an industrial nation with a long agrarian history.

Q: "It is easy to despise what you cannot get." Aesop

Q: "All the animals are equal, but some are more equal than others." George Orwell, *Animal Farm*

GLOBAL: The average black South African consumes about 10% of what the typical white person does; life expectancy for blacks is 58 years, compared to 70 years for whites.

Q: "If you think you can, you can. If you think you can't, you're right." Mary Kay Ash

NOTE: Leftists criticized capitalism for supporting the apartheid regime; defenders of capitalism claimed that this economic system is a progressive force indifferent to all castelike factors. (J. P. Morgan once said he might "only sail with a gentleman," but he was happy to do business with anyone.)

Seeing SOCIOLOGY in the NEWS

The New York Times

Languishing at the Bottom of Yemen's Ladder

By ROBERT F. WORTH
February 27, 2008

By day, they sweep the streets of the Old City, ragged, dark-skinned men in orange jump suits. By night, they retreat to fetid slums on the edge of town.

They are known as "Al Akhdam"—the servants. Set apart by their African features, they form a kind of hereditary caste at the very bottom of Yemen's social ladder.

Degrading myths pursue them: they eat their own dead, and their women are all prostitutes. Worst of all, they are reviled as outsiders in their own country, descendants of an Ethiopian army that is said to have crossed the Red Sea to oppress Yemen before the arrival of Islam.

"We are ready to work, but people say we are good for nothing but servants; they will not accept us," said Ali Izzil Muhammad Obaid, a 20-year-old man who lives in a filthy Akhdam shantytown on the edge of this capital. "So we have no hope."

In fact, the Akhdam—who prefer to be known as "Al Muhamasheen," or the marginalized ones—

may have been in this southern corner of the Arabian Peninsula for as long as anyone, and their ethnic origins are unclear. Their debased status is a remnant of Yemen's old social hierarchy, which collapsed after the 1962 revolution struck down the thousand-year-old Imamate.

But where Yemen's other hereditary social classes, the sayyids and the judges and the sheiks, and even the lower orders like butchers and iron-workers, slowly dissolved, the Akhdam retained their separate position. There are more than a million of them among Yemen's fast-growing population of 22 million, concentrated in segregated slums in the major cities.

"All the doors are closed to us except sweeping streets and begging," Mr. Obaid said. "We are surviving, but we are not living."

The Akhdam have not been offered the kind of affirmative action programs India's government has used to improve the lot of the Dalits, or untouchables, there. In part, that is because Yemen never had a formal caste system like India's.

As a result, the Akhdam have languished at the

margins of society, suffering a persistent discrimination that flouts the egalitarian maxims of the Yemeni state.

Even the recent waves of immigrants from Ethiopia and Somalia, many of them desperately poor, have fared better than the Akhdam, and do not share their stigma.

The Akhdam who work as street sweepers, for instance, are rarely granted contracts even after decades of work, despite the fact that all Yemeni civil servants are supposed to be granted contracts after six months, said Suha Bashren, a relief official with Oxfam here. They receive no benefits, and almost no time off.

"If supervisors want to dismiss them, they can do that," said Ali Abdullah Saeed Hawdal, who started working as a street sweeper in 1968. "The supervisors use violence against them with no fear of penalties. They treat them as people with no rights."

The living conditions of the Akhdam are appalling. . . . In one Akhdam shantytown on the edge of Sana, more than 7,000 people live crammed into a stinking warren of low concrete

---

Aristocratic England

In the Middle Ages, England had a castelike system of aristocracy. The aristocracy included the leading members of the church, who were thought to speak with the authority of God. Some clergy were local priests who were not members of the aristocracy and who lived simple lives. But the highest church officials lived in palaces and presided over an organization that owned much land, which was the major source of wealth. Church leaders, typically referred to as the *first estate* in France and other European countries, also had a great deal of power to shape the political events of the day.

The rest of the aristocracy, which in France and other European countries was known as the *second estate,* was a hereditary nobility that made up barely 5 percent of the population. The royal family—the king and queen at the top of the power structure—as well as lesser nobles (including several hundred families headed by men titled as dukes, earls, and barons) together owned most of the nation's land. Most of the men and women within the aristocracy were wealthy due to their holdings of land, and they had many servants for their homes as well as ordinary farmers to work their fields. With all their work done for them by others, members of the aristocracy had no occupation and came to believe that engaging in a trade or any other work for income was beneath them. Aristocrats used their leisure time to develop skills in horseback riding and warfare and to cultivate refined tastes in art, music, and literature.

To prevent their vast landholdings from being divided by heirs when they died, aristocrats devised the law of *primogeniture* (from the Latin meaning "firstborn"), which required that all property pass to the oldest son or other male relation. Younger sons had to find other means of support. Some of these men became leaders in the church—where they would live as well as they were used to—and helped tie together the church and the state by having members of the same families running both. Other younger sons within the aristocracy became military officers or judges or took up other professions considered honorable for gentlemen. In an age when no woman could inherit her father's property and few women had the opportunity to earn a living on their own, a noble daughter depended for her security on marrying well.

Below the high clergy and the rest of the aristocracy, the vast majority of men and women were simply called *commoners* or, in France and other European countries, the *third estate*. Most commoners were serfs working land owned by nobles or the church. Unlike members of the aristocracy, most commoners had little schooling and were illiterate.

As the Industrial Revolution expanded England's economy, some commoners living in cities made lots of money and were able to challenge the nobility. More emphasis on meritocracy, the growing importance of money, and the expansion of schooling and legal rights eventually blurred the difference between aristocrats and commoners and gave rise to a class system.

blocks next to a mountain of trash. Young children, many of them barefoot, run through narrow, muddy lanes full of human waste and garbage.

A young woman named Nouria Abdullah stood outside the tiny cubicle—perhaps 6 feet by 8 feet, with a ceiling too low to allow her to stand up—where she lives with her husband and six children. Inside, a thin plastic sheet covered a dirt floor. A small plastic mirror hung on the wall, and a single filthy pillow lay in the corner.

Nearby, a single latrine, in a room approximately 3 feet by 3 feet, serves about 50 people. The residents must carry water in plastic jugs from a tank on the edge of the slum, supplied by a charity group....

Ms. Abdullah said she and her family brought in no more than 1,000 Yemeni riyals a week, about $5. She begs for change, while her husband, Muhammad, gathers metal and electrical components from trash heaps and sells them.

Like most people in the shantytown, they have no documents, and they do not know how old they are. "We are living like animals," Ms. Abdullah said. "We cook and sleep and live in the same room. We need other shelters."

When the winter rains come, the houses are flooded, she said. On the cold days in winter, the family burns trash to stay warm.

Richard Bramble, a British doctor who works in a charity-sponsored clinic inside the shantytown, said half of the deaths there over the past year were of children under the age of 5, and one-quarter were in the first month of life....

Part of the problem, many members of the community say, is that most of the Akhdam have internalized their low status and do not try to better themselves, find real jobs or seek an education....

"They do not even push their children to become soldiers," said Muhammad Abdu Ali, the director of the medical clinic in the shantytown and one of the Akhdam. "They have given up on changing their situation." . . .

Mr. Hawdal pointed proudly to a plaque on the wall commemorating his long service as a sweeper. He has sent all of his children to school, unlike most of the Akhdam, and one of them made it as far as ninth grade.

But Mr. Hawdal acknowledged sadly that all of his children had since dropped out. He was running out of money, he said. But that was not the only reason.

"They had no hope of doing anything except street sweeping," he said.

WHAT DO YOU THINK?

1. Castes are set apart with cues visible in everyday life. What indicators of low-caste standing identify the people known as Al Akhdam?

2. What common stereotypes are used by people in Yemen to justify marginalizing Al Akhdam?

3. What, if anything, would you suggest the government do to assist the people known as Al Akhdam? Explain.

Perhaps it is a sign of the times that these days, traditional titles are put up for sale by aristocrats who need money. In 1996, for example, Earl Spencer—the brother of the late Princess Diana—sold one of his titles, Lord of Wimbledon, to raise the $300,000 he needed to redo the plumbing in one of his large homes (McKee, 1996).

The United Kingdom Today

The United Kingdom has a class system, but caste elements from England's aristocratic past are still evident. A small number of British families still hold considerable inherited wealth and enjoy high prestige, schooling at excellent universities, and substantial political influence. A traditional monarch, Queen Elizabeth II, is the United Kingdom's head of state, and Parliament's House of Lords is composed of "peers," about half of whom are aristocrats of noble birth. However, control of government has passed to the House of Commons, where the prime minister and other leaders reach their positions by achievement—winning an election—rather than by birth.

Lower in the class hierarchy, roughly one-fourth of the British people form the middle class. Many earn comfortable incomes from professions and business and are likely to have investments in the form of stocks and bonds. Below the middle class, perhaps half of all Britons consider themselves "working-class," earning modest incomes through manual labor. The remaining one-fourth of the British people make up the lower class, the poor who lack steady work or who work full time but are paid too little to live comfortably. Most lower-class Britons live in the nation's northern and western regions, which have been further impoverished by the closings of mines and factories.

The British mix of caste elements and meritocracy has produced a highly stratified society with some opportunity to move upward or downward, much the same as exists in the United States (Long & Ferrie, 2007). One result of centuries of aristocracy in the United Kingdom is great importance attached to linguistic accent. Distinctive patterns of speech develop in any society when people are set off from one another over several generations. People in the United States treat accent as a clue to where a person lives or grew up (we can easily identify a midwestern "twang" or a southern "drawl"). In the United Kingdom, however, accent is a mark of social class, with upper-class people speaking "the King's English" but most people speaking "like commoners." So different are these two accents that the British seem to be, as the saying goes, "a single people divided by a common language."

Another Example: Japan

Social stratification in Japan also mixes caste and meritocracy. Japan is both the world's oldest continuously operating monarchy and a modern society where wealth follows individual achievement.

Aristocratic Japan

By the fifth century C.E., Japan was an agrarian society with a rigid caste system, ruled by an imperial family, containing both aristocrats

NOTE: In 2009, top UK earner J. K. Rowling was worth about $1 billion, about twice as much as Queen Elizabeth.

NOTE: After September 11, 2001, Rudy Giuliani was knighted with the title "Knight Commander of the Most Excellent Order of the British Empire." Because he is not a British citizen, he is not permitted to use the title "Sir."

THEN AND NOW: Share of Britons who think the country would be worse off without the monarchy: 1984, 77%; 2007, 76% (Populus, 2007).

GLOBAL: The status or honor element of Japanese society is still evident in young people aspiring to join *ichi-ryu* ("first-class") corporations even if their income would be greater working elsewhere.

SEEING SOCIOLOGY
in Everyday Life

Are there any aristocratic elements of U.S. society? What are they?

SEEING SOCIOLOGY
in Everyday Life

In modern Japan, notice how elements of meritocracy (such as people going to school in order to get a better job) mix with elements of caste (such as the continuing importance of people's social background and differences in opportunities for women and men).

Following the centuries-old practice among aristocratic men in England, Prince Harry completed military training as part of his studies at Eton. He is part of a royal family that traces its ancestry back more than a thousand years—an element of caste that remains in the British class system.

and commoners. The emperor ruled by divine right (meaning that he claimed that God intended him to rule), and his military leader (*shogun*) enforced the emperor's rule with the help of regional nobles or warlords.

Below the nobility were the *samurai*, a warrior caste whose name means "to serve." This second rank of Japanese society was made up of soldiers who learned martial arts and who lived by a code of honor based on absolute loyalty to their leaders.

As in Great Britain, most people in Japan at this time in history were commoners who worked very hard to live from day to day. Unlike their European counterparts, however, Japanese commoners were not lowest in rank. At the bottom were the *burakumin*, or "outcasts," looked down on by both lord and commoner. Like the lowest-caste groups in India, these outcasts lived apart from others, performed the most distasteful work, and could not change their social standing.

Modern Japan

By the 1860s (the time of the Civil War in the United States), the nobles realized that Japan's traditional caste system would prevent the country from entering the modern industrial era. Besides, as in Britain, some nobles were happy to have their children marry wealthy commoners who had more money than they did. As Japan opened up to the larger world, the traditional caste system weakened. In 1871, the Japanese legally banned the social category of *burakumin*, although some people still looked down on those whose ancestors held this rank. After Japan's defeat in World War II, the nobles lost their privileges, so only the emperor remains as a symbol of Japan's traditions, but he has little real power.

Social stratification in Japan is very different from the rigid caste system of centuries ago. Today, Japanese society consists of "upper," "upper-middle," "lower-middle," and "lower" classes. The exact lines between these classes are unclear to most Japanese, and many people do move between classes over time. But because Japanese culture tends to respect tradition, family background is never far from the surface when sizing up someone's social standing. Officially, everyone is equal before the law, but in reality, many people still look at one another through the centuries-old lens of caste.

Finally, traditional ideas about gender continue to shape Japanese society. Legally, the two sexes are equal, but men dominate women in many ways. Because Japanese parents are more likely to send sons than daughters to college, there is a significant gender gap in education. With the recent economic downturn in Japan, many more women have entered the labor force. But most working women fill lower-level support positions in the corporate world, only rarely assuming leadership roles. In short, individual achievement in Japan's modern class system operates in the shadow of centuries of traditional male privilege (Norbeck, 1983; Brinton, 1988; H. W. French, 2002).

Classless Societies? The Former Soviet Union

Nowhere in the world do we find a society without some degree of social inequality. Yet some nations have claimed to be classless.

The Second Russian Revolution

The Union of Soviet Socialist Republics (USSR), which rivaled the United States as a military superpower in the mid- to late twentieth century, was born out of a revolution in Russia in 1917. The Russian Revolution ended the feudal aristocracy in which a nobility ruled the country and transferred farms, factories, and other productive property from private ownership to a new centralized state government.

The Russian Revolution was guided by the ideas of Karl Marx, who believed that private ownership of productive property was the basis of social classes (see Chapter 4, "Society"). When the state took control of the economy, Soviet officials boasted that they had created the first modern classless society.

Critics, however, pointed out that based on their jobs, the Soviet people were actually stratified into four unequal categories. At the top

GLOBAL: After World War II, General Douglas MacArthur represented the U.S. as the ruler of occupied Japan. MacArthur modeled the new Japanese government after that of the U.S. and advanced the rights and opportunities of women; he allowed the emperor to remain as a means of stabilizing the otherwise decimated society.

GLOBAL: Per capita income in Japan is below that in the U.S. (see Table 12–1 on page 307); to the observer, however, Japan seems a more middle-class society. There is little

of the striking urban poverty found in the U.S.; even so, the recent emergence of homelessness has challenged the positive view many Japanese have of their society.

DISCUSS: In the "Modern Japan" section, the text states that Japan's traditional caste system would prevent the country from becoming industrialized. Ask students to explain why.

structural social mobility a shift in the social position of large numbers of people due more to changes in society itself than to individual efforts

were high government officials, known as *apparatchiks*. Next came the Soviet intelligentsia, including lower government officials, college professors, scientists, physicians, and engineers. Below them were manual workers and, at the lowest level, the rural peasantry.

In reality, the Soviet Union was not classless at all. But putting factories, farms, colleges, and hospitals under state control did create more economic equality (although with sharp differences in power) than in capitalist societies such as the United States.

The Modern Russian Federation

In 1985, Mikhail Gorbachev came to power in the Soviet Union with a new economic program known as *perestroika* ("restructuring"). Gorbachev saw that although the Soviet system had reduced economic inequality, living standards were far behind those of other industrial nations. He tried to generate economic growth by reducing the inefficient centralized control of the economy.

Gorbachev's economic reforms turned into one of the most dramatic social movements in history. People in the Soviet Union and in other socialist countries of Eastern Europe blamed their poverty and their lack of basic freedoms on the repressive ruling class of Communist party officials. Beginning in 1989, people throughout Eastern Europe toppled their socialist governments, and at the end of 1991, the Soviet Union itself collapsed, with its largest republic remaking itself as the Russian Federation.

The Soviet Union's story shows that social inequality involves more than economic resources. Soviet society did not have the extremes of wealth and poverty found in the United Kingdom, Japan, and the United States. But an elite class existed all the same, based on political power rather than wealth.

What about social mobility in so-called classless societies? During the twentieth century, there was as much upward social mobility in the Soviet Union as in the United States. Rapidly expanding industry and government drew many poor rural peasants into factories and offices. This trend illustrates what sociologists call **structural social mobility**, *a shift in the social position of large numbers of people due more to changes in society itself than to individual efforts.*

One of the major events of the twentieth century was the socialist revolution in Russia, which led to the creation of the Soviet Union. Following the ideas of Karl Marx, the popular uprising overthrew a feudal aristocracy, as depicted in the 1920 painting *Bolshevik* by Boris Mikhailovich Kustodiev.

November 24, Odessa, Ukraine. The first snow of our voyage flies over the decks as our ship docks at Odessa, the former Soviet Union's southernmost port on the Black Sea. A short distance away, we gaze up the Potemkin Steps, the steep stairway up to the city, where bloody violence that eventually led to the Russian Revolution took place. It has been several years since our last visit, and much has changed; in fact, the Soviet Union itself has collapsed. Has life improved? For some people, certainly: There are now chic boutiques where well-dressed shoppers buy fine wines, designer clothes, and imported perfumes. But for most people, life seems much worse. Flea markets line the curbs as families sell their home furnishings. When meat costs $4 a pound and the average person earns about $30 a month, people become desperate. Even the city has to save money by turning off street lights after 8:00 p.m. The spirits of most people seem as dim as Odessa's streets.

During the 1990s, the forces of structural social mobility in the new Russian Federation turned downward. One indicator is that the average life span for Russian men dropped by eight years and for women by two years. Many factors are involved in this decline, including Russia's poor health care system, but the Russian people clearly have suffered in the turbulent period of economic change that began in 1991 (Gerber & Hout, 1998; Mason, 2003).

The hope was that in the long run, closing inefficient state industries would improve the nation's economic performance. The economy has expanded, but for many Russians, living standards have fallen, and millions face hard times. The few people who made huge

GLOBAL: The Soviet satellite states in Eastern Europe included the Baltic nations of Estonia, Latvia, and Lithuania (all three formally annexed to the USSR), as well as Poland, East Germany, Czechoslovakia, Romania, Hungary, and Bulgaria. Between 1989 and 1991, all established political independence.

NOTE: Estimates placed the fortune of the Soviet Communist party, dissolved in August 1991, at roughly $175 billion.

Q: "Soviet society follows the lead of Lenin toward becoming a classless, communist society." USSR high school textbook

NOTE: Popular Russian joke of the mid-1990s as capitalism expanded: "All the good things the Communists told us about communism turned out to be lies. And all the bad things they told us about capitalism turned out to be true."

fortunes have seen much of their new wealth vanish in the recent recession. This fact, along with more government control over the Russian economy, has caused economic inequality to decline. At the same time, however, many people wonder what a return to a more socialist society will mean for their living standards and political freedoms (Zuckerman, 2006; Wendle, 2009).

China: Emerging Social Classes

Sweeping political and economic change has affected not just the former Soviet Union but also the People's Republic of China. After the Communist revolution in 1949, the state took control of all farms, factories, and other productive property. Communist party leader

By allowing a market economy to expand, especially in the coastal regions, China has experienced remarkable economic growth. The gambling industry in Macao now rivals that of Las Vegas.

Mao Zedong declared all types of work to be equally important, so officially, social classes no longer existed.

The new program greatly reduced economic inequality. But as in the Soviet Union, social differences remained. The country was ruled by a political elite with enormous power and considerable privilege; below them were managers of large factories as well as skilled professionals; next came industrial workers; at the bottom were rural peasants, who were not even allowed to leave their villages and migrate to cities.

Further economic change came in 1978 when Mao died and Deng Xiaoping became China's leader. The state gradually loosened its hold on the economy, allowing a new class of business owners to emerge. Communist party leaders remain in control of the country, and some have prospered as they have joined the ranks of the small but wealthy elite who control new privately run industries. Much of this new economic growth has been concentrated in cities, especially in coastal areas, where living standards have soared far above those in China's rural interior (United Nations, 2008).

Since the late 1990s, the booming cities along China's coast have become home to many thousands of people made rich by the expanding economy. In addition, these cities have attracted more than 100 million young migrants from rural areas in search of better jobs and a better life. Many more have wanted to move to the booming cities, but the government still restricts movement, which has the effect of slowing upward social mobility. For those who have been able to move, the jobs that are available are generally better than the work that people knew before. But many of these new jobs are dangerous, and most pay wages that barely meet the higher costs of living in the city, so that the majority of the migrants remain poor. To make matters worse, the weakening global economy has caused many Chinese factories to lay off workers or even to shut down. As a result, beginning in 2008, some people began to migrate from cities back to the countryside—a case of downward social mobility (Atlas, 2007; Wu & Treiman, 2007; Chang, 2008; Powell, 2008).

A new category in China's social hierarchy consists of the *hai gui*, a term derived from words meaning "returned from overseas" or "sea turtles." The ranks of the "sea turtles" are increasing by tens of thousands each year as young women and men return from education in other countries, in many cases from college and university campuses in the United States. These young people, most of whom were from privileged families to begin with, typically return to China to find many opportunities and soon become very influential (Liu & Hewitt, 2008).

In sum, China displays a new and emerging class system that is a mix of the old political hierarchy and a new business hierarchy. Economic inequality in China has increased, and as Figure 10–1 shows, it is now about the same as in the United States. With so much

ideology cultural beliefs that justify particular social arrangements, including patterns of inequality

Davis-Moore thesis the functional analysis claiming that social stratification has beneficial consequences for the operation of society

change in China, that country's social stratification is likely to remain dynamic for some time to come (Bian, 2002).

Ideology: The Power behind Stratification

How do societies persist without sharing resources more equally? The highly stratified British aristocracy and the caste system in Japan each survived for centuries, and for 2,000 years, people in India accepted the idea that they should be privileged or poor based on the accident of birth.

A major reason that social hierarchies endure is **ideology**, *cultural beliefs that justify particular social arrangements, including patterns of inequality*. A belief—for example, the idea that rich people are smart and poor people are lazy—is ideological to the extent that it supports inequality by defining it as fair.

Plato and Marx on Ideology

According to the ancient Greek philosopher Plato (427–347 B.C.E.), every culture considers some type of inequality just. Although Karl Marx understood this, he was far more critical of inequality than Plato. Marx criticized capitalist societies for defending wealth and power in the hands of a few as "a law of the marketplace." Capitalist law, he continued, defines the right to own property and ensures that money stays within the same families from one generation to the next. In short, Marx concluded, culture and institutions combine to support a society's elite, which is why established hierarchies last such a long time.

Historical Patterns of Ideology

Ideology changes along with a society's economy and technology. Because agrarian societies depend on most people's lifelong labor, they develop caste systems that make carrying out the duties of a person's social position or "station" a moral responsibility. With the rise of industrial capitalism, an ideology of meritocracy emerges, defining wealth and power as prizes to be won by the individuals who perform the best. This change means that the poor—often given charity under feudalism—come to be looked down on as personally undeserving. This harsh view is found in the ideas of the early sociologist Herbert Spencer, as explained in the Thinking About Diversity box on page 258.

History shows how difficult it is to change social stratification. However, challenges to the status quo always arise. The traditional idea that "a woman's place is in the home," for example, has given way to increased economic opportunities for women in many societies today. The continuing progress toward racial equality in South Africa reflects widespread rejection of the ideology of apartheid.

Driving to work in São Paulo, Brazil, Fabio Campos passes both gated mansions of the very rich and rundown shacks of the very poor.

On her way to work in Stockholm, Sweden, Sylvia Arnbjörg passes through mostly middle-class neighborhoods.

Global Snapshot

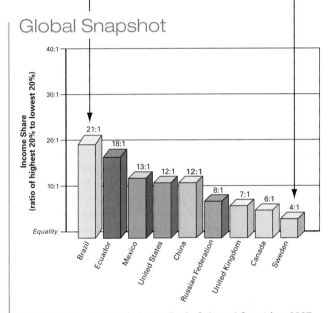

FIGURE 10–1 Economic Inequality in Selected Countries, 2007

Many low- and middle-income countries have greater economic inequality than the United States. But the United States has more economic inequality than most high-income nations.

Sources: U.S. Census Bureau (2008) and World Bank (2008).

The Functions of Social Stratification

Why does social stratification exist at all? One answer, consistent with the structural-functional approach, is that social inequality plays a vital part in the smooth operation of society. This argument was set forth more than sixty years ago by Kingsley Davis and Wilbert Moore (1945).

The Davis-Moore Thesis

The **Davis-Moore thesis** states that *social stratification has beneficial consequences for the operation of society*. How else, ask Davis and Moore, can we explain the fact that some form of social stratification has been found in every society?

Davis and Moore note that modern societies have hundreds of occupational positions of varying importance. Certain jobs—say, washing windows, cutting grass, or answering a telephone—are fairly easy and can be performed by almost anyone. Other jobs—such as designing new generations of computers or transplanting human

DIVERSITY: Justifications for inequality are embedded in gender. Among men, inequality is viewed more in terms of (classlike) individual merit; the subordination of women has been defended on the basis of (castelike) duty and natural order.

NOTE: Since every society has some kind of social stratification, ideology may be described as the assertion that specific kinds of inequality should not be defined as injustice.

DISCUSS: Davis and Moore's thesis suggests that agrarian societies, with little productive specialization, do not have to provide differential rewards to the mass of "commoners." However, such societies demand persistence; thus faithfully performing one's duty carries the reward of honor.

RESOURCE: Davis and Moore's analysis is one of the classics included in the companion reader *Seeing Ourselves*, 8th ed.

MAKING THE GRADE

Stratification systems produce ideas and beliefs that define their operation as just. In short, stratification involves not just who has what but also beliefs about justice—why people should have what they have.

THINKING ABOUT DIVERSITY: RACE, CLASS, & GENDER

The Meaning of Class: Is Getting Rich "the Survival of the Fittest"?

JAKE: "My dad is amazing. He's really smart!"

FRANK: "You mean he's rich. He owns I don't know how many businesses."

JAKE: "Do you think people get rich without being smart?"

It's a question we all wonder about. How much is our social position a matter of intelligence? What about hard work? Being born to the "right family"? Even "dumb luck"?

More than in most societies, in the United States we link social standing to personal abilities including intelligence. This idea goes back a long time. We have all heard the words "the survival of the fittest," which describes our society as a competitive jungle in which the "best" survive and the rest fall behind. The phrase was coined by one of sociology's pioneers, Herbert Spencer (1820–1903), whose ideas about social inequality are still widespread today.

Spencer, who lived in England, eagerly followed the work of the natural scientist Charles Darwin (1809–1882). Darwin's theory of biological evolution held that a species changes physically over many generations as it adapts to the natural environment. Spencer incorrectly applied Darwin's theory to the operation of society, which does not operate according to biological principles. In Spencer's distorted view, society became the "jungle," with the "fittest" people rising to wealth and the "failures" sinking into miserable poverty.

It is no surprise that Spencer's views, wrong as they were, were popular among the rising U.S. industrialists of the day. John D. Rockefeller (1839–1937), who made a vast fortune building the oil industry, recited Spencer's "social gospel" to young children in Sunday school. As Rockefeller saw it, the growth of giant corporations—and the astounding wealth of their owners—was merely the result of the survival of the fittest, a basic fact of nature. Neither Spencer nor Rockefeller had much sympathy for the poor, seeing poverty as evidence of individuals' failing to measure up in a competitive world. Spencer opposed social welfare programs because he thought they penalized society's "best" people (through taxes) and rewarded its "worst" members (through welfare benefits). By incorrectly using Darwin's theory,

the rich could turn their backs on everyone else, assuming that inequality was inevitable and somehow "natural."

Today, sociologists point out that our society is far from a meritocracy, as Spencer claimed. And it is not the case that companies or individuals who generate lots of money necessarily benefit society. The people who made hundreds of millions of dollars selling subprime mortgages in recent years certainly ended up hurting just about everyone. But Spencer's view that the "fittest" rise to the top remains widespread in our very unequal and individualistic culture.

WHAT DO YOU THINK?

1. How much do you think inequality in our society can correctly be described as "the survival of the fittest"? Why?

2. Why do you think Spencer's ideas are still popular in the United States today?

3. Is how much you earn a good measure of your importance to society? Why or why not?

---

organs—are difficult and demand the scarce talents of people with extensive and expensive training.

Therefore, Davis and Moore explain, the greater the functional importance of a position, the more rewards a society attaches to it. This strategy promotes productivity and efficiency because rewarding important work with income, prestige, power, and leisure encourages people to do these jobs and to work better, longer, and harder. In short, unequal rewards (which is what social stratification is) benefit society as a whole.

Davis and Moore claim that any society could be egalitarian, but only to the extent that people are willing to let *anyone* perform *any* job. Equality would also demand that someone who carries out a job poorly be rewarded the same as someone who performs it well. Such a system would clearly offer little incentive for people to try their best, reducing the society's productive efficiency.

The Davis-Moore thesis suggests the reason stratification exists; it does not state what rewards a society should give to any occupational position or how unequal the rewards should be. It merely points out that positions a society considers more important must offer enough rewards to draw talented people away from less important work.

CRITICAL REVIEW Although the Davis-Moore thesis is an important contribution to understanding social stratification, it has provoked criticism. Melvin Tumin (1953) wondered, first, how we assess the importance of a particular occupation. Perhaps the high rewards our society gives to physicians results partly from deliberate efforts by the medical profession to limit the supply of physicians and thereby increase the demand for their services.

NOTE: In light of the Davis-Moore thesis, seniority is not a uniformly positive principle. Most brain surgeons, for example, get better with time. Science professors, by contrast, do their best work early in their careers. The "term limits" debate suggests that legislators are more like the latter than the former (Pitney, 1995).

DISCUSS: According to one account, average salary in 2008 (including housing and utilities) for senior pastors in the U.S. was $139,000; Episcopalians typically earned more

than three times as much as Catholics. Does this pay disparity reflect differences in merit?

NOTE: Elvis Presley, deceased for nearly 30 years, earned about $42 million in 2006, according to *Forbes*. Michael Jackson's estate may well see earning rise in the years to come.

POP CULTURE: Are athletes, like soccer players David Beckham and Brian Rooney, baseball's Alex Rodriguez, and basketball's Michael Jordan, Kobe Bryant, and Kevin Garnett worth mega-millions?

● SEEING SOCIOLOGY
in Everyday Life

Following Davis and Moore's thinking, why do professors give grades from A to F? What would happen if they gave every student the same grade? Explain.

● MAKING THE GRADE

A more detailed discussion of Marx's theory of social inequality is found in Chapter 4 ("Society"). Reviewing that material will increase your understanding of this discussion.

Furthermore, do rewards actually reflect the contribution someone makes to society? With income of about $275 million per year, Oprah Winfrey earns more in one day than President Obama earns all year. Would anyone argue that hosting a talk show is more important than leading a country? And what about members of the U.S. military serving in Iraq or Afghanistan? Facing the risks of combat, a private first-class in the U.S. Army earned only $19,000 in 2008 (Defense Finance and Accounting Service, 2008; Kroll, 2008).

And what about the heads of the big Wall Street financial firms that collapsed in 2008? It seems reasonable to conclude that these corporate leaders made some bad decisions, yet their salaries were astronomical. Even after finishing its worst year ever, with losses of $27 billion, Merrill Lynch paid bonuses of more than $1 million to more than 700 employees (Fox, 2009). The top people in the financial industry made out even better. In 2007, James Dimon, head of JP Morgan Chase, had earnings of more than $55 million; the same year, Lloyd Blankfein, head of Goldman Sachs, made more than $70 million—an amount it would take the typical U.S. Army private more than 3,500 years to earn.

Even top executives who lose their jobs do surprisingly well. Chuck Prince was forced to resign as head at Citigroup, but not before receiving a "severance package" worth more than $30 million. When insurance giant AIG failed, corporate leader Martin Sullivan left the company, receiving $47 million on the way out (Beck & Simon, 2008; Scherer, 2008). Do corporate executives deserve such megasalaries for their contributions to society?

Second, Tumin claimed that Davis and Moore ignore how caste elements of social stratification can prevent the development of individual talent. Born to privilege, rich children have opportunities to develop their abilities that many gifted poor children never have.

Third, living in a society that places so much emphasis on money, we tend to overestimate the importance of high-paying work; what do stockbrokers or people who trade international currencies really contribute to society? For the same reason, it is difficult for us to see the value of work that is not oriented toward making money, such as parenting, creative writing, playing music in a symphony, or just being a good friend to someone in need (Packard, 2002).

Finally, by suggesting that social stratification benefits all of society, the Davis-Moore thesis ignores how social inequality promotes conflict and even outright revolution. This criticism leads us to the social-conflict approach, which provides a very different explanation for social inequality.

● **CHECK YOUR LEARNING** State the Davis-Moore thesis in your own words. What are Tumin's criticisms of this thesis?

Oprah Winfey reported income of $275 million in 2008 and enjoys fame to match her fortune. Guided by the Davis-Moore thesis, why would societies reward some people so much more than others? How would Karl Marx answer this question differently?

Stratification and Conflict

Social-conflict analysis argues that rather than benefiting society as a whole, social stratification benefits some people and disadvantages others. This analysis draws heavily on the ideas of Karl Marx, with contributions from Max Weber.

Karl Marx: Class Conflict

Karl Marx, whose ideas are discussed at length in Chapter 4 ("Society"), explained that most people have one of two basic relationships to the means of production: They either own productive property or labor for others. Different productive roles arise from different social classes. In medieval Europe, aristocratic families, including high church officials and titled nobles, owned the land on which peasants

SOCIAL SURVEY: "If someone has a high economic or social position, that indicates the person has special abilities or great accomplishments." (GSS 1984, *N* = 1,317; *Code-book*, 2005:143)

"Strongly agree"   11.7%   "Strongly disagree"   17.3%
"Somewhat agree"   36.2%   "Don't know"/No response   4.1%
"Somewhat disagree" 30.7%

NOTE: Peter Berger (1986) suggests that a flaw of Marxism is the empirical failure of the polarization thesis. Berger suggests that neo-Marxists have attempted to resolve this problem through global dependency theory (discussed in Chapter 12). Polarization, in short, has not occurred within industrial societies as much as it has among the world's nations as a whole.

blue-collar occupations lower-prestige jobs that involve mostly manual labor

white-collar occupations higher-prestige jobs that involve mostly mental activity

labored as farmers. In industrial class systems, the capitalists (or the bourgeoisie) own the factories, which use the labor of workers (the proletarians).

Marx lived during the nineteenth century, a time when a small number of industrialists in the United States were amassing great fortunes. Andrew Carnegie, J. P. Morgan, John D. Rockefeller, and John Jacob Astor (one of the few very rich passengers to drown on the *Titanic*) lived in fabulous mansions staffed by dozens of servants. Even by today's standards, their incomes were staggering. For example, Carnegie earned about $20 million a year in 1900 (more than $500 million in today's dollars), when the average worker earned roughly $500 a year (Baltzell, 1964; Pessen, 1990; Williamson, 2008).

Marx explained that capitalist society *reproduces the class structure* in each new generation. This happens as families gain wealth and pass it down from generation to generation. But, he predicted, oppression and misery would eventually drive the working majority to come together to overthrow capitalism in favor of a socialist system that would end class differences.

CRITICAL REVIEW Marx has had enormous influence on sociological thinking. But his revolutionary ideas, calling for the overthrow of capitalist society, also make his work highly controversial.

One of the strongest criticisms of Marxism is that it denies a central idea of the Davis-Moore thesis: that a system of unequal rewards is necessary to place talented people in the right jobs and to motivate them to work hard. Marx separated reward from performance; his egalitarian ideal was based on the principle "from each according to his ability; to each according to his needs" (Marx & Engels, 1972:388, orig. 1848). However, failure to reward individual performance may be precisely what caused the low productivity of the former Soviet Union and other socialist economies around the world. Defenders of Marxism respond to such criticism by asking why we assume that humanity is inherently selfish rather than social, noting that individual rewards are not the only way to motivate people to perform their social roles (M. S. Clark, 1991).

A second problem is that the revolutionary change Marx predicted has failed to happen, at least in advanced capitalist societies. The next section explains why.

CHECK YOUR LEARNING How does Marx's view of social stratification differ from the Davis-Moore thesis?

Why No Marxist Revolution?

Despite Marx's prediction, capitalism is still thriving. Why have industrial workers not overthrown capitalism? Ralf Dahrendorf (1959) suggested four reasons:

1. **Fragmentation of the capitalist class**. Today, millions of stockholders, rather than single families, own most large companies. Day-to-day corporate operations are in the hands of a large class of managers, who may or may not be major stockholders. With stock widely held—about half of U.S. households own stocks—more and more people have a direct stake in the capitalist system (U.S. Census Bureau, 2008).

2. **A higher standard of living**. As Chapter 16 ("The Economy and Work") explains, a century ago, most workers were in factories or on farms employed in **blue-collar occupations**, *lower-prestige jobs that involve mostly manual labor*. Today, most workers are engaged in **white-collar occupations**, *higher-prestige jobs that involve mostly mental activity*. These jobs are in sales, management, and other service fields. Most of today's white-collar workers do not think of themselves as an "industrial proletariat." Just as important, the average income in the

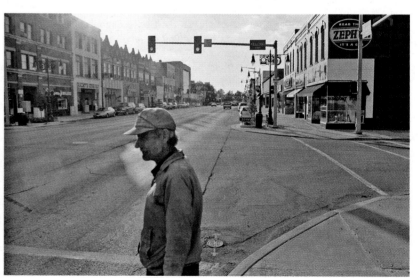

What is the main cause of social inequality? The Davis-Moore thesis suggests that societies attach unequal rewards to tasks of unequal importance. The social-conflict approach offers a different insight, claiming that the economic system determines the extent of stratification. Times have been tough in Galesburg, Illinois, since the Maytag corporation closed its factory in 2004. How would each theoretical approach explain the economic troubles of many of this town's people?

RESOURCE: Andrew Hacker's analysis of "who has how much and why" is included in the companion reader *Seeing Ourselves*, 8th ed.

Q: "That all men are born to equal rights is true . . . but to teach that all men are born with equal powers and faculties, to equal influence in society, to equal property and advantages through life is . . . gross fraud." John Adams

Q: "Weber preferred capitalism to socialism, which he feared would produce a grand, all-encompassing iron cage from which escape was impossible." George Ritzer (1998:4)

NOTE: "Mainstream" U.S. sociology has followed Weber in focusing on stratification as hierarchical differences in income and consumption. The political-economy approach derived from Marx, however, focuses on class, that is, differences in productive wealth.

SEEING SOCIOLOGY
in Everyday Life

Using what you have learned so far about social inequality in the United States, how correct do you think Marx was about capitalism? Explain your answer.

socioeconomic status (SES) a composite ranking based on various dimensions of social inequality

United States rose almost tenfold over the course of the twentieth century, even allowing for inflation, and the number of hours in the workweek decreased. In short, even in tough economic times, most of today's workers are better off than workers were a century ago, an example of structural social mobility. One result of this rising standard of living is that more people are content with the status quo and less likely to pressure for change.

3. **More worker organizations**. Workers today have the right to form labor unions, to make demands of management, and to back up their demands with threats of work slowdowns and strikes. As a result, labor disputes are settled without threatening the capitalist system.

4. **Greater legal protections**. Over the past century, the government passed laws to make workplaces safer. In addition, unemployment insurance, disability protection, and Social Security now provide workers with greater financial security.

A Counterpoint

These developments suggest that U.S. society has smoothed many of capitalism's rough edges. Yet some observers claim that Marx's analysis of capitalism is still largely valid (Domhoff, 1983; Boswell & Dixon, 1993; Hout, Brooks, & Manza, 1993). First, wealth remains highly concentrated, with 35 percent of all privately owned property in the hands of just 1 percent of the U.S. population (Keister, 2000; Wolff, 2007). Second, many of today's white-collar jobs offer no more income, security, or satisfaction than factory work did a century ago. Third, many benefits enjoyed by today's workers came about through the class conflict Marx described. Workers still struggle to hold on to what they have, and in recent years, many workers have actually lost pensions and other benefits. Fourth, although workers have gained some legal protections, ordinary people still face disadvantages that the law cannot overcome. Therefore, social-conflict theorists conclude, even without a socialist revolution in the United States, Marx was still mostly right about capitalism.

Max Weber: Class, Status, and Power

Max Weber, whose approach to social analysis is described in Chapter 4 ("Society"), agreed with Karl Marx that social stratification causes social conflict, but he viewed Marx's economics-based model as simplistic. Instead, he claimed that social stratification involves three distinct dimensions of inequality.

The first dimension is economic inequality—the issue so important to Marx—which Weber termed *class position*. Weber did not think of classes as well-defined categories but as a continuum ranging from

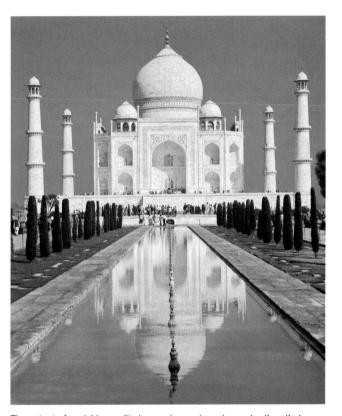

The extent of social inequality in agrarian systems is greater than that found in industrial societies. One indication of the unchallenged power of rulers is the monumental structures built over years with the unpaid labor of common people. Although the Taj Mahal in India is among the world's most beautiful buildings, it was built as a tomb for a single individual.

high to low. Weber's second dimension is *status*, or social prestige, and the third is *power*.

Weber's Socioeconomic Status Hierarchy

Marx viewed social prestige and power as simple reflections of economic position and did not treat them as distinct dimensions of inequality. But Weber noted that status consistency in modern societies is often quite low: A local official might exercise great power yet have little wealth or social prestige.

Weber, then, portrays social stratification in industrial societies as a multidimensional ranking rather than a hierarchy of clearly defined classes. In line with Weber's thinking, sociologists use the term **socioeconomic status (SES)** to refer to *a composite ranking based on various dimensions of social inequality*.

Q: "True education makes for inequality—the inequality of the individual, the inequality of success, the glorious inequality of talent, of genius. Inequality, not mediocrity; individual superiority, not standardization, is the measure of the progress of the world." Felix E. Schelling

Q: "It is the mark of the cultured man that he is aware of the fact that equality is an ethical and not a biological principle." Ashley Montagu

Q: "The chief vice of every egalitarian society is envy. . . . Such constant comparing is really the quintessence of vulgarity." Hannah Arendt

MAKING THE GRADE

Marx viewed social stratification in terms of classes. Weber viewed inequality in terms of a socioeconomic status hierarchy with multiple dimensions. Individuals stand higher on some dimensions and lower on others, so there are no clear-cut classes.

MAKING THE GRADE

Be sure you understand Weber's claim about the changing basis of stratification in agrarian (prestige), industrial-capitalist (money), and socialist (power) societies.

APPLYING THEORY

Social Stratification

	Structural-Functional Approach	Social-Conflict Approach	Symbolic-Interaction Approach
What is the level of analysis?	Macro-level	Macro-level	Micro-level
What is social stratification?	Stratification is a system of unequal rewards that benefits society as a whole.	Stratification is a division of a society's resources that benefits some people and harms others.	Stratification is a factor that guides people's interactions in everyday life.
What is the reason for our social position?	Social position reflects personal talents and abilities in a competitive economy.	Social position reflects the way society divides resources.	The products we consume all say something about social position.
Are unequal rewards fair?	Yes. Unequal rewards boost economic production by encouraging people to work harder and try new ideas. Linking greater rewards to more important work is widely accepted.	No. Unequal rewards only serve to divide society, creating "haves" and "have-nots." There is widespread opposition to social inequality.	Maybe. People may or may not define inequality as fair. People may view their social position as a measure of self-worth, justifying inequality in terms of personal differences.

Inequality in History

Weber claimed that each of his three dimensions of social inequality stands out at different points in the evolution of human societies. Status or social prestige is the main difference in agrarian societies, taking the form of honor. Members of these societies (whether nobles or servants) gain status by conforming to cultural norms that apply to their particular rank.

Industrialization and the development of capitalism eliminate traditional rankings based on birth but create striking financial inequality. Thus in an industrial society, the crucial difference between people is the economic dimension of class.

Over time, industrial societies witness the growth of a bureaucratic state. Bigger government and the spread of all sorts of other organizations make power more important in the stratification system. Especially in socialist societies, where government regulates many aspects of life, high-ranking officials become the new ruling elite.

This historical analysis points to a final difference between Weber and Marx. Marx thought societies could eliminate social stratification by abolishing the private ownership of productive property that is the basis of capitalism. Weber doubted that overthrowing capitalism would significantly lessen social stratification. It might reduce economic differences, he reasoned, but socialism would increase inequality by expanding government and concentrating power in the hands of a political elite. Popular uprisings against socialist bureaucracies in Eastern Europe and the former Soviet Union show that discontent can be generated by socialist political elites and thus support Weber's position.

CRITICAL REVIEW Max Weber's multidimensional view of social stratification has greatly influenced sociological thinking. But critics (particularly those who favor Marx's ideas) argue that although social class boundaries may have blurred, industrial and postindustrial societies still show striking patterns of social inequality.

As you will see in Chapter 11 ("Social Class in the United States"), income inequality has been increasing in the United States. Although some people still favor Weber's multidimensional hierarchy, in light of this trend, others think that Marx's view of the rich versus the poor is closer to the truth.

CHECK YOUR LEARNING What are Weber's three dimensions of social inequality? According to Weber, which of them would you expect to be most important in the United States? Why?

Q: "Men may not get all they pay for in this world; but they must certainly pay for all they get." Frederick Douglass

Q: "I have no respect for the passion for equality, which seems to me to be merely idealizing envy." Oliver Wendell Holmes

NOTE: The shrinking stature of the U.S. rich is suggested by this comparison: When William Henry Vanderbilt died in 1885, his obituary covered the entire front page of the *New York Times*. When Sam Walton died in 1992, his death was reported on 1/20th of a page.

conspicuous consumption buying and using products because of the "statement" they make about social position

SEEING SOCIOLOGY IN EVERYDAY LIFE

When Class Gets Personal: Picking (with) Your Friends

The sound of banjo music drifted across the field late one summer afternoon. I lay down my brush, climbed over the fence I had been painting, and walked toward the sound of the music to see what was going on. That's how I met my neighbor Max, a retired factory worker who lived just up the road. Max was a pretty good "picker," and within an hour, I was back on his porch with my guitar. I called Howard, a friend who teaches at the college, and he showed up a little while later, six-string in hand. The three of us jammed for a couple of hours, smiling all the while.

The next morning, I was mowing the grass in front of the house when Max came walking down the road. I turned off the mower as he got closer. "Hi, Max," I said. "Thanks for having us over last night. I really had fun."

"Don't mention it," Max responded with a wave. Then he stopped and shook his head a lit-

tle and added, "Ya know, I was thinkin' after you guys left. I mean, it was really somethin' how you

guys looked like you were having a great time. With somebody like *me!*"

"Well, yeah," I replied, not sure of what he meant. "You sure played better than we did."

Max looked down at the ground, embarrassed by the compliment. Then he added, "What I mean is that you guys were having a good time with somebody like *me.* You're both professors, right? *Doctors,* even . . ."

WHAT DO YOU THINK?

1. Why did Max assume that two college teachers would not enjoy spending time with him?

2. How does his reaction suggest that people take social position personally?

3. Can you think of a similar experience you have had with someone of a different social position?

Stratification and Interaction

Because social stratification has to do with the way an entire society is organized, sociologists (Marx and Weber included) typically treat it as a macro-level issue. But a micro-level analysis of social stratification is also important because people's social standing affects their everyday interactions. The Applying Theory table summarizes the contributions of the three approaches to an understanding of social stratification.

In most communities, people interact primarily with others of about the same social standing. To some extent, this is because we tend to live with others like ourselves. As we observe people during the course of our everyday activities, such as walking in a downtown shopping area, we see that couples or groups tend to be made up of individuals whose appearance and shopping habits are similar. People with very different social standing commonly keep their distance from one another. Well-dressed people walking down the street on their way to an expensive restaurant, for example, might move across the sidewalk or even cross the street to avoid getting close to others they think are homeless people. The Seeing Sociology in Everyday

Life box gives another example of how differences in social class position can affect interaction.

Finally, just about everyone realizes that the way we dress, the car we drive (or the bus we ride), and even the food and drink we order at the campus snack bar say something about our budget and personal tastes. Sociologists use the term **conspicuous consumption** to refer to *buying and using products because of the "statement" they make about social position.* Ignoring the water fountain in favor of paying for bottled water tells people you have extra money to spend. And no one needs a $100,000 automobile to get around, of course, but driving up in such a vehicle says "I have arrived" in more ways than one.

Stratification and Technology: A Global Pespective

We can weave together a number of observations made in this chapter to show that a society's technology affects its type of social stratification. This analysis draws on Gerhard Lenski's model of sociocultural evolution, detailed in Chapter 4 ("Society").

Q: "Suppose a man, having plowed and cultivated his farm, should take in his hand a bag of mixed seeds ... and walk straight across his land, sowing as he went. All pieces on his path would be sown alike: the rocks, the sandy ground, the good upland soil ... but there would be great variety in the result when harvest time came around. ... Something like this, I think, is the case with a stock of men passing through history." Charles Horton Cooley

NOTE: Technological revolutions tend to increase economic disparity because a small number of people control key innovations and the economy expands, benefiting those with wealth to invest.

DIVERSITY: In every society, income inequality ratios are greater for men than for women, who are underrepresented at the highest income levels (see Hout, Brooks, & Manza, 1993).

SEEING SOCIOLOGY
in Everyday Life

Can you identify aspects of everyday life that seem to suggest that economic inequality is increasing? Explain.

Industrial Societies

Industrialization turns the tide, pushing inequality downward. Prompted by the need to develop individual talents, meritocracy takes hold and weakens the power of traditional aristocracy. Industrial productivity also raises the standard of living of the historically poor majority. Specialized work demands schooling for all, sharply reducing illiteracy. A literate population, in turn, presses for a greater voice in political decision making, reducing social inequality and lessening men's domination of women.

Over time, even wealth becomes somewhat less concentrated (contradicting Marx's prediction). In the 1920s, the richest 1 percent of the U.S. population owned about 40 percent of all wealth, a figure that fell to 30 percent by the 1980s as higher taxes on the rich paid for new government programs benefiting the poor (Williamson & Lindert, 1980; Beeghley, 1989; U.S House of Representatives, 1991). Such trends help explain why Marxist revolutions occurred in *agrarian* societies—such as Russia (1917), Cuba (1959), and Nicaragua (1979)—where social inequality is most pronounced, rather than in industrial societies as Marx had predicted. However, wealth inequality in the United States turned upward again after 1990 and is once again about the same as it was in the 1920s (Keister, 2000; Wolff & Zacharias, 2006). With the goal of reducing this trend, the Obama administration has acted to raise federal income tax rates on high-income individuals.

The Kuznets Curve

In human history, then, technological advances first increase but then moderate the extent of social stratification. Greater inequality is functional for agrarian societies, but industrial societies benefit from a less unequal system. This historical trend, recognized by the Nobel Prize–winning economist Simon Kuznets (1955, 1966), is illustrated by the Kuznets curve, shown in Figure 10–2.

Social inequality around the world generally supports the Kuznets curve. Global Map 10–1 shows that high-income nations that have passed through the industrial era (including the United States, Canada, and the nations of Western Europe) have somewhat less income inequality than nations in which a larger share of the labor force remains in farming (as is common in Latin America and Africa). At the same time, it is important to remember that income inequality reflects not just technological development but also the political and economic priorities of a country. Income disparity in the United States may have declined during much of the last century, but this country still has more economic inequality than Canada, European nations, and Japan (although less than some other high-income nations, including Argentina, Saudi Arabia, and South Africa).

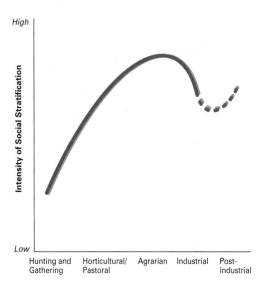

High

Intensity of Social Stratification

Low

Hunting and Gathering | Horticultural/ Pastoral | Agrarian | Industrial | Post-industrial

FIGURE 10–2 Social Stratification and Technological Development: The Kuznets Curve

The Kuznets curve shows that greater technological sophistication is generally accompanied by more pronounced social stratification. The trend reverses itself as industrial societies relax rigid, castelike distinctions in favor of greater opportunity and equality under the law. Political rights are more widely extended, and there is even some leveling of economic differences. However, the emergence of postindustrial society has brought an upturn in economic inequality, as indicated by the broken line added by the author.

Sources: Based on Kuznets (1955) and Lenski (1966).

Hunting and Gathering Societies

With simple technology, members of hunting and gathering societies produce only what is necessary for day-to-day living. Some people may produce more than others, but the group's survival depends on all sharing what they have. Thus no categories of people are better off than others.

Horticultural, Pastoral, and Agrarian Societies

As technological advances create a surplus, social inequality increases. In horticultural and pastoral societies, a small elite controls most of the surplus. Large-scale agriculture is more productive still, and striking inequality—as great as at any time in history—places the nobility in an almost godlike position over the masses.

Rocio Rodriguez is a university student in Santiago, Chile, a city marked by dramatic differences between rich and poor.

Torvold Johansson is a university student near Stockholm, Sweden, a city where economic differences are small by global standards.

Window on the World

GLOBAL MAP 10–1   Income Inequality in Global Perspective

Societies throughout the world differ in the rigidity and extent of their social stratification and their overall standard of living. This map highlights income inequality. Generally speaking, the United States stands out among high-income nations, such as Great Britain, Sweden, Japan, and Australia, as having greater income inequality. The less economically developed countries of Latin America and Africa, including Colombia, Brazil, and the Central African Republic, as well as much of the Arab world, exhibit the most pronounced inequality of income. Is this pattern consistent with the Kuznets curve?

Source: Based on Gini coefficients obtained from World Bank (2008).

Another criticism of the Kuznets curve is that it was developed by comparing societies at different levels of economic development (what sociologists call "cross-sectional data"). Such data do not tell us about the future of any one society. In the United States, recent trends showing increases in economic inequality suggest that the Kuznets curve may require serious revision—represented by the broken line in Figure 10–2. The fact that U.S. society is experiencing greater economic inequality as the Information Revolution moves forward (see Chapter 11) suggests that the long-term trend may differ from what Kuznets projected half a century ago.

Q: "There is probably less economic injustice and class conflict now than at any time since the Industrial Revolution began." E. Digby Baltzell (1964)

EXERCISE: Have students read Kurt Vonnegut's short story "Harrison Bergeron" in his collection *Welcome to the Monkey House*. How does Vonnegut describe a society where everyone is socially equal? Do students agree with his portrayal or not? Why?

Q: "Our thesis is that . . . the twenty-first [century] will open on a world in which cog-

nitive ability is the decisive dividing force." Richard Herrnstein and Charles Murray, *The Bell Curve*

GLOBAL: In 1994, and intriguing in light of the "bell curve" debate, the People's Republic of China adopted a policy to ban marriages between people deemed likely to produce physically or mentally defective children that would undermine the "quality of the population."

CONTROVERSY & DEBATE

The Bell Curve Debate: Are Rich People Really Smarter?

ELENA: (*with a smile*) So what do you think? Is going out with me giving you upward social mobility?

JOE: Give me a break. Your family is richer than mine. But that doesn't mean you're better or smarter. . . .

Are rich people smarter than the rest of us? Few books in sociology have taken on this question as directly as *The Bell Curve: Intelligence and Class Structure in American Life* (1994), by Richard J. Herrnstein and Charles Murray. The book ignited a firestorm of controversy over why social stratification divides our society and, just as important, what should be done about it.

    The Bell Curve is a long book that addresses many complex issues, but it makes eight major claims:

1. Something we can describe as "general intelligence" exists; people with more of it tend to be more successful in their careers than those with less.
2. At least half the variation in human intelligence is transmitted genetically from parents to children; the remaining variability is due to environmental factors that affect socialization.

3. During the past century—and especially since the Information Revolution began several decades ago—intelligence has become more necessary to perform our society's most important jobs.
4. At the same time, the most selective U.S. colleges and universities have shifted their admissions policies away from favoring children of inherited wealth to admitting young people with high grades and the highest scores on standardized tests such as the Scholastic Assessment Test (SAT), the American College Testing Program (ACT), and the Graduate Record Examination (GRE).
5. As a result of these changes in the workplace and on campus, our society is now dominated by a "cognitive elite," people who are not only better educated but actually more intelligent.
6. As very intelligent people interact with others similar to themselves, both on the campus and in the workplace, the odds are high that they will pair up, get married, and have intelligent children, extending the "cognitive elite" into another generation.
7. A similar process is at work at the other end of the social ladder: Poor people,

who, on average, have lower intelligence, have become socially segregated and tend to marry others like themselves, thus passing along their more modest abilities to their children.
8. Herrnstein and Murray therefore conclude that because membership in the affluent elite or the impoverished underclass is at least partly rooted in genetically inherited intelligence, we should not be surprised that the poor are more likely to have higher rates of crime and drug abuse. Further, we should expect that programs such as Head Start and affirmative action will do little to help the poor.

    Evaluating the claims made in *The Bell Curve* must begin with a hard look at the concept of intelligence. Critics of the book argue that most of what we call "intelligence" is the result not of genetic inheritance but of socialization. In other words, so-called intelligence tests do not measure cognitive *ability* as much as they measure cognitive *performance*. Average intelligence quotient (IQ) scores have been rising as the U.S. population becomes more educated. If schooling is so important to intelligence, then educational advantages alone

Social Stratification: Facts and Values

The year was 2081 and everybody was finally equal. They weren't only equal before God and the law. They were equal every which way. Nobody was smarter than anybody else. Nobody was better looking than anybody else. Nobody was stronger or quicker than anybody else. All this equality was due to the 211th, 212th, and 213th Amendments to the Constitution and the unceasing vigilance of agents of the Handicapper General.

With these words, the novelist Kurt Vonnegut Jr. (1968:7) begins the story of Harrison Bergeron, an imaginary account of a future United States in which all social inequality has been abolished. Vonnegut warns that although attractive in principle, equality can be a

dangerous concept in practice. His story describes a nightmare of social engineering in which every individual talent that makes one person different from another is systematically neutralized by the government.

To eliminate differences that make one person "better" than another, Vonnegut's state requires that physically attractive people wear masks that make them average-looking, that intelligent people wear earphones that generate distracting noise, and that the best athletes and dancers be fitted with weights to make them as clumsy as everyone else. In short, although we may imagine that social equality would liberate people to make the most of their talents, Vonnegut concludes that an egalitarian society could exist only if everyone is reduced to the lowest common denominator. In Vonnegut's view, this would amount not to liberation but to oppression.

Q: "The more complex a society becomes, the more valuable are the people who are especially good at dealing with complexity." Richard Herrnstein and Charles Murray, *The Bell Curve*

Q: "The very same people who scream freedom of expression for Snoop Doggy Dogg or Robert Mapplethorpe . . . would be only too happy to silence—or academically lynch—Charles Murray or his late partner, Richard Herrnstein." Leon R. Kass

Q: "I hate the impudence of a claim that in fifty minutes you can judge a human being's predestined fitness in life. . . . I hate the sense of superiority it creates and the sense of inferiority it imposes." Walter Lippmann, on IQ tests in 1922

NOTE: Two comprehensive critiques of the "bell curve thesis" are by Stephen Jay Gould (1994) and Melvin Kohn (1996).

would explain why rich children perform better on such tests.

Most researchers who study intelligence agree that genetics plays a part in children's intelligence, but most conclude that only 25 to 40 percent of intelligence is inherited—less than Herrnstein and Murray claim. *The Bell Curve* therefore misleads readers when it states that social stratification is a natural product of differences in inherited intelligence. Critics claim that this book echoes the social Darwinism popular a century ago, which justified the great wealth of industrial tycoons as "the survival of the fittest."

Could it be that the more today's competitive society seems like a jungle, the more people think of stratification as a matter of nature rather than nurture? But even if it is flawed, *The Bell Curve* raises important issues. If some people are smarter than others, shouldn't we expect them to end up in higher social positions? Shouldn't we expect the peo-ple who rise to the top in most fields to be at least a little smarter than the rest of us? If this is true, is it fair? Finally, what can our society do to ensure that all people will have the opportunity to develop their abilities as fully as possible?

How closely linked are social class position and personal intelligence? According to Herrnstein and Murray, in today's society birth matters less than in the past and personal ability matters more. Do you think the remarkable life story of Barack Obama, who was born to a single mother and went on to be president, reflects a more general trend? Why or why not?

WHAT DO YOU THINK?

1. Do you think there is such a thing as "general intelligence"? Why or why not?

2. Do you think that well-off people are, on average, more intelligent than people of low social position? If so, how do you know which factor is the cause and which the effect?

3. Do you think social scientists should study issues such as differences in human intelligence if their results could justify social inequality? Why or why not?

Sources: Herrnstein & Murray (1994), Jacoby & Glauberman (1995), Kohn (1996), and Arrow, Bowles, & Durlauf (2000).

Like Vonnegut's story, all of this chapter's explanations of social stratification involve value judgments. The Davis-Moore thesis states not only that social stratification is universal but also that it is necessary to make society highly productive. Class differences in U.S. society, from this point of view, reflect both variation in human abilities and the relatively unequal importance of different jobs. Taken together, these facts lead us to see complete equality as undesirable, because it could be achieved only in a rigid and inefficient society that cared little for developing individual talent and rewarding excellence.

Social-conflict analysis, advocated by Karl Marx, takes a much more positive view of equality. Marx thought that inequality is harmful because it causes both human suffering and conflict between haves and have-nots. As he saw it, social stratification springs from injus-tice and greed. As a result, Marx wanted people to share resources equally.

The Controversy & Debate box addresses the connection between intelligence and social class. This issue is among the most troublesome in social science, partly because of the difficulty in defining and measuring "intelligence" but also because the idea that elites are somehow "better" than others challenges our democratic culture.

The next chapter ("Social Class in the United States") examines inequality in our own nation, highlighting recent economic polarization. Then, Chapter 12 ("Global Stratification"), surveys social inequality throughout the world, explaining why some nations have so much more wealth than others. As you will learn, at all levels, the study of social stratification involves a mix of facts and values about the shape of a just society.

Seeing Sociology in Everyday Life

Chapter 10   Social Stratificattion

Can you find elements of caste and meritocracy in U.S. society?

This chapter explains that modern societies are class systems that combine elements of caste and meritocracy. Using the sociological perspective, you can see both caste and meritocracy in operation in many everyday situations. Here are three examples to get you started. Look at the photos below and then start your own list.

> **HINT**   The fact that parenting is not paid work means that people should not raise children for money but out of moral duty. "Fathering a child" may suggest only biological paternity; "mothering a child" implies deep involvement in a child's life, suggesting that gender has long been a caste element linking women to nurturing. Careers that emphasize merit, on the other hand, are typically those jobs that that are regarded as especially important and that require rare talents; even so, most successful musical performers are male. Judge Sotomayor is the first Hispanic and just the third woman (along with Sandra Day O'Connor and Ruth Bader Ginsburg) to serve on the U.S. Supreme Court. There have been just two African American justices (Thurgood Marshall and Clarence Thomas).

One of the most demanding jobs you can ever have is being a parent. And traditionally at least, most parenting is performed by women, with gender operating as a caste element. Why do you think our society does not pay parents for their work? What difference in meaning can you see between the phrases "fathering a child" and "mothering a child"?

Joel and Benji Madden grew up poor in a single-parent family and went on to find success in the band "Good Charlotte." Some careers, such as being a musician, an athlete, or an actor or actress, allow for a good deal of meritocracy. What do these careers have in common that explains the importance of meritocracy? Can you see elements of caste, as well, in these careers?

In 2009, Judge Sonia Sotomayor became the first Hispanic woman to join the U.S. Supreme Court. Her record of achievement began at Cardinal Spellman High School in the Bronx (New York), where she was valedictorian. Of more than 100 justices who have served on the Supreme Court, how many do you think have been Hispanic? How many have been women?

Applying SOCIOLOGY in Everyday Life

1. Identify three ways in which social stratification is evident in the everyday lives of students on your campus. In each case, explain exactly what is unequal and what difference it makes. Do you think individual talent or family background is more important in creating these social differences?

2. Sit down with parents, grandparents, or other relatives, and talk about how your family's social position has changed over the last three generations. Has social mobility taken place? If so, describe the change. Was it caused by the effort of individuals or changes in society itself?

3. The "seven deadly sins," the human failings recognized by the Roman Catholic Church during the Middle Ages, were pride, greed, envy, anger, lust, gluttony, and sloth. Why are these traits dangerous to an agrarian caste system? Are they a threat to a modern, capitalist class system? Why or why not?

MAKING THE GRADE

CHAPTER 10 Social Stratification

What Is Social Stratification?

SOCIAL STRATIFICATION is a system by which a society ranks categories of people in a hierarchy, so that some people have more money, power, and prestige than others.
Social stratification

- is a trait of society, not simply a reflection of individual differences
- is found in all societies but varies according to *what* is unequal and *how* unequal it is
- carries over from one generation to the next
- is supported by a system of cultural beliefs that defines certain kinds of inequality as just
- takes two general forms: caste systems and class systems

pp. 248–49

social stratification (p. 248) a system by which a society ranks categories of people in a hierarchy

social mobility (p. 249) a change in position within the social hierarchy

✓ Although some people, especially in high-income countries, may experience **social mobility,** the social standing of most people remains pretty much the same over their lifetime.

Caste and Class Systems

CASTE SYSTEMS

- are based on birth (ascription)
- permit little or no social mobility
- shape a person's entire life, including occupation and marriage
- are common in traditional, agrarian societies

pp. 249–50

CLASS SYSTEMS

- are based on both birth (ascription) and **MERITOCRACY** (individual achievement)
- permit some social mobility based on individual achievement
- are common in modern industrial and postindustrial societies

pp. 250–51

caste system (p. 249) social stratification based on ascription, or birth

class system (p. 250) social stratification based on both birth and individual achievement

meritocracy (p. 250) social stratification based on personal merit

status consistency (p. 250) the degree of uniformity in a person's social standing across various dimensions of social inequality

structural social mobility (p. 255) a shift in the social position of large numbers of people due more to changes in society itself than to individual efforts

ideology (p. 257) cultural beliefs that justify particular social arrangements, including patterns of inequality

AN ILLUSTRATION: INDIA
Although the caste system is formally outlawed in India, it is still observed in rural areas, where agriculture demands a lifetime of hard work and discipline.

- In traditional villages, people's caste determines the type of work they perform.
- People must interact with and marry others of the same ranking.
- Powerful cultural beliefs make observing caste rules a moral duty.

p. 249

- Class systems include elements of both caste and meritocracy.
- Class systems advance meritocracy to promote specialization, productivity, and efficiency.
- Class systems keep caste elements, such as family, to maintain order and social unity.
- **Status consistency** in class systems is low due to increased social mobility.

pp. 250–51

CASTE AND CLASS: THE UNITED KINGDOM

- In the Middle Ages, England had a castelike aristocracy, including the leading clergy and a hereditary nobility. The vast majority of people were commoners.
- Today's British class system mixes caste and meritocracy, producing a highly stratified society with some social mobility.

pp. 251–53

CASTE AND CLASS: JAPAN

- In the Middle Ages, Japan had a rigid caste system in which an imperial family ruled over nobles and commoners.
- Today's Japanese class system still places great importance on family background and traditional gender roles.

pp. 253–54

CLASSLESS SOCIETIES? THE FORMER SOVIET UNION

- Although the Russian Revolution in 1917 attempted to abolish social classes, the new Soviet Union was still stratified based on unequal job categories and the concentration of power in the new political elite. Economic development created new types of jobs, which resulted in **structural social mobility**.

- Since the collapse of the Soviet Union in the early 1990s, the forces of structural social mobility have turned downward and the gap between rich and poor has increased.

pp. 254–56

CHINA: EMERGING SOCIAL CLASSES

- Economic reforms introduced after the Communist revolution in 1949—including state control of factories and productive property—greatly reduced economic inequality, although social differences remained.

- In the last thirty years, China's government has loosened control of the economy, causing the emergence of a new class of business owners and an increase in economic inequality.

pp. 256–57

✓ Both caste and class systems are supported by *ideology*—cultural values and beliefs—that defines certain kinds of inequality as just (p. 257).

Theoretical Analysis of Social Stratification

The **STRUCTURAL-FUNCTIONAL APPROACH** points to ways social stratification helps society operate.

- The Davis-Moore thesis states that social stratification is universal because of its functional consequences.

- In caste systems, people are rewarded for performing the duties of their position at birth.

- In class systems, unequal rewards attract the ablest people to the most important jobs and encourage effort.

pp. 257–59

The **SOCIAL-CONFLICT APPROACH** claims that stratification divides societies in classes, benefiting some categories of people at the expense of others and causing social conflict.

- Karl Marx claimed that capitalism places economic production under the ownership of capitalists, who exploit the proletarians who sell their labor for wages.

- Max Weber identified three distinct dimensions of social stratification: economic class, social status or prestige, and power. Conflict exists between people at various positions on a multidimensional hierarchy of **Socioeconomic status (SES)**.

pp. 259–62

Davis-Moore thesis (p. 257) the functional analysis claiming that social stratification has beneficial consequences for the operation of society

blue-collar occupations (p. 260) lower-prestige jobs that involve mostly manual labor

white-collar occupations (p. 260) higher-prestige jobs that involve mostly mental activity

socioeconomic status (SES) (p. 261) a composite ranking based on various dimensions of social inequality

conspicuous consumption (p. 263) buying and using products because of the "statement" they make about social position

The **SYMBOLIC-INTERACTION APPROACH**, a micro-level analysis, explains that we size up people by looking for clues to their social standing. **Conspicuous consumption** refers to buying and displaying products that make a "statement" about social class. Most people tend to socialize with others whose social standing is similar to their own.

p. 263

See the Applying Theory table on page 262.

Social Stratification and Technology: A Global Perspective

Hunting and Gathering → Horticultural and Pastoral → Agrarian → Industrial → Postindustrial

- Gerhard Lenski explains that advancing technology initially increases social stratification, which is most intense in agrarian societies.

pp. 263–64

- Industrialization reverses the trend, reducing social stratification.

p. 264

- In postindustrial societies, social stratification again increases.

p. 264

See the Kuznets curve (Figure 10–2 on page 264).

Stratification: Facts and Values

People's beliefs about social inequality reflect not just facts but also politics and values concerning how a society should be organized.

pp. 266–67

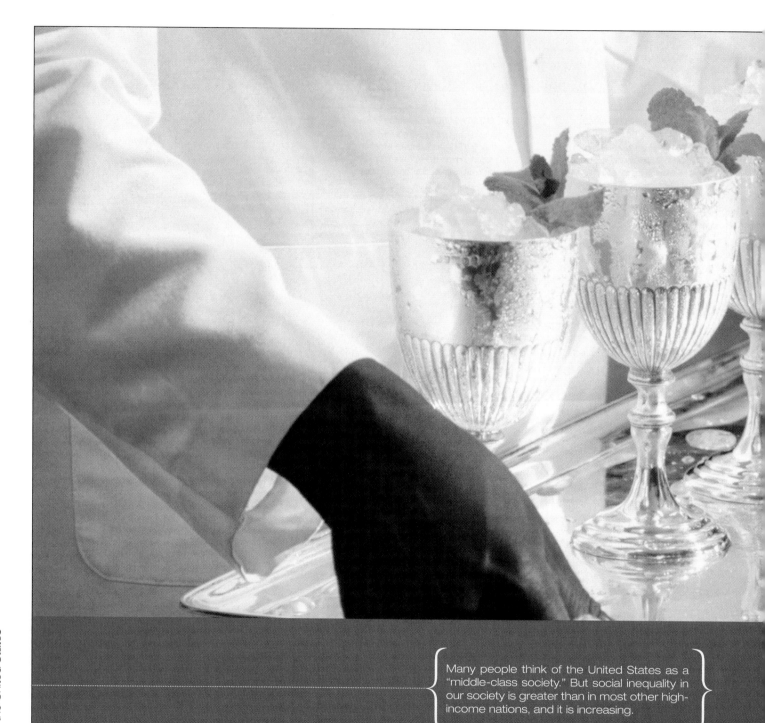

{ Many people think of the United States as a "middle-class society." But social inequality in our society is greater than in most other high-income nations, and it is increasing. }

CHAPTER 11

Social Class in the United States

SUPPLEMENTS: An outline of Chapter 11, along with supplementary lecture material and discussion topics, is found in the *Instructor's Manual.*

NOTE: Estimates suggest 70% to 90% of U.S. millionaires are first-generation millionaires.

Q: "It is easy to despise what you cannot get." Aesop

DIVERSITY: Some income inequality is the effect of age on earning power. The Census Bureau calculates median household income by age of householder: 25–34 years, $51,016; 35–44 years, $62,124, 45–54 years, $65,476; 55–64 years, $57,386; 65 years and older, $28,305 (U.S. Census Bureau, 2008).

CHAPTER OVERVIEW { This chapter surveys social stratification in the United States, beginning with a look at important measures of inequality. Many dimensions of inequality exist in our society, and inequality is greater than many people imagine.

Rosa Urias leans forward, pushing and pulling the vacuum cleaner across the hardwood floors, a motion she has repeated hundreds of times to the point that her right wrist and elbow are sore. It is now almost five o'clock in the afternoon, and this forty-five-year-old single mother of two is on her third cleaning job of the day. She works with her cousin Melitsa Sermiento, thirty-six, cleaning nine apartments and five houses each week. The two women, who both came to the United States from El Salvador, divide the money they earn, giving each one an annual income of about $28,000, barely enough to pay the bills in New York City.

But there is no shortage of work cleaning homes. Hundreds of thousands of New Yorkers make more than enough money to hire people like Rosa and Melitsa to dust their tables, mop their floors, and scrub their sinks and toilets while they are out doing their high-paying jobs, working out at the health club, or having lunch with friends.

Rosa reaches up over the bathroom sink to turn on a light so she can see better. She pulls the silver chain, but it breaks and she stands there with part of the chain hanging from her hand. She looks over at Melitsa, and both do their best to laugh it off. Then Rosa turns serious and says softly, in Spanish, "My daughter tells me I need some new dreams" (Eisenstadt, 2004).

New York may be a single large city, but the social world in which Rosa and Melitsa live is not the same as the social world of the people who hire these women. How different are the lives of the richest people in the United States and the lives of those who work hard all day just to get by? What about the lives of those who do not even have the security of work? This chapter answers all these questions, explaining some of the different "worlds" found in U.S. society, how different we are, and why the differences are getting bigger.

Dimensions of Social Inequality

The United States differs from most European nations and Japan in never having had a titled nobility. With the significant exception of our racial history, we have never known a caste system that rigidly ranks categories of people.

Even so, U.S. society is highly stratified. Not only do the rich have most of the money, but they also receive the most schooling, enjoy the best health, and consume the most goods and services. Such privilege contrasts sharply with the poverty of millions of women and men who worry about paying next month's rent or a doctor's bill when a child becomes ill. Many people think of the United States as a middle-class society, but is this really the case?

Income

One important dimension of inequality is **income**, *earnings from work or investments.* The Census Bureau reports that the median U.S. family income in 2007 was $61,355. The pie chart in the middle of Figure 11–1 illustrates the distribution of income among all U.S. families.[1] The richest 20 percent of families (earning at least $113,000 annually, with a mean of about $187,000) received 47.3 percent of all income, while the bottom 20 percent (earning less than $28,000, with a mean of about $16,000) received only 4.1 percent (U.S. Census Bureau, 2008).

The table at the left in Figure 11–1 provides a closer look at income distribution. In 2007, the highest-paid 5 percent of U.S. families earned at least $197,000 (averaging almost $317,000), or 20.1 percent of all income, more than the total earnings of the lowest-paid 40 percent. At the very top of the income pyramid, the richest half of 1 percent earned at least $1.8 million.

---

[1]The Census Bureau reports both mean and median incomes for families ("two or more persons related by blood, marriage, or adoption") and households ("two or more persons sharing a living unit"). In 2007, mean family income was $78,845, higher than the median ($61,355) because high-income families pull up the mean but not the median. For households, these figures are somewhat lower—a mean of $67,609 and a median of $50,233—largely because families average 3.15 people and households average 2.56.

NOTE: "Wealth" in this context means *privately held wealth* because public property (lands, forests, roads, transportation systems, and the military) is excluded from such considerations. According to the World Bank, if all public and private wealth in the U.S. were divided equally, each person would have about $500,000.

DISCUSS: We all think of being rich as having more money than we have now. But what do students think is a good definition of being rich in terms of income? Why?

THEN AND NOW: 1970 income data for comparison with Figure 11–1 for each quintile: 40.9%, 23.8%, 17.6%, 12.2%, 5.5%.

NOTE: Family size affects a child's share of resources and eventual accumulation of wealth. The Census Bureau reports that among people who were born between 1957 and 1964, those who grew up as an only child have a median net worth of $62,000; those with one sibling, $49,000; those with six or more siblings, $6,000.

income earnings from work or investments

wealth the total value of money and other assets, minus outstanding debts

SEEING SOCIOLOGY
in Everyday Life

Why do you think so many people view the United States as a middle-class society in which most people have more or less equal social standing?

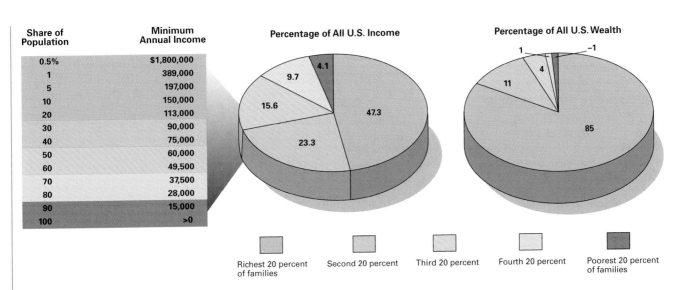

FIGURE 11–1   Distribution of Income and Wealth in the United States, 2007

Income, and especially wealth, is divided unequally in U.S. society.

Sources: Income data from U.S. Census Bureau (2008); wealth data based on Keister (2000), Bucks, Kennickell, & Moore (2006), Wolff (2007), and author estimates.

During recent decades, income inequality has increased. One part of this trend is that the very richest people now receive a much larger share of all income. For example, in 1978, the highest-paid 0.1 percent of all earners received 2.7 percent of all income. By 2007, this elite category (people making $7 million or more a year) took home more than four times as much, equaling 11.6 percent of all income (Internal Revenue Service, 2008; Fox, 2009).

Wealth

Income is only a part of a person's or family's **wealth,** *the total value of money and other assets, minus outstanding debts.* Wealth—including stocks, bonds, and real estate—is distributed more unequally than income. Recent reductions in taxes on income earned by individuals and on wealth passed from one generation to the next are likely to make this inequality even greater (Wahl, 2003).

The pie chart on the right in Figure 11–1 shows the distribution of wealth. The richest 20 percent of U.S. families own roughly 85 percent of the country's wealth. High up in this privileged category are the wealthiest 5 percent of families—the "very rich," who own 60 percent of all private property. Richer still, with wealth in the tens of millions of dollars, are the 1 percent of families that qualify as "super-rich" and possess about 35 percent of this nation's privately held resources (Keister, 2000; Keister & Moller, 2000; Bucks, Kennickell, & Moore, 2006;

Davies et al., 2006; Wolff, 2007). At the top of the wealth pyramid, the ten richest U.S. families have a combined net worth of more than $285 billion (Kroll, 2008). This amount equals the total property of 3 million average families, including enough people to fill the cities of Chicago, Houston, Philadelphia, Phoenix, and San Diego.

The wealth of the average U.S. family is currently about $100,000 (Bucks, Kennickell, & Moore, 2006; Federal Reserve Board, 2007). Family wealth reflects the value of homes, cars, investments, insurance policies, retirement pensions, furniture, clothing, and all other personal property, minus a home mortgage and other debts. The wealth of average people is not only less than that of the rich, however, but also different in kind. Most people's wealth centers on a home and a car—that is, property that generates no income—but the wealth of the rich is mostly in the form of stocks and other income-producing investments.

When financial assets are balanced against debts, the lowest-ranking 40 percent of U.S. families have virtually no wealth at all. The negative percentage shown in Figure 11–1 for the poorest 20 percent of the population means that these families actually live in debt.

Power

In the United States, wealth is an important source of power. The small proportion of families that control most of the nation's wealth

NOTE: The government has long curtailed inheritance using taxation. The first such tax existed from 1797 to 1802, another from 1862 to 1870, and a third from 1898 to 1902; all were intended to generate revenue. The current tax, exacted in 1916 to pay for World War I, was not later repealed. The tax reforms of 2001 will phase out estate taxes by 2011, although estate taxes will return in 2012 unless Congress enacts further legislation.

NOTE: How much money do people need to "get by"? The average person says $25,000; people in the top 1% (those with income over $250,000 or assets over $2.5 million) say $80,000. "To live in reasonable comfort"? Average: $41,000; rich: $150,000. "To fulfill all dreams"? Average: $102,000; rich: $500,000 ("Zandi Group Survey," 1998).

SEEING SOCIOLOGY
in Everyday Life

People of all social classes have the same right to vote. But can you think of ways in which the rich have more power to shape U.S. society than the rest of us?

MAKING THE GRADE

Notice in the sections below how ancestry, race and ethnicity, and gender can operate as caste elements.

also shape the agenda of the entire society. As explained in Chapter 17 ("Politics and Government"), some sociologists argue that such concentrated wealth weakens democracy because the political system serves the interests of the super-rich.

Occupational Prestige

In addition to generating income, work is also an important source of social prestige. We commonly evaluate each other according to the kind of work we do, giving greater respect to those who do what we consider important work and less respect to others with more modest jobs.

Sociologists measure the relative prestige of various occupations (NORC, 2007). Table 11–1 shows that people give high prestige to occupations such as physician, lawyer, and engineer that require extensive training and generate high income. By contrast, less prestigious work—as a waitress or janitor, for example—pays less and requires less schooling. Occupational prestige rankings are much the same in all high-income nations (Lin & Xie, 1988).

In any society, high-prestige occupations go to privileged categories of people. In Table 11–1, for example, the highest-ranking occupations are dominated by men. We have to go more than a dozen jobs down the list to find "secondary school teacher" and "registered nurse," careers chosen mostly by women. Similarly, many of the lowest-prestige jobs are commonly performed by people of color.

Schooling

Industrial societies have expanded opportunities for schooling, but some people still receive much more education than others. More than 85 percent of women and men aged twenty-five and older have completed high school. But just 29 percent of men and 30 percent of women have completed a four-year college degree.

Schooling affects both occupation and income, since most (but not all) of the better-paying white-collar jobs shown in Table 11–1 require a college degree or other advanced study. Most blue-collar jobs, which bring lower income and social prestige, require less schooling.

U.S. Stratification: Merit and Caste

As we discussed in Chapter 10 ("Social Stratification"), the U.S. class system is partly a meritocracy in that social position reflects individual talent and effort. But it also has caste elements, because birth plays a part in what we become later in life.

Ancestry

Nothing affects social standing in the United States as much as being born into a particular family, which has a strong bearing on schooling, occupation, and income. Research suggests that more than one-third of our country's richest individuals—those with hundreds of millions of dollars in wealth—acquired some of their fortunes from inheritance (Miller & Newcomb, 2005). Inherited poverty shapes the future of tens of millions of others.

Race and Ethnicity

Race is closely linked to social position in the United States. White people receive more schooling than African Americans and have higher overall occupational standing. The median African American family's income was $40,143 in 2007, just 57 percent of the $69,937 earned by non-Hispanic white families. This inequality in income makes a real difference in people's lives. For example, non-Hispanic white families are more likely to own their homes (75 percent do) than black families (47 percent) (U.S. Census Bureau, 2008).

Families that include married couples earn more than families with a single parent. With this fact in mind, some of the racial difference in income results from the larger share of single-parent families among African Americans. Comparing only families headed by married couples, African Americans earned 80 percent as much as non-Hispanic white families.

Members of our society tend to think of social class in terms of income and wealth, as if to say "I am what I own." For this reason, conspicuous consumption—buying and displaying various goods partly with an eye toward gaining social standing in the eyes of others—is a common pattern. How have you engaged in conspicuous consumption?

NOTE: The survey data in Table 11–2 show that people consider some jobs much more prestigious than others. Point out that most white-collar work is evaluated as more desirable than most blue-collar work. In addition, most jobs typically performed by women or minorities tend to fall lower in the rankings than jobs typically performed by white men.

DISCUSS: As we move into a postindustrial society, will prestige be less a matter of owning things and more a matter of developing personal creative potential?

NOTE: Among the reasons for the widening income gap in the United States are an increase in married couples with two people working for income and a widening pay gap between high school graduates and college graduates.

● SEEING SOCIOLOGY
in Everyday Life

Identify the jobs in Table 11–1 that have traditionally been performed by people of color. What pattern do you discover?

● SEEING SOCIOLOGY
in Everyday Life

Reading down from the top of Table 11-1, how far do you have to go before you see a job in which most workers would be women?

Table 11–1 The Relative Social Prestige of Selected Occupations in the United States

White-Collar Occupations	Prestige Score	Blue-Collar Occupations	White-Collar Occupations	Prestige Score	Blue-Collar Occupations
Physician	82		Real estate agent	49	
College or university professor	78		Bookkeeper	48	
Lawyer	76			48	Machinist
Dentist	74			48	Police officer
Physicist, astronomer	74		Musician, composer	46	
Architect	71			46	Secretary
Psychologist	71		Real estate agent or broker	44	
Airline pilot	70			42	Mail carrier
Electrical engineer	69		Photographer	41	
Member of the clergy	69			41	Tailor
Sociologist	66			40	Carpenter
Secondary school teacher	63			37	Auto body repairer
Optometrist	62			36	Bricklayer, stonemason
Registered nurse	62			33	Baker
Dental hygienist	61			33	Bulldozer operator
Pharmacist	61			33	Hairdresser
Elementary school teacher	60			32	Truck driver
Veterinarian	60		Cashier	31	
Actor	58		File clerk	30	
Accountant	57		Retail salesperson	29	
Economist	57			28	Waiter, waitress
Painter, sculptor	56			25	Bartender
Librarian	55			25	Child care worker
	53	Aircraft mechanic		23	Farm laborer
	53	Firefighter		23	Household laborer
Social worker	52			22	Door-to-door salesperson
Athlete	51			22	Janitor
Computer programmer	51			22	Taxi driver
Editor, reporter	51			17	Garbage collector
Radio or TV announcer	51			14	Bellhop
	49	Electrician		9	Shoe shiner

Source: Adapted from *General Social Surveys, 1972–2007: Cumulative Codebook* (Chicago: National Opinion Research Center, 2008).

Over time, the income difference builds into a huge wealth gap (Altonji, Doraszelski, & Segal, 2000). A recent survey of families by the Federal Reserve found that median wealth for minority families, including African Americans, Hispanics, and Asian Americans ($27,100), is just 19 percent of the median ($142,700) for non-Hispanic white families (Bucks, Kennickell, & Moore, 2006).

Social ranking involves ethnicity as well. People of English ancestry have always enjoyed the most wealth and the greatest power in

● SEEING SOCIOLOGY
in Everyday Life

To what extent is gender still an element of caste? That is, as you look around you, do women seem to have the same opportunities and privileges as men?

● MAKING THE GRADE

Pay attention to a key difference between the small number of "upper-uppers," who are almost always born (or occasionally marry) into "old money," and the much larger number of "lower-uppers," who move upward socially as they earn lots of "new money."

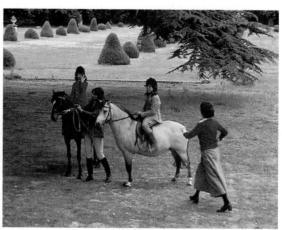

People often distinguish between the "new rich" and families with "old money." Men and women who suddenly begin to earn high incomes tend to spend their money on status symbols because they enjoy the new thrill of high-roller living and they want others to know of their success. Those who grow up surrounded by wealth, by contrast, are used to a privileged way of life and are more quiet about it. Thus the conspicuous consumption of the lower-upper class (*left*) can differ dramatically from the more private pursuits and understatement of the upper-upper class (*right*).

U.S. society. The Latino population—the largest U.S. racial or ethnic minority—has long been disadvantaged. In 2007, the median income among Hispanic families was $40,500, which is 58 percent of the median income for non-Hispanic white families. A detailed examination of how race and ethnicity affect social standing is presented in Chapter 14 ("Race and Ethnicity").

Gender

Of course, both men and women are found in families at every class level. Yet on average, women have less income, wealth, and occupational prestige than men. Among single-parent families, those headed by a woman are more than twice as likely to be poor than those headed by a man. Chapter 13 ("Gender Stratification") examines the link between gender and social stratification.

Social Classes in the United States

As Chapter 10 ("Social Stratification") explained, rankings in a caste system are rigid and obvious to all. Defining social categories in a more fluid class system such as ours, however, is not so easy.

There is an old joke about two guys who order a pizza, asking that it be cut into six slices because they aren't hungry enough to eat eight. Sociologists do the same thing with social class: Some divide the population into more classes than others. At one extreme, people find as many as six or even seven social classes; at the other, some follow Karl Marx and see two major classes: capitalists and proletarians. Still others side with Max Weber, claiming that stratification creates not clear-cut classes but a multidimensional status hierarchy.

Defining classes in U.S. society is difficult because of our relatively low level of status consistency. Especially toward the middle of the hierarchy, people's standing in one dimension may not be the same as their standing in another. For example, a government official may have the power to administer a multimillion-dollar budget yet may earn only a modest personal income. Similarly, many members of the clergy enjoy ample prestige but only moderate power and low pay. Or consider a lucky casino poker player who wins no special respect but makes a lot of money.

Finally, the social mobility characteristic of class systems—again, most pronounced around the middle—means that social position may change during a person's lifetime, further blurring class boundaries. With these issues in mind, we will examine four general rankings: the upper class, the middle class, the working class, and the lower class.

The Upper Class

Families in the upper class—5 percent of the U.S. population—earn at least $197,000 a year, and some earn ten times that much or more. As a general rule, the more a family's income comes from inherited

● SEEING SOCIOLOGY
in Everyday Life

When you think about the "American dream," you imagine rising to which part of the upper class? Explain your answer.

wealth in the form of stocks and bonds, real estate, and other investments, the stronger a family's claim to being upper-class.

In 2008, *Forbes* magazine profiled the richest 400 people in the country, who were worth at least $1.3 billion (and as much as $57 billion) (Miller & Greenberg, 2008). These people are the core of the upper class, or Karl Marx's "capitalists"—the owners of the means of production or most of the nation's private wealth. Many upper-class people are business owners, executives in large corporations, or senior government officials. Historically, the upper class has been composed mostly of white Anglo-Saxon Protestants, but this is less true today (Pyle & Koch, 2001).

Upper-Uppers

The *upper-upper class,* sometimes called "blue bloods" or simply "society," includes less than 1 percent of the U.S. population (Coleman & Neugarten, 1971; Baltzell, 1995). Membership is almost always the result of birth, as suggested by the joke that the easiest way to become an upper-upper is to be born one. Most of these families possess enormous wealth, which is primarily inherited. For this reason, members of the upper-upper class are said to have "old money."

Set apart by their wealth, upper-uppers live in old, exclusive neighborhoods, such as Beacon Hill in Boston, Rittenhouse Square in Philadelphia, the Gold Coast of Chicago, and Nob Hill in San Francisco. Their children typically attend private schools with others of similar background and complete their schooling at high-prestige colleges and universities. In the tradition of European aristocrats, they study liberal arts rather than vocational skills.

Women of the upper-upper class do volunteer work for charitable organizations. Such activities serve a dual purpose: They help the larger community, and they build networks that broaden this elite's power (Ostrander, 1980, 1984).

Lower-Uppers

Most upper-class people actually fall into the *lower-upper class.* The queen of England is in the upper-upper class based not on her fortune of $650 million but on her family tree. J. K. Rowling, author of the Harry Potter books, is probably worth twice as much—more than $1 billion—but this woman (who was once on welfare) is a member of the lower-upper class. The major difference, in other words, is that lower-uppers are the "working rich" who get their money mostly by earning it rather than inheritance. These well-to-do families—who make up 3 or 4 percent of the U.S. population—generally live in large homes in expensive neighborhoods, own vacation homes near the water or in the mountains, and send their children to private schools and good colleges. Yet most of the "new rich" do not gain entry into the clubs and associations of "old money" families.

In the United States, what we often call the American dream has been to earn enough to join the ranks of the lower-upper class. The athlete who signs a multimillion-dollar contract, the actress who

For decades, U.S. farm families who worked hard could expect to end up in the middle class. But the trend toward large-scale agribusiness has put the future of the small family farm in doubt. Although many young people in rural areas are turning away from farming toward other careers, some carry on, incorporating high technology into their farm management in their determined efforts to succeed.

lands a starring role in a Hollywood film, the computer whiz who creates the latest Internet site to capture the public's attention, and even the person who hits it big by winning a huge lottery jackpot are the talented achievers and lucky people who reach the lower-upper class.

The Middle Class

Made up of 40 to 45 percent of the U.S. population, the large middle class has a tremendous influence on our culture. Television programs and movies usually show middle-class people, and most commercial advertising is directed at these average consumers. The middle class contains far more racial and ethnic diversity than the upper class.

Upper-Middles

People in the top half of this category are called the *upper-middle class,* based on above-average income in the range of $113,000 to $197,000 a year. Such income allows upper-middle-class families to

THE MAP: Most of the 50 richest counties are found around large metropolitan areas, including New York (10), San Francisco (5), and Washington, D.C. (5). Although some rural counties are also rich, these tend to be areas popular as affluent getaways, including Pitkin County, Colorado (Aspen), and Nantucket, Massachusetts. Low-income counties are likely to be rural, and many also have a high immigrant population. Worth noting is that the patterns are very much the same as in maps in previous editions with data from 1990.

NOTE: The importance of a college education to middle-class standing is suggested by people placing college decals on car windows.

Q: "In our society, it is murder, psychologically, to deprive a man of a job or an income. You are in effect saying to that man that he has no right to exist." Martin Luther King Jr.

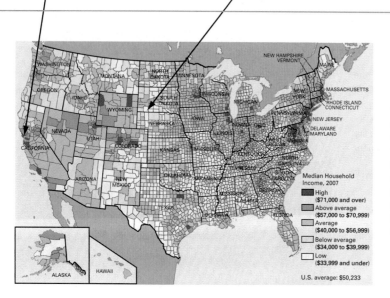

The Waehner family lives in Marin County, California, one of the highest-income communities in the United States, where annual household income averages more than $100,000.

Mitakuye Oyasin lives on the Pine Ridge Indian Reservation, one of the poorest communities in the United States, where annual household income averages less than $4,000.

Seeing Ourselves

NATIONAL MAP 11–1

Household Income across the United States, 2007

This map shows the median household income (that is, how much money, on average, a household earned) in the more than 3,000 counties that make up the United States, for the year 2007. The richest counties, shown in the darker shades of green, are not spread randomly across the country. Nor are the poorest U.S. counties, which are shown in the lightest green. Looking at the map, what patterns do you see in the distribution of wealth and poverty across the United States? What can you say about wealth and poverty in urban and rural areas?

Source: U.S. Census Bureau (2008).

Median Household Income, 2007
- High ($71,000 and over)
- Above average ($57,000 to $70,999)
- Average ($40,000 to $56,999)
- Below average ($34,000 to $39,999)
- Low ($33,999 and under)

U.S. average: $50,233

live in comfortable homes in fairly expensive areas, own several automobiles, and build investments. Two-thirds of upper-middle-class children graduate from college, and postgraduate degrees are common. Many go on to high-prestige careers as physicians, engineers, lawyers, accountants, and business executives. Lacking the power of the richest people to influence national or international events, upper-middles often play an important role in local political affairs.

Average-Middles

The rest of the middle class falls close to the center of the U.S. class structure. *Average-middles* typically work at less prestigious white-collar jobs as bank branch managers, high school teachers, and government office workers or in highly skilled blue-collar jobs such as electrical work and carpentry. Family income is between $50,000 and $112,000 a year, which is roughly the national average.[2] Middle-class people typically build up a small amount of wealth over the course of their working lives, mostly in the form of a house and a retirement account. Middle-class men and women are likely to be high school graduates, but the odds are just fifty-fifty that they will complete a college degree, usually at a less expensive, state-supported school.

The Working Class

About one-third of the population falls within the working class (sometimes called the *lower-middle class*). In Marxist terms, the working class forms the core of the industrial proletariat. The blue-collar

jobs held by members of the working class yield a family income of between $25,000 and $50,000 a year, somewhat below the national average. Working-class families have little or no wealth and are vulnerable to financial problems caused by unemployment or illness.

Many working-class jobs provide little personal satisfaction, require discipline but rarely imagination, and subject workers to continual supervision. These jobs also offer fewer benefits, such as medical insurance and pension plans. About two-thirds of working-class families own their own homes, usually in lower-cost neighborhoods. College becomes a reality for only about one-third of working-class children.

The Lower Class

The remaining 20 percent of our population make up the lower class. Low income makes their lives insecure and difficult. In 2007, the federal government classified 37 million people (12.5 percent of the population) as poor. Millions more—called the "working poor"—are slightly better off, holding low-prestige jobs that provide little satisfaction and minimal income. Barely half manage to complete high school, and only one in four ever reaches college.

Society segregates the lower class, especially when the poor are racial or ethnic minorities. About 45 percent of lower-class families own their own homes, typically in the least desirable neighborhoods. Although poor neighborhoods are usually found in our inner cities, lower-class families also live in rural communities, especially in the South.

Most communities contain people of various class levels. In the country as a whole, however, some areas are wealthier than others. National Map 11–1 shows one measure of social class—median household income—for all the counties in the United States.

[2]In some parts of the United States where the cost of living is very high (say, San Francisco), a family might need $150,000 or more in annual income to reach the middle class.

Q: "Class is for European democracies or something else; it isn't for the United States of America. We're not going to be divided by class." President George H. W. Bush

NOTE: A rough listing of upper-uppers is the *Social Register*, first published in 1887, which lists the home addresses and club affiliations of families. A rough listing of lower-uppers is the national edition of *Who's Who*, which lists the personal achievements of individuals.

Q: "A great many people are in the working class and don't know it." Marshal Berman

Q: "Underclass has become the code word for lower-income blacks and Puerto Ricans." Leslie Dunbar (1988:16)

DIVERSITY: The "underclass" includes only about 5% of the poor, who are chronically poor, living in inner-city areas, and dependent on welfare.

● SEEING SOCIOLOGY
in Everyday Life

If you wanted to assess someone's social class position and could ask only one question, what would it be? Explain your decision.

● MAKING THE GRADE

Be sure you understand how social class position involves not only money but also "cultural capital."

The Difference Class Makes

Social stratification affects nearly every dimension of our lives. We will briefly examine some of the ways social standing is linked to our health, values, politics, and family life.

Health

Health is closely related to social standing. Children born into poor families are three times more likely to die from disease, neglect, accidents, or violence during their first years of life than children born into privileged families. Among adults, people with above-average incomes are almost twice as likely as low-income people to describe their health as excellent. In addition, richer people live, on average, five years longer because they eat more nutritious food, live in safer and less stressful environments, and receive better medical care (Adams, Lucas, & Barnes, 2008).

Values and Attitudes

Some cultural values vary from class to class. The "old rich" have an unusually strong sense of family history because their social position is based on wealth passed down from generation to generation. Secure in their birthright privileges, upper-uppers also favor understated manners and tastes; many "new rich" engage in conspicuous consumption, using homes, cars, and even airplanes as status symbols to make a statement about their social position.

Affluent people with greater education and financial security are also more tolerant of controversial behavior such as homosexuality. Working-class people, who grow up in an atmosphere of greater supervision and discipline and are less likely to attend college, tend to be less tolerant (Lareau, 2002; NORC, 2007).

Social class has a great deal to do with self-concept. People with higher social standing experience more confidence in everyday interaction for the simple reason that others tend to view them as having greater importance. The Thinking About Diversity box on page 282 describes the challenges faced by one young woman from a poor family attending a college where most students are from elite families.

Politics

Do political attitudes follow class lines? The answer is yes, but the pattern is complex. A desire to protect their wealth prompts well-off people to be more conservative on *economic* issues, favoring, for example, lower taxes. But on *social* issues such as abortion and gay rights, highly educated, more affluent people are more liberal. People of lower social standing, by contrast, tend to be economic liberals, favoring government social programs that benefit them, but typically hold more conservative views on social issues (NORC, 2007).

A simple pattern emerges when it comes to political involvement. Higher-income people, who are better served by the system, are more likely to vote and to join political organizations than people with low incomes. In presidential elections, 80 percent of adults with family incomes of $75,000 vote, compared to about 60 percent of those with family incomes of $35,000 (U.S. Census Bureau, 2008).

Family and Gender

Social class also shapes family life. Generally, lower-class families are somewhat larger than middle-class families because of earlier marriage and less use of birth control. Another family pattern is that working-class parents encourage children to conform to conventional norms and to respect authority figures. Parents of higher social standing pass on different "cultural capital" to their children, teaching them to express their individuality and use their imagination more freely. In both cases, parents are looking to the future: The odds are that less privileged children will have jobs that require them to follow rules and that more privileged children will have careers that require more creativity (Kohn, 1977; McLeod, 1995; Lareau, 2002).

The more money a family has, the more parents can develop their children's talents and abilities. An affluent family earning an average

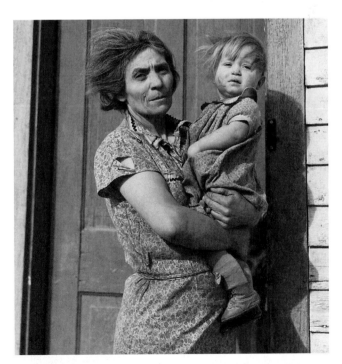

Compared to high-income people, low-income people are half as likely to report good health and, on average, live about five fewer years. The toll of low income—played out in inadequate nutrition, little medical care, and high stress—is easy to see on the faces of the poor, who look old before their time.

SEEING SOCIOLOGY
in Everyday Life

After reading the box below, think about times when you have felt out of place in some setting based on your social class position. Why did you feel this way? How do such feelings show that we often understand class differences in terms of personal worthiness?

THINKING ABOUT DIVERSITY: RACE, CLASS, & GENDER

The Power of Class: A Low-Income Student Asks, "Am I as Good as You?"

Marcella grew up without the privileges that most other students on the campus of this private, liberal arts college take for granted. During her senior year, she and I talked at length about her college experiences and why social class presented a huge challenge to her. Marcella is not her real name; she wishes to remain anonymous. I have summarized what she has said about her college life in the story that follows.

When I came here, I entered a new world. I found myself in a strange and dangerous place. All around me were people with habits and ideas I did not understand. A thousand times, I thought to myself, I hope all of you will realize that there are other worlds out there and that I am from one of them. Will you accept me?

I am a child of poverty, a young woman raised in a world of want and violence. I am now on the campus of an elite college. I may have a new identity as a college student. But my old life is still going on in my head. I have not been able to change how I think of myself.

Do you want to find out more about me? Learn more about the power of social class to shape how we feel about ourselves? Here is what I want to say to you.

When I was growing up, I envied most of you. You lived in a middle-class bubble, a world that held you, protected you, and comforted you. Not me. While your parents were discussing current events, planning family trips, and looking out for you, my father and mother were screaming at each other. I will never be able to forget summer nights when I lay in my bed, sticky with sweat, biting my fingernails as a telephone crashed against the wall that separated my room from theirs. My father was drunk and out of control; my mother ducked just in time.

Your fathers and mothers work in office buildings. They have good jobs, as doctors, lawyers, and architects; they are corporate managers; they run

small businesses. Your mothers and fathers are people who matter. My mom takes the bus to a hospital where she works for $10 an hour cleaning up after people. She spends her shift doing what she is told. My dad? Who knows. He was a deadbeat, a drunk, a drug addict. I don't know if he still is or not. I haven't heard from him in eight years.

You grew up in a neighborhood and probably lived for many years in one house. My family lived in low-cost rental housing. We moved a lot. When there was no money for rent, we packed up our stuff and moved to a new place. It seemed like we were always running away from something.

You grew up with books, with trips to the library, with parents who read to you. You learned how to speak well and have an impressive vocabulary. I never heard a bedtime story, and I had maybe one inspiring teacher. Most of what I know I had to learn on my own. Maybe that's why I always feel like I am trying to catch up to you.

You know how to use forks, knives, and spoons the right way. You know how to eat Chinese food and what to order at a Thai restaurant. You have favorite Italian dishes. You know how to order wine. You know about German beers, Danish cheeses, and French sauces. Me? I grew up having Thanksgiving

dinner on paper plates, eating turkey served by social service volunteers. When you ask me to go with you to some special restaurant, I make some excuse and stay home. I can't afford it. I am afraid you will find out how little I know about things you take for granted.

How did I ever get to this college? I remember one of my teachers telling me that I "have promise." The college admission office accepted me. But I am not sure why. I was given a scholarship that covers most of my tuition. That solved one big problem, and now I am here. But sometimes I am not sure I will stay. I have to study more than many of you to learn things you already know. I have to work two part-time jobs to make the money I needed to buy a used computer, clothes, and the occasional pizza at the corner place where many of you spend so much time.

It's amazing to me that I am here. I realize how lucky I am. But now that I am here, I realize that the road is so much longer than I thought it would be. Getting to this college was only part of the journey. The scholarship was only part of the answer. The biggest challenge for me is what goes on every day—the thousands of ways in which you live a life that I still don't really understand, the thousands of things that I won't know or that I will do wrong that will blow my cover, and show me up for the fraud I am.

WHAT DO YOU THINK?

1. How does this story show that social class involves much more than how much money a person has?

2. Why does Marcella worry that other people will think she is a "fraud"? If you could speak to her about this fear, what would you say?

3. Have you ever had similar feelings about being less important than—or better than—someone else based on social class position? Explain.

SOCIAL SURVEY: "On the whole, do you think it should or should not be the government's responsibility to reduce the differences between the rich and the poor?" (GSS 1998, N = 1,284; NORC, 2008)

"Definitely should be"   27.9%   "Definitely should not be"   20.5%
"Probably should be"   23.0%   "Don't know"/No response   2.6%
"Probably should not be"   26.0%

NOTE: Figure 11–2 shows changes in income for the five quintiles of the U.S. population. Explain to students that these quintiles do not contain all the same families over the 25-year period. In general, the top quintile has gotten richer over time, but every year some families enter this quintile and some families leave it.

NOTE: Bill Gates spent $53.4 million to build his current house.

intragenerational social mobility a change in social position occurring during a person's lifetime

intergenerational social mobility upward or downward social mobility of children in relation to their parents

● SEEING SOCIOLOGY
in Everyday Life

One reason for the increasing gap between high- and low-paid workers is the increasing value of a college degree in our postindustrial society.

of $115,400 a year will spend $298,680 raising a child born in 2007 to the age of eighteen. Middle-class people, with an average annual income of $61,000, will spend $204,060, and a lower-income family, earning less than $45,800, will spend $148,320 (Lino, 2008). Privilege leads to privilege as family life reproduces the class structure in each generation.

Class also shapes our world of relationships. In a classic study of married life, Elizabeth Bott (1971, orig. 1957) found that most working-class couples divide their responsibilities according to gender roles; middle-class couples, by contrast, are more egalitarian, sharing more activities and expressing greater intimacy. More recently, Karen Walker (1995) discovered that working-class friendships typically serve as sources of material assistance; middle-class friendships are likely to involve shared interests and leisure pursuits.

Social Mobility

Ours is a dynamic society marked by quite a bit of social movement. Earning a college degree, landing a higher-paying job, or marrying someone who earns a good income contributes to *upward social mobility;* dropping out of school, losing a job, or becoming divorced (especially for women) may result in *downward social mobility.*

Over the long term, social mobility is not so much a matter of changes in individuals as changes in society itself. In the first half of the twentieth century, for example, industrialization expanded the U.S. economy, pushing up living standards. Even people who were not good swimmers rode the rising tide of prosperity. In recent decades, the closing of U.S. factories has pushed *structural social mobility* in a downward direction, dealing economic setbacks to many people. The economic downturn that hit hard in 2008 and 2009 reduced the income and economic opportunities of millions of people.

Sociologists distinguish between shorter- and longer-term changes in social position. **Intragenerational social mobility** is *a change in social position occurring during a person's lifetime* (*intra* is Latin for "within"). **Intergenerational social mobility,** *upward or downward social mobility of children in relation to their parents,* is important because it usually reveals long-term changes in society, such as industrialization, that affect everyone (*inter* is Latin for "between").

Research on Mobility

In few societies do people think about "getting ahead" as much as in the United States. Moving up, after all, is the American dream. But is there as much social mobility as we like to think?

One recent study of intergenerational mobility shows that about 32 percent of U.S. men have the same type of work as their fathers, 37 percent have been upwardly mobile (for example, a son born to a father with a blue-collar job now does white-collar work), and 32 percent have been downwardly mobile (for example, the father has a white-collar job

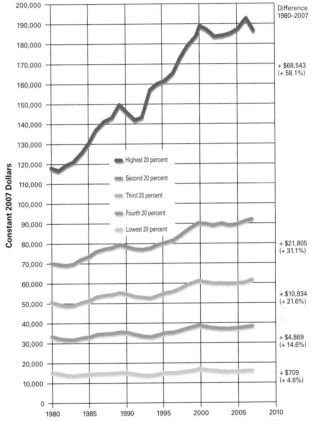

FIGURE 11–2   Mean Annual Income, U.S. Families, 1980–2007 (in 2007 dollars, adjusted for inflation)

The gap between high-income and low-income families is wider today than it was in 1980.

Source: U.S. Census Bureau (2008).

and the son does blue-collar work). Among women, 27 percent showed no change in relation to their fathers, 46 percent were upwardly mobile, and 28 percent were downwardly mobile (Beller & Hout, 2006).

Horizontal social mobility—changing jobs at the same class level—is even more common; overall, about 80 percent of children show at least some type of social mobility in relation to their fathers (Hout, 1998; Beller & Hout, 2006).

Research points to four general conclusions about social mobility in the United States:

1. **Social mobility over the past century has been fairly high.** A high level of mobility is what we would expect in an industrial class system.

Q: "I know of nothing more despicable and pathetic than a man who devotes all the hours of the waking day to the making of money for money's sake." John D. Rockefeller

NOTE: The share of U.S. families owning stock rose through the 1990s from about 20% to about 50% today.

SOCIAL SURVEY: "Differences in income in America are too large." (GSS 2000, N = 1,272; Codebook, 2005:1446)

"Strongly agree"	23.3%	"Disagree"	8.6%
"Agree"	38.4%	"Strongly disagree"	3.0%
"Neither agree nor disagree"	20.0%	"Don't know"/No response	6.6%

Seeing SOCIOLOGY in the NEWS

Newsweek

The End of Upward Mobility?

By JOEL KOTKIN
January 26, 2009

Barack Obama's ascension to the presidency won't end racism, but it does mean race is no longer the dominant issue in American politics. Instead, over the coming decades, class will likely constitute the major dividing line in our society—and the greatest threat to America's historic aspirations. This is a fundamental shift from the last century. Writing in the early 1900s, W.E.B. DuBois observed, "The problem of the 20th century is the problem of the color line." Developments in the ensuing years bore out this assertion. Indeed, before the 1960s, the decade of Barack Obama's birth, even the most talented people of color faced often insurmountable barriers to reaching their full potential. Today in a multiracial America, the path to success has opened up to an extent unimaginable in DuBois's time.

Obama's ascent reflects in particular the rise of the black bourgeoisie from tokens to a force at the heart of the meritocracy. Since the late 1960s, the proportion of African-American households living in poverty has shrunk from 70 percent to 46 percent, while the black middle class has grown from 27 percent to 37 percent. Perhaps more remarkable, the percentage who are considered prosperous—earning more than $107,000 a year in 2007 dollars—expanded from 3 percent to 17 percent.

Yet as racial equity has improved, class disparities between rich and poor, between the ultra-affluent and the middle class, have widened. This gap transcends race. African-Americans and Latinos may tend, on average, to be poorer than whites or Asians, but stagnant or even diminishing incomes affect all ethnic groups. (Most housecleaners are white, for instance—and the same goes for other low-wage professions.) Divisions may not be as visible as during the Gilded Age.

As Irving Kristol once noted, "Who doesn't wear blue jeans these days?" You can walk into a film studio or software firm and have trouble distinguishing upper management from midlevel employees.

But from the 1940s to the 1970s, the American middle class enjoyed steadily increasing incomes that stayed on a par with those in the upper classes. Since then, wages for most workers have lagged behind. As a result, the relatively small number of Americans with incomes seven times or more above the poverty level have achieved almost all the recent gains in wealth. Most disturbingly, the rate of upward mobility has stagnated overall, which means it is no easier for the poor to move up today than it was in the 1970s.

This disparity is strikingly evident in income data compiled by Citigroup, which shows that the top 1 percent of U.S. households now account for as much of the nation's total wealth . . . as they did

2. **Within a single generation, social mobility is usually small.** Most young families increase their income over time as they gain education and skills. For example, a typical family headed by a thirty-year-old earned about $57,000 in 2007; a typical family headed by a fifty-year-old earned $80,000 (U.S. Census Bureau, 2008). Yet only a few people move "from rags to riches" (the way J. K. Rowling did) or lose a lot of money (a number of rock stars who made it big had little money a few years later). Most social mobility involves limited movement within one class level rather than striking moves between classes.

3. **The long-term trend in social mobility has been upward.** Industrialization, which greatly expanded the U.S. economy, and the growth of white-collar work over the course of the twentieth century have raised living standards.

4. **Social mobility since the 1970s has been uneven.** Real income (adjusted for inflation) rose during the twentieth century until the 1970s. Between 1975 and 1985, gains were far smaller. During the 1980s, real income changed little for many people, rising slowly during the 1990s and falling slightly after 2000. The economic recession that began in 2008 is likely to result in downward social mobility for most U.S. families. Seeing Sociology in the News reports evidence that fewer people in this country are getting ahead.

Mobility by Income Level

The experience of social mobility depends on where in the social class system you happen to be. Figure 11–2 on page 283 shows how U.S.

families at different income levels made out between 1980 and 2007. Well-to-do families (the highest 20 percent, but not all the same families over the entire period) saw their incomes jump 58 percent, from an average $117,986 in 1980 to $186,529 in 2007. People in the middle of the population also had gains, but more modest ones. The lowest-income 20 percent saw only a 4.6 percent increase in earnings.

For families at the top of the income scale (the highest 5 percent), recent decades have brought a windfall. These families, with average income of more than $168,000 in 1980, were making $317,000 in 2007—almost twice as much (U.S. Census Bureau, 2008).

Mobility: Race, Ethnicity, and Gender

White people in the United States have always been in a more privileged position than people of African or Hispanic descent. Through the economic expansion of the 1980s and 1990s, many more African Americans entered the ranks of the wealthy. But overall, the real income of African Americans has changed little in three decades. African American family income as a percentage of white family income has fallen slightly to 57 percent in 2007 from 62 percent back in 1975. Compared with white families, Latino families in the United States lost even more ground, earning 66 percent as much as white families in 1975 and just 58 percent as much in 2007 (U.S. Census Bureau, 2008).

Feminists point out that historically, women in U.S. society have had limited opportunity for upward mobility because the clerical jobs (such as secretary) and service positions (such as food server) widely held by women offer few opportunities for advancement.

DISCUSS: What has caused the long-term rise in income disparity? Factors include a rising stock market (which boosted income and wealth to the richest 20% of the population), more two-income households (since higher-earning women tend to marry higher-earning men), and a low minimum wage. Some critics argue that new technology fosters a "winner takes most" climate. The recent recession has reduced the wealth of the rich, bringing a small reduction in the wealth gap.

Q: "What is important for democracy is not that great fortunes should not exist, but that great fortunes should not remain in the same hands." Alexis de Tocqueville

Q: "Nothing in the world can take the place of persistence. Talent will not. . . . Genius will not. . . . Education will not. . . . The slogan 'press on' will always solve the problems of the human race." Calvin Coolidge

in 1913, when monopolistic business practices were the order of the day. Their net worth is now greater than that of the bottom 90 percent of the nation's households combined. The top 20 percent of taxpayers realized nearly three quarters of all income gains from 1979 to 2000.

Even getting a colleges degree no longer guarantees upward mobility. The implicit American contract has always been that with education and hard work, anyone can get ahead. But since 2000, young people with college educations—except those who go to elite colleges and graduate schools—have seen their wages decline. The deepening recession will make this worse. According to a 2008 survey by the National Association of Colleges and Employers, half of all companies plan to cut the number of new graduates they hire this year, compared with last. But the problem goes well beyond the current crisis. For one thing, the growing number of graduates has flooded the job market at a time when many financially pressed boomers are postponing retirement. And college-educated workers today face unprecedented competition from skilled labor in other countries, particularly in the developing world.

The greatest challenge for Obama will be to change this trajectory for Americans under 30, who supported him by two to one. The promise that "anyone" can reach the highest levels of society is the basis of both our historic optimism and the stability of our political system. Yet even before the recession, growing inequality was undermining Americans' optimism about the future. In a 2006 Zogby poll, for example, nearly two thirds of adults did not think life would be better for their children. However inspirational the story of his ascent, Barack Obama will be judged largely by whether he can rebuild a ladder of upward mobility for the rest of America, too.

WHAT DO YOU THINK?

1. Do you think that class differences are emerging as the big issue of this century? Why or why not?

2. Most people in this country think it is only fair that, with schooling and hard work, people should be able to get ahead. How true is that idea today? Explain.

3. In your opinion, how optimistic or pessimistic are young people in the United States about their chances to get ahead in the years to come? Why?

Over time, however, the earnings gap between women and men has been narrowing. Women working full time in 1980 earned 60 percent as much as men working full time; by 2007, women were earning 78 percent as much (U.S. Census Bureau, 2008).

Mobility and Marriage

Research points to the conclusion that marriage has an important effect on social standing. In a study of women and men in their forties, Jay Zagorsky (2006) found that people who marry and stay married accumulate about twice as much wealth as people who remain single or who divorce. Reasons for this difference include the fact that couples who live together typically enjoy double incomes and also pay only half the bills they would have if they were single and living in separate households.

It is also likely that compared to single people, married men and women work harder in their jobs and save more money. Why? The main reason is that they are working not just for themselves but to support others who are counting on them (Popenoe, 2006).

Just as marriage pushes social standing upward, divorce usually makes social position go down. Couples who divorce take on the financial burden of supporting two households. After divorce, women are hurt more than men because it is typically the man who earns more. Many women who divorce lose not only most of their income but also benefits such as health care and insurance coverage (Weitzman, 1996).

Social mobility is a common theme in popular culture, including films. In *The Pursuit of Happyness,* Will Smith plays a man who struggles to "make it" and faces many challenges, such as caring for his son while he tries to succeed at a new job. In most such films, the main character eventually reaches his goal. In your opinion, how much truth is there in the idea that "everyone can get ahead through hard work"?

GLOBAL: An example of downward structural mobility was China's Cultural Revolution, which forced 17 million urban youths to relocate to rural areas (Zhou & Hou, 1999).

Q: "If we command our wealth, we shall be rich and free; if our wealth commands us, we are poor, indeed." Edmund Burke

Q: "When some learn that the American Dream does not fit all that is true about the realities of our life, they denounce the Dream and deny the truth of any of it. Fortunately, most of us are wiser and better adjusted to social reality; we recognize that, though it is called a Dream and some of it is false, by virtue of our firm belief in it we have made some of it true." W. Lloyd Warner, *Social Class in America*

SEEING SOCIOLOGY
in Everyday Life

Do you feel that you are likely to end up with a higher social position than your parents? The same? Lower? Why? How much of the mobility you expect is due to changes in U.S. society?

SEEING SOCIOLOGY
in Everyday Life

Big houses are an example of conspicuous consumption. Can you point to other examples of conspicuous consumption in everyday life?

SEEING SOCIOLOGY IN EVERYDAY LIFE

As CEOs Get Richer, the Great Mansions Return

I grew up in Elkins Park, Pennsylvania, an older suburban community just north of Philadelphia. Elkins Park was at that time and still is a mostly middle-class community, although, like most of suburbia, some neighborhoods boast bigger houses than others. What made Elkins Park special was that scattered over the area were a handful of great mansions, built a century ago by early Philadelphia industrialists. Back then, just about all there was to the town was these great "estates," along with fields and meadows. By about 1940, however, most of the land was split off into lots for the homes of newer middle-class suburbanites. The great mansions suddenly seemed out of place, with heirs trying to figure out how to pay the rising property taxes. As a result, many of the great mansions were sold, the buildings taken down, and the land subdivided.

In the 1960s, when I was a teenager, a short ride on my bicycle could take me past the Breyer estate (built by the founder of the ice-cream company, now the township police building), the Curtis estate (built by a magazine publisher and transformed into a community park), and the Wanamaker estate (built by the founder of a large Philadelphia department store, now the site of high-rise apartments). Probably the grandest of them all was the Wiedner estate, modeled after a French chateau, complete with doorknobs and window pulls covered in gold; it now stands empty.

In their day, these structures were not just homes to families with many servants; they also served as monuments to a time when the rich were, well, *really* rich. By contrast, the community that emerged on the grounds once owned by these wealthy families is middle-class, with modest homes on small lots.

But did the so-called Gilded Age of great wealth disappear forever? Hardly. By the 1980s, a new wave of great mansions was being built in the United States. Take the architect Thierry Despont, who designs huge houses for the super-rich. One of Despont's smaller homes might be 20,000 square feet (about ten times the size of the average U.S. house), and the larger ones go all the way up to 60,000 square feet (as big as any of the Elkins Park mansions built a century ago and almost the size of the White House). These mega-homes have kitchens as large as college classrooms, exercise rooms, indoor swimming pools, and even indoor tennis courts (Krugman, 2002).

Most of these megahouses have been built by newly rich chief executive officers (CEOs) of large corporations. CEOs have always made more money than most people, but recent years have seen executive pay soar. Between 1970 and 2007, the average U.S. family saw only a modest increase in income (about 30 percent after inflation is taken into account). Yet according to *Fortune* magazine, during the same period, the average annual compensation for the 100 highest-paid CEOs skyrocketed from $1.3 million (about 40 times the earnings of an average worker of that time) to $37.5 million (roughly a 2,800 percent increase and equal to 1,000 times as much as the earnings of today's average worker). Richer still, the twenty highest-earning investment fund managers in 2008 (a terrible year for the stock market) had, on average, $465 million *each* in income, earning more in ten minutes than the average worker made all year (Story, 2009).

WHAT DO YOU THINK?

1. Do you consider increasing economic inequality a problem? Why or why not?

2. How many times more than an average worker should a CEO earn? Explain your answer.

3. In light of the economic recession that began in 2008, with so many companies struggling, do you think we will enter an era of lower CEO pay or not? Explain your answer.

The American Dream: Still a Reality?

The expectation of upward social mobility is deeply rooted in U.S. culture. Through most of our history, the economy has grown steadily, raising living standards. Even today, for some people at least, the American dream is alive and well. In 2007, about one in four U.S. families earned $100,000 or more, compared with just one in twenty back in 1967 (in dollars controlled for inflation). There are now about 9 million millionaires in the United States, more than four times the number a decade ago (L. Eisenberg, 2007; R. Frank, 2008; U.S. Census Bureau, 2008).

Yet not all indicators are positive. Note these disturbing trends:

1. **For many workers, earnings have stalled.** The annual income of a fifty-year-old man working full time climbed by about 50 percent between 1958 and 1974 in constant dollars. Between 1974 and 2007, however, this worker's income rose by only 32 percent, even as the number of hours worked increased and the cost of

POP CULTURE: In an episode of *The Simpsons*, Bart wears a T-shirt characterizing the American dream as "money, donuts, and beer." Is this evidence of his own limited aspirations or of widespread cynicism among our young people about their chances for success?

NOTE: Looking at Figure 11–3, explain to students that median family income has generally gone up over time, which is a key reason most people have come to expect some rise in their living standards. These figures are controlled for inflation, meaning that the rise is not due to changes in the value of a dollar but are real changes in family income. The rise between 1950 and 1975 was clearly bigger than gains since 1975.

MAKING THE GRADE

The changes in median family income shown below in Figure 11–3 are examples of structural social mobility.

SEEING SOCIOLOGY
in Everyday Life

In your opinion, how significantly has the recent economic downturn affected people's optimism about their ability to realize the "American dream"?

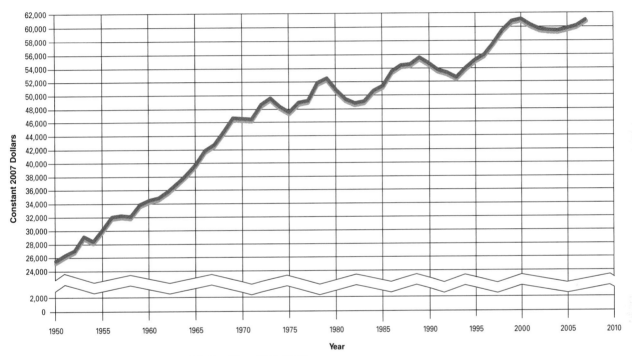

FIGURE 11–3 Median Annual Income, U.S. Families, 1950–2007

Average family income in the United States grew rapidly between 1950 and 1970. Since then, however, the increase has been smaller.

Source: U.S. Census Bureau (2008).

necessities like housing, education, and medical care went way up (Russell, 1995a; U.S. Census Bureau, 2008).

2. **More jobs offer little income.** The expanding global economy has moved many industrial jobs overseas, reducing the number of high-paying factory jobs here in the United States. At the same time, the expansion of our service economy means that more of today's jobs—in fast-food restaurants or large discount stores—offer relatively low wages.

3. **Young people are remaining at home.** Currently, more than half of young people aged eighteen to twenty-four are living with their parents. Since 1975, the average age at marriage has moved upward four years (to 25.6 years for women and 27.5 years for men).

Over the past generation, more people have become rich, and the rich have become richer. At the very top of the pile, as the Seeing Sociology in Everyday Life box explains, the highest-paid corporate executives have enjoyed a runaway rise in their earnings. Yet the increasing share of low-paying jobs has also brought downward mobility for millions of families, feeding the fear that the chance to enjoy a middle-class lifestyle is slipping away. As Figure 11–3 shows, although median income doubled between 1950 and 1973, it has grown by only 22 percent since then (U.S. Census Bureau, 2008).

The Global Economy and the U.S. Class Structure

Underlying the shifts in U.S. class structure is global economic change. Much of the industrial production that gave U.S. workers high-paying jobs a generation ago has moved overseas. With less industry at home, the United States now serves as a vast market for industrial goods such as cars and popular items like stereos, cameras, and computers made in China, Japan, South Korea, and elsewhere.

NOTE: The "log cabin president" claim began when William Henry Harrison (who won in 1840) circulated images of his log cabin, inviting people to think he was born poor. In fact, this son of a wealthy governor and signer of the Declaration of Independence was born on Virginia's Berkeley Plantation and lived in a mansion with 2,000 acres. In 1992, George H. W. Bush, son of a wealthy New England senator, used a Houston hotel address to claim he was a Texan.

NOTE: Some of the richest people in the U.S. gave away vast fortunes. Andrew Carnegie, the steel magnate, gave away $4.5 billion (in today's dollars) before his death in 1919; John D. Rockfeller, founder of Standard Oil, gave away $5.4 billion.

NOTE: In 2007, the average top executive of an S&P 500 corporation earned 344 times more than the average full-time male worker. Thirty years ago, the comparable figure was about 35 times as much (Anderson et al., 2008).

relative poverty the lack of resources of some people in relation to those who have more

absolute poverty a lack of resources that is life-threatening

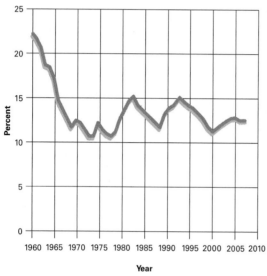

FIGURE 11–4 **The Poverty Rate in the United States, 1960–2007**

The share of our population in poverty fell dramatically between 1960 and 1970. Since then, the poverty rate has remained between 10 and 15 percent of the population.

Source: U.S. Census Bureau (2008).

Poverty in the United States

Social stratification creates both "haves" and "have-nots." All systems of social inequality create poverty, or at least **relative poverty,** *the lack of resources of some people in relation to those who have more.* A more serious but preventable problem is **absolute poverty,** *a lack of resources that is life-threatening.*

As Chapter 12 ("Global Stratification") explains, about 1 billion human beings—one person in six—are at risk of absolute poverty. Even in the affluent United States, families go hungry, live in inadequate housing, and suffer poor health because of a serious lack of resources.

The Extent of Poverty

In 2007, the government classified 37 million men, women, and children—12.5 percent of the population—as poor. This count of relative poverty refers to families with incomes below an official poverty line, which for a family of four in that year was set at $21,203. The poverty line is about three times what the government estimates people must spend for food. But the income of the average poor family was just 60 percent of this amount. This means that the typical poor family had to get by on less than $13,000 in 2007 (U.S. Census Bureau, 2008). Figure 11–4 shows that the official poverty rate fell during the 1960s and has stayed about the same since then.

Who Are the Poor?

Although no single description fits all poor people, poverty is pronounced among certain categories of our population. Where these categories overlap, the problem is especially serious.

Age

A generation ago, the elderly were at greatest risk for poverty. But thanks to better retirement programs offered today by private employers and the government, the poverty rate for people over age sixty-five fell from 30 percent in 1967 to 9.7 percent—well below the national average—in 2007. Looking at it from another angle, about 9.5 percent (3.6 million) of the poor are elderly (U.S. Census Bureau, 2008).

Today the burden of poverty falls more heavily on children. In 2007, 18.0 percent of people under age eighteen (13.3 million children) and 17.3 percent of people age eighteen to twenty-four (5 million young adults) were poor. Put another way, 49 percent of the U.S. poor are young people no older than twenty-four.

Race and Ethnicity

Two-thirds of all poor people are white; 25 percent are African Americans. But in relation to their overall numbers, African Americans are about three times as likely as non-Hispanic whites to be poor. In 2007,

High-paying jobs in manufacturing, held by 28 percent of the U.S. labor force in 1960, support only 10 percent of workers today (U.S. Department of Labor, 2008b). In their place, the economy now offers service work, which often pays far less. A traditionally high-paying corporation like USX (formerly United States Steel) now employs fewer people than the expanding McDonald's chain, and fast-food clerks make only a fraction of what steelworkers earn.

The global reorganization of work has not been bad news for everyone. On the contrary, the global economy is driving upward social mobility for educated people who specialize in law, finance, marketing, and computer technology. Even allowing for the downturn in 2008 and 2009, the global economic expansion helped push up the stock market about eightfold between 1980 and 2008, reaping profits for families with money to invest over this period.

But the same trend has hurt many average workers, who have lost their factory jobs and now perform low-wage service work. In addition, many companies (General Motors and Ford are recent examples) have downsized, cutting the ranks of their workforce in their efforts to stay competitive in world markets. As a result, even though more than 50 percent of all families contain two or more workers—more than twice the share in 1950—many families are working harder simply to hold on to what they have (U.S. Census Bureau, 2008).

DISCUSS: Looking at Figure 11–4, notice that the U.S. poverty rate has stayed between about 10 and 15 percent for the past three decades. Do students think that this country will ever reduce the poverty rate below 10 percent? Why or why not?

NOTE: Poverty is known to increase the risk of crime. Bruce Western (2002) notes that the reverse is also true because the "incarceration boom" of the last twenty years has disrupted career paths for millions of (mostly) men and increased economic inequality.

THE MAP: Appalachia is home to many poor whites, the Deep South to many poor African Americans, the Mexican border to poor Hispanics, and the "four corners" region and the Dakotas to poor American Indians.

NOTE: The poverty line does not reflect differences in cost of living from community to community.

Anna Mae Peters lives in Nitta Yuma, Mississippi. Almost everyone she knows lives below the government's poverty line.

Julie Garland lives in Greenwich, Connecticut, where people have very high income and there is little evidence of poverty.

feminization of poverty the trend of women making up an increasing proportion of the poor

Seeing Ourselves

NATIONAL MAP 11–2
Poverty across the United States, 2007

This map shows that the poorest counties in the United States—where the poverty rate is more than twice the national average—are in Appalachia, across the Deep South, along the border with Mexico, near the Four Corners region of the Southwest, and in the Dakotas. Can you suggest some reasons for this pattern?

Source: U.S. Census Bureau (2008).

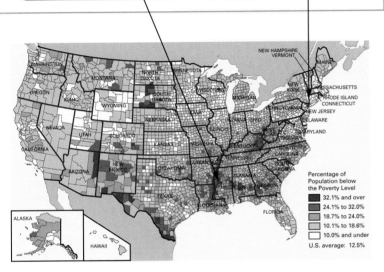

Percentage of Population below the Poverty Level

- 32.1% and over
- 24.1% to 32.0%
- 18.7% to 24.0%
- 10.1% to 18.6%
- 10.0% and under

U.S. average: 12.5%

24.5 percent of African Americans (9.2 million people) lived in poverty, compared to 21.5 percent of Hispanics (9.9 million), 10.2 percent of Asians and Pacific Islanders (1.3 million), and 8.2 percent of non-Hispanic whites (16 million). The poverty gap between whites and minorities has changed little since 1975.

People of color have especially high rates of child poverty. Among African American children, 34.5 percent are poor; the comparable figures are 28.6 percent among Hispanic children and 10.1 percent among non-Hispanic white children (U.S. Census Bureau, 2008).

Gender and Family Patterns

Of all poor people age eighteen or older, 56 percent are women and 44 percent are men. This difference reflects the fact that women who head households are at high risk of poverty. Of all poor families, 51 percent are headed by women with no husband present; just 8 percent of poor families are headed by single men.

The United States has thus experienced a **feminization of poverty**, *the trend of women making up an increasing proportion of the poor.* In 1960, only 25 percent of all poor households were headed by women; the majority of poor families had both wives and husbands in the home. By 2007, however, the share of poor households headed by a single woman had more than doubled to 51 percent.

The feminization of poverty is one result of a larger trend: the rapidly increasing number of households at all class levels headed by single women. This trend, coupled with the fact that households headed by women are at high risk of poverty, helps explain why women and their children make up an increasing share of the U.S. poor.

Urban and Rural Poverty

In the United States, the greatest concentration of poverty is found in central cities, where the 2007 poverty rate stood at 16.5 percent. The poverty rate in suburbs is 9 percent. Thus the poverty rate for urban areas as a whole is 11.9 percent—somewhat lower than the 15.4 percent found in rural areas. National Map 11–2 shows that most of the counties with the highest poverty rate in the United States are rural.

Explaining Poverty

The richest nation on Earth contains tens of millions of poor people, a fact that raises serious questions. It is true, as some analysts remind us, that most poor people in the United States are far better off than the poor in other countries: 35 percent of U.S. poor families own a home, 70 percent own a car, and only about 15 percent say they often go without food (U.S. Bureau of Agriculture, 2008; U.S. Census Bureau, 2008). But there is little doubt that poverty harms the overall well-being of millions of people in this country.

Why is there poverty in the first place? We will examine two opposing explanations for poverty that lead to a lively and important political debate.

One View: Blame the Poor

One approach holds that *the poor are mostly responsible for their own poverty.* Throughout this nation's history, people have placed a high value on self-reliance, convinced that social standing is mostly a matter of individual talent and effort. According to this view, society offers plenty of opportunities to anyone who is able and willing to take advantage of them, and the poor are those

SEEING SOCIOLOGY IN EVERYDAY LIFE

When Work Disappears, the Result Is Poverty

The U.S. economy has created tens of millions of new jobs in recent decades. Yet African Americans who live in inner cities have faced a catastrophic loss of work. William Julius Wilson points out that although people continue to talk about welfare reform, neither major political party (Democrats or Republicans) has said anything about the lack of work in central cities.

With the loss of inner-city jobs, Wilson continues, for the first time in U.S. history a large majority of the adults in our inner cities are not working. Studying the Washington Park area of Chicago, Wilson found a troubling trend. Back in 1950, most adults in this African American community had jobs, but by the mid-1990s, two-thirds did not. As one elderly woman who moved to the neighborhood in 1953 explained:

> When I moved in, the neighborhood was intact. It was intact with homes, beautiful homes, mini-mansions, with stores, laundromats, with Chinese cleaners. We had drugstores. We had hotels. We had doctors over on 39th Street. We had doctors' offices in the neighborhood. We had the middle class and the upper-middle class. It has gone from affluent to where it is today. (W.J. Wilson, 1996b:28)

Why has this neighborhood declined? Wilson's eight years of research point to one answer: There are barely any jobs. It is the loss of work that has pushed people into desperate poverty, weakened families, and made people turn to welfare. In nearby Woodlawn, Wilson identified more than

800 businesses that had operated in 1950; today, just 100 remain. In addition, a number of major employers in the past—including Western Electric and International Harvester—closed their plant doors in the late 1960s. The inner cities have fallen victim to economic change, including downsizing and the loss of industrial jobs that have moved overseas.

Wilson paints a grim picture. But he also believes the answer lies in creating new jobs. Wilson proposes attacking the problem in stages. First, the government could hire people to do all kinds of work, from clearing slums to putting up new housing. Such a program, modeled on the Works Progress Administration (WPA) created in 1935 during the Great Depression, would move people from welfare to work and in the process create much-needed hope. In addition, federal and

state governments must improve schools by enacting performance standards and providing more funding. Of special importance is teaching children language skills and computer skills to prepare them for the jobs being created by the Information Revolution. Improved regional public transportation would connect cities (where people need work) and suburbs (where most jobs now are). In addition, more affordable child care would help single mothers and fathers balance the responsibilities of employment and parenting.

Wilson claims that his proposals are well grounded in research. But he knows that politics revolves around other considerations as well. For one thing, if the public *thinks* there are jobs available, it is hard to change the perception that the poor are simply avoiding work. He also concedes that his proposals, at least in the short term, are more expensive than continuing to funnel welfare assistance to jobless communities.

But what are the long-term costs of allowing our cities to decay while suburbs prosper? On the other hand, what would be the benefits of giving everyone the hope and satisfaction that are supposed to define our way of life?

WHAT DO YOU THINK?

1. If Wilson were running for public office, do you think he would be elected? Why or why not?

2. In your opinion, why are people so reluctant to see inner-city poverty as a problem?

3. Where do you agree with Wilson's analysis of poverty? Where do you disagree?

William Julius Wilson spent years studying neighborhoods like this one in Chicago. He now teaches at Harvard University in Cambridge, Massachusetts.

people who cannot or will not work due to a lack of skills, schooling, or motivation.

In his study of poverty in Latin American cities, the anthropologist Oscar Lewis (1961) noted that many poor become trapped in a *culture of poverty,* a lower-class subculture that can destroy people's ambition to improve their lives. Raised in poor families, children

become resigned to their situation, producing a self-perpetuating cycle of poverty.

In 1996, hoping to break the cycle of poverty in the United States, Congress changed the welfare system, which had provided federal funds to assist poor people since 1935. The federal government continues to send money to the states to distribute to needy people, but

SOCIAL SURVEY: A U.S. Census Bureau survey (2008) of poor adults yielded these explanations for people not working: Ill/disabled, 35%; retired, 10%; family reasons, 28%; school/other, 21%; could not find work, 6%.

NOTE: About 35% of children of parents in the bottom wealth quintile remain there as adults, and 65% rise above that. Similarly, 35% of children born in the top quintile remain there as adults.

NOTE: One critic of Wilson notes that the population of the Chicago neighborhoods in Wilson's research declined from 250,000 in 1950 to 86,000 in 1990. This drop, suggests Marvin Kosters (1996), seems to indicate that most people succeeded over time in moving on and up.

Q: "To expose citizens to social problems beyond their capacity to remedy is to make moral insensitivity a requirement for daily living." Charles Krauthammer

● SEEING SOCIOLOGY
in Everyday Life

Our society has been more generous with the "worthy" poor (such as elderly people) than with the "unworthy" poor (such as able-bodied people who, we assume, should take care of themselves). Why do you think we have not done more to reduce poverty among children, who surely fall into the "worthy" category?

benefits carry strict time limits—in most cases, no more than two years at a stretch and a total of five years as an individual moves in and out of the welfare system. The stated purpose of this reform was to force people to be self-supporting and move them away from dependency on government.

Another View: Blame Society

A different position, argued by William Julius Wilson (1996a, 1996b; Mouw, 2000), holds that *society is mostly responsible for poverty.* Wilson points to the loss of jobs in the inner cities as the main cause of poverty, claiming that there is simply not enough work to support families. Wilson sees any apparent lack of trying on the part of poor people as a result of little opportunity rather than a cause of poverty. From Wilson's point of view, Lewis's analysis amounts to blaming the victims for their own suffering. The Seeing Sociology in Everyday Life box provides a closer look at Wilson's argument and how it would shape public policy.

○ **CRITICAL REVIEW**   The U.S. public is evenly divided over whether the government or people themselves should take responsibility for reducing poverty (NORC, 2007). And here's what we know about poverty and work: Government statistics show that 52 percent of the heads of poor households did not work at all during 2007, and an additional 29 percent worked only part time (U.S. Census Bureau, 2008). Such facts seem to support the "blame the poor" side of the argument, because one major cause of poverty is not holding a job.

But the *reasons* that people do not work seem more in step with the "blame society" position. Middle-class women may be able to combine working and child rearing, but this is much harder for poor women who cannot afford child care, and few employers provide child care programs. As Wilson explains, many people are idle not because they are avoiding work but because there are not enough jobs to go around. In short, the most effective way to reduce poverty is to ensure a greater supply of jobs as well as child care for parents who work (W. J. Wilson, 1996a; Bainbridge, Meyers, & Waldfogel, 2003).

○ **CHECK YOUR LEARNING**   Explain the view that the poor should take responsibility for poverty and the view that society is responsible for poverty. Which is closer to your own view?

The Working Poor

Not all poor people are jobless. The *working poor* command the sympathy and support of people on both sides of the poverty debate. In 2007, some 18 percent of heads of poor families (1.4 million women and men) worked at least fifty weeks of the year and yet could not escape poverty. Another 30 percent of these heads of families (2.2 million people) remained poor despite part-time employment. Put differently, 3.3 percent of full-time workers earn so little that they remain poor (U.S. Census Bureau, 2008). Congress set the minimum wage at $6.55 per hour in 2008, raising it to $7.25 per hour in July 2009. But even this increase cannot end working poverty—even at $8.00 an hour, a full-time worker still cannot lift an urban family of four above the poverty line.

Individual ability and personal effort do play a part in shaping social position. However, the weight of sociological evidence points to society, not individual character traits, as the primary cause of poverty because more and more of the jobs that are available offer only low wages. In addition, the poor are *categories* of people—female heads of families, people of color, people isolated from the larger society in inner-city areas—who face special barriers and limited opportunities.

The Controversy & Debate box on pages 292–93 takes a closer look at current welfare policy. Understanding this important social

The African American artist Henry Ossawa Tanner captured the humility and humanity of impoverished people in his painting *The Thankful Poor*. This insight is important in a society that tends to define poor people as morally unworthy and deserving of their bitter plight.
Henry Ossawa Tanner (1859–1937), *The Thankful Poor.* Private collection. Art Resource, New York.

Q: "Nobody talks more about free enterprise and competition and of the best man winning than the man who inherited his father's store or farm." C. Wright Mills

NOTE: The poverty rate among the entire U.S. population that works full time is 2.5%; among those (of all ages) with part-time work, 12.7%; among those with no work, 21.5% (DeNavas–Walt, Proctor, & Smith, 2008).

GLOBAL: In Japan, the law requires poor people to get help from kin before turning to the government for assistance; people physically able to work are not eligible for benefits in any case.

DISCUSS: Can students explain why most sociologists see poverty more as a problem of society than as a problem of specific individuals?

SEEING SOCIOLOGY
in Everyday Life

Do you see evidence of homelessness in your community? Has the problem become worse during the recent economic recession?

SEEING SOCIOLOGY
in Everyday Life

Do you think people in the United States consider homelessness to be a serious problem? Why or why not?

CONTROVERSY & DEBATE

The Welfare Dilemma

MARCO: (rushing in the door) Sorry I'm late. I stopped at the store and got stuck behind some welfare mother in the checkout line.

SERGI: (looking back with a confused grin) Exactly what does a person on welfare look like?

What is *your* image of a "welfare recipient"? If you are like many people in the United States, you might think of a middle-aged African American woman. But you would be wrong. In truth, the typical person receiving welfare in this country is a child who is white.

There is a lot of confusion about welfare. There is also disagreement about whether this type of assistance is a good or bad idea. In 1996, Congress debated the issue and enacted new law that ended the federal government's role in providing income assistance to poor households. In place of this federal program, new state-run programs now offer limited help to the poor, but they require people who receive aid to get job training or find work—or have their benefits cut off.

To understand how we got to where we are, let's begin by explaining what, exactly, welfare is. The term "welfare" refers to an assortment of policies and programs designed to improve the well-

being of some low-income people. Until the welfare reform of 1996, most people used the term to refer to just one part of the overall system, Aid for Families with Dependent Children (AFDC), a federal program of monthly financial support for parents (mostly single women) to care for themselves and their children. In 1996, about 5 million households received AFDC for some part of the year.

Conservatives opposed AFDC, claiming that rather than reducing child poverty, AFDC made

Is society responsible for poverty or are individuals themselves to blame? When it comes to homeless families, most people think society should do more.

the problem worse, in two ways. First, they claimed that AFDC weakened families, because for years after the program began, it paid benefits to poor mothers only if no husband lived in the home. As a result, the government was actually providing an economic incentive to women to have children outside of marriage, and they blame it for the rapid rise of out-of-wedlock births among poor people. To conservatives, marriage is one key to reducing poverty: Fewer than one in ten married-couple families are poor; more than nine in ten AFDC families were headed by an unmarried woman.

Second, conservatives believe that welfare encourages poor people to become dependent on government handouts, the main reason that eight out of ten poor heads of households did not have full-time jobs. Furthermore, only 5 percent of single mothers receiving AFDC worked full time, compared to more than half of nonpoor single mothers. Conservatives say that welfare gradually moved well beyond its original purpose of short-term help to nonworking women with children (say, after divorce or death of a husband) and gradually became a way of life. Once trapped

issue can help us decide how our society should respond to the problem of poverty, as well as the problem of homelessness, discussed next.

Homelessness

In 2005, the government's Department of Housing and Urban Development conducted a national survey of cities and towns to find out how many people in the United States were homeless at some time during that year. The answer was about 754,000, including people living in shelters, in transitional housing, and on the street (Ohlemacher, 2007). As with earlier estimates of the homeless population, critics claimed that the HUD survey undercounted the homeless, who may well number several million people. In addition, they add, evidence suggests that

the number of homeless people in the United States is increasing (L. Kaufman, 2004; National Coalition for the Homeless, 2007).

The familiar stereotypes of homeless people—men sleeping in doorways and women carrying everything they own in a shopping bag—have been replaced by the "new homeless": people thrown out of work because of plant closings, women who take their children and leave home to escape domestic violence, women and men forced out of apartments by rent increases, and others unable to meet mortgage or rent payments because of low wages or no work at all. Today, no stereotype paints a complete picture of the homeless.

The large majority of homeless people report that they do not work, although about 20 percent have at least a part-time job (U.S. Conference of Mayors, 2007). Working or not, all homeless people

NOTE: Due to factors including the negative stigma attached to receiving welfare and highly variable eligibility standards, roughly half the women and men eligible for welfare programs never apply for them.

NOTE: Welfare reform has not meant a reduction in government spending; rather, the government has shifted spending toward assisting low-income people who work. This spending totaled about $123 billion in 2006, exceeding spending for

the old AFDC program (Besharov & Germanis, 2007).

RESOURCE: The key conservative criticisms of public assistance are found in Charles Murray's *Breaking Ground* (1984); his thesis is that the outlay for welfare must continue to grow because the system fails to alleviate the problems it has set out to fix, actually making matters worse by fostering dependency. This claim is reflected in the 1996 reforms.

SEEING SOCIOLOGY
in Everyday Life

What are the arguments typically made by Democratic and Republican politicians on the issue of poverty?

in dependency, poor women would raise children who were themselves likely to be poor as adults.

Liberals have a different view. Why, they ask, do people object to government money going to poor mothers and children when most "welfare" actually goes to richer people? The cost of AFDC was as high as $25 billion annually—no small sum, to be sure, but much less than the $580 billion in annual Social Security benefits Uncle Sam provides to senior citizens, most of whom are not poor. And it is just a small fraction of the more than $1 trillion "bailout money" Congress voted in 2008 and 2009 to assist the struggling financial industry.

Liberals insist that most poor families who turn to public assistance are truly needy. Most of the people who are helped in this way are children. And they don't get very much. The typical household receives only about $400 per month in assistance, hardly enough to attract people to a life of welfare dependency. Even adding some additional money in the form of food stamps, households assisted by welfare still struggle well below the poverty line everywhere in the country. Therefore, liberals see public assistance as a "Band-Aid approach" to the serious social problems of too few jobs and too much income inequality in the United

States. As for the charge that public assistance weakens families, liberals agree that the share of families with one parent has gone up, but they see single parenting as a broad trend found at all class levels in many countries.

Back in 1996, the conservative arguments carried the day, ending the AFDC program. Our society's individualistic culture has always encouraged us to blame people themselves (rather than society) for poverty, which becomes a sign not of need but of laziness and personal failure. This view of the poor is probably the biggest reason that led Congress to replace the federal AFDC program with state-run programs called Temporary Assistance for Needy Families (TANF), requiring poor adults to get job training and limiting income assistance to two consecutive years with a lifetime limit of five years.

By 2008, the new TANF policy had reduced the number of households receiving income assistance by about 60 percent. This means that many single parents who were once on welfare have taken jobs or are receiving job training. In addition, the rate of out-of-wedlock births has fallen. With these facts in mind, conservatives who supported welfare reform see the new program as a huge success. The welfare rolls have been cut by more than half, and

more people have moved from receiving a check to working in order to support themselves. But liberals claim that the reform is far from successful. They point out that many of the people who are now working earn so little pay that they are hardly better off than before. In addition, half of these workers have no health insurance. In other words, the reform has greatly reduced the number of people receiving welfare but has done little to reduce the extent of poverty.

WHAT DO YOU THINK?

1. How does our cultural emphasis on self-reliance help explain the controversy surrounding public assistance? Why do people not criticize benefits (such as home mortgage interest deductions) for people who are better off?

2. Do you approve of the time limits on benefits built into the TANF program? Why or why not?

3. Do you think the Obama administration will reduce poverty? Explain your answer.

Sources: Lichter & Crowley (2002), Lichter & Jayakody (2002), U.S. Census Bureau (2008), and Von Drehle (2008).

have one thing in common: *poverty.* For that reason, the explanations of poverty just presented also apply to homelessness. Some (more conservative) people blame the *personal traits* of the homeless themselves. One-third of homeless people are substance abusers, and one-fourth are mentally ill. More broadly, a fraction of 1 percent of our population, for one reason or another, seems unable to cope with our complex and highly competitive society (U.S. Conference of Mayors, 2007; U.S. Department of Housing and Urban Development, 2007).

Other (more liberal) people see homelessness as resulting from *societal factors,* including low wages and a lack of low-income housing (Kozol, 1988; Bohannan, 1991; L. Kaufman, 2004). Supporters of this position note that one-third of the homeless consists of entire

families, and they point to children as the fastest-growing category of the homeless.

No one disputes that a large proportion of homeless people are personally impaired to some degree, but cause and effect are difficult to untangle. Long-term, structural changes in the U.S. economy, cutbacks in social service budgets, and the recent economic downturn have all contributed to the problem of homelessness.

Finally, social stratification extends far beyond the borders of the United States. In fact, the most striking social inequality is found not within any one nation but in the different living standards from nation to nation around the world. In Chapter 12 ("Global Stratification"), we broaden our investigation of stratification by looking at global inequality.

Seeing Sociology in Everyday Life

Chapter 11   Social Class in the United States

How do we understand inequality in our society?

This chapter sketches the class structure of the United States and also explains how factors such as race are linked to social standing. You already know, for example, that the rate of poverty is three times higher for African Americans than for whites, and you have also learned that the typical black family earns just 57 percent as much as the typical (non-Hispanic) white family. But rich people—here, we'll define "rich" as a family earning more than $75,000 a year—come in all colors. Here's a chance to test your sociological thinking by answering several questions about how race affects being rich. Look at each of the statements below: Does the statement reflect reality, or is it a myth?

1. In the United States, all rich people are white. *Reality or myth?*

2. Rich white families are actually richer than rich African American families. *Reality or myth?*

3. People in rich black families don't work as hard as members of rich white families. *Reality or myth?*

4. When you are rich, color doesn't matter. *Reality or myth?*

1. *Of course, in a nation that has an African American president, this is a myth.* But when it comes to being rich, race does matter: About 20 percent of African American families are affluent (Hispanic families, too), compared to about 46 percent of non-Hispanic white families.

2. *Reality.* Rich white, non-Hispanic families have a mean (average) income of almost $200,000 per year. Rich African American families average about $130,000 per year.

3. *Myth.* On average, rich black families are more likely to rely on multiple incomes (that is, they have more people working) than their white counterparts. In addition, rich white families receive more unearned income—that is, income from investments—than rich African American families.

4. *Myth.* Rich African Americans still face social barriers based on their race, just as rich whites benefit from the privileges linked to their color.

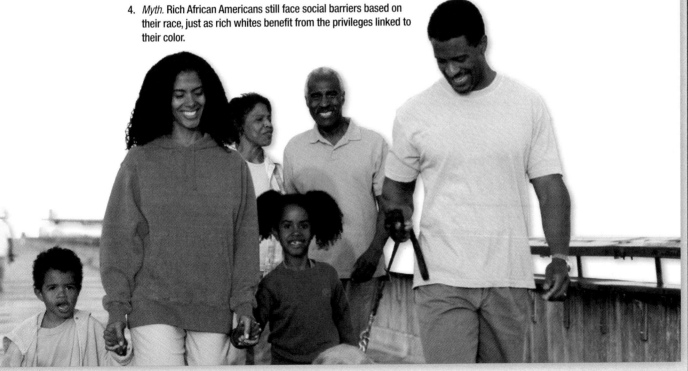

Applying SOCIOLOGY in Everyday Life

1. Develop several questions that together will let you measure social class position. The trick is to decide what you think social class really means. Then try your questions on several adults, refining the questions as you proceed.

2. During an evening of television viewing, assess the social class level of the characters you see on various shows. In each case, explain why you assign someone a particular social position. Do you find many clearly upper-class people? Middle-class people? Working-class people? Poor people? Describe the patterns you find.

3. Governor Arnold Schwarzenegger of California said, "In this country, it doesn't make any difference where you were born. It doesn't make any difference if, like me, you couldn't even speak English until you were in your twenties. America gave me opportunities, and my immigrant dreams came true. I want other people to get the same chances I did, the same opportunities. And I believe they can." Ask a number of people who came to the United States from another country the extent to which they agree or disagree with this statement.

MAKING THE GRADE

CHAPTER 11 Social Class in the United States

Dimensions of Social Inequality

SOCIAL STRATIFICATION involves many dimensions:

- *Income*—Earnings from work and investments are unequal, with the richest 20% of families earning twelve times as much as the poorest 20% of families.

- *Wealth*—The total value of all assets minus debts, wealth is distributed more unequally than income, with the richest 20% of families holding 85% of all wealth.

- *Power*—Income and wealth are important sources of power.

- *Schooling*—Schooling affects both occupation and income. Some categories of people have greater opportunities for schooling than others.

- *Occupational prestige*—Work generates not only income but also prestige. White-collar jobs generally offer more income and prestige than blue-collar jobs. Many lower-prestige jobs are performed by women and people of color.

pp. 274–76

income (p. 274) earnings from work or investments

wealth (p. 275) the total value of money and other assets, minus outstanding debts

U.S. Stratification: Merit and Caste

Although the United States is a meritocracy, social position in this country involves some caste elements.

ANCESTRY
Being born into a particular family affects a person's opportunities for schooling, occupation, and income.

p. 276

RACE AND ETHNICITY
Non-Hispanic white families enjoy high social standing based on income and wealth. By contrast, African American and Hispanic families remain disadvantaged.

pp. 276–78

GENDER
On average, women have less income, wealth, and occupational prestige than men.

p. 278

Social Classes in the United States

Defining **SOCIAL CLASSES** in the United States is difficult because of low status consistency and relatively high social mobility. But we can describe four general rankings:

- the upper class
- the middle class
- the working class
- the lower class

p. 278

$197,000
$197,000
$60,000
$60,000
$28,000
$28,000

UPPER CLASS—5% of the population. Most members of the *upper-upper class*, or "old rich," inherited their wealth; the *lower-upper class*, or "new rich," work at high-paying jobs.

MIDDLE CLASS—40% to 45% of the population. People in the *upper-middle class* have significant wealth; *average-middles* have less prestige, do white-collar work, and most attend college.

WORKING CLASS—30% to 35% of the population. People in the *lower-middle class* do blue-collar work; only about one-third of children attend college.

LOWER CLASS—20% of the population. Most people in the lower class lack financial security due to low income; many live below the poverty line; half do not complete high school.

pp. 278–80

The Difference Class Makes

HEALTH

- Rich people, on average, live longer and receive better health care than poor people.

  p. 281

VALUES AND ATTITUDES

- Affluent people, with greater education and financial security, display greater tolerance than working-class people.

  p. 281

POLITICS

- Affluent people tend to be more conservative on economic issues and more liberal on social issues than poor people.
- Affluent people, who are better served by the political system, are more likely to vote than poor people.

  p. 281

FAMILY AND GENDER

- Affluent families pass on advantages in the form of "cultural capital" to their children.
- Class also shapes the division of family responsibilities, with lower-class people maintaining more traditional gender roles.

  pp. 281–83

Social Mobility

- Social mobility is common in the United States, as it is in other high-income countries, but typically only small changes occur from one generation to the next.
- Between 1980 and 2007, the richest 20% of U.S. families enjoyed a 58% jump in annual income, while the 20% of families with the lowest income saw only a 4.6% increase.
- Historically, African Americans, Hispanic Americans, and women have had less opportunity for upward mobility in U.S. society than white men.
- The American dream—the expectation of upward social mobility—is deeply rooted in our culture. Although high-income families are earning more and more, many average families are struggling to hold on to what they have.
- Marriage encourages upward social mobility. Divorce lowers social standing.
- The global reorganization of work has created upward social mobility for educated people in the United States but has hurt average workers, whose factory jobs have moved overseas and who are forced to take low-wage service work.

  pp. 283–87

intragenerational social mobility (p. 283) a change in social position occurring during a person's lifetime

intergenerational social mobility (p. 283) upward or downward social mobility of children in relation to their parents

Poverty in the United States

POVERTY PROFILE

- The government classifies 37 million people, 12.5% of the population, as poor.
- About 49% of the poor are under age twenty-four.
- Two-thirds of the poor are white, but in relation to their population, African Americans and Hispanics are more likely to be poor.
- The **feminization of poverty** means that more poor families are headed by women.
- About 48% of the heads of poor families are among the "working poor" who work at least part time but do not earn enough to lift a family of four above the poverty line.
- An estimated 750,000 people are homeless at some time during the course of a year.

  pp. 288–93

EXPLANATIONS OF POVERTY

- Blame individuals: The *culture of poverty* thesis states that poverty is caused by shortcomings in the poor themselves (Oscar Lewis).
- Blame society: Poverty is caused by society's unequal disbribution of wealth and lack of good jobs (William Julius Wilson).

  pp. 289–91

relative poverty (p. 288) the lack of resources of some people in relation to those who have more

absolute poverty (p. 288) a lack of resources that is life-threatening

feminization of poverty (p. 289) the trend of women making up an increasing proportion of the poor

Around the world, social inequality is dramatic, with many people in low-income countries earning far less than people living elsewhere. Low wage levels is one reason many corporations that once produced their products in the United States now operate factories in other countries.

CHAPTER 12

Global Stratification

SUPPLEMENTS: The *Instructor's Manual* contains a detailed outline of Chapter 12, along with discussion topics and supplementary lecture material.

GLOBAL: In 2004, the world total GDP was about $40 trillion; total world wealth was about $750 trillion (United Nations Development Programme, 2006).

NOTE: The term "Third World" (and the three-worlds scheme) was first used in an August 14, 1952, article in *L'Observateur*, "Trois mondes, une planète," by the French demographer Alfred Sauvy.

CHAPTER OVERVIEW { This chapter shifts the focus from inequality within the United States to inequality in the world as a whole. The chapter begins by describing global inequality and then provides two theoretical models that explain global stratification.

More than 1,000 workers were busily sewing together polo shirts on the fourth floor of the garment factory in Narsingdi, a small town about 30 miles northeast of Bangladesh's capital city of Dhaka. The thumping of hundreds of sewing machines produced a steady roar throughout the long working day.

But in an instant everything changed when an electric gun used to shoot spot remover onto stained fabric gave off a spark. Suddenly, the worktable burst into flames. People rushed to smother the fire with shirts, but there was no stopping the blaze: In a room filled with combustible materials, the flames spread quickly.

The workers scrambled toward the narrow staircase that led to the street. At the bottom, however, the human wave pouring down the steep steps collided with a folding metal gate across the doorway that was kept locked to prevent workers from leaving during working hours. Panicked, the people turned, only to be pushed back by the hundreds behind them. In a single terrifying minute of screaming voices, thrusting legs, and pounding hearts, dozens were crushed and trampled. By the time the gates were opened and the fire put out, fifty-two garment workers lay dead.

Garment factories like this one are big business in Bangladesh, where clothing accounts for 75 percent of the country's total economic exports. Half of these garments end up in stores in the United States. The reason so much of the clothing we buy is made in poor countries like Bangladesh is simple economics: Bangladeshi garment workers labor for close to twelve hours a day, typically seven days a week, and yet earn only about $500 a year, which is just a few percent of what a garment worker makes in the United States.

Tanveer Chowdhury manages the garment factory owned by his family. Speaking to reporters, he complained bitterly about the tragedy. "This fire has cost me $586,373, and that does not include $70,000 for machinery and $20,000 for furniture. I made commitments to meet deadlines, and I still have the deadlines. I am now paying for air freight at $10 a dozen when I should be shipping by sea at 87 cents a dozen."

There was one other cost Chowdhury did not mention. To compensate families for the loss of their loved ones in the fire, he eventually agreed to pay $1,952 per person. In Bangladesh, life—like labor—is cheap (based on Bearak, 2001; Research and Markets, 2008).

Garment workers in Bangladesh are among the roughly 1.4 billion of the world's people who work hard every day and yet remain poor (Chen & Ravallion, 2008). As this chapter explains, although poverty is a reality in the United States and other nations, the greatest social inequality is not *within* nations but *between* them (Goesling, 2001). We can understand the full dimensions of poverty only by exploring **global stratification**, *patterns of social inequality in the world as a whole.*

Global Stratification: An Overview

Chapter 11 ("Social Class in the United States") described social inequality in the United States. In global perspective, however, social stratification is far greater. The pie chart at the left in Figure 12–1 divides the world's total income by fifths of the population. Recall

global stratification patterns of social inequality in the world as a whole

high-income countries the nations with the highest overall standards of living

middle-income countries nations with a standard of living about average for the world as a whole

low-income countries nations with a low standard of living in which most people are poor

from Chapter 11 that the richest 20 percent of the U.S. population earn about 48 percent of the national income (see Figure 11–1 on page 275). The richest 20 percent of global population, however, receive about 74 percent of world income. At the other extreme, the poorest 20 percent of the U.S. population earn about 4 percent of our national income; the poorest fifth of the world's people struggles to survive on just 2 percent of global income.

In terms of wealth, as the pie chart at the right in Figure 12–1 shows, global inequality is even greater. A rough estimate is that the richest 20 percent of the world's adults own more than 90 percent of the planet's wealth. About half of all wealth is owned by just 2 percent of the world's adult population; about 40 percent, by the richest 1 percent. On the other hand, the poorest half of the world's adults own barely 1 percent of all global wealth. In terms of dollars, about half the world's families have less than $2,500 in total wealth, far less than the $100,000 in wealth for the typical family in the United States (Bucks, Kennickell, & Moore, 2006; Porter, 2006; Davies et al., 2008).

Because the United States is among the world's richest countries, even people in the United States with income below the government's poverty line live far better than the majority of people on the planet. The average person living in a rich nation such as the United States is extremely well off by world standards. Any one of the world's richest people (in 2008, the world's three richest *people*—Bill Gates and Warren Buffett in the United States and Carlos Slim Helú in Mexico—were *each* worth more than $35 billion) has more personal wealth than the world's thirty-four poorest *countries* (United Nations Development Programme, 2007; Kroll, et al., 2009).

A Word about Terminology

Classifying the 194 independent nations on Earth into categories ignores many striking differences. These nations have rich and varied histories, speak different languages, and take pride in distinctive cultures. However, various models have been developed that help distinguish countries on the basis of global stratification.

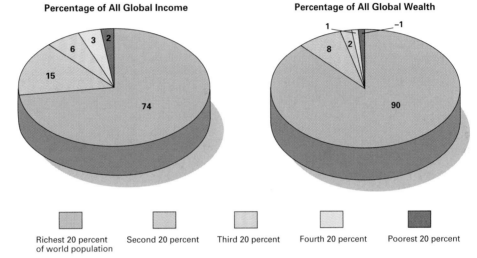

Percentage of All Global Income — 74, 15, 6, 3, 2

Percentage of All Global Wealth — 90, 8, 2, 1, 1, −1

Richest 20 percent of world population | Second 20 percent | Third 20 percent | Fourth 20 percent | Poorest 20 percent

FIGURE 12–1   **Distribution of Global Income and Wealth**

Global income is very unequal, with the richest 20 percent of the world's people earning almost forty times as much as the poorest 20 percent. Global wealth is even more unequally divided, with the richest 20 percent owning 90 percent of private wealth and the poorest half of the world's people having barely anything at all.

Sources: Based on United Nations Development Programme (2008, and Davies et al. (2006, 2008).

One such model, developed after World War II, labeled the rich, industrial countries the "First World"; the less industrialized, socialist countries the "Second World"; and nonindustrialized, poor countries the "Third World." But the "three worlds" model is now less useful. For one thing, it was a product of Cold War politics by which the capitalist West (the First World) faced off against the socialist East (the Second World) while other nations (the Third World) remained more or less on the sidelines. But as a result of the sweeping changes in Eastern Europe and the collapse of the former Soviet Union in the early 1990s, a distinctive Second World no longer exists.

Another problem is that the "three worlds" model lumped together more than 100 countries as the Third World. In reality, some relatively better-off nations of the Third World (such as Chile in South America) have thirteen times the per-person productivity of the poorest countries of the world (such as Ethiopia in East Africa).

These facts call for a modestly revised system of classification. The sixty-six **high-income countries** are defined as *the nations with the highest overall standards of living*. The world's seventy-two **middle-income countries** are not as rich; they are *nations with a standard of living about average for the world as a whole*. The remaining fifty-six **low-income countries** are *nations with a low standard*

GLOBAL: A country's level of economic development reflects the distribution of the labor force by sectors of the economy. The relative percentages in agriculture, industry, and services (men/women): low-income countries, 61/75, 15/10, 25/14; middle-income countries, 50/56, 23/17, 26/27; high-income countries, 4/2, 34/12, 62/96 (World Bank, 1999, 2007).

GLOBAL: The World Bank calculates that 100 million people in the Russian Federation and the nations of Eastern Europe were poor (about 25%) prior to the political reforms. It calculates that roughly the same number (but representing only 15%) of the people are poor in rich societies, including the U.S., Canada, and the nations of Western Europe.

Japan is among the world's high-income countries, in which industrial technology and economic expansion have produced material prosperity. The presence of market forces is evident in this view of downtown Tokyo (*above, left*). India has recently become one of the world's middle-income countries (*above, right*). An increasing number of motor vehicles fill city streets. Ethiopia (*left*) is among the world's low-income countries. As the photograph suggests, these nations have limited economic development and rapidly increasing populations. The result is widespread poverty.

of living in which most people are poor (United Nations Development Programme, 2008).

This model has two advantages over the older "three worlds" system. First, it focuses on economic development rather than political structure (capitalist or socialist). Second, it gives a better picture of the relative economic development of various countries because it does not lump together all less developed nations into a single "Third World."

When ranking countries, keep in mind that there is social stratification within every nation. In Bangladesh, for example, members of the Chowdhury family, who own the garment factory described in the chapter-opening story, earn as much as $1 million per year, which is several thousand times more than their workers earn. The full extent of global inequality is even greater, because the wealthiest people in rich countries such as the United States live worlds apart from the poorest people in low-income nations such as Bangladesh, Haiti, and Sudan.

High-Income Countries

In nations where the Industrial Revolution first took place more than two centuries ago, productivity increased more than 100-fold. To understand the power of industrial and computer technology, consider that the Netherlands—a small European nation slightly bigger than the state of Vermont—is more productive than the whole continent of Africa south of the Sahara.

Global Map 12–1 shows that the high-income nations of the world include the United States, Canada, Mexico, Argentina, Chile, the nations of Western Europe, Israel, Saudi Arabia, South Africa, Singapore, Hong Kong (part of the People's Republic of China),

Q: "Economic achievement and progress depend largely on human aptitudes and attitudes, on social and political institutions and arrangements which derive from these." P. T. Bauer

NOTE: A useful illustration here is to refer to the Thinking Globally box about the "global village" on page 8 in Chapter 1 ("The Sociological Perspective").

Q: "Half the world does not know how the other half lives." Rabelais

NOTE: Perhaps 5% of the U.S. population (15 million people) are poor enough to experience the life of most residents of low-income nations. (That's roughly the population of Angola or Kazakhstan.)

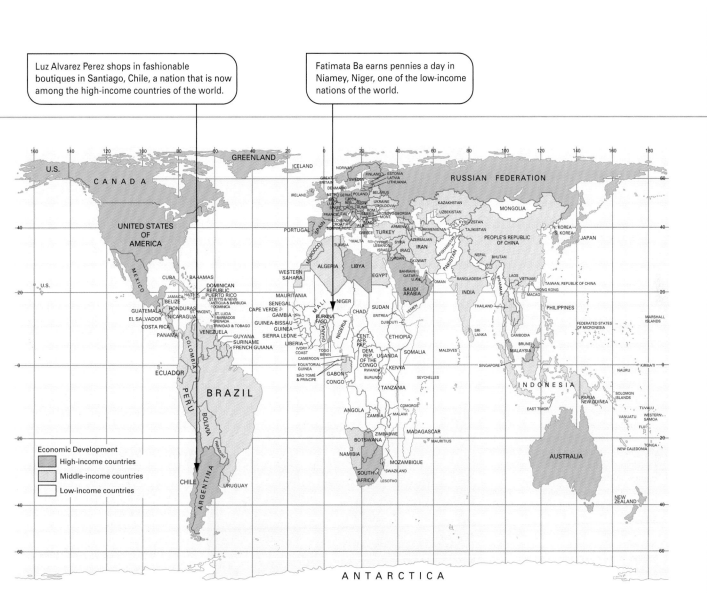

Luz Alvarez Perez shops in fashionable boutiques in Santiago, Chile, a nation that is now among the high-income countries of the world.

Fatimata Ba earns pennies a day in Niamey, Niger, one of the low-income nations of the world.

Economic Development
- High-income countries
- Middle-income countries
- Low-income countries

Window on the World

GLOBAL MAP 12–1 Economic Development in Global Perspective

In high-income countries—including the United States, Canada, Mexico, Chile, Argentina, the nations of Western Europe, South Africa, Israel, Saudi Arabia, Malaysia, Australia, the Russian Federation, and Japan—a highly productive economy provides people, on average, with material plenty. Middle-income countries—including most of Latin America and Asia—are less economically productive, with a standard of living about average for the world as a whole but far below that of the United States. These nations also have a significant share of poor people who are barely able to feed and house themselves. In the low-income countries of the world, poverty is severe and widespread. Although small numbers of elites live very well in the poorest nations, most people struggle to survive on a small fraction of the income common in the United States.

Note: Data for this map are provided by the United Nations. Each country's economic productivity is measured in terms of its gross domestic product (GDP), which is the total value of all the goods and services produced by a country's economy within its borders in a given year. Dividing each country's GDP by the country's population gives us the per capita (per-person) GDP and allows us to compare the economic performance of countries of different population sizes. High-income countries have a per capita GDP of more than $10,000. Many are far richer than this, however; the figure for the United States exceeds $41,000. Middle-income countries have a per capita GDP ranging from $2,500 to $10,000. Low-income countries have a per capita GDP of less than $2,500. Figures used here reflect the United Nations "purchasing power parities" system, which is an estimate of what people can buy using their income in the local economy.

Source: Data from United Nations Development Programme (2008).

GLOBAL: A society's mode of transportation is a shorthand index of development that is evident to a traveler. The poorest nations of the world depend on the muscle power of humans and their animals, illustrated by the waves of pedestrians and animals in the streets of Bangladesh. Developing nations (such as Taiwan) make extensive use of mopeds, motorcycles, and other lightweight, gasoline-powered vehicles. Rich societies employ high numbers of automobiles; in the U.S., the number of motor vehicles exceeds the number of adults. (And on college campuses, there is a curious return to low-tech walking and bicycling.)

NOTE: By and large, poor countries have more internal stratification than the U.S. Thus the chasm separating the rich of the U.S. and the world's poorest people is truly immense. One manifestation of this is the pattern of wealthy U.S. households employing immigrant service workers.

SEEING SOCIOLOGY
in Everyday Life

Why do you think most people from high-income countries who travel to middle- or low-income nations do so as tourists, but most who travel from middle- or low-income nations to high-income countries do so as immigrants?

THINKING ABOUT DIVERSITY: RACE, CLASS, & GENDER

Las Colonias: "America's Third World"

"We wanted to have something for ourselves," explains Olga Ruiz, who has lived in the border community of College Park, Texas, for eleven years. There is no college in College Park, nor does this dusty stretch of rural land have sewer lines or even running water. Yet this town is one of some 1,800 settlements that have sprouted up in southern Texas along the 1,200-mile border with Mexico that runs from El Paso to Brownsville. Together, they are home to at least 750,000 people, a number expected to pass 1 million in the near future.

Many people speak of *las colonias* (Spanish for "the colonies") as "America's Third World" because these desperately poor communities look much like their counterparts in Mexico or many other middle- or low-income nations. But this is the United States, and almost all of the people living in the *colonias* are Hispanic Americans, 85 percent of them legal residents and more than half U.S. citizens.

Anastacia Ledsema, now seventy-two years old, moved to a *colonia* called Sparks more than forty years ago. Born in Mexico, Ledsema married a Texas man, and together they paid $200 for a quarter-acre lot in a new border community. For months, they camped out on their land. Step by step, they invested their labor and their money to build a modest house. Not until 1995 did their small community get running water—a service that had been promised by developers years before. When the water line finally did arrive, however, things changed more than they expected. "When we got water," recalls Ledsema, "that's when so many people came in." The population of Sparks quickly doubled to about 3,000, overwhelming the water supply so that sometimes the faucet does not run at all.

The residents of all the *colonias* know that they are poor. Indeed, the Census Bureau declared the county surrounding one border community the poorest in the United States. Concerned over the lack of basic services in so many of these communities, Texas officials have banned new settlements. But most of the people who move here—even those who start off sleeping in their cars or trucks—see these communities as the first step on the path to the American dream. Oscar Solis, a neighborhood leader in Panorama Village, a community with a population of about 150, is proud to show visitors around the small but growing town. "All of this work we have done ourselves," he says with a smile, "to make our dream come true."

WHAT DO YOU THINK?

1. Are you surprised that such poverty exists in a rich country like the United States? Why or why not?

2. Why do you think such communities get little attention from the U.S. mass media?

3. To what extent do you think people living in these communities will have their "dreams come true"? Explain.

Source: Based on Schaffer (2002).

Japan, South Korea, the Russian Federation, Malaysia, Australia, and New Zealand.

These countries cover roughly 47 percent of Earth's land area, including parts of five continents, and they lie mostly in the Northern Hemisphere. In 2008, the total population of these nations was about 1.5 billion, or about 22 percent of the world's people. About three-fourths of the people in high-income countries live in or near cities (Population Reference Bureau, 2008 and World Bank, 2008).

Significant cultural differences exist among high-income countries; for example, the nations of Europe recognize more than thirty official languages. But these societies all produce enough economic goods and services to enable their people to lead comfortable lives.

Per capita income (that is, average income per person per year) ranges from about $10,000 annually (in Costa Rica and the Russian Federation) to more than $41,000 annually (in the United States and Norway). In fact, people in high-income countries enjoy 80 percent of the world's total income.

Keep in mind that high-income countries have many low-income people. The Thinking About Diversity box profiles the striking poverty that exists in *las colonias* along the southern border of the United States.

Production in rich nations is capital-intensive; it is based on factories, big machinery, and advanced technology. Most of the largest corporations that design and market computers, as well as

○ MAKING THE GRADE

The full extent of global stratification reflects both differences among countries and internal stratification.

most computer users, are located in high-income countries. High-income countries control the world's financial markets, so daily events in the financial exchanges of New York, London, and Tokyo affect people throughout the world. In short, rich nations are very productive because of their advanced technology and because they control the global economy.

Middle-Income Countries

Middle-income countries have a per capita income of between $2,500 and $10,000, roughly the median for the world's nations. About 55 percent of the people in middle-income countries live in or near cities, and industrial jobs are common. The remaining 45 percent of people live in rural areas, where most are poor and lack access to schools, medical care, adequate housing, and even safe drinking water.

Looking at Global Map 12–1, we see that seventy-two of the world's nations fall into the middle-income category. At the high end are Uruguay (Latin America), Bulgaria (Europe), and Thailand (Asia), where annual income is about $9,000. At the low end are Bolivia (Latin America), Lesotho (Africa), and Vietnam (Asia), with roughly $3,000 annually in per capita income.

One cluster of middle-income countries used to be part of the Second World. These countries, found in Eastern Europe and Western Asia, had mostly socialist economies until popular revolts between 1989 and 1991 swept their governments aside. Since then, these nations have introduced more free-market systems. These middle-income countries include Belarus, Ukraine, and Romania, as well as Kazakhstan, Georgia, and Turkmenistan.

Other middle-income nations include Peru and Brazil in South America and Namibia and Gabon in Africa. Both India and the People's Republic of China have entered the middle-income category, which now includes most of Asia.

Taken together, middle-income countries span roughly 33 percent of Earth's land area and are home to about 3.8 billion people, or about 58 percent of humanity. Some very large countries (such as China) are far less crowded than other smaller nations (such as El Salvador), but compared to high-income countries, these societies are densely populated.

Low-Income Countries

Low-income countries, where most people are very poor, are mostly agrarian societies with some industry. Fifty-six low-income countries, identified in Global Map 12–1, are spread across Central and East Africa and Asia. Low-income countries cover 20 percent of the

China has joined the ranks of middle-income nations, which is one reason this category now contains a majority of the world's people. In 2008, China hosted the Summer Olympics.

planet's land area and are home to about 1.3 billion people, or 19 percent of humanity. Population density is generally high, although it is greater in Asian countries (such as Bangladesh and Pakistan) than in Central African nations (such as Chad and the Democratic Republic of the Congo).

In poor countries, one-third of the people live in cities; most inhabit villages and farms as their ancestors have done for centuries. In fact, half the world's people are farmers, most of whom follow cultural traditions. With limited industrial technology, they cannot be very productive, one reason that many suffer severe poverty. Hunger, disease, and unsafe housing shape the lives of the world's poorest people.

Those of us who live in rich nations such as the United States find it hard to understand the scope of human need in much of the world. From time to time, televised pictures of famine in very poor countries such as Ethiopia and Bangladesh give us shocking glimpses of the poverty that makes every day a life-and-death struggle for many people in low-income nations. Behind these images lie cultural, historical, and economic forces that we shall explore in the remainder of this chapter.

Global Wealth and Poverty

 October 14, Manila, Philippines. What caught my eye was how clean she was—a girl no more than seven or eight years old. She was wearing a freshly laundered dress,

GLOBAL: Another way to describe the relationship in Figure 12–2 is that about four-fifths of the world's people account for just one-fifth of global GDP; the richest one-fifth account for about four-fifths of global GDP.

GLOBAL: The U.S., Japan, and Germany contain about 10% of the world's people but generate half the world's income.

GLOBAL: The world's labor force numbers more than 3 billion people; about 30% (almost 1 billion people) are unemployed or underemployed, almost all living in poor nations.

GLOBAL: Life expectancy at birth (2005) is a major indicator of quality of life: Japan, 82; Hong Kong, 81; Canada, 80; Germany, 79; U.K., 78; U.S., 78; Taiwan, 76; Poland, 75; China, 72; Romania, 71; Russia, 65; Ethiopia, 49; Uganda, 47; Nigeria, 44; Angola, 41 (Population Reference Bureau, 2006).

● SEEING SOCIOLOGY
in Everyday Life

Have you ever visited or lived in a middle- or low-income nation? If so, what can you say about everyday life there?

and her hair was carefully combed. She stopped to watch us, following us with her eyes: Camera-toting Americans stand out here, one of the poorest neighborhoods in the world.

Fed by methane from decomposing garbage, the fires never go out on Smokey Mountain, the vast garbage dump on the north side of Manila. Smoke covers the hills of refuse like a thick fog. But Smokey Mountain is more than a dump; it is a neighborhood that is home to thousands of people. It is hard to imagine a setting more hostile to human life. Amid the smoke and the squalor, men and women do what they can to survive. They pick plastic bags from the garbage and wash them in the river, and they collect cardboard boxes or anything else they can sell. What chance do their children have, coming from families that earn only a few hundred dollars a year, with hardly any opportunity for schooling, year after year breathing this foul air? Against this backdrop of human tragedy, one lovely little girl has put on a fresh dress and gone out to play.

Now our taxi driver threads his way through heavy traffic as we head for the other side of Manila. The change is

amazing: The smoke and smell of the dump give way to neighborhoods that could be in Miami or Los Angeles. A cluster of yachts floats on the bay in the distance. No more rutted streets; now we glide quietly along wide boulevards lined with trees and filled with expensive Japanese cars. We pass shopping plazas, upscale hotels, and high-rise office buildings. Every block or so we see the gated entrance to yet another exclusive residential community with security guards standing watch. Here, in large, air-conditioned homes, the rich of Manila live—and many of the poor work.

Low-income nations are home to some rich and many poor people. The fact that most people live with incomes of just a few hundred dollars a year means that the burden of poverty is far greater than among the poor of the United States. This is not to suggest that U.S. poverty is a minor problem. In so rich a country, too little food, substandard housing, and no medical care for tens of millions of people—almost half of them children—amount to a national tragedy.

The Severity of Poverty

Poverty in poor countries is more severe than it is in rich countries. A key reason that the quality of life differs so much around the world is that economic productivity is lowest in precisely the regions where population growth is highest. Figure 12–2 shows the proportion of world population and global income for countries at each level of economic development. High-income countries are by far the most advantaged, with 80 percent of global income supporting just 22 percent of humanity. In middle-income nations, 58 percent of the world's people earn 18 percent of global income. This leaves 19 percent of the planet's population with just 2 percent of global income. In short, for every dollar received by individuals in a low-income country, someone in a high-income country takes home $34.

Table 12–1 shows the extent of wealth and well-being in specific countries around the world. The first column of figures gives gross domestic product (GDP) for a number of high-, middle-, and low-income countries.[1] The United States, a large and highly productive nation, had a 2006 GDP of more than $12 trillion; Japan's GDP was approaching $5 trillion. A comparison of GDP figures shows that the world's richest nations are thousands of times more productive than the poorest countries.

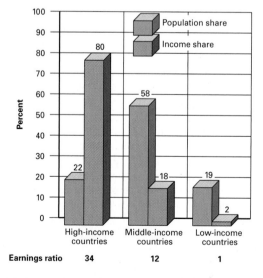

FIGURE 12–2 The Relative Share of Income and Population by Level of Economic Development

For every dollar earned by people in low-income countries, people in high-income countries earn $34.

Source: Based on United Nations Development Programme (2008).

[1]Gross domestic product is the value of all the goods and services produced by a country's economy within its borders in a given year.

The second column of figures in Table 12–1 divides GDP by the entire population size to give an estimate of what people can buy with their income in the local economy. The per capita GDP for rich countries like the United States, Sweden, and Canada is very high, exceeding $32,000. For middle-income countries, such as Uruguay and Bulgaria, the figures are in the $9,000 range. In the world's low-income countries, per capita GDP is just a few hundred dollars. In Niger or in Ethiopia, for example, a typical person labors all year to make what the average worker in the United States earns in a week.

The last column of Table 12–1 is a measure of the quality of life in the various nations. This index, calculated by the United Nations, is based on income, education (extent of adult literacy and average years of schooling), and longevity (how long people typically live). Index values are decimals that fall between extremes of 1 (highest) and 0 (lowest). By this calculation, Norwegians enjoy the highest quality of life (.968), with residents of the United States close behind (.951). At the other extreme, people in the African nation of Niger have the lowest quality of life (.374).

Relative versus Absolute Poverty

The distinction between relative and absolute poverty, made in Chapter 11 ("Social Class in the United States"), has an important application to global inequality. People living in rich countries generally focus on *relative poverty,* meaning that some people lack resources that are taken for granted by others. By definition, relative poverty exists in every society, rich or poor.

More important in global perspective, however, is *absolute poverty,* a lack of resources that is life-threatening. Human beings in absolute poverty lack the nutrition necessary for health and long-term survival. To be sure, some absolute poverty exists in the United States. But such immediately life-threatening poverty strikes only a very small proportion of the U.S. population; in low-income countries, by contrast, one-third or more of the people are in desperate need.

Because absolute poverty is deadly, one global indicator of this problem is median age at death. Global Map 12–2 identifies the age by which half of all people born in a nation die. In rich societies, most people die after the age of seventy-five; in poor countries, half of all deaths occur among children under the age of ten.

The Extent of Poverty

Poverty in poor countries is more widespread than it is in rich nations such as the United States. Chapter 11 ("Social Class in the United States") noted that the U.S. government officially classifies 12.5 percent of the population as poor. In low-income countries,

Table 12–1 Wealth and Well-Being in Global Perspective, 2006

Country	Gross Domestic Product (US$ billions)	GDP per Capita (PPP US$)*	Quality of Life Index
High-Income			
Norway	296	41,420	.968
Australia	733	31,794	.962
Canada	1,114	33,375	.961
Sweden	358	32,525	.956
Japan	4,534	31,267	.953
United States	12,417	41,890	.951
United Kingdom	2,199	33,238	.946
South Korea	788	22,029	.921
Middle-Income			
Eastern Europe			
Bulgaria	27	9,032	.824
Albania	8	5,316	.801
Ukraine	83	6,848	.788
Latin America			
Uruguay	17	9,962	.852
Brazil	796	8,402	.800
Ecuador	37	4,341	.772
Asia			
Thailand	177	8,677	.781
People's Republic of China	2,234	6,757	.777
India	806	3,452	.619
Middle East			
Iran	190	7,968	.759
Syria	26	3,808	.724
Africa			
Algeria	102	7,062	.733
Namibia	6	7,586	.650
Low-Income			
Latin America			
Haiti	4	1,663	.529
Asia			
Laos	3	2,039	.601
Pakistan	111	2,370	.551
Bangladesh	60	2,053	.547
Africa			
Kenya	19	1,240	.521
Guinea	3	2,316	.456
Ethiopia	11	1,055	.406
Mali	5	1,033	.380
Niger	3	781	.374

*These data are the United Nations' purchasing power parity (PPP) calculations, which avoid currency rate distortion by showing the local purchasing power of each domestic currency.

Source: United Nations Development Programme (2008).

THE MAP: The high mortality in low-income countries is all the more striking in light of the fact that infant mortality has actually dropped by half since 1965, from about 125 (per 1,000 live births) to 52 today.

THEN AND NOW: Life expectancy in sub-Saharan Africa has risen from about 37 in 1960 to 48 today, but that's still 30 years off the U.S. level.

Q: "The plight of women [in modernizing Bangladesh] is all too obvious in the streams of unattached mothers and children who pour into towns to beg, in the growth of prostitution, [and] in the desperation with which rural women have left the seclusion of their homes to seek work." Sultana Alam

Q: "Women-headed households are of fairly recent origin in the Third World." Sultana Alam

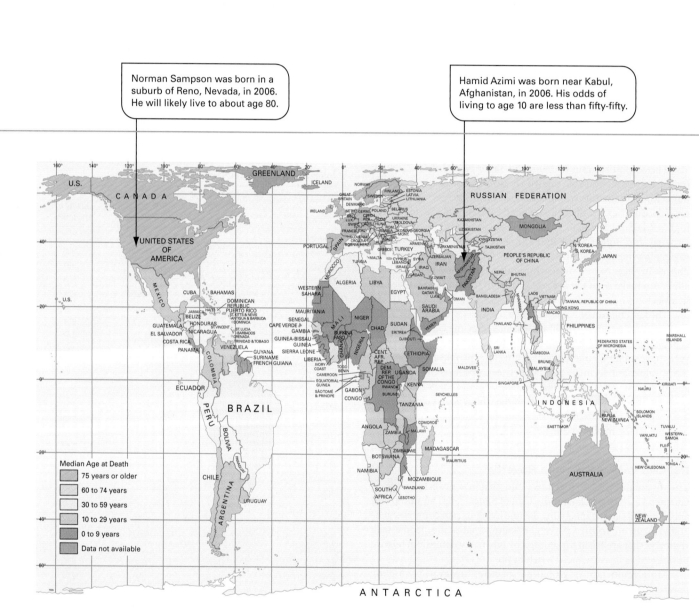

Window on the World

GLOBAL MAP 12–2   **Median Age at Death in Global Perspective**

This map identifies the age below which half of all deaths occur in any year. In the high-income countries of the world, including the United States, it is mostly the elderly who face death, that is, people aged seventy-five or older. In middle-income countries, including most of Latin America, most people die years or even decades earlier. In low-income countries, especially in Africa and parts of Asia, it is children who die, half of them never reaching their tenth birthday.

Source: World Bank (1993), with updates by the author.

however, most people live no better than the poor in the United States, and many are far worse off. As Global Map 12–2 shows, the high death rates among children in Africa indicate that absolute poverty is greatest there, where one-third of the population is malnourished. In the world as a whole, at any given time, 17 percent of the people—about 1.4 billion—suffer from chronic hunger, which leaves them less able to work and puts them at high risk of disease (Chen & Ravallion, 2008; United Nations Development Programme, 2008).

The typical adult in a rich nation such as the United States consumes about 3,500 calories a day, an excess that contributes to widespread obesity and related health problems. The typical adult

Q: "One billion more people are being fed today than in the early 1970s, but the number of hungry people continues to increase." John W. Helmuth

NOTE: The intensity of the problems of poor societies is most clearly evident in cities. Most of the largest cities of the world are now in poor countries, including Mexico City with some 25 million people.

GLOBAL: Illiteracy rates are high in poor societies (about half of all Africans and one-fourth of all Latin Americans can neither read nor write). Throughout the world, illiteracy is much more common among women than men. Examples (percent illiterate, 2006): Saudi Arabia, 13% of men, 31% of women; Cambodia, 15%, 36%; Algeria, 20%, 40%; India, 27%, 52%; Niger, 57%, 85%; Mali, 73%, 88% (World Bank, 2007).

SEEING SOCIOLOGY
in Everyday Life

How do you think the experience of childhood as a stage of the life course differs in high- and low-income countries?

MAKING THE GRADE

As explained below, gender inequality is greater in low-income countries than in high-income countries.

in a low-income country not only does more physical labor but consumes just 2,000 calories a day. The result is undernourishment: too little food or not enough of the right kinds of food (United Nations, 2006).

In the ten minutes it takes to read this section of the chapter, about 100 people in the world who are sick and weakened from hunger will die. This number amounts to about 25,000 people a day, or 9 million people each year. Clearly, easing world hunger is one of the most serious responsibilities facing humanity today (United Nations Development Programme, 2008).

Poverty and Children

Death comes early in poor societies, where families lack adequate food, safe water, secure housing, and access to medical care. In the world's low- and middle-income nations, one-third of all children do not receive enough nutrition to be healthy (Levinson & Bassett, 2007).

Poor children live in poor families, and many share in the struggle to get through each day. Organizations fighting child poverty estimate that as many as 100 million children living in cities in poor countries beg, steal, sell sex, or work for drug gangs to provide income for their families. Such a life almost always means dropping out of school and puts children at high risk of disease and violence. Many girls, with little or no access to medical assistance, become pregnant, a case of children who cannot support themselves having children of their own.

Analysts estimate that another 100 million of the world's children are orphaned or have left their families altogether, sleeping and living on the streets as best they can or perhaps trying to migrate to the United States. Roughly half of all street children are found in Latin American cities such as Mexico City and Rio de Janeiro, where half of all children grow up in poverty. Many people in the United States know these cities as exotic travel destinations, but they are also home to thousands of street children living in makeshift huts, under bridges, or in alleyways (Collymore, 2002; Leopold, 2007; Levinson & Bassett, 2007).

Poverty and Women

In rich societies, much of the work women do is undervalued, underpaid, or overlooked entirely. In poor societies, women face even greater disadvantages. Most of the people who work in sweatshops like the one described in the opening to this chapter are women.

To make matters worse, tradition keeps women out of many jobs in low-income nations; in Bangladesh, for example, women work in

Tens of millions of children fend for themselves every day on the streets of poor cities where many fall victim to disease, drug abuse, and violence. What do you think must be done to put an end to scenes like this one in Kolkata, India?

garment factories because that society's conservative Muslim religious norms bar them from most other paid work and limit their opportunity for advanced schooling (Bearak, 2001). At the same time, traditional norms in poor societies give women primary responsibility for child rearing and maintaining the household. The United Nations estimates that in poor countries, men own 90 percent of the land, a far greater gender disparity in wealth than is found in high-income nations. It is likely, then, that about 70 percent of the world's 1.4 billion people living near absolute poverty are women (C. Hymowitz, 1995; Moghadam, 2005).

Finally, most women in poor countries receive little or no reproductive health care. Limited access to birth control keeps women at home with their children, keeps the birth rate high, and limits the economic production of the country. In addition, the world's poorest women typically give birth without help from trained health care personnel. Figure 12–3 on page 310 illustrates a stark difference between low- and high-income countries in this regard.

Slavery

Poor societies have many problems in addition to hunger, including illiteracy, warfare, and even slavery. The British Empire banned slavery in 1833, followed by the United States in 1865. But slavery is a

GLOBAL: Refugees are on the rise, predominantly in the poorest regions of the world. Some 20 million people are displaced across international borders, with another 25 million uprooted within their own countries. As the numbers rise, rich countries are becoming more restrictive about admitting refugees.

GLOBAL: Starvation has been caused by social policies more than by natural forces such as droughts. Examples: 1846–50, Irish potato famine as food is diverted to England; 1932–34, some 5 million Soviet people die during Stalin's farm collectivization; 1958–61, perhaps 25 million starve during China's failed "Great Leap Forward."

DISCUSS: Do you think there should be a universal "right to food"?

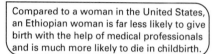

Compared to a woman in the United States, an Ethiopian woman is far less likely to give birth with the help of medical professionals and is much more likely to die in childbirth.

● MAKING THE GRADE

The list beginning on this page identifies six factors that play a part in explaining global poverty. As you read on, you will see that the first three are closer to modernization theory and the next three are closer to dependency theory.

Global Snapshot

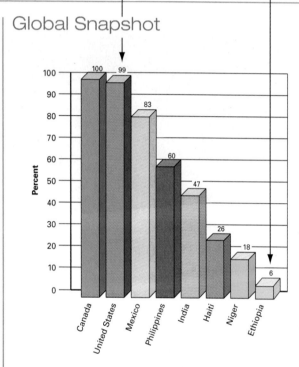

FIGURE 12–3 **Percentage of Births Attended by Skilled Health Staff**

In the United States, most women give birth with the help of medical professionals, but this is usually not the case in low-income nations.
Source: World Bank (2008).

Third, *debt bondage* is the practice by which an employer pays workers wages that are not enough to cover the food and housing provided by the employer; for practical purposes, they are enslaved. Many sweatshop workers in low-income nations fall into this category.

Fourth, *servile forms of marriage* may also amount to slavery. In India, Thailand, and some African nations, families marry off women against their will. Many end up as slaves working for their husband's family; some are forced into prostitution.

An additional form of slavery is *human trafficking,* the moving of men, women, and children from one place to another for the purpose of performing forced labor. Women or men are brought to a new country with the promise of a job and then forced to become prostitutes or farm laborers, or "parents" adopt children from another country and then force them to work in sweatshops. Such activity is big business: Next to trading in guns and drugs, trading in people brings the greatest profit to organized crime around the world (Orhant, 2002; Anti-Slavery International, 2008).

In 1948, the United Nations issued its Universal Declaration of Human Rights, which states, "No one shall be held in slavery or servitude; slavery and the slave trade shall be prohibited in all their forms." Unfortunately, more than six decades later, this social evil exists. Seeing Sociology in the News on pages 312–13 presents a case of forced labor currently taking place in Malaysia.

Explanations of Global Poverty

What accounts for severe and extensive poverty in so much of the world? The rest of this chapter provides answers using the following facts about poor societies:

1. **Technology**. About one-quarter of people in low-income countries farm the land using human muscle or animal power. With limited energy sources, economic production is modest.

2. **Population growth**. As Chapter 22 ("Population, Urbanization, and Environment") explains, the poorest countries have the world's highest birth rates. Despite the death toll from poverty, the populations of many poor countries in Africa, for example, double every twenty-five years. In these countries, half the people are teenagers or younger. With so many people entering their childbearing years, the wave of population growth will roll into the future. For example, the population of Uganda has swelled by almost 3 percent annually in recent years, so even with economic development, living standards there have fallen.

3. **Cultural patterns**. Poor societies are usually traditional. Holding on to long-established ways of life means resisting change— even change that promises a richer material life. The Seeing

reality for at least 20 million men, women, and children, and as many as 200 million people (about 3 percent of humanity) live in conditions that come close to slavery.

Anti-Slavery International describes four types of slavery. The first is *chattel slavery,* in which one person owns another. In spite of the fact that this practice is against the law almost everywhere in the world, about 20 million people fall into this category. The buying and selling of slaves still takes place in many countries throughout Asia, the Middle East, and especially Africa. The Thinking Globally box describes the reality of one slave's life in the African nation of Mauritania.

A second, more common form of bondage is *child slavery,* in which desperately poor families send their children out into the streets to beg or steal or do whatever they can to survive. Perhaps 100 million children—many in the poorest countries of Latin America and Africa—fall into this category.

NOTE: Points 1–3 below are part of modernization theory; points 4–6 are elements of dependency theory. Both theories are discussed later in this chapter.

NOTE: With a current rate of population growth of 1.7%, India's population passed the 1 billion mark in 2000 and will double again by 2046.

GLOBAL: Marlise Simons explains how economic development has undermined the cultural traditions of the Kaiapo in Brazil's Amazon region. See her article in the companion reader *Seeing Ourselves*, 8th ed., or the Thinking Globally box on pages 640–41 in Chapter 24.

colonialism the process by which some nations enrich themselves through political and economic control of other nations

neocolonialism a new form of global power relationships that involves not direct political control but economic exploitation by multinational corporations

multinational corporation a large business that operates in many countries

modernization theory (p. 312) a model of economic and social development that explains global inequality in terms of technological and cultural differences between nations

THINKING GLOBALLY

"God Made Me to Be a Slave"

Fatma Mint Mamadou is a young woman living in North Africa's Islamic Republic of Mauritania. Asked her age, she pauses, smiles, and shakes her head. She has no idea when she was born. Nor can she read or write. What she knows is tending camels, herding sheep, hauling bags of water, sweeping, and serving tea to her owners. This young woman is one of perhaps 90,000 slaves in Mauritania.

In the central region of this nation, having dark brown skin almost always means being a slave to an Arab owner. Fatma accepts her situation; she has known nothing else. She explains in a matter-of-fact voice that she is a slave like her mother before her and her grandmother before that. "Just as God created a camel to be a camel," she shrugs, "he created me to be a slave."

Fatma, her mother, and her brothers and sisters live in a squatter settlement on the edge of Nouakchott, Mauritania's capital city. Their home is a 9-by-12-foot hut that they built from wood scraps and other materials found at construction

sites. The roof is nothing more than a piece of cloth; there is no plumbing or furniture. The nearest water comes from a well a mile down the road.

In this region, slavery began more than 500 years ago, about the time Columbus sailed west toward the Americas. As Arab and Berber tribes raided local villages, they made slaves of the peo-

Human slavery continues to exist in the twenty-first century.

ple, and so it has been for dozens of generations ever since. In 1905, the French colonial rulers of Mauritania banned slavery. After the nation gained independence in 1961, the new government reaffirmed the ban. But such proclamations have done little to change strong traditions. Indeed, people like Fatma have no idea what "freedom to choose" means.

The next question is more personal: "Are you and other girls ever raped?" Again, Fatma hesitates. With no hint of emotion, she responds, "Of course, in the night the men come to breed us. Is that what you mean by rape?"

WHAT DO YOU THINK?

1. How does tradition play a part in keeping people in slavery?
2. What might explain the fact that the world still tolerates slavery?
3. Explain the connection between slavery and poverty.

Source: Based on Burkett (1997).

Sociology in Everyday Life box on page 314 explains why traditional people in India respond to their poverty differently than poor people in the United States.

4. **Social stratification**. Low-income societies distribute their wealth very unequally. Chapter 10 ("Social Stratification") explained that social inequality is greater in agrarian societies than in industrial societies. In Brazil, for example, 75 percent of all farmland is owned by just 4 percent of the people (Bergamo & Camarotti, 1996; Galano, 1998).

5. **Gender inequality**. Gender inequality in poor societies keeps women from holding jobs, which typically means they have many children. An expanding population, in turn, slows economic development. Many analysts conclude that raising living standards in much of the world depends on improving the social standing of women.

6. **Global power relationships**. A final cause of global poverty lies in the relationships between the nations of the world. Historically, wealth flowed from poor societies to rich nations through **colonialism**, *the process by which some nations enrich themselves through political and economic control of other nations*. The countries of Western Europe colonized much of Latin America beginning just over five centuries ago. Such global exploitation allowed some nations to develop economically at the expense of other nations.

Although 130 former colonies gained their independence over the course of the twentieth century, exploitation continues today through **neocolonialism** (*neo* is Greek for "new"), *a new form of global power relationships that involves not direct political control but economic exploitation by multinational corporations*. A **multinational corporation** is *a large business that operates in many*

GLOBAL: Types of foods change with rising income. People in low-income countries eat basic cereals; middle-income nations consume basic packaged foods; the availability of frozen foods marks high-income countries. In the highest-income countries, prepared foods are popular, with fresh foods and health foods enjoyed by the richest of the world's people.

GLOBAL: The British hand-over of Hong Kong to the People's Republic of China in 1997 marked the 68th such event in the 20th century. All the other former colonies are politically independent.

POP CULTURE: Celebrities including Sandra Bullock and Leonardo DiCaprio played an important part in the fundraising to assist victims of the 2004 earthquake and tsunami tragedy in South Asia.

Seeing SOCIOLOGY in the NEWS

Newsweek

Bottom of the Barrel

By GEORGE WEHRFRITZ, ERIKA KINETZ, AND JONATHAN KENT

March 24, 2008

Some of the world's leading computer makers don't want you to know about Local Technic Industry. It's a typical Malaysian company, one of many small makers of the cast-aluminum bodies for hard-disk drives used in just about every name-brand machine on the market. But that's precisely the problem: it's a typical Malaysian company. About 60 percent of Local Technic's 160 employees are from outside Malaysia—and a company executive says he pities those guest workers. "They have been fooled hook, line and sinker," he says. . . . It's not Local Technic's fault, he insists: sleazy labor brokers outside the country tricked the workers into paying huge placement fees for jobs that yield a net income close to zero. . . .

So why don't those foreign employees just quit? Because they can't, even if they find out they've been cheated by the very brokers who brought

them there. Malaysian law requires guest workers to sign multiple-year contracts and surrender their passports to their employers. Those who run away but stay in Malaysia are automatically classed as illegal aliens, subject to arrest, imprisonment and caning [beating with a cane rod] before being expelled from the country. "Passport, company take," says a Bangladeshi who has worked at Local Technic. . . . "They say, 'You come to this company, must work for this company and cannot work other place.' They say, 'If you work [for] someone else, the police will catch you.'" He paid a broker in Bangladesh $3,600 to get him a job at Local Technic. When he arrived, he says, he learned he was making $114 a month after deductions for room, board and taxes. The math is simple: minus the broker's fee, his net monthly pay is $14. If he never spends a penny on himself, three years of labor will earn him a grand total of $504.

This is the dark side of globalization: a vast work force trapped in conditions that verge on slavery. Most media coverage of human trafficking

tends to focus on crime, like the recent scandals involving migrant laborers who were kidnapped and forced to work at brick kilns in China. And forced prostitution, of course, which accounts for roughly 2 million people worldwide, according to the United Nations' International Labor Organization. . . . But the international market in "forced laborers" (the ILO's term) is far larger—and generally ignored. The ILO reckons the worldwide number of forced laborers today at some 12.3 million. It's a conservative estimate; other approximations rise as high as 27 million.

Forced labor has two defining features. First, the ILO says, the worker has not given informed consent, whether because of mental or physical duress, debt bondage or deceit. Second, there is a danger of punishment for refusing to do the job, including threats of violence, arrest, imprisonment or deportation. The market is controlled by predatory employment brokers who charge placement fees that average in the thousands of dollars. Even at that price, they find easy prey in poor lands like Bangladesh, Cambodia,

countries. Corporate leaders often impose their will on countries in which they do business to create favorable economic conditions for the operation of their corporations, just as colonizers did in the past (Bonanno, Constance, & Lorenz, 2000).

Global Stratification: Theoretical Analysis

There are two major explanations for the unequal distribution of the world's wealth and power: *modernization theory* and *dependency theory*. Each theory suggests a different solution to the suffering of hungry people in much of the world.

Modernization Theory

Modernization theory is *a model of economic and social development that explains global inequality in terms of technological and cultural differences between nations.* Modernization theory, which follows the structural-functional approach, emerged in the 1950s, a time when U.S. society was fascinated by new developments in technology. To showcase the power of productive technology and also to counter the growing influence of the Soviet Union, U.S. policymakers drafted a market-based foreign policy that has been with us ever since (Rostow,

1960, 1978; Bauer, 1981; Berger, 1986; Firebaugh, 1996; Firebaugh & Sandhu, 1998).

Historical Perspective

Until a few centuries ago, the entire world was poor. Because poverty is the norm throughout human history, modernization theory claims that it is *affluence* that demands an explanation.

Affluence came within reach of a growing share of people in Western Europe during the late Middle Ages as world exploration and trade expanded. Soon after, the Industrial Revolution transformed first Western Europe and then North America. Industrial technology and the spirit of capitalism created new wealth as never before. At first, this wealth benefited only a few individuals. But industrial technology was so productive that gradually the living standards of even the poorest people began to improve. Absolute poverty, which had plagued humanity throughout history, was finally in decline.

In high-income countries, where the Industrial Revolution began in the late 1700s or early 1800s, the standard of living jumped at least fourfold during the twentieth century. As middle-income nations in Asia and Latin America have industrialized, they too have become richer. But with limited industrial technology, low-income countries have changed much less.

Indonesia and the Philippines. Job seekers will do anything—sell whatever they own, cash in their savings, borrow the balance—in hope of making better lives for their families.

One of the most notorious host countries is Malaysia, with an estimated 2.5 million foreign workers, including many who fit the U.N. definition of forced laborers. . . . Malaysian law effectively makes every foreign worker a captive of the company that hired him or her. In the name of immigration control, employers like Local Technic are required to confiscate guest workers' passports and report any runaways to the police. No one blames company managers for lies told by independent labor recruiters inside or outside the country. Yet new recruits keep coming.

Professional spotters prowl Indonesia's neglected West Kalimantan province, collecting bounties as high as $100 for each mark they find for the brokers. Job touts then swoop down, offering gifts, cash and working papers. In Malaysia, just over the border, labor agencies pay the traffickers as much

as $1,000 a head on delivery—and new recruits are then told they'll have to pay that money back with interest before they can go home. . . .

And yet the nature of the global economy makes it nearly impossible to avoid buying products of forced labor. Trapped workers on plantations in Malaysia harvest basic commodities like rubber and palm oil (for toothpaste, cosmetics and biofuels). "It's like I'm out of hell," says one Indonesian who says he spent seven months at a Malaysian rubber plantation working 13 hours a day, seven days a week without pay until he escaped—only to be arrested, imprisoned, flogged and deported. His story is consistent with numerous accounts collected by nongovernmental organizations in Indonesia. But when that plantation's harvest goes to market, it looks just like rubber from anywhere else. . . .

So far, the international community has taken only small steps to control the traffic in forced labor. In response to complaints, Malaysia has called a temporary halt to imports of labor from

Bangladesh. . . . The Dhaka government has vowed to investigate charges that Bangladesh's labor exports effectively constitute legalized slavery. But emancipation remains only a dream.

WHAT DO YOU THINK?

1. How does the law in countries like Malaysia encourage labor practices that amount to slavery?

2. What should be done to ensure that workers in poor countries are treated fairly? Do you think change is likely? Why or why not?

3. According to the article, why is it "almost impossible" for people in high-income countries to avoid buying products made using forced labor? How much do you think about this issue when you buy products?

The Importance of Culture

Why didn't the Industrial Revolution sweep away poverty throughout the world? Modernization theory points out that not every society wants to adopt new technology. Doing so requires a cultural environment that emphasizes the benefits of material wealth and new ideas.

Modernization theory identifies *tradition* as the greatest barrier to economic development. In some societies, strong family systems and a reverence for the past discourage people from adopting new technologies that would raise their living standards. Even today, many traditional people—from the Amish in North America to Islamic people in the Middle East to the Semai of Malaysia—oppose new technology as a threat to their families, customs, and religious beliefs.

Max Weber (1958, orig. 1904–05) found that at the end of the Middle Ages, Western Europe's cultural environment favored change. As discussed in Chapter 4 ("Society"), the Protestant Reformation reshaped traditional Christian beliefs to generate a progress-oriented way of life. Wealth—looked on with suspicion by the Catholic church—became a sign of personal virtue, and the growing importance of individualism steadily replaced the traditional emphasis on family and community. Taken together, these new cultural patterns nurtured the Industrial Revolution.

Rostow's Stages of Modernization

Modernization theory holds that the door to affluence is open to all. As technological advances spread around the world, all societies should gradually industrialize. According to Walt Rostow (1960, 1978), modernization occurs in four stages:

1. **Traditional stage.** Socialized to honor the past, people in traditional societies cannot easily imagine that life could or should be any different. They therefore build their lives around families and local communities, following well-worn paths that allow little individual freedom or change. Life is often spiritually rich but lacking in material goods.

   A century ago, much of the world was in this initial stage of economic development. Nations such as Bangladesh, Niger, and Somalia are still at the traditional stage and remain poor. Even in countries, such as India, that have recently joined the ranks of middle-income nations, certain elements of the population have remained highly traditional. The Seeing Sociology in Everyday Life box on page 314 takes a look at traditional life in India.

2. **Take-off stage.** As a society shakes off the grip of tradition, people start to use their talents and imagination, sparking economic growth. A market emerges as people produce goods not just for

RESOURCE: The cultural value placed on achievement is regarded by some sociologists as the crucial factor in advancing or inhibiting development (see Lerner, 1958).

NOTE: The subtitle of Walt Whitman Rostow's (1960) work, "A Non-Communist Manifesto," suggests its opposition to Marx's thinking.

GLOBAL: During the 1990s, the population of poor countries increased by about 2% annually, versus 0.5% for rich nations; economic growth in poor countries was negative, against positive growth for rich societies.

GLOBAL: Hong Kong (about the size of Los Angeles) has twice the economic productivity of Egypt and three times that of Bangladesh.

MAKING THE GRADE

Rostow's stages of economic development describe an airplane, first on the ground, then moving fast down the runway, then climbing to cruising altitude, and then flying high. In the 1950s, when Rostow was writing, U.S. society was fascinated with jet planes, scientific achievement, and progress.

SEEING SOCIOLOGY IN EVERYDAY LIFE

"Happy Poverty" in India: Making Sense of a Strange Idea

Although India has become a middle-income nation, its per capita GDP is just $3,451, about one-twelfth that in the United States. For this reason, India is home to one-fourth of the world's hungry people.

But most North Americans do not readily understand the reality of poverty in India. Many of the country's 1.2 billion people live in conditions far worse than those our society labels "poor." A traveler's first experience of Indian life can be shocking. Chennai (formerly known as Madras), for example, one of India's largest cities with 7 million inhabitants, seems chaotic to an outsider—streets choked with motorbikes, trucks, carts pulled by oxen, and waves of people. Along the roadway, vendors sit on burlap cloths selling fruits, vegetables, and cooked food while people nearby talk, bathe, and sleep.

Although some people live well, Chennai is dotted with more than 1,000 shanty settlements, home to half a million people from rural villages who have come in search of a better life. Shantytowns are clusters of huts built with branches, leaves, and pieces of discarded cardboard and tin. These dwellings offer little privacy and have no refrigeration, running water, or bathrooms. A visitor from the United States may feel uneasy in such an area, knowing that the poorest sections of our own inner cities seethe with frustration and sometimes explode with violence.

But India's people understand poverty differently than we do. No restless young men hang out at the corner, no drug dealers work the streets, and there is little danger of violence. In the United States, poverty often means anger and isolation; in India, even shantytowns are organized around strong families—children, parents, and often grandparents—who offer a smile of welcome to a stranger.

For traditional people in India, life is shaped by *dharma,* the Hindu concept of duty and destiny that teaches people to accept their fate, whatever

it may be. Mother Teresa, who worked among the poorest of India's people, went to the heart of the cultural differences: "Americans have angry poverty," she explained. "In India, there is worse poverty, but it is a happy poverty."

Perhaps we should not describe anyone who clings to the edge of survival as happy. But poverty in India is eased by the strength and support of families and communities, a sense that life has a purpose, and a worldview that encourages each person to accept whatever life offers. As a result, a visitor may well come away from a first encounter with Indian poverty in confusion: "How can people be so poor and yet apparently content, active, and *joyful*?"

WHAT DO YOU THINK?

1. What did Mother Teresa mean when she said that in India there is "happy poverty"?
2. How might an experience like this in a very poor community change the way you think of being "rich"?
3. Do you know of any poor people in the United States who have attitudes toward poverty similar to these people in India? What would make people seem to accept being poor?

their own use but to trade with others for profit. Greater individualism, a willingness to take risks, and a desire for material goods also take hold, often at the expense of family ties and time-honored norms and values.

Great Britain reached take-off by about 1800, the United States by 1820. Thailand, a middle-income country in eastern Asia, is now in this stage. Such development is typically speeded by help from rich nations, including foreign aid, the availability of advanced technology and investment capital, and opportunities for schooling abroad.

3. **Drive to technological maturity.** As this stage begins, "growth" is a widely accepted idea that fuels a society's pursuit of higher living standards. A diversified economy drives a population eager to enjoy the benefits of industrial technology. At the same time, however, people begin to realize (and sometimes regret) that industrialization is eroding traditional family and local community life. Great Britain reached this point by about 1840, the United States by 1860. Today, Mexico, the U.S. territory of Puerto Rico, and South Korea are among the nations driving to technological maturity.

Q: "Capitalism has become one of the most dynamic forces in human history, transforming one society after another, and today it has become established as an international system determining the economic fate of most of mankind and, at least indirectly, its social, political, and cultural fate as well." Peter Berger (1986:115)

Q: "There is widespread agreement today, from Chile to China, that an economy allowing market forces the fullest feasible sway will perform better than one in which all decisions are centrally administered." Peter Berger (1986:130)

Q: "Wealth doesn't create poverty; wealth creates prosperity." George Gilder

MAKING THE GRADE

The photos below show us how stages of life—in this case, childhood—are constructed by society, as discussed in Chapter 5.

SEEING SOCIOLOGY
in Everyday Life

How would our society define work performed by children as young as those shown below?

In rich nations such as the United States, most parents expect their children to enjoy years of childhood, largely free from the responsibilities of adult life. This is not the case in poor nations across Latin America, Africa, and Asia. Poor families depend on whatever income their children can earn, and many children as young as six or seven work full days weaving or performing other kinds of manual labor. Child labor lies behind the low prices of many products imported for sale in this country.

At this stage of development, absolute poverty is greatly reduced. Cities swell with people who leave rural villages in search of economic opportunity. Specialization creates the wide range of jobs that we find in our economy today. An increasing focus on work makes relationships less personal. Growing individualism generates social movements demanding greater political rights. Societies approaching technological maturity also provide basic schooling for all their people and advanced training for some. The newly educated consider tradition "backward" and push for further change. The social position of women steadily approaches that of men.

4. **High mass consumption.** Economic development steadily raises living standards as mass production stimulates mass consumption. Simply put, people soon learn to "need" the expanding array of goods that their society produces. The United States, Japan, and other rich nations moved into this stage by 1900. Now entering this level of economic development are two former British colonies that are prosperous small societies of eastern Asia: Hong Kong (part of the People's Republic of China since 1997) and Singapore (independent since 1965).

The Role of Rich Nations

Modernization theory claims that high-income countries play four important roles in global economic development:

1. **Controlling population increase.** Because population growth is greatest in the poorest societies, rising population can overtake economic advances. Rich nations can help limit population growth by exporting birth control technology and promoting its use. Once economic development is under way, birth rates should decline, as they have in industrialized nations, because children are no longer an economic asset.

2. **Increasing food production.** Rich nations can export high-tech farming methods to poor nations to increase agricultural yields. Such techniques, collectively referred to as the Green Revolution, include new hybrid seeds, modern irrigation methods, chemical fertilizers, and pesticides for insect control.

3. **Introducing industrial technology.** Rich nations can encourage economic growth in poor societies by introducing machinery and information technology, which raise productivity. Industrialization also shifts the labor force from farming to skilled industrial and service jobs.

4. **Providing foreign aid.** Investment capital from rich nations can boost the prospects of poor societies trying to reach Rostow's take-off stage. Foreign aid can raise farm output by helping poor countries buy more fertilizer and build irrigation projects. In the same way, financial and technical assistance can help build power plants and factories to improve industrial output. Each year, the United States provides more than $25 billion in foreign aid to developing countries (U.S. Census Bureau, 2008).

DISCUSS: Do students realize that the U.S. spent more than one-third of its history (from 1607 to 1776) as a British colony?

GLOBAL: About 70% of global economic inequality is between-nation inequality; about 30% is within-nation inequality (Firebaugh, 2000).

Q: "I am convinced that the global economy makes it more difficult to devise and enact redistributive policies." Robert A. Dahl

Q: "The essence of neocolonialism is that the state subject to it is, in theory, independent and has all the trappings of international sovereignty. In reality, its economic system and thus its internal policy is directed from the outside." President Kwame Nkrumah of Ghana (1965; cited in Webster, 1984:79)

Q: "We now live in a global village." Marshall McLuhan (1969)

MAKING THE GRADE

Modernization theory is linked to structural-functional analysis; dependency theory is linked to social-conflict analysis.

dependency theory a model of economic and social development that explains global inequality in terms of the historical exploitation of poor nations by rich ones

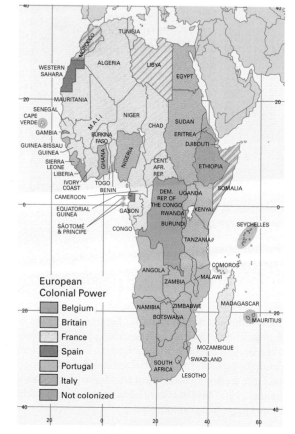

FIGURE 12–4 Africa's Colonial History

For more than a century, most of Africa was colonized by European nations, with France dominating in the northwest region of the continent and Great Britain dominating in the east and south.

European Colonial Power

- Belgium
- Britain
- France
- Spain
- Portugal
- Italy
- Not colonized

But modernization theory comes under fire from socialist countries (and left-leaning analysts in the West) as little more than a defense of capitalism. Its most serious flaw, according to critics, is that modernization simply has not occurred in many poor countries. Economic indicators reported by the United Nations show that living standards in a number of nations, including Haiti and Nicaragua in Latin America and Sudan, Ghana, and Rwanda in Africa, are little changed—and are in some cases worse—than in 1960 (United Nations Development Programme, 2008).

A second criticism of modernization theory is that it fails to recognize how rich nations, which benefit from the status quo, often block the path to development for poor countries. Centuries ago, critics charge, rich countries industrialized from a position of global strength. Can we expect poor countries today to do so from a position of global weakness?

Third, modernization theory treats rich and poor societies as separate worlds, ignoring the ways in which international relations have affected all nations. Many countries in Latin America and Asia are still struggling to overcome the harm caused by colonialism, which boosted the fortunes of Europe.

Fourth, modernization theory holds up the world's most developed countries as the standard for judging the rest of humanity, revealing an ethnocentric bias. We should remember that our Western idea of "progress" has caused us to rush headlong into a competitive, materialistic way of life, which uses up the world's scarce resources and pollutes the natural environment.

Fifth and finally, modernization theory suggests that the causes of global poverty lie almost entirely in the poor societies themselves. Critics see this analysis as little more than blaming the victims for their own problems. Instead, they argue, an analysis of global inequality should focus just as much on the behavior of rich nations as it does on the behavior of poor ones and also on the global economic system.

○ **CHECK YOUR LEARNING**   State the important ideas of modernization theory, including Rostow's four stages of economic development. Point to several strengths and weaknesses of this theory.

Concerns such as these reflect a second major approach to understanding global inequality, dependency theory.

Dependency Theory

Dependency theory is *a model of economic and social development that explains global inequality in terms of the historical exploitation of poor nations by rich ones*. This analysis, which follows the social-conflict approach, puts the main responsibility for global poverty on

○ **CRITICAL REVIEW**   Modernization theory has many influential supporters among social scientists (Parsons, 1966; W. E. Moore, 1977, 1979; Bauer, 1981; Berger, 1986; Firebaugh & Beck, 1994; Firebaugh, 1996, 1999; Firebaugh & Sandu, 1998). For decades, it has shaped the foreign policy of the United States and other rich nations. Supporters point to rapid economic development in Asia—especially in South Korea, Taiwan, Singapore, and Hong Kong—as proof that the affluence achieved in Western Europe and North America is within the reach of all countries.

MAKING THE GRADE

Be sure you understand the differences between colonialism and neocolonialism.

rich nations, which for centuries have systematically impoverished low-income countries and made them dependent on the rich ones—a destructive process that continues today.

Historical Perspective

Everyone agrees that before the Industrial Revolution, there was little affluence in the world. Dependency theory asserts, however, that people living in poor countries were actually better off economically in the past than their descendants are now. André Gunder Frank (1975), a noted supporter of this theory, argues that the colonial process that helped develop rich nations also *underdeveloped* poor societies.

Dependency theory is based on the idea that the economic positions of rich and poor nations of the world are linked and cannot be understood apart from each other. Poor nations are not simply lagging behind rich ones on the "path of progress"; rather, the prosperity of the most developed countries came largely at the expense of less developed ones. In short, some nations became rich only because others became poor. Both are products of the global commerce that began five centuries ago.

The Importance of Colonialism

Late in the fifteenth century, Europeans began exploring the Americas to the west, Africa to the south, and Asia to the east in order to establish colonies. They were so successful that a century ago, Great Britain controlled about one-fourth of the world's land, boasting that "the sun never sets on the British Empire." The United States, itself originally a collection of small British colonies on the eastern seaboard of North America, soon pushed across the continent, purchased Alaska, and gained control of Haiti, Puerto Rico, Guam, the Philippines, the Hawaiian Islands, part of Panama, and Guantanamo Bay in Cuba.

As colonialism spread, there emerged a brutal form of human exploitation—the international slave trade—beginning about 1500 and continuing until 1850. Even as the world was turning away from slavery, Europeans took control of most of the African continent, as Figure 12–4 shows, and dominated most of the continent until the early 1960s.

Formal colonialism has almost disappeared from the world. However, according to dependency theory, political liberation has not translated into economic independence. Far from it—the economic relationship between poor and rich nations continues the colonial pattern of domination. This neocolonialism is the heart of the capitalist world economy.

Modernization theory claims that corporations that build factories in low-income nations help people by providing them with jobs and higher wages than they had before; dependency theory views these factories as "sweatshops" that exploit workers. In response to the Olympic Games selling sports clothing produced by sweatshops, these women staged a protest in Athens, Greece; they are wearing white masks to symbolize the "faceless" workers who make much of what we wear. Is any of the clothing you wear made in sweatshop factories?

Wallerstein's Capitalist World Economy

Immanuel Wallerstein (1974, 1979, 1983, 1984) explains global stratification using a model of the "capitalist world economy." Wallerstein's term *world economy* suggests that the prosperity of some nations and the poverty and dependency of other countries result from a global economic system. He traces the roots of the global economy to the beginning of colonization more than 500 years ago, when Europeans began gathering wealth from the rest of the world. Because the world economy is based in the high-income countries, it is capitalist in character.[2]

Wallerstein calls the rich nations the *core* of the world economy. Colonialism enriched this core by funneling raw materials from around the world to Western Europe, where they fueled the Industrial Revolution. Today, multinational corporations operate profitably worldwide, channeling wealth to North America, Western Europe, Australia, and Japan.

[2]This discussion also draws on A. G. Frank (1980, 1981), Delacroix & Ragin (1981), Bergesen (1983), Dixon & Boswell (1996), and Kentor (1998).

NOTE: Arguing that the capitalist world economy is harmful to poor nations, André Gunder Frank maintains that the economies of poor countries have grown mostly during periods of global crisis, such as world wars.

GLOBAL: Generally speaking, striking political and economic transformations in recent years have been centered in Asia, including China and India—both now middle-income nations.

DISCUSS: Operating in 119 countries, McDonald's has more than 30,000 restaurants; KFC has more than 11,000 restaurants in 80 countries. Does this expansion constitute desirable development? Why or why not?

NOTE: Lenin attributed the failure of Marxist revolutions to occur in rich societies to the development of international capitalism that raised living standards at home based on exploitation of colonies abroad.

● MAKING THE GRADE

Modernization theory assumes that all of the world was poor before the Industrial Revolution and that some nations were able to become rich. Dependency theory assumes that today's poor countries were actually better off before colonialism drained them of their wealth.

Low-income countries represent the *periphery* of the world economy. Drawn into the world economy by colonial exploitation, poor nations continue to support rich ones by providing inexpensive labor and a vast market for industrial products. The remaining countries are considered the *semiperiphery* of the world economy. They include middle-income countries like India and Brazil that have closer ties to the global economic core.

According to Wallerstein, the world economy benefits rich societies (by generating profits) and harms the rest of the world (by causing poverty). The world economy thus makes poor nations dependent on rich ones. This dependency involves three factors:

1. **Narrow, export-oriented economies.** Poor nations produce only a few crops for export to rich countries. Examples include coffee and fruit from Latin American nations, oil from Nigeria, hardwoods from the Philippines, and palm oil from Malaysia. Today's multinational corporations purchase raw materials cheaply in poor societies and transport them to core nations, where factories process them for profitable sale. Thus poor nations develop few industries of their own.

2. **Lack of industrial capacity.** Without an industrial base, poor societies face a double bind: They count on rich nations to buy their inexpensive raw materials, and they must then try to buy from the rich nations the few expensive manufactured goods they can afford. In a classic example of this dependency, British colo-

nialists encouraged the people of India to raise cotton but prevented them from weaving their own cloth. Instead, the British shipped Indian cotton to their own textile mills in Birmingham and Manchester, manufactured the cloth, and shipped finished goods back to India, where the very people who harvested the cotton bought the garments.

Dependency theorists claim that the Green Revolution—widely praised by modernization theorists—works the same way. Poor countries sell cheap raw materials to rich nations and then must buy expensive fertilizers, pesticides, and machinery in return. Typically, rich countries profit from this exchange far more than poor nations.

3. **Foreign debt.** Unequal trade patterns have plunged poor countries into debt. Collectively, the poor nations of the world owe rich countries some $3 trillion; hundreds of billions of dollars are owed to the United States. Such staggering debt paralyzes a country, causing high unemployment and rampant inflation (World Bank, 2008).

The Role of Rich Nations

Modernization theory and dependency theory assign very different roles to rich nations. Modernization theory holds that rich countries *produce wealth* through capital investment and new technology. Dependency theory views global inequality in terms of how countries *distribute wealth*, arguing that rich nations have *overdeveloped* themselves as they have *underdeveloped* the rest of the world.

Dependency theorists dismiss the idea that programs developed by rich countries to control population and boost agricultural and industrial output raise living standards in poor countries. Instead, they claim, such programs actually benefit rich nations and the ruling elites, not the poor majority, in low-income countries (Kentor, 2001).

The hunger activists Frances Moore Lappé and Joseph Collins (1986; Lappé, Collins, & Rosset, 1998) maintain that the capitalist culture of the United States encourages people to think of poverty as somehow inevitable. In this line of reasoning, poverty results from "natural" processes, including having too many children, and natural disasters such as droughts. But global poverty is far from inevitable; in their view, it results from deliberate policies. Lappé and Collins point out that the world already produces enough food to allow every person on the planet to become quite fat. Moreover, India and most of Africa actually *export* food, even though many people in African nations go hungry.

According to Lappé and Collins, the contradiction of poverty amid plenty stems from the rich-

How does modernization theory view investment by global corporations such as Coca-Cola in low-income nations like Kenya? How does the view of dependency theory differ?

NOTE: Modernization theory is sometimes called "convergence theory" (especially by economists); dependency theory is also called "polarization theory."

NOTE: Although the economic gap between rich and poor countries has remained stable, the divide is narrowing between the two categories of nations on many social indicators. This is because rising income produces greater improvement in living standards for lower-income countries.

NOTE: Many products from rich countries—electricity, technology, communications equipment—are getting cheaper, which helps raise living standards abroad.

GLOBAL: "Divided" countries shed light on the merits of each theory. South Korea (well within the capitalist world economy) has per capita GDP of $20,499, compared to isolated North Korea's figure of $4,058. For West Germany in 1988, the figure was $14,730; for East Germany, $8,000.

MAKING THE GRADE

One key difference between modernization theory and dependency theory is their view of rich nations. The first approach sees rich nations as a solution to the problem of poverty; the second sees them as a cause of the problem.

nation policy of producing food for profit, not people. That is, corporations in rich nations cooperate with elites in poor countries to grow and export profitable crops such as coffee, which means using land that could otherwise produce basics such as beans and corn for local families. Governments of poor countries support the practice of growing for export because they need food profits to repay foreign debt. According to Lappé and Collins, the capitalist corporate structure of the global economy is at the core of this vicious cycle.

CRITICAL REVIEW The main idea of dependency theory is that no nation becomes rich or poor in isolation because a single global economy shapes the destiny of all nations. Pointing to continuing poverty in Latin America, Africa, and Asia, dependency theorists claim that development simply cannot proceed under the constraints now imposed by rich countries. Rather, they call for radical reform of the entire world economy so that it operates in the interests of the majority of people.

Critics charge that dependency theory wrongly treats wealth as if no one gets richer without someone else getting poorer. Corporations, small business owners, and farmers can and do create new wealth through hard work and imaginative use of new technology. After all, they point out, the entire world's wealth has increased sixfold since 1950.

Second, dependency theory is wrong in blaming rich nations for global poverty because many of the world's poorest countries (like Ethiopia) have had little contact with rich nations. On the contrary, a long history of trade with rich countries has dramatically improved the economies of many nations, including Sri Lanka, Singapore, and Hong Kong (all former British colonies), as well as South Korea and Japan. In short, say the critics, most evidence shows that foreign investment by rich nations encourages economic growth, as modernization theory claims, and not economic decline, as dependency theory holds (E. F. Vogel, 1991; Firebaugh, 1992).

Third, critics call dependency theory simplistic for pointing the finger at a single factor—the capitalist market system—as the cause of global inequality (Worsley, 1990). Dependency theory views poor societies as passive victims and ignores factors inside these countries that contribute to their economic problems. Sociologists have long recognized the vital role of culture in shaping people's willingness to embrace or resist change. Under the rule of the ultratraditional Muslim Taliban, for exam-

Although the world continues to grow richer, billions of people are being left behind. This shantytown in Lagos, Nigeria, is typical of many cities in low-income countries. What can you say about the quality of life in such a place?

ple, Afghanistan became economically isolated, and its living standards sank to among the lowest in the world. Is it reasonable to blame capitalist nations for that country's stagnation?

Nor can rich societies be held responsible for the reckless behavior of foreign leaders whose corruption and militarism impoverish their countries. Examples include the regimes of Ferdinand Marcos in the Philippines, François Duvalier in Haiti, Manuel Noriega in Panama, Mobutu Sese Seko in Zaire (today's Democratic Republic of the Congo), Robert Mugabe in Zimbabwe, and Saddam Hussein in Iraq. Some leaders even use food supplies as weapons in internal political struggles, leaving the masses starving, as in the African nations of Ethiopia, Sudan, and Somalia. Likewise, many countries throughout the world have done little to improve the status of women or control population growth.

Fourth, critics say that dependency theory is wrong to claim that global trade always makes rich nations richer and poor nations poorer. For example, in 2007, the United States had a trade deficit of $794 billion, meaning that this nation imports three-quarters of a trillion dollars' more goods than it sells abroad. The single greatest debt was owed to China, whose profitable trade has now pushed that country into the ranks of the world's middle-income nations (United Nations, 2008).

DISCUSS: Costa Rica, with average income at one-fourth the U.S. level, has the same life expectancy due largely to disbanding its army in 1949 and spending more on health and education. Brazil, with about the same average income as Costa Rica but different policies, has a life expectancy 10 years lower (Sachs, 1998).

DISCUSS: Longfellow said, "Out of the shadows of night, the world rolls into light. It is daybreak everywhere." Is he right?

DISCUSS: The mass media are a powerful force, making the world smaller. For example, Cable News Network (CNN) currently broadcasts to more than 60 nations. How do the media portray poor countries to us? How do they portray us to people abroad?

EXERCISE: Ask students to look over past issues of *National Geographic*. How accurately does this popular magazine portray life in poor nations?

● SEEING SOCIOLOGY
in Everyday Life

An increasingly popular idea is "fair trade," paying people in poor nations a fair price for their products. Would you pay more for a cup of coffee made using beans for which a farmer in a low-income country was paid a higher price? Why or why not?

● APPLYING THEORY ●

Global Poverty

	Modernization Theory	Dependency Theory
Which theoretical approach is applied?	Structural-functional approach	Social-conflict approach
How did global poverty come about?	The whole world was poor until some countries developed industrial technology, which allowed mass production and created affluence.	Colonialism moved wealth from some countries to others, making some nations poor as it made other nations rich.
What are the main causes of global poverty today?	Traditional culture and a lack of productive technology.	Neocolonialism—the operation of multinational corporations in the global, capitalist economy.
Are rich countries part of the problem or part of the solution?	Rich countries are part of the solution, contributing new technology, advanced schooling, and foreign aid.	Rich countries are part of the problem, making poor countries economically dependent and in debt.

Fifth, critics fault dependency theory for offering only vague solutions to global poverty. Most dependency theorists urge poor nations to end all contact with rich countries, and some call for nationalizing foreign-owned industries. In other words, dependency theory is really an argument for some sort of world socialism. In light of the difficulties that socialist societies (even better-off socialist countries such as Russia) have had in meeting the needs of their own people, critics ask, should we really expect such a system to rescue the entire world from poverty?

○ **CHECK YOUR LEARNING** State the main ideas of dependency theory. What are several of its strengths and weaknesses?

The Applying Theory table summarizes the main arguments of modernization theory and dependency theory.

Global Stratification: Looking Ahead

Among the most important trends in recent decades is the development of a global economy. In the United States, rising production and sales abroad bring profits to many corporations and their stockholders, especially those who already have substantial wealth. At the same time, the global economy has moved manufacturing jobs abroad, closing factories in this country and hurting many average workers. The net result: greater economic inequality in the United States.

People who support the global economy claim that the expansion of trade results in benefits for all countries involved. For this reason, they endorse policies like the North American Free Trade Agreement (NAFTA) signed by the United States, Canada, and Mexico. Critics of expanding globalization make other claims: Manufacturing jobs are being lost in the United States, and more manufacturing now takes place abroad in factories where workers are paid little and few laws ensure workplace safety. In addition, other critics of expanding globalization point to the ever-greater stresses that our economy places on the natural environment.

But perhaps the greatest concern is the vast economic inequality that exists between the world's countries. The concentration of wealth in high-income countries, coupled with the grinding poverty in low-income nations, may well be the biggest problem facing humanity in the twenty-first century.

Both modernization theory and dependency theory offer some understanding of this urgent problem. In evaluating these theories, we must consider empirical evidence. Over the course of the twentieth century, living standards rose in most of the world. Even the economic output of the poorest 25 percent of the world's people almost

NOTE: Figure 12–5 shows that both the rich and the poor are getting richer (as modernization theory claims) but the wealth gap is increasing (as dependency theory claims).

DISCUSS: How is raising the security of the world's poorest people in *our* interest?

● SEEING SOCIOLOGY
in Everyday Life

Based on what you have read here and elsewhere, do you think that, fifty years from now, the problem of global hunger will be more or less serious? Explain your answer.

tripled during those 100 years. As a result, the number of people living on less than $1.25 a day fell from about 1.9 billion in 1981 to about 1.4 billion in 2005 (Chen & Ravallion, 2008). In short, most people around the world are better off than ever before in *absolute* terms.

The greatest reduction in poverty has taken place in Asia, a region generally regarded as an economic success story. Back in 1981, almost 80 percent of global $1.25-per-day poverty was found in Asia; by 2005, that figure had fallen to 17 percent. Since then, two very large Asian countries—India and China—have joined the ranks of the middle-income nations. The economic growth in India and China has been so great that in the last two decades, global economic inequality has actually decreased as wealth has spread from Europe and North America to Asia (Sala-i-Martin, 2002; Bussollo et al., 2007; Chen & Ravallion, 2008; Davies et al., 2008).

Latin America represents a mixed case. During the 1970s, this region enjoyed significant economic growth; during the 1980s and 1990s, however, there was little overall improvement. The share of the global $1.25-per-day poverty was slightly higher in 2005 (3 percent) as it was in 1981 (2 percent) (Chen & Ravallion, 2008).

In Africa, about half of the nations are showing increasing economic growth. In many countries, however, especially those south of the Sahara, extreme poverty is getting worse. In 1981, sub-Saharan Africa accounted for 11 percent of $1.25-per-day poverty; by 2005, this share had risen to 28 percent (Sala-i-Martin, 2002; Chen & Ravillion, 2008).

Overall, then, most people are doing better than in the past. However, richer people in the world are moving ahead much faster than poor people, so that the world's *relative* poverty has been increasing (United Nations Development Programme, 2008). In 2005, the gap between the rich and the poor in the world was almost four times bigger than it was back in 1900. Figure 12–5 shows that the poorest people in the world are being left behind.

Recent trends suggest the need to look critically at both modernization and dependency theories. The fact that governments have played a large role in the economic growth that has occurred in Asia and elsewhere challenges modernization theory and its free-market approach to development. On the other hand, since the upheavals in the former Soviet Union and Eastern Europe, a global reevaluation of socialism has been taking place. Because socialist nations have a record of decades of poor economic performance and political repression, many low-income nations are unwilling to follow the advice of dependency theory and place economic development entirely under government control.

Although the world's future is uncertain, we have learned a great deal about global stratification. One insight offered by modernization theory is that poverty is partly a *problem of technology*. A higher standard of living for a surging world population depends on the

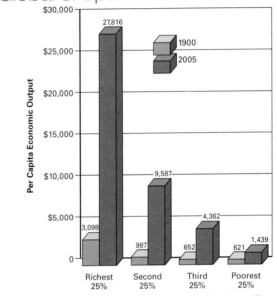

Global Snapshot

FIGURE 12–5 **The World's Increasing Economic Inequality**
The gap between the richest and poorest people in the world is almost four times bigger than it was a century ago.
Source: United Nations Development Programme (2008).

ability of poor nations to raise their agricultural and industrial productivity. A second insight, derived from dependency theory, is that global inequality is also a *political issue*. Even with higher productivity, the human community must address crucial questions concerning how resources are distributed, both within societies and around the globe.

Although economic development raises living standards, it also places greater strains on the natural environment. As nations such as India and China—with a combined population of 2.5 billion—become more affluent, their people will consume more energy and other resources (China has recently passed Japan to become the second-largest consumer of oil, behind the United States, which is one reason that oil prices and supplies have been under pressure). Richer nations also produce more solid waste and create more pollution.

Finally, the vast gulf that separates the world's richest and poorest people puts everyone at greater risk of war and terrorism as the poorest people challenge the social arrangements that threaten their existence (Lindauer & Weerapana, 2002). In the long run, we can achieve peace on this planet only by ensuring that all people enjoy a significant measure of dignity and security.

Seeing Sociology in Everyday Life

Chapter 12   Global Stratification

How much social inequality can we find if we look around the world?

This chapter explains that a global perspective reveals even more social stratification than we find here in the United States. Around the world, an increasing number of people in lower-income countries are traveling to higher-income nations in search of jobs. As "guest workers," they perform low-wage work that the country's own more well-off citizens do not wish to do. In such cases, the rich and poor truly live "worlds apart."

> **HINT**   Dubai's recent building boom has been accomplished using the labor of about 1 million guest workers, who actually make up about 85 percent of the population of the United Arab Emirates. Recent years have seen a rising level of social unrest, including labor strikes, which has led to some improvements in working and living conditions and better health care. But guest workers have no legal rights to form labor unions, nor do they have any chance to gain citizenship.

With so little income, many guest workers sleep six to a small room. How do you think living in a strange country, with few legal rights, affects these workers' ability to improve their working conditions?

Oil wealth has made some of the people of Dubai, in the United Arab Emirates, among the richest in the world. Dubai's wealthiest people can afford to ski on snow—in one of the hottest regions of the world—on enormous indoor ski slopes like this one. Is there anything about this picture that makes you uncomfortable? Explain your reaction.

Many guest workers come to Dubai from India to take jobs building this country's new high-rise hotels and business towers. Workers labor about twelve hours a day but earn only between $50 and $175 a month. Do you think the chance to take a job like this in a foreign country is an opportunity (income is typically twice what people can earn at home), or is it a form of exploitation?

Applying SOCIOLOGY in Everyday Life

1. What comparisons can you make between the pattern of guest workers coming to places like Dubai in the Middle East and workers coming to the United States from Mexico and other countries in Latin America?

2. Page through several issues of any current newsmagazine or travel magazine to find any stories or advertising mentioning lower-income countries (selling, say, coffee from Colombia or exotic vacations to India). What picture of life in low-income countries does the advertising present? In light of what you have learned in this chapter, how accurate does this image seem to you?

3. Millions of students from abroad study on U.S. campuses. Find a woman and a man on your campus who were raised in a low-income country. After explaining that you have been studying global inequality, ask if they are willing to share information about what life is like back home. If they are, ask about stratification in general, as well as their own social position, in their home country.

MAKING THE GRADE

CHAPTER 12 Global Stratification

Global Stratification: An Overview

HIGH-INCOME COUNTRIES

- contain 22% of the world's people
- receive 80% of global income
- have a high standard of living based on advanced technology
- produce enough economic goods to enable their people to lead comfortable lives
- include 66 nations, among them the United States, Canada, Mexico, Argentina, Chile, the nations of Western Europe, Israel, Saudi Arabia, South Africa, the Russian Federation, Japan, South Korea, Malaysia, and Australia

pp. 302–5

MIDDLE-INCOME COUNTRIES

- contain 58% of the world's people
- receive 18% of global income
- have a standard of living about average for the world as a whole
- include 72 nations, among them the nations of Eastern Europe, Peru, Brazil, Namibia, Egypt, Indonesia, India, and the People's Republic of China

p. 305

LOW-INCOME COUNTRIES

- contain 19% of the world's people
- receive 2% of global income
- have a low standard of living due to limited industrial technology
- include 57 nations, generally in Central and East Africa and Asia, among them Chad, the Democratic Republic of the Congo, Ethiopia, Bangladesh, and Pakistan

p. 305

See Global Map 12–1 on page 303.

✓ Although poverty is a reality in the United States and other nations, the greatest social inequality is *not* within nations but between *them*.

global stratification (p. 300) patterns of social inequality in the world as a whole

high-income countries (p. 301) the nations with the highest overall standards of living

middle-income countries (p. 301) nations with a standard of living about average for the world as a whole

low-income countries (p. 301) nations with a low standard of living in which most people are poor

Global Wealth and Poverty

All societies contain **RELATIVE POVERTY**, but low-income nations face widespread **ABSOLUTE POVERTY** that is life-threatening.

- Worldwide, about 1.4 billion people are at risk due to poor nutrition.
- About 9 million people, most of them children, die each year from diseases caused by poverty.
- Throughout the world, women are more likely than men to be poor. Gender bias is strongest in poor societies.
- As many as 200 million men, women, and children (about 3% of humanity) live in conditions that can be described as slavery.

pp. 305–10

FACTORS CAUSING POVERTY

- Lack of technology limits production.
- High birth rates produce rapid population increase.
- Traditional cultural patterns make people resist change.
- Extreme social inequality distributes wealth very unequally.
- Extreme gender inequality limits the opportunities of women.
- Colonialism allowed some nations to exploit other nations; neocolonialism continues today.

pp. 310–12

colonialism (p. 311) the process by which some nations enrich themselves through political and economic control of other nations

neocolonialism (p. 311) a new form of global power relationships that involves not direct political control but economic exploitation by multinational corporations

multinational corporation (p. 311) a large business that operates in many countries

Global Stratification: Theoretical Analysis

MODERNIZATION THEORY maintains that nations achieve affluence by developing advanced technology. This process depends on a culture that encourages innovation and change toward higher living standards.

Walt Rostow identified four stages of development:

- *Traditional stage*—People's lives are built around families and local communities. (Example: Bangladesh)
- *Take-off stage*—A market emerges as people produce goods not just for their own use but to trade with others for profit. (Example: Thailand)
- *Drive to technological maturity*—The ideas of economic growth and higher living standards gain widespread support; schooling is widely available; the social standing of women improves. (Example: Mexico)
- *High mass consumption*—Advanced technology fuels mass production and mass consumption as people now "need" countless goods. (Example: the United States)

pp. 312–15

MODERNIZATION THEORY CLAIMS

- Rich nations can help poor nations by providing technology to control population size, increase food production, and expand industrial and information economy output and by providing foreign aid to pay for new economic development.
- Rapid economic development in Asia shows that affluence is within reach of other nations of the world.

p. 315

CRITICS CLAIM

- Rich nations do little to help poor countries and benefit from the status quo. Low living standards in much of Africa and South America result from the policies of rich nations.
- Because rich nations, including the United States, control the global economy, many poor nations struggle to support their people and cannot follow the path to development taken by rich countries centuries ago.

p. 316

DEPENDENCY THEORY maintains that global wealth and poverty were created by the colonial process beginning 500 years ago that developed rich nations and underdeveloped poor nations. This capitalist process continues today in the form of neocolonialism—economic exploitation of poor nations by multinational corporations.

Immanuel Wallerstein's model of the capitalist world economy identified three categories of nations:

- *Core*—the world's high-income countries, which are home to multinational corporations
- *Semiperiphery*—the world's middle-income countries, with ties to core nations
- *Periphery*—the world's low-income countries, which provide low-cost labor and a vast market for industrial products

pp. 316–18

DEPENDENCY THEORY CLAIMS

- Three key factors—export-oriented economies, a lack of industrial capacity, and foreign debt—make poor countries dependent on rich nations and prevent their economic development.
- Radical reform of the entire world economy is needed so that it operates in the interests of the majority of people.

pp 318–19

CRITICS CLAIM

- Dependency theory overlooks the sixfold increase in global wealth since 1950 and the fact that the world's poorest countries have had weak, not strong, ties to rich countries.
- Rich nations are not responsible for cultural patterns or political corruption that block economic development in many poor nations.

p. 319–20

See the Applying Theory table on page 320.

modernization theory (p. 312) a model of economic and social development that explains global inequality in terms of technological and cultural differences between nations

dependency theory (p. 316) a model of economic and social development that explains global inequality in terms of the historical exploitation of poor nations by rich ones

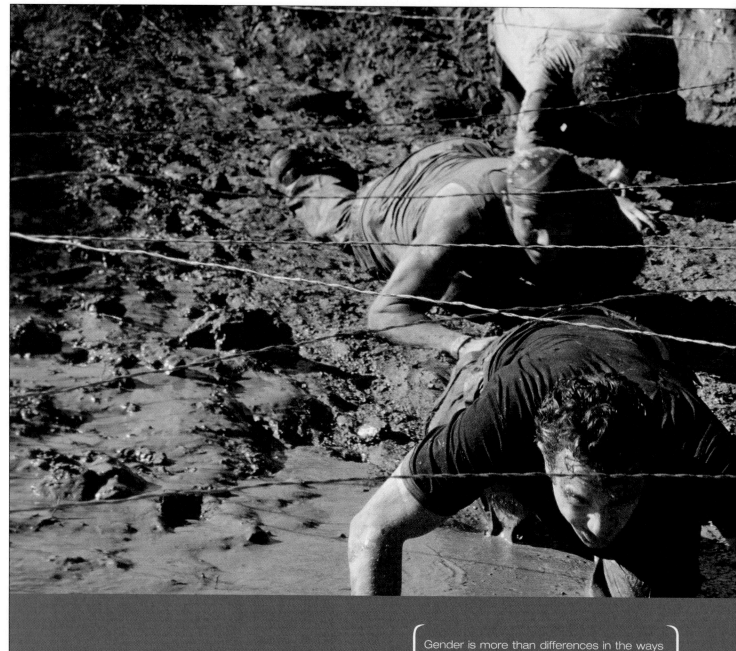

Gender is more than differences in the ways society expects women and men to behave. It is also a matter of social stratification, placing men in positions of power over women.

CHAPTER 13

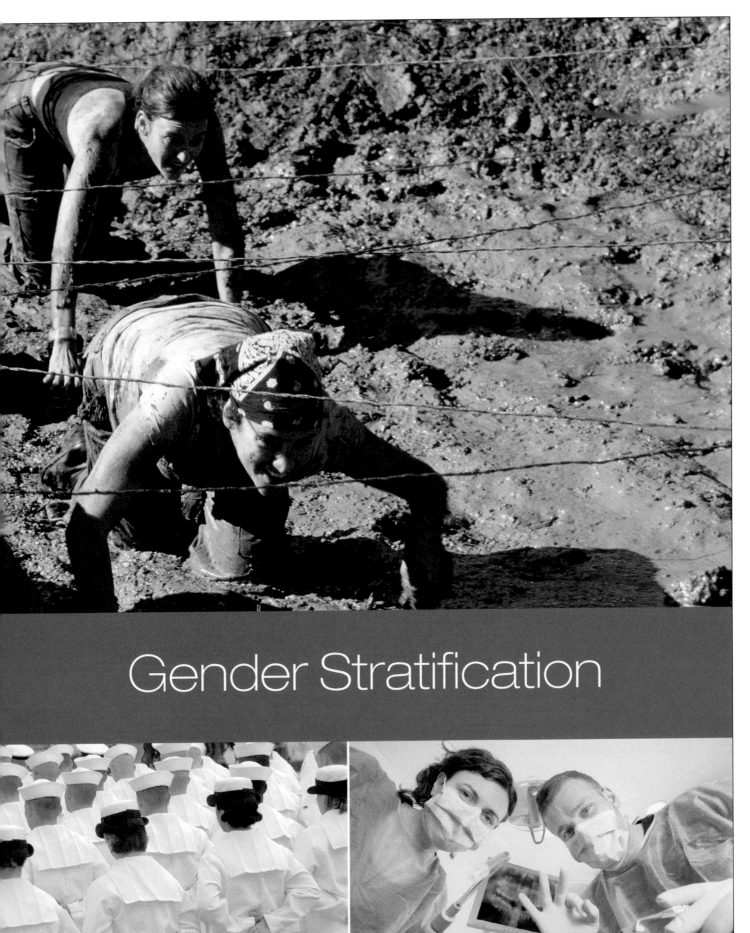

Gender Stratification

SUPPLEMENTS: An outline of this chapter, along with supplementary lecture material, is included in the *Instructor's Manual.*

Q: "The male is by nature fitter for command than the female, just as the elder and full-grown is fitter than the younger and immature.... The courage of a man is shown in commanding, of a woman in obeying." Aristotle, *Politics*

Q: "Most human beings live in single-sex worlds, women in a female world and men in a male world, and . . . the two are different from one another in a myriad of ways, both subjectively and objectively." Jessie Bernard (1981:3)

RESOURCE: An excerpt from Margaret Mead's *Sex and Temperament in Three Primitive Societies* (1963, orig. 1935) is one of the classic selections in the author's companion reader *Seeing Ourselves*, 8th ed.

CHAPTER OVERVIEW

This chapter examines gender, the meaning societies attach to being female or male, and explains how gender is an important dimension of social stratification.

At first we traveled quite alone . . . but before we had gone many miles, we came on other wagon-loads of women, bound in the same direction. As we reached different cross-roads, we saw wagons coming from every part of the country and, long before we reached Seneca Falls, we were a procession.

So wrote Charlotte Woodward in her journal as she made her way along the rutted dirt roads leading to Seneca Falls, a small town in upstate New York. The year was 1848, a time when slavery was legal in much of the United States and the social standing of all women, regardless of color, was far below that of men. Back then, in much of the country, women could not own property, keep their wages if they were married, draft a will, file lawsuits in a court (including lawsuits seeking custody of their children), or attend college, and husbands were widely viewed as having unquestioned authority over their wives and children.

Some 300 women gathered at Wesleyan Chapel in Seneca Falls to challenge this second-class citizenship. They listened as their leader, Elizabeth Cady Stanton, called for expanding women's rights and opportunities, including the right to vote. At that time, most people considered such a proposal absurd and outrageous. Even many attending the conference were shocked by the idea: Stanton's husband, Henry, rode out of town in protest (Gurnett, 1998).

Much has changed since the Seneca Falls convention, and many of Stanton's proposals are now widely accepted as matters of basic fairness. But as this chapter explains, women and men still lead different lives, in the United States and elsewhere in the world; in most respects, men are still in charge. This chapter explores the importance of gender and explains that gender, like class position, is a major dimension of social stratification.

Gender and Inequality

Chapter 8 ("Sexuality and Society") explained the biological differences based on sex that divide the human population into categories of female and male. **Gender** refers to *the personal traits and social positions that members of a society attach to being female or male.* Gender, then, is a dimension of social organization, shaping how we interact with others and how we think about ourselves. More important, gender also involves *hierarchy,* ranking men and women differently in terms of power, wealth, and other resources. This is why sociologists speak of **gender stratification**, *the unequal distribution of wealth, power, and privilege between men and women.*

In short, gender affects the opportunities and challenges we face throughout our lives.

Male-Female Differences

Many people think there is something "natural" about gender distinctions because biology does make one sex different from the other. But we must be careful not to think of social differences in biological terms. In 1848, for example, women were denied the vote because many people assumed that women did not have enough intelligence or interest in politics. Such attitudes had nothing to do with biology; they reflected the *cultural* patterns of that time and place.

Another example is athletic performance. In 1925, most people—women and men—believed that the best women runners could never compete with men in a marathon. Today, as Figure 13–1 shows, the gender gap has greatly narrowed, and the fastest women routinely post better times than the fastest men of decades past. Even here, most of the differences between men and women turn out to be socially created.

There are some differences in physical ability between the sexes. On average, males are 10 percent taller, 20 percent heavier, and

Q: "The [comparison of the three societies] suggests that . . . many, if not all, of the personality traits which we have called masculine or feminine are as lightly linked to sex as are the clothing, the manners, and the form of head-dress that a society at a given period assigns to either sex. . . . We are forced to conclude that human behavior is almost unbelievably malleable, responding accurately and contrastingly to contrasting cultural conditions." Margaret Mead

DISCUSS: Referring to Figure 13–1, point out that some biological differences between females and males affect athletic performance, but the converging pattern shows that most of what many people see as the "natural" differences between the two sexes are the creation not of biology but of society.

gender the personal traits and social positions that member of a society attach to being female or male

gender stratification the unequal distribution of wealth, power, and privilege between men and women

30 percent stronger, especially in the upper body. On the other hand, women outperform men in the ultimate game of life itself: Life expectancy for men in the United States is 75.4 years, and women can expect to live 80.7 years (Ehrenreich, 1999; Heron et al., 2008; McDowell et al., 2008).

In adolescence, males do a bit better in mathematics, and females show slightly stronger verbal skills, a difference that reflects both biology and socialization. However, research does not point to any difference in overall intelligence between males and females (Tavris & Wade, 2001; Lewin, 2008).

Biologically, then, men and women differ in limited ways; neither one is naturally superior. But culture can define the two sexes very differently, as the global study of gender described in the next section shows.

Gender in Global Perspective

The best way to see the cultural foundation of gender is by comparing one society to another. Three important studies highlight how societies can define "masculine" and "feminine" very differently.

The Israeli Kibbutz

In Israel, collective settlements are called *kibbutzim*. The *kibbutz* (the singular form of the word) has been an important setting for research because gender equality is one of its stated goals; men and women share in both work and decision making.

In recent decades, kibbutzim have become less collective and thus less distinctive organizations. But through much of their history, both sexes shared most everyday jobs. Many men joined women in taking care of children, and women joined men in repairing buildings and providing armed security. Both sexes made everyday decisions for the group. Girls and boys were raised in the same way; in many cases, young children were raised together in dormitories away from parents. Women and men in the kibbutzim have achieved remarkable (although not complete) social equality, evidence that cultures define what is feminine and what is masculine.

Margaret Mead's Research

The anthropologist Margaret Mead carried out groundbreaking research on gender. If gender is based on the biological differences between men and women, she reasoned, people everywhere should define "feminine" and "masculine" in the same way; if gender is cultural, these concepts should vary.

Mead (1963, orig. 1935) studied three societies in New Guinea. In the mountainous home of the Arapesh, Mead observed men and women with remarkably similar attitudes and behavior. Both sexes, she reported, were cooperative and sensitive to others—in short, what our culture would label "feminine."

The women's movement of the 1960s encouraged women to show their true abilities.

Diversity Snapshot

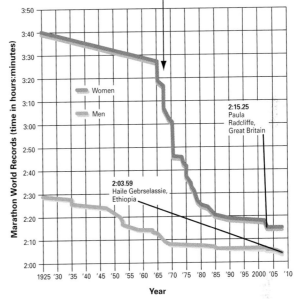

FIGURE 13–1 Men's and Women's Athletic Performance

Do men naturally outperform women in athletic competition? The answer is not obvious. Early in the twentieth century, men outpaced women by more than an hour in marathon races. But as opportunities for women in athletics have increased, women have been closing the performance gap. Only eleven minutes separate the current world marathon records for women (set in 2003) and for men (set in 2008).

Source: Marathonguide.com (2008).

Moving south, Mead then studied the Mundugumor, whose headhunting and cannibalism stood in striking contrast to the gentle ways of the Arapesh. In this culture, both sexes were typically selfish and aggressive, traits we define as "masculine."

Finally, traveling west to the Tchambuli, Mead discovered a culture that, like our own, defined females and males differently. But, Mead reported, the Tchambuli *reversed* many of our notions of gender: Females were dominant and rational, and males were submissive, emotional, and nurturing toward children. Based on her observations, Mead concluded that culture is the key to gender differences, because what one society defines as masculine another may see as feminine.

Some critics view Mead's findings as "too neat," as if she saw in these three societies just the patterns she was looking for. Deborah Gewertz (1981) challenged what she called Mead's "reversal hypothesis,"

NOTE: Patriarchy specifies paternity as the central social relationship. Note the Old Testament emphasis on "begats," a father begetting a son (Rothman, 1995).

DISCUSS: Gender is variable around the world, yet patriarchy is an almost universal pattern. Do students think that this means that to some degree, differences between females and males are rooted in biology? Why or why not?

Q: Differences between the male and female endocrine and central nervous sys-

tems "are such that—statistically speaking—males have a greater tendency to exhibit whatever behavior is necessary in any environment to attain dominance in hierarchies." Steven Goldberg

RESOURCE: Most sociologists reject the view that biology plays a significant role in gender formation. Goldberg's evidence is in "Reaffirming the Obvious" (1986a) and "Utopian Yearning versus Scientific Curiosity" (1986b).

SEEING SOCIOLOGY in Everyday Life

Do you think female and male athletes should compete on the same teams? Why or why not? Do you think men and women see this issue differently?

matriarchy a form of social organization in which females dominate males

patriarchy a form of social organization in which males dominate females

sexism the belief that one sex is innately superior to the other

pointing out that Tchambuli males are really the more aggressive sex. Gewertz explains that Mead visited the Tchambuli (who themselves spell their name Chambri) during the 1930s, after they had lost much of their property in tribal wars, and observed men rebuilding their homes, a temporary role for Chambri men.

George Murdock's Research

In a broader review of research on more than 200 preindustrial societies, George Murdock (1937) found some global agreement about which tasks are feminine and which are masculine. Hunting and warfare, Murdock concluded, generally fall to men, and home-centered tasks such as cooking and child care tend to be women's work. With their simple technology, preindustrial societies apparently assign roles reflecting men's and women's physical characteristics. With their greater size and strength, men hunt game and protect the group; because women bear children, they do most of the work in the home.

But beyond this general pattern, Murdock found much variety. Consider agriculture: Women did the farming in about the same number of societies as men; in most, the two sexes shared this work. When it came to many other tasks, from building shelters to tattooing the body, Murdock found that societies of the world were as likely to turn to one sex as the other.

CRITICAL REVIEW Global comparisons show that overall, societies do not consistently define tasks as either feminine or masculine. With industrialization, the importance of muscle power declines, further reducing gender differences (Nolan & Lenski, 2007). In sum, gender is too variable across cultures to be a simple expression of biology; what it means to be female and male is mostly a creation of society.

CHECK YOUR LEARNING By comparing many cultures, what do we learn about the origin of gender differences?

Patriarchy and Sexism

Conceptions of gender vary, and there is evidence of societies in which women have greater power than men. One example is the Musuo, a very small society in China's Yunnan province, in which women control most property, select their sexual partners, and make most decisions about everyday life. The Musuo appear to be a case of **matriarchy** ("rule of mothers"), *a form of social organization in which females dominate males,* which has only rarely been documented in human history.

The pattern found almost everywhere in the world is **patriarchy** ("rule of fathers"), *a form of social organization in which males dominate females.* Global Map 13–1 shows the great variation in the relative power and privilege of women that exists from country to country. According to the United Nations, Iceland, Australia, and Norway give women the highest social standing; by contrast, women in the African nations of Burkina Faso, Niger, Guinea-Bissau, and Sierra Leone have the lowest social standing in comparison to to men. Of all the world's nations, the United States ranks sixteenth in terms of gender equality (United Nations Development Programme, 2008).

The justification for patriarchy is **sexism**, *the belief that one sex is innately superior to the other.* Sexism is not just a matter of individual attitudes; it is built into the institutions of society. *Institutional sexism* is found throughout the economy, with women concentrated in low-paying jobs. Similarly, the legal system has long excused violence against women, especially on the part of boyfriends, husbands, and fathers.

The Costs of Sexism

Sexism limits the talents and ambitions of the half of the human population who are women. Although men benefit in some respects from sexism, their privilege comes at a high price. Masculinity in our culture encourages men to engage in many high-risk behaviors: using tobacco and alcohol, playing dangerous sports, and even driving recklessly. As Marilyn

In every society, people assume that certain jobs, patterns of behavior, and ways of dressing are "naturally" feminine while others are just as obviously masculine. But in global perspective, we see remarkable variety in such social definitions. These men, Wodaabe pastoral nomads who live in the African nation of Niger, are proud to engage in a display of beauty most people in our society would consider feminine.

GLOBAL: Women have the greatest relative political power in Norway, in which leaders of both major parties and half the members of the cabinet and parliament are women. A constitutional provision requires parties to ensure that 40% of their candidates are women.

DISCUSS: Ask students to compare Global Map 13–1 and Global Map 12–1. In general, the higher the level of economic output, the greater is the degree of equal-

ity between men and women. Discuss reasons for this correlation.

GLOBAL: Percentage of women in the labor force (2006): Denmark, 74%; U.S., 70%; U.K., 70%; Germany, 68%; France, 62%; Italy, 51%. Generally speaking, percentages are higher for northern and Western European nations, lower for southern and Eastern European countries.

Q: "Pregnancy and warfare test the limits of equality." Wendy Kaminer

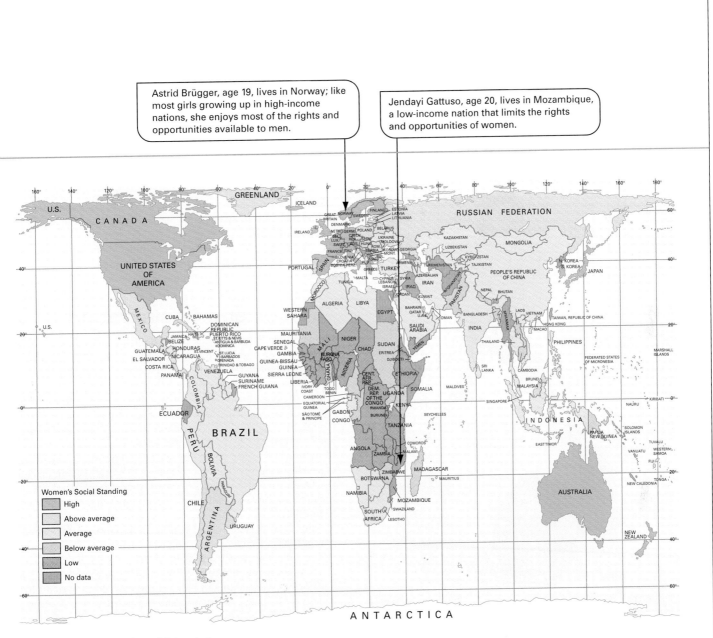

Astrid Brügger, age 19, lives in Norway; like most girls growing up in high-income nations, she enjoys most of the rights and opportunities available to men.

Jendayi Gattuso, age 20, lives in Mozambique, a low-income nation that limits the rights and opportunities of women.

Women's Social Standing
- High
- Above average
- Average
- Below average
- Low
- No data

Window on the World

GLOBAL MAP 13–1   **Women's Power in Global Perspective**

Women's social standing in relation to men's varies around the world. In general, women live better in rich countries than in poor countries. Even so, some nations stand out: In Iceland, Australia, and Norway, women come closest to social equality with men.

Source: Data from United Nations Development Programme (2008).

French (1985) argues, patriarchy leads men to seek control, not only of women but also of themselves and their world. This is why masculinity is closely linked not only to accidents but also to suicide, violence, and stress-related diseases. The *Type A personality*—marked by chronic impatience, driving ambition, competitiveness, and free-floating hostility—is a recipe for heart disease and almost perfectly matches the behavior that our culture considers masculine (Ehrenreich, 1983).

Finally, as men seek control over others, they lose opportunities for intimacy and trust. As one analyst put it, competition is supposed to "separate the men from the boys." In practice, however, it separates men from men and everyone else (Raphael, 1988).

Must Patriarchy Go On?

In preindustrial societies, women have little control over pregnancy and childbirth, which limits the scope of their lives. In those same

DISCUSS: Androgyny is the fusing of conventional traits of femininity and masculinity in a single personality. To what extent are most people androgynous? To what extent could we be? Is androgyny the fulfillment of "total humanity"? Why or why not?

RESOURCE: Judith Lorber takes a look at gender issues in "'Night to His Day': The Social Construction of Gender" in the companion reader *Seeing Ourselves*, 8th ed.

Q: "[Men] think themselves superior to women, but they mingle that with the notion of equality between men and women. It's very odd." Jean-Paul Sartre

DISCUSS: Of the following pairs, which term is applied to women, which to men? Aggressive/pushy; good on details/picky; not afraid to speak out/mouthy; handles authority/power-mad; a stern taskmaster/hard to work for (Haledjian, 1997).

gender roles (also known as **sex roles**) attitudes and activities that a society links to each sex

● SEEING SOCIOLOGY
in Everyday Life

Did you grow up in a home in which females and males had different jobs and responsibilities? How did this affect your view of gender?

Sex is a biological distinction that develops prior to birth. Gender is the meaning that a society attaches to being female or male. Gender differences are a matter of power, because what is defined as masculine typically has more importance than what is defined as feminine. Infants begin to learn the importance of gender by the way parents treat them. Do you think this child is a girl or a boy? Why?

societies, men's greater size and physical strength are valued resources that give them power. But industrialization, including birth control technology, increases people's choices about how to live. In societies like our own, biological differences offer little justification for patriarchy.

But males are dominant in the United States and elsewhere. Does this mean that patriarchy is inevitable? Some researchers claim that biological factors such as differences in hormones and slight differences in brain structure "wire" the two sexes with different motivations and behaviors—especially aggressiveness in males—making patriarchy difficult or perhaps even impossible to change (S. Goldberg, 1974; Rossi, 1985; Popenoe, 1993b; Udry,

2000). However, most sociologists believe that gender is socially constructed and *can* be changed. Just because no society has yet eliminated patriarchy does not mean that we must remain prisoners of the past.

To understand why patriarchy continues today, we must examine how gender is rooted and reproduced in society, a process that begins in childhood and continues throughout our lives.

Gender and Socialization

From birth until death, gender shapes human feelings, thoughts, and actions. Children quickly learn that their society considers females and males different kinds of people; by about age three, they begin to think of themselves in these terms.

In the past, many people in the United States traditionally described women using terms such as "emotional," "passive," and "cooperative." By contrast, men were described as "rational," "active," and "competitive." It is curious that we were taught for so long to think of gender in terms of one sex being opposite to the other, especially because women and men have so much in common and also because research suggests that most young people develop personalities that are some mix of these feminine and masculine traits (Bem, 1993).

Just as gender affects how we think of ourselves, so it teaches us how to behave. **Gender roles** (also known as **sex roles**) are *attitudes and activities that a society links to each sex.* A culture that defines males as ambitious and competitive encourages them to seek out positions of leadership and play team sports. To the extent that females are defined as deferential and emotional, they are expected to be supportive helpers and quick to show their feelings.

Gender and the Family

The first question people usually ask about a newborn—"Is it a boy or a girl?"—has great importance because the answer involves not just sex but the likely direction of the child's life. In fact, gender is at work even before the birth of a child, because especially in lower-income nations, parents hope that their firstborn will be a boy rather than a girl.

Soon after birth, family members welcome infants into the "pink world" of girls or the "blue world" of boys (Bernard, 1981). Parents even send gender messages in the way they handle infants. One researcher at an English university presented an infant dressed as either a boy or a girl to a number of women; her subjects handled the "female" child tenderly, with frequent hugs and caresses, and treated the "male" child more roughly, often lifting him up high in the air or bouncing him on a knee (Bonner, 1984; Tavris & Wade, 2001). The lesson is clear: The female world revolves around cooperation and emotion, and the male world puts a premium on independence and action.

GLOBAL: About 85% of U.S. parents express the desire that their children (regardless of sex) attend college. In Japan, 75% of parents want their sons to go to college, but only 30% voice this hope for daughters.

DISCUSS: Ask students to recall early experiences linked to gender in the family, peer group, and at school.

DISCUSS: Bring recent copies of *Sports Illustrated* and *Cosmopolitan* to class, and let students page through them. Ask the class to look for evidence that one magazine is "masculine" or "feminine." Discuss the evidence they find.

POP CULTURE: Films extending women's roles include *Charlie's Angels* (Drew Barrymore, Cameron Diaz, and Lucy Liu), *Elektra* (Jennifer Garner), and *Lara Croft: Tomb Raider* (Angelina Jolie). In addition to their masculine traits, these characters also display traditionally feminine beauty and sexuality.

SEEING SOCIOLOGY
in Everyday Life

Consider the statements "He fathered the child" and "She mothered the child." How do you think gender shapes the meaning of parenting?

SEEING SOCIOLOGY
in Everyday Life

What is your declared or likely major? Based on the classes you have taken, what share of students in this major are female and what share are male? Does this pattern agree with those described here?

Gender and the Peer Group

About the time they enter school, children begin to move outside the family and make friends with others of the same age. Considerable research shows that young children tend to form single-sex play groups (Martin & Fabes, 2001).

Peer groups teach additional lessons about gender. After spending a year observing children at play, Janet Lever (1978) concluded that boys favor team sports that have complex rules and clear objectives such as scoring runs or making touchdowns. Such games nearly always have winners and losers, reinforcing masculine traits of aggression and control.

Girls, too, play team sports. But, Lever explains, girls also play hopscotch, jump rope, or simply talk, sing, or dance. These activities have few rules, and rarely is victory the ultimate goal. Instead of teaching girls to be competitive, Lever explains, female peer groups promote the interpersonal skills of communication and cooperation, presumably the basis for girls' future roles as wives and mothers.

The games we play offer important lessons for our later lives. Lever's observations recall Carol Gilligan's gender-based theory of moral reasoning, discussed in Chapter 5 ("Socialization"). Boys, Gilligan (1982) claims, reason according to abstract principles. For them, "rightness" amounts to "playing by the rules." By contrast, girls consider morality a matter of responsibility to others.

Gender and Schooling

Gender shapes our interests and beliefs about our own abilities, guiding areas of study and, eventually, career choices (Correll, 2001). In high school, for instance, more girls than boys learn secretarial skills and take vocational classes such as cosmetology and food services. Classes in woodworking and auto mechanics attract mostly young men.

Women have now become a majority (57 percent) of the students on college campuses across the United States. As their numbers have increased, women have become well represented in many fields of study that once excluded them, including mathematics, chemistry, and biology. But men still predominate in many fields, including engineering, physics, and philosophy, and women cluster in the visual and performing arts (including music, dance, and drama), English, foreign languages, and the social sciences (including psychology, anthropology, and sociology). Newer areas of study are also gender-typed: More men than women take computer science, and courses in gender studies enroll mostly women (U.S. Department of Education, 2008).

The mass media typically present men in action, with women providing romantic interest. Can you find gender at work in the *Spiderman* films? What about other films?

Gender and the Mass Media

Since television first captured the public imagination in the 1950s, white males have held center stage; racial and ethnic minorities were all but absent from television until the early 1970s. Even when both sexes appeared on camera, men generally played the brilliant detectives, fearless explorers, and skilled surgeons. Women played the less capable characters, often unnecessary except for the sexual interest they added to the story.

Historically, advertisements have shown women in the home, cheerfully using cleaning products, serving food, and modeling clothes. Men predominate in ads for cars, travel, banking services, and alcoholic beverages. The authoritative voiceover—the faceless voice that describes a product on television and radio—is almost always male (D. M. Davis, 1993).

A careful study of gender in advertising reveals that men usually appear taller than women, implying male superiority. Women are more frequently presented lying down (on sofas and beds) or, like children, seated on the floor. Men's facial expressions and behavior give off an air of competence and imply dominance; women often appear child-like, submissive, and sexual. Men focus on the products being advertised; women often focus on the men (Goffman, 1979; Cortese, 1999).

Advertising also actively perpetuates what Naomi Wolf calls the "beauty myth." The Seeing Sociology in Everyday Life box on page 334 takes a closer look.

SEEING SOCIOLOGY
in Everyday Life

Do you think women on your campus are overly concerned with looking thin? Explain.

SEEING SOCIOLOGY IN EVERYDAY LIFE

The Beauty Myth

BETH: "I can't eat lunch. I need to be sure I can get into that black dress for tonight."

SARAH: "Maybe eating is more important than looking good for Tom."

BETH: "That's easy for you to say. You're a size 2 and Jake adores you!"

The Duchess of Windsor once remarked, "A woman cannot be too rich or too thin." The first half of her observation might apply to men as well, but certainly not the second. The answer lies in the fact that the vast majority of ads placed by the $10-billion-a-year cosmetics industry and the $35-billion diet industry target women.

According to Naomi Wolf (1990), certain cultural patterns create a "beauty myth" that is damaging to women. The beauty myth arises, first, because society teaches women to measure their worth in terms of physical appearance. Yet the standards of beauty embodied in the *Playboy* centerfold or the 100-pound New York fashion model are out of reach for most women.

The way society teaches women to prize relationships with men, whom they presumably attract with their beauty, also contributes to the beauty myth. Striving for beauty drives women to be extremely disciplined but also forces them to be highly attentive to and responsive to men. In short, beauty-minded women try to please men and avoid challenging male power.

Belief in the beauty myth is one reason that so many young women are focused on body

One way our culture supports the beauty myth is through beauty pageants for women; over the years, contestants have become thinner and thinner.

image, particularly being as thin as possible, often to the point of endangering their health. During the past several decades, the share of young women who develop an eating disorder such as anorexia nervosa (dieting to the point of starvation) or bulimia (binge eating followed by vomiting) has risen dramatically.

The beauty myth affects males as well: Men are told repeatedly that they should want to possess beautiful women. Such ideas about beauty reduce women to objects and motivate thinking about women as if they were dolls or pets rather than human beings.

There can be little doubt that the idea of beauty is important in everyday life. The question, according to Wolf, is whether beauty is about how we look or how we act.

WHAT DO YOU THINK?

1. Is there a "money myth" that states that people's income is a reflection of their worth? Does it apply more to one sex than to the other?

2. Can you see a connection between the beauty myth and the rise of eating disorders in young women in the United States? Explain the link.

3. Among people with physical disabilities, do you think that issues of "looking different" are more serious for women or for men? Why?

Gender and Social Stratification

Gender affects more than how people think and act. It is also about social hierarchy. The reality of gender stratification can be seen, first, in the world of working women and men.

Working Women and Men

Back in 1900, just 20 percent of U.S. women were in the labor force. Today, the figure has tripled to 60 percent, and 72 percent of these working women work full time (U.S. Department of Labor, 2008).

The once common view that earning income is a man's role no longer holds true.

Factors that have changed the U.S. labor force include the decline of farming, the growth of cities, shrinking family size, and a rising divorce rate. The United States, along with most other nations, considers women working for income the rule rather than the exception. Women make up almost half the U.S. paid labor force, and 52 percent of U.S. married couples depend on two incomes.

In the past, many women in the U.S. labor force were childless. But today, 60 percent of married women with children under age six are in the labor force, as are 73 percent of married women with children between six and seventeen years of age. For widowed, divorced,

SEEING SOCIOLOGY
in Everyday Life

As you look at Table 13–1, think about which jobs have a high concentration of men (some are noted in the text). How do they differ from the jobs in Table 13–1?

or separated women with children, the comparable figures are 65 percent of women with younger children and 78 percent of women with older children (U.S. Department of Labor, 2008).

Gender and Occupations

Although women are closing the gap with men as far as working for income is concerned, the work done by the two sexes remains very different. The U.S. Department of Labor (2008) reports a high concentration of women in two job types. Administrative support work draws 24 percent of working women, most of whom are secretaries or other office workers. These are often called "pink-collar jobs" because 75 percent are filled by women. Another 16 percent of employed women do service work. Most of these jobs are in food service industries, child care, and health care.

Table 13–1 shows the ten occupations with the highest concentrations of women. These jobs tend to be at the low end of the pay scale, with limited opportunities for advancement and with men as supervisors (U.S. Department of Labor, 2008).

Men dominate most other job categories, including the building trades, where 98 percent of brickmasons, stonemasons, and heavy equipment operators are men. Likewise, men make up 86 percent of police officers, 86 percent of engineers, 70 percent of physicians and surgeons, 67 percent of lawyers, and 67 percent of corporate managers. According to a recent survey, just twelve of the *Fortune* 500 companies in the United States have a woman chief executive officer, and just 15 percent of the seats of corporate boards of directors are held by women. The twenty-five highest-paid executives in the United States do not include any women at all. Even so, increasing the leadership role of women in the business world is not just a matter of fairness; research into the earnings of this country's 500 largest corporations showed that the companies with more women on the board are also the most profitable (Dickler, 2007; Graybow, 2007; Loomis, 2007; Catalyst, 2008; U.S. Department of Labor, 2008).

Gender stratification in everyday life is easy to see: Female nurses assist male physicians, female secretaries serve male executives, and female flight attendants are under the command of male airplane pilots. In any field, the greater the income and prestige associated with a job, the more likely it is to be held by a man. For example, women represent 97 percent of kindergarten teachers, 81 percent of elementary school teachers, 57 percent of secondary school educators, 46 percent of professors in colleges and universities, and 23 percent of college and university presidents (U.S. Department of Labor, 2008).

How are women kept out of certain jobs? By defining some kinds of work as "men's work," companies define women as less competent than men. In a study of coal mining in southern West Virginia, Suzanne Tallichet (2000) found that most men considered it "unnatural" for women to work in the mines. Women who did so were defined as deviant and subject to labeling as "sexually loose" or as lesbians. Such labeling made these women outcasts, presented a challenge to their holding the job, and made advancement all but impossible.

In the corporate world, as already noted, the higher in the company we look, the fewer women we find. You hardly ever hear anyone say that women don't belong at the top levels of a company. But many people seem to feel this way, which can prevent women from being promoted. Sociologists describe this barrier as a *glass ceiling* that is not easy to see but blocks women's careers all the same.

One challenge to male domination in the workplace comes from women who are entrepreneurs. In 2008, there were more than 10 million women-owned businesses in the United States, double the number of a decade ago; they employed more than 13 million people and generated $2 trillion in sales. Through starting their own businesses, women have shown that they can make opportunities for themselves apart from large, male-dominated companies (Center for Women's Business Research, 2008).

Men, too, are guided into some work and away from other jobs by gender. In Seeing Sociology in the News on page 336, one man explains the challenge of having a job that many people in our society define as feminine.

Gender, Income, and Wealth

In 2007, the median earnings of women working full time were $35,241, and men working full time earned $45,159. This means that for every dollar earned by men, women earned about 78 cents. This

Table 13–1 Jobs with the Highest Concentrations of Women, 2007

Occupation	Number of Women Employed	Percentage in Occupation Who Are Women
1. Dental hygienist	156,000	99.2
2. Speech-language pathologist	122,000	98.0
3. Preschool or kindergarten teacher	649,000	97.3
4. Secretary or administrative assistant	3,289,000	96.7
5. Dental assistant	265,000	96.3
6. Child care worker	1,269,000	94.6
7. Licensed practical or licensed vocational nurse	497,000	93.2
8. Receptionist or information clerk	1,340,000	93.0
9. Hairdresser, hairstylist, or cosmetologist	723,000	93.0
10. Medical records and health information technician	77,000	93.0

Source: U.S. Department of Labor (2008).

GLOBAL: The World Bank (2008) reports that young women have achieved earnings parity in several Latin American/Caribbean nations. Among high-income nations, Sweden comes closest with women earning 90% of men's income.

THEN AND NOW: The 1950 U.S. gender earnings ratio was 57% vs. 78% today.

DIVERSITY: The racial gap in earnings has changed little in recent decades, but the gender gap in earnings has been narrowing.

DIVERSITY: According to the 2000 census, during the 1990s, women's income rose 7.0%, whereas men's income fell 2.3%; men's income fell in 26 states; women's income increased in every state but Alaska.

SOCIAL SURVEY: "Women should take care of running their homes and leave running the country up to men." (GSS 1998, N = 1,871; NORC, 2008)

"Agree" 15.0%   "Disagree" 82.0%   "Don't know"/No response 3.0%

Seeing SOCIOLOGY in the NEWS

Newsweek

Don't Judge Me by My Tights

BY SASCHA RADETSKY
March 17, 2008

My business attire is a pair of tights. All right, there it is. I wear makeup onstage, and some of my colleagues are gay. Can we move on now? Can we leave behind the tired male-ballet-dancer stigma—that ballet is not a masculine pursuit—in order to move toward an appreciation of the athleticism and artistry involved in this line of work?

On an average day at the job, I handle lithe, lovely women, engage in duels and delight in the experience of an exotic locale. I move like a gymnast or martial artist and embody the vilest of pimps or the most chivalrous and passionate of lovers. I constantly expand the borders of my physical capabilities, and I hone my mind to a quick-learning, focused edge. Come 8 P.M., I'll fuse dynamic movement and storytelling with the grandeur of a full live orchestra.

Yes, I'm proud of my profession. Yet I find myself slightly guarded when I tell people what I do. Like some sort of incurable blight, the male-dancer stereotype has taken root . . . in our cultural consciousness. Pioneers like Baryshnikov or Nureyev might have opened some minds, but their days have long passed, and despite the noble efforts of a handful of current ballet leaders to expose fresh audiences to our art form, a whole new generation looks at male dancing with skewed vision. Some of my peers are foreigners; in many other countries male dancers are held in higher esteem. I studied in Russia for a year and always marveled

at the way Russians celebrated their artists, whether their medium was dance, music or the written word. But I'm American, and I want to live in my own country, as a dancer, with some respect.

The most irritating aspect of the male-dancer stereotype is the underlying insinuation that we in some way lack strength of character or a courageous spirit. Male and female, all dancers undergo strenuous training from a very young age, and constantly wrestle with injuries and fatigue. But male dancers must possess a special type of will and fortitude if they are to become professionals. . . . In our culture, girls are encouraged to take ballet; boys receive no such endorsement, except of course from ballet teachers or exceptionally supportive parents. The boy who perseveres in dance must have a genuine hunger for it, must be uniquely motivated and dedicated, and must develop a truly thick skin.

I started taking ballet when I was 5. My open-minded parents thought it was a good way to channel my rambunctious behavior. A few years later I was hooked. I loved the physicality and, of course, the girls, but I also learned that not everyone recognized the value of dance the way I did. I don't remember the first fight I got into for being a kid who took ballet, but I remember fighting a lot before I realized that maybe I should keep my extracurricular activities to myself. But ballet was rewarding enough to be worth a fat lip or a black eye, and I emerged from my years of dance training more focused than ever. . . . My American colleagues share similar stories of discouragement, harassment

and even violence. But these experiences served to harden resolve and develop courage, and I know I can always count on several of my dancer buddies for steadfast support—they got my back! Ironically, the stereotype of the sissy male dancer has given rise to a male dancer who is anything but. . . .

Exposure to ballet is all that is needed to open minds, for the combination of athletic movement, ardent drama and beautiful music can instill a profound appreciation in an audience. But for you out there who still feel compelled to malign male dancers with half-truths and petty stereotypes, well, maybe we need to step outside. I'll leave my tights on.

WHAT DO YOU THINK?

1. In the article, what qualities does the writer associate with being masculine?

2. Are you surprised at how difficult it can be for a man to do a job that many people see as not masculine? Explain.

3. Are there jobs that create similar problems for women? What jobs? Why?

difference is greater among older workers because older working women typically have less education and seniority than older working men. Earning differences are smaller among younger workers because younger men and women tend to have similar schooling and work experience.

Among all full-time workers of all ages, 26 percent of women earned less than $25,000 in 2006, compared with 17 percent of men. At the upper end of the income scale, men were more than twice as likely as women (20 percent versus 9 percent) to earn more than $75,000 (U.S. Census Bureau, 2008).

The main reason women earn less is the *type* of work they do, largely clerical and service jobs. In effect, jobs and gender interact. People still perceive jobs with less clout as "women's work," just as people devalue certain work simply because it is performed by women (England, Hermsen, & Cotter, 2000; Cohen & Huffman, 2003).

In recent decades, supporters of gender equality have proposed a policy of "comparable worth," paying people not according to the historical double standard but according to the level of skill and responsibility involved in the work. Several nations, including Great Britain and Australia, have adopted comparable worth policies, but such policies have found limited acceptance in the United States. As a result, women in this country lose as much as $1 billion in income annually.

A second cause of gender-based income disparity has to do with the family. Both men and women have children, of course, but our culture gives more responsibility for parenting to women. Pregnancy and raising small children keep many young women out of the labor force at a time when their male peers are making significant career advancements. When women workers return to the labor force, they have less job seniority than their male counterparts (Stier, 1996; Waldfogel, 1997).

DIVERSITY: In 2008, 15.1% of directors of *Fortune* 500 companies were women; 68 of these companies had no women directors (Catalyst, 2008).

NOTE: Since the first U.S. Congress, 11,699 people have served in the House or Senate, including 215 women (less than 2%).

GLOBAL: Austrian law requires that men equally share household chores and child care. The Austrian Women's Ministry claims that marriage is a private matter, but government "guidelines are needed."

SEEING SOCIOLOGY in Everyday Life

How is gender related to doing housework in your current home or in the home in which you grew up?

In addition, women who choose to have children may be unable or unwilling to take on demanding jobs that tie up their evenings and weekends. To avoid role strain, they may take jobs that offer shorter commuting distances, more flexible hours, and employer-provided child care services. Women pursuing both a career and a family are often torn between their dual responsibilities in ways that men are not. One study found that almost half of women in competitive jobs took time off to have children, compared to about 12 percent of men (Hewlett & Luce, 2005). Role conflict is also experienced by women on campus: One study concluded that young female professors with at least one child were at least 20 percent less likely to have tenure than male professors in the same field (Shea, 2002).

The two factors noted so far—type of work and family responsibilities—account for about two-thirds of the earnings difference between women and men. A third factor—discrimination against women—accounts for most of the remainder (Fuller & Schoenberger, 1991). Because overt discrimination is illegal, it is practiced in subtle ways. Women on their way up the corporate ladder often run into the glass ceiling described earlier; company officials may deny its existence, but it effectively prevents many women from rising above middle management.

For all these reasons, women earn less than men in all major occupational categories. Even so, many people think that women own most of this country's wealth, perhaps because women typically outlive men. Government statistics tell a different story: Fifty-seven percent of individuals with $1.5 million or more in assets are men, although widows are highly represented in this elite club (Johnson & Raub, 2006; Internal Revenue Service, 2008). Just 10 percent of the individuals identified in 2008 by *Forbes* magazine as the richest people in the United States were women (Miller & Greenberg, 2008).

Housework: Women's "Second Shift"

In the United States, we have always been of two minds about housework: We say that it is important to family life, but people get little reward for doing it (Bernard, 1981). Here, as around the world, taking care of the home and children has always been considered "women's work" (see Global Map 6–1 on page 142). As women have entered the labor force, the amount of housework women do has gone down, but the *share* done by women has stayed the same. Figure 13–2 shows that overall, women average 16.1 hours a week of housework, compared to 10.5 hours for men. As the figure shows, women in all categories do significantly more housework than men (Bureau of Labor Statistics, 2009).

Men do support the idea of women entering the paid labor force, and most husbands count on the money their wives earn. But many men resist taking on a more equal share of household duties (Heath & Bourne, 1995; Harpster & Monk-Turner, 1998; Stratton, 2001).

On average, women spend considerably more time doing housework than men.

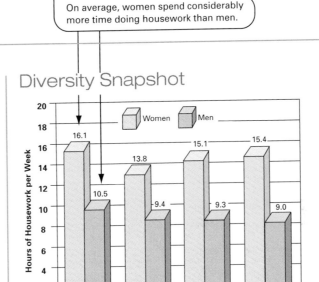

Diversity Snapshot

FIGURE 13–2 **Housework: Who Does How Much?**

Regardless of employment or family status, women do more housework than men. What effect do you think the added burden of housework has on women's ability to advance in the workplace?

Source: Adapted from Bureau of Labor Statistics (2009).

Gender and Education

In the past, our society considered schooling more necessary for men, who worked outside the home, than for women, who worked in the home. But times have changed. By 1980, women earned a majority of all associate's and bachelor's degrees; in 2007, that share was 59 percent (National Center for Education Statistics, 2009).

In recent decades, college doors have opened wider to women, and the differences in men's and women's majors are becoming smaller. In 1970, for example, women earned just 17 percent of bachelor's degrees in the natural sciences, computer science, and engineering; by 2007, their proportion had more than doubled to 36 percent.

In 1992, for the first time, women also earned a majority of postgraduate degrees, which often serve as a springboard to high-prestige jobs. In all areas of study in 2007, women earned 61 percent of master's degrees and 50 percent of doctorates (including 64 percent of all Ph.D. degrees in sociology). Women have also broken into many graduate fields that used to be almost all male. For example, in 1970, only a few hundred women earned a master's of business administration

DISCUSS: Ask students with experience living with a member of the other sex to describe, based on their own lives, how gender is linked to how much housework people do and what type of work people do.

DISCUSS: What share of students on your campus is female? What about in your program or major field of study?

DIVERSITY: Among non-Hispanic whites, women receive 54% of doctorates; among non-Hispanic African Americans, 65%; among Hispanics, 56%; Asians, 52%; Native Americans, 54%.

SEEING SOCIOLOGY
in Everyday Life

Sweden, Norway, Finland, and Denmark have laws that require at least 25 percent of candidates for elected office to be women. Do you think the United States should enact such a law? Why or why not?

Table 13–2   Significant "Firsts" for Women in U.S. Politics

1869	Law allows women to vote in Wyoming territory.
1872	First woman to run for the presidency (Victoria Woodhull) represents the Equal Rights party.
1917	First woman elected to the House of Representatives (Jeannette Rankin of Montana).
1924	First women elected state governors (Nellie Taylor Ross of Wyoming and Miriam "Ma" Ferguson of Texas); both followed their husbands into office. First woman to have her name placed in nomination for the vice-presidency at the convention of a major political party (Lena Jones Springs, a Democrat).
1931	First woman to serve in the Senate (Hattie Caraway of Arkansas); completed the term of her husband upon his death and won reelection in 1932.
1932	First woman appointed to the presidential cabinet (Frances Perkins, secretary of labor in the cabinet of President Franklin D. Roosevelt).
1964	First woman to have her name placed in nomination for the presidency at the convention of a major political party (Margaret Chase Smith, a Republican).
1972	First African American woman to have her name placed in nomination for the presidency at the convention of a major political party (Shirley Chisholm, a Democrat).
1981	First woman appointed to the U.S. Supreme Court (Sandra Day O'Connor).
1984	First woman to be successfully nominated for the vice-presidency (Geraldine Ferraro, a Democrat).
1988	First woman chief executive to be elected to a consecutive third term (Madeleine Kunin, governor of Vermont).
1992	Political "Year of the Woman" yields record number of women in the Senate (six) and the House (forty-eight), as well as (1) first African American woman to win election to the U.S. Senate (Carol Moseley-Braun of Illinois), (2) first state (California) to be served by two women senators (Barbara Boxer and Dianne Feinstein), and (3) first woman of Puerto Rican descent elected to the U.S. House of Representatives (Nydia Velazquez of New York).
1996	First woman appointed secretary of state (Madeleine Albright).
2000	First First Lady to win elected political office (Hillary Rodham Clinton, senator from New York).
2001	First woman to serve as national security adviser (Condoleezza Rice); first Asian American woman to serve in a presidential cabinet (Elaine Chao, secretary of labor).
2005	First African American woman appointed secretary of state (Condoleezza Rice).
2007	First woman elected as speaker of the House (Nancy Pelosi).
2008	For the first time, women make up a majority of a state legislature (New Hampshire).
2009	Record number of women in the Senate (seventeen) and the House (seventy-three).

Source: Compiled by the author.

55 percent of dental (D.D.S. and D.M.D.) degrees (National Center for Education Statistics, 2009). Our society once defined high-paying professions (and the drive and competitiveness needed to succeed in them) as masculine. But the share of women in all these professions has risen and is now close to half. When will parity be reached? It may not be in the next few years. For example, the American Bar Association (2008) reports that men still account for 53 percent of law school students across the United States.

Gender and Politics

A century ago, almost no women held elected office in the United States. In fact, women were legally barred from voting in national elections until the passage of the Nineteenth Amendment to the Constitution in 1920. However, a few women were candidates for political office even before they could vote. The Equal Rights party supported Victoria Woodhull for the U.S. presidency in 1872; perhaps it was a sign of the times that she spent election day in a New York City jail. Table 13–2 identifies milestones in women's gradual movement into U.S. political life.

Today, thousands of women serve as mayors of cities and towns across the United States, and tens of thousands hold responsible administrative posts in the federal government. At the state level, 24 percent of state legislators in 2009 were women (up from just 6 percent in 1970). National Map 13–1 shows where in the United States women have made the greatest political gains.

Change is coming more slowly at the highest levels of politics, although a majority of U.S. adults claim they would support a qualified woman for any office. In 2008, Hillary Clinton came close to gaining the presidential nomination of the Democratic party, losing out to Barack Obama, who became the nation's first African American president. In 2008, eight of fifty state governors were women (16 percent), and in Congress, women held 73 of 435 seats in the House of Representatives (17 percent) and 17 of 100 seats in the Senate (17 percent) (Center for American Women and Politics, 2009a).

Women make up half the world's population, but they hold just 18 percent of seats in the world's 188 parliaments. Although this percentage represents a rise from 3 percent fifty years ago, in only fourteen countries, among them Sweden and Norway, do women represent more than one-third of the members of parliament (Paxton, Hughes, & Green, 2006; Inter-Parliamentary Union, 2008).

Gender and the Military

Since colonial times, women have served in the U.S. armed forces. Yet in 1940, at the outset of World War II, just 2 percent of armed forces personnel were women. By the time of the war in Iraq, women represented about 14 percent of all U.S. military personnel, including deployed troops.

(M.B.A.) degree, compared to almost 66,000 in 2007 (44 percent of all such degrees) (National Center for Education Statistics, 2009).

Despite these advances for women, men still predominate in some professional fields. In 2007, men received 51 percent of medical (M.D.) degrees, 52 percent of law (LL.B. and J.D.) degrees, and

Q: "We can no longer go to war without women." General Colin Powell

THE MAP: Roughly speaking, women hold the most power in state government in the western states (the region in which women first became state governors). By contrast, the South remains the region in which women are least likely to be in the labor force and where the political clout of women is lowest.

SOCIAL SURVEY: Top ten nations in terms of share of women in national legislatures (mid-2007): (1) Rwanda, 56%; (2) Sweden, 47%; (3) Cuba, 43%; (4) Finland, 42.0%; (5) Argentina, 40%; (6) Netherlands, 39%; (7) Denmark, 38%; (8) Angola, 37%; (9) Costa Rica, 37%; (10) Spain, 36% (Inter-Parliamentary Union, 2008).

minority any category of people distinguished by physical or cultural difference that a society sets apart and subordinates

intersection theory analysis of the interplay of race, class, and gender, often resulting in multiple dimensions of disadvantage

In general, the western states have a higher percentage of legislators who are women than the southern states.

Seeing Ourselves

NATIONAL MAP 13–1
Women in State Government across the United States

Although women make up half of U.S. adults, just 24 percent of the seats in state legislatures are held by women. Look at the state-by-state variations in the map. In which regions of the country have women gained the greatest political power? What do you think accounts for this pattern?

Source: Center for American Women and Politics (2009).

Share of State Legislative Seats Held by Women

- High: 34.0% and over
- Above average: 27.0% to 33.9%
- Average: 20.0% to 26.9%
- Below average: 13.0% to 19.9%
- Low: 12.9% and under

U.S. average: 23.5%

Clearly, women make up a growing share of the U.S. military, and almost all military assignments are now open to both women and men. But law prevents women from engaging in offensive warfare. Even so, the line between troop support and outright combat is easily crossed, as the women serving in Iraq have learned. In fact, between March 2003 and March 2009, the war in Iraq claimed the lives of 101 women soldiers.

The debate on women's role in the military has been going on for centuries. Some people object to opening doors in this way, claiming that women lack the physical strength of men. Others reply that military women are better educated and score higher on intelligence tests than military men. But the heart of the issue is our society's deeply held view of women as *nurturers*—people who give life and help others—which clashes with the image of women trained to kill.

Whatever our views of women and men, the reality is that military women are in harm's way. In part, this fact reflects the strains experienced by a military short of personnel. In addition, the type of insurgency that surrounds our troops in Iraq can bring violent combat to any soldier at any time. Finally, our modern warfare technology blurs the distinction between combat and noncombat personnel. A combat pilot can fire missiles by radar at a target miles away; by contrast, noncombat medical evacuation teams routinely travel directly into the line of fire (Segal & Hansen, 1992; Kaminer, 1997; McGirk, 2006).

Are Women a Minority?

A **minority** is *any category of people distinguished by physical or cultural difference that a society sets apart and subordinates*. Given the economic disadvantage of being a woman in our society, it seems rea-

sonable to say that U.S. women are a minority even though they outnumber men.[1]

Even so, most white women do not think of themselves in this way (Lengermann & Wallace, 1985). This is partly because, unlike racial minorities (including African Americans) and ethnic minorities (say, Hispanics), white women are well represented at all levels of the class structure, including the very top.

Bear in mind, however, that at every class level, women typically have less income, wealth, education, and power than men. Patriarchy makes women dependent on men—first their fathers and later their husbands—for their social standing (Bernard, 1981).

Minority Women: Intersection Theory

If women are defined as a minority, what about minority women? Are they doubly handicapped? This question lies at the heart of **intersection theory**, *analysis of the interplay of race, class, and gender, often resulting in multiple dimensions of disadvantage*. Research shows that disadvantages linked to gender and race often combine to produce especially low social standing (Ovadia, 2001).

Income data illustrate the validity of this theory. Looking first at race and ethnicity, the median income in 2007 for African American women working full time was $31,114, which is 84 percent as much as the $36,891 earned by non-Hispanic white women

---

[1]Sociologists use the term "minority" instead of "minority group" because, as explained in Chapter 7 ("Groups and Organizations"), women make up a *category*, not a group. People in a category share a status or identity but generally do not know one another or interact.

SOCIAL SURVEY: "If your party nominated a woman for president, would you vote for her if she were qualified for the job?" (GSS 1998, *N* = 1,871; *Codebook*, 2005:277) [In a 1937 Gallup poll, 37% endorsed a qualified woman for president.]

"Yes" 90.2%   "No" 6.2%   "Don't know"/No response 3.6%

DIVERSITY: In 1992, the U.S. Senate chamber added a women's bathroom.

DIVERSITY: Of all families living below poverty level, 51% were headed by women in 2007. Of all poor African American families, 75% were headed by women; for Hispanics, the figure was 43%, and for non-Hispanic whites, 43% (U.S. Census Bureau, 2008).

MAKING THE GRADE

Feminists argue that rape is not about sex but about power. It is this claim that makes sexual violence against women not just a crime but a matter of gender stratification.

working full time; Hispanic women earned $26,695—just 72 percent as much as their white counterparts. Looking at gender, African American women earned only 86 percent as much as African American men, and Hispanic women earned only 89 percent as much as Hispanic men.

Combining these disadvantages, African American women earned 62 percent as much as non-Hispanic white men, and Hispanic women earned 53 percent as much (U.S. Census Bureau, 2008). These differences reflect minority women's lower positions in the occupational and educational hierarchies. These data confirm that although gender has a powerful effect on our lives, it does not operate alone. Class position, race and ethnicity, and gender form a multilayered system of disadvantage for some and privilege for others (Saint Jean & Feagin, 1998).

The basic insight of intersection theory is that various dimensions of social stratification—including race and gender—can add up to great disadvantages for some categories of people. Just as African Americans earn less than whites, women earn less than men. Thus African American women confront a "double disadvantage," earning just 62 cents for every dollar earned by non-Hispanic white men. How would you explain the fact that some categories of people are much more likely to end up in low-paying jobs like this one?

Violence against Women

In the nineteenth century, men claimed the right to rule their households, even to the point of using physical discipline against their wives, and a great deal of "manly" violence is still directed at women. A government report estimates that 587,000 aggravated assaults against women occur annually. To this number can be added 233,000 rapes or sexual assaults and perhaps 1.8 million simple assaults (U.S. Department of Justice, 2008).

Gender violence is also an issue on college and university campuses. According to research carried out by the U.S. Department of Justice, in a given academic year, about 3 percent of female college students become victims of rape (either attempted or completed). Projecting these figures over a typical five-year college career, about 20 percent of college women experience rape. In 90 percent of all cases, the victim knew the offender, and most of the assaults took place in the woman's living quarters (Karjane, Fisher, & Cullen, 2005).

Off campus, most gender-linked violence also occurs where most interaction between women and men takes place: in the home. Richard Gelles (cited in Roesch, 1984) argues that with the exception of the police and the military, the family is the most violent organization in the United States, and women suffer most of the injuries. The risk of violence is especially great for low-income women living in families that face a great deal of stress; low-income women also have fewer options to get out of a dangerous home (Gelles & Cornell, 1990; Smolowe, 1994; Frias & Angel, 2007).

Violence against women also occurs in casual relationships. As noted in Chapter 9 ("Deviance"), most rapes involve men known, and often trusted, by the victims. Dianne Herman (2001) claims that abuse of women is built into our way of life. All forms of violence against women—from the catcalls that intimidate women on city streets to a pinch in a crowded subway to physical assaults that occur at home—express what she calls a "rape culture" of men trying to dominate women. Sexual violence is fundamentally about *power*, not sex, and therefore should be understood as a dimension of gender stratification.

In global perspective, violence against women is built into different cultures in different ways. One case in point is the practice of female genital mutilation, a painful and often dangerous surgical procedure performed in more than forty countries and known to occur in the United States, as shown in Global Map 13–2. The Thinking About Diversity box on page 342 highlights a case of genital mutilation that took place in California and asks whether this practice, which some people defend as promoting "morality," amounts to a case of violence against women.

DIVERSITY: Gender involves not just difference but heirarchy. Sociology's recent emphasis on the "intersections" of class, gender, race, and ethnicity shows these to be cumulative dimensions of privilege or disadvantage.

DIVERSITY: Income figures for minority women link economic disadvantages to race and gender; a more complete picture would have to factor in differences in education, work histories, age, and other criteria.

DIVERSITY: Historically, the labor force participation of women of color was higher than that of white women. In 1940, for example, 40% of African American women worked for wages, compared to less than 30% of white women.

NOTE: In 2007, a total of 3,177 women died as a result of violence; 33% of them were victims of violence perpetrated by a spouse or intimate partner.

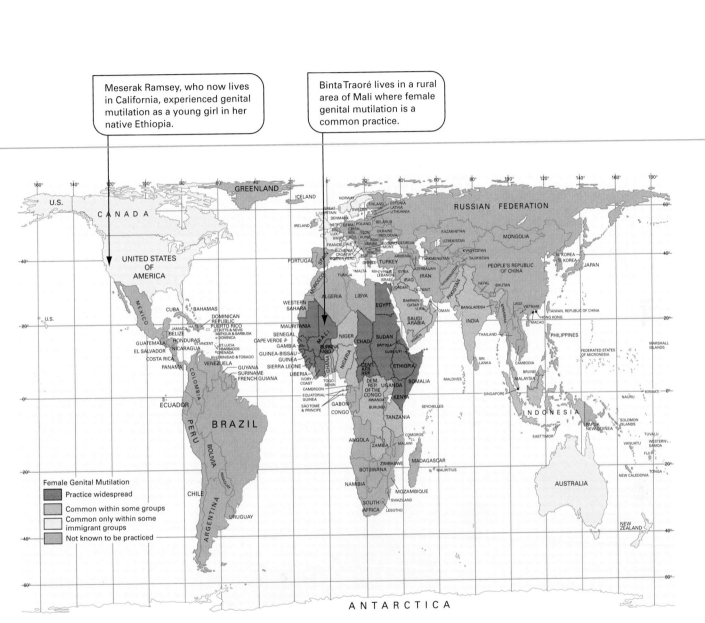

Meserak Ramsey, who now lives in California, experienced genital mutilation as a young girl in her native Ethiopia.

Binta Traoré lives in a rural area of Mali where female genital mutilation is a common practice.

Female Genital Mutilation
- Practice widespread
- Common within some groups
- Common only within some immigrant groups
- Not known to be practiced

Window on the World

GLOBAL MAP 13–2   **Female Genital Mutilation in Global Perspective**

Female genital mutilation is known to be performed in more than forty countries around the world. Across Africa, the practice is common and affects a majority of girls in the eastern African nations of Sudan, Ethiopia, and Somalia. In several Asian nations, including India, the practice is limited to a few ethnic minorities. In the United States, Canada, several European nations, and Australia, there are reports of the practice among some immigrants.

Sources: Data from Seager (2003), World Health Organization (2006), and UNICEF (2008).

Violence against Men

If our way of life encourages violence against women, it may encourage even more violence against men. As noted earlier in Chapter 9 ("Deviance"), in more than 80 percent of cases in which police make an arrest for a violent crime, including murder, robbery, and physical assault, the person arrested is a male. In addition, 53 percent of all

victims of violent crime are also men (U.S. Department of Justice, 2008).

Our culture tends to define masculinity in terms of aggression and violence. "Real men" work and play hard, speed on the highways, and let nothing stand in their way. A higher crime rate is one result. But even when no laws are broken, men's lives involve more stress and isolation than women's lives, which is one reason that the suicide rate for

Q: "To consider such traits as aggressiveness or passivity to be sex-linked is not possible in light of the facts." Margaret Mead

NOTE: Most people arrested for drunk driving are men, but the trend for men is downward and the trend for women is sharply upward.

DISCUSS: The box on female genital mutilation is a good issue to think about in terms of ethnocentrism and cultural relativism, discussed in Chapter 3 ("Culture"). Is our condemning this practice ethnocentric?

sexual harassment comments, gestures, or physical contacts of a sexual nature that are deliberate, repeated, and unwelcome

THINKING ABOUT DIVERSITY: RACE, CLASS, & GENDER

Female Genital Mutilation: Violence in the Name of Morality

Meserak Ramsey, a woman born in Ethiopia and now working as a nurse in California, paid a visit to an old friend's home. Soon after arriving, she noticed her friend's eighteen-month-old daughter huddled in the corner of a room in obvious distress. "What's wrong with her?" she asked.

Ramsey was shocked when the woman said her daughter had recently had a clitoridectomy, the surgical removal of the clitoris. This type of female genital mutilation—performed by a midwife, a tribal practitioner, or a doctor, and typically without anesthesia—is common in Nigeria, Sierra Leone, Senegal, Sudan, Ethiopia, Somalia, and Egypt and is known to exist in certain cultural groups in other nations around the world. It is illegal in the United States.

Among members of highly patriarchal societies, husbands demand that their wives be virgins at marriage and remain sexually faithful thereafter. The point of female genital mutilation is to eliminate sexual feeling, which, people assume, makes the girl less likely to violate sexual norms and thus be more desirable to men. In about one-fifth of all cases, an even more severe procedure, called infibulation, is performed, in which the entire external genital area is removed and the surfaces are stitched together, leaving only a small hole for urination and menstruation. Before marriage, a husband retains the right to open the wound and ensure himself of his bride's virginity.

How many women have undergone genital mutilation? Worldwide,

estimates place the number at more than 100 million (World Health Organization, 2006). In the United States, hundreds or even thousands of such procedures are performed every year. In most cases, immigrant mothers and grandmothers who have themselves been mutilated insist that young girls in their family follow their example. Indeed, many immigrant women demand the procedure *because* their daughters now live in the United States, where sexual mores are more lax. "I don't have to worry about her now," the girl's mother explained to Meserak Ramsey. "She'll be a good girl."

Medically, the consequences of genital mutilation include more than the loss of sexual pleasure. Pain is intense and can persist for years. There is also danger of infection, infertility, and even death. Ramsey knows this all too

well: She herself underwent genital mutilation as a young girl. She is one of the lucky ones who has had few medical problems since. But the extent of her suffering is suggested by this story: She invited a young U.S. couple to stay at her home. Late at night, she heard the woman cry out and burst into their room to investigate, only to learn that the couple was making love and the woman had just had an orgasm. "I didn't understand," Ramsey recalls. "I thought that there must be something wrong with American girls. But now I know that there is something wrong with me." Or with a system that inflicts such injury in the name of traditional morality.

WHAT DO YOU THINK?

1. Is female genital mutilation a medical procedure or a means of social control? Explain your answer.

2. Can you think of other examples of physical mutilation imposed on women? What are they?

3. What do you think should be done about female genital mutilation in places where it is widespread? Do you think respect for human rights should override respect for cultural differences in this case? Explain your answer.

These young women have just undergone female genital mutilation. What do you think should be done about this practice?

Sources: Crossette (1995) and Boyle, Songora, & Foss (2001).

men is four times higher than for women. In addition, as noted earlier, men live, on average, about five fewer years than women.

Violence is not simply a matter of choices made by individuals. It is built into our way of life, with resulting harm to both men and women. In short, the way any culture constructs gender plays an important part in how violent or peaceful a society will be.

Sexual Harassment

Sexual harassment refers to *comments, gestures, or physical contacts of a sexual nature that are deliberate, repeated, and unwelcome.* During the 1990s, sexual harassment became an issue of national importance that rewrote the rules for workplace interaction between women and men.

● SEEING SOCIOLOGY
in Everyday Life

The Internet has made pornography more accessible; do you think it has become more acceptable as well? Why or why not?

Most (but not all) victims of sexual harassment are women. The reason is that, first, our culture encourages men to be sexually assertive and to see women in sexual terms. As a result, social interaction in the workplace, on campus, and elsewhere can easily take on sexual overtones. Second, most people in positions of power—including business executives, doctors, bureau chiefs, assembly-line supervisors, professors, and military officers—are men who oversee the work of women. Surveys carried out in widely different work settings show that 5 percent of women claim that they have been harassed on the job during the past year and about half of women say they receive unwanted sexual attention (NORC, 2007).

Sexual harassment is sometimes obvious and direct: A supervisor may ask for sexual favors from an employee and make threats if the advances are refused. Courts have declared such *quid pro quo* sexual harassment (the Latin phrase means "one thing in return for another") to be a violation of civil rights.

More often, however, sexual harassment is a matter of subtle behavior—suggestive teasing, off-color jokes, comments about someone's looks—that may not even be intended to harass anyone. But based on the *effect* standard favored by many feminists, such actions add up to creating a *hostile environment*. Incidents of this kind are far more complex because they involve different perceptions of the same behavior. For example, a man may think that repeatedly complimenting a co-worker on her appearance is simply being friendly. The co-worker may believe that the man is thinking of her in sexual terms and is not taking her work seriously, an attitude that could harm her job performance and prospects for advancement.

Pornography

Chapter 8 ("Sexuality and Society") defined *pornography* as sexually explicit material that causes sexual arousal. Keep in mind, however, that people take different views of what is and what is not pornographic. The law gives local communities the power to define what sexually explicit materials violate "community standards of decency" and "lack any redeeming social value."

Traditionally, people have raised concerns about pornography as a *moral* issue. But pornography also plays a part in gender stratification. From this point of view, pornography is really a *power* issue because most pornography dehumanizes women, depicting them as the playthings of men.

In addition, there is widespread concern that pornography promotes violence against women by portraying them as weak and undeserving of respect. Men may show contempt for women defined this way by striking out against them. Surveys show that about half of U.S. adults think that pornography encourages men to commit rape (NORC, 2007:300).

In recent decades, our society has recognized sexual harassment as an important problem. As a result, at least officially, unwelcome sexual attention is no longer tolerated in the workplace. To what extent do you think sexual comments, off-color jokes, and unnecessary touching still take place on the job?

Like sexual harassment, pornography raises complex and conflicting issues. Despite the fact that some material may offend just about everybody, many people defend the rights of free speech and artistic expression. Pressure to restrict pornography has increased in recent decades, reflecting both the long-standing concern that pornography weakens morality and more recent concerns that it is demeaning and threatening to women.

Theoretical Analysis of Gender

Why does gender exist in the first place? Sociology's three main approaches offer insights about the importance of gender in social organization. The Applying Theory table on page 344 summarizes the important insights offered by these approaches.

Structural-Functional Analysis

The structural-functional approach views society as a complex system of many separate but integrated parts. From this point of view, gender serves as a means to organize social life.

As Chapter 4 ("Society") explained, members of hunting and gathering societies had little power over the forces of biology. Lacking effective birth control, women were frequently pregnant, and the responsibilities of child care kept them close to home. At the same

NOTE: The legal basis for charges of sexual harassment is Section 703 of Title VII of the 1964 Civil Rights Act, which outlaws workplace discrimination based on sex, and also on Title IX of the Education Amendments of 1972. In recent years, courts have ended the "see no evil" defense, declaring that organizations and companies are responsible for harassment if they have no programs or monitoring systems to combat it.

Q: "Sexual objectification is the primary process of the subjugation of women." Catharine MacKinnon

DISCUSS: Ask how the class distinguishes between "erotic" and "pornographic" material. Debate a proper balance among conservative moral concerns, liberal support for freedom of expression, and feminist opposition to the patriarchal dimensions of pornography.

● APPLYING THEORY ●

Gender

	Structural-Functional Approach	Symbolic-Interaction Approach	Social-Conflict Approach
What is the level of analysis?	Macro-level	Micro-level	Macro-level
What does gender mean?	Parsons described gender in terms of two complementary patterns of behavior: masculine and feminine.	Numerous sociologists have shown that gender is part of the reality that guides social interaction in everyday situations.	Engels described gender in terms of the power of one sex over the other.
Is gender helpful or harmful?	Helpful. Gender gives men and women distinctive roles and responsibilities that help society operate smoothly. Gender builds social unity as men and women come together to form families.	Hard to say; gender is both helpful and harmful. In everyday life, gender is one of the factors that helps us relate to one another. At the same time, gender shapes human behavior, placing men in control of social situations. Men tend to initiate most interactions, while women typically act in a more deferential manner.	Harmful. Gender limits people's personal development. Gender divides society by giving power to men to control the lives of women. Capitalism makes patriarchy stronger.

time, men's greater strength made them more suited for warfare and hunting game. Over the centuries, this sexual division of labor became institutionalized and largely taken for granted (Lengermann & Wallace, 1985; Freedman, 2002).

Industrial technology opens up a much greater range of cultural possibilities. With human muscles no longer the main energy source, the physical strength of men becomes less important. In addition, the ability to control reproduction gives women greater choices about how to live. Modern societies relax traditional gender roles as they become more meritocratic because such rigid roles waste an enormous amount of human talent. Yet change comes slowly because gender is deeply rooted in culture.

Gender and Social Integration

As Talcott Parsons (1942, 1951, 1954) observed, gender helps integrate society, at least in its traditional form. Gender establishes a *complementary* set of roles that link men and women into family units and give each sex responsibility for carrying out important tasks. Women take the lead in managing the household and raising children. Men connect the family to the larger world as they participate in the labor force.

Thus gender plays an important part in socialization. Society teaches boys—presumably destined for the labor force—to be rational, self-assured, and competitive. Parsons called this complex of traits *instrumental* qualities. To prepare girls for child rearing, their socialization stresses *expressive* qualities, such as emotional responsiveness and sensitivity to others.

Society encourages gender conformity by instilling in men and women a fear that straying too far from accepted standards of masculinity or femininity will cause rejection by the other sex. In simple terms, women learn to reject nonmasculine men as sexually unattractive, and men learn to reject unfeminine women. In sum, gender integrates society both structurally (in terms of what we do) and morally (in terms of what we believe).

○ **CRITICAL REVIEW** Influential in the 1950s, this approach has lost much of its standing today. First, functionalism assumes a singular vision of society that is not shared by everyone. Historically, many women have worked outside the home because of economic need, a fact not reflected in Parsons's conventional, middle-class view of family life. Second, Parsons's analysis ignores the personal strains and social costs of rigid, traditional gender

Q: "Consider, I address you as a legislator, whether, when men contend for their freedom, and to be allowed to judge for themselves their own happiness, it be not inconsistent and unjust to subjugate women, even though you firmly believe that you are acting in the manner best calculated to promote their happiness? Who made man the exclusive judge, if woman partake with him the gift of reason?" Mary Wollstonecraft, *A Vindication of the Rights of Woman* (1792)

Q: "We all live in single-sex worlds, and most of what we know—from history, the humanities, the social sciences—deals with the male world." Jessie Bernard

Q: "To be born a woman means to inhabit, from early infancy to the last day of life, a psychological world which differs from the world of man." Mirra Komarovsky

Q: "Conventionality is not morality." Charlotte Brontë

MAKING THE GRADE

The structural-functional approach is a more "horizontal" view of gender that emphasizes complementarity. The social-conflict approach is a more "vertical" view of gender that emphasizes inequality. The symbolic-interaction approach is the micro-level look at gender in everyday life.

roles. Third, in the eyes of those seeking sexual equality, Parsons's gender "complementarity" amounts to little more than women submitting to male domination.

CHECK YOUR LEARNING In Parsons's analysis, what functions does gender perform for society?

Symbolic-Interaction Analysis

The symbolic-interaction approach takes a micro-level view of society, focusing on face-to-face interaction in everyday life. As suggested in Chapter 6 ("Social Interaction in Everyday Life"), gender affects everyday interaction in a number of ways.

Gender and Everyday Life

If you watch women and men interacting, you will probably notice that women typically engage in more eye contact than men do. Why? Holding eye contact is a way of encouraging the conversation to continue; in addition, looking directly at someone clearly shows the other person that you are paying attention.

This pattern is an example of sex roles, defined earlier as the way a society defines how women and men should think and behave. To understand such patterns, consider the fact that people with more power tend to take charge of social encounters. When men and women engage one another, as they do in families and in the workplace, it is men who typically initiate the interaction. That is, men speak first, set the topics of discussion, and control the outcomes. With less power, women are expected to be more *deferential,* meaning that they show respect for others of higher social position. In many cases, this means that women (just like children or others with less power) spend more time being silent and also encouraging men (or others with more power) not just with eye contact but by smiling or nodding in agreement. As a technique to control a conversation, men often interrupt others, just as they typically feel less need to ask the opinions of other people, especially those with less power (Tannen, 1990, 1994; Henley, Hamilton, & Thorne, 1992; Ridgeway & Smith-Lovin, 1999).

CRITICAL REVIEW The strength of the symbolic-interaction approach is helping us see how gender plays a part in shaping almost all our everyday experiences. Because our society defines men (and everything that is defined as masculine) as having more value than women (and what is defined as feminine), just about every familiar social encounter is "gendered," so that men and women interact in distinctive and unequal ways.

The symbolic-interaction approach suggests that individuals socially construct the reality they experience as they interact, using gender as one element of their personal "performances." Gender can be a useful guide to how we behave. Yet gender, as a struc-

In the 1950s, Talcott Parsons proposed that sociologists interpret gender as a matter of *differences*. As he saw it, masculine men and feminine women formed strong families and made for an orderly society. In recent decades, however, social-conflict theory has reinterpreted gender as a matter of *inequality*. From this point of view, U.S. society places men in a position of dominance over women.

tural dimension of society, is beyond the immediate control of any of us as individuals and also gives some people power over others. Therefore, patterns of everyday social interaction reflect our society's gender stratification. Everyday interaction also helps reinforce this inequality. For example, to the extent that fathers take the lead in family discussions, the entire family learns to expect men to "display leadership" and "show their wisdom."

A limitation of the symbolic-interaction approach is that by focusing on situational social experience, it says little about the broad patterns of inequality that set the rules for our everyday lives. To understand the roots of gender stratification, we have to "look up" to see more closely how society makes men and women unequal. We will do this using the social-conflict approach.

CHECK YOUR LEARNING Point to ways that gender shapes the everyday face-to-face interactions of individuals.

Social-Conflict Analysis

From a social-conflict point of view, gender involves differences not just in behavior but in power as well. Consider the striking similarity between the way ideas about gender benefit men and the way

NOTE: E. Digby Baltzell points out that control of women's sexuality is not designed simply to ensure the domination of women; it is society's means of promoting endogamy, thus defending racial and class hegemony.

Q: "Differences of age and sex no longer have distinctive social validity for the working class. All [people] are instruments of labor, more or less expensive to use, according to their age and sex." Karl Marx and Friedrich Engels

DISCUSS: The term "transgendered" has emerged to refer to people, including transsexuals and cross-dressers, who violate gender norms. Why, according to Talcott Parsons, would such people encounter strong disapproval from others? Why, following a conflict approach, could such behavior be viewed as an act of resistance?

NOTE: The first Miss America beauty pageant was held in 1920, the same year that the 19th Amendment was passed, giving women the right to vote.

feminism support of social equality for women and men, in opposition to patriarchy and sexism

NASCAR racing has always been a masculine world. But Danica Patrick has made a name for herself as an outstanding driver. At the same time, she has made much of her income from trading on her good looks, including the 2009 *Sports Illustrated* swimsuit edition. Are men as likely to do the same? Why or why not?

oppression of racial and ethnic minorities benefits white people. Conventional ideas about gender do not make society operate smoothly; they create division and tension, with men seeking to protect their privileges as women challenge the status quo.

As earlier chapters noted, the social-conflict approach draws heavily on the ideas of Karl Marx. Yet as far as gender is concerned, Marx was a product of his time, and his writings focused almost entirely on men. However, his friend and collaborator Friedrich Engels did develop a theory of gender stratification.

Gender and Class Inequality

Looking back through history, Engels saw that in hunting and gathering societies, the activities of women and men, although different,

had equal importance. A successful hunt brought men great prestige, but the vegetation gathered by women provided most of a group's food supply. As technological advances led to a productive surplus, however, social equality and communal sharing gave way to private property and ultimately a class hierarchy, and men gained significant power over women. With surplus wealth to pass on to heirs, upper-class men needed to be sure their sons were their own, which led them to control the sexuality of women. The desire to control property brought about monogamous marriage and the family. Women were taught to remain virgins until marriage, to remain faithful to their husbands thereafter, and to build their lives around bearing and raising one man's children.

According to Engels (1902, orig. 1884), capitalism makes male domination even stronger. First, capitalism creates more wealth, which gives greater power to men as income earners and owners of property. Second, an expanding capitalist economy depends on turning people, especially women, into consumers who seek personal fulfillment through buying and using products. Third, society assigns women the task of maintaining the home to free men to work in factories. The double exploitation of capitalism, as Engels saw it, lies in paying men low wages for their labor and paying women no wages at all.

CRITICAL REVIEW Social-conflict analysis is critical of conventional ideas about gender, claiming that society would be better off if we minimized or even did away with this dimension of social structure. That is, this approach regards conventional families, which traditionalists consider personally and socially positive, as a social evil. A problem with social-conflict analysis, then, is that it minimizes the extent to which women and men live together cooperatively and often happily in families. A second problem lies in the assertion that capitalism is the basis of gender stratification. In fact, agrarian societies are typically more patriarchal than industrial-capitalist societies. Although socialist nations, including the People's Republic of China and the former Soviet Union, did move women into the workforce, by and large they provided women with very low pay in sex-segregated jobs (Rosendahl, 1997; Haney, 2002).

CHECK YOUR LEARNING According to Friedrich Engels, how does gender support social inequality in a capitalist class system?

Feminism

Feminism is *support of social equality for women and men, in opposition to patriarchy and sexism.* The first wave of feminism in the United States began in the 1840s as women opposed to slavery, including Elizabeth Cady Stanton and Lucretia Mott, drew parallels between

Q: "It is very little for me to have the right to vote, to own property, et cetera, if I may not keep my body, and its uses, in my absolute right." Lucy Stone (1855)

Q: "Anyone who knows anything about history knows that great social changes are impossible without the feminine ferment." Karl Marx

SOCIAL SURVEY: "Being born a man or a woman—how important is that for getting ahead in life?" (GSS 1987, N = 1,285; Codebook, 2005:1432)

"Essential"   2.7%   "Not very important"   32.8%
"Very important"   11.4%   "Not important at all"   26.5%
"Fairly important"   22.7%   "Don't know"/No response 3.9%

Q: "Everything Fred Astaire did, Ginger Rogers did backwards and in high heels." Bob Thaves

SEEING SOCIOLOGY
in Everyday Life

On your campus, do men's organizations (such as fraternities and athletic teams) enjoy any special privileges? What about women's organizations?

the oppression of African Americans and the oppression of women. Their main objective was obtaining the right to vote, which was finally achieved in 1920. But other disadvantages persisted, causing a second wave of feminism to arise in the 1960s that continues today.

Basic Feminist Ideas

Feminism views the personal experiences of women and men through the lens of gender. How we think of ourselves (gender identity), how we act (gender roles), and our sex's social standing (gender stratification) are all rooted in the operation of society.

Although feminists disagree about many things, most support five general principles:

1. **Working to increase equality**. Feminist thinking is political; it links ideas to action. Feminism is critical of the status quo, pushing for change toward social equality for women and men.

2. **Expanding human choice**. Feminists argue that cultural conceptions of gender divide the full range of human qualities into two opposing and limiting spheres: the female world of emotions and cooperation and the male world of rationality and competition. As an alternative, feminists propose a "reintegration of humanity" by which all individuals can develop all human traits (M. French, 1985).

3. **Eliminating gender stratification**. Feminism opposes laws and cultural norms that limit the education, income, and job opportunities of women. For this reason, feminists have long supported passage of the Equal Rights Amendment (ERA) to the U.S. Constitution, which states, in its entirety, "Equality of rights under the law shall not be denied or abridged by the United States or any State on account of sex." The ERA was first proposed in Congress in 1923. Although it has widespread support, it has yet to become law.

4. **Ending sexual violence**. Today's women's movement seeks to eliminate sexual violence. Feminists argue that patriarchy distorts the relationships between women and men, encouraging violence against women in the form of rape, domestic abuse, sexual harassment, and pornography (A. Dworkin, 1987; Freedman, 2002).

5. **Promoting sexual freedom**. Finally, feminism supports women's control over their sexuality and reproduction. Feminists support the free availability of birth control information. As Figure 13–3 shows, sixty-eight percent of married women of childbearing age in the United States use contraception; the use of contraceptives is far less common in many lower-income nations. Most feminists also support a woman's right to choose whether to bear children or end a pregnancy, rather than allowing men—husbands, physicians, and legislators—to

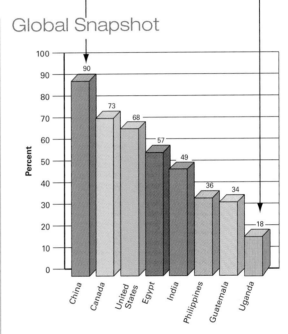

Achen Eke, age 24 and mother of three, lives in Uganda, where most women do not have access to contraception.

Chen-chi Bai, age 31 and the mother of one boy, lives in China, where contraception is encouraged and widely practiced.

Global Snapshot

FIGURE 13–3 **Use of Contraception by Married Women of Childbearing Age**

In the United States, most married women of childbearing age use contraception. In many lower-income countries, however, most women do not have the opportunity to make this choice.

Source: Population Reference Bureau (2009).

control their reproduction. Many feminists also support gay people's efforts to end prejudice and discrimination in a largely heterosexual culture (Ferree & Hess, 1995; Armstrong, 2002).

Types of Feminism

Although feminists agree on the importance of gender equality, they disagree on how to achieve it: through liberal feminism, socialist feminism, or radical feminism (Stacey, 1983; L. Vogel, 1983; Ferree & Hess, 1995; Armstrong, 2002; Freedman, 2002). The Applying Theory table on page 348 highlights the key arguments made by each type of feminist thinking.

Liberal Feminism

Liberal feminism is rooted in the classic liberal thinking that individuals should be free to develop their own talents and pursue their own

Q: "The early socialists often argued that problems associated with gender strat-ification would simply disappear under socialism. The leadership in socialist coun-tries still gives lip service to the ideal of gender equality and includes it among its long-term goals." Charlotte O'Kelly and Larry Carney

NOTE: Socialist feminists also oppose the family because living in isolated units discourages the solidarity that leads to collective action by women and men.

SOCIAL SURVEY: "If the husband in a family wants children, but the wife decides that she does not want any children, is it all right for the wife to refuse to have chil-dren?" (GSS 1996, N = 755; Codebook, 2005:318)

"Yes" 76.3%   "No" 16.3%   "Don't know"/No response 7.4%

NOTE: Radical feminism dovetails with the "children's rights" movement that aspires to free children from dependence on adults.

● MAKING THE GRADE

Feminism is one type of social-conflict approach to understanding gender.

● MAKING THE GRADE

The three types of feminism all agree on the importance of gender and the need to make women and men more socially equal. They disagree on the way to do that, with liberal femi-nism involving the least societal change and radical feminism involving the most.

● APPLYING THEORY ●

Feminism

	Liberal Feminism	Socialist Feminism	Radical Feminism
Does it accept the basic order of society?	Yes. Liberal feminism seeks change only to ensure equality of opportunity.	No. Socialist feminism supports an end to social classes and to family gender roles that encourage "domestic slavery."	No. Radical feminism supports an end to the family system.
How do women improve their social standing?	Individually, according to personal ability and effort.	Collectively, through socialist revolution.	Collectively, by working to eliminate gender itself.

interests. Liberal feminism accepts the basic organization of our society but seeks to expand the rights and opportunities of women, in part through passage of the Equal Rights Amendment. Liberal feminists also support reproductive freedom for all women. They respect the family as a social institution but seek changes, including more widely available maternity and paternity leave and child care for parents who work.

Given their belief in the rights of individuals, liberal feminists think that women should advance according to their own efforts, rather than working collectively for change. Both women and men, through their individual achievement, are capable of improving their lives, as long as society removes legal and cultural barriers.

Socialist Feminism

Socialist feminism evolved from the ideas of Karl Marx and Friedrich Engels. From this point of view, capitalism strengthens patriarchy by concentrating wealth and power in the hands of a small number of men. Socialist feminists do not think the reforms supported by liberal feminism go far enough. The family form created by capitalism must change if we are to replace "domestic slavery" with some collective means of carrying out housework and child care. Replacing the tra-ditional family can come about only through a socialist revolution that creates a state-centered economy to meet the needs of all.

Radical Feminism

Like socialist feminism, *radical feminism* finds liberal feminism inad-equate. Radical feminists believe that patriarchy is so deeply rooted in society that even a socialist revolution would not end it. Instead, reach-ing the goal of gender equality means that society must eliminate gender itself.

One possible way to achieve this goal is to use new reproduc-tive technology (see Chapter 18, "Families") to separate women's bodies from the process of childbearing. With an end to mother-hood, radical feminists reason, society could leave behind the entire family system, liberating women, men, and children from the oppres-sion of family, gender, and sex itself (A. Dworkin, 1987). Radical fem-inism seeks an egalitarian and gender-free society, a revolution more sweeping than that sought by Marx.

Opposition to Feminism

Because feminism calls for significant change, it has always been con-troversial. But today, just 20 percent of U.S. adults say they oppose fem-inism, a share that has declined over time (NORC, 2007). Figure 13–4 shows a similar downward trend in opposition to feminism among col-lege students after 1970. Note, however, that there has been little change in attitudes in recent years and that more men than women express antifeminist attitudes.

Feminism provokes criticism and resistance from both men and women who hold conventional ideas about gender. Some men oppose sexual equality for the same reason that many white people have his-torically opposed social equality for people of color: They do not want to give up their privileges. Other men and women, including those who are neither rich nor powerful, distrust a social movement (espe-cially its radical expressions) that attacks the traditional family and rejects patterns that have guided male-female relations for centuries.

Men who have been socialized to value strength and dominance may feel uneasy about the feminist ideal of men as gentle and warm (Doyle, 1983). Similarly, some women whose lives center on their husbands and children may think that feminism does not value the social roles that give meaning to their lives. In general, resistance to feminism is strongest among women who have the least education and those who do not work outside the home (Marshall, 1985; Ferree & Hess, 1995; CBS News, 2005).

SOCIAL SURVEY: "How important is the women's rights issue to you?" (GSS 1996, N = 1,460; Codebook, 2005:278)

"One of the most important"   11.2%   "Not important at all"   9.9%
"Important"   52.1%   "Don't know"/No response   1.8%
"Not very important"   25.1%

Q: "Gender is what gender means. It has no basis in anything other than the social reality its hegemony constructs." Catharine MacKinnon

Q: "We hold these truths to be self-evident: that all men and women are created equal; that they are endowed by their Creator with certain unalienable rights." Declaration of Sentiments, Seneca Falls, New York (1848)

Q: "I don't like a strident woman." Margaret Thatcher

SEEING SOCIOLOGY
in Everyday Life

Do you think women should get ahead through individual effort or by collective action? Explain.

Race and ethnicity play some part in shaping people's attitudes toward feminism. In general, African Americans (especially African American women) express the greatest support of feminist goals, followed by whites, with Hispanic Americans holding somewhat more traditional attitudes regarding gender (Kane, 2000).

Resistance to feminism is also found in academic circles. Some sociologists charge that feminism ignores a growing body of evidence that men and women do think and act in somewhat different ways, which may make complete gender equality impossible. Furthermore, say critics, with its drive to increase women's presence in the workplace, feminism undervalues the crucial and unique contribution women make to the development of children, especially in the first years of life (Baydar & Brooks-Gunn, 1991; Popenoe, 1993b; Gibbs, 2001).

Finally, there is the question of *how* women should go about improving their social standing. A large majority of U.S. adults believe that women should have equal rights, but 70 percent also say that women should advance individually, according to their abilities; only 10 percent favor women's rights groups or collective action (NORC, 2007: 430).

For these reasons, most opposition to feminism is directed toward its socialist and radical forms, while support for liberal feminism is widespread. In addition, there is an unmistakable trend toward greater gender equality. In 1977, some 65 percent of all adults endorsed the statement "It is much better for everyone involved if the man is the achiever outside the home and the woman takes care of the home and family." By 2006, the share supporting this statement had dropped sharply, to 36 percent (NORC, 2007:321).

Student Snapshot

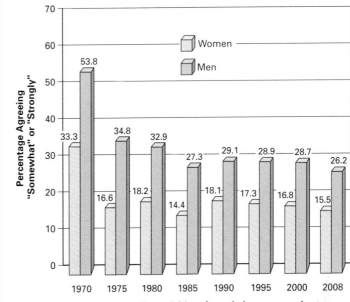

Statement: "The activities of married women are best confined to the home and family."

FIGURE 13–4   **Opposition to Feminism among First-Year College Students, 1970–2008**

The share of college students expressing antifeminist views declined after 1970. Men are still more likely than women to hold such attitudes.

Sources: Astin et al. (2002) and Pryor et al. (2008).

Gender: Looking Ahead

Predictions about the future are no more than educated guesses. Just as economists disagree about what the employment rate will be a year from now, sociologists can offer only general observations about the likely future of gender and society.

Change so far has been remarkable. A century ago, women were second-class citizens, without access to many jobs, barred from political office, and with no right to vote. Although women remain socially disadvantaged, the movement toward equality has surged ahead. Two-thirds of people entering the workforce during the 1990s were women, and in 2000, for the first time, a majority of U.S. families had both husband and wife in the paid labor force. Today's economy depends a great deal on the earnings of women.

Many factors have contributed to this transformation. Perhaps most important, industrialization and recent advances in computer technology have shifted the nature of work from physically demanding tasks that favor male strength to jobs that require thought and imagination. This change puts women and men on an even footing. Also, because birth control technology has given us greater control over reproduction, women's lives are less constrained by unwanted pregnancies.

Many women and men have also deliberately pursued social equality. For example, complaints of sexual harassment in the workplace are now taken much more seriously than they were a generation ago. As more women assume positions of power in the corporate and political worlds, social changes in the twenty-first century may be as great as those that have already taken place.

Seeing Sociology in Everyday Life

Chapter 13 Gender Stratification

Can you spot "gender messages" in the world around you?

As this chapter makes clear, gender is one of the basic organizing principles of everyday life. Most of the places we go and most of the activities we engage in as part of our daily routines are "gendered," meaning that they are defined as either more masculine or more feminine. Understanding this fact, corporations keep gender in mind when they market products to the public. Take a look at the ads below. In each case, can you explain how gender is at work in selling these products?

> **HINT** Looking for "gender messages" in ads is a process that involves several levels of analysis. Start on the surface by noting everything obvious in the ad, including the setting, the background, and especially the people. Then notice how the people are shown—what they are doing, how they are situated, their facial expressions, how they are dressed, and how they appear to relate to each other. Finally, state what you think is the message of the ad, based on both the ad itself and also what you know about the surrounding society.

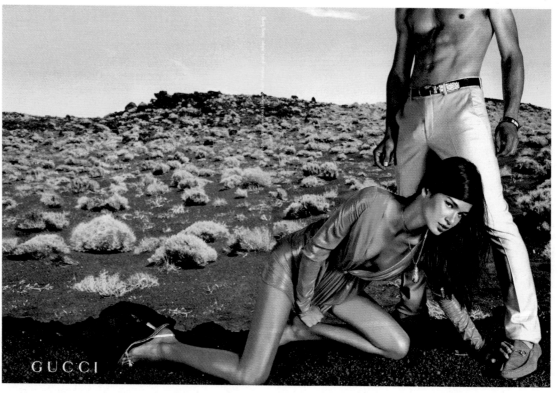

There are a lot of gender dynamics going on in this ad. What do you see?

Generally, our society defines cosmetics as feminine because most cosmetics are marketed toward women. How and why is this ad different?

What gender messages do you see in this ad?

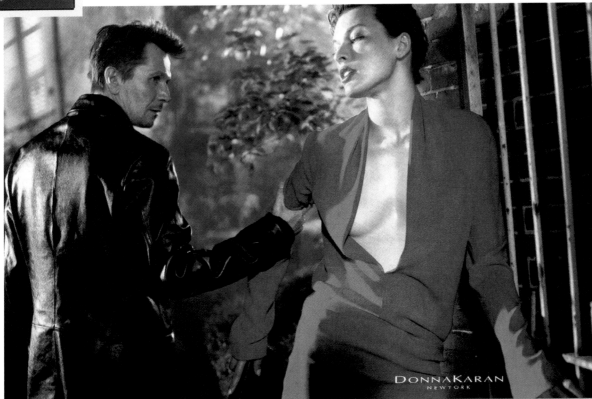

Applying SOCIOLOGY in Everyday Life

1. Look through some recent magazines and select three advertisements that involve gender. In each case, provide analysis of how gender is used in the ad.

2. Watch several hours of children's television programming on a Saturday morning. Notice the advertising, which mostly sells toys and breakfast cereal. Keep track of what share of toys are "gendered," that is, aimed at one sex or the other. What traits do you associate with toys intended for boys and those intended for girls?

3. Do some research on the history of women's issues in your state. When was the first woman sent to Congress? What laws once existed that restricted the work women could do? Do any such laws exist today? Did your state support the passage of the Equal Rights Amendment or not? What share of political officials today are women?

MAKING THE GRADE

CHAPTER 13 Gender Stratification

Gender and Inequality

GENDER refers to the meaning a culture attaches to being female or male.

- Evidence that gender is rooted in culture includes global comparisons by Margaret Mead and others showing how societies define what is feminine and masculine in various ways.
- Gender is not only about difference: Because societies give more power and other resources to men than to women, gender is an important dimension of social stratification. **Sexism** is built into the operation of social institutions.
- Although some degree of **patriarchy** is found almost everywhere, it varies throughout history and from society to society.

pp. 328–32

gender (p. 328) the personal traits and social positions that members of a society attach to being female or male

gender stratification (p. 328) the unequal distribution of wealth, power, and privilege between men and women

matriarchy (p. 330) a form of social organization in which females dominate males

patriarchy (p. 330) a form of social organization in which males dominate females

sexism (p. 330) the belief that one sex is innately superior to the other

Gender and Socialization

Through the socialization process, gender becomes part of our personalities (**gender identity**) and our actions (**gender roles**). All the major agents of socialization—family, peer groups, schools, and the mass media—reinforce cultural definitions of what is feminine and masculine.

pp. 332–33

gender roles (sex roles) (p. 332) attitudes and activities that a society links to each sex

Gender and Social Stratification

Gender stratification shapes **THE WORKPLACE**:

- A majority of women are now in the paid labor force, but 40% hold clerical or service jobs.
- Comparing full-time U.S. workers, women earn 78% as much as men.
- This gender difference in earnings results from differences in jobs, differences in family responsibilities, and discrimination.

pp. 334–37

Gender stratification shapes **FAMILY LIFE**:

- Most unpaid housework is performed by women, whether or not they hold jobs outside the home.
- Pregnancy and raising small children keep many women out of the labor force at a time when their male peers are making important career gains.

p. 337

Gender stratification shapes **EDUCATION**:

- Women now earn 59% of all associate's and bachelor's degrees.
- Women make up 47% of law school students and are an increasing share of graduates in professions traditionally dominated by men, including medicine and business administration.

pp. 337–38

minority (p. 339) any category of people distinguished by physical or cultural difference that a society sets apart and subordinates

intersection theory (p. 339) analysis of the interplay of race, class, and gender, often resulting in multiple dimensions of disadvantage

sexual harassment (p. 342) comments, gestures, or physical contacts of a sexual nature that are deliberate, repeated, and unwelcome

Gender stratification shapes **POLITICS**:

- Until a century ago, almost no women held any elected office in the United States.
- In recent decades, the number of women in politics has increased significantly.
- Even so, the vast majority of elected officials, especially at the national level, are men.
- Women make up only about 14% of U.S. military personnel.

pp. 338–39

INTERSECTION THEORY investigates the factors of race, class, and gender, which combine to cause special disadvantages for some categories of people.

- Women of color encounter greater social disadvantages than white women and earn much less than white men.
- Because all women have a distinctive social identity and are disadvantaged, they are a minority, although most white women do not think of themselves this way.

pp. 339–40

VIOLENCE AGAINST WOMEN AND MEN is a widespread problem that is linked to how a society defines gender. Related issues include

- **sexual harassment**, which mostly victimizes women because our culture encourages men to be assertive and to see women in sexual terms.
- **pornography**, which portrays women as sexual objects. Many see pornography as a moral issue; because pornography dehumanizes women, it is also a power issue.

pp. 340–43

Theoretical Analysis of Gender

The STRUCTURAL-FUNCTIONAL APPROACH suggests that

- in preindustrial societies, distinctive roles for males and females reflect biological differences between the sexes.
- in industrial societies, marked gender inequality becomes dysfunctional and gradually decreases.

Talcott Parsons described gender differences in terms of complementary roles that promote the social integration of families and society as a whole.

`pp. 343–45`

The SYMBOLIC-INTERACTION APPROACH suggests that

- individuals use gender as one element of their personal performances as they socially construct reality through everyday interactions.
- gender plays a part in shaping almost all our everyday experiences.

Because our society defines men as having more value than women, the sex roles that define how women and men should behave place men in control of social situations; women play a more deferential role.

`p. 345`

The SOCIAL-CONFLICT APPROACH suggests that

- gender is an important dimension of social inequality and social conflict.
- gender inequality benefits men and disadvantages women.

Friedrich Engels tied gender stratification to the rise of private property and a class hierarchy. Marriage and the family are strategies by which men control their property through control of the sexuality of women. Capitalism exploits everyone by paying men low wages and assigning women the task of maintaining the home.

`pp. 345–46`

See the Applying Theory table on page 344.

Feminism

FEMINISM

- endorses the social equality of women and men and opposes patriarchy and sexism.
- seeks to eliminate violence against women.
- advocates giving women control over their reproduction.

There are three types of feminism:

- Liberal feminism seeks equal opportunity for both sexes within the existing society.
- Socialist feminism claims that gender equality will come about by replacing capitalism with socialism.
- Radical feminism seeks to eliminate the concept of gender itself and to create an egalitarian and gender-free society.

Today, only 20% of U.S. adults say they oppose feminism. Most opposition is directed toward socialist and radical feminism. Support for liberal feminism is widespread.

`pp. 346–49`

feminism (p. 346) support of social equality for women and men, in opposition to patriarchy and sexism

See the Applying Theory table on page 348.

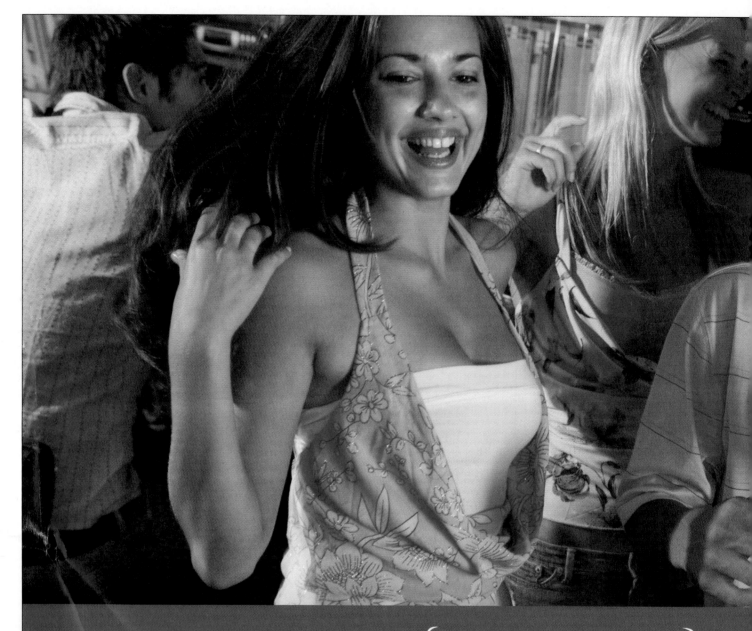

Ours is among the most racially and ethnically diverse of all societies. Racial and ethnic differences reflect people's traditional heritage and are a source of pride. At the same time, they are also an important foundation of social stratification.

CHAPTER 14

354

Race and Ethnicity

Q: "The world is now too small for anything but brotherhood." Arthur Powell Davies

GLOBAL: Of the world's 194 nations, 90% are ethnically heterogeneous. Among high-income countries, the U.S. is the most heterogeneous, and Japan stands out as the most homogeneous.

Q: "After all, there is but one race—humanity." George Moore

NOTE: *Race* is derived from the Latin, meaning "root"; *ethnic* is derived from the Greek, meaning "culture" or "people"; *minority* has a Latin root meaning "smaller" or "lesser."

GLOBAL: Morocco is a country with a high level of racial mix: African, European, and Middle Eastern. Brazil has a highly varied population descended from all parts of the world.

CHAPTER OVERVIEW { This chapter explains how race and ethnicity are created by society. Both race and ethnicity are not only matters of difference but also dimensions of social inequality.

On a cool November morning in New York City, the instructor of a sociology class at Bronx Community College is leading a small-group discussion of race and ethnicity. He explains that the meaning of both concepts is far less clear than most people think. Then he asks, "How do you describe yourself?"

Eva Rodriguez leans forward in her chair and is quick to respond. "Who am I? Or should I say what am I? This is hard for me to answer. Most people think of race as black and white. But it's not. I have both black and white ancestry in me, but you know what? I don't think of myself in that way. I don't think of myself in terms of race at all. It would be better to call me Puerto Rican or Hispanic. Personally, I prefer the term 'Latina.' Calling myself Latina says I have a mixed racial heritage, and that's what I am. I wish more people understood that race is not clear-cut."

This chapter examines the meaning of race and ethnicity. There are now millions of people in the United States who, like Eva Rodriguez, do not think of themselves in terms of a single category but as having a mix of ancestry.

The Social Meaning of Race and Ethnicity

As the opening to this chapter suggests, people frequently confuse race and ethnicity. For this reason, we begin with some definitions.

Race

A **race** is *a socially constructed category of people who share biologically transmitted traits that members of a society consider important.* People may classify one another racially based on physical characteristics such as skin color, facial features, hair texture, and body shape.

Racial diversity appeared among our human ancestors as the result of living in different geographic regions of the world. In regions of intense heat, for example, humans developed darker skin (from the natural pigment melanin) as protection from the sun; in regions with moderate climates, people have lighter skin. Such differences are literally only skin deep because human beings the world over are members of a single biological species.

The striking variety of physical traits found today is also the product of migration; genetic characteristics once common to a single place (such as light skin or curly hair) are now found in many lands. Especially pronounced is the racial mix in the Middle East (that is, western Asia), historically a crossroads of migration. Greater physical uniformity characterizes more isolated people, such as the island-dwelling Japanese. But every population has some genetic mixture, and increasing contact among the world's people ensures even more blending of physical characteristics in the future.

Although we think of race in terms of biological elements, race is a socially constructed concept. It is true that human beings differ in any number of ways involving physical traits, but a "race" comes into being only when the members of a society decide that some physical trait (such as skin color or eye shape) actually *matters.*

Because race is a matter of social definitions, it is a highly variable concept. For example, the members of U.S. society consider racial differences more important than people of many other countries. We also tend to "see" three racial categories—typically, black, white, and Asian—while people in other societies identify many more categories. People in Brazil, for example, distinguish between *branca* (white), *parda* (brown), *morena* (brunette), *mulata* (mulatto), *preta* (black), and *amarela* (yellow) (Inciardi, Surratt, & Telles, 2000).

In addition, race may be defined differently by various categories of people within a society. In the United States, for example, research shows that white people "see" black people as having darker skin than black people do (Hill, 2002).

The meanings and importance of race not only differ from place to place but also change over time. Back in 1900, for example, it was common in the United States to consider people of Irish, Italian, or

SEEING SOCIOLOGY
in Everyday Life

race a socially constructed category of people who share biologically transmitted traits that members of a society consider important

ethnicity (p. 358) a shared cultural heritage

Researchers have found that biracial and multiracial people choose different racial identities in different settings, depending on whom they are with (Harris & Sim, 2002). Have you ever experienced such a "racial shift"? Explain.

The range of biological variation in human beings is far greater than any system of racial classification allows. This fact is made obvious by trying to place all of the people pictured here into simple racial categories.

Jewish ancestry as "nonwhite." By 1950, however, this was no longer the case, and such people today are considered part of the "white" category (Loveman, 1999; Brodkin, 2007).

Today, the Census Bureau allows people to describe themselves using more than one racial category (offering six single-race options and fifty-seven multiracial options). Our society officially recognizes a wide range of multiracial people (U.S. Census Bureau, 2008).

Racial Types

Scientists invented the concept of "race" more than a century ago as they tried to organize the world's physical diversity into three racial types. They called people with relatively light skin and fine hair *Caucasoid*, people with darker skin and coarse hair *Negroid*, and people with yellow or brown skin and distinctive folds on the eyelids *Mongoloid*.

Sociologists consider such terms misleading at best and harmful at worst. For one thing, no society contains biologically "pure" people. The skin color of people we might call "Caucasoid" (or "Indo-European," "Caucasian," or more commonly, "white") ranges from very light (typical in Scandinavia) to very dark (in southern India). The same variation exists among so-called "Negroids" ("Africans" or more commonly, "black" people) and "Mongoloids" ("Asians"). In

fact, many "white" people (say, in southern India) actually have darker skin than many "black" people (the Aborigines of Australia). Overall, the three racial categories differ in just 6 percent of their genes, and there is actually more genetic variation *within* each category than *between* categories. This means that two people in the European nation of Sweden, randomly selected, are likely to have at least as much genetic difference as a Swede and a person in the African nation of Senegal (Harris & Sim, 2002; American Sociological Association, 2003; California Newsreel, 2003).

So how important is race? From a biological point of view, knowing people's racial category allows us to predict almost nothing about them. Why, then, do societies make so much of race? Such categories allow societies to rank people in a hierarchy, giving some people more money, power, and prestige than others and allowing some people to feel that they are inherently "better" than others. Because race may matter so much, societies may construct racial categories in extreme ways. Throughout much of the twentieth century, for example, many southern states labeled as "colored" anyone with as little as one thirty-second African ancestry (that is, one African American great-great-great-grandparent). Today, the law allows parents to declare the race of a child (or not) as they wish. Even so, most members of U.S. society are still very sensitive to people's racial backgrounds.

DISCUSS: Ask students what share of the U.S. population is in each major category identified in Table 14–1. Research shows that most people vastly overestimate the proportions. Discuss the results of the exercise with the class.

APPLIED: Check the advertising in any popular magazine, and note the share of ads that show people of two or more racial categories interacting. Do you think your results reflect social reality?

DISCUSS: Does "American" represent an ethnic identity?

GLOBAL: People the world over differ not only in skin color but also in height. The Masai of eastern Africa are tall and thin (which helps dissipate heat in that equatorial climate); the Eskimos and Aleuts of North America, by contrast, are short and stout, which serves to protect them in a far colder habitat.

SEEING SOCIOLOGY
in Everyday Life

Do you think all U.S. people of color, rich and poor alike, should be considered minorities? Why or why not?

minority any category of people distinguished by physical or cultural difference that a society sets apart and subordinates

prejudice (p. 360) a rigid and unfair generalization about an entire category of people

stereotype (p. 360) a simplified description applied to every person in some category

Table 14–1 Racial and Ethnic Categories in the United States, 2007

Racial or Ethnic Classification*	Approximate U.S. Population	Share of Total Population
Hispanic descent	**45,427,437**	**15.1%**
Mexican	29,166,981	9.7
Puerto Rican	4,120,205	1.4
Cuban	1,611,478	0.5
Other Hispanic	10,528,773	3.5
African descent	**38,756,452**	**12.8**
Nigerian	225,284	0.1
Ethiopian	159,809	0.1
Somalian	90,363	<
Other African	38,280,996	12.7
Native American descent	**2,365,347**	**0.8**
American Indian	1,922,043	0.6
Alaska Native Tribes	110,556	<
Other Native American	332,748	0.1
Asian or Pacific Island descent	**13,667,962**	**4.4**
Chinese	3,045,592	1.0
Asian Indian	2,570,166	0.9
Filipino	2,412,446	0.8
Vietnamese	1,508,489	0.5
Korean	1,344,171	0.4
Japanese	803,092	0.3
Cambodian	218,624	0.1
Other Asian or Pacific Islander	1,765,382	0.6
West Indian descent	**2,231,842**	**0.7**
Arab descent	**1,545,982**	**0.5**
Non-Hispanic European descent	**198,696,006**	**65.9**
German	50,756,529	16.8
Irish	36,495,800	12.1
English	28,178,670	9.3
Italian	17,849,848	5.9
Polish	9,976,358	3.3
French	9,616,662	3.2
Scottish	6,019,281	2.0
Dutch	5,071,425	1.7
Norwegian	4,655,711	1.5
Two or more races	**6,509,013**	**2.2**

*People of Hispanic descent may be of any race. Many people also identify with more than one ethnic category. Therefore, figures total more than 100 percent.
< indicates less than 1/10 of 1 percent.
Source: U.S. Census Bureau (2008).

A Trend toward Mixture

Over many generations and throughout the Americas, the genetic traits from around the world have become mixed. Many "black" people have a significant Caucasoid ancestry, just as many "white" people have some Negroid genes. Whatever people may think, race is not a black-and-white issue.

Today, people are more willing to define themselves as multiracial. On the most recent (2007) U.S. Census survey, almost 7 million people described themselves by checking two or more racial categories. And the official number of interracial births has tripled over the past twenty years to about 175,000 annually, almost 4 percent of all births.

Living in a multiracial family surely encourages people to think about the meaning of race. Seeing Sociology in the News on pages 360–61 provides one example.

Ethnicity

Ethnicity is *a shared cultural heritage*. People define themselves—or others—as members of an *ethnic category* based on common ancestry, language, or religion that gives them a distinctive social identity. The United States is a multiethnic society. Even though we favor the English language, more than 56 million people (20 percent of the U.S. population) speak Spanish, Italian, German, French, Chinese, or some other language in their homes. In California, about 45 percent of the population does so (U.S. Census Bureau, 2008).

With regard to religion, the United States is a predominantly Protestant nation, but most people of Spanish, Italian, and Polish descent are Roman Catholic, and many of Greek, Ukrainian, and Russian descent belong to the Eastern Orthodox church. More than 6 million Jewish Americans have ancestral ties to various nations around the world. The population of Muslim men and women is rapidly increasing and is generally estimated at between 2 and 3 million (Pew Research Center, 2007b).

Like race, the concept of "ethnicity" is socially constructed, becoming important only because society defines it that way. For example, U.S. society defines people of Spanish descent as "Latin," even though Italy probably has a more "Latin" culture than Spain. People of Italian descent are not viewed as Latin but as "European" and therefore less different (Camara, 2000; Brodkin, 2007). Like racial differences, the importance of ethnic differences can change over time. A century ago, Catholics and Jews were considered "different" in the mostly Protestant United States. This is much less true today.

Keep in mind that *race* is constructed from *biological* traits and *ethnicity* is constructed from *cultural* traits. However, the two often go hand in hand. For example, Japanese Americans have distinctive physical traits and, for those who hold to a traditional way of life, a

Marcos Chapa attends college in San Diego and lives in a community where most people are in some minority category.

Marianne Blumquist attends a community college in a small town an hour west of Minneapolis, where there are few racial or ethnic minorities.

● SEEING SOCIOLOGY in Everyday Life

Do you see stereotypes in common phrases such as "French kiss," "Dutch treat," "Indian giver," or being "gypped" (a reference to Gypsies)? Explain.

Seeing Ourselves

NATIONAL MAP 14–1
Where the Minority Majority Already Exists

Minorities are now in the majority in four states—Hawaii, California, New Mexico, and Texas—and the District of Columbia. At the other extreme, Vermont and Maine have the lowest share of racial and ethnic minorities (about 5 percent each). Why do you think states with high minority populations are located in the South and Southwest?

Source: U.S. Census Bureau (2008).

Percentage of Total Population Consisting of African Americans, Hispanics, Asians, Pacific Islanders, or Native Americans

- 50% or higher
- 40% to 49%
- 30% to 39%
- 20% to 29%
- 10% to 19%
- 9% or lower

distinctive culture as well. Table 14–1 presents the most recent data on the racial and ethnic diversity of the United States.

On an individual level, people play up or play down cultural traits, depending on whether they want to fit in or stand apart from the surrounding society. Immigrants may drop their cultural traditions or, like many people of Native American descent in recent years, try to revive their heritage. For most people, ethnicity is more complex than race because they identify with several ethnic backgrounds. The golf star Tiger Woods describes himself as one-eighth American Indian, one-fourth Thai, and one-fourth Chinese, as well as one-eighth white and one-fourth black (J. E. White, 1997).

Minorities

March 3, Dallas, Texas. The lobby of just about any hotel in a major U.S. city presents a lesson in contrasts: The majority of the guests checking in are white; the majority of hotel employees who carry luggage, serve food, and clean the rooms are racial or ethnic minorities.

As defined in Chapter 13 ("Gender Stratification"), a **minority** is *any category of people distinguished by physical or cultural difference that a society sets apart and subordinates.* Minority standing can be based on race, ethnicity, or both. As shown in Table 14–1, nonHispanic white people (66 percent of the total) are still a majority of the U.S. population. But the share of minorities is increasing. Today, minorities are a majority in four states (California, New Mexico, Texas, and Hawaii) and in sixteen of the country's 100 largest cities. By about 2050, minorities are likely to form a majority of the entire U.S. population. National Map 14–1 shows where a minority majority already exists.

Minorities have two important characteristics. First, they share a *distinctive identity,* which may be based on physical or cultural traits. Second, minorities experience *subordination.* As the rest of this chapter shows, U.S. minorities typically have lower income, lower occupational prestige, and limited schooling. These facts mean that class, race, and ethnicity, as well as gender, are overlapping and reinforcing dimensions of social stratification. The Thinking About Diversity box on page 362 profiles the struggles of recent Latin American immigrants.

Of course, not all members of any minority category are disadvantaged. Some Latinos are quite wealthy, certain Chinese Americans are celebrated business leaders, and African Americans are among our nation's political leaders. But even job success rarely allows individuals to escape their minority standing. As described in Chapter 6 ("Social Interaction in Everyday Life"), race or ethnicity often serves as a *master status* that overshadows personal accomplishments.

Minorities usually make up a small proportion of a society's population, but this is not always the case. Black South Africans are disadvantaged even though they are a numerical majority in their country. In the United States, women represent slightly more than half the population but are still struggling for all the opportunities and privileges enjoyed by men.

Prejudice and Stereotypes

November 19, Jerusalem, Israel. We are driving along the outskirts of this historical city—a holy place to Jews, Christians, and Muslims—when Razi, our taxi driver, spots a small group of Falasha—Ethiopian Jews—on a street corner. "Those people over there," he points as he

NOTE: *Prejudice* is derived from Latin words for "prejudgment."

DISCUSS: Do you think a sociologist has to be a member of a minority category to study that category? That is, do Hispanics have a special claim to study Hispanics, women to study women, and so on? Explain your position.

DIVERSITY: Among people over 35 years of age, 27% are racial or Hispanic minorities; among those under 35, 42% are. Thus young people will reach a minority-majority first (before 2050), and older people will remain mostly white. Similarly, during the 21st century, central cities will become minority-majority settings, and suburbs will remain mostly white.

Seeing SOCIOLOGY in the NEWS

Newsweek

Beyond Just Black and White: Why I Was So Eager to Claim My Biracial Son for My Own Side

By RAINA KELLEY
February 2, 2009

When I took my newly born son from the nurse's arms, I did the expected counting of his fingers and toes. I checked under his cap for hair and flexed his little limbs. Once confident he was whole and healthy, I began to wonder how dark his skin would get. As a black woman married to one of the world's fairest men, I worried that our son would be so light-skinned as to appear Caucasian, and I wanted him to look black. After we all came home from the hospital this past June, I Googled newborn eye color to reassure myself that Gabriel's eyes wouldn't change from my shade of brown to my husband's green. I brushed up on my genetics, and though I discovered that curly hair is a dominant trait, Gabe has straight brown locks that stick up in a cowlick just like his dad's—not the wild curls I struggle to keep under control. Undaunted by these failures to find Gabe's blackness, I inspected my son's skin daily

for the Mongolian spots common in African-American babies, but his skin was as smooth as . . . alabaster.

It was time to face facts. One day, I would be an old black lady hanging on the arm of a young white man who passersby would think was an obliging stranger but who was actually my offspring. It didn't help that everywhere my new nuclear family went, we were told that our son was the picture of his father, and, well, he is. So I began to wonder, if it's never much bothered me that I'm a different color from my husband, why was I as rigid as a Klan member when it came to identifying my son's race from birth?

It never occurred to me then that if people thought my son was white, it might make life easier on him. Obviously, I was not interested in logic. I just wanted to claim Gabriel for "my" side—in league with his mother against small minds, casual racism and discrimination. So even though Gabe still appeared Caucasian, I grew more obsessive in my racial cataloging. I'd ask my spouse embarrass-

ingly leading questions: "Do you think you have a black son?" "Is it weird having a black kid?" "Would it be strange for you if Gabe became the second African-American president?" To his credit, he tried to answer in good faith until a particularly brutal interrogation when I heard him jokingly mutter to Gabe that "Mommy's racist against us white people." It sounded absurd to hear Gabe described as white even though I myself had been saying things like "I hope he darkens up" and "He looks Dutch." Clearly, I had become so eager for my son to be black that I was tiptoeing across the line from mildly offensive to racist. . . . Can you imagine the reverse scenario? Gabe born dark-skinned and my husband saying, "I hope he gets whiter"?

But by his third month, Gabe's skin tone began to darken and my hormones leveled off; I can now report that, seven months after his birth, Gabriel is the exact shade you'd get if you mixed his father and me up in a paint can—a color I call golden. This has made me realize that I want Gabe to be

---

speaks, "they are different. They don't drive cars. They don't want to improve themselves. Even when our country offers them schooling, they don't take it." He shakes his head at the Ethiopians and drives on.

Prejudice is *a rigid and unfair generalization about an entire category of people.* Prejudice is unfair because *all* people in some category are described as the same, based on little or no direct evidence. Prejudice may target people of a particular social class, sex, sexual orientation, age, political affiliation, physical disability, race, or ethnicity.

Prejudices are *prejudgments* that can be either positive or negative. Our positive prejudices tend to exaggerate the virtues of people like ourselves, and our negative prejudices condemn those who differ from us. Negative prejudice can be expressed as anything from mild dislike to outright hostility. Because such attitudes are rooted in culture, everyone has at least some prejudice.

Prejudice often takes the form of a **stereotype** (*stereo* is derived from a Greek word meaning "solid"), *a simplified description applied to every person in some category.* Many white people hold stereotypical views of minorities. Stereotyping is especially harmful to minorities in the workplace. If company officials see workers only in terms of a stereotype, they will make assumptions about their abilities, steering them toward certain jobs and limiting their access to better opportunities (R. L. Kaufman, 2002).

Minorities, too, stereotype whites and other minorities (T. W. Smith, 1996; Cummings & Lambert, 1997). Surveys show, for example,

that more African Americans than whites express the belief that Asians engage in unfair business practices and that more Asians than whites criticize Hispanics for having too many children (Perlmutter, 2002).

Measuring Prejudice: The Social Distance Scale

One measure of prejudice is *social distance,* how closely people are willing to interact with members of some category. In the 1920s, Emory Bogardus developed the *social distance scale* shown in Figure 14–1 on page 363. Bogardus (1925) asked students at U.S. colleges and universities to look at this scale and indicate how closely they were willing to interact with people in thirty racial and ethnic categories. People express the greatest social distance (most negative prejudice) by declaring that a particular category of people should be barred from the country entirely (point 7); at the other extreme, people express the least social distance (most social acceptance) by saying they would accept members of a particular category into their family through marriage (point 1).

Bogardus (1925, 1967; Owen, Elsner, & McFaul, 1977) found that people felt much more social distance from some categories than from others. In general, students in his surveys expressed the most social distance from Hispanics, African Americans, Asians, and Turks, indicating that they would be willing to tolerate such people as co-workers but not as neighbors, friends, or family members. Students expressed the least social distance from those from northern and western Europe, including English and Scottish people, and also Canadians, indicating that they were willing to include them in their families by marriage.

proud of his entire heritage. Why does my son have to bear the legacy of a one-drop rule that is the direct intellectual descendant of slavery and Jim Crow? The very concept, that even the small-est amount of black blood in your ancestry makes you African-American, harks back to the early 20th century when states including Texas and Vir-ginia passed laws to protect the "purity" of the white race. Is this really a concept that needs to be perpetuated? . . .

For Gabriel's sake, I'm going to try to stop play-ing the black-vs.-white game, since my son is actually neither white nor black. He's biracial, and there are hundreds of thousands of little golden children out there just like him. One of them even grew up to be president of the United States. The latest U.S. Census numbers indicate that there are [almost 7] million biracial Americans. . . .

New mothers being insecure, I've now begun to wonder whether my constant harping about skin tone warped my infant son for life. Did I already doom him to rebel against my dichotomous racial regime, reject his blackness altogether and move to the Netherlands, the land of his father's people? Or maybe he'll grow up to look upon his father as the Man, his mother as a race traitor, and move to Namibia to start a new black-separatist movement? Or maybe he'll just be himself, because when you juxtapose Obama's comments about society with the reality of his election, isn't the real secret of American freedom that we don't have to accept the roles that society assigns us? Our newly elected president ignored the racial stereotyping that seemed to limit what he could accomplish in this country—and he didn't do it by passively accepting society's assessment of his skin tone. Perhaps as the number of multiracial Americans continues to grow, there will be a plurality of golden people who are impossible to positively identify as one race or the other. And the rest of us who can be easily cat-egorized will be forced to accept that color does not contribute to the content of one's character because we won't know which set of stereotypes to apply to whom. I want my son to grow up wearing his biracial heritage like an invisibility cloak, able to move unseen among people's prejudices—imper-vious to racial profiling. But I will prepare him for a world that may think he is black or white, even though he is golden.

WHAT DO YOU THINK?

1. When her son was born, did this mother make too much of trying to determine his race? Why or why not?

2. How is thinking about race a special challenge for mixed-race couples? Explain.

3. Do you think that as he goes through life, Gabe will decide to be one race at some times and another race at others? Explain.

What patterns of social distance do we find among college stu-dents today? A recent study using the same social distance scale reported three major findings (Parrillo & Donoghue, 2005):[1]

1. **Student opinion shows a trend toward greater social accept-ance.** Today's students express less social distance from all minorities than students did several decades ago. Figure 14–1 shows that the mean (average) score on the social distance scale declined from 2.14 in 1925 to 1.93 in 1977 and 1.44 in 2001. Respondents (81 percent of whom were white) showed notably greater acceptance of African Americans, a category that moved up from near the bottom in 1925 to the top one-third in 2001.

2. **People see less difference between various minorities.** The earliest studies found the difference between the highest- and lowest-ranked minorities (the range of averages) equal to almost three points on the scale. As the figure shows, the most recent research produced a range of averages of less than one point, indicating that today's students see fewer differences between various categories of people.

3. **The terrorist attacks of September 11, 2001, may have reduced social acceptance of Arabs and Muslims.** The most recent study was conducted just a few weeks after September 11, 2001. Perhaps the fact that the nineteen men who attacked the World Trade Cen-ter and the Pentagon were Arabs and Muslims is part of the reason that students ranked these categories last on the social distance scale. However, not a single student gave Arabs or Muslims a 7, indicating that they should be barred from the country. On the contrary, the 2001 mean scores (1.94 for Arabs and 1.88 for Mus-lims) show higher social acceptance than students in 1977 expressed toward eighteen of the thirty categories of people studied.

Racism

A powerful and harmful form of prejudice, **racism** is *the belief that one racial category is innately superior or inferior to another.* Racism has existed throughout world history. Despite their many achievements, the ancient Greeks, the peoples of India, and the Chinese all regarded people unlike themselves as inferior.

Racism has also been widespread throughout the history of the United States, where ideas about racial inferiority supported slavery. Today, overt racism in this country has decreased because more people believe in evaluating others, in Martin Luther King Jr.'s words, "not by the color of their skin but by the content of their character."

Even so, racism remains a serious social problem, as some peo-ple think that certain racial and ethnic categories are smarter than

[1] Parrillo and Donoghue dropped seven of the categories used by Bogardus (Armenians, Czechs, Finns, Norwegians, Scots, Swedes, and Turks), claiming they were no longer vis-ible minorities. They added nine new categories (Africans, Arabs, Cubans, Dominicans, Haitians, Jamaicans, Muslims, Puerto Ricans, and Vietnamese), claiming that these are visible minorities today. This change probably encouraged higher social distance scores, making the trend toward decreasing social distance all the more significant.

DIVERSITY: European stereotypes: Heaven is a place where the police are British, the cooks are French, the mechanics are German, the lovers are Italian, and the whole thing is organized by the Swiss. Hell is a place where the cooks are British, the mechanics are French, the lovers are Swiss, the police are German, and the whole thing is organized by the Italians.

NOTE: A century ago, people believed that race (and biology in general) directly affected human behavior; early anthropology and sociology were central in dispelling this view.

Q: "Race is not biologically definable; we are far too similar." Kenneth Kidd, Yale University geneticist

racism (p. 361) the belief that one racial category is innately superior or inferior to another

scapegoat a person or category of people, typically with little power, whom people unfairly blame for their own troubles

SEEING SOCIOLOGY
in Everyday Life

Do you think students on your campus have become more accepting of social diversity? Explain why or why not.

THINKING ABOUT DIVERSITY: RACE, CLASS, & GENDER

Hard Work: The Immigrant Life in the United States

Early in the morning, it is already hot on the streets of Houston as a line of pickup trucks snakes slowly into a dusty yard, where 200 laborers have been gathering since dawn, each hoping for a day's work. The driver of the first truck opens his window and tells the foreman that he is looking for a crew to spread boiling tar on a roof. Abdonel Cespedes, the foreman, turns to the crowd, and after a few minutes, three workers step forward and climb into the back of the truck. The next driver is looking for two experienced housepainters. The scene is repeated over and over as men and a few women leave to dig ditches, spread cement, hang drywall, open clogged septic tanks, or crawl under houses to poison rats.

As each driver pulls into the yard, the foreman asks, "How much?" Most offer $5 an hour. Cespedes automatically responds, "$7.25; the going rate is $7.25 for an hour's hard work." Sometimes he convinces them to pay that much, but usually not. The workers, who come from Mexico, El Salvador, and Guatemala, know that dozens of them will end up with no work at all this day. Most accept $5 or $6 an hour because they know that when the day is over, $50 is better than nothing.

Labor markets like this one are common in large cities, especially across the southwestern United States. The surge in immigration in recent years

has brought millions of people to this country in search of work, and most have little schooling and speak little English.

Manuel Barrera has taken a day's work moving the entire contents of a store to a storage site. He arrives at the boarded-up building and gazes at the mountains of heavy furniture that he must carry out to a moving van, drive across town, and then carry again. He sighs when he thinks about how hot it is outside and realizes that it is even hotter inside the building. He will have no break for lunch. No one says anything about toilets. Barrera shakes his head: "I will do this kind of work because it puts food on the table. But I did not foresee it would turn out like this."

These immigrants gather on a New York City street corner every morning hoping to be hired for construction work that pays about $60 a day with no benefits.

The hard truth is that immigrants to the United States do the jobs that no one else wants. At the bottom level of the national economy, they perform low-skill jobs in restaurants and hotels and on construction crews, and they work in private homes cooking, cleaning, and caring for children. Across the United States, about half of all housekeepers, household cooks, tailors, and restaurant waiters are men or women born abroad. Few immigrants make much more than the official minimum wage ($7.25 in 2009), and rarely do immigrant workers receive any health or pension benefits. Many well-off families take the labor of immigrants as much for granted as their air-conditioned cars and comfortable homes.

WHAT DO YOU THINK?

1. In what ways do you or members of your family depend on the low-paid labor of immigrants?

2. Do you favor allowing the 12 million people who entered this country illegally to earn citizenship? What should be done?

3. Should the U.S. government act to reduce the number of immigrants entering this country in the future? Why or why not?

Sources: Booth (1998), Tumulty (2006), and U.S. Department of Labor (2008a).

others. As the Seeing Sociology in Everyday Life box on page 364 explains, however, racial differences in mental abilities result from environment rather than biology.

Theories of Prejudice

Where does prejudice come from? Social scientists provide several answers to this question, focusing on frustration, personality, culture, and social conflict.

Scapegoat Theory

Scapegoat theory holds that prejudice springs from frustration among people who are themselves disadvantaged (Dollard et al., 1939). For instance, take the case of a white woman who is frustrated by the low pay she receives from her assembly-line job in a textile factory. Directing hostility at the powerful factory owners carries the obvious risk of being fired; therefore, she may blame her low pay on the presence of minority co-workers. Her prejudice does not improve her situation, but it is a relatively safe way to express anger, and it

Student Snapshot

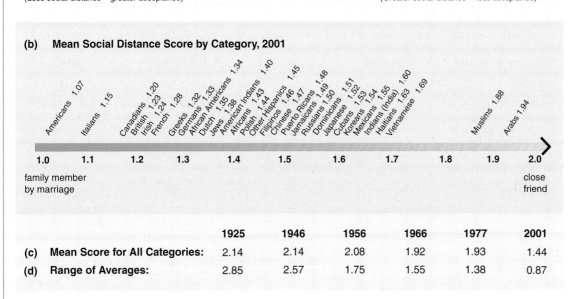

(a) Social Distance Scale

I would accept a [minority category] as a . . .

1	2	3	4	5	6	7
family member by marriage.	close friend.	neighbor.	co-worker.	speaking acquaintance.	visitor to my country.	I would bar from my country.

(Less social distance = greater acceptance)   *(Greater social distance = less acceptance)*

(b) Mean Social Distance Score by Category, 2001

Americans 1.07 · Italians 1.15 · Canadians 1.20 · British 1.23 · Irish 1.24 · French 1.28 · Greeks 1.32 · Germans 1.33 · African Americans 1.34 · Dutch 1.35 · Jews 1.38 · American Indians 1.40 · Africans 1.43 · Polish 1.44 · Other Hispanics 1.45 · Filipinos 1.46 · Chinese 1.47 · Puerto Ricans 1.48 · Jamaicans 1.49 · Russians 1.50 · Dominicans 1.51 · Japanese 1.52 · Cubans 1.53 · Koreans 1.54 · Mexicans 1.55 · Indians (India) 1.60 · Haitians 1.63 · Vietnamese 1.69 · Muslims 1.88 · Arabs 1.94

1.0	1.1	1.2	1.3	1.4	1.5	1.6	1.7	1.8	1.9	2.0

family member by marriage   close friend

		1925	1946	1956	1966	1977	2001
(c)	Mean Score for All Categories:	2.14	2.14	2.08	1.92	1.93	1.44
(d)	Range of Averages:	2.85	2.57	1.75	1.55	1.38	0.87

FIGURE 14–1 **Bogardus Social Distance Research**

The social distance scale is a good way to measure prejudice. Part (a) illustrates the complete social distance scale, from least social distance at the far left to greatest social distance at the far right. Part (b) shows the mean (average) social distance score received by each category of people in 2001. Part (c) presents the overall mean score (the average of the scores received by all racial and ethnic categories) in specific years. These scores have fallen from 2.14 in 1925 to 1.44 in 2001, showing that students express less social distance toward minorities today than they did in the past. Part (d) shows the range of averages, the difference between the highest and lowest scores in given years (in 2001, for instance, it was 0.87, the difference between the high score of 1.94 for Arabs and the low score of 1.07 for Americans). This figure has also become smaller since 1925, indicating that today's students tend to see fewer differences between various categories of people.

Source: Parrillo & Donoghue (2005).

may give her the comforting feeling that at least she is superior to someone.

A **scapegoat,** then, is *a person or category of people, typically with little power, whom people unfairly blame for their own troubles.* Because they have little power and thus are usually "safe targets," minorities often are used as scapegoats.

Authoritarian Personality Theory

Theodor Adorno and colleagues (1950) considered extreme prejudice a personality trait of certain individuals. This conclusion is supported by research showing that people who show strong prejudice toward one minority are usually intolerant of all minorities. These *authoritarian personalities* rigidly conform to conventional cultural

MAKING THE GRADE

The box links differences in intelligence between categories of people to culture, not biology. The point is that such differences are not genetic, and culture matters in the types of human achievement that figure into intelligence.

SEEING SOCIOLOGY IN EVERYDAY LIFE

Does Race Affect Intelligence?

As we go through an average day, we encounter people of various racial and ethnic categories. We also deal with people who are very intelligent as well as those whose abilities are more modest. Is there a connection between race or ethnicity and intelligence?

Common stereotypes say there is. Many people believe that Asian Americans are smarter than white people and that the typical white person is more intelligent than the average African American. These stereotypes are not new. Throughout the history of the United States, many people have assumed that some categories of people are smarter than others. Just as important, people have used this thinking to justify privileges for the allegedly superior category and even to bar supposedly inferior people from entering this country.

So what do we know about intelligence? We know that people, as individuals, differ in mental abilities. The distribution of human intelligence forms a "bell curve," as shown in the figure. A person's *intelligence quotient* (IQ) is calculated as the person's mental age in years, as measured by a test, divided by the person's actual age in years, with the result multiplied by 100. An eight-year-old who performs like a ten-year-old has an IQ of $10 \div 8 = 1.25 \times 100 = 125$. Average performance yields an IQ of 100.

In a controversial study of intelligence and social inequality, Richard Herrnstein and Charles Murray (1994) claimed that race was related to measures of intelligence. They said that the average IQ for people with European ancestry was 100; for people with East Asian ancestry, 103; and for people with African ancestry, 90.

Such assertions go against our democratic and egalitarian beliefs that no racial type is naturally better than another. Because these findings can increase prejudice, critics charge that

intelligence tests are not valid and even that the concept of intelligence has little real meaning.

Most social scientists believe that IQ tests do measure something important that we think of as intelligence, and they agree that *individuals* vary in intellectual aptitude. But they reject the idea that any *category* of people, on average, is naturally or biologically smarter than any other. So how do we explain the overall differences in IQ scores by race?

Thomas Sowell (1994, 1995) explains that most of this difference results not from biology but from environment. In some skillful sociological detective work, Sowell traced IQ scores for various racial and ethnic categories throughout the twentieth century. He found that on average, early-twentieth-century immigrants from European nations such as Poland, Lithuania, Italy, and Greece, as well as from Asian countries including China and Japan, scored 10 to 15 points below the U.S. average. But by the end of the twentieth century, people in these same categories had IQ scores that were average or above average. Among Italian Americans, for example, average IQ jumped almost 10 points; among Polish and Chinese Americans, the increase was almost 20 points.

Because genetic changes occur over thousands of years and most people in these categories marry others like themselves, biological factors cannot explain such a rapid rise in IQ scores. The only reasonable explanation is changing cultural patterns. The descendants of early immigrants improved their intellectual performance as their standard of living rose and their opportunity for schooling increased.

Sowell found that much the same was true of African Americans. Historically, the average IQ score of African Americans living in the North has been about 10 points higher than the average score of those living in the South. Among the descendants of African Americans who migrated from the South to the North after 1940, IQ scores went up, just as they did with descendants of European and Asian immigrants. Thus environmental factors appear to be critical in explaining differences in IQ among various categories of people.

According to Sowell, these test score differences tell us that *cultural patterns matter*. Asians who score high on tests are no smarter than other people, but they have been raised to value learning and pursue excellence. African Americans are no less intelligent than anyone else, but they carry a legacy of disadvantage that can undermine self-confidence and discourage achievement.

WHAT DO YOU THINK?

1. If IQ scores reflect people's environment, are they valid measures of intelligence? Could they be harmful?

2. According to Thomas Sowell, why do some racial and ethnic categories show dramatic short-term gains in average IQ scores?

3. Do you think parents and schools influence a child's IQ score? If so, how?

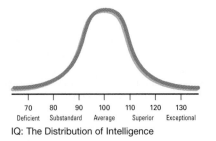

| 70 | 80 | 90 | 100 | 110 | 120 | 130 |
| Deficient | Substandard | Average | | Superior | | Exceptional |

IQ: The Distribution of Intelligence

values and see moral issues as clear-cut matters of right and wrong. People with authoritarian personalities also view society as naturally competitive and hierarchical, with "better" people (like themselves) inevitably dominating those who are weaker (all minorities).

Adorno and his colleagues also found the opposite pattern to be true: People who express tolerance toward one minority are likely to be accepting of all. They tend to be more flexible in their moral judgments and treat all people as equals.

prejudice (p. 360) a rigid and unfair generalization about an entire category of people

discrimination unequal treatment of various categories of people

institutional prejudice and discrimination bias built into the operation of society's institutions

MAKING THE GRADE

The importance of institutional prejudice and discrimination can be summed up like this: Prejudice and discrimination are found in individuals but are rooted in society itself.

Adorno thought that people with little schooling and those raised by cold and demanding parents tend to develop authoritarian personalities. Filled with anger and anxiety as children, they grow into hostile, aggressive adults who seek out scapegoats.

Culture Theory

A third theory claims that although extreme prejudice may be found in some people, some prejudice is found in everyone. Why? Because prejudice is part of the culture in which we all live and learn. The Bogardus social distance studies help prove the point. Bogardus found that students across the country had much the same attitudes toward specific racial and ethnic categories, feeling closer to some and more distant from others.

More evidence that prejudice is rooted in culture is the fact that minorities express the same attitudes as white people toward categories other than their own. Such patterns suggest that individuals hold prejudices because we live in a "culture of prejudice" that has taught us all to view certain categories of people as "better" or "worse" than others.

Conflict Theory

A fourth explanation proposes that prejudice is used as a tool by powerful people to oppress others. Anglos who look down on Latino immigrants in the Southwest, for example, can get away with paying the immigrants low wages for hard work. Similarly, all elites benefit when prejudice divides workers along racial and ethnic lines and discourages them from working together to advance their common interests (Geschwender, 1978; Olzak, 1989; Rothenberg, 2008).

According to another conflict-based argument, made by Shelby Steele (1990), minorities themselves encourage *race consciousness* to win greater power and privileges. Because of their historical disadvantage, minorities claim that they are victims entitled to special consideration based on their race. This strategy may bring short-term gains, but Steele cautions that such thinking often sparks a backlash from whites or others who oppose "special treatment" on the basis of race or ethnicity.

Discrimination

Closely related to prejudice is **discrimination,** *unequal treatment of various categories of people. Prejudice* refers to *attitudes,* but *discrimination* is a matter of *action.* Like prejudice, discrimination can be either positive (providing special advantages) or negative (creating obstacles) and ranges from subtle to extreme.

Institutional Prejudice and Discrimination

We typically think of prejudice and discrimination as the hateful ideas or actions of specific people. But Stokely Carmichael and Charles Hamil-

ton (1967) pointed out that far greater harm results from **institutional prejudice and discrimination,** *bias built into the operation of society's institutions,* including schools, hospitals, the police, and the workplace. For example, researchers have found that banks reject home mortgage applications from minorities at a higher rate than those from white people, even when income and quality of neighborhood are held constant (Gotham, 1998; Blanton, 2007).

According to Carmichael and Hamilton, people are slow to condemn or even recognize institutional prejudice and discrimination because it often involves respected public officials and long-established traditions. A case in point is *Brown* v. *Board of Education of Topeka,* the 1954 Supreme Court decision that ended the legal segregation of schools. The principle of "separate but equal" schooling had been the law of the land, supporting racial inequality by allowing school segregation. Despite this change in the law, half a century later, most U.S. students still attend schools in which one race overwhelmingly predominates (KewalRamani et al., 2007). In 1991, the courts pointed

Recent research measuring student attitudes confirms the trend of declining prejudice toward all racial and ethnic categories. On your campus, does race or ethnicity guide people's choice in romantic attachments? Do some racial and ethnic categories mix more often than others? Explain your answer.

Patterns of Majority and Minority Interaction

pluralism a state in which people of all races and ethnicities are distinct but have equal social standing

assimilation the process by which minorities gradually adopt patterns of the dominant culture

segregation the physical and social separation of categories of people

genocide the systematic killing of one category of people by another

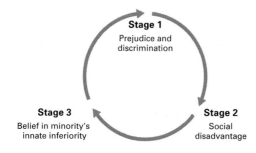

Stage 1
Prejudice and discrimination

Stage 3
Belief in minority's innate inferiority

Stage 2
Social disadvantage

Stage 1: Prejudice and discrimination begin, often as an expression of ethnocentrism or an attempt to justify economic exploitation.

Stage 2: As a result of prejudice and discrimination, a minority is socially disadvantaged, occupying a low position in the system of social stratification.

Stage 3: This social disadvantage is then interpreted not as the result of earlier prejudice and discrimination but as evidence that the minority is innately inferior, unleashing renewed prejudice and discrimination by which the cycle repeats itself.

FIGURE 14–2   Prejudice and Discrimination: The Vicious Circle
Prejudice and discrimination can form a vicious circle, perpetuating themselves.

out that neighborhood schools will never provide equal education as long as our population is segregated, with most African Americans living in central cities and most white people and Asian Americans living in suburbs.

Prejudice and Discrimination: The Vicious Circle

Prejudice and discrimination reinforce each other. The Thomas theorem, discussed in Chapter 6 ("Social Interaction in Everyday Life"), offers a simple explanation of this fact: *Situations that are defined as real become real in their consequences* (W. I. Thomas, 1966:301, orig. 1931).

As Thomas recognized, stereotypes become real to people who believe them and sometimes even to those who are victimized by them. Prejudice on the part of white people toward people of color does not produce *innate* inferiority, but it can produce *social* inferiority, pushing minorities into low-paying jobs, inferior schools, and racially segregated housing. Then, as white people interpret that social disadvantage as evidence that minorities do not measure up, they unleash a new round of prejudice and discrimination, giving rise to a vicious circle in which each perpetuates the other, as shown in Figure 14–2.

Majority and Minority: Patterns of Interaction

Sociologists describe patterns of interaction among racial and ethnic categories in a society in terms of four models: pluralism, assimilation, segregation, and genocide.

Pluralism

Pluralism is *a state in which people of all races and ethnicities are distinct but have equal social standing.* In other words, people who differ in appearance or social heritage all share resources roughly equally.

The United States is pluralistic to the extent that all people have equal standing under the law. In addition, large cities contain countless "ethnic villages," where people proudly display the traditions of their immigrant ancestors. These include New York's Spanish Harlem, Little Italy, and Chinatown; Philadelphia's Italian "South Philly"; Chicago's Little Saigon; and Latino East Los Angeles. New York City alone has more than 300 magazines, newspapers, and radio stations that publish in more than ninety languages (Logan, Alba, & Zhang, 2002; *Many Voices,* 2008; U.S. Department of Homeland Security, 2008b).

But the United States is not truly pluralistic, for three reasons. First, although most people value their cultural heritage, few want to live exclusively with others exactly like themselves (NORC, 2007). Second, our tolerance of social diversity goes only so far. One reaction to the rising number of U.S. minorities is a social movement to make English the nation's official language. Third, as you will see later in this chapter, people of various colors and cultures do *not* have equal social standing.

Assimilation

Many people think of the United States as a "melting pot" in which different nationalities blend together. But rather than everyone "melting" into some new cultural pattern, most minorities have adopted the dominant culture established by our earliest settlers. Why? Because doing so is both the path to upward social mobility and a way to escape the prejudice and discrimination directed at more visible foreigners. Sociologists use the term **assimilation** to describe *the process by which minorities gradually adopt patterns of the dominant culture.* Assimilation can involve changing modes of dress, values, religion, language, and friends.

The amount of assimilation varies by category. For example, Canadians have "melted" more than Cubans, the Dutch more than Dominicans, Germans more than the Japanese. Multiculturalists oppose making assimilation a goal because it suggests that minorities are a problem and the ones who need to do all the changing.

Note that assimilation involves changes in ethnicity but not in race. For example, many descendants of Japanese immigrants discard their ethnic traditions but retain their racial identity. For racial traits

DISCUSS: Discrimination always involves making distinctions; the question is which kinds of distinctions are deemed fair and just and which are viewed as unfair and wrong. Is a college wrong to admit students with better grades over those with lower grades?

POP CULTURE: The process of assimilation is shown in the 2004 film *Spanglish*, about the cultural changes experienced by a Mexican woman and her daughter who immigrated to the U.S. to work for an upper-class white family.

GLOBAL: In global perspective, Switzerland is a good example of pluralism. In this European nation of 7 million people, German, French, and Italian cultural traditions run deep. Swiss pluralism (albeit involving little difference in color) is based on officially recognizing all three ethnic languages and the fact that the three categories have roughly the same economic standing.

miscegenation biological reproduction by partners of different racial categories

to diminish over generations, **miscegenation,** or *biological reproduction by partners of different racial categories,* must occur. Although interracial marriage is becoming more common, it still amounts to only 4 percent of all U.S. marriages (U.S. Census Bureau, 2008).

Segregation

Segregation is *the physical and social separation of categories of people.* Some minorities, especially religious orders like the Amish, voluntarily segregate themselves. However, majorities usually segregate minorities by excluding them. Residential neighborhoods, schools, occupations, hospitals, and even cemeteries may be segregated. Pluralism encourages distinctiveness without disadvantage, but segregation enforces separation that harms a minority.

Racial segregation has a long history in the United States, beginning with slavery and evolving into racially separated housing, schools, buses, and trains. Court decisions such as the 1954 *Brown* case have reduced *de jure* (Latin, "by law") discrimination in this country. However, *de facto* ("in actual fact") segregation continues in the form of countless neighborhoods that are home to people of a single race.

Despite some recent decline, segregation persists in the United States. For example, Livonia, Michigan, is 91 percent white, and neighboring Detroit is 83 percent African American. Kurt Metzger (2001) explains, "Livonia was pretty much created by white flight [from Detroit]." Further, research shows that across the country, whites (especially those with young children) avoid neighborhoods where African Americans live (Emerson, Yancey, & Chai, 2001; Krysan, 2002). At the extreme, Douglas Massey and Nancy Denton (1989) document the *hypersegregation* of poor African Americans in some inner cities. Hypersegregation means having little contact of any kind with people outside the local community. Hypersegregation is the daily experience of about 20 percent of poor African Americans and is a pattern found in about twenty-five large U.S. cities (Wilkes & Iceland, 2004).

Genocide

Genocide is *the systematic killing of one category of people by another.* This deadly form of racism and ethnocentrism violates nearly every recognized moral standard, yet it has occurred time and again in human history.

Genocide was common in the history of contact between Europeans and the original inhabitants of the Americas. From the sixteenth century on, the Spanish, Portuguese, English, French, and Dutch forcibly colonized vast empires. Although most native people died from diseases brought by Europeans, against which they had no natural defenses, many who opposed the colonizers were killed deliberately (Matthiessen, 1984; Sale, 1990).

Genocide also occurred during the twentieth century. During World War I, at least 1 million Armenians in Eastern Europe per-

Should we expect people who come to the United States to change their language and other cultural patterns in order to "fit in," or should we expect them to hold onto their own traditions? Why?

ished under the rule of the Ottoman Empire. Soon after that, European Jews experienced a reign of terror known as the Holocaust during Adolf Hitler's rule in Germany. From about 1935 to 1945, the Nazis murdered more than 6 million Jewish men, women, and children, along with gay people, Gypsies, and people with handicaps. During the same period, the Soviet dictator Josef Stalin murdered on an even greater scale, killing perhaps 30 million real and imagined enemies during decades of violent rule. Between 1975 and 1980, Pol Pot's Communist regime in Cambodia butchered all "capitalists," a category that included anyone able to speak a Western language. In all, some 2 million people (one-fourth of the population) perished in the Cambodian "killing fields."

Tragically, genocide continues in the modern world. Recent examples include Hutus killing Tutsis in the African nation of Rwanda, Serbs killing Bosnians in the Balkans of Eastern Europe, and the killing of hundreds of thousands of people in the Darfur region of Sudan in Africa.

These four patterns of minority-majority interaction have all been played out in the United States. Although many people proudly point to patterns of pluralism and assimilation, it is also important to recognize the degree to which U.S. society has been built on segregation (of African Americans) and genocide (of Native Americans). The remainder of this chapter examines how these four patterns have shaped the history and present social standing of major racial and ethnic categories in the United States.

POP CULTURE: A notable case of genocide is featured in the 2004 film *Hotel Rwanda*. As shown in the film, thousands of Tutsis were killed by the Hutu militia in Rwanda.

RESOURCE: The author's companion reader *Seeing Ourselves*, 8th ed., includes "Out of Harmony: Health Problems and Young Native American Men" by Jennie R. Joe.

NOTE: In perhaps the most tragic eviction of American Indians from their land, thousands of Cherokees died on a forced march—the Trail of Tears—from their homes in the southeastern U.S. to reservations in Indian Territory, later Oklahoma, in 1838 and 1839.

● SEEING SOCIOLOGY
in Everyday Life

In your city or town, are there minority neighborhoods? Which categories of people live there? To what degree is your community racially or ethnically segregated?

In an effort to force assimilation, the U.S. Bureau of Indian Affairs took American Indian children from their families and placed them in boarding schools like this one, Oklahoma's Riverside Indian School. There they were taught to speak English by non-Indian teachers with the goal of making them into "Americans."

Race and Ethnicity in the United States

Give me your tired, your poor,
Your huddled masses yearning to breathe free,
The wretched refuse of your teeming shore,
Send these, the homeless, tempest-tossed to me:
I lift my lamp beside the golden door.

These words by Emma Lazarus, inscribed on the Statue of Liberty, express cultural ideals of human dignity, personal freedom, and economic opportunity. The United States has provided more of the "good life" to more immigrants than any other nation. About 1.5 million immigrants come to this country every year, and their many ways of life create a social mosaic that is especially evident in large cities with many distinctive racial and ethnic neighborhoods.

However, as a survey of this country's racial and ethnic minorities will show, our country's golden door has opened more widely for some than for others. We turn next to the history and current social standing of the major categories of the U.S. population.

Native Americans

The term "Native Americans" refers to the hundreds of societies—including the Aztec, Inca, Aleuts, Cherokee, Zuni, Sioux, and Mohawk—that first settled the Western Hemisphere. Some 30,000 years before Christopher Columbus landed in the Americas in 1492, migrating peoples crossed a land bridge from Asia to North America where the Bering Strait (off the coast of Alaska) lies today. Gradually, they spread throughout North and South America.

When the first Europeans arrived late in the fifteenth century, Native Americans numbered in the millions. But by 1900, after centuries of conflict and even acts of genocide, the "vanishing Americans" numbered just 250,000 (Dobyns, 1966; Tyler, 1973). The land they controlled also shrank dramatically, as National Map 14–2 shows.

Columbus first referred to Native Americans that he encountered as "Indians" because he mistakenly thought he had reached the coast of India. Columbus found the native people passive and peaceful, in stark contrast to the materialistic and competitive Europeans. Yet Europeans justified the seizure of Native American land by calling their victims thieves and murderers (Josephy, 1982; Matthiessen, 1984; Sale, 1990).

After the Revolutionary War, the new U.S. government took a pluralistic approach to Native American societies, seeking to gain more land through treaties. Payment for the land was far from fair, however, and when Native Americans resisted the surrender of their homelands, the U.S. government simply used its superior military power to evict them. By the early 1800s, few Native Americans remained east of the Mississippi River.

In 1871, the United States declared Native Americans wards of the government and adopted a strategy of forced assimilation. Relocated to specific territories designated as "reservations," Native Americans continued to lose their land and were well on their way to losing their culture as well. Reservation life encouraged dependency, replacing ancestral languages with English and traditional religion with Christianity. Officials of the Bureau of Indian Affairs took children from their parents and put them in boarding schools, where they were resocialized as "Americans." Authorities gave local control of reservation life to the few Native Americans who supported government policies, and they distributed reservation land, traditionally held collectively, as private property to individual families (Tyler, 1973).

Not until 1924 were Native Americans entitled to U.S. citizenship. After that, many migrated from reservations, adopting mainstream cultural patterns and marrying non–Native Americans. Today, almost half of Native Americans consider themselves biracial or multiracial (U. S. Census Bureau, 2008), and many large cities now contain sizable Native American populations. However, as Table 14–2 shows, Native American income is far below the U.S. average, and relatively few Native Americans earn a college degree.[2]

SEEING SOCIOLOGY
in Everyday Life

People tend to think about race and ethnicity when they deal with categories of people whom they think of as "other." WASPs have race and ethnicity, too, of course, but U.S. society does not construct these into a minority identity.

SEEING SOCIOLOGY
in Everyday Life

In what ways does being a WASP (or simply being white) confer privilege on people?

Seeing Ourselves

NATIONAL MAP 14–2

Land Controlled by Native Americans, 1790 to Today

In 1790, Native Americans controlled three-fourths of the land (blue-shaded areas) that eventually became the United States. Today, Native Americans control 304 reservations, scattered across the United States, that account for just 2 percent of the country's land area. How would you characterize these locations?

Source: Published in *The New York Times* on March 18, 1998. Copyright © 1998 by The New York Times Company. All rights reserved. Used by permission and protected by the copyright laws of the United States. The printing, copying, redistribution, or retransmission of this material without express written permission is prohibited.

1790

1850

1880

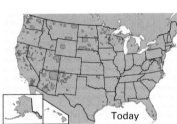
Today

From in-depth interviews with Native Americans in a western city, Joan Albon (1971) linked low Native American social standing to a range of cultural factors, including a noncompetitive view of life and a reluctance to pursue higher education. In addition, she noted, many Native Americans have dark skin, which makes them targets of prejudice and discrimination.

Members of more than 200 American Indian nations today are reclaiming pride in their cultural heritage. Traditional cultural organizations report a surge in new membership applications, and many children can speak native languages better than their parents. The legal right of Native Americans to govern their reservations has enabled some tribes to build profitable gaming casinos. But the wealth produced from gambling has enriched relatively few Native peoples, and most profits go to non-Indian investors (Bartlett & Steele, 2002). While some prosper, most Native Americans remain severely disadvantaged and share a profound sense of the injustice they have suffered at the hands of white people.

White Anglo-Saxon Protestants

White Anglo-Saxon Protestants (WASPs) were not the first people to inhabit the United States, but they soon dominated after European settlement began. Most WASPs are of English ancestry, but the category also includes people from Scotland and Wales. With some 36 million

people claiming English, Scottish, or Welsh ancestry, 12 percent of our society has some WASP background, and WASPs are found at all class levels (U.S. Census Bureau, 2008).

Many people associate WASPs with elite communities along the East and West Coasts. But the highest concentrations of WASPs are in Utah (because of migrations of Mormons with English ancestry), Appalachia, and northern New England (also due to historical patterns of immigration).

Looking back in time, WASP immigrants were highly skilled and motivated to achieve by what we now call the Protestant work ethic. Because of their high social standing, WASPs were not subject to the prejudice and discrimination experienced by other categories of immigrants. In fact, the historical dominance of WASPs has led others to want to become more like them (K. W. Jones, 2001).

WASPs were never one single group; especially in colonial times, considerable hostility separated English Anglicans and Scottish Presbyterians (Parrillo, 1994). But in the nineteenth century, most WASPs joined together to oppose the arrival of "undesirables" such as Germans in the 1840s and Italians in the 1880s. Those who could afford

---

[2]In making comparisons of education and especially income, keep in mind that various categories of the U.S. population have different median ages. In 2007, the median age for all U.S. people was 36.6 years; for Native Americans, the figure was 32.1 years. Because people's schooling and income increase over time, this age difference accounts for some of the disparities seen in Table 14–2.

Table 14–2   The Social Standing of Native Americans, 2007

	Native Americans	Entire U.S. Population
Median family income	$40,310	$61,355
Percentage in poverty	21.4%	12.5%
Completion of four or more years of college (age 25 and over)	12.7%	29.4%

Source: U.S. Census Bureau (2008).

NOTE: Native Americans had casinos in 29 states in 2008, earning more than $26 billion annually. Such financial clout commands growing attention from government leaders; unemployment is close to zero in reservations with casinos.

NOTE: E. Digby Baltzell, who coined the term "WASP," notes that, to many people in the U.S., a true WASP is a person whose first name is a last name.

NOTE: As non-WASP immigration increased, elite WASPs closed themselves off as an exclusive group, publishing the *Social Register* (1887), a list of members of "society," and establishing various genealogical organizations such as the Daughters of the American Revolution (1890) and the Society of Mayflower Descendents (1894). Such organizations further insulated wealthy WASPs from newly arrived immigrants (Baltzell, 1964).

● SEEING SOCIOLOGY
in Everyday Life

Do you think that Marian Anderson, who broke a "color line" by being invited to the White House, would have imagined our nation having an African American president?

● SEEING SOCIOLOGY
in Everyday Life

In your opinion, how much change has there been in racial prejudice and discrimination against African Americans during your lifetime? Explain your position.

The efforts of these four women greatly advanced the social standing of African Americans in the United States. Pictured from left to right: Sojourner Truth (1797–1883), born a slave, became an influential preacher and outspoken abolitionist who was honored by President Lincoln at the White House. Harriet Tubman (1820–1913), after escaping from slavery herself, masterminded the flight from bondage of hundreds of African American men and women via the "Underground Railroad." Ida Wells-Barnett (1862–1931), born to slave parents, became a partner in a Memphis newspaper and served as a tireless crusader against the terror of lynching. Marian Anderson (1902–1993), an exceptional singer whose early career was restrained by racial prejudice, broke symbolic "color lines" by singing in the White House in 1936 and on the steps of the Lincoln Memorial to a crowd of almost 100,000 people in 1939.

it sheltered themselves in exclusive suburbs and restrictive clubs. Thus the 1880s—the decade when the Statue of Liberty first welcomed immigrants to the United States—also saw the founding of the first country club with exclusively WASP members (Baltzell, 1964).

By about 1950, however, WASP wealth and power had peaked, as indicated by the 1960 election of John Fitzgerald Kennedy, the first Irish Catholic president. Yet the WASP cultural legacy remains. English is this country's dominant language and Protestantism its majority religion. Our legal system also reflects our English origins. But the historical dominance of WASPs is most evident in the widespread assumption that the terms "race" and "ethnicity" apply to everyone but them.

African Americans

Africans accompanied European explorers to the New World in the fifteenth century. But most accounts date the beginning of black history in the United States to 1619, when a Dutch trading ship brought twenty Africans to Jamestown, Virginia. Many more ships filled with African laborers followed. Whether these people arrived as slaves or as indentured servants (who paid for their passage by agreeing to work for a period of time), being of African descent on these shores soon became virtually synonymous with being a slave. In 1661, Virginia enacted the first law in the new colonies recognizing slavery (Sowell, 1981).

Slavery was the foundation of the southern colonies' plantation system. White people ran plantations using slave labor, and until 1808, some were also slave traders. Traders—Europeans, Africans, and North Americans—forcibly transported some 10 million Africans to various countries in the Americas, including 400,000 to the United States. On small sailing ships, hundreds of slaves were chained together for the several weeks it took to cross the Atlantic Ocean. Filth and disease killed many and drove others to suicide. Overall, perhaps half died en route (Franklin, 1967; Sowell, 1981).

The reward for surviving the miserable journey was a lifetime of servitude. Although some slaves worked in cities at various trades, most labored in the fields, often from daybreak until sunset and even longer during the harvest. The law allowed owners to use whatever disciplinary measures they deemed necessary to ensure that slaves were obedient and hardworking. Even killing a slave rarely prompted legal action. Owners also divided slave families at public auctions, where human beings were bought and sold as property. Unschooled and dependent on their owners for all their basic needs, slaves had little control over their lives (Franklin, 1967; Sowell, 1981).

Some free persons of color lived in both the North and the South, laboring as small-scale farmers, skilled workers, and small business owners. But the lives of most African Americans stood in glaring contradiction to the principles of equality and freedom on which the United States was founded. The Declaration of Independence states:

> We hold these Truths to be self-evident, that all Men are created equal, that they are endowed by their Creator with certain unalienable Rights, that among these are Life, Liberty, and the Pursuit of Happiness.

SOCIAL SURVEY: "On the average (Negroes/Blacks/African Americans) have worse jobs, income, and housing than white people. Do you think these differences are . . ." (GSS 2004, N = 906; *Codebook*, 2005:322–23)

	"Yes"	"No"	Don't Know"/ No Response
"mainly due to discrimination?"	33.4%	62.1%	4.4%

"because most blacks have less inborn ability to learn?"	8.8%	88.7%	2.4%
"because most blacks don't have the chance for education?"	41.2%	55.2%	3.6%
"because most blacks just don't have the motivation or willpower?"	47.0%	47.6%	5.4%

MAKING THE GRADE

Jim Crow laws are a clear example of institutional discrimination.

However, most white people did not apply these ideals to black people, and certainly not to slaves. In the *Dred Scott* case of 1857, the U.S. Supreme Court addressed the question "Are slaves citizens?" by writing, "We think they are not, and that they are not included, and were not intended to be included, under the word 'citizens' in the Constitution, and can therefore claim none of the rights and privileges which that instrument provides for and secures for citizens of the United States" (quoted in Blaustein & Zangrando, 1968:160). Thus arose what the Swedish sociologist Gunnar Myrdal (1944) called the "American dilemma": a democratic society's denial of basic rights and freedoms to one category of people. People would speak of equality, in other words, but do little to make all categories of people equal. Many white people resolved this dilemma by defining black people as naturally inferior and undeserving of equality (Leach, 2002).

In 1865, the Thirteenth Amendment to the Constitution outlawed slavery. Three years later, the Fourteenth Amendment reversed the *Dred Scott* ruling, giving citizenship to all people born in the United States. The Fifteenth Amendment, ratified in 1870, stated that neither race nor previous condition of servitude could deprive anyone of the right to vote. However, so-called *Jim Crow laws*—classic cases of institutional discrimination—segregated U.S. society into two racial castes. Especially in the South, white people beat and lynched black people (and some white people) who challenged the racial hierarchy.

The twentieth century brought dramatic changes for African Americans. After World War I, tens of thousands of men, women, and children left the rural South for jobs in northern factories. Although most did find economic opportunities, few escaped racial prejudice and discrimination, which placed them lower in the social hierarchy than white immigrants arriving from Europe.

In the 1950s and 1960s, a national civil rights movement led to landmark judicial decisions outlawing segregated schools and overt discrimination in employment and public accommodations. The Black Power movement gave African Americans a renewed sense of pride and purpose.

Despite these gains, people of African descent continue to occupy a lower social position in the United States, as shown in Table 14–3. The median income of African American families in 2007 ($40,143) was only 57 percent of non-Hispanic white family income ($69,937), a ratio that has changed little in thirty years.[3] Black families remain three times as likely as white families to be poor.

The number of African Americans securely in the middle class rose by more than half between 1980 and 2008; 41 percent earn

Table 14–3   The Social Standing of African Americans, 2007

	African Americans	Entire U.S. Population
Median family income	$40,143	$61,355
Percentage in poverty	24.5%	12.5%
Completion of four or more years of college (age 25 and over)	19.6%	29.4%

Source: U.S. Census Bureau (2008).

$50,000 or more. This means that the African American community is now economically diverse. Even so, a majority of African Americans are still working-class or poor. In recent years, many have seen earnings slip as urban factory jobs, vital to residents of central cities, have been lost to other countries where labor costs are lower. This is one reason that black unemployment is more than twice as high as white unemployment; among African American teenagers in many cities, the figure exceeds 40 percent (R. A. Smith, 2002; Pattillo, 2007; U.S. Department of Labor, 2008).

Since 1980, African Americans have made remarkable educational progress. The share of adults completing high school rose from half to more than three-fourths, nearly closing the gap between whites and blacks. Between 1980 and 2007, the share of African American adults with at least a college degree rose from 8 to 20 percent. But as Table 14–3 shows, African Americans are still well below the national standard when it comes to completing four years of college.

The political clout of African Americans has also increased. As a result of black migration to the cities and white flight to the suburbs, African Americans have gained greater political power in urban places, and half of this country's ten largest cities have elected African American mayors (Marshall & Ruhil, 2006). At the national level, the election of Barack Obama as this country's forty-fourth president—the first African American to hold this office—is a historic and hugely important event. It demonstrates that our society has moved beyond the assumption that race is a barrier to the highest office in the land (West, 2008). Yet in 2009, African Americans accounted for just 39 members of the House of Representatives (9 percent of the 435), one member of the Senate (out of 100), and only two of fifty state governors (National Governors Association, 2008).

In sum, for nearly 400 years, people of African ancestry in the United States have struggled for social equality. As a nation, we have come far in this pursuit. Overt discrimination is now illegal, and research documents a long-term decline in prejudice against African Americans (Firebaugh & Davis, 1988; J. Q. Wilson, 1992; NORC, 2007).

Fifty years after the abolition of slavery, W. E. B. Du Bois (1913) pointed to the extent of black achievement but cautioned that racial caste remained strong in the United States. Almost a century later, this racial hierarchy persists.

[3]Here again, a median age difference (non-Hispanic whites, 40.8; blacks, 31.1) accounts for some of the income and educational disparities. More important is a higher proportion of one-parent families among blacks than whites. If we compare only married-couple families, African Americans (median income $62,163 in 2007) earned 80 percent as much as non-Hispanic whites ($77,340).

DISCUSS: As the class reads through the history of African Americans, ask students to point out when (if at all) and how African Americans became "equal" to white people in U.S. society. Ask, too, about the significance of now having an African American president.

Q: "Never look down on anybody unless you are helping them up." Jesse Jackson

DISCUSS: In 2008, African American voter turnout (64.7%) was about that of whites (65.8%). What does this gain suggest about black aspirations?

Q: "Watch your thoughts; they become words.
   Watch your words; they become actions.
   Watch your actions; they become habits.
   Watch your habits; they become character.
   Watch your character; it becomes your destiny." Anonymous

● SEEING SOCIOLOGY
in Everyday Life

Don't assume that all Asian Americans (or Hispanics or members of any other minority category) are the same. The tables in this chapter highlight important differences among members of each minority category.

Table 14–4   The Social Standing of Asian Americans, 2007

	All Asian Americans	Chinese Americans	Japanese Americans	Asian Indian Americans	Filipino Americans	Entire U.S. Population
Median family income	$77,133	$78,258	$88,037	$92,925	$83,126	$61,355
Percentage in poverty	10.2%	12.0%	8.5%	8.1%	5.5%	12.5%
Completion of four or more years of college (age 25 and over)	52.6%	51.6%	46.5%	68.3%	48.0%	29.4%

Source: U.S. Census Bureau (2008).

Asian Americans

Although Asian Americans share some racial traits, enormous cultural diversity characterizes this category of people with ancestors from dozens of nations. In 2007, the total number of Asian Americans exceeded 13 million, or about 4.4 percent of the U.S. population. The largest category of Asian Americans is people of Chinese ancestry (3.1 million), followed by those of Asian Indian (2.6 million), Filipino (2.4 million), Vietnamese (1.5 million), Korean (1.3 million), and Japanese (800,000) descent. More than one-third of Asian Americans live in California.

Young Asian Americans command attention and respect as high achievers and are disproportionately represented at our country's best colleges and universities. Many of their elders, too, have made economic and social gains; most Asian Americans now live in middle-class suburbs, and an increasing number of Asian Americans live in some of the highest-income neighborhoods in the country. Yet despite (and sometimes because of) this achievement, Asian Americans often find that others are aloof or outright hostile toward them (O'Hare, Frey, & Fost, 1994; Chua-Eoan, 2000; Lee & Marlay, 2007).

The achievement of some Asian Americans has given rise to a "model minority" stereotype that is misleading because it hides the sharp differences in class standing found among their ranks. We will focus first on the history and current standing of Chinese Americans and Japanese Americans—the longest-established Asian American minorities—and conclude with a brief look at the more recent arrivals.

Chinese Americans

Chinese immigration to the United States began in 1849 with the economic boom of California's Gold Rush. New towns and businesses sprang up overnight, and the demand for cheap labor attracted some 100,000 Chinese immigrants. Most Chinese workers were young men willing to take difficult, low-status jobs that whites did not want. But the economy soured in the 1870s, and desperate whites began to compete with the Chinese for whatever work could be found. Suddenly, the hardworking Chinese were seen as a threat. Economic hard times led to prejudice and discrimination (Ling, 1971; Boswell, 1986). Soon laws were passed barring Chinese people from many occupations, and public opinion turned strongly against the "Yellow Peril."

In 1882, the U.S. government passed the first of several laws limiting Chinese immigration. This action caused domestic hardship because in the United States, Chinese men outnumbered Chinese women by twenty to one. This sex imbalance drove the Chinese population down to only 60,000 by 1920. Because Chinese women already in the United States were in high demand, they soon lost much of their traditional submissiveness to men (Hsu, 1971; Lai, 1980; Sowell, 1981).

Responding to racial hostility, some Chinese moved east; many more sought the relative safety of urban Chinatowns. There Chinese traditions flourished, and kinship networks, called *clans,* provided financial assistance to individuals and represented the interests of all. At the same time, however, living in an all-Chinese community discouraged residents from learning English, which limited their job opportunities (Wong, 1971).

A renewed need for labor during World War II prompted President Franklin Roosevelt to end the ban on Chinese immigration in 1943 and to extend the rights of citizenship to Chinese Americans born abroad. Many responded by moving out of Chinatowns and pursuing cultural assimilation. In Honolulu in 1900, for example, 70 percent of Chinese people lived in Chinatown; today, the figure is below 20 percent.

By 1950, many Chinese Americans had experienced upward social mobility. Today, people of Chinese ancestry are no longer limited to self-employment in laundries and restaurants; many hold high-prestige positions, especially in fields related to science and technology.

As shown in Table 14–4, the median family income of Chinese Americans in 2007 was $78,258, which is above the national average of $61,355. However, the higher income of all Asian Americans reflects a larger number of family members in the labor force.[4] Chinese Americans also have a record of educational achievement, with almost twice the national average of college graduates.

Despite their successes, many Chinese Americans still deal with subtle (and sometimes blatant) prejudice and discrimination. Such hostility is one reason that poverty remains a problem for many Chi-

---

[4]Median age for all Asian Americans in 2007 was 35.4 years, somewhat below the national median of 36.6 and the non-Hispanic white median of 40.8. But specific categories vary widely in median age: Japanese, 45.6; Filipino, 38.3; Chinese, 38.0; Korean, 35.8; Asian Indian, 32.2; Cambodian, 27.1; Hmong, 20.0 (U.S. Census Bureau, 2008).

Q: "There is no Negro problem in the United States; there is only a white problem." Richard Wright

NOTE: Before the Industrial Revolution, few people moved from one country to another. The word "immigrant" entered the English language only around 1790.

DIVERSITY: U.S. census breakdown of Asian Americans (2007): Chinese, 23%; Filipino, 18%; Indian, 19%; Vietnamese, 11%; Korean, 10%; Japanese, 6%.

NOTE: The current wave of immigration began in 1965 with liberalization of the old quota system dating from 1924. In essence, "country of origin" ceased to be a key criterion for admission to the U.S. in favor of special skills and family ties. This sparked a shift from Europe to Latin America and Asia as the source of immigrants and also allowed many families to join earlier immigrants.

● SEEING SOCIOLOGY
in Everyday Life

On your campus, do students of any one race or ethnic category tend to hang out together? Explain the patterns you see.

● SEEING SOCIOLOGY
in Everyday Life

Recent research on social distance (see pages 361–63) indicates that most of today's college students say they are more accepting of African Americans than Asian Americans. Does this square with your experiences? What about white people in the country as a whole—are they more accepting of Asian Americans or African Americans? Why?

nese Americans. The problem of poverty is most common among people who remain in the socially isolated Chinatowns working in restaurants or other low-paying jobs, raising the question of whether racial and ethnic enclaves help their residents or exploit them (Portes & Jensen, 1989; Kinkead, 1992; Gilbertson & Gurak, 1993).

Japanese Americans

Japanese immigration to the United States began slowly in the 1860s, reaching only 3,000 by 1890. Most were men who came to the Hawaiian Islands (annexed by the United States in 1898 and made a state in 1959) as a source of cheap labor. After 1900, however, as the number of Japanese immigrants to California rose (reaching 140,000 by 1915), white hostility increased (Takaki, 1998). In 1907, the United States signed an agreement with Japan curbing the entry of men—the chief economic threat—while allowing women to enter this country to ease the Japanese sex ratio imbalance. In the 1920s, state laws in California and elsewhere segregated the Japanese and banned interracial marriage, just about ending further Japanese immigration. Not until 1952 did the United States extend citizenship to foreign-born Japanese.

Immigrants from Japan and China differed in three important ways. First, there were fewer Japanese immigrants, so they escaped some of the hostility directed toward the more numerous Chinese. Second, the Japanese knew more about the United States than the Chinese did, which helped them assimilate (Sowell, 1981). Third, Japanese immigrants preferred rural farming to clustering in cities, which made them less visible. But many white people objected to Japanese ownership of farmland, so in 1913, California barred further purchases. Many foreign-born Japanese (called *Issei*) responded by placing farmland in the names of their U.S.-born children (*Nisei*), who were constitutionally entitled to citizenship.

Japanese Americans faced their greatest crisis after Japan bombed the U.S. naval fleet at Hawaii's Pearl Harbor on December 7, 1941. Rage was directed at the Japanese living in the United States. Some people feared that Japanese Americans would spy for Japan or commit acts of sabotage. Within a year, President Franklin Roosevelt signed Executive Order 9066, an unprecedented action designed to ensure national security by detaining people of Japanese ancestry in military camps. Authorities soon relocated 120,000 people of Japanese descent (90 percent of all U.S. Japanese) to remote inland reservations (Sun, 1998; Ewers, 2008).

Concern about national security always rises in times of war, but Japanese internment was sharply criticized. First, it targeted an entire category of people, not a single one of whom was known to have committed a disloyal act. Second, most of those imprisoned were *Nisei*, U.S. citizens by birth. Third, the United States was also at war with Germany and Italy, but no comparable action was taken against people of German or Italian ancestry.

On average, Asian Americans have income above the national median. At the same time, however, the poverty rate in many Asian American communities—including San Francisco's Chinatown—is well above average.

Relocation meant selling homes, furnishings, and businesses on short notice for pennies on the dollar. As a result, almost the entire Japanese American population was economically devastated. In military prisons—surrounded by barbed wire and guarded by armed soldiers—families crowded into single rooms, often in buildings that had previously sheltered livestock. The internment ended in 1944 when the U.S. Supreme Court declared it unconstitutional, although the last camp did not close until 1946 (after the war had ended). In 1988, Congress awarded $20,000 to each of the victims as token compensation for the hardships they endured.

After World War II, Japanese Americans staged a dramatic recovery. Having lost their traditional businesses, many entered new occupations; driven by cultural values stressing the importance of education and hard work, Japanese Americans have enjoyed remarkable success. In 2007, the median income of Japanese American families was more than 40 percent higher than the national average, and the rate of poverty among Japanese Americans was well below the national figure.

Upward social mobility has encouraged cultural assimilation and intermarriage. Younger generations of Japanese Americans rarely live

DIVERSITY: The sense that the Chinese would never assimilate is suggested by historic records such as this population count: "1,200 souls and two Chinamen".

NOTE: In 1943, the U.S. government extended the right of citizenship to Chinese Americans born abroad partly in response to China's status as a military ally in the war against Japan (Japanese Americans born abroad could not become U.S. citizens until 1952).

DIVERSITY: Percentage of Asian Americans who speak a language other than English at home: all Asians, 76%; Hmong, 93%; Chinese, 83%; Koreans, 80%; Indians, 80%; Filipinos, 67%; Japanese, 46% (U.S. Census Bureau, 2008).

DIVERSITY: Family size varies among Asian Americans, from 3 persons among Japanese Americans to 7 among the Hmong. Typically, income and family size are negatively correlated.

● SEEING SOCIOLOGY
in Everyday Life

Do you think Latinos are fairly represented in today's television shows and films? Explain your position.

Table 14–5 The Social Standing of Hispanic Americans, 2007

	All Hispanics	Mexican Americans	Puerto Ricans	Cuban Americans	Entire U.S. Population
Median family income	$40,566	$40,419	$42,300	$52,113	$61,355
Percentage in poverty	21.5%	22.0%	24.3%	13.8%	12.5%
Completion of four or more years of college (age 25 and over)	12.3%	8.6%	15.5%	25.0%	9.4%

Source: U.S. Census Bureau (2008).

in residential enclaves, as many Chinese Americans do, and most marry non-Japanese partners. In the process, some have abandoned their traditions, including the Japanese language. A high proportion of Japanese Americans, however, belong to ethnic associations as a way of maintaining their ethnic identity. Still, some appear to be caught between two worlds: no longer culturally Japanese yet, because of racial differences, not completely accepted in the larger society.

Recent Asian Immigrants

More recent immigrants from Asia include Filipinos, Indians, Koreans, Vietnamese, Guamanians, and Samoans. The Asian American population increased by 87 percent between 1990 and 2007 and currently accounts for more than one-third of all immigration to the United States (U.S. Department of Homeland Security, 2008b).

The entrepreneurial spirit is strong among Asian immigrants. In part this reflects cultural patterns that stress achievement and self-reliance, but having one's own small business is also a strategy for dealing with societal prejudice and discrimination. Small business success is one reason that Asian American family income is above the national average, but it is also true that in many of these businesses, a number of family members work long hours.

Another factor that raises the family income of Asian Americans is a high level of schooling. As shown in Table 14–4, for all categories of Asian Americans, the share of adults with a four-year college degree is well above the national average. Among Asian Indian Americans, who have the highest educational achievement of all Asian Americans, more than two-thirds of all men and women over the age of twenty-five have completed college, a proportion that is more than twice the national average. This remarkable educational achievement is one reason that Asian Indian Americans had a median family income of $92,925 in 2007, about 50 percent higher than the national average.

In sum, a survey of Asian Americans presents a complex picture. The Japanese come closest to having achieved social acceptance. But some surveys reveal greater prejudice against Asian Americans than against African Americans (Parrillo & Donahue, 2005). Median income data suggest that many Asian Americans have prospered. But these numbers reflect the fact that many Asian Americans live in Hawaii, California, or New York, where incomes are high but so are living costs.

Then, too, many Asian Americans remain poor. One thing is clear—their high immigration rate and their increasing political clout mean that people of Asian ancestry will play a central role in U.S. society in the decades to come (Takaki, 1998; Barbassa, 2009).

Hispanic Americans/Latinos

In 2007, the number of people of Hispanic descent in the United States topped 45 million (15.1 percent of the population), surpassing the number of Asian Americans (13.4 million, or 4.4 percent of the U.S. population) and even African Americans (39 million, or 12.8 percent) and making Hispanics the largest racial or ethnic minority. However, keep in mind that few people who fall into this category describe themselves as "Hispanic" or "Latino." Like Asian Americans, Hispanics are really a cluster of distinct populations, each of which identifies with a particular ancestral nation and particular families may or may not feel a part of a national Hispanic community (Marín & Marín, 1991; Jiménez, 2007). About two out of three Hispanics (some 29 million) are Mexican Americans, or "Chicanos." Puerto Ricans are next in population size (4 million), followed by Cuban Americans (1.6 million). Many other nations of Latin America are represented by smaller numbers.

Although the Hispanic population is increasing all over the country, most Hispanic Americans still live in the Southwest. One of three Californians is Latino (in greater Los Angeles, almost half the people are). National Map 14–3, on page 376 shows the distribution of the Hispanic, African American, Asian American, and Arab American populations across the United States.

Median family income for all Hispanics—$40,566 in 2007, as shown in Table 14–5,—is well below the national average.[5] As the following sections explain, however, some categories of Hispanics have fared better than others.

Mexican Americans

Some Mexican Americans are descendants of people who lived in a part of Mexico annexed by the United States after the Mexican Amer-

[5]The 2007 median age of the U.S. Hispanic population was 27.6 years, far below the non-Hispanic white median of 40.8 years. This difference accounts for some of the disparity in income and education.

● SEEING SOCIOLOGY
in Everyday Life

On your campus, do students ever seem to downplay their ethnicity as a way to "fit in"? Explain.

ican War (1846–48). Most, however, are more recent immigrants. Indeed, more immigrants now come to the United States from Mexico than from any other country.

Like many other immigrants, many Mexican Americans have worked as low-wage laborers, on farms and in factories. Table 14–5 shows that the 2007 median family income for Mexican Americans was $40,419, which is two-thirds of the national average. Almost one-fourth of Chicano families are poor—nearly twice the national average. Finally, despite gains since 1980, Mexican Americans still have a high dropout rate and receive much less schooling, on average, than the U.S. population as a whole.

Puerto Ricans

The island of Puerto Rico, like the Philippines, became a U.S. possession when the Spanish-American War ended in 1898. In 1917, Congress passed the Jones Act, which made Puerto Ricans (but not Filipinos) U.S. citizens and made Puerto Rico a territory of the United States.

New York City is home to nearly 1 million Puerto Ricans. However, about one-third of this community is severely disadvantaged. Adjusting to cultural patterns on the mainland—including, for many, learning English—is one major challenge; also, Puerto Ricans with dark skin encounter prejudice and discrimination. As a result, more people return to Puerto Rico each year than arrive. Between 1990 and 2007, the Puerto Rican population of New York actually fell by about 100,000 (Navarro, 2000; U.S. Census Bureau, 2008).

This "revolving door" pattern limits assimilation. About 70 percent of Puerto Rican families in the United States speak Spanish at home. Speaking Spanish keeps ethnic identity strong but limits economic opportunity. Puerto Ricans also have a higher incidence of woman-headed households than most other Hispanics, a pattern that puts families at greater risk of poverty (U.S. Census Bureau, 2007).

Table 14–5 shows that the 2007 median family income for Puerto Ricans was $42,300, or about 70 percent of the national average. Although long-term mainland residents have made economic gains, more recent immigrants from Puerto Rico continue to struggle to find work. Overall, Puerto Ricans remain the most socially disadvantaged Hispanic minority.

Cuban Americans

Within a decade after the 1959 Marxist revolution led by Fidel Castro, 400,000 Cubans had fled to the United States. Most settled with other Cuban Americans in Miami. Many were highly educated business and professional people who wasted little time becoming as successful in the United States as they had been in their homeland.

Table 14–5 shows that the 2007 median household income for Cuban Americans was $52,113, above that of other Hispanics but still well below the national average. The 1.6 million Cuban Americans living in the United States today have managed a delicate balancing act, achieving in the larger society while holding on to much of their traditional culture. Of all Hispanics, Cubans are the most likely to speak Spanish in their homes: Eight out of ten families do so. However, cultural distinctiveness and highly visible communities, such as Miami's Little Havana, provoke hostility from some people.

Arab Americans

Arab Americans are another U.S. minority that is increasing in size. Like Hispanic Americans, these are people whose ancestors lived in a variety of countries. What is sometimes called "the Arab world" includes twenty-two nations and stretches across northern Africa, from Mauritania and Morocco on Africa's west coast to Egypt and Sudan on Africa's east coast, and extends into the Middle East (western Asia), including Iraq and Saudi Arabia. Not all the people who live in these nations are Arabs, however; for example, the Berber people in Morocco and the Kurds of Iraq are not Arabs.

Arab cultures differ from society to society, but they share widespread use of the Arabic alphabet and language and have Islam as their dominant religion. But keep in mind that "Arab" (an ethnic

The strength of family bonds and neighborhood ties is evident in Carmen Lomas Garza's painting *Barbacoa para Cumpleaños* (Birthday Party Barbecue).

Carmen Lomas Garza, *Barbacoa para Cumpleaños* (Birthday Party Barbecue). Alkyds on canvas, 38 × 48 inches. © 1993 Carmen Lomas Garza (reg. 1994). Photo credit: M. Lee Fatherree. Collection of Federal Reserve Bank of Dallas.

DIVERSITY: About 20% of the U.S. population aged 5 and older speak a language other than English at home, a total of 55 million people in 2007. In 1980, the share was 11% and 23.5 million people. Most of these (62%) are Spanish speakers (in 1980: 48%); 15% (8.3 million) speak an Asian language (up from 2.2 million in 1980). About 40 percent of all non-English speakers live in Texas and California (U.S. Census Bureau, 2008).

THE MAP: Hispanics, African Americans, Asian Americans, and Arab Americans cluster in different regions of the U.S. Hispanics settle near the "Latin American" side of the country; similarly, most Asian immigrants come to California. Despite a marked northward migration after World War I, the highest concentrations of African Americans remain in the South. Metropolitan areas of the Northeast and Midwest are home to the highest proportions of Arab Americans.

SEEING SOCIOLOGY
in Everyday Life

Look closely at the maps. Can you explain why various categories of people tend to be concentrated in certain regions of the United States?

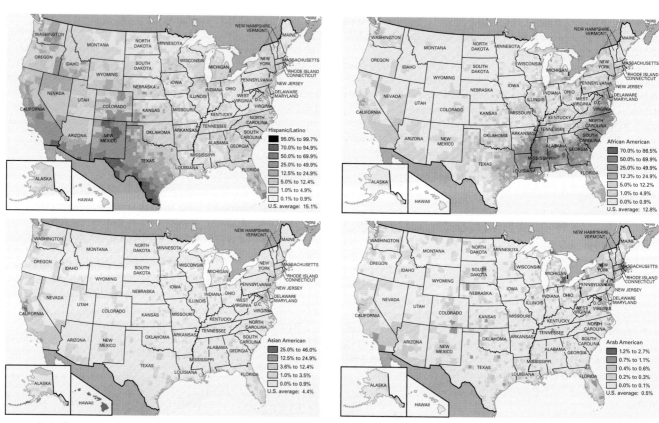

Seeing Ourselves

NATIONAL MAP 14–3

The Concentration of Hispanics or Latinos, African Americans, Asian Americans, and Arab Americans, by County

In 2007, people of Hispanic or Latino descent represented 15.1 percent of the U.S. population, compared with 12.8 percent African Americans, 4.4 percent Asian Americans, and 0.5 percent Arab Americans. These maps show the geographic distribution of these categories of people in 2000. Comparing them we see that the southern half of the United States is home to far more minorities than the northern half. But do they all concentrate in the same areas? What patterns do the maps reveal?

Source: U.S. Census Bureau (2008).

category) is not the same as "Muslim" (a follower of Islam). A majority of the people living in most Arab countries are Muslims, but some Arabs are Christians or followers of other religions. In addition, most of the world's Muslims do not live in Africa or the Middle East and are not Arabs.

Because many of the world's nations have large Arab populations, immigration to the United States has created a culturally diverse population of Arab Americans. Some Arab Americans are Muslims, and some are not; some speak Arabic, and some do not;

some maintain the traditions of their homeland, and some do not. As is the case with Hispanic Americans and Asian Americans, some are recent immigrants, and some have lived in this country for decades or even for generations.

As noted in Table 14–1, the government gives the official number of Arab Americans as 1.5 million, but because people may not declare their ethnic background, the actual number may be twice as high.[6] The largest populations of Arab Americans have ancestral ties to Lebanon (32 percent of all Arab Americans), Egypt (12 percent),

Q: "You cannot become thorough Americans if you think of yourselves in groups. America does not consist of groups. A man who thinks of himself as belonging to a particular national group has not yet become an American." Woodrow Wilson

Q: "Remember, remember always that all of us . . . are descended from immigrants and revolutionists." Franklin Delano Roosevelt

Q: "No one can make you feel inferior without your consent." Eleanor Roosevelt

DIVERSITY: Asian Americans are increasing in number primarily due to immigration, Latinos and Arab Americans because of both immigration and natural increase, and African Americans mainly due to natural increase.

SEEING SOCIOLOGY
in Everyday Life

Do you know of any highly educated immigrants who worked as professionals in their birth nations and who are now performing working-class jobs here in the United States? Why might immigrants have to do this?

and Syria (10 percent). Most Arab Americans (71 percent) report ancestral ties to one nation, but 29 percent report both Arab and non-Arab ancestry (U.S. Census Bureau, 2008). A look at National Map 14–3 shows the Arab American population is distributed throughout the United States.

Included in the Arab American population are people of all social classes. Some are highly educated professionals who work as physicians, engineers, and professors; others are working-class people who perform various skilled jobs in factories or on construction sites; still others do service work in restaurants, hospitals, or other settings or work in small family businesses. As shown in Table 14–6, median family income for Arab Americans is slightly above the national average ($65,291 compared to the national median of $61,355 in 2007), but Arab Americans have a much higher than average poverty rate (17.1 percent versus 12.5 percent for the population as a whole) (U.S. Census Bureau, 2008).

There are large, visible Arab American communities in a number of U.S. cities, including New York, Chicago, Los Angeles, Houston, and Dearborn (Michigan). Even so, Arab Americans may choose to downplay their ethnicity as a way to avoid prejudice and discrimination. The fact that many terrorist attacks against the United States and other nations have been carried out by Arabs has fueled a stereotype that links being Arab (or Muslim) with being a terrorist. This stereotype is unfair because it blames an entire category of people for actions by a few individuals. But it is probably the reason that the social distance research discussed earlier in this chapter shows students expressing more negative attitudes toward Arabs than toward any other racial or ethnic category. Its also helps explain why Arab Americans have been targets of an increasing number of hate crimes and why many Arab Americans feel that they are subject to "ethnic profiling" that threatens their privacy and freedom (Ali & Juarez, 2003; Ali, Lipper, & Mack, 2004; Hagopian, 2004).

White Ethnic Americans

The term "white ethnics" recognizes the ethnic heritage and social disadvantages of many white people. White ethnics are non-WASPs whose ancestors lived in Ireland, Poland, Germany, Italy, or other European countries. More than half the U.S. population falls into one or more white ethnic categories.

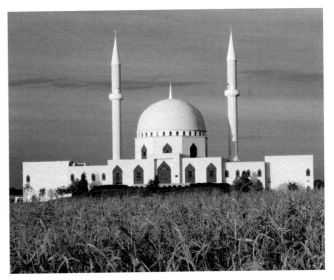

Arab American communities can be found in many large cities on the East and West Coasts of the United States, but the heaviest concentrations are found across the upper Midwest. This mosque rises above the cornfields in a rural area near Toledo, Ohio.

High rates of emigration from Europe during the nineteenth century first brought Germans and Irish and then Italians and Jews to our shores. Despite cultural differences, all shared the hope that the United States would offer greater political freedom and economic opportunity than their homelands. Most did live better in this country, but the belief that "the streets of America were paved with gold" turned out to be a far cry from reality. Most immigrants found only hard labor for low wages.

White ethnics also endured their share of prejudice and discrimination. Many employers shut their doors to immigrants, posting signs that warned "None need apply but Americans" (Handlin, 1941:67). In 1921, Congress enacted a quota system that greatly limited immigration, especially by southern and eastern Europeans, who were likely to have darker skin and different cultural backgrounds than the dominant WASPs. This quota system continued until 1968.

In response to prejudice and discrimination, many white ethnics formed supportive residential enclaves. Some also established footholds in certain businesses and trades: Italian Americans entered the construction industry; the Irish worked in construction and in civil service jobs; Jews predominated in the garment industry; many Greeks (like the Chinese) worked in the retail food business (W. M. Newman, 1973).

Table 14–6 The Social Standing of Arab Americans, 2007

	Arab Americans	Entire U.S. Population
Median family income	$65,291	$61,355
Percentage in poverty	17.1%	12.5%
Completion of four or more years of college (age 25 and over)	44.8%	29.4%

Source: U.S. Census Bureau (2008).

*The 2007 median age for Arab Americans was 30.8 years, below the national median of 36.6 years.

DISCUSS: How likely, in your opinion, is the election of a U.S. president who is Asian American? Hispanic American? Jewish? Give reasons for your opinion.

Q: "Once I thought to write a history of the immigrants in America. Then I discovered that the immigrants were American history." Oscar Handlin

DIVERSITY: The six leading states in attracting immigrants from abroad in 2007 were California, New York, Florida, Texas, New Jersey, and Illinois (U.S. Depart-

ment of Homeland Security, 2008).

DISCUSS: What do students see as the advantages and disadvantages of Arab Americans living in large cultural communities in cities such as Chicago, Dearborn, or Houston?

Q: "Illegal aliens have always been a problem in the United States; ask any Indian." Robert Orben

SEEING SOCIOLOGY
in Everyday Life

Do you know your school's policy on affirmative action?

CONTROVERSY & DEBATE

Affirmative Action: Solution or Problem?

STEPHANIE: I think Gruttner got, well, a raw deal. She should have been admitted.

GINA: Perhaps. But diversity is important. I believe in affirmative action.

MARCO: Maybe some people do get into college more easily. But that includes guys like me whose father went here.

Barbara Gruttner, who is white, claimed that she was the victim of racial discrimination. She maintained that the University of Michigan Law School had unfairly denied her application for admission while admitting many less qualified African American applicants. The basis of her claim was the fact that Michigan, a state university, admitted just 9 percent of white students with her grade point average and law school aptitude test scores while admitting 100 percent of African American applicants with comparable scores.

In 2003, the U.S. Supreme Court heard Gruttner's complaint in a review of the admissions policies of both the law school and the undergraduate program at the University of Michigan. In a 6–3 decision, the Court ruled against Gruttner, claiming that the University of Michigan Law School could use a policy of affirmative action that takes account of the race of applicants in the interest of creating a socially diverse student body. At the same

time, however, the Court struck down the university's undergraduate admissions policy, which awarded points not only for grades and college board scores but also for being a member of an underrepresented minority. A point system of this kind, the Court ruled, is too close to the rigid quota systems rejected by the Court in the past.

With this ruling, the Supreme Court continued to oppose quotalike systems while at the same time reaffirming the importance of racial diversity on campus. Thus colleges and universities can take account of race in order to increase the number of traditionally underrepresented students as long as race is treated as just one variable in a process that evaluates each applicant as an individual (Stout, 2003).

How did the controversial policy of affirmative action begin? The answer takes us back to the end of World War II, when the U.S. government funded higher education for veterans of all races. The so-called G.I. Bill held special promise for African Americans, most of whom needed financial assistance to enroll in college. By 1960, government funding helped 350,000 black men and women attend college.

There was just one problem: These individuals were not finding the kinds of jobs for which they were qualified. So the Kennedy administration devised a program of "affirmative action" to provide broader opportunities to qualified minorities. Employers were instructed to monitor hiring, promotion, and admissions policies to eliminate discrimination against minorities, even if unintended.

Defenders of affirmative action see it, first, as a sensible response to our nation's racial and eth-

Many working-class people still live in traditional neighborhoods, although those who prospered have gradually assimilated. Most descendants of immigrants who labored in sweatshops and lived in crowded tenements now lead more comfortable lives. As a result, their ethnic heritage has become a source of pride.

Race and Ethnicity: Looking Ahead

The United States has been and will remain a land of immigrants. Immigration has brought striking cultural diversity and tales of hope, struggle, and success told in hundreds of languages.

Millions of immigrants arrived in a great wave that peaked about 1910. The next two generations saw gradual economic gains and at least some assimilation into the larger society. The government also extended citizenship to Native Americans (1924), foreign-born Filipinos (1942), Chinese Americans (1943), and Japanese Americans (1952).

Another wave of immigration began after World War II and swelled as the government relaxed immigration laws in the 1960s. Today, about 1.5 million people come to the United States each year—about 1 million legally and another 500,000 illegally. Today's immigrants come not from Europe but from Latin America and Asia, with Mexicans, Asian Indians, and Filipinos arriving in the largest numbers.

Q: "Immigration is the sincerest form of flattery." Jack Paar

DISCUSS: Can minorities include affluent people? Certainly. More complex is the issue of whether affluent *categories* of people (say, Japanese) should be included along with less affluent categories (say, Native Americans). Ask the class.

DISCUSS: Do students consider white ethnics to be "minorities"? Why or why not?

RESOURCE: Karen Brodkin Sacks asks the question "How Did Jews Become White Folks?" in the author's companion reader *Seeing Ourselves*, 8th ed.

DIVERSITY: U.S. coins carry the Latin phrase *E Pluribus Unum* ("one formed from many"). Should our society emphasize the "unum" (which may favor a dominant cultural tradition) or the "pluribus" (which may cause division)? A multicultural credo might be *E Pluribus Plures*, "many from many."

SEEING SOCIOLOGY
in Everyday Life

Can you provide examples of xenophobia in our society today?

nic history, especially for African Americans, who suffered through two centuries of slavery and a century of segregation under Jim Crow laws. Throughout our history, they claim, being white gave people a big advantage. They see minority preference today as a step toward fair compensation for unfair majority preference in the past.

Second, given our racial history, many analysts doubt that the United States will ever become a color-blind society. They claim that because prejudice and discrimination are rooted deep in U.S. culture, simply claiming that we are color-blind does not mean that everyone will be treated fairly.

Third, supporters maintain that affirmative action has worked. Where would minorities be if the government had not enacted this policy in the 1960s? Major employers, such as fire and police departments in large cities, began hiring minorities and women for the first time only because of affirmative action. This program has helped expand the African American middle class and increased racial diversity on college campuses and in the workplace.

About 80 percent of African Americans support affirmative action. But 73 percent of white people and 56 percent of Hispanics *oppose* preferences for African Americans (NORC, 2007). Critics point out, first of all, that affirma-

tive action was intended as a temporary remedy to ensure fair competition but soon became a system of "group preferences" and quotas—in short, a form of "reverse discrimination," favoring people not because of performance but because of race, ethnicity, or sex.

Second, critics say, if racial preferences were wrong in the past, they are wrong now. Why should whites today, many of whom are far from privileged, be penalized for past discrimination that was in no way their fault? Our society has undone most of the institutional prejudice and discrimination of earlier times—doesn't the election of an African American president suggest that? Giving entire categories of people special treatment compromises standards of excellence and calls into question the real accomplishments of minorities.

A third argument against affirmative action is that it benefits those who need it least. Favoring minority-owned corporations or holding places in law school helps already privileged people. Affirmative action has done little for the African American underclass that needs the most help.

There are good arguments for and against affirmative action, and people who want our society to have more racial or ethnic equality fall on both sides of the debate. Voters in a number of states, including California, Washington,

Michigan, and Nebraska, have passed ballot initiatives banning the use of affirmative action based on gender or race. In 2008, however, voters in Colorado voted down such a proposal. So the country remains divided on this issue. The disagreement is not whether people of all colors should have equal opportunity but whether the current policy of affirmative action is part of the solution or part of the problem.

WHAT DO YOU THINK?

1. In view of the fact that society has historically favored males over females and whites over people of color, would you agree that white males have received more "affirmative action" than anyone? Why or why not?

2. Should affirmative action include only disadvantaged categories of minorities (say, African Americans and Native Americans) and exclude more affluent categories (such as Japanese Americans)? Why or why not?

3. Do you think the election of Barack Obama as the nation's first African American president suggests that affirmative action is no longer needed? Why or why not?

Sources: Bowen & Bok (1999), Kantrowitz & Wingert (2003), NORC (2007), Flynn (2008), and Leff (2008).

Many new arrivals face the same kind of prejudice and discrimination experienced by those who came before them. In fact, recent years have witnessed rising hostility toward foreigners (an expression of *xenophobia*, from Greek roots meaning "fear of what is strange"). In 1994, California voters passed Proposition 187, which stated that illegal immigrants should be denied health care, social services, and public education; it was later overturned in federal court. More recently, voters there mandated that all children learn English in school. Some landowners in the Southwest have taken up arms to discourage the large number of illegal immigrants crossing the border from Mexico, and our nation is increasing border security as we also wonder how to best deal with the more than 12 million illegal immigrants already here.

Even minorities who have been in the United States for generations feel the sting of prejudice and discrimination. Affirmative action, a policy meant to provide opportunities for members of racial and ethnic minorities, continues to be hotly debated in this country, as the Controversy & Debate box describes.

Like other minorities, today's immigrants hope to gain acceptance and to blend into U.S. society without completely giving up their traditional culture. Some still build racial and ethnic enclaves so that in many cities across the country, the Little Havanas and Koreatowns of today stand alongside the Little Italys and Chinatowns of the past. In addition, new arrivals still carry the traditional hope that their racial and ethnic identities can be a source of pride rather than a badge of inferiority.

Seeing Sociology in Everyday Life

Chapter 14   Race And Ethnicity

Is our society becoming more tolerant, more accepting of racially and ethnically mixed couples and friendship groups?

As the social distance research presented in this chapter shows, today's college students express greater acceptance of social diversity. Look at the two corporate advertisements shown here. What evidence of greater acceptance do you see? In your opinion, does this evidence mean that our society has really changed? Why or why not?

Here's an ad from 1957, when the civil rights movement was just getting under way. Based on what you have read in this chapter, how does this reflect what U.S. society was like fifty years ago in terms of racial segregation?

> **HINT**   On the face of it, today's ads suggest far greater racial and ethnic tolerance than was true fifty years ago, when we rarely saw images of people of different categories interacting with one another. The social distance research noted in this chapter also supports the idea that tolerance is increasing. Being more racially inclusive is also a smart business policy because of the increasing economic resources of various minority categories of the U.S. population.

UNITED COLORS OF BENETTON.

Especially in the case of advertising aimed at young people, racial and ethnic mixing has become the rule. How accurately does this image reflect everyday life? Do you think young people differ from older people in their degree of social tolerance? Explain.

Applying SOCIOLOGY in Everyday Life

1. Thinking about your own campus, can you point to ways in which race does not matter in students' lives? In what ways does race still matter? On balance, how important is race today?

2. Does your college or university take account of race and ethnicity in its admissions policies? Ask to speak with an admissions officer to see what you can learn about your school's use of race and ethnicity in admissions. Ask whether there is a "legacy" policy that favors children of parents who attended the school.

3. Give several of your friends or family members a quick quiz, asking them what share of the U.S. population is white, Hispanic, African American, and Asian (see Table 14-1 on page 358). Why do you think most white people exaggerate the African American population? (C. A. Gallagher, 2003)

MAKING THE GRADE

CHAPTER 14 Race and Ethnicity

The Social Meaning of Race and Ethnicity

RACE refers to socially constructed categories based on biological traits a society defines as important.

- The meaning and importance of race vary from place to place and over time.
- Societies use racial categories to rank people in a hierarchy, giving some people more money, power, and prestige than others.
- In the past, scientists created three broad categories—Caucasoids, Mongoloids, and Negroids—but there are no biologically pure races.

pp. 356–58

ETHNICITY refers to socially constructed categories based on cultural traits a society defines as important.

- Ethnicity reflects common ancestors, language, and religion.
- The importance of ethnicity varies from place to place and over time.
- People choose to play up or play down their ethnicity.
- Societies may or may not set categories of people apart based on differences in ethnicity.

pp. 358–59

race (p. 356) a socially constructed category of people who share biologically transmitted traits that members of a society consider important

ethnicity (p. 358) a shared cultural heritage

minority (p. 359) any category of people distinguished by physical or cultural difference that a society sets apart and subordinates

Minorities are people of various racial and ethnic categories who are visually distinctive and disadvantaged by a society (p. 359).

Prejudice and Stereotypes

PREJUDICE is a rigid and unfair generalization about a category of people.

- The social distance scale is one measure of prejudice.
- One type of prejudice is the **STEREOTYPE**, an exaggerated description applied to every person in some category.
- **RACISM**, a very destructive type of prejudice, asserts that one race is innately superior or inferior to another.

pp. 360–62

There are four **THEORIES OF PREJUDICE**:

- **Scapegoat theory** claims that prejudice results from frustration among people who are disadvantaged.
- **Authoritarian personality theory** (Adorno) claims that prejudice is a personality trait of certain individuals, especially those with little education and those raised by cold and demanding parents.
- **Culture theory** (Bogardus) claims that prejudice is rooted in culture; we learn to feel greater social distance from some categories of people.
- **Conflict theory** claims that prejudice is a tool used by powerful people to divide and control the population.

pp. 362–65

prejudice (p. 360) a rigid and unfair generalization about an entire category of people

stereotype (p. 360) a simplified description applied to every person in some category

racism (p. 361) the belief that one racial category is innately superior or inferior to another

scapegoat (p. 363) a person or category of people, typically with little power, whom people unfairly blame for their own troubles

Discrimination

DISCRIMINATION refers to actions by which a person treats various categories of people unequally.

- Prejudice refers to *attitudes*; discrimination involves *actions*.
- Institutional prejudice and discrimination are biases built into the operation of society's institutions, including schools, hospitals, the police, and the workplace.
- Prejudice and discrimination perpetuate themselves in a vicious circle, resulting in social disadvantage that fuels additional prejudice and discrimination.

pp. 365–66

discrimination (p. 365) unequal treatment of various categories of people

institutional prejudice and discrimination (p. 365) bias built into the operation of society's institutions

Majority and Minority: Patterns of Interaction

PLURALISM means that racial and ethnic categories, although distinct, have roughly equal social standing.

- U.S. society is pluralistic in that all people in the United States, regardless of race or ethnicity, have equal standing under the law.
- U.S. society is not pluralistic in that all racial and ethnic categories do not have equal social standing.

p. 366

ASSIMILATION is a process by which minorities gradually adopt the patterns of the dominant culture.

- Assimilation involves changes in dress, language, religion, values, and friends.
- Assimilation is a strategy to escape prejudice and discrimination and to achieve upward social mobility.
- Some categories of people have assimilated more than others.

pp. 366–67

pluralism (p. 366) a state in which people of all races and ethnicities are distinct but have equal social standing

assimilation (p. 369) the process by which minorities gradually adopt patterns of the dominant culture

miscegenation (p. 367) biological reproduction by partners of different racial categories

segregation (p. 367) the physical and social separation of categories of people

genocide (p. 367) the systematic killing of one category of people by another

SEGREGATION is the physical and social separation of categories of people.

- Although some segregation is voluntary (as by the Amish), majorities usually segregate minorities by excluding them from neighborhoods, schools, and occupations.
- *De jure* segregation is segregation by law; *de facto* segregation describes settings that contain only people of one category.
- Hypersegregation means having little social contact with people beyond the local community.

p. 367

GENOCIDE is the systematic killing of one category of people by another.

- Historical examples of genocide include the extermination of Jews by the Nazis and the killing of Western-leaning people in Cambodia by Pol Pot.
- Recent examples of genocide include Hutus killing Tutsis in the African nation of Rwanda, Serbs killing Bosnians in the Balkans of Eastern Europe, and systematic killing in the Darfur region of Sudan.

p. 367

Race and Ethnicity in the United States

NATIVE AMERICANS, the earliest human inhabitants of the Americas, have endured genocide, segregation, and forced assimilation. Today, the social standing of Native Americans is well below the national average.

pp. 368–69

WHITE ANGLO-SAXON PROTESTANTS (WASPs) were most of the original European settlers of the United States, and many continue to enjoy high social position today.

pp. 369–70

AFRICAN AMERICANS experienced more than two centuries of slavery. Emancipation in 1865 gave way to segregation by law (the so-called Jim Crow laws). In the 1950s and 1960s, a national civil rights movement resulted in legislation that outlawed segregated schools and overt discrimination in employment and public accommodations. Today, despite legal equality, African Americans are still disadvantaged.

pp. 370–71

ASIAN AMERICANS have suffered both racial and ethnic hostility. Although some prejudice and discrimination continue, both Chinese and Japanese Americans now have above-average income and schooling. Asian immigrants—especially Koreans, Indians, and Filipinos—now account for more than one-third of all immigration to the United States.

pp. 372–74

HISPANIC AMERICANS/LATINOS, the largest U.S. minority, include many ethnicities sharing a Spanish heritage. Mexican Americans, the largest Hispanic minority, are concentrated in the southwest region of the country and are the poorest Hispanic category. Cubans, concentrated in Miami, are the most affluent Hispanic category.

pp. 374–75

ARAB AMERICANS are a growing U.S. minority. Because they come to the United States from so many different nations, Arab Americans are a culturally diverse population, and they are represented in all social classes. They have been a target of prejudice and hate crimes in recent years as a result of a stereotype that links all Arab Americans with terrorism.

pp. 375–77

WHITE ETHNIC AMERICANS are non-WASPs whose ancestors emigrated from Europe in the nineteenth and twentieth centuries. In response to prejudice and discrimination, many white ethnics formed supportive residential enclaves.

pp. 377–78

{ Growing older involves changes to our bodies. But societies shape our experiences at every stage of life, defining older people in distinctive ways that involve important disadvantages. }

CHAPTER 15

Aging and the Elderly

NOTE: If today's longevity were the same as it was in 1900, half of the U.S. population would not be here at all; half of that share would have already died, and the other half would never have been born (White & Preston, 1996).

POP CULTURE: In general, elderly people have a very limited presence in U.S. popular culture, which is largely a youth culture.

POP CULTURE: It is rare for one of Hollywood's Academy Awards to go to an elderly actor. This is especially true for women, with winners typically in their thirties. Older people who have won the Best Actor or Best Actress award include Jack Nicholson (won at ages 39 and 61), Henry Fonda (won at age 76), Jessica Tandy (won at age 80), and Katharine Hepburn (won at ages 26, 60, 61, and 74).

CHAPTER OVERVIEW

This chapter explores the process of growing old and explains why aging is a dimension of social stratification. The importance of understanding aging is increasing along with the elderly share of our population.

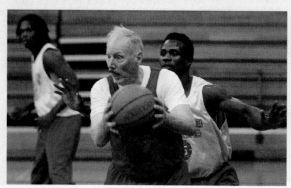

It was a good game for the basketball team at Roane State Community College in Tennessee as hundreds of students cheered as the clock ran out and the team posted a big victory over rival King College. But it was a special night for team member Ken Mink, who late in the game scored two points from the free-throw line. What's so unusual about that? Mink, a full-time student at Roane State, is seventy-three years old. Returning to college for a degree he never completed when he was younger, Mink began practicing with the basketball team and finally got the chance to play his first game in fifty-two years (Associated Press, 2008).

Does it seem odd for someone in his seventies to be playing a sport? Or even being enrolled in college? In our society, it is certainly not the norm. As we age, our lives change, and not simply in ways that reflect our biology. Society, too, is at work. In fact, society organizes our lives in patterned ways that correspond to being a child, an adolescent, an adult, and an older person. As this chapter explains, growing old in the United States brings with it distinctive experiences and also significant disadvantages, including lower income, prejudice, and discrimination in the workplace. For this reason, like class, gender, and race, growing old is a dimension of social stratification. The importance of learning about old age is increasing all the time because the number of older people in the U.S. population is greater than ever and rising rapidly.

The Graying of the United States

A quiet but powerful revolution is reshaping the United States. As shown in Figure 15–1, in 1900, the United States was a young nation, with half the population under age twenty-three; just 4 percent had reached sixty-five. But the number of elderly people—women and men aged sixty-five or older—increased tenfold during the last century. By 2009, the number of seniors exceeded 38 million and half the population was over thirty-seven. Seniors now outnumber teenagers, and they account for 12.7 percent of the entire population. By 2035, the number of seniors will double again to more than 77 million, and about half the country's people will be over forty (U.S. Census Bureau, 2008).

In nearly all high-income nations, the share of elderly people is increasing rapidly. There are two reasons for this increase: low birth rates (people are having fewer children) and increasing longevity (people are living longer).

In the United States, the ranks of the elderly will swell even more rapidly as the first of the baby boomers—some 78 million strong—reach age sixty-five in 2011. As recent political debate shows, there are serious questions about the ability of the current Social Security system to meet the needs of so many older people.

Birth Rate: Going Down

The U.S. birth rate has been falling for more than a century. This is the usual trend as societies industrialize. Why? Because in industrial societies, children are more likely to survive into adulthood, and so couples have fewer children. In addition, although to farming families children are an economic asset, to families in industrial societies children are an economic liability. In other words, children no longer add to their family's financial income but instead are a major expense.

Finally, as more and more women work outside the home, they choose to have fewer children. This trend reflects both the rising standing of women and advances in birth control technology over the past century.

Life Expectancy: Going Up

Life expectancy in the United States is going up. In 1900, a typical female born here could expect to live just forty-eight years, and a male, forty-six years. By contrast, females born in 2006 can look forward to living 80.7 years, and males can expect to live 75.4 years (Heron et al., 2008).

● SEEING SOCIOLOGY
in Everyday Life

In what specific ways would you expect campus life to change as more older people return to college for retraining? Do you see these changes as positive or not? Why?

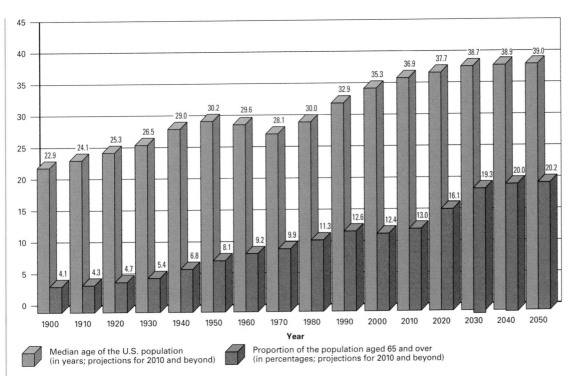

FIGURE 15–1 **The Graying of U.S. Society**

The proportion of the U.S. population over the age of sixty-five tripled during the last century. The median age of the U.S. population has now passed thirty-five years and will continue to rise.

Source: U.S. Census Bureau (2008).

This longer life span is one result of the Industrial Revolution. Greater material wealth and advances in medicine have raised living standards so that people benefit from better housing and nutrition. In addition, medical advances have almost eliminated infectious diseases—such as smallpox, diphtheria, and measles—that killed many infants and children a century ago. Other medical advances help us fend off cancer and heart disease, which claim most of the U.S. population, but now later in life.

As life becomes longer, the oldest segment of the U.S. population—people over eighty-five—is increasing rapidly and is already forty times greater than in 1900. These men and women now number 5.4 million (about 1.8 percent of the total population). Their numbers will grow to almost 20 million (about 4.3 percent of the total) by the year 2050 (U.S. Census Bureau, 2008).

This major increase in the elderly population will change our society in many ways. As the number of older people retiring from the labor force goes up, the proportion of nonworking adults—already about ten times greater than in 1900—will demand ever more health care and other resources. The ratio of working-age adults to non-working elderly people, called the *old-age dependency ratio,* will fall from the current level of five to one to about three to one by the year 2030 (U.S. Social Security Administration, 2008). With fewer and fewer workers to support tomorrow's swelling elderly population, what security can today's young people expect in their old age? The Thinking Globally box on page 388 takes a closer look at a country where the graying of the population is taking place even faster than in the United States: Japan.

An Aging Society: Cultural Change

As the average age of the population rises and the share over age sixty-five climbs ever higher, cultural patterns are likely to change. Through much of the twentieth century, the young rarely mixed with the old, so most people learned little about old age. But as this country's elderly population steadily increases, age segregation will decline. Younger

MAKING THE GRADE

The average age of the U.S. population is about thirty-seven; Japan's average age is forty-four.

gerontology the study of aging and the elderly

THINKING GLOBALLY

Can Too Many Be Too Old? A Report from Japan

With an average age of forty-four, the population of Japan is among the oldest in the world. One cause of the aging Japanese population is a declining birth rate, which has fallen to just 1.2 children born for every woman. A second cause of Japan's aging population is the nation's increasing life expectancy. Girls born in Japan in 2008 can expect to live, on average, eighty-six years, and boys can expect to live seventy-nine years.

Looking ahead, Japan's future population patterns are setting off alarms. First, the low birth rate is not enough to replace the country's population. This means that the number of Japanese people—now 127 million—will steadily fall to about 94 million by 2050. Second, by 2050, half the Japanese population will be older than fifty-five. This means that the country's labor force will shrink by millions of people, a change that may well reduce economic output and lower living standards. Third, the Japanese worry about how their society will support

their increasing population of seniors. In 2008, some 23 percent of Japan's people were sixty-five or older; this share will rise to about one-third by 2030. Today, three workers support every person over sixty-five. But this ratio is falling so that by 2050, the old-age dependency ratio will be about one to one. At this point, elderly people would not receive nearly as much income as they currently enjoy.

The Japanese case is all the more important because it is not unique. Other nations, including Italy and Spain, have populations almost as old as Japan's, and by 2050, they will face the same problems. The United States is among the "youngest" of the high-income countries. But what happens elsewhere will happen here, too. It is just a matter of time.

WHAT DO YOU THINK?

1. Living longer is generally thought to be a good thing. What are some of the problems that come with an aging population?

2. When a nation's average age passes fifty, what changes to popular culture might you expect?

3. How might immigration be a strategy to raise the old-age dependency ratio?

Sources: Porter (2004), Haub (2008), and U.S. Census Bureau (2008).

---

people will see more seniors on the highways, at shopping malls, and at sporting events. In addition, the design of buildings—including homes, stores, stadiums, and college classrooms—is likely to change to ease access for older shoppers, sports fans, and students.

As the chapter-opening story of Ken Mink suggests, colleges are also opening their doors to more older people, and seniors are becoming a familiar sight on many campuses. As baby boomers (people born between 1946 and 1964) enter old age, many are deciding to put off retirement and complete degrees or train for new careers. Community colleges, which offer extensive programs that prepare people for new types of work, are now offering a wide range of "second career" programs that attract older people (Olson, 2006).

Of course, the extent of contact with older people depends a great deal on where in the country you live. The elderly represent a far greater share of the population in some regions, especially in the midsection, from North Dakota and Minnesota down to Texas, as shown in National Map 15–1.

When thinking about how an aging population will change our ways of life, keep in mind that seniors are socially diverse. Being "elderly" is a category open to everyone, if we are lucky enough to live that long. Elders in the United States are women and men of all classes, races, and ethnic backgrounds.

The "Young Old" and the "Old Old"

Analysts sometimes distinguish two cohorts of the elderly, roughly equal in size (Himes, 2001). The younger elderly are between sixty-five and seventy-five and typically live independently with good health and financial security; they are likely to be living as couples. The older elderly are past age seventy-five and are more likely to have health and money problems and to be dependent on others. Because of their greater longevity, women outnumber men in the elderly population, an imbalance that grows greater with advancing age. Among the "oldest old," those over age eighty-five, 67 percent are women.

THE MAP: Because young people migrate to regions of the country where jobs are plentiful, counties with high proportions of elderly people are those that are economically contracting (especially rural counties in the middle of the country).

NOTE: Between 1960 and 2000, the overall U.S. population grew 56%; the over-65 population increased 116%, and the 85 and older population soared 367%.

DISCUSS: The journal entry on this page suggests that the van driver in Sri Lanka thought many of us in the United States really did not want our aging parents around. Do students think this is a fair assumption or not? Why?

Q: "The older I grow, the more I distrust the familiar doctrine that age brings wisdom." H. L. Mencken

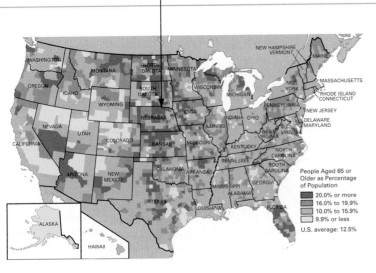

Sheila Markham and her many elderly friends in rural Boyd County, Nebraska, have a hard time finding young people to shovel their winter snow.

Seeing Ourselves

NATIONAL MAP 15–1

The Elderly Population across the United States

Common sense suggests that elderly people live in the Sunbelt, enjoying the warmer climate of the South and Southwest. Although it is true that Florida has a disproportionate share of people over age sixty-five, it turns out that most counties with high percentages of older people are in the Midwest. What do you think accounts for this pattern? Hint: Which regions of the United States do younger people leave in search of jobs?

Source: U.S. Census Bureau (2008).

People Aged 65 or Older as Percentage of Population
- 20.0% or more
- 16.0% to 19.9%
- 10.0% to 15.9%
- 9.9% or less

U.S. average: 12.5%

Growing Old: Biology and Culture

Studying the graying of a society's population is the focus of **gerontology** (derived from the Greek word *geron*, meaning "old person"), *the study of aging and the elderly*. Gerontologists—who work in many disciplines, including medicine, psychology, and sociology—investigate not only how people change as they grow old but also the different ways in which societies around the world define old age.

Biological Changes

Aging consists of gradual, ongoing changes in the body. But how we experience life's transitions—whether we welcome our maturity or complain about physical decline—depends largely on how our cultural system defines the various stages of life. In general, U.S. culture takes a positive view of biological changes that occur early in life. Through childhood and adolescence, people look forward to expanding opportunities and responsibilities.

But today's youth-oriented culture takes a dimmer view of the biological changes that happen later on. Few people receive congratulations for getting old, at least not until they reach eighty-five or ninety. Rather, we offer sympathy to friends as they turn forty, fifty, and sixty and make jokes to avoid facing up to the fact that advancing age will put us all on a slippery slope of physical and mental decline. In short, we assume that by age fifty or sixty, people stop growing *up* and begin growing *down*.

Growing old brings on predictable changes: gray hair, wrinkles, height and weight loss, and declining strength and vitality. After age fifty, bones become more brittle, and the older people get, the longer it takes for injuries to heal. In addition, advancing age means that the odds of developing a chronic illness (such as arthritis or diabetes) or a life-threatening condition (like heart disease or cancer) rise. The senses—taste, sight, touch, smell, and especially hearing—become less sharp with advancing age (Treas, 1995; Metz & Miner, 1998).

Though health becomes more fragile as people get older, most elderly men and women are not disabled by their physical condition. Only about one in ten seniors reports trouble walking, and fewer than one in five needs intensive care in a hospital or nursing home. About 11 percent need help with shopping, chores, or other daily activities. Overall, only 31 percent of people over age seventy-five characterize their health as "fair" or "poor"; 69 percent consider their overall condition "good" or "excellent." In fact, the share of seniors reporting good or excellent health is going up (Pleis & Lethbridge-Çejku, 2006; Centers for Disease Control and Prevention, 2007; Adams, Barnes, & Vickerie, 2008).

Of course, some elders have better health than others. Health problems become more common after people reach the age of seventy-five. In addition, because women typically live longer than men, they suffer more from chronic disabilities like arthritis. Well-to-do people also fare better because they live and work in safer and more healthful environments and can afford better medical care. Almost 80 percent of elderly people with annual incomes over $35,000 assess their own health as "excellent" or "good," but that figure drops below half for people with incomes under $20,000. Lower income and stress linked to prejudice and discrimination also explain why only 60 percent of older African Americans assess their health in positive terms, compared to 76 percent of elderly white

MAKING THE GRADE

Carefully read the discussion below explaining two key ways that culture shapes the process of aging.

people (Federal Interagency Forum, 2008; National Center for Health Statistics, 2009).

Psychological Changes

Just as we tend to overstate the physical problems of old age, we sometimes exaggerate the psychological changes that accompany growing old. The common view about intelligence over the life course can be summed up as "What goes up must come down."

If we measure skills such as sensorimotor coordination—the ability to arrange objects to match a drawing—we do find a steady decline after midlife. The ability to learn new material and to think quickly also declines, although not until around age seventy. Even then, only about 9 percent of adults over age seventy suffer symptoms ranging from mild memory loss to more serious mental conditions. For most, the ability to apply familiar ideas holds steady with advancing age, and the capacity for thoughtful reflection and spiritual growth actually increases (Baltes & Schaie, 1974; Metz & Miner, 1998; Cortez, 2008).

We all wonder if we will think or feel differently as we get older. Gerontologists report that for better or worse, the answer is usually no. The most common personality changes with advancing age are becoming less materialistic, more mellow in attitudes, and more thoughtful. Generally, two elderly people who had been childhood friends would recognize in each other the same personality traits that brought them together as youngsters (Neugarten, 1977; Wolfe, 1994).

Aging and Culture

November 1, Kandy, Sri Lanka. Our little van struggles up the steep mountain incline. Breaks in the lush vegetation offer spectacular views that interrupt our conversation about growing old. "Then there are no old-age homes in your country?" I ask. "In Colombo and other cities, I am sure," our driver responds, "but not many. We are not like you Americans." "And how is that?" I counter, stiffening a bit. His eyes remain fixed on the road: "We would not leave our fathers and mothers to live alone."

When do people grow old? How do younger people regard society's oldest members? How do elderly people view themselves? The answers people give to these questions vary from society to society, showing that although aging is a biological process, it is also a matter of culture.

How long and how well people live depend, first, on a society's technology and standard of living. Through most of human history, as the English philosopher Thomas Hobbes (1588–1679) famously put it, people's lives were "nasty, brutish, and short" (although Hobbes himself made it to the ripe old age of ninety-one). In his day, most people married and had children as teenagers, became middle-aged in their twenties, and died from various illnesses in their thirties and forties. Many of history's great men and women never reached what we would call old age at all: The English poet Keats died at age twenty-

The reality of growing old is as much a matter of culture as it is of biology. In the United States, being elderly often means being inactive; yet in many other countries of the world, elders often continue many familiar and productive routines.

THE MAP: Life expectancy closely parallels level of economic development; compare this map to Global Map 12–1 on page 303.

GLOBAL: In a ranking of the oldest countries (defined in terms of share of population aged 60 and over), the U.S. (14%) ranks below most European nations and Japan.

GLOBAL: In almost every nation, there are more elderly women than men. Exceptions include Bahrain, Bhutan, and Kuwait, probably due to sex-selective abortion and strong patriarchy.

NOTE: Life expectancy is affected by changes in infant mortality and tends to exaggerate the change in life span for those who reach old age. In 1900, Americans reaching age 65 typically lived to age 77; by 2004, they could expect to reach 84.

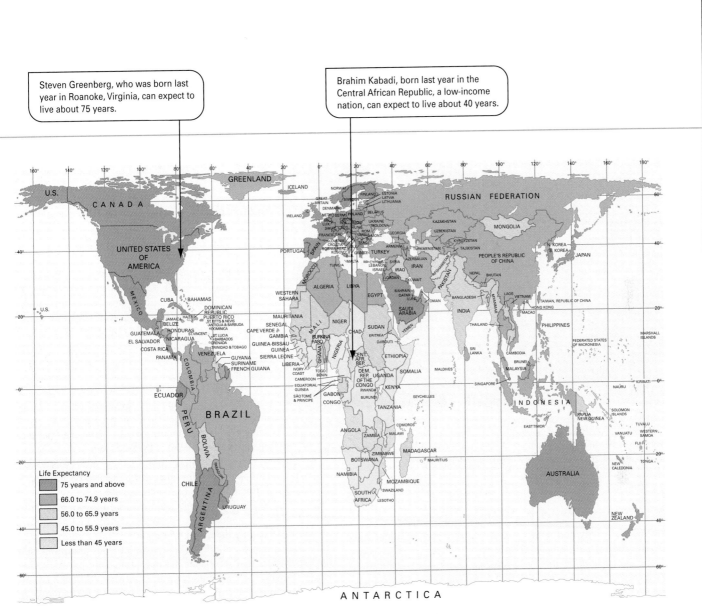

Steven Greenberg, who was born last year in Roanoke, Virginia, can expect to live about 75 years.

Brahim Kabadi, born last year in the Central African Republic, a low-income nation, can expect to live about 40 years.

Life Expectancy

- 75 years and above
- 66.0 to 74.9 years
- 56.0 to 65.9 years
- 45.0 to 55.9 years
- Less than 45 years

Window on the World

GLOBAL MAP 15–1 Life Expectancy in Global Perspective

Life expectancy shot up during the twentieth century in high-income countries, including Canada, the United States, Western Europe, Japan, and Australia. A newborn in the United States can now expect to live about seventy-eight years, and our life expectancy would be greater still were it not for the high risk of death among infants born into poverty. Because poverty is the rule in much of the world, lives are correspondingly shorter, especially in parts of Africa, where life expectancy may be less than forty years.

Source: Population Reference Bureau (2008).

six; Mozart, the Austrian composer, at thirty-five. Among famous writers, none of the three Brontë sisters lived to the end of her thirties; Edgar Allan Poe died at forty, Henry David Thoreau at forty-five, Oscar Wilde at forty-six, and William Shakespeare at fifty-two.

By about 1900, however, rising living standards and advancing medical technology in the United States and Western Europe combined to extend longevity to about age fifty. As Global Map 15–1 shows, this is still the figure in many low-income countries today. In high-income nations, however, increasing affluence has added almost thirty years to the average life span.

Just as important as longevity is the value societies attach to their senior members. As Chapter 10 ("Social Stratification") explains, all societies distribute basic resources unequally. We now turn to the importance of age in this process.

NOTE: The social clout of the baby boom generation is evident in the fact that they defined the 1960s, brought an end to the Vietnam War, got the vote by the time many of them were 18, initiated the second wave of feminism, celebrated the first Earth Day, and then raised the drinking age before their own children turned 18 (Longino, 1994).

Q: "Let us recognize ourselves in this old man or in that old woman." Simone de Beauvoir

NOTE: Research suggests that among adult subjects aged 25 to 74, subjective happiness rises with advancing age (Mroczek & Kolarz, 1998).

age stratification the unequal distribution of wealth, power, and privilege among people at different stages of the life course

gerontocracy a form of social organization in which the elderly have the most wealth, power, and prestige

SEEING SOCIOLOGY
in Everyday Life

Our society is sometimes described as a "youth culture." Why do people say this? Do you agree? Explain your answer.

In 2008, Hollywood actor Clint Eastwood, who is known for his tough-guy roles in films over past decades, directed, produced, and starred in *Gran Torino* at the age of seventy-eight. The film, which explores the challenges of growing older in a modern society, ended up being the biggest money-maker of his long career.

Age Stratification: A Global Survey

Like race, ethnicity, and gender, age is a basis for social ranking. **Age stratification** is *the unequal distribution of wealth, power, and privilege among people at different stages of the life course.* Age stratification varies according to a society's level of technological development.

Hunting and Gathering Societies

As Chapter 4 ("Society") explains, without the technology to produce a surplus of food, hunters and gatherers must be nomadic. This means that survival depends on physical strength and stamina. As members of these societies grow old (in this case, about age thirty), they become less active and may even be considered an economic burden and, when food is in short supply, abandoned (Sheehan, 1976).

Pastoral, Horticultural, and Agrarian Societies

Once societies develop the technology to raise their own crops and animals, they produce a surplus. In such societies, some individuals build up considerable wealth over a lifetime. Of all age categories, the most privileged are typically the elderly, a pattern called **gerontocracy**, *a form of social organization in which the elderly have the most wealth, power, and prestige.* Old people, particularly men, are honored and sometimes feared by their families, and they remain active leaders of society until they die. This respect for the elderly also explains the widespread practice of ancestor worship in agrarian societies.

Industrial and Postindustrial Societies

Industrialization pushes living standards upward and advances medical technology, both of which increase human life expectancy. But although industrialization adds to the *quantity* of life, it can harm the *quality* of life for older people. Contrary to the practice in traditional societies, industrial societies give little power and prestige to the elderly. The reason is that with industrialization, the prime source of wealth shifts from land (typically controlled by the oldest members of society) to businesses and other goods (usually owned and managed by younger people). For all low-income nations, 35 percent of men and 19 percent of women over the age of sixty-five remain in the labor force. In high-income countries, these percentages are far smaller: 14 percent of men and 8 percent of women. The fact that older people move out of the paid labor force is one reason that the peak earning years for U.S. workers are around age fifty-five, after which earnings decline (International Labour Organization, 2009).

In high-income countries, younger people move away from their parents to pursue careers, depending less on their parents and more on their own earning power. In addition, because industrial, urban societies change rapidly, the skills, traditions, and life experiences that served the old may seem unimportant to the young. Finally, the tremendous productivity of industrial nations means that not all members of a society need to work, so most of the very old and the very young play nonproductive roles.

The long-term effect of all these factors transforms *elders* (a word with positive connotations) into *the elderly* (a term that carries far less prestige). In postindustrial societies such as the United States and Canada, economic and political leaders are usually people between the ages of forty and sixty who combine experience with up-to-date skills. Even as the U.S. population, on average, is getting older, the country's corporate executives are getting younger, declining from an average age of fifty-nine in 1980 to fifty-five today (Herring, 2005).

In rapidly changing sectors of the economy, especially the high-tech fields, many key executives are younger still, sometimes barely out of college. Industrial societies often give older people only marginal participation in the economy because they lack the knowledge and training demanded in a fast-changing marketplace.

Some occupations are dominated by older people. The average farmer is fifty-five; the average age of the entire U.S. labor force is only forty-one. More than one-fourth of today's farmers are over the age of

DISCUSS: To what extent do students think problems such as finding meaning in life, social isolation, and poverty are caused by biological factors? To what extent are they caused by the way society is organized? Explain.

DIVERSITY: By age 75, 46% of women but only 19% of men live alone. By 85: 57% and 32%. At no age do most men live alone.

NOTE: Academics are older than the adult population as a whole. With increasing college enrollments and many coming retirements, our colleagues should be in rising demand.

MAKING THE GRADE

Notice the big differences between women and men in living arrangements.

sixty-five. Older people also predominate in other traditional occupations, working as barbers, tailors, and shop clerks, and in jobs that involve minimal physical activity, such as night security guards (Yudelman & Kealy, 2000; U.S. Department of Agriculture, 2004).

Japan: An Exceptional Case

Throughout the last century, Japan stood out as an exception to the rule that industrialization lowers the social standing of older people. Not only is the share of seniors in Japan increasing as fast as anywhere in the world, but Japan's more traditional culture gives older people great importance. Most elders in Japan live with an adult daughter or son, and they play a significant role in family life. Elderly men in Japan are also more likely than their U.S. counterparts to stay in the labor force, and in many Japanese corporations, the oldest employees enjoy the greatest respect. But Japan is becoming more like other industrial nations, where growing old means giving up some measure of social importance. In addition, a long economic downturn has left Japanese families less able to care for their older members, which may further weaken the traditional importance of elders (Ogawa & Retherford, 1997; Onishi, 2006; Lah, 2008).

Transitions and Challenges of Aging

We confront change at each stage of life. Old age has its rewards, but of all stages of the life course, it presents the greatest challenges.

Physical decline in old age is less serious than most younger people think. But even so, older people endure pain, limit their activities, increase their dependency on others, lose dear friends and relatives, and face up to their own mortality. Because our culture places such a high value on youthfulness, aging in the United States often means added fear and self-doubt. As one retired psychologist quipped about old age, "Don't let the current hype about the joys of retirement fool you. They are not the best of times. It's just that the alternative is even worse" (Rubenstein, 1991).

Finding Meaning

Chapter 5 ("Socialization") presented Erik Erikson's theory that elderly people must resolve a tension of "integrity versus despair." No matter how much they still may be learning and achieving, older people recognize that their lives are nearing an end. Thus elderly people spend more time reflecting on their past, remembering disappointments as well as accomplishments. Integrity, to Erikson (1963, orig. 1950; 1980), means assessing your life realistically. Without such honesty, this stage of life may turn into a time of despair—a dead end with little positive meaning.

Table 15–1   Living Arrangements of the Elderly, 2007

	Men	Women
Living alone	19.0%	38.6%
Living with spouse	72.8	42.2
Living with other relatives or nonrelatives	8.2	19.2

In 2007, some 3.5 percent of elderly people lived in nursing homes. This number includes people from all of these categories.

Source: U.S. Census Bureau (2008).

In a classic study of people in their seventies, Bernice Neugarten (1971) found that some people cope with growing older better than others. Worst off are those who fail to come to terms with aging; they develop *disintegrated and disorganized personalities* marked by despair. Many of these people end up as passive residents of hospitals or nursing homes.

Slightly better off are people with *passive-dependent personalities.* They have little confidence in their abilities to cope with daily events, sometimes seeking help even if they do not really need it. Always in danger of social withdrawal, their life satisfaction level is relatively low.

A third category develops *defended personalities,* living independently but fearful of aging. They try to shield themselves from the reality of old age by fighting to stay youthful and physically fit. Although it is good to be concerned about health, setting unrealistic standards breeds stress and disappointment.

Most of Neugarten's subjects, however, displayed what she termed *integrated personalities,* coping well with the challenges of growing old. As Neugarten sees it, the key to successful aging lies in keeping personal dignity and self-confidence while accepting growing old.

Social Isolation

Being alone can cause anxiety at any age, but isolation is most common among elderly people. Retirement closes off one source of social interaction, physical problems may limit mobility, and negative stereotypes of the elderly as "over the hill" may discourage younger people from close social contact with them.

But the greatest cause of social isolation is the death of significant others, especially the death of a spouse. One study found that almost three-fourths of widows and widowers cited loneliness as their most serious problem (Lund, 1989).

The problem of social isolation falls more heavily on women because they typically outlive their husbands. Table 15–1 shows that 73 percent of men aged sixty-five and over live with spouses, but only 42 percent of elderly women do. In addition, 39 percent of older

RESOURCE: The author's companion reader *Seeing Ourselves*, 8th ed., includes an examination of how the grandparent role is changing by Roseann Giarrusso, Merril Silverstein, and Vern Bengston.

RESOURCE: For information on the role of grandparents in children's lives, see the Census Bureau report *Grandparents Living with Grandchildren: 2000* at http://www.census.gov/prod/2003pubs/c2kbr-31.pdf

Seeing SOCIOLOGY in the NEWS

Grandparents Raising Grandkids: "Everybody Understands"

BY STACY BYRNE
April 6, 2009

At a brown-bag lunch meeting earlier this year, Elaine Steiger told how her eight-year-old great-grandson Micah has been acting rebellious lately.

"He won't go to church with me," Steiger said. "He's mad at me."

Steiger and her husband, Emil, who recently died, have raised the boy since he was a baby. They eventually adopted him.

"Both of his parents landed in prison," she said. "Since he turned eight it seems like he's having more problems. He's not seeing his mother as much as he'd like to."

Steiger is not able to vent about the daily frustrations of parenthood to her co-workers; she is seventy-two and retired seven years ago from working in the kitchen at Benefis Health System.

So she finds others who are experiencing the same ups and downs that come with parenting grandchildren—people who understand and might have advice or just an open ear and a shoulder to cry on—at the Grandparents Raising Grandchildren Support Group that meets monthly at Westgate Mall.

"I have one of those, too," said Mariellen Ritts, who also is raising an eight-year-old grandson. "His problem is the kids he's hanging out with at school."

As the discussion continued, some of the others—grandparents, great-grandparents and foster grandparents—threw in whatever advice they had to offer. Then Ritts, who acts as the group leader, said she would arrange for a speaker to come in and talk about behavioral issues among elementary school kids.

Another grandparent then brought up the grandparent-rights bills being presented at the Legislature. She explained what the bills were and told when they would be heard.

The group also made plans for a chili feed and talked about some of the speakers and events in the months to come.

"When I first got into that group (about five years ago), I didn't realize there were that many (other grandparents) out there," said Ritts, adding there are more than sixty members, though usually less than half attend the meetings.

Ritts said they discuss problems they or their grandchildren are having, they support each other during court battles, and they lean on each other when they find themselves lacking parental rights.

"It's just a good group because we understand each other," said Steiger, adding it's comforting to hear other people's stories. "We shed many tears, but everybody understands when you break down. We're all in the same boat."

Dr. Sandra Bailey started the Grandparents Raising Grandchildren Project through Montana State University Extension after seeing the need to provide grandparents with resources to help with the challenges associated with raising their grandchildren. . . .

The network of grandparents raising grandchildren support groups popping up around the

women (especially the "older elderly") live alone, compared to 19 percent of older men (U.S. Census Bureau, 2008).

For most older people, family members are the major source of social support. The majority of U.S. seniors have at least one adult child living no more than 10 miles away. About half of these nearby children visit their parents at least once a week, although research confirms that daughters are more likely than sons to visit regularly (Lin & Rogerson, 1994; Rimer, 1998). In addition, older people are playing an increasing role in the lives of not only their children but also their grandchildren. Seeing Sociology in the News takes a closer look.

Retirement

Beyond earnings, work provides us with an important part of our personal identity. Therefore, retirement means not only a reduction in income but also less social prestige and perhaps some loss of purpose in life.

Some organizations help ease this transition. Colleges and universities, for example, confer the title "professor emeritus" (*emeritus* in Latin means "fully earned") on retired faculty members, many of whom are permitted to keep library privileges, a parking space, and an e-mail account. These highly experienced faculty can be a valuable resource not only to students but to younger professors as well (Parini, 2001).

Because seniors are socially diverse, there is no single formula for successful retirement. Part-time work occupies many people entering old age and provides some extra cash as well. Grandparenting is an enormous source of pleasure for many older people. Volunteer work is another path to rewarding activity, especially for those who have saved enough so that they do not have to work—one reason that volunteerism is increasing more among seniors than in any other age category (Gardyn, 2000; Savishinsky, 2000; Shapiro, 2001).

Although retirement is a familiar idea, the concept developed only within the past century or so in high-income countries. High-income societies are so productive that not everyone needs to work; in addition, advanced technology places a premium on up-to-date skills. Therefore, retirement emerged as a strategy to permit younger workers—presumably those with the most current knowledge and training—to have the largest presence in the labor force. Fifty years ago, most companies in the United States even had a mandatory retirement age, typically between sixty-five and seventy, although in the 1970s, Congress enacted laws phasing out such policies so that they apply to only a few occupations today. For example, air traffic controllers hired after 1972 must retire at age fifty-six, commercial airline pilots must retire at age sixty, and most police officers and firefighters must retire between fifty-five and sixty (Gokhale, 2004). In most high-income societies, then, retirement is a personal choice made possible by private and government pension programs. In low-income nations, most people do not have the opportunity to retire from paid work.

Even in high-income nations, of course, people can choose to retire only if they can afford to do so. Generally speaking, when eco-

DISCUSS: Do students think most workers will find retirement to be an improvement in their lives or not? How does the type of work you do affect the experience of retirement?

DIVERSITY: Poverty rates for the elderly by race and ethnicity, 2005: ages 65–74: all, 8.8%; non-Hispanic white, 6.1%; African American, 23.5%; Hispanic, 16.5%;

ages 75 and over: all, 10.6%; non-Hispanic white, 8.8%; African American, 22.8%; Hispanic, 18.0% (U.S. Census Bureau, 2008).

DISCUSS: Retirement provides the potential to do some of life's most important work. Consider the activism and accomplishments of Jimmy Carter since he left the presidency in 1981.

state is an example of how the project is helping. The project, with the help of AARP and several state agencies, also offers parent education classes, coordinates a statewide task force to address grandparents' needs, produces fact sheets and newsletters, and operates a library of reference materials on family and parenting.

Through the project, grandparents can find information about the Women Infant Children (WIC) program, Temporary Assistance for Needy Families (TANF), Children's Health Insurance Plan (CHIP), DPHHS Senior and Long Term Care (SLTC), plus everything from food stamps to Medicaid to finding child care.

Jona McNamee, extension agent at the Cascade County Extension office, said some people make quilts for the grandparents and others donate meals or various services, such as haircuts and manicures. . . .

Marion Mullins was raised by her grandmother, and now she is raising three of her own grandchildren. . . .

Mullins leads the Busy Beavers 4-H Club that meets every other Saturday at the First English Lutheran Church, "unless there's a wedding or something," she said. She's been teaching the kids how to sew, cook, garden and do ceramics and woodworking.

"I'm drawing on what I learned when I was in 4-H," she said. "I had an excellent teacher; I remember everything she taught me."

Most of the kids in the group are being raised by their grandparents, though the group is open to anyone ages 6 to 18 who would like to join. It only costs $5 a year, plus the occasional cost of supplies, to join a 4-H club, where kids can learn skills that will help them throughout their lives.

"They're getting some sort of direction; they're learning new tasks," Mullins said. "My guys, they've learned to do their own laundry; they're learning how to cook. One of my kids is ADHD, and he excels with his cooking. Also I've let him sew a little bit and he excels at that."

Mullins said many of the kids in the Busy Beavers come from families that don't have a lot of money. But people donate to the group ("someone donated the wood for the woodworking"), and she has the molds and is able to fire the ceramics and supply the paint.

"If someone wanted to donate materials for sewing, they could take it to the extension office," she said.

WHAT DO YOU THINK?

1. Do you think that, in general, grandparents should have specific rights with respect to their grandchildren? If so, what rights? Why?

2. Why do you think the number of grandparents raising young children is going up?

3. What benefits do grandparents gain by raising grandchildren?

Adapted from the original article, "Grandparents Raising Grandkids: Everybody Understands," by Stacy Byrne, *Great Falls Tribune*, April 6, 2009, www.greatfallstribune.com.

nomic times are good, people save more and think about retiring early. This was generally the case in the United States during the second half of the twentieth century. By 2005, the median net worth of senior households was about $200,000. Greater wealth permitted more people to retire earlier, and so the median retirement age fell from sixty-eight in 1950 to sixty-three by 2005.

However, the economic downturn that began in 2007 has had the opposite effect, forcing older people to confront the harsh reality that their retirement "nest egg" has been cracked by the sinking stock market and disappearing pensions. With so much wealth suddenly gone, many find that they must continue to work. A recent policy to deal with hard times is "staged retirement," in which people continue working well past the age of sixty-five, reducing their hours at work to a point that allows them to build greater financial security (Kadlec, 2002; McCartney, 2005; Koskela, 2008).

Some retired people, including many whose investments have declined in value or who now face expenses that they cannot afford, are being forced to go back to paid work. The Seeing Sociology in Everyday Life box on page 396 takes a closer look.

Aging and Poverty

By the time they reach sixty-five, most people have paid off their home mortgages and their children's college expenses. But the costs of medical care, household help, and home utilities (like heat) typically go up. At the same time, retirement often means a significant decline in income. The good news is that over recent decades, seniors have built up more wealth than ever before (as noted, a median net worth of about $200,000 in 2005). However, most of this is tied up in the value of their homes, which has fallen in recent years. And home values do not provide income for everyday expenses. The economic downturn has also hurt many seniors, as employers have cut back retirement pensions and benefits at the same time that investment income has declined. Today's reality, then, is that most people over age sixty-five get most of their income from the government in the form of Social Security. This helps explain why the risk of poverty rises after midlife, as shown in Figure 15–2 on page 397.

Looking back in time, the poverty rate among the elderly fell from about 35 percent in 1960 to 9.7 percent in 2007—below the 12.5 percent rate for the entire population. The long-term trend since about 1980 shows that seniors have posted a 35 percent increase in average income (in constant dollars), double the increase in income of people under thirty-five (U.S. Census Bureau, 2008).

Several factors have boosted the financial strength of seniors. Better health now allows people who want to work to stay in the labor force, and more of today's older couples earn two incomes. Government policy, too, has helped older people, because programs benefiting the elderly—including Social Security—now amount to almost half of all government spending, even as spending on children has remained flat. But the recent economic downturn has canceled out many of these advantages as people have lost some of the pension income they were counting on, and as more companies reduce

NOTE: Point out to the class that the poverty rate is at or below the national aver-age for every age category above young people under 25. That is one good way of highlighting how much of the poverty problem involves children and young adults.

NOTE: The costs of prescription drugs were about $161 billion in 2003, and sen-iors consume much of this. By 2010, this cost is projected to rise to $360 billion

(Fetto, 2003a).

NOTE: Despite the present trend toward greater affluence for the elderly, several factors may undermine their future financial security: (1) the shift toward lower-income jobs noted in Chapter 11, (2) an increase in people reaching 65 with liv-ing parents who need support, and (3) reliance on an increasingly minority workforce that historically has been underpaid to support the retirement system.

SEEING SOCIOLOGY
in Everyday Life

The argument supporting a mandatory retirement age for airline pilots rests on the fact that the lives of hundreds of people are, literally, in their hands. What about surgeons, who currently are not subject to mandatory retirement? Should there be such a requirement or not? Why?

SEEING SOCIOLOGY
in Everyday Life

Do you think that the adult children of elderly people should be expected to help with the financial needs of their parents? Why or why not?

SEEING SOCIOLOGY IN EVERYDAY LIFE

Back to Work! Will We Ever Get to Retire?

Sixty-year-old Martha Perry used to think about old age as the "golden years." Perry had worked hard for decades, and it had paid off. The sale of her small business, added to years of regular sav-ings, netted her a total of about $1 million, which she invested. Based on the projected earnings from her investments, with additional income from Social Security, Perry figured she was set for the rest of her life. She looked forward to playing golf, enjoying an active social life, and traveling.

That was before the stock market tumble that began in 2008. A year later, her accountant gave her some bad news: Her nest egg had lost half its value. With barely half the income she expected—only about $16,000 a year—Perry's travel plans have been put on hold. "I'm going to have to look for part-time work," she says, shaking her head. "But something tells me it's going to end up being full-time work."

The severe recession that began in 2007 has sent stock prices tumbling and caused home values to fall. This economic downturn has hit everyone hard, but older people who rely on investment income have suffered more than most. Many have seen their retire-

ment vanish as quickly as the money in their 401(k) investment portfolios. Still others have lost retirement investments as a result of corpo-rate scandals. That explains why millions of older people who had hoped to retire are still working and millions of retirees who can no longer make ends meet are now reading the want ads and once again looking for work.

This trend helps explain why the share of older people in the labor force is now going

People used to believe that if they "played by the rules" and worked hard for decades, they could expect a comfortable retirement. What has the recent economic downturn done to this idea?

up. Certainly, some seniors are happy to con-tinue their careers, and others enjoy working part time. But in the past, many seniors did so by choice, enjoying their jobs while knowing they could retire whenever they wanted to. Now millions of people realize that they no longer have a choice. Worse, they wonder whether they will ever be able to step out of the labor force. For those who do not like the jobs they have, of course, the future will be far less happy. The bottom line: The dream of "early retirement," widespread a decade ago, is all but gone.

WHAT DO YOU THINK?

1. What is the relationship between how well the economy is doing and people's retirement plans?

2. Why does "phased retirement" for many older people really mean "delayed retirement"?

3. Do you know anyone who has had a pension reduced or canceled by a corporation? How has that affected the person's financial security?

Sources: Kadlec (2002) and Koskela (2008).

---

or cancel retirement benefits, workers and retirees are receiving less to fund their future.

As we have seen in earlier chapters, some categories of people face particular challenges. Disadvantages linked to race and ethnic-ity throughout the life course persist in old age. In 2007, the poverty rate among elderly Hispanics (17.1 percent) and African Americans (23.2 percent) was two to three times higher than the rate for elderly non-Hispanic whites (7.4 percent) (U.S. Census Bureau, 2008).

Gender also shapes the lives of people as they age. Among full-time workers, women over sixty-five had median earnings of $31,517 in 2007, compared to $45,340 for men over sixty-five. A quick calcu-lation shows that these older full-time working women earned just 70 percent as much as comparable men. Thus the income gap linked

to gender is greater among older people than among younger peo-ple (recall from Chapter 13, "Gender Stratification," that *all* working women earn 78 percent as much as *all* working men). This is because older women typically have much less schooling than men their age, so they hold lower-paying jobs, which are also less likely to provide pensions later on.

But because most elderly people have retired from the labor force, a more realistic financial picture must take account of all sen-iors. When we include both those who are working and those who are not, median individual income is far lower: $15,714 for women, which is 57 percent of the $27,454 earned by men (U.S. Census Bureau, 2008). In light of these low averages, it is easy to see why seniors—and especially women, who are less likely to have pensions

Q: "Aging is the neglected stepchild of the human life cycle." Robert Butler

SOCIAL SURVEY: The National Center on Elder Abuse reports that in about one-third of cases, seniors are abused by spouses; adult children at home come next, with self-abuse through neglect third.

GLOBAL: In a 1994 effort to strengthen "family values," Singapore passed legislation allowing elderly people to sue their children for support.

DISCUSS: Why is most eldercare provided by women?

SOCIAL SURVEY: "As you know, many older people share a home with their grown children. Do you think this is generally a good idea or a bad idea?" (GSS 2004, N = 876; Codebook, 2006:263)

"A good idea"   47.1%   "Depends"   21.5%
"A bad idea"   30.9%   "Don't know"/No response   0.5%

caregiving information and unpaid care provided to a dependent person by family members, other relatives, or friends

ageism prejudice and discrimination against older people

Growing old means increased risk of poverty because by age 60, average income goes down.

or income other than Social Security—are concerned about expenses such as the costs of health care and prescription drugs, both of which are rising fast (Fetto, 2003a; Institute for Women's Policy Research, 2007).

In the United States, today as in decades past, growing old (especially for women and other minorities) increases the risk of poverty. One government study found that elderly households typically spend about 80 percent of their income on housing, food, health care, and other basic necessities. This points to the conclusion that most seniors are just getting by (Federal Interagency Forum, 2008).

Finally, poverty among the elderly is often hidden from view. Because of personal pride and a desire to remain independent, many elderly people hide financial problems, even from their own families. People who have supported their children for years find it difficult to admit that they can no longer provide for themselves.

Caregiving

In an aging society, the need for caregiving is bound to increase. **Caregiving** refers to *informal and unpaid care provided to a dependent person by family members, other relatives, or friends*. Although parents provide caregiving to children, the term is more often applied to the needs of elderly men and women. Indeed, today's middle-aged adults are called the "sandwich generation" because many will spend as much time caring for their aging parents as for their own children.[1]

Who Are the Caregivers?

Surveys show that 80 percent of caregiving to elders is provided by family members, in most cases by one person. Most caregivers live close to the older person. In addition, most caregiving is provided by women, most often daughters or wives. This gender norm is so strong that daughters-in-law are more likely than blood-related sons to care for an aging parent (National Alliance for Caregiving and AARP, 2004; U.S. Department of Health and Human Services, 2004).

About two-thirds of caregivers are married, and one-third are also responsible for young children. When we add the fact that half of all caregivers also have a part- or full-time job, it is clear that caregiving is a responsibility over and above what most people already consider a full day's work. Half of all primary caregivers spend more than twenty hours per week providing elder care.

Elder Abuse

Abuse of older people takes many forms, from passive neglect to active torment; it includes verbal, emotional, financial, and physical harm.

Diversity Snapshot

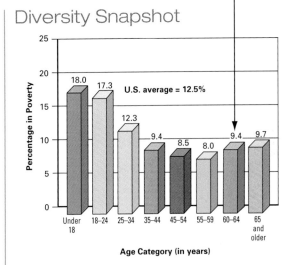

FIGURE 15–2   **U.S. Poverty Rates, by Age, 2007**
The highest poverty rate is for young people. But among older people, the rate rises once again.
Source: U.S. Census Bureau (2008).

At least 1 million elderly people (3 percent of the total) suffer serious maltreatment each year, and three times as many (about 10 percent) suffer abuse at some point. Like other forms of family violence, abuse of the elderly often goes unreported because the victims are reluctant to talk about their plight (Holmstrom, 1994; M. Thompson, 1997, 1998; National Center on Elder Abuse, 2005).

Many caregivers experience fatigue, emotional distress, and guilt over not being able to do more. Abuse is most likely to occur if the caregiver not only finds the work difficult but also (1) works full time, (2) cares for young children, (3) is poor, (4) feels little affection for the older person, (5) finds the elderly person very difficult, and (6) gets no support or help from others.

But the relatively small share of cases involving abuse should not overshadow the positive side of caregiving. Helping another person is a selfless act of human kindness that affirms the best in us and provides a source of personal enrichment and satisfaction (Lund, 1993).

Ageism

Earlier chapters explained how ideology—including racism and sexism—serves to justify the social disadvantages of minorities. In the same way, sociologists use the term **ageism** for *prejudice and*

---

[1]This discussion of caregiving is based on Lund (1993) and additional information provided by Dale Lund.

NOTE: Robert Butler coined the term "ageism" in 1969.

RESOURCE: Robert Butler's statement "The Tragedy of Old Age in America," which challenges various myths about old age, is included among the classics in the Macionis and Benokraitis reader *Seeing Ourselves*, 8th ed.

SOCIAL SURVEY: Surveys show 7% of Internet users are 64–72; 4% are 73 and older, with 45% of these seniors online.

DISCUSS: Was John Glenn's 1999 flight into space at age 77 an important statement about the abilities of older people? At the same age Clint Eastwood recently starred in and directed his most successful movie (*Gran Torino*).

DIVERSITY: The Age Discrimination in Employment Act (1967) prohibits discrimination against workers or job applicants aged 40 to 65. In 1986, an additional change banned mandatory retirement in almost all types of jobs.

SEEING SOCIOLOGY
in Everyday Life

On your campus, are the most popular faculty members younger instructors or older instructors? Do you think that age plays into a professor's student evaluations? If so, how?

SEEING SOCIOLOGY
in Everyday Life

Do you think elderly people should be considered a minority? Explain why or why not.

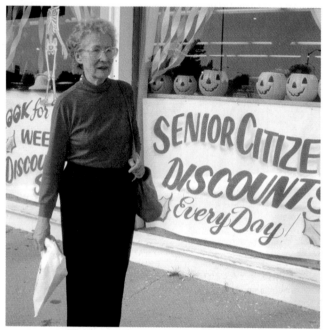

In the United States, it is common for businesses to offer a "senior discount" to people over sixty-five (sometimes even fifty-five). What is the reason for this practice? Would you prefer a policy of offering discounts to single parents with children, a category of people at much higher risk of poverty?

discrimination against older people. Elderly people are the primary targets of ageism, although middle-aged people can suffer as well. Examples of ageism include passing over qualified older job applicants in favor of younger workers or firing older workers first.

Like racism and sexism, ageism can be blatant (as when a company decides not to hire a sixty-year-old applicant because of her age) or subtle (as when a nurse speaks to elderly patients in a condescending tone, as if they were children). Also like racism and sexism, ageism builds physical traits into stereotypes. In the case of the elderly, some people consider gray hair, wrinkled skin, and stooped posture signs of personal incompetence. Negative stereotypes portray the aged as helpless, confused, unable to deal with change, and generally unhappy. Even "positive" images of sweet little old ladies and eccentric old gentlemen are stereotypes that gloss over individuality and ignore years of experience and accomplishment (Butler, 1975; E. Cohen, 2001).

Sometimes ageism reflects a bit of truth. Statistically speaking, older people are more likely than younger people to be mentally and physically impaired. But we slip into ageism when we make unfair generalizations about an entire category of people.

Betty Friedan (1993), a pioneer of the modern feminist movement, believes that ageism is deeply rooted in our culture. She points out that few elderly people appear in the mass media; only a small percentage of television shows, for example, feature main characters over age sixty. More generally, when most of us think about older people, it is often in negative terms: This older man *lacks* a job, that older woman has *lost* her vitality, and seniors *look back* to their youth. In short, says Friedan, we often treat being old as if it were a disease, marked by decline and deterioration, for which there is no cure.

Even so, Friedan believes that older women and men in the United States are discovering that they have more to contribute than others give them credit for. Advising small business owners, designing housing for the poor, teaching children to read—there are countless ways in which older people can help others and at the same time enhance their own lives.

The Elderly: A Minority?

Elderly people in the United States face social disadvantages. Does that mean that the elderly are a minority in the same way as, say, African Americans or women?

The elderly appear to meet the definition of a minority because they have a clear social identity based on their age and they are subject to prejudice and discrimination. But Gordon Streib (1968) counters that we should not think of elderly people as a minority. First, minority status is usually both permanent and exclusive. That is, a person is an African American or a woman *for life* and cannot become part of the dominant category of whites or men. But being elderly is an *open* status because people are elderly for only part of their lives, and everyone who has the good fortune to live long enough grows old.

Second, the seniors at highest risk of being poor or otherwise disadvantaged fall into categories of people—women, African Americans, Hispanics—who are at highest risk of being poor throughout the life course. As Streib sees it, it is not so much that the old grow poor as that the poor grow old.

If so, old people are not a minority in the same sense as other categories. It might be better to say that the elderly are a part of our population that faces special challenges as they age.

Theoretical Analysis of Aging

Let us now apply sociology's theoretical approaches to gain insight into how society shapes the lives of the elderly. We will consider the structural-functional, symbolic-interaction, and social-conflict approaches in turn.

DIVERSITY: On average, a male born in the U.S. can look forward to 60 years of good health, a female to 63.

NOTE: The cultural value of individualism encourages elderly people to fend for themselves in order to be self-reliant. This kind of social disengagement is vividly evident in the single-room occupancy (SRO) hotels inhabited by many poor, elderly men (Cowgill, 1986:49).

NOTE: Another limitation of activity theory is putting too much emphasis on physical activity (Dale Lund).

DIVERSITY: The elderly are politically active: three-fourths of seniors voted in the 2008 national elections, compared to about 60% of people aged 25–34. Seniors supported McCain over Obama 51% to 47%.

disengagement theory the idea that society functions in an orderly way by removing people from positions of responsibility as they reach old age

activity theory the idea that a high level of activity increases personal satisfation in old age

Structural-Functional Analysis: Aging and Disengagement

Drawing on the ideas of Talcott Parsons—an architect of the structural-functional approach—Elaine Cumming and William Henry (1961) explain that the physical decline and death that accompany aging can disrupt society. In response, society *disengages* the elderly, gradually transferring statuses and roles from the old to the young so that tasks are performed with minimal interruption. **Disengagement theory** is *the idea that society functions in an orderly way by removing people from positions of responsibility as they reach old age.*

Disengagement ensures the orderly operation of society by removing aging people from productive roles before they are no longer able to perform them. Another benefit of disengagement in a rapidly changing society is that it makes room for young workers, who typically have the most up-to-date skills and training. Disengagement provides benefits to aging people as well. Although most sixty-year-olds in the United States wish to keep working, most begin to think about retirement and perhaps cut back a bit on their workload. Exactly when people begin to disengage from their careers, of course, depends on their health, enjoyment of the job, and financial situation.

Retiring does not mean being inactive. Some people start a new career and others pursue hobbies or engage in volunteer work. In general, people in their sixties start to think less about what they *have been doing* and begin to think more about what they *want to do* with the rest of their lives (Palmore, 1979; Schultz & Heckhausen, 1996).

Disengagement theory suggests that society gradually removes responsibilities from people as they grow old. Activity theory counters that like people at any stage of life, elders find life worthwhile to the extent that they stay active. As a result, many older men and women seek out new jobs, hobbies, and social activities.

○ **CRITICAL REVIEW** Disengagement theory explains why rapidly changing high-income societies tend to define their oldest members as socially marginal. But there are several limitations to this approach.

First, especially in recent years, many workers have found that they cannot disengage from paid work because they need the income. Second, some elderly people, rich or poor, do not want to disengage from work they enjoy. Disengagement may also mean losing friends and social prestige. Third, it is not clear that the societal benefits of disengagement outweigh its social costs, which include the loss of human resources and the need to take care of people who might otherwise be able to support themselves. As the number of elderly people swells, finding ways to help seniors remain independent is a high priority. Fourth, any rigid system of disengagement does not take account of the widely differing abilities of the elderly. This concern leads us to the symbolic-interaction approach.

○ **CHECK YOUR LEARNING** State clearly the basic idea behind disengagement theory. How does disengagement benefit the aging individual? How does it benefit society?

Symbolic-Interaction Analysis: Aging and Activity

Drawing on the symbolic-interaction approach, **activity theory** is *the idea that a high level of activity increases personal satisfaction in old age.* Because everyone bases social identity on many roles, disengagement is bound to reduce satisfaction and meaning in the lives of older people. What seniors need is not to be pushed out of roles but to have many productive or recreational options. The importance of having choices is especially great for today's sixty-five-year-old, who can look forward to about twenty more years of life (Smart, 2001; M. W. Walsh, 2001).

Activity theory does not reject the idea of job disengagement; it simply says that people need to find new roles to replace those they leave behind. Research confirms that elderly people who maintain a high activity level find the most satisfaction in their lives.

Activity theory also recognizes that the elderly are diverse, with a variety of interests, needs, and physical abilities. For this reason, the activities that people choose and the pace at which they pursue them are always an individual matter (Neugarten, 1977; Moen, Dempster-McClain, & Williams, 1992).

○ **CRITICAL REVIEW** Activity theory shifts the focus of analysis from the needs of society (as stated in disengagement theory) to the needs of the elderly themselves. It emphasizes the

399

NOTE: A grim demographic fact is that after age 30, a person's chance of death doubles every eight years (Waldrop, 1992).

NOTE: The modern avoidance of death is evident in the loss of the traditional custom of writing one's own epitaph. Today, even writing a will is considered to be a matter for late in life and is avoided entirely by two-thirds of U.S. people, who die without one.

GLOBAL: Death practices display remarkable cultural variety. Societies burn, bury, leave out in the weather, embalm, smoke, and even pickle their dead members. Similarly, funerals are times for laughter, tears, revelry, solemnity, fighting, or even sex—depending on the culture.

Q: "One can experience an unconditional affirmation of life only when one has accepted death, not as contrary to life, but as an aspect of it." Joseph Campbell

● MAKING THE GRADE

In one important sense, activity theory, which says that people must be active to find meaning in life, is a direct challenge to disengagement theory.

● APPLYING THEORY ●

Aging and the Elderly

	Structural-Functional Approach	Symbolic-Interaction Approach	Social-Conflict Approach
What is the level of analysis?	Macro-level	Micro-level	Macro-level
How do we understand growing old?	The fact that people grow old and eventually die can disrupt the operation of society. Therefore, societies disengage the elderly from important tasks and other responsibilities as they reach old age.	For elders, like everyone else, being active encourages both health and happiness. Therefore, elders strive to maintain a high activity level, replacing roles they leave with new roles.	Aging is one dimension of social stratification. Generally, middle-aged people have the most wealth and power. Poor people, women, and other minorities face the greatest disadvantages as they grow old.

social diversity of elderly people and highlights the importance of choice in any government policy.

A limitation of this approach is that it assumes that elders are both healthy and competent, which may or may not be the case. Another problem with this approach is that it ignores the fact that many of the problems older people face—such as poverty—have more to do with society than with themselves. We turn now to that point of view: social-conflict theory.

──○ **CHECK YOUR LEARNING** Explain what activity theory says about aging. How does this approach challenge disengagement theory?

Social-Conflict Analysis: Aging and Inequality

A social-conflict analysis is based on the idea that access to opportunities and social resources differs for people in different age categories. For this reason, age is a dimension of social stratification. In the United States, middle-aged people enjoy the greatest power and the most opportunities and privileges, and the elderly and people under the age of twenty-five have a higher risk of poverty. Employers who replace senior workers with younger men and women in order to keep wages low may not intend to discriminate against older people. However, according to recent court rulings, if such policies have the effect of causing special harm to older people, they amount to discrimination.

The social-conflict approach claims that our industrial-capitalist economy creates an age-based hierarchy. In line with Marxist

thought, Steven Spitzer (1980) points out that a profit-oriented society devalues any category of people that is less productive. To the extent that older people do not work, our society labels them as mildly deviant.

Social-conflict analysis also draws attention to various dimensions of social inequality within the elderly population. Differences of class, race, ethnicity, and gender divide older people as they do everyone else. For this reason, some seniors have far greater economic security, access to better medical care, and more options for personal satisfaction in old age than others. Elderly white people typically enjoy advantages denied to older minorities. And women—an increasing majority as people age—suffer the social and economic disadvantages of both sexism and ageism.

──○ **CRITICAL REVIEW** The social-conflict approach adds to our understanding of the aging process by highlighting age-based inequality and pointing out that capitalism devalues elderly people who are less productive. But critics claim that the real culprit is *industrialization*. As evidence they point to the fact that the elderly are not better off under a socialist system, as a Marxist analysis implies. Furthermore, the idea that either industrialization or capitalism necessarily causes the elderly to suffer is challenged by the long-term rise in income and well-being experienced by seniors in the United States. The Applying Theory table summarizes what we learn from each of the theoretical approaches.

──○ **CHECK YOUR LEARNING** What does Marxist theory teach us about aging in a capitalist society?

NOTE: In 1963, Jessica Mitford's book *The American Way of Death* pointed out this culture's extravagant funeral rituals. Today, we spend half as much on funerals, largely because of the increasing popularity of cremation, up to about 33% of deaths from about 3% in 1960.

Q: "Let us endeavor to live so that when we come to die even the undertaker will be sorry." Mark Twain

NOTE: Philosophically, the right-to-die debate breaks down this way: Those who categorically view life—even with suffering—as preferable to death reject euthanasia. Those who recognize circumstances under which death is preferable to life endorse euthanasia, but they must determine when life should be ended.

NOTE: In Oregon, from 1997 to 2008, 341 terminally ill people had physicians assist in a suicide.

● SEEING SOCIOLOGY in Everyday Life

Ask members of your class if they have ever seen a person die. Do the responses support the idea that modern society separates death from life?

Death and Dying

To every thing there is a season,
And a time for every matter under heaven:
A time to be born and a time to die . . .

These lines from the biblical book of Ecclesiastes state two basic truths about human existence: the fact of birth and the inevitability of death. Just as life varies throughout history and around the world, death has many faces. We conclude this chapter with a brief look at the changing character of death, the final stage in the process of growing old.

Historical Patterns of Death

In the past, death was a familiar part of life. Many children died soon after birth, a fact that led many parents to delay naming children until they were one or two years old. For those fortunate enough to survive infancy, illness, accidents, and natural catastrophes made life uncertain at best.

Sometimes food shortages forced societies to protect the majority by sacrificing the least productive members. *Infanticide* is the killing of newborn infants, and *geronticide* is the killing of the elderly.

Because death was commonplace, it was readily accepted. Medieval Christianity assured believers that death fit into the divine plan for human existence. Here is how the historian Philippe Ariès describes Sir Lancelot, one of King Arthur's knights of the Round Table, preparing for death when he thinks he is mortally wounded:

> His gestures were fixed by old customs, ritual gestures which must be carried out when one is about to die. He removed his weapons and lay quietly upon the ground. . . . He spread his arms out, his body forming a cross . . . in such a way that his head faced east toward Jerusalem. (1974:7–8)

As societies gradually learned more about health and medicine, death became less of an everyday experience. Fewer children died at birth, and accidents and disease took a smaller toll among adults. As a result, most people living in high-income societies today view dying as extraordinary, something that happens to the very old or to younger people in rare and tragic cases. Back in 1900, about one-third of all deaths in the United States occurred before the age of five and fully two-thirds before the age of fifty-five. Today, by contrast, 84 percent of people in the United States die *after* reaching the age of fifty-five. Death and old age are closely linked in our culture.

The Modern Separation of Life and Death

Now removed from everyday experience, death seems somehow unnatural. Social conditions prepared our ancestors to accept death, but modern society's youth culture and aggressive medical technol-

In many traditional societies, people express great respect not only for elders but also for their ancestors. Dani villagers in New Guinea mummified the body of this elder in a sitting position so that they could continue to honor him and feel his presence in their daily lives.

ogy foster a desire for eternal youth and immortality. Death has become separated from life.

Death is also *physically* removed from everyday activities. The clearest evidence of this is that many of us have never seen a person actually die. Our ancestors typically died at home in the presence of family and friends, but most deaths today occur in impersonal settings such as hospitals and nursing homes. Even in hospitals, dying patients occupy a special part of the building, and hospital morgues are located well out of sight of patients and visitors alike (Ariès, 1974; Lee, 2002).

Ethical Issues: Confronting Death

In a society in which technology gives us the power to prolong life, moral questions about when and how people should die are more pressing than ever. For example, the national debate in 2005 surrounding the death of Terri Schiavo, who was kept alive by mechanical means for fifteen years, was not just about the fate of one woman; many people feel we need a better understanding of what the "right to die" rules should be.

Q: "We must wait until the evening to see how splendid the day has been." Sophocles

Q: "Death is a subject that is evaded, ignored, and denied by our youth-worshiping, progress-oriented society. It is almost as if we have taken on death as just another disease to be conquered." Braga & Braga (1975:x)

Q: "Death, after all, is the only reality that never lets you down." Pico Iyer

NOTE: People with one year or less to live consume 30% of all Medicare funds; the average person in the U.S. receives more than one-third of all medical care in the last six months of life.

NOTE: The first cyber-funeral service has begun operation: For about $6,500, Cybermourn will set up a camera at the funeral and post the live video to a Web site for anyone invited to "participate."

● MAKING THE GRADE

Even death is now a cultural factor; in many cases, it results from a decision.

● SEEING SOCIOLOGY
in Everyday Life

Where do you stand on the right-to-die debate? Why?

THINKING GLOBALLY

Death on Demand: Euthanasia in the Netherlands

Marcus Erich picked up the telephone and called his brother Arjen. In a quiet voice, thirty-two-year-old Marcus announced, "Friday at five o'clock." When the time came, Arjen was there, having driven to his brother's farmhouse south of Amsterdam. They said their final good-byes. Soon afterward, Marcus's physician arrived. Marcus and the doctor spoke for a few moments, and then the doctor prepared a "cocktail" of barbiturates and other drugs. As Marcus drank the mixture, he made a face, joking, "Can't you make this sweeter?"

As the minutes passed, Marcus lay back and his eyes closed. But after half an hour, he was still breathing. At that point, according to their earlier agreement, the physician administered a lethal injection. Minutes later, Marcus's life came to an end.

Events like this take us to the heart of the belief that people have a "right to die." Marcus Erich was dying of AIDS. For five years, his body had been wasting away, and he was suffering greatly with no hope of recovery. He wanted his doctor to end his life.

The Netherlands, a small nation in northwestern Europe, has gone further than any other in the world in allowing mercy killing, or euthanasia. A 1981 Dutch law allows a physician to assist in a suicide if the following five conditions are met:

1. The patient must make a voluntary, well-considered, and repeated request to a doctor for help in dying.

2. The patient's suffering must be unbearable and without hope of improvement.

3. The doctor and the patient must discuss alternatives.

4. The doctor must consult with at least one colleague who has access to the patient and the patient's medical records.

5. The assisted suicide must be performed in accordance with sound medical practice.

Official records indicate that doctors end about 2,000 lives a year in the Netherlands, and the number has been rising slowly but steadily. But because many cases are never reported, the actual number may be two or three times as high. Critics point to the fact that in recent years, Dutch doctors have brought about the death of people who, due to their illness, were not able to clearly state their desire to die. Although the Dutch policy of euthanasia enjoys widespread popular support in the Netherlands, it remains controversial in the world as a whole.

WHAT DO YOU THINK?

1. What advantages and benefits do you see in the Dutch law permitting physician-assisted suicide?

2. What are the disadvantages or dangers of such a law?

3. What about cases in which a person is very ill and cannot state the desire to die or not to die? Should euthanasia be permitted in such cases? If so, when and why?

The Netherlands has been at the forefront of the movement to extend active euthanasia. Recently, a doctor administering a fatal injection to a man suffering from Lou Gehrig's disease was shown on Dutch national television. Where do you stand on this issue?

Sources: Della Cava (1997), Mauro (1997), and B. Barr (2004).

When Does Death Occur?

Perhaps the most basic question is the most difficult: Exactly how do we define death? Common sense suggests that life ceases when breathing and heartbeat stop. But the ability of medical personnel to resuscitate someone after a heart attack and artificially sustain breathing makes such definitions of death obsolete. Medical and legal experts in the United States continue to debate the meaning of death, but many now consider death an *irreversible* state involving no response to stimulation, no movement or breathing, no reflexes, and no indication of brain activity (Wall, 1980; D. G. Jones, 1998).

The Right-to-Die Debate

Terri Schiavo remained alive without evidence of being conscious or responsive to her surroundings for fifteen years following a heart attack that cut off blood to her brain. Debate surrounding this case, which ended with her death after her feeding tube was removed, shows that many people are less afraid of death than of the prospect of being kept alive at all costs. In other words, medical technology that can sustain life also threatens personal freedom by letting doctors or others rather than the dying person decide when life is to end. In response, people who support a "right to die" seek control over

Q: "Out of life comes death; and out of death, life; / Out of the young, the old; and out of the old, the young; / Out of waking, sleep; out of sleep, waking; / The stream of creation and dissolution never stops." Heraclitus

Q: "Do not go gentle into that good night; / . . . Rage, rage against the dying of the light." Dylan Thomas

Q: "There may be some good in coming to death at least as well prepared as we go on our vacations, our driving tests, or our weddings." Pico Iyer

Q: "I'm not afraid to die; I just don't want to be there when it happens." Woody Allen

EXERCISE: Ask students to prepare a list of social changes they might expect were life expectancy to increase another 20 years during the 21st century, much as it did during the 20th.

euthanasia assisting in the death of a person suffering from an incurable disease

their own deaths just as they seek control over their lives (Ogden, 2001).

After thoughtful discussion, patients, families, and physicians may decide not to take "heroic measures" to keep a person alive. Physicians and family members may issue a "do not resuscitate" order, which will allow a patient who stops breathing to die. *Living wills*—documents stating which medical procedures an individual wants and does not want under specific conditions—are now widely used.

A more difficult issue involves mercy killing, or **euthanasia** (also known as "mercy killing")—*assisting in the death of a person suffering from an incurable disease.* Euthanasia (from the Greek, meaning "a good death") poses an ethical dilemma because it involves not just refusing treatment but actively taking steps to end life. Some people see euthanasia as an act of kindness, while others consider it a form of murder.

Is there a right to die? People with incurable diseases can choose not to have treatment that might prolong their lives. But whether a doctor should be allowed to help bring about death is a matter of debate. In 1997, voters in Oregon passed a right-to-die initiative (the Death with Dignity Act). Although this law has been challenged repeatedly ever since, Oregon physicians can legally assist in ending the lives of patients; since then, Oregon physicians have legally assisted in the deaths of about 350 patients (Leff, 2008.) In 1997, the U.S. Supreme Court, in *Vacco v. Quill,* declared that the U.S. Constitution recognizes no right to die. This decision discouraged other states from considering laws similar to the one in Oregon; only in neighboring Washington in 2008 did voters pass a ballot initiative permitting physician-assisted suicide (Leff, 2008).

Supporters of the right-to-die movement hold up as a model the Netherlands, which has the most permissive euthanasia law in the world. How does the Dutch system operate? The Thinking Globally box takes a closer look.

Should the United States hold the line on euthanasia or follow the lead of the Dutch? Right-to-die advocates maintain that a person facing extreme suffering should be able to choose to live or die. And if death is the choice, medical assistance can help people toward a "good death." Surveys show that two-thirds of U.S. adults support giving people the option of dying with a doctor's help (NORC, 2007).

On the other side of the debate, opponents fear that laws allowing physician-assisted suicide invite abuse. Pointing to the Netherlands, critics cite surveys indicating that in most cases, the five conditions for physician-assisted suicide are not met. In particular, most physicians do not consult with another doctor or even report the euthanasia to authorities. Of greater concern is the fact that in about one-fifth of all physician-assisted suicides, the patient never explic-

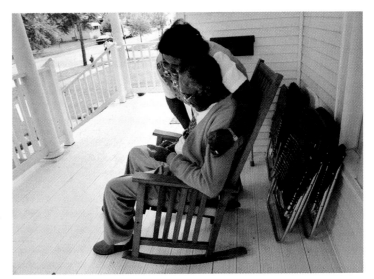

Unlike a hospital, which tries to save and extend life, the hospice movement tries to give dying people greater comfort, including the companionship and support of family members.

itly asks to die. This is so even though half of these patients are conscious and capable of making decisions themselves (Gillon, 1999). This fact—and the steadily rising number of physician-assisted suicides in the Netherlands—leads opponents to argue that legalizing physician-assisted suicide puts a nation on a slippery slope toward more and more euthanasia. How can we be sure, they ask, that ill people won't be pushed into accepting death by doctors who consider suicide the right choice for the terminally ill or by family members who are weary of caring for them or want to avoid the expenses of medical treatment?

Evidence drawn from the United States does not raise fears in the same way. In Oregon, the number of annual cases of physician-assisted suicide has remained low—around thirty a year. No matter how the right-to-die debate eventually turns out, we have entered a new era when it comes to dying. Today, individuals, family members, and medical personnel must face death not as a medical fact but as a negotiated outcome.

Bereavement

Elisabeth Kübler-Ross (1969) found that most people usually confront their own death in stages (see Chapter 5, "Socialization"). Initially, individuals react with *denial,* followed by *anger;* then they try *negotiation,* hoping for divine intervention. Gradually, they fall into *resignation* and finally reach *acceptance.*

Q: Daniel Callahan (1987:223) advocates "an understanding of the process of aging and death that looks to our obligations to the young and to the future, that sees old age as a source of knowledge and insight of value to other age groups, that recognizes the necessity of limits and the acceptance of decline and death, and that values the old for their age and not their continuing youthful vitality."

NOTE: Daniel Callahan's analysis raises important questions: Is getting older good for everyone? Is it even possible for everyone?

● SEEING SOCIOLOGY
in Everyday Life

How might recent efforts to extend health care to everyone figure into the "limits" debate?

CONTROVERSY & DEBATE

Setting Limits: Must We "Pull the Plug" on Old Age?

SIMONE: I'm almost sixty now. When I'm eighty-five, I want the best medical care I can find. Why shouldn't I get it?

JUAN: I'll tell you why—because our society can't spend more and more money on extending the lives of old people when so many children are at risk.

SERGIO: I guess the answer depends on whether you're young or old.

As the U.S. elderly population soars, as new technology gives us more power to prolong life, and as medical care gets increasingly expensive, many people now wonder just how much old age we can afford. Currently, about half the average person's lifetime spending for medical care occurs during the final years of life, and the share is rising. Against the spiraling costs of prolonging life, we well may ask if what is medically *possible* is morally *desirable*. In the decades to come, warns the gerontologist Daniel Callahan (1987), an elderly population ready and eager to extend their lives will eventually force us either to "pull the plug" on old age or to shortchange everyone else.

Just raising this issue, Callahan admits, seems cold and heartless. But consider that the bill for the elderly's health topped $400 billion in 2007—more than four times what it cost in 1980. This dramatic increase reflects the current policy of directing more and more medical resources to studying and treating the diseases and disabilities of old age.

So Callahan makes the case for limits. First, the more we spend on behalf of the elderly, the less we can provide for others. With poverty a growing problem among children, can we afford to spend more and more on the oldest members of our society?

Second, a *longer* life does not necessarily mean a *better* life. Cost aside, does heart surgery that prolongs the life of an eighty-four-year-old woman a year or two necessarily improve the quality of her life? Cost considered, would those resources yield more "quality of life" if used, say, to give a ten-year-old child a kidney transplant? Or to provide basic care and comfort to hundreds of low-income seniors?

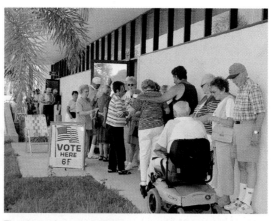

The share of our population over the age of sixty-five is going up. in addition, older people are very likely to vote. What do these facts lead you to predict about government policy dealing with health care for the elderly?

Third, we need to reconsider our view of death as an enemy to be conquered at all costs. Rather, he suggests, a more realistic position for an aging society is to treat death as a natural end to the life course. If we cannot make peace with death for our own well-being, then in a society with limited resources, we must do it for the benefit of others.

But not everyone agrees. Shouldn't people who have worked all their lives and made our society what it is enjoy our generosity in their final years? Would it be right to deny medical care to aging people who are able and willing to pay for it?

Today, we face questions that few people would have imagined even fifty years ago: Is peak longevity good for everyone? Is it even *possible* for everyone?

WHAT DO YOU THINK?

1. Should doctors and hospitals use a double standard, offering more complete care to the youngest people and limited care to society's oldest members? Why or why not?

2. Do you think that a goal of the medical establishment should be to extend life at all costs? Explain your position.

3. How should society balance the needs of high-income seniors with the needs of those with little or no money to pay for medical care as they age?

Sources: Callahan (1987), and U.S. Census Bureau (2008).

According to some researchers, bereavement follows the same pattern of stages. The people closest to a dying person may initially deny the reality of impending death and then gradually reach a point of acceptance. Other investigators, however, question any linear "stage theory," arguing that bereavement is a very personal and unpredictable process (Lund, Caserta, & Dimond, 1986; Lund, 1989; Cut-cliffe, 1998). What experts do agree on, however, is the fact that how family and friends view an impending death has an effect on the person who is dying. By accepting an approaching death, others can help the dying person do the same; denying the death isolates the dying person, who is not able to share feelings and experiences with others.

Many dying people find support in the *hospice movement.* Unlike a hospital, which is designed to cure disease, a hospice helps people have a good death. These care centers for dying people try to minimize pain and suffering—either at the center or at home—and encourage family members to stay close by. Most hospices also provide social support for family members experiencing bereavement (Foliart & Clausen, 2001).

Under the best of circumstances, bereavement often involves profound grief. Research documents that bereavement is less intense for someone who accepts the death of a loved one and has brought satisfactory closure to the relationship. Such closure also allows family and friends to comfort one another more effectively after a death occurs.

Reaching closure is not possible when a death is unexpected, and survivors' social disorientation may last for years. One study of middle-aged women who had recently experienced the death of their husbands found that many felt they had lost not only a spouse but also their reason for living. Therefore, dealing successfully with bereavement requires the time and social support necessary to form a new sense of self and recognize new life options (Atchley, 1983; Danforth & Glass, 2001). With the number of older people in the United States increasing so fast, understanding death and dying is taking on greater importance.

Aging: Looking Ahead

This chapter has explored the graying of the United States and other high-income nations. By 2050, the number of elderly people in this country will exceed the entire country's population in 1900. In addition, one in four of tomorrow's seniors will be over age eighty-five. In decades to come, then, society's oldest members will gain a far greater voice in everyday life. Younger people will find that careers relating to gerontology—the study of the elderly—are sure to gain in importance.

With more elderly people living longer, will our society have the support services to sustain them? Remember that as the needs of the elderly increase, a smaller share of younger people will be there to respond and pay the bills with their taxes. What about the spiraling medical costs of an aging society? As the baby boomers enter old age, some analysts paint a doomsday picture of the United States, with desperate and dying elderly people everywhere (Longino, 1994). Addressing the need for health care—for old and young alike—is one important task facing the Obama administration.

But there is also good news. For one thing, the health of tomorrow's elderly people—today's middle-aged adults—will be better than ever: Smoking is way down, and more people are becoming

In the 2007 film *The Bucket List*, two terminally ill men, played by Jack Nicholson (shown above) and Morgan Freeman, set out to experience many grand adventures before they "kick the bucket." Approaching the end of life—if we see it coming—can provide opportunities to resolve many issues that we have carried with us for decades.

aware of the national problem of obesity and are eating more healthfully. Such trends suggest that the elderly may well become more vigorous and independent. Tomorrow's seniors will also enjoy the benefits of steadily advancing medical technology, although, as the Controversy & Debate box explains, how much of the country's medical resources older people can claim is already being hotly debated.

Another positive sign over the past several decades is the growing financial strength of the elderly. The economic downturn after 2000, which intensified in 2008, has been stressful, and many elderly people have lost income, retirement benefits, and equity in their homes. But it is likely that the long-term trend will remain fairly bright for most seniors, and it may turn out that tomorrow's elderly—the baby boomers—will be more affluent than ever. Why? One important fact is that the baby boomers are the first generation of the U.S. population whose women have been in the labor force most of their lives. For this reason, the boomers are likely to have substantial savings and pension income.

At the same time, younger adults will face a mounting responsibility to care for aging parents. A falling birth rate coupled with a growing elderly population will demand that middle-aged people perform an increasing share of caregiving for the very old.

Most of us need to learn more about caring for aging parents, which includes far more than meeting physical needs. More important lessons involve communicating, expressing love, and facing up to eventual death. In caring for our parents, we will also teach important lessons to our children, including the skills they will need, one day, to care for us.

Seeing Sociology in Everyday Life

Chapter 15   Aging and the Elderly

How are older adults changing today's society?

A lot has been said about the baby boomers—the women and men born between 1945 and 1964—who were the driving force behind many of the changes that took place in the 1960s and 1970s. Civil rights, women's rights, and gay rights reflect just some of the social movements they invented or carried on. Now, as this cohort begins to enter old age, they are rewriting the rules once again, this time about what it means to be old.

> **HINT**   The baby boomers have been a cohort making change, and as they have aged they have redefined every stage of life. As elders, they appear determined to maintain active lives well beyond the traditional time of retirement. The celebrities pictured here also suggest that older people can be sexy—and the generation that brought sex out into the open for young people is defining sex as a part of growing old. The social justice values that defined the boomers as young people seem to still drive them as seniors. Most of all, they appear determined that their political voice will be heard.

Mick Jagger and Keith Richard launched the "Rolling Stones" almost fifty years ago and they continue to perform as they reach their late sixties. What do these stars of popular culture say about older men?

A much younger Paul McCartney wrote the lyrics to "When I'm Sixty-Four," probably never imagining that he would still be still be writing music and performing today—he will reach age seventy in 2012. In what ways is he a role model for elders?

Judy Collins turned seventy in 2009 and continues a busy career as a folk singer and political activist. In what ways do you expect older people to reshape U.S. politics?

Joan Baez has also been a folk singer and political activist for more than half a century. These women have supported numerous social movements, ranging from opposition to the use of land mines to the antiwar movement. In what ways do you expect older people to reshape U.S. politics?

Applying SOCIOLOGY in Everyday Life

1. Ask several faculty nearing retirement and several who have already retired about the practices and policies of your college or university for helping older faculty when they retire. Based on what you learn, decide whether retiring from an academic career is harder or easier than retiring from other types of work (say, construction work or a job as a corporate manager), and explain why.

2. Look through an issue of a popular magazine, such as *Time, Newsweek,* or *People,* and study the pictures of men and women in news stories and advertising. What share of the pictures show elderly people? In what types of advertising are they featured?

3. Obtain a copy of a living will (do an online search), and try to respond to all the questions it asks. How does filling out this form affect your thinking about death?

MAKING THE GRADE

CHAPTER 15 Aging and the Elderly

The Graying of the United States

The "graying of the United States" means that the average age of the U.S. population is steadily going up.

- In 1900, the median age was 23, and elderly people were 4% of the population.
- By 2030, the median age will be almost 40, and elderly people will be 19% of the population.

p. 386

In high-income countries like the United States, the share of elderly people has been increasing for two reasons:

- Birth rates have been falling as families choose to have fewer children.
- Life expectancy has been rising as living standards improve and medical advances reduce deaths from infectious diseases.

pp. 386–87

✓ As the U.S. population ages, cultural patterns are likely to change, with elderly people becoming more evident in everyday life.

Growing Old: Biology and Culture

BIOLOGICAL AND PSYCHOLOGICAL CHANGES are associated with aging.

- Although people's health becomes more fragile with advancing age, affluent elderly people experience fewer health problems than poor people, who cannot afford quality medical care.
- Psychological research confirms that growing old does not result in overall loss of intelligence or major changes in personality.

pp. 389–90

Although aging is a biological process, how elderly people are regarded by society is a matter of **CULTURE**. The age at which people are defined as old varies:

- Until several centuries ago, old age began as early as 30.
- In poor societies today, where life expectancy is low, people become old at 50 or even 40.

pp. 390–91

gerontology (p. 389) the study of aging and the elderly

age stratification (p. 392) the unequal distribution of wealth, power, and privilege among people at different stages of the life course

gerontocracy (p. 392) a form of social organization in which the elderly have the most wealth, power, and prestige

AGE STRATIFICATION: A GLOBAL SURVEY

In *hunting and gathering societies*, where survival depends on physical stamina, both the very young and the very old contribute less to society.

p. 392

In *agrarian societies*, elders are typically the most privileged and respected members of society, a pattern known as **gerontocracy**.

p. 392

In *industrial* and *postindustrial societies*, the social standing of the elderly is low because the fast pace of social change is dominated by the young.

pp. 392–93

Transitions and Challenges of Aging

PERSONAL CHALLENGES that elderly people face include

- the realization that one's life is nearing an end
- social isolation caused by the death of friends or a spouse, physical disability, or retirement from one's job
- reduced social prestige and a loss of purpose in life due to retirement

pp. 393–95

A person's risk of **POVERTY** rises after midlife, although since 1960, the poverty rate for the elderly has fallen and is now below the poverty rate for the population as a whole.

- The aged poor include categories of people—such as single women and people of color—who are at high risk of poverty at any age.
- Some retired people have had to return to work in order to make ends meet, a result of the recent economic downturn.

pp. 395–97

caregiving (p. 397) informal and unpaid care provided to a dependent person by family members, other relatives, or friends

ageism (p. 397) prejudice and discrimination against older people

The need for **CAREGIVING** is increasing in our aging society.

- Most caregiving for the elderly is performed by family members, typically women.
- About 1 to 2 million elderly people are victims of **ELDER ABUSE** each year.

p. 397

AGEISM—prejudice and discrimination against older people—is used to justify age stratification.

- Like racism and sexism, ageism builds physical traits into stereotypes that make unfair generalizations about all elderly people.

pp. 397–98

✓ The fact that the elderly include men and women of all races, ethnicities, and social classes suggests that older people are not a minority (p. 398).

Theoretical Analysis of Aging

The **STRUCTURAL-FUNCTIONAL APPROACH** points to the role that aging plays in the orderly operation of society.

- **Disengagement theory** suggests that society helps the elderly disengage from positions of social responsibility before the onset of disability or death.
- The process of disengagement provides for the orderly transfer of statuses and roles from the older to the younger generation.

p. 399

The **SYMBOLIC-INTERACTION APPROACH** focuses on the meanings that people attach to growing old.

- **Activity theory** claims that a high level of activity increases people's personal satisfaction in old age.
- People must find new roles in old age to replace the ones they left behind.

pp. 399–400

disengagement theory (p. 399) the idea that society functions in an orderly way by removing people from positions of responsibility as they reach old age

activity theory (p. 399) the idea that a high level of activity increases personal satisfaction in old age

The **SOCIAL-CONFLICT APPROACH** highlights the inequalities in opportunities and social resources available to people in different age categories.

- A capitalist society's emphasis on economic efficiency leads to the devaluation of those who are less productive, including the elderly.
- Some categories of elderly people—namely, women and other minorities—have less economic security, less access to quality medical care, and fewer options for personal satisfaction in old age than others.

p. 400

See the Applying Theory table on page 400.

Death and Dying

HISTORICAL PERSPECTIVE

- In the past, death was a familiar part of everyday life and was accepted as a natural event that might occur at any age.
- Modern society has set death physically apart from everyday activities, and advances in medical technology have resulted in people's inability or unwillingness to accept death.
- This avoidance of death also reflects the fact that most people in high-income societies die in old age.

p. 401

ETHICAL ISSUES: CONFRONTING DEATH

- Our society's power to prolong life has sparked a debate as to the circumstances under which a dying person should be kept alive by medical means.
- People who support a person's right to die seek control over the process of their own dying.
- **Euthanasia** poses an ethical dilemma because it involves not just refusing treatment but actively taking steps to end a person's life.

pp. 401–3

euthanasia (p. 403) assisting in the death of a person suffering from an incurable disease; also known as *mercy killing*

BEREAVEMENT

- Some researchers believe that the process of bereavement follows the same pattern of stages as a dying person coming to accept approaching death: denial, anger, negotiation, resignation, and acceptance.
- The **hospice movement** offers support to dying people and their families.

pp. 403–5

✓ *The fact that more people today are living longer raises questions about society's ability and responsibility to care for them as they age (p. 405).*

The economy is the social institution that organizes how a society produces, distributes, and consumes goods and services. Our nation's economy is changing, reshaping the type of work that people do. At the same time, many longstanding debates about how the economy ought to operate are likely to continue.

CHAPTER 16

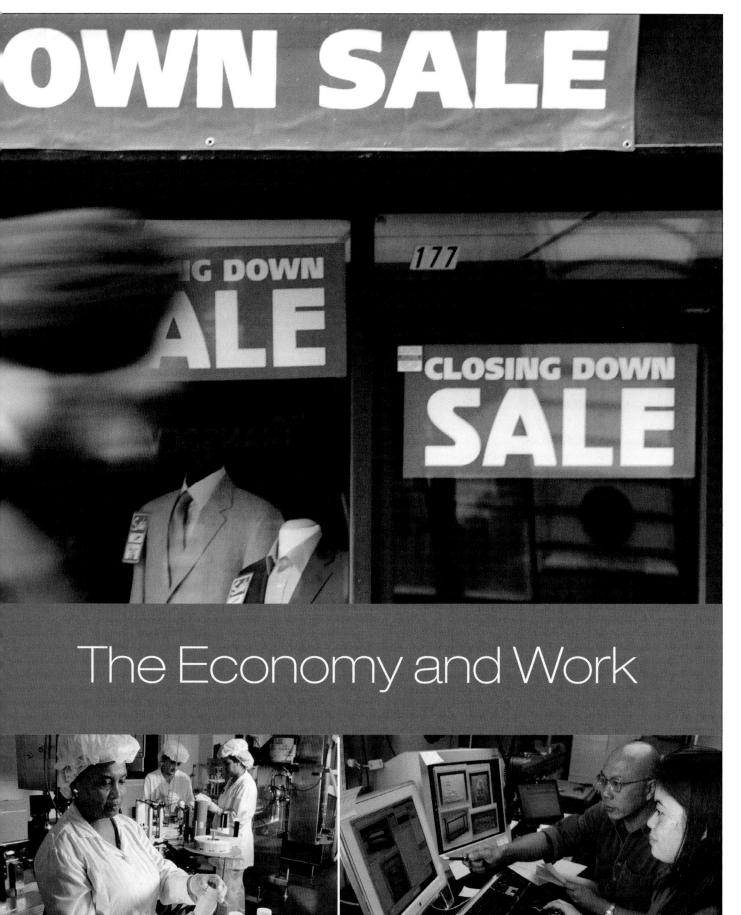

The Economy and Work

SUPPLEMENTS: An outline of this chapter, supplementary minilectures, and suggested topics for discussion are found in the *Instructor's Manual*.

DISCUSS: The Industrial Revolution went far beyond mere technological upheaval. What was it for Marx? A capitalist revolution. For Weber? The triumph of rationality. For Durkheim? A process of expanding specialization.

Q: "[The preindustrial economy] was limited to what could be organized within a family, and within the lifetime of its head." Peter Laslett (1984)

Q: "A fundamental characteristic of the world we have lost was the scene of labor, which was universally supposed to be the home." Peter Laslett (1984)

CHAPTER OVERVIEW { This chapter explores the operation of the economy, a major social institution; it begins with a look at how changes in economic production have reshaped society.

Here's a quick quiz about the U.S. economy. (Hint: All six questions have the same answer.)

- Which business do more than 130 million people in the United States visit each week?
- Which business sells products made by more than 60,000 companies?
- Which U.S. company, on average, opens a new store every day?
- Which U.S. company is the country's biggest corporation in terms of annual sales?
- Which U.S. company will create nearly 800,000 new jobs over the next five years?
- Which single company actually grew in size during the recent economic downturn, accounting for 25 percent of all the growth in U.S. economic output in the last few years?

You have probably guessed that the correct answer is Wal-Mart, the global discount chain founded by Sam Walton, who opened his first store in Arkansas in 1962. In 2008, Wal-Mart announced revenues of $375 billion from more than 4,100 stores in the United States and 3,416 stores in other countries from Brazil to China.

But not everyone is pleased with the expansion of Wal-Mart. Across the United States, many people have joined a social movement to keep Wal-Mart out of their local communities, fearing the loss of local businesses and, in some cases, local culture. Critics also claim that the merchandising giant pays low wages, keeps out labor unions, and sells many products made in sweatshops abroad (Saporito, 2003; Walsh, 2007; Wal-Mart, 2008).

This chapter examines the economy, widely considered the most influential of all social institutions. (The other major social institutions are examined in the chapters that follow.) As the story of Wal-Mart's expansion suggests, the economy of the United States—and the economic system of the entire world—is dominated by a number of giant corporations. Who benefits from these megabusinesses? Who loses? What is it like to work for one of these corporations? To answer these questions, sociologists study how the economy operates as well as the nature of work and what jobs mean to each of us.

The Economy: Historical Overview

The **economy** is *the social institution that organizes a society's production, distribution, and consumption of goods and services*. As an institution, the economy operates, for better or worse, in a generally predictable manner. *Goods* are commodities ranging from necessities (food, clothing, shelter) to luxury items (cars, swimming pools, yachts). *Services* are activities that benefit others (for example, the work of priests, physicians, teachers, and computer software specialists).

We value goods and services because they ensure survival or because they make life easier or more interesting. Also, what people produce as workers and what they buy as consumers are important parts of social identity, as when we say, "He's a steelworker," or "She drives a Mercedes." How goods and services are distributed, too, shapes the lives of everyone by giving more resources to some and fewer to others.

The economies of modern high-income nations are the result of centuries of social change. We turn now to three technological revolutions that reorganized production and, in the process, transformed social life.

The Agricultural Revolution

The earliest human societies were made up of hunters and gatherers living off the land. In these technologically simple societies, there was no distinct economy. Rather, producing and consuming were part of family life.

As Chapter 4 ("Society") explained, when people harnessed animals to plows, beginning some 5,000 years ago, a new agricultural economy was created that was fifty times more productive than hunting and gathering. The resulting surplus meant that not everyone had

NOTE: The effects of technological advancement are summarized in the first section of Chapter 4, "Gerhard Lenski: Society and Technology." Marvin Harris (1987) estimates the rising productive capacity linked to societies at various stages of technological development in terms of the ratio of calories expended to calories produced: hunting and gathering, 1:3; horticultural and pastoral, 1:5; agrarian, 1:50; industrial, 1:5,000.

EXERCISE: To help students become familiar with economic data, direct them to *Statistical Abstract of the United States* (U.S. Census Bureau), *Human Development Report* (United Nations), and *World Development Report* (World Bank). These three annual publications provide extensive data about the economies of the U.S. and other nations.

● SEEING SOCIOLOGY in Everyday Life

Look back at the Chapter 12 opening story on page 300 about the fire in the Bangladesh sweatshop. What was the factory owner's biggest concern?

economy the social institution that organizes a society's production, distribution, and consumption of goods and services

postindustrial economy a productive system based on service work and high technology

to produce food, so many took on specialized work: making tools, raising animals, or building dwellings. Soon towns sprang up, linked by networks of traders dealing in food, animals, and other goods. These four factors—agricultural technology, job specialization, permanent settlements, and trade—made the economy a distinct social institution.

The Industrial Revolution

By the mid-eighteenth century, a second technological revolution was under way, first in England and then in North America. The development of industry was even more powerful than the rise of agriculture in bringing change to the economy. Industrialization changed the economy in five fundamental ways:

1. **New sources of energy**. Throughout history, "energy" had meant the muscle power of people or animals. But in 1765, the English inventor James Watt introduced the steam engine. One hundred times more powerful than animal muscles, early steam engines soon drove heavy machinery.

2. **Centralization of work in factories**. Steam-powered machines soon moved work from homes to factories, the centralized and impersonal workplaces that housed the machines.

3. **Manufacturing and mass production**. Before the Industrial Revolution, most people grew or gathered raw materials such as grain, wood, or wool. In an industrial economy, the focus shifts so that most people work to turn raw materials into a wide range of finished products such as furniture and clothing.

4. **Specialization**. Centuries ago, people worked at home, making products from start to finish. In the factory, a worker repeats a single task over and over, making only a small contribution to the finished product.

5. **Wage labor**. Instead of working for themselves, factory workers became wage laborers working for strangers, who often cared less for them than for the machines they operated.

The Industrial Revolution gradually raised the standard of living as countless new products and services fueled an expanding marketplace. Yet the benefits of industrial technology were shared very unequally, especially at the beginning. Some factory owners made vast fortunes, while the majority of industrial workers lived close to poverty. Children, too, worked in factories or in coal mines for pennies a day. Women working in factories were among the lowest paid, and they endured special problems, as the Thinking About Diversity box on page 414 explains.

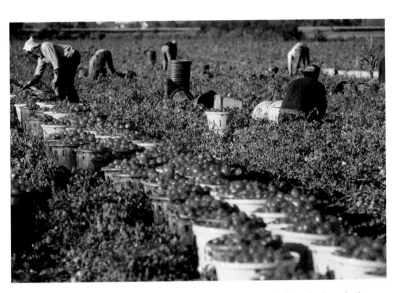

As societies industrialize, a smaller share of the labor force works in agriculture. In the United States, much of the agricultural work that remains is performed by immigrants from lower-income nations. These farmer workers from Mexico travel throughout Florida during the tomato harvest.

The Information Revolution and Postindustrial Society

By about 1950, the nature of production was changing once again. The United States was creating a **postindustrial economy**, *a productive system based on service work and high technology*. Automated machinery (and later, robotics) reduced the role of human labor in factory production and expanded the ranks of clerical workers and managers. The postindustrial era is marked by a shift from industrial work to service work.

Driving this change is a third technological breakthrough: the computer. Just as the Industrial Revolution did two-and-a-half centuries ago, the Information Revolution has introduced new kinds of products and new forms of communication and has altered the character of work. In general, there have been three significant changes:

1. **From tangible products to ideas**. The industrial era was defined by the production of goods; in the postindustrial era, people work with symbols. Computer programmers, writers, financial analysts, advertising executives, architects, editors, and all sorts of consultants make up more of the labor force in the information age.

2. **From mechanical skills to literacy skills**. The Industrial Revolution required mechanical skills, but the Information Revolution requires literacy skills: speaking and writing well and, of course, knowing how to use a computer. People able to communicate

Q: "Women have always worked in factories. Indeed it was women's labor that was initially responsible for the very beginnings of the Industrial Revolution." Ellen Israel Rosen (1987:18)

NOTE: Because of the low wages and strict control endured by women in early factories, people sometimes called wagons traveling across New England in search of these workers "slavers," a comparison to slave ships.

DISCUSS: After the class reads the box on women in the textile mills, ask students if they can understand why, in decades past, unmarried women were sometimes called "spinsters."

Q: Despite the toil, we all agree, / Or out of mills or in; / Dependent on others we ne'er will be, / So long as we're able to spin. "Song of the Spinners" from *The Lowell Offering* (1842)

primary sector   the part of the economy that draws raw materials from the natural environment

secondary sector   the part of the economy that transforms raw materials into manufactured goods

MAKING THE GRADE

Be sure you understand the three sectors of the economy.

tertiary sector   the part of the economy that involves services rather than goods

---

THINKING ABOUT DIVERSITY: RACE, CLASS, & GENDER

Women in the Mills of Lowell, Massachusetts

Back in 1810, few people paid much attention as Francis Cabot Lowell, ancestor of two prominent Boston families, the Cabots and the Lowells, stepped off a ship returning from England. But Lowell carried with him documents that would change the course of the U.S. economy: plans, based on machinery operating in England, for this country's first power loom textile factory (Eisler, 1977; Wertheimer, 1982).

Lowell built his factory beside a waterfall on the Merrimack River in Massachusetts so that he could use waterpower to operate large looms to weave cloth. Soon the productive factory had transformed a small farming village into a thriving industrial town that at his death was renamed in his honor.

From the outset, 90 percent of the mill workers were women. Factory owners preferred women because they could be paid $2 to $3 a week, half the wages men received. Many immigrant men were willing to work for such low wages, but often prejudice disqualified "foreigners" from any job at all.

Recruiters, driving wagons through the small towns of New England, urged parents to send their daughters to the mills, where, they promised, the young women would be

properly supervised as they learned skills and discipline. The offer appealed to many parents, who could barely provide for their children, and the prospect of getting out on their own surely excited many young women. Back then, there were few occupations open to women, and those that were—primarily teaching and household service—paid even less than factory work.

At the Lowell factory, young women lived in dormitories, paying one-third of their wages for room and board. They were subject to a curfew

and, as a condition of employment, regularly attended church. Any morally questionable conduct (such as bringing men to their rooms) resulted in firm disciplinary action.

Besides fulfilling their promise to parents, factory owners had another motive for their strict rules: They knew that closely supervised women were not able to organize. Working twelve or thirteen hours a day, six days a week, the Lowell employees had good reason to seek improvements in their working conditions. Yet any public criticism of the factory, or even possession of "radical" literature, could cost a worker her job.

WHAT DO YOU THINK?

1. How did race, ethnicity, and gender shape the workforce in the early textile mills?

2. Why were women workers so closely supervised? Can you think of similarly close supervision in the workplace today?

3. Compare the textile mills in Lowell to the Bangladeshi sweatshop described in the opening of Chapter 12. How are they similar? How do they differ?

---

effectively are likely to do well; people without these skills face fewer opportunities.

3. **From factories to almost anywhere.** Industrial technology drew workers into factories located near power sources, but computer technology allows people to work almost anywhere. Laptop and wireless computers and cell phones now turn the home, a car, or even an airplane into a "virtual office." What this means for everyday life is that new information technology blurs the line between our lives at work and at home.

Sectors of the Economy

The three revolutions just described reflect a shifting balance among the three sectors of a society's economy. The **primary sector** is *the part of the economy that draws raw materials from the natural environment*.

The primary sector—agriculture, raising animals, fishing, forestry, and mining—is largest in low-income nations. Figure 16–1 shows that 25 percent of the economic output of low-income countries is from the primary sector, compared with 9 percent of economic activity in middle-income nations and just 2 percent in high-income countries such as the United States.

The **secondary sector** is *the part of the economy that transforms raw materials into manufactured goods*. This sector grows quickly as societies industrialize. It includes operations such as refining petroleum into gasoline and turning metals into tools and automobiles. The globalization of industry means that just about all the world's countries have a significant share of their workers in the secondary sector. Figure 16–1 shows that the secondary sector now accounts for a greater share of economic output in low-income nations than it does in high-income countries.

global economy   economic activity that crosses national borders

The **tertiary sector** is *the part of the economy that involves services rather than goods*. The tertiary sector grows with industrialization, accounting for 48 percent of economic output in low-income countries, 60 percent in middle-income countries, and 72 percent in high-income nations. About 78 percent of the U.S. labor force is in service work, including secretarial and clerical work and positions in food service, sales, law, health care, law enforcement, advertising, and teaching.

The Global Economy

New information technology is drawing people around the world closer together and creating a **global economy**, *economic activity that crosses national borders*. The development of a global economy has five major consequences.

First, we see a global division of labor: Different regions of the world specialize in one sector of economic activity. As Global Map 16–1 on page 416 shows, agriculture represents about half the total economic output of the world's poorest countries. Global Map 16–2 indicates that most of the economic output of high-income countries, including the United States, is in the service sector. In short, the world's poorest nations specialize in producing raw materials, and the richest nations specialize in the production of services.

Second, an increasing number of products pass through more than one nation. Look no further than your morning coffee: The beans may have been grown in Colombia and transported to New Orleans on a freighter registered in Liberia, made in a shipyard in Japan using steel from Korea, and fueled by oil from Venezuela.

Third, national governments no longer control the economic activity that takes place within their borders. In fact, governments cannot even regulate the value of their national currencies because dollars, euros, pounds sterling, and yen are traded around the clock in the financial markets of New York, London, and Tokyo.

A fourth consequence of the global economy is that a small number of businesses, operating internationally, now controls a vast share of the world's economic activity. Based on the latest available data, the 1,000 largest multinational companies account for half the world's economic output (DeCarlo, 2008; World Bank, 2008).

Fifth and finally, the globalization of the economy raises concerns about the rights and opportunities of workers. Critics of this trend claim that the United States is losing jobs—especially factory jobs—to low-income nations. This means that workers here face lower wages and higher unemployment; many workers abroad are paid extremely low wages. As a result, say critics, the global expansion of capitalism threatens the well-being of workers throughout the world.

The world is still divided into 194 politically distinct nations. But increasing international economic activity makes nationhood less significant than it was even a decade ago.

In high-income nations such as the United States, almost three out of four jobs are in the tertiary or service sector of the economy.

Global Snapshot

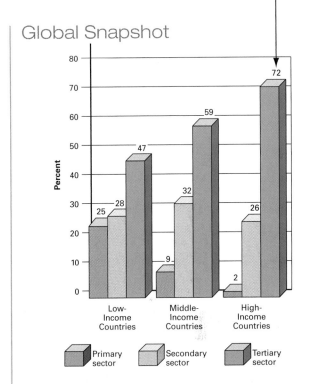

FIGURE 16–1   **The Size of Economic Sectors, by Income Level of Country**

As countries become richer, the primary sector becomes a smaller part of the economy and the tertiary or service sector becomes larger.

Source: Estimates based on World Bank (2008).

Economic Systems: Paths to Justice

October 20, Saigon, Vietnam. Sailing up the narrow Saigon River is an unsettling experience for anyone who came of age during the 1960s. People like me need to remember that Vietnam is a country, not a war, and that almost forty years have passed since the last U.S. helicopter lifted off the rooftop of the U.S. embassy, ending our country's presence there.

Saigon is now a boomtown. Neon signs bathe the city's waterfront in color; hotels, bankrolled by Western corporations, push skyward from a dozen construction sites; taxi meters record fares in U.S. dollars, not Vietnamese dong; Visa and American

THE MAP: The first map shows that the economies of low-income nations are significantly agrarian. In middle- and high-income countries, however, agriculture represents a very small share of economic output. The second global map is virtually a negative image of the first.

NOTE: The shift from an industrial to a service economy can be seen in the falling number of U.S. homes with a workshop and the rising number with a home office.

Q: "I believe that the most important, the most fundamental human right is how to ensure that the 1.2 billion Chinese people have adequate food and clothing." Jiang Zemin, president of the PRC, when asked about human rights in 1997

GLOBAL: A 1995 Gallup poll in China found that 4% of respondents supported the statement "Never think of yourself; give everything in service to society"; 68% endorsed the statement "Work hard and get rich."

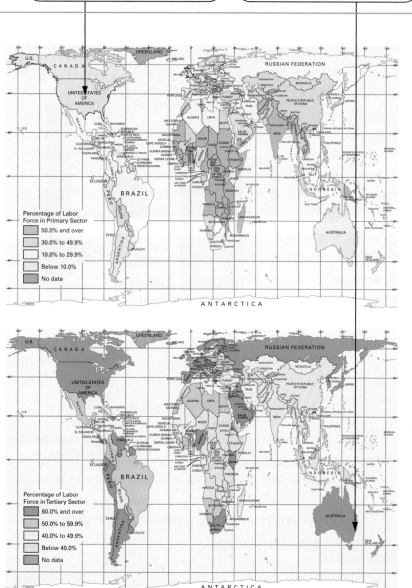

Sandra Johanson is a hygiene technician on a large corporate-owned farm in Kansas. She is one of the relatively few people in the United States working in agriculture.

Lily May Vale is an investment analyst in Sydney, Australia. Like most people in high-income nations, she works in the service sector.

Percentage of Labor Force in Primary Sector
- 50.0% and over
- 30.0% to 49.9%
- 10.0% to 29.9%
- Below 10.0%
- No data

Percentage of Labor Force in Tertiary Sector
- 60.0% and over
- 50.0% to 59.9%
- 40.0% to 49.9%
- Below 40.0%
- No data

Window on the World

GLOBAL MAP 16–1
Agricultural Employment in Global Perspective

The primary sector of the economy is largest in the nations that are least developed. Thus in the poor countries of Africa and Asia, up to half of all workers are farmers. This picture is altogether different in the world's most economically developed countries—including the United States, Canada, Great Britain, and Australia—which have a mere 2 percent of their labor force in agriculture.

Source: Data from International Labor Organization (2009).

GLOBAL MAP 16–2
Service-Sector Employment in Global Perspective

The tertiary sector of the economy becomes ever larger as a nation's income level rises. In the United States, Canada, the countries of Western Europe, much of South America, Australia, and Japan, about two-thirds of the labor force performs service work.

Source: Data from International Labor Organization (2009).

Express stickers decorate the doors of fashionable shops that cater to tourists from Japan, France, and the United States.
There is an irony here: After decades of fighting, the loss of millions of human lives, and the victory of Communist forces, the Vietnamese are doing an about-face and turning toward capitalism. What we see today is what might well have happened had the U.S. forces won the war.

Every society's economic system makes a statement about *justice* by determining who is entitled to what. Two general economic models are capitalism and socialism. No nation anywhere in the world has an economy that is completely one or the other; capitalism and socialism represent two ends of a continuum along which all real-world economies can be located. We will look at each of these two models in turn.

NOTE: The *Oxford English Dictionary* indicates that the word "capitalism" entered the English language in the late 18th century. Peter Berger claims that Adam Smith never used the term. The etymology of the word reveals a Latin root, *caput,* meaning "head."

DISCUSS: Capitalist societies make consumption key to social and personal identity. The United States has twice as many shopping malls as it does high schools.

DISCUSS: How does morality figure in the market system? Some analysts say there is no morality in a market economy, only profit; the political left describes the market as implicitly immoral because it ignores social good; the political right says that self-seeking is inherently moral because it represents people freely serving their own chosen ends. Also, a market system offers people freedoms as producers and consumers and bridges national, religious, racial, ethnic, and other traditional divides.

capitalism an economic system in which natural resources and the means of producing goods and services are privately owned

socialism an economic system in which natural resources and the means of producing goods and services are collectively owned

communism a hypothetical economic and political system in which all members of a society are socially equal

SEEING SOCIOLOGY
in Everyday Life

Supporters of Wal-Mart sometimes make the claim that this store has done a lot to reduce poverty in the United States by giving working people low prices for things they need. Do you agree with this view? Why or why not?

Capitalism

Capitalism is *an economic system in which natural resources and the means of producing goods and services are privately owned.* An ideal capitalist economy has three distinctive features:

1. **Private ownership of property**. In a capitalist economy, individuals can own almost anything. The more capitalist an economy is, the more private ownership there is of wealth-producing property, such as factories, real estate, and natural resources.

2. **Pursuit of personal profit**. A capitalist society seeks to create profit and wealth. The profit motive is the reason people take new jobs, open new businesses, or try to improve products. Making money is considered the natural way of economic life. Just as important, the Scottish philosopher Adam Smith (1723–1790) claimed that as individuals pursue their self-interest, the entire society prospers (1937, orig. 1776).

3. **Competition and consumer choice**. A purely capitalist economy is a free-market system with no government interference (sometimes called a *laissez-faire economy,* from the French words meaning "leave it alone"). Adam Smith stated that a freely competitive economy regulates itself by the "invisible hand" of the law of supply and demand.

   Consumers regulate a free-market economy, Smith explained, by selecting the goods and services offering the greatest value. As producers compete for the customer's business, they provide the highest-quality goods at the lowest possible prices. In Smith's time-honored phrase, from narrow self-interest comes the "greatest good for the greatest number of people." Government control of an economy, on the other hand, distorts market forces by reducing the quantity and quality of goods, shortchanging consumers in the process.

Justice in a capitalist system amounts to freedom of the marketplace, where a person can produce, invest, and buy according to individual self-interest. The increasing popularity of Wal-Mart, described in the opening to this chapter, reflects the fact that people think they get a lot for their money when shopping there.

The United States is considered a capitalist nation because most businesses are privately owned. However, it is not purely capitalist because government plays a large role in the economy. The government owns and operates a number of businesses, including almost all of this country's schools, roads, parks and museums, the U.S. Postal Service, the Amtrak railroad system, and the entire U.S. military. The U.S. government also had a major hand in building the Internet. In addition, governments use taxation and other forms of regulation to influence what companies produce, control the quality and cost of merchandise, and motivate consumers to conserve natural resources.

The U.S. government also sets minimum wage levels, enforces workplace safety standards, regulates corporate mergers, provides farm price supports, and supplements the income of a majority of its people in the form of Social Security, public assistance, student loans, and veterans' benefits. Local, state, and federal governments combined are the country's biggest employer, with 16 percent of the nonfarm labor force on their payrolls (U.S. Department of Labor, 2008b).

Socialism

Socialism is *an economic system in which natural resources and the means of producing goods and services are collectively owned.* In its ideal form, a socialist economy rejects each of the three characteristics of capitalism just described in favor of three opposite features:

1. **Collective ownership of property**. A socialist economy limits rights to private property, especially property used to generate income. Government controls such property and makes housing and other goods available to all, not just to the people with the most money.

2. **Pursuit of collective goals**. The individualistic pursuit of profit goes against the collective orientation of socialism. What capitalism celebrates as the "entrepreneurial spirit," socialism condemns as greed; individuals are expected to work for the common good of all.

3. **Government control of the economy**. Socialism rejects capitalism's laissez-faire approach in favor of a *centrally controlled* or *command economy* operated by the government. Commercial advertising thus plays little role in socialist economies.

Justice in a socialist context means not competing to gain wealth but meeting everyone's basic needs in a roughly equal manner. From a socialist point of view, the common capitalist practice of giving workers as little in pay and benefits as possible to boost company earnings is unjust because it puts profits before people.

The People's Republic of China and some two dozen other nations in Asia, Africa, and Latin America model their economies on socialism, placing almost all wealth-generating property under state control (Miller & Holmes, 2009). The extent of world socialism has declined during the1990s as most of the countries in Eastern Europe and the former Soviet Union have geared their economies toward a market system. More recently, however, voters in Bolivia, Venezuela, Ecuador, and other nations in South America have elected leaders who have moved the national economies in a socialist direction.

Socialism and Communism

Many people think of *socialism* and *communism* as the same thing, but they are not. **Communism** is *a hypothetical economic and political*

417

SOCIAL SURVEY: "How do you feel about communism as a form of government?" (GSS 1994, *N* = 484; *Codebook*, 2005:164)

"It's the worst kind of all"	51.7%
"It's bad, but no worse than some others"	32.4%
"It's all right for some countries"	12.0%
"It's a good form of government"	1.0%

"Don't know"/No response   2.9%

NOTE: For Adam Smith, there is no explicit category of the social; social good springs from individual interests. By contrast, for Karl Marx, there is no explicit category of the individual; individual satisfaction springs from collective action.

Q: "Under capitalism, man exploits man. Under socialism, the reverse is true." Polish proverb

welfare capitalism an economic and political system that combines a mostly market-based economy with extensive social welfare programs

state capitalism an economic and political system in which companies are privately owned but cooperate closely with the government

Capitalism still thrives in Hong Kong (*left*), evident in streets choked with advertising and shoppers. Socialism is more the rule in China's capital, Beijing (*right*), a city dominated by government buildings rather than a downtown business district.

system in which all members of a society are socially equal. Karl Marx viewed socialism as one important step on the path toward the ideal of a communist society that abolishes all class divisions. In many socialist societies today, the dominant political party describes itself as communist, but the communist goal has not been achieved in any country.

Why? For one thing, social stratification involves differences in power as well as wealth. Socialist societies have reduced economic differences by regulating people's range of choices. In the process, government did not "wither away," as Marx imagined it would. Rather, government has grown, giving socialist political elites enormous power and privilege.

Marx might have agreed that a communist society is a *utopia* (from Greek words meaning "no place"). Yet Marx considered communism a worthy goal and might well have objected to so-called Marxist societies such as North Korea, the People's Republic of China, and Cuba for falling short of the promise of communism.

Welfare Capitalism and State Capitalism

Some nations of Western Europe, including Sweden and Italy, have market-based economies but also offer broad social welfare programs. Analysts call this type of economic system **welfare capitalism**, *an economic and political system that combines a mostly market-based economy with extensive social welfare programs.*

Under welfare capitalism, the government owns some of the largest industries and services, such as transportation, the mass media, and health care. In Sweden and Italy, about 12 percent of economic production is "nationalized," or state-controlled. Most industry is left in private hands, although it is subject to extensive government regulation. High taxation (aimed especially at the rich) funds a wide range of social welfare programs, including universal health care and child care. In Sweden, for example, social services represent one-third of all economic output, twice the share in the United States (OECD, 2009).

Another blend of capitalism and socialism is **state capitalism**, *an economic and political system in which companies are privately owned but cooperate closely with the government.* State capitalism is the rule among the nations along the Pacific Rim. Japan, South Korea, and Singapore are all capitalist countries, but their governments work in partnership with large companies, supplying financial assistance and controlling foreign imports to help their businesses compete in world markets (Gerlach, 1992).

Relative Advantages of Capitalism and Socialism

Which economic system works best? Comparing economic models is difficult because all countries mix capitalism and socialism to varying degrees. In addition, nations differ in cultural attitudes toward work, access to natural resources, levels of technological development, and patterns of trade. Despite such complicating factors, some crude comparisons are revealing.

Economic Productivity

One key dimension of economic performance is productivity. A commonly used measure of economic output is gross domestic product (GDP), the total value of all goods and services produced annually.

Q: "To get rich is glorious." Deng Xiaoping to President Jimmy Carter (1979)

GLOBAL: South Korean state capitalism has concentrated more than half of all economic production in just four major corporations, including Hyundai.

DISCUSS: Does socialism's lower productivity result from Marx's separation of reward from effort, implied in his famous call, "From each according to ability; to each according to need"?

NOTE: In the U.S. (and even more in Europe) the government controls much of the "market" economy through taxation. A household earning $60,000 pays 35% to 40% in federal, state, and local income taxes, plus another 5% to 7% in sales tax, as well as property taxes. At a person's death, the government taxes estates worth more than $2 million at half their value. Thus the richest one-third of Americans surrender more than half their lifetime earnings to taxes.

MAKING THE GRADE

Both capitalism and socialism have advantages and disadvantages. One general point on which most experts agree is that capitalism is more productive and socialism generates more social equality.

SEEING SOCIOLOGY
in Everyday Life

Do you think the United States could ever become a socialist nation? Explain.

Per capita (per-person) GDP allows us to compare the economic performance of nations of different population sizes.

The output of mostly capitalist countries at the end of the 1980s—before the fall of the socialist systems in the Soviet Union and Eastern Europe—varied somewhat but averaged about $13,500 per person. The comparable figure for the mostly socialist former Soviet Union and nations of Eastern Europe was about $5,000. This means that the capitalist countries outproduced the socialist nations by a ratio of 2.7 to 1 (United Nations Development Programme, 1990). A recent comparison of socialist North Korea (per capita GDP of $1,700) and capitalist South Korea ($22,985) provides an even sharper contrast (United Nations Development Programme, 2008).

Economic Equality

The distribution of resources within a population is another important measure of how well an economic system works. A comparative study of Europe in the mid-1970s, when that region was split between mostly capitalist and mostly socialist countries, compared the earnings of the richest 5 percent of the population and the poorest 5 percent (Wiles, 1977). Societies with capitalist economies had an income ratio of about 10 to 1; the ratio for socialist countries was about 5 to 1. In other words, capitalist economies support a higher overall standard of living, but with greater income inequality; socialist economies create more economic equality but with a lower overall living standard.

Personal Freedom

One additional consideration in evaluating capitalism and socialism is the personal freedom each gives its people. Capitalism emphasizes the *freedom to pursue self-interest* and depends on the ability of producers and consumers to interact with little interference by the state. Socialism, by contrast, emphasizes *freedom from basic want*. The goal of equality requires the state to regulate the economy, which in turn limits personal choices and opportunities for citizens.

Can a single society offer both political freedom and economic equality? In the capitalist United States, our political system offers many personal freedoms, but the economy generates a lot of inequality, and freedom is not worth as much to a poor person as to a rich one. By contrast, North Korea or Cuba has considerable economic equality, but people cannot speak out or travel freely within or outside of the country. Perhaps the closest any country has come to "having it all" is Denmark—the Thinking Globally box on page 420 takes a closer look.

Changes in Socialist and Capitalist Countries

In 1989 and 1990, the nations of Eastern Europe, which had been seized by the Soviet Union at the end of World War II, overthrew their socialist regimes. These nations—including the former German

Directly comparing the economic performance of capitalism and socialism is difficult because nations differ in many ways. But a satellite image of socialist North Korea and capitalist South Korea at night shows the dramatically different electrical output of the two nations, one indication of economic activity.

Democratic Republic (reunited with Germany), the Czech Republic, Slovakia, Hungary, Romania, and Bulgaria—have been moving toward capitalist market systems after decades of state-controlled economies. In 1991, the Soviet Union itself formally dissolved, and many of its former republics introduced some free-market principles. Within a decade, three-fourths of former Soviet government enterprises were partly or entirely in private hands (Montaigne, 2001).

There were many reasons for these sweeping changes. First, the capitalist economies far outproduced their socialist counterparts. The socialist economies were successful in achieving economic equality, but living standards were low compared to those of Western Europe. Second, Soviet socialism was heavy-handed, rigidly controlling the media and restricting individual freedoms. In short, socialism did away with *economic* elites, as Karl Marx predicted, but as Max Weber foresaw, socialism increased the power of *political* elites.

So far, the market reforms in Eastern Europe are proceeding unevenly. Some nations (the Czech Republic, Slovakia, Poland, and

● SEEING SOCIOLOGY
in Everyday Life

Do you think the world would be better off with more capitalism or more socialism? Why?

primary labor market jobs that provide extensive benefits to workers

secondary labor market jobs that provide minimal benefits to workers

---

THINKING GLOBALLY

Want Equality and Freedom? Try Denmark

Denmark is a small nation in northwestern Europe with about 5.5 million people. This country is a good example of the economic and political system called welfare capitalism in which a market economy is mixed with broad government programs that provide for the welfare of all citizens.

Most Danes consider life in their country to be very good. There is a high standard of living—Denmark's per-person GDP is $37,000, not far behind the figure of $42,000 in the United States. But Denmark has only one-third as much income inequality as we have in this country. Its unemployment rate is about 2 percent lower than in the United States.

Low inequality and low unemployment are largely the result of government regulation of the economy. Taxes in Denmark are among the highest in the world, with most people paying about 40 percent of their income in taxes and those earning over about $70,000 paying more than 60 percent. That's in addition to a sales tax of 25 percent on everything people buy. These high taxes increase economic equality (by taking more taxes from the rich and giving more benefits to the poor), and they also allow the government to fund the social welfare programs

that provide benefits to everyone. For example, every Danish citizen is entitled to government-funded schooling and government-funded health

To enable men and women to work for income, the government of Denmark grants paid child-care leave to both fathers and mothers.

care, and each worker receives at least five weeks of paid vacation leave each year. People who are out of work receive about 90 percent of their income from the government for up to four years.

Many people—especially the Danes themselves—feel that Denmark offers an ideal mix of political freedom (Danes have extensive political rights and elect their leaders) as well as economic security (all citizens can benefit from extensive government services and programs).

WHAT DO YOU THINK?

1. What evidence of less income inequality might you expect to see in Denmark if you were to visit that country?

2. Would you be willing to pay most of your income in taxes if the government provided you with benefits such as schooling and health care? Why or why not?

3. Do you think most people in the United States would like to have our society become more like Denmark? Why or why not?

Source: Based on Fox (2007).

---

the Baltic states of Latvia, Estonia, and Lithuania) are doing relatively well, but others (Romania, Bulgaria, and the Russian Federation) have been buffeted by price increases and falling living standards. Officials hope that expanding production will eventually bring a turnaround. However, the introduction of a market economy has brought with it an increase in economic inequality (Ignatius, 2007; World Bank, 2008).

A number of other countries have recently begun moving toward more socialist economies. In 2005, the people of Bolivia elected Evo Morales, a former farmer, union leader, and activist, as their new president, over a wealthy business leader who was educated in the United States. This election placed Bolivia in a group of nations—including Ecuador, Venezuela, Brazil, Chile, and Uruguay—that are moving toward more socialist economies. The reasons for this shift vary from country to country, but the common element is economic inequality. In Bolivia, for example, economic production has increased in recent decades, but most of the benefits have gone to a wealthy business elite.

By contrast, more than half of the country's people remain very poor (Howden, 2005).

Work in the Postindustrial U.S. Economy

Economic change is occurring not just in the socialist world but in the United States as well. In 2008, a total of 143 million people in the United States—61 percent of those aged sixteen and over—were working for income. A larger share of men (66.7 percent) than women (55.7 percent) had jobs, a gap that has been holding steady over time. Among men, 60.9 percent of African Americans were employed, compared with 70.5 percent of whites, 72.8 percent of Asians, and 76.0 percent of Hispanics. Among women, 58.7 percent of African Americans were employed, compared to 57.5 percent of whites, 56.6

DISCUSS: Is there a link between the rise of a service economy and the increasing number of overly committed two-career couples who use services ranging from housecleaning to take-out food?

THEN AND NOW: The decline of farming can be seen in the falling number of farms owned by African Americans: 926,000 in 1920 compared to 18,000 in 2000.

THEN AND NOW: U.S. union membership in 2008 was 16 million, up 400,000

from the year before. Only 12% of all workers (one in eight) are union members, well below the peak of 35.5% (more than one in three) in 1945.

SOCIAL SURVEY: "How much confidence do you have in people running organized labor?" (GSS 2004, *N* = 876; NORC, 2008)

| "A great deal" | 11.8% | "Hardly any" | 28.4% |
| "Only some" | 54.6% | "Don't know"/No response | 5.3% |

labor union organizations of workers that seek to improve wages and working conditions through various strategies, including negotiations and strikes

profession (p. 422) a prestigious white-collar occupation that requires extensive formal education

SEEING SOCIOLOGY
in Everyday Life

Do you think the jobs provided by colleges to students as part of their financial aid offer a fair level of pay and benefits? Explain your view.

percent of Asians, and 54.2 percent of Hispanics (U.S. Department of Labor, 2009).

The Decline of Agricultural Work

In 1900, roughly 40 percent of U.S. workers were farmers. In 2008, just 1.5 percent were in agriculture. Although recent years have seen a small resurgence of family farms—reflecting the growing popularity of organic and locally grown foods—the larger trend is that the family farm of a century ago has been replaced by *corporate agribusinesses.* Farmland is now more productive, but this change in output has caused painful adjustments across the country as a traditional way of life is lost (Dudley, 2000; A. Carlson, 2008). Figure 16–2 illustrates the shrinking role of the primary sector in the U.S. economy.

From Factory Work to Service Work

A century ago, industrialization swelled the ranks of blue-collar workers. By 1950, however, a white-collar revolution had moved a majority of workers into service occupations. By 2008, fully 78 percent of the labor force worked in the service sector, and almost all of this country's new jobs were being created in this sector (U.S. Department of Labor, 2009).

As Chapter 11 ("Social Class in the United States") explained, the expansion of service work is one reason many people call the United States a middle-class society. But much service work—including sales and clerical positions and jobs in hospitals and restaurants—pays much less than older factory jobs. This means that many of the jobs in today's postindustrial society provide only a modest standard of living. Women and other minorities, as well as many young people just starting their working careers, are the most likely to have jobs doing low-paying service work (Kalleberg, Reskin, & Hudson, 2000; Greenhouse, 2006).

The economic trends affect the job prospects of college graduates, especially in today's uncertain economy. "Seeing Sociology in the News on pages 422–23 looks at some of the challenges graduates are facing.

The Dual Labor Market

Sociologists see the jobs in today's economy falling into two categories. The **primary labor market** offers *jobs that provide extensive benefits to workers.* This segment of the labor market includes the traditional white-collar professions such as medicine and law, as well as upper-management positions. These are jobs that people think of as *careers,* interesting work that provides high income, job security, and opportunity for advancement.

Few of these advantages apply to work in the **secondary labor market,** *jobs that provide minimal benefits to workers.* This segment of the labor force is employed in low-skilled, blue-collar assembly-line

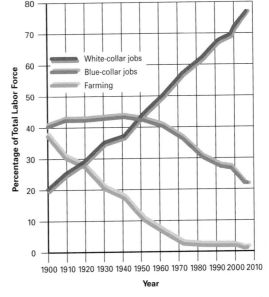

FIGURE 16–2 **The Changing Pattern of Work in the United States, 1900–2008**

Compared to a century ago, when the economy involved a larger share of factory and farm work, making a living in the United States now involves mostly white-collar service jobs.

Source: Estimates based on U.S. Department of Labor (2009b).

operations and low-level service-sector jobs, including clerical positions. Workers in the secondary labor market receive lower income, have less job security and fewer benefits, and find less satisfaction in their work. Women and other minorities are overly represented in the secondary labor market workforce (J. I. Nelson, 1994; Kalleberg, Reskin, & Hudson, 2000).

Labor Unions

The changing U.S. economy has seen a decline in **labor unions,** *organizations of workers that seek to improve wages and working conditions through various strategies, including negotiations and strikes.* During the Great Depression of the 1930s, union membership increased rapidly; by 1950, it had reached more than one-third of nonfarm workers. Union rolls peaked at almost 25 million around 1970. Since then, membership has declined to about 12 percent of nonfarm workers, or some 15.7 million men and women. Looking more closely, 36 percent of government workers are members of unions, compared to just 8 percent of private-sector (nongovernment) workers (Clawson & Clawson, 1999; U.S. Department of Labor, 2008b).

DISCUSS: How many of your students work? The University of Michigan's Institute for Social Research estimates that three-fourths of high school seniors worked for income; 40% of all seniors work more than 20 hours a week.

RESOURCE: Karl Marx's analysis of "alienated labor" is one of the classic selections included in the author's companion reader *Seeing Ourselves*, 8th ed.

Q: "Opportunity is missed by most people because it is dressed in overalls and looks like work." Thomas Edison

Seeing SOCIOLOGY in the

College Students Look to Future with Worry, Hope

BY CHRIS WELCH
April 2, 2009

It's traditionally seen as a time for celebration, but these days Hamline University senior Emily Amici looks at graduation day with nothing but uncertainty.

"If I don't have a job, I'll be panicking," the St. Paul, Minnesota, student says.

Amici wants to dive head-first into the business world, but with the economy hurting, that can be a bit daunting. Amici is majoring in international management with a minor in Spanish, and until mid-school year she thought she'd be just fine.

"I had already started interviewing with companies back in like October, and I was like 'Wow, they're already looking to hire people and it's only October, so that's a good sign.' But then right around December things just started going downhill, and it's been kind of rough."

The numbers bear her out, with the unemployment rate among college graduates at a record high. In February, almost 1.9 million college graduates were unemployed, according to the Bureau of Labor Statistics.

Amici had her sights set on an entry-level position with a Minnesota-based international food company that she says has traditionally hired between 10 and 20 recent grads each year. She'd gone through three separate rounds of interviews with the food company and things were looking positive—for a little while.

"They were really interested in hiring me, but due to staffing changes or economic conditions, they couldn't extend offers at this time," she explains. . . .

She's sent out about 100 resumes. Four of those have produced interviews, two of which, however, ended similarly.

"They just couldn't hire," she says, admitting it's been frustrating—especially for someone with a 3.9 grade point average.

"I guess when I look at it, I'm a pretty good student," Amici says shyly. "I just feel like if I can't get a job . . . it's just going to be impossible for a lot of people to get jobs."

She says she's even been to job fairs recently where the majority of companies have openly said they aren't even hiring, just merely taking applications for future consideration. But Amici still keeps a positive outlook.

"They have to hire eventually, though," she says. "I mean, I don't know if that'll be in April or August or two years from now."

Mike Brinda is a junior studying applied economics at the University of Minnesota. He's decided to let the job world wait for him. He's continuing his education by going to graduate school in finance—an idea some might shudder at given today's economic climate.

"I know finance is pretty bad right now," Brinda admits. "But hopefully it's in the upswing, and probably with more education it might be easier to get a job."

Claudia Parliament, a University of Minnesota professor in the Department of Applied Economics, . . . says she was a bit surprised when Brinda told her of his plans.

The pattern of union decline holds in other high-income countries, yet unions claim a far smaller share of workers in the United States than elsewhere. From about 20 percent in Japan, union membership climbs to 28 percent in Canada, between 20 and 40 percent in much of Europe, and a high of 78 percent in Sweden (Visser, 2006).

The widespread decline in union memberships reflects the shrinking industrial sector of the economy. Newer service jobs—such as sales jobs at retailers like Wal-Mart, described in the chapter opening—have generally not become unionized. Citing low wages and numerous worker complaints, unions are trying to organize Wal-Mart employees, so far without winning over a single store. The weak economy of the past few years has given unions a short-term boost. The Obama administration is supporting new laws that may make it easier for workers to form unions. But long-term gains probably depend on the ability of unions to adapt to the new global economy. Union members in the United States, used to seeing foreign workers as "the enemy," will have to build new international alliances (Rousseau, 2002; Dalmia, 2008; Allen, 2009).

Professions

All kinds of jobs today are called *professional*—we hear of professional tennis players, professional housecleaners, even professional exterminators. As distinct from *amateur* (from the Latin for "lover," meaning someone who does something just for the love of doing it), a professional performs some task to make a living. But what exactly is a profession?

A **profession** is *a prestigious white-collar occupation that requires extensive formal education*. People performing this kind of work make a *profession*, or public declaration, of their willingness to work according to certain principles. Professions include the ministry, medicine, law, academia, architecture, accountancy, and social work. An occupation is considered a profession to the extent that it demonstrates the following four basic characteristics (W. J. Goode, 1960; Ritzer & Walczak, 1990):

1. **Theoretical knowledge.** Professionals have a theoretical understanding of their field rather than mere technical training. Anyone can master first-aid skills, for example, but physicians have a theoretical understanding of human health. This means that tennis players, housecleaners, and exterminators do not really qualify as professionals.

2. **Self-regulating practice.** The typical professional is self-employed, "in private practice" rather than working for a company. Professionals oversee their own work and observe a code of ethics.

3. **Authority over clients.** Because of their expertise, professionals are sought out by clients, who value their advice and follow their directions.

4. **Community orientation rather than self-interest.** The traditional professing of duty states an intention to serve others rather than merely to seek income.

Q: "A profession is a conspiracy against the layman." George Bernard Shaw

NOTE: The original meaning of the word "profession" was "the taking of a vow." A professor was thus a person who took a religious vow, revealing the ecclesiastical origins of the European universities. This helps explain why ethics and public responsibility continue to figure in professional life.

Q: "Economics is the study of money and why it is good." Woody Allen

NOTE: In the U.S., there are about 3,680 working sociologists, compared to 106,830 architects, 555,770 lawyers, and 1,115,000 accountants; annually, about 500 doctorates in sociology are awarded, compared to 15,000 medical doctorates and 43,000 law doctorates (U.S. Department of Labor, 2008).

"When he first told me he wanted to go into business, I said, 'Whoa, that's interesting,'" Parliament says. "I would think that people would be leery of a major in that field."

Still, Parliament says she supports Brinda's decision because she knows he has a passion for personal finance, and, in her opinion, it's never a bad option to further your education.

"I think it's a good time to be in school right now because you're investing in your own skills," Parliament says. "And right now when there's not as many job prospects it's a good time for you to make those kinds of investments." . . .

Coincidentally or not, both Hamline University and the University of Minnesota are seeing slight growth among students studying business. Despite the dismal economic outlook, there still seems to be a genuine interest and curiosity about the recession and in business-related fields in general, faculty members say.

Wayne Sigler, the director of admissions for the University of Minnesota, says business has always been a strong area for the school. He says it's only "continuing to grow."

Julian Schuster, dean of Hamline University's School of Business, echoes Sigler's words and adds that, in a sense, learning economics is "fashionable."

He says Hamline business classes have been filling quickly because there's an interest in what's current, such as economics and finance.

"The process of understanding empowers them to comprehend that actually a big portion of what is going to happen they can address by their own actions," Schuster says. "And that mood is something which I see at the end of our classes."

Emily Amici may have a better understanding of business, but if she can't find a job in her field of study, she'll have to settle with her current position as a waitress until she does. She says she's not planning to go to grad school at the moment.

"Right now, I'm just taking it as it comes," she says.

And perhaps the best thing for business students to do is follow the lead of Hamline junior Erik Gusaas, who's in the process of finding internships that may lead to jobs.

"I just try to keep a positive attitude toward it. [I] just keep knocking at the door and figure something has to eventually fall my way. I have to try to keep a stiff upper lip."

WHAT DO YOU THINK?

1. How does this article show that the success or failure we experience in our everyday lives is often caused by larger societal forces?

2. Do you think students who understand about the surrounding society will end up making better choices in their lives? Explain.

3. Is it a wise decision to go after a career in a field you feel passionate about, even if the immediate prospects for success seem limited? Explain your own views.

Excerpted by permission from "College Students Look to the Future with Worry, Hope" by Chris Welch, April 2, 2006, from cnn.com <http://cnn.com>

In almost all cases, professional work requires not just a college degree but also a graduate degree. Not surprisingly, therefore, professions are well represented among the occupations beginning college students say they hope to enter after graduation, as shown in Figure 16–3 on page 424.

Many occupations that do not qualify as true professions nonetheless seek to *professionalize* their services. Claiming professional standing often begins by renaming the work to suggest special, theoretical knowledge, moving the field away from its original, lesser reputation. Stockroom workers become "inventory supply managers," and exterminators are reborn as "insect control specialists."

Interested parties may also form a professional association that certifies their skills. This organization then licenses its members, writes a code of ethics, and emphasizes the work's importance in the community. To win public acceptance, a professional association may also establish schools or other training facilities and perhaps start a professional journal. Not all occupations try to claim professional status. Some *paraprofessionals*, including paralegals and medical technicians, possess specialized skills but lack the extensive theoretical education required of full professionals.

Self-Employment

Self-employment—earning a living without being on the payroll of a large organization—was once common in the United States. About 80 percent of the labor force was self-employed in 1800, compared to just 7.2 percent of workers today (8.9 percent of men and 5.4 percent of women) (U.S. Department of Labor, 2009).

Lawyers, physicians, and other professionals are well represented among the ranks of the self-employed. But most self-employed workers are small business owners, plumbers, carpenters, freelance writers, editors, artists, and long-distance truck drivers. In all, the self-employed are more likely to have blue-collar than white-collar jobs.

Women own 28 percent of this country's businesses, and the share is rising. The 6.5 million firms owned by U.S. women employ 7 percent of the labor force and generate close to $1 trillion in annual sales (U.S. Small Business Administration, 2006).

Unemployment and Underemployment

Every society has some unemployment. Few young people entering the labor force find a job right away; workers may leave their jobs to seek new work or stay at home raising children; others may be on strike or suffer from long-term illnesses; still others lack the skills to perform useful work.

But unemployment is not just an individual problem; it is also caused by the economy. Jobs disappear as occupations become obsolete and companies change the way they operate. Since 1980, the 500 largest U.S. businesses eliminated more than 5 million jobs while creating even more new ones.

Generally, companies downsize to become more competitive, or firms close in the face of foreign competition or economic recession.

DISCUSS: Is the home-based "virtual office" a good thing? Pluses include more freedom, no commute, more flexibility; minuses include isolation, harder-to-get help, and blurring between home and work life.

NOTE: The U.S. economy is very dynamic. One study estimated that between 1993 and 2002, U.S. companies eliminated 310 million jobs and created 328 million new ones (Irwin, 2004).

DISCUSS: Consider ways in which unemployment is socially detrimental (undermining families) as well as economically harmful.

GLOBAL: Sweden and other Nordic countries have responded to rising unemployment by cutting the average workday (to about 6 hours) to maintain full employment. This flex-time pattern also encourages more women with family responsibilities into the workplace.

> In a society such as ours, with so many different types of work, no one career attracts the interest of more than a small share of today's students.

underground economy economic activity involving income not reported to the government as required

corporation an organization with a legal existence, including rights and liabilities, separate from that of its members

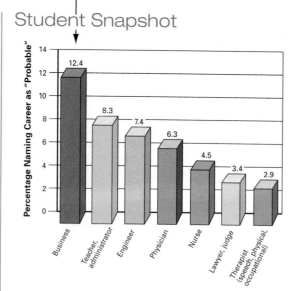

Student Snapshot

FIGURE 16–3 **The Careers Most Commonly Named as Probable by First-Year College Students, 2008**

Today's college students expect to enter careers that pay well and carry high prestige.

Source: Pryor et al. (2008).

During the recession that began in 2008 in the United States, several million jobs were lost, with unemployment rising in just about every part of the economy. Jobs have been lost not only by blue-collar workers but also by white-collar workers who had typically weathered downturns in the past.

In 2008, just as the economy was falling into recession, 7 million people over the age of sixteen were unemployed, about 4.6 percent of the civilian labor force (U.S. Department of Labor, 2008b). But during 2008, more than 2.5 million people lost their jobs, pushing the unemployment rate above 9 percent by mid-2009. In some regions of the country, especially rural areas, unemployment rates are usually far worse—about double the national average.

Figure 16–4 shows that in 2008, unemployment among African Americans (11.9 percent) was more than twice the rate among white people (6.6 percent). Regardless of sex or age, unemployment is lower among whites than among African Americans; the gap between white and black teenagers was especially large. For all categories of people, one of the best ways to avoid unemployment is to earn a college degree: As the figure shows, the unemployment rate for college graduates was below 4 percent—well below the national average.

Underemployment is also a problem for millions of workers. In an era of corporate bankruptcy, the failure of large banks, and downsiz-

ing by companies throughout the U.S. economy, millions of workers—the lucky ones who still have their jobs—have been left with lower salaries, fewer benefits such as health insurance, and disappearing pensions. Rising global competition, weaker worker organizations, and economic recession have combined to allow many people to keep their jobs only by agreeing to cutbacks in pay or to the loss of other benefits (K. Clark, 2002; Gutierrez, 2007; McGeehan, 2009).

In addition, the government reports that more than 27 million people work part time, defined as less than thirty-five hours a week. Although most say they are satisfied with this arrangement, at least one-third claim that they want more work but cannot find it (U.S. Department of Labor, 2007).

The Underground Economy

The U.S. government requires individuals and businesses to report their economic activity, especially earnings. Unreported income makes a transaction part of the **underground economy**, *economic activity involving income not reported to the government as required by law.*

Most of us participate in the underground economy in small ways from time to time: A family makes extra money by holding a garage sale, or teenagers baby-sit for neighbors without reporting the income. Much more of the underground economy is due to criminal activity, such as prostitution, bribery, theft, illegal gambling, loan-sharking, and the sale of illegal drugs.

But the largest segment of contributors to the underground economy is people who fail to report some or all of their legally earned income when it comes time to file income tax returns. Self-employed persons such as carpenters, physicians, and small business owners may understate their income on tax forms; food servers and other service workers may not report their earnings from tips. Individually, the amounts people do not report may be small, but taken together, U.S. taxpayers fail to pay as much as $345 billion annually in federal taxes (Internal Revenue Service, 2006).

Workplace Diversity: Race and Gender

In the past, white men have been the mainstay of the U.S. labor force. However, the nation's proportion of minorities is rising rapidly. The African American population is increasing faster than the population of non-Hispanic white people. The rate of increase in the Asian American and Hispanic populations is even greater.

Such dramatic changes are likely to affect U.S. society in countless ways. Not only will more and more workers be women and other minorities, but the workplace will have to develop programs and policies that meet the needs of a socially diverse workforce and also encourage everyone to work together effectively and respectfully. The Thinking About Diversity box on page 426 takes a closer look at some of the issues involved in our changing workplace.

NOTE: For young people, at least one of the jobs they will hold has yet to be invented!

POP CULTURE: One lasting pop culture image of the increasing diversity of the workforce is "Rosie the Riveter," depicting the movement of women into the labor force during World War II.

NOTE: National Maps 14–1 and 14–3, on pages 359 and 376, illustrate the areas of the country in which the character of the workforce is most affected by racial and ethnic diversity.

RESOURCE: "Getting a Job in Harlem: Experiences of African American, Puerto Rican, and Dominican Youth," by Katherine S. Newman, appears in the author's companion reader *Seeing Ourselves*, 8th ed.

SEEING SOCIOLOGY
in Everyday Life

Can you think of advantages and disadvantages of being able to work almost anywhere? Do the benefits of the "anywhere office" outweigh the downsides?

The best strategy to reduce your risk of being without a job is to complete a college education.

Information Technology and Work

July 2, Ticonderoga, New York. The manager of the local hardware store scans the bar codes of a bag-ful of items. "The computer doesn't just total the costs," she explains. "It also keeps track of inventory, placing orders from the warehouse and deciding which products to continue to sell and which to drop." "Sounds like what you used to do, Maureen," I respond with a smile. "Yep," she nods, with no smile at all.

Another workplace issue is the increasing role of computers and other information technology. The Information Revolution is changing what people do in a number of ways (Rule & Brantley, 1992; Vallas & Beck, 1996):

1. **Computers are deskilling labor.** Just as industrial machinery replaced the master craftsworkers of an earlier era, computers now threaten the skills of managers. More business operations are based not on executive decisions but on computer modeling. In other words, a machine decides whether to place an order, stock a dress in a certain size and color, or approve a loan application.

2. **Computers are making work more abstract.** Most industrial workers have a hands-on relationship with their product. Postindustrial workers use symbols to perform abstract tasks, such as making a company more profitable or making software more user-friendly.

3. **Computers limit workplace interaction.** As workers spend more time at computer terminals, they become increasingly isolated from one another.

4. **Computers increase employers' control of workers.** Computers allow supervisors to monitor employees' output continuously, whether they work at computer terminals or on assembly lines.

5. **Computers allow companies to relocate work.** Because computer technology allows information to flow almost anywhere instantly, the symbolic work in today's economy may not take place where we might think. We have all had the experience of calling a business (say, a hotel or bookstore) located in our own town only to find that we are talking to a person at a computer workstation thousands of miles away. Computer technology provides the means to outsource many jobs to other places where wages may be lower.

Perhaps, in the wake of widespread failures on Wall Street, there will be a trend away from allowing computers to manage risk, putting responsibility for business decisions back in the hands of people (Kivant, 2008). Or perhaps both computers and people have flaws that will always prevent us from living in a perfect world. But the

Diversity Snapshot

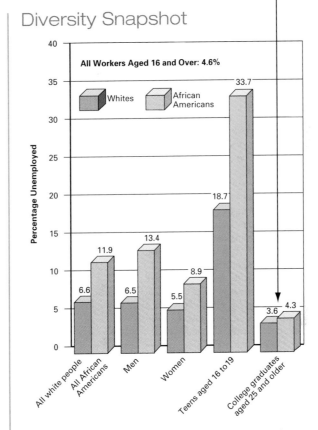

All Workers Aged 16 and Over: 4.6%

FIGURE 16–4 **Official U.S. Unemployment Rates for Various Categories of Adults, 2008**

Although college graduates have a low risk of unemployment, race is related to unemployment for all categories of people.

Source: U.S. Department of Labor (2009).

rapidly increasing reliance on computers in business reminds us that new technology is never socially neutral. It changes the relationships between people in the workplace, shapes the way we work, and often alters the balance of power between employers and employees. Understandably, then, people welcome some aspects of the Information Revolution and oppose others.

Corporations

At the core of today's capitalist economy lies the **corporation**, *an organization with a legal existence, including rights and liabilities, separate from that of its members.* Incorporating makes an organization a

RESOURCE: A selection from William Julius Wilson's research, "When Work Disappears," is in the companion reader *Seeing Ourselves*, 8th ed.

NOTE: Economic uncertainty has made federal government jobs more popular in recent years. Average pay for a federal job nationwide now exceeds $60,000 plus benefits and pension.

Q: "Banks are more dangerous than standing armies." Thomas Jefferson

SOCIAL SURVEY: "How much confidence do you have in the people running banks and financial institutions?" (GSS 2006, *N* = 876; *Codebook*, 2006:235)

"A great deal"	29.7%	"Hardly any"	13.3%
"Only some"	55.8%	"Don't know"/No response	1.3%

Q: "Among the purposes of a society should be to try to arrange for a continuous supply of work at all times and seasons." Pope Leo XIII

conglomerate a giant corporation composed of many smaller corporations

---

THINKING ABOUT DIVERSITY: RACE, CLASS, & GENDER

Twenty-First-Century Diversity: Changes in the Workplace

An upward trend in the U.S. minority population is changing the workplace. As the figure shows, the number of non-Hispanic white men in the U.S. labor force will rise by just 1 percent by 2016, the number of African American men will increase by 12 percent, the number of Hispanic men by 23 percent, and the number of Asian American men by 24 percent.

Among non-Hispanic white women, the projected rise is 1 percent; among African American women, 14 percent; and among Asian women, 29 percent. Hispanic women will show the greatest gains, estimated at 31 percent.

Within a decade, non-Hispanic white men will represent just 35 percent of all workers, a figure that will continue to drop. As a result, companies that welcome social diversity will tap the largest pool of talent and enjoy a competitive advantage leading to higher profits (Graybow, 2007; Toossi, 2007; Harford, 2008; U.S. Department of Labor, 2008b).

Welcoming social diversity means, first, recruiting talented workers of both sexes and all racial and cultural backgrounds. But developing the potential of all employees requires meeting the needs of women and other minorities, which may not be the same as those of white men. For example, child care at the workplace is a big issue for working mothers with small children.

Second, businesses must develop effective ways to deal with tensions that arise from social differences. They will have to work harder to ensure that workers are treated equally and respectfully, which means having zero tolerance for racial or sexual harassment.

Third, companies will have to rethink current promotion practices. At present, 72 percent of the directors of *Fortune* 100 companies are white men; 28 percent are women or other minorities (Executive Leadership Council, 2008). In a survey of U.S. companies, the U.S. Equal Employment Opportunity Commission (2008) confirmed that non-Hispanic white men, who make up 33 percent of adults aged twenty to sixty-four, hold 54 percent of management jobs; the comparable figures are 34 and 29 percent, respectively, for non-Hispanic white women, 12 and 7 percent for non-Hispanic African Americans, and 15 and 6 percent for Hispanics.

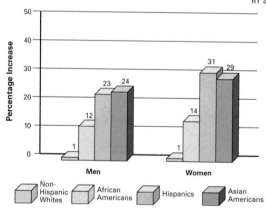

Projected Increase in the Number of People in the U.S. Labor Force, 2007–2016

Looking ahead, the share of minorities in the U.S. labor force will increase much faster than the share of white men and women.

Source: U.S. Department of Labor (2008)

WHAT DO YOU THINK?

1. What underlying factors are increasing the diversity of the U.S. workplace?

2. In what specific ways do you think businesses should support minority workers?

3. In what other settings (such as schools) is social diversity becoming more important?

---

legal entity, able to enter into contracts and own property. Of the more than 30 million businesses in the United States, 5.7 million are incorporated (U.S. Census Bureau, 2008). Incorporating protects the wealth of owners from lawsuits that result from business debts or harm to consumers; it can also mean a lower tax rate on the company's profits.

Economic Concentration

Most U.S. corporations are small, with assets of less than $500,000, so it is the largest corporations that dominate our nation's economy. In 2005, the government listed 2,405 corporations with assets exceeding $2.5 billion, representing three-fourths of all corporate assets (Internal Revenue Service, 2008).

The largest U.S. corporation in terms of sales is Wal-Mart. Its annual sales ($375 billion in 2008) equal the combined tax revenues of more than 80 percent of the states.

Conglomerates and Corporate Linkages

Economic concentration has created the **conglomerate**, *a giant corporation composed of many smaller corporations*. Conglomerates form as corporations enter new markets, spin off new companies,

NOTE: GM, Ford, and Chrysler would probably disagree that the corporate world lacks competition. They have seen their U.S. market share slide to less than half of all auto sales in recent decades in the face of rising competition from Japan and Korea. In 2009, GM and Chrysler went through bankruptcy.

GLOBAL: Fueling the deindustrialization of the U.S. are the relatively low wage rates typical of poor societies: from $7.95 an hour in Taiwan to $3.72 an hour in Mexico.

POP CULTURE: Activists use the mass media to heighten awareness of unethical labor practices by large corporations in low-income countries. One example is Nikewatch, whose recent campaign "What's the Story behind Your Sports Shoes?" shows the plight of the children working to make popular products such as Nike sneakers.

SEEING SOCIOLOGY
in Everyday Life

Do you think being very big benefits the public by making a corporation efficient? Or does being very big make a corporation so powerful that it doesn't need to be accountable to the public? Explain your position.

monopoly the domination of a market by a single producer

oligopoly the domination of a market by a few producers

or merge with other companies. For example, PepsiCo is a conglomerate that includes Pepsi-Cola, Frito-Lay, Gatorade, Tropicana, and Quaker.

Many conglomerates are linked because they own each other's stock, the result being worldwide corporate alliances of staggering size. Until 2009, General Motors owned Opel (Germany), Vauxhall (Great Britain), Saab (Sweden), and still owns part of Daewoo (South Korea) and has partnerships with Suzuki and Toyota (Japan). Similarly, Ford owns Volvo (Sweden) and a share of Mazda (Japan).

Corporations are also linked through *interlocking directorates,* networks of people who serve as directors of many corporations (Weidenbaum, 1995; Kono et al., 1998). These boardroom connections give corporations access to valuable information about other companies' products and marketing strategies. While perfectly legal, such linkages may encourage illegal activity, such as price fixing, as the companies share information about their pricing policies.

Corporations: Are They Competitive?

According to the capitalist model, businesses operate independently in a competitive market. But in light of the extensive linkages that exist between them, it is obvious that large corporations do not operate independently. Also, a few large corporations dominate many markets, so they are not truly competitive.

Federal law forbids any company from establishing a **monopoly**, *the domination of a market by a single producer,* because with no competition, such a company could simply charge whatever it wanted for its products. But **oligopoly**, *the domination of a market by a few producers,* is both legal and common. Oligopoly arises because the huge investment needed to enter a major market, such as the auto industry, is beyond the reach of all but the biggest companies. In addition, competition means risk, which big business tries to avoid.

The federal government seeks to regulate corporations in order to protect the public interest. Yet as recent corporate scandals have shown—most recently involving the housing mortgage business and the collapse of so many banks—regulation is often too little too late, resulting in companies harming millions of people. The U.S. government is the corporate world's single biggest customer, and in 2008 and 2009 it stepped in to support many struggling corporations with multibillion-dollar bailout programs. Especially during tough economic times, the public tends to support a greater role for the government in the economy (Sachs, 2009).

Corporations and the Global Economy

Corporations have grown so large that they now account for most of the world's economic output. The biggest corporations are based in the United States, Japan, and Western Europe, but their marketplace

In today's corporate world, computers are changing the nature of work just as factories did more than a century ago. In what ways is computer-based work different from factory work? In what ways do you think it is very much the same?

is the entire world. In fact, many large U.S. companies such as McDonald's and the chipmaker Intel earn most of their money outside the United States.

Global corporations know that poor countries contain most of the world's people and resources. In addition, labor costs are attractively low: A manufacturing worker in Mexico earns about $3.72 an hour and labors for more than a week to earn what a worker in Japan (who averages about $24 an hour) or the United States ($30 per hour) earns in a single day.

As Chapter 12 ("Global Stratification") explained, the impact of multinational corporations on poor countries is controversial. Modernization theorists claim that by unleashing the great productive power of capitalism, multinational corporations help to raise living standards in poor nations, offering them tax revenues, new jobs, and advanced technology that together accelerate economic growth (Berger, 1986; Firebaugh & Beck, 1994; Firebaugh & Sandu, 1998).

Dependency theorists respond that multinationals make global inequality worse by blocking the development of local industries and

NOTE: In 2009, polls showed public support for more government regulation: 55% favoring and 37% opposing (Polling Report, 2009).

Q: "Growth for the sake of growth is the ideology of the cancer cell." John Nichols

Q: "The general rule is that while property may be regulated to a certain extent, if regulation goes too far, it will be recognized as a taking." Oliver Wendell Holmes

DISCUSS: Advocates of government regulation argue that such supervision guards against monopoly. Defenders of the market claim that allowing free international trade forces large companies to be competitive (witness how the Japanese automakers successfully challenged the U.S. Big Three). What do students think? What did we learn from the recent housing crisis?

Q: "The business of the United States is business." President Warren G. Harding

● MAKING THE GRADE

Supporters of a market economy point to the productive efficiency of the market; critics point to the market's effects in generating economic inequality.

CONTROVERSY & DEBATE

The Market: Does the "Invisible Hand" Lift Us Up or Pick Our Pockets?

The market or government planning? Governments rely on one or the other to determine the products and services companies will produce and what people will consume. So important is this question that the answer has much to do with how nations define themselves, choose their allies, and identify their enemies.

Historically, U.S. society has relied on the "invisible hand" of the market to make economic decisions. Market dynamics move prices up or down according to the supply of products and buyer demand. The market thus links the efforts of countless people, each of whom—to restate Adam Smith's insight—is motivated only by self-interest. Defenders of the market system—most notably the economists Milton Friedman and Rose Friedman (1980)—claim that a more or less freely operating market system is the key to this country's high standard of living.

But others point to the contributions government makes to the U.S. economy. First, government must step in to carry out tasks that no private company could do as well, such as defending the country against enemies abroad or terrorists at home. Government (in partnership with private companies) also plays a key role in building and maintaining public projects such as roads, utilities, schools, libraries, and museums.

The Friedmans counter that whatever the task, government usually ends up being very inefficient. They claim that for most people, the least satisfying goods and services available today—public schools, the postal service, and passenger railroad service—are government-operated. The products we enjoy most—household appliances, computers and other new electronics, fashionable clothes—are products of the market. The Friedmans and other supporters of free markets believe that minimal state regulation serves the public interest best.

But supporters of government intervention in the economy make other arguments. First,

they claim that the market has incentives to produce only what is profitable. Few private companies set out to meet the needs of poor people because by definition, poor people have little money to spend.

Second, the market has certain self-destructive tendencies that only the government can curb. In 1890, for example, the government passed the Sherman Antitrust Act to break up the monopolies that controlled the nation's oil and steel production. In the decades since then—especially after President Franklin Roosevelt's New Deal of the 1930s—government has taken a strong regulatory role to control inflation (by setting interest rates), enhance the well-being of workers (by imposing workplace safety standards), and benefit consumers (by setting standards for product quality). When the market failed to prevent the serious economic downturn in 2008, the public voiced support for

To what extent do you think government regulation of the economy is necessary?

a larger government presence in the national economy.

Third, because the market magnifies social inequality, the government must step in on the side of social justice. Since capitalist economies concentrate income and wealth in the hands of a few, it is necessary for government to tax the rich at a higher rate to ensure that wealth reaches more of the population.

Does the market's "invisible hand" look out for us or pick our pockets? Although most people in the United States favor a free market, they also support government intervention that benefits the public. In recent years, public confidence in corporations has fallen, and confidence in the federal government has gone up. Government's job is not only to ensure national security but also to maintain economic stability. The Obama administration claims that the government needs to expand its efforts to put people to work by, for example, repairing the nation's roads and bridges as well as developing alternative sources of energy.

During the 1980s, support for the free market was strong; today, we see a swing back to support for a larger government role in the economy. In the decades to come, we should expect to see people in the United States, and also around the world, continuing to debate the best balance of market forces and government decision making.

WHAT DO YOU THINK?

1. Do you agree or disagree with the statement that "a government is best that governs least"? Why?

2. Do you think people favor less government control of the economy in good times and more government control in bad times? Why or why not?

3. In what ways has the Obama administration expanded the role of government in the economy?

THE MAP: The midsection of the U.S. is losing young people and has a high share of the elderly. People are moving to coastal areas and almost all of the West, where tourism is booming and natural beauty abounds.

GLOBAL: In 2007, foreign interests invested an estimated $2 trillion in the U.S.; by region, the largest investor was Europe ($1.5 trillion), followed by Asia ($320 billion). The list of individual investor nations was topped by the U.K. ($411 billion), Japan ($233 billion), and the Netherlands ($209 billion) (U.S. Bureau of Economic Analysis, 2008).

● SEEING SOCIOLOGY
in Everyday Life

Compare National Map 16–1 with National Map 22–1 on page 570. The regions losing jobs (such as the Great Plains) are also losing population (especially young people), which is why the average person there is older.

Leon Acosta, age 23 and just out of college, has relocated to Park City, Utah, where he has found a good job and lots of friends his own age.

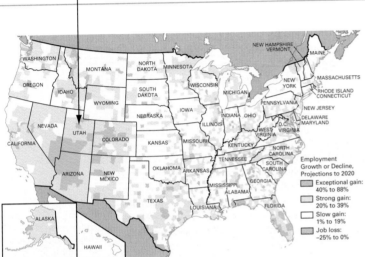

Seeing Ourselves

NATIONAL MAP 16–1
Where the Jobs Will Be: Projections to 2020

The economic prospects for people living in counties across the United States are not the same. Gains in jobs are projected to be strong for most areas in the western states as well as for Florida; some areas in the East and the Midwest are also expected to gain jobs. But job growth will be slow at best in the midsection of the country, with a number of counties even projected to lose jobs in the years to come.

Source: Woods & Poole Economics, Washington, D.C. Copyright © 2007.

Employment Growth or Decline, Projections to 2020
- Exceptional gain: 40% to 88%
- Strong gain: 20% to 39%
- Slow gain: 1% to 19%
- Job loss: –25% to 0%

pushing poor countries to make goods for export rather than food and other products for local people. From this standpoint, multinationals make poor nations increasingly dependent on rich nations (Wallerstein, 1979; Dixon & Boswell, 1996; Kentor, 1998).

In short, modernization theory praises the market as the key to progress and affluence for all the world's people, and dependency theory calls for replacing market systems with government-based economic policies. The Controversy & Debate box on page 428 takes a closer look at the issue of market versus government economies.

The Economy: Looking Ahead

Social institutions are a society's way of meeting people's needs. But as we have seen, the U.S. economy only partly succeeds in this mission. Over the years, our national economy experiences expansion but also recession. In addition, in both good times and bad, our economy provides for some people much better than for others.

One important trend that underlies change in the economy is the Information Revolution. First, the share of the U.S. labor force in manufacturing is less than half what it was in 1960; service work, especially computer-related jobs, makes up the difference. For industrial workers, the postindustrial economy has brought rising unemployment and declining wages. Our society must face up to the challenge of providing millions of men and women with the language and computer skills they need to succeed in the new economy. Yet in recent years, millions of people in "good" service jobs have found themselves out of work. In addition, there are regional differences in the economic outlook: National Map 16–1 shows which

regions are projected to gain jobs and which are expected to lose them by the year 2020.

A second transformation of recent years is the expansion of the global economy. Two centuries ago, the ups and downs people experienced reflected events and trends in their own town. One century ago, communities were economically linked so that one town's prosperity depended on producing goods demanded by people elsewhere in the country. Today, we have to look beyond the national economy because, for example, the historical rise in the cost of gasoline in our local communities has much to do with increasing demand for oil around the world, especially in China and India. As both producers and consumers, we are now responding to factors and forces that are both distant and unseen.

Finally, analysts around the world are rethinking conventional economic models. The global economy shows that socialism is less productive than capitalism, one important reason behind the collapse of the socialist regimes in Eastern Europe and the Soviet Union. But capitalism has its own problems, including high levels of inequality and a steady stream of corporate scandal—two important reasons that the economy now operates with significant government regulation.

What will be the long-term effects of all these changes? Two conclusions seem certain. First, the economic future of the United States and other nations will be played out in a global arena. The new postindustrial economy in the United States has emerged as more industrial production has moved to other nations. Second, it is imperative that we address the related issues of global inequality and population increase. Whether the world reduces or enlarges the gap between rich and poor societies may well steer our planet toward peace or war.

Seeing Sociology in Everyday Life

Chapter 16   The Economy and Work

Why is the economy important?

As this chapter explains, the economy is the social institution that guides what a society produces as well as how it distributes and consumes these goods and services. The photos below show families living in low-, middle-, and high-income regions of the world. Looking at each photo, what can you say about that nation's economy? What is each family's level of material affluence? What else in each photo strikes you as significant?

> **HINT**   For many families in low-income regions of the world, life is centered on tilling the fields close to home. By contrast, people living in middle- and high-income societies with industrial and postindustrial economies typically work in factories or in offices. Socialism generated considerable economic equality, but it also produced a relatively low level of material affluence. Even in high-income nations such as Japan, people still consume less than the average family in the United States. In Japan, for example, most families live in smaller homes and apartments. In Japanese cities, ownership of motor vehicles is limited, and most people rely on the country's excellent public transportation systems.

Bhutan is a lower-income nation high in the Himalayan Mountains. The Namgay family was photographed by a team of photographers who traveled around the world, asking families in various countries to pose with all the things they own assembled in front of their homes. How do you think the members of this family make a living? What else can you say about their way of life?

The Ukita family lives in Tokyo, the largest city of Japan, one of the world's most productive nations. Because mountains make up much of their country, the Japanese people are densely packed into urban areas. What do you see in this photo of the Ukita family— also shown with all their possessions assembled in front of their home— that differs from what you might expect to find in a comparable photo taken in the United States?

The Nguyen family lives in Vietnam, a middle-income country that remains mostly socialist. How does living within such an economic system shape everyday life?

Applying SOCIOLOGY in Everyday Life

1. Imagine that your family were to assemble for a photo similar to those above. What differences in possessions would stand out?

2. Visit a discount store such as Wal-Mart or Kmart and do a little "fieldwork" in an area of the store that interests you. Pick ten products, and see where each is made. Do the results support the existence of a global economy?

3. Do some research to learn about the economy of your state, including the type of work people do, the unemployment rate, and what trends are under way. A good place to start is the Web site for the U.S. Bureau of Labor Statistics at http://www.bls/org.

MAKING THE GRADE

CHAPTER 16 The Economy and Work

The Economy: Historical Overview

The **ECONOMY** is the major social institution through which a society produces, distributes, and consumes goods and services.

p. 412

In technologically simple societies, economic activity is simply part of family life.

p. 412

The **AGRICULTURAL REVOLUTION** (5,000 years ago) made the economy a distinct social institution based on
- agricultural technology
- specialized work
- permanent settlements
- trade

pp. 412–13

The **INDUSTRIAL REVOLUTION** (beginning around 1750) expanded the economy based on
- new sources of energy
- centralization of work in factories
- specialization and mass production
- wage labor

p. 413

The **POSTINDUSTRIAL ECONOMY**, propelled by the **INFORMATION REVOLUTION**, which began around 1950, is based on
- a shift from industrial work to service work
- computer technology

pp. 413–14

economy (p. 412) the social institution that organizes a society's production, distribution, and consumption of goods and services

postindustrial economy (p. 413) a productive system based on service work and high technology

primary sector (p. 414) the part of the economy that draws raw materials from the natural environment

secondary sector (p. 414) the part of the economy that transforms raw materials into manufactured goods

tertiary sector (p. 415) the part of the economy that involves services rather than goods

global economy (p. 415) economic activity that crosses national borders

Three Sectors of the Economy

The **PRIMARY SECTOR**
- draws raw materials from the natural environment
- is of greatest importance (25% of the economy) in low-income nations

Examples: agriculture, fishing, mining

p. 414

The **SECONDARY SECTOR**
- transforms raw materials into manufactured goods
- is a significant share (26%–32%) of the economy in low-, middle-, and high-income nations

Examples: automobile and clothing manufacturing

p. 414

The **TERTIARY SECTOR**
- produces services rather than goods
- is the largest sector (47%–72%) in low-, middle-, and high-income countries

Examples: secretarial work, sales, teaching

p. 415

✓ Today's expanding global economy produces and consumes products and services with little regard for national borders. Globalization also means that the world's 1,000 largest corporations account for half of the world's economic output (p. 415).

Economic Systems: Paths to Justice

CAPITALISM is based on private ownership of property and the pursuit of profit in a competitive marketplace. Capitalism results in
- greater productivity ⟷
- higher overall standard of living ⟷
- greater income inequality ⟷
- freedom to act according to self-interest ⟷

Example: The United States has a mostly capitalist economy.

SOCIALISM is grounded in collective ownership of productive property through government control of the economy. Socialism results in
- less productivity
- lower overall standard of living
- less income inequality
- freedom from basic want

Examples: The People's Republic of China and Venezuela have mostly socialist economies.

pp. 415–18

Under **WELFARE CAPITALISM,**
- government may own some large industries such as transportation and the mass media
- most industry is privately owned but highly regulated by government
- high taxation of the rich helps pay for extensive government services for all

Examples: Sweden and Italy have welfare capitalist economies.

p. 418

Under **STATE CAPITALISM,**
government works in partnership with large companies by
- supplying financial assistance
- controlling foreign imports

Examples: Japan and Singapore have state capitalist economies.

p. 418

capitalism (p. 417) an economic system in which natural resources and the means of producing goods and services are privately owned

socialism (p. 417) an economic system in which natural resources and the means of producing goods and services are collectively owned

communism (p. 417) a hypothetical economic and political system in which all members of a society are socially equal

welfare capitalism (p. 418) an economic and political system that combines a mostly market-based economy with extensive social welfare programs

state capitalism (p. 418) an economic and political system in which companies are privately owned but cooperate closely with the government

Work in the Postindustrial U.S. Economy

JOBS

- Agricultural work represents only 1.5% of jobs.
- Blue-collar, industrial work has declined to 21% of jobs.
- White-collar, service work has increased to 78% of jobs.

pp. 420–21

THE DUAL LABOR MARKET

- Jobs in the primary labor market involve interesting work that provides high income, benefits, and job security.
- Jobs in the secondary labor market have lower pay, less job security, and fewer benefits and provide less personal satisfaction.

p. 421

primary labor market (p. 421) jobs that provide extensive benefits to workers

secondary labor market (p. 421) jobs that provide minimal benefits to workers

labor unions (p. 421) organizations of workers that seek to improve wages and working conditions through various strategies, including negotiations and strikes

profession (p. 422) a prestigious white-collar occupation that requires extensive formal education

underground economy (p. 424) economic activity involving income not reported to the government as required by law

SELF-EMPLOYMENT

- 7.2% of U.S. workers are self-employed.
- Many professionals fall into this category, but most self-employed people have blue-collar jobs.

p. 423

UNEMPLOYMENT

- Unemployment has many causes, including the operation of the economy itself.
- In 2008, more than 8% of the country's labor force was unemployed.
- At highest risk for unemployment are young people and African Americans.

pp. 423–24

INFORMATION TECHNOLOGY

Information technology is changing the workplace and how people work. Computers are
- deskillling labor
- making work more abstract
- limiting interaction among workers
- increasing employers' control over workers
- allowing companies to relocate work

p. 425

- ✓ A decline in labor unions over the past 50 years reflects the shrinking industrial sector of the economy (pp. 421–22).
- ✓ The underground economy—some of which involves criminal activity but most of which involves citizens failing to report some or all legally earned income on tax forms—accounts for a $345 billion loss in federal taxes annually (p. 424).
- ✓ U.S. companies must adapt to an increasing share of minorities in the workforce in order to recruit talented workers and maintain a competitive edge (p. 424).

Corporations

CORPORATIONS form the core of the U.S. economy. Incorporation
- makes an organization a legal entity
- shields owners' wealth from lawsuits brought against the company
- can result in a lower tax rate on the company's profits

pp. 425–26

ECONOMIC CONCENTRATION AND COMPETITION

The largest corporations, which are **conglomerates**, account for most corporate assets and profits (examples: PepsiCo, General Motors).

- Corporations are linked through interlocking directorates.
- Recognizing that corporate linkages and the domination of certain markets by large corporations reduce competition, federal laws forbid **monopoly** and price fixing.

pp. 426–27

CORPORATIONS AND THE GLOBAL ECONOMY

Many large corporations operate as multinationals, producing and distributing products in nations around the world.

- Modernization theorists claim that multinationals raise living standards in poor countries by offering them more jobs and advanced technology.
- Dependency theorists claim that multinationals make global inequality worse by pushing poor countries to produce goods for export and making them more dependent on rich nations.

pp. 427–29

corporation (p. 425) an organization with a legal existence, including rights and liabilities, separate from that of its members

conglomerate (p. 426) a giant corporation composed of many smaller corporations

monopoly (p. 427) the domination of a market by a single producer

oligopoly (p. 427) the domination of a market by a few producers

{ Politics is the social institution that distributes power, sets goals, and makes decisions. Despite the fact that many people in the United States think government is not doing a very good job, almost half of young people in this country are not even registered to vote! }

CHAPTER

17

Politics and Government

NOTE: As Hannah Arendt explained, the concept of authority is Roman in origin with roots in the Latin verb *augere*, meaning "to augment." Thus authority involves steadily augmenting some past foundation.

NOTE: Ferdinand Tönnies, too, described the social roots of authority. He linked authority to advanced age, force, and wisdom or spirit.

NOTE: Another reason for the routinization of charisma is to prevent the rise of new charismatics.

CHAPTER OVERVIEW { This chapter explores politics, a major social institution, and also analyzes the character and causes of war and terrorism.

It was late at night, but the many powerful lights made Chicago's Grant Park almost as bright as a summer afternoon. The crowd, estimated at close to 100,000 people, was lit up as well, and a thunderous outpouring of approval rose as the candidate walked out on the stage to give his victory speech. His broad smile continued until the roar subsided. Then he began to speak:

> If there is anyone out there who still doubts that America is a
> place where all things are possible, who still wonders if the
> dream of our Founders is alive in our time, who still questions
> the power of our democracy, tonight is your answer.

And so it was that Barack Obama—a relative newcomer to politics, an African American, raised by a single mother—accepted his role as the forty-fourth president of the United States. For millions of people, Obama's election to the highest office in the land signifies that "the system" works, that ordinary people can and do select their leaders. But regardless of who sits in the White House, many people still have little trust in our government. As millions of others see it, our political system is rigged by the importance of money, by "special interests" that usually get their way, and by a lack of concern among our leaders for the problems of ordinary women and men.

How power is exercised within a society—who has it and how it is used—is the focus of this chapter. What we call **politics**—or more formally, the "polity"—is *the social institution that distributes power, sets a society's goals, and makes decisions*. We will examine the political system in the United States and, from various points of view, assess the extent to which our society is truly democratic. Then we will turn our attention to the world as a whole, including the international use of power in the form of war and terrorism.

Power and Authority

The sociologist Max Weber (1978, orig. 1921) claimed that every society is based on **power**, which he defined as *the ability to achieve desired ends despite resistance from others*. The use of power is the business of **government**, *a formal organization that directs the political life of a society*. Governments demand compliance on the part of a population; yet Weber noted that most governments do not openly threaten their people. Most of the time, people respect, or at least accept, their society's political system.

Weber pointed out that no government is likely to keep its power for long if compliance came *only* from the threat of brute force. After all, there could never be enough police to watch everyone—and who would watch the police? Every government, therefore, tries to make itself seem legitimate in the eyes of the people. This fact brings us to Weber's concept of **authority**, *power that people perceive as legitimate rather than coercive*. How do governments transform raw power into more stable authority? Weber pointed to three ways: traditional authority, rational-legal authority, and charismatic authority.

Traditional Authority

Preindustrial societies, said Weber, rely on **traditional authority**, *power legitimized by respect for long-established cultural patterns*. Woven into a population's collective memory, traditional authority means that people accept a system, usually one of hereditary leadership, simply because it has always been that way. Chinese emperors in centuries past were legitimized by tradition, as were aristocratic rulers in medieval Europe. The power of tradition can be so strong that for better or worse, people typically come to view traditional rulers as almost godlike.

Traditional authority declines as societies industrialize. Hannah Arendt (1963) pointed out that traditional authority remains strong only as long as everyone shares the same beliefs and way of life. Modern scientific thinking, the specialization demanded by industrial production, and the social changes and cultural diversity resulting from immigration all combine to weaken tradition. Therefore, a U.S. president would never claim to rule "by the grace of God,"

DIVERSITY: Most people recognized as charismatic have been men. But the 20th century saw the rise of many exceptional women, from Amelia Earhart to Princess Diana. In politics, charismatic women leaders included Indira Gandhi of India, Golda Meir of Israel, Benazir Bhutto of Pakistan, and Margaret Thatcher of the U.K. Notice that most charismatics do not die of old age.

RESOURCE: The classic analysis of monarchy, aristocracy, and democracy is found in Aristotle's *Politics*. He favors aristocracy—the rule of the most able—but warns of its corruption into self-serving class rule. His critique of democracy focuses on this system's granting of an equal voice in government to all people, learned and unlearned, virtuous and nonvirtuous alike.

politics the social institution that distributes power, sets a society's goals, and makes decisions

government a formal organization that directs the political life of a society

power the ability to achieve desired ends despite resistance from others

authority power that people perceive as legitimate rather than coercive

traditional authority power legitimized by respect for long-established cultural patterns

rational-legal authority power legitimized by legally enacted rules and regulations (also known as *bureaucratic authority*)

charismatic authority power legitimized by extraordinary personal abilities that inspire devotion and obedience

routinization of charisma the transformation of charismatic authority into some combination of traditional and bureaucratic authority

as many rulers in the ancient world did. Even so, some upper-class families with names like Bush, Kennedy, Roosevelt, and Rockefeller are so well established in our country's political life that their members may enter the political arena with some measure of traditional authority (Baltzell, 1964).

Traditional authority is also a source of strength for *patriarchy,* the domination of women by men. This traditional form of power is still widespread, although it is increasingly challenged. Less controversial is the traditional authority parents have over their children. As children, most of us can remember challenging a parent's demand by asking "Why?" only to hear the response "Because I said so!" Answering this way, the parent makes clear that the demand is not open to debate; to respond otherwise would ignore the parent's traditional authority over the child and put the two on an equal footing.

Rational-Legal Authority

Weber defined **rational-legal authority** (sometimes called *bureaucratic authority*) as *power legitimized by legally enacted rules and regulations.* Rational-legal authority is power legitimized in the operation of lawful government.

As Chapter 7 ("Groups and Organizations") explains, Weber viewed bureaucracy as the type of organization that dominates in rational-thinking, modern societies. The same rational worldview that promotes bureaucracy also erodes traditional customs and practices. Instead of looking to the past, members of today's high-income societies seek justice through formally enacted rules of law.

Rationally enacted rules also guide the use of power in everyday life. The authority of deans and classroom teachers, for example, rests on the offices they hold in bureaucratic colleges and universities. The police, too, depend on rational-legal authority. In contrast to traditional authority, rational-legal authority comes not from family background but from a position in government organization. A traditional monarch rules for life, but a modern president or prime minister accepts and gives up power according to law, which shows that presidential authority lies in the office, not in the person.

Charismatic Authority

Finally, Weber claimed that power can turn into authority through charisma. **Charismatic authority** is *power legitimized by extraordinary personal abilities that inspire devotion and obedience.* Unlike traditional and rational-legal authority, charismatic authority depends less on a person's ancestry or office and more on personality.

Charismatic leaders have surfaced throughout history, using their personal skills to turn an audience into followers. Often they make their own rules and challenge the status quo. Examples of charismatic leaders can be as different as Jesus of Nazareth and Adolf Hitler. The fact that they and others, such as India's liberator, Mahatma Gandhi, and the U.S. civil rights leader Martin Luther King Jr., succeeded in transforming the society around them explains why charismatics are almost always highly controversial and why few of them die of old age.

Because charismatic authority flows from a single individual, the leader's death creates a crisis. Survival of a charismatic movement, Weber explained, requires the **routinization of charisma,** *the transformation of charismatic authority into some combination of traditional and bureaucratic authority.* After the death of Jesus, for example, followers institutionalized his teachings in a church, built on tradition and bureaucracy. Routinized in this way, the Roman Catholic Church has lasted for 2,000 years.

Politics in Global Perspective

Political systems have changed over the course of history. Technologically simple hunting and gathering societies, once found all over the planet, operated like large families without formal governments. Leadership generally fell to a man with unusual strength, hunting skill, or personal charisma. But with few resources, such leaders might control their own people but could never rule a large area (Nolan & Lenski, 2007).

Agrarian societies are larger, with specialized jobs and material surpluses. In these societies, a small elite gains control of most of the wealth and power, moving politics from the family so that it becomes a social institution in its own right. This is the point in history when leaders start to claim a divine right to rule, gaining some measure of Weber's traditional authority. Leaders may also benefit from rational-legal authority to the extent that their rule is supported by law.

As societies grow bigger, politics takes the form of a national government, or *political state.* But the effectiveness of a political state depends on the available technology. Centuries ago, armies moved slowly on foot, and communication over even short distances was uncertain. For this reason, the early political empires—such as Mesopotamia in the Middle East about 5,000 years ago—took the form of many small *city-states.*

More complex technology brings about the larger-scale system of *nation-states.* Currently, the world has 194 independent nation-states, each with a somewhat distinctive political system. Generally, however, these political systems fall into four categories: monarchy, democracy, authoritarianism, and totalitarianism.

Monarchy

Monarchy (with Latin and Greek roots meaning "one ruler") is *a political system in which a single family rules from generation to generation.*

NOTE: The word "democracy" has Greek roots meaning "rule of the people" or "popular authority."

Q: "Democracy presumes a dialogue between people and between nations." Olof Palme

GLOBAL: Economic development and democracy go together, but which comes first varies around the world. In the U.S., political democracy came first; in Asia, however, many nations have industrialized and prospered without being very democratic.

SEEING SOCIOLOGY
in Everyday Life

Why do you think there are no monarchies in North and South America?

monarchy (p. 437) a political system in which a single family rules from generation to generation

democracy a political system that gives power to the people as a whole

Monarchy is linked to both religion and family. In 2004, the coronation ceremony of Cambodia's first new king in fifty years, Norodom Sihamoni, included a religious ritual performed by his father.

Monarchy is commonly found in the ancient agrarian societies; the Bible, for example, tells of great kings such as David and Solomon. In the world today, twenty-seven nations have royal families;[1] some trace their ancestry back for centuries. In Weber's terms, then, monarchy is legitimized by tradition.

During the Middle Ages, *absolute monarchs* in much of the world claimed a monopoly of power based on divine right. Today, claims of divine right are rare, although monarchs in a number of nations—

including Kuwait, Saudi Arabia, and Oman—still exercise almost absolute control over their people.

With industrialization, however, monarchs gradually pass from the scene in favor of elected officials. All the European nations with royal families today are *constitutional monarchies,* meaning that their monarchs are little more than *symbolic* heads of state; actual governing is the responsibility of elected officials, led by a prime minister and guided by a constitution. In these nations, nobility formally reigns, but elected officials actually rule.

Democracy

The historical trend in the modern world has been toward **democracy**, *a political system that gives power to the people as a whole.* More accurately, because it would be impossible for *all* citizens to act as leaders, we have devised a system of *representative democracy* that puts authority in the hands of leaders chosen by the people in elections.

Most high-income countries of the world, including those that still have royal families, claim to be democratic. Industrialization and democratic government go together because both require a literate populace. Also, with industrialization, the legitimization of power in a tradition-based monarchy gives way to rational-legal authority. Thus democracy and rational-legal authority go together, just like monarchy and traditional authority.

But high-income countries such as the United States are not truly democratic for two reasons. First, there is the problem of bureaucracy. The U.S. federal government has 2.7 million regular employees, 1.4 million uniformed military personnel, and 8 million employees paid by various grants and special funding—about 12 million workers in all. Another 19 million people work in almost 90,000 local governments across the country. Most people who run the government are never elected by anyone and do not have to answer directly to the people.

The second problem involves economic inequality, since rich people have far more political power than poor people. Both of the 2008 presidential candidates—John McCain (mostly through his wife's fortune) and Barack Obama (who has earned millions from book sales)—are wealthy men, and in the game of politics, "money talks." Given the even greater resources of billion-dollar corporations, how well does our "democratic" system hear the voices of "average people"?

Still, democratic nations do provide many rights and freedoms. Global Map 17–1 shows one assessment of the extent of political freedom around the world. According to Freedom House, an organization that tracks political trends, eighty-nine of the world's nations (with 46 percent of the global population) were "free," respecting many civil liberties, in 2008. This represents a gain for freedom: Just eighty-one nations were considered free a decade earlier (Freedom House, 2009).

[1]In Europe: Sweden, Norway, Denmark, Great Britain, the Netherlands, Liechtenstein, Luxembourg, Belgium, Spain, and Monaco; in the Middle East: Jordan, Saudi Arabia, Oman, Qatar, Bahrain, and Kuwait; in Africa: Lesotho, Swaziland, and Morocco; in Asia: Brunei, Tonga, Tuvalu, Thailand, Malaysia, Cambodia, Bhutan, and Japan (U.S. Department of State, 2009).

THEN AND NOW: In 1985, according to Freedom House, 34.9% of the world's people were "free," 23.3% were "partly free," and 41.8% were "not free."

Q: Winston Churchill pronounced democracy "the worst form of government—except for all the rest."

GLOBAL: Worldwide, many more nations describe themselves as "democratic" than really are. As examples, the Democratic People's Republic of Korea has one party and is rigidly ruled by dictator Kim Jong-il. Similarly, the Democratic Republic of the Congo is ruled by a repressive government and is racked by warring factions.

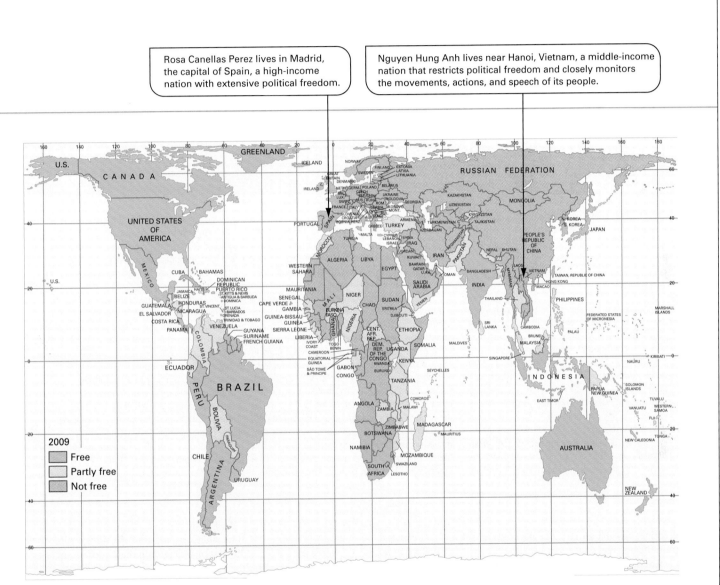

Rosa Canellas Perez lives in Madrid, the capital of Spain, a high-income nation with extensive political freedom.

Nguyen Hung Anh lives near Hanoi, Vietnam, a middle-income nation that restricts political freedom and closely monitors the movements, actions, and speech of its people.

2009
- Free
- Partly free
- Not free

Window on the World

GLOBAL MAP 17–1   **Political Freedom in Global Perspective**

In 2008, a total of 90 of the world's 194 nations at that time, containing 46 percent of all people, were politically "free"; that is, they offered their citizens extensive political rights and civil liberties. Another 62 countries, which included 18 percent of the world's people, were "partly free," with more limited rights and liberties. The remaining 42 nations, home to 36 percent of humanity, fall into the category of "not free." In these countries, government sharply restricts individual initiative. Between 1980 and 2008, democracy made significant gains, largely in Latin America and Eastern Europe. In Asia, India (containing 1.1 billion people) returned to the "free" category in 1999. In 2000, Mexico joined the ranks of nations considered "free" for the first time.

Source: Freedom House (2009).

Democracy and Freedom: Capitalist and Socialist Approaches

Despite the problems just described, rich capitalist nations such as the United States claim to operate as democracies. Of course, socialist countries like Cuba and the People's Republic of China make the same claim. This curious fact suggests that we need to look more closely at *political economy,* the interplay of politics and economics.

The political life of the United States, Canada, and the nations of Europe is largely shaped by the economic principles of capitalism,

NOTE: Generally speaking, the political left (following Rousseau and Marx) seeks to lessen inequality, viewing inequality as equivalent to injustice. The political right (following Plato) defends dimensions of inequality as legitimate or just. Thus the concept of "authority" has been of more interest to the right, whereas the left has critiqued legitimizing "ideologies."

NOTE: Authoritarian regimes are concerned mostly with overt compliance; totalitarian regimes seek to win the "hearts and minds" of their people.

NOTE: Totalitarianism opposes all pluralism. As an example, anti-Semitism in the former Soviet Union probably was less about religion and more an attempt to quash all loyalties except loyalty to the state.

SEEING SOCIOLOGY
in Everyday Life

In your opinion, what is the most important way in which people can be "free"? Are civil liberties or economic security more important? Explain your answer.

authoritarianism a political system that denies the people participation in government

totalitarianism a highly centralized political system that extensively regulates people's lives

THINKING GLOBALLY

"Soft Authoritarianism" or Planned Prosperity? A Report from Singapore

JAKE: If people have plenty to eat and a comfortable place to sleep, they'll be happy.

SERENA: I think being free is more important than being well-off economically.

NOOR: Let me tell you a little about Singapore, where I live. . . .

Singapore is on the tip of the Malay peninsula and has a population of 4.6 million. To many of its people, the tiny nation seems an Asian paradise. Surrounded by poor societies grappling with rapidly growing populations, rising crime rates, and dirty, sprawling cities, Singapore stands apart with its affluence, cleanliness, and safety. Visitors from the United States sometimes say it seems more of a theme park than a country.

Since gaining its independence from Malaysia in 1965, Singapore has startled the world with its economic development and its

high per capita income. In contrast to the United States, Singapore has scarcely any social problems such as crime, slums, unemployment, or children living in poverty. There are hardly any traffic jams, and you won't find graffiti on subway cars or litter in the streets.

The key to Singapore's orderly environment is the ever-present government, which actively promotes traditional morality and regulates just about everything. The state owns and manages most of the country's housing and has a hand in many businesses. It provides tax breaks for family planning and for the completion of additional years of schooling. To limit traffic, the government slaps hefty surcharges on cars, pushing the price of a basic sedan up to around $40,000.

Singapore has tough anticrime laws that mandate death by hanging for drug dealing and permit police to hold a person suspected of a crime without charge or trial. The government

has outlawed some religious groups (including Jehovah's Witnesses) and bans pornography outright. To keep the city clean, the state forbids smoking in public, bans eating on its subways, imposes stiff fines for littering, and even regulates the use of chewing gum.

In economic terms, Singapore does not fit the familiar categories. Government control of many businesses, including television stations, telephone service, airlines, and taxis, seems socialist. Yet unlike most socialist enterprises, these businesses operate efficiently and very profitably. Singapore's capitalist culture applauds economic growth (although the government cautions people against being too materialistic), and hundreds of multinational corporations are based here.

Singapore's political climate is as unusual as its economy. Freedom House (2009) characterizes Singapore as "partly free." The law pro-

described in Chapter 16 ("The Economy and Work"). The pursuit of profit in a market system requires that "freedom" be defined in terms of people's right to act in their own self-interest. Thus the capitalist approach to political freedom translates into personal liberty, the freedom to act in whatever ways maximize profit or other personal advantage. From this point of view, political "democracy" means that individuals have the right to select their leaders from among those running for office.

However, capitalist societies are marked by a striking inequality of income and wealth. If everyone acts according to self-interest, the inevitable result is that some people have much more power to get their way than others. Critics of capitalism claim that a wealthy elite dominates the economic and political life of the society.

By contrast, socialist systems claim they are democratic because their economies meet everyone's basic needs for housing, schooling, work, and medical care. Despite being a much poorer country than the United States, for example, Cuba provides basic medical care to all its people regardless of their ability to pay.

But critics of socialism counter that the extensive government regulation of social life in these countries is oppressive. The social-

ist governments of China and Cuba, for example, do not allow their people to move freely across or even within their borders and tolerate no organized political opposition.

These contrasting approaches to democracy and freedom raise an important question: Can economic equality and political liberty go together? To foster economic equality, socialism limits the choices of individuals. Capitalism, on the other hand, provides broad political liberties, which in practice mean little to the poor.

Authoritarianism

Some nations prevent their people from having a voice in politics. **Authoritarianism** is *a political system that denies the people participation in government.* An authoritarian government is indifferent to people's needs, offers them no voice in selecting leaders, and uses force in response to dissent or opposition. The absolute monarchies in Saudi Arabia and Oman are authoritarian, as is the military junta in Ethiopia. Usually, people resist heavy-handed government. But not always. The Thinking Globally box looks at the "soft authoritarianism" that thrives in the small Asian nation of Singapore.

GLOBAL: The People's Republic of China installed wired radio soon after the communist revolution there. Although broadcast radio would have allowed more than one channel, the government provided only one message, hence the wiring strategy.

DISCUSS: Will new information technology enhance democracy by expanding available information or promote totalitarianism by increasing social control?

Q: In *Democracy in America*, Tocqueville foresaw totalitarian regimes with remark-

able accuracy almost a century before they appeared, describing "an innumerable multitude of men, all equal and alike . . . each a stranger to the fate of all the rest." Ruling this mass is "an immense and tutelary power, which takes upon itself alone to secure their gratifications . . . [seeking] to keep them in perpetual childhood."

Q: "Man is born free, and everywhere he is in chains." Jean-Jacques Rousseau, *The Social Contract* (1762)

MAKING THE GRADE

Authoritarianism and totalitarianism are not the same. All totalitarian systems are authoritarian, but not all authoritarian systems are totalitarian. (Monarchy, for example, is authoritarian but not totalitarian.)

vides for elections of political leaders, but one party—the People's Action party—has dominated the political process since independence and controls almost all the seats in the country's parliament.

Singapore is not a democratic country in the conventional sense. But most people in this prospering nation are quite happy with their way of life. Singapore's political system offers a simple bargain: Government demands loyalty from its people; in return, it gives them security and prosperity. Critics charge that this system amounts to a "soft authoritarianism" that controls people's lives and stifles political dissent. But most of the people of Singapore know the struggles of living else-

where and, for now at least, consider the trade-off a good one.

WHAT DO YOU THINK?

1. What aspects of political life in Singapore do you like? Why?
2. What aspects of political life in Singapore do you not like? Why?
3. Would you say that Singapore offers a better life than the United States? Why or why not?

Totalitarianism

October 30, Beijing, China. Several U.S. students are sitting around a computer in the lounge of a Chinese university dormitory. They are taking turns running Google searches on keywords such as "democracy" and "Amnesty International." They soon realize that China's government filters the results of Internet searches, permitting only officially approved sites to appear. One Chinese student who is watching points out that things could be worse—in North Korea, she explains, the typical person has no access to computers at all.

The most intensely controlled political form is **totalitarianism,** *a highly centralized political system that extensively regulates people's lives.* Totalitarianism emerged in the twentieth century as technological advances gave governments the ability to rigidly control their populations. The Vietnamese government closely monitors

the activities of not just visitors but all its citizens. Similarly, the government of North Korea uses surveillance equipment and powerful computers to control its people by collecting and storing information about them.

Although some totalitarian governments claim to represent the will of the people, most seek to bend people to the will of the government. As the term itself implies, such governments have a *total* concentration of power, allowing no organized opposition. Denying the people the right to assemble and controlling access to information, these governments create an atmosphere of personal isolation and fear. In the final decades of the Soviet Union, for example, ordinary citizens had no access to telephone directories, copying equipment, fax machines, or even accurate city maps.

Socialization in totalitarian societies is intensely political, with the goal of obedience and commitment to the system. In North Korea, one of the world's most totalitarian states, pictures of leaders and political messages are everywhere, reminding citizens that they owe total allegiance to the state. Government-controlled schools and mass media present only official versions of events.

NOTE: In 2008, the IRS took in $927 billion in individual income taxes, 48% of government revenue; corporate taxes, 14%; Social Security, retirement, and insurance premiums, 36%; excise, customs, gift, and estate taxes, 2%. Where it goes: Social Security, Medicare, and other retirement programs, 48%; national defense and veterans' benefits, 24%; health and education, 13%; debt interest, 8%; physical and community development, 3%; law enforcement, 2%; natural environment, 1%.

GLOBAL: In the U.S. in 1900, taxpayers labored until January 22 to pay their taxes for the year. In 2008, "tax freedom day" was April 23. Tax freedom day in global perspective: India (2000), March 14; Australia (2007), April 24; U.K. (2007), June 1; Canada (2007), June 20 (Tax Foundation, 2008).

NOTE: Generally speaking, Republicans use government power to regulate the moral environment, and Democrats use government in regulate the economy.

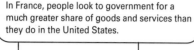

In France, people look to government for a much greater share of goods and services than they do in the United States.

welfare state a system of government agencies and programs that provides benefits to the population

Global Snapshot

FIGURE 17–1   The Size of Government, 2007

Government activity accounts for a smaller share of economic output in the United States than in other high-income countries.

Source: U.S. Census Bureau (2009).

Totalitarian governments span the political spectrum from fascist (as in Nazi Germany) to communist (as in North Korea). In all cases, however, one party claims total control of the society and permits no opposition.

A Global Political System?

Chapter 16 ("The Economy and Work") described the emergence of a global economy, in which large corporations operate with little regard to national boundaries. Is globalization changing politics in the same way? On one level, the answer is no. Although most of the world's economic activity is international, the planet remains divided into nation-states, just as it has been for centuries. The United Nations (founded in 1945) was a small step in the direction of global government, but to date its political role in the world has been limited.

On another level, however, politics has become a global process. For some analysts, multinational corporations have created a new political order because of their enormous power to shape events

throughout the world. In other words, politics is dissolving into business as corporations grow larger than governments.

Also, the Information Revolution has moved national politics onto the world stage. E-mail, text messaging, and cellular phones mean that few countries can conduct their political affairs in complete privacy.

Finally, several thousand *nongovernmental organizations* (NGOs) seek to advance global issues, such as human rights (Amnesty International) or an ecologically sustainable world (Greenpeace). NGOs will continue to play a key part in expanding the global political culture.

To sum up, just as individual nations are losing control of their own economies, governments cannot fully manage the political events occurring within their borders.

Politics in the United States

After fighting a war against Britain to gain political independence, the United States replaced the British monarchy with a representative democracy. Our nation's political development reflects a cultural history as well as its capitalist economy.

U.S. Culture and the Rise of the Welfare State

The political culture of the United States can be summed up in a word: individualism. This emphasis is found in the Bill of Rights, which guarantees freedom from undue government interference. It was this individualism that the nineteenth-century poet and essayist Ralph Waldo Emerson had in mind when he said, "The government that governs best is the government that governs least."

But most people stop short of Emerson's position, believing that government is necessary to defend the country, operate highway systems and schools, maintain law and order, and help people in need. To accomplish these things, the U.S. government has grown into a vast and complex **welfare state**, *a system of government agencies and programs that provides benefits to the population*. Government benefits begin even before birth (through prenatal nutrition programs) and continue during old age (through Social Security and Medicare). Some programs are especially important to the poor, who are not well served by our capitalist economic system; but students, farmers, homeowners, small business operators, veterans, performing artists, and even executives of giant corporations get various subsidies and supports. In fact, a majority of U.S. adults look to government for at least part of their income.

Today's welfare state is the result of a gradual increase in the size and scope of government. In 1789, the presence of the federal gov-

SOCIAL SURVEY: "Do you consider the amount of federal income tax which you have to pay as too high, about right, or too low?" (GSS 2006, N = 898; *Codebook*, 2006:153)

| "Too high" | 56.9% | "Too low" | 0.8% |
| "About right" | 39.9% | "Don't know"/No response | 2.3% |

Q: "The less government we have, the better." Ralph Waldo Emerson

Q: "Government exists to protect us from each other. We cannot afford the government it would take to protect us from ourselves." Ronald Reagan

NOTE: The policies of the major U.S. parties shift over time. Republicans were the party of civil rights for decades; now Democrats claim that mantle. Democrats supported large deficits; so did Reagan. Democrats endorsed intervention in foreign wars until 1950; now Republicans tend to (Dennis Dedrick).

● SEEING SOCIOLOGY
in Everyday Life

Where do you fall on the political spectrum? On social issues, are you more liberal or more conservative? What about on economic issues?

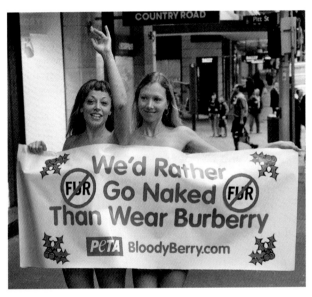

Lower-income people have more pressing financial needs, and so they tend to focus on economic issues, such as job wages and benefits. Higher-income people, by conrast, provide support for many social issues, such as animal rights.

ernment amounted to little more than a flag in most communities, and the entire federal budget was a mere $4.5 million ($1.50 for each person in the nation). Since then, it has risen steadily, reaching $3.1 trillion in 2009 ($10,218 per person) (U.S. Office of Management of Budget, 2008).

Similarly, when our nation was founded, one government employee served every 1,800 citizens. Today, about one in seven workers in the United States is a government employee, which is more people than are engaged in manufacturing (U.S. Census Bureau, 2008).

Despite this growth, the U.S. welfare state is still smaller than those of many other high-income nations. Figure 17–1 shows that government is larger in most of Europe, especially in France and the Scandinavian countries such as Denmark and Sweden.

The Political Spectrum

Who supports a bigger welfare state? Who wants to cut it back? Answers to these questions reveal attitudes that form the *political spectrum,* beliefs that range from extremely liberal to extremely conservative. About one-fourth of adults in the United States fall on the liberal, or "left," side, and one-third say they are conservative, placing themselves on the political "right"; the remaining 40 percent claim to be moderates, in the political "middle" (NORC, 2007:132; Horowitz, 2008).

The political spectrum helps us understand two types of issues: *Economic issues* focus on economic inequality; *social issues* involve moral questions about how people ought to live.

Economic Issues

Economic liberals support both extensive government regulation of the economy and a larger welfare state in order to reduce income inequality. The government can reduce inequality by taxing the rich more heavily and providing more benefits to the poor. Economic conservatives want to limit the hand of government in the economy and allow market forces more freedom, claiming that this produces more jobs and makes the economy more productive.

Social Issues

Social issues are moral questions about how people ought to live, ranging from abortion and the death penalty to gay rights and the treatment of minorities. Social liberals support equal rights and opportunities for all categories of people, view abortion as a matter of individual choice, and oppose the death penalty because it has been unfairly applied to minorities. The "family values" agenda of social conservatives supports traditional gender roles and opposes gay marriage, affirmative action, and other "special programs" for minorities. At the same time, social conservatives condemn abortion as morally wrong and support the death penalty.

443

SEEING SOCIOLOGY
in Everyday Life

As Figure 17–2 suggests, college students have always been more liberal than the population as a whole.

special-interest group people organized to address some economic or social issue

Of the two major political parties in the United States, the Republican party is more conservative on both economic and social issues, and the Democratic party is more liberal. But both political parties favor big government when it advances their particular aims. During the 2008 presidential campaign, for example, Republican John McCain supported bigger government in the form of a stronger military; Democrat Barack Obama also favored enlarging government to expand the social "safety net" that would provide, for example, health care coverage for all.

Class, Race, and Gender

Most people hold a mix of conservative and liberal attitudes. With wealth to protect, well-to-do people tend to be conservative on economic issues. But their extensive schooling and secure social standing lead most to be social liberals. Low-income people display the opposite pattern, with most being liberal on economic issues but supporting a socially conservative agenda (NORC, 2007; Ohlemacher, 2008).

African Americans, both rich and poor, tend to be more liberal than whites (especially on economic issues) and for half a century have voted Democratic (95 percent cast ballots for the Democratic candidate, Barack Obama, in 2008). Historically, Latinos, Asian Americans, and Jews have also supported the Democratic party (Kohut, 2008).

Women tend to be somewhat more liberal than men. Among U.S. adults, more women lean toward the Democrats, and more men vote for Republican candidates. In 2008, for example, 56 percent of women but just 49 percent of men voted for Barack Obama. Figure 17–2 shows how this pattern has changed over time among college students. Although there have been shifts in student attitudes—to the right in the 1970s and to the left beginning in the late 1990s—college women have remained more liberal than college men (Astin et al., 2002; Sax et al., 2003; NORC, 2007; Pryor et al., 2007).

Party Identification

Because many people hold mixed political attitudes, with liberal views on some issues and conservative stands on others, party identification in this country is weak. Surveys conducted in 2009 after the national election show that about 35 percent favor the Democratic party, 23 percent favor the Republican party, and about 36 percent say they are "independent" (Pew, 2009). This lack of strong party identification is one reason each of the two major parties gains or loses power from election to election. Democrats held the White House in 1996 and gained ground in Congress in 1996, 1998, and 2000. In 2002 and 2004, the tide turned as Republicans made gains in Congress and kept control of the White House. In 2006, the tide turned again, with Democrats gaining control of Congress and winning the White House in 2008.

There is also an urban-rural divide in U.S. politics: People in urban areas typically vote Democratic and those in rural areas Republican. The Seeing Sociology in Everyday Life box takes a closer look at the national political scene, and National Map 17–1 shows the county-by-county results for the 2008 presidential election.

Special-Interest Groups

For years, a debate has raged across the United States about the private ownership of firearms. Organizations such as the Brady Campaign to Prevent Gun Violence support stricter gun laws; other organizations, including the National Rifle Association, strongly oppose such measures. Each of these organizations is an example of a **special-interest group**, *people organized to address some economic or social issue*. Special-interest groups, which include associations of older adults, fireworks producers, and environmentalists, are strong in nations where political parties tend to be weak. Special-interest groups employ *lobbyists* to work on their behalf, trying to get members of Congress to support their goals. Washington, D.C., is home to about 15,000 lobbyists (Secretary of the U.S. Senate, 2009).

Student Snapshot

FIGURE 17–2 Left-Right Political Identification of College Students, 1970–2006

Student attitudes moved to the right after 1970 and shifted left in the late 1990s. College women tend to be more liberal than college men.

Sources: Astin et al. (2002), Sax et al. (2003), and Pryor et al. (2009).

THE MAP: Urban areas tend to be Democratic; rural counties tend to be Republican. Immigrants, who tend to be young and vote Democratic, settle in urban areas; rural counties have, on average, older and more conservative populations.

POP CULTURE: In 2004, despite the media-based "Rock the Vote" campaign led by music celebrities, young people turned out on election day in numbers no greater than in 2000. In 2008, however, the youth vote did increase.

Q: "How come we choose from fifty people for Miss America and just two for president?" Anonymous

NOTE: Voting among young people is most common in states where (1) education levels are high (the Midwest has the highest level of high school graduation); (2) young people discuss politics with parents (at meals); and (3) parents are likely to vote (the Midwest has high senior turnout).

SEEING SOCIOLOGY
in Everyday Life

Do you identify with a political party? Which one? Has your party identification changed over time?

SEEING SOCIOLOGY IN EVERYDAY LIFE

The Rural-Urban Divide: Election 2008

JORGE: Just about everyone I know in L.A. voted Democratic. I mean, *nobody* voted for McCain!

HARRY: If you lived in my county in rural Ohio, you'd see the exact opposite. Obama did not do well there at all.

As this conversation suggests, the reality of everyday politics in the United States depends on where you live. Political attitudes and voting patterns in rural and urban places are quite different. Sociologists have long debated why these differences exist.

Take a look at National Map 17–1, which shows the county-by-county results for the 2008 presidential election. The first thing that stands out is that the Republican candidate, John McCain, won 72 percent of U.S. counties—2,250 out of 3,115 ("McCain" counties appear in red on the map). Democrat Barack Obama won in 865 counties ("Obama" counties appear in blue).

How did Obama win the election when McCain won so many more counties? Obama won 53 percent of the popular vote, doing well in counties with large populations. Democrats do very well in large cities, for example, where Obama won 70 percent of the popular vote in 2008. Rural counties, with relatively small populations, tend to lean Republican. McCain received 53 percent of the rural vote in 2008. In many states, it is easy to see the rural-urban divide. In Ohio, for example, Obama won enough votes in and around Cleveland, Columbus, and Cincinnati to carry the entire state even though most of the state's counties went for McCain.

The national pattern has led many political analysts to distinguish urban "blue states" that vote Democratic and rural "red states" that vote Republican. Looking more closely, at the county level, there appears to be a political divide between "liberal, urban America" and "conservative, rural America."

What accounts for this difference? Typically, rural counties are home to people who have lived in one place for a long time, are more traditional and family-oriented in their values, and are more likely to be religious. Such people tend to vote Republican. By contrast, urban areas are home to more minorities, young and single people, college students, and lower-income people, all of whom are more likely to vote Democratic.

WHAT DO YOU THINK?

1. Can you find your county on the map? Which way did most people vote? Can you explain why?

2. In most elections, more Republicans than Democrats claim they are concerned about "moral values"; more Democrats than Republicans say they care about "the economy and jobs." Can you explain why?

3. How might Democratic candidates do better in rural areas? How might Republican candidates do better in urban areas?

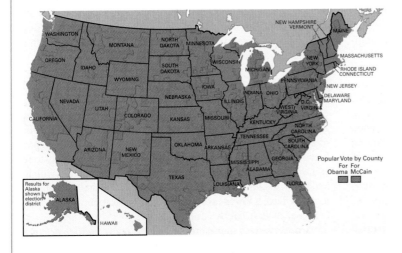

Seeing Ourselves

NATIONAL MAP 17–1

The Presidential Election, 2008: Popular Vote by County

Barack Obama won the 2008 presidential election with 53 percent of the total popular vote, but he received a majority of the vote in only about one-fourth of the nation's counties. Obama and other Democrats did well in more densely populated urban areas, while John McCain and other Republicans did well in less populated rural areas. Can you explain why urban areas are mostly Democratic and rural areas are mostly Republican? What other social characteristics do you think distinguish the people who vote Democratic from those who vote Republican?

Politics and Government **CHAPTER 17**

Q: "If voting changed anything, they'd make it illegal." Cousin Woodman

NOTE: Recent high point of voter turnout was 63% in 1960 (Kennedy beat Nixon); all-time peak was 82.4% in 1876 (Rutherford Hayes beat Samuel Tilden and only men voted) (D.C. Johnston, 1996).

Q: "Politics are almost as exciting as war, and even more dangerous. In war, you can die once; but in politics, many times." Winston Churchill

SOCIAL SURVEY: "How much confidence do you have in Congress?" (GSS 2006, N = 1,989; Codebook, 2006:238)

| "A great deal" | 10.5% | "Hardly any" | 35.3% |
| "Only some" | 51.6% | "Don't know/No response" | 2.6% |

political action committee (PAC) an organization formed by a special-interest group, independent of political parties, to raise and spend money in support of political goals

The 2008 campaign for the White House succeeded in drawing a larger share of young people into the political process than ever before. On the night of his election, Barack Obama thanked his young supporters by hosting a youth inaugural ball.

A **political action committee (PAC)** is *an organization formed by a special-interest group, independent of political parties, to raise and spend money in support of political goals*. Political action committees channel most of their funds directly to candidates likely to support their interests. Since they were created in the 1970s, the number of PACs has grown rapidly to more than 4,200 (Federal Election Commission, 2008).

Because of the rising costs of political campaigns, most candidates eagerly accept support from political action committees. In the 2006 congressional elections, 26 percent of all campaign funding came from PACs, and senators seeking reelection received, on average, at least $1 million each in PAC contributions. Spending rose again in 2008, in the most expensive presidential election in history, with Barack Obama and John McCain spending more than $1 billion in their campaigns. Other candidates spent a total of $5 billion on their campaigns (Center for Responsive Politics, 2008; Pickler & Sidoti, 2008).

Supporters of this practice claim that PACs represent the interests of a vast assortment of businesses, unions, and church groups, thereby increasing political participation. Critics counter that organizations supplying cash to politicians expect to be treated favorably in return, so in effect, PACs are attempting to buy political influence ("Abramoff Effect," 2006; Center for Responsive Politics, 2008).

Does having the most money matter? The answer is yes—in 94 percent of the congressional races, the candidate with the most money ended up winning the election. Concerns about the power of money have led to much discussion of campaign financing. In 2002, Congress passed a modest campaign finance reform, limiting the amount of unregulated money that candidates are allowed to collect. Despite this change, both presidential races since then set new records for campaign spending (Center for Responsive Politics, 2008).

Voter Apathy

A disturbing fact of U.S. political life is that many people in this country do not vote. In fact, U.S. citizens are less likely to vote today than they were a century ago. In the 2000 presidential election, which was decided by a few hundred votes, only half the people eligible to vote went to the polls. In 2008, participation rose to 63 percent (the highest turnout since 1960), still lower than in almost all other high-income countries (Center for the Study of the American Electorate, 2008).

Who is and is not likely to vote? Research shows that women are slightly more likely than men to cast a ballot. People over sixty-five are much more likely to vote than college-age adults (almost half of whom have not even registered). Non-Hispanic white people are just slightly more likely to vote (66 percent voted in 2008) than African Americans (65 percent), and Hispanics (50 percent) are the least likely of all to vote. Generally speaking, people with a bigger stake in U.S. society—homeowners, parents with young children, people with more schooling and good jobs—are more likely to vote. Income matters, too: People earning more than $75,000 are twice as likely to vote (79 percent in 2008) as people earning less than $10,000 (50 percent) (U.S. Census Bureau, 2009).

Of course, we should expect some nonvoting because at any given time, millions of people are sick or away from home or have recently moved to a new neighborhood and have forgotten to reregister. In addition, registering and voting depend on the ability to read and write, which discourages tens of millions of U.S. adults with limited literacy skills. Finally, people with physical disabilities that limit mobility have a lower turnout than the general population (Schur & Kruse, 2000; Brians & Grofman, 2001).

Conservatives suggest that apathy is really *indifference to politics* among people who are, by and large, content with their lives. Liberals and especially radicals on the far left of the political spectrum counter that apathy reflects *alienation from politics* among

DISCUSS: Ask the class if convicted criminals should or should not vote. Should any categories of people lose their political voice?

RESOURCE: An excerpt from C. Wright Mills's *Power Elite* is among the classics included in the author's companion reader *Seeing Ourselves*, 8th ed.

NOTE: A more traditionally Marxist view of politics argues that elites need not circulate through the three sectors as Mills claims; the power of the capitalists is sufficient to ensure that politicians serve their interests.

SEEING SOCIOLOGY
in Everyday Life

Why do you think that almost half of today's young people do not vote? Have you registered to vote?

MAKING THE GRADE

Use the Applying Theory table to review the three political models.

APPLYING THEORY

Politics

	Pluralist Model	Power-Elite Model	Marxist Political-Economy Model
Which theoretical approach is applied?	Structural-functional approach	Social-conflict approach	Social-conflict approach
How is power spread throughout society?	Power is spread widely so that all groups have some voice.	Power is concentrated in the hands of top business, political, and military leaders.	Power is directed by the operation of the capitalist economy.
Is the United States a democracy?	Yes. Power is spread widely enough to make the country a democracy.	No. Power is too concentrated for the country to be a democracy.	No. The capitalist economy sets political decision making, so the country is not a democracy.

people who are so deeply dissatisfied with society that they doubt that elections make any real difference. Because disadvantaged and powerless people are least likely to vote, and because the candidacy of Barack Obama raised the level of participation among minorities, the liberal explanation for apathy is probably closer to the truth.

Should Convicted Criminals Vote?

Although the right to vote is at the very foundation of our country's claim to being democratic, all states except Vermont and Maine have laws that bar people in prison from voting. Thirty states do not allow people on probation after committing a felony to vote; thirty-five states do the same for people on parole. Eleven states ban voting even after people have completed their sentences, subject to various appeals to restore voting rights. Overall, 5.3 million people (including 1.4 million African American men) in the United States do not have the right to vote (Sentencing Project, 2008).

Should government take away political rights as a type of punishment? The legislatures of most of our fifty states have said yes. But critics point out that this practice may be politically motivated, because preventing convicted criminals from voting makes a difference in the way elections in this country turn out. Convicted felons (who tend to be lower-income people) show better than a two-to-one preference for Democratic over Republican candidates. Even taking into account expected voter apathy, one recent study concluded that if these laws had not been in force in 2000, Democrat

Al Gore would have defeated George W. Bush for the presidency (Uggen & Manza, 2002).

Theoretical Analysis of Power in Society

Sociologists have long debated how power is spread throughout the U.S. population. Power is a very difficult topic to study because decision making is complex and often takes place behind closed doors. Despite this difficulty, researchers have developed three competing models of power in the United States. The Applying Theory table provides a summary of each.

The Pluralist Model: The People Rule

The **pluralist model**, closely linked to structural-functional theory, is *an analysis of politics that sees power as spread among many competing interest groups.* Pluralists claim, first, that politics is an arena of negotiation. With limited resources, no organization can expect to achieve all its goals. Organizations therefore operate as *veto groups,* realizing some success but mostly keeping opponents from achieving all their ends. The political process relies heavily on creating alliances and compromises among numerous interest groups so that policies gain wide support. In short, pluralists see power as spread widely throughout society, with all people having

Q: "The power elite is composed of men whose positions enable them to transcend the ordinary environments of ordinary men and women; they are in positions to make decisions having major consequences." C. Wright Mills (1956:3–4).

Q: "The executive of the modern state is but a committee for managing the common affairs of the whole bourgeoisie." Marx and Engels

Q: "Since all political systems were created by [people], it follows that [people] can also change them." Peter Berger (1963:128)

Q: "A fanatic is one who can't change his mind and won't change the subject." Winston Churchill

pluralist model (p. 447) an analysis of politics that sees power as spread among many competing interest groups

power-elite model an analysis of politics that sees power as concentrated among the rich

Marxist political-economy model an analysis that explains politics in terms of the operation of a society's economic system

MAKING THE GRADE

Generally, the pluralist model is close to sociology's structural-functional approach; the power-elite model is based on social-conflict theory, as is the Marxist political-economy model, which is more radical because it implies that changes in basic social institutions are needed to make the country truly democratic.

at least some voice in the political system (Dahl, 1961, 1982; Rothman & Black, 1998).

The Power-Elite Model: A Few People Rule

The **power-elite model**, based on social-conflict theory, is *an analysis of politics that sees power as concentrated among the rich.* The term *power elite* was coined by C. Wright Mills (1956), who argued that a small upper class holds most of society's wealth, prestige, and power.

Mills claimed that members of the power elite head up the three major sectors of U.S. society: the economy, the government, and the military. The power elite is made up of the "super-rich" (corporate executives and major stockholders); top officials in Washington, D.C., and state capitals around the country; and the highest-ranking officers in the U.S. military.

Further, Mills explained, these elites move from one sector to another, building power as they go. Former Vice President Dick Cheney, for example, has moved back and forth between powerful positions in the corporate world and the federal government. Colin Powell moved from a top position in the U.S. military to become secretary of state. More broadly, when presidents pick cabinet officials, most of these powerful public officials are millionaires. This was true in the Bush administration and is probably the case for about half of those in the Obama administration.

Power-elite theorists say that the United States is not a democracy because the influence of a few people with great wealth and power is so strong that the average person's voice cannot be heard. They reject the pluralist idea that various centers of power serve as checks and balances on one another. According to the power-elite model, those at the top are so powerful that they face no real opposition (Bartlett & Steele, 2000; Moore et al., 2002).

The Marxist Model: The System Is Biased

A third approach to understanding U.S. politics is the **Marxist political-economy model**, *an analysis that explains politics in terms of the operation of a society's economic system.* Like the power-elite model, the Marxist model rejects the idea that the United States operates as a political democracy. But the power-elite model focuses on just the enormous wealth and power of certain individuals; the Marxist model goes further and sees bias rooted in the nation's institutions, especially its economy. As noted in Chapter 4 ("Society"), Karl Marx claimed that a society's economic system (capitalist or socialist) shapes its political system. Therefore, the power elites do not simply appear out of nowhere; they are creations of the capitalist economy.

From this point of view, reforming the political system—say, by limiting the amount of money that rich people can contribute to political candidates—is unlikely to bring about true democracy. The problem does not lie in the people who exercise great power or the people who don't vote; the problem is rooted in the system itself, what Marxists call the "political economy of capitalism." In other words, as long as the United States has a mostly capitalist economy, the majority of people will be shut out of politics, just as they are exploited in the workplace.

CRITICAL REVIEW Which of the three models is most accurate? Over the years, research has shown support for each one. In the end, how you think our political system ought to work is as much a matter of political values as of scientific fact.

Classic research by Nelson Polsby (1959) supports the pluralist model. Polsby studied the political scene in New Haven, Connecticut, and concluded that key decisions on various issues—including education, urban renewal, and the electoral nominating process—were made by different groups. Polsby concluded that in New Haven, no one group—not even the upper class—ruled all the others.

Robert Lynd and Helen Lynd (1937) studied Muncie, Indiana (which they called "Middletown," to suggest that it was a typical city), and documented the fortune amassed by a single family, the Balls, from their business manufacturing glass canning jars. Their findings support the power-elite position. The Lynds showed how the Ball family dominated the city's life, pointing to that family's name on a local bank, a university, a hospital, and a department store. In Muncie, according to the Lynds, the power elite boiled down, more or less, to a single family.

From the Marxist perspective, the point is not to look at which individuals make decisions. Rather, as Alexander Liazos (1982:13) explains in his analysis of the United States, "The basic tenets of capitalist society shape everyone's life: the inequalities of social classes and the importance of profits over people." As long as the basic institutions of society are organized to meet the needs of the few rather than the many, Liazos concludes, a democratic society is impossible.

Clearly, the U.S. political system gives almost everyone the right to participate in the political process through elections. But the power-elite and Marxist models point out that at the very least, the U.S. political system is far less democratic than most people think. Most citizens may have the right to vote, but the major political parties and their candidates typically support only positions that are acceptable to the most powerful segments of society and consistent with the operation of our capitalist economy.

Whatever the reasons, many people in the United States appear to be losing confidence in their leaders. More than 80 per-

NOTE: The word "radical" is derived from the Latin meaning "of the root" (a radish is also a root). Hence radical politics seeks not reform but a change in the system itself.

Q: "Political power grows out of the barrel of a gun." Chinese leader Mao Zedong

NOTE: "An oppressive government is more to be feared than a tiger." Confucius

NOTE: Be sure to clearly contrast the terms *reform, coup d'état,* and *revolution.*

● MAKING THE GRADE

Revolution, in which one political system is replaced by another, involves far greater change than reform, which implies change within the present system.

political revolution the overthrow of one political system in order to establish another

cent of U.S. adults report having, at best, only "some confidence" that members of Congress and other government officials will do what is best for the country (NORC, 2007:1526, 1719).

○ **CHECK YOUR LEARNING** What is the main argument of the pluralist model of power? What about the power-elite model? The Marxist political-economy model?

Power beyond the Rules

In politics, there is always disagreement over a society's goals and the means to achieve them. A political system tries to resolve these controversies within a system of rules. But political activity sometimes breaks the rules or tries to do away with the entire system.

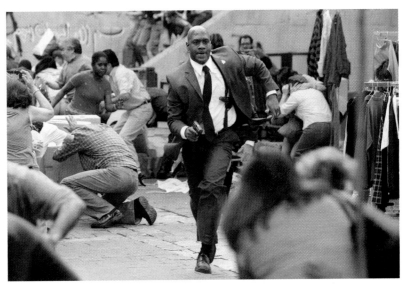

The 2007 film *Vantage Point* shows that whether violence is seen as justified or is defined as terrorism depends on your political point of view.

Revolution

Political revolution is *the overthrow of one political system in order to establish another.* Reform involves change *within* a system, either through modification of the law or, in the extreme case, through a *coup d'état* (in French, literally, "blow to the state"), in which one leader topples another. Revolution involves change in the type of system itself.

No political system is immune to revolution, nor does revolution produce any one kind of government. Our country's Revolutionary War (1775–83) replaced colonial rule by the British monarchy with a representative democracy. French revolutionaries in 1789 also overthrew a monarch, only to set the stage for the return of monarchy in the person of Napoleon. In 1917, the Russian Revolution replaced monarchy with a socialist government built on the ideas of Karl Marx. In 1991, a new Russian revolution dismantled the socialist Soviet Union, and the nation was reborn as fifteen independent republics, the largest of which—known as the Russian Federation—has moved closer to a market system and given a somewhat greater political voice to its people.

Despite their striking variety, revolutions share a number of traits (Tocqueville, 1955, orig. 1856; Skocpol, 1979; Tilly, 1986):

1. **Rising expectations.** Common sense suggests that revolution would be more likely when people are severely deprived, but history shows that most revolutions occur when people's lives are improving. Rising expectations, rather than bitterness and despair, make revolution more likely.

2. **Unresponsive government.** Revolutions become more likely when a government is unwilling to reform itself, especially when demands for reform by powerful segments of society are ignored.

3. **Radical leadership by intellectuals.** The English philosopher Thomas Hobbes (1588–1679) claimed that intellectuals provide the justification for revolution, and universities are often the center of political change. Students played a critical role in China's prodemocracy movement in the 1990s and the uprisings in Eastern Europe.

4. **Establishing a new legitimacy.** Overthrowing a political system is not easy, but ensuring a revolution's long-term success is harder still. Some revolutionary movements are held together mostly by hatred of the past regime and fall apart once new leaders are installed. Revolutionaries must also guard against counterrevolutionary drives led by overthrown leaders. This explains the speed and ruthlessness with which victorious revolutionaries typically dispose of former leaders.

Scientific analysis cannot declare that a revolution is good or bad. The full consequences of such an upheaval depend on personal values and typically become evident only after many years. For example, nearly two decades after the revolutions that toppled their governments in the early 1990s, the future of many of the former Soviet states remains uncertain.

Q: "Politics makes strange bedfellows." Charles Dudley Warner

NOTE: The U.S. State Department's definition of terrorism: "Premeditated, politically motivated violence perpetrated against noncombatant targets by subnational groups or clandestine state agents, normally intended to influence an audience."

GLOBAL: In 2008, the U.S. government listed the following nations as supporting state-sponsored terrorism: Iran, Syria, Cuba, North Korea, and Sudan.

NOTE: It is difficult to fight terrorism in an open (porous) society. Each day, the United States receives 60,000 cargo shipments, 300,000 vehicles, and 1.3 million people (Mitchell, 2002).

terrorism refers to acts of violence or the threat of violence used as a political strategy by an individual or a group

SEEING SOCIOLOGY
in Everyday Life

Do you think you will live to see a world free from terrorism? What will have to happen to create such a world?

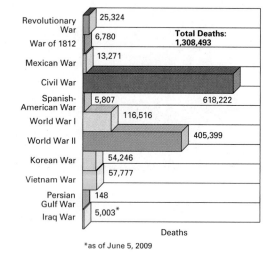

FIGURE 17–3 **Deaths of Americans in Eleven U.S. Wars**

Almost half of all U.S. deaths in war occurred during the Civil War (1861–65).

Sources: Compiled from various sources by Maris A. Vinovskis (1989) and the author.

Terrorism

The terrorist attacks on the United States on September 11, 2001, involving four commercial airliners, killed nearly 3,000 innocent people, injured many thousands more, completely destroyed the twin towers of the World Trade Center in New York City, and seriously damaged the Pentagon in Washington, D.C. Not since the attack on Pearl Harbor at the outbreak of World War II had the United States suffered such a blow. Indeed, this event was the most serious terrorist act ever recorded.

Terrorism refers to *acts of violence or the threat of violence used as a political strategy by an individual or a group.* Like revolution, terrorism is a political act beyond the rules of established political systems. According to Paul Johnson (1981), terrorism has four distinguishing characteristics.

First, terrorists try to paint violence as a legitimate political tactic, even though such acts are condemned by virtually every nation. Terrorists also bypass (or are excluded from) established channels of political negotiation. Therefore, terrorism is a weaker organization's strategy against a stronger enemy. In recent decades, terrorism has become commonplace in international politics. In 2007, there were more than 14,000 acts of terrorism worldwide, which claimed more than 22,000 lives and injured more than 44,000 people. Most of those killed were in Iraq, but major terrorist attacks took place in

many nations, including Afghanistan, India, and the Philippines (U.S. Department of State, 2008).

Second, terrorism is used not just by groups but also by governments against their own people. *State terrorism* is the use of violence, generally without support of law, by government officials as a way to control the population. State terrorism is lawful in some authoritarian and totalitarian states, which survive by creating widespread fear and intimidation among the population. The dictator Saddam Hussein, for example, relied on secret police and state terror to protect his power in Iraq.

Third, democratic societies reject terrorism in principle, but they are especially vulnerable to terrorists because they give broad civil liberties to people and have less extensive police networks. In contrast, totalitarian regimes make widespread use of state terrorism, but their extensive police power gives individuals few opportunities to commit acts of terror against the government.

Fourth and finally, terrorism is always a matter of definition. Governments claim the right to maintain order, even by force, and may label opposition groups that use violence as "terrorists." Political differences may explain why one person's "terrorist" is another's "freedom fighter" (Jenkins, 2003).

Although hostage taking and outright killing provoke popular anger, taking action against terrorists is difficult. Because most terrorist groups are shadowy organizations with no formal connection to any established state, identifying the parties responsible may be difficult. In addition, any military response risks confrontation with other governments. Yet as the terrorism expert Brian Jenkins warns, the failure to respond "encourages other terrorist groups, who begin to realize that this can be a pretty cheap way to wage war" (quoted in Whitaker, 1985:29).

War and Peace

Perhaps the most critical political issue is **war**, *organized, armed conflict among the people of two or more nations, directed by their governments.* War is as old as humanity, but understanding it is crucial today because humanity now has weapons that can destroy the entire planet.

At almost any moment during the twentieth century, nations somewhere in the world were engaged in violent conflict. In its short history, the United States has participated in eleven large-scale wars. From the Revolutionary War to the Iraq War, more than 1.3 million U.S. men and women have been killed in armed conflicts, as shown in Figure 17–3, and many times that number have been injured. Thousands more died in "undeclared wars" and limited military actions in the Dominican Republic, Nicaragua, Lebanon, Grenada, Panama, Haiti, Bosnia, Afghanistan, and elsewhere.

SEEING SOCIOLOGY
in Everyday Life

war organized, armed conflict among the people of two or more nations, directed by their governments

Does it seem fair or unfair that the defense of this country falls heavily on working-class people? Explain your position.

The Causes of War

Wars occur so often that we might think that there is something natural about armed confrontation. But there is no evidence that human beings must wage war under any particular circumstances. On the contrary, governments around the world usually have to force their people to go to war.

Like all forms of social behavior, warfare is a product of *society* that is more common in some places than in others. The Semai of Malaysia, among the most peace-loving of the world's peoples, rarely resort to violence. In contrast, the Yanomamö (see the box on page 61) are quick to wage war.

If society holds the key to war or peace, under what circumstances do humans go to battle? Quincy Wright (1987) cites five factors that promote war:

1. **Perceived threats**. Nations mobilize in response to a perceived threat to their people, territory, or culture. Leaders justified the U.S.-led military campaign to disarm Iraq, for example, by stressing the threat that Saddam Hussein posed to the United States.

2. **Social problems**. When internal problems generate widespread frustration at home, a nation's leaders may divert public attention by attacking an external "enemy" as a form of scapegoating. Although U.S. leaders claimed that the war in Iraq was a matter of national security, there is little doubt that the onset of the war diverted attention from the struggling national economy and boosted the popularity of President George W. Bush.

3. **Political objectives**. Poor nations, such as Vietnam, have used wars to end foreign domination. Powerful countries, such as the United States, may benefit from a periodic show of force (recall the deployments of troops in Somalia, Haiti, Bosnia, and Afghanistan) to increase global political standing.

4. **Moral objectives**. Nations rarely claim that they are going to war to gain wealth and power. Instead, their leaders infuse military campaigns with moral urgency. By calling the 2003 invasion of Iraq "Operation Iraqi Freedom," U.S. leaders portrayed the mission as a morally justified war of liberation from an evil tyrant.

5. **The absence of alternatives**. A fifth factor promoting war is the absence of alternatives. Although the goal of the United Nations is to maintain international peace by finding alternatives to war, the UN has had limited success in preventing conflict between nations.

There is an old saying that all is fair in love and war, but wars (like relationships) are actually carried out according to rules. The war on terrorism has raised questions about the rights of captured enemy combatants, most of whom are not soldiers in any nation's army. Should the prisoners who have been held at the U.S. base in Guantanamo Bay, Cuba, be treated according to the rules of war as spelled out in the United Nations' Geneva Convention? Should they have access to the U.S. courts as U.S. citizens do?

Social Class and the Military

In World War II, three-fourths of the men in the United States in their late teens and twenties served in the military, either voluntarily or by being *drafted*—called to service. Only those who had some physical or mental impairment were freed from the obligation to serve. Today, by contrast, there is no draft, and fighting is done by a volunteer military. But not every member of our society is equally likely to volunteer.

One study revealed that the military has few young people who are rich and also few who are very poor. Rather, it is primarily working-class people who look to the military for a job, to earn some money to go to college, or simply to get out of the small town they grew up in. In addition, the largest number of young enlistees comes from the South, where local culture is more supportive of the military and where most military bases are located. As two analysts put it, "America's military seems to resemble the makeup of a two-year commuter or trade school outside Birmingham or Biloxi far more than that of a ghetto or barrio or four-year university in Boston" (Halbfinger & Holmes, 2003:1).

Q: "Someday they will give a war and nobody will come." Carl Sandburg

SOCIAL SURVEY: "How much confidence do you have in the U.S. militrary?"
(GSS 2006, *N* = 876; *Codebook*, 2006:238)

"A great deal"	47.1%	"Hardly any"	12.3%
"Only some"	39.1%	"Don't know"/No response	1.4%

Q: "When we discuss national security, we tend too often to give it a military label. It is, in fact, much broader than military power and much more complex. There can be no security without social betterment." Hubert H. Humphrey

Q: "I am the first to admit that a war is waged in pursuance of political aims." Dwight D. Eisenhower

Q: "True individual freedom cannot exist without economic security." FDR

Seeing SOCIOLOGY in the NEWS

The New York Times

Taking the War Out of a Child Soldier

BY NINA BERNSTEIN
May 13, 2007

The teenager stepped off an airplane at Kennedy International Airport on Nov. 8 and asked for asylum. Days before, he had been wielding an automatic weapon as a child soldier in Ivory Coast. Now he had only his name, Salifou Yankene, and a phrase in halting English: "I want to make refugee."

Eventually Salifou's story would emerge, and in granting him asylum, one of the system's toughest judges would find it credible: the assassination of his father and older sister when he was 12; the family's flight to a makeshift camp for the displaced; his conscription at 15 by rebel troops who chopped off his younger brother's hand; and an extraordinary escape two years later, when his mother risked her life to try to save him.

But when a lawyer took the case without fee in January, Salifou, then 17, was almost ready to give up. Detained in a New Jersey jail, overtaken by guilt, anger and despair, he resisted painful questions, sometimes crying, "Send me back!" And the lawyer soon realized that saving Salifou would require much more than winning him asylum.

There are 300,000 child soldiers worldwide, human rights groups say. Only a few have ever made it to the United States. . . .

No one has really grappled with how to handle those who make it to this country seeking refuge.

Their violent pasts pose hard questions: Should they be legally barred from asylum as persecutors or protected as victims? How can they be healed, and who will help them? . . .

Less than three weeks ago, days after his 18th birthday, immigration authorities abruptly

released Salifou alone, at 10 p.m., on a street corner in Lower Manhattan.

"They say, 'You free to go,'" he recalled, eyes wide. "I say, 'Go where?'"

Salifou could still be deported. At his asylum hearing in April, the government argued that based solely on his own account, he was a persecutor, and thus legally barred from refuge. . . .

Salifou testified that to satisfy leaders who punished disobedience with death, he had looted during raids, grabbed new child conscripts and hit and kicked civilians without pity if they resisted. He maintained, though, that while he had shot at people, he had never knowingly killed anyone. . . .

In one sense, Salifou's childhood ended on Aug. 6, 2001, according to the 25-page affidavit he signed. That was the day his father and older sister were shot to death within earshot of the family home in Man, a market town in northwestern Ivory Coast. He remains tormented that as a 12-year-old

Is Terrorism a New Kind of War?

In recent years, we have heard government officials speak of terrorism as a new kind of war. War has historically followed certain patterns: It is played out according to some basic rules, the warring parties are known to each other, and the objectives of the warring parties—which generally involve control of territory—are clearly stated.

Terrorism breaks from these patterns. The identity of terrorist individuals and organizations may not be known, those involved may deny their responsibility, and their goals may be unclear. The 2001 terrorist attacks against the United States were not attempts to defeat the nation militarily or to secure territory. They were carried out by people representing not a country but a cause, one not well understood in the United States. In short, they were expressions of anger and hate, an effort to destabilize the country and create widespread fear.

Conventional warfare is symmetrical, with two nations sending their armies into battle. By contrast, terrorism is an unconventional form of warfare, an asymmetrical conflict in which a small number of attackers uses terror and their own willingness to die to level the playing field against a much more powerful enemy. Although the terrorists may be ruthless, the nation under attack must exercise restraint in its response to terrorism because little may be known about the identity and location of the parties responsible.

The Costs and Causes of Militarism

The cost of armed conflict extends far beyond battlefield casualties. Together, the world's nations spend almost $1.6 trillion annually for

military purposes (Central Intelligence Agency, 2009). Spending this much diverts resources from the desperate struggle for survival by hundreds of millions of poor people.

Defense is the U.S. government's second largest expenditure (after Social Security), accounting for 22 percent of all federal spending, which amounted to more than $675 billion in 2009. The war on terrorism and the Iraq War continue to push this number higher. In recent years, the United States has emerged as the world's only superpower, accounting for almost half the world's military spending. Put another way, the United States spends as much on the military as the rest of the world's nations combined (Stockholm International Peace Research Institute, 2007; U.S. Office of Management and Budget, 2009).

For decades, military spending went up as a result of the *arms race* between the United States and the Soviet Union, which ended with the collapse of the USSR in 1991. But some analysts (those who support power-elite theory) link high military spending to the domination of U.S. society by a **military-industrial complex**, *the close association of the federal government, the military, and defense industries.* The roots of militarism, then, lie not just in external threats to our security but also in the institutional structures here at home (Marullo, 1987; Barnes, 2002b).

A final reason for continuing militarism is regional conflict. During the 1990s, for example, localized wars broke out in Bosnia, Chechnya, and Zambia, and tensions today run high between Israel and the Palestinians and between India and Pakistan. Even limited wars have the potential to grow and draw in other countries, including the United

Q: "Forgive your enemies, but never forget their names." Ed Koch

GLOBAL: Among the most damaging elements of war are land mines. Experts estimate that more than 100 million mines remain in the ground in 70 countries, killing or maiming some 5,000 people annually, mostly civilians (Landmine Monitor, 2008).

NOTE: The "doomsday clock," created in 1947 at the outset of the Cold War, was initially set at 7 minutes to midnight. In 2009, it stood at 5 minutes to midnight (but was 17 minutes to midnight in 1991).

Q: "One of the keys to our thinking in New Zealand is that the nuclear weapons of so-called allies are as dangerous as those of so-called enemies." Helen Clark, member of parliament

he was powerless to protect his family when armed men ransacked the house and assaulted his mother.

His father, a civil servant in the defense ministry, had been politically active with an opposition party, but may also have dealt in arms and diamonds. He had been able to afford to send Salifou to a French school, where he excelled.

But after the murders of his father and sister, he fled with his mother, brother and two younger sisters. For three years, they lived in a roving camp for the displaced, and it was all they could do to stay alive.

Late in 2004, troops of the Mouvement Patriotique, the rebel faction that controlled the north, raided the camp for new recruits. As rebels grabbed Salifou and his younger brother, Abdul Razack, then about 13, their mother held on to Abdul's arm, yelling that he was too young to take. To punish her, Salifou testified, one rebel chopped off Abdul's hand with a machete.

Abdul was left behind, but Salifou was thrown in the back of a truck with other boys and began two years as an unwilling child soldier among thousands—trained, armed, drugged and growing numb to violence.

"There are some who can't be healed anymore," he said two days after his release, confessing that firing a machine gun had seemed "cool," the power, heady. "There are some who can't stop killing and giving orders. There are people who hate people. If you had a terrible childhood, if you hated your parents." He added, "I loved my parents."

In the end, he said, his mother helped him persuade his chief to let him visit her briefly after one of his raids stumbled on her village camp again. Later, with a well-timed gift of a yam for his leader, she had Salifou return and meet Father William, a friend of his father's who would take him to safety.

"I told her that I wasn't going to leave," he said, mindful that the rebels often hurt or killed the families of those who escaped. "But she forced me."

He has had no contact with his family since. . . .

WHAT DO YOU THINK?

1. What makes the idea of children fighting in military combat troubling?

2. In this article, how did Salifou become a soldier? Did he have any choice about it?

3. What do you think will be the long-term effects of being a child soldier for people like Salifou?

States. India and Pakistan—both nuclear powers—moved to the brink of war in 2002 and then pulled back. In 2003, the announcement by North Korea that it, too, had nuclear weapons raised tensions in Asia. Iran continues to develop nuclear technology, raising fears that this nation may soon have an atomic bomb.

The dangers of war affect everyone on the planet. But the burden of fighting is especially high for hundreds of thousands of children who take part—typically against their will—in combat. Seeing Sociology in the News looks at the case of one young man forced into combat at the age of fifteen.

Nuclear Weapons

Despite the easing of superpower tensions, the world still contains more than 10,000 operational nuclear warheads, representing a destructive power of several tons of TNT for every person on the planet. If even a small fraction of this stockpile is used in war, life as we know it would end. Albert Einstein, whose genius contributed to the development of nuclear weapons, reflected, "The unleashed power of the atom has changed everything *save our modes of thinking,* and we thus drift toward unparalleled catastrophe." In short, nuclear weapons make unrestrained war unthinkable in a world not yet capable of peace.

The United States, the Russian Federation, Great Britain, France, the People's Republic of China, Israel, India, Pakistan, and probably North Korea all have nuclear weapons. The danger of catastrophic war increases with **nuclear proliferation,** *the acquisition of nuclear weapons technology by more and more nations.* A few nations stopped the development of nuclear weapons—Argentina and Brazil halted work in 1990, and South Africa dismantled its arsenal in 1991. But by 2015, there could be ten new nations in the "nuclear club," and as many as fifty nations by 2025 (Grier, 2006). Such a trend makes even the smallest regional conflict very dangerous to the entire planet.

Mass Media and War

The Iraq War was the first war in which television crews traveled with U.S. troops, reporting as the campaign unfolded. The mass media provided ongoing and detailed reports of events; cable television made available live coverage of the war twenty-four hours a day, seven days a week.

Media outlets critical of the war—especially the Arab news channel Al-Jazeera—tended to report the slow pace of the conflict, the casualties to the U.S. and allied forces, and the deaths and injuries suffered by Iraqi civilians, information that would increase pressure to end the war. Media outlets supportive of the war—including most news organizations in the United States—tended to report the rapid pace of the war and the casualties to Saddam Hussein's forces and to downplay harm to Iraqi civilians as minimal and unintended. In short, the power of the mass media to provide selective information to a worldwide audience means that television and other media are almost as important to the outcome of a conflict as the military forces who are doing the actual fighting.

GLOBAL: The Nuclear Nonproliferation Treaty has been signed by 183 nations, including the United States. It bans other countries from developing atomic weapons and requires nations with this technology to work toward reducing their armaments. Nuclear powers that have not signed the treaty include India, Pakistan, and Israel.

Q: "A fear of weapons is a sign of sexual immaturity." Sigmund Freud

Q: "In the Third World, where one child in ten dies before the age of five, there are six times as many soldiers as there are physicians." Ruth Leger Sivard (1993:6)

Q: "Just be glad you're not getting all the government you're paying for." Will Rogers

Q: "Idealism is the noble toga that political gentlemen drape over the will to power." Aldous Huxley.

military-industrial complex (p. 452) the close association of the federal government, the military, and defense industries

nuclear proliferation (p. 453) the acquisition of nuclear weapons technology by more and more nations

Pursuing Peace

How can the world reduce the dangers of war? Here are the most recent approaches to peace:

Deterrence

The logic of the arms race linked security to a "balance of terror" between the superpowers. The principle of *mutual assured destruction* (MAD) means that the side launching a first-strike nuclear attack against the other will face greater retaliation. This deterrence policy kept the peace during more than fifty years of the Cold War between the United States and the Soviet Union. But this strategy fueled an enormously expensive arms race and had little effect on nuclear proliferation, which represents a growing threat to peace. Deterrence also does little to stop terrorism or to prevent war started by a powerful nation (such as the United States) against a weaker foe (such as the Taliban regime in Afghanistan or Saddam Hussein's Iraq).

High-Technology Defense

If technology created the weapons, perhaps it can also protect us from them. Such is the claim of the *strategic defense initiative* (SDI). Under SDI, satellites and ground installations would destroy enemy missiles soon after they were launched (Thompson & Waller, 2001). In response to a survey taken shortly after the 2001 terrorist attacks, two-thirds of U.S. adults expressed support for SDI ("Female Opinion," 2002). However, critics claim that the system, which they refer to as "Star Wars," would be, at best, a leaky umbrella. Others worry that building such a system will spark another massive arms race. In 2009, the Obama administration stated that it is unlikely to support further development of SDI.

Diplomacy and Disarmament

Some analysts believe that the best path to peace is diplomacy rather than technology (Dedrick & Yinger, 1990). Teams of diplomats working together can increase security by reducing, rather than building, weapons stockpiles.

But disarmament has limitations. No nation wants to be weakened by letting down its defenses. Successful diplomacy depends on everyone involved making efforts to resolve a common problem (Fisher & Ury, 1988). Although the United States and the Soviet Union succeeded in negotiating arms reduction agreements, the world now faces increasing threats from nations such as North Korea and Iran.

Resolving Underlying Conflict

In the end, reducing the dangers of war may depend on resolving underlying conflicts by promoting a more just world. Poverty, hunger, and illiteracy are all root causes of war. Perhaps the world needs to reconsider the wisdom of spending thousands of times as much money on militarism as we do on efforts to find peaceful solutions (Sivard, 1988; Kaplan & Schaffer, 2001).

Politics: Looking Ahead

Change in political systems is ongoing. Several problems and trends are likely to be important as the twenty-first century unfolds.

One troublesome problem in the United States is the inconsistency between our democratic ideals and our low turnout at the polls. Perhaps, as conservative pluralist theorists say, many people do not bother to vote because they are content with their lives. On the other hand, liberal power-elite theorists may be right in their view that people withdraw from a system that concentrates wealth and power in the hands of so few people. Or perhaps, as radical Marxist critics claim, people find that our political system gives little real choice, limiting options and policies to those that support our capitalist economy. In any case, the current high level of apathy indicates that significant political reform is needed.

A second issue is the global rethinking of political models. The Cold War between the United States and the Soviet Union encouraged people to think of politics in terms of the two opposing models, capitalism and socialism. Today, however, people are more likely to consider a broader range of political systems that links government to the economy in various ways. "Welfare capitalism," as found in Sweden,

One reason to pursue peace is the rising toll of death and mutilation caused by millions of land mines placed in the ground during wartime and left there afterward. Civilians—many of them children—maimed by land mines receive treatment in this Kabul, Afghanistan, clinic.

Q: "I would remind you that extremism in the defense of liberty is no vice . . . and moderation in the pursuit of justice is no virtue." Barry Goldwater

Q: "A single death is a tragedy; a million deaths is a statistic." Josef Stalin

Q: "Politics is supposed to be the second oldest profession. I have come to realize that it bears a very close resemblance to the first." Ronald Reagan

Q: "Power corrupts. Absolute power is kind of neat." John Lehman

Q: "Democracy is the recurrent suspicion that more than half of the people are right more than half of the time." E. B. White

Q: "Democracy is a device that guarantees that we will be governed no better than we deserve." George Bernard Shaw

SEEING SOCIOLOGY
in Everyday Life

Do you think the world is getting better at avoiding war? Explain.

CONTROVERSY & DEBATE

Islam and Freedom: A "Democracy Gap"?

One of the reasons given by the U.S. government for sending military troops to Iraq was to encourage the spread of democracy in the Middle East, especially in countries with mostly Islamic populations.

But what about the claim of the Middle East needing democracy? Is democracy a goal that is sought—and equated with freedom—everywhere? The answer is "not exactly," because various nations have very different political histories, and "freedom" means different things in different cultural settings; political freedom, however, is a basic element of all democracies.

Freedom House, an organization that monitors political freedom around the world, tracks people's right to vote, to express ideas, and to move about without undue interference from government. It reports that the part of the world with the least political freedom stretches from Africa through the Middle East to Asia (look back at Global Map 17–1 on page 439).

Many of the nations that Freedom House characterizes as "not free" have populations that are largely Islamic. This organization reports that in 2009, 48 of the world's 194 nations had an Islamic majority population. As the figure shows, just 9 (19 percent) of these 48 countries had democratic governments, and Freedom House rated only two—Indonesia and Mali—as "free." Of the remainder, 21 were rated "partly free" and 25 were rated "not free." Of the 146 nations without a majority Islamic population, 109 (75 percent) had democratic governments, and 84 were rated as "free." In other words, countries without Islamic majorities were three times more likely to have democratic govern-

ments than countries with Islamic majorities. Freedom House concluded that countries with an Islamic majority display a "democracy gap" (Karatnycky, 2002; Freedom House, 2009).

This relative lack of democracy was found in all world regions that contain Islamic-majority nations—Africa, central Europe, the Middle East, and Asia. The pattern was especially strong among the sixteen Islamic-majority states in the Middle East and North Africa that are ethnically Arabic—none is an electoral democracy.

What explains this "democracy gap"? Freedom House points to four factors. First, countries with Islamic-majority populations are typically less developed economically, with limited schooling for their people and widespread poverty. Second, these countries have cultural traditions that rigidly control the lives of women, providing them with few economic, educational, or political opportunities. Third, although most other countries limit the power of religious elites in government, and some (including the United States) even require a "separation of church and state," Islamic-majority nations support giving Islamic leaders political power. In just two recent cases—Iran and Afghanistan under the Taliban—Islamic leaders have actually taken formal control of the government; more commonly, religious leaders do not hold office but exert considerable influence on political outcomes.

Fourth and finally, the enormous wealth that comes from Middle Eastern oil also plays a part in preventing democratic government. In Iraq, Saudi Arabia, Kuwait, Qatar, and other

nations, this resource has provided astounding riches to a small number of families, money that they can use to shore up their political control. In addition, oil wealth permits elites to build airports and other modern facilities without encouraging broader economic development that would raise the living standards of the majority.

For all these reasons, Freedom House concludes that the road to democracy for Islamic-majority nations is likely to be long. But today's patterns may not predict those of tomorrow. In 1950, very few Catholic-majority countries (mostly in Europe and Latin America) had democratic governments. Today, however, most of these nations are democratic. Note, too, that a majority of the world's Muslims—who live in Nigeria, Turkey, Bangladesh, India, Indonesia, and the United States—already live under democratic governments. But perhaps the best indicator that change is under way is that by 2009, Freedom House had added two more countries with Islamic majorities to the list of "free" nations of the world.

WHAT DO YOU THINK?

1. Do you think the United States is right or wrong in the way it is seeking to bring about a democratic political system in Iraq? Why?

2. Do you expect greater democracy in Islamic-majority countries fifty years from now? Why or why not?

3. Can you point to several reasons that Muslim people might object to the kind of political system we call "democracy"? Explain.

---

or "state capitalism," as found in Japan and South Korea, are just two possibilities. In all cases, promoting the broadest democratic participation is an important goal. The Controversy & Debate box takes a look at the debate over the chances for democratic governments emerging in the world's Islamic countries.

Third, we still face the danger of war in many parts of the world. Even as the United States and the Russian Federation dismantle some

warheads, vast stockpiles of nuclear weapons remain, and nuclear technology continues to spread around the world. In addition, new superpowers are likely to arise (the People's Republic of China and India are likely candidates), and regional conflicts and terrorism are likely to continue. We can only hope for—*and vote for*—leaders who will find nonviolent solutions to the age-old problems that provoke war, putting us on the road to world peace.

Seeing Sociology in Everyday Life

Chapter 17 Politics and Government

How important are you to the political process?

Historically, as this chapter explains, young people have been less likely than older people to take part in politics. But, as a study of the 2008 election suggests, that trend may be changing as evidence builds that young people intend to have their voices heard.

> **HINT** In the 2008 presidential campaign, thousands of young people served as volunteers for both major political candidates, telephoning voters or walking door to door in an effort to increase public interest, raise money, and get people to the polls on Election Day. Many celebrities—including musicians and members of the Hollywood entertainment scene—also spoke out in favor of a candidate, most of them favoring the Democratic Party. But most important of all is voting, and your vote counts as much as that of any celebrity. Are you registered to vote? Will you turn out next Election Day?

Thousands of young people volunteered to assist the 2008 presidential candidates in their campaigns. In what ways do you think young people helped their candidates simply by using the telephone?

You don't need to be a campaign worker to make a difference. What is the easiest—and in the end, the most important—way to be a part of the political process?

Tom Morello, guitarist for "Rage Against the Machine" and other bands, has made political activism a central part of his career as a musician, speaking for various left-of-center causes. Can you identify other celebrities who have tried to shape public opinion?

Applying SOCIOLOGY in Everyday Life

1. The following Web site provides data on how people voted in the 2008 presidential election by gender, age, race, income, religion, and other variables: http://www.cnn.com/ELECTION/2008. Visit this site, and develop a profile of the typical Democratic voter and the typical Republican voter. Which variables best predict differences in voting preference?

2. With several classmates or friends, make a list of political leaders who have personal charisma. Discuss why each person is on the list. Do you think personal charisma today is something

more than "being good on television"? If so, precisely what is it? Which candidates in the 2008 presidential election had the most charisma?

3. Freedom House, an organization that studies civil rights and political liberty around the world, publishes an annual report, "Freedom in the World." Find a copy in the library, or examine global trends and the political profile of any country on the Web at http://www.freedomhouse.org.

MAKING THE GRADE

CHAPTER 17 Politics and Government

Politics: Power and Authority

POLITICS is the major social institution by which a society distributes power and organizes decision making. Max Weber claimed that raw power is transformed into *legitimate authority* in three ways:

- Preindustrial societies rely on tradition to transform power into authority. **Traditional authority** is closely linked to kinship.
- As societies industrialize, tradition gives way to rationality. **Rational-legal authority** underlies the operation of bureaucratic offices as well as the law.
- At any time, however, some individuals transform power into authority through charisma. **Charismatic authority** is based on extraordinary personal qualities (as found in Jesus of Nazareth, Adolf Hitler, and Mahatma Gandhi).

pp. 436–37

Politics in Global Perspective

MONARCHY is common in agrarian societies.
- Leadership is based on kinship.
- During the Middle Ages, absolute monarchs claimed to rule by divine right.

pp. 437–38

DEMOCRACY is common in modern societies.
- Leadership is linked to elective office.
- Bureaucracy and economic inequality limit true democracy in high-income countries today.

p. 438

AUTHORITARIANISM is any political system that denies the people participation in government.
- Absolute monarchies and military juntas are examples of authoritarian regimes.

p. 440

TOTALITARIANISM concentrates all political power in one centralized leadership.
- Totalitarian governments allow no organized opposition, and they rule by fear.

pp. 441–42

POLITICAL FREEDOM

The world is divided into 194 politically independent nation-states, 90 of which were politically "free" in 2008. Another 62 countries were "partly free," and the remaining 42 countries were "not free." Compared to a decade ago, more of the world's nations are "free."

pp. 438–40

A GLOBAL POLITICAL SYSTEM?

The world remains divided into 194 independent countries, but

- multinational corporations have created a new political oder because their enormous wealth gives them power to shape world events
- in an age of computers and other new information technology, governments can no longer control the flow of information across their borders

p. 442

Politics in the United States

THE RISE OF THE WELFARE STATE

U.S. government has expanded over the past two centuries, although the welfare state in the United States is smaller than in most other high-income nations.

pp. 442–43

THE POLITICAL SPECTRUM
- The political spectrum, from the liberal left to the conservative right, involves attitudes on both economic issues and social issues.
- Affluent people tend to be conservative on economic issues and liberal on social issues.
- Party identification in the United States is weak.

pp. 443–44

SPECIAL-INTEREST GROUPS
- Special-interest groups advance the political aims of specific segments of the population.
- **Political action committees** play a powerful role in electoral politics.

pp. 444–46

VOTER APATHY
- Voter apathy runs high in the United States.
- Only 63% of eligible voters went to the polls in the 2008 presidential election.

pp. 446–47

---

politics (p. 436) the social institution that distributes power, sets a society's goals, and makes decisions

power (p. 436) the ability to achieve desired ends despite resistance from others

government (p. 436) a formal organization that directs the political life of a society

authority (p. 436) power that people perceive as legitimate rather than coercive

traditional authority (p. 436) power legitimized by respect for long-established cultural patterns

rational-legal authority (p. 437) power legitimized by legally enacted rules and regulations; also known as *bureaucratic authority*

charismatic authority (p. 437) power legitimized by extraordinary personal abilities that inspire devotion and obedience

routinization of charisma (p. 437) the transformation of charismatic authority into some combination of traditional and bureaucratic authority

monarchy (p. 437) a political system in which a single family rules from generation to generation

democracy (p. 438) a political system that gives power to the people as a whole

authoritarianism (p. 440) a political system that denies the people participation in government

totalitarianism (p. 441) a highly centralized political system that extensively regulates people's lives

welfare state (p. 442) a system of government agencies and programs that provides benefits to the population

special-interest group (p. 444) people organized to address some economic or social issue

political action committee (PAC) (p. 446) an organization formed by a special-interest group, independent of political parties, to raise and spend money in support of political goals

Theoretical Analysis of Power in Society

The PLURALIST MODEL

- claims that political power is spread widely in the United States
- is linked to structural-functional theory

pp. 447–48

The POWER-ELITE MODEL

- claims that power is concentrated in a small, wealthy segment of the population
- is based on the ideas of C. Wright Mills
- is linked to social-conflict theory

p. 448

The MARXIST POLITICAL-ECONOMY MODEL

- claims that our political agenda is determined by a capitalist economy, so true democracy is impossible
- is based on the ideas of Karl Marx
- is linked to social-conflict theory

pp. 448–49

pluralist model (p. 447) an analysis of politics that sees power as spread among many competing interest groups

power-elite model (p. 448) an analysis of politics that sees power as concentrated among the rich

Marxist political-economy model (p. 448) an analysis that explains politics in terms of the operation of a society's economic system

See the Applying Theory table on page 447.

Power beyond the Rules

REVOLUTION radically transforms a political system. Revolutions

- occur during periods of rising expectations and when governments are unwilling to reform themselves
- are usually led by intellectuals
- must establish a new legitimacy in the eyes of the people

p. 449

TERRORISM employs violence in the pursuit of political goals and is used by a group against a much more powerful enemy.

- State terrorism is the use of violence by government officials as a way to control the population.
- Who or what is defined as terrorist depends on one's political perspective.
- Terrorism is an unconventional form of warfare.

p. 450

political revolution (p. 449) the overthrow of one political system in order to establish another

terrorism (p. 450) acts of violence or the threat of violence used as a political strategy by an individual or a group

War and Peace

CAUSES OF WAR

Like all forms of social behavior, war is a product of society. Societies go to war when

- they perceive a threat to their way of life
- governments want to divert public attention from social problems at home
- they want to achieve a specific political or moral objective
- they can find no alternatives to resolving conflicts

p. 451

MILITARISM IN THE WORLD TODAY

- The U.S. military is composed mainly of members of the working class.
- Military spending rose dramatically in the second half of the twentieth century because of the *arms race* between the United States and the former Soviet Union.
- Some analysts point to the domination of U.S. society by a **military-industrial complex**.
- The development and spread of nuclear weapons have increased the threat of global catastrophe.

pp. 451–53

war (p. 450) organized, armed conflict among the people of two or more nations, directed by their governments

military-industrial complex (p. 452) the close association of the federal government, the military, and defense industries

nuclear proliferation (p. 453) the acquisition of nuclear weapons technology by more and more nations

PURSUING PEACE

The most recent approaches to peace include

- deterrence
- high-technology defense
- diplomacy and disarmament
- resolving underlying conflict

In the end, pursuing peace means ending poverty, hunger, and illiteracy and promoting social justice for all people.

p. 454

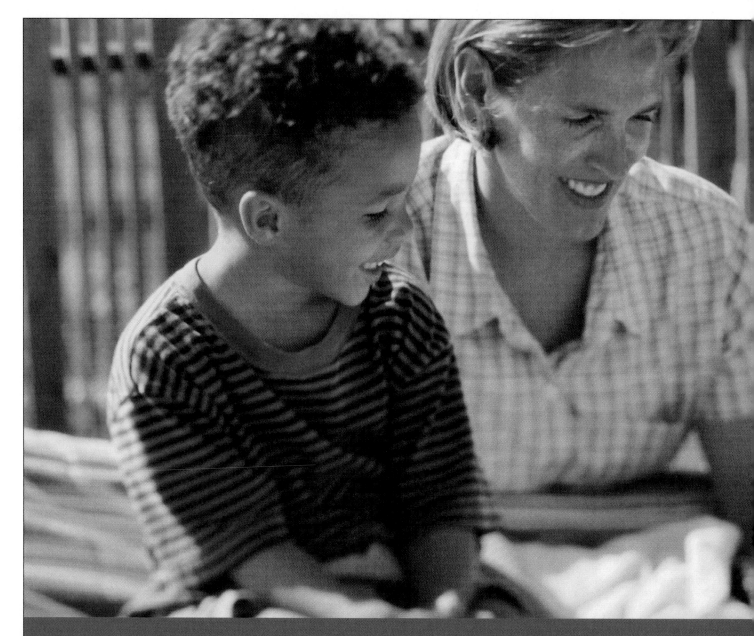

{ Families are an important social institution in every society, guiding the behavior of both young and old as well as playing a part in continuing social inequality. Many debates surround today's families, including exactly what relationships should be considered families. }

CHAPTER 18

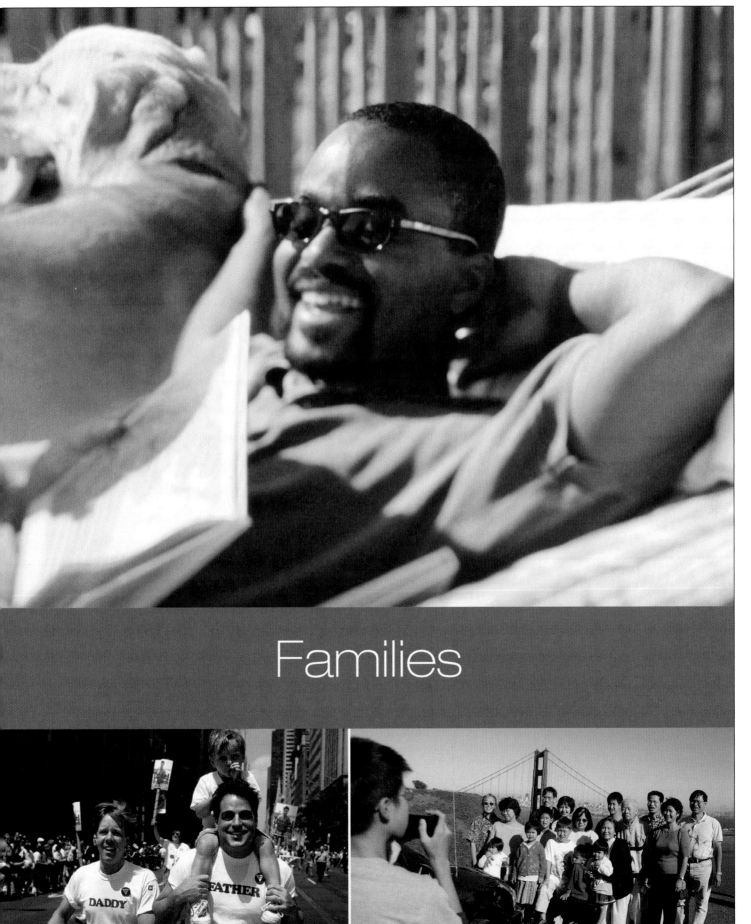

Families

CHAPTER OVERVIEW

This chapter explores the family, a major social institution. The chapter begins by introducing a number of important concepts that sociologists use to describe and analyze families.

Rosa Yniguez is one of seven children who grew up in Jalisco, Mexico, in a world in which families worked hard, went to church regularly, and were proud of having many children. Rosa remembers visiting the home of friends of her parents who had a clock in their living room with a picture of each of their twelve children where the numbers on the clock face would be.

Now thirty-five years old, Rosa is living in San Francisco and working as a cashier in a department store. In some respects, she has carried on her parents' traditions— but not in every way. Recalling her childhood, she says, "In Mexico, many of the families I knew had six, eight, ten children. Sometimes more. But I came to this country to get ahead. That is simply impossible with too many kids." As a result of her desire to keep her job and make a better life for her family, Yniguez has decided to have no more than the three children she has now.

A tradition of having large families has helped make Hispanics the largest ethnic minority in the United States. But today more and more Latinas are making the same decision as Rosa Yniguez and opting to have fewer children. Studies show that the birth rate for all immigrant women has been dropping during the past decade (Navarro, 2004; U.S. Census Bureau, 2008).

Families have been with us for a very long time. But as this story indicates, U.S. families are changing in response to a number of factors, including the desire of women to have more career options and to provide better lives for their children. In fact, the family is changing faster than any other social institution (Bianchi & Spain, 1996). This chapter explores the changes in family life, as well as the diversity of families both around the world and here in the United States.

Families: Basic Concepts

The **family** is *a social institution found in all societies that unites people in cooperative groups to care for one another, including any children.* Family ties are also called **kinship**, *a social bond based on common ancestry, marriage, or adoption.* All societies contain families, but exactly who people call their kin has varied through history and varies today from one culture to another. From the point of view of any individual, families change as we grow up, leaving the family into which we were born to form a family of our own.

Here as in other countries, families form around **marriage**, *a legal relationship, usually involving economic cooperation, sexual activity, and childbearing.* The traditional belief in the United States is that people should marry before having children; this expectation is found in the word *matrimony,* which in Latin means "the condition of motherhood." Today, 61 percent of children are born to married couples, but 39 percent are born to single women who may or may not live with a partner.

Families, then, have become more diverse. Which relationships are and are not considered a family can have important consequences, because employers typically extend benefits such as health care only to family members. The U.S. Census Bureau, which collects data used by sociologists, counts as families only people living together who are linked by "blood, marriage, or adoption."[1] All Census Bureau data on families in this chapter are based on that definition. However, the trend in the United States is toward a broader definition of families to include both homosexual and heterosexual partners and unmarried as well as married couples who live together. These *families of affinity* are made up of people who think of themselves as a family and wish others to see them that way.

---

[1] According to the U.S. Census Bureau, there were 116 million U.S. households in 2007. Of these, 78.4 million (68 percent) met the bureau's definition of "family." The remaining living units contained single people or unrelated individuals living together. In 1950, fully 90 percent of all households were families.

family a social institution found in all societies that unites people in cooperative groups to care for one another, including any children

kinship a social bond based on common ancestry, marriage, or adoption

extended family a family composed of parents and children as well as other kin; also known as a *consanguine family*

nuclear family a family composed of one or two parents and their children; also known as a *conjugal family*

marriage a legal relationship, usually involving economic cooperation, sexual activity, and childbearing

endogamy marriage between people of the same social category

exogamy marriage between people of different social categories

monogamy marriage that unites two partners

polygamy marriage that unites a person with two or more spouses

polygyny marriage that unites one man and two or more women

polyandry marriage that unites one woman and two or more men

Families: Global Variations

How closely related do people have to be to consider themselves a "family"? In preindustrial societies, people commonly recognize the **extended family**, *a family consisting of parents and children as well as other kin.* This group is sometimes called the *consanguine family* because it includes everyone with "shared blood." With industrialization, however, increased social mobility and geographic migration give rise to the **nuclear family**, *a family composed of one or two parents and their children.* The nuclear family is also called the *conjugal family* (*conjugal* means "based on marriage"). Although many people in our society think of kinship in terms of extended families, most people carry out their everyday routines within a nuclear family.

The family is changing most quickly in nations that have a large welfare state (see Chapter 17, "Politics and Government"). In the Thinking Globally box on page 464, the sociologist David Popenoe takes a look at Sweden, which, he claims, is home to the weakest families in the world.

Families in the United States have diverse forms, and celebrity couples represent them all. Although same-sex couples can marry in only six states, they are becoming more common across the country; television personality Rosie O'Donnell lives with her partner, Kelli Carpenter, and their four children. Cohabitation without marriage is also becoming more common in our society; Brad Pitt and Angelina Jolie live together and have three adopted children and three biological children.

Marriage Patterns

Cultural norms, and often laws, identify people as suitable or unsuitable marriage partners. Some marital norms promote **endogamy**, *marriage between people of the same social category.* Endogamy limits potential partners to people of the same age, race, religion, or social class. By contrast, **exogamy** is *marriage between people of different social categories.* In rural areas of India, for example, people are expected to marry someone of the same caste (endogamy) but from a different village (exogamy). The reason for endogamy is that people of similar position pass along their standing to their offspring, maintaining the traditional social hierarchy. Exogamy, on the other hand, links communities and encourages the spread of culture.

In high-income nations, laws permit only **monogamy** (from the Greek, meaning "one union"), *marriage that unites two partners.* Global Map 18–1 on page 465 shows that monogamy is the rule throughout North and South America as well as Europe, although many countries in Africa and southern Asia permit **polygamy** (from the Greek, meaning "many unions"), *marriage that unites a person with two or more spouses.* Polygamy has two forms. By far the more common form is **polygyny** (from the Greek, meaning "many women"), *marriage that unites one man and two or more women.* For example, Islamic nations in the Middle East and Africa permit men up to four wives. Even so, most Islamic families are monogamous because few men can afford to support several wives and even more children.

Polyandry (from the Greek, meaning "many men" or "many husbands") is *marriage that unites one woman and two or more men.* This extremely rare pattern exists in Tibet, a mountainous land where agriculture is difficult. There, polyandry discourages the division of land into parcels too small to support a family and divides the hard work of farming among many men.

Most of the world's societies have at some time permitted more than one marital pattern. Even so, most marriages have been monogamous (Murdock, 1965, orig. 1949). This historical preference for monogamy reflects two facts of life: Supporting several spouses is very expensive, and the number of men and women in most societies is roughly equal.

Residential Patterns

Just as societies regulate mate selection, they also designate where a couple lives. In preindustrial societies, most newlyweds live with one set of parents who offer them protection, support, and assistance. Most common is the norm of **patrilocality** (Greek for "place of the father"), *a residential pattern in which a married couple lives with or near the husband's family.* But some societies (such as the North American Iroquois) favor **matrilocality** (meaning "place of

patrilocality (p. 463) a residential pattern in which a married couple lives with or near the husband's family

matrilocality (p. 463) a residential pattern in which a married couple lives with or near the wife's family

neolocality a residential pattern in which a married couple lives apart from both sets of parents

descent the system by which members of a society trace kinship over generations

patrilineal descent a system tracing kinship through men

matrilineal descent a system tracing kinship through women

bilateral descent (p. 466) a system tracing kinship through both men and women

THINKING GLOBALLY

The Weakest Families on Earth? A Report from Sweden

INGE: In Sweden, we have a government that takes care of every person!

SAM: In the United States, we have families to do that. . . .

We in the United States can envy the Swedes for avoiding many of our worst social problems, including violent crime, drug abuse, and savage poverty. Instead, this Scandinavian nation seems to fulfill the promise of the modern welfare state, with a large and professional government bureaucracy that sees to virtually all human needs.

But one drawback of such a large welfare state, according to David Popenoe (1991, 1994), is that Sweden has the weakest families on Earth. Because people look to the government, not spouses, for economic assistance, Swedes are less likely to marry than members of almost all other high-income societies. For the same reason, Sweden also has a high share of adults living alone (42 percent, compared to 27 percent in the United States). In addition, a large proportion of couples live together outside marriage (27 percent, versus 9 percent in the United States), and 55 percent of all Swedish children (compared to 39 percent in the United States) are born to unmarried parents. Average household size in Sweden is almost the smallest in the world (2.1 persons, versus 2.6 in the United States). Finally, Swedish couples, whether married or not, are more likely to break up than partners in the United States or any other high-income nation.

Popenoe claims that a growing culture of individualism and self-fulfillment,

along with the declining influence of religion, began eroding Swedish families in the 1960s. The movement of women into the labor force also played a part. Today, Sweden has the lowest proportion of women who are homemakers (10 percent, versus 22 percent in the United States) and the highest percentage of women in the labor force (68 percent, versus 59 percent in the United States).

But most important, according to Popenoe, is the expansion of the welfare state. The Swedish government offers its citizens a lifetime of services. Swedes can count on the government to deliver and school their children, provide comprehensive health care, support them when they are out of work, and pay for their funerals.

Many Swedes supported this welfare state, thinking it would strengthen families. But as Popenoe sees it, government is really *replacing* families. Take the case of child care: The Swedish government operates child care centers that are

staffed by professionals and available regardless of parents' income. However, the government gives nothing to parents who wish to care for their children in their own home. In effect, government benefits encourage people to let the state do what family members used to do for themselves.

But if Sweden's system has solved so many social problems, why should anyone care about the family getting weaker? For two reasons, says Popenoe. First, it is very expensive for government to provide many "family" services; this is the main reason that Sweden has one of the highest rates of taxation in the world. Second, at any price, Popenoe says that government employees in large child care centers cannot provide children with the same love and emotional security given by two parents living as a family. When it comes to taking care of people—especially young children—small, intimate groups do the job better than large, impersonal organizations.

WHAT DO YOU THINK?

1. Do you agree with Popenoe that government should not replace families? Explain your answer.

2. In the United States, we have a much smaller welfare state than Sweden has. Should our government do more for its people? Why or why not?

3. With regard to children, list two specific things that government can do better than parents and two things that parents do better than government.

the mother"), *a residential pattern in which a married couple lives with or near the wife's family.* Societies that engage in frequent local warfare tend toward patrilocality, so sons are close to home to offer protection. On the other hand, societies that engage only in distant warfare may be either patrilocal or matrilocal, depending on

whether its sons or daughters have greater economic value (Ember & Ember, 1971, 1991).

Industrial societies show yet another pattern. Finances permitting, they favor **neolocality** (from the Greek, meaning "new place"), *a residential pattern in which a married couple lives apart from both sets of parents.*

GLOBAL: Teen pregnancy is increasing in poor societies, perhaps one indication of the breakdown of tradition. In Botswana, a southern African nation, one-fifth of female teens become pregnant, most unintentionally due to lack of knowledge about birth control.

DIVERSITY: Statistically speaking, the typical U.S. family is a married couple, both of whom are high school graduates and in the labor force, with one child (mean) or no children (mode), living in a (mortgaged) home that they own. At any given point in time, about 20% of all households have a wife, husband, and one or more children at home, although more than half take this form during the life course; at any given time, about one in twenty households includes a working man, homemaker woman, and one or more children, although, again, about 25% take this form at some point.

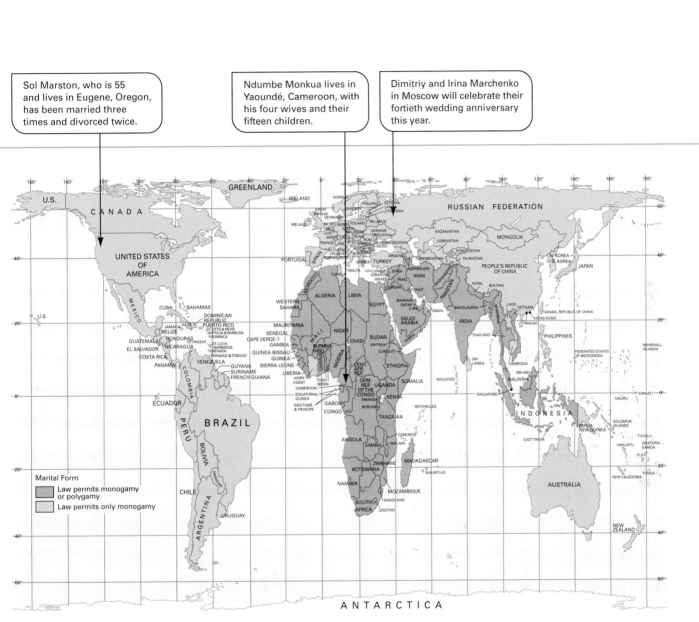

Sol Marston, who is 55 and lives in Eugene, Oregon, has been married three times and divorced twice.

Ndumbe Monkua lives in Yaoundé, Cameroon, with his four wives and their fifteen children.

Dimitriy and Irina Marchenko in Moscow will celebrate their fortieth wedding anniversary this year.

Window on the World

GLOBAL MAP 18–1 **Marital Form in Global Perspective**

Monogamy is the only legal form of marriage throughout the Western Hemisphere and in much of the rest of the world. In most African nations and in southern Asia, however, polygamy is permitted by law. In many cases, this practice reflects the influence of Islam, a religion that allows a man to have up to four wives. Even so, most marriages in these countries are monogamous, primarily for financial reasons.

Source: *Peters Atlas of the World* (1990) with updates by the author.

Patterns of Descent

Descent refers to *the system by which members of a society trace kinship over generations.* Most preindustrial societies trace kinship through either the father's side or the mother's side of the family. **Patrilineal descent**, the more common pattern, is *a system tracing kinship through men.* In this pattern, children are related to others only through their fathers. Tracing kinship through patrilineal descent ensures that fathers pass property on to their sons. Patrilineal descent characterizes most pastoral and agrarian societies, in which men produce the most valued resources. A less common pattern is **matrilineal descent**, *a system tracing kinship through women.* Matrilineal descent, in which mothers pass property to their daughters, is found more frequently in horticultural societies, where women are the main food producers.

NOTE: The incest taboo limits kinship confusion. A few years back, Rolling Stone Bill Wyman's (then age 58) son, Stephen (age 32), announced his intention to marry the mother (age 45) of his father's ex-wife (age 24). Such a union would have made Stephen stepfather to his former stepmother, and Bill stepgrandfather to his former wife. Bill would also be his son's son-in-law and the father of his father-in-law!

GLOBAL: Royals often play loose with the incest taboo. In Egyptian mythology, for example, the god Isis married her brother Osiris.

DISCUSS: To help students appreciate how important the functions of the family are for society, ask them to look at the list of functions on these pages and try to find an alternative social setting (friends, clubs, or government) for each one. How well can other settings take over family functions?

SEEING SOCIOLOGY
in Everyday Life

In terms of patterns of descent, how would you describe the common practice in the United States of a woman adopting her husband's last name after marriage?

incest taboo   a norm forbidding sexual relations or marriage between certain relatives

APPLYING THEORY

Family

	Structural-Functional Approach	Social-Conflict and Feminist Approaches	Symbolic-Interaction and Social-Exchange Approaches
What is the level of analysis?	Macro-level	Macro-level	Micro-level
What is the importance of family for society?	The family performs vital tasks, including socializing the young and providing emotional and financial support for members. The family helps regulate sexual activity.	The family perpetuates social inequality by handing down wealth from one generation to the next. The family supports patriarchy as well as racial and ethnic inequality.	The symbolic-interaction approach explains that the reality of family life is constructed by members in their interaction. The social-exchange approach shows that courtship typically brings together people who offer the same level of advantages.

Industrial societies with greater gender equality recognize **bilateral descent** ("two-sided descent"), *a system tracing kinship through both men and women.* In this pattern, children include people on both the father's side and the mother's side among their relatives.

Patterns of Authority

Worldwide, polygyny, patrilocality, and patrilineal descent are dominant and reflect the common global pattern of patriarchy. In industrial societies like the United States, men are still typically heads of households, and most U.S. parents give children their father's last name. However, more egalitarian family patterns are evolving, especially as the share of women in the labor force goes up.

Theoretical Analysis of Families

As in earlier chapters, the three major theoretical approaches offer a range of insights about the family. The Applying Theory table summarizes what we can learn from each approach.

Functions of the Family: Structural-Functional Analysis

According to the structural-functional approach, the family performs many vital tasks. For this reason, the family is often called the "backbone of society."

1. **Socialization.** As explained in Chapter 5 ("Socialization"), the family is the first and most important setting for child rearing. Ideally, parents help children become well-integrated, contributing members of society. Of course, family socialization continues throughout the life cycle. Adults change within marriage, and as any parent knows, mothers and fathers learn as much from their children as their children learn from them.

2. **Regulation of sexual activity.** Every culture regulates sexual activity in the interest of maintaining kinship organization and property rights. The **incest taboo** is *a norm forbidding sexual relations or marriage between certain relatives.* Although the incest taboo exists in every society, exactly which relatives cannot marry varies from one culture to another. The matrilineal Navajo, for example, forbid marrying any relative of one's mother. Our bilateral society applies the incest taboo to both sides of the family but limits it to close relatives, including parents, grandparents, siblings, aunts, and uncles (National Map 8–1 on page 191 shows which states allow or forbid first-cousin marriages). But even brother-sister (but not parent-child) marriages existed among the ancient Egyptian, Incan, and Hawaiian nobility (Murdock, 1965, orig. 1949).

   Reproduction between close relatives of any species can result in mental and physical damage to offspring. Yet only human beings observe an incest taboo, a fact suggesting that the key reason for controlling incest is social. Why? First, the incest taboo limits sexual competition in families by restricting sex to

Q: "Marriage is not a statement of a public love affair, but a public institution for the nurture and socialization of children." Melanie Phillips

DISCUSS: Primary groups are not immune to conflict. Discuss the meaning of the common sayings "You always hurt the ones you love" and "Familiarity breeds contempt."

Q: "There are two marriages, then, in every marital union, his and hers. And his . . . is better than hers." Jessie Bernard

Q: In *The Republic*, Plato advocates the abolition of the "private" family: "All these women are to belong to all these men in common, and no woman is to live privately with any man. And the children, in their turn, will be in common, and neither will a parent know his own offspring, nor a child his parent." (Book V)

SEEING SOCIOLOGY
in Everyday Life

Thinking about the "marriage marketplace," why do you think women have traditionally been less willing than men to reveal their age?

spouses. Second, because kinship defines people's rights and obligations toward one another, reproduction among close relatives would hopelessly confuse kinship ties and threaten social order. Third, forcing people to marry outside their immediate families ties together the larger society.

3. **Social placement**. Families are not needed for people to reproduce, but they do help maintain social organization. Parents pass on their own social identity—in terms of race, ethnicity, religion, and social class—to their children at birth.

4. **Material and emotional security**. Many people view the family as a "haven in a heartless world," offering physical protection, emotional support, and financial assistance. Perhaps this is why people living in families tend to be happier, healthier, and wealthier than people living alone (Goldstein & Kenney, 2001; U.S. Census Bureau, 2008).

○ **CRITICAL REVIEW** Structural-functional analysis explains why society, at least as we know it, is built on families. But this approach glosses over the diversity of U.S. family life and ignores how other social institutions (such as government) could meet some of the same human needs. Finally, structural-functionalism overlooks negative aspects of family life, including patriarchy and family violence.

○ **CHECK YOUR LEARNING** Identify four important functions of the family for society.

Inequality and the Family: Social-Conflict and Feminist Analysis

Like the structural-functional approach, the social-conflict approach, including feminist analysis, considers the family central to our way of life. But rather than focusing on ways that kinship benefits society, this approach points out how the family perpetuates social inequality.

1. **Property and inheritance**. Friedrich Engels (1902, orig. 1884) traced the origin of the family to men's need (especially in the upper classes) to identify heirs so that they could hand down property to their sons. Families thus concentrate wealth and reproduce the class structure in each new generation.

2. **Patriarchy**. Feminists link the family to patriarchy. To know their heirs, men must control the sexuality of women. Families therefore transform women into the sexual and economic property of men. A century ago in the United States, most wives' earnings belonged to their husbands. Today, women still bear most of the responsibility for child rearing and housework (Benokraitis & Feagin, 1995; Stapinski, 1998; England, 2001).

Women have long been taught to see marriage as the key to a happy life. Social-conflict theory, however, points to the fact that marriage often means a lifetime sentence of unpaid domestic labor. Susan Pyzow's painting *Bridal Bouquet* makes the point.

© Susan Pyzow, *Bridal Bouquet,* watercolor on paper, 10×13.5 in. Studio SPM Inc.

3. **Race and ethnicity**. Racial and ethnic categories persist over generations because most people marry others like themselves. Endogamous marriage supports racial and ethnic hierarchies.

○ **CRITICAL REVIEW** Social-conflict and feminist analysis shows another side of family life: its role in social stratification. Engels criticized the family for its support of capitalism. But noncapitalist societies also have families (and family problems). The family may be linked to social inequality, as Engels argued, but the family carries out societal functions not easily accomplished by other means.

○ **CHECK YOUR LEARNING** Point to ways in which families support social inequality.

NOTE: Social-exchange analysis is a kind of rational-choice theory.

NOTE: Social-exchange analysis also explains why people who perceive more potential new partners in their surroundings have higher divorce rates (see South & Lloyd, 1995).

RESOURCE: Among the classics included in the author's companion reader *Seeing Ourselves*, 8th ed., is Jessie Bernard's "'His' and 'Her' Marriage."

RESOURCE: See Bron B. Ingoldsby's article "Mate Selection and Marriage around the World" in the companion reader.

POP CULTURE: In middle-income nations in Asia, the basis of marriage has shifted from family arrangement to romantic love, a trend encouraged by Bollywood, the Indian film industry, and stars such as Aishwayra Rai.

● SEEING SOCIOLOGY
in Everyday Life

How similar are your parents (or you and your spouse) in terms of age, social class, race, ethnicity, and education?

According to social exchange theory, people form relationships based on what each offers to the other. Generally partners see the exchange as fair or "about even." What do you think is the exchange involved in this marriage?

Constructing Family Life: Micro-Level Analysis

Both structural-functional and social-conflict analyses view the family as a structural system. By contrast, micro-level analysis explores how individuals shape and experience family life.

The Symbolic-Interaction Approach

Ideally, family living offers an opportunity for *intimacy*, a word with Latin roots meaning "sharing fear." As family members share many activities over time, they identify with each other and build emotional bonds. Of course, the fact that parents act as authority figures often limits their closeness with younger children. But as children approach adulthood, kinship ties typically open up to include sharing confidences with greater intimacy (Macionis, 1978).

The Social-Exchange Approach

Social-exchange analysis, another micro-level approach, describes courtship and marriage as forms of negotiation (Blau, 1964). Dating allows each person to assess the advantages and disadvantages of a potential spouse. In essence, exchange analysts suggest, people "shop around" for partners to make the best "deal" they can.

In patriarchal societies, gender roles dictate the elements of exchange: Men bring wealth and power to the marriage marketplace, and women bring beauty. The importance of beauty explains women's traditional concern with their appearance. But as women have joined the labor force, they are less dependent on men to support them, and so the terms of exchange are converging for men and women.

─○ **CRITICAL REVIEW** Micro-level analysis balances structural-functional and social-conflict visions of the family as an institutional system. Both the interaction and exchange viewpoints focus on the individual experience of family life. However, micro-level analysis misses the bigger picture: Family life is similar for people in the same social and economic categories. The Applying Theory table summarizes what we can learn by applying each of the theoretical approaches to family life.

─○ **CHECK YOUR LEARNING** How does a micro-level approach to understanding family differ from a macro-level approach? State the main ideas of the symbolic-interaction approach and the social-exchange approach.

Stages of Family Life

The family is a dynamic institution, with marked changes across the life course. New families begin with courtship and evolve as the new partners settle into the realities of married life. Next, for most couples at least, come the years spent developing careers and raising children, leading to the later years of marriage, after the children have left home to form families of their own. We will look briefly at each of these four stages.

Courtship

November 2, Kandy, Sri Lanka. Winding through the rain forest of this beautiful island, our van driver, Harry, recounts how he met his wife. Actually, he explains, it was more of an arrangement: The two families were both Buddhist and of the same caste. "We got along well, right from the start," recalls Harry. "We had the same background. I suppose she or I could have said no. But love marriages happen in the city, not in the village where I grew up."

In rural Sri Lanka, as in rural areas of low- and middle-income countries throughout the world, most people consider courtship too important to be left to the young (Stone, 1977). *Arranged marriages* are alliances between extended families of similar social standing and usually involve an exchange not just of children but also of wealth and favors. Romantic love has little to do with marriage, and parents may make such arrangements when their children are very

MAKING THE GRADE

Recall from Chapter 10 ("Social Stratification") that arranged marriage is a pattern associated with caste systems. A greater emphasis on love and personal choice in mate selection arises in class systems.

homogamy (p. 470) marriage between people with the same social characteristics

infidelity (p. 470) sexual activity outside one's marriage

THINKING GLOBALLY

Early to Wed: A Report from Rural India

Sumitra Jogi cries as her wedding is about to begin. Are they tears of joy? Not exactly. This "bride" is an eighteen-month-old squirming in the arms of her mother. The groom? A boy of seven.

In a remote, rural village in India's western state of Rajasthan, two families gather at midnight to celebrate a traditional wedding ritual. It is May 2, in Hindu tradition an especially good day to marry. Sumitra's father smiles as the ceremony begins; her mother cradles the infant, who has fallen asleep. The groom, dressed in a special costume with a red and gold turban on his head, gently reaches up and grasps the baby's hand. Then, as the ceremony reaches its conclusion, the young boy leads the child and mother around the wedding fire three-and-one-half times as the audience beams at the couple's first steps together as husband and wife.

Child weddings are illegal in India, but in the rural regions, traditions are strong and marriage laws are hard to enforce. As a result, thousands of children marry each year. "In rural Rajasthan," explains one social welfare worker, "all the girls are married by age fourteen. These are poor, illiterate families, and they don't want to keep girls past their first menstrual cycle."

For the immediate future, Sumitra Jogi will remain with her parents. But in eight or ten years, a second ceremony will send her to live

The eighteen-month-old girl on the left is breastfeeding during her wedding ceremony in a small village in the state of Rajasthan, India; her new husband is seven years old. Although outlawed, such arranged marriages involving children are still known to take place in traditional, remote areas of India.

with her husband's family, and her married life will begin.

If the responsibilities of marriage lie years in the future, why do families push their children to marry at such an early age? Parents of girls know that the younger the bride, the smaller the dowry offered to the groom's family. Then, too, when girls marry this young, there is no question about their virginity, which raises their value on the marriage market. Arranged marriages are an alliance between families. No one thinks about love or the fact that the children are too young to understand what is taking place (J. W. Anderson, 1995).

WHAT DO YOU THINK?

1. Why are arranged marriages common in very traditional regions?

2. List several advantages and disadvantages of arranged marriages from the point of view of the families involved.

3. Can you point to ways in which mate selection in the United States is "arranged" by society?

---

young. A century ago in Sri Lanka and India, for example, half of all girls married before reaching age fifteen (Mayo, 1927; Mace & Mace, 1960). As the Thinking Globally box explains, child marriage is still found in some parts of the world today.

Because traditional societies are more culturally homogeneous, almost all young men and women have been well socialized to be good spouses. Therefore, parents can arrange marriages with little thought about whether or not the two individuals involved are *personally* compatible because they know that the partners will be *culturally* compatible.

Industrialization both erodes the importance of extended families and weakens tradition. As young people begin the process of choosing their own mate, dating sharpens courtship skills and allows sexual experimentation. Marriage is delayed until young people complete their schooling, build the financial security needed to live apart from their parents, and gain the experience needed to select a suitable partner.

Romantic Love

Our culture celebrates *romantic love*—affection and sexual passion for another person—as the basis for marriage. We find it hard to imagine marriage without love, and popular culture—from fairy tales like "Cinderella" to today's television sitcoms and dramas—portrays love as the key to a successful marriage.

Our society's emphasis on romance motivates young people to "leave the nest" to form new families of their own, and physical passion can help a new couple through the often difficult adjustments of living together (W. J. Goode, 1959). On the other hand, because feelings change over time, romantic love is a less stable foundation for marriage than social and economic considerations, which is one reason that the divorce rate is much higher in the United States than in nations in which culture is a stronger guide in the choice of a partner.

DISCUSS: Distinguish homogamy (marriage between partners of similar background) from endogamy (marriage within some specific category).

NOTE: In a society with a high divorce rate, people sometimes refer to first marriages at a young age (lasting no more than five years and producing no children) as "starter marriages."

Q: "Marriage is the beginning and the pinnacle of all culture. It makes the savage gentle." Johann Wolfgang von Goethe

Q: "Love makes time pass, and time makes love pass." French saying

Q: "Marriage changes passion: Suddenly you're in bed with a relative." Anonymous

Seeing SOCIOLOGY in the NEWS

American Dating—Muslim Style

BY TOM A. PETER
April 28, 2008

It was an all-American college moment on the Michigan State University campus in East Lansing: Tosif Khatri was laughing and chatting with two fellow students—both women—as they walked to a local cafe.

But the buzz of Mr. Khatri's cellphone popped the bubble. It was his cousin calling to invoke a bit of the family's old country Indian-Muslim traditions. "Not that it's any of my business or anything like that," the cousin said, "but are you, like, hanging out with girls right now?"

"I said 'Oh, no . . . it's nothing silly or anything like that, it's just for the sake of a student event,'" Khatri recalls.

"Okay. I was just checking," signed off the suspicious cousin.

From an Islamic perspective, Khatri hadn't done anything wrong. He was hanging with two female colleagues to discuss organizational matters for the Muslim Student Association (MSA). But

the line blurs when Khatri admits that the outing was also an excuse to socialize. Many Muslims would even call such a mixed-sex meeting haram, sinful.

. . . Outings like this happen increasingly among American Muslims as they integrate into the United States. Reactions like Khatri's watchful cousin's illustrate the challenge young Muslim men and women face trying to interact, let alone "date."

The careful rules that dictate male-female interaction and courtship quite simply can't be applied in the United States as they are in predominately Muslim countries. What's more, Islamic teachings lay out few undisputable guidelines when it comes to finding and meeting a mate; every Muslim tradition has its own interpretation. So, what an Indian Muslim might find permissible could be off-limits for an Arab Muslim.

The result: U.S. Muslims are pioneering ways to read Muslim rules in ways that make sense in an American context.

While Muslim courtship rules vary around the globe—from arranged marriages (possibly never

seeing your partner's face before the wedding night) to looser versions (spending time with each other in the company of family)—most Muslims would agree that a guy and a girl going out alone doesn't fly. A popular Hadith, or saying of the prophet Muhammad, warns that when an unwed man and woman are left alone, Satan is the third person in the room.

When Sofia Begg-Latif, the daughter of Indian immigrants, first met Farhan Latif, a Pakistani-American, the two were officers of University of Michigan at Dearborn's MSA. Often MSA leaders spent late nights together organizing events, and as will happen, the longer they worked, the less they talked about work. . . .

When it became clear that both wanted more than a working relationship, Latif couldn't respectably just ask Begg-Latif out for dinner and a movie. Instead, he told her that he'd like to speak with her parents for permission to court. She agreed, and they began a traditional courtship in the presence of their families, never spending time alone or kissing until they were married. . . .

But even in our country, sociologists point out, society aims Cupid's arrow more than we like to think. Most people fall in love with others of the same race, of comparable age, and of similar social class. Our society "arranges" marriages by encouraging **homogamy** (literally, "like marrying like"), *marriage between people with the same social characteristics.*

The extent of homogamy is greater for some categories of our population (such as younger people and immigrants from traditional societies) than for others (older people and those who do not live according to strict traditions). Seeing Sociology in the News describes courtship patterns among young Muslims on the campuses of U.S. colleges and universities.

Settling In: Ideal and Real Marriage

Our culture gives the young an idealized, "happily ever after" picture of marriage. Such optimism can lead to disappointment, especially for women, who are taught to view marriage as the key to personal happiness. Also, romantic love involves a good deal of fantasy: We fall in love with others not always as they are but as we want them to be.

Sexuality, too, can be a source of disappointment. In the romantic haze of falling in love, people may see marriage as an endless sexual honeymoon, only to face the sobering realization that sex becomes a less-than-all-consuming passion. Although the frequency of marital sex does decline over time, about two in three married people report that they are satisfied with the sexual dimension of their relationship.

In general, couples with the best sexual relationships experience the most satisfaction in their marriages. Sex may not be the key to marital bliss, but more often than not, good sex and good relationships usually go together (Laumann et al., 1994; T. W. Smith, 2006).

Infidelity—*sexual activity outside one's marriage*—is another area where the reality of marriage does not match our cultural ideal. In a recent survey, 91 percent of U.S. adults said sex outside of marriage is "always wrong" or "almost always wrong." Even so, 16 percent of men and 13 percent of women indicated on a private, written questionnaire that they had been sexually unfaithful to their partners at least once (NORC, 2007:298, 1877).

Child Rearing

Despite the demands children make on us, adults in this country overwhelmingly identify raising children as one of life's greatest joys. Today, about half of U.S. adults say that two children is the ideal number, and few people want more than three (NORC, 2007:294, 574). This is a change from two centuries ago, when *eight* children was the average.

Big families pay off in preindustrial societies because children supply needed labor. People therefore regard having children as a wife's duty, and without effective birth control, childbearing is a regular event. Of course, a high death rate in preindustrial societies prevents many children from reaching adulthood; as late as 1900, one-third of children born in the United States died by age ten.

Q: "We think of ourselves as a nation that cherishes its children, but, in fact, America treats its children like excess baggage. Our tax code offers greater incentives for breeding horses than for raising children. We slash school budgets and deny working parents the right to spend even a few weeks with their newborns. We spend 23% of the federal budget on the elderly but less than 5% on children." Sylvia Ann Hewlett

NOTE: The share of latchkey children rises with age, the number of hours a mother works, and parental income.

NOTE: One study estimated that the employer costs of child care have a significant effect on the employment rate of women with young children; providing more child care, in short, would cut some jobs (see Han & Waldfogel, 2001).

While the romantic attraction that provided the initial sparks may help them blend into the American cultural landscape, there's a negative stigma in the Muslim community that they married for love.

"People always say, 'Was it a love marriage or an arranged marriage?' " says Begg-Latif. . . .

Just as the MSA provided a key social forum for the Latifs to negotiate their love connection, it has proved such a successful Muslim matchmaker that it's been nicknamed the "Matrimonial Student Association." It provides a place for single Muslims to meet without getting too personal and it's always under the safety net of working toward Islamic goals. On many university campuses, MSA members like Khatri ruffle conservatives' feathers by going out for group dinners or social outings after meetings.

While these informal meetings happen, the concept of dating for fun simply does not exist in Islam. Any potential match is judged, pursued, or abandoned based on marriage potential.

In the United States, however, many Muslims—especially Arabs—have re-interpreted parts of the courtship process to allow for something closer to the American way.

"I think it's widely accepted now among Muslims in America that things are not the same as they were in their country of origin, whether it's Sudan, Pakistan, or Egypt," says Imam Mohamed Magid, the executive director of the All Dulles Area Muslim Society in Sterling, Va. . . .

Hanaa Soltan, a newlywed in her late 20s, is grateful for the new dating flexibility. Her family allowed her to take advantage of nikah, an old tradition that allows something close to American dating. Under Islamic law, nikah is a legal marriage that entitles couples to all the privileges of marriage. In practice, most using a nikah remain chaste until their wedding night. If the couple decides to break up during the nikah, there's far less stigma than getting divorced after the marriage ceremony. . . .

For Soltan, a nikah allowed her to spend time alone with her fiancé. . . . They could go out to dinner alone and Soltan could even remove her veil in front of her husband-to-be.

"We have our religious beliefs and we have Arab culture to a certain extent, but at the end of the day we're all born and raised here . . . and you don't have to stick to what your parents did," says Soltan, who's now happily married.

WHAT DO YOU THINK?

1. How does leaving one country to live in another raise problems concerning proper behavior involving dating and other activities?

2. How do campus religious and cultural organizations in the United States help many young people from traditional societies engage in courtship that meets traditional standards?

3. From a sociological point of view, why do traditional societies try to control the dating behavior of young people? Why do less traditional societies (such as the United States) give young people more dating freedom?

By Tom A. Peter. Reproduced with permission from the April 28, 2008, issue of *The Christian Science Monitor* (www.csmonitor.com). © 2008 The Christian Science Monitor. All rights reserved.

Economically speaking, industrialization transforms children from an asset to a liability. It now costs almost $300,000 to raise one child, including college tuition (Lino, 2008). No wonder the average size of the U.S. family dropped steadily during the twentieth century to one child per family![2]

The trend toward smaller families is most evident in high-income nations. The picture differs in low-income countries in Latin America, Asia, and especially Africa, where many women have few alternatives to bearing children. In such societies, as a glance back at Global Map 1–1 on page 4 shows, between four and six children is still the norm.

Parenting is a very expensive, lifelong commitment. As our society has given people greater choices about family life, more U.S. adults have decided to delay childbirth or to remain childless. In 1960, almost 90 percent of women between twenty-five and twenty-nine who had ever married had at least one child; today, this proportion is just 69 percent (U.S. Census Bureau, 2008).

No one doubts that almost all parents care deeply about their children, but about two-thirds of parents in the United States say they don't have enough time to spend with their kids (K. Clark, 2002; Cohn, 2007). But unless we accept a lower standard of living, economic realities demand that most parents pursue careers outside the home, even if that means devoting less time to their children. For many families, including the Yniguez family described in the opening to this chapter, having fewer children is an important step toward resolving the tension between work and parenting (Gilbert, 2005).

Children of working parents spend most of the day at school. But after school, some 5.6 million children (14 percent of five- to fourteen-year-olds) are *latchkey kids* who are left to fend for themselves (U. S. Census Bureau, 2008). Traditionalists in the "family values" debate charge that many mothers work at the expense of their children, who receive less parenting. Progressives counter that such criticism targets women for wanting the same opportunities men have long enjoyed.

Congress took a step toward easing the conflict between family and job responsibilities by passing the Family and Medical Leave Act in 1993. This law allows up to ninety days of unpaid leave from work to care for a new child or to deal with a serious family emergency. Still, most adults in this country have to juggle parental and job responsibilities. When parents work, who cares for the kids? The Seeing Sociology in Everyday Life box on page 473 provides the answer.

The Family in Later Life

Increasing life expectancy in the United States means that couples who remain married will stay together for a long time. By about age

---

[2]According to the U.S. Census Bureau, the median number of children per family was 0.93 in 2007. Among all families, the medians were 0.80 for whites, 1.22 for African Americans, and 1.40 for Hispanics.

● SEEING SOCIOLOGY
in Everyday Life

Have other family members paid for any of your schooling?

● SEEING SOCIOLOGY
in Everyday Life

After the death of a spouse, men are more likely than women to remarry. Can you explain why?

"Son, you're all grown up now. You owe me two hundred and fourteen thousand dollars."

sixty, most have finished the task of raising children. At this point, marriage brings a return to living with only a spouse.

Like the birth of children, their departure—creating an "empty nest"—requires adjustments, although a marriage often becomes closer and more satisfying. Years of living together may have less-ened a couple's sexual passion, but understanding and commitment often increase.

Personal contact with children usually continues because most older adults live a short distance from at least one of their children. One-third of all U.S. adults (56 million) are grandparents. Most grandparents help with child care and other responsibilities. Among African Americans, who have a high rate of single parenting, grand-mothers have an especially important position in family life (U.S. Census Bureau, 2006; AARP Foundation, 2007).

The other side of the coin is that more adults in midlife now care for aging parents. The empty nest may not be filled by a parent coming to live in the home, but many adults find that caring for par-ents, who now live to eighty, ninety, and beyond, can be as taxing as raising young children. The oldest of the baby boomers—now past

sixty—are called the "sandwich generation" because many (especially women) will spend as many years caring for their aging parents as they did caring for their children (Lund, 1993).

The final and surely the most difficult transition in married life comes with the death of a spouse. Wives typically outlive their hus-bands because of their greater life expectancy and the fact that women usually marry men several years older than themselves. Wives can thus expect to spend some years as widows. The challenge of living alone following the death of a spouse is especially great for men, who usu-ally have fewer friends than widows and may lack housekeeping skills.

U.S. Families: Class, Race, and Gender

Dimensions of inequality—social class, ethnicity and race, and gender—are powerful forces that shape marriage and family life. This discussion addresses each factor in turn, but bear in mind that they overlap in our lives.

Social Class

Social class determines both a family's financial security and its range of opportunities. Interviewing working-class women, Lillian Rubin (1976) found that wives thought a good husband was one who held a steady job, did not drink too much, and was not violent. Rubin's middle-class respondents, by contrast, never mentioned such things; these women simply *assumed* that a husband would provide a safe and secure home. Their ideal husband was someone they could talk to easily, sharing feelings and experiences.

Clearly, what women (and men) think they can hope for in mar-riage—and what they end up with—is linked to their social class. Much the same holds for children; boys and girls lucky enough to be born into more affluent families enjoy better mental and physical health, develop more self-confidence, and go on to greater achieve-ment than children born to poor parents (McLeod & Shanahan, 1993; Duncan et al., 1998).

Ethnicity and Race

As Chapter 14 ("Race and Ethnicity") discusses, ethnicity and race are powerful social forces that can affect family life. Keep in mind, however, that American Indian, Latino, and African American fami-lies (like all families) do not fit any single generalization or stereo-type (Allen, 1995).

American Indian Families

American Indians display a wide variety of family types. Some pat-terns emerge, however, among people who migrate from tribal reser-

MAKING THE GRADE

Remember that family patterns for American Indians, Latinos, or any other racial or ethnic category vary by social class and that the experiences of family life may also differ for women and men.

SEEING SOCIOLOGY
in Everyday Life

Looking at the figure below, which arrangement for child care do you prefer? Why?

SEEING SOCIOLOGY IN EVERYDAY LIFE

Who's Minding the Kids?

Traditionally, the task of providing daily care for young children fell to stay-at-home mothers. But with a majority of mothers and fathers now in the labor force, finding quality, affordable child care is a high priority for parents.

The figure shows the various arrangements reported by working mothers to care for children under the age of five. Half of these children receive care at home from a parent (23 percent) or a relative (27 percent). Of the remaining half of these children, 25 percent attend preschool or a day care program, 9 percent are cared for in a nonrelative's home, 8 percent are cared for in their own home by a nanny or babysitter, and 8 percent have no regular arrangement (U.S. Census Bureau, 2008).

The use of day care programs has doubled over the past decade because many parents cannot find affordable in-home care for their children. Some day

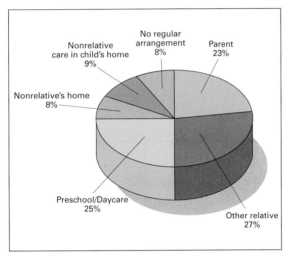

Working mothers report that a majority of their young children receive care in the home.

care centers are so big that they amount to "tot lots" where parents "park" their children for the day. The impersonality of such settings and the rapid turnover in staff prevent the warm and consistent nurturing that young children need to develop a sense of trust. But other child care centers offer a secure and healthful environment. Research suggests that *good* care centers are good for children; *bad* facilities are not.

WHAT DO YOU THINK?

1. Why do so many parents have trouble finding affordable child care? Should employers do more?

2. As parents, would you and your partner be willing to limit your working hours to allow child care at home? Why or why not?

3. How can parents assess the quality of a child care center? What should they look for?

---

vations to cities. Women and men who arrive in cities often seek out others—especially kin and members of the same tribe—for help getting settled. One study, for example, tells the story of two women migrants to the San Francisco area who met at a meeting of an Indian organization and realized that they were of the same tribe. The women and their children decided to share an apartment, and soon after, the children began to refer to one another as brothers, sisters, and cousins. As the months passed, the two mothers came to think of themselves as sisters (Lobo, 2002).

Migration also creates many "fluid households" with changing membership. In another case from the same research, a large apartment in San Francisco was rented by a woman, her aunt, and their children. Over the course of the next month, however, they welcomed into their home more than thirty other urban migrants, who stayed for a short time until they found housing of their own. Such patterns of mutual assistance, often involving real and fictional kinship, are common among all low-income people.

American Indians who leave tribal reservations for the cities are typically better off than those who stay behind. Because people on

reservations have a hard time finding work, they cannot easily form stable marriages, and problems such as alcoholism and drug abuse can shatter the ties between parent and child.

Latino Families

Many Latinos enjoy the loyalty and support of extended families. Traditionally, too, Latino parents exercise considerable control over children's courtship, considering marriage an alliance of families, not just a union based on romantic love. Some Latino families also follow conventional gender roles, encouraging *machismo*—strength, daring, and sexual conquest—among men and treating women with respect but also close supervision.

However, assimilation into the larger society is changing these traditional patterns. As the story opening this chapter explained, many women who come to California from Mexico favor smaller families. Similarly, many Puerto Ricans who migrate to New York do not maintain the strong extended family ties they knew in Puerto Rico. Traditional male authority over women has also lessened, especially among affluent Latino families, whose number has tripled in

DIVERSITY: The Census Bureau reports that in 2007, 61% of the 11.3 million African American children under 18 lived with only one parent. Those families with a woman heading the household (almost all of them) had a median income of $24,328, 39% of the comparable figure for black married-couple families ($62,163).

DIVERSITY: One-parent African American families represent more than half the total but receive only one-third of all black family income.

THEN AND NOW: African American households with female heads: *1940*, 18%; *2005*, 45%; two-parent households: *1940*, 77%; *2007*, 49%. Percentage of African American children residing with both parents: *1960*, 75%; *2007*, 39% (U.S. Census Bureau, 2008).

● SEEING SOCIOLOGY
in Everyday Life

Surveys report that most U.S. teens now claim they have dated someone of another race. Do you think the proportion of mixed-race marriages will rise in the next twenty years? Why or why not?

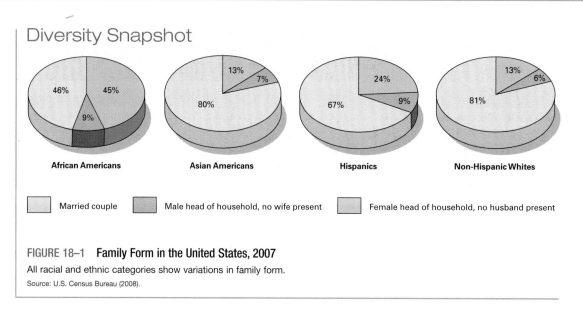

Diversity Snapshot

FIGURE 18–1   **Family Form in the United States, 2007**

All racial and ethnic categories show variations in family form.

Source: U.S. Census Bureau (2008).

the past twenty years (Lach, 1999; Navarro, 2004; Raley, Durden, & Wildsmith, 2004).

Overall, however, the typical Hispanic family had an income of $40,566 in 2007, or 66 percent of the national average (U.S. Census Bureau, 2008). Many Hispanic families suffer the stress of unemployment and other poverty-related problems.

African American Families

African American families face economic disadvantages: The typical African American family earned $40,143 in 2007, which was 65 percent of the national average. People of African ancestry are three times as likely as non-Hispanic whites to be poor, and poverty means that both parents and children are likely to experience unemployment, substandard housing, and poor health.

Under these circumstances, maintaining a stable marriage is difficult. Consider that 29 percent of African American women in their forties have never married, compared to about 9 percent of white women of the same age. This means that African American women—often with children—are more likely to be single heads of households. Figure 18–1 shows that women headed 45 percent of all African American families in 2007, compared to 24 percent of Hispanic families, 13 percent of non-Hispanic white families, and 13 percent of Asian or Pacific Islander families (U.S. Census Bureau, 2008).

Regardless of race, single-mother families are always at high risk of poverty. Twenty-one percent of single families headed by non-Hispanic white women are poor. Higher yet, the poverty rate among families headed by African American women (37 percent) and His-panic women (38 percent) is strong evidence of how the intersec-tion of class, race, and gender can put women at a disadvantage. African American families with both wife and husband in the home, which represent 46 percent of the total, are much stronger economically, earning 80 percent as much as comparable non-Hispanic white families. But 70 percent of African American children are born to single women, and 35 percent of African American boys and girls are growing up poor today, meaning that these families carry much of the burden of child poverty in the United States (U.S. Census Bureau, 2008; Martin et al., 2009).

Ethnically and Racially Mixed Marriages

Most spouses have similar social backgrounds with regard to class and race. But over the course of the twentieth century, when it came to choosing a marriage partner, ethnicity came to matter less and less. In recent decades, for example, a woman of German and French ancestry might readily marry a man of Irish and English background without inviting any particular reaction from their families or from society in general.

Even so, race remains a powerful factor in mate selection. Before a 1967 Supreme Court decision (*Loving* v. *Virginia*), interracial marriage was actually illegal in sixteen states. Today, African, Asian, and Native Americans represent 18 percent of the U.S. population; if people ignored race in choosing spouses, we would expect about the same share of marriages to be mixed. The actual proportion of mixed marriages is 4 percent, showing that race remains important in social relations. But most people claim that race and ethnicity should not matter in choosing a partner. In addition, the age at first marriage has been rising to an average of 27.5 for men and 25.6 for women. Young people who marry when they are older are more likely to make

NOTE: Racially mixed marriages are most common in urban areas. In addition, the West Coast (especially California) has the greatest number of racially mixed marriages, reflecting both high minority populations and a relatively tolerant culture.

DIVERSITY: In 2007, there were 2,336,000 interracial couples and 4,306,000 interracial/Hispanic couples, up from 651,000 in 1980. About 5% of U.S. births are children of mixed race (U.S. Census Bureau, 2009).

DISCUSS: States vary sharply, from banning interracial adoption to promoting it. The National Association of Black Social Workers encourages the placement of children first with biological parents, then in "community of origin," then with others (of another race). About 40% of adopted children are African American.

DISCUSS: What are some of the effects of the high rate of intermarriage among ethnic categories on U.S. cultural diversity?

● SEEING SOCIOLOGY
in Everyday Life

Given the high level of divorce in the United States, do you think it would be more accurate to call our marriage system "serial monogamy" (one partner after another)? Explain.

choices about partners with less input from parents. One consequence of this increasing freedom of choice is that the share of ethnically and racially mixed marriages is increasing (Rosenfeld & Kim, 2005; U.S. Census Bureau, 2008).

The most common type of "mixed" couple includes one partner who is Hispanic (the largest racial or ethnic minority category) and one who is not, but today's couples include just about every imaginable combination. In about half of all "mixed" marriages, one or both partners claim to have a multiracial or multiethnic identity. Such couples are likely to live in the West; in five states—Hawaii, Alaska, California, Nevada, and Oklahoma—more than 10 percent of all married couples are interracial (Lee & Edmonston, 2005; U.S. Census Bureau, 2008).

Gender

The sociologist Jessie Bernard (1982) claimed that every marriage is actually two different relationships: the woman's marriage and the man's marriage. The reason is that few marriages have two equal partners. Although patriarchy has weakened, most people still expect husbands to be older and taller than their wives and to have more important, better-paid jobs.

Why, then, do many people think that marriage benefits women more than men? The positive stereotype of the carefree bachelor contrasts sharply with the negative image of the lonely spinster, suggesting that women are fulfilled only through being wives and mothers.

However, Bernard claimed, married women actually have poorer mental health, less happiness, and more passive attitudes toward life than single women. Married men, on the other hand, generally live longer, are mentally better off, and report being happier overall than single men. These differences suggest why, after divorce, men are more eager than women to find a new partner.

Bernard concluded that there is no better assurance of long life, health, and happiness for a man than a woman well socialized to devote her life to taking care of him and providing the security of a well-ordered home. She is quick to add that marriage *could* be healthful for women if husbands did not dominate wives and expect them to do almost all the housework. Survey responses confirm that couples rank "sharing household chores" as among the most important factors that contribute to a successful marriage (Pew Research Center, 2007a).

Transitions and Problems in Family Life

The newspaper columnist Ann Landers once remarked that one marriage in twenty is wonderful, five in twenty are good, ten in twenty are tolerable, and the remaining four are "pure hell." Families can be a source of joy, but for some, the reality falls far short of the ideal.

For most of our nation's history, interracial marriage was illegal. Although the last of these laws was struck down forty years ago, race and ethnicity continue to guide the process of courtship and marriage. Even so, interracial relationships are becoming more and more common.

Divorce

U.S. society strongly supports marriage, and about nine out of ten people at some point "tie the knot." But many of today's marriages unravel. Figure 18–2 on page 476 shows the tenfold increase in the U.S. divorce rate over the past century. By 2007, almost four marriages in ten were eventually ending in divorce (for African Americans, the rate was about six in ten). From another angle, of all people over the age of fifteen, 21 percent of men and 23 percent of women have been divorced at some point. Ours is the highest divorce rate in the world; it is more than $1\frac{1}{2}$ times as high as in Canada and Japan and more than four times higher than in Italy and Ireland (European Union, 2009).

The high U.S. divorce rate has many causes (Furstenberg & Cherlin, 1991; Etzioni, 1993; Popenoe, 1999; Greenspan, 2001):

1. **Individualism is on the rise**. Today's family members spend less time together. We have become more individualistic and more concerned about personal happiness and earning income than about the well-being of our partners and children.

A century ago, many people regarded divorce as a mark of personal failure.

The divorce rate rose during World War II, when many couples were separated for long periods of time.

● SEEING SOCIOLOGY
in Everyday Life

Reading about "who divorces," point to ways in which society shapes individual choice.

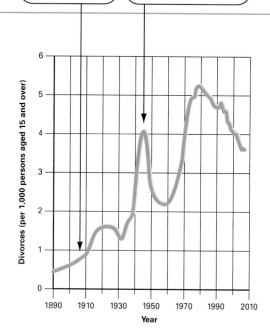

FIGURE 18–2 Divorce Rate for the United States, 1890–2007

Over the long term, the U.S. divorce rate has gone up. Since about 1980, however, the trend has been downward.

Source: U.S. Census Bureau (2009).

2. **Romantic love fades**. Because our culture bases marriage on romantic love, relationships may fail as sexual passion fades. Many people end a marriage in favor of a new relationship that promises renewed excitement and romance.

3. **Women are less dependent on men**. Women's increasing participation in the labor force has reduced wives' financial dependence on husbands. Therefore, women find it easier to leave unhappy marriages.

4. **Many of today's marriages are stressful**. With both partners working outside the home in most cases, jobs leave less time and energy for family life. This makes raising children harder than ever. Children do stabilize some marriages, but divorce is most common during the early years of marriage, when many couples have young children.

5. **Divorce has become socially acceptable**. Divorce no longer carries the powerful stigma it did several generations ago. Family and friends are now less likely to discourage couples in conflict from divorcing.

6. **Legally, a divorce is easier to get**. In the past, courts required divorcing couples to show that one or both were guilty of

behavior such as adultery or physical abuse. Today, all states allow divorce if a couple simply declares that the marriage has failed. Concern about easy divorces, shared by more than half of U.S. adults, has led some states to consider rewriting their marriage laws (Phillips, 2001; NORC, 2007).

Who Divorces?

At greatest risk of divorce are young spouses—especially those who marry after a brief courtship—who lack money and emotional maturity. The chance of divorce also rises if the couple marries after an unexpected pregnancy or if one or both partners have substance abuse problems. People whose parents divorced also have a higher divorce rate themselves. Researchers suggest that a role-modeling effect is at work: Children who see parents go through divorce are more likely to consider divorce themselves (Amato, 2001). Finally, people who are not religious are more likely to divorce than those who have strong religious beliefs (Amato, 2001; Pew Research Center, 2008).

Divorce is also more common when both partners have successful careers, perhaps because of the strains of a two-career marriage but also because financially secure people do not feel that they have to remain in an unhappy home. Finally, men and women who divorce once are more likely to divorce again, probably because high-risk factors follow them from one marriage to another (Glenn & Shelton, 1985).

Divorce and Children

Because mothers usually gain custody of children but fathers typically earn more income, the well-being of children often depends on fathers' making court-ordered child support payments. As Figure 18–3 indicates, courts award child support in 57 percent of all divorces involving children. Yet in any given year, almost half the children legally entitled to support receive only partial payments or no payments at all. Some 3.2 million "deadbeat dads" fail to support their youngsters. In response, federal legislation now mandates that employers withhold money from the earnings of fathers or mothers who fail to pay up; it is a serious crime to refuse to make child support payments or to move to another state to avoid making them (U.S. Census Bureau, 2008).

The effects of divorce on children go beyond financial support. Divorce can tear young people from familiar surroundings, entangle them in bitter feuding, and distance them from a parent they love. Most serious of all, many children blame themselves for their parents' breakup. Divorce changes the course of many children's lives, causing emotional and behavioral problems and raising the risk of dropping out of school and getting into trouble with the law. Many experts counter that divorce is better for children than staying in a family torn by tension and violence. In any case, parents should remember that if they consider divorce, more than their own well-being is at stake (Wallerstein & Blakeslee, 1989; Amato & Sobolewski, 2001).

GLOBAL: Divorce rates for selected countries (2007; per 1,000 people aged 15–64 years): U.S., 3.6; Japan, 2.2; Canada, 2.2; Ireland, 0.8; Italy 0.8 (OECD, 2009).

THEN AND NOW: Divorces per 1,000 people: *1970*, 3.5; *2007*, 3.6. Share of 30- to 34-year-old women not married: *1970*, 6.2%; *2006*, 25%. Share of 30- to 34-year-old women who have not had a child: *1970*, 8.3%; *2006*, 26.2%.

NOTE: First marriages have a median duration of about eight years; second marriages typically last eight years as well.

DISCUSS: The complexity of family violence is that it mixes economic dependency, trust, emotional ties, history, and children with physical conflict. The answers to the question "Why does she go back?" are easier to understand in this broader context.

● SEEING SOCIOLOGY
in Everyday Life

A girl who has been an only child becomes part of a "blended family" and suddenly has two older brothers. What adjustments might she have to make?

family violence   emotional, physical, or sexual abuse of one family member by another

Remarriage and Blended Families

Four out of five people who divorce remarry, most within four years. Nationwide, more than one-third of all new marriages are now remarriages for at least one partner. Men, who benefit more from wedlock, are more likely than women to remarry (U.S. Census Bureau, 2008).

Remarriage often creates *blended families,* composed of children and some combination of biological parents and stepparents. With brothers, sisters, half-siblings, a stepparent—not to mention a biological parent who may live elsewhere and be married to someone else with other children—young people in blended families face the challenge of defining many new relationships and deciding just who is part of the nuclear family. Parents often have trouble defining responsibilities for household work among people unsure of their relationships to each other. When the custody of children is an issue, exspouses can be an unwelcome presence for people in a new marriage. Although blended families require that members adjust to their new circumstances, they offer both young and old the chance to relax rigid family roles (Furstenberg & Cherlin, 2001; McLanahan, 2002).

Family Violence

The ideal family is a source of pleasure and support. However, the disturbing reality of many homes is **family violence**, *emotional, physical, or sexual abuse of one family member by another*. With the exception of the police and the military, says the sociologist Richard J. Gelles, the family is "the most violent group in society" (quoted in Roesch, 1984:75).

Violence against Women

Family brutality often goes unreported to police. Even so, the U.S. Department of Justice (2008) estimates that about 700,000 adults are victims of domestic violence each year. Of this total, 73 percent of cases involve violence against women, and the remaining 27 percent involve violence against men. Fully 33 percent of women who are victims of homicide (but just 3 percent of men) are killed by spouses, partners, or ex-partners. Nationwide, the death toll from family violence is about 1,400 women each year. Overall, women are more likely to be injured by a family member than to be mugged or raped by a stranger or hurt in an automobile accident (Shupe, Stacey, & Hazlewood, 1987; Blankenhorn, 1995; U.S. Department of Justice, 2008).

Historically, the law defined wives as the property of their husbands, so no man could be charged with raping his wife. Today, however, all states have enacted *marital rape laws.* The law no longer regards domestic violence as a private family matter; it gives victims more options. Now, even without a formal separation or divorce, a woman can obtain court protection from an abusive spouse, and all states have "stalking laws" that forbid one ex-partner from following or otherwise threatening the other. Communities across the United

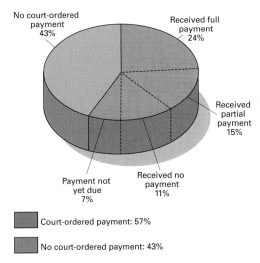

FIGURE 18–3   Payment of Child Support after Divorce

In almost half of all cases of court-ordered child support, the full payment is never received.

Source: U.S. Census Bureau (2008).

States have established shelters to provide counseling and temporary housing for women and children driven from their homes by domestic violence.

Finally, the harm caused by domestic violence goes beyond the physical injuries. Victims often lose their ability to trust others. One study found that women who had been physically or sexually abused were much less likely than nonvictims to form stable relationships later on (Cherlin et al., 2004).

Violence against Children

Family violence also victimizes children. Each year, there are more than 3 million reports of alleged child abuse or neglect, about 1,500 of them involving a child's death. Child abuse entails more than physical injury; abusive adults misuse power and trust to damage a child's emotional well-being. Child abuse and neglect are most common among the youngest and most vulnerable children (Besharov & Laumann, 1996; U.S. Department of Health and Human Services, 2008).

Although child abusers conform to no simple stereotype, they are more likely to be women (58 percent) than men (42 percent). But almost all abusers share one trait—having been abused themselves as children. Research shows that violent behavior in close relationships is learned; in families, violence begets violence (S. Levine, 2001; U.S. Department of Health and Human Services, 2008).

Families   CHAPTER 18

477

NOTE: Alan Booth and James Dabbs (1992) investigated records of 4,500 male veterans held by the Centers for Disease Control and Prevention and found that those with relatively high levels of testosterone were 50% less likely to marry than men in the relatively low category. The high-testosterone men who married were 43% more likely to divorce, 38% more likely to have extramarital sex, and 12% more likely to abuse their wives.

NOTE: A Census Bureau study of the U.S. poor in 2000 found that 30.7% of people in female-headed households were poor vs. 5.8% of people in married-couple households. Of the chronic poor—people poor all year long—only 1.4% lived in married-couple households. Thus one of the clearest predictors of whether a child will live in poverty is the marital status of the child's parents.

SEEING SOCIOLOGY
in Everyday Life

In what ways do children benefit from growing up in a household with both biological parents?

cohabitation   the sharing of a household by an unmarried couple

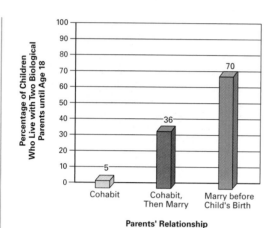

FIGURE 18–4   **Parental Involvement in Children's Lives: Cohabiting and Married Parents**

Marriage increases the odds that children will remain in the same household with both biological parents as they grow up.

Source: Phillips (2001).

Alternative Family Forms

Most families in the United States are composed of a married couple who raise children. But in recent decades, our society has displayed increasing diversity in family life.

One-Parent Families

Twenty-nine percent of U.S. families with children under eighteen have only one parent in the household, a proportion that more than doubled during the last generation. Put another way, 26 percent of U.S. children now live with only one parent, and almost half will do so before reaching eighteen. One-parent families, 85 percent of which are headed by a single mother, result from divorce, death, or an unmarried woman's decision to have a child (U.S. Census Bureau, 2008).

Single parenthood increases a woman's risk of poverty because it limits her ability to work and to further her education. The opposite is also true: Poverty raises the odds that a young woman will become a single mother. But single parenthood goes well beyond the poor: One-third of women in the United States become pregnant as teenagers, and many decide to raise their children whether they marry or not. Even more important, the number of unmarried women in their twenties, thirties, and forties who decide to have a child is increasing (Pew Research Center, 2007a; Martin et al., 2009).

Looking back at Figure 18–1 on page 474, note that 54 percent of African American families are headed by a single parent. Single parenting is less common among Hispanics (33 percent), Asian Americans (20 percent), and non-Hispanic whites (19 percent). In many single-parent families, mothers turn to their own mothers for support. In the United States, then, the rise in single parenting is tied to a declining role for fathers and the growing importance of grandparenting.

Research shows that growing up in a one-parent family usually puts children at a disadvantage. Some studies claim that because a father and a mother each make distinctive contributions to a child's social development, one parent has a hard time doing as good a job alone. But the most serious problem for one-parent families, especially if that parent is a woman, is poverty. On average, children growing up in a single-parent family start out poorer, get less schooling, and end up with lower incomes as adults. Such children are also more likely to be single parents themselves (Blankenhorn, 1995; Kantrowitz & Wingert, 2001; McLanahan, 2002; U.S. Census Bureau, 2008).

Cohabitation

Cohabitation is *the sharing of a household by an unmarried couple.* As a long-term form of family life, with or without children, cohabitation is especially common in the Scandinavian countries and gaining popularity in other European nations. In the United States, the number of cohabiting couples increased from about 500,000 in 1970 to more than 6.2 million today (5.5 million heterosexual couples and 750,000 homosexual couples), or about 6 percent of all households. Almost half of all people between twenty-five and forty-four years of age have cohabited at some point (U.S. Census Bureau, 2008).

Cohabiting tends to appeal to more independent-minded individuals as well as those who favor gender equality (Brines & Joyner, 1999). Most couples cohabit for no more than a few years; at that point, about half decide to marry and half split up. Mounting evidence suggests that living together may actually discourage marriage because partners (especially men) become used to low-commitment relationships. For this reason, cohabiting couples who have children—currently representing about one in eight births in the United States—may not always be long-term parents. Figure 18–4 shows that just 5 percent of children born to cohabiting couples will live until age eighteen with both biological parents if the parents remain unmarried. The share rises to 36 percent among children whose parents marry at some point, but even this is half of the 70 percent figure among children whose parents married before they were born. When cohabiting couples with children separate, the involvement of both parents, including financial support, is highly uncertain (Popenoe & Whitehead, 1999; Booth & Crouter, 2002; Scommegna, 2002).

Gay and Lesbian Couples

In 1989, Denmark became the first country to permit registered partnerships with the benefits of marriage for same-sex couples. This change

NOTE: In 2000, about 60% of gay families and 45% of lesbian families lived in the largest 20 U.S. cities, which contained 26% of the overall U.S. population (Bianchi & Casper, 2000).

POP CULTURE: The film and television industries typically depict families in highly diverse forms. The television show *Star Trek: The Next Generation*, for example, had few families and even fewer that might be termed "conventional." See the photo essay on pages 482–83.

GLOBAL: Denmark legalized homosexual activity in 1930. The Danes, Norwegians, and Swedes allow gay and nongay couples equal rights with regard to marriage, inheritance, taxation, and property ownership but not with regard to adoption of children.

● SEEING SOCIOLOGY
in Everyday Life

Have you ever lived with a partner? How does cohabitation differ from marriage?

extended social legitimacy to gay and lesbian couples and equalized advantages in inheritance, taxation, and joint property ownership. Since then, Norway (1993), Sweden (1994), Iceland (1996), Finland (2001), the United Kingdom (2004), and Australia (2008) have followed suit. However, only five countries have extended marriage—in name as well as practice—to same-sex couples: the Netherlands (2001), Belgium (2003), Canada (2005), Spain (2005), and South Africa (2006).

In the United States, Massachusetts became the first state to legalize same-sex marriage in 2004. As of 2009, Iowa, Connecticut, Vermont, New Hampshire, and Maine have also changed their laws to allow same-sex marriage. New Jersey, Oregon, and Washington permit same-sex unions with all the rights of marriage.

Back in 1996, the U.S. Congress passed a law defining marriage as joining one man and one woman. Since then, a total of thirty states have amended their constitutions to permit marriage only between one man and one woman. Nonetheless, the trend in public opinion is toward greater acceptance of same-sex marriage. Currently, about one-third of U.S. adults support gay marriage, and half support civil unions providing same-sex couples with the rights enjoyed by married people (Newport, 2005; NORC, 2007:1643; Leff, 2008).

Most gay couples with children in the United States are raising the offspring of previous heterosexual unions; others have adopted children. But many gay parents are quiet about their sexual orientation, not wishing to draw unwelcome attention to their children or to themselves. In several widely publicized cases, courts have removed children from the custody of homosexual couples, citing a concern for the "best interests" of the children.

Gay parenting challenges many traditional ideas. But it also shows that many gay people value family life as highly as heterosexuals do.

Singlehood

Because nine out of ten people in the United States marry, we tend to view singlehood as a temporary stage of life. However, increasing numbers of people are choosing to live alone. In 1950, only one household in ten contained a single person. By 2007, this share had risen to 27 percent, a total of 31 million single adults (U.S. Census Bureau, 2008).

Most striking is the rising number of single young women. In 1960, 28 percent of U.S. women aged twenty to twenty-four were single; by 2007, the proportion had soared to 76 percent. Underlying this trend is women's greater participation in the labor force. Although most of these women will marry later on, women who are economically secure view a husband as a matter of choice rather than a financial necessity and marry later or, in some cases, not at all (Edwards, 2000).

In 2009, Iowa joined the growing number of states that allow same-sex couples to marry. Some people oppose any same-sex relationships; others support civil unions; still others believe that same-sex marriage should be lawful throughout the United States. Where do you stand on this issue? Why?

By midlife, many unmarried women sense a lack of available men. Because we expect a woman to "marry up," the older a woman is, the more education she has, and the better her job, the more difficulty she has finding a suitable husband.

New Reproductive Technologies and Families

Medical advances involving reproductive technologies are also changing families. In 1978, England's Louise Brown became the world's first "test-tube baby"; since then, tens of thousands of children have been conceived outside the womb.

Test-tube babies are the product of *in vitro fertilization,* in which doctors unite a woman's egg and a man's sperm "in glass" (usually not a test tube but a shallow dish) rather than in a woman's body. Doctors then either implant the resulting embryo in the womb of the woman who is to bear the child or freeze it for implantation at a later time.

Modern reproductive technologies allow some couples who cannot conceive by conventional means to have children. These techniques may also eventually help reduce the incidence of birth defects. Genetic screening of sperm and eggs allows medical specialists to increase the odds of having a healthy baby. But new reproductive technologies also raise difficult and troubling questions: When one woman carries an

Q: "The happiest moments of my life have been the few which I have passed at home in the bosom of my family." Thomas Jefferson

NOTE: Some of the changes in our thinking about family life involve a shift from family *form* to family *function*. Rather than defining the family as a single, traditional form, more people (especially sociologists) seem to be saying, "If it works like a family, it is a family." The Latin root *familia* means simply "household."

Q: "Neither the pessimists who believe that the family is falling apart nor the unbridled optimists who claim that the family has never been in better shape provide an accurate picture of family life in the near future. But . . . what we have come to view as the 'traditional' family will no longer predominate." Andrew Cherlin and Frank F. Furstenberg Jr.

● MAKING THE GRADE

Whatever your view of traditional families, be sure you can point to ways U.S. families have changed since 1960.

CONTROVERSY & DEBATE

Should We Save the Traditional Family?

AARON: My parents were really goin' at each other last night. Man, I don't know whether they're going to stay together.

ABDUL: I hope they do, my friend. Families are what ties society together.

TAWNEESHA: Listen to you guys! The important thing is for each person to be happy. If being married does it for you, great. But there's lots of different ways for people to find happiness.

What are "traditional families"? Are they vital to our way of life or a barrier to progress? People use the term *traditional family* to mean a married man and woman who at some point in their lives raise children. Statistically speaking, traditional families are less common than they used to be. In 1950, as the figure shows, 90 percent of U.S. households were families—using the Census Bureau's definition of two or more persons related by blood, marriage, or adoption. By 2007, just 68 percent of households were families, due to rising levels of divorce, cohabitation, and singlehood.

"Traditional family" is more than just a handy expression; it is also a moral statement. Belief in the traditional family implies giving high value to becoming and staying married, putting children ahead of careers, and favoring two-parent families over various alternatives.

"Traditional Families Are the Solution"

On one side of the debate, David Popenoe (1993a) has warned of a serious erosion of the traditional family since 1960. At that time, married couples with young children accounted for almost half of all households; today, the figure is 23 percent.

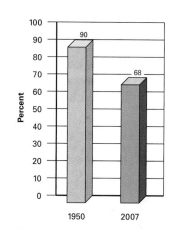

Share of U.S. Households That the Census Bureau Classified as Families, 1950 and 2007

Families were a smaller share of all U.S. households in 2007 compared to 1950.

Singlehood is up, from 10 percent of households in 1960 to 27 percent today. And the divorce rate has risen by 64 percent since 1960, so that nearly four in ten of today's marriages end in permanent separation. Because of both divorce and the increasing number of children born to single women, the share of youngsters who will live with just one parent before age eighteen has almost tripled since 1960 to 26 percent. In other words, just one in four of today's children will grow up with two parents and go on to maintain a stable marriage as an adult (U.S. Census Bureau, 2008).

In light of such data, Popenoe suggests that it may not be an exaggeration to say that the family is falling apart. He sees a fundamental shift from a "culture of marriage" to a "culture of divorce," where traditional vows of marital commitment— "till death do us part"—now amount to little more than "as long as I am happy." The negative consequences of the cultural trend toward weaker families, Popenoe continues, are obvious and can be found everywhere: As we pay less and less attention to children, the crime rate among young people goes up, along with a host of other problem behaviors including underage smoking and drinking, premarital sex, and teen suicide.

As Popenoe sees it, we must work hard and act quickly to reverse current trends. Government cannot be the solution and may even be part of

---

embryo developed from the egg of another, who is the mother? When a couple divorces, which spouse is entitled to use, or destroy, their frozen embryos? Should parents use genetic screening to select the traits of their child? Such questions remind us that technology changes faster than our ability to understand the consequences of its use (A. Cohen, 1998; Nock, Wright, & Sanchez, 1999).

Families: Looking Ahead

Family life in the United States will continue to change in the years to come, and with change comes controversy. Advocates of "traditional family values" line up against those who support greater personal choice; the Controversy & Debate box outlines some of the issues.

Sociologists cannot predict the outcome of this debate, but we can suggest five likely future trends.

First, the divorce rate is likely to remain high, even in the face of evidence that marital breakups harm children. Today's marriages are about as durable as they were a century ago, when many were cut short by death. The difference is that now more couples *choose* to end marriages that fail to live up to their expectations. So even though the divorce rate has declined since 1980, it is unlikely to return to the low rates that marked the early decades of the twentieth century.

Second, family life in the twenty-first century will be more diverse than ever. Cohabiting couples, one-parent families, gay and lesbian families, and blended families are all on the rise. Most families are still based on marriage, and most married couples still have

Q: "As long as the term 'family' is used to cover both the 'real' family and its antithe-sis—the single-parent version—the question of whether a society can do without families is hopelessly obfuscated. Moreover, a challenging thesis is hidden: the thesis that it does not matter which social arrangements adults devise to bring up children." Amitai Etzioni

Q: "Home is the place that, if you have to go there, they have to take you in." Robert Frost

DISCUSS: Child psychiatrist Stanley Greenspan (2001) suggests that parents limit their workweek to four-thirds time—that is, each working two-thirds time, or one working full time and the other one-third time—so that they may devote two-thirds of the working day to their children. Ask students what they think of this idea.

SEEING SOCIOLOGY
in Everyday Life

How important do you think strong families are to the health of our society? What makes a family "strong"?

the problem: Since 1960, as families have weakened, government spending on social programs has soared. To save the traditional family, says Popenoe, we need a cultural turnaround similar to what happened with regard to cigarette smoking. In this case, we must replace our "me first" attitudes with commitment to our spouse and children and publicly endorse the two-parent family as best for the well-being of children.

"Traditional Families Are the Problem"

Judith Stacey (1993) provides a feminist viewpoint, saying "good riddance" to the traditional family. In her view, the traditional family is more problem than solution: "The family is not here to stay. Nor should we wish it were. On the contrary, I believe that all democratic people, whatever their kinship preferences, should work to hasten its demise" (Stacey, 1990:269).

The main reason for rejecting the traditional family, Stacey explains, is that it perpetuates social inequality. Families play a key role in maintaining the class hierarchy by transferring wealth as well as "cultural capital" from one generation to another. Feminists criticize the traditional family's patriarchal form, which subjects women to their husbands' authority and

gives them most of the responsibility for housework and child care. From a gay rights perspective, she adds, a society that values traditional families also denies homosexual men and women equal participation in social life.

Stacey thus applauds the breakdown of the family as social progress. She does not view the family as a necessary social institution but as a political construction that elevates one category of people—affluent white males—above others, including women, homosexuals, and poor people.

Whether the traditional family is a positive force in U.S. society or a negative one depends on your point of view.

Stacey also claims that the concept of the "traditional family" is increasingly irrelevant in a diverse society in which both men and women work for income. What our society needs, Stacey concludes, is not a return to some golden age of the family but political and economic change, including income parity for women, universal health care and child care, programs to reduce unemployment, and expanded sex education in the schools. Such measures not only help families but also ensure that people in diverse family forms receive the respect and dignity they deserve.

WHAT DO YOU THINK?

1. To strengthen families, David Popenoe suggests that parents put children ahead of their own careers by limiting their joint workweek to sixty hours. Do you agree? Why or why not?

2. Judith Stacey thinks that marriage is weaker today because women are rejecting patriarchal relationships. What do you think about this argument?

3. Do we need to change family patterns for the well-being of our children? As you see it, what specific changes are called for?

children. But the diversity of family forms implies a trend toward more personal choice.

Third, men will play a limited role in child rearing. In the 1950s, a decade that many people view as the "golden age" of families, men began to withdraw from active parenting (Snell, 1990; Stacey, 1990). In recent years, a countertrend has become evident, with some older, highly educated men staying at home with young children, many using computer technology to continue their work. But the stay-at-home dad represents no more than 10 percent of fathers with young children (U.S. Census Bureau, 2008). The bigger picture is that the high U.S. divorce rate and the increase in single motherhood are weakening children's ties to fathers and increasing children's risk of poverty.

Fourth, families will continue to feel the effects of economic changes. In many homes today, both household partners work,

reducing marriage and family life to the interaction of weary men and women who must try to fit a little "quality time" with their children into an already full schedule. The long-term effects of the two-career couple on families as we have known them are likely to be mixed.

Fifth and finally, the importance of new reproductive technologies will increase. Ethical concerns about whether what *can* be done *should* be done will slow these developments, but new approaches to reproduction will continue to alter the traditional experience of parenthood.

Despite the changes and controversies that have shaken the family in the United States, most people still report being happy as partners and parents. Marriage and family life are likely to remain foundations of our society for generations to come.

Seeing Sociology in Everyday Life

Chapter 18   Families

How do the mass media portray the family?

Everybody is familiar with the traditional families portrayed in popular 1950s television shows such as *Ozzie Harriet* and *Leave It To Beaver*. Both of these shows had a working father, homemaker mother, and two (wonderful) sons. But, as the images below suggest, today's television shows are not as family-centered.

> **HINT** The general pattern found in the mass media today is certainly different from that common in the 1950s, the so-called "golden age of families." Today's television shows emphasize that careers often leave little time for family (*House*) or that, for a variety of reasons, stable marriages are the exception rather than the rule (all the shows illustrated here). Does Hollywood have an anti-family bias? This is hard to answer; perhaps script writers find that nonconventional family forms make for more interesting stories. In any case, most television shows make clear that people of all ages (well, maybe not Gregory House) are capable of finding and maintaining satisfying relationships, whether or not those relationsips conform to a traditional family form.

The most popular television show of 2009 is *House*, which revolves around a brainy but belligerent physician and his colleagues at an upscale New Jersey hospital. None of the main characters in the show is married; none has children; and none gets along well with parents. Why might this be the case?

Another hit television series is *Gossip Girl*, about a group of young people from well-off families in New York. Other than their wealth, what can you say about the families that these young people come from?

Another popular show is *Two and a Half Men*, in which Charlie Sheen plays a young bachelor who is joined by his twice-divorced brother and his brother's young son. What can you say about the way this show presents family life?

Applying SOCIOLOGY in Everyday Life

1. List your favorite television shows and, in each case, describe the importance the show gives to family life. What family forms are presented in the show? Are families a source of happiness to people or not?

2. Relationships with various family members differ. With which family member—mother, father, brother, sister—do you most readily share confidences? Why? Which family member would you turn to first in a crisis, and why? Who in your family would be the last to know?

3. Parents and grandparents can be a wonderful source of information about changes in marriage and the family. Ask them at what ages they married, what their married lives have been like, and what changes in family life today stand out for them. Compare the answers of two or more relatives. Are they very different?

MAKING THE GRADE

CHAPTER 18 Families

Families: Basic Concepts

All societies are built on *kinship*. The **FAMILY** varies across cultures and over time:

- In industrialized societies such as the United States, *marriage* is monogamous.
- Preindustrial societies recognize the *extended family*; industrialization gives rise to the *nuclear family*.
- Many preindustrial societies permit *polygamy*, of which there are two types: *polygyny* and *polyandry*.
- In global perspective, *patrilocality* is most common, but industrial societies favor *neolocality* and a few societies have *matrilocal residence*.
- Industrial societies use *bilateral descent*; preindustrial societies are either *patrilineal* or *matrilineal*.

pp. 462–66

Theoretical Analysis of Families

The **STRUCTURAL-FUNCTIONAL APPROACH** identifies major family functions that help society operate smoothly:

- socialization of children to help them become well-integrated members of society
- regulation of sexual activity in order to maintain kinship organization and property rights
- giving children a social identity within society in terms of race, ethnicity, religion, and social class
- providing material and emotional support to family members

pp. 466–67

The **SOCIAL-CONFLICT APPROACH** and **FEMINIST APPROACH** point to ways in which families perpetuate social inequality

- Families ensure the continuation of the class structure by passing on wealth to their children.
- Families perpetuate gender roles by establishing men as the heads of the household and by assigning the responsibility for child rearing and housework to women.
- The tendency of people to marry others like themselves supports racial and ethnic hierarchies.

p. 467

The **incest taboo**, which restricts sexual relations between certain relatives, exists in all societies (p. 466).

- The **SYMBOLIC-INTERACTION APPROACH** explores how family members build emotional bonds in the course of everyday family life.
- The **SOCIAL-EXCHANGE APPROACH** sees courtship and marriage as a process of negotiation in which each person weighs the advantages and disadvantages of a potential partner.

p. 468

See the Applying Theory table on page 466.

Stages of Family Life

COURTSHIP AND ROMANTIC LOVE

- Arranged marriages are common in preindustrial societies.
- Courtship based on romantic love is central to mate selection in the United States and leads to the formation of new families.
- The contrast between our culture's idealized vision of marriage and the everyday realities of married life can lead to disappointment and failed marriages.

pp. 468–70

CHILD REARING

- Large families are necessary in preindustrial societies because children are a source of needed labor.
- Family size has decreased over time as industrialization increases the costs of raising children.
- As more women choose to go to school or join the labor force, fewer children are born.
- The "family values" debate revolves around who cares for children when both parents work outside the home.

pp. 470–71

family (p. 462) a social institution found in all societies that unites people in cooperative groups to care for one another, including any children

kinship (p. 462) a social bond based on common ancestry, marriage, or adoption

marriage (p. 462) a legal relationship, usually involving economic cooperation, sexual activity, and childbearing

extended family (p. 463) a family consisting of parents and children as well as other kin; also known as a *consanguine family*

nuclear family (p. 463) a family composed of one or two parents and their children; also known as a *conjugal family*

endogamy (p. 463) marriage between people of the same social category

exogamy (p. 463) marriage between people of different social categories

monogamy (p. 463) marriage that unites two partners

polygamy (p. 463) marriage that unites a person with two or more spouses

polygyny (p. 463) marriage that unites one man and two or more women

polyandry (p. 463) marriage that unites one woman and two or more men

patrilocality (p. 463) a residential pattern in which a married couple lives with or near the husband's familiy

matrilocality (p. 463) a residential pattern in which a married couple lives with or near the wife's familiy

neolocality (p. 464) a residential pattern in which a married couple lives apart from both sets of parents

descent (p. 465) the system by which members of a society trace kinship over generations

patrilineal descent (p. 465) a system tracing kinship through men

matrilineal descent (p. 465) a system tracing kinship through women

bilateral descent (p. 466) a system tracing kinship through both men and women

incest taboo (p. 466) a norm forbidding sexual relations or marriage between certain relatives

homogamy (p. 470) marriage between people with the same social characteristics

infidelity (p. 470) sexual activity outside one's marriage

THE FAMILY IN LATER LIFE

- The departure of children, known as the "empty nest," requires adjustments to family life.
- Many middle-aged couples care for aging parents, and many older couples are active grandparents.
- The final transition in marriage begins with the death of a spouse.

p. 471–72

U.S. Families: Class, Gender, and Race

SOCIAL CLASS is a powerful force that shapes family life.

- Social class determines a family's financial security and opportunities available to family members.
- Children born into rich families typically have better mental and physical health and go on to achieve more in life than children born into poor families.

p. 472

GENDER affects family dynamics because husbands dominate in most marriages.

- Research suggests that marriage provides more benefits for men than for women.
- After divorce, men are more likely than women to remarry.

p. 475

ETHNICITY AND RACE can affect a person's experience of family life, although no single generalization fits all families within a particular category.

- Migration of American Indians from reservations to cities creates many "fluid households" with changing membership.
- The traditional pattern of extended families common to Latinos is changing as Latinos assimilate into the larger U.S. society.
- African American families face severe economic disadvantages, and more than one-third of African American children are growing up poor.

pp. 472–75

Most married couples have similar social background with regard to class and race, but over the past century, ethnicity has mattered less and less (pp. 474–75).

Transitions and Problems in Family Life

DIVORCE

The divorce rate is seven times what it was a century ago; four in ten of today's marriages will end in divorce. Researchers point to six causes:

- Individualism is on the rise.
- Romantic love fades.
- Women are less dependent on men.
- Many of today's marriages are stressful.
- Divorce is socially acceptable.
- Legally, a divorce is easier to get.

pp. 475–76

FAMILY VIOLENCE

- Family violence, which victimizes mostly women and children, is far more common than official records indicate.
- Most adults who abuse family members were themselves abused as children.

p. 477

REMARRIAGE

- Four out of five people who divorce eventually remarry.
- Remarriage creates blended families that include children from previous marriages.

p. 477

family violence (p. 477) emotional, physical, or sexual abuse of one family member by another

cohabitation (p. 478) the sharing of a household by an unmarried couple

Alternative Family Forms

ONE-PARENT FAMILIES

- The proportion of one-parent families—now 29% of all families in the United States—more than doubled during the last generation.
- Single parenthood increases a woman's risk of poverty, which puts children at a disadvantage.

p. 478

GAY AND LESBIAN COUPLES

- Although only Massachusetts, Connecticut, Vermont, New Hampshire, Maine, and Iowa allow same-sex marriage, many gay men and lesbians form long-lasting relationships and, increasingly, are becoming parents.

pp. 478–79

COHABITATION

- Almost half of all people 25 to 44 years of age have cohabited at some point.
- Research shows that children born to cohabiting couples are less likely to live with both biological parents until age 18 than children born to married parents.

p. 478

SINGLEHOOD

- One in four households today—up from one in ten in 1950—contains a single person.
- The number of young women who are single is rising dramatically, a result of women's greater participation in the workforce and lessened dependence on men for material supoort.

p. 479

New Reproductive Technologies

- Although ethically controversial, new reproductive technologies are changing conventional ideas of parenthood.

pp. 479–80

{ Religion is the social institution involving beliefs and practices based on recognizing what is sacred. There are many world religions, just as there are many different religious organizations within U.S. society. }

CHAPTER 19

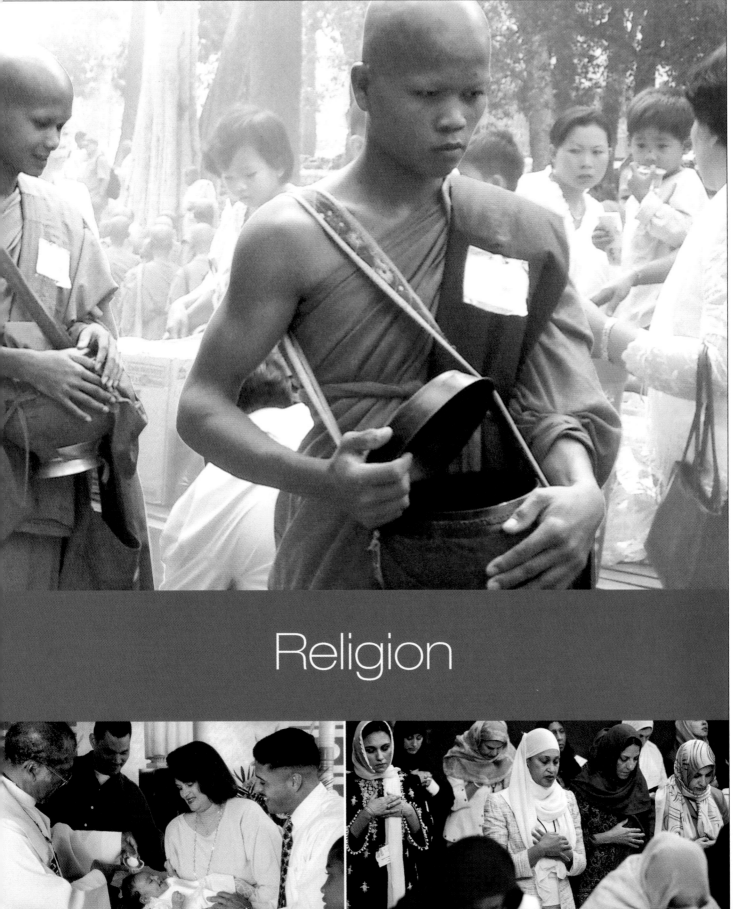

Religion

NOTE: The Latin root of "religion" is *religare*, "to be tied back," suggesting the link between religion and tradition.

Q: "We are not human beings on a spiritual journey; we are spiritual beings on a human journey." Stephen Covey

EXERCISE: Ask students to attend a worship service of an unfamiliar religious organization; a good discussion will follow. Another idea: Direct students to campus religious leaders to discuss the role of religion in a college education.

CHAPTER OVERVIEW { This chapter explores the meaning and importance of religion, a major social institution, which is based on the concept of the sacred.

With its many churches, synagogues, temples, and mosques (a recent study put the figure at one house of worship for every 1,000 people), one country stands out as among the most religious countries on Earth.

- For its entire history, its leaders have proclaimed that God is responsible for its prosperity and liberty.

- Today, four out of five of this nation's people say they have "experienced God's presence or a spiritual force."

- Together, its people give more than $65 billion each year to religious organizations—more than the total economic output of most low-income countries.

- Written on its money is the official national motto, "In God We Trust."

- And in schools, children stand before the national flag and pledge their allegiance to "one nation under God" (Sheler, 2002; Aprill, 2004).

You have already guessed that the country described is the United States. But although the United States is a religious nation, it is also a country of immigrants, and as a result, its people have many different images of God. In countless places of worship—from soaring Gothic cathedrals in New York City to small storefront tabernacles in Los Angeles—Christians, Muslims, Jews, Buddhists, Hindus, Sikhs, Jains, Zoroastrians, and followers of dozens of other religions can be found (Yang & Ebaugh, 2001; Sheler, 2002). One scholar described the United States as the world's most religiously diverse nation, a country in which Hindu and Jewish children go to school together and Muslims and Buddhists, Sikhs and Jains work in the same factories and offices as Protestants and Catholics (Eck, 2001). And as you will see, many people in the United States today are spiritual without being part of any organized religion.

This chapter begins by explaining what religion is from a sociological point of view. We then explore the changing face of religious belief throughout history and around the world and examine the vital and sometimes controversial place of religion in today's society.

Religion: Basic Concepts

The French sociologist Emile Durkheim stated that religion involves "things that surpass the limits of our knowledge" (1965:62, orig. 1915). We define most objects, events, or experiences as **profane** (from Latin, meaning "outside the temple"), *included as an ordinary element*

of everyday life. But we also consider some things **sacred**, *set apart as extraordinary, inspiring awe and reverence*. Setting the sacred apart from the profane is the essence of all religious belief. **Religion**, then, is *a social institution involving beliefs and practices based on recognizing the sacred*.

There is great diversity in matters of faith, and nothing is sacred to everyone on Earth. Although people regard most books as profane, Jews believe that the Torah (the first five books of the Hebrew Bible or Old Testament) is sacred, in the same way that Christians revere the Old and New Testaments of the Bible and Muslims exalt the Qur'an (Koran).

But no matter how a community of believers draws religious lines, Durkheim explained, people understand profane things in terms of their everyday usefulness: We log on to the Internet with our laptop or turn a key to start our car. What is sacred we reverently set apart from daily life, giving it a "forbidden" or "holy" aura. Marking the boundary between the sacred and the profane, for example, Muslims remove their shoes before entering a mosque, to avoid defiling a sacred place with soles that have touched the profane ground outside.

The sacred is embodied in **ritual**, or *formal, ceremonial behavior*. Holy Communion is the central ritual of Christianity; to the Christian faithful, the wafer and wine consumed during Communion are never treated in a profane way as food but as the sacred symbols of the body and blood of Jesus Christ.

DISCUSS: Do the following two pronouncements of the Roman Catholic church favor Marxism or market capitalism?

Q: "The needs of the poor must take priority over the desires of the rich; and the rights of workers over the maximization of profits." John Paul II

Q: "In today's world . . . the right of economic initiative is often suppressed. Yet it is a right which is important not only for the individual but for the common good. Experience shows that the denial of this right, or its limitation in the name of alleged 'equality' of everyone in society, diminishes, or in practice absolutely destroys the spirit of initiative." John Paul II

Leading this flock calls for improvisation. Imams must unify diverse congregations with often-clashing Islamic traditions. They must grapple with the threat of terrorism, answering to law enforcement agents without losing the trust of their fellow Muslims. Sometimes they must set aside conservative beliefs that prevail in the Middle East, the birthplace of Islam.

Islam is a legalistic faith: Muslims believe in a divine law that guides their daily lives, including what they should eat, drink and wear. In countries where the religion reigns, this is largely the accepted way. . . .

The religion's *fiqh*, or jurisprudence, is built on 14 centuries of scholarship, but imams in Europe and America often find this body of law insufficient to address life in the West. The quandaries of America were foreign to Mr. Shata.

Pornography was rampant, prompting a question Mr. Shata had never heard in Egypt: Is oral sex lawful? Pork and alcohol are forbidden in Islam, raising questions about whether Muslims could sell beer or bacon. Tired of the menacing stares in the subway, women wanted to know if they could remove their headscarves. Muslims were navigating their way through problems Mr. Shata had never fathomed.

For a while, the imam called his fellow sheiks in Egypt with requests for *fatwas*, or nonbinding legal rulings. But their views carried little relevance to life in America. Some issues, like oral sex, he dared not raise. Over time, he began to find his own answers and became, as he put it, flexible.

Is a Big Mac permissible? Yes, the imam says, but not a bacon cheeseburger.

It is a woman's right, Mr. Shata believes, to remove her *hijab* if she feels threatened. Muslims can take jobs serving alcohol and pork, he says, but only if other work cannot be found. Oral sex is acceptable, but only between married couples. Mortgages, he says, are necessary to move forward in America.

"Islam is supposed to make a person's life easier, not harder," Mr. Shata explained. . . .

WHAT DO YOU THINK?

1. In your own words, how would you describe Sheik Reda Shata's function as imam in his Brooklyn congregation?

2. In what ways do Muslim traditions blend well with U.S. cultural traditions? In what ways do they conflict? How does Sheik Reda deal with these conflicts?

3. Has religion helped guide your own everyday life behavior and decisions? If so, give some examples.

Today, the British monarch is the formal head of the Church of England, illustrating the close ties between religious and political elites. In practical terms, linking the church and the state means that opposing the government amounts to opposing the church and, by implication, God. Religion also encourages people to accept the social problems of this world while they look hopefully to a "better world to come." In a well-known statement, Marx dismissed religion as preventing revolutionary change; religion is, in his words, "the sigh of the oppressed creature, the sentiment of a heartless world, and the soul of soulless conditions. It is the opium of the people" (1964:27, orig. 1848).

Religion and social inequality are also linked through gender. Virtually all the world's major religions are patriarchal, as the Thinking About Diversity box on page 492 explains.

CRITICAL REVIEW Social-conflict analysis emphasizes the power of religion to support social inequality. Yet religion also promotes change toward equality. For example, nineteenth-century religious groups in the United States played an important part in the movement to abolish slavery. In the 1950s and 1960s, religious organizations and their leaders were the core of the civil rights movement. In the 1960s and 1970s, many clergy opposed the Vietnam War, and today many support any number of progressive causes such as feminism and gay rights.

CHECK YOUR LEARNING How does religion help maintain class inequality and gender stratification?

The Applying Theory table on page 493 summarizes the three theoretical approaches to understanding religion.

Religion and Social Change

Religion can be the conservative force portrayed by Karl Marx. But at some points in history, as Max Weber (1958, orig. 1904–05) explained, religion has promoted dramatic social change.

Max Weber: Protestantism and Capitalism

Weber argued that particular religious ideas set into motion a wave of change that brought about the Industrial Revolution in Western Europe. The rise of industrial capitalism was encouraged by Calvinism, a movement within the Protestant Reformation.

As Chapter 4 ("Society") explains in detail, John Calvin (1509–1564) was a leader in the Reformation who preached the doctrine of *predestination*. According to Calvin, an all-powerful and all-knowing God had selected some people for salvation but condemned most to eternal damnation. Each individual's fate, sealed before birth and known only to God, was either eternal glory or endless hellfire.

Driven by anxiety over their fate, Calvinists understandably looked for signs of God's favor in this world and came to see prosperity as a sign of divine blessing. Religious conviction and a rigid devotion to duty led Calvinists to work hard, and many amassed great wealth. But money was not for selfish spending or even for sharing with the poor, whose plight they saw as a mark of God's rejection. As agents of God's work on Earth, Calvinists believed that

Religion CHAPTER 19

491

DIVERSITY: The proportion of women serving as clergy in Protestant denominations ranges from 14% for Presbyterians to 35% for Unitarians.

Q: "Every man thinks God is on his side. The rich and powerful know he is." Jean Anouilh.

SOCIAL SURVEY: "Where would you place your image of God on the scale [between (1) Mother and (7) Father]?" (GSS 1998, *N* = 1,445; *Codebook*, 2005:185)

(1) 2.9%	(4) 24.5%	(7) 47.1%
(2) 1.1%	(5) 8.2%	"Don't know"/No response 4.4%
(3) 2.1%	(6) 9.6%	

● SEEING SOCIOLOGY
in Everyday Life

Can you think of an example of one society using the idea of "converting heathens" to justify controlling another society? Explain.

THINKING ABOUT DIVERSITY: RACE, CLASS, & GENDER

Religion and Patriarchy: Does God Favor Males?

Why do two-thirds of adults in the United States say they think of God as "father" rather than "mother" (NORC, 2007:190)? It is probably because we link godly traits such as wisdom and power to men. Just about all the world's religions tend to favor males, a fact evident in passages from their sacred writings.

The Qur'an (Koran), the sacred text of Islam, declares that men are to dominate women: "Men are in charge of women. . . . Hence good women are obedient. . . . As for those whose rebelliousness you fear, admonish them, banish them from your bed, and scourge them" (quoted in W. Kaufman, 1976:163).

Christianity, the major religion of the Western world, also supports patriarchy. Many Christians revere Mary, the mother of Jesus, but the New Testament also includes the following passages:

A man . . . is the image and glory of God; but woman is the glory of man. For man was not made from woman, but woman from man. Neither was man created for woman, but woman for man. (1 Corinthians 11:7–9)

As in all the churches of the saints, the women should keep silence in the churches. For they are not permitted to speak, but should be subordinate, as even the law says. If there is anything they desire to know, let them ask their husbands at home. For it is shameful for a woman to speak in church. (1 Corinthians 14:33–35)

Wives, be subject to your husbands, as to the Lord. For the husband is the head of the wife as Christ is the head of the church. . . . As the church is subject to Christ, so let

wives also be subject in everything to their husbands. (Ephesians 5:22–24)

Let a woman learn in silence with all submissiveness. I permit no woman to teach or to have authority over men; she is to keep silent. For Adam was formed first, then Eve; and Adam was not deceived, but the woman was deceived and became a transgressor. Yet woman will be saved through bearing children, if she continues in faith and love and holiness, with modesty. (1 Timothy 2:11–15)

Judaism has also traditionally supported patriarchy. Male Orthodox Jews say the following words in daily prayer:

Blessed art thou, O Lord our God, King of the Universe, that I was not born a gentile.

Blessed art thou, O Lord our God, King of the Universe, that I was not born a slave.

Patriarchy is a characteristic of all the world's major religions, including Christianity, Judaism, and Islam. Male dominance can be seen in restrictions that limit religious leadership to men and also in regulations that prohibit women from worshiping alongside men.

Blessed art thou, O Lord our God, King of the Universe, that I was not born a woman.

Many patriarchal religions also exclude women from the clergy. Today, Islam and the Roman Catholic Church ban women from the priesthood, as do about half of Protestant denominations. But a growing number of Protestant religious organizations do ordain women, who now represent more than one-third of U.S. clergy. Orthodox Judaism upholds the traditional prohibition against women serving as rabbis, but Reform and Conservative Judaism look to both men and women as spiritual leaders. Across the United States, the proportion of women in seminaries has never been higher (now roughly one-third), which is more evidence of a trend toward greater equality (Association of Theological Seminaries, 2009; Hartford Institute, 2009).

Feminists argue that unless traditional ideas of gender are removed from our understanding of God, women will never be equal to men in the church. The theologian Mary Daly puts the matter bluntly: "If God is male, then male is God" (quoted in Woodward, 1989:58).

WHAT DO YOU THINK?

1. Are you or other members of your family affiliated with a religious organization? If so, what evidence of patriarchy do you see in this religion?

2. Why do you think many religions encourage people to think of God as male?

3. Can you think of God in terms that do not include gender? Explain your answer.

they best fulfilled their "calling" by reinvesting profits and achieving ever-greater success in the process.

All the while, Calvinists lived thrifty lives and adopted technological advances, which laid the groundwork for the rise of industrial

capitalism. In time, the religious fervor that motivated early Calvinists weakened, leaving a profane "Protestant work ethic." To Max Weber, industrial capitalism itself arose as a "disenchanted" religion, further showing the power of religion to alter the shape of society.

RESOURCE: An excerpt from Max Weber's *Protestant Ethic and the Spirit of Capitalism* is among the classics included in the author's companion reader *Seeing Ourselves*, 8th ed.

Q: Rationalization "means that principally there are no mysterious, incalculable forces that come into play, but rather that one can, in principle, master all things by calculation." Max Weber

NOTE: Churches, with formally ordained (rather than charismatic) leaders, exemplify the routinization of charisma that, as Simmel might have said, favors form over content.

GLOBAL: In Japan, the emperor has traditionally been the head priest of the Shinto religion.

GLOBAL: With a state church, Pakistan named its capital Islamabad ("City of Islam").

church a religious organization that is well integrated into the larger society

state church a church formally linked to the state

denomination a church, independent of the state, that recognizes religious pluralism

liberation theology the combining of Christian principles with political activism, often Marxist in character

APPLYING THEORY

Religion

	Structural-Functional Approach	Symbolic-Interaction Approach	Social-Conflict Approach
What is the level of analysis?	Macro-level	Micro-level	Macro-level
What is the importance of religion for society?	Religion performs vital tasks, including uniting people and controlling behavior. Religion gives life meaning and purpose.	Religion strengthens marriage by giving it (and family life) sacred meaning. People often turn to sacred symbols for comfort when facing danger and uncertainty.	Religion supports social inequality by claiming that the social order is just. Religion turns attention from problems in this world to a "better world to come."

Liberation Theology

Historically, Christianity has reached out to oppressed people, urging all to a stronger faith in a better life to come. In recent decades, however, some church leaders and theologians have taken a decidedly political approach and endorsed **liberation theology**, *the combining of Christian principles with political activism, often Marxist in character.*

This social movement started in the 1960s in Latin America's Roman Catholic Church. Today, Christian activists continue to help people in poor nations liberate themselves from abysmal poverty. Their message is simple: Social oppression runs counter to Christian morality, so as a matter of faith and justice, Christians must promote greater social equality.

Pope Benedict XVI, like Pope John Paul II before him, condemns liberation theology for distorting traditional church doctrine with left-wing politics. Nevertheless, the liberation theology movement has gained strength in the poorest countries of Latin America, where many people's Christian faith drives them to improve conditions for the poor and oppressed (Neuhouser, 1989; J. E. Williams, 2002).

Types of Religious Organizations

Sociologists categorize the hundreds of different religious organizations found in the United States along a continuum, with *churches* at one end and *sects* at the other. We can describe any actual religious organization in relation to these two ideal types by locating it on the church-sect continuum.

Church

Drawing on the ideas of his teacher Max Weber, Ernst Troeltsch (1931) defined a **church** as *a type of religious organization that is well integrated into the larger society.* Churchlike organizations usually persist for centuries and include generations of the same families. Churches have well-established rules and regulations and expect leaders to be formally trained and ordained.

Though concerned with the sacred, a church accepts the ways of the profane world. Church members think of God in intellectual terms (say, as a force for good) and favor abstract moral standards ("Do unto others as you would have them do unto you") over specific rules for day-to-day living. By teaching morality in safely abstract terms, church leaders avoid social controversy. For example, many congregations celebrate the unity of all peoples but say little about their own lack of racial diversity. By downplaying this type of conflict, a church makes peace with the status quo (Troeltsch, 1931).

A church may operate with or apart from the state. As its name implies, a **state church** is *a church formally allied with the state.* State churches have existed throughout human history. For centuries, Roman Catholicism was the official religion of the Roman Empire, and Confucianism was the official religion of China until early in the twentieth century. Today, the Anglican Church is the official church of England, and Islam is the official religion of Pakistan and Iran. State churches count everyone in the society as a member, which sharply limits tolerance of religious differences.

A **denomination**, by contrast, is *a church, independent of the state, that recognizes religious pluralism.* Denominations exist in nations, including the United States, that formally separate church

GLOBAL: The Church of Sweden (the Lutheran church) counts all Swedes among its members, unless they officially withdraw from it. The state owns church property and pays clergy as state employees.

GLOBAL: Some members of a society with a state church see denominations as chaotic. "If Protestantism is a true religion," one Moroccan commented, "why do you Americans have hundreds of denominations?"

sect a religious organization that stands apart from the larger society

charisma extraordinary personal qualities that can infuse people with emotion and turn them into followers

cult a religious organization that is largely outside a society's cultural traditions

MAKING THE GRADE

In general, the importance of charisma is greatest in cults, less so in sects, and least important in churches.

and state. This country has dozens of Christian denominations—including Catholics, Baptists, Episcopalians, Presbyterians, and Lutherans—as well as various categories of Judaism, Islam, and other traditions. Although members of any denomination hold to their own doctrine, they recognize the right of others to have other beliefs.

Sect

The second general religious form is the **sect**, *a type of religious organization that stands apart from the larger society.* Sect members have rigid religious convictions and deny the beliefs of others. Compared

In global perspective, the range of religious activity is truly astonishing. Members of this Southeast Asian cult show their devotion to God by suspending themselves in the air using ropes and sharp hooks that pierce their skin. What religious practices that are common in the United States might seem astonishing to people living in other countries?

to churches, which try to appeal to everyone (the term *catholic* also means "universal"), a sect forms an exclusive group. To members of a sect, religion is not just one aspect of life but a firm plan for living. In extreme cases, members of a sect withdraw completely from society in order to practice their religion without interference. The Amish community is one example of a North American sect that isolates itself. Because our culture generally considers religious tolerance a virtue, members of sects are sometimes accused of being narrow-minded in insisting that they alone follow the true religion (Kraybill, 1994; P. W. Williams, 2002).

In organizational terms, sects are less formal than churches. Sect members may be highly spontaneous and emotional in worship, compared to members of churches, who tend to listen passively to their leaders. Sects also reject the intellectualized religion of churches, stressing instead the personal experience of divine power. Rodney Stark (1985:314) contrasts a church's vision of a distant God ("Our Father, who art in Heaven") with a sect's more immediate God ("Lord, bless this poor sinner kneeling before you now").

Churches and sects also have different patterns of leadership. The more churchlike an organization, the more likely that its leaders are formally trained and ordained. Sectlike organizations, which celebrate the personal presence of God, expect their leaders to exhibit divine inspiration in the form of **charisma** (from Greek, meaning "divine favor"), *extraordinary personal qualities that can infuse people with emotion and turn them into followers.*

Sects generally form as breakaway groups from established religious organizations (Stark & Bainbridge, 1979). Their psychic intensity and informal structure make them less stable than churches, and many sects blossom only to disappear soon after. The sects that do endure typically become more like churches, with declining emphasis on charismatic leadership as they become more bureaucratic.

To sustain their membership, many sects actively recruit, or *proselytize,* new members. Sects highly value the experience of *conversion,* a personal transformation or religious rebirth. For example, members of Jehovah's Witnesses go door to door to share their faith with others in the hope of attracting new members.

Finally, churches and sects differ in their social composition. Because they are more closely tied to the world, well-established churches tend to include people of high social standing. Sects attract more disadvantaged people. A sect's openness to new members and its promise of salvation and personal fulfillment appeal to people who feel they are social outsiders.

Cult

A **cult** is *a religious organization that is largely outside a society's cultural traditions.* Most sects spin off from conventional religious organizations. However, a cult typically forms around a highly charismatic

GLOBAL: Singapore bans Jehovah's Witnesses as disruptive; in 1995, that government seized 66 of the sect's Bibles.

Q: "The Kingdom of God is not a matter of talk, but of power." 1 Corinthians 4:20–21

DISCUSS: Are "Deadheads" a cult? Following the death of Jerry Garcia in 1995,

the news media compared the musician to a priest or god and his band, the Grateful Dead, to a church.

GLOBAL: Similar to the Heaven's Gate suicides, since 1994, some 74 members of the Order of the Solar Temple have killed themselves in Canada, Switzerland, and France. Some analysts point out that the approach of the year 2000 stimulated cult formation around the world.

● SEEING SOCIOLOGY
in Everyday Life

Can you think of ways in which a religious organization that began as a cult becomes a church? What has to change?

animism the belief that elements of the natural world are conscious life forms that affect humanity

leader who offers a compelling message about a new and very different way of life. As many as 5,000 cults exist in the United States (Marquand & Wood, 1997).

Because some cult principles or practices are unconventional, the popular view is that they are deviant or even evil. The suicides of thirty-nine members of California's Heaven's Gate cult in 1997—people who claimed that dying was a doorway to a higher existence, perhaps in the company of aliens from outer space—confirmed the negative image the public holds of most cults. In short, calling any religious community a "cult" amounts to dismissing its members as crazy (Shupe, 1995; Gleick, 1997).

This charge is unfair because there is nothing basically wrong with this kind of religious organization. Many longstanding religions—Christianity, Islam, and Judaism included—began as cults. Of course, few cults exist for very long. One reason is that they are even more at odds with the larger society than sects. Many cults demand that members not only accept their doctrine but also adopt a radically new lifestyle. This is why people sometimes accuse cults of brainwashing their members, although research suggests that most people who join cults experience no psychological harm (Kilbourne, 1983; P. W. Williams, 2002).

Religion in History

Like other social institutions, religion shows marked variation according to time and place. Let us look at several ways in which religion has changed over the course of history.

Religion in Preindustrial Societies

Early hunters and gatherers practiced **animism** (from a Latin word meaning "breath of life"), *the belief that elements of the natural world are conscious life forms that affect humanity.* Animists view forests, oceans, mountains, and even the wind as spiritual forces. Many Native American societies are animistic, which explains their reverence for the natural environment.

Belief in a single divine power responsible for creating the world began with pastoral and horticultural societies, which first appeared 10,000 to 12,000 years ago. The conception of God as a "shepherd" arose because Christianity, Judaism, and Islam all began among pastoral peoples.

Religion becomes more important in agrarian societies, which develop a specialized priesthood in charge of religious rituals and organizations. The huge cathedrals that dominated the towns of medieval Europe—many of which remian standing today—are evidence of the central role of religion in the social life of medieval agrarian society.

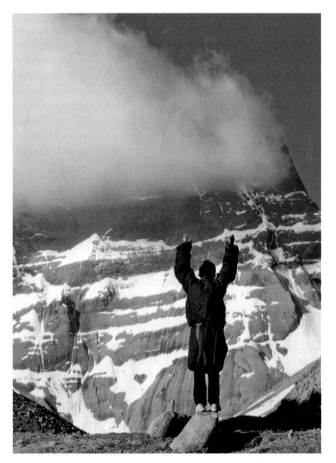

Animism is widespread in traditional societies, whose members live respectfully within the natural world on which they depend for their survival. Animists see a divine presence not just in themselves but in everything around them. Their example has inspired "New Age" spirituality, described on pages 506–7.

Religion in Industrial Societies

The Industrial Revolution introduced a growing emphasis on science. More and more, people looked to doctors and scientists for the knowledge and comfort they used to get from priests. But as Durkheim (1965, orig. 1915) predicted almost a century ago, religion persists in industrial societies because science is powerless to address issues of ultimate meaning in human life. In other words, learning *how* the world works is a matter for scientists, but *why* we and the rest of the universe exist at all is a question of faith. In addition, as already noted, the United States stands out as a modern society in which religion has remained especially strong (McClay, 2007; Greeley, 2008).

● MAKING THE GRADE

As you read through the discussions of world religions, keep in mind that the first three are Western religions and the second three are Eastern religions. Later in the chapter, you'll find a summary of the differences between Western and Eastern religions.

monotheism belief in a single divine power

polytheism belief in many gods

Although it began as a cult, Christianity's 2 billion followers makes it now the most widespread of the world's religions.

World Religions

The diversity of religions in the world is almost as wide-ranging as the diversity of culture itself. Many of the thousands of different religions are found in just one place and have few followers. But there are a number of *world religions*, with millions of adherents. We shall briefly examine six world religions, which together claim at least 4 billion believers—more than two-thirds of humanity.

Christianity

Christianity is the most widespread religion, with 2 billion followers, one-third of the world's people. Most Christians live in Europe or the Americas; more than 85 percent of the people in the United States and Canada identify with Christianity. As shown in Global Map 19–1, people who think of themselves as Christian represent a large share of the population in many world regions, with the notable exceptions of northern Africa and Asia. European colonization spread Christianity throughout much of the world over the past 500 years. Its dominance in the West is shown by the fact that our calendar numbers years from the birth of Jesus Christ.

As noted earlier, Christianity began as a cult, drawing elements from Judaism, a much older religion. Like many cults, Christianity was built on the personal charisma of a leader, Jesus of Nazareth, who preached a message of personal salvation. Jesus did not directly challenge the political power of his day, the Roman Empire, telling his followers to "render therefore to Caesar the things that are Caesar's" (Matthew 22:21). But his message was a revolutionary one all the same, promising that faith and love would triumph over sin and death.

Christianity is one example of **monotheism**, *belief in a single divine power*. This new religion was quite different from the Roman Empire's traditional **polytheism**, *belief in many gods*. Yet Christianity views the Supreme Being as a sacred Trinity: God the Creator; Jesus Christ, Son of God and Redeemer; and the Holy Spirit, a Christian's personal experience of God's presence.

The claim that Jesus was divine rests on accounts of his final days on Earth. Brought to trial as a threat to established political leaders, Jesus was tried in Jerusalem and sentenced to death by crucifixion, a common means of execution at the time. This explains why the cross became a sacred Christian symbol. According to Christian belief, three days after his execution, Jesus rose from the dead, revealing that he was the Son of God.

Jesus' followers, especially his twelve closest associates, known as the apostles, spread Christianity throughout the Mediterranean region. At first, the Roman Empire persecuted Christians. But by the fourth century, the empire had adopted Christianity as a state church, the official religion of what became known as the Holy Roman Empire.

Christianity took various forms, including the Roman Catholic Church and the Eastern Orthodox Church, based in Constantinople (now Istanbul, Turkey). Toward the end of the Middle Ages, the Protestant Reformation in Europe gave rise to hundreds of new denominations. In the United States, dozens of these denominations—the Baptists and Methodists are the two largest—command sizable followings (W. Kaufman, 1976; Jacquet & Jones, 1991).

Islam

Islam has about 1.3 billion followers, which is one-fifth of humanity. Followers of Islam are called Muslims. A majority of people in the Middle East are Muslims, so we tend to associate Islam with Arabs in that region of the world. But most of the world's Muslims live elsewhere: Global Map 19–2 shows that most people in northern Africa and Indonesia are Muslims. In addition, large concentrations of Muslims are found in western Asia in Pakistan, India, Bangladesh, and the southern republics of the former Soviet Union. Because Muslims have a higher birth rate than followers of any other major religion, it is possible that Islam could become the world's dominant religion by the end of this century.

Most estimates put the Muslim population of the United States at about 2 million, although a few sources place the number as high as 8 million. In any case, Islam is clearly an important part of our country's religious life. The Muslim population is not only large but quite diverse. It includes Arab Americans and others with Middle Eastern ancestry, Asian Americans, and African Americans (Eck, 2001; Pew Research Center, 2007b).

MAKING THE GRADE

To learn the most from reading maps, compare all four in this chapter—shown below and on page 500.

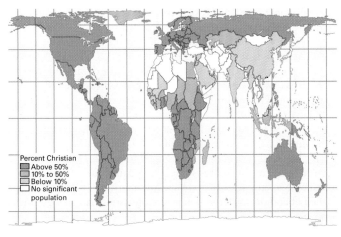

Window on the World

GLOBAL MAP 19–1 **Christianity in Global Perspective**

Christianity is the dominant religion of Western Europe and became the dominant religion of the Americas. Can you explain this pattern?

Source: Association of Religion Data Archives (2009).

Percent Christian
- Above 50%
- 10% to 50%
- Below 10%
- No significant population

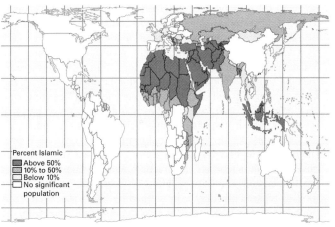

Window on the World

GLOBAL MAP 19–2 **Islam in Global Perspective**

Islam is the dominant religion of the Middle East, but most of the world's Muslims live in North Africa and Southeast Asia.

Source: Association of Religion Data Archives (2009).

Percent Islamic
- Above 50%
- 10% to 50%
- Below 10%
- No significant population

Islam is the word of God as revealed to Muhammad, who was born in the city of Mecca (in what is now Saudi Arabia) about the year 570. To Muslims, Muhammad is a prophet, not a divine being as Jesus is to Christians. The text of the Qur'an (Koran), which is sacred to Muslims, is the word of Allah (Arabic for "God") as transmitted through Muhammad, Allah's messenger. In Arabic, the word *islam* means both "submission" and "peace," and the Qur'an urges submission to Allah as the path to inner peace. Muslims express this personal devotion in a ritual of prayers five times each day.

After the death of Muhammad, Islam spread rapidly. Although divisions arose among Muslims, all accept the Five Pillars of Islam: (1) recognizing Allah as the one, true God and Muhammad as God's messenger; (2) ritual prayer; (3) giving alms to the poor; (4) fasting during the month of Ramadan; and (5) making a pilgrimage at least once in one's life to the Sacred House of Allah in Mecca (Weeks, 1988; El-

Attar, 1991). Like Christianity, Islam holds people accountable to God for their deeds on Earth. Those who live obediently will be rewarded in heaven, and evildoers will suffer unending punishment.

Muslims are also required to defend their faith, which has led to calls for holy wars against unbelievers (in roughly the same way that medieval Christians fought in the Crusades). Recent decades have witnessed a rise in militancy and anti-Western feeling in much of the Muslim world, where many people see the United States as both militarily threatening and representing a way of life that they view as materialistic and immoral. Many Westerners—who typically know little about Islam and often stereotype all Muslims on the basis of the terrorist actions of a few—respond with confusion and sometimes hostility (Eck, 2001; Ryan, 2001).

Many people in the United States also view Muslim women as socially oppressed. There are differences among Muslim nations in

MAKING THE GRADE

Can you name the sacred texts of the three world religions that are widespread in the West?

Many religions promote literacy because they demand that followers study sacred texts. As part of their upbringing, most Muslim parents teach their children lessons from the Qur'an; later, the children will do the same for a new generation of believers.

terms of rights given to women: Tunisia allows women far more opportunities than, say, Saudi Arabia, which does not allow women to vote or even drive a car. It is true that many Muslim women lack some of the personal freedoms enjoyed by Muslim men. Yet many—perhaps even most—accept the mandates of their religion and find security in a system that guides the behavior of both women and men (Peterson, 1996). Defenders of Islam also point out that patriarchy was well established in the Middle East long before the birth of Muhammad and that Islam actually improved the social position of women by requiring husbands to deal justly with their wives. For example, Islam permits a man to have up to four wives, but it requires men to have only one wife if having more would cause him to treat any woman unjustly (Qur'an, "The Women," v. 3).

Judaism

In terms of numbers, Judaism's 15 million followers worldwide make it something less than a world religion. Jews make up a majority of the population in only one country—Israel. But Judaism has special importance to the United States because the largest concentration of Jews (6 million people) is found in North America.

Jews look to the past as a source of guidance in the present and for the future. Judaism has deep historical roots that extend 4,000 years before the birth of Christ to the ancient societies of Mesopotamia. At this time, Jews were animistic, but this belief changed after Jacob—grandson of Abraham, the earliest great ancestor—led his people to Egypt.

Jews survived centuries of slavery in Egypt. In the thirteenth century B.C.E., Moses, the adopted son of an Egyptian princess, was called by God to lead the Jews from bondage. This exodus (a word with Latin and Greek roots mean "marching out") from Egypt is remembered by Jews today in the annual ritual of Passover. After their liberation, the Jews became monotheistic, recognizing a single, all-powerful God.

A distinctive concept of Judaism is the *covenant,* a special relationship with God by which the Jews became God's "chosen people." The covenant implies a duty to observe God's law, especially the Ten Commandments as revealed to Moses on Mount Sinai. Jews regard the Old Testament of the Bible as both a record of their history and a statement of the obligations of Jewish life. Of special importance are the Bible's first five books (Genesis, Exodus, Leviticus, Numbers, and Deuteronomy), called the *Torah* (a word meaning "teaching" and "law"). In contrast to Christianity's central concern with personal salvation, Judaism emphasizes moral behavior in this world.

Judaism has three main denominations. Orthodox Jews (including roughly 600,000 people in the United States) strictly observe traditional beliefs and practices, wear traditional dress, segregate men and women at religious services, and eat only kosher foods (prepared precisely as prescribed in the Torah). Such traditional practices set off Orthodox Jews in the United States from the larger society, making them the most sectlike. In the mid-nineteenth century, many Jews wanted to join in with the larger society, which led to the formation of more churchlike Reform Judaism (now including about 2 million people in this country). A third segment, Conservative Judaism (with more than 1.5 million U.S. adherents), has established a middle ground between the other two denominations (Grim & Masci, 2008).

Whatever the denomination, Jews share a cultural history of oppression as a result of prejudice and discrimination. A collective memory of centuries of slavery in Egypt, conquest by Rome, and persecution in Europe has shaped the Jewish identity. It was Jews in Italy who first lived in an urban ghetto (this word comes from the Italian *borghetto,* meaning "settlement outside the city walls"), and this residential segregation soon spread to other parts of Europe.

Jewish immigration to the United States began in the mid-1600s. The early immigrants who prospered were assimilated into largely Christian communities. But as great numbers entered the country

NOTE: Orthodox Jews also look to the Talmud—which consists of the Mishnah (text) and Gemorrah (commentary)—for explicit guidance in everyday life.

NOTE: Although Judaism and Christianity are both monotheistic religions, they may have polytheistic origins. In the original Hebrew, the accounts of creation in Genesis used plural pronouns ("Then God said, Let us make man in our image" 1:26), leading scholars to speculate that the religion evolved from polytheistic roots.

NOTE: As members of many religions have done, the ancient Hebrews distinguished between the sacred and the secular through practices such as keeping the Sabbath, observing dietary restrictions, and maintaining holy places.

NOTE: The precise meaning of "Semite" is a person with ancestral roots in southwest Asia, including both Arabs and Jews. In the U.S., however, people commonly use the term to refer only to Jews.

SEEING SOCIOLOGY
in Everyday Life

Hinduism and Buddhism have influenced New Age spirituality in the United States, as explained later in this chapter on pages 506–7.

at the end of the nineteenth century, prejudice and discrimination against Jews—commonly termed *anti-Semitism*—increased. Before and during World War II, anti-Semitism reached a vicious peak as the Nazi regime in Germany systematically annihilated 6 million Jews.

Today, the social standing of Jews is well above average. Still, many Jews are concerned about the future of their religion because in the United States, only half the children growing up in Jewish households are learning Jewish culture and ritual, and more than half marry non-Jews. Others are more optimistic, suggesting that a rising number of "mixed marriages" may attract new people to Judaism (Dershowitz, 1997; Keister, 2003; Goldscheider, 2004).

Hinduism

Hinduism is the oldest of all the world religions, originating in the Indus River valley about 4,500 years ago. Today, there are about 870 million Hindus, which is almost 14 percent of the world's people. Global Map 19–3 on page 500 shows that Hinduism remains an Eastern religion, mostly practiced in India and Pakistan but with a significant presence in southern Africa and Indonesia.

Over the centuries, Hinduism and the culture of India have blended so that now one is not easily described apart from the other (although India also has a sizable Muslim population). This connection also explains why Hinduism, unlike Christianity, Islam, and Judaism, has not diffused widely to other nations. But with 1.3 million followers in the United States, Hinduism is an important part of our country's cultural diversity.

Hinduism differs from most other religions in that it is not linked to the life of any single person. In addition, Hinduism envisions God as a universal moral force rather than a specific entity. For this reason, Hinduism—like other Eastern religions, as you will see shortly—is sometimes described as an "ethical religion." Hindu beliefs and practices vary widely, but all Hindus believe that they have moral responsibilities, called *dharma*. Dharma, for example, calls people to observe the traditional caste system, described in Chapter 10 ("Social Stratification").

Another Hindu principle, *karma,* involves a belief in the spiritual progress of the human soul. To a Hindu, each action has spiritual consequences, and proper living results in moral development. Karma works through *reincarnation,* a cycle of death and rebirth by which a person is born into a spiritual state corresponding to the moral quality of a previous life. Unlike Christianity and Islam, Hinduism recognizes no ultimate judgment at the hands of a supreme god. But in the ongoing cycle of rebirth, it may be said that people get what they deserve. For those who reach *moksha,* the state of spiritual perfection, the soul has no further need to be reborn.

The case of Hinduism shows that not all religions can be neatly labeled as monotheistic or polytheistic. Hinduism is monotheistic

The Dalai Lama is the religious and political leader of the Tibetan people and is the best-known Buddhist teacher in the world. He received the Nobel Peace Prize in 1989 for his efforts to liberate his people from Chinese control through nonviolent means.

insofar as it views the universe as a single moral system; yet Hindus see this moral force at work in every element of nature. Hindus connect to this moral force through their private meditation and rituals, which vary from village to village across the vast nation of India. Many also participate in public events, such as the *Kumbh Mela,* which every twelve years brings some 20 million pilgrims to bathe in the purifying waters of the sacred Ganges River.

Hinduism is not well understood by most people in the United States, although elements of Hindu thought have entered the New Age movement, discussed later in this chapter. But more than 2.5 million people in this country claim Asian Indian ancestry, and the number of immigrants from India is rising, which is making Hinduism more and more important in the United States (Larson, 2000; Eck, 2001; U.S. Census Bureau, 2008).

Buddhism

Twenty-five hundred years ago, the rich culture of India gave rise to Buddhism. Today, some 380 million people, or 6 percent of humanity, are Buddhists, and almost all live in Asia. As shown in Global Map 19–4 on page 500, Buddhists are a majority of the population in Myanmar (Burma), Thailand, Cambodia, and Japan. Buddhism is also widespread in India and the People's Republic of China. Buddhism has

POP CULTURE: Buddhist ideas are widespread in popular culture. For example, movies such as *The Matrix* make use of Buddhist symbols and beliefs.

GLOBAL: Eastern religions—Buddhism, Hinduism, Confucianism, Shintoism—are sometimes called "ethical religions" because they have no gods in the Western sense. Another difference is that Eastern religions have a cyclical framework of birth and rebirth; most Western religions use a linear sense of time.

DIVERSITY: Today, 2,700 chaplains in the U.S. armed forces represent more than 100 religious organizations, including one Buddhist chaplain (some 2,500 military personnel are adherents of this religion).

NOTE: Buddhism's "eightfold path" to enlightenment encompasses proper views, resolve, speech, action, livelihood, effort, mindfulness, and concentration.

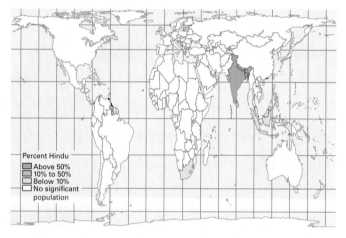

Window on the World

GLOBAL MAP 19–3   **Hinduism in Global Perspective**

Hinduism is closely linked to the culture of India.

Source: Association of Religion Data Archives (2009).

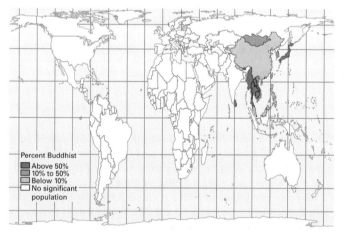

Window on the World

GLOBAL MAP 19–4   **Buddhism in Global Perspective**

Buddhists represent a large part of the populations of most Asian nations.

Source: Association of Religion Data Archives (2009).

much in common with Hinduism: It recognizes no god of judgment, sees each daily action as having spiritual consequences, and believes in reincarnation. But like Christianity, Buddhism has origins in the life of one person.

Siddhartha Gautama was born to a high-caste family in Nepal in 563 B.C.E. Even as a young man, he was deeply spiritual. At the age of twenty-nine, he experienced a personal transformation, which led him to years of travel and meditation. By the end of this journey, he achieved what Buddhists describe as *bodhi,* or enlightenment. By gaining an understanding of the essence of life, Gautama became the Buddha.

Drawn by his personal charisma, followers spread the Buddha's teachings—the *dhamma*—across India. In the third century B.C.E., India's ruler became a Buddhist and sent missionaries throughout Asia, transforming Buddhism into a world religion.

Buddhists believe that much of life in this world involves suffering. This idea is rooted in the Buddha's own travels in a very poor society. But, the Buddha claimed, the solution to suffering is not worldly wealth and power. On the contrary, a concern with worldly things holds back spiritual development. Instead, the Buddha taught that we must use meditation to move beyond selfish concerns and material desires. Only by quieting the mind can people connect with the power of the larger universe—the goal described as *nirvana,* a state of enlightenment and peace (E. J. Thomas, 1975; Van Biema, 1997; Eck, 2001).

Confucianism

From about 200 B.C.E. until the beginning of the twentieth century, Confucianism was a state church—the official religion of China.

MAKING THE GRADE

Pay attention to the two main differences between Eastern and Western religions.

After the 1949 revolution, the Communist government of the new People's Republic of China repressed all religious expression. But even today, hundreds of millions of Chinese are still influenced by Confucianism. China is still home to Confucian thought, although Chinese immigration has spread this religion to other nations in Southeast Asia. Perhaps 100,000 followers of Confucius live in North America.

Confucius, whose Chinese name was K'ung Fu-tzu, lived between 551 and 479 B.C.E. Like the Buddha, Confucius was deeply moved by people's suffering. The Buddha's response was sectlike—a spiritual withdrawal from the world. Confucius took a more churchlike approach, instructing his followers to engage the world according to a code of moral conduct. In the same way that Hinduism became part of the Indian way of life, Confucianism became linked to the traditional culture of China.

A central idea of Confucianism is *jen,* meaning "humaneness." In practice, this means that we must always place moral principle above our self-interest, looking to tradition for guidance in how to live. In the family, Confucius taught, each of us must be loyal and considerate. For their part, families must remember their duties toward the larger community. In this model, layers of moral obligation unite society as a whole.

Of all world religions, Confucianism stands out as lacking a clear sense of the sacred. Perhaps Durkheim would have said that Confucianism is the celebration of the sacred character of society itself. Others might call Confucianism less a religion than a model of disciplined living. However you look at it, Confucianism shares with religion a body of beliefs and practices through which its followers seek moral goodness and social harmony (Schmidt, 1980; McGuire, 1987; Ellwood, 2000).

Religion: East and West

You may already have noticed two general differences between the belief systems of Eastern and Western societies. First, religions that arose in the West (Christianity, Islam, Judaism) have a clear focus on God as a distinct entity. Eastern religions (Hinduism, Buddhism, Confucianism), however, see divine power in everything, so that these religions make little distinction between the sacred and the profane and seem more like ethical codes for living.

Second, followers of Western religions form congregations, worshiping together in a special place at a regular time. Followers of Eastern religions, by contrast, express their religion anywhere and everywhere in their daily lives. Religious temples do exist, but they are used by individuals as part of their daily routines rather than by groups according to a rigid schedule. This is why visitors to a country like Japan are as likely to find temples there filled with tourists as with worshipers.

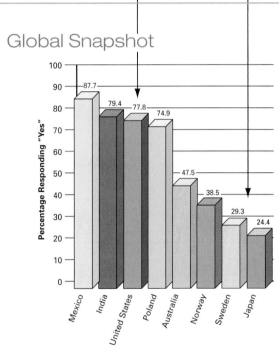

In general, people in higher-income countries are less religious than those in lower-income nations. (The U.S. population is an important exception to this pattern.)

Global Snapshot

Survey Question: "Do you gain comfort and strength from religion?"

FIGURE 19–1   Religiosity in Global Perspective

Religion is stronger in the United States than in many other nations.

Source: Inglehart et al. (2006).

Despite these two differences, however, all religions have a common element: a call to move beyond selfish, everyday concerns in pursuit of a higher moral purpose. Religions may take different paths to this goal, but they all encourage a spiritual sense that there is more to life than what we see around us.

Religion in the United States

As noted in the opening to this chapter, the United States is one of the most religious high-income nations in the world (World Values Survey, 2006; McClay, 2007). As Figure 19–1 shows, nearly eight in ten members of our society say they gain "comfort and strength from religion," a higher share than in most other countries.

That said, scholars debate exactly how religious we are. Some claim that religion remains central to our way of life, but others conclude that a decline of the traditional family and the growing importance of science are weakening religious faith (Hadaway, Marler, & Chaves, 1993; Greeley, 2008).

Q: "A myth is a religion in which no one any longer believes." James Feibleman

GLOBAL: Many Marxist states have been intentionally nonreligious. When Mikhail Gorbachev was sworn in as the president of the Soviet Union in 1985, he placed his hand on a copy of that nation's constitution. Albania outlaws any religious gesture; crossing oneself can bring a prison sentence.

GLOBAL: Andrew Greeley (2002) notes a religious revival in Russia, with 60% claiming to believe in God, and a majority of Russians say they want baptisms, weddings, and funerals in the church.

GLOBAL: Proportion describing the personal significance of religion as very important or rather important: Brazil, 89.3%; U.S., 83.3%; Switzerland, 43.5%; Russia, 39.9%; Germany, 38.2%; Sweden, 29.2%; Japan, 23.3% (Inglehart et al., 2000).

MAKING THE GRADE

How religious the U.S. population is depends on how you operationalize this concept, a process explained on pages 32–33 in Chapter 2 ("Sociological Investigation").

religiosity the importance of religion in a person's life

Table 19–1 Religious Identification in the United States, 2006

Religion	Share of Respondents Indicating a Preference
Protestant denominations	**52.1%**
Baptist	17.5
Methodist	6.6
Lutheran	4.0
Presbyterian	2.8
Episcopalian	1.7
All others or no denomination	19.4
Catholic	**24.9**
Jewish	**1.7**
Other or no answer	**4.7**
No religious preference	**16.5**

Source: *General Social Surveys, 1972–2006: Cumulative Codebook* (Chicago: National Opinion Research Center, 2007), pp. 172–73.

Religious Affiliation

National surveys show that about 85 percent of U.S. adults identify with a religion (NORC, 2007:172). Table 19–1 shows that more than half of U.S. adults consider themselves Protestants, one-fourth are Catholics, and fewer than 2 percent are Jews. Large numbers of people follow dozens of other religions, from animism to Zen Buddhism, making our society the most religiously diverse on Earth (Eck, 2001). The remarkable religious diversity of the United States results from a constitutional ban on any government-sponsored religion and from our historically high numbers of immigrants from all over the world.

About 90 percent of U.S. adults report that they had at least some formal religious instruction when growing up, and 60 percent say they belong to a religious organization (NORC, 2007:442, 1815). National Map 19–1 shows the share of people who claim to belong to any church across the United States.

National Map 19–2 goes a step further, showing that the religion most people identify with varies by region. New England and the Southwest are mostly Catholic, the South is mostly Baptist, and in the northern Plains states, Lutherans predominate. In and around Utah, most people belong to the Church of Jesus Christ of Latter-Day Saints, whose followers are more commonly known as Mormons.

Religiosity

Religiosity is *the importance of religion in a person's life.* However, exactly how religious we are depends on how we operationalize this concept. For example, 93 percent of U.S. adults claim to believe in a divine power, although just 63 percent claim that they "know that God exists and have no doubts about it" (NORC, 2007:445). Fifty-nine percent of adults say they pray at least once a day, but just 31 percent

report attending religious services on a weekly or almost weekly basis (NORC, 2007:183, 175).

Clearly, the question "How religious are we?" has no easy answer, and it is likely that many people in the United States claim to be more religious than they really are. Although most people in the United States say they are at least somewhat religious, probably no more than about one-third actually are. Religiosity also varies among denominations. Members of sects are the most religious of all, followed by Catholics and then "mainstream" Protestant denominations such as Episcopalians, Methodists, and Presbyterians. In general, older people are more religious than younger people, and women are more religious than men (Sherkat & Ellison, 1999; Miller & Stark, 2002).

What difference does being more religious make? Researchers have linked a number of social patterns to strong religious beliefs, including low rates of delinquency among young people and low rates of divorce among adults. According to one study, religiosity helps unite children, parents, and local communities in ways that benefit young people, enhancing their educational achievement (Muller & Ellison, 2001).

Religion: Class, Ethnicity, and Race

Religious affiliation is related to a number of other factors, including social class, ethnicity, and race.

Social Class

A study of *Who's Who in America,* which profiles U.S. high achievers, showed that 33 percent of the people who gave a religious affiliation were Episcopalians, Presbyterians, and United Church of Christ members, denominations that together account for less than 10 percent of the population. Jews, too, enjoy high social position, with this 1.7 percent of the population accounting for 12 percent of the listings in *Who's Who.*

Research shows that other denominations, including Congregationalists, Methodists, and Catholics, have moderate social standing. Lower social standing is typical of Baptists, Lutherans, and members of sects. Of course, there is considerable variation within all denominations (Waters, Heath, & Watson, 1995; Keister, 2003; Pyle, 2006).

Ethnicity

Throughout the world, religion is tied to ethnicity, mostly because one religion stands out in a single nation or geographic region. Islam predominates in the Arab societies of the Middle East, Hinduism is fused with the culture of India, and Confucianism runs deep in Chinese society. Christianity and Judaism do not follow this pattern; although these religions are mostly Western, Christians and Jews are found all over the world.

THE MAP: High church membership characterizes the Mormon region of Utah, the South and Southwest (where fundamentalism and Hispanic immigrants are concentrated), and the Plains states (where there is a high percentage of small-town elderly people).

THE MAP: Immigration (of Lutherans to the upper Midwest) and migration (of Mormons to Utah) shaped much of the religious diversity of the U.S.

Q: "All civilizations are based on religion." Arnold Toynbee

Q: "Religious insanity is very common in the United States." Alexis de Tocqueville

MAKING THE GRADE

Class, ethnicity, and race affect religion as they affect many other social patterns. In the map below, any areas of high religiosity are also those with an older population.

SEEING SOCIOLOGY
in Everyday Life

The United States is religiously diverse, but because certain religions predominate in particular regions of the country, most people do not experience the full range of this diversity in their everyday lives.

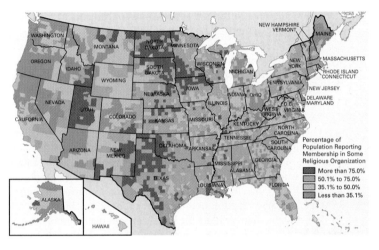

Seeing Ourselves

NATIONAL MAP 19–1

Religious Membership across the United States

In general, people in the United States are more religious than people in other high-income nations. Yet membership in a religious organization is more common in some parts of the country than in others. What pattern do you see in the map? Can you explain the pattern?

Source: Glenmary Research Center (2002).

Percentage of Population Reporting Membership in Some Religious Organization

- More than 75.0%
- 50.1% to 75.0%
- 35.1% to 50.0%
- Less than 35.1%

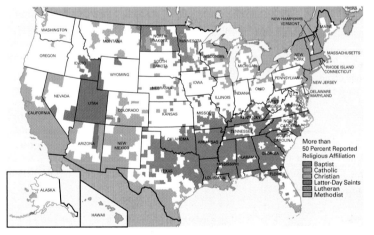

Seeing Ourselves

NATIONAL MAP 19–2

Religious Diversity across the United States

In most counties, a large share of people who report having an affiliation are members of the same religious organization. So although the United States is religiously diverse at the national level, most people live in communities where one denomination predominates. What historical facts might account for this pattern?

Source: Glenmary Research Center (2002).

More than 50 Percent Reported Religious Affiliation

- Baptist
- Catholic
- Christian
- Latter-Day Saints
- Lutheran
- Methodist

Religion and national identity are joined in the United States as well. For example, we have Anglo-Saxon Protestants, Irish Catholics, Russian Jews, and people of Greek Orthodox heritage. This linking of nation and creed results from the influx of immigrants from nations with a single major religion. Still, nearly every ethnic category displays some religious diversity. For example, people of English ancestry may be Protestants, Roman Catholics, Jews, Hindus, Muslims, or followers of other religions.

Race

Scholars claim that the church is both the oldest and the most important social institution in the African American community. Transported to the Western Hemisphere in slave ships, most Africans became Christians, the dominant religion in the Americas, but they blended Christian belief with elements of African religions. Guided by this religious mix, African American Christians have developed rituals that seem, by European standards, far more spontaneous and emotional (Frazier, 1965; Paris, 2000; McRoberts, 2003).

When African Americans started moving from the rural South to the industrial cities of the North around 1940, the church played a major role in addressing the problems of dislocation, poverty, and prejudice (Pattillo, 1998). Black churches have also provided an important avenue of achievement for talented men and women. Ralph Abernathy, Martin Luther King Jr., and Jesse Jackson have all achieved world recognition for their work as religious leaders.

Today, with 87 percent of African Americans claiming a religious affiliation, this category is somewhat more religious than

GLOBAL: Secularization has proceeded further in Europe than in the U.S. In the U.K., for example, whereas law required everyone to attend communion in the 17th century, today just 2% of the population goes to church regularly (Barr, 2003).

Q: "The more of himself man attributes to God, the less he has left in himself." Karl Marx

NOTE: One index of secularization is cremations, which are replacing traditional burials as religious and ethnic traditions weaken. They are also most popular in regions of the country—including California and Florida—where the population is most geographically mobile. Four percent of people chose cremation in 1972, according to the Cremation Association of North America; the current figure is 25%.

SEEING SOCIOLOGY
in Everyday Life

Do you think our society would be better off if more people were religious? Or would it be worse off? Explain your answer.

secularization the historical decline in the importance of the supernatural and sacred

civil religion a quasi-religious loyalty linking individuals in a basically secular society

Religious affiliation in the United States is surprisingly dynamic. In the last fifty years, traditional, "mainstream" religious organizations have lost about half their membership; during the same period, fundamentalist and new spiritualist movements have increased their numbers. As a result, recent research shows that about 44 percent of U.S. adults report having changed their religious affiliation at some point in their lives.

the population as a whole. The vast majority favor a Protestant denomination. However, there is an increasing number of non-Christian African Americans, especially in large U.S. cities. Among them, the most common non-Christian religion is Islam, with as many as 1 million African American followers (Paris, 2000; Pew Forum, 2009).

Religion in a Changing Society

Like family life, religion is also changing in the United States. In the following sections, we look at two major aspects of change: changing affiliations over time and the process of secularization.

Changing Affiliation

A lot of change is going on within the world of religion. Within the United States, membership in established, mainstream churches such as the Episcopalian and Presbyterian denominations has fallen by almost 50 percent since 1960. During this period, as we shall see shortly, other religious categories (including both the "New Age" spir-

itual movement and conservative fundamentalist organizations) have increased in popularity.

Many people are moving from one religious organization to another. A survey by the Pew Forum on Religious & Public Life (2008) shows that 44 percent of adults in the United States report that they have switched religious affiliation at some point in their lives. The pattern by which people are born and raised with a religious affiliation they keep throughout their lives is no longer the case for almost half of the U.S. population.

Such personal changes mean that religious organizations experience a pattern of people coming and going. Catholics, for example, have represented almost one-fourth of the U.S. adult population for some time. But this fairly stable statistic hides the fact that about one-third of all people raised Catholic have left the church. At the same time, about the same number of people—including many immigrants—have joined this church. A more extreme example is the Jehovah's Witnesses: Two-thirds of the people raised in this church have left, but their numbers have been more than replaced by converts recruited by members who travel door-to-door spreading their message.

This pattern of religious "churn" means that there is an active and competitive marketplace of religious organizations in the United States. Perhaps one result of this active competition for members is that U.S. society remains among the most religious in the world. But it also reflects a loosening of ties to the religious organizations people are born into, so men and women now have more choice about their religious beliefs and affiliation.

June 4, Ticonderoga, New York. Our summer church is small—maybe forty people attend on a typical Sunday. These days, Ed Keller says, it's tough for churches to survive with kids' sports teams scheduling practices and games on Sunday morning, Wal-Mart and the other discount stores open for shopping, and many dog-tired people taking advantage of the chance to sleep a little later. Ed thinks that our modern world sometimes seems less than "church-friendly."

Secularization

Secularization is *the historical decline in the importance of the supernatural and the sacred.* Secularization (from a Latin word for "worldly," meaning literally "of the present age") is commonly associated with modern, technologically advanced societies in which science is the major way of understanding.

NOTE: Civil religion is evident in the writing of Jean-Jacques Rousseau, who hated the church but wanted to keep a spirit and discipline in citizenship; curiously, secular conservatives, too, wish to maintain religion's capacity to legitimize public order and maintain the social fabric.

Q: In humans, "social causes substitute themselves for organic causes. The organism is spiritualized." Emile Durkheim

GLOBAL: One measure of the strength of civil religion is the number of national holidays each year: U.S., 32; Japan, 19; Germany, 13; Canada and France, 11; Sweden and Great Britain, 10 (Baker, 1997).

● MAKING THE GRADE

The development of sociology itself as a rational view of the world may be one expression of historical secularization.

Today, we are more likely to experience the transitions of birth, illness, and death in the presence of physicians (people with scientific knowledge) than in the company of religious leaders (whose knowledge is based on faith). This shift alone suggests that religion's relevance to our everyday lives has declined. Harvey Cox (1971:3) explains:

> The world looks less and less to religious rules and rituals for its morality or its meanings. For some [people], religion provides a hobby, for others a mark of national or ethnic identification, for still others an aesthetic delight. For fewer and fewer does it provide an inclusive and commanding system of personal and cosmic values and explanations.

If Cox is right, should we expect religion to disappear someday? Most sociologists say no. The vast majority of people in the United States still say they believe in God, and as many people claim to pray each day as vote in national elections. In fact, the share of people with a religious affiliation is actually higher today than it was back in 1850.

Our society does not seem to be moving steadily toward secularization. It is true that some dimensions of religiosity (such as belief in life after death) have declined, but others (such as religious affiliation) have increased. Similarly, some religious organizations have lost members, but others find their membership increasing. Among college students, as Figure 19–2 shows, the share of first-year students saying they have no religious preference has gone up, more than doubling between 1980 and 2008 (a trend mirrored in the larger adult population). But this share is still just a minority. Putting all this together, the claim that religion is declining in this country may be off the mark (Hout & Fischer, 2002; McClay, 2007; Greeley, 2008; Pryor et al., 2008).

Religious patterns are clearly changing, but people disagree whether this is good or bad. Conservatives tend to see any weakening of religion as a mark of moral decline. Progressives view secularization in more positive terms, as liberation from the dictatorial beliefs of the past, giving people greater choice about what to believe. Secularization has also helped bring some practices of many religious organizations, such as ordaining only men, into line with widespread support for greater gender equality.

An important event that helped spark the secularization debate took place in 1963, when the U.S. Supreme Court banned prayer in public schools as a violation of the constitutional separation of church and state. In recent years, however, religion has returned to many public schools; the Seeing Sociology in Everyday Life box on page 506 takes a closer look at this trend.

According to the secularization thesis, religion should weaken in high-income nations as people enjoy higher living standards and greater security. A global perspective shows that this thesis holds for the countries of Western Europe, where most measures of religios-

Fewer than one-quarter of women and men on U.S. campuses claim no religious affiliation.

Student Snapshot

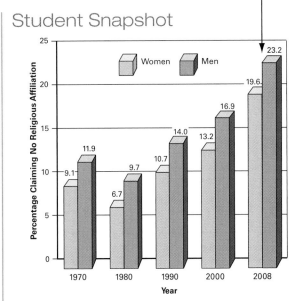

FIGURE 19–2 **Religious Nonaffiliation among First-Year College Students, 1970–2008**

The share of students claiming no religious affiliation has risen in recent decades.

Sources: Astin et al. (2002) and Pryor et al. (2008).

ity have declined and are now low. But the United States—the richest country of all—is an exception; religion remains quite strong here and may even be getting stronger.

Civil Religion

One expression of secularization in the world is the rise of what the sociologist Robert Bellah (1975) calls **civil religion**, *a quasi-religious loyalty linking individuals in a basically secular society.* In other words, formal religion may lose power, but citizenship takes on religious qualities. Most people in the United States consider our way of life a force for moral good in the world. Many people also find religious qualities in political movements, whether liberal or conservative (Williams & Demerath, 1991).

Civil religion also involves a wide range of rituals, from singing the national anthem at major sporting events to waving the flag in public parades. At all such events, the U.S. flag serves as a sacred symbol of our national identity, and we expect people to treat it with respect.

Religion CHAPTER 19

505

Q: "Politics and the pulpit are terms that have no agreement." Edmund Burke

NOTE: The "vital force" noted by New Agers is the *prana* in Yoga, the Chinese concept of *chi*, and the Islamic concept of *baraka*. Another difference: Conventional religion sees a God of moral judgment, but New Age spiritualism sees God as a supportive power in all of us.

SOCIAL SURVEY: "How important is following one's conscience even if it means going against what the churches or synagogues say and do?" (GSS 1998, *N* = 1,445; *Codebook*, 2005:449)

(1) "Very important" 39.9%   (4) 7.4%
(2) 16.2%   (5) "Not very important" 9.5%
(3) 21.7%   "Don't know"/No response 6.4%

● SEEING SOCIOLOGY
in Everyday Life

Do you think that the rise of New Age spirituality is evidence of secularization or evidence of the continuing importance of religion in everyday life? Explain your view.

SEEING SOCIOLOGY IN EVERYDAY LIFE

Should Students Pray in School?

It is late afternoon on a cloudy spring day in Minneapolis, and two dozen teenagers have come together to pray. They share warm smiles as they enter the room. As soon as everyone is seated, the prayers begin, with one voice following another. One girl prays for her brother; a boy prays for the success of an upcoming food drive; another asks God to comfort a favorite teacher who is having a hard time. Then they join their voices to pray for all the teachers at their school who are not Christians. Following the prayers, the young people sing Christian songs, discuss a Scripture lesson, and bring their meeting to a close with a group hug (Van Biema, 1998, 1999).

What is so unusual about this prayer meeting is that it is taking place in Room 133 of Patrick Henry High School, a public institution. In public schools from coast to coast, something of a religious revival is taking place as more and more students hold meetings like this one.

You would have to be at least fifty years old to remember when it was routine for public school students to start the day with Bible reading and prayer. In 1963, the Supreme Court ruled that religion in the schools violated the constitutional ban on government-sponsored religion, and this decision soon put an end to all religious activies in public schools.

But from the moment the ruling was announced, critics charged that by supporting a wide range of other activities

and clubs while banning religious activities, schools were really being *antireligious*. Critics also point out that nowhere does the U.S. Constitution demand a separation of church and state; the First Amendment states that "Congress shall make no law respecting an establishment of religion, or prohibiting the free exercise thereof." So why can't students meet to participate in religious activities if they choose to do so? In 1990, such thinking led the Supreme Court to hand down a new ruling, stating that religious groups can meet on school property as long as group membership is voluntary, the meetings are held outside regular class hours, and students rather than adults run them.

Although some U.S. colleges and universities are operated by religious organizations, most offer a secular education. At secular schools, do you think religious groups should be treated the same in terms of funding as any other groups? Why or why not?

In recent years, student religious groups have formed in perhaps one-fourth of all public schools. Evangelical Christian organizations such as First Priority and National Network of Youth are using the Internet as well as word of mouth in an effort to expand the place of religion in every public school across the country. However, opponents of school prayer worry that religious enthusiasm may lead some students to pressure others to join their groups. Such disagreements ensure that the debate over prayer in school will continue.

WHAT DO YOU THINK?

1. Do you think that religious clubs should have the same freedom to operate on school grounds as other organizations? Why or why not?

2. The First Amendment to the U.S. Constitution states that Congress must not establish any official religion and must also pass no law that would interfere with the free practice of religion. How would you apply this principle to the issue of prayer in school?

3. Schools support the mental and physical development of students; should they also support their spiritual development? If you were a member of the local school board, what would be your position on the place of religion in public schools?

"New Age" Seekers: Spirituality without Formal Religion

December 29, Machu Picchu, Peru. We are ending the first day exploring this magnificent city built by the Inca people high in the Andes Mountains. Lucas, a local shaman, or religious leader, is leading a group of twelve travelers in a ceremony of thanks. He kneels on the dirt floor of the

small stone building and places offerings—corn and beans, sugar, plants of all colors, and even bits of gold and silver—in front of him as gifts to Mother Earth as he prays for harmony, joy, and the will to do good for one another. His words and the magical setting make the ceremony a very powerful experience.

In recent decades, more and more people have been seeking spiritual development outside of established religious organizations. This trend has led some analysts to suggest that the United States is becom-

NOTE: Fundamentalism is, in part, a product of our frontier history, when circuit preachers made dramatic presentations in hopes of prompting an immediate conversion by those attending. Fundamentalism is less pronounced in Europe because European churches are more established and usually linked to the state.

Q: "There is a bias among some of our political elites, that if you're willing to die for the Bible, you're a fanatic." Nina Shea

NOTE: Literal interpretation of the sacred texts of any religion sharply limits debate among adherents about religious truth, thereby fostering consensus. But literal readings may still reveal inconsistencies; for example, there are two creation stories in Genesis.

MAKING THE GRADE

"New age" religion is more Eastern than Western in focus. See page 501.

fundamentalism a conservative religious doctrine that opposes intellectualism and worldly accommodation in favor of restoring traditional, otherworldly religion

ing a *postdenominational society.* In simple terms, more people seem to be spiritual seekers, believing in a vital spiritual dimension to human existence that they pursue more or less separately from membership in any formal denomination.

What exactly is the difference between this so-called New Age focus on spirituality and a traditional concern with religion? As one analysis (Cimino & Lattin, 1999:62) puts it, spirituality is

> the search for . . . a religion of the heart, not the head. It . . . downplays doctrine and dogma, and revels in direct experience of the divine—whether it's called the "holy spirit" or "divine consciousness" or "true self." It's practical and personal, more about stress reduction than salvation, more therapeutic than theological. It's about feeling good rather than being good. It's as much about the body as the soul.

Millions of people in the United States take part in New Age spirituality. Hank Wesselman (2001:39–42), an anthropologist and spiritual teacher, identifies five core values that define this approach:

1. **Seekers believe in a higher power**. There exists a higher power, a vital force that is within all things and all people. Humans, then, are partly divine.

2. **Seekers believe we're all connected**. Everything and everyone is interconnected as part of a universal divine pattern.

3. **Seekers believe in a spirit world**. The physical world is not all there is; a more important spiritual reality (or "spirit world") also exists.

4. **Seekers want to experience the spirit world**. Spiritual development means gaining the ability to experience the spirit world. Many seekers come to understand that helpers and teachers (traditionally called "angels") dwell in the spirit world and can touch their lives.

5. **Seekers pursue transcendence**. Various techniques (such as yoga, meditation, and prayer) give people an increasing ability to rise above the immediate physical world (the experience of "transcendence"), which is seen as the larger purpose of life.

From a traditional point of view, this New Age spirituality may seem more like psychology than religion. It avoids judgments about right and wrong in favor of encouraging all of us to grow as we move along our life's journey. It has become an important new form of religious expression in the modern world—one that blends traditional belief with modern tolerance and rationality—that is gaining popularity, especially among highly educated people (Tucker, 2002; Wuthnow, 2003; Besecke, 2003, 2005).

New Age "seekers" are people in pursuit of spiritual growth, often using the age-old technique of meditation. The goal of this activity is to quiet the mind so that by moving away from everyday concerns, one can hear an inner, divine voice. Countless people attest to the spiritual value of meditation; it has also been linked to improved physical health.

Religious Revival: "Good Old-Time Religion"

At the same time as New Age spirituality is becoming more popular, a great deal of change has been going on in the world of organized religion. In the United States, membership in liberal mainstream denominations such as Episcopalian and Presbyterian has dropped by almost 50 percent since 1960. During the same period, affiliation with more conservative religious organizations (including the Mormons, the Seventh-Day Adventists, and Christian sects) has risen just as fast.

These opposing trends suggest that secularization may be self-limiting: As many churchlike organizations become more worldly, many people leave them in favor of more sectlike communities offering a more intense religious experience (Stark & Bainbridge, 1981; Jacquet & Jones, 1991; Iannaccone, 1994; Hout, Greeley, & Wilde, 2001).

Religious Fundamentalism

Fundamentalism is *a conservative religious doctrine that opposes intellectualism and worldly accommodation in favor of restoring traditional, otherworldly religion.* In the United States, fundamentalism has made the greatest gains among Protestants. Southern Baptists, for example, are the largest religious community in the country. But fundamentalist groups have also grown among Roman Catholics, Jews, and Muslims.

In response to what they see as the growing influence of science and the weakening of the conventional family, religious fundamentalists

SOCIAL SURVEY: "The U.S. Supreme Court has ruled that no state or local government may require the reading of the Lord's Prayer or Bible verses in public schools. What are your views on this?" (GSS 2004, N = 906; Codebook, 2005:196)

"Approve" 35.2%   "Disapprove" 61.6%   "Don't know"/No response 3.2%

Q: "If we do discover a complete theory [of physics] . . . it would be the ultimate triumph of human reason—for then we would truly know the mind of God." Stephen Hawking

Q: "Science without religion is lame; religion without science is blind." Albert Einstein

SEEING SOCIOLOGY
in Everyday Life

Do you think the rise of fundamentalist Islam in some parts of the world challenges the secularization thesis? Why or why not?

CONTROVERSY & DEBATE

Does Science Threaten Religion?

CIHAN: I think someday science will prove religion to be false.

RASHEED: I don't think science and religion are talking about the same thing at all.

About 400 years ago, the Italian physicist and astronomer Galileo (1564–1642) helped launch the Scientific Revolution with a series of startling discoveries. Dropping objects from the Leaning Tower of Pisa, he discovered some of the laws of gravity; making his own telescope, he observed the stars and found that Earth orbited the sun, not the other way around.

For his trouble, Galileo was challenged by the Roman Catholic Church, which had preached for centuries that Earth stood motionless at the center of the universe. Galileo only made matters worse by responding that religious leaders had no business talking about matters of science.

Before long, he found his work banned and himself under house arrest.

As Galileo's treatment shows, right from the start, science has had an uneasy relationship with religion. In the twentieth century, the two clashed again over the issue of creation. Charles Darwin's masterwork, *On the Origin of Species,* states that humanity evolved from lower forms of life over a billion years. Yet this theory seems to fly in the face of the biblical account of creation

found in Genesis, which states that "God created the heavens and the earth," introducing life on the third day and, on the fifth and sixth days, animal life, including human beings fashioned in God's own image.

Galileo would certainly have been an eager observer of the famous "Scopes monkey trial." In 1925, the state of Tennessee put a small-town science teacher named John Thomas Scopes on trial for teaching Darwinian evolution in the local high school. State law forbade teaching "any theory that denies the story of the Divine Creation of man as taught in the Bible" and especially the idea that "man descended from a lower order of animals." Scopes was found guilty and fined $100. His conviction was reversed on appeal, so the case never reached the U.S. Supreme Court, and the Tennessee law stayed on the books until 1967. A year later, the Supreme Court, in *Epperson v. Arkansas,* struck down

---

defend what they call "traditional values." As they see it, liberal churches are simply too open to compromise and diversity (and religious "seekers" are even more tolerant and open to change). Religious fundamentalism is distinctive in five ways (Hunter, 1983, 1985, 1987):

1. **Fundamentalists take the words of sacred texts literally.** Fundamentalists insist on a literal reading of sacred texts such as the Bible to counter what they see as excessive intellectualism among more liberal religious organizations. For example, fundamentalist Christians believe that God created the world in seven days precisely as described in the biblical book of Genesis.

2. **Fundamentalists reject religious pluralism.** Fundamentalists believe that tolerance and relativism water down personal faith. Therefore, they maintain that their religious beliefs are true and other beliefs are not.

3. **Fundamentalists pursue the personal experience of God's presence.** In contrast to the worldliness and intellectualism of other religious organizations, fundamentalism seeks a return to "good old-time religion" and spiritual revival. To fundamentalist Christians, being "born again" and having a personal relationship with Jesus Christ should be evident in a person's everyday life.

4. **Fundamentalists oppose "secular humanism."** Fundamentalists think that accommodation to the changing world weakens religious faith. They reject "secular humanism," our society's tendency to look to scientific experts rather than to God for guidance about how we should live. There is nothing new in this tension between science and religion; it has existed for centuries, as the Controversy & Debate box explains.

5. **Many fundamentalists endorse conservative political goals.** Although fundamentalism tends to back away from worldly concerns, some fundamentalist leaders (including Ralph Reed, Pat Robertson, and Gary Bauer) have entered politics to oppose what they call the "liberal agenda," including feminism and gay rights. Fundamentalists oppose abortion and gay marriage; they support the traditional two-parent family, seek a return of prayer in schools, and criticize the mass media for coloring stories with a liberal bias (Manza & Brooks, 1997; Thomma, 1997; Rozell, Wilcox, & Green, 1998).

Opponents regard fundamentalism as judgmental, rigid, and self-righteous. But many find in fundamentalism, with its greater religious certainty and emphasis on the emotional experience of God's

DISCUSS: Why do almost all presidents describe themselves as religious? Would a self-declared atheist be electable as president in the U.S. today? Why or why not?

Q: "We have too many men of science, too few of God. We have grasped the mystery of the atom and rejected the Sermon on the Mount. . . . Ours is a world of nuclear giants and ethical infants. We know more about war than about peace, more about killing than about living." General Omar N. Bradley (1948)

SEEING SOCIOLOGY
in Everyday Life

Were you raised in a particular religious tradition? If yes, would you describe it as "fundamentalist," "moderate," or "liberal"? What beliefs do you hold now?

all such laws as unconstitutional government support of religion.

Today, almost four centuries after Galileo was silenced, many people still debate the apparently conflicting claims of science and religion. A third of U.S. adults believe that the Bible is the literal word of God, and many of them reject any scientific findings that run counter to it (NORC, 2007:203). In 2005, all eight members of the school board in Dover, Pennsylvania, were voted out of office after they took a stand that many townspeople saw as weakening the teaching of evolution; at the same time, the Kansas state school board ordered the teaching of evolution to include its weaknesses and limitations from a religious point of view ("Much Ado about Evolution," 2005).

But a middle ground is emerging: Half of U.S. adults (and also many church leaders) say that the Bible is a book of truths inspired by God without being accurate in a literal, scientific

sense. That is, science and religion are two different ways of understanding that answer different questions. Both Galileo and Darwin devoted their lives to investigating *how* the natural world works. Yet only religion can address *why* we and the natural world exist in the first place.

This basic difference between science and religion helps explain why our nation is both the most scientific and the most religious in the world. As one scientist noted, the mathematical odds that a cosmic "big bang" 12 billion years ago created the universe and led to the formation of life as we know it are even smaller than the chance of winning a state lottery twenty weeks in a row. Doesn't such a scientific fact suggest an intelligent and purposeful power in our creation? Can't a person be a religious believer and at the same time a scientific investigator?

In 1992, a Vatican commission concluded that the church's silencing of Galileo was wrong.

Today, most scientific and religious leaders agree that science and religion represent important but different truths. Many also believe that in today's rush to scientific discovery, our world has never been more in need of the moral guidance provided by religion.

WHAT DO YOU THINK?

1. Why do you think some scientific people reject religious accounts of human creation? Why do some religious people reject scientific accounts?

2. Does the sociological study of religion challenge anyone's faith? Why or why not?

3. About half of U.S. adults think science is changing our way of life too fast. Do you agree? Why or why not?

Sources: Gould (1981), Huchingson (1994), Applebome (1996), and Greely (2008).

presence, an appealing alternative to the more intellectual, tolerant, and worldly "mainstream" denominations (Marquand, 1997).

Which religions are fundamentalist? In recent years, the world has become familiar with an extreme form of fundamentalist Islam that supports violence directed against Western culture. In the United States, the term is most correctly applied to conservative Christian organizations in the evangelical tradition, including Pentecostals, Southern Baptists, Seventh-Day Adventists, and Assemblies of God. Several national religious movements, including Promise Keepers (a men's organization) and Chosen Women, have a fundamentalist orientation. In national surveys, 28 percent of U.S. adults describe their religious upbringing as "fundamentalist," 39 percent claim a "moderate" upbringing, and 29 percent, a "liberal" background (NORC, 2007:174).

The Electronic Church

In contrast to local congregations of years past, some religious organizations, especially fundamentalist ones, have become electronic churches featuring "prime-time preachers" (Hadden & Swain, 1981). Electronic religion is found only in the United States. It has made James Dobson, Joel Osteen, Franklin Graham, Robert Schuller, and others

more famous than all but a few clergy of the past. About 5 percent of the national television audience (some 10 million people) regularly view religious television, and 20 percent (about 40 million) watch or listen to some religious programming every week (NORC, 2007:444).

Religion: Looking Ahead

The popularity of media ministries, the growth of fundamentalism, new forms of spirituality, and the connection of millions of people to mainstream churches show that religion will remain a major part of modern society for decades to come. High levels of immigration from many religious countries (in Latin America and elsewhere) should intensify as well as diversify the religious character of U.S. society in the twenty-first century (Yang & Ebaugh, 2001).

The world is becoming more complex, and change seems to move more rapidly than our ability to make sense of it all. But rather than weakening religion, this process fires the religious imagination. As new technology gives us the power to change, extend, and even create life, we are faced with increasingly difficult moral questions. Against this backdrop of uncertainty, it is little wonder that many people look to their faith for guidance and hope.

Seeing Sociology in Everyday Life

Chapter 19   Religion

How religious is our society?

Compared to most other high-income nations, the United States has a relatively high level of religious belief and activity. We consider ourselves to be a modern, secular society, yet as this chapter explains, most people claim to be religious and at least one-third of the population is. Civil religion is also evident in many aspects of our everyday lives. Look at the photos below: Can you point to elements of civil religion in each of these familiar situations?

> **HINT**   As this chapter explains, civil religion is a quasi-religious loyalty linking members of a mostly secular society. Important events that qualify as civil religion are not formally religious but are typically defined as holidays (a word derived from "holy days"); involve gatherings of family, neighbors, and friends; and include ritual activities and the sharing of specific foods and beverages.

On Thanksgiving Day, most families across the United States gather to share a special dinner and give thanks for their good fortune. What religious or quasi-religious elements are part of a typical Thanksgiving celebration?

What about the Fourth of July? How is this special day an example of civil religion?

In recent decades, football's Super Bowl has emerged as an important annual event. What elements of civil religion can you find in Super Bowl Sunday?

Applying SOCIOLOGY in Everyday Life

1. Make a list of other events, activities, and pastimes that might be considered examples of civil religion. (Start off with Election Day; what about baseball?) Are there any local college events or rituals that might be included? In each case, explain the religious element that you see and the way the event or activity affects members of a community.

2. Develop five questions that might be used on a questionnaire or in an interview to measure how religious people are. Present them to several people. Use the results to show that how reli-

gious people appear to be depends on exactly what questions you ask them.

3. Is religion in the United States getting weaker? To evaluate the claim that our society is undergoing secularization, go to the library or local newspaper office and obtain an issue of your local newspaper published fifty years ago and, if possible, one published 100 years ago. Compare the amount of attention given to religious issues then and now. What pattern do you see?

MAKING THE GRADE

CHAPTER 19 Religion

Religion: Basic Concepts

- **RELIGION** is a major social institution based on setting the *sacred* apart from the *profane*.
- Religion is grounded in *faith* rather than scientific evidence, and people express their religious beliefs through various rituals.

p. 488

✓ Sociologists study how religion is linked to other social patterns but make no claims about the truth of any religious belief (p. 489).

profane (p. 488) included as an ordinary element of everyday life

sacred (p. 488) set apart as extraordinary, inspiring awe and reverence

religion (p. 488) a social institution involving beliefs and practices based on recognizing the sacred

ritual (p. 488) formal, ceremonial behavior

faith (p. 489) belief based on conviction rather than on scientific evidence

Theoretical Analysis of Religion

The **STRUCTURAL-FUNCTIONAL APPROACH** desribes how people celebrate the power of society through religion. Emile Durkheim identified three major functions of religion:

- Religion unites people, promoting social cohesion.
- Religion encourages people to obey cultural norms, promoting conformity.
- Religion gives meaning and purpose to life.

pp. 489–90

The **SYMBOLIC-INTERACTION APPROACH** explains that people use religion to give everyday life sacred meaning.

- People create rituals that separate the sacred from the profane.
- Peter Berger claimed that people are especially likely to seek religious meaning when faced with life's uncertainties and disruptions.

p. 490

The **SOCIAL-CONFLICT APPROACH** highlights religion's support of social inequality.

- Karl Marx claimed that religion justifies the status quo and diverts people's attention from social injustice.
- In this way, religion discourages change toward a more just and equal society.
- Religion is also linked to gender inequality: The world's major religions are all patriarchal.

pp. 490–91

totem (p. 489) an object in the natural world collectively defined as sacred

📖 See the Applying Theory table on page 493.

Religion and Social Change

- Max Weber argued, in opposition to Marx, that religion can encourage social change. He showed how Calvinism became "disenchanted," leading to a profane "Protestant work ethic" that contributed to the rise of industrial capitalism.
- **LIBERATION THEOLOGY,** a fusion of Christian principles and political activism, tries to encourage social change.

pp. 491–93

liberation theology (p. 493) the combining of Christian principles with political activism, often Marxist in character

Types of Religious Organizations

CHURCHES are religious organizations well integrated into their society. Churches fall into two categories: state churches (examples: the Anglican Church in England and Islam in Morocco), and denominations (examples: Christian denominations such as Baptists and Lutherans, as well as various categories of Judaism, Islam, and other traditions).

pp. 493–94

SECTS are the result of religious division. They are marked by charismatic leadership and members' suspicion of the larger society.

p. 494

CULTS are religious organizations based on new and unconventional beliefs and practices.

pp. 494–95

church (p. 493) a type of religious organization that is well integrated into the larger society

state church (p. 493) a church formally allied with the state

denomination (p. 493) a church, independent of the state, that recognizes religious pluralism

sect (p. 494) a type of religious organization that stands apart from the larger society

charisma (p. 494) extraordinary personal qualities that can infuse people with emotion and turn them into followers

cult (p. 494) a religious organization that is largely outside a society's cultural traditions

Sociologists categorize religious organizations in the United States along a continuum, with churches at one end and sects at the other.

Churches ←————————————————→ Sects	
try to appeal to everyone	hold rigid religious convictions
have a highly formal style of worship	have a spontaneous and emotional style of worship
formally train and ordain leaders	follow highly charismatic leaders
are long-established and organizationally stable	form as breakaway groups and are less stable
attract members of high social standing	attract members who are social outsiders

Religion in History

- Hunting and gathering societies practiced *animism*, viewing elements of the natural world as spiritual forces.
- Belief in a single divine power began in pastoral and horticultural societies.
- Organized religion gained importance in agrarian societies.
- In industrial societies, scientific knowledge explains *how* the world works, but people look to religion to answer questions about *why* the world exists.

p. 495

animism (p. 495) the belief that elements of the natural world are conscious life forms that affect humanity

World Religions

WESTERN RELIGIONS

CHRISTIANITY
- Christianity is the most widespread religion, with 2 billion followers—almost one-third of the world's people.
- Christianity began as a cult built on the personal charisma of Jesus of Nazareth; Christians believe Jesus is the Son of God and follow his teachings.

pp. 496

ISLAM
- Islam has about 1.3 billion followers, who are known as Muslims—almost one-fifth of the world's people.
- Muslims follow the word of God as revealed to the prophet Muhammad and written in the Qur'an, the sacred text of Islam.

pp. 496–498

JUDAISM
- Judaism's 15 million followers are mainly in Israel and the United States.
- Jewish belief rests on the covenant between God and his chosen people, embodied in the Ten Commandments and the Old Testament of the Bible.

pp. 498-99

EASTERN RELIGIONS

HINDUISM
- Hinduism is the oldest world religion and today has about 870 million adherents.
- Hindus see God as a universal moral force rather than a specific being and believe in the principles of *dharma* (moral responsibilities) and *karma* (the spiritual progress of the human soul).

pp. 499

BUDDHISM
- Buddhists number about 390 million people.
- Buddhist teachings are similar to Hindu beliefs, but Buddhism is based on the life of one person, Siddhartha Gautama, who taught the use of meditation as a way to move beyond selfish desires to achieve *nirvana*, a state of enlightenment and peace.

pp. 499–500

CONFUCIANISM
- Confucianism was the state church of China until the 1949 Communist revolution repressed religious expression. It is still strongly linked to Chinese culture.
- Confucianism teaches *jen*, or "humaneness," meaning that people must place moral principles above self-interest. Layers of moral obligations unite society as a whole.

pp. 500-501

✓ *Western religions share a focus on God and have well-defined congregations. Eastern religions tend to be ethical codes largely fused with the broader culture.*

monotheism (p. 496) belief in a single divine power

polytheism (p. 496) belief in many gods

Religion in the United States

The United States is one of the most religious and religiously diverse nations. How researchers operationalize "religiosity" affects how "religious" our people seem to be:
- 85% of adults identify with a religion
- 63% profess a firm belief in God and belong to a religious organization
- 59% of adults say they pray at least once a day
- just 31% say they attend religious services weekly

pp. 501–2

Religious affiliation is tied to *social class*, *ethnicity*, and *race*:
- On average, Episcopalians, Presbyterians, and Jews enjoy high standing; lower social standing is typical of Baptists, Lutherans, and members of sects.
- Religion is often linked to ethnic background because people came to the United States from countries that have or had a major religion.
- Transported to this country in slave ships, most Africans became Christians, but they blended Christian beliefs with elements of African religions they brought with them.

pp. 502–4

religiosity (p. 502) the importance of religion in a person's life

Religion in a Changing Society

- **SECULARIZATION** is a decline in the importance of the supernatural and sacred.
- In the United States, while some indicators of religiosity (like membership in mainstream churches) have declined, others (such as membership in sects) have increased.
- Today, **CIVIL RELIGION** takes the form of a quasi-religious patriotism that ties people to their society.

pp. 504–5

- *Spiritual seekers* are part of the New Age movement, which pursues spiritual development outside conventional religious organizations.
- **FUNDAMENTALISM** opposes religious accommodation to the world, interprets religious texts literally, and rejects religious diversity.

pp. 506–9

secularization (p. 504) the historical decline in the importance of the supernatural and the sacred

civil religion (p. 505) a quasi-religious loyalty linking individuals in a basically secular society

fundamentalism (p. 507) a conservative religious doctrine that opposes intellectualism and worldly accommodation in favor of restoring traditional, otherworldly religion

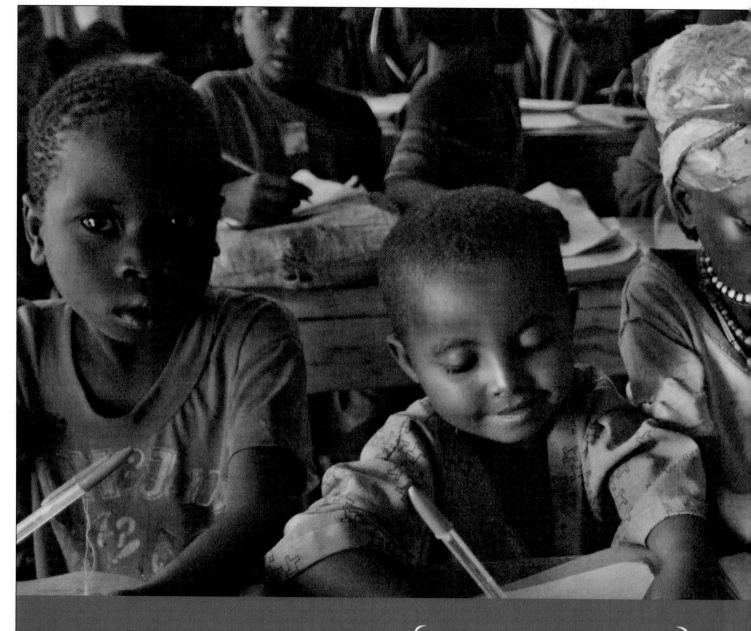

In the modern world, education emerges as a new social institution as societies develop schooling to prepare people for future work. Earning a college degree has a powerful and positive effect on future earnings.

CHAPTER 20

Education

SUPPLEMENTS: An outline for this chapter, supplementary lecture material, and discussion topics are found in the *Instructor's Manual*.

NOTE: Since 1970, significant improvements in elementary school enrollment have been reported by most nations in sub-Saharan Africa. Still, many of these societies have a level of schooling that is comparable to that offered in the U.S. in 1850.

NOTE: The world's oldest university was founded in Bologna, Italy, in the late 11th century. In England, the oldest is Oxford, founded in the early 12th century. By the 13th century, historical notes mention "university chests," funds for the assistance of poor students—the earliest form of financial aid.

CHAPTER OVERVIEW

This chapter explains the operation of education, a major social institution. The chapter begins with a global survey of schooling and then focuses on education in the United States.

When Lisa Addison was growing up in Baltimore, her teachers always said she was smart and should go to college. "I liked hearing that," she recalls. "But I didn't know what to do about it. No one in my family had ever gone to college. I didn't know what courses to take in high school. I had no idea of how to apply to a college. How would I pay for it? What would it be like if I got there?"

Discouraged and uncertain, Addison found herself "kind of goofing off in school." After finishing high school, she spent the next fifteen years working as a waitress in a restaurant and then as a kitchen helper in a catering company. Now, at the age of thirty-eight, Addison has decided to go back to school. "I don't want to do this kind of work for the rest of my life. I *am* smart. I can do better. At this point, I *am* ready for college."

Addison took a giant step through the door of the Community College of Baltimore County, speaking to counselors and setting her sights on an associate's degree in business. When she finishes the two-year program, she plans to transfer to a four-year university to complete a bachelor's degree. Then she hopes to go back into the food service industry—but this time as manager at higher pay (Toppo & DeBarros, 2005).

Higher education is part of the American dream for almost all young people in the United States. But many face the types of challenges that delayed Lisa Addison in her journey toward a college degree. Especially for people growing up in low-income families, often with parents who are not college graduates, the odds of getting to college can be small.

Who goes to college in the United States? What difference does higher education make in the type of job you get or the money you make? This chapter answers these questions by focusing on **education**, *the social institution through which society provides its members with important knowledge, including basic facts, job skills, and cultural norms and values.* In high-income nations such as the United States, education is largely a matter of **schooling**, *formal instruction under the direction of specially trained teachers.*

Education: A Global Survey

In the United States, young people expect to spend most of their first eighteen years in school. This was not the case a century ago, when just a small elite had the privilege of attending school. Even today, most young people in poor countries receive only a few years of formal schooling.

Schooling and Economic Development

The extent of schooling in any society is tied to its level of economic development. In low- and middle-income countries, which are home to most of the world's people, families and communities teach young people important knowledge and skills. Formal schooling, especially learning that is not directly connected to survival, is available mainly to wealthy people who may not need to work and who can pursue personal enrichment. The word *school* is from a Greek root that means "leisure." In ancient Greece, famous teachers such as Socrates, Plato, and Aristotle taught aristocratic, upper-class men who had plenty of spare time. The same was true in ancient China, where the famous philosopher K'ung Fu-tzu (Confucius) shared his wisdom with a privileged few.

> **December 30, the Cuzco region, Peru.** High in the Andes Mountains of Peru, families send their children to the local school. But "local" can mean 3 miles away or more, and there are no buses, so these children, almost all from poor families, walk at least an hour each way. Schooling is required by law, but in the rural highlands, some parents prefer to keep their children at home where they can help with the farming and livestock.

GLOBAL: A classic example of a foreign nation structuring an educational system is the U.S. remaking of Japanese schooling during the occupation after World War II.

GLOBAL: Research explains the U.S.-Asian "math gap" in terms of parental attitudes: Most U.S. parents are satisfied with their children's learning and amount of homework; most Asian parents are not and are more demanding of their children.

RESOURCE: The author's companion reader Seeing Ourselves, 8th ed., includes "The English Only Debate" by Alejandro Portes.

GLOBAL: One key to Japanese educational achievement is powerful cultural discipline. Such collective pressure generates collective distinction but produces fewer highly innovative individuals. To illustrate, U.S. men and women have received proportionately more Nobel Prizes than the Japanese have.

education the social institution through which society provides its members with important knowledge, including basic facts, job skills, and cultural norms and values

schooling formal instruction under the direction of specially trained teachers

SEEING SOCIOLOGY
in Everyday Life

The extent of schooling is one good measure of economic development.

Today, the limited schooling that takes place in lower-income countries reflects the national culture. In Iran, for example, schooling is closely tied to Islam. Similarly, schooling in Bangladesh (Asia), Zimbabwe (Africa), and Nicaragua (Latin America) has been shaped by the distinctive cultural traditions of these nations.

All lower-income countries have one trait in common when it comes to schooling: There is not much of it. In the world's poorest nations (including several in Central Africa), more than one-fourth of all children never get to school (World Bank, 2009). Worldwide, more than one-third of all children never reach the secondary grades (what we call *high school*). As a result, about one-fifth of the world's people cannot read or write. Global Map 20–1 on page 518 shows the extent of illiteracy around the world, and the following national comparisons illustrate the link between the extent of schooling and economic development.

In many low-income nations, children are as likely to work as they are to attend school, and girls receive less schooling than boys. But the doors to schooling are now opening to more girls and women. These young women are studying nursing at Somalia University in downtown Mogadishu.

Schooling in India

India has recently become a middle-income country, but people there still earn only about 6 percent of U.S. average income, and most poor families depend on the earnings of children. Even though India has outlawed child labor, many children continue to work in factories—weaving rugs or making handicrafts—up to sixty hours per week, which greatly limits their opportunities for schooling.

Today, almost 90 percent of children in India complete primary school, typically in crowded schoolrooms where one teacher may face as many as sixty children, twice as many as in the average U.S. public school classroom. Barely half of Indian children go on to secondary school, and very few enter college. As a result, 34 percent of India's people are not able to read and write (UNESCO, 2009).

Patriarchy also shapes Indian education. Indian parents are joyful at the birth of a boy because he and his future wife will both contribute income to the family. But there are economic costs to raising a girl: Parents must provide a dowry (a gift of wealth to the groom's family), and after her marriage, a daughter's work benefits her husband's family. Therefore, many Indians see less reason to invest in the schooling of girls, so only 49 percent of girls (compared to 59 percent of boys) reach the secondary grades. What do the girls do while the boys are in school? Most of the children working in Indian factories are girls—a family's way of benefiting from their daughters while they can (UNESCO, 2008).

Schooling in Japan

Schooling has not always been part of the Japanese way of life. Before industrialization brought mandatory education in 1872, only a privileged few attended school. Today, Japan's educational system is widely praised for producing some of the world's highest achievers.

The early grades concentrate on transmitting Japanese traditions, especially a sense of obligation to family. Starting in their early teens, students take a series of difficult and highly competitive examinations. Their scores on these written tests, which are like the Scholastic Assessment Test (SAT) in the United States, decide the future of all Japanese students.

More men and women graduate from high school in Japan (93 percent) than in the United States (87 percent). But competitive examinations allow just half of high school graduates—compared to 66 percent in the United States—to enter college. Understandably, Japanese students (and their parents) take entrance examinations very seriously. About half attend "cram schools" to prepare for the exams, which means very late nights completing homework. Such hard work is one reason that Japanese students often nap in class—seen by teachers as the mark of a serious student (Steger, 2006; UNESCO, 2008).

Japanese schooling produces impressive results. In a number of fields, notably mathematics and science, Japanese students outperform students in almost every other high-income nation, including the United States (OECD, 2009).

Schooling in Great Britain

During the Middle Ages, schooling was a privilege of the British nobility, who studied classical subjects, having little concern for the practical skills needed to earn a living. But as the Industrial Revolution

Q: "A human being is not, in any proper sense, a human being until he is educated."
Horace Mann

Q: "It is well to remember from time to time that nothing that is worth knowing can be taught." Oscar Wilde

GLOBAL: British "public" schools number about 1,000 and cost at least $30,000 a year. They are similar to private boarding schools here in the United States. The "Harry Potter" films offer one view of such schools.

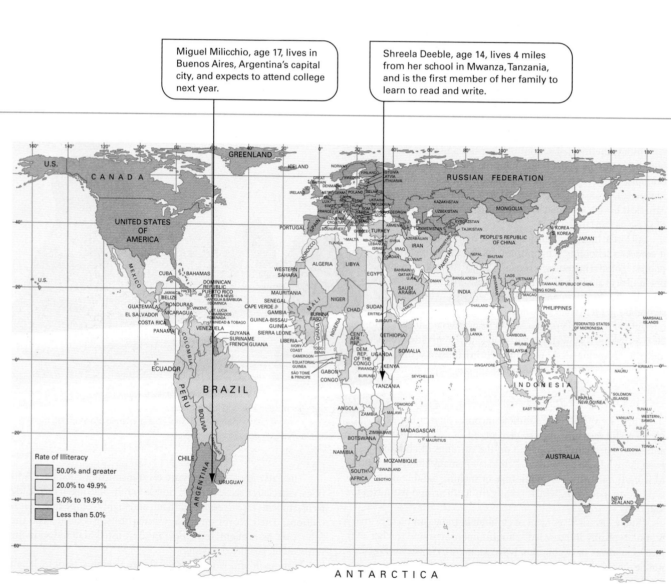

Miguel Milicchio, age 17, lives in Buenos Aires, Argentina's capital city, and expects to attend college next year.

Shreela Deeble, age 14, lives 4 miles from her school in Mwanza, Tanzania, and is the first member of her family to learn to read and write.

Rate of Illiteracy

- 50.0% and greater
- 20.0% to 49.9%
- 5.0% to 19.9%
- Less than 5.0%

Window on the World

GLOBAL MAP 20–1   **Illiteracy in Global Perspective**

Reading and writing skills are widespread in high-income countries, where illiteracy rates generally are below 5 percent. In much of Latin America, however, illiteracy is more common, one consequence of limited economic development. In fifteen nations—fourteen of them in Africa—illiteracy is the rule rather than the exception; there people rely on the oral tradition of face-to-face communication rather than the written word.

Source: UNESCO (2009).

created a need for an educated labor force, and as working-class people demanded access to schools, a rising share of the population entered the classroom. British law now requires every child to attend school until age sixteen.

Traditional class differences still affect British schooling. Most wealthy families send their children to what the British call *public schools*, which we would refer to as private boarding schools. These elite

schools enroll about 7 percent of British students and teach not only academic subjects but also the special patterns of speech, mannerisms, and social graces of the British upper class. Because these academies are very expensive, most British students attend state-supported day schools (Department for Children, Schools, and Families, 2008).

The British have tried to reduce the importance of social background in schooling by expanding their university system and linking

NOTE: Thomas Jefferson was among the first proponents of mandatory public education. The public often resisted such laws in the 19th century, so troops were sometimes called out to escort children to school.

DIVERSITY: College completion (in 2007, aged 25 and over), as in Table 20–1, by sex: 29.5% for men, 28.0% for women; African American men, 18.0%, African American women, 19.0%; Hispanic men, 11.8%, Hispanic women, 13.7%.

NOTE: Mandatory education laws helped establish our conception of childhood as young people left the world of work on farms and in factories to study in classrooms.

NOTE: Regarding the U.S. emphasis on "relevant" education: After the recent recession began, students turned to career tracks promising greater security. These include teaching and government jobs, including the military.

MAKING THE GRADE

Our country's expansion of schooling has been not only to prepare people for jobs, but in pursuit of the goal of equal opportunity.

SEEING SOCIOLOGY
in Everyday Life

What is your career goal? Are the courses you are taking geared to helping you realize this goal?

admission to competitive entrance examinations. For the students who score the highest, the government pays most of the college costs. But many well-to-do children who do not score very well still manage to get into Oxford or Cambridge, the most prestigious British universities, on a par with our own Yale, Harvard, and Princeton. Many "Oxbridge" graduates go on to positions at the top of the British power elite: Most of the highest-ranking members of the British government have "Oxbridge" degrees.

These brief sketches of schooling in India, Japan, and Great Britain show the crucial importance of economic development. In poor countries, many children—especially girls—work rather than go to school. Rich nations enact mandatory education laws to prepare an industrial workforce as well as to satisfy demands for greater equality. But a nation's history and culture still matter, as we see in the intense competition of Japanese schools, the traditional social stratification that shapes schools in Great Britain, and, in the next section, the practical emphasis found in the schools of the United States.

Schooling in the United States

The United States was among the first countries to set a goal of mass education. By 1850, about half the young people between the ages of five and nineteen were enrolled in school. By 1918, all states had passed a *mandatory education law* requiring children to attend school until the age of sixteen or completion of the eighth grade. Table 20–1 shows that a milestone was reached in the mid-1960s when for the first time a majority of U.S. adults had a high school diploma. Today, 86.6 percent have completed high school, and 29.4 percent have a four-year college degree (U.S. Census Bureau, 2009).

The U.S. educational system is shaped by both our high standard of living (which means that young people typically do not have to work) and our democratic principles (the idea that schooling should be provided to everyone). Thomas Jefferson thought the new nation could become democratic only if people learned to read. Today, the United States has an outstanding record of higher education for its people: No other country has as large a share of adults with university degrees (U.S. Census Bureau, 2008).

Schooling in the United States also tries to promote *equal opportunity*. National surveys show that most people think schooling is crucial to personal success, and a majority also believe that everyone has the chance to get an education consistent with personal ability and talent (NORC, 2007). However, this opinion expresses our cultural ideals rather than reality. A century ago, for example, few women had the chance to go to college, and even today, most men and women who attend college come from families with above-average incomes.

In the United States, the educational system stresses the value of *practical* learning, knowledge that prepares people for future jobs. This emphasis is in line with what the educational philosopher John

	Table 20–1 Educational Achievement in the United States, 1910–2008		
Year	**High School Graduates**	**College Graduates**	**Median Years of Schooling**
1910	13.5%	2.7%	8.1
1920	16.4	3.3	8.2
1930	19.1	3.9	8.4
1940	24.1	4.6	8.6
1950	33.4	6.0	9.3
1960	41.1	7.7	10.5
1970	55.2	11.0	12.2
1980	68.7	17.0	12.5
1990	77.6	21.3	12.4
2000	84.1	25.6	12.7
2008	86.6	29.4	N.A.

Notes: Figures are for people 25 years of age and over. Percentage of high school graduates includes those who go on to college. Percentage of high school dropouts can be calculated by subtracting the percentage of high school graduates from 100 percent. N.A. = not available.

Source: U.S. Census Bureau (2009).

Dewey (1859–1952) called *progressive education,* having the schools make learning relevant to people's lives. Similarly, students seek out subjects of study that they feel will give them an advantage when they are ready to compete in the job market. For example, as concerns about international terrorism have risen in recent years, so have the numbers of students choosing to study geography, international conflict, and Middle Eastern history and culture (M. Lord, 2001).

The Functions of Schooling

Structural-functional analysis looks at ways in which formal education supports the operation and stability of society. We look briefly at five ways in which this happens.

Socialization

Technologically simple societies look to families to teach skills and values and thus transmit a way of life from one generation to the next. As societies gain more complex technology, they turn to trained teachers to develop and pass on the more specialized knowledge that adults will need to take their place in the workforce.

In primary school, children learn language and basic mathematical skills. Secondary school builds on this foundation, and for many students, college allows further specialization. In addition, all schooling teaches cultural values and norms. For example, civics classes instruct students in our political way of life, and rituals such as saluting the flag foster patriotism. Likewise, activities such as spelling bees develop competitive individualism and a sense of fair play.

DIVERSITY: Dovetailing with the social integration function of schooling is the multiculturalism debate, examined in Chapter 3 ("Culture").

NOTE: The U.S. has 17.5 million college students, 13% of the world's total. About 200 very selective schools accept fewer than 40% of applicants; 1500 accept 41%–90%; 200 accept more than 90%.

DISCUSS: Discuss the cultural values implicit in the classroom spelling bee (including competition, individual performance, and specific standards of achievement).

POP CULTURE: The importance of higher education has long influenced the mass media. Comedians from the Marx Brothers to John Belushi to Rodney Dangerfield set movies on the college campus.

◉ MAKING THE GRADE

Manifest functions refer to consequences that are widely understood; *latent functions* refer to those less commonly recognized.

Graduation from college is an important event in the lives of an ever-increasing number of people in the United States. Look over the discussion of the functions of schooling. How many of these functions do you think people in college are aware of? Can you think of other social consequences of going to college?

Cultural Innovation

Faculty at colleges and universities create culture as well as pass it on to students. Research in the sciences, the social sciences, the humanities, and the fine arts leads to discovery and changes in our way of life. For example, medical research at major universities has helped increase life expectancy, just as research by sociologists and psychologists helps us learn how to enjoy life more so that we can take advantage of our longevity.

Social Integration

Schooling molds a diverse population into one society sharing norms and values. This is one reason that states enacted mandatory education laws a century ago at a time when immigration was very high. In light of the ethnic diversity of many urban areas today, schooling continues to serve this purpose.

Social Placement

Schools identify talent and match instruction to ability. Schooling increases meritocracy by rewarding talent and hard work regardless of social background and provides a path to upward social mobility.

Latent Functions of Schooling

Schooling also serves several less widely recognized functions. It provides child care for the growing number of one-parent and two-career families. In addition, schooling occupies thousands of young people in their teens and twenties who would otherwise be competing for limited opportunities in the job market. High schools, colleges, and universities also bring together people of marriageable age. Finally, schools establish networks that serve as a valuable career resource throughout life.

○ **CRITICAL REVIEW** Structural-functional analysis stresses ways in which formal education supports the operation of a modern society. However, this approach overlooks how the classroom behavior of teachers and students can vary from one setting to another, a focus of the symbolic-interaction approach discussed next. In addition, structural-functional analysis says little about many problems of our educational system and how schooling helps reproduce the class structure in each generation, which is the focus of social-conflict analysis found in the final theoretical section of the chapter.

○ **CHECK YOUR LEARNING** Identify the five functions of schooling for the operation of society.

Schooling and Social Interaction

The basic idea of the symbolic-interaction approach is that people create the reality they experience in their day-to-day interaction. We use this approach to explain how stereotypes can shape what goes on in the classroom.

The Self-Fulfilling Prophecy

Chapter 6 ("Social Interaction in Everyday Life") presented the Thomas theorem, which states that situations that people define as real become real in their consequences. Put another way, people who expect others to act in certain ways often encourage that very behavior. Doing so, people set up a *self-fulfilling prophecy.*

Jane Elliott, an elementary school teacher in the all-white community of Riceville, Iowa, carried out a simple experiment that showed how a self-fulfilling prophecy can take place in the classroom. In 1968, Elliot was teaching a fourth-grade class when Dr. Martin Luther King Jr. was assassinated. Her students were puzzled and asked why a national hero had been brutally shot. Elliott responded by asking her white students what they thought about people of color, and she was stunned to find out that they held many powerful negative stereotypes.

POP CULTURE: Because of the power of the mass media to influence the young, controversy has often arisen over media portrayals of unconventional social patterns. Recently, U.S. Secretary of Education Margaret Spellings objected to the PBS program *Postcards from Buster* because the leading character, Buster the Bunny, learned cooking from two lesbian couples. In response, PBS pulled the episode.

SOCIAL SURVEY: "How important for getting ahead in life is having a good education?" (GSS 1987, *N* = 1,285; *Codebook*, 2005:1429)

"Essential"	34.7%	"Not very important"	1.3%
"Very important"	48.2%	"Not important at all"	0%
"Fairly important"	14.3%	"Don't know"/No response	1.5%

MAKING THE GRADE

This discussion of the symbolic-interaction approach to education echoes the labeling approach to deviance in Chapter 9 ("Deviance"). Review pages 221–24.

To show the class the harmful effects of such stereotypes, Elliott performed a classroom experiment. She found that almost all of the children in her class had either blue eyes or brown eyes. She told the class that children with brown eyes were smarter and worked harder than children with blue eyes. To be sure everyone could easily tell which category a child fell into, pieces of brown or blue colored cloth were pinned to every student's collar.

Elliott recalls the effect of this "lesson" on the way students behaved: "It was just horrifying how quickly they became what I told them they were." Within half an hour, Elliot continued, a blue-eyed girl named Carol had changed from a "brilliant, carefree, excited little girl to a frightened, timid, uncertain, almost-person." Not surprisingly, in the hours that followed, the brown-eyed students came to life, speaking up more and performing better than they had done before. The prophecy had been fulfilled: Because the brown-eyed children thought they were superior, they became superior in their classroom performance—as well as "arrogant, ugly, and domineering" toward the blue-eyed children. For their part, the blue-eyed children began underperforming, becoming the inferior people they believed themselves to be.

At the end of the day, Elliott took time to explain to everyone what they had experienced. She applied the lesson to race, pointing out that if white children thought they were superior to black children, they would expect to do better in school, just as many children of color who live in the shadow of the same stereotypes would underperform in school. The children also realized that the society that teaches these stereotypes, as well as the hate that often goes with them, encourages the kind of violence that ended the life of Dr. King (Kral, 2000).

CRITICAL REVIEW The symbolic-interaction approach explains how we all build reality in our everyday interactions with others. When school officials define some students as "gifted," for example, we can expect teachers to treat them differently and the students themselves to behave differently as a result of having been labeled in this way. If students and teachers come to believe that one race is academically superior to another, the behavior that follows may be a self-fulfilling prophecy.

One limitation of this approach is that people do not just make up such beliefs about superiority and inferiority. Rather, these beliefs are built into a society's system of social inequality, which brings us to the social-conflict approach.

CHECK YOUR LEARNING How can the labels that schools place on some students affect the students' actual performance and the reactions of others?

How well young people perform in school depends a lot on what people expect of them. The 2007 film *The Great Debaters* is based on the true story of a coach at an all-black college in Texas during the 1930s. Believing in the abilities of his students, he guides them to become one of the best debate teams in the country.

Schooling and Social Inequality

Social-conflict analysis explains how schooling both causes and perpetuates social inequality. In this way, it can explain how stereotypes of "good" and "bad" students described in the symbolic-interaction discussion arise in the first place. In addition, a social-conflict approach challenges the structural-functional idea that schooling develops everybody's talents and abilities by claiming that schooling plays a part in social stratification.

Social Control

Schooling is a way of controlling people, reinforcing acceptance of the status quo. Samuel Bowles and Herbert Gintis (1976) claim that the rise of public education in the late nineteenth century came at exactly the same time that factory owners needed an obedient and disciplined workforce. Once in school, immigrants learned not only the English language but also the importance of following orders.

Standardized Testing

Here is a question of the kind historically used to measure the academic ability of school-age children in the United States:

Painter is to *painting* as _____ is to *sonnet*.
(a) driver (b) poet (c) priest (d) carpenter

521

Q: "A classification scheme is meant to provide ways of grouping learners for instructional purposes through a series of labels such as *slow learner, underachiever, late bloomer, disadvantaged,* and *deprived*. These labels become an intrinsic part of the normal operation of the organization. Teachers, administrators, and counselors do not expect as much from those who are classified as slow as we do from those who are classified as fast." Mario D. Fantini

DISCUSS: Discuss Herrnstein and Murray's contention in *The Bell Curve* (1994) that higher education became more meritocratic during the 20th century, with the effect of segregating an emerging "cognitive elite."

DISCUSS: Ask students to think about all the standardized tests they have taken over the years. Do they think such tests are biased against certain categories of people or not? Explain.

tracking assigning students to different types of educational programs

MAKING THE GRADE

For more on school inequality, see this chapter's photo essay on pages 436–37.

The correct answer is "(b) poet": A painter creates a painting just as a poet creates a sonnet. This question supposedly measures logical reasoning, but getting the right answer also depends on knowing what each term means. Students who are unfamiliar with the sonnet as a Western European form of written verse are not likely to answer the question correctly.

The organizations that create standardized tests claim that this type of bias has been all but eliminated because they carefully study response patterns and drop any question that favors one racial or ethnic category. But critics insist that some bias based on class, race, or ethnicity will always exist in formal testing. Because test questions will always reflect our society's dominant culture, minority students are placed at a disadvantage (Crouse & Trusheim, 1988; Putka, 1990).

School Tracking

Despite controversy over standardized tests, most schools in the United States use them for **tracking**, *assigning students to different types of educational programs*, such as college preparatory classes, general education, and vocational and technical training.

Tracking supposedly helps teachers meet each student's individual needs and abilities. However, one education critic, Jonathan Kozol (1992), considers tracking an example of "savage inequalities" in our school system. Most students from privileged backgrounds do well

on standardized tests and get into higher tracks, where they receive the best the school can offer. Students from disadvantaged backgrounds typically do less well on these tests and end up in lower tracks, where teachers stress memorization and put little focus on creativity.

Based on these concerns, schools across the United States are cautious about making tracking assignments and give students the chance to move from one track to another. Some schools have even dropped tracking entirely. Tracking can help match instruction with students' abilities, but rigid tracking can have a powerful impact on students' learning and self-concept. Young people who spend years in higher tracks tend to see themselves as bright and able; students in lower tracks end up with less ambition and low self-esteem (Bowles & Gintis, 1976; Oakes, 1985; Kilgore, 1991; Kozol, 1992).

Inequality among Schools

Just as students are treated differently within schools, schools themselves differ in important ways. The biggest difference is between public and private schools.

Public and Private Schools

Across the United States, about 90 percent of the 56 million primary and secondary school children attend state-funded public schools. The rest go to private schools.

Sociological research has documented the fact that young children living in low-income communities typically learn in classrooms like the one on the left, with large class sizes and low budgets that do not provide for high technology and other instructional materials. Children from high-income communities typically enjoy classroom experiences such as the one shown on the right, with small classes and the latest learning technology.

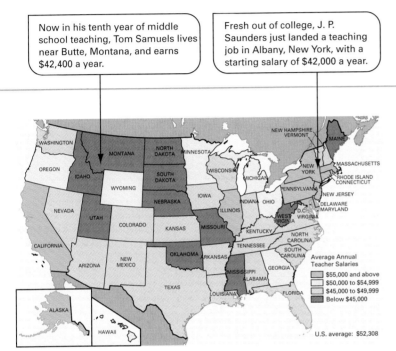

Now in his tenth year of middle school teaching, Tom Samuels lives near Butte, Montana, and earns $42,400 a year.

Fresh out of college, J. P. Saunders just landed a teaching job in Albany, New York, with a starting salary of $42,000 a year.

Seeing Ourselves

NATIONAL MAP 20–1

Teachers' Salaries across the United States

In 2008, the average public school teacher in the United States earned $52,308. The map shows the average teacher salary for all the states; they range from a low of $36,674 in South Dakota to a high of $64,424 in California. Looking at the map, what pat-tern do you see? What do high-salary (and low-salary) states have in common?

Source: National Education Association, *Rankings and Estimates: Rankings of the States, 2007, and Estimates of School Statistics, 2008*. Washington, D.C.: National Education Association, 2008.

Average Annual Teacher Salaries
$55,000 and above
$50,000 to $54,999
$45,000 to $49,999
Below $45,000

U.S. average: $52,308

Most private school students attend one of the 7,500 *parochial schools* (*parochial* is from Latin, meaning "of the parish") operated by the Roman Catholic Church. The Catholic school system grew rapidly a century ago as cities swelled with immigrants. Enrolling their children in Catholic schools helped the new arrivals hold onto their religious heritage in a new and mostly Protestant society. Today, after decades of flight from the inner city by white people, many parochial schools enroll non-Catholics, including a growing number of African Americans whose families seek an alternative to the neigh-borhood public school.

Protestants also have private schools, often known as Christian academies. These schools are favored by parents who want religious instruction for their children as well as higher academic and disci-plinary standards.

There are also about 6,800 nonreligious private schools in the United States that enroll mostly young people from well-to-do fam-ilies. These are typically prestigious and expensive preparatory ("prep") schools, modeled on British boarding schools, that not only provide strong academic programs but also convey the values and teach the way of life of the upper class. Many "preppies" maintain lifelong school-based social networks that provide numerous social advantages.

Are private schools qualitatively better than public schools? Research shows that holding family social background constant, stu-dents in private schools do outperform those in public schools on standard measures of academic success. The advantages of private schools include smaller classes, more demanding coursework, and greater discipline (Coleman & Hoffer, 1987; Peterson & Llaudet, 2006).

Inequality in Public Schooling

But even public schools are not all the same. Differences in funding result in unequal resources; consequently, children in more affluent areas receive a better education than children living in poor commu-nities. National Map 20–1 shows one key way in which resources differ: Average yearly teacher salaries vary by as much as $25,000 in state-by-state comparisons.

At the local level, differences in school funding can be dramatic. Winnetka, Illinois, one of the richest suburbs in the United States, spends more than $13,000 a year on each of its students, compared to less than $8,000 in poor areas like Laredo, Texas, and in recent years, these differences have grown (Winter, 2004). The Thinking About Diversity box on page 524 shows the effects of funding differ-ences in the everyday lives of students.

Because schools are typically funded through local property taxes, schools in more affluent areas will offer a better education than schools in poor communities. This difference also benefits whites over minorities, which is why some districts enacted a pol-icy of *busing*, transporting students to achieve racial balance and equal opportunity in schools. Although only 5 percent of U.S. schoolchildren are bused to schools outside their neighborhoods, this policy is controversial. Supporters claim that given the reality of racial segregation, the only way government will adequately fund schools in poor, minority neighborhoods is if white children from richer areas attend. Critics respond that busing is expensive and undermines the concept of neighborhood schools. But almost everyone agreed on one thing: Given the racial imbalance of most urban areas, an effective busing scheme would have to join inner cities and suburbs, a plan that has never been politically possible.

RESOURCE: An excerpt by Jonathan Kozol, "Savage Inequalities: Children in U.S. Schools," is included in the author's companion reader *Seeing Ourselves*, 8th ed.

NOTE: Stanford, Calif., is the most educated town in the U.S.; 90% of adult residents have a B.A. degree or higher. In Massachusetts, 40% of people aged 25 or older have completed four years of college.

NOTE: Catholic schools generally outperform public schools, despite spending only about one-third as much per student (Stern, 1996).

NOTE: Sixty-three percent of people aged 25 years or older who are high school graduates have attained some college education. About 75% of these attended public schools; government funding covers about 48% of their costs. Among college matriculants, only 58% complete a bachelor's degree after six years.

SEEING SOCIOLOGY
in Everyday Life

Do you think all children in the community in which you grew up received equal schooling? Explain.

THINKING ABOUT DIVERSITY: RACE, CLASS, & GENDER

Schooling in the United States: Savage Inequality

"Public School 261? Head down Jerome Avenue and look for the mortician's office." Off for a day studying the New York City schools, Jonathan Kozol parks his car and walks toward PS 261. Finding PS 261 is not easy because the school has no sign. In fact, the building is a former roller rink and doesn't look much like a school at all.

The principal explains that this is in a minority area of the North Bronx, so the population of PS 261 is 90 percent African American and Hispanic. Officially, the school should serve 900 students, but it actually enrolls 1,300. The rules say class size should not exceed thirty-two, but Kozol observes that it sometimes approaches forty. Because the school has just one small cafeteria, the children must eat in three shifts. After lunch, with no place to play, students squirm in their seats until told to return to their classrooms. Only one classroom in the entire school has a window to the world outside.

Toward the end of the day, Kozol remarks to a teacher about the overcrowding and the poor condition of the building. She sums up her thoughts: "I had an awful room last year. In the winter, it was 56 degrees. In the summer, it was up to 90."

"Do the children ever comment on the building?" Kozol asks.

"They don't say," she responds, "but they know. All these kids see TV. They know what suburban schools are like. Then they look around them at their school. They don't comment on it, but you see it in their eyes. They understand."

Several months later, Kozol visits PS 24, in the affluent Riverdale section of New York City. This school is set back from the road, beyond a lawn planted with magnolia and dogwood trees, which are now in full bloom. On one side of the building is a playground for the youngest children; behind the school are playing fields for the older kids. Many people pay the high price of a house in Riverdale because the local schools have such an excellent reputation. There are 825 children here; most are white and a few are Asian, Hispanic, or African American. The building is in good repair. It has a large library and even a planetarium. All the classrooms have windows with bright curtains.

Entering one of the many classes for gifted students, Kozol asks the children what they are doing today. A young girl answers confidently, "My name is Laurie, and we're doing problem solving." A tall, good-natured boy continues, "I'm David. One thing that we do is logical thinking. Some problems, we find, have more than one good answer." Kozol asks if such reasoning is innate or if it is something a child learns. Susan, whose smile reveals her braces, responds, "You know some things to start with when you enter school. But we learn some things that other children don't. We learn certain things that other children don't know because we're *taught* them."

WHAT DO YOU THINK?

1. Are there differences between schools in your city or town? Explain.

2. Why do you think there is little public concern about schooling inequality?

3. What changes would our society have to make to eliminate schooling inequality?

Source: Adapted from Kozol (1992:85–88, 92–96).

Across the United States, many inner-city schools lack the facilities to provide a good education.

Since the 1990s, busing students to achieve racial balance in schools has sharply declined. Although there was some modest decline in racial segregation in U.S. public schools between 1970 and 1990, there has been little change since then (Logan, Oakley, & Stowell, 2008).

But other policies to address unequal schools have emerged. One plan is to provide money equally across a state. This is the approach taken by Vermont, which passed a law that distributes per-student tax money equally to all communities.

But not everyone thinks that money is the key to good schooling. A classic report by a research team headed by James Coleman (1966) confirmed that students in mostly minority schools suffer from larger class size, insufficient libraries, and fewer science labs. But the Coleman report cautioned that more money by itself would

DIVERSITY: Race and ethnicity continue to account for significant differences in SAT performance. Combined scores in 2008: Asian American/Pacific Islander: 1,610; white, 1,583; American Indian, 1,446; Mexican American, 1,364; African American, 1,280 (College Board, 2009).

DIVERSITY: Gary Orfield (1994) reports that the percentage of African Americans attending predominantly minority schools was 64% in 1972–73; in 1991–92 it was 66%. Comparable data for Hispanics, 57% and 73%. Among blacks, 39% attended 90%–100% minority schools in 1972–73; 34% in 1991–92. Comparable data for Hispanics, 23% and 34%.

MAKING THE GRADE

Kozol's account in the box is a "reproduction theory" stating that schooling transmits advantage or disadvantage from parents to children. Downey's research confirms that schooling cannot overcome differences in family resources but it does reduce the gap between rich and poor.

not magically improve schooling. More important are the cooperative efforts and enthusiasm of teachers, parents, and the students themselves. In other words, even if school funding were exactly the same everywhere (as in Vermont), students who benefit from more *cultural capital*—that is, those whose parents value schooling, read to their children, and encourage the development of imagination—would still perform better. In short, we should not expect schools alone to overcome marked social inequality in the United States (Schneider et al., 1998; Israel, Beaulieu, & Hartless, 2001).

Further research confirms the difference that home environment makes in a student's school performance. A research team studied the rate at which school-age children gain skills in reading and mathematics (Downey, von Hippel, & Broh, 2004). Because U.S. children go to school six to seven hours a day, five days a week, and do not attend school during summer months, the researchers calculate that children spend only about 13 percent of their waking hours in school. During the school year, high-income children learn somewhat more quickly than low-income children, but the learning gap is far greater during the summer season when children are not in school. The researchers conclude that when it comes to student performance, schools matter, but the home and local neighborhood matter more. Put another way, schools close some of the learning gap that is created by differences in family resources, but they do not "level the playing field" between rich and poor children the way we like to think they do.

Access to Higher Education

Schooling is the main path to good jobs. But only 67 percent of U.S. high school graduates enroll in college immediately after graduation. Among young people eighteen to twenty-four years old, about 39 percent are enrolled in college (National Center for Education Statistics, 2009).

A crucial factor affecting access to U.S. higher education is family income. College is expensive: Even at state-supported institutions, annual tuition averages about $6,600, and admission to the most exclusive private colleges and universities exceeds $45,000 a year. As shown in Figure 20–1, nearly two-thirds of children from families with incomes above $75,000 annually (roughly the richest 30 percent, who fall within the upper-middle class and upper class) attend college, but only 25 percent of young people from families earning less than $20,000 go on to higher education (U.S. Census Bureau, 2008).

These economic differences are one reason that the education gap between whites and minorities widens at the college level. As Figure 20–2 on page 526 shows, African Americans are not quite as likely as non-Hispanic whites to graduate from high school and are much less likely to complete four or more years of college. Hispan-

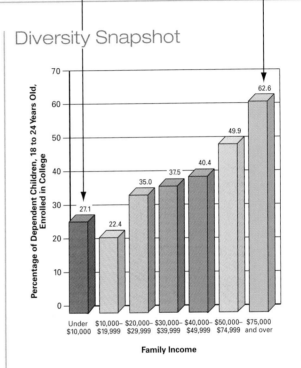

A young person whose family earns more than $75,000 a year is more than twice as likely to attend college as one whose family earns less than $10,000.

Diversity Snapshot

FIGURE 20–1 **College Attendance and Family Income, 2005**

The higher a family's income, the more likely it is that children will attend college.

Source: U.S. Census Bureau (2006).

ics, many of whom speak Spanish as their first language, have a lower rate of high school graduation, and again, the gap is much greater when it comes to college degrees. Schooling is an important path to social mobility in our society, but the promise of schooling has not overcome the racial inequality that exists in the United States.

Completing college brings many rewards, including higher earnings. In the past forty years, as our economy has shifted to work that requires processing information, the gap in average income between people who complete only high school and those who earn a four-year college degree has more than doubled. In fact, today, a college degree adds as much as $1 million to a person's lifetime income. In simple terms, higher education is a good investment.

Table 20–2 on page 526 gives details. In 2007, men who were high school graduates averaged $37,855, and college graduates averaged $62,087. The ratios in parentheses show that a man with a bachelor's degree earns 2.7 times as much in annual income as a man with eight or fewer years of schooling. Across the board, women earn

SEEING SOCIOLOGY
in Everyday Life

Are there specific things parents can do to improve their children's learning? How did your parents affect your learning?

SEEING SOCIOLOGY
in Everyday Life

In Table 20–2, compare the earnings of college graduates with high school graduates to see the value of a college degree.

Diversity Snapshot

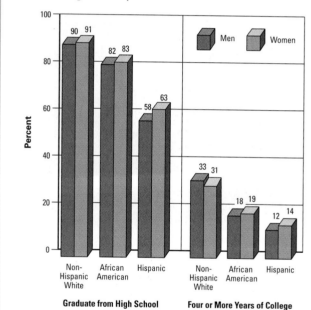

FIGURE 20–2   Educational Achievement for Various Categories of People, Aged 25 Years and Over, 2007

U.S. society still provides less education to minorities.

Source: U.S. Census Bureau (2007).

Some two-year colleges are private, but most are publicly funded community colleges that serve a local area (usually a city or a county) and charge a low tuition (National Center for Education Statistics, 2008).

Because higher education is a key path to better jobs and higher income, the government makes money available to help certain categories of people pay the costs of college. After World War II, the GI Bill provided college funds to veterans, with the result that tens of thousands of men and women were able to attend college. Some branches of the military continue to offer college money to enlistees; in addition, veterans continue to benefit from a number of government grants and scholarships.

Community Colleges

Since the 1960s, the expansion of state-funded community colleges has further increased access to higher education. According to the National Center for Education Statistics (2008), the 1,685 two-year colleges across the United States now enroll 37 percent of all college undergraduates.

Community colleges provide a number of specific benefits. First, their relatively low tuition cost places college courses and degrees within the reach of millions of families that could not otherwise afford them. Many students at community colleges today are the first in their families to pursue a college degree. The lower cost of community colleges is especially important during periods of economic recession. When the economy slumps and people lose their jobs, college enrollments soar, especially at community colleges.

Second, community colleges have special importance for minorities. Currently, almost half of all African American and Hispanic undergraduates in the United States attend community colleges.

less than men, although as with men, added years of schooling boosts their income, although not quite as much. Keep in mind that for both men and women, some of the greater earnings have to do with social background, because those with the most schooling are likely to come from relatively well-off families to begin with.

Greater Opportunity: Expanding Higher Education

With some 18.2 million people enrolled in colleges and universities, the United States is the world leader in providing a college education to its people. This country also enrolls more students from abroad than any other.

One reason for this achievement is that there are 4,314 colleges and universities in the United States. This number includes 2,629 four-year institutions (which award bachelor's degrees) as well as 1,685 two-year colleges (which award associate's degrees).

Table 20–2   Median Income by Sex and Educational Attainment, 2007

Education	Men	Women
Professional degree	$100,000 (4.3)	$71,098 (3.9)
Doctorate	92,089 (3.9)	68,989 (3.8)
Master's degree	76,284 (3.3)	55,426 (3.0)
Bachelor's degree	62,087 (2.7)	45,773 (2.5)
1–3 years of college	44,899 (1.9)	32,837 (1.8)
4 years of high school	37,855 (1.6)	27,240 (1.5)
9–11 years of school	29,317 (1.3)	20,398 (1.1)
0–8 years of school	23,375 (1.0)	18,261 (1.0)

Notes: Figures are for persons aged 25 years and over working full time. The earnings ratio, in parentheses, indicates what multiple of the lowest income level a person with the indicated amount of additional schooling earns.

Source: U.S. Census Bureau (2008).

NOTE: A bit of sociological trivia: The legality of free, public-sponsored education was decided in 1874 by the Michigan Supreme Court, under the control of Justice Thomas Cooley, Charles Horton Cooley's father.

NOTE: Another angle on earnings and education: A male high school graduate earns 61% as much as a male with a college degree, and this gap is increasing.

EXERCISE: Have students investigate a Web site discussing the performance of U.S. students in global context: http://www.edexcellence.net

Q: Asked to describe the most miserable state for humanity, Benjamin Franklin responded, "A lonely man on a rainy day who cannot read."

MAKING THE GRADE

The social-conflict approach claims that schooling transforms family privilege into personal merit. This means that, although we understand that earning a college degree is a personal achievement, family privilege plays a major part in getting people to college in the first place.

SEEING SOCIOLOGY
in Everyday Life

Are you the first in your family to attend college? If not, for how many generations before you have family members attended college?

APPLYING THEORY

Education

	Structural-Functional Approach	Symbolic-Interaction Approach	Social-Conflict Approach
What is the level of analysis?	Macro-level	Micro-level	Macro-level
What is the importance of education for society?	Schooling performs many vital tasks for the operation of society, including socializing the young and encouraging discovery and invention to improve our lives. Schooling helps unite a diverse society by teaching shared norms and values.	How teachers define their students—as well as how students think of themselves—can become real to everyone and affect students' educational performance.	Schooling maintains social inequality through unequal schooling for rich and poor. Within individual schools, tracking provides privileged children with a better education than poor children.

Third, although it is true that community colleges serve local populations, two-year colleges also attract students from around the world. Many community colleges recruit students from abroad, and about 20 percent of all foreign students enrolled on a U.S. campus are studying at community colleges (National Center for Education Statistics, 2008).

Fourth, the top priority of faculty who work at large universities is typically research, but the most important job for community college faculty is teaching. Thus although teaching loads are high (typically four or five classes each semester), community colleges appeal to faculty who find their greatest pleasure in the classroom. Community college students often get more attention from faculty than students at large universities (Jacobson, 2003).

Finally, community colleges teach the knowledge and career skills that countless people depend on to find the jobs they want. Seeing Sociology in the News on pages 528–29 takes a closer look.

Privilege and Personal Merit

If attending college is a rite of passage for rich men and women, as social-conflict analysis suggests, then *schooling transforms social privilege into personal merit*. Given our cultural emphasis on individualism, we tend to see credentials as badges of ability rather than as symbols of family affluence (Sennett & Cobb, 1973).

When we congratulate the new graduate, we rarely recognize the resources—in terms of both money and cultural capital—that made this achievement possible. Yet young people from families with incomes exceeding $200,000 a year average more than 350 points higher on the SAT college entrance examination than young people from families with less than $20,000 in annual income (College Board, 2009). The richer students are more likely to get into college; once there, they are also more likely to complete their studies and get a degree. In a *credential society*—one that evaluates people on the basis of their schooling—companies hire job applicants with the best education. This process ends up helping people with advantages to begin with and harming those who are already disadvantaged (Collins, 1979).

CRITICAL REVIEW Social-conflict analysis links formal education to social inequality to show how schooling transforms privilege into personal worthiness and social disadvantage into personal deficiency. However, the social-conflict approach overlooks the extent to which finishing a degree reflects plenty of hard work and the extent to which schooling provides upward social mobility for talented women and men from all backgrounds. In addition, despite the claims that schooling supports the status quo, today's college curricula challenge social inequality on many fronts.

CHECK YOUR LEARNING Explain several ways in which education is linked to social inequality.

The Applying Theory table sums up what the theoretical approaches show us about education.

Q: "The actual success of a teacher depends in large measure on the capacity to state the subject matter of instruction in terms of the experience of the [student]." George Herbert Mead

Q: "Don't let school interfere with your education." Mark Twain

Q: "There has come to be a recognition that many of the issues in education today are not in the domain of educational psychologists, but have to do with the social structure of the school and the world outside the school." James S. Coleman

Q: "Education, then, beyond all other devices of human origin, is a great equalizer of conditions of men—the balance wheel of the social machinery." Horace Mann (1948)

Seeing SOCIOLOGY in the NEWS

The New York Times

Community College: Dream Catchers

By JOHN MERROW

April 22, 2007

Matters were simpler 100 years ago, when junior colleges were created to prepare deserving students for the final two years of a university. In fact, the very first public junior college, in Joliet, Ill., was set up in a high school, as the equivalent of grades 13 and 14.

Community colleges today do far more than offer a ladder to the final years. They train the people who repair your furnace, install your plumbing, take your pulse. They prepare retiring baby boomers for second or third careers, and provide opportunities for a growing number of college-age students turning away from the high cost and competition at universities. And charged with doing the heavy remedial lifting, community colleges are now as much 10th and 11th grade as 13th and 14th.

It's a long to-do list on a tightening public purse. Two-year colleges receive less than 30 percent of state and local financing for higher education, according to the American Association of Community Colleges. Yet they are growing much faster than four-year colleges and universities, enrolling nearly half of all undergraduates. That's 6.6 million students. Add those taking just a course or two, and the total reaches some 12 million.

Kay M. McClenney, director of the annual Community College Survey of Student Engagement, calls America's two-year colleges "today's Ellis Island," because they serve a disproportionate number of immigrants, first-generation citizens and minorities. . . .

Midlife, Starting Over

. . . At 51, [Brian Bullas] is determined to redefine himself. With his wife working days, bartending seemed a logical career choice when his son was small. Today, he has a different view. . . . "Bartending has been a pretty stagnant job," he said. "I think I can give more to myself and to my family

and to society by trying a new career that I think I'm going to be good at."

After graduating from San Diego City College next month and passing the licensing exam, Mr. Bullas will be a registered nurse. He will be in great demand, because the country desperately needs nurses. The national shortfall, of about 6 percent, is particularly acute in California. A 2006 report by the Hospital Association of Southern California estimates that the state currently needs 22,500 registered nurses and predicted a shortage of 116,000 by 2020. Two-year institutions train some 60 percent of the nation's new nurses.

Mr. Bullas says he "won the lottery" when he was able to start classes. He did get lucky: three of four applicants to City's nursing program are accepted but are immediately placed on a waiting list. There just isn't enough room.

"They're qualified, we tell them they're qualified, but then they have to go off and flip burgers or tend bar or do whatever, until their number comes up," says Terrence Burgess, the college president.

Problems in the Schools

An intense debate revolves around the quality of schooling in the United States. Perhaps because we expect our schools to do so much—teach, equalize opportunity, instill discipline, and fire our children's imagination—people are divided on whether public schools are doing their job. Although almost half of adults give schools in their local community a performance grade of A or B, just about the same number give a grade of C or below (Bushaw & Gallup, 2008).

Discipline and Violence

When many of today's older teachers think back to their own student days, school "problems" consisted of talking out of turn, chewing gum, breaking the dress code, or cutting class. Today, schools are grappling with serious issues such as drug and alcohol abuse, teenage pregnancy, and outright violence. Although almost everyone agrees that schools should teach personal discipline, many think the job is no longer being done.

Schools do not create violence; in most cases, violence spills into the schools from the surrounding society. In the wake of a number of school shootings in recent years, many school districts have adopted zero-tolerance policies that require suspension or expulsion for serious misbehavior or bringing weapons on campus.

Deadly school shootings—including the deaths of thirty-three students at Virginia Tech University in 2007 and the deaths of eight students at Northern Illinois University in 2008—have shocked the nation. Such tragic incidents also raise serious questions about balancing students' right to privacy (typically, laws forbid colleges from informing parents of a student's grades or mental health issues) and the need to ensure the safety of the campus population. In the Virginia Tech case, had the university been able to bring the young man's mental health problems to the attention of the police or his family, the tragedy might have been prevented (Gibbs, 2007; Shedden, 2008).

Student Passivity

If some schools are plagued by violence, many more are filled with students who are bored. Some of the blame for passivity can be placed on the fact that electronic devices, from television to iPods, now consume more of young people's time than school, parents, and community activities. But schools must share the blame because the educational system itself encourages student passivity (Coleman, Hoffer, & Kilgore, 1981).

Bureaucracy

The small, personal schools that served countless local communities a century ago have evolved into huge educational factories. In a study

Q: "Discipline is the ultimate tenet of education. Discipline establishes the format, the environment for academic achievement to occur." Joe Clark, controversial principal of Eastside High School in Paterson, N.J.

NOTE: Research suggests that one-third of parents are "seriously disengaged" from their adolescent children's lives (Steinberg, 1996).

DISCUSS: How might the following factors correlate with the recent outbursts of school violence? Compared to 1960, the average child spends 11 fewer hours with parents each week, depression among children has increased tenfold, and teen suicide has risen fourfold (Cloud, 1999).

"It's not uncommon up and down the state to have wait lists that go two and three years out." . . .

Mr. Bullas chose this route because City's nursing classes are scheduled for the convenience of working adults and because the cost is low.

Community colleges attract a lot of men and women like Brian Bullas. In a study conducted by ACT Inc. and the American Association of Community Colleges, more than 35 percent of students indicated that changing careers was the major reason they were taking classes.

Mr. Bullas already has a degree in sociology from the University of San Diego, where he played varsity baseball. He was drafted by the Oakland A's but played only in the minors and Canada, he says, before turning to restaurant work and bartending. The road to where he is today has been a triathlon of classwork and clinical and personal responsibilities—eight hours two days a week at the hospital and two in the classroom; four or five nights, eight hours a night, at the Marine Room. "I have a couple of days where I carpool kids to school, do the shopping, and help out with homework when I can with my son," he said.

The stress, just getting through it, shows in his face. It helps that his wife ("a saint") has a good job managing a health club. "I do keep in contact with her to let her know where I am and what I'm doing," he said, laughing.

Mr. Bullas has studied in a parking lot, waiting for his son at baseball or basketball or water polo; he does schoolwork behind the bar when it's slow. "They let you know that you should have a book in your car at all times," he said.

He is a focused learner who furiously takes notes during a demonstration of an IV pole. Afterward, he goes up to the teacher to ask questions.

He thinks about that day when he will enter a patient's room for the first time on his own. "I know I'm going to have support," he said. "But I also know that the patient's life is in my hands, and I want to be sure I've done my homework."

WHAT DO YOU THINK?

1. In your opinion, what are the most important contributions of community colleges to our society?

2. Why do some people describe community colleges as "today's Ellis Island," referring to the place where tens of millions of immigrants got their start in the United States?

3. Have you or someone you know attended a community college? If so, does the story of Brian Bullas ring true?

of high schools across the United States, Theodore Sizer (1984:207–9) identified five ways in which large, bureaucratic schools undermine education:

1. **Rigid uniformity**. Bureaucratic schools run by outside specialists (such as state education officials) generally ignore the cultural character of local communities and the personal needs of their children.

2. **Numerical ratings**. School officials define success in terms of numerical attendance records and dropout rates and "teach to the tests," hoping to raise achievement test scores. In the process, they overlook dimensions of schooling that are difficult to quantify, such as creativity and enthusiasm.

3. **Rigid expectations**. Officials expect fifteen-year-olds to be in the tenth grade and eleventh-graders to score at a certain level on a standardized verbal achievement test. Rarely are exceptionally bright and motivated students permitted to advance more quickly or graduate early. Similarly, poor performers are pushed from grade to grade, doomed to fail year after year.

4. **Specialization**. Students in middle school and high school learn Spanish from one teacher, receive guidance from another, and are coached in sports by still others. Students shuffle between fifty-minute periods throughout the school day. As a result, no school official comes to know the child well.

5. **Little individual responsibility**. Highly bureaucratic schools do not empower students to learn on their own. Similarly, teachers have little say in what they teach in their classes and how they do it; any change in the pace of learning risks disrupting the system.

Of course, with 56 million schoolchildren in the United States, schools must be bureaucratic to get the job done. But Sizer recommends that we "humanize" schools by reducing rigid scheduling, cutting class size, and training teachers more broadly so that they become more involved in the lives of their students. Overall, as James Coleman (1993) has suggested, schools need to be less "administratively driven" and more "output-driven." Perhaps this transformation could begin by ensuring that graduation from high school depends on what students have learned rather than simply on the number of years they have spent in the building.

College: The Silent Classroom

Passivity is also common among college and university students. Sociologists rarely study the college classroom—a curious fact, considering how much time they spend there. One exception was a study at a coeducational university where David Karp and William Yoels (1976) found that even in small classes, only a few students spoke up. Passivity seems to be a classroom norm, and students may even become irritated if one of their number is especially talkative.

POP CULTURE: Epitomizing today's apathetic student, Bobby of *King of the Hill* is unfocused and without particular talent, yet still insightful, comical, and lovable.

NOTE: The blackboard, which may encourage passivity among college students, was first used at Bowdoin College in 1823.

DISCUSS: What factors do students think are responsible for widespread student passivity in the classroom?

Q: "Instructors who want dialogue to return to the classroom must take it upon themselves to challenge students with a freer, more reflexive form of learning. Professors who rely solely on [lecture-oriented] teaching techniques—but then slouch on their podiums and lament that 'teaching is dead' when these techniques fail—are guilty of murder." Richard A. Wright (1985)

SEEING SOCIOLOGY
in Everyday Life

How many of your classes encourage active student discussion? Is participation more common in some disciplines than in others? Why?

For all categories of people in the United States, dropping out of school greatly reduces the chances of getting a good job and earning a secure income. Why is the dropout rate particularly high among Hispanic Americans?

According to Karp and Yoels, most students think classroom passivity is their own fault. Yet as anyone who observes young people outside the classroom knows, they are usually active and vocal. It is clearly the schools that teach students to be passive and to view instructors as experts who serve up "knowledge" and "truth." Most college students find little value in classroom discussion and see their proper role as listening quietly and taking notes. As a result, the researchers estimate, just 10 percent of college class time is used for discussion.

Faculty can bring students to life in their classrooms by making use of four teaching strategies: (1) calling on students by name when they volunteer, (2) positively reinforcing student participation, (3) asking analytical rather than factual questions and giving students time to answer, and (4) asking for student opinions even when no one volunteers a response (Auster & MacRone, 1994).

Dropping Out

If many students are passive in class, others are not there at all. The problem of *dropping out*—quitting school before earning a high school diploma—leaves young people (many of whom are disadvantaged to begin with) unprepared for the world of work and at high risk of poverty. For example, school dropouts account for more than 50 percent of all people receiving welfare assistance and more than 80 percent of the prison population (Christle, Jolivette, & Nelson, 2007).

Although the dropout rate has declined slightly in recent decades, a sad fact is that today's children are actually less likely to complete high school than their parents were (Ripley, 2008). Currently, 8.7 percent of people between the ages of sixteen and twenty-four have dropped out of school, a total of some 3.5 million young women and men. Dropping out is least pronounced among non-Hispanic whites (5.3 percent), higher among non-Hispanic African Americans (8.4 percent), and highest of all among Hispanics (21.4 percent) (National Center for Education Statistics, 2009). These are the official statistics, which include young people who are known to have left school. But a number of researchers estimate that the actual dropout rates are probably at least twice the government's numbers (Thornburgh, 2006).

Some students drop out because of problems with the English language, others because of pregnancy, and some because they must work to help support their family. For children growing up in families with income in the bottom 25 percent, the dropout rate is more than five times higher than for children living in high-income families (National Center for Education Statistics, 2009). These data suggest that many dropouts are young people whose parents also have little schooling, revealing a multigenerational cycle of disadvantage.

Academic Standards

Perhaps the most serious educational issue confronting our society is the quality of schooling. In 1983, a comprehensive report on the quality of U.S. schools, titled *A Nation at Risk,* was issued by the National Commission on Excellence in Education (NCEE). It begins with this alarming statement:

> If an unfriendly foreign power had attempted to impose on America the mediocre educational performance that exists today, we might well have viewed it as an act of war. As it stands, we have allowed this to happen to ourselves. (1983:5)

Supporting this claim, the report notes that "nearly 40 percent of seventeen-year-olds cannot draw inferences from written material; only one-fifth can write a persuasive essay; and only one-third can solve mathematical problems requiring several steps" (NCEE, 1983:9). Furthermore, scores on the SAT have shown little improvement over time. In 1967, mean scores for students were 516 on the mathematical test and 543 on the verbal test; by 2008, the average in mathematics had dropped 1 point to 515, and the verbal average had plunged to just 502. Nationwide, one-third of high school students—and more

functional illiteracy a lack of the reading and writing skills needed for everyday living.

than half in urban schools—fail to master even the basics in reading, math, and science on the National Assessment of Educational Progress examination (Barnes, 2002a; National Assessment of Education Progress, 2007; College Board, 2009).

For many people, even basic literacy is at issue. **Functional illiteracy,** *a lack of the reading and writing skills needed for everyday living,* is a problem for one in four U.S. children. For older people, about 30 million U.S. adults (about 14 percent of the total) lack basic skills in reading and writing.

A Nation at Risk recommended drastic reform. First, it called for schools to require *all* students to complete several years of English, mathematics, social studies, general science, and computer science. Second, schools should not promote students until they meet achievement standards. Third, teacher training must improve, and teachers' salaries must be raised to draw talent into the profession. The report concluded that schools must meet public expectations and that citizens must be prepared to pay for a job well done.

What has happened in the years since this report was issued? In some respects, schools have improved. A report by the National Center for Education Statistics (2008) noted some decline in the dropout rate, a trend toward schools' offering more challenging courses, and a larger share of high school graduates going to college. At the same time, the evidence suggests that a majority of elementary school students are falling below standards in reading; in many cases, they can't read at all. In short, although some improvement is evident, much remains to be done.

The United States spends more on schooling its children than almost any other nation—half again more than in Japan and double the average in Europe. Even so, a recent government report comparing the academic performance of fifteen-year-olds in fifty-seven countries found that the United States placed twenty-ninth in science and thirty-fifth in mathematics. Such statistics fuel fears that our country is losing its leadership in science to other nations, including China, India, and South Korea (OECD, 2007b).

Cultural values also play a part in how hard students work at their schooling. For example, U.S. students are generally less motivated and do less homework than students in Japan. Japanese young people also spend sixty more days in school each year than U.S students. Perhaps one approach to improving academic performance is simply to have students spend more time in school.

Grade Inflation

Academic standards depend on using grades that have clear meaning and are awarded for work of appropriate quality. Yet recent decades have seen substantial *grade inflation,* the awarding of ever-higher grades for average work. Though not necessarily found in every

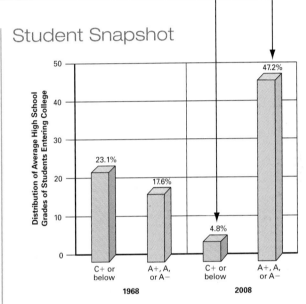

Student Snapshot

> Few grades of C+ or below are given to today's students, and almost half of all grades are now A's.

FIGURE 20–3   Grade Inflation in U.S. High Schools

In recent decades, teachers have given higher and higher grades to students.

Sources: Astin et al. (2002) and Pryor et al. (2008).

school, the trend toward grade inflation is evident across the country in both high schools and colleges.

One study of high school grades revealed a dramatic change in grades between 1968 and 2008. In 1968, as shown in Figure 20–3, the high school records of students who had just entered college included more grades of C+ and below than grades of A−, A, and A+. By 2008, however, these A grades outnumbered grades of C+ and below by almost ten to one (Pryor et al., 2008).

A few colleges and universities have enacted policies that limit the share of A's (generally to one-third of all grades). But there is little evidence that grade inflation will slow down anytime soon. As a result, the C grade (which used to mean "average") may all but disappear, making just about every student "above average."

What accounts for grade inflation? In part, today's teachers are concerned about the morale and self-esteem of their students and perhaps their own popularity. In any case, teachers clearly are not as "tough" as they used to be. At the same time, the ever more competitive process of getting into college and graduate school puts increasing pressure on high schools and colleges to award high grades (Astin et al., 2002).

NOTE: Math achievement level of U.S. 8th graders: 71% at or above basic level, 29% below basic, 32% at or above proficient, and 7% advanced (National Assessment of Educational Progress, 2005).

DISCUSS: Is grade inflation a problem? Since 1970, 93% of Stanford University's grades have been A's and B's—and no F's. In 1995, Stanford reintroduced failing grades (NP for "not passed").

NOTE: Edison Schools, which had been the largest for-profit school company, has recently moved away from managing schools and now focuses on testing, summer school, and tutoring.

NOTE: The most powerful opponent of school choice programs is the National Education Association (NEA), with more than 2 million members, most of them teachers.

● SEEING SOCIOLOGY
in Everyday Life

Recall that U.S. students spend only about 13 percent of their waking hours in school. Do you think they should spend more time in school? Explain your answer.

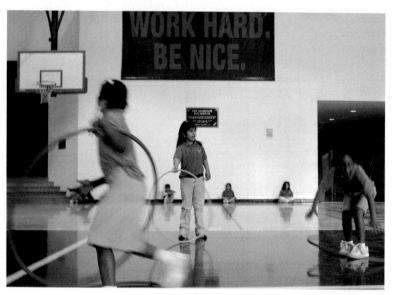

Charter schools, one part of the school choice movement, encourage personal discipline and academic excellence. Do you support school choice? Why or why not?

Current Issues in U.S. Education

Our society's schools continuously confront new challenges. This section explores several recent and important educational issues.

School Choice

Some analysts claim that our public schools teach poorly because they have no competition. Giving parents options for schooling their children might force all schools to do a better job. This is the essence of a policy called *school choice.*

The goal of school choice is to create a market for schooling so that parents and students can shop for the best value. According to one proposal, the government would give vouchers to families with school-age children and allow them to spend that money at public, private, or parochial schools. In recent years, major cities, including Indianapolis, Minneapolis, Milwaukee, Cleveland, Chicago, and Washington, D.C., as well as the states of Florida and Illinois, have experimented with choice plans aimed at making public schools perform better to win the confidence of families.

Supporters claim that giving parents a choice about where to enroll their children is the only sure way to improve all schools. But critics (including teachers' unions) charge that school choice

amounts to giving up on our nation's commitment to public education and that it will do little to improve schools in central cities, where the need is greatest (A. Cohen, 1999; Morse, 2002).

In 2002, President George W. Bush signed a new education bill that downplayed vouchers in favor of another approach to greater choice. Starting in the 2005–06 school year, all public schools began testing every child in reading, mathematics, and science in grades three through eight. Although the federal government will provide more aid to schools where students do not perform well, if those schools do not show improvements in test scores over a period of time, their students will have the choice of either special tutoring or transportation to another school. This program, called "No Child Left Behind," has succeeded in showing which schools are not doing a good job educating children and has raised some measures of student performance. At the same time, however, there has been little change in many of the worst-performing schools (Lindlaw, 2002; Wallis & Steptoe, 2007).

A more modest type of school choice involves *magnet schools,* almost 2,700 of which now exist across the country. Magnet schools offer special facilities and programs that promote educational excellence in a particular field, such as computer science, foreign languages, science and mathematics, or the arts. In school districts with magnet schools, parents can choose the school best suited to their child's particular talents and interests.

Another school choice strategy involves *charter schools,* public schools that are given more freedom to try out new policies and programs. There are more than 4,000 such schools in forty-one states, Washington, D.C., and Puerto Rico; they enroll 1.2 million students, 60 percent of whom are minorities. In many of these schools, students have demonstrated high academic achievement— a requirement for renewal of the charter (U.S. Charter Schools, 2008).

A final development in the school choice movement is *schooling for profit.* Advocates of this plan say that school systems can be operated by private profit-making companies more efficiently than by local governments. Private schooling is nothing new, of course; more than 28,000 schools in the United States are currently run by private organizations and religious groups. What is new is that hundreds of public schools, enrolling hundreds of thousands of students, are now run by private businesses for profit.

Research confirms that many public school systems suffer from bureaucratic bloat, spending too much and teaching too little. And our society has long looked to competition to improve quality. Evidence suggests that for-profit schools have greatly reduced adminis-

DIVERSITY: In 2005, the enrollment of charter schools was 42% white, 31% black, 22% Hispanic, 3% American Indian, and 3% Asian. Traditional public schools are 58% white, 17% black, 19% Hispanic, 5% Asian, and 1% American Indian (U.S. Department of Education, 2008).

NOTE: The increasing number of home computers is pushing up the number of home schoolers.

Q: "In the first place, God made idiots. That was for practice. Then he made school boards." Mark Twain

NOTE: Twenty-five years after publication of *A Nation at Risk*, average teacher salaries have climbed and a number of states have initiated examinations for promotion and graduation, but the dropout rate has changed little, and achievement test scores have risen only slightly.

● SEEING SOCIOLOGY
in Everyday Life

Have you ever attended a magnet school, charter school, or for-profit school? If so, was it a good experience?

mainstreaming integrating students with disabilities or special needs into the overall educational program.

trative costs, but the educational results appear mixed. Although several companies claim to have improved student learning, some cities have cut back on business-run schools. In recent years, school boards in Baltimore, Miami, Hartford, and Boston have canceled the contracts of for-profit schooling corporations. But other cities are deciding to give for-profit schooling a try. For example, after Philadelphia's public school system failed to graduate one-third of its students, the state of Pennsylvania took over that city's schools and turned over most of them to for-profit companies, and student test scores have gone up. In light of conflicting evidence about the performance of for-profit schools, emotions among both supporters and critics of this policy continue to run high, with each side claiming to speak for the well-being of the schoolchildren caught in the middle (Sizer, 2003; Garland, 2007; Richburg, 2008).

Home Schooling

Home schooling is gaining popularity across the United States. About 1.5 million children (almost 3 percent of all school-age children) receive their formal schooling at home.

Why do parents undertake the enormous challenge of schooling their own children? Some twenty years ago, most of the parents who pioneered home schooling (which is now legal in every state) wanted to give their children a strongly religious upbringing. Today, however, many are mothers and fathers who simply do not believe that public schools are doing a good job, and they think they can do better. To benefit their children, they are willing to alter work schedules and relearn algebra or other necessary subjects. Many belong to groups in which parents pool their efforts, specializing in what each knows best.

Advocates of home schooling point out that given the poor performance of many public schools, no one should be surprised that a growing number of parents are stepping up to teach their own children. In addition, this system works—on average, students who learn at home outperform those who learn in school. Critics argue that home schooling reduces the amount of funding going to local public schools, which ends up hurting the majority of students. In addition, as one critic point out, home schooling "takes some of the most affluent and articulate parents out of the system. These are the parents who know how to get things done with administrators" (Chris Lubienski, quoted in Cloud & Morse, 2001:48).

Schooling People with Disabilities

Many of the 6.7 million children with disabilities in the United States face special challenges getting to and from school; once there, many with crutches or wheelchairs cannot negotiate stairs and other obstacles inside school buildings. Other children with developmental disabilities such as mental retardation require extensive personal

Educators have long debated the best way to teach children with disabilities. On one hand, such children may benefit from separate facilities staffed by specially trained teachers. On the other hand, children are less likely to be stigmatized as "different" if they are included in regular classrooms. One way to "mainstream" children with special needs is to provide them with teaching assistants who offer the help they need throughout the day.

attention from specially trained teachers. Because of these challenges, many children with mental and physical disabilities have received a public education only after persistent efforts by parents and other concerned citizens (Horn & Tynan, 2001; U.S. Department of Education, 2008).

About half of all children with disabilities are schooled in special facilities; the rest attend public schools, many in regular classes. Most schools avoid expensive "special education" in favor of **mainstreaming**, *integrating students with disabilities or special needs into the overall educational program*. Mainstreaming is a form of *inclusive education* that works best for physically impaired students who have no difficulty keeping up academically with the rest of the class. A benefit of putting children with and without disabilities in the same classroom is allowing everyone to learn to interact with people who are different from themselves.

Education CHAPTER 20

533

NOTE: Since 1970, the number of U.S. students with "specific learning disabilities" has increased rapidly from 796,000 to 5.4 million in 2007, down a bit from 6 million in 2000.

NOTE: With greater resources going to gifted as well as learning disabled students, the share of budgets going to "ordinary" students fell from 80% in 1967 to 59% in 1998 (Ratnesar, 1998).

DIVERSITY: Relatively few U.S. students learn a language other than English. The percentage of high schoolers who take one or more years of: Spanish, 30%; French, 8%; German, 2% (U.S. Census Bureau, 2006).

DISCUSS: In 2007, some 66% of two- and four-year colleges offered distance learning courses enrolling 12.2 million students. What are the benefits and drawbacks of distance courses?

SEEING SOCIOLOGY
in Everyday Life

Have you considered a career in teaching? If so, why? If not, what changes might make the field more appealing to you?

SEEING SOCIOLOGY IN EVERYDAY LIFE

The Twenty-First-Century Campus: Where Are the Men?

MEG: I mean, what's with this campus not having enough men?
TRICIA: It's no big deal. I'd rather focus on my work.
MARK: I think it's, like, really cool for us guys.

A century ago, the campuses of colleges and universities across the United States might as well have hung out a sign that read "Men Only." Almost all of the students and faculty were male. There were a small number of women's colleges, but many more schools—including some of the best-known U.S. universities such as Yale, Harvard, and Princeton—barred women outright.

Since then, women have won greater social equality. By 1980, the number of women enrolled at U.S. colleges finally matched the number of men.

In a surprising trend, however, the share of women on campus has continued to increase. As a result, in 2005, men accounted for only 43 percent of all U.S. undergraduates. Meg DeLong noticed the gender imbalance right away when she moved into her dorm at the University of Georgia at Athens; she soon learned that just 39 percent of her first-year classmates were men. In some classes, there were few men, and women usually dominated discussions. Out of class, DeLong and many other women soon complained that having so few men on campus hurt their social life. Not surprisingly, most of the men felt otherwise (Fonda, 2000).

What accounts for the shifting gender balance on U.S. campuses? One theory is that young men are drawn away from college by the lure of jobs, especially in high technology. This pattern is sometimes termed the "Bill Gates syndrome," after the man who dropped out of college and soon became the world's richest person by helping to found Microsoft. In addition, analysts point to an anti-intellectual male culture. Young women are drawn to learning and seek to do well in school, but young men attach less importance to studying. Rightly or wrongly, more men seem to think they can get a good job without investing years of their lives and a considerable amount of money in getting a college degree.

The gender gap is evident in all racial and ethnic categories and at all class levels. Among African Americans on campus, only 33 percent are men. The lower the income level, the greater the gender gap in college attendance.

Many college officials are concerned about the lack of men on campus. In an effort to attract more balanced enrollments, some colleges are adopting what amounts to affirmative action programs for males. But courts in several states have already ruled such policies illegal. Many colleges, therefore, are turning to more active recruitment; admissions officers are paying special attention to male applicants and stressing a college's strength in mathematics and science—areas traditionally popular with men. In the same way that colleges across the country are striving to increase their share of minority students, the hope is that they can also succeed in attracting a larger share of men.

WHAT DO YOU THINK?

1. Among high school students, are men less concerned than women about academic achievement? Why or why not?

2. Is there a gender imbalance on your campus? Does it create problems? What problems? For whom?

3. What programs or policies do you think might increase the number of men going to college?

Adult Education

In 2005, more than 94 million U.S. adults over twenty-five were enrolled in some type of schooling. These older students range in age from the mid-twenties to the seventies and beyond and make up 39 percent of students in degree-granting programs. Adults in school are more likely to be women than men, and most have above-average incomes.

Why do adults return to the classroom? The most obvious reasons given are to advance a career or train for a new job, but many are in class simply for personal enrichment (U.S. Census Bureau, 2006).

The Teacher Shortage

A major challenge for U.S. schools is hiring enough teachers to fill the classrooms. A number of factors—including low salaries, frustration, and retirement, as well as rising enrollment and reductions in class size—have combined to create more than 300,000 teaching vacancies in the United States each year.

How will these slots be filled? About the same number of people graduate with education degrees each year. Most of them do not have a degree in a specific field, such as mathematics, biology, or

DISCUSS: Is there enough intellectual diversity on U.S. college campuses? A report from the American Enterprise Institute found large majorities of Democrats and members of other left-leaning parties among the faculties of major universities. For example, Cornell had 166 Democrats/other left parties and 6 Republicans/other parties of the right; U. Colorado, Boulder: 116 Democrats/left, 5 Republicans/right; Stanford: 151, 17; Brown: 54, 3; UC-San Diego: 99, 6.

Q: "A university is what a college becomes when the faculty loses interest in the students." John Ciardi

Q: "I am always ready to learn, although I do not always like being taught." Winston Churchill

Q: "I find that the three major administrative problems on a campus are sex for the students, athletics for the alumni, and parking for the faculty." Clark Kerr

English, and many have trouble passing state certification tests in the subject they want to teach. As a result, many schools, especially in low-income neighborhoods, are taught by teachers who may be just one chapter ahead of their students (Quaid, 2008).

This means that the teacher shortage is really a shortage of *good* teachers. For our nation's public schools to improve, two things must happen: First, teachers who do not teach well must receive additional training or lose their jobs, and second, well-qualified people need to be attracted into the classroom (Ripley, 2008).

Getting rid of bad teachers (and perhaps bad principals, too) means changing rules that make it difficult or impossible to fire someone after a few years on the job. Gaining well-qualified teachers depends on adopting various recruitment strategies. Some schools offer incentives such as higher salaries (the average salary for a thirty-year-old teacher in public schools is only about $37,000 a year) to draw into teaching people who already have had successful careers. Some schools provide signing bonuses (especially for hard-to-fill positions in mathematics and chemistry) or give housing allowances (in cities such as New York, where the cost of housing is often out of the reach of teachers). President Obama (2007) has written that he believes that school districts should pay highly qualified and effective teachers as much as $100,000 a year—but, he adds, they must also be able to dismiss unqualified and ineffective teachers.

Other policy ideas include having community colleges play a larger role in teacher education and having government and school boards make it easier for well-trained people to get the certification they need to enter the classroom. Finally, many school districts are going global, actively recruiting in countries such as Spain, India, and the Philippines to bring talented women and men from around the world to teach in U.S. classrooms (Philadelphia, 2001; Evelyn, 2002; Ripley, 2008; Wallis, 2008).

Debate about education in the United States extends beyond the issues noted here. The Seeing Sociology in Everyday Life box highlights the declining share of college students who are men.

Schooling: Looking Ahead

Although the United States still leads the world in sending people to college, the public school system continues to struggle with serious problems. In terms of quality of schooling, this country has fallen behind many other high-income nations, a fact that calls into question the future strength of the United States on the world stage.

Many of the problems of schooling discussed in this chapter have their roots in the larger society. We cannot expect schools *by*

Because our public schools face many challenges, controversy over education policy is likely to continue in the years to come. What recent issues have been debated in your state?

themselves to provide high-quality education. Schools will improve only to the extent that students, teachers, parents, and local communities commit themselves to educational excellence. In short, educational problems are *social* problems for which there is no quick fix.

For much of the twentieth century, there were just two models for education in the United States: public schools run by the government and private schools operated by nongovernmental organizations. In recent decades, however, many new ideas about schooling have emerged, including schooling for profit and a wide range of school choice programs. In the decades ahead, we are likely to see some significant changes in mass education, guided in part by social science research into the outcomes of different strategies.

Another factor that will continue to reshape schools is new information technology. Today, all but the poorest primary and secondary schools use computers for instruction. Computers encourage students to be more active and allow them to progress at their own pace. Even so, computers will never bring to the educational process the personal insights and imagination of a motivated human teacher.

Nor will technology ever solve all the problems that plague our schools, including violence and rigid bureaucracy. What we need is a broad plan for social change that renews this country's early ambition to provide universal schooling of high quality—a goal that we have yet to achieve.

535

Seeing Sociology in Everyday Life

How big is our society's inequality in schooling?

All schools, of course, differ in many ways. But there are several tiers of schooling in the United States, and these reflect the social class standing of the students they enroll. The images below provide a closer look at this educational hierarchy.

At the top of the schooling hierarchy are private boarding schools. The best of these schools, such as Lawrenceville School in New Jersey, have large endowments, small classes with extremely well-trained and very dedicated teachers, and magnificent campuses with facilities that rival those of the nation's top colleges. What do you estimate is the annual cost to attend such a school?

> **HINT**   Private boarding schools provide an outstanding education, and the independent living experience also helps students prepare for success in a good college or university. Although schools like Lawrenceville provide financial aid to many students, the cost of a single year at such a school for most students is about $50,000, which is just about as much as the average family earns in a year. Suburban high schools are supported through tax money; yet the cost of homes in these affluent communities is typically hundreds of thousands of dollars, putting this level of schooling out of reach for a large share of U.S. families. Public schools in the inner city enroll students from families with below-average incomes, which means these schools have the highest percentage of minority students. Liberal Democrats such as the Obamas strongly support public education, but they, like most other residents of the White House (Amy Carter went to public school), have chosen private schooling for their children, whether for educational or security reasons.

In the middle of the educational hierarchy are the best public high schools, most of which are found in suburban communities. This classroom in Briarcliff High School in Briarcliff Manor, New York, has small classes with good teachers and offers many extra-curricular activities. What level of income do you think is typical of the families who are able to send their children to schools such as this?

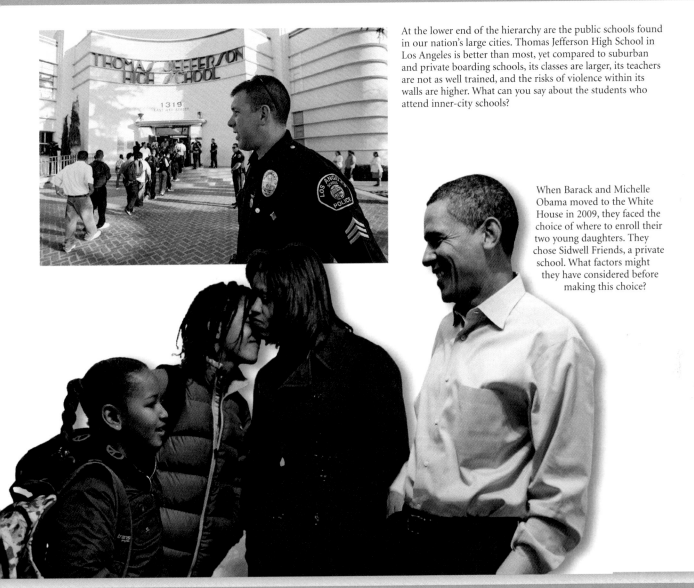

At the lower end of the hierarchy are the public schools found in our nation's large cities. Thomas Jefferson High School in Los Angeles is better than most, yet compared to suburban and private boarding schools, its classes are larger, its teachers are not as well trained, and the risks of violence within its walls are higher. What can you say about the students who attend inner-city schools?

When Barack and Michelle Obama moved to the White House in 2009, they faced the choice of where to enroll their two young daughters. They chose Sidwell Friends, a private school. What factors might they have considered before making this choice?

Applying SOCIOLOGY in Everyday Life

1. Make a visit to a public or private secondary school near your college or home. What is the typical social background of students enrolled there? Does the school have a tracking policy? If so, find out how it works. How much importance does a student's social background have in making a tracking assignment?

2. Most people agree that teaching our children is important work. Yet teachers earn relatively low salaries. Check the prestige ranking for teachers in Table 11–1 on page 277. See what you can learn about the average salary of teachers in your community, and compare it to the pay of other workers. Do you think teachers are paid enough?

3. Since the passage of the Americans with Disabilities Act of 1990, schools have tried to "accommodate" students with a broader range of physical and mental disabilities. Talk to officials on your campus about policies at your school and how laws of this kind are changing education.

MAKING THE GRADE

CHAPTER 20 Education

Education: A Global Survey

EDUCATION is the social institution for transmitting knowledge and skills, as well as teaching cultural norms and values.

- In preindustrial societies, education occurs informally within the family.
- Industrial societies develop formal systems of schooling to educate their children.
- Differences in schooling in societies around the world today reflect both cultural values and each country's level of economic development.

pp. 516–17

education (p. 516) the social institution through which society provides its members with important knowledge, including basic facts, job skills, and cultural norms and values

schooling (p. 516) formal instruction under the direction of specially trained teachers

SCHOOLING IN INDIA

- Despite the fact that India is now a middle-income country, patriarchy continues to shape education in India. Many more boys attend school than girls, who are often expected to work in factories at young ages.
- Today, almost 90% of children in India complete primary school, but barely half of them go on to secondary school.

p. 517

SCHOOLING IN JAPAN

- The earliest years of schooling in Japan concentrate on transmitting Japanese cultural traditions.
- More men and women graduate from high school in Japan (93%) than in the United States (87%), but only half of high school graduates gain college admission, which is determined by highly competitive examinations.

p. 517

SCHOOLING IN GREAT BRITAIN

- During the Middle Ages, schooling was a privilege of the British nobility. The Industrial Revolution created a need for a literate workforce.
- Traditional class differences still affect British schooling; elite schools, which enroll 7% of British students, provide a path for admission to the most prestigious universities.

pp. 517–19

SCHOOLING IN THE UNITED STATES

- The United States was among the first countries to undertake compulsory mass education, reflecting both democratic political ideals and the needs of the industrial-capitalist economy.
- Schooling in the United States claims to promote equal opportunity, but the opportunity to go to college is closely tied to family income.
- The U.S. educational system stresses the value of practical learning that prepares young people for their place in the workforce.

p. 519

The Functions of Schooling

The **STRUCTURAL-FUNCTIONAL APPROACH** focuses on the ways in which schooling contributes to the orderly operation of society. Key functions of schooling include:

- *Socialization*—teaching the skills that young people need to succeed in life, as well as cultural values and norms
- *Cultural innovation*—providing the opportunity for academic research that leads to important discoveries
- *Social integration*—molding a diverse population into one society by teaching cultural norms and values
- *Social placement*—reinforcing meritocracy and providing a path for upward social mobility
- *Latent functions*—providing child care and the opportunity for building social networks

pp. 519–20

Schooling and Social Interaction

The **SYMBOLIC-INTERACTION APPROACH** looks at how we build reality in our day-to-day interactions.

- The "self-fulfilling prophecy" describes how self-image can have important consequences for how students perform in school. If students think they are academically superior, they are likely to perform better; students who think they are inferior are likely to perform less well.

pp. 520–21

Schooling and Social Inequality

The **SOCIAL-CONFLICT APPROACH** links schooling to inequality involving class, race, and gender.

- Formal education serves as a means of generating conformity to produce obedient adult workers.
- Standardized tests have been criticized as culturally biased tools that may lead to labeling less privileged students as personally deficient.
- **Tracking** has been challenged by critics as a program that gives a better education to privileged youngsters.
- The majority of young people in the United States attend state-funded public schools. A small proportion of students—usually the most well-to-do—attend elite private college preparatory schools.
- Differences in school funding affect the quality of education: Public schools in more affluent areas offer a better education than schools in poor areas.
- Largely due to the high cost of college, only 66% of U.S. students enroll in college directly after high school graduation; the higher a family's income, the more likely it is that children will attend college.
- Earning a college degree today adds as much as $1 million to a person's lifetime income.

pp. 521–27

tracking (p. 522) assigning students to different types of educational programs

📖 See the Applying Theory table on page 527.

Problems in the Schools

VIOLENCE permeates many schools, especially in poor neighborhoods.

- Critics charge that schools today fall short in their efforts to teach personal discipline.

p. 528

The bureaucratic character of schools fosters **STUDENT PASSIVITY**. Schools have evolved into huge educational factories that

- demand rigid uniformity
- define success in terms of numerical ratings
- hold rigid expectations of students
- require too much specialization
- instill little individual responsibility in students

pp. 528–30

The high school **DROPOUT RATE**—currently 8.7% of young people—leaves many young people unprepared for the world of work and at high risk of poverty.

- The dropout rate for children in families with income in the bottom 25% is more than four times higher than for children living in high-income families.

p. 530

DECLINING ACADEMIC STANDARDS are reflected in

- today's lower average scores on achievement tests
- the functional illiteracy of a significant proportion of high school graduates
- grade inflation

pp. 530–31

functional illiteracy (p. 531) a lack of the reading and writing skills needed for everyday living

Current Issues in U.S. Education

The **SCHOOL CHOICE MOVEMENT** seeks to make schools more accountable to the public. Innovative school choice options include

- magnet schools
- schooling for profit
- charter schools

pp. 532–33

HOME SCHOOLING

- The original pioneers of home schooling did not believe in public education because they wanted to give their children a strongly religious upbringing.
- Home schooling advocates today point to the poor performance of public schools.

p. 533

SCHOOLING PEOPLE WITH DISABILITIES

- In the past, children with mental or physical disabilities were schooled in special classes.
- **Mainstreaming** affords them broader opportunities and exposes all children to a more diverse student population.

p. 533

ADULT EDUCATION

- Adults represent a growing proportion of students in the United States.
- Most older learners are women who are engaged in job-related study.

p. 534

THE TEACHER SHORTAGE

- More than 300,000 teaching positions go unfilled in the United States each year due to low salaries, frustration, retirement, rising enrollments, and reduced class size.
- To address this shortage, many school districts are recruiting teachers from abroad.

pp. 534–35

mainstreaming (p. 533) integrating students with disabilities or special needs into the overall educational program

- ✓ Because the problems of our schools have their roots in the larger society, improvement will require a national commitment.
- ✓ The widespread use of computers in schools today is evidence that the Information Revolution is changing the way we learn.

Improving human health is an important concern, especially in modern societies, which create medical systems to promote well-being. But like many resources, health is spread unequally throughout the U.S. population as well as around the world.

CHAPTER 21

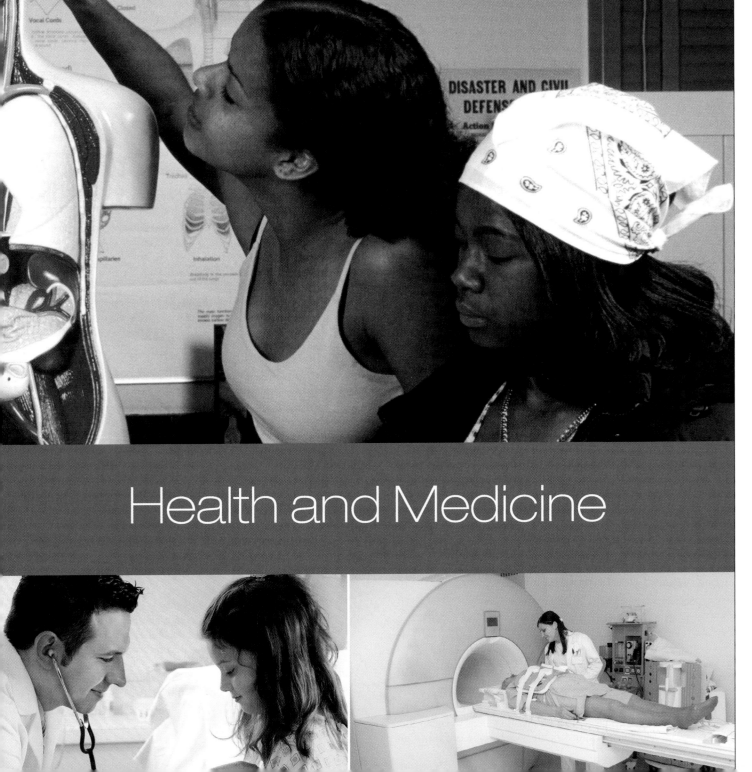

Health and Medicine

THEN AND NOW: Technology has rapidly changed the character of modern medicine. The first map of the circulatory system was made in 1628. The first heart transplant was done in 1961; for several years thereafter, each transplant was a major media event. Today, such procedures are commonplace and covered by Medicare.

GLOBAL: In only four countries do men, on average, outlive women: Niger, Namibia, Zambia, and Botswana.

NOTE: One sign of long-term improvement in nutrition: Lucy, the 3-million-year-old adult fossilized skeleton found in Ethiopia, stood only about 3 feet 6 inches tall; she would have weighed 65 pounds.

CHAPTER OVERVIEW { This chapter explores health care, including medicine, a social institution of major importance. The chapter begins by explaining why health is a social issue and why sociologists have much to say about human health.

Krista Peters cannot remember a time in her life when she was not on a diet. The sixteen-year-old, who lives in a small Pennsylvania town, shakes her head. "It's, like, I can't do anything about it. I know I don't look good. My mom says I shouldn't eat so much; the nurse at school says the same thing. But if it's up to me, then why can't I ever lose any weight?"

Peters does have a weight problem. Although she stands just 5 feet 2 inches tall, she weighs 240 pounds. Doctors would call her seriously obese, and the longer she remains so heavy, the greater her odds of serious disease and even death at a young age.

Krista Peters is not alone. In a society where fast food has become something of a national dish and people use the word "supersize" as a verb, men and women all across the United States are getting fat. Not some people—*most* people. According to the experts, about two-thirds of U.S. adults are overweight. In response to the rising level of obesity among young people, the government is currently considering a ban on junk food in school cafeterias.

Being overweight is a serious health issue. People like Krista Peters are at high risk for heart disease, stroke, and diabetes. Each year, several hundred thousand people in the United States die early from diseases related to being overweight. Obesity is not just a personal problem; it is also a *social* problem. The choices people make do matter, but members of our society are up against some powerful cultural forces. Consider the fact that the U.S. population is confronted with unhealthy fast food at every turn. Our national consumption of salty potato chips, sugar-rich soft drinks, high-calorie pizza, and chocolate candy bars rises every year. Car companies and airlines have even had to design larger seats to fit more "supersized" people (Bellandi, 2003; Witt, 2004; Bennett, 2006; CDC, 2009).

What Is Health?

In ideal terms, according to the World Health Organization (1946:3), **health** is *a state of complete physical, mental, and social well-being*. This definition underscores the major theme of this chapter: Health is not just a matter of personal choice, nor it is only a biological issue; patterns of well-being and illness are rooted in the organization of society.

Health and Society

Society shapes people's health in four major ways:

1. **Cultural patterns define health.** Standards of health vary from place to place. A century ago, yaws, a contagious skin disease, was so common in sub-Saharan Africa that people there considered it normal (Dubos, 1980). In the United States, a rich diet is so common that most adults and about one-fifth of children are overweight. "Health," therefore, is sometimes a matter of having the same disease as your neighbors (Pinhey, Rubinstein, & Colfax, 1997).

   What people see as healthful also reflects what they think is morally good. Members of our society (especially men) think a competitive way of life is "healthy" because it fits our cultural mores, but stress contributes to heart disease and many other illnesses. People who object to homosexuality on moral grounds call this sexual orientation "sick," even though it is natural from a biological point of view. Thus ideas about health act as a form of social control, encouraging conformity to cultural norms.

2. **Cultural standards of health change over time.** In the early twentieth century, some doctors warned women not to go to college because higher education would strain the female brain. Others claimed that masturbation was a threat to health. We know now that both of these ideas are false. Fifty years ago, on the other hand, few doctors understood the dangers of cigarette smoking or too much sun exposure, practices that we now recognize as serious health risks. Even patterns of basic hygiene change over time. Today, most people in the United States bathe every day; this is three times as often as fifty years ago (Gillespie, 2000).

3. **A society's technology affects people's health.** In poor nations, infectious diseases are widespread because of malnutrition and poor sanitation. As industrialization raises living

GLOBAL: Only about one-third of the world's people tap into a safe water supply. Worldwide, more than 500,000 women, almost all in poor countries, die each year from pregnancy-related causes.

GLOBAL: Illustrating high mortality from infectious disease early in the 20th century, a 1918 flu epidemic killed millions worldwide, including 500,000 in the U.S. This was the world's deadliest pandemic.

GLOBAL: The leading causes of death in the U.S. in 1900, as presented in Table 21–1, are leading causes of death in poor societies today.

DIVERSITY: Leading causes of death by age—under 1: congenital abnormalities; for all age categories between 1 and 44: unintentional injuries; 45–64: cancer; 65 and older: heart disease (Heron & Smith, 2007).

MAKING THE GRADE

health a state of complete physical, mental, and social well-being

In high-income societies today, few deaths result from infectious diseases; most deaths result from chronic illnesses.

standards, people become healthier. But industrial technology also creates new threats to health. As Chapter 22 ("Population, Urbanization, and Environment") explains, high-income ways of life threaten human health by overtaxing the world's resources and creating pollution.

4. **Social inequality affects people's health**. All societies distribute resources unequally. In general, the rich have far better physical and mental health than the poor.

Health: A Global Survey

We see the close link between health and social life in the fact that human well-being improved over the long course of history as societies developed more advanced technology. Differences in societal development are also the cause of striking differences in health around the world today.

Health in Low-Income Countries

December 25, Yucay, Peru. We're attending the Christmas Day street festival in this small village in the Andes Mountains. There is much excitement and happiness everywhere. Oddly, perhaps, I notice that not one of the hundreds of people who have passed by along the main street is wearing glasses. One Peruvian friend says that in this poor community, there are no optometrists or eye doctors, and no one has any extra money to afford glasses.

In much of the world, severe poverty cuts decades off the long life expectancy typical of rich countries. A look back at Global Map 15–1 on page 391 shows that people in most parts of Africa have a life expectancy of barely fifty years, and in the poorest countries, most people die before reaching their teens (Population Reference Bureau, 2009).

The World Health Organization reports that 1 billion people around the world—about one person in six—suffer from serious illness due to poverty. Bad health can result from eating only a single type of food or more commonly from simply having too little to eat. Malnutrition kills people of all ages, especially children.

In low-income countries, poor sanitation is also a killer. Safe drinking water is as hard to come by as a balanced diet, and bad water carries a number of infectious diseases, including influenza, pneumonia, and tuberculosis, which are widespread killers in poor societies today. To make matters worse, medical personnel are few and far between; as a result, the world's poorest people—many of whom live in Central Africa—never see a physician.

In poor nations with minimal medical care, it is no wonder that almost 10 percent of children die within a year of their birth (World Bank, 2009). In some countries, half the children never reach adulthood. For those who do grow up, illness and poverty form a vicious circle: Poverty breeds disease, which in turn undermines the ability to work. When medical technology does control infectious disease, the populations of poor nations rise. Without resources to ensure the well-being of the people they have now, poor societies can ill afford population increases. Therefore, programs that lower death rates in poor countries will succeed only if they are coupled with programs that reduce birth rates.

Health in High-Income Countries

By 1800, as the Industrial Revolution took hold, factory jobs in the cities attracted people from all over the countryside. Cities quickly became overcrowded, causing serious sanitation problems. Factories fouled the air with smoke, which few people recognized as a health threat until well into the twentieth century. Workplace accidents were common.

Gradually, industrialization improved health in Western Europe and North America by providing better nutrition and safer housing for most people, so that by about 1850, health began to improve. Around this time, medical advances began to control infectious diseases. In 1854, for example, a physician named John Snow mapped the street addresses of London's cholera victims and found that they had all drunk contaminated water from the same well. Not long afterward, scientists linked cholera to a specific bacterium and developed a vaccine against the deadly disease. Armed with scientific knowledge, early environmentalists campaigned against common practices such as discharging raw sewage into the same rivers used for drinking water. By the early twentieth century, death rates from infectious diseases had fallen sharply.

A glance at Table 21–1 shows that the leading killers in 1900 were infectious diseases, such as influenza and pneumonia. Today,

Table 21–1 Leading Causes of Death in the United States, 1900 and 2006

1900	2006
1. Influenza and pneumonia	1. Heart disease
2. Tuberculosis	2. Cancer
3. Stomach and intestinal disease	3. Stroke
4. Heart disease	4. Lung disease (noncancerous)
5. Cerebral hemorrhage	5. Accidents
6. Kidney disease	6. Alzheimer's disease
7. Accidents	7. Diabetes
8. Cancer	8. Influenza and pneumonia
9. Disease in early infancy	9. Kidney disease
10. Diphtheria	10. Blood disease

Sources: Information for 1900 is from William C. Cockerham, *Medical Sociology*, 2nd ed. (Englewood Cliffs, N.J.: Prentice Hall, 1986), p. 24; information for 2006 is from Centers for Disease Control and Prevention (2008).

THE MAP: Urbanites do indeed have better health than rural people. Across the country, almost all the excellent health areas are in major metropolitan regions (where incomes are high).

DIVERSITY: Interestingly, prior to the Industrial Revolution, men and women had about the same longevity.

NOTE: One component of health differences is income: People in Fairfax County, Va. (a Washington, D.C., suburb), live about 15 years longer than people living in the downtown capital, 12 miles away. Race, too, is at work, with African Americans and Native Americans worse off than whites, even controlling for income.

Parker Jeeter lives in McCurtain County, Oklahoma, a low-income community, where health problems are common among his neighbors.

Marina Treleaven lives in an affluent neighborhood of Chester County, Pennsylvania, where health indicators are well above the national average.

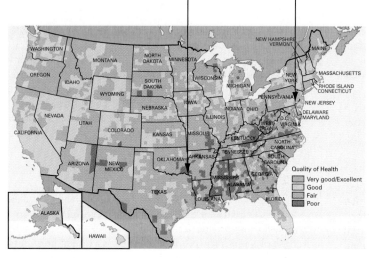

Seeing Ourselves

NATIONAL MAP 21–1
Health across the United States

Average health varies from place to place throughout the United States. This map shows the results of a survey that asked people across the country about their personal health, including their smoking habits, nutritional diet, and frequency of illness. Looking at the map, what pattern do you see? Can you explain it?

Source: *American Demographics*, October 2000, p. 50. Reprinted with permission from *American Demographics*. © 2004 by Crain Communications, Inc.

Quality of Health
Very good/Excellent
Good
Fair
Poor

in high-income countries such as the United States, such diseases account for just a small percentage of deaths. It is now chronic illnesses, such as heart disease, cancer, and stroke, that cause most deaths, usually in old age.

Health in the United States

Because the United States is a rich nation, health is generally good by world standards. Still, some categories of people are better off than others.

Who Is Healthy? Age, Gender, Class, and Race

Social epidemiology is *the study of how health and disease are distributed throughout a society's population.* Just as early social epidemiologists traced the spread of diseases, researchers today examine the connection between health and our physical and social environments. National Map 21–1 surveys the health of the population of the United States, where there is a twenty-year difference in average life expectancy between the richest and poorest communities. Patterns of health can be viewed in terms of age, gender, social class, and race.

Age and Gender

Death is now rare among young people. Still, young people do fall victim to accidents and, more recently, to acquired immune deficiency syndrome (AIDS).

Across the life course, women have better health than men. First, girls are less likely than boys to die before or immediately after birth.

Then, as socialization begins, males become more aggressive and individualistic, which contributes to their higher rates of accidents, violence, and suicide. As the Seeing Sociology in Everyday Life box explains, the combination of chronic impatience, uncontrolled ambition, and frequent outbursts of hostility that doctors call "coronary-prone behavior" is a fairly close match with our culture's definition of masculinity.

Social Class and Race

Government researchers tell us that 79 percent of adults in families with incomes over $75,000 think their health is excellent or very good, but only 52 percent of adults in families earning less than $35,000 say the same. Conversely, only about 4 percent of higher-income people describe their health as either fair or poor, compared with 18 percent of low-income people. Having a higher income and greater wealth boosts people's health by improving their nutrition, enabling them to receive better health care, and allowing them to live in safer and less stressful surroundings (Adams, Barnes, & Vickerie, 2008).

Research suggests that African Americans are no different from whites in terms of their desire for good health and willingness to seek medical help. But poverty among African Americans—at three times the rate for whites—shapes people's everyday options and helps explain why black people are more likely to die in infancy and, as adults, are more likely to suffer the effects of violence, drug abuse, and poor health (Schnittker, Pescosolido, & Croghan, 2005; U.S. Census Bureau, 2008).

The life expectancy of white children born in 2006 is five years greater than that of African Americans (78.5 years versus 73.6). Gender is an even stronger predictor of health than race because African

DISCUSS: Is competition "natural," even though high levels of stress contribute to heart disease, which is the leading killer in the U.S. (see Table 21–1)? Heart disease kills 630,000 people annually, more than the total killed in all U.S. wars over the course of the 20th century.

NOTE: The Harvard School of Public Health's projections of the top 10 killers of the U.S. population in 2020: (1) heart disease, (2) severe depression, (3) traffic accidents, (4) stroke, (5) chronic pulmonary disease, (6) respiratory infections, (7) tuberculosis, (8) war injuries, (9) diarrheal infections, (10) HIV/AIDS.

SEEING SOCIOLOGY
in Everyday Life

social epidemiology the study of how health and disease are distributed throughout a society's population.

Have you ever thought about gender as a health issue? Explain.

SEEING SOCIOLOGY IN EVERYDAY LIFE

Masculinity: A Threat to Health?

JEFF: Cindy! If you don't get out of there in ten seconds, I'm gonna beat you up!

CINDY: Chill out! I have as much right to be in the bathroom as you do. I'm not finished.

JEFF: Are you going to take *all day?*

CINDY: Why are you guys always in such a hurry?

Doctors call it "coronary-prone behavior." Psychologists call it the "Type A personality." Sociologists recognize it as our culture's concept of masculinity. This combination of attitudes and behavior, common among men in our society, includes not just impatience ("C'mon! Get outta my bathroom!") but also uncontrolled ambition ("I've gotta have it—I *need* that!") and free-floating hostility ("Why are people *such idiots?*").

This pattern, although normal from a cultural point of view, is one major reason that men who are driven to succeed are at high risk of heart disease. By acting out the Type A personality, we may get the job done, but we set in motion complex biochemical processes that are very hard on the human heart.

Here are a few questions to help you assess your own degree of risk (or that of someone important to you):

1. **Do you believe you have to be aggressive to succeed?** Do "nice guys finish last"? If your answer to this question is yes, for your heart's sake, try to remove hostility from your life. Here's a place to start: Eliminate profanity from your speech. Whenever someone in everyday life starts getting to you, try replacing aggression with compassion, which can be surprisingly effective in dealing with other people. Medically speaking, compassion and humor—rather than irritation and aggravation—will improve your health.

2. **How well do you handle uncertainty and opposition?** Do you have moments when you fume "Why won't the waiter take my order?" or "This customer just doesn't get it!"? We all like to know what's going on,

and we like others to agree with us. But the world often doesn't work that way. Accepting uncertainty and opposition makes us more mature and certainly healthier.

3. **Are you uncomfortable showing positive emotions?** Many men think giving and accepting love—from women, from children, and from other men—is a sign of weakness. But the medical truth is that love supports health and anger damages it.

As human beings, we have a great deal of choice about how to live. Think about the choices you make, and reflect on how our society's idea of masculinity often makes us hard on others (including those we love) and, just as important, hard on ourselves.

WHAT DO YOU THINK?

1. What aspects of masculinity are harmful to health? Why?

2. If aspects of masculine behavior are harmful, why do you think they are so common?

3. How can sociology play a part in changing men's behavior for the better?

Sources: Friedman & Rosenman (1974) and M. P. Levine (1990).

American women outlive men of either race. From another angle, 81 percent of white men but just 67 percent of African American men will live to age sixty-five. The comparable figures for women are 88 percent for whites and 79 percent for African Americans (Arias, 2007; Centers for Disease Control and Prevention, 2008).

Infant mortality—the death rate among children under one year of age—is twice as high for disadvantaged children as for children born into privileged families. Although the health of the richest children in our nation is the best in the world, our poorest children are as vulnerable to disease as those in low-income nations such as Nigeria and Vietnam.

Cigarette Smoking

Cigarette smoking tops the list of preventable health hazards in the United States. Only after World War I did smoking become popular in this country. Despite growing evidence of its dangers, smoking remained fashionable until around a generation ago. Today, however, an increasing number of people consider smoking a mild form of social deviance, and an increasing number of states have banned smoking in public buildings (Niesse, 2007).

The popularity of cigarettes peaked in 1960, when 45 percent of U.S. adults smoked. By 2007, only 20 percent were still lighting up, according to the Centers for Disease Control and Prevention (CDC,

SEEING SOCIOLOGY
in Everyday Life

Sixteen states have enacted laws banning smoking in all public buildings. Would you support making this ban a national policy? Why or why not?

eating disorder an intense form of dieting or other unhealthy method of weight control driven by the desire to be very thin

---

THINKING ABOUT DIVERSITY: RACE, CLASS, & GENDER

Gender and Eating Disorders: A Report from Fiji

In 1995, television came to Fiji, a small group of islands in the South Pacific Ocean. A single cable channel carried programming from the United States, Great Britain, and Australia. Anne Becker (1999, 2004), a Harvard researcher specializing in eating disorders, read the news with great interest, wondering what effect the global spread of culture from the United States via television would have on young women there.

Traditionally, Fijian culture emphasizes good nutrition and looking strong and healthy. The idea of dieting to look very thin was almost unknown. So it is not surprising that in 1995, Becker found that just 3 percent of teenage girls reported ever vomiting to control their weight.

By 1998, however, a striking change was taking place, with 15 percent of teenage girls—a fivefold increase—reporting this practice. Becker also found that 62 percent of girls claimed they had dieted during the previous month and 74 percent reported feeling "too big" or "fat."

The rapid rise in eating disorders in Fiji, which Becker linked to the introduction of television, shows the power of culture to shape patterns of health. Eating disorders, including anorexia nervosa and bulimia, are even more common in the United States, where about half of college women report engaging in such behavior, even though most of these women, medically speaking, are not overweight. Fijian women are now

being taught what many women in the United States already believe: "You are never too thin to feel fat."

WHAT DO YOU THINK?

1. Why are eating disorders a social issue as well as a medical issue?

2. At what age do you think that young girls learn that "you are never too thin to feel fat"? How do they learn this?

3. How big a role do you think the mass media play in the problem of eating disorders?

2008). Quitting is difficult because cigarette smoke contains nicotine, a physically addictive drug. Many people smoke to cope with stress: Divorced and separated people, the unemployed, and people serving in the armed forces are likely to smoke. Smoking is much more common among working-class people than among those with more income and education. A larger share of men (22 percent) than women (17 percent) smoke. But cigarettes, the only form of tobacco popular with women, have taken a toll on women's health. By 1987, lung cancer surpassed breast cancer as a cause of death among U.S. women, who now account for 39 percent of all smoking-related deaths (Pampel, 2006; CDC, 2008).

More than 440,000 men and women in the United States die prematurely each year as a direct result of cigarette smoking, a figure that exceeds the death toll from alcohol, cocaine, heroin, homicide, suicide, automobile accidents, and AIDS combined (CDC, 2008). Smokers also suffer more frequent minor illnesses such as the flu, and pregnant women who smoke increase the likelihood of spontaneous abortion and low-birthweight babies. Even nonsmokers exposed to cigarette smoke have a higher risk of smoking-related diseases.

Tobacco is an $89 billion industry in the United States. In 1997, the tobacco industry admitted that cigarette smoking is harmful to health and agreed to stop marketing cigarettes to young people. Despite the antismoking trend in the United States, research shows that the percentage of college students who smoke is approaching 30 percent and is rising (College Tobacco Prevention Resource, 2006).

In addition, the use of chewing tobacco—known to cause cancers of the mouth and throat—is increasing among the young.

The tobacco industry has increased its sales abroad, especially in low- and middle-income countries where there is less regulation of tobacco products. In many countries, especially in Asia, a large majority of men smoke. India and China, for example, contain about 40 percent of the world's cigarette smokers. Worldwide, more than 1 billion adults (about 25 percent of the total) smoke, consuming some 6 trillion cigarettes annually, and smoking is on the rise. One result of the rise in global smoking is that cancer is likely to overtake heart disease as the world's number one killer in the next year or two (Stobbe, 2008).

The harm that can come from cigarette smoking is real. But the good news is that about ten years after quitting, an ex-smoker's health is about as good as that of someone who never smoked at all.

Eating Disorders

An **eating disorder** is *an intense form of dieting or other unhealthy method of weight control driven by the desire to be very thin.* One eating disorder, *anorexia nervosa,* is characterized by dieting to the point of starvation; another is *bulimia,* which involves binge eating followed by induced vomiting to avoid weight gain.

Eating disorders have a significant cultural component; 95 percent of people who suffer from anorexia nervosa or bulimia are women, mostly from white, affluent families. For women, U.S. culture equates

SEEING SOCIOLOGY
in Everyday Life

Calculate your *body mass index* (BMI): Divide your weight in pounds by the square of your height in inches, and multiply the result by 703 (or go to http://www.nhlbisupport.com/bmi). A BMI of 18.5 to 24.9 is normal, 25.0 to 29.9 is considered overweight, and 30.0 and above is obese. What is your BMI? Are you surprised by the results?

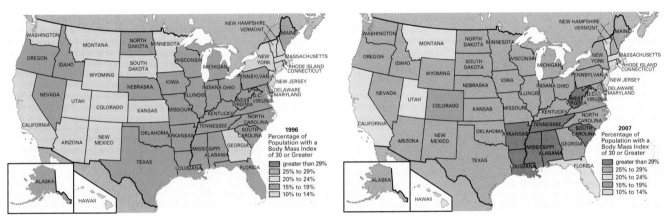

Seeing Ourselves

NATIONAL MAP 21–2   Obesity across the United States, 1996 and 2007

The map on the left shows the percentage of each state's population that was medically obese in 1996. Notice the increased percentages of obese people evident by 2007. What factors do you think are responsible for the trend toward more and more obesity in our country?

Source: Centers for Disease Control and Prevention (2008).

slimness with being successful and attractive to men. Conversely, we tend to stereotype overweight women (and to a lesser extent men) as lazy, sloppy, and even stupid (M. P. Levine, 1987; A. E. Becker, 1999).

Research shows that most college-age women believe that "guys like thin girls," that being thin is critical to physical attractiveness, and that they are not as thin as men would like. In fact, most college women want to be even thinner than most college men want them to be. Men typically express greater satisfaction with their own body shape (Fallon & Rozin, 1985).

Because few women are able to meet our culture's unrealistic standards of beauty, many women develop a low self-image. This feeling may encourage the sales of makeup, clothes, and various beauty aids, as does the mass media's focus on people's appearance. But it also leads many young women to diet to the point of risking their health and even their lives. The Thinking About Diversity box explains how the introduction of U.S. culture to the island of Fiji resulted in a sharp increase in eating disorders among women in that far-off part of the world.

Obesity

Eating disorders such as anorexia nervosa and bulimia are serious, but they are not the biggest eating-related problem in the United States. Obesity in the population as a whole is rapidly reaching crisis propor-

tions. As noted in the opening to this chapter, the government reports that two-thirds of U.S. adults are overweight, which is defined in terms of a *body mass index* (BMI) of 25.0 to 29.9, or roughly 10 to 30 pounds over a healthy weight. Half of all overweight people in the United States are clinically obese, with a BMI over 30, which means that they are at least 30 pounds over their healthy weight. National Map 21–2 shows the trend toward more and more obesity in the United States.

Being overweight can limit physical activity and raises the risk of a number of serious diseases, including heart disease, stroke, and diabetes. According to the U.S. government, the cost of treating diseases caused by obesity plus the cost of lost days at work due to such illnesses is about $118 billion every year. Most seriously, several hundred thousand people die each year in the United States from disease related to being overweight (Ferraro & Kelley-Moore, 2003; CDC, 2008).

A cause for national concern is the fact that about one in five young people in this country is already overweight, and the proportion is increasing. This trend suggests that the medical problems of this new generation will be even greater as they reach middle age and may ultimately reverse the historical trend toward greater life expectancy.

What are the social causes of obesity? One factor is that we live in a society in which more and more people have jobs that keep them sitting in front of computer screens rather than engaging in the type of physical labor that was common a century ago. Even when we are not on the job, most of the work around the house is done by

Health and Medicine   CHAPTER 21

547

Seeing SOCIOLOGY in the { NEWS }

Newsweek

How Fat Went Global

By MARY CARMICHAEL
December 18, 2008

Two years ago, when Barry Popkin announced that more than a billion people worldwide were overweight—easily outnumbering the 800 million who were malnourished—folks looked up from their Big Macs in shock. Then they went back to eating, pushing the number of overweight people to its current number, an astonishing 1.6 billion. And it's not just Americans, or even Western cultures; obesity has become a global problem. [Popkin's] new book, . . . *The World Is Fat* (Avery), pins the blame for the ever-growing obesity crisis on some well-known villains: sugary drinks, couch-potato lifestyles and yes, cheeseburgers. But Popkin also reveals some less obvious culprits: evolutionary biology, for instance, and a host of other forces beyond any individual's control. A professor of global nutrition at the University of North Carolina at Chapel Hill, he spoke with *Newsweek*'s Mary Carmichael. Excerpts:

Q: Your thesis is that we're all getting fat because we're eating more and moving less. That makes sense for individuals: if I sit around eating donuts, I'll gain weight. But you're talking about whole countries—the whole world, really. So what is going on?

A: The constant thing we've heard in America for the last 20 years is "You fat, gluttonous Americans, you should feel guilty. You're overweight and it's your fault." But all of a sudden, we're seeing the same problems in places where 20 years ago all they worried about was hunger: in Egypt, and among blacks in South Africa, and in China, where a third of adults now are overweight and obese. In Mexico, nobody was overweight 15 years ago; now 71 percent of Mexican women and 66 percent of men are. When you get to this kind of point, you've got to step back and say, "Wait, what is going on?"

What's happened is that from 30 years ago to today, we've had an exponential explosion in what we can think of as the "obesogenic environment." You see food available everywhere. You can't move

more than 100 feet without seeing a caloric beverage. . . . The average American has not changed the amount of water he consumes in the last 30 years or so. But he's added 22 ounces of caloric beverages to his diet, and that's 300 extra calories per day. Then you match that kind of diet with human biology. We naturally prefer sweet and fatty foods because of what those foods used to mean for survival when we were hunter-gatherers. They had the nutrients we needed, and they let us store more energy for the hungry season.

Q: And now, for most people, there is no hungry season.

A: Right. But we're still eating the same kinds of foods. From the beginning of humanity, we've always wanted to have tastier food and less work to do. These are innate drives, and we can't change our biology.

It's not just about what we eat. People around the world are less active now, too. When I started working in China in the '80s, everyone biked to work. Today it's dangerous to bike, so people take mass transit or cars or motorcycles, and kids

machines (or other people). Children spend more of their time sitting as well—watching television or playing video games.

Then, of course, there is diet. The typical person in the United States is eating more salty and fatty food than ever before (Wells & Buzby, 2008). And meals are also getting bigger: The Department of Agriculture reported that in 2000, the typical U.S. adult consumed 140 more pounds of food in a year than was true a decade earlier. Comparing old and new editions of cookbooks, recipes that used to say they would feed six now say they will feed four. The odds of being overweight go up among people with lower incomes partly because they may lack the education to make healthy choices and partly because stores in low-income communities offer a greater selection of low-cost, high-fat snack foods and fewer healthful fruits and vegetables (Hellmich, 2002).

Obesity is a problem not only in the United States but around the world. Seeing Sociology in the News takes a look at the global obesity crisis.

Sexually Transmitted Diseases

Sexual activity is both pleasurable and vital to the continuation of our species. But sexual activity can transmit more than fifty kinds of *sexually transmitted diseases* (STDs). Because our culture associates sex with sin, some people regard these diseases not only as illnesses but also as marks of immorality.

STDs grabbed national attention during the "sexual revolution" of the 1960s, when infection rates rose dramatically as people began sexual activity earlier and with a greater number of partners. This means that the rise in STDs is an exception to the general decline of infectious diseases during the twentieth century. By the late 1980s, the rising dangers of STDs, especially AIDS, generated a sexual counterrevolution as people moved away from casual sex (Kain, 1987; Laumann et al., 1994). The following sections briefly describe several common STDs.

Gonorrhea and Syphilis

Gonorrhea and syphilis, among the oldest known diseases, are caused by microscopic organisms that are almost always transmitted by sexual contact. Untreated, gonorrhea causes sterility; syphilis damages major organs and can result in blindness, mental disorders, and death.

In 2007, some 356,000 cases of gonorrhea and 11,500 cases of syphilis were officially recorded in the United States, although the actual numbers may be several times higher. Most cases are contracted by non-Hispanic African Americans (70 percent), with lower numbers among non-Hispanic whites (20 percent), Latinos (9 percent), and Asian Americans and Native Americans (1 percent) (CDC, 2009).

Both gonorrhea and syphilis can easily be cured with antibiotics such as penicillin. Thus neither is a major health problem in the United States.

under 12 are banned from biking because it's not safe. They don't walk, either.

Q: How important a factor is globalization? . . .

A: Well, let's take an example. Up until three years ago, there was no snacking in China. Now it's exploding. Why? Because all of a sudden, there are Chinese equivalents of Wal-Mart. A lot of people used to live in a subsistence world, a more primitive world. . . . But now we have supermarkets everywhere, and everybody sees the same TV we see and wants the same things we want. . . .

Q: So, the big question: What do we do about this? How should we be rethinking policies to combat obesity around the world?

A: In this country, at least, the first thing we can do is what we're starting in New York right now, which is a beverage tax. . . . Juice, soft drinks, fruit drinks, energy drinks, all caloric beverages except skim milk—all of these have [little] value except calories. So I'd start by taxing them. It's a lot harder with fatty foods. They may have some important nutritional value. Besides, it's not fat we really care about, it's calories. So I would prefer not

to do a "fat tax," but to have an added-sugar tax, as well as a tax on fried foods and certain junk foods that are really energy-dense.

Q: Wouldn't you also want to make healthy foods cheaper? How do you do that?

A: That's a critical step. . . . Beans and fruits and vegetables—we have essentially ignored those crops, and instead we have made certain foods, staples like grains and animal foods, dirt-cheap by creating a whole system around them, with big agribusinesses and government funding and lobbyists. . . . If it were up to me, we would cut out half of the subsidies we currently put into the grain sector. . . .

Q: Some people are going to respond to all this by saying it should be a matter of individual responsibility—that diet and weight are a matter of choice and the government shouldn't meddle.

A: That's OK if those people want to pay for the extra health-care costs that come with obesity. But right now this is affecting everyone in America, because we all pay those costs. It's the same issue we had with seatbelts. People who didn't use them were only hurting themselves, physically, but in the process,

they were raising insurance costs for everyone. Now we are at a point where people can't even walk and they need scooters to get around, . . . where we're taking toes and feet off people that have diabetes. If the government is going to pay for all of this, that affects everyone, and we need to do something about it. . . .

WHAT DO YOU THINK?

1. On what grounds does the author claim that obesity is a societal issue rather than simply a matter of individual choice?

2. Do you think obesity is "beyond an individual's control"? Why or why not?

3. What societal action does the author suggest to combat obesity? What other policies or strategies would you suggest?

Genital Herpes

Genital herpes is a virus that is fairly common, infecting at least 45 million adolescents and adults in the United States (one in five). Though far less dangerous than gonorrhea and syphilis, herpes is incurable. People with genital herpes may not have any symptoms, or they may experience periodic, painful blisters on the genitals accompanied by fever and headache. Although not fatal to adults, pregnant women with genital herpes can transmit the disease during a vaginal delivery, and it can be deadly to a newborn. Therefore, women with active infections usually give birth by cesarean section (Sobel, 2001; CDC, 2009).

AIDS

The most serious of all sexually transmitted diseases is *acquired immune deficiency syndrome* (AIDS). Identified in 1981, it is incurable and almost always fatal. AIDS is caused by the *human immunodeficiency virus* (HIV), which attacks white blood cells, weakening the immune system. AIDS thus makes a person vulnerable to a wide range of diseases that eventually cause death.

AIDS deaths in the United States numbered 14,110 in 2007. But officials recorded 35,962 new cases in the United States that year, raising the total number of cases on the official record to 1,018,428. Of these people, 562,793 have died (CDC, 2009).

Globally, HIV infects some 33 million people—half of them under the age of twenty-five—and the number continues to rise.

The global AIDS death toll now exceeds 25 million, with about 1 percent of the 2 million deaths in 2007 here in the United States (UNAIDS, 2008). Global Map 21–1 on page 550 shows that Africa (especially south of the Sahara) has the highest HIV infection rate and accounts for 68 percent of all world cases. A recent United Nations study found that in the nations of southern Africa, fifteen-year-olds face a fifty-fifty chance of becoming infected with HIV. The risk is especially high for girls, not only because HIV is transmitted more easily from men to women but also because many African cultures encourage women to be submissive to men. According to some analysts, the AIDS crisis now threatens the political and economic security of Africa, which affects the entire world (Ashford, 2002; UNAIDS, 2008).

Upon infection, people with HIV display no symptoms at all, so most are unaware of their condition. Symptoms of AIDS may not appear for a year or longer, but during this time an infected person may infect others. Within five years, one-third of infected people in the United States develop full-blown AIDS; half develop AIDS within ten years; and almost all become sick within twenty years. In low-income countries, the progression of this illness is much more rapid, with many people dying within a few years of becoming infected.

HIV is infectious but not contagious. That means that HIV is transmitted from person to person through direct contact with blood, semen, or breast milk but not through casual contact such as shaking hands, hugging, sharing towels or dishes, swimming together,

GLOBAL: In global perspective, the use of condoms is highest in Japan (the "pill" has not been widely available there); lowest use is in sub-Saharan Africa (where the AIDS epidemic is worst).

NOTE: The UN estimates that more than 2 million children in the world are now living with AIDS; most have already lost one or both parents to the disease. Almost all are in sub-Saharan Africa.

GLOBAL: UNAIDS estimates that as many as 20 million people in China could be infected with HIV by 2010 if the current trend persists (vs. 25 million infected in Africa in 2006).

GLOBAL: The AIDS death toll may well overtake the 40 million killed by the Black Death in Europe during the 14th century.

Window on the World

GLOBAL MAP 21–1 **HIV/AIDS Infection of Adults in Global Perspective**

Sixty-eight percent of all global HIV infections are in sub-Saharan Africa. In Swaziland, one-fourth of people between the ages of fifteen and forty-nine are infected with HIV/AIDS. This very high infection rate reflects the prevalence of other sexually transmitted diseases and infrequent use of condoms, two factors that promote transmission of HIV. South and Southeast Asia account for about 13 percent of global HIV infections. In Thailand, 1.4 percent of people aged fifteen to forty-nine are now infected. All of North and South America taken together account for 9 percent of global HIV infections. In the United States, 0.6 percent of people aged fifteen to forty-nine are infected. The incidence of infection in Muslim nations is extremely low by world standards.

Sources: Population Reference Bureau (2009).

or even coughing and sneezing. The risk of transmitting the virus through saliva (as in kissing) is extremely low. The chance of transmitting HIV through sexual activity is greatly reduced by the use of latex condoms. However, abstinence or an exclusive relationship with an uninfected person are the only sure ways to avoid infection.

Specific behaviors put people at high risk of HIV infection. The first is *anal sex* with an infected person because anal sex can cause rec-

tal bleeding, allowing easy transmission of HIV from one individual to another. The fact that many homosexual and bisexual men engage in anal sex helps explain why these categories of people account for 48 percent of AIDS cases in the United States.

Sharing needles used to inject drugs is a second high-risk behavior. At present, intravenous drug users account for 28 percent of persons with AIDS. Sex with an intravenous drug user is also very risky.

NOTE: 2007 state rates for new AIDS cases range from a high of 148 per 100,000 people in Washington, D.C., to 25 in New York, 29 in Maryland, 22 in Florida, and 20 in Georgia, down to 1 in Vermont.

DISCUSS: What policies or practices on your campus might help reduce the spread of HIV?

NOTE: The term "a negotiated death" has emerged to indicate the decision by

family members, medical, legal, religious, and ethical specialists, and sometimes patients themselves, about how and when death should occur. Such negotiation often results in a doctor issuing a "do not resuscitate" order for a terminally ill patient.

NOTE: The first "wrongful life" suit against a hospital was brought in 1990 by a man who claims he was revived against his will.

MAKING THE GRADE

The increase in sexually transmitted diseases is one exception to the downward trend in infectious diseases.

SEEING SOCIOLOGY
in Everyday Life

Have you considered writing your own will? Why or why not?

Because intravenous drug use is more common among poor people in the United States, AIDS is now becoming a disease of the socially disadvantaged. Minorities make up the majority of people with AIDS: African Americans (who are 12.8 percent of the total population) account for 46 percent of people with AIDS, and Latinos (15 percent of the population) represent 18 percent of AIDS cases. Almost 80 percent of all women and children with the disease are African American or Latino. By contrast, Asian Americans and Native Americans together account for only about 1 percent of people with AIDS (CDC, 2008).

Use of any drug, including alcohol, also increases the risk of HIV infection to the extent that it impairs judgment. In other words, even people who understand what places them at risk of infection may act less responsibly if they are under the influence of alcohol, marijuana, or some other drug.

As Figure 21–1 on page 552 shows, 47 percent of people with AIDS in the United States became infected through homosexual contact, although heterosexuals, infected in various ways, account for about 27 percent of AIDS cases. But heterosexual activity can transmit HIV, and the danger rises with the number of sexual partners one has, especially if they fall into high-risk categories. Worldwide, heterosexual relations are the primary means of HIV transmission, accounting for two-thirds of all infections.

In the United States, treating just one person with AIDS can cost hundreds of thousands of dollars, and this figure may rise as new therapies appear. Government health programs, private insurance, and personal savings rarely cover more than a fraction of the cost of treatment. In addition, there is the mounting cost of caring for at least 75,000 children orphaned by AIDS (worldwide, the number is around 15 million). Overall, there is little doubt that AIDS represents both a medical and a social problem of monumental proportions.

In the early 1980s, the U.S. government responded slowly to the AIDS crisis, largely because the earliest people to be infected, gay men and intravenous drug users, were widely viewed as deviant. But funds allocated for AIDS research and education have increased rapidly (now totaling some $24 billion annually), and researchers have identified some drugs, including protease inhibitors, that suppress the symptoms of the disease enough to greatly extend the lives of people infected with HIV. But educational programs remain the most effective weapon against AIDS, since prevention is the only way to stop the spread of a disease that so far has no cure.

Ethical Issues surrounding Death

Now that technological advances are giving human beings the power to draw the line separating life and death, we must decide how and when to do so. In other words, questions about the use of medical technology have added an ethical dimension to health and illness.

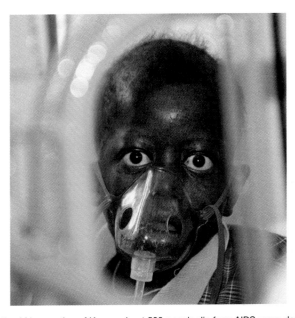

In the African nation of Kenya, about 500 people die from AIDS every day. In parts of sub-Saharan Africa, the epidemic is so great that half of all children will eventually become infected with HIV. This young Nairobi child, who already has AIDS, is fighting for his life.

When Does Death Occur?

Common sense suggests that life ceases when breathing and heartbeat stop. But the ability to replace a heart and artificially sustain respiration makes that definition of death obsolete. Medical and legal experts in the United States now define death as an *irreversible* state involving no response to stimulation, no movement or breathing, no reflexes, and no indication of brain activity (Wall, 1980; D. G. Jones, 1998).

Do People Have a Right to Die?

Today, medical personnel, family members, and patients themselves face the burden of deciding when a terminally ill person should die. Among the most difficult cases are the roughly 10,000 people in the United States in a permanent vegetative state who cannot express their desires about life and death.

Generally speaking, the first duty of physicians and hospitals is to protect a patient's life. Even so, a mentally competent person in the process of dying may refuse medical treatment and even nutrition, either at the time or, in advance, through a document called a *living will* that states the extent of medical care a person would or would not want in the event of an illness or injury that leaves the person unable to make decisions.

Health and Medicine CHAPTER 21

551

GLOBAL: The 2002 Dutch euthanasia law permits doctors to administer euthanasia to nonresidents, which raised the possibility of "euthanasia tourism," although no such trend has materialized.

DISCUSS: Some proponents of euthanasia claim that we act more humanely toward dying pets than toward dying parents. Ask the class.

Q: "Medicine, a synthesis of many disciplines, is essentially the practice of knowl-

edge and skills and attitudes helpful in the care of the sick." Patricia L. Kendall and George G. Reader

Q: "Physicians have exceedingly high prestige in American society. . . . Medicine thus attracts those who value status and income, who seek a challenging and interesting occupation, who enjoy exercising judgment, and who seek to do good." David Mechanic

euthanasia assisting in the death of a person suffering from an incurable disease

SEEING SOCIOLOGY
in Everyday Life

Do you believe people have a "right to die"? Under what circumstances?

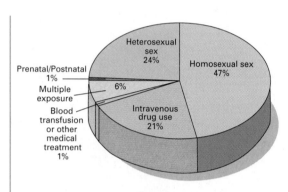

FIGURE 21–1 **Types of Transmission for Reported U.S. AIDS Cases as of 2007**

There are several ways in which people can be infected with HIV.

Source: Centers for Disease Control and Prevention (2008).

What about Mercy Killing?

Mercy killing is the common term for **euthanasia,** *assisting in the death of a person suffering from an incurable disease.* Euthanasia (from the Greek, meaning "a good death") poses an ethical dilemma, being at once an act of kindness and a form of killing.

Whether there is a "right to die" is one of today's most difficult issues. All people with incurable diseases have a right to refuse treatment that might prolong their lives. But whether a doctor should be allowed to help bring about death is at the heart of the debate. In 1994, three states—Washington, California, and Oregon—asked voters whether doctors should be able to help people who wanted to die. Only Oregon's proposition passed, and the law was quickly challenged and remained tied up in state court until 1997, when Oregon voters again endorsed it. Since then, Oregon doctors have legally assisted in the death of about 350 terminally ill patients. In 1997, however, the U.S. Supreme Court decided that under the U.S. Constitution, there is no "right to die," a decision that has slowed the spread of such laws. Only in 2008 did Washington became the second state to allow physician-assisted suicide (Leff, 2008).

Supporters of *active* euthanasia—allowing a dying person to enlist the services of a physician to bring on a quick death—argue that there are circumstances (as when a dying person suffers great pain) that make death preferable to life. Critics counter that permitting active euthanasia invites abuse (see Chapter 15, "Aging and the Elderly"). They fear that patients will feel pressure to end their lives in order to spare family members the burden of caring for them and the high costs of hospitalization. Research in the Netherlands, where physician-assisted suicide is legal, indicates that about one-fifth of all such deaths have occurred without a patient explicitly requesting to die (Gillon, 1999).

In the United States, a majority of adults express support for giving terminally ill people the right to choose to die with a doctor's help (NORC, 2007). Therefore, the right-to-die debate is sure to continue.

The Medical Establishment

Medicine is *the social institution that focuses on fighting disease and improving health.* Through most of human history, health care was the responsibility of individuals and their families. Medicine emerges as a social institution only as societies become more productive and people take on specialized work.

Members of agrarian societies today still turn to various traditional health practitioners, including acupuncturists and herbalists, who play a central part in improving health. In industrial societies, medical care falls to specially trained and licensed professionals, from anesthesiologists to X-ray technicians. Today's medical establishment in the United States took form over the past 200 years.

The Rise of Scientific Medicine

In colonial times, physicians, herbalists, druggists, barbers, midwives, and ministers practiced the healing arts. But not all were effective: Unsanitary instruments, lack of anesthesia, and simple ignorance made surgery a terrible ordeal, and physicians probably killed as many people as they saved.

Physicians made medicine into a science by studying the human body and how it works and emphasizing surgery to repair the body and the use of drugs to fight disease. Pointing to their specialized knowledge, these doctors gradually established themselves as professionals who earned medical degrees. The American Medical Association (AMA) was founded in 1847 and symbolized the growing acceptance of a scientific model of medicine.

Still, traditional approaches to health care had their supporters. The AMA opposed them by seeking control of the certification process. In the early 1900s, state licensing boards agreed to certify only doctors trained in scientific programs approved by the AMA. As a result, schools teaching other healing skills began to close, which soon limited the practice of medicine to individuals holding an M.D. degree. In the process, both the prestige and the income of physicians rose dramatically; today, men and women with M.D. degrees earn, on average, $250,000 annually.

Practitioners who did things differently, such as osteopathic physicians, concluded that they had no choice but to fall in line with AMA standards. Thus osteopaths (with D.O. degrees), originally trained to treat illness by manipulating the skeleton and muscles, today treat illness with drugs in much the same way as medical doctors (with M.D. degrees). Chiropractors, herbal healers, and mid-

THEN AND NOW: The American Medical Association (AMA) has been losing clout. By 1999, just 30% of physicians belonged to the organization, down from 70% in 1960.

NOTE: There are some 973,000 physicians in the U.S.; 72% are men (92% of all nurses are women). Men now receive 51% of medical degrees, so gender balance in this profession is increasing.

NOTE: The importance of the natural environment to health is addressed in Chapter 22 ("Population, Urbanization, and Environment").

Q: "Proper treatment will cure a cold in seven days; left to its own, however, a cold will hang on for a week." Henry G. Felson

medicine the social institution that focuses on fighting disease and improving health

holistic medicine an approach to health care that emphasizes the prevention of illness and takes into account a person's entire physical and social environment

SEEING SOCIOLOGY
in Everyday Life

Point to specific ways in which people should take personal responsibility for their own health. In what ways should society change to promote public health?

wives still practice using traditional methods, but they have lower standing within the medical profession. The tension and conflict between scientific medicine and traditional healing continues today, both in the United States and in many other countries.

Scientific medicine, taught in expensive, urban medical schools, also changed the social profile of doctors such that most came from privileged backgrounds and practiced in cities. Women, who had played a large part in many fields of healing, were pushed aside by the AMA. Some early medical schools did focus on the training of women and African Americans, but gradually most of these schools ran out of money and closed. Only in recent decades has the social diversity of medical doctors increased, with women and African Americans representing 30 percent and 6 percent, respectively, of all physicians (U.S. Department of Labor, 2008).

Holistic Medicine

In recent decades, the scientific model of medicine has been combined with the more traditional model of **holistic medicine,** *an approach to health care that emphasizes the prevention of illness and takes into account a person's entire physical and social environment.* Holistic practitioners agree on the need for drugs, surgery, artificial organs, and high technology, but they emphasize treatment of the whole person rather than symptoms and focus on health rather than disease. There are three foundations of holistic health care (Gordon, 1980; Patterson, 1998):

1. **Treat patients as people.** Holistic practitioners concern themselves not only with symptoms but also with how environment and lifestyle affect their patients. Holistic practitioners extend the bounds of conventional medicine, taking an active role in fighting poverty, environmental pollution, and other dangers to public health.

2. **Encourage responsibility, not dependency**. In the scientific model, patients are dependent on physicians. Holistic medicine tries to shift some responsibility for health from physicians to people themselves by encouraging health-promoting behavior. Holistic medicine thus favors an *active* approach to *health* rather than a *reactive* approach to *illness.*

3. **Provide personal treatment**. Scientific medicine locates medical care in impersonal offices and hospitals, both disease-centered settings. By contrast, holistic practitioners favor, as much as possible, a personal and relaxed environment such as the home.

In sum, holistic care does not oppose scientific medicine but shifts the emphasis from treating disease toward achieving the greatest well-being for everyone. Because the AMA currently recognizes more than fifty medical specialties, it is clear that there is a need for practitioners who are concerned with the whole patient.

Traditional healers work to improve people's health throughout the world. This patient is receiving a traditional needle therapy in Suining, a city in China's Sichuan province. Do you think people in the United States are accepting of traditional healing practices? Why or why not?

Paying for Medical Care: A Global Survey

As medicine has come to rely on high technology, the costs of providing medical care have skyrocketed. Countries throughout the world use various strategies to meet these costs.

Medicine in Socialist Nations

In nations with mostly socialist economies, government provides medical care directly to the people. These countries hold that all citizens have the right to basic medical care. The state owns and operates medical facilities and uses public funds to pay salaries to doctors and other medical care workers, who are government employees.

People's Republic of China This economically growing but mostly agrarian nation faces the immense task of providing for the health of more than 1.3 billion people. China has experimented with private medicine, but the government controls most medical care.

China's "barefoot doctors," roughly comparable to U.S. paramedics, bring some modern methods of medical care to millions of peasants in rural villages. Otherwise, traditional healing arts, including acupuncture and the use of medicinal herbs, are still widely practiced in China. The Chinese approach to health is based on a holistic concern for the interplay of mind and body (Kaptchuk, 1985).

Russian Federation The Russian Federation has transformed what was a state-dominated economy into more of a market system, so

Health and Medicine CHAPTER 21

553

GLOBAL: Physicians in most poor societies of the world do not share diagnostic information freely with patients.

GLOBAL: Costs for medical care in Great Britain and other European countries are rising as their populations age.

DISCUSS: Another way in which the Russian Federation stands out is its low use of effective birth control and its very high rate of abortion. A recent report of the International Planned Parenthood Federation claims there are 9 million abortions there per year, which is 25,000 per day and more than 1,000 per hour.

socialized medicine a medical care system in which the government owns and operates most medical facilities and employs most physicians

THINKING GLOBALLY

When Health Fails: A Report from Russia

Night is falling in Pitkyaranta, a small town on the western edge of Russia, near the Finnish border. Andrei, a thirty-year-old man with a weathered face and a long ponytail, weaves his way through the deepening shadows along a busy street. He has spent much of the afternoon in a bar with friends watching music videos, smoking cigarettes, and drinking vodka. Andrei is a railroad worker, but several months ago he was laid off. "Now," he explains bitterly, "I have nothing to do but drink and smoke." Andrei shrugs off a question about his health. "The only thing I care about is finding a job. I am a grown man. I don't want to be supported by my mother and father." Andrei still thinks of himself as young, yet according to current health patterns in Russia, his life is half over (Landsberg, 1998).

After the collapse of the Soviet Union in 1991, living conditions worsened steadily. One result, say doctors, is lots of stress—especially on men who earn too little to support their families or are out of work entirely. Few people eat well anymore, but Russian men now drink and smoke more than ever. The World Health Organization (2007)

reports that alcohol abuse is Russia's number one killer, with cigarette smoking not far behind.

In towns like Pitkyaranta, signs of poor health are everywhere: Women no longer breast-feed their babies, adults suffer higher rates of accidents and illness, and like Andrei,

people look old before their time. Doctors work to stop the health slide, but with poorly equipped hospitals, they are simply overwhelmed. Life expectancy has dropped several years for women and even more dramatically for men, who now live an average of just fifty-nine years, about the same as two generations ago. A mere 100 miles to the west in Finland, where economic trends are far better, men live an average of seventy-five years.

Among young Russian men like Andrei, a joke is making the rounds. Their health may be failing, they say, but this cloud has a silver lining: At least they no longer have to worry about retirement.

WHAT DO YOU THINK?

1. Based on this report, in what ways is health in Russia a social issue as well as a medical matter?

2. In general, how does a society's economic health relate to the physical health of its people?

3. Can you think of stories similar to this one that involve the United States?

medical care, like so much else, is in transition. But the state remains in charge of health care, and the government claims that everyone has a right to basic medical care.

As in China, people in the Russian Federation do not choose a physician but report to a local government-operated health facility. Physicians have much lower incomes than medical doctors in the United States, earning about the same salary as skilled industrial workers (by contrast, doctors earn roughly five times as much as industrial workers in the United States). Also, about 70 percent of Russian doctors are women, compared to 30 percent in the United States. As in our society, occupations dominated by women in the Russian Federation offer lower pay.

In recent years, the Russian Federation has suffered setbacks in health care, partly because of a falling standard of living, as the Thinking Globally box explains. A rising demand for medical attention has strained a bureaucratic system that at best provides highly standardized and impersonal care. The optimistic view is that as market reforms proceed, both living standards and the quality of medical

services will improve. In Russia's uncertain times, what does seem certain is that inequalities in medical care will increase (Specter, 1995; Landsberg, 1998; Mason, 2003; Zuckerman, 2006).

Medicine in Capitalist Nations

People living in nations with mostly capitalist economies usually pay for medical care out of their own pockets. However, because high cost puts medical care beyond the reach of many people, government programs underwrite much of the expense.

Sweden In 1891, Sweden began a mandatory, comprehensive system of government medical care. Citizens pay for this program with their taxes, which are among the highest in the world. Typically, physicians are government employees, and most hospitals are government-managed. Because this medical system resembles that found in socialist societies, Sweden's system is called **socialized medicine**, *a medical care system in which the government owns and operates most medical facilities and employs most physicians.*

GLOBAL: Great Britain's National Health program has suffered severe financial problems in recent years, and delays in treatment are common. Liberals claim that privatization has meant disastrous cutbacks in government funding; conservatives counter that the system has become bloated with bureaucrats, with about three administrators for every medical practitioner.

NOTE: Several European countries, including the U.K. and France, have enacted laws prohibiting the genital mutilation of women; to date, Minnesota and North Dakota have as well.

RESOURCE: Efua Dorkenoo and Scilla Elworthy's article "Female Genital Mutilation" is included in the author's companion reader *Seeing Ourselves*, 8th ed.

direct-fee system a medical care system in which patients pay directly for the services of physicians and hospitals

SEEING SOCIOLOGY
in Everyday Life

The head of the Ford Motor Company said recently that in building a car, the cost of medical care for workers is now greater than the cost of steel. How do you think the rising cost of medical care affects an average family's budget?

Great Britain In 1948, Great Britain also established socialized medicine by creating a dual system of medical service. All British citizens are entitled to medical care provided by the National Health Service, but those who can afford to do so may go to doctors and hospitals that operate privately.

Canada Since 1972, Canada has had a "single-payer" model of medical care that provides health services to all Canadians. Like a giant insurance company, the Canadian government pays doctors and hospitals according to a set schedule of fees. Like Great Britain, Canada also has some physicians working outside the government-funded system and setting their own fees, although costs are regulated by the government.

Canada boasts of providing care for everyone at a lower cost than the (nonuniversal) medical system in the United States. However, the Canadian system uses less state-of-the-art technology and responds more slowly, meaning that people may wait months for major surgery. But the Canadian system provides care for all citizens, regardless of income, unlike the United States, where lower-income people are often denied medical care (Rosenthal, 1991; Macionis & Gerber, 2008).

> **July 31, Montreal, Canada.** I am visiting the home of an oral surgeon who appears (judging by the large home) to be doing pretty well. Yet he complains that the Canadian government, in an effort to hold down medical costs, caps doctors' annual salaries at the equivalent of about U.S. $125,000. Therefore, he explains, many specialists have left Canada for the United States, where they can earn much more; other doctors and dentists simply limit their practices.

Japan Physicians in Japan operate privately, but a combination of government programs and private insurance pays their patients' medical costs. As shown in Figure 21–2, the Japanese approach medical care much as the Europeans do, with most medical expenses paid through the government.

Paying for Medical Care: The United States

The United States stands alone among industrialized nations in having no universal, government-sponsored program of medical care. Ours is a **direct-fee system,** *a medical care system in which patients pay directly for the services of physicians and hospitals.* Europeans look to government to fund from 70 to nearly 90 percent of their medical costs (paid for through taxation), but the U.S. government pays just 45 percent of this country's medical costs (U.S. Department of Health and Human Services, 2009).

Global Snapshot

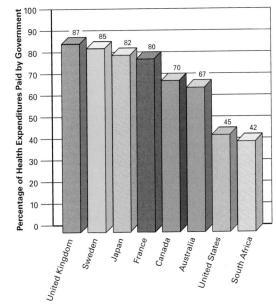

FIGURE 21–2 **Extent of Socialized Medicine in Selected Countries**
The governments of most high-income countries pay a greater share of their people's medical costs than the U.S. government does.
Source: World Bank (2008).

In the United States, rich people can purchase the best medical care in the world. Yet the poor are worse off than their counterparts in Europe. This difference explains the relatively high death rates among both infants and adults in the United States compared to those in many European countries (United Nations Development Programme, 2009).

Several states, including Maine, Vermont, and Massachusetts, have enacted programs that provide health care to everyone. Why does the United States have no national program that provides universal care? First, back during World War II, the government froze worker earnings. As a way to increase pay within the wage freeze, more employers began providing health care benefits. Second, labor unions tried to expand health care benefits from employers rather than go after government programs. Third, the public generally favors a private, worker-and-employer system rather than a government-based system because our culture stresses individual self-reliance. Fourth and finally, the AMA and the health insurance industry have strongly and consistently opposed national medical care. Even so,

SOCIAL SURVEY: "In general, some people think that it is the responsibility of the government in Washington to see to it that people have help in paying for doctors and hospital bills. Others think that these matters are not the responsibility of the federal government and that people should take care of these things themselves. Where do you place yourself on this scale?" (GSS 2006, N = 1989; *Codebook*, 2006:369)

(1) "Government should help" 33.0%
(2) 19.0%
(3) "Agree with both views" 32.0%
(4) 8.0%
(5) "People should take care of themselves" 7.0%
"Don't know"/No response 1.0%

health maintenance organization (HMO) an organization that provides comprehensive medical care to subscribers for a fixed fee

SEEING SOCIOLOGY
in Everyday Life

Should the United States follow the lead of other high-income countries and enact a government program of medical care for everyone? Why or why not?

the Obama administration took office in 2009 with the promise of making health care available to all people in the United States.

There is no question that health care in this country is very expensive. The cost of medical care increased dramatically from $12 billion in 1950 to more than $2.2 trillion in 2007. This sum amounts to more than $7,500 per person, more than any other nation in the world spends for medical care. Who pays the medical bills?

Private Insurance Programs

In 2007, about 177 million people (59 percent) received some medical care benefits from a family member's employer or labor union. Another 27 million people (9 percent) purchased private coverage on their own. Combining these figures, 68 percent of the U.S. population has private insurance, although few such programs pay all medical costs (U.S. Census Bureau, 2008).

Public Insurance Programs

In 1965, Congress created Medicare and Medicaid. Medicare pays a portion of the medical costs of men and women over age sixty-five; in 2007, it covered 41 million women and men, 14 percent of the population. In the same year, Medicaid, a medical insurance program for the poor, provided benefits to 40 million people, about 13 percent of the population. An additional 11 million veterans, 4 percent of the population, can obtain free care in government-operated hospitals. In all, 28 percent of this country's people get medical benefits from the government, but most also have private insurance (U.S. Census Bureau, 2008).

Health Maintenance Organizations

About 65 million people (22 percent) in the United States belong to a **health maintenance organization** (HMO), *an organization that provides comprehensive medical care to subscribers for a fixed fee.* HMOs vary in their costs and benefits, and none provides full coverage. Fixed fees make these organizations profitable to the extent that their subscribers stay healthy; therefore, many take a preventive approach to health. At the same time, HMOs have been criticized for refusing to pay for medical procedures that they consider unnecessary. Congress is currently debating the extent to which patients can sue HMOs to obtain better care.

In all, 85 percent of the U.S. population has some medical care coverage, either private or public. Yet most plans do not provide full coverage, so a serious illness threatens even middle-class people with financial hardship. Most programs also exclude certain medical services, such as dental care and treatment for mental health and substance abuse problems. Worse, 46 million people (about 15 percent of the population) have no medical insurance at all, even though 73 percent of these people are working. Almost as many lose their medical coverage temporarily each year due to layoffs or job changes. Caught in the medical care bind are mostly low- to moderate-

income people who do not qualify for Medicaid yet cannot afford the cost of the preventive medical care they need to stay healthy (Brink, 2002; U.S. Census Bureau, 2008).

Religious Health Collectives

A recent development in the United States has been *religious health collectives*, which currently serve less than 1 million people. In such cases, families organize their own health care system, which operates as a private insurance system. Members pay a monthly fee that gives them coverage for most medical expenses. Most of the member families are religious, and each collective requires its members to agree to conform to rules of "healthy behavior" as a condition for participating. For example, most collectives ban the use of tobacco, limit the use of alcohol, and forbid any use of illegal drugs as well as sex outside of marriage (Andrews, 2008).

The Nursing Shortage

Another important issue in medical care is the shortage of nurses across the United States. In 2007, there were some 2.5 million registered nurses (who hold the R.N. degree), but about 8 percent of the available jobs (roughly 116,000 positions) were unfilled (U.S. Department of Labor, 2008).

The main cause of the shortage is that fewer people are entering the nursing profession. During the past decade, enrollments in nursing programs have dropped by one-third, even as the need for nurses, driven by the aging of the U.S. population, goes up. What accounts for this decline? One factor is that today's young women have a wide range of occupational choices, and fewer are drawn to the traditionally female occupation of nursing. This fact is evident in the rising median age of working nurses, which is now forty-seven. Another is that many of today's nurses are unhappy with their working conditions, citing heavy patient loads, too much required overtime, a stressful working environment, and a lack of recognition and respect from supervisors, physicians, and hospital managers. In fact, one recent survey found that a majority of working nurses say they would not recommend the field to others, and many R.N.'s are leaving the field for other jobs.

The nursing shortage is harming health care. One study estimates that more than 6,000 hospital patients die each year for lack of immediate treatment due to the shortage of nurses. Such facts are bringing change to the profession. Salaries, which range from about $45,000 for general-duty nurses to $100,000 for certified nurse-anesthetists, are rising, although slowly. Some hospitals and physicians are also offering signing bonuses in efforts to attract new nurses. In addition, nursing programs are trying harder to recruit a more diverse population, seeking more minorities (which are currently underrepresented) and more men, who now make up only 7 percent of R.N.'s (Yin, 2002;

sick role patterns of behavior defined as appropriate for people who are ill

Marquez, 2006; American Association of Colleges of Nursing, 2008; U.S. Department of Labor, 2008).

Theoretical Analysis of Health and Medicine

Each of sociology's major theoretical approaches helps us organize and interpret facts and issues concerning human health.

Structural-Functional Analysis: Role Theory

Talcott Parsons (1951) viewed medicine as society's strategy to keep its members healthy. According to this model, illness is dysfunctional because it undermines people's abilities to perform their roles.

The Sick Role

Society responds to sickness not only by providing medical care but also by affording people a **sick role**, *patterns of behavior defined as appropriate for people who are ill.* According to Parsons, the sick role releases people from normal obligations such as going to work or attending classes. To prevent abuse of this privilege, however, people cannot simply claim to be ill; they must "look the part" and, in serious cases, get the help of a medical expert. After assuming the sick role, the patient must want to get better and must do whatever is needed to regain good health, including cooperating with health professionals.

The Physician's Role

Physicians evaluate people's claims of sickness and help restore the sick to normal routines. To do this, physicians use their specialized knowledge and expect patients to cooperate with them, providing necessary information and following "doctor's orders" to complete the treatment.

CRITICAL REVIEW Parsons's analysis links illness and medicine to the broader organization of society. Others have extended the concept of the sick role to some nonillness situations such as pregnancy (Myers & Grasmick, 1989).

One limitation of the sick-role concept is that it applies to acute conditions (like the flu or a broken leg) better than to chronic illnesses (like heart disease), which may not be reversible. In addition, a sick person's ability to assume the sick role (to take time off from work to regain health) depends on the patient's resources; many working poor, for example, cannot afford to assume a sick role. Finally, illness is not entirely dysfunctional; it can have some positive consequences: Many people who

Throughout the United States, there is a serious shortage of nurses. One strategy for filling this need is to recruit more men into this profession; currently, men account for only 7 percent of nurses with R.N. degrees.

experience serious illness find that it provides the opportunity to reevaluate their lives and gain a better sense of what is truly important (D. G. Myers, 2000; Ehrenreich, 2001).

Finally, critics point out that Parsons's analysis gives doctors, rather than patients, the primary responsibility for health. A more prevention-oriented approach gives each of us as individuals the responsibility to pursue health.

CHECK YOUR LEARNING Define the sick role. How does turning illness into a role in this way help society operate?

Symbolic-Interaction Analysis: The Meaning of Health

According to the symbolic-interaction approach, society is less a grand system than a complex and changing reality. In this model, health and medical care are socially constructed by people in everyday interaction.

The Social Construction of Illness

If both health and illness are socially constructed, people in a poor society may view hunger and malnutrition as normal. Similarly, many members of our own society give little thought to the harmful effects of a rich diet.

Our response to illness is also based on social definitions that may or may not square with medical facts. People with AIDS may

THEN AND NOW: In 1975, the average length of a hospital stay for childbirth was four days; today, it is two days. Among the reasons: drugs, better equipment, and cost pressures from insurance companies.

RESOURCE: A discussion of the sick role by Talcott Parsons is included among the classics in the author's companion reader *Seeing Ourselves*, 8th ed.

NOTE: More than 50% of U.S. adults take at least one sick day each year; half of respondents indicated taking at least one "sick day" when they were not really ill (Lach, 1999).

NOTE: A latent function of illness is forcing us to reexamine our lives and priorities. For some, a more spiritual orientation results, perhaps even recognizing that our essence lies not in our body at all.

SEEING SOCIOLOGY
in Everyday Life

Have you ever had, or even considered, cosmetic surgery? Explain your reasons.

Definitions of health are based on cultural standards, including ideas about beauty. Every year, millions of people undergo cosmetic surgery to bring their appearance into line with societal definitions of how people ought to look.

be forced to deal with fear and prejudice that have no medical basis. Likewise, students may pay no attention to signs of real illness on the eve of a vacation but head for the infirmary hours before a midterm examination with a case of the sniffles. In short, health is less an objective fact than a negotiated outcome.

How people define a medical situation may actually affect how they feel. Medical experts marvel at *psychosomatic* disorders (a fusion of Greek words for "mind" and "body"), when state of mind guides physical sensations (Hamrick, Anspaugh, & Ezell, 1986). Applying the sociologist W. I. Thomas's theorem (presented in Chapter 6, "Social Interaction in Everyday Life"), we can say that once health or illness is defined as real, it can become real in its consequences.

The Social Construction of Treatment

Also in Chapter 6, we used Erving Goffman's dramaturgical approach to explain how physicians tailor their physical surroundings (their office) and their behavior (the "presentation of self") so that others see them as competent and in charge.

The sociologist Joan Emerson (1970) further illustrates this process of reality construction in her analysis of the gynecological examination carried out by a male doctor. This situation is vulnerable to serious misinterpretation, since a man's touching of a woman's genitals is conventionally viewed as a sexual act and possibly an assault.

To ensure that people define the situation as impersonal and professional, the medical staff wear uniforms and furnish the examination room with nothing but medical equipment. The doctor's manner and

overall performance are designed to make the patient feel that to him, examining the genital area is no different from treating any other part of the body. A female nurse is usually present during the examination, not only to assist the physician but also to avoid any impression that a man and a woman are "alone together."

Managing situational definitions in this way is only rarely taught in medical schools. The oversight is unfortunate, because as Emerson's analysis shows, understanding how people construct reality in the examining room is as important as mastering the medical skills required for treatment.

The Social Construction of Personal Identity

A final insight provided by the symbolic-interaction approach is how surgery can affect people's social identity. The reason that medical procedures can have a major effect on how we think of ourselves is that our culture places great symbolic importance on some organs and other parts of our bodies. People who lose a limb (say, in military combat) typically experience serious doubts about being "as much of a person" as before. The effects of surgery can be important even when there is no obvious change in physical appearance. For example, Jean Elson (2004) points out that one out of three women in the United States eventually has her uterus surgically removed in a procedure known as a *hysterectomy*. In interviews with women who had undergone the procedure, Elson found that the typical woman faced serious self-doubt about gender identity, asking, in effect, "Am I still a woman?" Only 10 percent of hysterectomies are for cancer; most are for pain, bleeding, or cysts—serious conditions but not so dangerous that other types of treatment might not be considered. Perhaps, Elson points out, doctors might be more willing to consider alternative treatment if they were aware of how symbolically important the loss of the uterus is to many women.

Many women who undergo breast surgery have much the same reaction, doubting their own feminine identity and worrying that men will no longer find them attractive. For men to understand the significance of such medical procedures, it is only necessary to imagine how a male might react to the surgical loss of any or all of his genitals.

CRITICAL REVIEW The symbolic-interaction approach reveals that what people view as healthful or harmful depends on numerous factors that are not, strictly speaking, medical. This approach also shows that in any medical procedure, both patient and medical staff engage in a subtle process of reality construction. Finally, this approach has helped us understand the symbolic importance of limbs and other bodily organs; the loss of any part of the body—through accident or elective surgery—can have important consequences for personal identity.

By directing attention to the meanings people attach to health and illness, the symbolic-interaction approach draws crit-

DISCUSS: Defining death is a good symbolic-interaction issue. Who participates in the definition of death? When may this definition be a negotiation among parties with various interests? What kinds of power are exercised by patients, family members, clergy, and physicians?

DISCUSS: Ask students if they have ever had an illness, accident, or other health issue that changed personal identity in any way.

NOTE: Supporting the validity of self-assessments of health, one study found people who characterize their health as "poor" were seven times more likely to die in the subsequent 12 years than those who described their health as "excellent" (Goleman, 1991).

SEEING SOCIOLOGY
in Everyday Life

How do you think soldiers who lose a hand, an arm, or a leg feel about themselves afterward? In terms of personal and social identity, what healing and rebuilding are needed?

MAKING THE GRADE

In general, the social-conflict approach claims that any institution (in this case, medicine) would operate more in the interest of the population as a whole if it were under government rather than market control.

icism for implying that there are no objective standards of well-being. Certain physical conditions do indeed cause definite changes in people, regardless of how we view those conditions. People who lack sufficient nutrition and safe water, for example, suffer from their unhealthy environment, whether they define their surroundings as normal or not.

As Figure 21–3 shows, the share of first-year college students in the United States who describe their physical health as "above average" is lower today than it was in 1985. Do you think this trend reflects changing perceptions or a real decline in health (due, say, to eating more unhealthy food)?

○ **CHECK YOUR LEARNING** Explain what it means to say that health, the treatment of illness, and personal identity are all socially constructed.

Social-Conflict and Feminist Analysis: Health and Inequality

Social-conflict analysis points out the connection between health and social inequality and, taking a cue from Karl Marx, ties medicine to the operation of capitalism. Researchers have focused on three main issues: access to medical care, the effects of the profit motive, and the politics of medicine.

Access to Care

Health is important to everyone. Yet by requiring individuals to pay for medical care, capitalist societies allow the richest people to have the best health. The access problem is more serious in the United States than in other high-income nations because we do not have a universal medical care system.

Conflict theorists argue that the capitalist system provides excellent medical care for the rich but not for the rest of the population. Most of the 46 million people who lack medical care coverage at present have moderate to low incomes. When a serious illness strikes, the experience is starkly different for rich and poor people in our society.

The Profit Motive

Some conflict analysts go further, arguing that the real problem is not access to medical care but the nature of capitalist medicine itself. The profit motive turns physicians, hospitals, and the pharmaceutical industry into money-hungry corporations. The drive for higher profits encourages physicians to recommend unnecessary tests and surgery and to rely too much on expensive drugs and treatments rather than focusing on helping people improve their living conditions and lifestyles.

Of about 25 million surgical operations performed in the United States each year, three-fourths are elective, which means that they

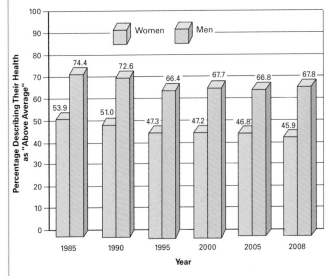

Student Snapshot

FIGURE 21–3 **Self-Assessment of Physical Health by First-Year College Students, 1985–2008**

Since 1985, a smaller share of students have described their health as "above average."

Sources: Astin et al. (2002) and Pryor et al. (2008).

are intended to promote long-term health and are not prompted by a medical emergency. Of course, any medical procedure or use of drugs is risky, and between 5 and 10 percent of patients are harmed each year as a result. Therefore, the decision to perform surgery, social-conflict theorists argue, reflects not just the medical needs of patients but also the financial interests of surgeons and hospitals (Cowley, 1995; Nuland, 1999).

Finally, say conflict theorists, our society is too tolerant of physicians' having a direct financial interest in the tests and procedures they order for their patients (Pear & Eckholm, 1991). Medical care should be motivated by a concern for people, not profits.

Medicine as Politics

Although science claims to be politically neutral, feminists feel that scientific medicine often takes sides on significant social issues. For example, the medical establishment has always strongly opposed government medical care programs and only recently allowed a significant number of women to join the ranks of physicians. The history of medicine itself shows that racial and sexual discrimination have kept women and other minorities out of medicine, but discrimination has been supported by

Q: "If you treat a sick child like an adult and a sick adult like a child, everything usually works out pretty well." Ruth Carlisle

Q: "Less access to the present health system would, contrary to popular rhetoric, benefit the poor." Ivan Illich

DIVERSITY: As late as 1969, some localities in the U.S. legally required blood products to be labeled with the race of the donor.

Q: "A great doctor kills more people than a great general." G. W. Leibniz

DISCUSS: Are racial disparities in health biological or social? One bit of evidence supporting a social hypothesis is that indigenous and immigrant people of one race often differ dramatically in health. For example, foreign-born blacks have very good health profiles, but U.S.-born blacks have relatively poor health profiles (Hummer et al., 1999).

MAKING THE GRADE

The Apply Theory table below is a learning tool to help you understand theoretical approaches to health.

APPLYING THEORY

Health

	Structural-Functional Approach	Symbolic-Interaction Approach	Social-Conflict and Feminist Approaches
What is the level of analysis?	Macro-level	Micro-level	Macro-level
How is health related to society?	Illness is dysfunctional for society because it prevents people from carrying out their daily roles.	Societies define "health" and "illness" differently according to their living standards.	Health is linked to social inequality, with rich people having more access to care than poor people.
	The sick role releases people who are ill from responsibilities while they try to get well.	How people define their own health affects how they actually feel (psychosomatic conditions).	Capitalist medical care places the drive for profits over the needs of people, treating symptoms rather than addressing poverty and sexism as causes of illness.

"scientific" opinions about, say, the inferiority of certain categories of people (Leavitt, 1984). Consider the diagnosis of "hysteria," a term that has its origins in the Greek word *hyster,* meaning "uterus." In choosing this word to describe a wild, emotional state, the medical profession suggested that being a woman is somehow the same as being irrational.

Even today, according to conflict theory, scientific medicine explains illness exclusively in terms of bacteria and viruses, ignoring the damaging effects of poverty. In effect, scientific medicine hides the bias in our medical system by transforming this social issue into simple biology.

CRITICAL REVIEW   Social-conflict analysis provides still another view of how health, medicine, and society are related. According to this approach, social inequality is the reason some people have better health than others.

The most common objection to the conflict approach is that it minimizes the gains in U.S. health brought about by scientific medicine and higher living standards. Although there is plenty of room for improvement, health indicators for our population as a whole rose steadily over the course of the twentieth century and compare well with those of other industrial nations.

CHECK YOUR LEARNING   Explain how health and medical care are related to social classes, to capitalism, and to gender stratification.

In sum, sociology's three major theoretical approaches explain why health and medicine are social issues. The Applying Theory table sums up what they teach us.

But advancing technology will not solve every health problem. On the contrary, as the Controversy & Debate box explains, today's advancing technology is raising new questions and concerns.

The renowned French scientist Louis Pasteur (1822–1895), who spent much of his life studying how bacteria cause disease, said just before he died that health depends less on bacteria than on the social environment in which the bacteria are found (Gordon, 1980:7). Explaining Pasteur's insight is sociology's contribution to human health.

Health and Medicine: Looking Ahead

In the early 1900s, deaths from infectious diseases like diphtheria and measles were widespread. Because scientists had yet to develop penicillin and other antibiotics, even a small wound might become infected, and a simple infection from a minor wound was sometimes life-threatening. Today, a century later, most members of U.S. society take good health and long life for granted. Although the increasing obesity epidemic is cause for concern, it seems reasonable to expect the improvements in U.S. health to continue throughout the twenty-first century.

Another encouraging trend is that more people are taking responsibility for their own health. Every one of us can live better and longer if we avoid tobacco, eat sensibly, and exercise regularly.

Many health problems will continue to plague U.S. society in the decades to come. The biggest problem, discussed throughout this chapter, is this nation's double standard in health: greater well-being for the rich and higher rates of disease for the poor. International compar-

Q: "In the USA—the richest country in the world—even the relatively affluent are now concerned about their ability to pay for medical care, while the poor have always been acutely aware of the gross deficiencies in the medical facilities available to them." Lesley Doyal

SOCIAL SURVEY: "Would you like to know, through genetic profiling, what harmful diseases you might suffer from later in life?" Yes, 81%; no, 11% (Harris poll, 2002).

THEN AND NOW: In the past, urban living was less healthful than rural living because cities had no sanitation and many urban residents faced extreme poverty. Gradually, however, the quality of urban life improved. Today, cities pose some risks to health (air pollution, crime, high stress) but also offer extensive medical care.

Q: "The ways in which the poor die reflect the conditions of their lives." Carol Stack (1975)

● MAKING THE GRADE

The box below presents a case of cultural lag: Our scientific ability has progressed beyond our certainty about when or even if we should act on what we know.

CONTROVERSY & DEBATE

The Genetic Crystal Ball: Do We Really Want to Look?

FELISHA: Before I get married, I want my partner to have a genetic screening. It's like buying a house or a car—you should check it out before you sign on the line.

EVA: Do you expect to get a warranty, too?

The liquid in the laboratory test tube seems ordinary enough, like a syrupy form of water. But this liquid is one of the greatest medical breakthroughs of all time; it may even hold the key to life itself. The liquid is deoxyribonucleic acid, or DNA, the spiraling molecule found in cells of the human body that contains the blueprint for making each one of us human as well as different from every other person.

The human body is composed of some 100 trillion cells, most of which contain a nucleus of twenty-three pairs of chromosomes (one of each pair comes from each parent). Each chromosome is packed with DNA, in segments called genes. Genes guide the production of protein, the building block of the human body.

If genetics sounds complicated (and it is), the social implications of genetic knowledge are even more complex. Scientists discovered the structure of the DNA molecule in 1952, and in recent years they have made great gains in "mapping" the human genome. Charting the genetic landscape may lead to understanding how each bit of DNA shapes our being.

But do we really want to turn the key to unlock the secrets of life itself? And what do we do with this knowledge once we have it? Research has already identified genetic abnormalities that cause sickle-cell anemia, muscular dystrophy, Huntington's disease, cystic fibrosis, some forms of cancer, and other crippling and deadly afflictions. Genetic screening—gazing into a person's genetic "crystal ball"—could let people know their medical destiny and allow doctors to manipulate segments of DNA to prevent diseases before they appear.

But many people urge caution in such research, warning that genetic information can easily be abused. At its worst, genetic mapping opens the door to Nazi-like efforts to breed a "super-race." In 1994, the People's Republic of China began to use genetic information to regulate marriage and childbirth with the purpose of avoiding "new births of inferior quality."

It seems inevitable that some parents will want to use genetic testing to evaluate the health (or even the eye color) of their future children.

Scientists are learning more and more about the genetic factors that prompt the eventual development of serious diseases. If offered the opportunity, would you want to undergo a genetic screening that would predict the long-term future of your own health?

What if they want to abort a fetus because it falls short of their standards? Should parents be allowed to use genetic manipulation to create "designer children"?

Then there is the issue of "genetic privacy." Can a prospective spouse request a genetic evaluation of her fiancé before agreeing to marry? Can a life insurance company demand genetic testing before issuing a policy? Can an employer screen job applicants to weed out those whose future illnesses might drain the company's health care funds? Clearly, what is scientifically possible is not always morally desirable. Society is already struggling with questions about the proper use of our expanding knowledge of human genetics. Such ethical dilemmas will multiply as genetic research moves forward in the years to come.

WHAT DO YOU THINK?

1. Traditional wedding vows join couples "in sickness and in health." Do you think individuals have a right to know the future health of their potential partner before tying the knot? Why or why not?

2. Do you think parents should be able to genetically "design" their children? Why or why not?

3. Is it right that private companies doing genetic research are able to patent their discoveries so that they can profit from the results, or should this information be made available to everyone? Explain your answer.

Sources: D. Thompson (1999) and Golden & Lemonick (2000).

isons show that the United States lags in some measures of human health because we neglect the people at the margins of our society. An important question, then, is how a rich society can afford to let millions of its members face life without the security of medical care.

Finally, we know that health problems are far greater in low-income nations than they are in the United States. The good news is that life expectancy for the world as a whole has been on the rise—from forty-eight years in 1950 to sixty-eight years today—and the biggest gains have occurred in poor countries (Population Reference Bureau, 2009). But in much of Latin America, Asia, and especially Africa, hundreds of millions of adults and children lack not only medical attention but also adequate food and safe drinking water. Improving the health of the world's poorest people is a critical challenge for us in the years to come.

Seeing Sociology in Everyday Life

Chapter 21   Health and Medicine

How does society affect patterns of health?

Certain occupations put people at higher-than-average risk of accident or death. One example is coal mining, which has long been one of the deadliest jobs. Although the death toll from mining accidents in the United States has gone down over time, even miners who manage to avoid mine collapses or explosions typically suffer harm from years of breathing coal dust. Look at the photos below: How do they link health to a way of life?

> **HINT**   Among the most dangerous jobs in the United States are farming (dangers come from using power equipment), mining, timber cutting, truck driving, and constructing tall buildings. Many members of the military also face danger on a daily basis. In general, people in the working class are at greater risk than middle-class people, who typically work in offices; men also predominate in the most dangerous jobs. Overall, about 6,000 U.S. (nonmilitary) workers lose their lives every year in workplace accidents.

Crews on fishing boats such as this one spend months at a time battling high seas and often frigid temperatures. As documented on the television show *The Deadliest Catch*, it is a rare and fortunate fishing season that brings no death or serious injury. What other jobs threaten the health and well-being of U.S. workers?

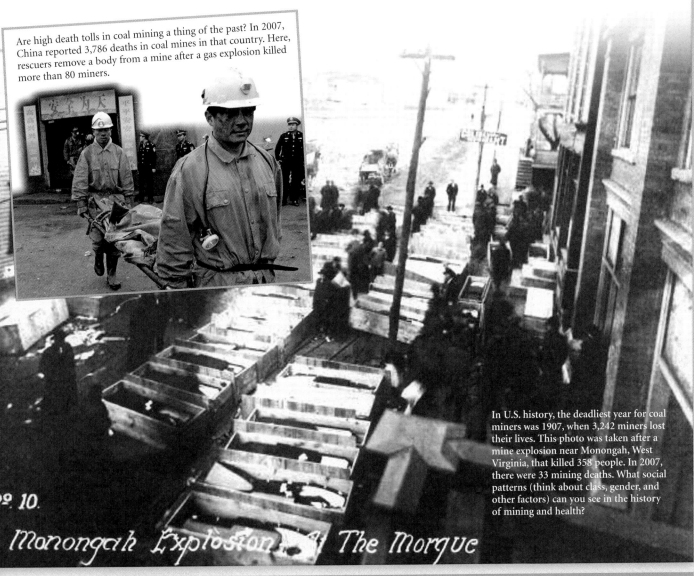

Are high death tolls in coal mining a thing of the past? In 2007, China reported 3,786 deaths in coal mines in that country. Here, rescuers remove a body from a mine after a gas explosion killed more than 80 miners.

In U.S. history, the deadliest year for coal miners was 1907, when 3,242 miners lost their lives. This photo was taken after a mine explosion near Monongah, West Virginia, that killed 358 people. In 2007, there were 33 mining deaths. What social patterns (think about class, gender, and other factors) can you see in the history of mining and health?

Monongah Explosion At The Morgue

Applying SOCIOLOGY in Everyday Life

1. Take a trip to the local courthouse or city hall to find public records showing people's cause of death and age at death. Compare the records for 1905 and 2005. What patterns do you find in life expectancy and causes of death?

2. Get a course catalogue from a medical school (or visit a school's Web site) and see how much, if any, of the curriculum deals with the social dimensions of medical care.

3. Interview a midwife (many list their services in the Yellow Pages) about her work helping women deliver babies. How do midwives differ from medical obstetricians in their approach?

MAKING THE GRADE

CHAPTER 21   Health and Medicine

What Is Health?

HEALTH AND SOCIETY

Health is a social issue because personal well-being depends on a society's level of technology and its distribution of resources.

- A society's culture shapes definitions of health, which change over time.
- A society's technology affects people's health.
- Social inequality affects people's health.

pp. 542–43

health (p. 542) a state of complete physical, mental, and social well-being

Health: A Global Survey

HEALTH IN LOW-INCOME COUNTRIES

- Poor nations suffer from inadequate sanitation, hunger, and other problems linked to poverty.
- Life expectancy in low-income nations is about twenty years less than in the United States; in the poorest nations, 10% of children die within a year of birth, and half the children do not survive to adulthood.

p. 543

HEALTH IN HIGH-INCOME COUNTRIES

- In the nineteenth century, industrialization improved health dramatically in Western Europe and North America.
- A century ago, infectious diseases were leading killers; today, most people in the United States die in old age of chronic illnesses such as heart disease, cancer, or stroke.

pp. 543–44

Health in the United States

WHO IS HEALTHY? AGE, GENDER, CLASS, AND RACE

- More than three-fourths of U.S. children born today will live to at least age sixty-five.
- Throughout the life course, women have better health than men. Our culture's definition of masculinity promotes aggressive and individualistic behavior that contributes to men's higher rate of coronary disease as well as accidents and violence.
- People of high social position enjoy better health than the poor, a result of better nutrition, wider access to health care, and safer and less stressful living conditions.
- Poverty among African Americans, which is three times the rate for whites, helps explain why black people are more likely to die in infancy and to suffer the effects of violence, drug abuse, and poor health.

pp. 544–45

CIGARETTE SMOKING

- Cigarette smoking is the greatest preventable cause of death; more than 440,000 people in the United States die prematurely each year as a result of smoking cigarettes.
- Many people smoke as a way to relieve stress. Smoking is more common among men, working-class people, divorced people, the unemployed, and those serving in the armed forces.
- Tobacco is an $89 billion industry in the United States; the tobacco industry has increased its sales abroad, especially in low-income countries.

pp. 545–46

social epidemiology (p. 544) the study of how health and disease are distributed throughout a society's population

eating disorder (p. 546) an intense form of dieting or other unhealthy method of weight control driven by the desire to be very thin

euthanasia (p. 552) assisting in the death of a person suffering from an incurable disease; also known as *mercy killing*

EATING DISORDERS AND OBESITY

- Eating disorders—anorexia nervosa and bulimia—are tied to cultural expectations of thinness; 95% of people who suffer from eating disorders are women.
- Two-thirds of U.S. adults are overweight; being overweight raises the risk of heart disease, stroke, and diabetes.
- Social causes of obesity include an inactive lifestyle and a diet heavy in salt and fatty foods.

pp. 546–48

SEXUALLY TRANSMITTED DISEASES

- STDs became a matter of national concern during the "sexual revolution" beginning in the 1960s; by the late 1980s, the dangers of STDs, especially AIDS, caused a sexual counterrevolution as people turned away from casual sex.
- Specific behaviors that put people at risk of AIDS include anal sex, sharing needles, and use of any drug.

pp. 548–51

ETHICAL ISSUES SURROUNDING DEATH

- Questions about the use of medical technology have added an ethical dimension to health and illness.
- Supporters of a "right to die" argue that individuals should be able to decide for themselves when to use or refuse medical treatment to prolong their lives.

pp. 551–52

The Medical Establishment

THE RISE OF SCIENTIFIC MEDICINE

- Health care was historically a family concern but with industrialization became the responsibility of trained specialists.
- The model of scientific medicine is the foundation of the U.S. medical establishment.

pp. 552–53

HOLISTIC MEDICINE

- Holistic medicine, focusing on prevention of illness, takes a broader and more traditional approach than scientific medicine.
- Holistic practitioners focus on health rather than disease; they emphasize treating patients as people, encourage people to take responsibility for their own health, and provide treatment in personal, relaxed surroundings.

p. 553

medicine (p. 552) the social institution that focuses on fighting disease and improving health

holistic medicine (p. 553) an approach to health care that emphasizes prevention of illness and takes into account a person's entire physical and social environment

socialized medicine (p. 554) a medical care system in which the government owns and operates most medical facilities and employs most physicians

direct-fee system (p. 555) a medical care system in which patients pay directly for the services of physicians and hospitals

health maintenance organization (HMO) (p. 556) an organization that provides comprehensive medical care to subscribers for a fixed fee

PAYING FOR MEDICAL CARE: A GLOBAL SURVEY

- Socialist societies define medical care as a right; governments offer basic care equally to everyone.
- Capitalist societies view medical care as a commodity to be purchased, although most capitalist governments help pay for medical care through socialized medicine or national health insurance.

pp. 553–55

PAYING FOR MEDICAL CARE: THE UNITED STATES

- The United States, with a direct-fee system, is the only high-income nation with no universal medical care program.
- Most people have private or government health insurance, but about 46 million people in the United States do not have medical insurance.

pp. 555–56

THE NURSING SHORTAGE

- Roughly 8% of jobs for registered nurses in the United States are currently unfilled.
- The wider range of occupational choices for women today has resulted in fewer young women choosing this traditonally female job. Efforts to raise salary levels and to recruit more men to the profession are under way.

pp. 556–57

Theoretical Analysis of Health and Medicine

The **STRUCTURAL-FUNCTIONAL APPROACH** considers illness to be dysfunctional because it reduces people's abilities to perform their roles. According to Talcott Parsons, society responds to illness by defining roles:

- The *sick role* excuses the ill person from routine social responsibilities.
- The *physician's role* is to use specialized knowledge to take charge of the patient's recovery.

p. 557

The **SYMBOLIC-INTERACTION APPROACH** investigates how health and medical care are socially constructed by people in everyday interaction:

- Our response to illness is not always based on medical facts.
- How people define a medical situation may affect how they feel.

pp. 557–59

The **SOCIAL-CONFLICT** and **FEMINIST APPROACHES** focus on the unequal distribution of health and medical care. They criticize the U.S. medical establishment for

- its overreliance on drugs and surgery
- the dominance of the profit motive
- overemphasis on the biological rather than the social causes of illness

pp. 559–60

sick role (p. 557) patterns of behavior defined as appropriate for people who are ill

See the Applying Theory table on page 560.

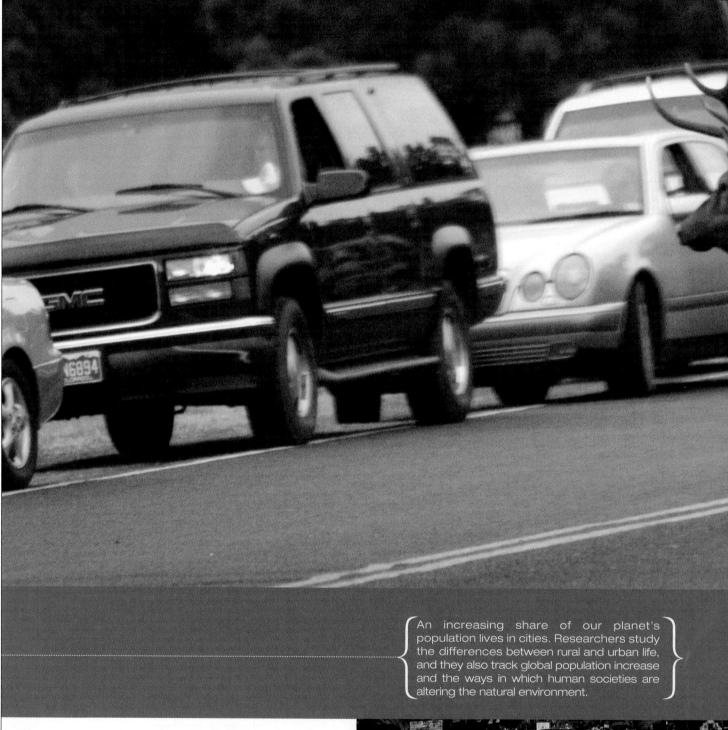

An increasing share of our planet's population lives in cities. Researchers study the differences between rural and urban life, and they also track global population increase and the ways in which human societies are altering the natural environment.

CHAPTER 22

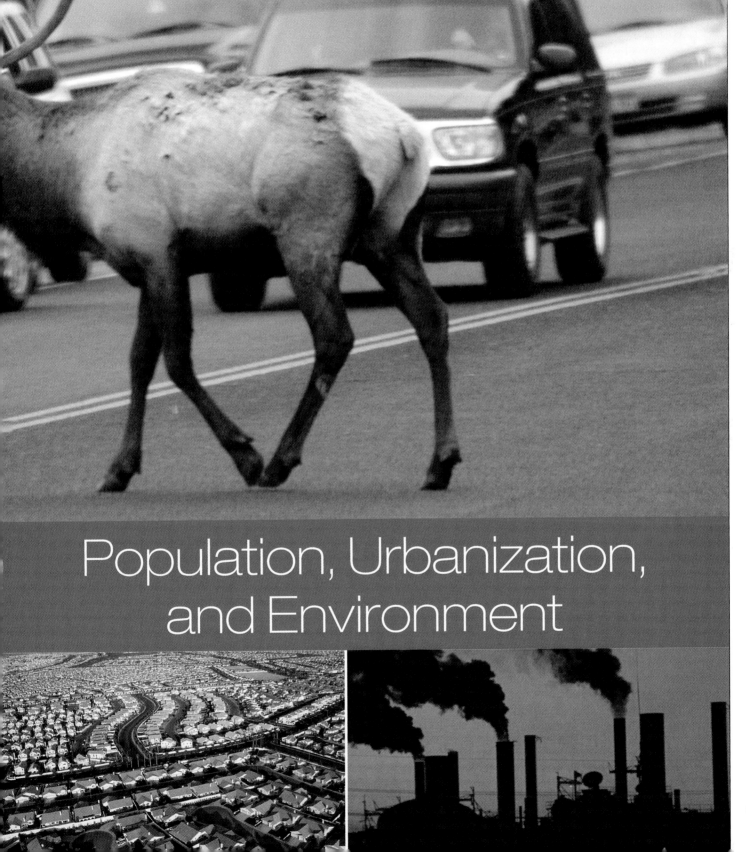

Population, Urbanization, and Environment

SUPPLEMENTS: An outline of this chapter, supplementary lecture material, and suggested discussion topics are found in the *Instructor's Manual*.

Q: "Children are poor men's riches." Old proverb

DIVERSITY: Birth rates per 1,000 population, by category, for 2006: non-Hispanic white, 11.6; American Indian, Eskimo, and Aleut, 14.9; non-Hispanic black, 16.5; Asian and Pacific Islander, 16.6; Hispanic, 23.4 (Martin et al., 2009).

NOTE: Fertility in the U.S. has declined despite rising tax deductions for children.

CHAPTER OVERVIEW { This chapter explores three related dimensions of social change: population dynamics, urbanization, and increasing threats to the natural environment.

Looking for a new place to live after you finish college? Crosby, North Dakota, would really like you to call it home. The town's officials will do more than welcome you—they will give you a free piece of land on which to build a house. As a bonus, they will throw in a free membership in the local country club.

Ellsworth, Kansas, also wants you. The town leaders will match Crosby's offer of free land and go one better, paying you $1,000 cash to get you started on building your new home.

Perhaps the best deal of all is found in Plainville, Kansas. In addition to free land, you can forget about property taxes for the next ten years!

Why are these towns so eager to attract new residents? The answer is that they are all in the Great Plains, the central region of the United States extending from North Dakota all the way down to Texas that has lost much of its population in recent decades. The town leaders of Crosby (current population 1,100), Ellsworth (2,500), and Plainville (2,000) are offering these fantastic deals because they are worried that unless there is a turnaround, their towns may disappear, as hundreds of nearby communities already have (Greene, 2005).

All across the Great Plains, towns are hanging on by a thread. This chapter investigates population patterns, explaining why people move from place to place, why some cities get so large, and why small towns sometimes die. It also looks at the effects on the physical environment of population change and our entire way of life.

Demography: The Study of Population

When humans first began to cultivate plants some 12,000 years ago, Earth's entire *Homo sapiens* population was around 5 million, about the number living in Minnesota today. Very slow growth pushed the global total in 1 C.E. to perhaps 300 million, or about the population of the United States today.

Starting around 1750, world population began to spike upward. We now add more than 80 million people to the planet each year; today, the world holds 6.7 billion people (Population Reference Bureau, 2008).

The causes and consequences of this drama are the basis of **demography,** *the study of human population.* Demography (from Greek, meaning "description of people") is a cousin of sociology that analyzes the size and composition of a population and studies how and why people move from place to place. Demographers not only collect statistics but also raise important questions about the effects of population growth and suggest how it might be controlled. The following sections present basic demographic concepts.

Fertility

The study of human population begins with how many people are born. **Fertility** is *the incidence of childbearing in a country's population.* During her childbearing years, from the onset of menstruation (typically in the early teens) to menopause (usually in the late forties), a woman is capable of bearing more than twenty children. But *fecundity,* or maximum possible childbearing, is sharply reduced by cultural norms, finances, and personal choice.

Demographers describe fertility using the **crude birth rate,** *the number of live births in a given year for every 1,000 people in a population.* To calculate a crude birth rate, divide the number of live births in a year by the society's total population, and multiply the result by 1,000. In the United States in 2007, there were 4.3 million live births in a population of 301 million, yielding a crude birth rate of 14.3 (Tejada-Vera & Sutton, 2008).

> **January 18, Coshocton County, Ohio.** Having just finished the mountains of meat and potatoes that make up a typical Amish meal, we have gathered in the living room of Jacob Raber, a member of this rural Amish community. Mrs. Raber, a mother of four, is telling us about Amish life. "Most of the women I know have five or six children," she says with a smile, "but certainly not everybody—some have eleven or twelve!"

A country's birth rate is described as "crude" because it is based on the entire population, not just women in their childbearing years.

NOTE: *Life expectancy* is calculated at birth for people born in a given year. Because it is reduced by infant mortality, this term should be distinguished from *longevity*, or how long people can live. For example, when the U.S. was founded, life expectancy was about 35 years due to high death rates from infectious diseases, although living to 65 and beyond was not unheard of. (George Washington died at age 67, Martha Washington at age 70.)

DISCUSS: Ask students to account for this trend: U.S. death rates peak in January (just after the holidays) and remain high through April; birth rates rise in May and remain high through October.

EXERCISE: Trace the regional migration of the U.S. population by looking at the shifting location of Major League Baseball teams. In 1956, 14 of 16 teams were in the Northeast or Midwest; in 2009, 14 of 30 teams were elsewhere.

● SEEING SOCIOLOGY
in Everyday Life

How do you think low-fertility societies differ from high-fertility societies with respect to (1) age at first marriage, (2) opportunities available to women, and (3) attitudes toward homosexuality? Explain your responses.

demography the study of human population

fertility the incidence of childbearing in a country's population

crude birth rate the number of live births in a given year for every 1,000 people in a population

mortality the incidence of death in a country's population

crude death rate the number of deaths in a given year for every 1,000 people in a population

Global Snapshot

(a)

(b)

(c)

FIGURE 22–1   (a) Crude Birth Rates and Crude Death Rates, (b) Infant Mortality Rates, and (c) Life Expectancy around the World, 2008

By world standards, North America has a low birth rate, an average death rate, a very low infant mortality rate, and high life expectancy.

[1] United States and Canada.

[2] Australia, New Zealand, and South Pacific Islands.

Source: Population Reference Bureau (2009).

In addition, this measure ignores differences between various categories of the population: Fertility among the Amish, for example, is quite high, and fertility among Asian Americans is low. But the crude measure is easy to calculate and allows rough comparisons of the fertility of one country or region in relation to others. Part (a) of Figure 22–1 shows that on a global scale, the crude birth rate of North America is low.

Mortality

Population size also reflects **mortality,** *the incidence of death in a country's population.* To measure mortality, demographers use the **crude death rate,** *the number of deaths in a given year for every 1,000 people in a population.* This time, we take the number of deaths in a year, divide by the total population, and multiply the result by 1,000. In 2007, there were 2.4 million deaths in the U.S. population of 301 million, yielding a crude death rate of 8.0 (Tejada-Vera & Sutton, 2008). Part (a) of Figure 22–1 shows that this rate is about average.

A third useful demographic measure is the **infant mortality rate,** *the number of deaths among infants under one year of age for each 1,000 live births in a given year.* To compute infant mortality, divide the number of deaths of children under one year of age by the number

of live births during the same year, and multiply the result by 1,000. In 2007, there were 28,600 infant deaths and 4.3 million live births in the United States. Dividing the first number by the second and multiplying the result by 1,000 yields an infant mortality rate of 6.6. Part (b) of Figure 22–1 indicates that by world standards, North American infant mortality is very low.

But remember that differences exist among various categories of people. For example, African Americans, with nearly three times the burden of poverty as whites, have an infant mortality rate of 13.3—more than twice the white rate of 5.6.

Low infant mortality greatly raises **life expectancy,** *the average life span of a country's population.* U.S. males born in 2006 can expect to live 75.4 years, and females can look forward to 80.7 years. As part (c) of Figure 22–1 shows, life expectancy in North America is twenty-four years greater than is typical of low-income countries of Africa.

Migration

Population size is also affected by **migration,** *the movement of people into and out of a specified territory.* Movement into a territory, or *immigration,* is measured as an *in-migration rate,* calculated as the number of people entering an area for every 1,000 people in the

THE MAP: The main reason for internal migration is the search for economic opportunity. People leave economically depressed areas for those that promise better jobs. Migrants tend to be younger people; those who remain are older, on average, and have less schooling.

NOTE: The table in the end-of-chapter box sketches global birth, death, and natural increase rates over time.

GLOBAL: Sex-ratio imbalance in Asia is especially high for second and third births. In South Korea, for example, 108 boys are born for every 100 girls as second children; for fourth children, the figure soars to 128 boys for every 100 girls.

DIVERSITY: Sex ratios differ by race: at birth, whites = 105, blacks = 104; at ages 20–24: whites = 108, blacks = 103; at ages 40–44: whites = 102, blacks = 88 (U.S. Census Bureau, 2009).

infant mortality rate (p. 569) the number of deaths among infants under one year of age for each 1,000 live births in a given year

life expectancy (p. 569) the average life span of a country's population

migration (p. 569) the movement of people into and out of a specified territory

sex ratio the number of males for every 100 females in a nation's population

age-sex pyramid a graphic representation of the age and sex of a population

Cheryl Richardson, age 36, has just moved to Las Vegas to work in the expanding tourism industry, which has boosted the region's population.

Tom and Ellen Posten, in their sixties, live in Wichita County, Kansas; like many other families in the area, their children have all moved out of the county in search of better jobs.

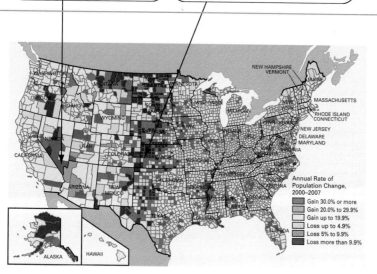

Seeing Ourselves

NATIONAL MAP 22–1

Population Change across the United States

This map shows that since 2000, population has been moving from the heartland of the United States toward the coasts. What do you think is causing this internal migration? What types of people do you think remain in counties that are losing population?

Source: U.S. Census Bureau (2009).

Annual Rate of Population Change, 2000–2007
- Gain 30.0% or more
- Gain 20.0% to 29.9%
- Gain up to 19.9%
- Loss up to 4.9%
- Loss 5% to 9.9%
- Loss more than 9.9%

population. Movement out of a territory, or *emigration,* is measured in terms of an *out-migration rate,* the number leaving for every 1,000 people. Both types of migration usually occur at the same time; the difference between them is the *net migration rate.*

All nations experience internal migration, that is, movement within their borders from one region to another. National Map 22–1 shows where the U.S. population is moving and the places left behind (as suggested by the chapter opening, notice the heavy losses in the Plains States in the middle of the country).

Migration is sometimes voluntary, as when people leave a small town and move to a larger city. In such cases, "push-pull" factors are typically at work; a lack of jobs "pushes" people to move, and more opportunity elsewhere "pulls" them to a larger city. Migration can also be involuntary, as during the forced transport of 10 million Africans to the Western Hemisphere as slaves or when Hurricane Katrina forced tens of thousands of people to flee New Orleans.

Population Growth

Fertility, mortality, and migration all affect the size of a society's population. In general, rich nations (such as the United States) grow as much from immigration as from natural increase; poorer nations (such as Pakistan) grow almost entirely from natural increase.

To calculate a population's natural growth rate, demographers subtract the crude death rate from the crude birth rate. The natural growth rate of the U.S. population in 2007 was 6.3 per 1,000 (the crude birth rate of 14.3 minus the crude death rate of 8.0), or about 0.6 percent annual growth.

Global Map 22–1 shows that population growth in the United States and other high-income nations is well below the world average of 1.2 percent. Earth's low-growth continents are Europe (currently

posting a slight decline, expressed as a *negative* 0.1 percent annual rate), North America (0.6 percent), and Oceania (1.1 percent). Close to the global average are Asia (1.2 percent) and Latin America (1.5 percent). The highest growth region in the world is Africa (2.4 percent).

A handy rule of thumb for estimating a nation or region's growth is to divide the number 70 by the population growth rate; this yields the *doubling time* in years. Thus an annual growth rate of 2 percent (found in parts of Latin America) doubles a population in thirty-five years, and a 3 percent growth rate (found in some countries in Africa) drops the doubling time to just twenty-three years. The rapid population growth of the poorest countries is deeply troubling because these countries can barely support the populations they have now.

Population Composition

Demographers also study the makeup of a society's population at a given point in time. One variable is the **sex ratio,** *the number of males for every 100 females in a nation's population.* In 2007, the sex ratio in the United States was 97 (97 males for every 100 females). Sex ratios are usually below 100 because, on average, women outlive men. Because Plainville, Kansas, has an aging population, its sex ratio is 89, or 89 males for every 100 females. In India, however, the sex ratio is 106 because many parents value sons more than daughters and may either abort a female fetus or, after birth, give more care to their male children, raising the odds that a female child will die.

A more complex measure is the **age-sex pyramid,** *a graphic representation of the age and sex of a population.* Figure 22–2 on page 572 presents the age-sex pyramids for the populations of the United States and Mexico. Higher mortality with advancing age gives these figures

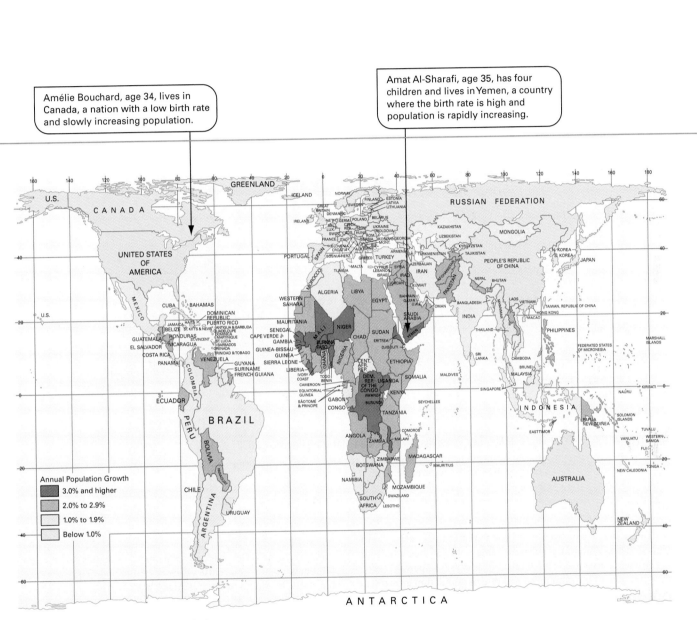

Amélie Bouchard, age 34, lives in Canada, a nation with a low birth rate and slowly increasing population.

Amat Al-Sharafi, age 35, has four children and lives in Yemen, a country where the birth rate is high and population is rapidly increasing.

Window on the World

GLOBAL MAP 22–1   Population Growth in Global Perspective

The richest countries of the world—including the United States, Canada, and the nations of Europe—have growth rates below 1 percent. The nations of Latin America and Asia typically have growth rates around 1.5 percent, a rate that doubles a population in forty-seven years. Africa has an overall growth rate of 2.4 percent (despite only small increases in countries with a high rate of AIDS), which cuts the doubling time to twenty-nine years. In global perspective, we see that a society's standard of living is closely related to its rate of population growth: Population is rising fastest in the world regions that can least afford to support more people.

Source: Population Reference Bureau (2009).

a rough pyramid shape. In the U.S. pyramid, the bulge in the middle reflects high birth rates during the *baby boom* from the mid-1940s to the mid-1960s. The contraction for people in their twenties and thirties reflects the subsequent *baby bust*. The birth rate of 14.3 in 2007 is still well below the high of 25.3 in 1957.

Comparing the U.S. and Mexican age-sex pyramids reveals different demographic trends. The pyramid for Mexico, like that of other lower-income nations, is wide at the bottom (reflecting higher birth rates) and narrows quickly by what we would term middle age (due to higher mortality). In short, Mexico is a much younger society,

GLOBAL: Economic development shapes a nation's population pyramid. India has four times the U.S. population, but we have 3.5 million more people aged 80 and over. Although the U.S. has twice the population of Nigeria, that nation has more children aged 5 and under.

NOTE: A greater proportion of U.S. babies born today will reach age 65 than survived a single year in 1900.

DISCUSS: What share of people ever born are alive today? Modern *Homo sapiens* have existed for 50,000 years (2,500 generations), but because global population is so high today, the best estimate—5.8%—is surprisingly high (Haub, 2002).

RESOURCE: Malthus's population thesis is included in the author's companion reader *Seeing Ourselves*, 8th ed.

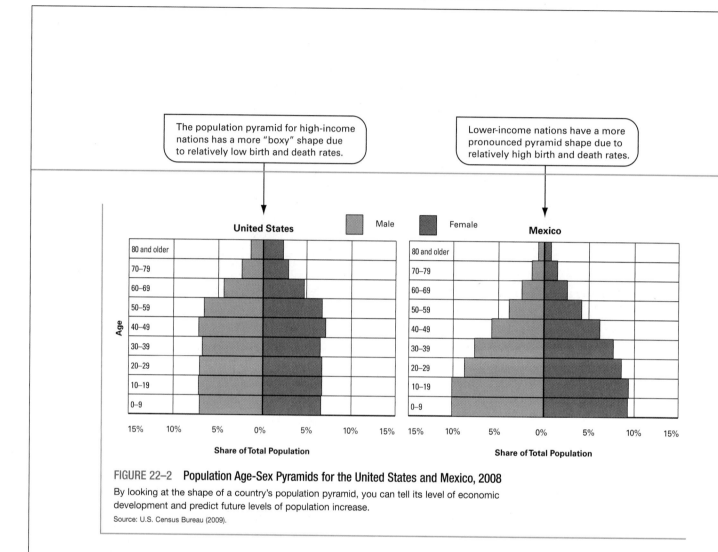

The population pyramid for high-income nations has a more "boxy" shape due to relatively low birth and death rates.

Lower-income nations have a more pronounced pyramid shape due to relatively high birth and death rates.

FIGURE 22–2 **Population Age-Sex Pyramids for the United States and Mexico, 2008**

By looking at the shape of a country's population pyramid, you can tell its level of economic development and predict future levels of population increase.

Source: U.S. Census Bureau (2009).

with a median age of twenty-six, compared to thirty-seven in the United States. With a larger share of females still in their childbearing years, Mexico's crude birth rate (20) is nearly 50 percent higher than our own (14.3), and its annual rate of population growth (1.1 percent) is almost twice the U.S. rate (0.6 percent).

History and Theory of Population Growth

In the past, people wanted large families because human labor was the key to productivity. In addition, until rubber condoms were invented in the mid-1800s, prevention of pregnancy was uncertain at best. But high death rates from infectious diseases put a constant brake on population growth.

A major demographic shift began about 1750 as the world's population turned upward, reaching the 1 billion mark by 1800. This milestone (which took all of human history to reach) was repeated barely a century later in 1930, when a second billion people were added to the planet. In other words, not only was population increasing, but the *rate* of growth was accelerating. Global population reached 3 billion by 1962 (just thirty-two years later) and 4 billion by 1974 (only twelve years after that). The rate of world population

increase has slowed recently, but our planet passed the 5 billion mark in 1987, the 6 billion mark in 1999, and now stands at 6.8 billion (2009). In no previous century did the world's population even double; in the twentieth century, it *quadrupled*.

Currently, the world is gaining 80 million people each year; 97 percent of this increase is in poor countries. Experts predict that Earth's population will reach 7 billion very soon and will climb more slowly to about 9 billion by 2050 (United Nations Population Reference Division, 2009). Given the world's troubles feeding the present population, such an increase is a matter of urgent concern.

Malthusian Theory

The sudden population spurt 250 years ago sparked the development of demography. Thomas Robert Malthus (1766–1834), an English economist and clergyman, warned that population increase would soon lead to social chaos. Malthus (1926, orig. 1798) calculated that population would increase in what mathematicians call a *geometric progression*, illustrated by the series of numbers 2, 4, 8, 16, 32, and so on. At such a rate, Malthus concluded, world population would soon soar out of control.

Food production would also increase, Malthus explained, but only in *arithmetic progression* (as in the series 2, 3, 4, 5, 6, and so on)

SEEING SOCIOLOGY
in Everyday Life

Using the age-sex pyramid for the United States shown in Figure 22–2, why do you think many people are concerned that there will not be enough workers to pay for the retirement of the baby boom generation? How does the pyramid shape change as more and more baby boomers enter retirement?

demographic transition theory a thesis that links population patterns to a society's level of technological development

because even with new agricultural technology, farmland is limited. Thus Malthus presented a distressing vision of the future: people reproducing beyond what the planet could feed, leading ultimately to widespread starvation and war over what resources were left.

Malthus recognized that artificial birth control or abstinence might change his prediction. But he considered one morally wrong and the other impractical. Famine and war therefore stalked humanity in Malthus's mind, and he was justly known as "the dismal parson."

CRITICAL REVIEW Fortunately, Malthus's prediction was flawed. First, by 1850, the European birth rate began to drop, partly because children were becoming an economic liability rather than an asset and partly because people began using artificial birth control. Second, Malthus underestimated human ingenuity: Modern irrigation techniques, fertilizers, and pesticides increased farm production far more than he could have imagined.

Some people criticized Malthus for ignoring the role of social inequality in world abundance and famine. For example, Karl Marx (1967, orig. 1867) objected to viewing suffering as a "law of nature" rather than the curse of capitalism. More recently, "critical demographers" have claimed that saying poverty is caused by high birth rates in low-income countries amounts to blaming the victims. On the contrary, they see global inequality as the real issue (Horton, 1999; Kuumba, 1999).

Still, Malthus offers an important lesson. Habitable land, clean water, and fresh air are limited resources, and greater economic productivity has taken a heavy toll on the natural environment. In addition, medical advances have lowered death rates, pushing up world population. Common sense tells us that no level of population growth can go on forever. People everywhere must become aware of the dangers of population increase.

CHECK YOUR LEARNING What did Malthus predict about human population increase? About food production? What was his overall conclusion?

Demographic Transition Theory

A more complex analysis of population change is **demographic transition theory,** *a thesis that links population patterns to a society's level of technological development.* Figure 22–3 on page 574 shows the demographic consequences at four levels of technological development.

Preindustrial, agrarian societies (Stage 1) have high birth rates because of the economic value of children and the absence of birth control. Death rates are also high because of low living standards and limited medical technology. Deaths from outbreaks of disease cancel out births, so population rises and falls only slightly over time. This was the case for thousands of years in Europe before the Industrial Revolution.

This street scene in Kolkata (Calcutta), India, conveys the vision of the future found in the work of Thomas Robert Malthus, who feared that population increase would overwhelm the world's resources. Can you explain why Malthus had such a serious concern about population? How is demographic transition theory a more hopeful analysis?

Stage 2, the onset of industrialization, brings a demographic transition as death rates fall due to greater food supplies and scientific medicine. But birth rates remain high, resulting in rapid population growth. It was during Europe's Stage 2 that Malthus formulated his ideas, which accounts for his pessimistic view of the future. The world's poorest countries today are in this high-growth stage.

In Stage 3, a mature industrial economy, the birth rate drops, curbing population growth once again. Fertility falls because most children survive to adulthood and because high living standards make raising children expensive. In short, affluence transforms children from economic assets into economic liabilities. Smaller families, made possible by effective birth control, are also favored by women working outside the home. As birth rates follow death rates downward, population growth slows further.

NOTE: Voluntary sterilization has increased dramatically to become the most common form of birth control in the U.S. In addition, U.S. Catholics, whose religious doctrine prohibits artificial birth control, do not differ from others in contraceptive practices.

NOTE: Abortion, legal in the U.S. since 1973, contributes to low fertility. Some 1.2 million pregnancies end this way each year in the U.S.

GLOBAL: China has a legal minimum age of marriage: 22 years for men and 20 for women. In some cities, such as Beijing, the ages are higher: 28 and 25, respectively.

GLOBAL: In rich societies, women average just under one child during their reproductive lifetimes (counting only those who have children, the median is just under two). In poor societies, virtually all women have children, averaging almost four.

The United States is in this historical stage, with both a low birth rate and a low death rate.

MAKING THE GRADE

Demographic transition theory is linked to modernization theory, discussed in Chapter 12 ("Global Stratification").

FIGURE 22–3 Demographic Transition Theory

Demographic transition theory links population change to a society's level of technological development.

Stage 4 corresponds to a postindustrial economy in which the demographic transition is complete. The birth rate keeps falling, partly because dual-income couples gradually become the norm and partly because the cost of raising children continues to increase. This trend, linked to steady death rates, means that population grows only very slowly or even decreases. This is the case today in Japan, Europe, and the United States.

CRITICAL REVIEW Demographic transition theory suggests that the key to population control lies in technology. Instead of the runaway population increase feared by Malthus, this theory sees technology slowing growth and spreading material plenty.

Demographic transition theory is linked to modernization theory, one approach to global development discussed in Chapter 12 ("Global Stratification"). Modernization theorists are optimistic that poor countries will solve their population problems as they industrialize. But critics, notably dependency theorists, strongly disagree. Unless there is a redistribution of global resources, they maintain, our planet will become increasingly divided into industrialized "haves," enjoying low population growth, and nonindustrialized "have-nots," struggling in vain to feed more and more people.

CHECK YOUR LEARNING Explain the four stages of demographic transition theory.

Global Population Today: A Brief Survey

What can we say about population in today's world? Drawing on the discussion so far, we can identify important patterns and reach several conclusions.

The Low-Growth North

When the Industrial Revolution began in the Northern Hemisphere, the population increase in Western Europe and North America was a high 3 percent annually. But in the centuries since, the growth rate has steadily declined, and in 1970, it fell below 1 percent. As our postindustrial society settles into Stage 4, the U.S. birth rate is at about the replacement level of 2.1 children per woman, a point demographers term **zero population growth,** *the rate of reproduction that maintains population at a steady level.* More than eighty nations, almost all of them rich, are at or below the point of zero population growth.

Among the factors that serve to hold down population in these postindustrial societies include a high proportion of men and women in the labor force, rising costs of raising children, trends toward later marriage and singlehood, and widespread use of contraceptives and abortion.

In high-income nations, then, population increase is not the pressing problem that it is in poor countries. On the contrary, many governments in high-income countries, including Italy and Japan, are concerned about a future problem of *underpopulation* because declining population size may be difficult to reverse and because the swelling ranks of the elderly can look to fewer and fewer young people for support (Kent & Mather, 2002; Population Reference Bureau, 2009).

The High-Growth South

Population is a critical problem in poor nations of the Southern Hemisphere. No nation of the world lacks industrial technology entirely; demographic transition theory's Stage 1 applies today to remote rural areas of low-income nations. But much of Latin America, Africa, and Asia is at Stage 2, with a mix of agrarian and industrial economies. Advanced medical technology, supplied by rich countries, has sharply reduced death rates, but birth rates remain high. This is why poor countries now account for two-thirds of Earth's people and 97 percent of global population increase.

In some of the world poorest countries, such as the Democratic Republic of the Congo in Africa, women still have, on average, more than six children during their lifetimes. But in most poor countries, birth rates have fallen from about six children per woman (typical in 1950) to about three. But this level of fertility is still high enough to make global poverty much worse. This is why leaders in the battle against global poverty point to the importance of reducing fertility rates in low-income nations.

Notice, too, that a key element in controlling world population growth is improving the status of women. Why? Because of this simple truth: Give women more life choices and they will have fewer children. History has shown that women who are free to decide when

● SEEING SOCIOLOGY
in Everyday Life

Typically, immigrants are younger than most people in their new country. What is the likely effect of high immigration on a country's ability to support more and more older people?

zero population growth the rate of reproduction that maintains population at a steady level

urbanization the concentration of population into cities

and where to marry, bear children as a matter of choice, and have access to education and to good jobs will limit their own fertility (Axinn & Barber, 2001; Roudi-Fahimi & Kent, 2007).

The Demographic Divide

High- and low-income nations display very different population dynamics, a gap that is sometimes called the *demographic divide.* In Italy, a high-income nation with very low growth, women average just over one child in their lifetimes. Such a low birthrate means that the number of annual births is less than the number of deaths. This means that at the moment, Italy is actually *losing* population. Looking ahead to 2050, and even assuming some gains from immigration, Italy's population is projected to be about the same as it is today. But the share of elderly people in Italy—now 20 percent—will only increase as time goes on.

How different the patterns are in a low-income nation such as the Democratic Republic of the Congo. There, women still average six to seven children, so even with a high mortality rate, this nation's population will triple by 2050. The share of elderly people is extremely low—about 3 percent—and half that country's people are below the age of fifteen. With such a high growth rate, it is no surprise that the problem of poverty is bad and getting worse: About three-fourths of the people are undernourished (Population Reference Bureau, 2009).

In sum, a demographic divide now separates rich countries with low birth rates and aging populations from poor countries with high birth rates and very young population. Just as humanity has devised ways to reduce deaths around the world, it must now bring down population growth, especially in poor countries where projections suggest a future as bleak as that imagined by Thomas Malthus centuries ago.

China stands out as a nation that that has taken a strong stand on reducing population increase. That country's one-child policy, enacted back in the 1970s, has reduced China's population by about 250 million. Yet as the Thinking About Diversity box on page 576 explains, this policy has been controversial.

Urbanization: The Growth of Cities

October 8, Hong Kong. The cable train grinds to the top of Victoria Peak, where we behold one of the world's most spectacular vistas: the city of Hong Kong at night! A million bright, colorful lights ring the harbor as ships,

Fertility in the United States has fallen during the past century and is now quite low. But some categories of the U.S. population have much higher fertility rates. One example is the Amish, a religious society living in rural areas of Ohio, Pennsylvania, and other states. It is common for Amish couples to have five, six, or more children. Why do you think the Amish favor large families?

ferries, and traditional Chinese junks slowly slip by. Day or night, few places match Hong Kong for sheer energy: This small city is as economically productive as the state of Wisconsin or the nation of Finland. We could sit here for hours entranced by the spectacle of Hong Kong.

Throughout most of human history, the sights and sounds of great cities such as Hong Kong, Paris, and New York were simply unimaginable. Our distant ancestors lived in small, nomadic groups, moving as they depleted vegetation or hunted migratory game. The tiny settlements that marked the emergence of civilization in the Middle East some 12,000 years ago held only a small fraction of Earth's people. Today, the largest three or four cities of the world hold as many people as the entire planet did back then.

Urbanization is *the concentration of population into cities.* Urbanization redistributes population within a society and transforms many patterns of social life. We will trace these changes in terms of three urban revolutions: the emergence of cities 10,000 years ago, the development of industrial cities after 1750, and the explosive growth of cities in poor countries today.

The Evolution of Cities

Cities are a relatively new development in human history. Only about 12,000 years ago did our ancestors begin living in permanent settlements, which set the stage for the *first urban revolution.*

Q: "Although individual women [worldwide] are having fewer children, on average, than their mothers, there are simply more women having children, resulting in continuing increases in additions to world population." Population Reference Bureau

Q: "The central problem of the sociologist of the city is to discover the forms of social action and organization that typically emerge in relatively permanent, compact settlements of large numbers of heterogeneous individuals." Louis Wirth (1938)

Q: "The main population of the city that boasted its world conquests lived in cramped, noisy, airless, foul smelling, infected quarters, paying extortionate rents to merciless landlords, undergoing daily indignities and terrors that coarsened and brutalized them." Lewis Mumford (1961:221)

SEEING SOCIOLOGY
in Everyday Life

With global population increasing, would you support expanding the one-child policy to other countries? Why or why not?

THINKING ABOUT DIVERSITY: RACE, CLASS, & GENDER

Where Are the Girls? China's One-Child Policy

The parents had argued for hours. But Yang, the father, was determined, and Jianying, the mother, was exhausted. Finally, Yang wrested the baby from Jianying's arms. The decision was made; the girl had to go. Yang put several extra layers of clothing on his daughter and lay the newborn in a cardboard box lined with blankets. Next to her, he placed a small bottle of milk. Then Yang lifted the box and carried it off into the dark night toward the distant village, leaving behind his wife sobbing, "Yang, I beg you, bring back my baby!"

Yet in her heart, she too knew that this must be done. Half an hour later, Yang arrived in the village and found his way to the local school. He kissed his daughter goodbye and set her makeshift crib on the steps of the school, knowing that when dawn broke she would be found by school officials and cared for. With tears in his eyes, Yang said a quick prayer to his ancestors to keep the baby safe from harm. Then he turned and again disappeared into the night, knowing that he would never see or hear from her again.

This story may be heartbreaking, but it is one that has occurred tens of thousands of times in China. What would prompt parents to give up a child? Why would a father abandon his daughter in a public place? The answer lies in China's population control policy and the nation's cultural traditions.

Back in the 1970s, the high Chinese birth rate was fueling a rapid population increase. Government leaders could see that the country's economic development depended on controlling population growth. As a result, they passed a law stating that a family can have only one child. Couples who follow the one-child policy can expect rewards such as a better job, a higher salary, and maybe even a larger apartment. On the other hand, parents who violate the law by having a second child face a stiff fine, and their second child may not be eligible for educational and health care benefits.

The government actively promotes the one-child message in the mass media, in popular songs, and in the schools. But education is not the government's only tactic; enforcement officials can be found in most neighborhoods and workplaces. Most Chinese willingly comply with the policy, praising it as good for the country. Those who do not must face the consequences.

Modern China is determined to control population increase. But China is also a country steeped in a tradition of male dominance. If government rules permit only one child, most families would prefer a boy. Why? Parents see boys as a better investment because sons will carry on the family name and will honor the obligation to care for their aging parents. On the other hand, girls will end up caring for their *husbands'* parents, leading most Chinese to see raising daughters as a waste of precious resources. The Chinese government has expanded women's rights and opportunities, but patriarchal traditions are deeply rooted in the country's history, and attitudes change slowly.

Around the world, the one-child policy has attracted both praise and condemnation. On the positive side, analysts agree that it has succeeded in its goal of reducing the rate of population increase. This trend, in turn, has helped raise living standards and lifted China to the ranks of middle-income nations. Many one-child families are happy with the added income from women who now work outside the home, and parents now have more to spend on a child's schooling.

But the one-child policy also has a dark side, which is shown in the story that began this box. Since the law was passed, as many as 1 million girls have "disappeared." In some cases, parents who learn the woman is carrying a female fetus may choose abortion so they can "try again." In other cases, family members decide to kill a female infant soon after birth. In still other cases, girls survive but are never recorded in the birth statistics, so that parents can try again to have a son. Such girls grow up as "noncitizens" who can never go to school or receive treatment at a local health clinic. Finally, some parents, like those described earlier, give up or abandon their daughter in the hope that the child may find a home elsewhere.

China's one-child policy has certainly held population increase in check. But it has had a dramatic toll on the female population of China. In one recent year, the nation's birth records showed almost 1 million fewer girls than boys. The Chinese population is now about 250 million lower than it would have been without the one-child policy, but the country's population is also steadily becoming more and more male.

WHAT DO YOU THINK?

1. Point to the reasons China's one-child policy has attracted praise and also blame. On balance, do you think this is a good policy? Can you think of a better way to control population? Explain.

2. What about cases where parents think they can afford additional children? Should family size be a couple's decision? Or does government have a responsibility to look out for the entire country's well-being?

3. Do you now understand why almost all of the babies U.S. parents adopt from China are girls?

China's one-child policy is advertised on billboards throughout the country.

Sources: Hesketh, Lu, & Xing (2005), Baochang et al. (2007), and Yardley (2008).

Q: "The bourgeoisie has subjected the country to the rule of the towns. It has created enormous cities, has greatly increased the urban population as compared to the rural, and has thus rescued a considerable part of the population from the idiocy of rural life." Karl Marx and Friedrich Engels

GLOBAL: London was the first city to reach 2 million population, about 1840; by 1900, only 4 cities had this number of people (London, Berlin, Paris, and New York). In 1985, there were 85 cities with 2 million or more people; by 2009, 206 cities were over this mark.

NOTE: Urban growth late in the 19th century was nothing less than staggering, contributing to the birth of urban sociology. Chicago, the first city of urban sociology, grew 12-fold between 1870 and 1920.

● SEEING SOCIOLOGY
in Everyday Life

As the sections describing preindustrial and industrial cities explain, the size and shape of a city provide clues to a society's technology and culture.

The First Cities

As explained in Chapter 4 ("Society"), hunting and gathering forced people to move all the time; however, once our ancestors discovered how to domesticate animals and cultivate crops, they were able to stay in one place. Raising their own food also created a material surplus, which freed some people from food production and allowed them to build shelters, make tools, weave cloth, and take part in religious rituals. The emergence of cities led to both higher living standards and job specialization.

The first city that we know of was Jericho, which lies to the north of the Dead Sea in what is now the West Bank. When first settled some 10,000 years ago, it was home to only 600 people. But as the centuries passed, cities grew to tens of thousands of people and became the centers of vast empires. By 3000 B.C.E., Egyptian cities flourished, as did cities in China about 2000 B.C.E. and in Central and South America about 1500 B.C.E. In North America, however, only a few Native American societies formed settlements; widespread urbanization had to await the arrival of European settlers in the seventeenth century.

Preindustrial European Cities

European cities date back some 5,000 years to the Greeks and later the Romans, both of whom created great empires and founded cities across Europe, including Vienna, Paris, and London. With the fall of the Roman Empire, the so-called Dark Ages began as people withdrew into defensive walled settlements and warlords battled for territory. Only in the eleventh century did Europe become more peaceful; trade flourished once again, allowing cities to grow.

Medieval cities were quite different from those familiar to us today. Beneath towering cathedrals, the narrow and winding streets of London, Brussels, and Florence teemed with merchants, artisans, priests, peddlers, jugglers, nobles, and servants. Occupational groups such as bakers, carpenters, and metalworkers clustered together in distinct sections or "quarters." Ethnicity also defined communities as residents tried to keep out people who differed from themselves. The term "ghetto" (from the Italian *borghetto,* meaning "outside the city walls") was first used to describe the neighborhood in which the Jews of Venice were segregated.

Industrial European Cities

As the Middle Ages came to a close, steadily increasing commerce enriched a new urban middle class, or *bourgeoisie* (French, meaning "townspeople"). With more and more money, the bourgeoisie soon rivaled the hereditary aristocracy.

By about 1750, the Industrial Revolution triggered a *second urban revolution,* first in Europe and then in North America. Factories unleashed tremendous productive power, causing cities to grow bigger than ever before. London, the largest European city, reached 550,000 people by 1700 and exploded to 6.5 million by 1900 (A. F. Weber, 1963, orig. 1899; Chandler & Fox, 1974).

Cities not only grew but changed shape as well. Older winding streets gave way to broad, straight boulevards to handle the increasing flow of commercial traffic. Steam and electric trolleys soon crisscrossed the expanding cities. Because land was now a commodity to be bought and sold, developers divided cities into regular-sized lots (Mumford, 1961). The center of the city was no longer the cathedral but a bustling central business district filled with banks, retail stores, and tall office buildings.

With a new focus on business, cities became more crowded and impersonal. Crime rates rose. Especially at the outset, a few industrialists lived in grand style, but most men, women, and children barely survived by working in factories.

Organized efforts by workers to improve their lives eventually brought changes to the workplace, better housing, and the right to vote. Public services such as water, sewer systems, and electricity further improved urban living. Today, some urbanites still live in poverty, but a rising standard of living has partly fulfilled the city's historical promise of a better life.

The Growth of U.S. Cities

Most of the Native Americans who inhabited North America for thousands of years before the arrival of Europeans were migratory people who formed few permanent settlements. The spread of villages and towns came after European colonization.

Colonial Settlement, 1565–1800

In 1565, the Spanish built a settlement at Saint Augustine, Florida, and in 1607, the English founded Jamestown, Virginia. The first lasting settlement came in 1624, when the Dutch established New Amsterdam, later renamed New York.

New York and Boston (founded by the English in 1630) started out as tiny villages in a vast wilderness. They resembled medieval towns in Europe, with narrow, winding streets that still curve through lower Manhattan and downtown Boston. When the first census was completed in 1790, as Table 22–1 on page 578 shows, just 5 percent of the nation's people lived in cities.

Urban Expansion, 1800–1860

Early in the nineteenth century, as cities along the East Coast grew bigger, towns sprang up along the transportation routes that opened the American West. By 1860, Buffalo, Cleveland, Detroit, and Chicago were changing the face of the Midwest, and about one-fifth of the U.S. population lived in cities.

Urban expansion was greatest in the northern states; New York City, for example, had ten times the population of Charleston, South

NOTE: Cities grew upward, propelled by advances in building technology. In 1848, 5-story iron frame buildings were big news; by 1884, a steel structure in Chicago reached 10 stories, and buildings began to use elevators (devised in the 1850s). By 1900, skylines reached 30 stories and, on the eve of World War I, New York had 61 buildings more than 20 stories tall. Today, Taiwan's Taipei 101 Tower is the world's tallest (1,482 feet). Next world's tallest: Burj Dubai. The technology exists to raise towers to a mile or more, restrained by high cost, the inability to control fire, and people's general reluctance to live that high above the ground.

metropolis a large city that socially and economically dominates an urban area

suburbs urban areas beyond the political boundaries of a city

megalopolis a vast urban region containing a number of cities and their surrounding suburbs

SEEING SOCIOLOGY
in Everyday Life

Is there a class difference in people's use of the streets as a place to meet and greet others? For example, do you think working-class people are more likely to use the streets in this way than middle-class suburbanites?

Table 22–1   Urban Population of the United States, 1790–2000

Year	Population (in millions)	Percentage Living in Cities
1790	3.9	5.1%
1800	5.3	6.1
1820	9.6	7.3
1840	17.1	10.5
1860	31.4	19.7
1880	50.2	28.1
1900	76.0	39.7
1920	105.7	51.3
1940	131.7	56.5
1960	179.3	69.9
1980	226.5	73.7
2000	281.4	79.0

Source: U.S. Census Bureau (2009).

Carolina. The division of the United States into the industrial-urban North and the agrarian-rural South was one major cause of the Civil War (Schlesinger, 1969).

The Metropolitan Era, 1860–1950

The Civil War (1861–65) gave an enormous boost to urbanization as factories strained to produce weapons. Waves of people deserted the countryside for cities in hopes of finding better jobs. Joining them were tens of millions of immigrants, mostly from Europe, forming a culturally diverse urban mix.

In 1900, New York's population soared past the 4 million mark, and Chicago, a city of only 100,000 people in 1860, was closing in on 2 million. Such growth marked the era of the **metropolis** (from the Greek, meaning "mother city"), *a large city that socially and economically dominates an urban area.* Metropolises became the economic centers of the United States. By 1920, urban areas were home to a majority of the U.S. population.

Industrial technology pushed the urban skyline ever higher. In the 1880s, steel girders and mechanical elevators permitted buildings to rise more than ten stories high. In 1930, New York's Empire State Building was hailed as an urban wonder, reaching 102 stories into the clouds.

Urban Decentralization, 1950–Present

The industrial metropolis reached its peak about 1950. Since then, something of a turnaround—termed *urban decentralization*—has occurred as people have left downtown areas for outlying **suburbs,** *urban areas beyond the political boundaries of a city.* The old industrial cities of the Northeast and Midwest stopped growing, and some lost considerable population in the decades after 1950. At the same time,

suburban populations increased rapidly. The urban landscape of densely packed central cities evolved into sprawling suburban regions.

Suburbs and Urban Decline

Imitating the European aristocracy, some of the rich had town houses in the city as well as large country homes beyond the city limits. But not until after World War II did ordinary people find a suburban home within their reach. With more and more cars in circulation, new four-lane highways, government-backed mortgages, and inexpensive tract homes, the suburbs grew rapidly. By 1999, most of the U.S. population lived in the suburbs and shopped at nearby malls rather than in the older and more distant downtown shopping districts (Pederson, Smith, & Adler, 1999; Macionis & Parrillo, 2010).

As many older cities of the Snowbelt—the Northeast and Midwest—lost higher-income taxpayers to the suburbs, they struggled to pay for expensive social programs for the poor who remained. Many cities fell into financial crisis, and urban decay became severe. Soon the inner city came to be synonymous with slums, crime, drugs, unemployment, poverty, and minorities.

The urban critic Paul Goldberger (2002) points out that the decline of central cities has also led to a decline in the importance of public space. Historically, the heart of city life was played out on the streets. The French word for a sophisticated person is *boulevardier,* which literally means "street person"—a term that has a negative meaning in the United States today. The active life that once took place on public streets and in public squares now takes place in shopping malls, the lobbies of cineplex theaters, and gated residential communities—all privately owned spaces. Further reducing the vitality of today's urban places is the spread of television, the Internet, and other media that people use without leaving home.

Postindustrial Sunbelt Cities

As older Snowbelt cities fell into decline, Sunbelt cities in the South and the West began to grow rapidly. The soaring populations of cities such as Los Angeles and Houston reflect a population shift to the Sunbelt, where 60 percent of U.S. people now live. In addition, most of today's immigrants enter the country in the Sunbelt region. In 1950, nine of the ten biggest U.S. cities were in the Snowbelt; in 2007, seven of the top ten were in the Sunbelt (U.S. Census Bureau, 2008).

Unlike their colder counterparts, Sunbelt cities came of age after urban decentralization began. So although cities like Chicago have long been enclosed by a ring of politically independent suburbs, cities like Houston have pushed their boundaries outward to include suburban communities. Chicago covers 227 square miles; Houston is more than twice that size, and the greater Houston urban area covers almost 9,000 square miles—an area the size of the state of New Jersey.

○ MAKING THE GRADE

The megalopolis, edge cities, and the "rural rebound" are all aspects of population decentralization as cities spread outward after 1950.

The great sprawl of Sunbelt cities has drawbacks. Many people in cities such as Atlanta, Dallas, Phoenix, and Los Angeles complain that unplanned growth results in traffic-clogged roads, poorly planned housing developments, and schools that cannot keep up with the inflow of children. Not surprisingly, voters in many communities across the United States have passed ballot initiatives seeking to limit urban sprawl (Lacayo, 1999; Romero & Liserio, 2002; W. Sullivan, 2007).

Megalopolis: The Regional City

Another result of urban decentralization is urban regions or regional cities. The U.S. Census Bureau (2009) recognizes 374 *metropolitan statistical areas* (MSAs). Each includes at least one city with 50,000 or more people. The bureau also recognizes 579 *micropolitan statistical areas*, urban areas with at least one city of 10,000 to 50,000 people. *Core-based statistical areas* (CBSAs) include both metropolitan and micropolitan statistical areas.

The biggest CBSAs contain millions of people and cover large areas that extend into several states. In 2008, the largest MSA was New York and its adjacent urban areas in Long Island, western Connecticut, northern New Jersey, and eastern Pennsylvania, with a total population of 22 million. Next in size is the CBSA in southern California that includes Los Angeles, Riverside, and Long Beach, with a population of almost 18 million.

As regional cities grow, they begin to overlap. In the early 1960s, the French geographer Jean Gottmann (1961) coined the term **megalopolis** to designate *a vast urban region containing a number of cities and their surrounding suburbs*. Along the East Coast, a 400-mile megalopolis stretches all the way from New England to Virginia. Other supercities cover the eastern coast of Florida and stretch from Cleveland west to Chicago.

Edge Cities

Urban decentralization has also created *edge cities*, business centers some distance from the old downtowns. Edge cities—a mix of corporate office buildings, shopping malls, hotels, and entertainment complexes—differ from suburbs, which contain mostly homes. The population of suburbs peaks at night, but the population of edge cities peaks during the workday.

As part of expanding urban regions, most edge cities have no clear physical boundaries. Some do have names, including Las Colinas (near the Dallas–Fort Worth airport), Tyson's Corner (in Virginia, near Washington, D.C.), and King of Prussia (northwest of Philadelphia). Other edge cities are known only by the major

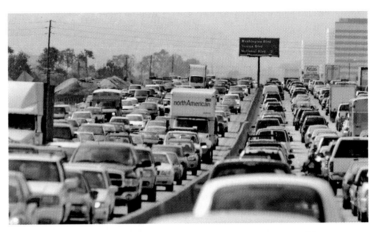

In recent decades, many U.S. cities in the Sunbelt have spread outward in a process called urban sprawl. Los Angeles, for example, now covers about 500 square miles, and even with a vast system of freeways, people moving around the city often find themselves stuck in slow-moving traffic. What are other disadvantages of urban sprawl?

highways that flow through them, including Route 1 in Princeton, New Jersey, and Route 128 near Boston (Garreau, 1991; Macionis & Parrillo, 2010).

The Rural Rebound

Over the course of U.S. history, as shown by the data in Table 22–1, the urban population of the nation has increased steadily. Immigration has played a part in this increase because most newcomers settle in cities. At the same time, there has been considerable migration from rural areas to urban places, typically by people seeking greater social, educational, and economic opportunity.

However, since about 1990, three-fourths of the rural counties across the United States gained population, a trend analysts have called the "rural rebound." Most of this gain resulted from the migration of people from urban areas. This trend has not affected all rural places: As the opening to this chapter explains, many small towns in rural areas (especially in the Plains States) are struggling to stay alive. But even there, losses slowed during the 1990s.

The greatest gains have come to rural communities that offer scenic and recreational attractions, such as lakes, mountains, and ski areas. People are drawn to rural communities not only by their natural beauty but also by their slower pace of life: less traffic, less crime, and cleaner air. A number of companies have relocated to rural counties, which has increased economic opportunity for the rural population (K. M. Johnson, 1999; Johnson & Fuguitt, 2000; D. Johnson, 2001).

NOTE: As part of the rural rebound, average time driving to work rose. New York became the first state where residents had a one-way commute that averaged more than half an hour.

Q: "In *Gemeinschaft* [people] remain essentially united in spite of all separating factors, whereas in *Gesellschaft* they are essentially separated in spite of all uniting factors." Ferdinand Tönnies

Q: "Empirically, pure *Gemeinschaft* is impossible, because all *Gemeinschaften* have rational aspects; likewise, pure *Gesellschaft* is impossible, because man's social conduct can never be entirely determined by intellect and reason." Rudolf Heberle

POP CULTURE: Seeking community is an important theme of popular culture. In the 1980s and 1990s, the rave phenomenon was popular among young people seeking a short-lived experience of *Gemeinschaft* or mechanical solidarity.

Gemeinschaft a type of social organization in which people are closely tied by kinship and tradition

Gesellschaft a type of social organization in which people come together only on the basis of individual self-interest

SEEING SOCIOLOGY
in Everyday Life

How might Tönnies explain social patterns such as our high rate of divorce, widespread fear of crime, and incidents of "road rage" on the highways?

The rural rebound has been most pronounced in towns that offer spectacular natural beauty. There are times when people living in the scenic town of Park City, Utah, cannot even find a parking space.

Urbanism as a Way of Life

Early sociologists in Europe and the United States focused their attention on the rise of cities and how urban life differed from rural life. We briefly examine their accounts of urbanism as a way of life.

Ferdinand Tönnies: *Gemeinschaft* and *Gesellschaft*

In the late nineteenth century, the German sociologist Ferdinand Tönnies (1855–1937) studied how life in the new industrial metropolis differed from life in rural villages. From this contrast, he developed two concepts that have become a lasting part of sociology's terminology.

Tönnies (1963, orig. 1887) used the German word **Gemeinschaft** ("community") to refer to *a type of social organization in which people are closely tied by kinship and tradition.* The *Gemeinschaft* of the rural village joins people in what amounts to a single primary group.

By and large, argued Tönnies, *Gemeinschaft* is absent in the modern city. On the contrary, urbanization creates **Gesellschaft** ("association"), *a type of social organization in which people come together only on the basis of individual self-interest.* In the *Gesellschaft* way of life, individuals are motivated by their own needs rather than by a desire to help improve the well-being of everyone. By and large, city dwellers have little sense of community or common identity and look to others mainly when they need something. Tönnies saw in urbanization a weakening of close, long-lasting social relations in favor of the brief and impersonal ties or secondary relationships typical of business.

Emile Durkheim: Mechanical and Organic Solidarity

The French sociologist Emile Durkheim (see Chapter 4, "Society") agreed with much of Tönnies's thinking about cities. However, Durkheim countered that urbanites do not lack social bonds; they simply organize social life differently than rural people.

Durkheim described traditional, rural life as *mechanical solidarity,* social bonds based on common sentiments and shared moral values. With its emphasis on tradition, Durkheim's concept of mechanical solidarity bears a striking similarity to Tönnies's *Gemeinschaft.* Urbanization erodes mechanical solidarity, Durkheim explained, but it also generates a new type of bonding, which he called *organic solidarity,* social bonds based on specialization and interdependence. This concept, which parallels Tönnies's *Gesellschaft,* reveals an important difference between the two thinkers. Both thought the growth of industrial cities weakened tradition, but Durkheim optimistically pointed to a new kind of solidarity. Where societies had been built on *likeness* (mechanical solidarity), Durkheim now saw social life based on *difference* (organic solidarity).

For Durkheim, urban society offered more individual choice, moral tolerance, and personal privacy than people find in rural villages. In sum, Durkheim thought that something is lost in the process of urbanization, but much is gained.

Georg Simmel: The Blasé Urbanite

The German sociologist Georg Simmel (1858–1918) offered a microanalysis of cities, studying how urban life shapes the everyday experience of individuals. According to Simmel, individuals perceive the city as a crush of people, objects, and events. To prevent being overwhelmed by all this stimulation, urbanites develop a *blasé attitude,* tuning out

Q: "Thus the metropolitan type of man ... develops an organ protecting him against the threatening currents and discrepancies of his external environment which would uproot him. He reacts with his head instead of his heart." Georg Simmel

Q: "The city, and particularly the great city, is ... where human relationships are likely to be impersonal and rational, defined in terms of interest and in terms of cash." Robert Park

Q: "Characteristically, urbanites meet one another in highly segmental roles. They are, to be sure, dependent on more people for the satisfactions of their life needs than are rural people ... but they are less dependent upon particular persons, and their dependence upon others is confined to a highly fractionalized aspect of the other's round of activity. This is essentially what is meant by saying that the city is characterized by secondary rather than primary contacts." Louis Wirth

SEEING SOCIOLOGY
in Everyday Life

How would Simmel explain cases of people turning away from others in need on the grounds that they simply "don't want to get involved"?

MAKING THE GRADE

Tönnies's concept of *Gemeinschaft* corresponds to Durkheim's mechanical solidarity; *Gesellschaft* corresponds to organic solidarity.

Peasant Dance (left, c. 1565), by Pieter Breughel the Elder, conveys the essential unity of rural life forged by generations of kinship and neighborhood. By contrast, Lily Furedi's *Subway (right)* communicates the impersonality common to urban areas. Taken together, these paintings capture Tönnies's distinction between *Gemeinschaft* and *Gesellschaft.*

Pieter Breughel the Elder (c. 1525/30–1569), *Peasant Dance,* c. 1565, Kunsthistorisches Museum, Vienna/Superstock. Lily Furedi, American. *Subway.* Oil on canvas, 99 x 123 cm. National Collection of Fine Arts, Washington, D.C./Smithsonian Institute.

much of what goes on around them. Such detachment does not mean that city dwellers lack compassion for others; they simply keep their distance as a survival strategy so that they can focus their time and energy on the people and things that really matter to them.

The Chicago School: Robert Park and Louis Wirth

Sociologists in the United States soon joined the study of rapidly growing cities. Robert Park, a leader of the first U.S. sociology program at the University of Chicago, sought to add a street-level perspective by getting out and studying real cities. As he said of himself, "I suspect that I have actually covered more ground, tramping about in cities in different parts of the world, than any other living man" (1950:viii). Walking the streets, Park found the city to be an organized mosaic of distinctive ethnic communities, commercial centers, and industrial districts. Over time, he observed, these "natural areas" develop and change in relation to one another. To Park, the city was a living organism—a human kaleidoscope.

Another major figure in the Chicago School of urban sociology was Louis Wirth (1897–1952). Wirth (1938) is best known for blending the ideas of Tönnies, Durkheim, Simmel, and Park into a comprehensive theory of urban life.

Wirth began by defining the city as a setting with a large, dense, and socially diverse population. These traits result in an impersonal, superficial, and transitory way of life. Living among millions

of others, urbanites come into contact with many more people than residents of rural areas. So when city people notice others at all, they usually know them not in terms of *who they are* but *what they do*—as, for instance, the bus driver, the florist, or the grocery store clerk. Specialized urban relationships are pleasant for all concerned, but self-interest rather than friendship is usually the main reason behind the interaction.

The impersonal nature of urban relationships, together with the great social diversity found in cities today, makes city dwellers more tolerant than rural villagers. Rural communities often jealously enforce their narrow traditions, but the heterogeneous population of a city rarely shares any single code of moral conduct (T. C. Wilson, 1985, 1995).

CRITICAL REVIEW In both Europe and the United States, early sociologists presented a mixed view of urban living. Rapid urbanization troubled Tönnies, and Wirth saw personal ties and traditional morality lost in the anonymous rush of the city. Durkheim and Park emphasized urbanism's positive face, pointing to more personal freedom and greater personal choice.

One problem with all these views is that they paint urbanism in broad strokes that overlook the effects of class, race, and gender. There are many kinds of urbanites—rich and poor, black and white, Anglo and Latino, women and men—all leading distinctive lives (Gans, 1968). As the Thinking About Diversity box on page 582 explains, the share of minorities in the largest U.S.

Q: "Having seen it, I urgently desire never to see it again. It is inhabited by savages." Rudyard Kipling, on Chicago

Q: "We must restore to the city the maternal, life-nurturing functions, the autonomous activities, the symbiotic associations that have been neglected or suppressed. For the city should be an organ of love." Lewis Mumford (1961:575)

DIVERSITY: Age cohorts play a part in the trend toward the coming "minority majority." Among people under 35 years of age, 42 percent are minorities; above 35, 27 percent are minorities.

GLOBAL: In the U.S., "urban" means living in a settlement of at least 2,500 people; in some nations, urban refers to smaller villages. In Colombia, urban places are as small as 1,500 people.

urban ecology the study of the link between the physical and social dimensions of cities

THINKING ABOUT DIVERSITY: RACE, CLASS, & GENDER

Minorities Now a Majority in the Largest U.S. Cities

According to the results of the 2000 census, minorities—Hispanics, African Americans, and Asians—are now a majority of the population in 48 of the 100 largest U.S. cities, up from 30 in 1990.

What accounts for the change? One reason is that large cities have been losing their non-Hispanic white population. Santa Ana, California, for example, lost 38 percent of its 1990 white population; the drop was 40 percent in Birmingham, Alabama, and a whopping 53 percent in Detroit, Michigan. The white share of the population of all 100 of the largest cities fell from 52.1 percent in 1990 to 43.8 percent in 2000, as the figure shows.

But an even bigger reason for the minority-majority trend is the increase in immigration. Immigration, coupled with higher birth rates among new immigrants, resulted in a 43 percent gain in the Hispanic population (almost 4 million people) of the largest 100 cities between 1990 and 2000. The Asian population also surged by 40 percent (more than 1.1 million people). The

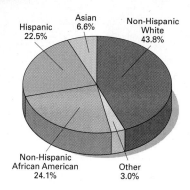

Population Profile for the 100 Largest U.S. Cities, 2000

Racial and ethnic minorities make up a majority of the population of this country's 100 largest cities.

Source: U.S. Census Bureau (2001).

African American population was steady over the course of the 1990s. Political officials and other policymakers have been watching these figures closely, for the future vitality of the largest U.S. cities depends on meeting the needs and welcoming the contributions of the swelling minority populations.

WHAT DO YOU THINK?

1. Why are the minority populations of large U.S. cities increasing?

2. What positive changes and what challenges does a minority majority bring to a city?

3. Before Hurricane Katrina, African Americans represented 60 percent of the population of New Orleans; afterward, the share was about 40 percent. What difference might this change make in the city's immediate future?

Sources: Schmitt (2001) and U.S. Census Bureau (2008).

cities increased sharply during the 1990s. We see social diversity most clearly in cities, where various categories of people are large enough to form distinct, visible communities (Macionis & Parrillo, 2010).

○ **CHECK YOUR LEARNING** Of these urban sociologists—Tönnies, Durkheim, Park, and Wirth—which were more positive about urban life? Which were more negative? In each case, explain why.

Urban Ecology

Sociologists (especially members of the Chicago School) developed **urban ecology,** *the study of the link between the physical and social dimensions of cities.* One issue of interest to urban ecologists is why cities are located where they are. Broadly speaking, the first cities emerged in fertile regions where the ecology favored raising crops. In addition, preindustrial people were concerned with defense, so they built their cities on mountains (ancient Athens was perched on an outcropping of rock) or surrounded by water (Paris and Mexico City

were founded on islands). With the coming of the Industrial Revolution, economic considerations gained importance, which explains why all the major U.S. cities were situated near rivers or natural harbors that facilitated trade.

Urban ecologists also study the physical design of cities. In 1925, Ernest W. Burgess, a student and colleague of Robert Park's, described land use in Chicago in terms of *concentric zones.* City centers, Burgess observed, are business districts bordered by a ring of factories, followed by residential rings with housing that becomes more expensive the farther it is from the noise and pollution of the city's center.

Homer Hoyt (1939) refined Burgess's observations, noting that distinctive districts sometimes form *wedge-shaped sectors.* For example, one fashionable area may develop next to another, or an industrial district may extend outward from a city's center along a train or trolley line.

Chauncy Harris and Edward Ullman (1945) added yet another insight: As cities decentralize, they lose their single-center form in favor of a *multicentered model.* As cities grow, residential areas, indus-

RESOURCE: The author's companion reader *Seeing Ourselves*, 8th ed., includes three urban classics: Ferdinand Tönnies's "*Gemeinschaft* and *Gesellschaft*," Georg Simmel's "The Metropolis and Mental Life," and Louis Wirth's "Urbanism as a Way of Life."

THEN AND NOW: Share of U.S. population by region, *1900*: Northeast, 28%; Midwest, 34%; South, 32%; West, 6%; *2000*: Northeast, 19%; Midwest, 23%; South, 36%; West, 22% (U.S. Census Bureau).

NOTE: The criticism that urban ecology ignores the role of political and economic elites stands at the core of what has become known as the "new" urban sociology.

SEEING SOCIOLOGY
in Everyday Life

The decline of industrial production is evident in the decline of industrial cities, such as Detroit.

trial parks, and shopping districts typically push away from one another. Few people wish to live close to industrial areas, for example, so the city becomes a mosaic of distinct districts.

Social area analysis investigates what people in particular neighborhoods have in common. Three factors seem to explain most of the variation: family patterns, social class, and race and ethnicity (Shevky & Bell, 1955; Johnston, 1976). Families with children look for areas with single-family homes or large apartments and good schools. The rich seek high-prestige neighborhoods, often in the central city near cultural attractions. People with a common race or ethnic heritage tend to cluster in distinctive communities.

Brian Berry and Philip Rees (1969) tie together many of these insights. They explain that distinct family types tend to settle in the concentric zones described by Burgess. Specifically, households with many children tend to live in the outer areas of a city, while "young singles" cluster toward the city's center. Social class differences are primarily responsible for the sector-shaped districts described by Hoyt—for instance, the rich occupy one "side of the tracks" and the poor the other. And racial and ethnic neighborhoods are found at various points throughout the city, consistent with Harris and Ullman's multicentered model.

The industrial revolution created great cities across the United States. In recent decades, however, the movement of industry abroad has brought decline to Detroit and other older cities in the "rustbelt." From this abandoned warehouse, we see the headquarters of General Motors, which, in 2009, declared bankruptcy. What do you see as the future of such cities?

Urban Political Economy

In the late 1960s, many large U.S. cities were rocked by riots. In the wake of this unrest, some analysts turned away from the ecological approach to a social-conflict understanding of city life. The *urban political economy* model applies Karl Marx's analysis of conflict in the workplace to conflict in the city (Lindstrom, 1995).

Political economists reject the ecological approach's view of the city as a natural organism with particular districts and neighborhoods developing according to an internal logic. They claim that city life is defined by larger institutional structures, especially the economy. Capitalism, which transforms the city into real estate traded for profit and concentrates wealth and power in the hands of the few, is the key to understanding city life. From this point of view, for example, the decline in industrial Snowbelt cities after 1950 was the result of deliberate decisions by the corporate elite to move their production facilities to the Sunbelt (where labor is cheaper and less likely to be unionized) or to move them out of the country entirely to low-income nations (Molotch, 1976; Castells, 1977, 1983; Lefebvre, 1991; Jones & Wilson, 1999).

CRITICAL REVIEW The fact that many U.S. cities are in crisis, with widespread poverty, high crime, and barely functioning schools, seems to favor the political economy model over the urban ecology approach. But one criticism applies to both: They

focus on U.S. cities during a limited period of history. Much of what we know about industrial cities does not apply to preindustrial U.S. towns in our own past or to the rapidly growing cities in many poor nations today. It is unlikely that any single model of cities can account for the full range of urban diversity.

CHECK YOUR LEARNING In your own words, explain what the urban ecology theories and the urban political economy theory teach us about cities.

Urbanization in Poor Nations

November 16, Cairo, Egypt. People call the vast Muslim cemetery in Old Cairo the "City of the Dead". In truth, it is very much alive: Tens of thousands of squatters have moved into the mausoleums, making this place an eerie mix of life and death. Children run across the stone floors, clotheslines stretch between the monuments, and an occasional television antenna protrudes from a tomb roof. With Cairo's population increasing at the rate of 1,000 people a day, families live where they can.

GLOBAL: Selected population densities (people per square mile): Macao, 50,475; Hong Kong, 17,445; Taiwan, 1,840; Lebanon, 1,006; Israel, 1,000; India, 906; Japan, 880; Haiti, 834; U.K., 653; China, 369; Mexico, 148; U.S., 86; Brazil, 60; Canada, 10.

Q: "In the course of my own lifetime, Earth's population has increased two-and-a-half times, and most of this increase is now to be found in the exploding urban centers, especially in the slums and shantytowns of Africa, Asia, and Latin America." Isaac Asimov

ecology the study of the interaction of living organisms and the natural environment

natural environment Earth's surface and atmosphere, including living organisms, air, water, soil, and other resources necessary to sustain life

ecosystem a system composed of the interaction of all living organisms and their natural environment

environmental deficit profound long-term harm to the natural environment caused by humanity's focus on short-term material affluence

MAKING THE GRADE

Be sure you understand when and where the three urban revolutions occurred.

As noted earlier, twice in its history, the world has experienced a revolutionary expansion of cities. The first urban revolution began about 8000 B.C.E. with the first urban settlements and continued until permanent settlements were in place on several continents. About 1750, the second urban revolution took off; it lasted for two centuries as the Industrial Revolution spurred rapid growth of cities in Europe and North America.

A third urban revolution is now under way. Today, approximately 75 percent of people in industrial societies are already city dwellers. But extreme urban growth is occurring in low-income nations. In 1950, about 25 percent of the people in poor countries lived in cities. In 2008, the world became mostly urban for the first time in history with more than half of humanity living in cities (Population Reference Bureau, 2009).

Not only are more people urban; cities are also getting bigger. In 1950, only seven cities in the world had populations over 5 million, and only two of these were in low-income countries. By 2008, forty-nine cities had passed this mark, and thirty-two of them were in less developed nations (Brockerhoff, 2000; United Nations, 2008).

This third urban revolution is taking place because many poor nations have entered the high-growth Stage 2 of the demographic transition. Falling death rates have fueled population increases in Latin America, Asia, and especially Africa. For urban areas, the rate of increase is *twice* as high because in addition to natural increase, millions of people leave the countryside each year in search of jobs, health care, education, and conveniences such as running water and electricity.

Cities do offer more opportunities than rural areas, but they provide no quick fix for the massive problems of escalating population and grinding poverty. Many cities in less economically developed nations—including Mexico City, Egypt's Cairo, India's Kolkata (formerly Calcutta), and Manila in the Philippines—are simply unable to meet the basic needs of much of their populations. All these cities are surrounded by wretched shantytowns—settlements of makeshift homes built from discarded materials. As noted in Chapter 12 ("Global Stratification"), even city dumps are home to thousands of poor people, who pick through the piles of waste hoping to find enough to eat or sell to make it through another day.

Environment and Society

The human species has prospered, rapidly expanding over the entire planet. An increasing share of the global population now lives in cities, complex settlements that offer the promise of a better life than that found in rural villages.

But these advances have come at a high price. Never before in history have human beings placed such demands on the planet. This disturbing development brings us to the final section of this chapter:

the interplay between the natural environment and society. Like demography, **ecology** is another cousin of sociology, formally defined as *the study of the interaction of living organisms and the natural environment*. Ecology rests on the research of natural scientists as well as social scientists. This text focuses on the aspects of ecology that involve familiar sociological concepts and issues.

The **natural environment** is *Earth's surface and atmosphere, including living organisms, air, water, soil, and other resources necessary to sustain life*. Like every other species, humans depend on the natural environment to survive. Yet with our capacity for culture, humans stand apart from other species; we alone take deliberate action to remake the world according to our own interests and desires, for better and for worse.

Why is the environment of interest to sociologists? Simply because environmental problems, from pollution to acid rain to global warming, do not arise from the natural world operating on its own. Such problems result from the specific actions of human beings, which means they are *social* problems.

The Global Dimension

The study of the natural environment requires a global perspective. The reason is simple: Regardless of political divisions among nations, the planet is a single **ecosystem**, *a system composed of the interaction of all living organisms and their natural environment*.

The Greek meaning of *eco* is "house," reminding us that this planet is our home and that all living things and their natural environment are interrelated. A change in any part of the natural environment ripples throughout the entire global ecosystem.

Consider, from an ecological point of view, our national love of hamburgers. People in North America (and, increasingly, around the world) have created a huge demand for beef, which has greatly expanded the ranching industry in Brazil, Costa Rica, and other Latin American nations. To produce the lean meat sought by fast-food corporations, cattle in Latin America feed on grass, which uses a great deal of land. Latin American ranchers get the land for grazing by clearing thousands of square miles of forests each year. These tropical forests are vital to maintaining Earth's atmosphere. Deforestation ends up threatening everyone, including people in the United States enjoying their hamburgers (N. Myers, 1984a).

Technology and the Environmental Deficit

Sociologists point to a simple formula: $I = PAT$, where environmental impact (I) reflects a society's population (P), its level of affluence (A), and its level of technology (T). Members of societies with simple technology—the hunters and gatherers described in Chapter 4

MAKING THE GRADE

I = PAT is an important environmental idea; be sure you understand its meaning.

SEEING SOCIOLOGY
in Everyday Life

Can you identify ways in which the mass media and our popular culture (music, films, and television) encourage people to support the logic of growth?

("Society")—hardly affect the environment because they are few in number, are poor, and have only simple technology. On the contrary, nature affects their lives as they follow the migration of game, watch the rhythm of the seasons, and suffer from natural catastrophes such as fires, floods, droughts, and storms.

Societies at intermediate stages of technological development have a somewhat greater capacity to affect the environment. Such societies are both larger and richer. But the environmental impact of horticulture (small-scale farming), pastoralism (the herding of animals), and even agriculture (the use of animal-drawn plows) is limited because people still rely on muscle power for producing food and other goods.

Humans' ability to control the natural environment increased dramatically with the Industrial Revolution. Muscle power gave way to engines that burn fossil fuels: coal at first and then oil. Such machinery affects the environment in two ways: We consume more natural resources, and we release more pollutants into the atmosphere. Even more important, armed with industrial technology, we are able to bend nature to our will, tunneling through mountains, damming rivers, irrigating deserts, and drilling for oil in the arctic wilderness and on the ocean floor. This explains why people in rich nations, who represent just 22 percent of humanity, account for half of the world's energy use (World Bank, 2008).

Not only do high-income societies use more energy, but they produce 100 times more goods than people in agrarian societies do. Higher living standards in turn increase the problem of solid waste (because people ultimately throw away most of what they produce) and pollution (industrial production generates smoke and other toxic substances).

From the start, people recognized the material benefits of industrial technology. But only a century later did they begin to see the long-term effects on the natural environment. Today, we realize that the technological power to make our lives better can also put the lives of future generations at risk, and there is a national debate about how to address this issue. Seeing Sociology in the News on pages 586–87 describes one high school's efforts to address environmental issues.

Evidence is mounting that we are running up an **environmental deficit,** *profound long-term harm to the natural environment caused by humanity's focus on short-term material affluence* (Bormann, 1990). The concept of environmental deficit is important for three reasons. First, it reminds us that environmental concerns are *sociological,* reflecting societies' priorities about how people should live. Second, it suggests that much environmental damage—to the air, land, and water—is *unintended.* By focusing on the short-term benefits of, say, cutting down forests, strip mining, or using throwaway packaging, we fail to see their long-term environmental effects. Third, in some respects, the environmental deficit is *reversible.* Societies have created environmental problems but can also undo many of them.

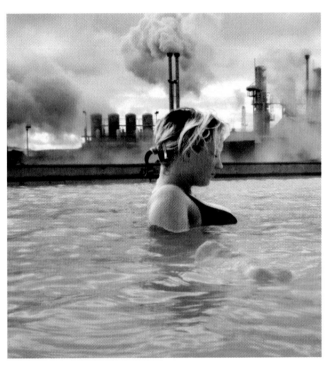

The most important insight sociology offers about our physical world is that environmental problems do not simply "happen." Rather, the state of the natural environment reflects the ways in which social life is organized—how people live and what they think is important. The greater the technological power of a society, the greater that society's ability to threaten the natural environment.

Culture: Growth and Limits

Whether we recognize environmental dangers and decide to do something about them is a cultural matter. Thus along with technology, culture has powerful environmental consequences.

The Logic of Growth

When you turn on the television news, you might hear a story like this: "The government reported bad economic news today, with the economy growing by only half a percent during the first quarter of the year." If you stop to think about it, our culture defines an economy that isn't growing as "stagnant" (which is bad) and an economy that is getting smaller as a "recession" or a "depression" (which is *very* bad). What is "good" is *growth*—the economy getting bigger and bigger. More cars, bigger homes, more income, more spending—the idea of *more* is at the heart of our cultural definition of living well (McKibben, 2007).

NOTE: Environmentalists use the term "overshoot" to refer to exceeding the carrying capacity of an environment (intentionally or otherwise).

Q: "We stand where two roads diverge. But unlike the roads in Robert Frost's poem, they are not equally fair. The road we have long been traveling is deceptively easy, a smooth superhighway on which we progress with great speed, but at its end lies disaster. The other fork in the road, the one 'less traveled by,' offers our last,

and only, chance to reach a destination that assures the preservation of our Earth." Rachel Carson (1962:277)

DISCUSS: A widespread view holds that only "modern" people are concerned about the environment. Do students agree? The conventional view is challenged by Brechin and Kempton (1994), who argue that "folk societies" are typically environmentally aware.

Seeing SOCIOLOGY in the NEWS

Boyz Under the Hood

By DAVID KUSHNER
December 18, 2008

Even among the roughest schools in the country, West Philadelphia High School stands out. Situated among boarded-up abandoned buildings and graffiti-covered crack houses, the school has had dozens of arson fires. A Spanish teacher was beaten bloody with a fire extinguisher. A music instructor got a broken jaw after being slugged by a pupil for trying to take away a cell phone. One 15-year-old girl was left for dead after having her face slashed while waiting for her school bus. She survived, but needed 114 stitches.

But in the automotive shop class in a garage next door, a group of African American students and their scrappy white teacher are making their school famous for something else: building the world's greenest car. Kids in baggy jeans and sideways hats mill around a sleek purple car they built that runs on biodiesel. Sparks fly from a chainsaw as one boy cuts through an aluminum plate, his long afro held back by the strap of his scuffed goggles.

Behind a windowed wall, half a dozen girls are busy at their iMacs. Samantha Wright ... boots up a solar charging station she designed using an image of a rundown Philadelphia parking lot from Google Earth, and augmented it with green roofs and cars. "The photoactive panels convert the sunlight into direct energy," she explains, pointing to a carport onscreen. "We're changing the world, man. I never expected to be doing that."

Like the other kids in the shop, Wright, the daughter of a phone sex worker and absentee dad, overcame incredible odds to find a haven here at the Electric Vehicle X Club, an after-school program that has been turning these cars and kids around, and that's not all. While Washington and Detroit hit the skids on delivering alternative fuel cars for the masses, these inner-city teens are churning out some of the most badass and competitive eco-wheels on the planet for as little as $15,000. As the blog Treehugger puts it, they're "sending a message to the major U.S. auto manufacturers: if we can do it, why can't you?"

In addition to clocking their suburban opponents at state science fairs, the EVX Club has crushed colleges and high-financed corporate start-ups with back-to-back titles in the coveted Northeast Sustainable Energy Association's Tour De Sol, a prestigious eco-car challenge. They modified a Saturn to run on soybean fuel, and transformed a Slovakian kit car into a wildly sporty hybrid called the Hybrid X. "Hybrids don't have to be slow and ugly like a Prius," says 18-year-old EV member, Lawrence Jones-Mahoney. "They can be efficient and cool."

Now the team is racing to prove their cars—and themselves—to the world. They're the dark horse entrants in the Progressive Automotive X-Prize: a worldwide contest to build a car, suitable for mass production, that gets 100 miles per gallon. The contest runs through summer 2010, and the winner gets $10 million....

Simon Hauger, the 38-year-old neighborhood hero who runs the West Philly High auto school, is working overtime with his students to win. But the checkered flag is theirs. "The fact that

---

One of the reasons we define growth in positive terms is that we value *material comfort,* believing that money and the things it buys improve our lives. We also believe in the idea of *progress,* thinking the future will be better than the present. In addition, we look to *science* to make our lives easier and more rewarding. In simple terms, "having things is good," "life gets better," and "people are clever." Taken together, such cultural values form the *logic of growth.*

An optimistic view of the world, the logic of growth holds that more powerful technology has improved our lives and that new discoveries will continue to do so in the future. Throughout the history of the United States and other high-income nations, the logic of growth has been the driving force behind settling the wilderness, building towns and roads, and pursuing material affluence.

However, "progress" can lead to unexpected problems, including strain on the environment. The logic of growth responds by arguing that people (especially scientists and other technology experts) will find a way out of any problem that growth places in our path. For example, before the world runs short of oil, we will come up with hydrogen, solar, or nuclear engines or some other as yet unknown technology to meet the world's energy needs.

Environmentalists counter that the logic of growth is flawed because it assumes that natural resources such as oil, clean air, fresh water, and topsoil will always be plentiful. We can and will exhaust

these *finite* resources if we continue to pursue growth at any cost. Echoing Malthus, environmentalists warn that if we call on Earth to support increasing numbers of people, we will surely deplete finite resources, destroying the environment—and ourselves—in the process.

The Limits to Growth

If we cannot invent our way out of the problems created by the logic of growth, perhaps we need another way of thinking about the world. Environmentalists therefore counter that growth must have limits. Stated simply, the *limits-to-growth thesis* is that humanity must put in place policies to control the growth of population, production, and use of resources in order to avoid environmental collapse.

In *The Limits to Growth,* a controversial book that was influential in launching the environmental movement, Donella Meadows and her colleagues (1972) used a computer model to calculate the planet's available resources, rates of population growth, amount of land available for cultivation, levels of industrial and food production, and amount of pollutants released into the atmosphere. The authors concede that any long-range predictions are speculative, and some critics think they are plain wrong (Simon, 1981). But right or wrong, the conclusions of the study call for serious consideration. First, the authors claim that we are quickly consum-

DISCUSS: Ask the class to point out specific ways in which our culture encourages economic growth. What specific changes are called for by the limits-to-growth approach?

NOTE: Discuss ways in which economic growth is understood in our culture as good. For example, news broadcasts might say, "Good news on the economic front: housing starts were up 12% in June." Never would we hear economic growth characterized as "bad."

NOTE: The *Limits to Growth* authors called themselves the "Club of Rome." Their arguments bring to mind the earlier contentions of Thomas Robert Malthus; hence, they are also known as "neo-Malthusians."

Q: "We all live downwind." Bumper sticker

we've come this far," Hauger says, looking around the room, "we've already won." . . .

When a go-kart was donated to the school, Hauger decided to start an after-school science group that would work on building an electric motor for the kart. He called it the Electric Vehicle Club. One by one, kids trickled in after school—gang members, drug dealers. One kid had a 150 IQ, but a mom on crack and a dad dying of AIDS. The kid was bouncing between foster homes and stealing credit cards on the side. But when Hauger slapped a wrench in the kid's hand, he was transformed. "When he would work on a project, he would block out all the crap in his life," Hauger recalls, "and he became a mad scientist. Working on this made all the math and science hands on." . . .

As word of Hauger's club spread, kids got turned on not only by getting under the hood, but by making cars that can better the planet—and busting labels along the way. "There's a stereotype that urban kids are just violent and don't care about anything," says Wright, "but we know the environment is important, and we can do something about it."

For the EV club's next project, they modified a silver Jeep Wrangler to go electric. Clueless how to proceed, they hit the Net—downloading instructions from an obscure eco-geek magazine called *Mother Earth*. With Hauger guiding them and improvising plenty, they ripped out the gas engine and stored 217 lead acid batteries in a custom aluminum casing. When they drove their electric hot rod Jeep into the city's science fair of microscopes and Bunsen burners, jaws dropped. "The judges didn't know what to do with it," Hauger recalls. Then they gave West Philly High the top prize. . . .

As the current 15 kids on the EVX team mill around the garage, talk turns to the plans for the Auto X prize. "As crazy as it sounds, I think we have a shot at winning," Hauger says. While the competition is focusing on high-priced cars that look like the Jetsons, the EVX team is taking a decidedly more accessible—and they hope—winning approach. . . .

. . . The EVX team's legacy is already spreading among those in the eco-car pursuit. "It's inspiring that a contest can inspire a group like that to

compete," says Darryl Siry, spokesperson for Tesla, "it says something about who they are. I recommend they not listen to people who tell them this is how it's done. Innovation comes from figuring out solutions and answers to problems in new ways."

WHAT DO YOU THINK?

1. Do you think that many people think of environmental issues as the concerns mainly of more well-off people? Explain.

2. Would you make environmental study part of the curriculum of every school in the country? Why or why not?

3. What specific strategies or policies would you suggest to encourage greater environmental understanding on the part of this country's young people?

ing Earth's finite resources. Supplies of oil, natural gas, and other energy sources are declining, and will continue to drop, a little faster or slower depending on the conservation policies of rich nations and the speed with which other nations such as India and China continue to industrialize. Within the next 100 years, resources will run out, crippling industrial output and causing a decline in food production.

This limits-to-growth theory shares Malthus's pessimism about the future. People who accept it doubt that current patterns of life are sustainable for even another century. Perhaps we all can learn to live with less. This may not be as hard as you might think: Research shows, for example, that as material consumption has gone up in recent decades, there has been no increase in levels of personal happiness (D. G. Myers, 2000). In the end, environmentalists warn, either make fundamental changes in how we live, placing less strain on the natural environment, or widespread hunger and conflict will force change on us.

Solid Waste: The Disposable Society

Across the United States, people generate a massive amount of solid waste—about 1.4 billion pounds *every day*. Figure 22–4 on page 588 shows the average composition of a typical community's trash.

As a rich nation of people who value convenience, the United States has become a *disposable society*. We consume more products than virtually any other nation, and many of these products have throwaway packaging. For example, fast food is served with cardboard, plastic, and Styrofoam containers that we throw away within minutes. Countless other products, from film to fishhooks, are elaborately packaged to make the products more attractive to the customer and to discourage tampering and theft.

Manufacturers market soft drinks, beer, and fruit juices in aluminum cans, glass jars, and plastic containers, which not only consume finite resources but also generate mountains of solid waste. Then there are countless items intentionally designed to be disposable: pens, razors, flashlights, batteries, even cameras. Other products, from light bulbs to automobiles, are designed to have a limited useful life and then become unwanted junk. As Paul Connett (1991) points out, even the words we use to describe what we throw away— *waste, litter, trash, refuse, garbage, rubbish*—show how little we value what we cannot immediately use. But this was not always the case, as the Seeing Sociology in Everyday Life box on page 589 explains.

Living in a rich society, the average person in the United States consumes hundreds of times more energy, plastics, lumber, water, and other resources than someone living in a low-income country such as Bangladesh or Tanzania and nearly twice as much as people

SOCIAL SURVEY: "It is just too difficult for someone like me to do much about the environment." (GSS 2000, *N* = 1,276; *Codebook*, 2006:1755)

"Strongly agree"	5.7%	"Disagree"	40.2%
"Agree"	21.0%	"Strongly disagree"	7.2%
"Neither agree nor disagree"	20.1%	"Don't know"/No response	6.9%

GLOBAL: Heavy reliance on landfills is typical of some industrial nations (U.S., U.K., Australia, Canada) but not others, where incineration is the favored means of disposal (Japan, Sweden, Switzerland, Luxembourg).

NOTE: In 1993, the space shuttle *Endeavour* had to change course quickly to avoid a large piece of "space junk" (an old Soviet rocket). Currently, more than 17,000 objects measuring 4 inches or more are circling Earth.

SEEING SOCIOLOGY in Everyday Life

Do you think that having more, in a materialistic sense, is the path to personal happiness? Why or why not?

SEEING SOCIOLOGY in Everyday Life

Think about how specific ways we live put more or less strain on the natural environment.

FIGURE 22–4 **Composition of Community Trash**

We throw away a wide range of material, with paper the single largest part of our trash.

Source: U.S. Environmental Protection Agency (2008).

in some other high-income countries such as Sweden and Japan. This high level of consumption means not only that we in the United States use a disproportionate share of the planet's natural resources but also that we generate most of the world's refuse.

We like to say that we throw things "away." But most of our solid waste never goes away. Rather, it ends up in landfills, which are, literally, filling up. Material in landfills can pollute underground water supplies. Although in most places, laws now regulate what can be discarded in a landfill, the Environmental Protection Agency has identified 1,331 dump sites across the United States containing hazardous materials that are polluting water both above and below the ground. In addition, what goes into landfills all too often stays there, sometimes for centuries. Tens of millions of tires, diapers, and other items we bury in landfills each year do not decompose but will remain as an unwelcome legacy for future generations.

Environmentalists argue that we should address the problem of solid waste by doing what many of our grandparents did: Use less and turn "waste" into a resource. Part of the solution is *recycling*, reusing resources we would otherwise discard. Recycling is an accepted practice in Japan and many other nations, and it is becoming more common in the United States, where we now reuse about one-third of waste materials (U.S. Environmental Protection Agency, 2008). The share is increasing as laws require the recovery and reuse of certain materials such as glass bottles and aluminum cans and as the business of recycling becomes more profitable.

Water and Air

Oceans, lakes, and streams are the lifeblood of the global ecosystem. Humans depend on water for drinking, bathing, cooking, cleaning, recreation, and a host of other activities.

According to what scientists call the *hydrologic cycle,* Earth naturally recycles water and refreshes the land. The process begins as heat from the sun causes Earth's water, 97 percent of which is in the oceans, to evaporate and form clouds. Because water evaporates at lower temperatures than most pollutants, the water vapor that rises from the seas is relatively pure, leaving various contaminants behind. Water then falls to the Earth as rain, which drains into streams and rivers and finally returns to the sea. Two major concerns about water, then, are supply and pollution.

Water Supply

Less than 1 percent of Earth's water is suitable for drinking. It is not surprising, then, that for thousands of years, water rights have figured prominently in laws around the world. Today, some regions of the world, especially the tropics, enjoy plentiful fresh water, using a small share of the available supply. However, high demand, coupled with modest reserves, makes water supply a matter of concern in much of North America and Asia, where people look to rivers rather than rainfall for their water. In China, aquifers are dropping rapidly. In the Middle East, water supply is reaching a critical level. Iran is rationing water in its capital city. In Egypt, the Nile River provides just one-sixth as much water per person as it did in 1900. Across northern Africa and the Middle East, as many as 1 billion people may lack the water they need for irrigation and drinking by 2025 (United Nations Environmental Programme, 2008).

Rising population and the development of more complex technology have greatly increased the world's appetite for water. The global consumption of water (now estimated at 150 billion cubic feet per year) has tripled since 1950 and is rising steadily. As a result, even in parts of the world that receive plenty of rainfall, people are using groundwater faster than it can be replenished naturally. In the Tamil Nadu region of southern India, for example, so much groundwater is being used that the water table has fallen 100 feet over the last several decades. Mexico City—which has sprawled to some 1,400 square miles—has pumped so much water from its underground aquifer that the city has sunk 30 feet during the past century and continues to drop about 2 inches per year. Farther north in the United States, the Ogallala aquifer, which lies below seven states from South Dakota to Texas, is now being pumped so rapidly that some experts fear it could run dry in just a few decades.

In light of such developments, we must face the reality that water is a valuable and finite resource. Greater conservation of water by individuals (the average person consumes 359,000 gallons in a life-

SEEING SOCIOLOGY
in Everyday Life

Las Vegas is one of the fastest-growing U.S. cities—and it is built in a desert. Do you think the future water needs of this city's people (and those of the entire Southwest) are ensured? What will we do if the answer turns out to be no?

SEEING SOCIOLOGY IN EVERYDAY LIFE

Why Grandma Macionis Had No Trash

Grandma Macionis, we always used to say, never threw anything away. She was born and raised in Lithuania—the "old country"—where life in a poor village shaped her in ways that never changed, even after she came to the United States as a young woman and settled in Philadelphia.

In her later years, when I knew her, I can remember the family traveling together to her house to celebrate her birthday. We never knew what to get Grandma, because she never seemed to need anything. She lived a simple life and had simple clothes and showed little interest in "fancy things." She used everything until it wore out. Her kitchen knives, for example, were worn narrow from decades of sharpening. And she hardly ever threw anything away—she recycled all her garbage as compost for her vegetable garden.

After opening a birthday present, she would carefully save the box, wrapping paper, and ribbon, which meant as much to her as whatever gift they surrounded. We all expected her to save every bit of whatever she was given, smiling to each other as we watched her put everything

away, knowing she would find a way to use it all again and again.

As strange as Grandma sometimes seemed to her grandchildren, she was a product of her culture. A century ago, in fact, there was little "trash." If socks wore thin, people mended them, probably more than once. When they were beyond repair,

they were used as rags for cleaning or sewn with bits of other old clothing into a quilt. Everything had value—if not in one way, then in another.

During the twentieth century, as women joined men in working outside the home, income went up, and families began buying more and more "time-saving" products. Before long, few people cared about the kind of recycling that Grandma practiced. Soon cities sent crews from block to block to pick up truckloads of discarded material. The era of "trash" had begun.

WHAT DO YOU THINK?

1. Just as Grandma Macionis was a product of her culture, so are we. Do you know people who have plenty but never seem to think they have enough?

2. What cultural values make people today demand time-saving products and "convenience" packaging?

3. In what ways does this box show that the state of the natural environment is a social issue?

---

time) is part of the answer. However, households around the world account for just 5 percent of water use. It is even more crucial that we curb water consumption by industry, which uses 20 percent of the global total, and farming, which consumes 75 percent of the total for irrigation.

Perhaps new irrigation technology will reduce the future demand for water. But here again, we see how population increase, as well as economic growth, strains our ecosystem (Population Action International, 2000; United Nations Environmental Programme, 2008).

Water Pollution

In large cities from Mexico City to Cairo to Shanghai, many people have no choice but to drink contaminated water. Infectious diseases such as typhoid, cholera, and dysentery, all caused by waterborne microorganisms, spread rapidly through these populations. Besides ensuring ample *supplies* of water, then, we must also protect the *quality* of water.

Water quality in the United States is generally good by global standards. However, even here the problem of water pollution is steadily growing. According to the Sierra Club (2009), an environmental activist organization, U.S. society produces some 500 million pounds of toxic waste each year, and much of it ends up in our rivers and streams. This pollution results not just from intentional dumping but also from the runoff of agricultural fertilizers and lawn chemicals.

A special problem is *acid rain*—precipitation made acidic by air pollution—which destroys plant and animal life. Acid rain begins with power plants burning fossil fuels (oil and coal) to generate electricity; this burning releases sulfuric and nitrous oxides into the air. As the wind sweeps these gases into the atmosphere, they react with the air to form sulfuric and nitric acids, which turns atmospheric moisture acidic.

This is a clear case of one type of pollution causing another: Air pollution (from smokestacks) ends up contaminating water (in lakes and streams that collect acid rain). Acid rain is truly a global phenomenon because the regions that suffer the harmful effects may be

GLOBAL: Irrigation is not only the main source of water use but also a major source of energy consumption. In India, for example, some 8 million irrigation pumps consume one-fourth of that nation's power.

GLOBAL: The Aral Sea, between Kazakhstan and Uzbekistan in central Asia, is disappearing because of badly planned irrigation projects. It is now almost half its original size.

DISCUSS: If 70% of the planet is covered with water, why do environmentalists claim that the supply of water is a serious concern?

GLOBAL: Costa Rica leads the world's tropical countries in the rate at which it is cutting down its rain forest—7% annually. Brazil, however, is cutting the most forest in absolute terms, about 3.2 million acres annually. Throughout the world, about 100 acres of rain forest disappear *every minute*.

SEEING SOCIOLOGY
in Everyday Life

Have you experienced changes in your own world resulting from global warming or other issues discussed here?

rain forests regions of dense forestation, most of which circle the globe close to the equator

global warming a rise in Earth's average temperature due to an increasing concentration of carbon dioxide in the atmosphere

Water is vital to life, and it is also in short supply. The state of Gujarat, in western India, has experienced a long drought. In the village of Natwarghad, people crowd together, lowering pots into the local well, taking what little water is left.

improved human health: Experts estimate that improvement in U.S. air quality over the past several decades has added almost half a year to the average life span (Chang, 2009).

If high-income countries can breathe a bit more easily than they once did, the problem of air pollution in poor societies is becoming more serious. One reason is that people in low-income countries still rely on wood, coal, peat, and other "dirty" fuels to cook their food and heat their homes. In addition, nations eager to encourage short-term industrial development may pay little attention to the longer-term dangers of air pollution. As a result, many cities in Latin America, Eastern Europe, and Asia are plagued by air pollution as bad as London's "pea soup" back in the 1950s.

The Rain Forests

Rain forests are *regions of dense forestation, most of which circle the globe close to the equator*. The largest tropical rain forests are in South America (notably Brazil), west-central Africa, and Southeast Asia. In all, the world's rain forests cover some 1.5 billion acres, or 4.5 percent of Earth's total land surface.

Like other global resources, rain forests are falling victim to the needs and appetites of the surging world population. As noted earlier, to meet the demand for beef, ranchers in Latin America burn forested areas to increase their supply of grazing land. We are also losing rain forests to the hardwood trade. People in rich nations pay high prices for mahogany and other woods because, as the environmentalist Norman Myers (1984b:88) puts it, they have "a penchant for parquet floors, fine furniture, fancy paneling, weekend yachts, and high-grade coffins." Under such economic pressure, the world's rain forests are now just half their original size, and they continue to shrink by at least 1 percent (58,000 square miles) annually, which amounts to about an acre every second. Unless we stop this loss, the rain forests will vanish before the end of this century, and with them will go protection for Earth's biodiversity and climate (Rainforest Foundation, 2009).

Global Warming

Why are rain forests so important? One reason is that they cleanse the atmosphere of carbon dioxide (CO_2). Since the beginning of the Industrial Revolution, the amount of carbon dioxide produced by humans, mostly from factories and automobiles, has risen sharply. Much of this carbon dioxide is absorbed by the oceans. But plants also take in carbon dioxide and expel oxygen. This is why rain forests are vital to maintaining the chemical balance of the atmosphere.

The problem is that production of carbon dioxide is rising while the amount of plant life on Earth is shrinking. To make matters worse,

thousands of miles from the source of the original pollution. For instance, British power plants have caused acid rain that has devastated forests and fish in Norway and Sweden, up to 1,000 miles to the northeast. In the United States, we see a similar pattern as midwestern smokestacks have harmed the natural environment of upstate New York and New England.

Air Pollution

Because we are surrounded by air, most people in the United States are more aware of air pollution than contaminated water. One of the unexpected consequences of industrial technology, especially the factory and the motor vehicle, has been a decline in air quality. In London in the mid-twentieth century, factory smokestacks, automobiles, and coal fires used to heat homes all added up to what was probably the worst urban air quality the world has ever known. The fog that some British jokingly called "pea soup" was in reality a deadly mix of pollutants: In 1952, an especially thick haze that hung over London for five days killed 4,000 people.

Air quality improved in the final decades of the twentieth century. Rich nations passed laws that banned high-pollution heating, including the coal fires that choked London. In addition, scientists devised ways to make factories and motor vehicles operate much more cleanly. In fact, today's vehicles produce only a fraction of the pollution that spewed from models of the 1950s and 1960s. And cleaner air has

POP CULTURE: The dangers of global warming are vividly portrayed in the Hollywood film *The Day After Tomorrow* and Al Gore's documentary *An Inconvenient Truth*.

NOTE: Reforestation programs can significantly help in reducing the buildup of atmospheric carbon dioxide.

NOTE: A significant forest region, which contains substantial biological diver-

sity, is found in the temperate climate of the U.S. Pacific Northwest.

SOCIAL SURVEY: "Modern science will solve our environmental problems with little change to our way of life." (GSS 2000, N = 1,276; *Codebook*, 2006:1750)

"Strongly agree"	2.8%	"Disagree"	35.1%
"Agree"	18.1%	"Strongly disagree"	7.7%
"Neither agree nor disagree"	26.3%	"Don't know"/No response	9.9%

SEEING SOCIOLOGY
in Everyday Life

Do you worry much about global warming? Why or why not?
Do you think global warming could affect you personally? How?

environmental racism patterns of development that expose poor people, especially minorities, to environmental hazards

rain forests are being destroyed mostly by burning, which releases even more carbon dioxide into the atmosphere. Experts estimate that the atmospheric concentration of carbon dioxide is now 40 percent higher than it was 150 years ago and rising rapidly (Gore, 2006; Adam, 2008).

High above Earth, carbon dioxide acts like the glass roof of a greenhouse, letting heat from the sun pass through to the surface while preventing much of it from radiating away from the planet. The result of this *greenhouse effect,* say ecologists, is **global warming,** *a rise in Earth's average temperature due to an increasing concentration of carbon dioxide in the atmosphere.* Over the past century, the global temperature has risen about 1.3° Fahrenheit (to an average of 58° F). Scientists warn that it could rise by 5° to 10° F during this century. Already, the polar ice caps are melting, and scientists predict that increasing average temperatures could melt so much ice that the sea level would rise enough to cover low-lying land all around the world: Water would cover all of Bangladesh, for example, and much of the coastal United States, including Washington, D.C., right up to the steps of the White House. On the other hand, the U.S. Midwest, currently one of the most productive agricultural regions in the world, would probably become more arid.

Some scientists point out that we cannot be sure of the consequences of global warming. Others point to the fact that global temperature changes have been taking place throughout history, apparently having little or nothing to do with rain forests or human activity. A few are optimistic, suggesting that higher concentrations of carbon dioxide in the atmosphere might speed up plant growth (since plants thrive on this gas), and this increase would correct the imbalance and push Earth's temperature downward once again. But the consensus of scientists is now clear: Global warming is a serious problem that threatens the future of all of us (Kerr, 2005; Gore, 2006; International Panel on Climate Change, 2007; Singer, 2007).

Declining Biodiversity

Our planet is home to as many as 30 million species of animals, plants, and microorganisms. As rain forests are cleared and humans extend their control over nature, several dozen unique species of plants and animals cease to exist each day, reducing the planet's *biodiversity*.

But given the vast number of living species, why should we be concerned by the loss of a few? Environmentalists give four reasons. First, our planet's biodiversity provides a varied source of human food. Using agricultural high technology, scientists can "splice" familiar crops with more exotic plant life, making food more bountiful as well as more resistant to insects and disease. Thus biodiversity helps feed our planet's rapidly increasing population.

Second, Earth's biodiversity is a vital genetic resource used by medical and pharmaceutical researchers to produce hundreds of new

compounds each year that cure disease and improve our lives. For example, children in the United States now have a good chance of surviving leukemia, a disease that was almost a sure killer two generations ago, because of a compound derived from a tropical flower called the rosy periwinkle. The oral birth control pill, used by tens of millions of women in this country, is another product of plant research involving the Mexican forest yam.

Third, with the loss of any species of life—whether it is the magnificent California condor, the famed Chinese panda, the spotted owl, or even a single species of ant—the beauty and complexity of our natural environment are diminished. And there are clear warning signs of such loss: Three-fourths of the world's 10,000 species of birds are declining in number.

Finally, unlike pollution, the extinction of any species is irreversible and final. An important ethical question, then, is whether we who live today have the right to impoverish the world for those who live tomorrow (E. O. Wilson, 1991; Brown et al., 1993).

Environmental Racism

Conflict theory has given rise to the concept of **environmental racism,** *patterns of development that expose poor people, especially minorities, to environmental hazards.* Historically, factories that spew pollution have stood near neighborhoods of the poor and people of color. Why? In part, the poor themselves were drawn to factories in

Members of small, simple societies, such as the Mentawi in Indonesia, live in harmony with nature; they do not have the technological means to greatly affect the natural world. Although we in complex societies like to think of ourselves as superior to such people, the truth is that there is much we can—indeed, must—learn from them.

DISCUSS: Ask students if they are surprised that the world gains almost 80 million people a year. Should this increase be seen as a sign of human success or human failure? Why?

GLOBAL: As a personal solution to the myriad problems of poor nations, tens of millions of people are migrating toward richer northern countries. In response, many rich societies are tightening restrictions on immigration.

NOTE: The neo-Malthusians fall within the environmental movement, arguing that growth is a social danger. The anti-Malthusians tend to be economists who follow Adam Smith in viewing growth as good.

GLOBAL: A study by the Pakistani government concludes that nation can support some 200 million people, up from the present 162 million, but not the 295 million projected by 2050.

● MAKING THE GRADE

With its focus on inequality, environmental racism is linked to the social-conflict approach.

ecologically sustainable culture a way of life that meets the needs of the present generation without threatening the environmental legacy of future generations

search of work, and their low incomes often meant they could afford housing only in undesirable neighborhoods. Sometimes the only housing that fit their budgets stood in the very shadow of the plants and mills where they worked.

Nobody wants a factory or dump nearby, but the poor have little power to resist. Through the years, the most serious environmental hazards have been located near Newark, New Jersey (not in upscale Bergen County), in southside Chicago (not wealthy Lake Forest), or on Native American reservations in the West (not in affluent suburbs of Denver or Phoenix) (Commission for Racial Justice, 1994; Bohon & Humphrey, 2000).

Looking Ahead: Toward a Sustainable Society and World

The demographic analysis presented in this chapter reveals some disturbing trends. We see, first, that Earth's population has reached record levels because birth rates remain high in poor nations and death rates have fallen just about everywhere. Reducing fertility will remain a pressing need throughout this century. Even with some recent decline in the rate of population increase, the nightmare Thomas Malthus described is still a real possibility, as the Controversy & Debate box explains.

If human ingenuity created the threats to our environment we now face, can humans also solve these problems? In recent years, a number of designs for small, environmentally friendly cars show the promise of new technology. But do such innovations go far enough? Will we have to make more basic changes to our way of life to ensure human survival in the centuries to come?

Further, population growth remains greatest in the poorest countries of the world, which cannot meet the needs of their present populations, much less future ones. Supporting 80 million additional people on our planet each year, 78 million of them in low-income countries, will require a global commitment to provide not just food but housing, schools, and employment as well. The well-being of the entire world may ultimately depend on resolving the economic and social problems of poor, overly populated countries and bridging the widening gulf between "have" and "have-not" nations.

Urbanization is continuing, especially in poor countries. For thousands of years, people have sought out cities in the hope of finding a better life. But the sheer numbers of people who live in today's supercities—including Mexico City, São Paulo (Brazil), Kinshasa (Democratic Republic of the Congo), Mumbai (India), and Manila (Philippines)—have created urban problems on a massive scale.

Around the world, humanity is facing a serious environmental challenge. Part of this problem is population increase, which is greatest in poor countries. But part of the problem is the high levels of consumption in rich nations such as our own. By increasing the planet's environmental deficit, our present way of life is borrowing against the well-being of our children and their children. Globally, members of rich societies, who currently consume so much of Earth's resources, are mortgaging the future security of the poor countries of the world.

The answer, in principle, is to create an **ecologically sustainable culture,** *a way of life that meets the needs of the present generation without threatening the environmental legacy of future generations.* Sustainable living depends on three strategies.

First, the world needs to *bring population growth under control.* The current population of 6.7 billion is already straining the natural environment. Clearly, the higher the world's population climbs, the more difficult environmental problems will become. Even if the recent slowing of population growth continues, the world will have about 9 billion people by 2050. Few analysts think that the planet can support this many people; most argue that we must hold the line at about 7 billion, and some argue that we must *decrease* population in the coming decades (Smail, 2007).

A second strategy is to *conserve finite resources.* This means meeting our needs with a responsible eye toward the future by using resources efficiently, seeking alternative sources of energy, and in some cases, learning to live with less.

A third strategy is to *reduce waste.* Whenever possible, simply using less is the best solution. Learning to live with less is not likely to come easily, but keep in mind the research that suggests that as our society has consumed more and more, people have not become any happier (D. G. Myers, 2000). Recycling programs, too, are part of

DISCUSS: Do all species have a part to play in the world? If so, the significance of humans may lie in our ability to care for all forms of life. In the process, will we decide our own future?

DIVERSITY: The concept of "environmental racism" partly reflects the movement's concern over its largely white, middle-class membership. (One recent survey found that 43% of readers of the Sierra Club's magazine have postgraduate degrees.)

SOCIAL SURVEY: "Are you willing to accept cuts in your standard of living in order to protect the environment?" (GSS 2000, N = 1,276; *Codebook*, 2006:1754)

"Very willing"	5.4%	"Not very willing"	18.6%
"Fairly willing"	22.0%	"Not at all willing"	21.6%
"Neither willing nor unwilling"	23.9%	"Don't know"/No response	8.4%

● SEEING SOCIOLOGY
in Everyday Life

What share of the world's people do you think are concerned about global population increase?

CONTROVERSY & DEBATE

Apocalypse: Will People Overwhelm the Planet?

NUSHAWN: I'm telling you, there are too many people already! Where is everyone going to live?

TABITHA: Have you ever been to Kansas? Or Wyoming? There's plenty of empty space out there.

MARCO: Maybe now. But I'm not so sure about our children—or their children. . . .

Are you worried about the world's increasing population? Think about this: By the time you finish reading this box, more than 1,000 people will have been added to our planet. By this time tomorrow, global population will have risen by nearly 220,000. Currently, as the table shows, there are more than four births for every two deaths on the planet, pushing the world's population upward by 80 million annually. Put another way, global population growth amounts to adding another Ethiopia to the world each year.

It is no wonder that many demographers and environmentalists are deeply concerned about the future. Earth has an unprecedented population: The 2.7 billion people we have added since 1974 alone exceed the planet's total in 1900. Might Thomas Robert Malthus, who predicted that overpopulation would push the world into war and suffering, be right after all? Lester Brown and other *neo-Malthusians* predict a coming apocalypse if we do not change our ways. Brown admits that Malthus failed to imagine how much technology (especially fertilizers and altering plant genetics) could boost the planet's agricultural output. But he maintains that Earth's rising population is rapidly outstripping its finite resources. Families in many poor countries can find little firewood, members of rich countries are depleting the oil reserves, and everyone is draining our supply of clean water and poisoning the planet with waste. Some analysts argue that we have already passed Earth's "carrying capacity" for

population and we need to hold the line or even reduce global population to ensure our long-term survival.

But other analysts, the *anti-Malthusians*, sharply disagree. Julian Simon points out that two centuries after Malthus predicted catastrophe, Earth supports almost six times as many people who, on average, live longer, healthier lives than ever before. With more advanced technology, people have devised ways to increase productivity and limit population increase. As Simon sees it, this is cause for celebration. Human ingenuity has consistently proved the doomsayers wrong, and Simon is betting it will continue to do so.

WHAT DO YOU THINK?

1. Where do you place your bet? Do you think Earth can support 8 or 10 billion people? Explain your reasoning.

2. Fully 97% percent of current population growth is in poor countries. What does this mean for the future of rich nations? For the future of poor ones?

3. What should people in rich countries do to ensure the future of children everywhere?

Global Population Increase, 2009

	Births	Deaths	Net Increase
Per year	135,474,672	55,644,164	79,810,508
Per month	11,289,556	4,638,680	6,650,876
Per day	371,163	152,505	218,659
Per hour	15,465	6,354	9,111
Per minute	258	106	152
Per second	4.3	1.8	2.5

Sources: Brown (1995), Simon (1995), Scanlon (2001), Smail (2007), and U.S. Census Bureau (2009).

---

the answer, and recycling can make everyone part of the solution to our environmental problems.

In the end, making all these strategies work depends on a basic change in the way we think about ourselves and our world. Our *egocentric* outlook sets our own interests as standards for how to live, but a sustainable environment demands an *ecocentric* outlook that helps us see how the present is tied to the future and why everyone must work together. Most nations in the southern half of the world are *underdeveloped,* unable to meet the basic needs of their people. At the same time, most countries in the northern half of the world are *overdeveloped,* using more resources than the planet can sustain over time. The changes needed to create a sustainable ecosystem will

not come easily, and they will be costly. But the price of not responding to the growing environmental deficit will certainly be greater (Kellert & Bormann, 1991; Brown et al., 1993; Population Action International, 2000; Gore, 2006).

Finally, consider that the great dinosaurs dominated this planet for some 160 million years and then perished forever. Humanity is far younger, having existed for a mere 250,000 years. Compared to the rather dimwitted dinosaurs, our species has the gift of great intelligence. But how will we use this ability? What are the chances that our species will continue to flourish 160 million years—or even 160 years—from now? The answer depends on the choices that will be made by one of the 30 million species living on Earth: human beings.

Seeing Sociology in Everyday Life

Chapter 22   Population, Urbanization, and Environment

Why is the environment a social issue?

As this chapter explains, the state of the natural environment depends on how society is organized, especially the importance a culture attaches to consumption and economic growth.

> **HINT**   If expansion is "good times," then contraction is a "recession" or perhaps even a "depression." Such a worldview means that it is normal—or even desirable—to live in a way that increases stress on the natural environment. Sustainability, an idea that is especially important as world population increases, depends on learning to live with what we have or maybe even learning to live with less. Although many people seem to think so, it really doesn't require a 6,000-pound SUV to move around urban areas. Actually, it might not require a car at all. This new way of thinking requires that we do not define social standing and personal success in terms of what we own and what we consume. Can you imagine a society like that? What would it be like?

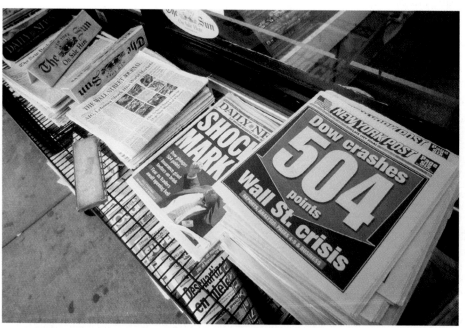

We learn to see economic expansion as natural and good. When the economy stays the same for a number of months, we say we are experiencing "stagnation." How do we define a period when the economy gets smaller, as happened during the fall of 2008?

What would it take to convince members of our society that smaller (rather than bigger) might be better? Why do we seem to prefer not just bigger cars but bigger homes and more and more material possessions?

Applying SOCIOLOGY in Everyday Life

1. Here is an illustration of the problem of runaway growth (Milbrath, 1989:10): "A pond has a single water lily growing on it. The lily doubles in size each day. In thirty days, it covers the entire pond. On which day does it cover half the pond?" When you realize the answer, discuss the implications of this example for population increase.

2. Draw a mental map of a city familiar to you with as much detail of specific places, districts, roads, and transportation facilities as you can. Compare your map to a real one or, better yet, a map drawn by someone else. Try to account for the differences.

3. As an interesting exercise, carry a trash bag around for a single day, and collect everything you throw away. Most people are surprised to find that the average person in the United States discards close to 5 pounds of paper, metal, plastic, and other materials daily (over a lifetime, that's about 50 tons).

MAKING THE GRADE

CHAPTER 22 Population, Urbanization, and Environment

Demography: The Study of Population

✓ Demography analyzes the size and composition of a population and how and why people move from place to place. Demographers collect data and study several factors that affect population (p. 568).

FERTILITY
- Fertility is the incidence of childbearing in a country's population.
- Demographers describe fertility using the **crude birth rate**.

pp. 568–69

MORTALITY
- Mortality is the incidence of death in a country's population.
- Demographers measure mortality using both the **crude death rate** and the **infant mortality rate.**

p. 569

MIGRATION
The **net migration rate** is the difference between the in-migration rate and the out-migration rate.

pp. 569–70

POPULATION GROWTH
In general, rich nations grow almost as much from immigration as from natural increase; poorer nations grow almost entirely from natural increase.

p. 570

POPULATION COMPOSITION
Demographers use **age-sex pyramids** to show the composition of a population graphically and to project population trends.

pp. 570–72

demography (p. 568) the study of human population

fertility (p. 568) the incidence of childbearing in a country's population

crude birth rate (p. 568) the number of live births in a given year for every 1,000 people in a population

mortality (p. 569) the incidence of death in a country's population

crude death rate (p. 569) the number of deaths in a given year for every 1,000 people in a population

infant mortality rate (p. 569) the number of deaths among infants under one year of age for each 1,000 live births in a given year

life expectancy (p. 569) the average life span of a country's population

migration (p. 569) the movement of people into and out of a specified territory

sex ratio (p. 570) the number of males for every 100 females in a nation's population

age-sex pyramid (p. 570) a graphic representation of the age and sex of a population

History and Theory of Population Growth

- Historically, world population grew slowly because high birth rates were offset by high death rates.
- About 1750, a demographic transition began as world population rose sharply, mostly due to falling death rates.
- In the late 1700s, Thomas Robert Malthus warned that population growth would outpace food production, resulting in social calamity.
- **Demographic transition theory** contends that technological advances gradually slow population increase.
- World population is expected to reach between 8 billion and 9 billion by 2050.

pp. 572–74

demographic transition theory (p. 573) a thesis that links population patterns to a society's level of technological development

zero population growth (p. 574) the rate of reproduction that maintains population at a steady level

✓ Currently, the world is gaining 80 million people each year, with 97% of this increase taking place in poor countries (p. 572).

Urbanization: The Growth of Cities

The **FIRST URBAN REVOLUTION** began with the appearance of cities about 10,000 years ago.
- By about 2,000 years ago, cities had emerged in most regions of the world except North America and Antarctica.
- Preindustrial cities have low-rise buildings; narrow, winding streets; and personal social ties.

pp. 575–77

A **SECOND URBAN REVOLUTION** began about 1750 as the Industrial Revolution propelled rapid urban growth in Europe.
- The physical form of cities changed as planners created wide, regular streets to facilitate commerce.
- The emphasis on business, as well as the increasing size of cities, made urban life more impersonal.

p. 577

urbanization (p. 575) the concentration of population into cities

metropolis (p. 578) a large city that socially and economically dominates an urban area

suburbs (p. 578) urban areas beyond the political boundaries of a city

megalopolis (p. 579) a vast urban region containing a number of cities and their surrounding suburbs

IN THE UNITED STATES, urbanization has been going on for more than 400 years and continues today.
- Urbanization came to North America with European colonists.
- By 1850, hundreds of new cities had been founded from coast to coast.
- By 1920, a majority of the U.S. population lived in urban areas.
- Since 1950, the decentralization of cities has resulted in the growth of suburbs and edge cities and a "rebound" in rural population.
- Nationally, Sunbelt cities—but not the older Snowbelt cities—are increasing in size and population.

pp. 577–79

Urbanism as a Way of Life

✓ *Rapid urbanization during the nineteenth century led early sociologists to study the differences between rural and urban life. These early sociologists included, in Europe, Tönnies, Durkheim, and Simmel, and in the United States, Park and Wirth.*

FERDINAND TÖNNIES built his analysis on the concepts of *Gemeinschaft* and *Gesellschaft*.

- *Gemeinschaft*, typical of the rural village, joins people in what amounts to a single primary group.
- *Gesellschaft*, typical of the modern city, describes individuals motivated by their own needs rather than by a desire to help improve the well-being of the community.

p. 580

EMILE DURKHEIM agreed with much of Tönnies's thinking but claimed that urbanites do not lack social bonds; the basis of social solidarity simply differs in the two settings. He described

- **mechanical solidarity**—social bonds based on common sentiments and shared moral values. This type of social solidarity is typical of traditional, rural life.
- **organic solidarity**—social bonds based on specialization and interdependence. This type of social solidarity is typical of modern, urban life.

p. 580

Gemeinschaft (p. 580) a type of social organization in which people are closely tied by kinship and tradition

Gesellschaft (p. 580) a type of social organization in which people come together only on the basis of individual self-interest

urban ecology (p. 582) the study of the link between the physical and social dimensions of cities

GEORG SIMMEL claimed that the overstimulation of city life produced a blasé attitude in urbanites.

pp. 580–81

ROBERT PARK, at the University of Chicago, claimed that cities permit greater social freedom.

pp. 581–82

LOUIS WIRTH saw large, dense, heterogeneous populations creating an impersonal and self-interested, though tolerant, way of life.

pp. 581–82

Urbanization in Poor Nations

- The world's first urban revolution took place about 8000 B.C.E. with the first urban settlements.
- The second urban revolution took place after 1750 in Europe and North America with the Industrial Revolution.
- A third urban revolution is now occurring in poor countries. Today, most of the world's largest cities are found in less developed nations.

pp. 583–84

Environment and Society

The state of the **ENVIRONMENT** is a social issue because it reflects how human beings organize social life.

- Societies increase the **environmental deficit** by focusing on short-term benefits and ignoring the long-term consequences brought on by their way of life.
- The more complex a society's technology, the greater its capacity to alter the natural environment.

pp. 584–85

- The *logic-of-growth thesis* supports economic development, claiming that people can solve environmental problems as they arise.
- The *limits-to-growth thesis* states that societies must curb development to prevent eventual environmental collapse.

pp. 585–87

ecology (p. 584) the study of the interaction of living organisms and the natural environment

natural environment (p. 584) Earth's surface and atmosphere, including living organisms, air, water, soil, and other resources necessary to sustain life

ecosystem (p. 584) a system composed of the interaction of all living organisms and their natural environment

environmental deficit (p. 585) profound long-term harm to the natural environment caused by humanity's focus on short-term material affluence

rain forests (p. 590) regions of dense forestation, most of which circle the globe close to the equator

global warming (p. 591) a rise in Earth's average temperature due to an increasing concentration of carbon dioxide in the atmosphere

environmental racism (p. 591) patterns of development that expose poor people, especially minorities, to environmental hazards

ecologically sustainable culture (p. 592) a way of life that meets the needs of the present generation without threatening the environmental legacy of future generations

ENVIRONMENTAL ISSUES include

- **Disposing of solid waste**—54% of what we throw away ends up in landfills, which are filling up and can pollute groundwater.
- **Protecting the quality of water and air**—The supply of clean water is already low in some parts of the world. Industrial technology has caused a decline in air quality.
- **Protecting the rain forests**—Rain forests help remove carbon dioxide from the atmosphere and are home to a large share of this planet's living species. Under pressure from development, the world's rain forests are now half their original size and are shrinking by about 1% annually.
- **Environmental racism**—Conflict theory has drawn attention to the pattern by which the poor, especially minorities, suffer most from environmental hazards.

pp. 587–92

Collective behavior takes many forms, from silent vigils to loud political protests, and sociologists study them all. One especially important form is social movements, organized efforts to bring about—and sometimes to prevent—social change.

CHAPTER 23

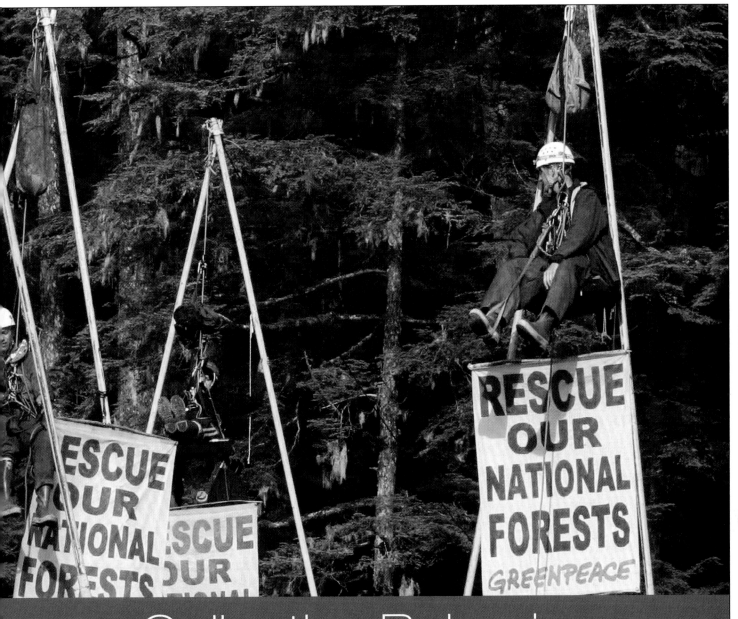

Collective Behavior and Social Movements

SUPPLEMENTS: An outline of this chapter, suggested discussion topics, and supplementary lecture material are found in the *Instructor's Manual*.

Q: "Never confuse motion with action." Ernest Hemingway

NOTE: The term "collective behavior" was coined by Robert E. Park; in fact, Park
defined sociology as "the science of collective behavior," suggesting a focus on
dynamic rather than stable social patterns (see Turner, 1967).

CHAPTER OVERVIEW { This chapter explores collective behavior, which is wide-ranging and includes crowd behavior, rumor and gossip, panics, disasters, and social movements.

Few people who lived along the Gulf Coast of the United States will ever forget the events that began on the morning of August 29, 2005. Hurricane Katrina roared ashore, packing winds of more than 125 miles per hour. The monster storm, extending 200 miles from one edge to the other, devastated coastal communities all across Louisiana, Mississippi, and Alabama.

In the city of New Orleans, events went from bad to worse when the levees that held back the waters of Lake Ponchartrain gave way, flooding about 80 percent of the city, which lies almost entirely below sea level. As the water rose, people were caught in their homes and fled upstairs. The lucky ones managed to break through the roof and climb out to await rescue. Others were trapped and drowned. In all, some 1,500 people in New Orleans died.

People across the country were stunned by television and newspaper images of thousands of people, waist-deep in water or floating on makeshift rafts, desperately trying to reach higher ground. The public was reminded how vulnerable we are to the forces of nature, even in a major city, and also how the poor—many of whom had no way to flee the storm—ended up suffering the most, as they so often do. In addition, we had a chance to observe how people at all levels in society react to a major disaster, coping with both physical devastation and social disintegration as entire communities are torn apart.

Studying disasters such as Hurricane Katrina is one example of the work sociologists do when they investigate **collective behavior,** *activity involving a large number of people that is unplanned, often controversial, and sometimes dangerous.* This chapter investigates various types of collective behavior, including what happens when people must deal with not only disasters but also mobs and riots, panic and mass hysteria, rumor and gossip, and fashions and fads. In addition, it will examine social movements, a type of collective behavior aimed at changing people's lives in some important way.

Studying Collective Behavior

Collective behavior is complex and difficult to study for three reasons:

1. **Collective behavior is diverse**. Collective behavior involves a wide range of human action. At first glance, it is difficult to see what disasters have in common with fads, rumors, and mob behavior.

2. **Collective behavior is variable**. Sometimes a rumor, like the fear that one or more major auto manufacturers might declare bankruptcy, spreads across the United States. But other rumors quickly die out. Why does one rumor catch on but others do not?

3. **Much collective behavior is transitory**. Sociologists have long studied social institutions such as the family because they are continuing parts of society. Disasters, rumors, and fads, however, come and go quickly.

Some researchers are quick to point out that these problems apply not just to collective behavior but to most forms of human behavior (Aguirre & Quarantelli, 1983). In addition, collective behavior is not always so surprising; anyone can predict that crowds will form at sporting events and music festivals, and sociologists can study these gatherings at first hand or record them on videotape to study later. Researchers can even anticipate some natural disasters such as tornadoes, which are common in some parts of the United States, and be ready to study how people respond to such events (D. L. Miller, 1985).

As a result of their efforts, sociologists now know a great deal about collective behavior. The first lesson to learn is that all collective behavior involves the action of some **collectivity,** *a large number of people whose minimal interaction occurs in the absence of well-defined and conventional norms.* Collectivities are of two types. A *localized collectivity* refers to people physically close to one another, as in the case of crowds and riots. A *dispersed collectivity* or *mass behavior* involves people who influence one another despite being spread over a large area. Examples of this type of collective behavior include rumors, public opinion, and fashion.

NOTE: Peter Dahlgren characterizes collective behavior as the breakdown of "the smooth rationality upon which the social order rests." Enrico Quarantelli, by contrast, counters that most collective behavior is both continuous and rational.

GLOBAL: The 1998 visit of Pope John Paul II gave Cuba its first large crowd since the 1959 revolution to hear a speaker other than Fidel Castro.

Q: "Collective behavior is not merely identical with the study of groups.... Organizational behavior is the behavior of groups that are governed by established rules or procedures, which have the force of tradition behind them.... Collectivities, or the groups within which collective behavior takes place, are not guided in a straightforward fashion by the culture of the society." Ralph Turner and Lewis Killian (1987:4)

collective behavior activity involving a large number of people that is unplanned, often controversial, and sometimes dangerous

collectivity a large number of people whose minimal interaction occurs in the absence of well-defined and conventional norms

crowd a temporary gathering of people who share a common focus of attention and who influence one another

SEEING SOCIOLOGY
in Everyday Life

Do you think people go to athletic games or musical events in part because they enjoy the experience of being in a large crowd? Explain your answer.

Be sure to keep in mind how collectivities differ from the already familiar concept of social groups (see Chapter 7, "Groups and Organizations"). Here are three key differences:

1. **People in collectivities have little or no social interaction**. People in groups interact frequently and directly; by contrast, people in mobs or other localized collectivities interact very little. Most people taking part in dispersed collectivities, such as a fad, do not interact at all.

2. **Collectivities have no clear social boundaries**. Group members share a sense of identity, but people engaged in collective behavior usually do not. People in a local crowd may have the same object of their attention, such as someone on a ledge threatening to jump, but they feel little sense of unity. Individuals involved in dispersed collectivities, such as students worried about the possibility of a military draft, have almost no awareness of shared membership. To give another example, people may share concerns over many issues, but usually it is difficult to say exactly who falls within the ranks of, say, the environmental or feminist movement.

3. **Collectivities generate weak and unconventional norms**. Conventional cultural norms usually regulate the behavior of people in groups. Some collectivities, such as people traveling together on an airplane, do observe conventional norms, but their interaction is usually limited to polite small talk with respect for the privacy of others sitting nearby. Other collectivities—such as excited fans after a game who take to the streets drinking and overturning cars—behave according to no clear guidelines (Weller & Quarantelli, 1973; Turner & Killian, 1987).

Localized Collectivities: Crowds

One major form of collective behavior is the **crowd**, *a temporary gathering of people who share a common focus of attention and who influence one another*. Crowds are a fairly new development: Most of our ancestors never saw a large crowd. In medieval Europe, for example, about the only time large numbers of people gathered in one place was when armies faced off on the battlefield (Laslettt, 1984). Today, however, crowds of 25,000 or more are common at rock concerts, sporting events, political demonstrations, and even the registration halls of large universities. Estimates placed the size of the crowd at President

On election night in 2008, a crowd formed spontaneously in New York's Times Square to await the election results. Reading the description in the text, which type of crowd behavior is this?

Obama's inauguration ceremony in Washington, D.C., at about 1.5 million (M. Tucker, 2009).

All crowds include a lot of people, but they differ in their social dynamics. Herbert Blumer (1969) identified four categories of crowds:

A *casual crowd* is a loose collection of people who interact little, if at all. People lying on a beach or people who rush to the scene of an automobile accident have only a passing awareness of one another.

A *conventional crowd* results from deliberate planning, as illustrated by a country auction, a college lecture, or a presidential inauguration. In each case, the behavior of people involved follows a clear set of norms.

An *expressive crowd* forms around an event with emotional appeal, such as a religious revival, an AC/DC concert, or the New Year's Eve celebration in New York City's Times Square. Excitement is the main reason people join expressive crowds, which makes this spontaneous experience exhilarating for those involved.

An *acting crowd* is a collectivity motivated by an intense, single-minded purpose, such as an audience rushing the doors of a concert hall or fleeing from a mall after hearing gunshots. Acting crowds are set in motion by powerful emotions, which can sometimes trigger mob violence.

Any crowd can change from one type to another. In 2001, for example, a conventional crowd of more than 10,000 fans filed into a soccer stadium in Johannesburg, South Africa, to watch a match

NOTE: The term "mob" is derived from the Latin *mobile vulgus*, meaning the "movable or changeable common people." Note the historical association of mobs with common people.

NOTE: The word "riot" was used in medieval Europe to refer to a dispute or quarrel; its likely Latin root is *rugire*, meaning "to roar."

Q: "For freedom and justice and so the troopers can't hit us anymore." An African American schoolgirl explaining why she was joining the Selma march (1965)

DIVERSITY: Racial violence has a long history in the U.S. Most common were white attacks on black people, Asians, and Native Americans. The pattern of African Americans rioting against whites emerged later, in the 1960s.

● MAKING THE GRADE

There are five types of crowds; be sure you understand each one. Notice, too, that an "acting crowd" and a "mob" are the same thing.

mob a highly emotional crowd that pursues a violent or destructive goal

riot a social eruption that is highly emotional, violent, and undirected

between two rival teams. After a goal was scored, the crowd erupted, and people began to push toward the field. Within seconds, an acting crowd had formed, and a stampede began, which ended up crushing forty-seven people to death (Nessman, 2001). In 2009, when a USAir jet crash-landed in the Hudson River minutes after taking off from a New York airport, some passengers briefly panicked, creating an acting crowd. But by the time the plane came to rest, people followed directions and evacuated the plane in a surprisingly quiet and conventional manner (Ripley, 2009).

Deliberate action by a crowd is not simply the product of rising emotions. Participants in *protest crowds*—a fifth category we can add to Blumer's list—may stage marches, boycotts, sit-ins, and strikes for political purposes (McPhail & Wohlstein, 1983). The antiwar demonstrations that took place on many campuses and in many large cities since the beginning of the Iraq War are examples of protest crowds. Sometimes protest crowds have the low-level energy characteristic of a conventional crowd; at other times, people become emotional enough to form an acting crowd.

Mobs and Riots

When an acting crowd turns violent, the result may be the birth of a **mob**, *a highly emotional crowd that pursues a violent or destructive goal.* Despite, or perhaps because of, their intense emotions, mobs tend to dissipate quickly. How long a mob continues to exist depends on its precise goals and whether its leadership tries to inflame or calm the crowd.

Lynching is the most notorious example of mob behavior in the United States. William Lynch, who lived in Virginia during the colonial period, took it upon himself to enforce law and order in his community before there were formal police and courts. His name soon came to be associated with violence and murder carried out beyond the law.

In the United States, lynching has always been colored by race. After the Civil War, so-called lynch mobs terrorized newly freed African Americans. Any person of color who challenged white superiority risked being hanged or burned alive by hate-filled whites.

Lynch mobs—typically composed of poor whites who felt threatened by competition from freed slaves—reached their peak between 1880 and 1930. Police recorded some 5,000 lynchings in that period, though many more undoubtedly occurred. Often lynchings were popular events, attracting hundreds of spectators; sometimes victims were killed quickly, but others were tortured before being put to death. Most of these terrorist killings took place in the Deep South, where the farming economy depended on a cheap and obedient labor force. On the western frontier, lynch mobs targeted people of Mexican and Asian descent. In about 25 percent of reported lynchings, whites killed other whites. Lynching women was rare; only about 100 such cases are known, almost all involving women of color (W. White, 1969, orig. 1929; Grant, 1975; Lacayo, 2000).

A highly energized crowd with no particular purpose is a **riot**, *a social eruption that is highly emotional, violent, and undirected.* Unlike the action of a mob, a riot usually has no clear goal, except perhaps to express dissatisfaction. The cause of most riots is some long-standing anger or grievance; violent action is ignited by some minor incident that causes people to start destroying property and harming other persons (Smelser, 1962; M. Rosenfeld, 1997). A mob action usually ends when some specific violent goal is accomplished (such as a lynching); a riot tends to go on until participants run out of steam or police and community leaders gradually bring participants under control.

Throughout our nation's history, riots have been sparked by social injustice. Industrial workers, for example, have rioted to vent rage over unfair working conditions. In 1886, a bitter struggle by Chicago factory workers for an eight-hour workday led to the explosive Haymarket Riot, which left eleven dead and scores injured. Prison inmates sometimes express anger and despair through riots.

In addition, race riots have occurred in this country with striking regularity. Early in the twentieth century, crowds of whites attacked African Americans in Chicago, Detroit, and other cities. In the 1960s, seemingly trivial events sparked rage at continuing prejudice and discrimination, causing violent riots in numerous inner-city ghettos. In Los Angeles in 1992, the acquittal of white police officers involved in the beating of a black motorist, Rodney King, set off an explosive riot. Violence and fires killed more than fifty people, injured thousands, and destroyed property worth hundreds of millions of dollars.

Not all riots are fired by hate. They can also begin with very positive feelings. In 2000, for example, young men celebrating New York City's National Puerto Rican Day began spraying water on young women in the crowd. During the next few hours, sexual violence erupted as dozens of women were groped, stripped, and assaulted—apparently resulting, as one report put it, from a mixture of "marijuana, alcohol, hot weather, testosterone idiocy, and lapses in police [protection]" (Barstow & Chivers, 2000:1). On a number of state university campuses, a win by the home sports team was all it took to send hundreds of students into the streets, drinking alcohol and soon lighting fires and battling with police. As one analyst put it, in an "anything goes" culture, some people think they can do whatever they feel like doing (Pitts, 2000; Madensen & Eck, 2006).

Crowds, Mobs, and Social Change

What does a riot accomplish? One answer is "power." Ordinary people can gain power when they act collectively. In recent years, demonstrators in New York, Cincinnati, Los Angeles, and numerous other cities have called national attention to their claim of racial bias on the part of police and caused police departments to carefully review

Q: "The age we are about to enter will in truth be the era of crowds." Gustave Le Bon (1895)

Q: "What constituted a people, a unity, a whole, becomes in the end an agglomeration of individualities lacking cohesion." Gustave Le Bon (1895)

Q: "The nearer the people are drawn to the common level of an equal and similar condition, the less prone does each man become to place implicit faith in a certain man or a certain class of men. But his readiness to believe the multitude increases, and opinion is more than ever the mistress of the world." Alexis de Tocqueville

officer conduct. The power of the crowd to challenge the status quo and sometimes to force social change is the reason crowds are controversial. Throughout history, defenders of the status quo have feared "the mob" as a threat. By contrast, those seeking change have supported collective action.

Explaining Crowd Behavior

What accounts for the behavior of crowds? Social scientists have developed several explanations.

Contagion Theory

An early explanation of collective behavior was offered by the French sociologist Gustave Le Bon (1841–1931). According to Le Bon's *contagion theory* (1960, orig. 1895), crowds have a hypnotic influence on their members. Shielded by the anonymity found in large numbers, people forget about personal responsibility and give in to the contagious emotions of the crowd. A crowd thus assumes a life of its own, stirring up emotions and driving people toward irrational, even violent, action.

In the wake of a mass shooting that left fourteen people dead at an immigration services center in Binghamton, New York, in 2009, neighbors gathered to hold a candlelight vigil. After reading the theories of crowd behavior on pages 603–4, try to apply each theory to an event such as this one. Which approach makes the most sense to you? Why?

○ **CRITICAL REVIEW** Le Bon's idea that crowds provide anonymity and can generate strong emotions is surely true. Yet as Clark McPhail (1991) points out, a considerable body of research shows that "the madding crowd" does not take on a life of its own; its actions result from the policies and decisions made by specific individuals. In the case of the 2003 nightclub fire in Rhode Island that killed ninety-seven people, the high death toll did not result simply from the crowd "going wild," piling up at the doors and becoming trapped inside the flaming building. Later investigation showed that the band had used dangerous fireworks onstage, flames ignited flammable soundproofing material on the ceiling, and the room had no sprinkler system. As a result, fire engulfed the entire building in minutes, before many people realized what was happening (Apuzzo, 2003; Forliti, 2003).

Finally, although collective behavior may involve strong emotions, such feelings may not be irrational, as contagion theory suggests. Emotions—as well as action—can reflect real fear (as in the nightclub fire) or result from a sense of injustice (as in the police bias protests) (Jasper, 1998).

○ **CHECK YOUR LEARNING** State the contagion theory of crowd behavior. What are several criticisms of this theory?

Convergence Theory

Convergence theory holds that crowd behavior comes not from the crowd itself but from the particular people who join in. From this point of view, a crowd is a convergence of like-minded individuals.

Contagion theory states that crowds cause people to act in a certain way; convergence theory says the opposite, claiming that people who wish to act in a certain way come together to form crowds.

In recent years, the crowds that formed at demonstrations opposing the Iraq War, for example, did not cause participants to become antiwar. On the contrary, participants came together because of their political attitudes.

○ **CRITICAL REVIEW** By linking crowds to broader social forces, convergence theory rejects Le Bon's claim that crowd behavior is irrational in favor of the view that people in crowds express existing beliefs and values. But in fairness to Le Bon, people sometimes do things in a crowd that they would not have the courage to do alone, because crowds can spread responsibility among many people. In addition, crowds can intensify an emotion simply by creating a critical mass of like-minded people.

○ **CHECK YOUR LEARNING** State the convergence theory of crowd behavior. What are two criticisms of this theory?

Emergent-Norm Theory

Ralph Turner and Lewis Killian (1987) developed the *emergent-norm theory* of crowd dynamics. These researchers admit that social behavior

Q: "Usually the judgment that someone has acted irrationally is made in hindsight or by someone who is not in the situation of the actor and thus has a different perspective." Ralph Turner and Lewis Killian

Q: "The public is the only critic whose opinion is worth anything at all." Mark Twain

POP CULTURE: Gossip is a mainstay of popular culture, and newspapers like the *Star* and magazines like *People* and *Us* spew a torrent of gossip. In some cases, people fight the media, as in Paul McCartney's recent divorce.

THEN AND NOW: Public opinion changes over time. Support for women's right to abortion rose steadily from 1973 to 1992 (reaching about 50% of adults) and fell after that, rising again to about 54% in 2008 (NORC, 2008).

mass behavior collective behavior among people spread over a wide geographic area

rumor unconfined information that people spread informally, often by word of mouth

gossip rumor about people's personal affairs

public opinion widespread attitudes about controversial issues

propaganda (p. 606) information presented with the intention of shaping public opinion

fashion (p. 606) a social pattern favored by a large number of people

fad (p. 606) an unconventional social pattern that people embrace briefly but enthusiastically

panic (p. 606) a form of collective behavior in which people in one place react to a threat or other stimulus with irrational, frantic, and often self-destructive behavior

mass hysteria or **moral panic** (p. 606) a form of dispersed collective behavior in which people react to a real or imagined event with irrational and even frantic fear

is never entirely predictable, but if similar interests draw people into a crowd, distinctive patterns of behavior may emerge.

According to Turner and Killian, crowds begin as collectivities containing people with mixed interests and motives. Especially in the case of expressive, acting, and protest crowds, norms may be vague and changing. Consider how many Iraqi citizens began looting government buildings after U.S. troops toppled Saddam Hussein; after a while, however, although some continued to steal anything they could carry, others tried to stop the lawlessness. In short, people in crowds make their own rules as they go along.

○ **CRITICAL REVIEW** Emergent-norm theory represents a middle-ground approach to crowd dynamics. Turner and Killian (1993) explain that crowd behavior is neither as irrational as contagion theory suggests nor as deliberate as convergence theory implies. Certainly, crowd behavior reflects the desires of participants, but it is also guided by norms that emerge as the situation unfolds.

Decision making does play a role in crowd behavior, although people watching from the sidelines may not realize it. For example, frightened people clogging the exits of a burning nightclub may appear to be victims of irrational panic, but from their point of view, fleeing a rapidly spreading fire makes a lot of sense.

Emergent-norm theory points out that people in a crowd take on different roles. Some step forward as leaders; others become lieutenants, rank-and-file followers, inactive bystanders, and even opponents (Weller & Quarantelli, 1973; Zurcher & Snow, 1981).

○ **CRITICAL REVIEW** State the emergent-norm theory of crowd behavior. What are several criticisms of this theory?

Dispersed Collectivities: Mass Behavior

It is not just people clustered together in crowds who take part in collective behavior. **Mass behavior** refers to *collective behavior among people spread over a wide geographic area.*

Rumor and Gossip

A common type of mass behavior is **rumor,** *unconfirmed information that people spread informally, often by word of mouth.* People pass along rumors through face-to-face communication, of course, but today's modern technology—including telephones, the mass media, e-mail, text messaging, and the Internet—spreads rumors faster and farther than ever before.

Rumor has three main characteristics:

1. **Rumor thrives in a climate of uncertainty**. Rumors arise when people lack clear and certain information about an issue. The fact that no one really understood why a young gunman killed thirty-three students and professors on the campus of Virginia Tech in 2007 helps explain why rumors were flying on many other campuses that the same type of violence might erupt there.

2. **Rumor is unstable**. People change a rumor as they pass it along, usually giving it a "spin" that serves their own interests. Conservative "law and order" people had one explanation of Virginia Tech violence; more liberal "gun control" advocates had another.

3. **Rumor is difficult to stop**. The number of people aware of a rumor increases very quickly because each person spreads information to many others. The mass media and the Internet can quickly spread local issues and events across the country and around the world. Rumors go away eventually, but in general, the only way to control rumors is for a believable source to issue a clear and convincing statement of the facts.

Rumor can trigger the formation of crowds or other collective behavior. For this reason, officials establish rumor control centers during a crisis in order to manage information. Yet some rumors persist for generations, perhaps just because people enjoy them; the Seeing Sociology in Everyday Life box gives a classic example.

Gossip is *rumor about people's personal affairs.* Charles Horton Cooley (1962, orig. 1909) explained that rumor involves some issue many people care about, but gossip interests only a small circle of people who know a particular person. This is why rumors spread widely but gossip tends to be localized.

Communities use gossip as a means of social control, using praise and blame to encourage people to conform to local norms. Also, people gossip about others to put them down and to raise their own standing as social "insiders" (Baumgartner, 1998; Nicholson, 2001). At the same time, no community wants gossip to get out of control to the point that no one knows what to believe, which is why people who gossip too much are criticized as "busybodies."

Public Opinion and Propaganda

Another type of dispersed collective behavior is **public opinion,** *widespread attitudes about controversial issues.* Exactly who is, or is not, included in any "public" depends on the issue involved. Over the years in the United States, publics have formed over numerous controversial issues, from global warming and air pollution to handguns and health care. More recently, the public has debated affirmative action, campaign finance reform, and government funding of public radio and television.

Whatever the issue, a small share of people have no opinion at all; this may be due to either ignorance or indifference. Even on some important issues, a majority of people have no clear opinion. One

NOTE: Delbert Miller claimed that in 1945, only a small number of people on his campus learned of the death of President Roosevelt directly from radio reports. Within 30 minutes, however, about 90% of the people had been informed by word of mouth. Obviously, today's more powerful mass media reduce the significance of word of mouth in spreading national rumors.

NOTE: Jack Levin and Arnold Arluke spread a rumor on their campus by widely distributing flyers announcing a fictitious wedding. The flyers were not circulated until a day before the supposed event. Still, the researchers found that one week later, 52% of a campus sample had heard about the wedding, and 12% claimed to have actually attended it (1987:14–15).

● SEEING SOCIOLOGY in Everyday Life

Rumors travel through social networks (described in Chapter 7, "Groups and Organizations") and more rapidly and widely through the Internet and other mass media.

SEEING SOCIOLOGY IN EVERYDAY LIFE

The Rumor Mill: Paul Is Dead!

Probably the best-known rock group of the twentieth century was the Beatles—Paul McCartney, John Lennon, George Harrison, and Ringo Starr—whose music caused a cultural revolution in the 1960s. However, today's young people may not know the rumor that circulated about Paul McCartney at the height of the group's popularity (Rosnow & Fine, 1976; Kapferer, 1992).

On October 12, 1969, a young man telephoned a Detroit disk jockey to say that he had discovered the following "evidence" that Paul McCartney was dead:

1. At the end of the song "Strawberry Fields Forever" on the *Magical Mystery Tour* album, if you filter out the background noise, you can hear a voice saying, "I buried Paul!"

2. The phrase "Number 9, Number 9, Number 9" from the song "Revolution 9" on *The Beatles* (commonly known as the "White Album"), when played backward, seems to say, "Turn me on, dead man!"

Two days later, the University of Michigan student newspaper ran a story titled "McCartney Is Dead: Further Clues Found." It sent millions of Beatles fans racing for their albums to confirm the following "tip-offs":

3. A picture inside the *Magical Mystery Tour* album shows John, George, and Ringo wearing red carnations, but Paul is wearing a black flower.

4. The cover of the *Sergeant Pepper's Lonely Hearts Club Band* album shows a grave with yellow flowers arranged in the shape of Paul's bass guitar.

5. On the inside of that album, McCartney wears an armpatch with the letters "OPD." Is this the initials of some police department or confirmation that Paul had been "officially pronounced dead"?

6. On the back cover of the same album, three Beatles are facing forward but McCartney has his back to the camera.

7. On the album cover of *Abbey Road,* John Lennon is clothed as a clergyman, Ringo Starr wears an undertaker's black tie, and George Harrison is clad in workman's attire as if ready to dig a grave. McCartney is barefoot, which is how Tibetan ritual says to prepare a corpse for burial.

8. Also on the cover of *Abbey Road,* John Lennon's Volkswagen appears behind Paul with the license plate "28 IF," as if to say

that McCartney would be *28 if* he were alive.

The rumor that began to circulate was that McCartney had died of head injuries suffered in an automobile accident in November 1966 and that after the accident, record company executives had secretly replaced him with a double. This "news" left fans grief-stricken all around the world.

Of course, McCartney was and still is very much alive. He enjoys jokes about the "Paul is dead" episode, and few doubt that he dreamed up some of the details of his own "death," with a little help from his friends. But the story has a serious side, showing how quickly rumors can arise and how they spread in a climate of distrust. In the late 1960s, many young people were quite ready to believe that the media and other powerful interests were conspiring to conceal McCartney's death.

Back in 1969, McCartney himself denied the rumor in a *Life* magazine interview. But thousands of suspicious readers noticed that on the back of the page on which McCartney's picture appeared was an ad for an automobile. Holding this page up to the light, the car lay across McCartney's chest and blocked his head. Another clue!

WHAT DO YOU THINK?

1. What kinds of issues give rise to rumors?

2. What types of rumors have circulated recently on your campus? What got them started? What made them go away?

3. Overall, do you think rumors are helpful, harmful, or harmless? Why?

recent study, for example, found that 60 percent of U.S. adults claimed they did not understand our country's income tax system well enough to know if they supported it or not (Rosenbaum, 2003).

Also, not everyone's opinion carries the same weight. Some categories of people are more likely to be asked for their opinion, and what they say will have more clout because they are better educated, wealthier, or better connected. By forming an organization, various categories of people can increase their voice. Through the American Medical Association, for example, physicians have a lot to say about medical care in the United States, just as members of the National Education Association have a great deal of influence on public education.

POP CULTURE: All governments use propaganda for a wide range of goals. In the 1930s, the U.S. government created something of a moral panic in order to enact the Marijuana Tax Act of 1937. Help from Hollywood came in the form of the film *Reefer Madness*.

SOCIAL SURVEY: Scanning the General Social Survey data reveals that a significant proportion of respondents have no opinion about many issues: Should authorities prevent parents from showing pornographic films to their 10-year-old child? (17% express no opinion.) Does the average person influence government decisions? (8% voice no opinion.) Is the world getting better? (19% express no opinion.) Is there life after death? (8% have no opinion.)

SEEING SOCIOLOGY
in Everyday Life

Have you ever taken a course in which the information presented by the professor, some of the class readings, or perhaps a film seemed to be propaganda? What made it seem that way? Ask some of your classmates if they agree with you.

Special-interest groups and political leaders all try to shape public tastes and attitudes by using **propaganda,** *information presented with the intention of shaping public opinion.* Although we tend to think of propaganda in negative terms, it is not necessarily false. A thin line separates information from propaganda; the difference depends mostly on the presenter's intention. We offer *information* to enlighten others; we use *propaganda* to sway people toward our own point of view. Political speeches, commercial advertising, and even some college lectures may include propaganda in an effort to steer people toward thinking or acting in some specific way.

Fashions and Fads

Fashions and fads also involve people spread over a large area. A **fashion** is *a social pattern favored by a large number of people.* People's tastes in clothing, music, and automobiles, as well as ideas about politics, change often, going in and out of fashion.

In preindustrial societies, clothing and personal appearance change very little, reflecting traditional *style.* Women and men, the rich and the poor, lawyers and carpenters wear distinctive clothes and hairstyles that reflect their occupations and social standing (Lofland, 1973; Crane, 2000).

In industrial societies, however, established style gives way to changing fashion. For one thing, modern people care less about tradition and are often eager to try out new "lifestyles." Higher rates of social mobility also cause people to use their appearance to make a statement about themselves. The German sociologist Georg Simmel (1971, orig. 1904) explained that rich people usually stand out as the trendsetters; with plenty of money to spend on luxuries, they attract lots of attention. As the U.S. sociologist Thorstein Veblen (1953, orig. 1899) put it, fashion involves *conspicuous consumption* as people buy expensive products (from designer handbags to Hummers) not because they need them but simply to show off their wealth.

Ordinary people who want to look wealthy are eager to buy less expensive copies of what the rich make fashionable. In this way, a fashion moves downward through the class structure. But eventually, the fashion loses its prestige when too many average people now share "the look," so the rich move on to something new. In short, fashions are born along the Fifth Avenues and Rodeo Drives of the rich, gain popularity in Targets and Wal-Marts across the country, and are eventually pushed aside in favor of something new.

Since the 1960s, however, there has been a reversal of this pattern in the United States, and many fashions favored by rich people are drawn from people of lower social position. This pattern began with blue jeans, which have long been worn by people doing manual labor. During the civil rights and antiwar movements of the 1960s, denim jeans became popular among college students who wanted to identify with "ordinary people." Today, emblems of the hip-hop culture allow even the most affluent entertainers and celebrities to mimic styles that began among the inner-city poor. Even rich and famous people often identify with their ordinary roots: In one of her songs, Jennifer Lopez sings, "Don't be fooled by the rocks that I've got, I'm still, I'm still Jenny from the block."

A **fad** is *an unconventional social pattern that people embrace briefly but enthusiastically.* Fads, sometimes called *crazes,* are common in high-income societies, where many people have the money to spend on amusing, if often frivolous, things. During the 1950s, two young Californians produced a brightly colored plastic hoop, a version of a toy popular in Australia, that you can swing around your waist by gyrating your hips. The "hula hoop" became a national craze. In less than a year, hula hoops all but vanished, only to reappear from time to time. Pokémon cards are another example of the rise and fall of a fad (Aguirre, Quarantelli, & Mendoza, 1988).

How do fads differ from fashions? Fads capture the public imagination but quickly burn out. Because fashions reflect basic cultural values like individuality and sexual attractiveness, they tend to stay around for a while. Therefore, a fashion—but rarely a fad—becomes a more lasting part of popular culture. Streaking, for instance, was a fad that came out of nowhere and soon vanished; denim clothing, however, is an example of fashion that originated in the rough mining camps of Gold Rush California in the 1870s and is still popular today.

Panic and Mass Hysteria

A **panic** is *a form of collective behavior in which people in one place react to a threat or other stimulus with irrational, frantic, and often self-destructive behavior.* The classic illustration of a panic is people streaming toward the exits of a crowded theater after someone yells, "Fire!" As they flee, they trample one another, blocking the exits so that few actually escape.

Closely related to panic is **mass hysteria** or **moral panic,** *a form of dispersed collective behavior in which people react to a real or imagined event with irrational and even frantic fear.* Whether the cause of the hysteria is real or not, a large number of people take it very seriously.

One example of a moral panic is the controversy set off by flag burning during the Vietnam War; a more recent example is fear of AIDS or of people with AIDS. Sometimes such situations pose little real danger to anyone: There is almost no chance of becoming infected with HIV by simply interacting with someone who has AIDS. At another level, however, a fear of AIDS can become a danger if it were to give rise to a hate crime targeting a person with AIDS.

One factor that makes moral panics common in our society is the influence of the mass media. Diseases, disasters, and deadly crime all get intense coverage by television and other media, which hope to gain an audience. As Erich Goode (2000:549) points out, "The mass media *thrive* on scares; contributing to moral panics is the media's stock in trade."

Q: "Fashions fade; style is eternal." Yves St. Laurent

DISCUSS: A long-lived fad is Rubik's cube, invented in 1974 by Erno Rubik, a Hungarian architect. By 1982, sales exceeded 30 million cubes (and 10 million books on how to solve it); later, it fizzled. Another example is the troll doll, created by a Danish woodcutter as a gift for his daughter in 1959; it became a hit in 1964 and lasted for a number of years. What other fads can students identify?

NOTE: Contrast transient fads with more lasting trends, which are rooted in a basic cultural pattern. One such trend is McDonaldization, discussed in Chapter 7, involving fast food, fast oil changes, and packaged vacations, which responds to our need for quick products on the go.

disaster an event, generally unexpected, that causes extensive harm to people and damage to property

MAKING THE GRADE

Be sure you understand the three types of disasters—natural disaster, technological disaster, and intentional disaster—and can give an example of each.

Sociologists classify disasters into three types. Hurricane Katrina, which brought massive flooding to New Orleans, is an example of a natural disaster. The 1989 grounding of the tanker ship *Exxon Valdez*, which spilled 11 million gallons of crude oil off the coast of Alaska, was a technological disaster. The slaughter of hundreds of thousands of people and the displacement of millions more from their homes in the Darfur region of Sudan since 2003 is an example of an intentional disaster.

Mass hysteria is sometimes triggered by an event that, at the extreme, sends people into chaotic flight. Of course, people who see others overcome by fear may become more afraid themselves, and the hysteria feeds on itself. When a presidential 747 chased by an Air Force jet flew low over New York City in a 2009 "photo op," it sent thousands of people who remembered the 9/11 attacks running into the streets, although at the time there was no real danger.

Disasters

A **disaster** is *an event, generally unexpected, that causes extensive harm to people and damage to property*. Disasters are of three types. Floods, hurricanes, earthquakes, and forest fires are all examples of *natural disasters* (K. T. Erikson, 2005a). A second type is the *technological disaster,* which is widely regarded as an accident but is more accurately a failure to control technology (K. T. Erikson, 2005a). The oil spill resulting when the *Exxon Valdez* tanker ran aground off the coast of Alaska in 1989, dumping 11 million gallons of oil into the water, and the 1986 nuclear accident at the Chernobyl power plant in Ukraine, which released 400 times more radiation than the nuclear bomb that

destroyed Hiroshima at the end of World War II, were both technological disasters. A third type of disaster is the *intentional disaster,* in which one or more organized groups deliberately harm others. War, terrorist attacks, and the genocide in Yugoslavia (1992–95), in Rwanda (1994), and currently in the Darfur region of Sudan are examples of intentional disasters.

The full scope of the harm caused by disasters may become evident only many years after the event takes place. The Thinking Globally box on page 608 provides an example of a technological disaster that is still affecting people and their descendants more than fifty years after it occurred.

Kai Erikson (1976, 1994, 2005a) has investigated dozens of disasters of all types. From the study of floods, nuclear contamination, oil spills, and genocide, Erikson reached three major conclusions about the consequences of disasters.

First, disasters are *social* events. We all know that disasters harm people and destroy property, but what most people don't realize is that disasters also damage human community. In 1972, when a dam burst and sent a mountain of water down West Virginia's Buffalo Creek, it killed 125 people, destroyed 1,000 homes, and left 4,000

SEEING SOCIOLOGY
in Everyday Life

Many people who were forced from New Orleans when Hurricane Katrina hit believed that government officials had not done all they could to help them. How does such a belief intensify the effects of a disaster?

SEEING SOCIOLOGY
in Everyday Life

What social damage do you think was caused by the 1986 explosion and massive radiation leak at the Chernobyl nuclear plant in Ukraine?

THINKING GLOBALLY

A Never-Ending Atomic Disaster

It was just after dawn on March 1, 1954, and the air was already warm on Utrik Island, a small bit of coral and volcanic rock in the South Pacific that is one of the Marshall Islands. The island was home to 159 people, who lived by fishing much as their ancestors had done for centuries. The population knew only a little about the outside world—a missionary from the United States taught the local children, and two dozen military personnel lived at a small U.S. weather station with an airstrip that received one plane each week.

At 6:45 A.M., the western sky suddenly lit up brighter than anyone had ever seen, and seconds later, a rumble like a massive earthquake rolled across the island. Some of the Utrik people thought the world was coming to an end. And truly, the world they had always known was gone forever.

About 160 miles to the west, on Bikini Island, the United States military had just detonated an atomic bomb, a huge device with 1,000 times the power of the bomb used at the end of World War II to destroy the Japanese city of Hiroshima. The enormous blast vaporized the entire island and sent a massive cloud of dust and radiation into the atmosphere. The military expected the winds to take the cloud north into an open area of the ocean, but the cloud blew east instead. By noon, the radiation cloud had engulfed a Japanese fishing boat ironically called the *Lucky Dragon,* exposing the twenty-three people on board to a dose of radiation that would eventually sicken or kill them all. By the end of the afternoon, the deadly cloud reached Utrik Island.

The cloud was made up of coral and rock dust, all that was left of Bikini Island. The dust fell softly on Utrik Island, and the children, who remembered pictures of snow shown to them by their missionary teacher, ran out to play in the white powder that was piling up everywhere. No one realized that it was contaminated with deadly radiation.

Three-and-one-half days later, the U.S. military landed planes on Utrik Island and informed all the people that they would have to leave immediately, bringing nothing with them. For three months, the island people were housed at

another military base, and then they were returned home.

Many of the people who were on the island that fateful morning died young, typically from cancer or some other disease associated with radiation exposure. But even today, those who survived consider themselves and their island poisoned by the radiation, and they believe that the poison will never go away. The radiation may or may not still be in their bodies and in the soil and sand on the island, but it has certainly worked its way deep into their culture. More than fifty years after the bomb exploded, people still talk about the morning that "everything changed." The damage from this disaster turned out to be much more than medical—it was a social transformation that left the people with a deep belief that they are all sick, that life will never be the same, and that powerful people who live on the other side of the world could have prevented the disaster but did not.

WHAT DO YOU THINK?

1. In what sense is a disaster like this one never really over?

2. In what ways did the atomic bomb test change the culture of the Utrik people?

3. The U.S. government never formally took responsibility for what happened. What elements of global stratification do you see in what happened to the people of Utrik Island?

Source: Based on K. T. Erikson (2005a).

people homeless. After the waters had returned to normal and help was streaming into the area, the people were paralyzed not only by the loss of family members and friends but also by the loss of their entire way of life. Despite nearly forty years of effort, they have not been able to rebuild the community life they once knew. We can pinpoint when disasters start, but as Erikson points out, we cannot predict when their effects will end. And when disaster strikes, it is almost always the poor who suffer the most. This lesson was made clear, as

noted at the start of this chapter, when Hurricane Katrina struck New Orleans in 2005.

Second, Erikson discovered that the social damage is more serious when an event involves some toxic substance, as is usually the case with technological disasters. As the case of radiation falling on Utrik Island shows us, people feel "poisoned" when they have been exposed to a dangerous substance that they fear and over which they have no control.

Q: "Interest in the field [of collective behavior and social movements] has hardly been constant, tending instead to wax and wane partly in response to the level of movement activity in society." Doug McAdam, John D. McCarthy, and Mayer N. Zald (1996)

Q: "Do not make the mistake of thinking that a concerned group of people cannot change the world; it's the only thing that ever has." Margaret Mead

EXERCISE: Ask students to identify what social movements are represented by organizations on your campus. The class might invite several leaders to describe their groups' goals and strategies.

social movement an organized activity that encourages or discourages social change

claims making (p. 610) the process of trying to convince the public and public officials of the importance of joining a social movement to address a particular issue

SEEING SOCIOLOGY
in Everyday Life

Have you ever taken part in a social movement or witnessed one in action on your campus? If so, which of the four types best describes the movement?

Third, the social damage is most serious when the disaster is caused by the actions of other people. This can happen through negligence or carelessness (in the case of technological disasters) or through willful action (in the case of intentional disasters). Our belief that "other people will do us no harm" is a basic foundation of social life, Erikson claims. But when others act carelessly (as in the case of the *Exxon Valdez* oil spill) or intentionally in ways that harm us (as in the case of genocide in Yugoslavia), those who survive typically lose their trust in others to a degree that may never go away.

Social Movements

A **social movement** is *an organized activity that encourages or discourages social change.* Social movements are among the most important types of collective behavior because they often have lasting effects on our society.

Social movements are common in the modern world, but this was not always the case. Preindustrial societies are tightly bound by tradition, making social movements extremely rare. However, the many subcultures and countercultures found in industrial and postindustrial societies encourage social movements dealing with a wide range of public issues. In recent decades, for example, the gay rights movement has won legal changes in numerous cities and several states, forbidding discrimination based on sexual orientation and allowing formal domestic partnership and in some places even legal gay marriage. Like any social movement that seeks change, the gay rights movement has prompted a countermovement made up of traditionalists who want to limit the social acceptance of homosexuality. In today's society, almost every important public issue gives rise to a social movement favoring change and an opposing countermovement resisting it.

Types of Social Movements

Sociologists classify social movements according to several variables (Aberle, 1966; Cameron, 1966; Blumer, 1969). One variable asks, *Who is changed?* Some movements target selected people, and others try to change everyone. A second variable asks, *How much change?* Some movements seek only limited change in our lives, and others pursue radical transformation of society. Combining these variables results in four types of social movements, shown in Figure 23–1.

Alterative social movements are the least threatening to the status quo because they seek limited change in only a part of the population. Their aim is to help certain people *alter* their lives. Promise Keepers, one example of an alterative social movement, encourages men to live more spiritual lives and be more supportive of their families.

Redemptive social movements also target specific people, but they seek radical change. Their aim is to help certain people *redeem* their

FIGURE 23–1 Four Types of Social Movements

There are four types of social movements, reflecting who is changed and how great the change is.

Source: Based on Aberle (1966).

lives. For example, Alcoholics Anonymous is an organization that helps people with an alcohol addiction achieve a sober life.

Reformative social movements aim for only limited social change but target everyone. Multiculturalism, described in Chapter 3 ("Culture"), is an educational and political movement that advocates working toward social equality for people of all races and ethnicities. Reformative social movements generally work inside the existing political system. Some are *progressive,* promoting a new social pattern, and others are *reactionary,* opposing those who seek change by trying to preserve the status quo or to revive past social patterns. Thus just as multiculturalists push for greater racial equality, white supremacist organizations try to maintain the historical dominance of white people.

Revolutionary social movements are the most extreme of all, seeking the transformation of an entire society. Sometimes pursuing specific goals, sometimes spinning utopian dreams, these social movements reject existing social institutions as flawed in favor of a radically new alternative. Both the left-wing Communist party (pushing for government control of the entire economy) and the right-wing militia groups (advocating the destruction of "big government") seek to radically change our way of life (van Dyke & Soule, 2002).

Claims Making

In 1981, the Centers for Disease Control and Prevention began to track a strange disease that was rapidly killing people, most of them homosexual men. The disease came to be known as AIDS (acquired immune deficiency syndrome). Although this is a deadly disease, there was little public attention and few stories in the mass media. It was only

GLOBAL: To illustrate the concept of relative deprivation, consider the experience of this young man who finished college and took part in a Peace Corps program in Nepal (cited in D. G. Myers, 2000:134–5): "In rural Nepal, my one-room house had no electricity, no heat, no indoor toilet, no running water. . . . But although my living conditions in Nepal were a bit startling at first, the most [interesting] feature of my experience was how quickly they came to seem normal. Within a matter of weeks, I lost all sense of impoverishment. Indeed, my $40 monthly stipend was more than most others had in my village. . . . I experienced a feeling of prosperity."

●○ MAKING THE GRADE

All social movements engage in claims making, which is really what politics is all about. The idea is simply that the better a movement can get its message out in a convincing way, the more likely it is to succeed in its goals.

●○ MAKING THE GRADE

The discussion beginning on this page presents seven theories of why social movements come into being and why they may succeed or fail. They each add to our understanding of social movements.

about five years later that the public became aware of the rising number of deaths and began to think of AIDS as a serious social threat.

The change in public thinking was the result of **claims making**, *the process of trying to convince the public and public officials of the importance of joining a social movement to address a particular issue.* In other words, for a social movement to form, some issue has to be defined as a problem that demands public attention. Usually, claims making begins with a small number of people. In the case of AIDS, the gay community in large cities (notably San Francisco and New York) mobilized to convince people of the dangers posed by this deadly disease. Over time, if the mass media give the issue attention and public officials speak out on behalf of the problem, it is likely that the social movement will gain strength. Some new college programs also make claims about what should and should not be defined as a problem.

Considerable public attention has now been given to AIDS, and there is ongoing research aimed at finding a cure for this deadly disease. The process of claims making goes on all the time for dozens of issues. Today, for example, a movement to ban the use of cellular telephones in automobiles has pointed to the thousands of automobile accidents each year related to the use of phones while driving; so far, five states have passed laws banning this practice, seventeen others ban cell phones for new drivers, and debate continues elsewhere (McVeigh, Welch, & Bjarnason, 2003; Macionis, 2008; Governors' Highway Safety Association, 2009).

Political debate is a matter of claims making by various organizations. After the insurance giant AIG was saved from collapse by a massive government bailout, executives took millions of dollars in bonuses for themselves, claiming this served the interest of the company. The action prompted one organization to visit the executives' homes, denouncing the bonuses as little more than greed and demanding that the money be returned.

Explaining Social Movements

Because social movements are intentional and long-lasting, sociologists find this type of collective behavior easier to explain than brief episodes of mob behavior or mass hysteria described earlier in the chapter. Several theories have gained importance.

Deprivation Theory

Deprivation theory holds that social movements seeking change arise among people who feel deprived. People who feel they lack enough income, safe working conditions, basic political rights, or plain human dignity may organize a social movement to bring about a more just state of affairs (Morrison, 1978; J. D. Rose, 1982).

The rise of the Ku Klux Klan and the passage of Jim Crow laws by whites intent on enforcing segregation in the South after the Civil War illustrate deprivation theory. With the end of slavery, white landowners lost a source of free labor, and poorer whites lost the claim that they were socially superior to African Americans. This change produced a sense of deprivation, prompting whites to try to keep all people of color "in their place" (Dollard et al., 1939). African Americans' deprivation was far greater, of course, but as minorities in a racist society, they had little opportunity to organize. During the twentieth century, however, African Americans did organize successfully in pursuit of racial equality.

As Chapter 7 ("Groups and Organizations") explains, deprivation is a relative concept. Regardless of anyone's absolute amount of money and power, people feel either good or bad about their situation only by comparing themselves to some other category of people. **Relative deprivation,** then, is *a perceived disadvantage arising from some specific comparison* (Stouffer et al., 1949; Merton, 1968).

Alexis de Tocqueville's study of the French Revolution offers a classic illustration of relative deprivation (1955, orig. 1856). Why did rebellion occur in progressive France, where feudalism was breaking down, rather than in more traditional Germany, where peasants were much worse off? Tocqueville's answer was that as bad as their condition was, German peasants had known nothing but feudal servitude, and so they could imagine little else and had no basis for feeling deprived. French peasants, by contrast, had seen improvements in their lives that made them eager for more change. Consequently, the French—but not the Germans—felt relative deprivation. As Tocqueville saw it, increasing freedom and prosperity did not satisfy people as much as it sparked their desire for an even better life.

Closer to home, Tocqueville's insight helps explain patterns of rioting during the 1960s. Protest riots involving African Americans took place not in the South, where many black people lived in miserable poverty, but in Detroit, at a time when the city's auto industry was booming, black unemployment was low, and black home

Q: "Psychological attributes of individuals, such as frustration and alienation, have minimal direct impact for explaining the occurrence of rebellion and revolution per se." Carol Mueller

DIVERSITY: Although some social movements that challenge the status quo have been dominated by men, not all have: The abolition, suffrage, child care, and anti–drunk driving movements are only a few examples of movements dominated by women.

relative deprivation a perceived disadvantage arising from some specific comparison

MAKING THE GRADE

Review the discussion in Chapter 7 ("Groups and Organizations") on page 166 to see how we use reference groups to decide whether we are being deprived or not.

ownership was the highest in the country (Thernstrom & Thernstrom, 1998).

CRITICAL REVIEW Deprivation theory challenges our commonsense assumption that the worst-off people are the most likely to organize for change. People do not organize simply because they suffer in an absolute sense; rather, social movements arise out of a sense of *relative* deprivation. Both Tocqueville and Marx—as different as they were in many ways—agreed on the importance of relative deprivation in the formation of social movements.

But most people experience some discontent all the time, so deprivation theory leaves us wondering why social movements arise among some categories of people and not others. A second problem is that deprivation theory suffers from circular reasoning: We assume that deprivation causes social movements, but often the only evidence of deprivation is the social movement itself (Jenkins & Perrow, 1977). A third limitation is that this approach focuses on the cause of a social movement and tells us little about what happens after movements take form (McAdam, McCarthy, & Zald, 1988).

CHECK YOUR LEARNING State the basic idea of the deprivation theory of social movements. What are several criticisms of this theory?

Mass-Society Theory

William Kornhauser's *mass-society theory* (1959) argues that socially isolated people seek out social movements as a way to gain a sense of belonging and importance. From this point of view, social movements are most likely to arise in impersonal, *mass* societies. This theory points out the *personal* as well as the *political* consequences of social movements that offer a sense of community to people otherwise adrift in society (Melucci, 1989).

It follows, says Kornhauser, that categories of people with weak social ties are those most eager to join a social movement. People who are well integrated socially, by contrast, are unlikely to seek membership in a social movement.

Kornhauser concludes that activists tend to be psychologically vulnerable people who eagerly join groups and can be manipulated by group leaders. For this reason, Kornhauser claims, social movements are rarely very democratic.

A curious fact is that rioting by African Americans in U.S. cities during the 1960s was more common in the North (here, in Detroit), where good factory jobs were available and living standards were higher, than in the South, where a larger share of people lived in rural areas with lower incomes. Relative deprivation theory explains this apparent contradiction by pointing out that it was in the North, where life had improved, that people came to expect equality. Relative to that goal, the reality of second-class citizenship became intolerable.

CRITICAL REVIEW To Kornhauser's credit, his theory focuses on both the kind of society that produces social movements and the kinds of people who join them. But one criticism is that there is no clear standard for measuring the extent to which we live in a "mass society," so his thesis is difficult to test.

A second criticism is that explaining social movements in terms of people hungry to belong ignores the social-justice issues that movements address. Put otherwise, mass-society theory suggests that flawed people, rather than a flawed society, are responsible for social movements.

What does research show about mass-society theory? The record is mixed. Research by Frances Piven and Richard Cloward (1977) supports Kornhauser's approach. Piven and Cloward found that a breakdown of routine social patterns has encouraged poor people to form social movements. Also, a study of the New Mexico State Penitentiary found that when prison programs that promoted social ties among inmates were suspended, inmates were more likely to protest their conditions (Useem & Goldstone, 2002).

But other studies cast doubt on this approach. Some researchers conclude that the Nazi movement in Germany did not draw heavily from socially isolated people (Lipset, 1963; Oberschall, 1973). Similarly, many of the people who took part

NOTE: Mass-society theory has much in common with Hirschi's control theory of deviance (see Chapter 9, "Deviance"): Both suggest that the behavior in question arises among people with few social attachments.

NOTE: The importance of coming forward with personal testimonies within the movement to end sexual violence can be used to illustrate culture theory. Key phrases ("glass ceiling" or "date rape") also focus a movement.

NOTE: The conservative character of mass-society theory stems from the implication that it is the loss of traditional social ties (and not social inequality) that leads to social movements. Kornhauser follows Tocqueville rather than Marx in focusing on mass movements rather than on class movements. The distinction between mass society and class society is developed further in Chapter 24.

MAKING THE GRADE

Notice that culture theory says that people react to images and other elements of nonmaterial culture; political-economy theory (p.615) states that people react to economic or material factors.

Social movements are often given great energy by powerful visual images, which is one key idea of culture theory. During World War II, this photo of six soldiers raising the U.S. flag on the tiny Pacific island of Iwo Jima increased morale at home and was the inspiration for a memorial sculpture. Some twenty-five years later, newspapers published the photo on the right, showing children running from a napalm strike by U.S. planes in South Vietnam. The girl in the middle of the picture had ripped the flaming clothes from her body. This photo increased the strength of the social movement against the war in Vietnam.

in urban riots during the 1960s had strong ties to their communities (Sears & McConahay, 1973). Evidence also suggests that most young people who join religious movements have fairly normal family ties (Wright & Piper, 1986). Finally, researchers who have examined the biographies of 1960s' political activists find evidence of deep and continuing commitment to political goals rather than isolation from society (McAdam, 1988, 1989; Whalen & Flacks, 1989).

○ **CHECK YOUR LEARNING** State the basic idea of the mass-society theory of social movements. What are several criticisms of this theory?

Culture Theory

In recent years, sociologists have developed *culture theory,* the recognition that social movements depend not only on material resources and the structure of political power but also on cultural symbols. That is, people in any particular situation are likely to mobilize to form a social movement only to the extent that they develop "shared understandings of the world that legitimate and motivate collective action" (McAdam, McCarthy, & Zald, 1996:6; see also J. E. Williams, 2002).

In part, mobilization depends on a sense of injustice, as suggested by deprivation theory. In addition, people must come to believe that they are not able to respond to their situation effectively by acting alone.

Finally, social movements gain strength as they develop symbols and a sense of community that both build strong feelings and direct energy into organized action. Media images of the burning World Trade Center towers after the terrorist attacks on September 11, 2001, helped mobilize people to support the "war against terrorism." Likewise, photos of gay couples celebrating their weddings have helped fuel both the gay rights movement and the countermovement trying to prevent the spread of gay marriage. Colorful, rubber bracelets are now used by at least a dozen social movements to encourage people to show support for various causes.

○ **CRITICAL REVIEW** A strength of culture theory is reminding us that social movements depend not just on material resources but also on cultural symbols. At the same time, powerful symbols (such as the flag and ideas about patriotism and respecting our leaders) help support the status quo. How and when symbols turn people from supporting the system toward protest against it are questions in need of further research.

○ **CHECK YOUR LEARNING** State the basic idea of the culture theory of social movements. What is the main criticism of this theory?

Resource-Mobilization Theory

Resource-mobilization theory points out that no social movement is likely to succeed—or even get off the ground—without substantial

THE MAP: In general, opposition to the war in Iraq is greatest in large urban areas where most voters support the more liberal Democratic party. Mobilization was less effective in rural areas, especially in the older and more Republican Plains States.

DISCUSS: Illustrating the importance of resources to social movements, consider the contribution academics have made to the growing success of the feminist movement.

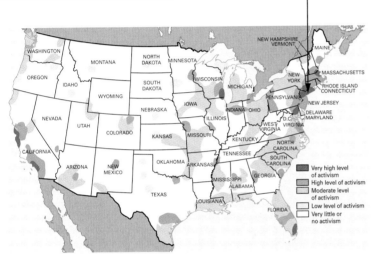

Sarah Goldberg and many of her friends in New York City took part in the 2007 virtual march against the war in Iraq.

Very high level of activism
High level of activism
Moderate level of activism
Low level of activism
Very little or no activism

Seeing Ourselves

NATIONAL MAP 23–1

Virtual March: Political Mobilization across the United States

In early 2007, the political action group MoveOn.org organized a "virtual march on Washington," urging people across the country to call their representatives in Congress to express opposition to the U.S. buildup of troops in Iraq. The map shows the areas in which the most telephone calls were made. What can you say about the places where the mobilization was most and least effective?

Source: MoveOn.org (2007).

resources, including money, human labor, office and communications equipment, access to the mass media, and a positive public image. In short, any social movement rises or falls on how well it attracts resources, mobilizes people, and forges alliances.

Outsiders can be just as important as insiders in affecting the outcome of a social movement. Because socially disadvantaged people, by definition, lack the money, contacts, leadership skills, and organizational know-how that a successful movement requires, sympathetic outsiders fill the resource gap. In U.S. history, well-to-do white people, including college students, performed a vital service to the black civil rights movement in the 1960s, and affluent men have joined women as leaders of the women's movement.

Resources connecting people are also vital. The 1989 prodemocracy movement in China was fueled by students whose location on campuses clustered together in Beijing allowed them to build networks and recruit new members (Zhao, 1998). More recently, the Internet and cell phones have been important resources that help organizations link hundreds of thousands of people across the country or around the world. In early 2007, the liberal activist organization MoveOn.org used the Internet to create a "virtual march" in which people across the country telephoned their representatives in Congress to oppose the troop "surge" in Iraq. National Map 23–1 shows where that organization had more or less success in mobilizing opposition to the war in Iraq. In the 2008 presidential campaign, YouTube videos of Barack Obama were viewed almost 2 billion times, surely contributing to his success. Almost one-third of U.S. voters say they now get most of their political news from the Internet (Ramirez, 2008). High technology has helped social movements to develop in other countries as well. Seeing Sociology in the News on pages 614–15 describes one recent case in Egypt.

The availability of organizing ideas online has helped people on campuses and elsewhere increase support for various social movements. For example, Take Back the Night is an annual occasion for rallies at which people speak out in opposition to violence against women, children, and families. Using resources available online, even a small number of people can plan and carry out an effective political event (Passy & Giugni, 2001; Packer, 2003).

CRITICAL REVIEW Resource-mobilization theory recognizes that both resources and discontent are necessary to the success of a social movement. Research confirms the importance of forging alliances to gaining resources and notes that movements with few resources may, in desperation, turn to violence to call attention to their cause (Grant & Wallace, 1991; Jenkins, Jacobs, & Agone, 2003).

Critics of this theory counter that "outside" people and resources are not always needed to ensure a movement's success. They argue that even relatively powerless segments of a population can promote change if they are able to organize effectively and have strongly committed members (Donnelly & Majka, 1998). Aldon Morris (1981) adds that the success of the civil rights movement of the 1950s and 1960s was due to people of color who drew mostly on their own skills and resources. A second problem with this theory is that it overstates the extent to which powerful people are willing to challenge the status quo. Some rich white people did provide valuable resources to the black civil rights movement, but probably more often, elites were indifferent or opposed to significant change (McAdam, 1982, 1983; Pichardo, 1995).

CHECK YOUR LEARNING State the basic idea of resource-mobilization theory. What are two criticisms of this theory?

DISCUSS: The women's movement illustrates the stages of Smelser's theory. (1) Historical pattern of patriarchy; women can organize in opposition. (2) Strain between U.S. ideal of equality and reality of patriarchy. (3) Early feminist scholarship and organization. (4) First wave of feminism—passage of 13th, 14th, and 15th Amendments extended rights to African American men but ignored women of both races; second wave of feminism—African American civil rights movement (led predominantly by men) and the increasing proportion of women in the labor force. (5) Mobilization spearheaded by organizations such as the National Organization for Women (NOW); widespread publication of feminist ideas (as in *Ms.* magazine). (6) Passage of 19th Amendment slowed the women's movement; ERA remains unratified, but legislation has advanced women's social and economic rights.

Seeing SOCIOLOGY in the NEWS

Wired

Cairo Activists Use Facebook to Rattle Regime

By DAVID WOLMAN
October 20, 2008

Under the scorching sun on a beach in Alexandria, Egypt, a few dozen political activists snap digital pictures and chatter nervously. Many of them wear white T-shirts emblazoned with the image of a fist raised in solidarity and the words "April 6 Youth" splashed across the back. A few of them get to work constructing a giant kite out of bamboo poles and a sheet of plastic painted to look like the Egyptian flag. Most are in their twenties, some younger; one teenage girl wears a teddy bear backpack.

Before the group can get the kite aloft, and well before they have a chance to distribute their prodemocracy leaflets, state security agents swarm across the sand. The cops shout threats to break up what is, by Western standards, a tiny demonstration.

The activists disperse from the beach, feeling hot and frustrated; they didn't even get a chance to fly their kite. Joining up with other friends, they walk together, . . . singing patriotic songs. . . .

A group of security agents jump out of nowhere. It's a coordinated assault that explodes into a frenzy of punches and shoves. There are screams and grunts as about a dozen kids fall or are knocked to the ground. The other 30 or so scatter, sprinting for blocks in all directions before slowing enough to send each other hurried text messages: Where are you? What happened?

Those who didn't get away are hustled into a van and two cars. The security men are shouting at them: "Where is Ahmed Maher?"

Three hours before the scuffle and arrests, Ahmed Maher walks briskly toward a dilapidated office building on Alexandria's Abu-Qir Street. . . .

He speaks softly to fellow activists . . . but his arrival has an electrifying effect: He's here. Back in March, Maher and a friend launched a Facebook group to promote a protest planned for April 6. It became an Internet phenomenon, quickly attracting more than 70,000 members. The April 6 Youth Movement . . . blossomed within days into something influential enough to arouse the ire of Egypt's internal security forces. Maher is part of a new generation in the Middle East that, through blogs, YouTube, Flickr, Twitter, and now Facebook, is using virtual reality to combat corrupt and oppressive governments. Their nascent, tech-fired rebellion has triggered a government backlash and captured the world's attention.

Two ceiling fans do little to relieve the stifling summer heat. Forty people are squeezed into the office. . . . Many of the attendees are connecting for the first time—in the real world, that is. Most know each other only through Facebook, and they're finally matching names and aliases to actual faces. Taped to the wall at the front of the room is a yellow piece of construction paper. The makeshift sign, written in Arabic lettering, reads: "Welcome to the first dialog meeting of the April 6 Youth Movement." Young women, some with head scarves and some without, sit in green plastic chairs, while guys in their twenties stand in silence. . . .

Facebook is the third-most visited Web site in Egypt, after Google and Yahoo. . . . Today, close to 1 million Egyptians are on the site, about 11 percent of the total online population. . . .

Structural-Strain Theory

One of the most influential theories about social movements was developed by Neil Smelser (1962). *Structural-strain theory* identifies six factors that encourage the development of social movements. Smelser's theory also suggests which factors encourage unorganized mobs or riots and which encourage highly organized social movements. The prodemocracy movement that transformed Eastern Europe during the late 1980s illustrates Smelser's theory.

1. **Structural conduciveness.** Social movements begin to emerge when people come to think their society has some serious problems. In Eastern Europe, these problems included low living standards and political repression by national governments.

2. **Structural strain.** People begin to experience relative deprivation when society fails to meet their expectations. Eastern Europeans joined the prodemocracy movement because they compared their living standards to the higher ones in Western Europe; they also knew that their standard of living was lower than what years of socialist propaganda had led them to expect.

3. **Growth and spread of an explanation.** Forming a well-organized social movement requires a clear statement of not just the problem but also its causes and its solutions. If people are confused about why they are suffering, they will probably express their dissatisfaction in an unorganized way through rioting. In the case of Eastern Europe, intellectuals played a key role in the prodemocracy movement by pointing out economic and political flaws in the socialist system and proposing strategies to increase democracy.

4. **Precipitating factors.** Discontent may exist for a long time before some specific event sparks collective action. Such an event occurred in 1985 when Mikhail Gorbachev came to power in the Soviet Union and began his program of *perestroika* (restructuring). As Moscow relaxed its rigid control over Eastern Europe, people there saw a historic opportunity to reorganize political and economic life and claim greater freedom.

5. **Mobilization for action.** Once people share a concern about some issue, they are ready to take action—to distribute leaflets, stage rallies, and build alliances with sympathetic groups. The initial success of the Solidarity movement in Poland—supported by the Reagan administration in the United States and by Pope John Paul II in the Vatican—mobilized people throughout Eastern Europe to press for change. The rate of change became faster and faster: What had taken a decade in Poland required only months in Hungary and only weeks in other Eastern European nations.

6. **Lack of social control.** The success of any social movement depends in large part on the response of political officials, police, and the military. Sometimes the state moves swiftly to crush a social movement, as happened in the case of prodemocracy forces in the People's Republic of China. But Gorbachev adopted a policy of nonintervention in Eastern Europe, open-

SOCIAL SURVEY: "Should organizing a nationwide strike of all workers against the government be allowed or not?" (GSS 2006, *N* = 1,519; *Codebook*, 2006:1488)

"Definitely allowed"   17.5%   "Definitely not allowed"   28.4%
"Probably allowed"   23.7%   "Don't know"/No response   1.5%
"Probably not allowed" 28.9%

Q: "You cannot put a rope around the neck of an idea." Sean O'Casey

Q: "All previous historical movements were movements of minorities, or in the interests of minorities. The proletarian movement is the self-conscious, independent movement of the immense majority, in the interest of the immense majority." Karl Marx and Friedrich Engels

In March, [Maher and Israa Abdel Fattah] learned that workers in the industrial city of El-Mahalla el-Kobra were planning a strike on April 6 to protest paltry wages and soaring food prices. [They] were sympathetic to the cause and wondered whether Facebook might be a way to spread the word about the strike, arrange more demonstrations in Cairo, and enlist support for a nationwide shopping boycott.

The duo launched the April 6 group on March 23. They used their real names for their Facebook profiles, and they were both listed as administrators for the group. That night, they sent out 300 invitations urging people to join. By the next morning, 3,000 people had signed up. Invitees weren't just joining—they were recruiting everyone they knew. It was the kind of viral growth Silicon Valley executives fantasize about, and the chain reaction was just beginning. . . .

The group's message was inclusive and earnest, factors that proved essential for amplifying interest and participation in the boycott and scattered demonstrations. Like minority opposition groups

everywhere, Egypt's are rife with infighting. The April 6 group, in contrast, benefited from a constituency of young people—many of whom had little or no political experience—and a broad message of solidarity for workers and the poor that made it easy for people to say, "Yeah, I'm into that." Click. . . .

In places like Egypt, these virtual gatherings are a big deal. Although freedom of speech and freedom of religion may be democracy's headliners, it's the less sexy-sounding freedom of assembly that, when prohibited, can effectively asphyxiate political organization. Uniting 70,000 people is no easy feat in a country where collective action is so risky. Social networking has changed that. In turn, it is changing the dynamics of political dissent. . . .

Government retaliation against the youth movement has embarrassed the regime. Many Egyptian citizens are rooting for the idealistic Facebook kids, and the international media look favorably on their cause. . . .

Maher thinks back to his arrest in May. Agents let him go after he gave up the password—a fake one. Payback seems inevitable. In any case, he has

a better plan in place this time: He has given one of his friends his password, with instructions to change it immediately if Maher is arrested. That way, even if Maher is broken by torture, he won't be able to give the authorities the information they need to take control of the April 6 network.

WHAT DO YOU THINK?

1. How is high technology a vital resource for today's social movements? How is it especially important in countries with limited freedom of assembly?

2. Have you been involved in a social movement that was based on an electronic network? If so, describe the importance of this technology to the movement's goals.

3. Overall, do you think that high technology will be a force for positive change in the world? Explain.

Adapted from the original article, "Cairo Activists Use Facebook to Rattle Regime" by David Wolman, *Wired* magazine online, October 20, 2008. Reprinted by permission of the author.

ing the door for change. Ironically, the movements that began in Eastern Europe soon spread to the Soviet Union itself, ending the historical domination of the Communist party in 1991 and producing a new and much looser political confederation.

○ **CRITICAL REVIEW**   Smelser's analysis explains how various factors help or hurt the development of social movements. Structural-strain theory also explains why people may respond to their problems either by forming organized social movements or through spontaneous mob action.

Yet Smelser's theory contains some of the same circularity of argument found in Kornhauser's analysis. A social movement is caused by strain, says Smelser, but the only evidence of underlying strain is often the social movement itself. What's more, structural-strain theory is incomplete, overlooking the important role that resources like the mass media or international alliances play in the success or failure of a social movement (Jenkins & Perrow, 1977; McCarthy & Zald, 1977; Olzak & West, 1991).

○ **CHECK YOUR LEARNING**   According to structural-strain theory, what six factors encourage the formation of social movements? What are two criticisms of this theory?

Political-Economy Theory

Marxist *political-economy theory* also has something to say about social movements. From this point of view, social movements arise

in capitalist societies because the capitalist economic system fails to meet the needs of the majority of people. Despite great economic productivity, U.S. society is in crisis, with millions of people unable to find good jobs, living below the poverty line, and living without health insurance.

Social movements arise as a response to such conditions. Workers organize to demand higher wages, citizens rally for a health policy that will protect everyone, and people march in opposition to spending billions to fund wars at the expense of social welfare programs (Buechler, 2000).

○ **CRITICAL REVIEW**   A strength of political-economy theory is its macro-level approach. Other theories explain the rise of social movements in terms of traits of individuals (such as weak social ties or a sense of relative deprivation) or traits of movements (such as their available resources), but this approach focuses on the institutional structures (the economy and political system) of society itself.

This approach explains social movements concerned with economic issues. But it is less helpful in accounting for the recent rise of social movements concerned with noneconomic issues such as obesity, animal rights, or the state of the natural environment.

○ **CHECK YOUR LEARNING**   State the basic idea of the political-economy theory of social movements. What is the main criticism of this theory?

Q: "No man can be a patriot on an empty stomach." William Cowper Brann

Q: "Social movements and their goals represent, respectively, actual and potential social changes." C. Wendell King

NOTE: A Marxist view of new social movements sees people and the state as entering more and more areas of private life in an effort to resolve the contradictions of 21st-century capitalist economies.

SOCIAL SURVEY: "Should organizing protest marches and demonstrations against the government be allowed?" (GSS 2006, *N* = 1,518; *Codebook*, 2006:1487)

"Definitely allowed"   53.1%   "Definitely not allowed"   5.8%
"Probably allowed"   29.8%   "Don't know"/No response   1.1%
"Probably not allowed"   10.3%

SEEING SOCIOLOGY
in Everyday Life

Have you been involved in a social movement? If so, did gender play a part in the movement's operation in terms of leadership? In some other way?

Efforts to control the process of global warming are a current example of a new social movement. This movement has gained ground because of the involvement of former vice president Al Gore, who has focused public attention on the harmful effects of change to Earth's climate.

New Social Movements Theory

A final theoretical approach addresses what are often called "new social movements." *New social movements theory* suggests that recent social movements in the postindustrial societies of North America and Western Europe have a new focus (McAdam, McCarthy, & Zald, 1988; Pakulski, 1993; Jenkins & Wallace, 1996).

First, older social movements, such as those led by labor organizations, are concerned mostly with economic issues, but new social movements tend to focus on improving our social and physical surroundings. The environmental movement, for example, is trying to stop global warming and address other environmental dangers.

Second, most of today's social movements are international, focusing on global ecology, the social standing of women and gay people, animal rights, and opposition to war. In other words, as the process of globalization links the world's nations, social movements are becoming global.

Third, most social movements of the past drew strong support from working-class people, but new social movements that focus on noneconomic issues usually draw support from the middle and upper-middle classes. As discussed in Chapter 17 ("Politics and Government"), more affluent people tend to be more conservative on economic issues (because they have wealth to protect) but more liberal on social issues (partly as a result of extensive education). In the United States and other rich nations, the number of highly educated

professionals—the people who are most likely to support "new social movements"—is increasing, a fact suggesting that these movements will grow (Jenkins & Wallace, 1996; F. Rose, 1997).

CRITICAL REVIEW   One strength of new social movements theory is recognizing that social movements have become international along with the global economy. This theory also highlights the power of the mass media and new information technology to unite people around the world in pursuit of political goals.

However, critics claim that this approach exaggerates the differences between past and present social movements. The women's movement, for example, focuses on many of the same issues—workplace conditions and pay—that have concerned labor organizations for decades. Similarly, many people protesting the use of U.S. military power consider economic equality around the world their primary goal.

CHECK YOUR LEARNING   How do "new" social movements differ from "old" social movements?

Each of the seven theories presented here offers some explanation of the emergence of social movements. The Summing Up table summarizes them all.

Gender and Social Movements

Gender figures prominently in the operation of social movements. In keeping with traditional ideas about gender in the United States, more men than women tend to take part in public life, including spearheading social movements.

Investigating Freedom Summer, a 1964 voter registration project in Mississippi, Doug McAdam (1992) found that movement members considered the job of registering African American voters in a hostile white community dangerous and therefore defined it as "men's work." Many of the women in the movement, despite more years of activist experience, ended up working in clerical or teaching assignments behind the scenes. Only the most exceptionally talented and committed women, McAdam found, were able to overcome the movement's gender barriers. In short, women have played leading roles in many social movements (including the abolitionist and feminist movements in the United States), but male dominance has been the norm even in social movements that otherwise oppose the status quo (Herda-Rapp, 1998).

Stages in Social Movements

Despite the many differences that set one social movement apart from another, all unfold in roughly the same way, as shown in Figure 23–2 on page 618. Researchers have identified four stages in the life of the typical social movement (Blumer, 1969; Mauss, 1975; Tilly, 1978):

NOTE: A key contention of new social movements theory is that recruitment into social movements is based more on symbolism (in Weberian terms) than on class interests (in Marxist terms). Indeed, Stanley Aronowitz (1992) suggests that minorities, lesbians, and environmentalists—adherents of the new social movements of the left—may take over the working classes' historic mission to over-

throw capitalism. New social movements are found in postindustrial societies, conventional social movements in industrial societies.

Q: "Mass movements can rise and spread without belief in a God, but never without belief in a devil." Eric Hoffer

MAKING THE GRADE

Use the Summing Up table to review all seven theories of social movements.

SUMMING UP

Theories of Social Movements

Deprivation Theory	People experiencing relative deprivation begin social movements. The social movement is a means of seeking change that brings participants greater benefits. Social movements are especially likely when rising expectations are frustrated.
Mass-Society Theory	People who lack established social ties are mobilized into social movements. Periods of social breakdown are likely to spawn social movements. The social movement gives members a sense of belonging and social participation.
Culture Theory	People are drawn to a social movement by cultural symbols that define some cause as just. The movement itself usually becomes a symbol of power and justice.
Resource-Mobilization Theory	People may join for all the reasons noted for the first three theories and also because of social ties to existing members. But the success or failure of a social movement depends largely on the resources available to it. Also important is the extent of opposition within the larger society.
Structural-Strain Theory	People come together because of their shared concern about the inability of society to operate as they believe it should. The growth of a social movement reflects many factors, including a belief in its legitimacy and some precipitating event that provokes action.
Political-Economy Theory	People unite to address the societal ills caused by capitalism, including unemployment, poverty, and lack of health care. Social movements are necessary because a capitalist economy inevitably fails to meet people's basic needs.
New Social Movements Theory	People who join social movements are motivated by quality-of-life issues, not necessarily economic concerns. Mobilization is national or international in scope. New social movements arise in response to the expansion of the mass media and new information technology.

Stage 1: Emergence

Social movements are driven by the perception that all is not well. Some, such as the civil rights and women's movements, are born of widespread dissatisfaction. Others emerge only as a small vanguard group increases public awareness of some issue. Gay activists, for example, helped raise public concern about the threat posed by AIDS.

Stage 2: Coalescence

After emerging, a social movement must define itself and develop a strategy for "going public." Leaders must determine policies, decide on tactics to be used, build morale, and recruit new members. At this stage, the movement may engage in collective action, such as rallies or demonstrations, to attract the attention of the media and increase public awareness. The movement may also form alliances with other organizations to acquire necessary resources.

Stage 3: Bureaucratization

To become a political force, a social movement must become an established, bureaucratic organization, as described in Chapter 7 ("Groups and Organizations"). As this happens, the movement relies less on the charisma and talents of a few leaders and more on a capable staff. When social movements do not become established in this way, they risk dissolving if the leader steps down, as is the case with many organ-

izations of college activists. By contrast, the National Organization for Women (NOW) is well established and can be counted on to speak for feminists despite its changing leadership.

But becoming more bureaucratic can also hurt a social movement. Surveying the fate of various social movements in U.S. history, Piven and Cloward (1977) found that leaders sometimes become so engrossed in building an organization that they neglect the need to keep people "fired up" for change. In such cases, the radical edge of protest is lost.

Stage 4: Decline

Eventually, most social movements begin to decline. Frederick Miller (1983) suggests four reasons this can occur.

First, if members have met their goals, decline may simply signal success. For example, the women's suffrage movement disbanded after it won the right for women to vote. But as is the case with the modern women's movement, winning one victory leads to new goals.

Second, a social movement may fold because of organizational failures, such as poor leadership, loss of interest among members, insufficient funds, or repression by authorities. Some people lose interest when the excitement of early efforts is replaced by day-to-day routine. Fragmentation due to internal conflicts over goals and strategies is another common problem. Students for a Democratic

NOTE: Since 1975, women have been overly represented as candidates for offices in the American Sociological Association (ASA) and have also had higher odds of winning than men, holding qualifications constant. Organizations such as Sociologists for Women in Society have played a part in boosting women's power in the ASA (Rosenfeld, Cunningham, & Schmidt, 1997).

NOTE: Many social movements fall into one of two categories: equality movements seeking social equality for various categories of people (based on class, race, sexual orientation, etc.) and specific protest movements targeting gun control, nuclear power, animal experimentation, etc. (Caplow et al., 1991).

NOTE: Joan Fitzgerald and Louise Simmons (1991) point out that to evaluate the success of any social movement, we must look beyond immediate effects to assess the movement's contribution to future social change.

● SEEING SOCIOLOGY
in Everyday Life

Can you think of social movements on your campus that illustrate the patterns shown in Figure 23–2?

Society (SDS), a student movement opposing the war in Vietnam, splintered into several small factions by the end of the 1960s as members disagreed over goals and strategies for change.

Third, a social movement can fall apart if leaders are attracted by offers of money, prestige, or power from within the "system." This type of "selling out" is one example of the iron law of oligarchy, discussed in Chapter 7 ("Groups and Organizations"): Organizational leaders can use their position to serve their own interests. For example, Vernon Jordan, once head of the activist National Urban League, became a close adviser to President Clinton and a rich and powerful Washington insider. But this process can also work the other way: Some people give up high-paying careers to become activists. Cat Stevens, a rock star of the 1970s, became a Muslim, changed his name to Yusuf Islam, and since then has devoted his life to the spread of his religion.

Fourth and finally, a social movement can be crushed by repression. Officials may destroy a social movement by frightening away participants, discouraging new recruits, and even imprisoning leaders. In general, the more revolutionary the social movement is, the more officials try to repress it. Until 1990, the government of South Africa banned the African National Congress (ANC), a political organization seeking to overthrow the state-supported system of apartheid. Even suspected members of the ANC were subject to arrest. Only after 1990, when the government lifted the decades-old ban and released from prison ANC leader Nelson Mandela (who was elected the country's president in 1994) did South Africa begin the journey away from apartheid.

Beyond the reasons noted by Miller, a fifth cause of decline is that a social movement may "go mainstream." Some movements become an accepted part of the system—typically, after realizing some of their goals—so that they continue to flourish but no longer challenge the status quo. The U.S. labor movement, for example, is now well established; its leaders control vast sums of money and, according to some critics, now have more in common with the business tycoons they opposed in the past than with rank-and-file workers.

Social Movements and Social Change

Social movements exist to encourage or to resist social change. The political life of our society is based largely on the claims and counterclaims of social movements about what the problems are and which are the right solutions.

But there is little doubt that social movements have changed our way of life. Sometimes we overlook the success of past social movements and take for granted the changes that other people struggled so hard to win. Beginning a century ago, workers' movements in the United States fought to end child labor in factories, limit working hours, make the workplace safer, and establish workers' right to bargain collectively with employers. Today's laws protecting the environment are another product of successful social movements. In addition, women now enjoy greater legal rights and economic opportunities because of the battles won by earlier generations of women.

As the Controversy & Debate box explains, some college students become part of movements seeking social and political goals. Keeping in mind the importance of social movements to the future direction of society, what about you? Are you willing to take a stand?

Social Movements: Looking Ahead

Especially since the turbulent 1960s—a decade marked by widespread social protests—U.S. society has been pushed and pulled by many social movements and countermovements calling attention to issues from abortion to financing political campaigns to medical care to war. Of course, different people define the problems in different ways, just as they are likely to settle on different policies as solutions. In short, social movements and the problems they address are always political (Macionis, 2010).

For three reasons, the scope of social movements is likely to increase. First, protest should increase as women, African Americans, gay people, and other historically marginalized categories of our population gain a

FIGURE 23–2 Stages in the Lives of Social Movements
Social movements typically go through four stages. The last is decline, which may occur for any of five reasons.

THEN AND NOW: Percentage of first-year college students who claim to "frequently discuss politics": *1967, 27%; 2008, 36%*. Percentage who view "keeping up to date with political affairs" as an important life goal: *1967, 55%; 2008, 40%*. Percentage who identify "being very well off financially" as an important life goal: *1967, 42%; 2006, 77%* (Pryor et al., 2008).

SOCIAL SURVEY: "In general, would you say that people should obey the law without exception, or are there exceptional occasions on which people should follow their consciences even if it means breaking the law?" (GSS 2006, *N* = 1,518; *Codebook*, 2006:1486)

"Obey the law"   52.6%   "Follow conscience"   46.7%
"Don't know"/No response   0.7%

SEEING SOCIOLOGY
in Everyday Life

The 2008 presidential election increased political activity of young people. Do you see this trend on your campus?

CONTROVERSY & DEBATE

Are You Willing to Take a Stand?

MYISHA: Why don't more students on this campus get involved?

DEANNA: I have more to do now than I can handle. Who's got time to save the world?

JUSTIN: Somebody had better care. The world needs a lot of help!

Are you satisfied with our society as it is? Surely, everyone would change some things about our way of life. Indeed, surveys show that if they could, a lot of people would change plenty! There is considerable pessimism about the state of U.S. society: Two-thirds of U.S. adults think that the average person's situation is "getting worse, not better," and three-fourths of respondents stated that most government officials are "not interested" in the average person's problems (NORC, 2007:267–68).

But in light of such concerns, few people are willing to stand up and try to bring about change. In recent years, 23 percent report giving money to some organization seeking social change, and just 6 percent of U.S. adults say they joined a rally or a march in the last five years (NORC, 2007:1176, 1523).

Many college students probably suspect that age has something to do with such apathy. That is, young people have the interest and idealism to challenge the status quo, but older adults worry only about their families and their jobs. Indeed, one of the popular sayings of the activist 1960s was "You can't trust anyone over thirty." But the facts are otherwise: Students entering college in 2006 expressed less interest in political issues than their parents.

Asked to select important goals in life from a list, 40 percent of first-year students included "keeping up with political affairs" and just 30 percent checked off "participat-ing in community action programs." As the figure shows, just 36 percent of students claimed to discuss politics frequently in the past year, and only 23 percent said they voted in a student election (Pryor at al., 2008).

Certainly, people cite some good reasons to avoid political controversy. Anytime we challenge the system—whether on campus or in the national political arena—we risk making enemies, losing a job, or perhaps even sustaining physical injury.

But the most important reason that people in the United States avoid joining in social movements may have to do with cultural norms about how change should occur. In our individualistic culture, people favor taking personal responsibility over collective action as a means of addressing social problems. For example, when asked about the best way to deal with problems of inequality linked to race, class, and gender, most U.S. adults say that individuals should rely on hard work and their own efforts, and only a few point to social movements and political activism as the best way to bring about change. This individualistic orientation helps explain why adults in this country are only half as likely as their European counterparts to join in lawful demonstrations (Inglehart et al., 2000; NORC, 2007).

Sociology, of course, poses a counterpoint to our cultural individualism As C. Wright Mills (1959) explained decades ago, many of the problems we encounter as individuals are caused by the structure of society. As a result, said Mills, solutions to many of life's problems depend on collective effort—that is, on people willing to take a stand for what they believe.

WHAT DO YOU THINK?

1. Do you think the reluctance of people in the United States to address problems through collective action shows that they are basically satisfied with their lives or that they think individuals acting together can't make a difference? Explain your answer.

2. Have you ever participated in a political demonstration? What were its goals? What did it accomplish?

3. Does it surprise you that most eighteen- to twenty-four-year-olds in the United States do not bother to vote? How do you explain such political apathy?

Student Snapshot

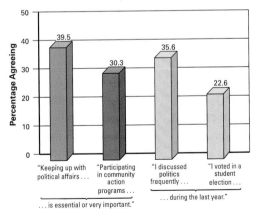

Political Involvement of Students Entering College in 2008: A Survey

First-year college students are mostly younger people who express limited interest in politics.

Source: Pryor et al. (2008).

greater political voice. Second, at a global level, the technology of the Information Revolution means that anyone with a television or a personal computer can be well informed about political events, often as soon as they happen. Third, new technology and the emerging global economy mean that social movements are now uniting people throughout the entire world. Because many problems are global in scope, we can expect the formation of international social movements seeking to solve them.

Seeing Sociology in Everyday Life

Chapter 23   Collective Behavior and Social Movements

What is the scope of today's social movements?

Social movements are about trying to create (or resist) change. Some movements have a local focus, others are national in scope, and still others tackle international or global issues.

> **HINT**   Every social movement makes a claim about how the world should be. In just about every case, some people disagree, perhaps giving rise to a countermovement. Certainly, many people might agree that tobacco products are harmful, but they also might argue that the best way to reduce tobacco use is not government action (reducing people's freedom) but educating people to make better choices or instituting programs to help people who try to quit. Likewise, "diversity" movements may attract opposition from people opposed to affirmative action or other programs that they see as favoring some racial category. Finally, almost all global issues are also local issues, in that they affect life here at home. After all, a disease spreading around the world is a threat to everyone. Countries ravaged by AIDS or hunger can become unstable, threatening global peace.

This group of high school students in Austin, Texas, recently took to the streets as part of an "Up in Smoke" movement seeking higher cigarette taxes and other government action to reduce the use of tobacco products by Texans. Can you imagine a countermovement on this issue? What might its goal be?

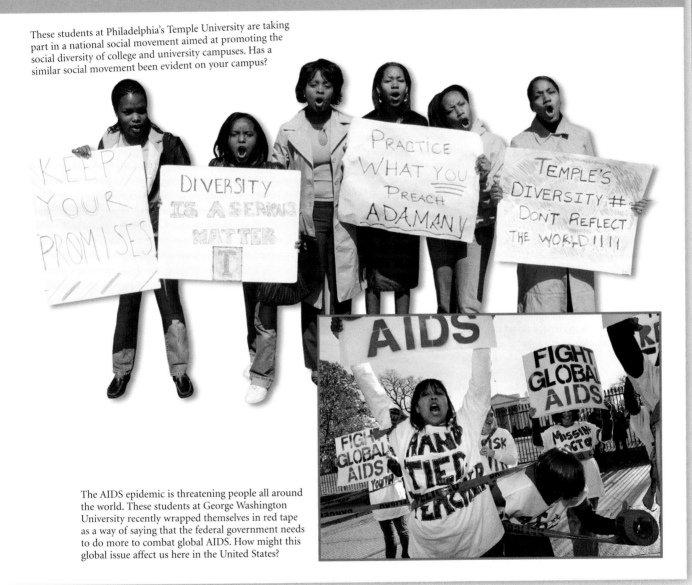

These students at Philadelphia's Temple University are taking part in a national social movement aimed at promoting the social diversity of college and university campuses. Has a similar social movement been evident on your campus?

The AIDS epidemic is threatening people all around the world. These students at George Washington University recently wrapped themselves in red tape as a way of saying that the federal government needs to do more to combat global AIDS. How might this global issue affect us here in the United States?

Applying SOCIOLOGY in Everyday Life

1. What social movements are represented by organizations on your campus? Invite several leaders to describe their group's goals and strategies to your class.

2. With ten friends, try this experiment: One person writes down a detailed "rumor" about someone important and then whispers it to the second person, who whispers it to a third, and so on.

The last person to hear the rumor writes it down again. Compare the two versions of the rumor. Are you surprised by the results of your experiment? Why or why not?

3. With other members of the class, identify recent fad products. What makes people want them? Why do people lose interest in them so quickly?

MAKING THE GRADE

CHAPTER 23 Collective Behavior and Social Movements

Studying Collective Behavior

COLLECTIVE BEHAVIOR differs from group behavior:
- Collectivities contain people who have little or no social interaction.
- Collectivities have no clear social boundaries.
- Collectivities generate weak and unconventional norms.

`pp. 600–601`

collective behavior (p. 600) activity involving a large number of people that is unplanned, often controversial, and sometimes dangerous

collectivity (p. 600) a large number of people whose minimal interaction occurs in the absence of well-defined and conventional norms

Localized Collectivities: Crowds

CROWDS, an important type of collective behavior, take various forms:
- casual crowds
- conventional crowds
- expressive crowds
- acting crowds
- protest crowds

`pp. 601–602`

MOBS AND RIOTS
Crowds that become emotionally intense can create violent mobs and riots.
- **Mobs** pursue a specific goal; **rioting** involves unfocused destruction.
- Crowd behavior can threaten the status quo, which is why crowds have figured heavily in social change throughout history.

`pp. 602–3`

crowd (p. 601) a temporary gathering of people who share a common focus of attention and who influence one another

mob (p. 602) a highly emotional crowd that pursues a violent or destructive goal

riot (p. 602) a social eruption that is highly emotional, violent, and undirected

EXPLAINING CROWD BEHAVIOR
Social scientists have developed several explanations of crowd behavior:
- **Contagion theory** views crowds as anonymous, suggestible, and swayed by rising emotions.
- **Convergence theory** states that crowd behavior reflects the desires people bring to them.
- **Emergent-norm theory** suggests that crowds develop their own behavior as events unfold.

`pp. 603–4`

Dispersed Collectivities: Mass Behavior

RUMOR AND GOSSIP
Rumor—unconfirmed information that people spread informally—thrives in a climate of uncertainty and is difficult to stop.
- Rumor, which involves public issues, can trigger the formation of crowds or other collective behavior.
- **Gossip** is rumor about people's personal affairs.

`p. 604`

PUBLIC OPINION AND PROPAGANDA
Public opinion consists of people's positions on important, controversial issues.
- Public attitudes change over time, and at any time on any given issue, a small share of people hold no opinion at all.
- Special-interest groups and political leaders try to shape public attitudes by using **propaganda.**

`pp. 604–6`

mass behavior (p. 604) collective behavior among people spread over a wide geographic area

rumor (p. 604) unconfirmed information that people spread informally, often by word of mouth

gossip (p. 604) rumor about people's personal affairs

public opinion (p. 604) widespread attitudes about controversial issues

propaganda (p. 606) information presented with the intention of shaping public opinion

fashion (p. 606) a social pattern favored by a large number of people

fad (p. 606) an unconventional social pattern that people embrace briefly but enthusiastically

panic (p. 606) a form of collective behavior in which people in one place react to a threat or other stimulus with irrational, frantic, and often self-destructive behavior

mass hysteria (moral panic) (p. 606) a form of dispersed collective behavior in which people react to a real or imagined event with irrational and even frantic fear

disaster (p. 607) an event, generally unexpected, that causes extensive harm to people and damage to property

FASHIONS AND FADS
People living in industrial societies use **fashion** as a source of social prestige.
- **Fads** are more unconventional than fashions; although people may follow a fad with enthusiasm, it usually goes away in a short time.
- Fashions reflect basic cultural values, which makes them more enduring.

`p. 606`

PANIC AND MASS HYSTERIA
A **panic** (in a local area) and **mass hysteria** (across an entire society) are types of collective behavior in which people respond to a significant event, real or imagined, with irrational, frantic, and often self-destructive behavior.

`pp. 606–7`

DISASTERS
Disasters are generally unexpected events that cause great harm to many people. Disasters are of three types:
- *natural disasters* (Example: Hurricane Katrina)
- *technological disasters* (Example: nuclear accident at the Chernobyl power plant)
- *intentional disasters* (Example: Darfur genocide)

`pp. 607–9`

Social Movements

SOCIAL MOVEMENTS are an important type of collective behavior.

- Social movements try to promote or discourage change, and they often have a lasting effect on society.

p. 609

social movement (p. 609) an organized activity that encourages or discourages social change

claims making (p. 610) the process of trying to convince the public and public officials of the importance of joining a social movement to address a particular issue

relative deprivation (p. 610) a perceived disadvantage arising from some specific comparison

TYPES OF SOCIAL MOVEMENTS

Sociologists classify social movements according to the range of people they try to involve and the extent of change they try to accomplish:

- *Alterative social movements* seek limited change in specific individuals. (Example: Promise Keepers)
- *Redemptive social movements* seek radical change in specific individuals. (Example: Alcoholics Anonymous)
- *Reformative social movements* seek limited change in the whole society. (Example: the environmental movement)
- *Revolutionary social movements* seek radical change in the whole society. (Example: the Communist party)

p. 609

✓ Social movements engage in **claims making** to try to convince people that a particular issue should be a matter of public attention (p. 610).

EXPLANATIONS OF SOCIAL MOVEMENTS

- **Deprivation theory:** Social movements arise among people who feel deprived of something, such as income, safe working conditions, or political rights.
- **Mass-society theory:** Social movements attract socially isolated people who join a movement in order to gain a sense of identity and purpose.
- **Culture theory:** Social movements depend not only on money and resources but also on cultural symbols that motivate people.
- **Resource-mobilization theory:** Success of a social movement is linked to available resources, including money, labor, and the mass media.
- **Structural-strain theory:** A social movement develops as the result of six factors. Clearly stated grievances encourage the formation of social movements; undirected anger, by contrast, promotes rioting.
- **Political-economy theory:** Social movements arise within capitalist societies that fail to meet the needs of a majority of people.
- **New social movements theory:** Social movements in postindustrial societies are typically international in scope and focus on quality-of-life issues.

pp. 610–16

See the Summing Up table on page 617.

✓ Traditional ideas about gender in U.S. society figure prominently in the organization of social movements (p. 616).

STAGES IN SOCIAL MOVEMENTS

A typical social movement proceeds through consecutive stages:

- *emergence* (defining the public issue)
- *coalescence* (entering the public arena)
- *bureaucratization* (becoming formally organized)
- *decline* (due to failure or, sometimes, success)

pp. 616–18

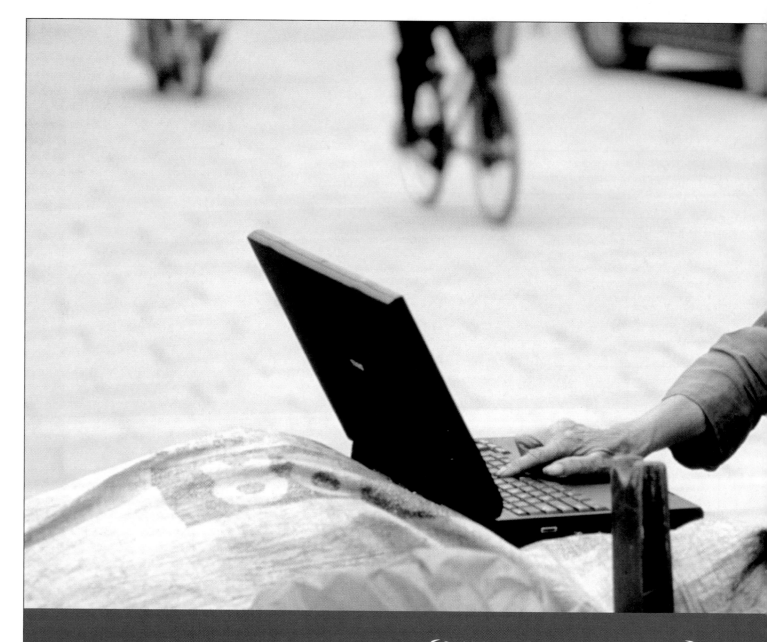

Social change often brings together traditional and moden ways of life. Sociologists study the process of social change, pointing to its causes and to the fact that the consequences of change are both expected and unexpected as well as both helpful and harmful.

CHAPTER 24

Social Change: Traditional, Modern, and Postmodern Societies

SUPPLEMENTS: An outline of this chapter, suggested discussion topics, and supplementary lecture material are found in the *Instructor's Manual.*

DISCUSS: Consider ways in which the university diffuses knowledge, thereby promoting social change (see Wilkinson, 1994).

Q: "After all is said and done, more is said than done." Anonymous

DISCUSS: Are "great people" or "average people" primarily responsible for social change? Historically, conservatives argued the former, since this individualistic position favored traditional hierarchy and elites. Liberals tended toward the more egalitarian, collectivist view.

CHAPTER OVERVIEW

This chapter explores social change, explaining how modern societies differ from earlier, traditional societies. It begins by describing the process of social change and some of its causes.

The five-story, red brick apartment building at 253 East Tenth Street in New York City has been standing for more than a century. In 1900, one of the twenty small apartments in the building was occupied by thirty-nine-year-old Julius Streicher; Christine Streicher, age thirty-three; and their four young children. The Streichers were immigrants, having come in 1885 from their native Germany to New York, where they met and married.

The Streichers probably considered themselves successful. Julius operated a small clothing shop a few blocks from his apartment; Christine stayed at home, raised the children, and did the housework. Like most people in the country at that time, neither Julius nor Christine had graduated from high school, and they worked ten to twelve hours a day, six days a week. Their income—which was average for that time—was about $35 a month, or roughly $425 a year. (In today's dollars, that would be slightly more than $11,000, which would put the family well below the poverty line.) They spent almost half of their income for food; most of the rest went for rent.

Today, Dorothy Sabo resides at 253 East Tenth Street, living alone in the same apartment where the Streichers spent much of their lives. Now eighty-seven, she is retired from a career teaching art at a nearby museum. In many respects, Sabo's life has been far easier than the life the Streichers knew. For one thing, when the Streichers lived there, the building had no electricity (people used kerosene lamps and candles) and no running water (Christine Streicher spent most of every Monday doing laundry, using water she carried from a public fountain at the end of the block). There were no telephones, no television, and of course no computers. Today, Dorothy Sabo takes all these conveniences for granted. Although she is hardly rich, her pension and Social Security amount to several times as much (in constant dollars) as the Streichers earned.

But Sabo has her own worries. She is concerned about the environment and often speaks out about global warming. A century ago, if the Streichers and their neighbors were concerned about "the environment," they probably would have meant the smell coming up from the street. At a time when motor vehicles were just beginning to appear in New York City, carriages, trucks, and trolleys were all pulled by horses—thousands of them. These animals dumped 60,000 gallons of urine and 2.5 million pounds of manure on the streets each and every day (Simon & Cannon, 2001).

It is difficult for most people today to imagine how different life was a century ago. Not only was life much harder back then, but it was also much shorter. Statistical records show that a century ago, life expectancy was just forty-six years for men and forty-eight years for women, compared to about seventy-five and eighty-one years today (Heron et al., 2008).

Over the past 100 years, much has changed for the better. Yet as this chapter explains, social change is not all positive. Even changes for the better can have negative consequences, creating unexpected new problems. As you will see, early sociologists were mixed in their assessment of *modernity,* changes brought about by the Industrial Revolution. Likewise, today's sociologists point to both good and bad aspects of *postmodernity,* the recent transformations of society caused by the Information Revolution and the postindustrial economy. One thing is clear: For better and worse, the rate of change has never been faster than it is now.

NOTE: In 1900, the entire U.S. had just 8,000 cars and recorded just 38 automobile fatalities.

NOTE: The French artist (Eugene Henri) Paul Gauguin lived from 1848 to 1903; his primitive paintings depicting life in Tahiti stood in stark contrast to the tremendous change that Western Europe was undergoing during this time of industrialization.

NOTE: In 1999, Joyce and Paul Bowler and their children were selected by a British TV show to spend a month living as a middle-class family did in 1900. After one week of getting up at 5:30 A.M., cooking and cleaning with no electricity, wearing corsets, and playing parlor games at night by gaslight, they were ready to give up (D. G. Myers, 2000:3).

social change the transformation of culture and social institutions over time

What Is Social Change?

In earlier chapters, we examined relatively fixed or *static* social patterns, including status and role, social stratification, and social institutions. We also looked at the *dynamic* forces that have shaped our way of life, ranging from innovations in technology to the growth of bureaucracy and the expansion of cities. These are all dimensions of **social change**, *the transformation of culture and social institutions over time*. The process of social change has four major characteristics:

1. **Social change happens all the time**. "Nothing is constant except death and taxes" goes the old saying. Yet even our thoughts about death have changed dramatically as life expectancy in the United States has doubled over the past 100 or so years. And back in the Streichers' day, people in the United States paid no taxes on their earnings; taxation increased dramatically over the course of the twentieth century, along with the size and scope of government. In short, even the things that seem constant are subject to the twists and turns of change.

   Still, some societies change faster than others. As Chapter 4 ("Society") explained, hunting and gathering societies change quite slowly; members of today's high-income societies, by contrast, experience significant change within a single lifetime.

   It is also true that in a given society, some cultural elements change faster than others. William Ogburn's theory of *cultural lag* (1964; see Chapter 3, "Culture") states that material culture (that is, things) usually changes faster than nonmaterial culture (ideas and attitudes). For example, the genetic technology that allows scientists to alter and perhaps even create life has developed more rapidly than our ethical standards for deciding when and how to use it.

2. **Social change is sometimes intentional but often it is unplanned**. Industrial societies actively promote many kinds of change. For example, scientists seek more efficient forms of energy, and advertisers try to convince us that life is incomplete without an iPod or some other gadget. Yet rarely can anyone envision all the consequences of the changes that are set in motion.

   Back in 1900, when the country still relied on horses for transportation, many people looked ahead to motorized vehicles that would carry them in a single day distances that used to take weeks or months. But no one could see how much the mobility provided by automobiles would alter everyday life in the United States, scattering family members, threatening the environment, and reshaping cities and suburbs. Nor could automotive pioneers have predicted the more than 41,000 deaths that occur in car accidents each year in the United

States alone (National Highway Traffic Safety Administration, 2008).

3. **Social change is controversial**. The history of the automobile shows that social change brings both good and bad consequences. Capitalists welcomed the Industrial Revolution because new technology increased productivity and swelled profits. However, workers feared that machines would make their skills obsolete and resisted the push toward "progress."

   Today, as in the past, changing patterns of social interaction between black people and white people, women and men, and gays and heterosexuals are welcomed by some people and opposed by others.

4. **Some changes matter more than others**. Some changes (such as clothing fads) have only passing significance; others (like the invention of computers) may change the world. Will the Information Revolution turn out to be as important as the Industrial Revolution? Like the automobile and television, the computer has both positive and negative effects, providing new kinds of jobs while eliminating old ones, isolating people in offices while linking people in global electronic networks, offering vast amounts of information while threatening personal privacy.

In response to the accelerating pace of change in the nineteenth century, Paul Gauguin left his native France for the South Pacific, where he was captivated by a simpler and seemingly timeless way of life. He romanticized this environment in many paintings, including *Nave Nave Moe (Sacred Spring)*.

Paul Gauguin, French (1848–1903), *Nave Nave Moe (Sacred Spring)*, 1894. Hermitage, Saint Petersburg, Russia. Oil on canvas, 73 × 98 cm. © The Bridgeman Art Library International Ltd.

NOTE: In modern, rapidly changing societies, the origins of cultural elements are often forgotten. Lucky Strike cigarettes were named for a California gold strike; Baby Ruth candy bars were named for the birth of Grover Cleveland's daughter.

DISCUSS: In a *Time*/CNN poll, more people thought the world would be in better shape (41%) at the end of the 21st century than feared it would be worse (32%). "About the same," 15% replied. Are students optimistic or pessimistic?

SEEING SOCIOLOGY
in Everyday Life

Look at the various changes in the United States over the past century. In each case, think about how the change affected everyday social life.

modernity social patterns resulting from industrialization

modernization the process of social change begun by industrialization

These young men are performing in a hip-hop dance marathon in Hong Kong. Hip-hop music, dress style, and dancing have become popular in Asia, a clear case of cultural diffusion. Social change occurs as cultural patterns move from place to place, but people in different societies don't always have the same understanding of what these patterns mean. How might Chinese youth understand hip-hop differently from the young African Americans in the United States who originated it?

Causes of Social Change

Social change has many causes. In a world linked by sophisticated communication and transportation technology, change in one place often sets off change elsewhere.

Culture and Change

Chapter 3 ("Culture") identified three important sources of cultural change. First, *invention* produces new objects, ideas, and social patterns. Rocket propulsion research, which began in the 1940s, has produced spacecraft that reach toward the stars. Today we take such technology for granted; during this century, a significant number of people may well travel in space.

Second, *discovery* occurs when people take note of existing elements of the world. For example, medical advances offer a growing understanding of the human body. Beyond the direct effects on human health, medical discoveries have stretched life expectancy, setting in motion the "graying" of U.S. society (see Chapter 15, "Aging and the Elderly").

Third, *diffusion* creates change as products, people, and information spread from one society to another. Ralph Linton (1937a) recognized that many familiar elements of our culture came from other lands. For example, the cloth used to make our clothing was developed in Asia, the clocks we see all around us were invented in Europe,

and the coins we carry in our pockets were devised in what is now Turkey.

In general, material things change more quickly than cultural ideas. That is, breakthroughs such as the science of cloning occur faster than our understanding of when—and even whether—they are morally desirable.

Conflict and Change

Inequality and conflict in a society also produce change. Karl Marx saw class conflict as the engine that drives societies from one historical era to another (see Chapter 4, "Society," and Chapter 10, "Social Stratification"). In industrial-capitalist societies, he maintained, the struggle between capitalists and workers pushes society toward a socialist system of production.

In the more than 125 years since Marx's death, this model has proved simplistic. Yet Marx correctly foresaw that social conflict arising from inequality (involving not just class but also race and gender) would force changes in every society, including our own, to improve the lives of working people.

Ideas and Change

Max Weber also contributed to our understanding of social change. Although Weber agreed that conflict could bring about change, he traced the roots of most social change to ideas. For example, people with charisma (Martin Luther King Jr. was one example) can carry a message that changes the world.

Weber also highlighted the importance of ideas by showing how the religious beliefs of early Protestants set the stage for the spread of industrial capitalism (see Chapter 4, "Society"). The fact that industrial capitalism developed primarily in areas of Western Europe where the Protestant work ethic was strong proved to Weber (1958, orig. 1904–05) the power of ideas to bring about change.

Ideas also direct social movements. Chapter 23 ("Collective Behavior and Social Movements") explained how change occurs when people join together in the pursuit of a common goal, such as cleaning up the environment or improving the lives of oppressed people.

Demographic Change

Population patterns also play a part in social change. A century ago, as the chapter opening suggested, the typical household (4.8 people) was almost twice as large as it is today (2.6 people). Women are hav-

NOTE: In light of how quickly today's information becomes obsolete, note that Euclidian mathematics texts remained up-to-date and more or less unchanged for 23 centuries.

Q: "All of us are taking a journey into the future that will last every day of our lives. What will we be seeing and doing? How will we live?" Isaac Asimov

THE MAP: Signaling the mobility and growth of U.S. society: The average age of housing stock is 30 years—below the median age of the population (35 years). The counties with more long-term residents typically have an older population, and they are also places where economic growth is limited or stagnant. Many of them have lost young people to urban areas offering greater economic prospects. Thus few counties have escaped change of one kind or another.

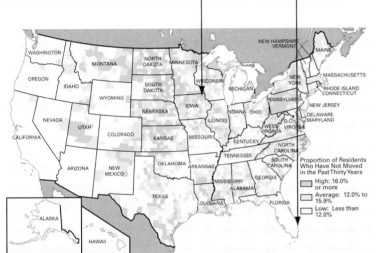

Martina Serfass, age 54, is a nurse who lives near Decorah, Iowa; most of the people in her community have lived there all their lives.

Serge Smith-Heiser, age 27, lives in an apartment complex in Fort Lauderdale, Florida, and thinks of his city as a place where people come and go. He arrived two years ago in search of a new job.

● MAKING THE GRADE

Be sure you understand the four traits of modernization identified by Peter Berger.

Seeing Ourselves

NATIONAL MAP 24–1

Who Stays Put? Residential Stability across the United States

Overall, only about 9 percent of U.S. residents have not moved during the past thirty years. Counties with a higher proportion of "long-termers" typically have experienced less change over recent decades: Many neighborhoods have been in place since before World War II, and many of the same families live in them. As you look at the map, what can you say about these stable areas? What accounts for the fact that most of these counties are rural and at some distance from the coasts?

Source: U.S. Census Bureau (1996).

Proportion of Residents Who Have Not Moved in the Past Thirty Years
- High: 16.0% or more
- Average: 12.0% to 15.9%
- Low: Less than 12.0%

ing fewer children, and more people are living alone. In addition, change is taking place as our population grows older. As Chapter 15 ("Aging and the Elderly") explained, 13 percent of the U.S. population was over age sixty-five in 2008, three times the proportion in 1900. By the year 2030, seniors will account for 20 percent of the total (U.S. Census Bureau, 2008). Medical research and health care services already focus extensively on the elderly, and life will change in countless additional ways as homes and household products are redesigned to meet the needs of older consumers.

Migration within and among societies is another demographic factor that promotes change. Between 1870 and 1930, tens of millions of immigrants entered the industrial cities in the United States. Millions more from rural areas joined the rush. As a result, farm communities declined, cities expanded, and for the first time, the United States became a mostly urban nation. Similar changes are taking place today as people move from the Snowbelt to the Sunbelt and mix with new immigrants from Latin America and Asia.

Where in the United States have demographic changes been greatest, and which areas have been least affected? National Map 24–1 provides one answer, showing counties where the largest share of people have lived in their present homes for thirty years or more.

One community that has recently experienced striking demographic change is the small city of Lewiston, Maine. Seeing Sociology in the News on pages 630–31 explains what is happening there.

Modernity

A central concept in the study of social change is **modernity,** *social patterns resulting from industrialization.* In everyday usage, *modernity* (its Latin root means "lately") refers to the present in relation to the past. Sociologists include in this catchall concept all of the social patterns that were set in motion by the Industrial Revolution, which began in Western Europe in the 1750s. **Modernization,** then, is *the process of social change begun by industrialization.* The timeline inside the back cover of this text highlights important events that mark the emergence of modernity. Table 24–1 on page 632 provides a snapshot of some of the changes that took place during the twentieth century.

Four Dimensions of Modernization

Peter Berger (1977) identified four major characteristics of modernization:

1. **The decline of small, traditional communities**. Modernity involves "the progressive weakening, if not destruction, of the . . . relatively cohesive communities in which human beings have found solidarity and meaning throughout most of history" (1977:72). For thousands of years, in the camps of hunters and gatherers and in the rural villages of Europe and North America, people lived in small communities where social life revolved around family and neighborhood. Such traditional worlds gave each person a well-defined place that, although limiting the range of choice, offered a strong sense of identity, belonging, and purpose.

   Small, isolated communities still exist in remote corners of the United States, of course, but they are home to only a small percentage of our nation's people. These days, their isolation is only geographic: Cars, telephones, television, and the Internet give rural families the pulse of the larger society and connect them to the entire world.

Q: "The philosophers have attempted to understand the world. The point, however, is to change it." Karl Marx

NOTE: Two sections of Chapter 4 ("Society") introduced Marx's materialist analysis of change and Weber's idealist analysis.

DISCUSS: Do students tend to criticize people from other cultures who take a
more casual attitude toward time?

Q: "Every era redefines what of the past remains relevant and what needs to be discarded." Irving Horowitz

Seeing SOCIOLOGY in the NEWS

Newsweek

The Refugees Who Saved Lewiston

By JESSE ELLISON
January 26, 2009

Barely a decade ago, Lewiston, Maine, was dying. The once bustling mill town's population had been shrinking since the 1970s; most jobs had vanished long before, and residents (those who hadn't already fled) called the decaying center of town "the combat zone." That was before a family of Somali refugees discovered Lewiston in 2001 and began spreading the word to immigrant friends and relatives that housing was cheap and it looked like a good place to build new lives and raise children in peace. Since then, the place has been transformed. Per capita income has soared, and crime rates have dropped. In 2004, *Inc.* magazine named Lewiston one of the best places to do business in America, and in 2007, it was named an "All-America City" by the National Civic League, the first time any town in Maine had received that honor in roughly 40 years. . . .

Immigrants from Somalia may sound like improbable rescuers for a place like Lewiston.

Maine is one of the whitest states in the country, second only to Vermont, and its old families have a reputation for distinct chilliness toward "outsiders." And many of the immigrants spoke no English at all when they arrived. But even beyond the obvious racial, cultural and religious differences between the Muslim newcomers and the locals, the town's image had become so negative that it was hard to imagine people choosing to move there. "Nothing could have rightfully prepared them," says Paul Badeau of the Lewiston-Auburn Economic Growth Council. "And nothing could have rightfully prepared us, either." It wasn't easy at first. Townspeople feared for the few jobs that remained in the area, and they warned that the strangers would overload local social services. In 2002, the then Mayor Laurier Raymond wrote an open letter to the Somali community begging them to stop encouraging friends and family to follow them to Maine.

But the Somalis kept coming, followed by Sudanese, Congolese and other Africans. By some estimates, 4,000 new immigrants have moved to

Lewiston since 2001, and dozens are still arriving every month. Eight years ago, the town's adult-education center had only 76 students learning English as a second language. Now some 950 pass through every year. . . . Today, Somali women and children in donated winter parkas carefully navigate the snowbanks in the town's formerly crime-ridden low-income residential area.

The center of town still has pawnbrokers and bars, but now there are also shops with names like Mogadishu and Baracka, with signs advertising halal foods and selling headscarves and prepaid African phone cards. "Generally, refugees or migrants that come into a town give a new injection of energy," says Karen Jacobsen, director of the Forced Migration Program at Tufts University's Feinstein International Famine Center. "Somalis particularly. They have a very good network [with strong] trading links, and new economic activities they bring with them." Retailers sell clothes and spices imported from Africa; other entrepreneurs have launched restaurants and

2. **The expansion of personal choice**. Members of traditional, preindustrial societies view their lives as shaped by forces beyond human control—gods, spirits, fate. As the power of tradition weakens, people come to see their lives as an unending series of options, a process Berger calls *individualization*. Many people in the United States, for example, choose a "lifestyle" (sometimes adopting one after another), showing an openness to change. Indeed, a common belief in our modern culture is that people *should* take control of their lives.

3. **Increasing social diversity**. In preindustrial societies, strong family ties and powerful religious beliefs enforce conformity and discourage diversity and change. Modernization promotes a more rational, scientific worldview as tradition loses its hold and people gain more and more individual choice. The growth of cities, the expansion of impersonal bureaucracy, and the social mix of people from various backgrounds combine to encourage diverse beliefs and behavior.

4. **Orientation toward the future and a growing awareness of time**. Premodern people model their lives on the past, but people in modern societies think more about the future. Modern people are not only forward-looking but also optimistic that new inventions and discoveries will improve their lives.

Modern people organize their daily routines down to the very minute. With the introduction of clocks in the late Middle Ages, Europeans began to think not in terms of sunlight and seasons but in terms of hours and minutes. Preoccupied with efficiency and personal gain, modern people demand precise measurement of time and are likely to agree that "time is money." Berger points out that one good indicator of a society's degree of modernization is the share of people wearing wristwatches.

Finally, recall that modernization touched off the development of sociology itself. As Chapter 1 ("The Sociological Perspective") explained, the discipline originated in the wake of the Industrial Revolution in Western Europe, where social change was proceeding most rapidly. Early European and U.S. sociologists tried to analyze the rise of modern society and its consequences, both good and bad, for human beings.

Ferdinand Tönnies: The Loss of Community

The German sociologist Ferdinand Tönnies (1855–1937) produced a lasting account of modernization in his theory of *Gemeinschaft* and *Gesellschaft* (see Chapter 22, "Population, Urbanization, and Environment"). Like Peter Berger, whose work he influenced, Tönnies (1963, orig. 1887) viewed modernization as the progressive loss of *Gemeinschaft*, or human community. As Tönnies saw it, the Industrial Revolution weakened the social fabric of family and tradition by small businesses providing translation services, in-home care for the elderly and other social services. There's even a business consultant. "Increasingly, there's an acceptance that immigration is associated with good economic growth," says urban-studies specialist Richard Florida, director of the University of Toronto's Martin Prosperity Institute. "How is Maine going to grow? It's a big state with a sparse population. One of the ways to grow quickly is import people."

Commerce isn't all the Somalis are reshaping. Maine has America's highest median age and the lowest percentage of residents under 18. Throughout the 1990s, the state's population of 20- to 30-year-olds fell an average of 3,000 a year. Demographers predict that by 2030, the state will have only two workers for each retiree. "In many small Maine towns they're looking at having to close schools for lack of schoolchildren," says State Economist Catherine Reilly. "It will snowball.... In ten or fifteen years that's going to be the difficulty of businesses finding workers." The

same ominous trend is seen in other states with similarly homogenous demographics and low numbers of foreign-born residents—states like Montana, North Dakota and West Virginia. Reilly adds: "If you told a demographer just our racial composition, they would be able to guess that we're an old state with a low birthrate."

Lewiston's sudden jolt is reflected even in enrollment at local universities. Although University of Maine enrollment has dropped systemwide since 2002, the student population at its Lewiston campus jumped 16 percent between 2002 and 2007. And Andover College, which opened a campus in Lewiston in 2004, had to start expanding almost immediately to accommodate a boom in applications. Enrollment doubled in two years. The reason? "Young people didn't want to go to a place that's all white," says Morrison. Practically everyone in Lewiston credits the Somalis' discovery of their town with much of its newfound success. "It's been an absolute blessing in many ways," says Badeau. "Just to have an infusion of diversity,

an infusion of culture and of youth. Cultural diversity was the missing piece." The question is whether the rest of Maine—and other states like it—can find their own missing pieces.

WHAT DO YOU THINK?

1. What was the initial reaction of the people of Lewiston, Maine, to the prospect of thousands of immigrants settling in their town? What actually happened?

2. What are some of the changes that immigration brought to this city and state?

3. Do you think young people are more attracted to towns that are more racially and ethnically diverse? Explain.

introducing a businesslike emphasis on facts, efficiency, and money. European and North American societies gradually became rootless and impersonal as people came to associate mostly on the basis of self-interest—the state Tönnies termed *Gesellschaft*.

Early in the twentieth century, at least some parts of the United States could be described using Tönnies's concept of *Gemeinschaft*. Families that had lived for generations in small villages and towns were bound together in a hardworking, slow-moving way of life. Telephones (invented in 1876) were rare; not until 1915 could a person place a coast-to-coast call. Living without television (introduced commercially in the 1920s and not widespread until after 1950), families entertained themselves, often gathering with friends in the evening to share stories, sorrows, or song. Lacking rapid transportation (Henry Ford's assembly line began in 1908, but cars became common only after World War II), many people knew little of the world beyond their hometown.

Inevitable tensions and conflicts divided these communities of the past. But according to Tönnies, because of the traditional spirit of *Gemeinschaft*, people were "essentially united in spite of all separating factors" (1963:65, orig. 1887).

Modernity turns societies inside out so that, as Tönnies put it, people are "essentially separated in spite of uniting factors" (1963:65, orig. 1887). This is the world of *Gesellschaft*, where, especially in large cities, most people live among strangers and ignore the people they pass on the street. Trust is hard to come by in a mobile and anony-

mous society where people tend to put their personal needs ahead of group loyalty and an increasing majority of adults believe "you can't be too careful" in dealing with people (NORC, 2007:1743). No wonder researchers conclude that even as we become more affluent, the social health of modern societies has declined (D. G. Myers, 2000).

○ **CRITICAL REVIEW** Tönnies's theory of *Gemeinschaft* and *Gesellschaft* is the most widely cited model of modernization. The theory's strength lies in combining various dimensions of change: growing population, the rise of cities, and increasing impersonality in social interaction. But modern life, though often impersonal, still has some degree of *Gemeinschaft*. Even in a world of strangers, modern friendships can be strong and lasting. Some analysts also think that Tönnies favored—perhaps even romanticized—traditional societies while overlooking bonds of family, neighborhood, and friendship that continue to flourish in modern societies.

○ **CHECK YOUR LEARNING** As types of social organization, how do *Gemeinschaft* and *Gesellschaft* differ?

Emile Durkheim: The Division of Labor

The French sociologist Emile Durkheim, whose work is discussed in Chapter 4 ("Society"), shared Tönnies's interest in the profound social changes that resulted from the Industrial Revolution. For Durkheim

NOTE: A characteristic of modernity is the rise of tolerance (from the Latin *tolerare*, meaning "to bear"). For most of us, the virtues of tolerance are easy to enumerate, if not always to act on. Contemporary people tend to embrace cultural relativism (especially as their schooling increases); traditional people (and those with less schooling) generally adopt a more ethnocentric, absolutist worldview.

Q: "Only the wisest and the stupidest do not change." Confucius

NOTE: Durkheim's concept of "mechanical solidarity" implies that we can learn the workings of an entire society by examining any one component of it, just as we can understand a physical substance through analysis of a single molecule. This is not true of internally differentiated, organic bodies.

division of labor specialized economic activity

anomie a condition in which society provides little moral guidance to individuals

MAKING THE GRADE

Durkheim's concepts match up with those of Tönnies, but be sure to get it right: Mechanical solidarity corresponds to *Gemeinschaft*, and organic solidarity is the same as *Gesellschaft*.

Table 24–1 The United States: A Century of Change

	1900	2000
National population	76 million	281 million
Share living in cities	40%	80%
Life expectancy	46 years (men), 48 years (women)	74 years (men), 79 years (women)
Median age	22.9 years	35.3 years
Average household income	$8,000 (in 2000 dollars)	$40,000 (in 2000 dollars)
Share of income spent on food	43%	15%
Share of homes with flush toilets	10%	98%
Average number of cars	1 car for every 2,000 households	1.3 cars for every household
Divorce rate	about 1 in 20 marriages	about 8 in 20 marriages
Average gallons of petroleum products consumed	34 per person per year	1,100 per person per year

(1964a, orig. 1893), modernization is defined by an increasing **division of labor**, or *specialized economic activity*. Every member of a traditional society performs more or less the same daily round of activities; modern societies function by having people perform highly specific roles.

Durkheim explained that preindustrial societies are held together by *mechanical solidarity,* or shared moral sentiments. In other words, members of preindustrial societies view everyone as basically alike, doing the same kind of work and belonging together. Durkheim's concept of mechanical solidarity is virtually the same as Tönnies's *Gemeinschaft.*

With modernization, the division of labor becomes more and more pronounced. To Durkheim, this change means less mechanical solidarity but more of another kind of tie: *organic solidarity,* or mutual dependency between people engaged in specialized work. Put simply, modern societies are held together not by likeness but by difference: All of us must depend on others to meet most of our needs. Organic solidarity corresponds to Tönnies's concept of *Gesellschaft.*

Despite obvious similarities in their thinking, Durkheim and Tönnies viewed modernity somewhat differently. To Tönnies, modern *Gesellschaft* amounts to the loss of social solidarity, because modern people lose the "natural" and "organic" bonds of the rural village, leaving only the "artificial" and "mechanical" ties of the big, industrial city. Durkheim had a different view of modernity, even reversing Tönnies's language to bring home the point. Durkheim labeled modern society "organic," arguing that modern society is no less natural than any other, and he described traditional societies as "mechanical" because they are so regimented. Durkheim viewed modernization not as the loss of community but as a change from community based on bonds of likeness (kinship and neighborhood) to community based on economic interdependence (the division of

labor). Durkheim's view of modernity is thus both more complex and more positive than Tönnies's view.

CRITICAL REVIEW Durkheim's work, which resembles that of Tönnies, is a highly influential analysis of modernity. Of the two, Durkheim was more optimistic; still, he feared that modern societies might become so diverse that they would collapse into **anomie**, *a condition in which society provides little moral guidance to individuals.* Living with weak moral norms and values, modern people can become egocentric, placing their own needs above those of others and finding little purpose in life.

The suicide rate—which Durkheim considered a good index of anomie—did in fact increase in the United States over the course of the twentieth century, and the vast majority of U.S. adults report that they see moral questions not in clear terms of right and wrong but in confusing "shades of gray" (NORC, 2007:447). Yet shared norms and values still seem strong enough to give most individuals some sense of meaning and purpose. Whatever the hazards of anomie, most people seem to value the personal freedom modern society gives us.

CHECK YOUR LEARNING Define mechanical solidarity and organic solidarity. In his view of the modern world, what makes Durkheim more optimistic than Tönnies?

Max Weber: Rationalization

For Max Weber (also discussed in Chapter 4, "Society"), modernity meant replacing a traditional worldview with a rational way of thinking. In preindustrial societies, tradition acts as a constant brake on change. To traditional people, "truth" is roughly the same as "what has always been" (1978:36, orig. 1921). To modern peo-

Q: "With the loss of tradition we have lost the thread that safely guided us through the vast realms of the past." Hannah Arendt

RESOURCE: Emile Durkheim's "Anomy and Modern Life" and Max Weber's "The Disenchantment of Modern Life" are among the classics in the author's companion reader *Seeing Ourselves*, 8th ed.

DISCUSS: Consider the limits of science implied by Leo Tolstoy's observation that "science is meaningless because it gives no answer to the question, the only question of importance for us: 'What shall we do and how shall we live?'"

WEB: For more on Tönnies, Durkheim, Weber, and Marx, visit the Gallery of Sociologists at http://www.TheSociologyPage.com

MAKING THE GRADE

Be sure you see what, from Max Weber's point of view, the scientist, the capitalist, and the bureaucrat have in common.

Max Weber maintained that the distinctive character of modern society was its rational worldview. Virtually all of Weber's work on modernity centered on types of people he considered typical of their age: the scientist, the capitalist, and the bureaucrat. Each is rational to the core: The scientist is committed to the orderly discovery of truth, the capitalist to the orderly pursuit of profit, and the bureaucrat to orderly conformity to a system of rules.

ple, however, "truth" is the result of rational calculation. Because they value efficiency and have little reverence for the past, modern people adopt whatever social patterns allow them to achieve their goals.

Echoing Tönnies and Durkheim, who held that industrialization weakens tradition, Weber declared modern society to be "disenchanted." The unquestioned truths of an earlier time had been challenged by rational thinking. In short, modern society turns away from the gods. Throughout his life, Weber studied various modern "types"—the capitalist, the scientist, the bureaucrat—all of whom share the detached worldview that Weber believed was coming to dominate humanity.

CRITICAL REVIEW Compared with Tönnies and especially Durkheim, Weber was very critical of modern society. He knew that science could produce technological and organizational wonders but worried that science was turning us away from more basic questions about the meaning and purpose of human existence. Weber feared that rationalization, especially in bureaucracies, would erode the human spirit with endless rules and regulations.

CHECK YOUR LEARNING How did Weber understand modernity? What does it mean to say that modern society (think of the scientists, capitalists, and bureaucrats) is "disenchanted"?

Some of Weber's critics think that the alienation he attributed to bureaucracy actually stemmed from social inequality. That criticism leads us to the ideas of Karl Marx.

Karl Marx: Capitalism

For Karl Marx, modern society was synonymous with capitalism; he saw the Industrial Revolution as primarily a *capitalist revolution.* Marx traced the emergence of the bourgeoisie in medieval Europe to the expansion of commerce. The bourgeoisie gradually displaced the feudal aristocracy as the Industrial Revolution gave it a powerful new productive system.

Marx agreed that modernity weakened small communities (as described by Tönnies), sharpened the division of labor (as noted by Durkheim), and encouraged a rational worldview (as Weber claimed). But he saw these simply as conditions necessary for capitalism to flourish. Capitalism, according to Marx, draws population from farms and small towns into an ever-expanding market system centered in cities; specialization is needed for efficient factories; and rationality is exemplified by the capitalists' endless pursuit of profit.

Earlier chapters have painted Marx as a spirited critic of capitalist society, but his vision of modernity also includes a good bit of optimism. Unlike Weber, who viewed modern society as an "iron cage" of bureaucracy, Marx believed that social conflict in capitalist societies would sow seeds of revolutionary change, leading to an

DISCUSS: Pose to the class the Weberian irony that the more we learn about the natural world, the more uncertainty we feel about ultimate cause and meaning.

Q: "The bourgeoisie, during its rule of scarcely one hundred years, has created more massive and more colossal productive forces than have all preceding generations together." Karl Marx and Friedrich Engels

NOTE: The term "individual," with a Latin root meaning "indivisible," first became widely used in early 19th-century Europe, at a time when traditional social ties were weakening.

Q: "Things do not change; we change." Henry David Thoreau

MAKING THE GRADE

This table is a good summary of trends that define our modern society. It also reviews much of what you have studied in earlier chapters.

SUMMING UP

Traditional and Modern Societies: The Big Picture

Elements of Society	Traditional Societies	Modern Societies
Cultural Patterns		
Values	Homogeneous; sacred character; few subcultures and countercultures	Heterogeneous; secular character; many subcultures and countercultures
Norms	Great moral significance; little tolerance of diversity	Variable moral significance; high tolerance of diversity
Time orientation	Present linked to past	Present linked to future
Technology	Preindustrial; human and animal energy	Industrial; advanced energy sources
Social Structure		
Status and role	Few statuses, most ascribed; few specialized roles	Many statuses, some ascribed and some achieved; many specialized roles
Relationships	Typically primary; little anonymity or privacy	Typically secondary; much anonymity and privacy
Communication	Face to face	Face-to-face communication supplemented by mass media
Social control	Informal gossip	Formal police and legal system
Social stratification	Rigid patterns of social inequality; little mobility	Fluid patterns of social inequality; high mobility
Gender patterns	Pronounced patriarchy; women's lives centered on the home	Declining patriarchy; increasing number of women in the paid labor force
Settlement patterns	Small-scale; population typically small and widely dispersed in rural villages and small towns	Large-scale; population typically large and concentrated in cities
Social Institutions		
Economy	Based on agriculture; much manufacturing in the home; little white-collar work	Based on industrial mass production; factories become centers of production; increasing white-collar work
State	Small-scale government; little state intervention in society	Large-scale government; much state intervention in society
Family	Extended family as the primary means of socialization and economic production	Nuclear family retains some socialization functions but is more a unit of consumption than of production
Religion	Religion guides worldview; little religious pluralism	Religion weakens with the rise of science; extensive religious pluralism
Education	Formal schooling limited to elites	Basic schooling becomes universal, with growing proportion receiving advanced education
Health	High birth and death rates; short life expectancy because of low standard of living and simple medical technology	Low birth and death rates; longer life expectancy because of higher standard of living and sophisticated medical technology
Social Change	Slow; change evident over many generations	Rapid; change evident within a single generation

egalitarian socialism. Such a society, as he saw it, would harness the wonders of industrial technology to enrich people's lives and also rid the world of social classes, the source of social conflict and suffering. Although Marx's evaluation of modern, capitalist society was negative, he imagined a future of human freedom, creativity, and community.

CRITICAL REVIEW Marx's theory of modernization is a complex theory of capitalism. But he underestimated the dominance of bureaucracy in modern societies. In socialist societies in particular, the stifling effects of bureaucracy turned out to be as bad as, or even worse than, the dehumanizing aspects of capitalism. The upheavals in Eastern Europe and the former Soviet

Q: "Kites fly highest against the wind." Winston Churchill

DISCUSS: Graphically contrast traditional society (strong social surroundings, weak individualism) with modern society (opposite pattern) using these figures: (from E. Digby Baltzell).

Q: "Our lives make sense in a thousand ways, most of which we are unaware of, because of traditions that are centuries, if not millennia, old." Robert N. Bellah et al. (1985:282)

RESOURCE: An excerpt from David Myers's *American Paradox: Spiritual Hunger in an Age of Plenty* is included in the author's companion reader *Seeing Ourselves*, 8th ed.

mass society a society in which prosperity and bureaucracy have weakened traditional social ties

class society (p. 636) a capitalist society with pronounced social stratification

SEEING SOCIOLOGY
in Everyday Life

Identify five examples of "mass culture" that are the same throughout the United States. Name five more that differ from region to region.

Union in the late 1980s and early 1990s reveal the depth of popular opposition to oppressive state bureaucracies.

○ **CHECK YOUR LEARNING** How did Marx understand modern society? Of the four theorists just discussed—Tönnies, Durkheim, Weber, and Marx—who was the most optimistic about modern society? Who was the most pessimistic? Explain your responses.

Theoretical Analysis of Modernity

The rise of modernity is a complex process involving many dimensions of change, as described in earlier chapters and summarized in the Summing Up table. How can we make sense of so many changes going on all at once? Sociologists have developed two broad explanations of modern society, one guided by the structural-functional approach and the other based on social-conflict theory.

Structural-Functional Theory: Modernity as Mass Society

One broad approach—drawing on the ideas of Ferdinand Tönnies, Emile Durkheim, and Max Weber—understands modernization as the emergence of *mass society* (Kornhauser, 1959; Nisbet, 1966; Berger, Berger, & Kellner, 1974; Pearson, 1993). A **mass society** is *a society in which prosperity and bureaucracy have weakened traditional social ties*. A mass society is highly productive; on average, people have more income than ever. At the same time, it is marked by weak kinship and impersonal neighborhoods, leaving individuals to feel socially isolated. Although many people have material plenty, they are spiritually weak and often experience moral uncertainty about how to live.

The Mass Scale of Modern Life

November 11, on Interstate 275. From the car window, we see BP and Sunoco gas stations, a Kmart and a Wal-Mart, an AmeriSuites hotel, a Bob Evans, a Chi-Chi's Mexican restaurant, and a McDonald's. This road happens to circle Cincinnati, Ohio. But it could be in Boston, Saint Louis, Denver, San Diego, or almost anywhere else in the United States.

George Tooker's 1950 painting *The Subway* depicts a common problem of modern life: Weakening social ties and eroding traditions create a generic humanity in which everyone is alike yet each person is an anxious stranger in the midst of others.

Source: George Tooker, *The Subway*, 1950, egg tempera on gesso panel, 18 1/8 × 36 1/8 inches, Whitney Museum of American Art, New York. Purchased with funds from the Juliana Force Purchase Award, 50.23. Photograph © Whitney Museum of American Art

Mass-society theory argues, first, that the scale of modern life has greatly increased. Before the Industrial Revolution, Europe and North America formed a mosaic of rural villages and small towns. In these local communities, which inspired Tönnies's concept of *Gemeinschaft*, people lived out their lives surrounded by kin and guided by a shared heritage. Gossip was an informal yet highly effective way of ensuring conformity to community standards. These small communities, with their strong moral values and their low tolerance of social diversity, exemplified the state of mechanical solidarity described by Durkheim.

For example, before 1690, English law demanded that everyone participate regularly in the Christian ritual of Holy Communion (Laslett, 1984). On the North American continent, only Rhode Island among the New England colonies tolerated religious dissent. Because social differences were repressed in favor of conformity to established norms, subcultures and countercultures were few, and change proceeded slowly.

Increasing population, the growth of cities, and specialized economic activity driven by the Industrial Revolution gradually altered this pattern. People came to know one another by their jobs (for example, as "the doctor" or "the bank clerk") rather than by their kinship group or hometown. People looked on most others as strangers. The face-to-face communication of the village was eventually replaced by the impersonal mass media: newspapers, radio, television, and computer networks. Large organizations steadily

DISCUSS: What does "success" mean? We have come to use the word *succeed* in a notably nonspecific manner. Its traditional meaning—to follow or replace another by descent—made sense in a relatively fixed social order with strong social ties. The term's contemporary meaning of achieving individual goals, whatever they may be, suggests a far more fluid social order.

Q: "While I take inspiration from the past, like most Americans, I live for the future." Ronald Reagan (1992)

NOTE: The conservative implication of mass-society theory is that social inequality still persists, but it is not as severe a problem as it was in the 19th century. Instead, the growing state is problematic.

MAKING THE GRADE

Mass-society theory is critical of the expansion of the modern state, claiming that large bureaucracies encourage dehumanization. Class-society theory takes a more positive view of the expanding state, claiming that it helps reduce social inequality.

assumed more and more responsibility for seeing to the daily tasks that had once been carried out by family, friends, and neighbors; public education drew more and more people to schools; police, lawyers, and courts supervised a formal criminal justice system. Even charity became the work of faceless bureaucrats working for various social welfare agencies.

Geographic mobility and exposure to diverse ways of life all weaken traditional values. People become more tolerant of social diversity, defending individual rights and freedom of choice. Treating people differently because of their race, sex, or religion comes to be defined as backward and unjust. In the process, minorities at the margins of society gain greater power and broader participation in public life. The election of Barack Obama—an African American—to the highest office in the United States is surely one indicator that ours is now a modern society (West, 2008).

The mass media give rise to a national culture that washes over traditional differences that used to set off one region from another. As one analyst put it, "Even in Baton Rouge, La., the local kids don't say 'y'all' anymore; they say 'you guys' just like on TV" (Gibbs, 2000:42). In this way, mass-society theorists fear, transforming people of various backgrounds into a generic mass may end up dehumanizing everyone.

The Ever-Expanding State

In the small-scale preindustrial societies of Europe, government amounted to little more than a local noble. A royal family formally reigned over an entire nation, but without efficient transportation and efficient communication, even absolute monarchs had far less power than today's political leaders.

As technological innovation allowed government to expand, the centralized state grew in size and importance. At the time the United States gained independence from Great Britain, the federal government was a tiny organization with the main purpose of providing national defense. Since then, government has assumed responsibility for more and more areas of social life: schooling the population, regulating wages and working conditions, establishing standards for products of all sorts, offering financial assistance to the ill and the unemployed, providing loans to students, and recently, bailing out corporations facing economic ruin. To pay for such programs, taxes have soared: Today's average worker labors about four months each year to pay for the broad array of services that government provides.

In a mass society, power resides in large bureaucracies, leaving people in local communities with little control over their lives. For example, state officials mandate that local schools must have a standardized educational program, local products must be government-certified, and every citizen must maintain extensive tax records.

Although such regulations may protect people and advance social equality, they also force us to deal more and more with nameless officials in distant and often unresponsive bureaucracies, and they undermine the autonomy of families and local communities.

CRITICAL REVIEW The growing scale of modern life certainly has positive aspects, but only at the price of losing some of our cultural heritage. Modern societies increase individual rights, tolerate greater social differences, and raise standards of living (Inglehart & Baker, 2000). But they are prone to what Weber feared most—excessive bureaucracy—as well as Tönnies's self-centeredness and Durkheim's anomie. Modern society's size, complexity, and tolerance of diversity all but doom traditional values and family patterns, leaving individuals isolated, powerless, and materialistic. As Chapter 17 ("Politics and Government") notes, voter apathy is a serious problem in the United States. But should we be surprised that individuals in vast, impersonal societies think no one person can make much of a difference?

Critics sometimes say that mass-society theory romanticizes the past. They remind us that many people in small towns were actually eager to set out for a better standard of living in cities. This approach also ignores problems of social inequality. Critics say this theory attracts conservatives who defend conventional morality and overlook the historical inequality of women and other minorities.

CHECK YOUR LEARNING In your own words, state the mass-society theory of modernity. What are two criticisms of it?

Social-Conflict Theory: Modernity as Class Society

The second interpretation of modernity derives largely from the ideas of Karl Marx. From a social-conflict perspective, modernity takes the form of a **class society**, *a capitalist society with pronounced social stratification.* That is, although agreeing that modern societies have expanded to a mass scale, this approach views the heart of modernization as an expanding capitalist economy, marked with inequality (Habermas, 1970; Harrington, 1984; Buechler, 2000).

Capitalism

Class-society theory follows Marx in claiming that the increasing scale of social life in modern society results from the growth and greed unleashed by capitalism. Because a capitalist economy pursues ever-greater profits, both production and consumption steadily increase.

According to Marx, capitalism rests on "naked self-interest" (Marx & Engels, 1972:337, orig. 1848). This self-centeredness weakens the social ties that once united small communities. Capitalism

Q: "The road leading out from our bewilderment and despair is of course political." Olof Palme

Q: "A case can be made that the central question of sociology, from its inception in the rather fanciful philosophy of Auguste Comte, has been the question about the nature of modernity." Peter Berger (1986:28)

Q: "The bourgeoisie . . . has pitilessly torn asunder the motley feudal ties that

bound man to his 'natural superiors,' and has left remaining no other nexus between man and man than naked self-interest, than callous 'cash payment.'" Karl Marx and Friedrich Engels

Q: "The need for a constantly expanding market for its products chases the bourgeoisie over the whole surface of the globe. It must nestle everywhere, settle everywhere, establish connections everywhere." Karl Marx and Friedrich Engels

MAKING THE GRADE

Both mass- and class-society theories are critical of modernity: the first because of what is lost (traditional social ties), the second because of what remains (persistent social inequality).

also treats people as commodities: a source of labor and a market for capitalist products.

Capitalism supports science, not just as the key to greater productivity but as an ideology that justifies the status quo. That is, modern societies encourage people to view human well-being as a technical puzzle to be solved by engineers and other experts rather than through the pursuit of social justice. For example, a capitalist culture seeks to improve health through scientific medicine rather than by eliminating poverty, which is a core cause of poor health.

Business also raises the banner of scientific logic, trying to increase profits through greater efficiency. As Chapter 16 ("The Economy and Work") explains, today's capitalist corporations have reached enormous size and control unimaginable wealth as a result of globalization. From the class-society point of view, the expanding scale of life is less a function of *Gesellschaft* than the inevitable and destructive consequence of capitalism.

Persistent Inequality

Modernity has gradually worn away the rigid categories that set nobles apart from commoners in preindustrial societies. But class-society theory points out that elites are still with us, in the form of capitalist millionaires rather than the nobles of an earlier era. In short, a few people are still born to wealth and power. The United States may have no hereditary monarchy, but the richest 5 percent of the population controls about 60 percent of all privately held property.

What of the state? Mass-society theorists argue that the state works to increase equality and fight social problems. Marx disagreed; he doubted that the state could accomplish more than minor reforms because as he saw it, the real power lies in the hands of capitalists, who control the economy. Other class-society theorists add that to the extent that working people and minorities do enjoy greater political rights and a higher standard of living today, these changes were the result of political struggle, not government goodwill. In short, they conclude, despite our pretensions of democracy, our political economy leaves most people powerless in the face of wealthy elites.

CRITICAL REVIEW Class-society theory dismisses Durkheim's argument that people in modern societies suffer from anomie, claiming instead that they suffer from alienation and powerlessness. Not surprisingly, then, the class-society interpretation of modernity enjoys widespread support among liberals and radicals who favor greater equality and call for extensive regulation (or abolition) of the capitalist marketplace.

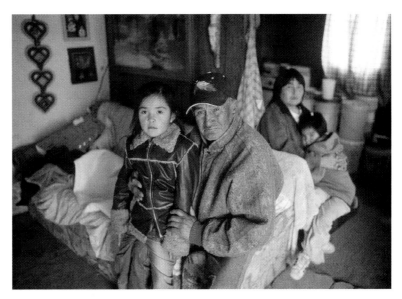

Social-conflict theory sees modernity not as an impersonal mass society but as an unequal class society in which some categories of people are second-class citizens. This Arizona family, like many Native Americans, lives on a reservation, where poverty is widespread and many trailer homes do not have electricity or running water.

A basic criticism of class-society theory is that it overlooks the long-term increasing prosperity of modern societies and the fact that discrimination based on race, ethnicity, and gender is now illegal and is widely regarded as a social problem. In addition, most people in the United States do not want an egalitarian society; they prefer a system of unequal rewards that reflects personal differences in talent and effort.

Based on socialism's failure to generate a high standard of living, few observers think that a centralized economy would cure the ills of modernity. The United States may face a number of social problems—from unemployment to hunger and industrial pollution to war—but these problems are also found in socialist nations.

CHECK YOUR LEARNING In your own words, state the class-society theory of modernity. What are several criticisms of it?

The Summing Up table on page 638 contrasts the two interpretations of modernity. Mass-society theory focuses on the increasing scale of life and the growth of government; class-society theory stresses the expansion of capitalism and the persistence of inequality.

NOTE: For mass-society theorists, the essential problem of modernity is anomie (as noted by Durkheim); for class-society theorists, it is alienation (following Marx).

POP CULTURE: Reflecting class-society theory, two recent films, *The Incredibles* and *Sideways*, explore the experience of powerlessness in modern society.

POP CULTURE: The widespread notion of having an "identity crisis" suggests the extent to which U.S. society has become a mass society.

Q: "Identity is a coherent sense of self. It depends upon the awareness that one's endeavors and one's life make sense, that they are meaningful in the context in which life is lived. It depends also upon stable values, and upon the conviction that one's actions and values are harmoniously related. It is a sense of wholeness, of integration, of knowing what is right and what is wrong and of being able to choose." Allen Wheelis (1958:18)

social character personality patterns common to members of a particular society

tradition-directedness rigid conformity to time-honored ways of living

other-directedness openness to the latest trends and fashions, often expressed by imitating others

● MAKING THE GRADE

Riesman's tradition-directedness corresponds to Tönnies's *Gemeinschaft* and Durkheim's mechanical solidarity. Other-directedness is linked to *Gesellschaft* and organic solidarity.

SUMMING UP

Two Interpretations of Modernity

	Mass Society	Class Society
Process of modernization	Industrialization; growth of bureaucracy	Rise of capitalism
Effects of modernization	Increasing scale of life; rise of the state and other formal organizations	Expansion of the capitalist economy; persistence of social inequality

Modernity and the Individual

Both mass- and class-society theories look at the broad societal changes that have taken place since the Industrial Revolution. But from these macro-level approaches we can also draw micro-level insights into how modernity shapes individual lives.

Mass Society: Problems of Identity

Modernity freed individuals from the small, tightly knit communities of the past. Most people in modern societies have the privacy and freedom to express their individuality. However, mass-society theory suggests that so much social diversity, widespread isolation, and rapid social change make it difficult for many people to establish any coherent identity at all (Wheelis, 1958; Berger, Berger, & Kellner, 1974).

As Chapter 5 ("Socialization") explains, people's personalities are largely a product of their social experiences. The small, homogeneous, and slowly changing societies of the past provided a firm, if narrow, foundation for building a personal identity. Even today, the Amish communities that flourish in the United States and Canada teach young men and women "correct" ways to think and behave. Not everyone born into an Amish community can tolerate strict demands for conformity, but most members establish a well-integrated and satisfying personal identity (Kraybill & Olshan, 1994; Kraybill & Hurd, 2006).

Mass societies are quite another story. Socially diverse and rapidly changing, they offer only shifting sands on which to build a personal identity. Left to make many life decisions on their own, many people—especially those with greater wealth—face a bewildering array of options. The freedom to choose has little value without standards to help us make good choices, and in a tolerant mass society, people may find little reason to choose one path over another. As a result, many people shuttle from one identity to another, changing their lifestyles, relationships, and even religions in search of an elusive "true self." Given the widespread "relativism" of modern societies, people without a moral compass lack the security and certainty once provided by tradition.

To David Riesman (1970, orig. 1950), modernization brings changes in **social character**, *personality patterns common to members of a particular society*. Preindustrial societies promote what Riesman calls **tradition-directedness**, *rigid conformity to time-honored ways of living*. Members of traditional societies model their lives on those of their ancestors, so that "living a good life" amounts to "doing what our people have always done."

Tradition-directedness corresponds to Tönnies's *Gemeinschaft* and Durkheim's mechanical solidarity. Culturally conservative, tradition-directed people think and act alike. Unlike the conformity sometimes found in modern societies, the uniformity of tradition-directedness is not an effort to imitate a popular celebrity or follow the latest fashions. Instead, people are alike because they all draw on the same solid cultural foundation. Amish women and men exemplify tradition-directedness; in Amish culture, tradition ties everyone to ancestors and descendants in an unbroken chain of righteous living.

Members of diverse and rapidly changing societies consider a tradition-directed personality deviant because it seems so rigid. Modern people, by and large, prize personal flexibility, the capacity to adapt, and sensitivity to others. Riesman calls this type of social character **other-directedness**, *openness to the latest trends and fashions, often expressed by imitating others*. Because their socialization occurs in societies that are continuously in flux, other-directed people develop fluid identities marked by superficiality, inconsistency, and change. They try on different "selves" almost like new clothing, seek out role models, and engage in varied performances as they move from setting to setting (Goffman, 1959). In a traditional society, such "shiftiness" makes a person untrustworthy, but in a changing, modern society, the chameleonlike ability to fit in virtually anywhere is very useful.

NOTE: David Reisman used the expression "social character" to mean "mode of conformity." Tradition-directedness is conformity based on categorical memberships; inner-directedness (not addressed in this chapter) is conformity to inwardly held values in the absence of strong tradition; other-directedness is conformity to one's contemporaries.

NOTE: The "lonely crowd" thesis includes the argument that the family has lost its socialization function to schools, various specialists, and the mass media, prompting more other-directedness in children.

DISCUSS: Our society is witnessing a rise in mild personality disorders. Do you think that the weaker moral structure of today's society, which fails to provide the guidance and support found in earlier times, plays a part in this rise?

SEEING SOCIOLOGY
in Everyday Life

Have you ever felt difficulty deciding "who you are"? Do you try to be a different person in different settings?

MAKING THE GRADE

In a sense, mass-society theory claims that modern people have too much freedom and choice; class-society theory claims that we have too little.

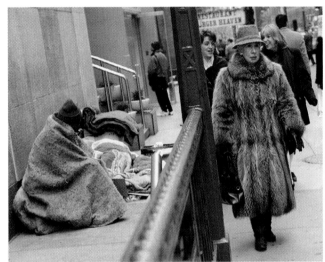

Mass-society theory relates feelings of anxiety and lack of meaning in the modern world to rapid social change that washes away tradition. This notion of modern emptiness is captured in the photo at the left. Class-society theory, by contrast, ties such feelings to social inequality, by which some categories of people are made into second-class citizens (or not made citizens at all), an idea expressed in the photo at the right.

In societies that value the up-to-date rather than the traditional, people look to others for approval, using members of their own generation rather than elders as role models. Peer pressure can be irresistible to people without strong standards to guide them. Our society urges individuals to be true to themselves. But when social surroundings change so rapidly, how can people develop the self to which they should be true? This problem lies at the root of the identity crisis so widespread in industrial societies today. "Who am I?" is a nagging question that many of us struggle to answer. In truth, this problem is not so much us as the inherently unstable mass society in which we live.

Class Society: Problems of Powerlessness

Class-society theory paints a different picture of modernity's effects on individuals. This approach maintains that persistent social inequality undermines modern society's promise of individual freedom. For some people, modernity serves up great privilege, but for many, everyday life means coping with economic uncertainty and a growing sense of powerlessness (K. S. Newman, 1993; Ehrenreich, 2001).

For racial and ethnic minorities, the problem of relative disadvantage looms even larger. Similarly, although women participate more broadly in modern societies, they continue to run up against traditional barriers of sexism. This approach rejects mass-society theory's claim that people suffer from too much freedom. According to class-society theory, our society still denies a majority of people full participation in social life.

As Chapter 12 ("Global Stratification") explains, the expanding scope of world capitalism has placed more of Earth's population under the influence of multinational corporations. As a result, more than three-fourths of the world's income is concentrated in the high-income nations, where just 22 percent of its people live. Is it any wonder, class-society theorists ask, that people in poor nations seek greater power to shape their own lives?

The problem of widespread powerlessness led Herbert Marcuse (1964) to challenge Max Weber's statement that modern society is rational. Marcuse condemned modern society as irrational for failing to meet the needs of so many people. Although modern capitalist societies produce unparalleled wealth, poverty remains the daily plight of more than 1 billion people. Marcuse adds that technological advances further reduce people's control over their own lives. High technology gives a great deal of power to a small core of specialists—not the majority of people—who now dominate the discussion of when to go to war, what our energy policy should be, and how people should pay for health care. Countering the common view that technology *solves* the world's problems, Marcuse believed that science *causes* them. In sum, class-society theory asserts that people suffer because modern societies concentrate knowledge, wealth, and power in the hands of a privileged few.

SEEING SOCIOLOGY
in Everyday Life

In 1970, Alvin Toffler coined the phrase "future shock" to describe the effect of social change that comes so rapidly that it overwhelms us. Do you think the pace of change has become overwhelming? Does our world need more change, or do we have too much already? Explain your answers.

| THINKING GLOBALLY | Does "Modernity" Mean "Progress"? The Kaiapo of the Amazon and the Gullah of Georgia |

The firelight flickers in the gathering darkness. Chief Kanhonk sits, as he has done at the end of the day for many years, ready to begin an evening of animated storytelling (Simons, 2007). This is the hour when the Kaiapo, a small society in Brazil's lush Amazon region, celebrate their heritage. Because the Kaiapo are a traditional people with no written language, the elders rely on evenings by the fire to pass along their culture to their children and grandchildren. In the past, evenings like this have been filled with tales of brave Kaiapo warriors fighting off Portuguese traders who were in pursuit of slaves and gold.

But as the minutes pass, only a few older villagers assemble for the evening ritual. "It is the Big Ghost," one man grumbles, explaining the poor turnout. The "Big Ghost" has indeed descended on them; its bluish glow spills from windows throughout the village. The Kaiapo children—and many adults as well—are watching sitcoms on television. The installation of a satellite dish in the village several years ago has had consequences far greater than anyone

imagined. In the end, what their enemies failed to do with guns, the Kaiapo may well do to themselves with prime-time programming.

The Kaiapo are among the 230,000 native peoples who inhabit Brazil. They stand out because of their striking body paint and ornate ceremonial dress. During the 1980s, they became rich from gold mining and harvesting mahogany trees. Now they must decide whether their newfound fortune is a blessing or a curse.

To some, affluence means the opportunity to learn about the outside world through travel and television. Others, like Chief Kanhonk, are not so sure. Sitting by the fire, he thinks aloud: "I have been saying that people must buy useful things like knives and fishing hooks. Television does not fill the stomach. It only shows our children and grandchildren white people's things." Bebtopup, the oldest priest, nods in agreement: "The night is the time the old people teach the young people. Television has stolen the night" (Simons, 2007:522).

Far to the north, in the United States, half an hour by ferry from the coast of Georgia, lies the swampy island community of Hog Hammock. The seventy African American residents of the island today trace their ancestry back to the first slaves who settled there in 1802.

Walking past the colorful houses nestled among pine trees draped with Spanish moss, visitors feel transported back in time. The local people, known as Gullahs (or in some places, Geechees)

Modernity and Progress

In modern societies, most people expect, and applaud, social change. We link modernity to the idea of *progress* (from the Latin, meaning "moving forward"), a state of continual improvement. We see stability as stagnation.

Given our bias in favor of change, our society tends to regard traditional cultures as backward. But change, particularly toward material affluence, is a mixed blessing. As the Thinking Globally box shows, social change is too complex simply to equate with progress.

Even getting rich has both advantages and disadvantages, as the cases of the Kaiapo and the Gullah show. Historically, among people in the United States, a rising standard of living has made lives longer and materially more comfortable. At the same time, many people wonder if today's routines are too stressful, with families often having little time to relax or simply be together. Perhaps this is why, in the United States, even as material prosperity has increased, measures

of happiness have declined (D. G. Myers, 2000; Inglehart, Welzel, & Foa, 2009).

Science, too, has its pluses and minuses. People in the United States are more confident than people in other nations that science improves our lives (Inglehart et al., 2000). But surveys also show that many adults in the United States feel that science "makes our way of life change too fast" (NORC, 2007).

New technology has always sparked controversy. A century ago, the introduction of automobiles and telephones allowed more rapid transportation and more efficient communication. But at the same time, such technology weakened traditional attachments to hometowns and even to families. Today, people might well wonder whether computer technology will do the same thing, giving us access to people around the world but shielding us from the community right outside our doors; providing more information than ever before but in the process threatening personal privacy. In short,

DISCUSS: Honor is a matter of specific status; dignity is generically human. One loses honor by violating normative roles; one loses dignity by giving up (or giving away) autonomy. Discuss the differences between "dying with honor" and "dying with dignity."

Q: "He was a bold man that first ate an oyster." Jonathan Swift

Q: "Let us not look backward in anger or forward in fear, but around in awareness." James Thurber

NOTE: The saying "You can't argue with progress" suggests the inevitable and linear nature of change as our culture sees it.

Q: "The major advances in civilization are processes that all but wreck the societies in which they occur." Alfred North Whitehead

● MAKING THE GRADE

The importance of a global perspective is seeing that "tradition" and "modernity" are not simply opposites but are often found in unexpected combinations in societies around the world.

speak a mixture of English and West African languages. They fish, living much as they have for hundreds of years.

But the future of this way of life is now in doubt. Few young people who are raised in Hog Hammock can find work beyond fishing and making traditional crafts. "We have been here nine generations and we are still here," says one local. Then, referring to the island's nineteen children, she adds, "It's not that they don't want to be here, it's that there's nothing here for them—they need to have jobs" (Curry, 2001:41).

Just as important, with people on the mainland looking for waterside homes for vacations or year-round living, the island has become prime real estate. Not long ago, one of the larger houses went up for sale, and the community was shocked to learn that its asking price was more than $1 million. The locals know only too well that higher property values will mean high taxes that few can afford to pay. In short, Hog Hammock is likely to become another Hilton Head, once a Gullah community on the South Carolina coast that is now home to well-to-do people from the mainland.

The odds are that the people of Hog Hammock will be selling their homes and moving inland. But few people are happy at the thought of selling out, even for a good price. After all, moving away will mean the end of their cultural heritage.

The stories of both the Kaiapo and the people of Hog Hammock show us that change is not a simple path toward "progress." These people may be moving toward modernity, but this process will have both positive and negative consequences. In the end, both groups of people may enjoy a higher standard of living with better homes, more schooling, and new technology. But their new affluence will come at the price of their traditions. The drama of these people is now being played out around the world as more and more traditional cultures are being lured away from their heritage by the affluence and materialism of rich societies.

WHAT DO YOU THINK?

1. Why is social change both a winning and a losing proposition for traditional peoples?

2. Do the changes described here improve the lives of the Kaiapo? What about the Gullah community?

3. Do traditional people have any choice about becoming modern? Explain your answer.

we all realize that social change comes faster all the time, but we may disagree about whether a particular change is good or bad for society.

Modernity: Global Variation

October 1, Kobe, Japan. Riding the computer-controlled monorail high above the streets of Kobe or the 200-mile-per-hour bullet train to Tokyo, we see Japan as the society of the future; its people are in love with high technology. But in other ways, the Japanese remain strikingly traditional: Few corporate executives and almost no senior politicians are women, young people still show seniors great respect, and public orderliness contrasts with the relative chaos of many U.S. cities.

Japan is a nation at once traditional and modern. This contradiction reminds us that although it is useful to contrast traditional and modern societies, the old and the new often coexist in unexpected ways. In the People's Republic of China, ancient Confucian principles are mixed with contemporary socialist thinking. In Saudi Arabia and Qatar, the embrace of modern technology is mixed with respect for the ancient principles of Islam. Likewise, in Mexico and much of Latin America, people observe centuries-old Christian rituals even as they struggle to move ahead economically. In short, combinations of traditional and modern are far from unusual; rather, they are found throughout the world.

Q: "'Postmodernism' usually refers to a certain constellation of styles and tones in cultural works; pastiche; blankness; a sense of exhaustion; a mixture of levels, forms, stylish; a relish of copies and repetitions; a knowingness that dissolves commitment into irony; acute self-consciousness about the constructed nature of the work; pleasure in the play of surfaces; a rejection of history." Todd Gitlin ("Postmodernism: Roots and Politics," *Dissent*, Winter 1989:100–8)

DISCUSS: Other postmodern changes include the collapse of culture into various "lifestyles"; the dissolution of social stratification into a mosaic of class, gender, and racial categories; weakening political parties; the rise of smaller organizational work groups, suggesting the erosion of traditional bureaucracy; and weakening faith in science (see Crook, Pakulski, & Waters, 1992).

postmodernity social patterns characteristic of postindustrial societies

SEEING SOCIOLOGY IN EVERYDAY LIFE

Tracking Change: Is Life in the United States Getting Better or Worse?

FLORENCE: I think life is great! Don't you?

SAMANTHA: I guess it depends on what you mean by "life."

FLORENCE: Hey, I'm feeling good, and you want to make everything complicated!

SAMANTHA: Well, sorry to sound like a sociology major, but it is. In some ways life is getting better; in other ways, it's not. . . .

We began this chapter with a look at what life was like in a large U.S. city in 1900, more than a century ago. It is easy to see that in many ways, life is far better for us today than it was for our grandparents and great-grandparents. In recent decades, however, not all indicators have been good. Here is a look at some trends shaping the United States since 1970 (Miringoff & Miringoff, 1999; D. G. Myers, 2000).

First, the good news: By some measures, life in this country is clearly improving. Infant mortality has been falling steadily, meaning that fewer and fewer children die soon after birth. In addition, an increasing share of people are reaching old age, and after reaching sixty-five, they are living longer than ever. More good news: The poverty rate among the elderly is well below what it was in 1970. Schooling is another area of improvement: The share of people dropping out of high school is down, and the share completing a college education is up. Even alcohol-related traffic deaths on the highways are down.

Next, a number of indicators show that life is about the same as it was in the 1970s. For example, teenage drug use is about the same now as it was a generation earlier. Unemployment has been way up in the past year or two, but over the past three decades the overall level has stayed about the same. Finally, there is about the same amount of affordable housing in the United States now as there was back in 1970.

Then there is the bad news. By some measures, several having to do with children, the quality of life in the United States has actually fallen. The official rate of child abuse is up, as is the rate of suicide among young people. Although the level of violent crime has fallen

over the past fifteen years, it remains above the 1970 level. Average hourly wages, one measure of economic security, show a downward trend, meaning that more families today have to rely on two or more earners to maintain family income. As far as jobs and income are concerned, people's confidence in the future is not as great as it used to be. The number of people without health insurance is also on the rise. And economic inequality in this country—the gap between the rich and the poor—has been increasing.

Overall, the evidence does not support any simple ideas about "progress over time." Social change has been and will continue to be a complex process that reflects the kinds of priorities we set for this nation as well as our will to achieve them.

Research shows that people in the United States today are better off economically than were past generations. At the same time, measures of personal happiness appear to be going down. How can you explain this contradiction?

WHAT DO YOU THINK?

1. Some analysts claim that U.S. society embodies a paradox: Over the past three decades, we see increasing economic health but declining social health. Based on the data presented here, do you agree or disagree? Explain your answer.

2. Which of the trends noted in this box do you find most important? Why?

3. Overall, do you think the quality of life in the United States is improving or not? Explain.

Source: U.S. Census Bureau (2008).

Postmodernity

If modernity was the product of the Industrial Revolution, is the Information Revolution creating a postmodern era? A number of scholars think so, and they use the term **postmodernity** to refer to *social patterns characteristic of postindustrial societies.*

The term *postmodernism* has been used for decades in literary, philosophical, and even architectural circles. It moved into sociology on a wave of social criticism that has been building since the spread of left-leaning politics in the 1960s. Although there are many variants of postmodern thinking, all share the following five themes (Hall & Neitz, 1993; Inglehart, 1997; Rudel & Gerson, 1999):

NOTE: Maureen T. Hallinan (1997) suggests thinking about social change without assuming that trends are continuous and linear in an effort to better explain
"dramatic social upheavals."

Q: "Change is one thing, progress is another. Change is scientific, progress is ethical; change is indubitable, whereas progress is a matter of controversy." Bertrand
Russell

DISCUSS: What do changes in popular magazines suggest about social change?
In the 1950s, *Life* was big; by 1974, *People* was popular; by 1979, *Self* was launched;
in 1986, *Child*. Does this trend show a narrowing of our interests?

DISCUSS: We often describe changes in shorthand terms—for instance, the
"activist 1960s" or "the go-go and greedy 1980s." How do students characterize
recent decades of our history?

1. **In important respects, modernity has failed**. The promise of modernity was a life free from want. As postmodernist critics see it, however, the twentieth century was unsuccessful in solving social problems like poverty. This fact is evident in today's high poverty rates, as well as the spreading sense of financial insecurity.

2. **The bright light of "progress" is fading**. Modern people look to the future, expecting that their lives will improve in significant ways. Members (and even leaders) of postmodern societies, however, are less confident about what the future holds. The strong optimism that carried society into the modern era more than a century ago has given way to widespread pessimism; even before the recent economic downturn, most U.S. adults believed that life was getting worse (NORC, 2007:259).

3. **Science no longer holds the answers**. The defining trait of the modern era was a scientific outlook and a confident belief that technology would make life better. But postmodern critics argue that science has not solved many old problems (such as poor health) and has even created new problems (such as pollution and global warming).

   Postmodernist thinkers discredit science, claiming that it implies a singular truth. On the contrary, they maintain, there is no one truth. This means that objective reality does not exist; rather, many realities can result from how we socially construct the world.

4. **Cultural debates are intensifying**. Now that more people have all the material things they really need, ideas are taking on more importance. In this sense, postmodernity is also a post-materialist era, in which more careers involve working with symbols and in which issues such as social justice, the state of the natural environment, and animal rights command more and more public attention.

5. **Social institutions are changing**. Just as industrialization brought a sweeping transformation to social institutions, the rise of a postindustrial society is remaking society again. For example, the postmodern family no longer conforms to any single pattern; on the contrary, individuals are choosing among many new family forms.

⊸ **CRITICAL REVIEW** Analysts who claim that the United States and other high-income societies are entering a postmodern era criticize modernity for failing to meet human needs. In defense of modernity, there have been marked increases in longevity and living standards over the course of the past century.

Based on everything you have read in this chapter, do you think that, on balance, our society is changing for better or worse? Why?

Even if we accept postmodernist views that science is bankrupt and progress is a sham, what are the alternatives?

⊸ **CHECK YOUR LEARNING** In your own words, state the characteristics of a postmodern society.

Is society getting better or not? The Seeing Sociology in Everyday Life box offers evidence suggesting that life in the United States is getting better in some ways but not in others.

Looking Ahead: Modernization and Our Global Future

Back in Chapter 1 (see page 8), we imagined the entire world reduced to a village of 1,000 people. About 200 residents of this "global village" come from high-income countries. Another 200 people are so poor that their lives are at risk.

The tragic plight of the world's poor shows that the planet is in desperate need of change. Chapter 12 ("Global Stratification") presented two competing views of why more than 1 billion people around the world are so poor. *Modernization theory* claims that in the past, the entire world was poor and that technological change, especially the Industrial Revolution, enhanced human productivity and raised living standards in many nations. From this point of view, the solution

DISCUSS: Etzioni maintains that U.S. moral revival is possible without the new puritanism of the right or the danger of totalitarianism from the left. Although he believes that family is vital, he supports women's equal access to the workplace. He also proposes that schools teach morality but without indoctrination.

Q: "And in the end, the love you take is equal to the love you make." The Beatles

Q: Communitarians are "people committed to creating a new moral, social, and political order based on restored communities, without allowing puritanism or oppression." Amitai Etzioni

Q: "Nobody makes a greater mistake than he who does nothing because he could only do a little." Edmund Burke

● SEEING SOCIOLOGY
in Everyday Life

Do you think there is too much of a "me first" attitude in today's world? Explain your view.

CONTROVERSY & DEBATE

Personal Freedom and Social Responsibility: Can We Have It Both Ways?

SAMUEL: I feel that being free is the most important thing. Let me do what I want!

SANJI: But if everyone felt that way, what would the world be like?

DOREEN: Isn't there a way to be true to ourselves and also take account of other people?

One issue we all have to work out is making decisions that take account of other people. But what, exactly, do we owe others? To see the problem, consider an event that took place in New York City in 1964.

Shortly after midnight on a crisp March evening, Kitty Genovese drove into the parking lot of her apartment complex. She turned off the engine, locked the doors of her vehicle, and headed across the blacktop toward the entrance to her building. Out of nowhere, a man holding a knife lunged at her, and as she screamed in terror and pain, he stabbed her repeatedly. Windows opened above as curious neighbors looked down to see what

was going on. But the attack continued for more than thirty minutes until Genovese lay dead in the doorway. The police never identified her killer,

In today's world, people can find new ways to express age-old virtues such as extending a helping hand to their neighbors in need. In the wake of Hurricane Katrina, thousands of college students from across the country converged on New Orleans to help repair the damage to the stricken city. Are there opportunities for you to get involved in your own community?

and their investigation revealed a stunning fact: *Not one* of the dozens of neighbors who witnessed the attack on Kitty Genovese went to her aid or even called the police.

Decades after this tragic event, we still confront the question of what we owe others. We prize our individual rights and personal privacy, but sometimes we turn a cold shoulder to people in need. When a cry for help is met with indifference, have we pushed our modern idea of personal freedom too far? In a society of expanding individual rights, can we keep a sense of human community?

These questions highlight the tension between traditional and modern social systems, which we can see in the writings of all the sociologists discussed in this chapter. Tönnies, Durkheim, and others concluded that in some respects, traditional community and modern individualism don't mix. That is, society can unite its members in a moral community only by limiting their

---

to global poverty is to promote technological development and market economies around the world.

For reasons suggested earlier, however, global modernization may be difficult. Recall that David Riesman portrayed preindustrial people as *tradition-directed* and likely to resist change. So modernization theorists advocate that the world's rich societies help poor countries grow economically. Industrial nations can speed development by exporting technology to poor regions, welcoming students from these countries, and providing foreign aid to stimulate economic growth.

The review of modernization theory in Chapter 12 points to some success with policies in Latin America and to greater success in the small Asian countries of Taiwan, South Korea, Singapore, and Hong Kong (since 1997 part of the People's Republic of China). But jump-starting development in the poorest countries of the world poses greater chal-

lenges. And even where dramatic change has occurred, modernization involves a trade-off. Traditional people, such as Brazil's Kaiapo, may gain wealth through economic development, but they lose their cultural identity and values as they are drawn into a global "McCulture" based on Western materialism, pop music, trendy clothes, and fast food. One Brazilian anthropologist expressed hope about the future of the Kaiapo: "At least they quickly understood the consequences of watching television. . . . Now [they] can make a choice" (Simons, 2007:523).

But not everyone thinks that modernization is really an option. According to a second approach to global stratification, *dependency theory*, today's poor societies have little ability to modernize, even if they want to. From this point of view, the major barrier to economic development is not traditionalism but global domination by rich capitalist societies.

POP CULTURE: Much celebrity philanthropy targets inequality around the world. For example, Sharon Stone raised funds to fight malaria, Angelina Jolie helped the United Nations feed and clothe war survivors, Richard Gere has tried to combat AIDS in India, and Bono has worked for years to get more aid to Africa.

Q: "The optimist proclaims that we live in the best of all possible worlds, and the pessimist fears this is true." James Cabell

Q: "No sooner is a thing brought to sight than it is swept by and another takes its place—and this too will be swept away." Marcus Aurelius

NOTE: Mahatma Gandhi noted seven great dangers to human virtue: wealth without work, pleasure without conscience, knowledge without character, business without ethics, science without humanity, religion without sacrifice, and politics without principle.

SEEING SOCIOLOGY
in Everyday Life

Does the balance between individual freedom and personal responsibility differ for men and women? If so, how, and why?

range of personal choices about how to live. In short, although we value both community and freedom, we can't have it both ways.

The sociologist Amitai Etzioni (1993, 1996, 2003) has tried to strike a middle ground. The *communitarian movement* rests on the simple idea that with rights must come responsibilities. Put another way, our pursuit of self-interest must be balanced by a commitment to the larger community.

Etzioni claims that modern people have become too concerned about individual rights. We expect the system to work for us, but we are reluctant to support the system. For example, we believe that people accused of a crime have the right to their day in court, but fewer and fewer of us are willing to perform jury duty; similarly, we are quick to accept government services but resent having to support these services with our taxes.

The communitarians advance four proposals to balance individual rights and public responsibilities. First, our society should halt the expanding "culture of rights" by which we put our own interests ahead of social responsibility. The U.S. Constitution, which is quoted so often when discussing individual rights, does not guarantee us

the right to do whatever we want. Second, we must remember that all rights involve responsibilities; for society to work, we must all play a part. Third, the well-being of everyone may require limiting our individual rights; for example, pilots and bus drivers who are responsible for public safety may be asked to take drug tests. Fourth, no one can ignore key responsibilities such as upholding the law and responding to a cry for help from someone like Kitty Genovese.

The communitarian movement appeals to many people who believe in both personal freedom and social responsibility. But Etzioni's proposals have drawn criticism from both sides of the political spectrum. To those on the left, serious problems ranging from voter apathy and street crime to disappearing pensions and millions of workers without medical care cannot be solved with some vague notion of "social responsibility." As they see it, what we need is expanded government programs to protect people and lessen inequality.

Conservatives, on the political right, see different problems in Etzioni's proposals (Pearson, 1995). As they see it, the communitarian movement favors liberal goals, such as confronting

prejudice and protecting the environment, but ignores conservative goals such as strengthening religious belief and supporting traditional families.

Etzioni responds that the criticism coming from both sides suggests that he has found a moderate, sensible answer to a serious problem. But the debate may also indicate that in a society as diverse as the United States, people who are so quick to assert their rights are not so quick to agree on their responsibilities.

WHAT DO YOU THINK?

1. Have you ever failed to come to the aid of someone in need or danger? Why?

2. Half a century ago, President John F. Kennedy stated, "Ask not what your country can do for you; ask what you can do for your country." Do you think that people today support this idea? Why or why not?

3. Are you willing to serve on a jury? Do you mind paying your fair share of taxes? Would you be willing to perform a year of national service after you graduate from college? Explain your answers.

Dependency theory asserts that rich nations achieved modernization at the expense of poor ones, by taking poor nations' natural resources and exploiting their human labor. Even today, the world's poorest countries remain locked in a disadvantageous economic relationship with rich nations, dependent on wealthy countries to buy their raw materials and in return provide them with whatever manufactured products they can afford. According to this view, continuing ties with rich societies only perpetuates current patterns of global inequality.

Whichever approach you find more convincing, keep in mind that change in the United States is no longer separate from change in the rest of the world. At the beginning of the twentieth century, most people in today's high-income countries lived in relatively small settlements with limited awareness of the larger world. Today, the world

has become one huge village because the lives of all people are increasingly interconnected.

The twentieth century witnessed unprecedented human achievement. Yet solutions to many problems of human existence—including finding meaning in life, resolving conflicts between nations, and eliminating poverty—have eluded us. The Controversy & Debate box examines one dilemma: balancing individual freedom and personal responsibility. To this list of pressing matters have been added new concerns, such as controlling population growth and establishing an environmentally sustainable society. In the coming years, we must be prepared to tackle such problems with imagination, compassion, and determination. Our growing understanding of human society gives us reason to be hopeful that we can get the job done.

Q: "Somewhere ages and ages hence:
Two roads diverged in a wood, and I—
I took the one less traveled by,
And that has made all the difference."

Robert Frost

Thank you for making this text part of your course. Please be in touch (macionis@kenyon.edu) with comments or suggestions. Visit http://www .TheSociologyPage.com for more good stuff and some of my rock and roll—my small gift to you. JJM

Seeing Sociology in Everyday Life

Chapter 24   Social Change: Traditional, Modern, and Postmodern Societies

Is tradition the opposite of modernity?

Conceptually, this may be true. But as this chapter explains, traditional and modern social patterns combine in all sorts of interesting ways in our everyday lives. Look at the photographs below, and identify elements of tradition and modernity. Do they seem to go together, or are they in conflict? Why?

> **HINT**   Although sociologists analyze tradition and modernity as conceptual opposites, every society combines these elements in various ways. People may debate the virtues of traditional and modern life, but the two patterns are found almost everywhere. Technological change always has social consequences—for example, the use of cell phones changes people's social networks and economic opportunities; similarly, the spread of McDonald's changes not only what people eat but where and with whom they share meals.

These young girls live in the city of Istanbul in Turkey, a country that has long debated the merits of traditional and modern life. What sets off traditional and modern ways of dressing? Do you think such differences are likely to affect patterns of friendship? Would the same be true in the United States?

When the first McDonald's restaurant opened in the city of Kiev in Ukraine, many people stopped by to taste a hamburger and see what "fast food" was all about. As large corporations expand their operations around the world, do they tip the balance away from tradition in favor of modernity? How?

In Riyadh, Saudi Arabia, these young men are shopping for the latest in cell phones. Does such modern technology threaten a society's traditions?

Applying SOCIOLOGY in Everyday Life

1. How do tradition and modernity combine in your life? Point to several ways in which you are traditional and several ways in which you are thoroughly modern.

2. Ask people in your class or friendship group to make five predictions about U.S. society in the year 2050, when today's twenty-year-olds will be senior citizens. Compare notes. On what issues is there agreement?

3. Do you think the rate of social change has been increasing? Do some research about modes of travel—including walking, riding animals, bicycles, trains, cars, airplanes, and rockets. At what point in history did each of these ways of moving come into being? What pattern do you see?

MAKING THE GRADE

CHAPTER 24   Social Change: Traditional, Modern, and Postmodern Societies

What Is Social Change?

SOCIAL CHANGE is the transformation of culture and social institutions over time. Every society changes all the time, sometimes faster, sometimes more slowly. Social change often generates controversy.

p. 627

social change (p. 627) the transformation of culture and social institutions over time

Causes of Social Change

CULTURE
- *Invention* produces new objects, ideas, and social patterns.
- *Discovery* occurs when people take notice of existing elements of the world.
- *Diffusion* creates change as products, people, and information spread from one society to another.

p. 628

SOCIAL CONFLICT
- Karl Marx claimed that class conflict between capitalists and workers pushes society toward a socialist system of production.
- Social conflict arising from class, race, and gender inequality has resulted in social changes that have improved the lives of working people.

p. 628

IDEAS
Max Weber traced the roots of most social changes to ideas:
- The fact that industrial capitalism developed first in areas of Western Europe where the Protestant work ethic was strong demonstrates the power of ideas to bring about change.

p. 628

DEMOGRAPHIC FACTORS
Population patterns play a part in social change:
- The aging of U.S. society has resulted in changes to family life and the development of consumer products to meet the needs of the elderly.
- Migration within and between societies promotes change.

pp. 628–29

Modernity

MODERNITY refers to the social consequences of industrialization, which include
- the decline of traditional communities
- the expansion of personal choice
- increasing social diversity
- focus on the future

pp. 629–30

modernity (p. 629) social patterns resulting from industrialization

modernization (p. 629) the process of social change begun by industrialization

division of labor (p. 632) specialized economic activity

anomie (p. 632) Durkheim's term for a condition in which society provides little moral guidance to individuals

FERDINAND TÖNNIES described modernization as the transition from *Gemeinschaft* to *Gesellschaft*, a process characterized by the loss of traditional community and the rise of individualism.

pp. 630–31

EMILE DURKHEIM saw modernization as a society's expanding division of labor. *Mechanical solidarity*, based on shared activities and beliefs, is gradually replaced by *organic solidarity*, in which specialization makes people interdependent.

pp. 631–32

MAX WEBER saw modernity as the decline of a traditional worldview and the rise of rationality. Weber feared the dehumanizing effects of modern rational organization.

pp. 632–33

KARL MARX saw modernity as the triumph of capitalism over feudalism. Capitalism creates social conflict, which Marx claimed would bring about revolutionary change leading to an egalitarian socialist society.

pp. 633–35

Analysis of Modernity

STRUCTURAL-FUNCTIONAL THEORY: MODERNITY AS MASS SOCIETY

- According to **mass-society theory**, modernity increases the scale of life, enlarging the role of government and other formal organizations in carrying out tasks previously performed by families in local communities.

- Cultural diversity and rapid social change make it difficult for people in modern societies to develop stable identities and to find meaning in their lives.

pp. 635–36

SOCIAL-CONFLICT THEORY: MODERNITY AS CLASS SOCIETY

- According to **class-society theory**, modernity involves the rise of capitalism into a global economic system resulting in persistent social inequality.

- By concentrating wealth in the hands of a few, modern capitalist societies generate widespread feelings of alienation and powerlessness.

pp. 636–37

mass society (p. 635) a society in which prosperity and bureaucracy have weakened traditional social ties

class society (p. 636) a capitalist society with pronounced social stratification

social character (p. 638) personality patterns common to members of a particular society

tradition-directedness (p. 638) rigid conformity to time-honored ways of living

other-directedness (p. 638) openness to the latest trends and fashions, often expressed by imitating others

See the Summing Up tables on pages 634 and 638.

Modernity and the Individual

Both mass-society theory and class-society theory are macro-level approaches; from them, however, we can also draw micro-level insights into how modernity shapes individual lives.

MASS SOCIETY: PROBLEMS OF IDENTITY

- Mass-society theory suggests that the great social diversity, widespread isolation, and rapid social change of modern societies make it difficult for individuals to establish a stable social identity.

David Riesman described the changes in social character that modernity causes:

- Preindustrial societies exhibit **tradition-directedness**: Everyone in society draws on the same solid cultural foundation, and people model their lives on those of their ancestors.

- Modern societies exhibit **other-directedness**: Because their socialization occurs in societies that are continuously in flux, other-directed people develop fluid identities marked by superficiality, inconsistency, and change.

pp. 638–39

CLASS SOCIETY: PROBLEMS OF POWERLESSNESS

- Class-society theory claims that the problem facing most people today is economic uncertainty and powerlessness.

- Herbert Marcuse claimed that modern society is irrational because it fails to meet the needs of so many people.

- Marcuse also believed that technological advances further reduce people's control over their own lives.

- People suffer because modern societies have concentrated both wealth and power in the hands of a privileged few.

p. 639

Modernity and Progress

Social change is too complex and controversial simply to be equated with progress:

- A rising standard of living has made lives longer and materially more comfortable; at the same time, many people are stressed and have little time to relax with their families; measures of happiness have declined over recent decades.

- Science and technology have brought many conveniences to our everyday lives, yet many people are concerned that life is changing too fast; the introduction of automobiles and advanced communications technology has weakened traditional attachments to hometowns and even to families.

pp. 640–41

Looking Ahead: Modernization and Our Global Future

Modernization theory links global poverty to the power of tradition. Rich nations can help poor countries develop their economies.

pp. 643–44

Dependency theory explains global poverty as the product of the world economic system. The operation of multinational corporations makes poor nations economically dependent on rich nations.

pp. 644–45

✓ *Although we often think of tradition and modernity as opposites, traditional and modern elements coexist in most societies.*

Postmodernity

POSTMODERNITY refers to the cultural traits of postindustrial societies. Postmodern criticism of society centers on the failure of modernity, and specifically science, to fulfill its promise of prosperity and well-being.

pp. 642–43

postmodernity (p. 642) social patterns characteristic of postindustrial societies

ESSAYS: The essay questions provided in this section may be used for exams, for class discussion and review, or as paper topics. Brief answers to the essay questions are given here. Additional essay questions are found in the *Instructor's Manual* that accompanies this text.

ESSAY 1: We may seem less in control of our lives to the extent that the sociologi-

cal perspective points to the power of society over us. Yet understanding the opportunities and constraints we face ends up giving us greater power over our lives.

ESSAY 2: Structural-functional questions deal with the functions of each for the operation of society as a whole. Symbolic-interaction questions explore the variable and changing meanings individuals find in particular settings. Social-conflict questions point to how each both reflects and perpetuates social inequality.

MAKING THE GRADE
Sample Test Questions

These questions are similar to those found in the test bank that accompanies this textbook.

Chapter 1   The Sociological Perspective

Multiple-Choice Questions

1. **What does the sociological perspective tell us about whom any individual chooses to marry?**
   a. There is no explaining personal feelings like love.
   b. People's actions reflect human free will.
   c. The operation of society guides many of our personal choices.
   d. In the case of love, opposites attract.

2. **Which early sociologist studied patterns of suicide?**
   a. Peter Berger
   b. Emile Durkheim
   c. Auguste Comte
   d. Karl Marx

3. **The personal value of studying sociology includes**
   a. seeing the opportunities and constraints in our lives.
   b. the fact that it is good preparation for a number of jobs.
   c. being more active participants in society.
   d. All of the above are correct.

4. **The discipline of sociology first developed in**
   a. countries experiencing rapid social change.
   b. countries with little social change.
   c. countries with a history of warfare.
   d. the world's poorest countries.

5. **Which early sociologist coined the term *sociology* in 1838?**
   a. Karl Marx
   b. Herbert Spencer
   c. Adam Smith
   d. Auguste Comte

6. **Which theoretical approach is closest to that taken by early sociologists Auguste Comte and Emile Durkheim?**
   a. the symbolic-interaction approach
   b. the structural-functional approach
   c. the social-conflict approach
   d. None of the above is correct.

7. **Which term refers to the recognized and intended consequences of a social pattern?**
   a. manifest functions
   b. latent functions
   c. eufunctions
   d. dysfunctions

8. **Sociology's social-conflict approach draws attention to**
   a. how structure contributes to the overall operation of society.
   b. how people construct meaning through interaction.
   c. patterns of social inequality.
   d. the stable aspects of society.

9. **Which woman, among the first sociologists, studied the evils of slavery and also translated the writings of Auguste Comte?**
   a. Elizabeth Cady Stanton
   b. Jane Addams
   c. Harriet Martineau
   d. Margaret Mead

10. **Which of the following illustrates a micro-level focus?**
    a. analyzing the operation of the U.S. political system
    b. studying patterns of global terrorism
    c. describing class inequality in the armed forces
    d. observing two new dormitory roommates getting to know one another

ANSWERS: 1 (c); 2 (b); 3 (d); 4 (a); 5 (d); 6 (b); 7 (a); 8 (c); 9 (c); 10 (d).

Essay Questions

1. Explain why applying the sociological perspective can make us seem less in control of our lives. In what ways does it actually give us greater power over our lives?

2. Guided by the discipline's three major theoretical approaches, come up with sociological questions about (a) television, (b) war, and (c) colleges and universities.

Chapter 2   Sociological Investigation

Multiple-Choice Questions

1. *Science* **is defined as**
   a. a logical system that bases knowledge on direct, systematic observation.
   b. belief based on faith in some ultimate truth.
   c. knowledge based on a society's traditions.
   d. information that comes from recognized "experts."

2. *Empirical evidence* **refers to**
   a. quantitative rather than qualitative data.
   b. what people consider "common sense."
   c. information people can verify with their senses.
   d. patterns found in every known society.

3. **When trying to measure people's "social class," you would have to keep in mind that**
   a. your measurement can never be both reliable and valid.
   b. there are many ways to operationalize this variable.
   c. there is no way to measure "social class."
   d. in the United States, everyone agrees on what "social class" means.

4. **What is the term for the value that occurs most often in a series of numbers?**
   a. the mode
   b. the median
   c. the mean
   d. All of the above are correct.

5. **When measuring any variable, *reliability* refers to**
   a. whether you are really measuring what you want to measure.
   b. how dependable the researcher is.
   c. results that everyone would agree with.
   d. whether repeating the measurement yields consistent results.

6. **We can correctly say that two variables are *correlated* if**
   a. change in one causes no change in the other.
   b. one occurs before the other.
   c. their values vary together.
   d. both measure the same thing.

7. **Which of the following is *not* a defining trait of a cause-and-effect relationship?**
   a. The independent variable must happen before the dependent variable.
   b. Each variable must be shown to be independent of the other.
   c. The two variables must display correlation.
   d. There must be no evidence that the correlation is spurious.

8. **Interpretive sociology is a research orientation that**
   a. focuses on action.
   b. sees an objective reality "out there."
   c. focuses on the meanings people attach to behavior.
   d. seeks to increase social justice.

9. **To study the effects on test performance of playing soft music during an exam, a researcher conducts an experiment in which one test-taking class hears music and another does not. According to the chapter discussion of the experiment, the class hearing the music is called**
   a. the placebo.
   b. the control group.
   c. the dependent variable.
   d. the experimental group.

10. **In participant observation, the problem of "breaking in" to a setting is often solved with the help of a**
    a. key informant.
    b. research assistant.
    c. bigger budget.
    d. All of the above are correct.

Essay Questions

1. Explain the idea that there are various types of truth. What are the advantages and limitations of science as a way of discovering truth?

2. Compare and contrast scientific sociology, interpretive sociology, and critical sociology. Which of these approaches best describes the work of Durkheim, Weber, and Marx?

Chapter 3   Culture

Multiple-Choice Questions

1. **Of all the world's countries, the United States is the most**
   a. multicultural.
   b. culturally uniform.
   c. slowly changing.
   d. resistant to cultural diversity.

2. **Ideas created by members of a society are part of**
   a. high culture.
   b. material culture.
   c. norms.
   d. nonmaterial culture.

3. **Sociologists define a symbol as**
   a. any gesture that insults others.
   b. any element of material culture.
   c. anything that has meaning to people who share a culture.
   d. any pattern that causes culture shock.

4. **U.S. culture holds a strong belief in**
   a. the traditions of the past.
   b. individuality.
   c. equality of condition for all.
   d. All of the above are correct.

5. **Cheating on a final examination is an example of violating campus**
   a. folkways.
   b. symbols.
   c. mores.
   d. high culture.

6. **Subculture refers to**
   a. a part of the population lacking culture.
   b. elements of popular culture.
   c. people who embrace high culture.
   d. cultural patterns that set apart a segment of a society's population.

ANSWERS: 1 (a); 2 (c); 3 (b); 4 (a); 5 (d); 6 (c); 7 (b); 8 (c); 9 (d); 10 (a).

ESSAY 1: These foods all came from different countries, showing the cultural diversity of the U.S. In addition, all are easily and quickly consumed ("fast foods"), suggesting our cultural emphasis on efficiency.

ESSAY 2: The chapter explains that the world is now sharing more cultural patterns but also points to limitations to the "global cultural" idea. Whether this trend is positive or negative is for each person to decide.

7. Which region of the United States has the largest share of people who speak a language other than English at home?
   a. the Southwest
   b. the Northeast
   c. the Northwest
   d. the South

8. Sociologists use the term "cultural lag" to refer to
   a. the slowing of cultural change in the United States.
   b. the fact that some societies change faster than others do.
   c. that fact that some elements of culture change faster than others.
   d. people who are less cultured than others.

9. Which of the following is a description of ethnocentrism?
   a. taking pride in your ethnicity
   b. judging another culture using the standards of your own culture
   c. seeing another culture as better than your own
   d. judging another culture by its own standards

10. Which theoretical approach focuses on the link between culture and social inequality?
    a. the structural-functional approach
    b. the social-conflict approach
    c. the symbolic-interaction approach
    d. the sociobiology approach

ANSWERS: 1 (a); 2 (d); 3 (c); 4 (b); 5 (c); 6 (d); 7 (a); 8 (c); 9 (b); 10 (b).

Essay Questions

1. In the United States, hot dogs, hamburgers, French fries, and ice cream have long been considered national favorites. What cultural patterns help explain the love of these kinds of foods?

2. From what you have learned in this chapter, do you think that a global culture is emerging? Do you regard the prospect of a global culture as positive or negative? Why?

Chapter 4   Society

Multiple-Choice Questions

1. Which of the following would Lenski highlight as a cause of change in society?
   a. new religious movements
   b. conflict between workers and factory owners
   c. the steam engine
   d. the extent to which people share moral values

2. Horticultural societies are those in which
   a. people hunt animals and gather vegetation.
   b. people are nomadic.
   c. people have learned to raise animals.
   d. people use simple hand tools to raise crops.

3. Lenski claims that the development of more complex technology
   a. has both positive and negative effects.
   b. is entirely positive.
   c. is mostly negative.
   d. has little or no effect on society.

4. Marx believed that the industrial-capitalist economic system
   a. was very productive.
   b. concentrated wealth in the hands of a few.
   c. created conflict between two great classes: capitalists and proletarians.
   d. All of the above are correct.

5. Marx considered which of the following to be the "foundation" of society?
   a. technology
   b. the economy
   c. dominant ideas
   d. type of solidarity

6. Unlike Marx, Weber thought alienation was caused by
   a. social change that is too rapid.
   b. extensive social inequality.
   c. the high level of rationality in modern society.
   d. All of the above are correct.

7. What Lenski called the "industrial" society and Marx called the "capitalist" society, Weber called
   a. the "rational" society.
   b. the "ideal" society.
   c. the "traditional" society.
   d. the "technological" society.

8. Marx's "materialist" analysis contrasts with Weber's
   a. "optimistic" analysis.
   b. "idealist" analysis.
   c. "traditional" analysis.
   d. "technological" analysis.

9. Durkheim thought of society as
   a. existing only in people's minds.
   b. constantly changing.
   c. an objective reality.
   d. having no clear existence at all.

ESSAY 1: Marx would certainly be concerned about class inequality and would look forward to a class revolution overthrowing capitalism. Weber would wonder about the pace of rationalization and perhaps regard socialism not as a solution but as adding to the problem of rationalization. Durkheim would ask about how well society "hangs together" and the basis of societal solidarity; he would also wonder about the extent of anomie.

ESSAY 2: Marx is clearly following the social-conflict approach. Weber is harder to characterize, but his focus on the meaning people find in the world links him to the symbolic-interaction approach. Durkheim is clearly following the structural-functional approach.

ESSAY 1: The "nature" side says our behavior is directed by human biology; the "nurture" side says we learn how to behave from the social environment. The two positions are not opposed if we argue that human biology does not rigidly direct behavior through instincts, making it essential that we nurture young people.

ESSAY 2: All stress the importance of social experience. Freud and Piaget place more emphasis on biological traits: Freud's id is presocial, and Piagets's view of development utilizes stages linked to biological maturation.

10. **Which of the following questions might Durkheim ask about the ongoing war on terror?**
    a. Would the war on terror unite people across the United States?
    b. Which class benefits most from the war on terror?
    c. How does war lead to new kinds of technology?
    d. How does war increase the scope of bureaucracy?

ANSWERS: 1 (c); 2 (d); 3 (a); 4 (d); 5 (b); 6 (c); 7 (a); 8 (b); 9 (c); 10 (a)

Essay Questions

1. How would Marx, Weber, and Durkheim imagine U.S. society a century from now? What kinds of questions or concerns would each thinker have?

2. Link Marx, Weber, and Durkheim to one of sociology's theoretical approaches, and explain your choices.

Chapter 5   Socialization

Multiple-Choice Questions

1. **Kingsley Davis's study of Anna, the girl isolated for five years, shows that**
   a. humans have all the same instincts found in other animal species.
   b. without social experience, a child never develops personality.
   c. personality is present in all humans at birth.
   d. many human instincts disappear in the first few years of life.

2. **Most sociologists take the position that**
   a. humans have instincts that direct behavior.
   b. biological instincts develop in humans at puberty.
   c. it is human nature to nurture.
   d. All of the above are correct.

3. **Lawrence Kohlberg explored socialization by studying**
   a. cognition.
   b. the importance of gender in socialization.
   c. the development of biological instincts.
   d. moral reasoning.

4. **Carol Gilligan added to Kohlberg's findings by showing that**
   a. girls and boys typically use different standards in deciding what is right and wrong.
   b. girls are more interested in right and wrong than boys are.
   c. boys are more interested in right and wrong than girls are.
   d. today's children are far less interested in right and wrong than their parents are.

5. **The "self," said George Herbert Mead, is**
   a. the part of the human personality made up of self-awareness and self-image.
   b. the presence of culture within the individual.
   c. basic drives that are self-centered.
   d. present in infants from birth.

6. **Why is the family so important to the socialization process?**
   a. Family members provide vital caregiving to infants and children.
   b. Families give children social identity in terms of class, ethnicity, and religion.
   c. Parents' behavior can greatly affect a child's self-concept.
   d. All of the above are correct.

7. **Social class position affects socialization: Lower-class parents tend to stress _____, and well-to-do parents stress _____.**
   a. independence; protecting children
   b. independence; dependence
   c. obedience; creativity
   d. creativity; obedience

8. **In global perspective, which statement about childhood is correct?**
   a. In every society, the first ten years of life are a time of play and learning.
   b. Rich societies extend childhood much longer than poor societies do.
   c. Poor societies extend childhood much longer than rich societies do.
   d. Childhood is defined by being biologically immature.

9. **Modern, high-income societies typically define people in old age as**
   a. the wisest of all.
   b. the most up-to-date on current fashion and trends.
   c. less socially important than younger adults.
   d. All of the above are correct.

10. **According to Erving Goffman, the purpose of a total institution is**
    a. to reward someone for achievement in the outside world.
    b. to give a person more choices about how to live.
    c. to encourage lifelong learning in a supervised context.
    d. to change a person's personality or behavior.

ANSWERS: 1 (b); 2 (c); 3 (d); 4 (a); 5 (a); 6 (d); 7 (c); 8 (b); 9 (c); 10 (d).

Essay Questions

1. State the two sides of the "nature-nurture" debate. In what important way are nature and nurture not opposed to each other?

2. What are common themes in the ideas of Freud, Piaget, Kohlberg, Gilligan, Mead, and Erikson? In what ways do their theories differ?

ESSAY 1: Key elements to include are presentation of self, performances, front and back regions, idealization, embarrassment, and tact, and also gender. To analyze a professor teaching a class, review the discussion of the doctor's office in the chapter.

ESSAY 2: Emotions are rooted in biology because all people display six basic emotions and people everywhere use the same facial expressions to convey them. Such commonalities suggest that emotions are "wired" into human behavior. At the same time, what triggers an emotion, the rules for the display of emotions, and the value people attach to emotion all vary as elements of human culture.

Chapter 6   Social Interaction in Everyday Life

Multiple-Choice Questions

1. **Which term defines who and what we are in relation to others?**
   a. role
   b. status
   c. role set
   d. master status

2. **In U.S. society, which of the following is often a master status?**
   a. occupation
   b. physical or mental disability
   c. race or color
   d. All of the above are correct.

3. **"Role set" refers to**
   a. a number of roles found in any one society.
   b. a number of roles attached to a single status.
   c. a number of roles that are more or less the same.
   d. a number of roles within any one organization.

4. **Frank excels at football at his college, but he doesn't have enough time to study as much as he wants to. This problem is an example of**
   a. role set.
   b. role strain.
   c. role conflict.
   d. role exit.

5. **The Thomas theorem states that**
   a. our statuses and roles are the keys to our personality.
   b. most people rise to their level of incompetence.
   c. people know the world only through their language.
   d. situations defined as real are real in their consequences.

6. **Which of the following is the correct meaning of "presentation of self"?**
   a. efforts to create impressions in the minds of others
   b. acting out a master status
   c. thinking back over the process of role exit
   d. trying to take attention away from others

7. **Paul Ekman points to what as an important clue to deception by another person?**
   a. smiling
   b. using tact
   c. inconsistencies in a presentation
   d. All of the above are correct.

8. **In terms of dramaturgical analysis, tact is understood as**
   a. helping someone take on a new role.
   b. helping another person "save face."
   c. making it hard for someone to perform a role.
   d. negotiating a situation to get your own way.

9. **In her study of human emotion, Arlie Hochschild explains that companies typically**
   a. try to regulate the emotions of workers.
   b. want workers to be unemotional.
   c. encourage people to express their true emotions.
   d. profit from making customers more emotional.

10. **People are likely to "get" a joke when they**
    a. know something about more than one culture.
    b. have a different social background than the joke teller.
    c. understand the two different realities being presented.
    d. know why someone wants to tell the joke.

ANSWERS: 1 (b); 2 (d); 3 (b); 4 (c); 5 (d); 6 (a); 7 (c); 8 (b); 9 (a); 10 (c).

Essay Questions

1. Explain Erving Goffman's idea that we engage in a "presentation of self." What are the elements of this presentation? Apply this approach to an analysis of a professor teaching a class.

2. In what ways are human emotions rooted in biology? In what ways are emotions guided by culture?

Chapter 7   Groups and Organizations

Multiple-Choice Questions

1. **What term did Charles Cooley give to a small social group whose members share personal and lasting relationships?**
   a. expressive group
   b. in-group
   c. primary group
   d. secondary group

2. **Which type of group leadership is concerned with getting the job done?**
   a. laissez-faire leadership
   b. secondary group leadership
   c. expressive leadership
   d. instrumental leadership

ESSAY 1: Primary groups are the opposite of secondary groups on several dimensions. See the discussion on pages 162–63 and the Summing Up table on page 164.

ESSAY 2: See the discussion on pages 170–71. The advantage of the organizational form is the promise of efficiency. The disadvantages are discussed in the "Problem of Bureaucracy" section on pages 173–74. To Weber, the rationalization of society was largely negative in that the rigidity and narrow focus of formal organizations saps us of our deep humanity. (The Weber section of Chapter 4 provides added detail.)

3. The research done by Solomon Asch, in which subjects were asked to pick lines of the same length, showed that
   a. groups encourage their members to conform.
   b. most people are stubborn and refuse to change their minds.
   c. groups often generate conflict.
   d. group members rarely agree on everything.

4. What term refers to a social group that someone uses as a point of reference in making an evaluation or decision?
   a. out-group
   b. reference group
   c. in-group
   d. primary group

5. A network is correctly thought of as
   a. the most close-knit social group.
   b. a category of people with something in common.
   c. a social group in which most people know one another.
   d. a web of weak social ties.

6. From the point of view of a nurse, a hospital is a
   a. normative organization.
   b. coercive organization.
   c. utilitarian organization.
   d. All of the above are correct.

7. Bureaucracy is a type of social organization characterized by
   a. specialized jobs.
   b. offices arranged in a hierarchy.
   c. lots of rules and regulations.
   d. All of the above are correct.

8. According to Robert Michels, bureaucracy always means
   a. inefficiency.
   b. oligarchy.
   c. alienation.
   d. specialization.

9. Rosabeth Moss Kanter claims that large business organizations
   a. need to "open up" opportunity to encourage workers to perform well.
   b. must have clear and stable rules to survive in a changing world.
   c. do well or badly depending on how talented the leader is.
   d. suffer if they do not adopt the latest technology.

10. The "McDonaldization of society" implies that
    a. organizations can provide food for people more efficiently than families can.
    b. impersonal organizations concerned with efficiency, uniformity, and control are becoming more and more common.

   c. it is possible for organizations to both do their job and meet human needs.
   d. society today is one vast social network.

ANSWERS: 1 (c); 2 (d); 3 (a); 4 (b); 5 (d); 6 (c); 7 (d); 8 (b); 9 (a); 10 (b).

Essay Questions

1. How do primary groups differ from secondary groups? Give examples of each in your own life.

2. According to Max Weber, what are the six traits that define bureaucracy? What is the advantage of this organizational form? What are several problems that often go along with it?

Chapter 8   Sexuality and Society

Multiple-Choice Questions

1. What is the term for humans who have some combination of female and male genitalia?
   a. asexual people
   b. bisexual people
   c. transsexual people
   d. intersexual people

2. A global perspective on human sexuality shows us that
   a. although sex involves our biology, it is also a cultural trait that varies from place to place.
   b. people everywhere in the world have the same sexual practices.
   c. people in all societies are uncomfortable talking about sex.
   d. All of the above are correct.

3. Why is the incest taboo found in every society?
   a. It limits sexual competition between members of families.
   b. It helps define people's rights and obligations toward one another.
   c. It integrates members of a family within the larger society.
   d. All of the above are correct.

4. The sexual revolution reached its peak during the
   a. 1890s.
   b. 1920s.
   c. 1960s.
   d. 1980s.

ESSAY 1: See the discussion on pages 193–94. Attitudes toward sexuality became more open, and sexual activity became more casual. Causes of these changes included greater geographic and social mobility that removed young people from their parents and their "roots"; the Kinsey studies, which increased discussion of and knowledge about sexuality; the 1960s youth culture, which encouraged sexual activity; and the development of birth control technology that reduced the risk of pregnancy associated with being sexually active.

ESSAY 2: This is largely a matter of personal values and opinion. See the discussion of these topics on pages 200–204.

5. Survey data show that the largest share of U.S. adults reject which of the following?
   a. extramarital sex
   b. homosexuality
   c. premarital sex
   d. sex simply for pleasure

6. According to the Laumann study of sexuality in the United States,
   a. only one-third of the adult population is sexually active.
   b. there is great diversity in levels of sexual activity, so no one stereotype is correct.
   c. single people have more sex than married people.
   d. most married men admit to cheating on their wives at some point in their marriage.

7. What is the term meaning "sexual attraction to people of both sexes"?
   a. heterosexuality
   b. homosexuality
   c. bisexuality
   d. asexuality

8. Compared to 1950, the U.S. rate of teenage pregnancy today is
   a. higher.
   b. the same, but more teens become pregnant by choice.
   c. the same, but more pregnant teens are married.
   d. lower.

9. By what point in their lives do most young people in the United States today become sexually active?
   a. when they marry
   b. by the middle of college
   c. by the end of high school
   d. by age thirteen

10. If we look back in history, we see that once a society develops birth control technology,
    a. social control of sexuality becomes more strict.
    b. the birth rate actually goes up.
    c. attitudes about sexuality become more permissive.
    d. people no longer care about incest.

ANSWERS: 1 (d); 2 (a); 3 (d); 4 (c); 5 (a); 6 (b); 7 (c); 8 (d); 9 (c); 10 (c).

Essay Questions

1. What was the "sexual revolution"? What changed? Can you point to reasons for the change?

2. Of the issues discussed in this chapter (prostitution, teen pregnancy, pornography, sexual violence, and abortion), which do you think is the most important for U.S. society today? Why?

Chapter 9   Deviance

Multiple-Choice Questions

1. Crime is a special type of deviance that
   a. refers to violations of law.
   b. involves punishment.
   c. refers to any violation of a society's norms.
   d. always involves a particular person as the offender.

2. Emile Durkheim explains that deviance is
   a. defined by the rich and used against the poor.
   b. harmful not just to victims but to society as a whole.
   c. often at odds with public morality.
   d. found in every society.

3. Applying Robert Merton's strain theory, a person selling illegal drugs for a living would be an example of which of the following categories?
   a. conformist
   b. innovator
   c. retreatist
   d. ritualist

4. Labeling theory states that deviance
   a. is a normal part of social life.
   b. always changes people's social identity.
   c. arises not from what people do as much as how others respond.
   d. All of the above are correct.

5. When Jake's friends began calling him a "dope-head," he left the group and spent more time smoking marijuana. He also began hanging out with others who used drugs, and by the end of the term, he had dropped out of college. Edwin Lemert would call this situation an example of
   a. primary deviance.
   b. the development of secondary deviance.
   c. the formation of a deviant subculture.
   d. the beginning of retreatism.

6. A social-conflict approach claims that who a society calls deviant depends on
   a. who has and does not have power.
   b. a society's moral values.
   c. how often the behavior occurs.
   d. how harmful the behavior is.

7. Stealing a laptop computer from the study lounge in a college dorm is an example of which criminal offense?
   a. burglary
   b. motor vehicle theft
   c. robbery
   d. larceny-theft

8. The FBI's criminal statistics used in this chapter to create a profile of the street criminal reflect
   a. all crimes that occur.
   b. offenses known to the police.
   c. offenses that involve violence.
   d. offenses resulting in a criminal conviction.

9. Most people arrested for a violent crime in the United States are
   a. white.
   b. African American.
   c. Hispanic.
   d. Asian.

10. Which of the following is the oldest justification for punishing an offender?
    a. deterrence
    b. retribution
    c. societal protection
    d. rehabilitation

ANSWERS: 1 (a); 2 (d); 3 (b); 4 (c); 5 (b); 6 (a); 7 (d); 8 (b); 9 (a); 10 (b).

Essay Questions

1. How does a sociological view of deviance differ from the common-sense idea that bad people do bad things?

2. Research (Mauer, 1999) shows that one in three black men between the ages of twenty and twenty-nine is in jail, on probation, or on parole. What factors, noted in this chapter, help explain this pattern?

Chapter 10   Social Stratification

Multiple-Choice Questions

1. *Social stratification* refers to
   a. job specialization.
   b. ranking categories of people in a hierarchy.
   c. the fact that some people work harder than others.
   d. inequality of personal talent and individual effort.

2. Looking back in history and around the world today, we see that social stratification may involve differences in
   a. how unequal people are.
   b. what resources are unequally distributed.
   c. why a society claims people should be unequal.
   d. All of the above are correct.

3. A caste system is social stratification
   a. based on individual achievement.
   b. based on meritocracy.
   c. based on birth.
   d. in which a person's social position is likely to change over time.

4. Sally has two advanced degrees, earns an average salary, and is working at a low-prestige job. Which concept best describes her situation?
   a. low status consistency
   b. horizontal social mobility
   c. upward social mobility
   d. high status consistency

5. According to the Davis-Moore thesis,
   a. equality is functional for society.
   b. the more inequality a society has, the more productive it is.
   c. more important jobs must offer enough rewards to draw talent from less important work.
   d. societies with more meritocracy are less productive than those with caste systems.

6. Karl Marx claimed that society "reproduces the class structure." By this, he meant that
   a. society benefits from inequality.
   b. class differences are passed on from one generation to the next.
   c. class differences are the same everywhere.
   d. a society without classes is impossible.

7. Max Weber claimed that social stratification is based on
   a. economic class.
   b. social status or prestige.
   c. power.
   d. All of the above are correct.

8. A society with which type of productive technology has the least amount of social stratification?
   a. hunting and gathering
   b. horticultural/pastoral
   c. industrial
   d. postindustrial

ESSAY 1: Individual effort does matter to the extent that a society is meritocratic. But no society is or has ever been entirely meritocratic. See the discussion on pages 248–49.

ESSAY 2: Caste and class systems differ in terms of (1) how "closed" or "open" they are to allowing social mobility, (2) the key dimensions of inequality (prestige versus money), and (3) the ideological justification for inequality (fate or God's will versus merit). Remember that class systems blend caste and meritocracy.

9. Keeping the Kuznets curve in mind, which type of society has the most social stratification?
   a. hunting and gathering
   b. horticultural/pastoral
   c. agrarian
   d. industrial

10. The "bell curve" thesis suggests that which of the following is more important than ever to social position in the United States?
    a. family background
    b. intelligence
    c. hard work
    d. whom you know

ANSWERS: 1 (b); 2 (d); 3 (c); 4 (a); 5 (c); 6 (b); 7 (d); 8 (a); 9 (c); 10 (b).

Essay Questions

1. Explain why social stratification is a creation of society, not just a reflection of individual differences.

2. How do caste and class systems differ? How are they the same? Why does industrialization introduce a measure of meritocracy into social stratification?

Chapter 11   Social Class in the United States

Multiple-Choice Questions

1. Which of the following terms refers to earnings from work or investments?
   a. income
   b. assets
   c. wealth
   d. power

2. The wealthiest 20 percent of people in the United States own about how much of the country's privately owned wealth?
   a. 35 percent
   b. 55 percent
   c. 85 percent
   d. 95 percent

3. About what share of U.S. adults over the age of twenty-five are college graduates?
   a. 10 percent
   b. 29 percent
   c. 40 percent
   d. 68 percent

4. In the United States, average income for African American families is what share of average income for non-Hispanic white families?
   a. 87 percent
   b. 77 percent
   c. 67 percent
   d. 57 percent

5. Which of the following is another term for the "working class"?
   a. upper-middle class
   b. average-middle class
   c. lower-middle class
   d. lower class

6. In terms of health, people living in high-income families
   a. live in safer and less stressful environments.
   b. are more likely to describe their own health as "excellent."
   c. live longer lives.
   d. All of the above are correct.

7. Which quintile (20 percent) of the U.S. population has seen the greatest change in income over the last generation?
   a. the top quintile
   b. the middle quintile
   c. the lowest quintile
   d. All quintiles have seen the same change.

8. Change in social position during a person's own lifetime is called
   a. intergenerational social mobility.
   b. intragenerational social mobility.
   c. structural social mobility.
   d. horizontal social mobility.

9. In 2006, about what share of the U.S. population was officially counted as poor?
   a. 42.3 percent
   b. 22.3 percent
   c. 12.3 percent
   d. 2.3 percent

ESSAY 1: Early in the chapter, the text states that people claim the U.S. is a middle-class society because we have never had a formal aristocracy as we find in Europe. Other important reasons are that we all tend to interact primarily with others more or less like ourselves and that middle-class images are widely spread by the mass media.

ESSAY 2: Both the statistical picture of poverty and the profile of those at high risk of poverty are found on pages 288–89. Keep in mind that some categories (such as African Americans) are at higher risk of poverty even though most poor people are white.

10. Which age category of the U.S. population has the highest percentage of people in poverty?
    a. seniors over age sixty-five
    b. middle-aged people
    c. young people aged eighteen to twenty-four
    d. children under age eighteen

ANSWERS: 1 (a); 2 (c); 3 (b); 4 (d); 5 (c); 6 (d); 7 (a); 8 (b); 9 (c); 10 (c).

Essay Questions

1. We often hear people say that the United States is a "middle-class society." Where does this idea come from? Based on what you have read in this chapter, how true do you think this claim is? Why?

2. What is the extent of poverty in the United States? Who are the poor in terms of age, race and ethnicity, and gender?

Chapter 12   Global Stratification

Multiple-Choice Questions

1. In global perspective, the richest 20 percent of all people earn about what share of the entire world's income?
    a. 20 percent
    b. 40 percent
    c. 60 percent
    d. 80 percent

2. The United States, Canada, and Japan are all
    a. high-income countries.
    b. middle-income countries.
    c. low-income countries.
    d. in different income categories.

3. Low-income nations
    a. are evenly spread in all world regions.
    b. are found mostly in Africa and Asia.
    c. are all in Latin America.
    d. contain a majority of the world's people.

4. China and India are now
    a. the world's poorest countries.
    b. counted among the world's low-income nations.
    c. counted among the world's middle-income nations.
    d. counted among the world's high-income nations.

5. Which of the following is the range of annual personal income for people living in middle-income nations?
    a. $250 to $1,000
    b. $1,000 to $2,500
    c. $2,500 to $10,000
    d. $10,000 to $25,000

6. How does poverty in poor nations compare to poverty in the United States?
    a. In poor nations, poverty is more likely to involve men.
    b. In most poor nations, the problem of poverty has been all but solved.
    c. In poor nations, most people do not consider poverty a problem.
    d. In poor nations, there is far more absolute poverty.

7. *Neocolonialism* refers to the process by which
    a. rich countries gain new colonies to replace older ones.
    b. multinational corporations dominate the economy of a poor country.
    c. rich countries grant independence to their former colonies.
    d. more and more large corporations do business in many countries at once.

8. Which of the following statements is the basis of modernization theory?
    a. The main cause of poverty in the world is low productivity due to simple technology and traditional culture.
    b. Poor nations can never become rich if they remain part of the global capitalist economy.
    c. The main cause of poverty in the world is the operation of multi-national corporations.
    d. Most poor nations were richer in the past than they are today.

9. According to Walt Rostow, which is the final stage of economic development?
    a. drive to technological maturity
    b. traditional
    c. high mass consumption
    d. take-off

10. Dependency theory differs from modernization theory by saying that
    a. poor nations are responsible for their own poverty.
    b. capitalism is the best way to produce economic development.
    c. economic development is not a good idea for poor countries.
    d. global stratification results from the exploitation of poor countries by rich countries.

ANSWERS: 1 (d); 2 (a); 3 (b); 4 (c); 5 (c); 6 (d); 7 (b); 8 (a); 9 (c); 10 (d).

ESSAY 1: The differences are defined on page 307. Relative poverty is found everywhere, in rich and poor countries alike. Absolute poverty exists in rich countries, but it is a far more serious problem in low-income nations, contributing to the deaths of about 15 million people each year.

ESSAY 2: Gender stratification is greater in low-income nations than it is in high-income countries. If women do not have choices about how to live, including both educational and economic opportunities, they cannot be economically as productive, contributing to economic growth. In addition, women who must remain in the home have more children, which increases population. More people with less economic output clearly reduces economic growth.

ESSAY 1: "Sex" refers to biological differences between females and males. "Gender" refers to how societies attach meaning to these differences. While some researchers claim that biological differences do encourage the sexes to behave in slightly different ways, most sociologists claim that sex and gender are not directly related.

ESSAY 2: Gender is a dimension of social stratification because women have less income, wealth, and power than men do. Gender combines with class, as well as race and ethnicity, to produce multiple disadvantages as explained by intersection theory, discussed on pages 339–40.

Essay Questions

1. What are the differences between relative poverty and absolute poverty? Describe global social stratification using both concepts.

2. Why do many analysts believe that economic development in low-income countries depends on raising the social standing of women?

Chapter 13   Gender Stratification

Multiple-Choice Questions

1. **Gender is not just a matter of difference but also a matter of**
   a. power.
   b. wealth.
   c. prestige.
   d. All of the above are correct.

2. **The anthropologist Margaret Mead studied gender in three societies in New Guinea and found that**
   a. all societies define femininity in much the same way.
   b. all societies define masculinity in much the same way.
   c. what is feminine in one society may be masculine in another.
   d. the meaning of gender is changing everywhere toward greater equality.

3. **For all of us raised in U.S. society, gender shapes our**
   a. feelings.
   b. thoughts.
   c. actions.
   d. All of the above are correct.

4. **There is a "beauty myth" in U.S. society that encourages**
   a. women to believe that their personal importance depends on their looks.
   b. beautiful women to think that they do not need men.
   c. men to improve their physical appearance to get the attention of women.
   d. women to think they are as physically attractive as today's men are.

5. **In the United States, what share of women work for income?**
   a. 80 percent
   b. 60 percent
   c. 50 percent
   d. 30 percent

6. **In the U.S. labor force,**
   a. men and women have the same types of jobs.
   b. men and women have the same pay.
   c. women are still concentrated in several types of jobs.
   d. almost all working women hold "pink-collar jobs."

7. **For which of the following categories of people in the United States is it true that women do more housework than men?**
   a. people who work for income
   b. people who are married
   c. people who have children
   d. All of the above are correct.

8. **In the United States, women in the labor force working full time earn how much for every dollar earned by men working full time?**
   a. 78 cents
   b. 86 cents
   c. 90 cents
   d. 98 cents

9. **After the 2008 elections, women held about what percentage of seats in Congress?**
   a. 7 percent
   b. 17 percent
   c. 37 percent
   d. 57 percent

10. **Which type of feminism accepts U.S. society as it is but wants to give women the same rights and opportunities as men?**
    a. socialist feminism
    b. liberal feminism
    c. radical feminism
    d. All of the above are correct.

ANSWERS: 1 (d); 2 (c); 3 (d); 4 (a); 5 (b); 6 (c); 7 (d); 8 (a); 9 (b); 10 (b).

Essay Questions

1. How do the concepts "sex" and "gender" differ? In what ways are they related?

2. Why is gender considered a dimension of social stratification? How does gender intersect with other dimensions of inequality such as class, race, and ethnicity?

Chapter 14   Race and Ethnicity

Multiple-Choice Questions

1. *Race* refers to _____ considered important by a society, and *ethnicity* refers to _____.
   a. biological traits; cultural traits
   b. cultural traits; biological traits
   c. differences; what we have in common
   d. what we have in common; differences

2. What share of the U.S. population consists of people of Hispanic ancestry?
   a. 45.1 percent
   b. 35.1 percent
   c. 25.1 percent
   d. 15.1 percent

3. A minority is defined as a category of people who
   a. have physical traits that make them different.
   b. are less than half the society's population.
   c. are defined as both different and disadvantaged.
   d. are below average in terms of income.

4. In this country, four states now have a "minority majority." Which of the following is not one of them?
   a. California
   b. Florida
   c. Hawaii
   d. New Mexico

5. Research using the Bogardus social distance scale shows that U.S. college students
   a. are less prejudiced than students fifty years ago.
   b. believe that Arabs and Muslims should be kept out of the country.
   c. have the strongest prejudice against African Americans.
   d. All of the above are correct.

6. *Prejudice* is a matter of _____, and *discrimination* is a matter of _____.
   a. biology; culture
   b. attitudes; behavior
   c. choice; social structure
   d. what rich people think; what rich people do

7. The United States is not truly pluralistic because
   a. part of our population lives in "ethnic enclaves."
   b. this country has a history of slavery.
   c. different racial and ethnic categories are unequal in social standing.
   d. All of the above are correct.

8. Which term is illustrated by immigrants from Ecuador learning to speak the English language?
   a. genocide
   b. segregation
   c. assimilation
   d. pluralism

9. During the late 1400s, the first Europeans came to the Americas; Native Americans
   a. followed shortly thereafter.
   b. had just migrated from Asia.
   c. came with them from Europe.
   d. had inhabited this land for 30,000 years.

10. Which of the following is the largest category of Asian Americans in the United States?
    a. Chinese Americans
    b. Japanese Americans
    c. Korean Americans
    d. Vietnamese Americans

ANSWERS: 1 (a); 2 (d); 3 (c); 4 (b); 5 (a); 6 (b); 7 (c); 8 (c); 9 (d); 10 (a).

Essay Questions

1. What is the difference between race and ethnicity? What does it mean to say that race and ethnicity are socially constructed?

2. What is a minority? Support the claim that African Americans and Arab Americans are both minorities in the United States, using specific facts from the chapter.

Chapter 15   Aging and the Elderly

Multiple-Choice Questions

1. Where in the world is the share of the elderly population increasing most quickly?
   a. low-income nations
   b. all the world's nations
   c. high-income nations
   d. the United States

2. What is the average (median) age of the U.S. population?
   a. sixty-seven years
   b. fifty-seven years
   c. forty-seven years
   d. thirty-seven years

3. As we look at older people in the United States, we find a larger share of
   a. men.
   b. women.
   c. well-off people.
   d. married people.

4. **What effect does industrialization have on the social standing of the oldest members of a society?**
   a. Social standing goes down.
   b. There is little or no effect.
   c. Social standing goes up.
   d. Social standing goes up for men and down for women.

5. **The term *gerontocracy* refers to a society where**
   a. there is a lot of social inequality.
   b. men dominate women.
   c. religious leaders are in charge.
   d. the oldest people have the most wealth, power, and prestige.

6. **The idea of retirement first appears in which type of society?**
   a. hunting and gathering
   b. pastoral
   c. industrial
   d. postindustrial

7. **In the United States, the poverty rate for people over the age of sixty-five is**
   a. higher than the national average.
   b. the same as the national average.
   c. lower than the national average.
   d. higher than among any other age category.

8. **Which category of people in the United States provides most of the caregiving to elderly people?**
   a. professionals working in the home
   b. nurses
   c. other elderly people
   d. women

9. **The structural-functional approach to aging involves**
   a. disengagement theory.
   b. activity theory.
   c. social inequality.
   d. All of the above are correct.

10. **A document in which a person states which medical procedures he or she wishes to be used or avoided under specific conditions is known as a**
    a. death wish.
    b. living will.
    c. legal trust.
    d. power of attorney.

Essay Questions

1. What is the "graying of the United States"? What two factors are causing this trend? What are some of the likely consequences of this trend for our way of life?

2. How is ageism like sexism and racism? How is it different? If older people are disadvantaged, should they be considered a minority? Why or why not?

Chapter 16   The Economy and Work

Multiple-Choice Questions

1. **The economy is the social institution that guides**
   a. the production of goods and services.
   b. the distribution of goods and services.
   c. the consumption of goods and services.
   d. All of the above are correct.

2. **The early textile factories in New England, which marked the start of the Industrial Revolution in the United States, employed**
   a. mostly women who were paid half the wages earned by men.
   b. mostly immigrants who had just arrived from Asia and Latin America.
   c. people who had been in the United States the longest.
   d. All of the above are correct.

3. **Building houses and making cars are examples of production in which economic sector?**
   a. the primary sector
   b. the secondary sector
   c. the tertiary sector
   d. the service sector

4. **Which of the following marks the rise of a postindustrial economy?**
   a. the spread of factories
   b. declining rates of consumption
   c. the development of computer technology
   d. larger machinery

5. **Today, about what share of the U.S. labor force has industrial (secondary-sector) jobs?**
   a. one-fifth
   b. one-half
   c. two-thirds
   d. nine-tenths

ANSWERS: 1 (c); 2 (d); 3 (b); 4 (a); 5 (d); 6 (c); 7 (c); 8 (d); 9 (a); 10 (b).

ESSAY 1: The Industrial Revolution (see factors listed on page 413) made the U.S. economy much more productive, moved production from the primary to secondary sector of the economy, moved production from farm and home to factories where workers received wages for their labor, and increased worker specialization. The Information Revolution (see pages 413–14) shifted production from the secondary to the tertiary sector, demanded not mechanical skills but literacy skills, and decentralized work from factories to almost anywhere.

ESSAY 2: The economic models of capitalism and socialism differ in terms of private versus collective ownership of property, pursuit of private versus collective goals, and competition and consumer choice versus government control of the economy. In general, capitalism is more productive than socialism, generates more economic inequality (but not necessarily less inequality in terms of power), and supports a wider range of personal freedoms (see pages 418–19).

6. What is a result of the globalization of the economy?
   a. Certain areas of the world are specializing in one sector of economic activity.
   b. Industrial jobs in the United States are being lost.
   c. More and more products pass through several nations on their way to consumers.
   d. All of the above are correct.

7. A capitalist society's approach to economic "justice" amounts to
   a. doing what is best for society's poorest members.
   b. freedom of the marketplace.
   c. making everyone more or less socially equal.
   d. All of the above are correct.

8. Socialist economies differ from capitalist economies in that they
   a. are more productive.
   b. create less economic equality.
   c. create more economic equality.
   d. make greater use of commercial advertising.

9. In the United States, what percentage of nonfarm workers are members of a labor union?
   a. 12 percent
   b. 32 percent
   c. 52 percent
   d. 72 percent

10. The largest 2,405 corporations, each with assets exceeding $2.5 billion, represent about what share of all corporate assets in the United States?
    a. 10 percent
    b. 25 percent
    c. 50 percent
    d. 75 percent

ANSWERS: 1 (d); 2 (a); 3 (b); 4 (c); 5 (a); 6 (d); 7 (b); 8 (c); 9 (a); 10 (d).

Essay Questions

1. In what specific ways did the Industrial Revolution change the U.S. economy? How is the Information Revolution changing the economy once again?

2. What key characteristics distinguish capitalism from socialism? Compare these two systems in terms of productivity, economic inequality, and extent of personal freedoms.

Chapter 17   Politics and Government

Multiple-Choice Questions

1. According to Max Weber, power is defined as
   a. "the shadow of wealth."
   b. the ability to achieve desired ends despite resistance from others.
   c. a society's form of government.
   d. the creation of bureaucracy.

2. Max Weber claimed that the main difference between power and authority is that
   a. power is a better way to hold a society together.
   b. authority is based on brute force.
   c. power involves a special claim to justice.
   d. people typically view authority as legitimate rather than coercive.

3. Modern societies, including the United States, rely mostly on which type of authority?
   a. charismatic authority
   b. traditional authority
   c. rational-legal authority
   d. no authority

4. In which type of political system does power reside in the hands of the people as a whole?
   a. democracy
   b. aristocracy
   c. totalitarianism
   d. monarchy

5. When sociologists use the term "political economy," they are referring to
   a. the fact that people "vote with their pocketbook."
   b. the fact that the political and economic systems are linked.
   c. any democratic political system.
   d. the most efficient form of government.

6. The claim that socialist societies are democratic is typically based on the fact that
   a. their members have considerable personal liberty.
   b. these societies have no elite.
   c. these societies meet the basic economic needs of everyone.
   d. these societies have a high standard of living.

7. Which type of government concentrates all power in one place and rigidly regulates people's lives?
   a. an aristocratic government
   b. a democratic government
   c. an authoritarian government
   d. a totalitarian government

8. In the 2004 U.S. presidential election, about what share of registered voters actually cast a vote?
   a. close to 100 percent
   b. about 81 percent
   c. about 63 percent
   d. about 27 percent

9. The Marxist political-economy model suggests that
   a. power is concentrated in the hands of a small "power elite."
   b. an antidemocratic bias is built into the capitalist system.
   c. power is spread widely throughout society.
   d. many people do not vote because they are basically satisfied with their lives.

10. Which war resulted in the greatest loss of American lives?
   a. the Civil War
   b. World War II
   c. the Korean War
   d. the Vietnam War

ANSWERS: 1 (b); 2 (d); 3 (c); 4 (a); 5 (b); 6 (c); 7 (d); 8 (c); 9 (b); 10 (a).

Essay Questions

1. What is the difference between authority and power? How do preindustrial and industrial societies create authority in different ways?

2. Compare and contrast the pluralist, power-elite, and Marxist political-economy models of political power. Which of these models do you think makes the most sense? Why?

Chapter 18   Families

Multiple-Choice Questions

1. The family is a social institution that is found in
   a. most but not all societies.
   b. low-income nations but typically not in high-income nations.
   c. high-income nations but typically not in low-income nations.
   d. every society.

2. What is the term sociologists use for a family containing parents, children, and other kin?
   a. a nuclear family
   b. an extended family
   c. a family of affinity
   d. a conjugal family

3. A system of marriage that unites one woman with two or more men is called
   a. polygamy.
   b. polygyny.
   c. polyandry.
   d. bilateral marriage.

4. Sociologists claim that marriage in the United States follows the principle of homogamy, which means that partners are
   a. people of the same sex.
   b. people who are socially alike in terms of class, age, and race.
   c. people who marry due to social pressure.
   d. selected based on love rather than by parents.

5. Which of the following are included among the functions of the family?
   a. socialization of children
   b. regulation of sexual activity
   c. social placement of children
   d. All of the above are correct.

6. Which theoretical approach states that people select partners who have about the same to offer as they do?
   a. the structural-functional approach
   b. the social-exchange approach
   c. the social-conflict approach
   d. the feminist approach

7. Which of the following transitions in married life is usually the hardest for people?
   a. birth of the second child
   b. last child leaving home
   c. death of a spouse
   d. retiring from the labor force

8. In the United States, many Latino families are characterized by
   a. strong extended kinship.
   b. parents exerting a great deal of control over their children's courtship.
   c. traditional gender roles.
   d. All of the above are correct.

9. For which category of the U.S. population is the highest proportion of children born to single women?
   a. African Americans
   b. Asian Americans
   c. Hispanic Americans
   d. non-Hispanic white Americans

ESSAY 1: Examples include all the patterns of family life discussed on pages 463–66. In addition, race, ethnicity, social class, and gender all shape the experience of family life. Finally, the rising and fall divorce rate reflects events and changes in society.

ESSAY 2: The facts can support either assessment, which reflects political values as well. Generally, conservatives see families getting weaker; liberals see families changing and becoming more diverse. The Controversy & Debate box on pages 480–81 summarizes much of this debate.

ESSAY 1: Durkheim explained that people define certain things as sacred, setting them apart from everyday life as extraordinary and inspiring awe and reverence. People define as profane everything that they regard as an ordinary element of everyday life.

ESSAY 2: Churches, sects, and cults differ in how well they are integrated into the larger society. Another difference involves how the religion's leaders are recognized (as a result of formal training or personal charisma). See the discussion on pages 493–95.

10. Which category of people in the United States is at the highest risk of divorce?
    a. gay and lesbian couples
    b. young people who marry after a short courtship
    c. a couple whose parents never experienced divorce
    d. a couple facing a wanted and expected pregnancy

ANSWERS: 1 (d); 2 (b); 3 (c); 4 (b); 5 (d); 6 (b); 7 (c); 8 (d); 9 (a); 10 (b).

Essay Questions

1. Sociologists point to ways in which family life reflects not just individual choices but the structure of society as well. Provide three examples of how society shapes family life.

2. Overall, do you think families in the United States are becoming weaker or simply more diverse? Support your position.

Chapter 19   Religion

Multiple-Choice Questions

1. What term did Emile Durkheim use to refer to the everyday elements of our lives?
   a. religion
   b. profane
   c. sacred
   d. ritual

2. Faith, or belief in religious matters, is best described as
   a. what we learn from science.
   b. what our senses tell us.
   c. our cultural traditions.
   d. conviction in things unseen.

3. The reason sociologists study religion is to learn
   a. the meaning of life.
   b. whether a particular religion is true or not.
   c. how patterns of religious activity affect society.
   d. which religious organization they wish to join.

4. Which of the following is *not* one of the important functions of religion, according to Durkheim?
   a. generating social conflict
   b. generating social cohesion
   c. providing social control
   d. providing meaning and purpose

5. Peter Berger claims that we are most likely to turn to religion when we experience
   a. social conflict.
   b. the best of times.
   c. familiar, everyday routines.
   d. important events that are out of our control.

6. Which sociologist explained how religion helps support social inequality?
   a. Emile Durkheim
   b. Karl Marx
   c. Max Weber
   d. Ernst Troeltsch

7. Which type of religious organization is most integrated into the larger society?
   a. cult
   b. church
   c. sect
   d. New Age spirituality

8. A sect is a type of religious organization that
   a. has formally trained leaders.
   b. is well integrated into the larger society.
   c. rejects the importance of charisma.
   d. stands apart from the larger society.

9. Which of the following religions is found in the United States?
   a. Islam
   b. Judaism
   c. Christianity
   d. All of the above are correct.

10. The term "secularization" refers to which of the following?
    a. religion becoming more important in people's lives
    b. increasing popularity of fundamentalism
    c. the decline in the importance of religion and the sacred
    d. churches resisting social change

ANSWERS: 1 (b); 2 (d); 3 (c); 4 (a); 5 (d); 6 (b); 7 (b); 8 (d); 9 (d); 10 (c).

Essay Questions

1. What is the basic distinction between the sacred and the profane that underlies all religious belief?

2. In what ways do churches, sects, and cults differ?

ESSAY 1: Industrialization expands the division of labor, which requires that education move outside of a family into the hands of specially trained teachers. To see the effect of political and cultural systems on schooling, review the global material on pages 516–19.

ESSAY 2: Functional analysis states that education contributes to socialization, cultural innovation, cultural integration, social placement, and performs various latent functions, such as child care. Conflict analysis claims schooling reflects social standing and, therefore, reproduces social inequality in each generation. See pages 519–27.

Chapter 20   Education

Multiple-Choice Questions

1. In the United States and other countries, laws requiring all children to attend school were enacted following
   a. national independence.
   b. the Industrial Revolution.
   c. World War II.
   d. the computer age.

2. Japan differs from the United States in that getting into college depends more on
   a. athletic ability.
   b. race and ethnicity.
   c. family money.
   d. scores on achievement tests.

3. What share of the U.S. adult population has completed high school?
   a. 45.3 percent
   b. 65.5 percent
   c. 85.7 percent
   d. 99.9 percent

4. Using a structural-functional approach, schooling carries out the task of
   a. tying together a diverse population.
   b. creating new culture.
   c. socializing young people.
   d. All of the above are correct.

5. A social-conflict approach highlights how education
   a. reflects and reinforces social inequality.
   b. helps prepare students for their future careers.
   c. has both latent and manifest functions.
   d. All of the above are correct.

6. The importance of community colleges to U.S. higher education is reflected in the fact that they
   a. greatly expand the opportunity to attend college.
   b. enroll almost 40 percent of all U.S. college students.
   c. enroll half of all African American and Hispanic college students.
   d. All of the above are correct.

7. What share of people in the United States between the ages of sixteen and twenty-four drop out before completing high school?
   a. 1.3 percent
   b. 9.3 percent
   c. 29.3 percent
   d. 39.3 percent

8. Support for the school choice movement is based on the claim that U.S. public schools perform poorly because
   a. they have no competition.
   b. many schools lack enough funding.
   c. the national poverty rate is high.
   d. too many parents are not involved in the schools.

9. This chapter provides lots of evidence to support the claim that
   a. U.S. schools are better than those in other high-income nations.
   b. most public schools perform well and most private schools do not.
   c. without involving the entire society, schools cannot improve the quality of education.
   d. All of the above are correct.

10. About what share of all U.S. college students today are men?
    a. 63 percent
    b. 53 percent
    c. 43 percent
    d. 33 percent

ANSWERS: 1 (b); 2 (d); 3 (c); 4 (d); 5 (a); 6 (d); 7 (b); 8 (a); 9 (c); 10 (c).

Essay Questions

1. Why does industrialization lead societies to expand their systems of schooling? In what ways has schooling in the United States been shaped by our economic, political, and cultural systems?

2. From a structural-functional perspective, why is schooling important to the operation of society? From a social-conflict point of view, how does schooling reproduce social inequality in each generation?

Chapter 21   Health and Medicine

Multiple-Choice Questions

1. Health is a social issue because
   a. cultural patterns define what people view as healthy.
   b. social inequality affects people's health.
   c. a society's technology affects people's health.
   d. All of the above are correct.

2. In the very poorest nations of the world today, a majority of people die before reaching
   a. their teens.
   b. the age of fifty.
   c. the age of sixty-five.
   d. the age of seventy-five.

ESSAY 1: Health is a social concept because culture defines health, with definitions changing over time; a society's technology affects health; and social inequality shapes public health. See pages 542–43.

ESSAY 2: The sick role is the central concept in Parsons's structural-functional theory of health and illness. See the discussion on page 557.

3. The Industrial Revolution reduced deaths caused by _____, which increased the share of deaths caused by _____.
   a. disease; war
   b. starvation; accidents
   c. infectious diseases such as influenza; chronic conditions such as heart disease
   d. chronic conditions such as heart disease; infectious diseases such as influenza

4. Social epidemiology is the study of
   a. which bacteria cause a specific disease.
   b. the distribution of health and illness in a population.
   c. what categories of people become doctors.
   d. the distribution of doctors around the world.

5. What is the largest cause of death among young people in the United States?
   a. cancer   c. accidents
   b. influenza   d. AIDS

6. In the United States, which category of people has the highest life expectancy?
   a. African American men
   b. white men
   c. African American women
   d. white women

7. In the United States, the greatest preventable cause of death is
   a. sexually transmitted diseases.
   b. automobile accidents.
   c. cigarette smoking.
   d. AIDS.

8. About what share of U.S. adults are overweight?
   a. two-thirds   c. one-third
   b. half   d. one-fifth

9. Which sexually transmitted disease is most common among U.S. adults?
   a. AIDS   c. gonorrhea
   b. genital herpes d. syphilis

10. A social-conflict analysis claims that capitalism harms human health because
    a. it does not encourage people to take control of their own health.
    b. it gives physicians little financial incentive to work.
    c. it reduces average living standards.
    d. it makes quality of care dependent on income.

Essay Questions

1. Why is health as much a social as a biological issue? How does a social-conflict analysis of health and medicine point to the need to define health as a social issue?

2. Describe Talcott Parsons's structural-functional analysis of health and illness. What is the sick role? When and how is it used?

Chapter 22 Population, Urbanization, and Environment

Multiple-Choice Questions

1. *Demography* is defined as the study of
   a. democratic political systems.
   b. human culture.
   c. human population.
   d. the natural environment.

2. Which region of the world has *both* the lowest birth rate and the lowest infant mortality rate?
   a. Latin America   c. Africa
   b. Europe   d. Asia

3. Typically, high-income nations grow mostly from _____, and low-income nations grow from _____.
   a. immigration; natural increase
   b. emigration; natural increase
   c. natural increase; immigration
   d. internal migration; natural increase

4. In general, the higher the average income of a country,
   a. the faster the population increases.
   b. the slower the population increases.
   c. the lower the level of immigration.
   d. the lower the level of urbanization.

5. In the United States, urban decentralization has caused
   a. the expansion of suburbs.
   b. the development of vast urban regions.
   c. the growth of edge cities.
   d. All of the above are correct.

6. Which term was used by Ferdinand Tönnies to refer to a type of social organization in which people come together on the basis of individual self-interest?
   a. mechanical solidarity
   b. organic solidarity
   c. *Gesellschaft*
   d. *Gemeinschaft*

ANSWERS: 1 (d); 2 (a); 3 (a); 4 (c); 5 (b); 6 (c); 7 (c); 8 (a); 9 (b); 10 (d).

ESSAY 1: In brief, economic development reduces death rates first and then reduces birth rates, resulting in very slow population increase. See the discussion on pages 573–74.

ESSAY 2: Urbanism was linked by Tönnies to *Gesellschaft*; by Durkheim to organic solidarity with increased privacy and tolerance of moral differences; and by Simmel to a blasé attitude. Wirth defined urbanism as large, dense, heterogeneous settlements that promote a superficial, impersonal, and transitory social life. See the discussion on pages 580–81.

7. The world's third urban revolution is now taking place in
   a. the United States.
   b. Europe and Japan.
   c. middle-income nations.
   d. low-income nations.

8. The *environmental deficit* refers to
   a. long-term harm to the environment caused by a shortsighted focus on material affluence.
   b. the public's lack of interest in the natural environment.
   c. the fact that natural scientists ignore the social dimensions of environmental problems.
   d. the lack of funding for important environmental programs.

9. Which of the following statements reflects the "limits to growth" thesis?
   a. People are rapidly consuming Earth's finite resources.
   b. Whatever problems technology creates, technology can solve.
   c. The quality of life on Earth is getting better.
   d. Higher living standards today will benefit future generations.

10. *Environmental racism* is the idea that
    a. few minorities are found within the environmental movement.
    b. prejudice is the major cause of pollution and other environmental problems.
    c. environmental dangers are greatest for the poor and minorities.
    d. All of the above are correct.

ANSWERS: 1 (c); 2 (b); 3 (a); 4 (b); 5 (d); 6 (c); 7 (d); 8 (a); 9 (a); 10 (c).

Essay Questions

1. According to demographic transition theory, how does economic development affect population patterns?
2. According to Ferdinand Tönnies, Emile Durkheim, Georg Simmel, and Louis Wirth, what characterizes urbanism as a way of life? Note several differences in the ideas of these thinkers.

Chapter 23 Collective Behavior and Social Movements

Multiple-Choice Questions

1. Which of the following is true about collective behavior?
   a. It usually involves a large number of people.
   b. It is often spontaneous.
   c. It is often controversial.
   d. All of the above are correct.

2. Which of the following is a good example of a collectivity?
   a. students quietly working out in the college weight room
   b. excited soccer fans throwing bottles as they leave a stadium
   c. students in line in the cafeteria waiting to be served
   d. All of the above are correct.

3. A mob differs from a riot in that the mob
   a. typically has a clear objective.
   b. is not violent.
   c. does not involve people with intense emotion.
   d. lasts a long time.

4. Which theory says that "crowds can make people go crazy"?
   a. emergent-norm theory
   b. convergence theory
   c. contagion theory
   d. subcultural theory

5. When sociologists speak of "mass behavior," they have in mind
   a. people taking part in a riot or mob.
   b. many people spread over a large area thinking or acting in a particular way.
   c. irrational behavior on the part of people in a crowd.
   d. people imitating what they see others do.

6. Which of the following is an example of a technological disaster?
   a. the collapse of the World Trade Center towers on September 11, 2001
   b. the deaths of millions of civilians during World War II
   c. Hurricane Katrina slamming into the Gulf Coast
   d. the radiation leak from the Chernobyl nuclear power plant

7. Hula hoops, streaking, and collecting Pokémon cards are all examples of
   a. style.   c. fads.
   b. fashion.   d. popular social movements.

8. Deprivation theory explains that social movements arise among people who
   a. feel adrift in society.
   b. are poor and feel they have little more to lose.
   c. believe that they lack rights, income, or something else that they think they should have.
   d. are moved to action by particular cultural symbols.

9. The claim that social movements cannot arise without factors such as effort, money, and leadership is made by which theory?
   a. resource-mobilization theory
   b. deprivation theory
   c. mass-society theory
   d. political-economy theory

ESSAY 1: Most collective behavior is transitory (although social movements can be lasting) and involves collectivities that are either local (crowds, mobs, riots, gossip, and panic) or dispersed (rumor, fashion, fads, mass hysteria). All collective behavior involves weak and unconventional norms, but the various types differ in many other respects, which makes this area of social life difficult to study and explain. See pages 600–607.

ESSAY 2: "Old social movements" focus on economic issues and have great importance in industrial societies. Typically led by labor organizations, they draw strong support from working-class people. "New social movements" focus on social and environmental issues, draw support from middle- and upper-middle-class people, and are likely to be global in scope. See page 616.

ESSAY 1: Tönnies described modernity in terms of the transition from *Gemeinschaft* to *Gesellschaft*; Durkheim, in terms of change from mechanical to organic solidarity; Weber, in terms of the rise of rationality; and Marx, in terms of the rise of capitalism. Discussion of differences and similarities is found on pages 630–35.

ESSAY 2: Claims of a mass society point to loss of local community and the rise of impersonal bureaucracy (especially the state). Mass-society theory has links to structural-functional analysis and tends to be politically conservative. Claims of a class society point to the rise of capitalism and persistent inequality. Class-society theory has links to the social-conflict approach and is politically left of center.

10. The effect of gender on the operation of social movements in the United States is demonstrated by the fact that
    a. few women are interested in most public issues.
    b. men have usually taken leadership roles.
    c. men tend to avoid participation in social movements.
    d. women typically have taken leadership roles.

ANSWERS: 1 (d); 2 (b); 3 (a); 4 (c); 5 (b); 6 (d); 7 (c); 8 (c); 9 (a); 10 (b).

Essay Questions

1. The concept of collective behavior encompasses a broad range of social patterns. List some of these patterns. What traits do they have in common? How do they differ?

2. In what respects do some recent social movements (the environment, animal rights, and gun control) differ from older crusades (the right of workers to form unions or the right of women to vote)?

Chapter 24   Social Change: Traditional, Modern, and Postmodern Societies

Multiple-Choice Questions

1. Sociologists use the term "modernity" to refer to social patterns that emerged
   a. with the first human civilizations.
   b. after the fall of Rome.
   c. after the Industrial Revolution.
   d. along with the Information Revolution.

2. Which of the following are common causes of social change?
   a. invention of new ideas and things
   b. diffusion from one cultural system to another
   c. discovery of existing things
   d. All of the above are correct.

3. Karl Marx highlighted the importance of which of the following in the process of social change?
   a. immigration and demographic factors
   b. ideas
   c. social conflict
   d. cultural diffusion

4. Max Weber's analysis of how Calvinism helped create the spirit of capitalism highlighted the importance of which of the following in the process of social change?
   a. invention
   b. ideas
   c. social conflict
   d. cultural diffusion

5. Which term was used by Ferdinand Tönnies to describe a traditional society?
   a. *Gemeinschaft*
   b. *Gesellschaft*
   c. mechanical solidarity
   d. organic solidarity

6. According to Emile Durkheim, modern societies have
   a. respect for established tradition.
   b. widespread alienation.
   c. common values and beliefs.
   d. an increasing division of labor.

7. For Max Weber, modernity meant the rise of _____; for Karl Marx, modernity meant _____.
   a. capitalism, anomie
   b. rationality, capitalism
   c. tradition, self-interest
   d. specialization, *Gesellschaft*

8. Which of the following statements about modernity as a mass society is *not* correct?
   a. There is more poverty today than in past centuries.
   b. Kinship ties have become weaker.
   c. Bureaucracy, including government, has increased in size.
   d. People experience moral uncertainty about how to live.

9. Sociologists who describe modernity in terms of class society focus on which of the following?
   a. rationality as a way of thinking about the world
   b. mutual dependency
   c. the rise of capitalism
   d. the high risk of anomie

10. David Riesman described the other-directed social character typical of modern people as
    a. rigid conformity to tradition.
    b. eagerness to follow the latest fashions and fads.
    c. strong individualism.
    d. All of the above are correct.

ANSWERS: 1 (c); 2 (d); 3 (c); 4 (b); 5 (a); 6 (d); 7 (b); 8 (a); 9 (c); 10 (b).

Essay Questions

1. Discuss how Tönnies, Durkheim, Weber, and Marx described modern society. What are the similarities and differences in their understandings of modernity?

2. What traits lead some analysts to call the United States a "mass society"? Why do other analysts describe the United States as a "class society"?

Glossary

abortion   the deliberate termination of a pregnancy

absolute poverty   a lack of resources that is life-threatening

achieved status   a social position a person assumes voluntarily that reflects personal ability and effort

activity theory   the idea that a high level of activity increases personal satisfaction in old age

Afrocentrism   emphasizing and promoting African cultural patterns

ageism   prejudice and discrimination against older people

age-sex pyramid   a graphic representation of the age and sex of a population

age stratification   the unequal distribution of wealth, power, and privilege among people at different stages of the life course

agriculture   large-scale cultivation using plows harnessed to animals or more powerful energy sources

alienation   the experience of isolation and misery resulting from powerlessness

animism   the belief that elements of the natural world are conscious life forms that affect humanity

anomie   Durkheim's term for a condition in which society provides little moral guidance to individuals

anticipatory socialization   learning that helps a person achieve a desired position

ascribed status   a social position a person receives at birth or takes on involuntarily later in life

asexuality   a lack of sexual attraction to people of either sex

assimilation   the process by which minorities gradually adopt patterns of the dominant culture

authoritarianism   a political system that denies people participation in government

authority   power that people perceive as legitimate rather than coercive

beliefs   specific thoughts or ideas that people hold to be true

bilateral descent   a system tracing kinship through both men and women

bisexuality   sexual attraction to people of both sexes

blue-collar occupations   lower-prestige jobs that involve mostly manual labor

bureaucracy   an organizational model rationally designed to perform tasks efficiently

bureaucratic authority   see *rational-legal authority*

bureaucratic inertia   the tendency of bureaucratic organizations to perpetuate themselves

bureaucratic ritualism   a focus on rules and regulations to the point of undermining an organization's goals

capitalism   an economic system in which natural resources and the means of producing goods and services are privately owned

capitalists   people who own and operate factories and other businesses in pursuit of profits

caregiving   informal and unpaid care provided to a dependent person by family members, other relatives, or friends

caste system   social stratification based on ascription, or birth

cause and effect   a relationship in which change in one variable causes change in another

charisma   extraordinary personal qualities that can infuse people with emotion and turn them into followers

charismatic authority   power legitimized through extraordinary personal abilities that inspire devotion and obedience

church   a type of religious organization that is well integrated into the larger society

civil religion   a quasi-religious loyalty binding individuals in a basically secular society

claims making   the process of trying to convince the public and public officials of the importance of joining a social movement to address a particular issue

class conflict   conflict between entire classes over the distribution of a society's wealth and power

class consciousness   Marx's term for workers' recognition of themselves as a class unified in opposition to capitalists and ultimately to capitalism itself

class society   a capitalist society with pronounced social stratification

class system   social stratification based on both birth and individual achievement

cohabitation   the sharing of a household by an unmarried couple

cohort   a category of people with something in common, usually their age

collective behavior   activity involving a large number of people that is unplanned, often controversial, and sometimes dangerous

collectivity   a large number of people whose minimal interaction occurs in the absence of well-defined and conventional norms

colonialism   the process by which some nations enrich themselves through political and economic control of other nations

communism   a hypothetical economic and political system in which all members of a society are socially equal

community-based corrections   correctional programs operating within society at large rather than behind prison walls

concept   a mental construct that represents some part of the world in a simplified form

concrete operational stage   Piaget's term for the level of human development at which individuals first see causal connections in their surroundings

conglomerate   a giant corporation composed of many smaller corporations

conjugal family   see *nuclear family*

consanguine family   see *extended family*

conspicuous consumption   buying and using products because of the "statement" they make about social position

control   holding constant all variables except one in order to see clearly the effect of that variable

corporate crime   the illegal actions of a corporation or people acting on its behalf

corporation   an organization with a legal existence, including rights and liabilities, separate from that of its members

correlation   a relationship in which two (or more) variables change together

counterculture   cultural patterns that strongly oppose those widely accepted within a society

crime   the violation of a society's formally enacted criminal law

crimes against the person   crimes that direct violence or the threat of violence against others; also known as *violent crimes*

crimes against property   crimes that involve theft of property belonging to others; also known as *property crimes*

criminal justice system   the organizations—police, courts, and prison officials—that respond to alleged violations of the law

criminal recidivism   later offenses by people previously convicted of crimes

critical sociology   the study of society that focuses on the need for social change

crowd   a temporary gathering of people who share a common focus of attention and who influence one another

crude birth rate the number of live births in a given year for every 1,000 people in a population

crude death rate the number of deaths in a given year for every 1,000 people in a population

cult a religious organization that is largely outside a society's cultural traditions

cultural integration the close relationships among various elements of a cultural system

cultural lag the fact that some cultural elements change more quickly than others, disrupting a cultural system

cultural relativism the practice of judging a culture by its own standards

cultural transmission the process by which one generation passes culture to the next

cultural universals traits that are part of every known culture

culture the ways of thinking, the ways of acting, and the material objects that together form a people's way of life

culture shock personal disorientation when experiencing an unfamiliar way of life

Davis-Moore thesis the assertion that social stratification has beneficial consequences for the operation of a society

deductive logical thought reasoning that transforms general theory into specific hypotheses suitable for testing

democracy a political system that gives power to the people as a whole

demographic transition theory a thesis that links population patterns to a society's level of technological development

demography the study of human population

denomination a church, independent of the state, that recognizes religious pluralism

dependency theory a model of economic and social development that explains global inequality in terms of the historical exploitation of poor nations by rich ones

dependent variable the variable that changes

descent the system by which members of a society trace kinship over generations

deterrence the attempt to discourage criminality through the use of punishment

deviance the recognized violation of cultural norms

direct-fee system a medical care system in which patients pay directly for the services of physicians and hospitals

disaster an event, generally unexpected, that causes extensive harm to people and damage to property

discrimination unequal treatment of various categories of people

disengagement theory the idea that society enhances its orderly operation by removing people from positions of responsibility as they reach old age

division of labor specialized economic activity

dramaturgical analysis Erving Goffman's term for the study of social interaction in terms of theatrical performance

dyad a social group with two members

eating disorder an intense form of dieting or other unhealthy method of weight control driven by the desire to be very thin

ecologically sustainable culture a way of life that meets the needs of the present generation without threatening the environmental legacy of future generations

ecology the study of the interaction of living organisms and the natural environment

economy the social institution that organizes a society's production, distribution, and consumption of goods and services

ecosystem a system composed of the interaction of all living organisms and their natural environment

education the social institution through which society provides its members with important knowledge, including basic facts, job skills, and cultural norms and values

ego Freud's term for a person's conscious efforts to balance innate pleasure-seeking drives with the demands of society

empirical evidence information we can verify with our senses

endogamy marriage between people of the same social category

environmental deficit profound long-term harm to the natural environment caused by humanity's focus on short-term material affluence

environmental racism patterns of development that expose poor people, especially minorities, to environmental hazards

ethnicity a shared cultural heritage

ethnocentrism the practice of judging another culture by the standards of one's own culture

ethnomethodology Harold Garfinkel's term for the study of the way people make sense of their everyday surroundings

Eurocentrism the dominance of European (especially English) cultural patterns

euthanasia assisting in the death of a person suffering from an incurable disease; also known as *mercy killing*

exogamy marriage between people of different social categories

experiment a research method for investigating cause and effect under highly controlled conditions

expressive leadership group leadership that focuses on the group's well-being

extended family a family consisting of parents and children as well as other kin; also known as a *consanguine family*

fad an unconventional social pattern that people embrace briefly but enthusiastically

faith belief based on conviction rather than on scientific evidence

false consciousness Marx's term for explanations of social problems as the shortcomings of individuals rather than as the flaws of society

family a social institution found in all societies that unites people in cooperative groups to care for one another, including any children

family violence emotional, physical, or sexual abuse of one family member by another

fashion a social pattern favored by a large number of people

feminism support of social equality for women and men, in opposition to patriarchy and sexism

feminization of poverty the trend of women making up an increasing proportion of the poor

fertility the incidence of childbearing in a country's population

folkways norms for routine or casual interaction

formal operational stage Piaget's term for the level of human development at which individuals think abstractly and critically

formal organization a large secondary group organized to achieve its goals efficiently

functional illiteracy a lack of the reading and writing skills needed for everyday living

fundamentalism a conservative religious doctrine that opposes intellectualism and worldly accommodation in favor of restoring traditional, otherworldly religion

Gemeinschaft a type of social organization in which people are closely tied by kinship and tradition

gender the personal traits and social positions that members of a society attach to being female or male

gender-conflict approach a point of view that focuses on inequality and conflict between women and men

gender roles (sex roles) attitudes and activities that a society links to each sex

gender stratification the unequal distribution of wealth, power, and privilege between men and women

generalized other George Herbert Mead's term for widespread cultural norms and values we use as a reference in evaluating ourselves

genocide the systematic killing of one category of people by another

gerontocracy a form of social organization in which the elderly have the most wealth, power, and prestige

gerontology the study of aging and the elderly

Gesellschaft a type of social organization in which people come together only on the basis of individual self-interest

global economy economic activity that crosses national borders

global perspective the study of the larger world and our society's place in it

global stratification patterns of social inequality in the world as a whole

global warming a rise in Earth's average temperature due to an increasing concentration of carbon dioxide in the atmosphere

gossip rumor about people's personal affairs

government a formal organization that directs the political life of a society

groupthink the tendency of group members to conform, resulting in a narrow view of some issue

hate crime a criminal act against a person or a person's property by an offender motivated by racial or other bias

Hawthorne effect a change in a subject's behavior caused simply by the awareness of being studied

health a state of complete physical, mental, and social well-being

health maintenance organization (HMO) an organization that provides comprehensive medical care to subscribers for a fixed fee

heterosexism a view that labels anyone who is not heterosexual as "queer"

heterosexuality sexual attraction to someone of the other sex

high culture cultural patterns that distinguish a society's elite

high-income countries nations with the highest overall standards of living

holistic medicine an approach to health care that emphasizes the prevention of illness and takes into account a person's entire physical and social environment

homogamy marriage between people with the same social characteristics

homophobia discomfort over close personal interaction with people thought to be gay, lesbian, or bisexual

homosexuality sexual attraction to someone of the same sex

horticulture the use of hand tools to raise crops

hunting and gathering making use of simple tools to hunt animals and gather vegetation for food

hypothesis a statement of a possible relationship between two (or more) variables

id Freud's term for the human being's basic drives

ideal type an abstract statement of the essential characteristics of any social phenomenon

ideology cultural beliefs that justify particular social arrangements, including patterns of inequality

incest taboo a norm forbidding sexual relations or marriage between certain relatives

income earnings from work or investments

independent variable the variable that causes the change

inductive logical thought reasoning that transforms specific observations into general theory

industrialism the production of goods using advanced sources of energy to drive large machinery

infant mortality rate the number of deaths among infants under one year of age for each 1,000 live births in a given year

infidelity sexual activity outside one's marriage

in-group a social group toward which a member feels respect and loyalty

institutional prejudice and discrimination bias built into the operation of society's institutions

instrumental leadership group leadership that focuses on the completion of tasks

intergenerational social mobility upward or downward social mobility of children in relation to their parents

interpretive sociology the study of society that focuses on the meanings people attach to their social world

intersection theory analysis of the interplay of race, class, and gender, often resulting in multiple dimensions of disadvantage

intersexual people people whose bodies (including genitals) have both female and male characteristics

interview a series of questions a researcher asks respondents in person

intragenerational social mobility a change in social position occurring during a person's lifetime

kinship a social bond based on common ancestry, marriage, or adoption

labeling theory the idea that deviance and conformity result not so much from what people do as from how others respond to those actions

labor unions organizations of workers that seek to improve wages and working conditions through various strategies, including negotiations and strikes

language a system of symbols that allows people to communicate with one another

latent functions the unrecognized and unintended consequences of any social pattern

liberation theology the combining of Christian principles with political activism, often Marxist in character

life expectancy the average life span of a country's population

looking-glass self Cooley's term for a self-image based on how we think others see us

low-income countries nations with a low standard of living in which most people are poor

macro-level orientation a broad focus on social structures that shape society as a whole

mainstreaming integrating students with disabilities or special needs into the overall educational program

manifest functions the recognized and intended consequences of any social pattern

marriage a legal relationship, usually involving economic cooperation, sexual activity, and childbearing

Marxist political-economy model an analysis that explains politics in terms of the operation of a society's economic system

mass behavior collective behavior among people spread over a wide geographic area

mass hysteria (moral panic) a form of dispersed collective behavior in which people react to a real or imagined event with irrational and even frantic fear

mass media the means for delivering impersonal communications to a vast audience

mass society a society in which prosperity and bureaucracy have weakened traditional social ties

master status a status that has special importance for social identity, often shaping a person's entire life

material culture the physical things created by members of a society

matriarchy a form of social organization in which females dominate males

matrilineal descent a system tracing kinship through women

matrilocality a residential pattern in which a married couple lives with or near the wife's family

measurement a procedure for determining the value of a variable in a specific case

mechanical solidarity Durkheim's term for social bonds, based on common sentiments and shared moral values, that are strong among members of preindustrial societies

medicalization of deviance the transformation of moral and legal deviance into a medical condition

medicine the social institution that focuses on fighting disease and improving health

megalopolis a vast urban region containing a number of cities and their surrounding suburbs

mercy killing see *euthanasia*

meritocracy social stratification based on personal merit

metropolis a large city that socially and economically dominates an urban area

micro-level orientation a close-up focus on social interaction in specific situations

middle-income countries nations with a standard of living about average for the world as a whole

migration the movement of people into and out of a specified territory

military-industrial complex the close association of the federal government, the military, and defense industries

minority any category of people distinguished by physical or cultural difference that a society sets apart and subordinates

miscegenation biological reproduction by partners of different racial categories

mob a highly emotional crowd that pursues a violent or destructive goal

modernity social patterns resulting from industrialization

modernization the process of social change begun by industrialization

modernization theory a model of economic and social development that explains global inequality in terms of technological and cultural differences between nations

monarchy a political system in which a single family rules from generation to generation

monogamy marriage that unites two partners

monopoly the domination of a market by a single producer

monotheism belief in a single divine power

moral panic see *mass hysteria*

mores norms that are widely observed and have great moral significance

mortality the incidence of death in a country's population

multiculturalism a perspective recognizing the cultural diversity of the United States and promoting equal standing for all cultural traditions

multinational corporation a large business that operates in many countries

natural environment Earth's surface and atmosphere, including living organisms, air, water, soil, and other resources necessary to sustain life

neocolonialism a new form of global power relationships that involves no direct political control but economic exploitation by multinational corporations

neolocality a residential pattern in which a married couple lives apart from both sets of parents

network a web of weak social ties

nonmaterial culture the ideas created by members of a society

nonverbal communication communication using body movements, gestures, and facial expressions rather than speech

norms rules and expectations by which a society guides the behavior of its members

nuclear family a family composed of one or two parents and their children; also known as a *conjugal family*

nuclear proliferation the acquisition of nuclear weapons technology by more and more nations

objectivity personal neutrality in conducting research

oligarchy the rule of the many by the few

oligopoly the domination of a market by a few producers

operationalize a variable specifying exactly what is to be measured before assigning a value to a variable

organic solidarity Durkheim's term for social bonds, based on specialization and interdependence, that are strong among members of industrial societies

organizational environment factors outside an organization that affect its operation

organized crime a business supplying illegal goods or services

other-directedness openness to the latest trends and fashions, often expressed by imitating others

out-group a social group toward which a person feels a sense of competition or opposition

panic a form of collective behavior in which people in one place react to a threat or other stimulus with irrational, frantic, and often self-destructive behavior

participant observation a research method in which investigators systematically observe people while joining them in their routine activities

pastoralism the domestication of animals

patriarchy a form of social organization in which males dominate females

patrilineal descent a system tracing kinship through men

patrilocality a residential pattern in which a married couple lives with or near the husband's family

peer group a social group whose members have interests, social position, and age in common

personality a person's fairly consistent patterns of acting, thinking, and feeling

personal space the surrounding area over which a person makes some claim to privacy

plea bargaining a legal negotiation in which a prosecutor reduces a charge in exchange for a defendant's guilty plea

pluralism a state in which people of all races and ethnicities are distinct but have equal social standing

pluralist model an analysis of politics that sees power as spread among many competing interest groups

political action committee (PAC) an organization formed by a special-interest group, independent of political parties, to raise and spend money in support of political goals

political revolution the overthrow of one political system in order to establish another

politics the social institution that distributes power, sets a society's goals, and makes decisions

polyandry marriage that unites one woman and two or more men

polygamy marriage that unites a person with two or more spouses

polygyny marriage that unites one man and two or more women

polytheism belief in many gods

popular culture cultural patterns that are widespread among a society's population

population the people who are the focus of research

pornography sexually explicit material intended to cause sexual arousal

positivism a way of understanding based on science

positivist sociology the study of society based on systematic observation of social behavior

postindustrial economy a productive system based on service work and high technology

postindustrialism the production of information using computer technology

postmodernity social patterns characteristic of postindustrial societies

power the ability to achieve desired ends despite resistance from others

power-elite model an analysis of politics that sees power as concentrated among the rich

prejudice a rigid and unfair generalization about an entire category of people

preoperational stage Piaget's term for the level of human development at which individuals first use language and other symbols

presentation of self Erving Goffman's term for a person's efforts to create specific impressions in the minds of others

primary group a small social group whose members share personal and lasting relationships

primary labor market jobs that provide extensive benefits to workers

primary sector the part of the economy that draws raw materials from the natural environment

primary sex characteristics the genitals, organs used for reproduction

profane included as an ordinary element of everyday life

profession a prestigious white-collar occupation that requires extensive formal education

proletarians people who sell their labor for wages

propaganda information presented with the intention of shaping public opinion

property crimes see *crimes against property*

prostitution the selling of sexual services

public opinion widespread attitudes about controversial issues

queer theory a body of research findings that challenges the heterosexual bias in U.S. society

questionnaire a series of written questions a researcher presents to subjects

race a socially constructed category of people who share biologically transmitted traits that members of a society consider important

race-conflict approach a point of view that focuses on inequality and conflict between people of different racial and ethnic categories

racism the belief that one racial category is innately superior or inferior to another

rain forests regions of dense forestation, most of which circle the globe close to the equator

rationality a way of thinking that emphasizes deliberate, matter-of-fact calculation of the most efficient way to accomplish a particular task

rationalization of society Weber's term for the historical change from tradition to rationality as the main type of human thought

rational-legal authority power legitimized by legally enacted rules and regulations; also known as *bureaucratic authority*

reference group a social group that serves as a point of reference in making evaluations and decisions

rehabilitation a program for reforming the offender to prevent later offenses

relative deprivation a perceived disadvantage arising from some specific comparison

relative poverty the lack of resources of some people in relation to those who have more

reliability consistency in measurement

religion a social institution involving beliefs and practices based on recognizing the sacred

religiosity the importance of religion in a person's life

replication repetition of research by other investigators

research method a systematic plan for doing research

resocialization radically changing an inmate's personality by carefully controlling the environment

retribution an act of moral vengeance by which society makes the offender suffer as much as the suffering caused by the crime

riot a social eruption that is highly emotional, violent, and undirected

ritual formal, ceremonial behavior

role behavior expected of someone who holds a particular status

role conflict conflict among the roles connected to two or more statuses

role set a number of roles attached to a single status

role strain tension among the roles connected to a single status

routinization of charisma the transformation of charismatic authority into some combination of traditional and bureaucratic authority

rumor unconfirmed information that people spread informally, often by word of mouth

sacred set apart as extraordinary, inspiring awe and reverence

sample a part of a population that represents the whole

Sapir-Whorf thesis the idea that people see and understand the world through the cultural lens of language

scapegoat a person or category of people, typically with little power, whom people unfairly blame for their own troubles

schooling formal instruction under the direction of specially trained teachers

science a logical system that bases knowledge on direct, systematic observation

scientific management Frederick Taylor's term for the application of scientific principles to the operation of a business or other large organization

secondary group a large and impersonal social group whose members pursue a specific goal or activity

secondary labor market jobs that provide minimal benefits to workers

secondary sector the part of the economy that transforms raw materials into manufactured goods

secondary sex characteristics bodily development, apart from the genitals, that distinguishes biologically mature females and males

sect a type of religious organization that stands apart from the larger society

secularization the historical decline in the importance of the supernatural and the sacred

segregation the physical and social separation of categories of people

self George Herbert Mead's term for the part of an individual's personality composed of self-awareness and self-image

sensorimotor stage Piaget's term for the level of human development at which individuals experience the world only through their senses

sex the biological distinction between females and males

sexism the belief that one sex is innately superior to the other

sex ratio the number of males for every 100 females in a nation's population

sex roles see *gender roles*

sexual harassment comments, gestures, or physical contacts of a sexual nature that are deliberate, repeated, and unwelcome

sexual orientation a person's romantic and emotional attraction to another person

sick role patterns of behavior defined as appropriate for people who are ill

significant others people, such as parents, who have special importance for socialization

social change the transformation of culture and social institutions over time

social character personality patterns common to members of a particular society

social conflict the struggle between segments of society over valued resources

social-conflict approach a framework for building theory that sees society as an arena of inequality that generates conflict and change

social construction of reality the process by which people creatively shape reality through social interaction

social control attempts by society to regulate people's thoughts and behavior

social dysfunction any social pattern that may disrupt the operation of society

social epidemiology the study of how health and disease are distributed throughout a society's population

social functions the consequences of any social pattern for the operation of society as a whole

social group two or more people who identify with and interact with one another

social institutions the major spheres of social life, or societal subsystems, organized to meet human needs

social interaction the process by which people act and react in relation to others

socialism an economic system in which natural resources and the means of producing goods and services are collectively owned

socialization the lifelong social experience by which people develop their human potential and learn culture

socialized medicine a medical care system in which the government owns and operates most medical facilities and employs most physicians

social mobility a change in position within the social hierarchy

social movement an organized activity that encourages or discourages social change

social stratification a system by which a society ranks categories of people in a hierarchy

social structure any relatively stable pattern of social behavior

societal protection rendering an offender incapable of further offenses temporarily through imprisonment or permanently by execution

society people who interact in a defined territory and share a culture

sociobiology a theoretical approach that explores ways in which human biology affects how we create culture

sociocultural evolution Lenski's term for the changes that occur as a society gains new technology

socioeconomic status (SES) a composite ranking based on various dimensions of social inequality

sociological perspective the special point of view of sociology that sees general patterns of society in the lives of particular people

sociology the systematic study of human society

special-interest group people organized to address some economic or social issue

spurious correlation an apparent but false relationship between two (or more) variables that is caused by some other variable

state capitalism an economic and political system in which companies are privately owned but cooperate closely with the government

state church a church formally allied with the state

status a social position that a person holds

status consistency the degree of uniformity in a person's social standing across various dimensions of social inequality

status set all the statuses a person holds at a given time

stereotype a simplified description applied to every person in some category

stigma a powerfully negative label that greatly changes a person's self-concept and social identity

structural-functional approach a framework for building theory that sees society as a complex system whose parts work together to promote solidarity and stability

structural social mobility a shift in the social position of large numbers of people due more to changes in society itself than to individual efforts

subculture cultural patterns that set apart some segment of a society's population

suburbs urban areas beyond the political boundaries of a city

superego Freud's term for the cultural values and norms internalized by an individual

survey a research method in which subjects respond to a series of statements or questions on a questionnaire or in an interview

symbol anything that carries a particular meaning recognized by people who share a culture

symbolic-interaction approach a framework for building theory that sees society as the product of the everyday interactions of individuals

technology knowledge that people use to make a way of life in their surroundings

terrorism acts of violence or the threat of violence used as a political strategy by an individual or a group

tertiary sector the part of the economy that involves services rather than goods

theoretical approach a basic image of society that guides thinking and research

theory a statement of how and why specific facts are related

Thomas theorem W. I. Thomas's observation that situations that are defined as real are real in their consequences

total institution a setting in which people are isolated from the rest of society and manipulated by an administrative staff

totalitarianism a highly centralized political system that extensively regulates people's lives

totem an object in the natural world collectively defined as sacred

tracking assigning students to different types of educational programs

tradition values and beliefs passed from generation to generation

traditional authority power legitimized by respect for long-established cultural patterns

tradition-directedness rigid conformity to time-honored ways of living

transsexuals people who feel they are one sex even though biologically they are the other

triad a social group with three members

underground economy economic activity involving income not reported to the government as required by law

urban ecology the study of the link between the physical and social dimensions of cities

urbanization the concentration of population into cities

validity actually measuring exactly what you intend to measure

values culturally defined standards that people use to decide what is desirable, good, and beautiful and that serve as broad guidelines for social living

variable a concept whose value changes from case to case

victimless crimes violations of law in which there are no obvious victims

violent crimes see *crimes against the person*

war organized, armed conflict among the people of two or more nations, directed by their governments

wealth the total value of money and other assets, minus outstanding debts

welfare capitalism an economic and political system that combines a mostly market-based economy with extensive social welfare programs

welfare state a system of government agencies and programs that provides benefits to the population

white-collar crime crime committed by people of high social position in the course of their occupations

white-collar occupations higher-prestige jobs that involve mostly mental activity

zero population growth the rate of reproduction that maintains population at a steady level

References

*Blue type denotes reference citations new to this thirteenth edition.

AARP FOUNDATION. "GrandFacts." October 2007. [Online] Available July 3, 2008, at http://www.grandfactsheets.org/doc/National%20Resources%20Fact%20Sheet.pdf

ABERLE, DAVID F. *The Peyote Religion among the Navaho.* Chicago: Aldine, 1966.

"Abramoff Effect: Leaping out of Bed with the Lobbyists." *New York Times* (January 16, 2006). [Online] Available May 2, 2009, at http://query.nytimes.com/gst/fullpage.html?res=9D04EEDC143FF935A25752C0A9609C8B63&sec=&spon=

ADAM, DAVID. "World CO₂ Levels at Record High, Scientists Warn." *Guardian* (May 12, 2008). [Online] Available July 16, 2008, at http://www.guardian.co.uk/environment/2008/may/12/climatechange.carbonemissions

ADAMS, PATRICIA F., PATRICIA M. BARNES, and JACKLINE L. VICKERIE. *Summary Health Statistics for the U.S. Population: National Health Survey, 2007.* Vital and Health Statistics. Series 10, No. 238. (November 2008). [Online] Available February 3, 2009, at http://www.cdc.gov/nchs/data/series/sr_10/sr10_238.pdf

ADAMS, PATRICIA F., JACQUELINE WILSON LUCAS, and PATRICIA M. BARNES. *Summary Health Statistics for the U.S. Population: National Health Interview Survey, 2006.* Vital and Health Statistics. Series 10, No. 236. (January 2008). [Online] Available November 22, 2008, at http://www.cdc.gov/nchs/data/series/sr_10/sr10_236.pdf

ADLER, JERRY. "When Harry Called Sally . . ." *Newsweek* (October 1, 1990):74.

ADORNO, THEODORE W., ELSE FRENKEL-BRUNSWIK, DANIEL J. LEVINSON, and R. NEVITT SANFORD. *The Authoritarian Personality.* New York: Harper & Brothers, 1950.

AGUIRRE, BENIGNO E., and E. L. QUARANTELLI. "Methodological, Ideological, and Conceptual-Theoretical Criticisms of Collective Behavior: A Critical Evaluation and Implications for Future Study." *Sociological Focus.* Vol. 16, No. 3 (August 1983):195–216.

AGUIRRE, BENIGNO E., E. L. QUARANTELLI, and JORGE L. MENDOZA. "The Collective Behavior of Fads: Characteristics, Effects, and Career of Streaking." *American Sociological Review.* Vol. 53, No. 4 (August 1988):569–84.

AKERS, RONALD L., MARVIN D. KROHN, LONN LANZA-KADUCE, and MARCIA RADOSEVICH. "Social Learning and Deviant Behavior." *American Sociological Review.* Vol. 44, No. 4 (August 1979):636–55.

ALAN GUTTMACHER INSTITUTE. "Teen Pregnancy: Trends and Lessons Learned." *Issues in Brief.* 2002 Series, No. 1. 2002. [Online] Available May 30, 2005, at http://www.agi-usa.org/pubs/ib_1-02.pdf

———. "U.S. Teenage Pregnancy Statistics: National and State Trends and Trends by Race and Ethnicity." Rev. September 2006. [Online] Available May 8, 2007, at http://www.guttmacher.org/pubs/2006/09/12/USTPstats.pdf

ALBON, JOAN. "Retention of Cultural Values and Differential Urban Adaptation: Samoans and American Indians in a West Coast City." *Social Forces.* Vol. 49, No. 3 (March 1971):385–93.

ALI, LORRAINE, and VANESSA JUAREZ. "We Love This Country." *Newsweek.* April 7, 2003.

ALI, LORRAINE, TAMARA LIPPER, and MOHAMMED MACK. "Voters: A Demographic Shift." *Newsweek.* October 25, 2004.

ALLAN, EMILIE ANDERSEN, and DARRELL J. STEFFENSMEIER. "Youth, Underemployment, and Property Crime: Differential Effects of Job Availability and Job Quality on Juvenile and Young Adult Arrest Rates." *American Sociological Review.* Vol. 54, No. 1 (February 1989):107–23.

ALLEN, MIKE. "Card Check Battle Starts Tomorrow." *Politico* (March 9, 2009). [Online] Available May 8, 2009, at http://www.politico.com/news/stories/0309/19786.html

ALLEN, THOMAS B., and CHARLES O. HYMAN. *We Americans: Celebrating a Nation, Its People, and Its Past.* Washington, D.C.: National Geographic Society, 1999.

ALLEN, WALTER R. "African American Family Life in Social Context: Crisis and Hope." *Sociological Forum.* Vol. 10, No. 4 (December 1995):569–92.

ALTONJI, JOSEPH G., ULRICH DORASZELSKI, and LEWIS SEGAL. "Black/White Differences in Wealth." *Economic Perspectives.* Vol. 24, No. 1 (2000):38–50.

AMATO, PAUL R. "What Children Learn from Divorce." *Population Today.* Vol. 29, No. 1 (January 2001):1, 4.

AMATO, PAUL R., and JULIANA M. SOBOLEWSKI. "The Effects of Divorce and Marital Discord on Adult Children's Psychological Well-Being." *American Sociological Review.* Vol. 66, No. 6 (December 2001):900–21.

AMERICAN ASSOCIATION OF COLLEGES OF NURSING. "Fact Sheet: Nursing Shortage." September 2008. [Online] Available February 6, 2009, at http://www.aacn.nche.edu/Media/FactSheets/NursingShortage.htm

AMERICAN BAR ASSOCIATION. "First-Year and Total J.D. Enrollment by Gender, 1947–2007." 2008. [Online] Available May 12, 2008, at http://www.abanet.org/legaled/statistics/charts/stats%20-%206.pdf

AMERICAN GAMING ASSOCIATION. "2008 State of the States: AGA Survey of Casino Entertainment." [Online] Available November 12, 2008, at http://www.americangaming.org/assets/files/aga_2008_sos.pdf

AMERICAN PSYCHOLOGICAL ASSOCIATION. *Violence and Youth: Psychology's Response.* Washington, D.C.: American Psychological Association, 1993.

AMERICAN SOCIOLOGICAL ASSOCIATION. "Code of Ethics." Washington, D.C.: American Sociological Association, 1997.

———. *Careers in Sociology.* 6th ed. Washington, D.C.: American Sociological Association, 2002.

———. *The Importance of Collecting Data and Doing Social Scientific Research on Race.* Washington, D.C.: American Sociological Association, 2003.

AMIN, AASHA MEHREEN, and ELITA KARIM. "Nailing the 'If' Factor." *Daily Star* (April 4, 2008). [Online] Available December 3, 2008, at http://www.thedailystar.net/magazine/2008/04/01/index.htm

AMNESTY INTERNATIONAL. "Secrecy Surrounds Death Penalty." 2008. [Online] Available April 16, 2008, at http://www.amnesty.org/en/news-and-updates/report/secrecy-surrounds-death-penalty-20080415

———. "Abolitionist and Retentionist Countries." 2009. [Online] Available June 21, 2009, at http://www.amnesty.org/en/death-penalty/abolitionist-and-retentionist-countries

ANDERSON, ELIJAH. "The Code of the Streets." *Atlantic Monthly* (May 1994):81–94.

———. "The Ideologically Driven Critique." *American Journal of Sociology.* Vol. 197, No. 6 (May 2002):1533–50.

ANDERSON, JOHN WARD. "Early to Wed: The Child Brides of India." *Washington Post* (May 24, 1995):A27, A30.

ANDREWS, MICHELLE. "In God They Trust." *U.S. News & World Report* (July 7, 2008):58–59.

ANTI-DEFAMATION LEAGUE. "State Hate Crime Statutory Provisions, 2008." 2008. [Online] at http://www.adl.org/99hatecrime/state_hate_crime_laws.pdf

ANTI-SLAVERY INTERNATIONAL. "Slavery Remains Despite Year of Successes." December 2, 2008. [Online] Available November 12, 2008, at http://www.antislavery.org/archive/press/latestpressrelease.htm

ANTLFINGER, CARRIE. "Homicides Down in Some Large U.S. Cities." *Yahoo News.* January 3, 2009. [Online] Available January 3, 2009, at http://news.yahoo.com/s/ap/20090103/ap_on_re_us/urban_homicides

APPLEBOME, PETER. "70 Years after Scopes Trial, Creation Debate Lives." *New York Times* (March 10, 1996):1, 10.

APRILL, ELLEN P. "Churches, Politics, and the Charitable Contribution Deduction." *Boston College Law Review.* Vol. 42, No. 4 (2004):843–874. [Online] Available April 19, 2009, at http://www.bc.edu/bc_org/avp/law/lwsch/journals/bclawr/42_4/04_FMS.htm

APUZZO, ALAN. "R.I. Official: Club Owners Not Helpful." [Online] Available February 24, 2003, at http://news.yahoo.com

ARENDT, HANNAH. *Between Past and Future: Six Exercises in Political Thought.* Cleveland, Ohio: Meridian Books, 1963.

ARIAS, ELIZABETH. "United States Life Tables, 2004." *National Vital Statistics Reports.* Vol. 56, No. 9 (December 28, 2007). [Online] Available May 2, 2009, at http://www.cdc.gov/nchs/data/nvsr/nvsr56/nvsr56_09.pdf

ARIÈS, PHILIPPE. *Centuries of Childhood: A Social History of Family Life.* New York: Vintage Books, 1965.

———. *Western Attitudes toward Death: From the Middle Ages to the Present.* Baltimore: Johns Hopkins University Press, 1974.

ARMSTRONG, ELISABETH. *The Retreat from Organization: U.S. Feminism Reconceptualized.* Albany: State University of New York Press, 2002.

"Army Apologizes over Salutation." *USA Today* (January 8, 2009):6A.

ARROW, KENNETH, SAMUEL BOWLES, and STEVEN DURLAUF. *Meritocracy and Economic Inequality.* Princeton, N.J.: Princeton University Press, 2000.

ASANTE, MOLEFI KETE. *Afrocentricity.* Trenton, N.J.: Africa World Press, 1988.

ASCH, SOLOMON. *Social Psychology.* Englewood Cliffs, N.J.: Prentice Hall, 1952.

ASHFORD, LORI S. "New Perspectives on Population: Lessons from Cairo." *Population Bulletin.* Vol. 50, No. 1 (March 1995).

———. "Young Women in Sub-Saharan Africa Face a High Risk of HIV Infection." *Population Today.* Vol. 30, No. 2 (February/March 2002):3, 6.

ASSOCIATED PRESS. "Man, 73, Scores Two Points in College Hoops Game." November 4, 2008. [Online] Available April 19, 2009, at http://www.breitbart.com/article.php?id=D948A1MO0&show_article=1&catnum=9

ASSOCIATION OF THEOLOGICAL SEMINARIES. "Annual Data Tables/Factbooks." 2009. [Online] Available February 23, 2009, at http://www.ats.edu/Resources/Documents/AnnualDataTables/2007-08AnnualDataTables.pdf

ASTIN, ALEXANDER W., LETICIA OSEGUERA, LINDA J. SAX, and WILLIAM S. KORN. *The American Freshman: Thirty-Five Year Trends.* Los Angeles: UCLA Higher Education Research Institute, 2002.

ATCHLEY, ROBERT C. *Aging: Continuity and Change.* Belmont, Calif.: Wadsworth, 1983.

ATLAS, TERRY. "The Human Cost of China's Boom Times." *U.S. News & World Report* (March 12, 2007):21.

AUSTER, CAROL J., and MINDY MACRONE. "The Classroom as a Negotiated Social Setting: An Empirical Study of the Effects of Faculty Members' Behavior on Students' Participation." *Teaching Sociology.* Vol. 22, No. 4 (October 1994):289–300.

AXINN, WILLIAM G., and JENNIFER S. BARBER. "Mass Education and Fertility Transition." *American Sociological Review.* Vol. 66, No. 4 (August 2001):481–505.

BAINBRIDGE, JAY, MARCIA K. MEYERS, and JANE WALDFOGEL. "Childcare Reform and the Employment of Single Mothers." *Social Science Quarterly.* Vol. 84, No. 4 (December 2003):771–91.

BAKALAR, NICHOLAS. "Reactions: Go On, Laugh Your Heart Out." *New York Times* (March 8, 2005). [Online] Available March 11, 2005, at http://www.nytimes.com/2005/03/08/health/08reac.html

BAKER, PATRICIA S., WILLIAM C. YOELS, JEFFREY M. CLAIR, and RICHARD M. ALLMAN. "Laughter in the Triadic Geriatric Encounters: A Transcript-Based Analysis." In REBECCA J. ERIKSON and BEVERLY CUTHBERTSON-JOHNSON, eds., *Social Perspectives on Emotion.* Vol. 4. Greenwich, Conn.: JAI Press, 1997:179–207.

BALTES, PAUL B., and K. WARNER SCHAIE. "The Myth of the Twilight Years." *Psychology Today.* Vol. 7, No. 10 (March 1974):35–39.

BALTZELL, E. DIGBY. *The Protestant Establishment: Aristocracy and Caste in America.* New York: Vintage Books, 1964.

———. "Introduction to the 1967 Edition." In W. E. B. DU BOIS, *The Philadelphia Negro: A Social Study.* New York: Schocken Books, 1967; orig. 1899.

———. *Puritan Boston and Quaker Philadelphia.* New York: Free Press, 1979.

———. *Sporting Gentlemen: From the Age of Honor to the Cult of the Superstar.* New York: Free Press, 1995.

BAOCHANG, GU, WANG FENG, GUO ZHIGANG, and ERLI ZHANG. "China's Local and National Fertility Policies at the End of the Twentieth Century." *Population and Development Review.* Vol. 33, No. 1 (2007):129–48.

BARASH, DAVID P. *The Whisperings Within.* New York: Penguin Books, 1981.

BARBASSA, JULIANA. "Asian-American Political Profile Rising in U.S." *Yahoo News* (January 18, 2009). [Online] Available January 18, 2009, at http://news.yahoo.com/s/ap/20090118/ap_on_re_us/asian_american_politics

BARNES, JULIAN E. "Wanted: Readers." *U.S. News & World Report* (September 9, 2002a):44–45.

———. "War Profiteering." *U.S. News & World Report* (May 13, 2002b):20–24.

———. "Unequal Education." *U.S. News & World Report* (March 22, 2004):66–75.

BARON, JAMES N., MICHAEL T. HANNAN, and M. DIANE BURTON. "Building the Iron Cage: Determinants of Managerial Intensity in the Early Years of Organizations." *American Sociological Review.* Vol. 64, No. 4 (August 1999):527–47.

BARONE, MICHAEL. "Cultures Aren't Equal." *U.S. News & World Report.* Vol. 139, No. 6 (August 22, 2005):26.

BAROVICK, HARRIET. "Tongues That Go Out of Style." *Time* (June 10, 2002):22.

BARR, BOB. "Euthanasia . . . or a 'Dutch Treat'?" *Washington Times* (December 26, 2004). [Online] Available July 29, 2007, at http://www.bobbarr.org/default.asp?pt=newsdescr&RI=585

BARSTOW, DAVID, and C. J. CHIVERS. "A Volatile Mixture Exploded into Rampage in Central Park." *New York Times* (June 17, 2000):A1, B7.

BARTLETT, DONALD L., and JAMES B. STEELE. "Corporate Welfare." *Time* (November 9, 1998):36–54.

———. "How the Little Guy Gets Crunched." *Time* (February 7, 2000):38–41.

———. "Wheel of Misfortune." *Time* (December 16, 2002):44–58.

BARTON, BERNADETTE. *Stripped: Inside the Lives of Exotic Dancers.* New York: New York University Press, 2006.

BAUER, P. T. *Equality, the Third World, and Economic Delusion.* Cambridge, Mass.: Harvard University Press, 1981.

BAUMGARTNER, M. P. "Introduction: The Moral Voice of the Community." *Sociological Focus.* Vol. 31, No. 2 (May 1998):105–17.

BAYDAR, NAZLI, and JEANNE BROOKS-GUNN. "Effect of Maternal Employment and Child-Care Arrangements on Preschoolers' Cognitive and Behavioral Outcomes: Evidence from Children from the National Longitudinal Survey of Youth." *Developmental Psychology.* Vol. 27, No. 6 (November 1991):932–35.

BEARAK, BARRY. "Lives Held Cheap in Bangladesh Sweatshops." *New York Times* (April 15, 2001):A1, A12.

BEARMAN, PETER S., JAMES MOODY, and KATHERINE STOVEL. "Chains of Affection." *American Journal of Sociology.* Vol. 110, No. 1 (July 2004):44–91.

BECK, RACHEL, and ELLEN SIMON. "CEOs Who Got Out before Crisis Left with Millions." *Yahoo News* (September 25, 2008). [Online] Available September 25, 2008, at http://news.yahoo.com/s/ap/20080925/ap_on_bi_ge/bailout_ceo_pay&printer=1;_ylt=Ak3oDhhSUwYZqhuaJh10BZ9v24cA

BECKER, ANNE E. "The Association of Television Exposure with Disordered Eating Among Ethnic Fijian Adolescent Girls." Paper presented at the annual meeting of the American Psychiatric Association, Washington, D.C., May 19, 1999.

———. "New Global Perspectives on Eating Disorders." *Culture, Medicine, and Psychiatry.* Vol. 28, No. 4 (December 2004):434–37.

BECKER, HOWARD S. *Outside: Studies in the Sociology of Deviance.* New York: Free Press, 1966.

BEDARD, PAUL. "Washington Whispers." *U.S. News & World Report* (March 25, 2002):2.

BEEGHLEY, LEONARD. *The Structure of Social Stratification in the United States.* Needham Heights, Mass.: Allyn & Bacon, 1989.

BEGLEY, SHARON. "Gray Matters." *Newsweek* (March 7, 1995):48–54.

Bell, Daniel (1973). *The Coming of Postindustrial Society: A Venture in Social Forecasting.* New York: Basic Books, 1973.

BELLANDI, DEANNA. "Study Finds Meal Portion Sizes Growing." [Online] Available January 3, 2003, at http://www.yahoo.com

BELLER, EMILY, and MICHAEL HOUT. "Intergenerational Social Mobility: The United States in Comparative Perspective." *The Future of Children.* Vol. 16, No. 2 (Fall 2006). [Online] Available April 30, 2008, at http://www.futureofchildren.org/information2826/information_show.htm?doc_id=389282

BEM, SANDRA LIPSITZ. *The Lenses of Gender: Transforming the Debate on Sexual Inequality.* New Haven, Conn.: Yale University Press, 1993.

BENEDICT, RUTH. "Continuities and Discontinuities in Cultural Conditioning." *Psychiatry.* Vol. 1, No. 2 (May 1938):161–67.

BENJAMIN, LOIS. *The Black Elite: Facing the Color Line in the Twilight of the Twentieth Century.* Chicago: Nelson-Hall, 1991.

BENNETT, JESSICA. "No More Junk." *Newsweek* (April 18, 2006). [Online] Available April 25, 2007, at http://www.msnbc.msn.com/id/12359367/site/newsweek

BENOKRAITIS, NIJOLE, and JOE R. FEAGIN. *Modern Sexism: Blatant, Subtle, and Overt Discrimination.* 2nd ed. Englewood Cliffs, N.J.: Prentice Hall, 1995.

BERGAMO, MONICA, and GERSON CAMAROTTI. "Brazil's Landless Millions." *World Press Review.* Vol. 43, No. 7 (July 1996):46–47.

BERGEN, RAQUEL KENNEDY. "Interviewing Survivors of Marital Rape: Doing Feminist Research on Sensitive Topics." In CLAIRE M. RENZETTI and RAYMOND M. LEE, eds., *Researching Sensitive Topics.* Thousand Oaks, Calif.: Sage, 1993.

BERGER, PETER L. *Invitation to Sociology.* New York: Anchor Books, 1963.

———. *The Sacred Canopy: Elements of a Sociological Theory of Religion.* Garden City, N.Y.: Doubleday, 1967.

———. *Facing Up to Modernity: Excursions in Society, Politics, and Religion.* New York: Basic Books, 1977.

———. *The Capitalist Revolution: Fifty Propositions about Prosperity, Equality, and Liberty.* New York: Basic Books, 1986.

BERGER, PETER L., BRIGITTE BERGER, and HANSFRIED KELLNER. *The Homeless Mind: Modernization and Consciousness.* New York: Vintage Books, 1974.

BERGESEN, ALBERT, ed. *Crises in the World-System.* Beverly Hills, Calif.: Sage, 1983.

BERNARD, JESSIE. *The Female World.* New York: Free Press, 1981.

———. *The Future of Marriage,* 2nd ed. New Haven, Conn.: Yale University Press, 1982.

BERRY, BRIAN L., and PHILIP H. REES. "The Factorial Ecology of Calcutta." *American Journal of Sociology.* Vol. 74, No. 5 (March 1969):445–91.

BERTEAU, CELESTE. "Disconnected Intimacy: AOL Instant Messenger Use among Kenyon College Students." Senior thesis. Kenyon College, 2005.

BESECKE, KELLY. "Speaking of Meaning in Modernity: Reflexive Spirituality as a Cultural Resource." *Sociology of Religion.* Vol. 62, No. 3 (2003):365–81.

———. "Seeing Invisible Religion: Religion as a Societal Conversation about Transcendent Meaning." *Sociological Theory.* Vol. 23, No. 2 (June 2005):179–96.

BESHAROV, DOUGLAS J., and LISA A. LAUMANN. "Child Abuse Reporting." *Society.* Vol. 34, No. 4 (May/June 1996):40–46.

BEST, RAPHAELA. *We've All Got Scars: What Boys and Girls Learn in Elementary School.* Bloomington: Indiana University Press, 1983.

BIAN, YANJIE. "Chinese Social Stratification and Social Mobility." *Annual Review of Sociology.* Vol. 28 (2002):91–116.

BIANCHI, SUZANNE M., and DAPHNE SPAIN. "Women, Work, and Family in America." *Population Bulletin.* Vol. 51, No. 3 (December 1996).

BLACK, CASSANDRA. "Survey Reports More Women Are Having Extramarital Affairs." *Associated Content* (May 4, 2007). [Online] Available April 19, 2009, at http://www.associatedcontent.com/article/231316/survey_reports_more_women_are_having.html

BLACKWOOD, EVELYN, and SASKIA WIERINGA, eds. *Female Desires: Same-Sex Relations and Transgender Practices across Cultures.* New York: Columbia University Press, 1999.

BLANKENHORN, DAVID. *Fatherless America: Confronting Our Most Urgent Social Problem.* New York: HarperCollins, 1995.

BLANTON, KIMBERLY. "Borrowers Sue Subprime Lender, Allege Race Bias." *Boston Globe.* July 13, 2007. [Online] Available March 9, 2008, at http://www.boston.com/business/personalfinance/articles/2007/07/13/borrowers_sue_subprime_lender_allege_race_bias/

BLAU, JUDITH R., and PETER M. BLAU. "The Cost of Inequality: Metropolitan Structure and Violent Crime." *American Sociological Review.* Vol. 47, No. 1 (February 1982):114–29.

BLAU, PETER M. *Exchange and Power in Social Life.* New York: Wiley, 1964.

———. *Inequality and Heterogeneity: A Primitive Theory of Social Structure.* New York: Free Press, 1977.

BLAU, PETER M., TERRY C. BLUM, and JOSEPH E. SCHWARTZ. "Heterogeneity and Intermarriage." *American Sociological Review.* Vol. 47, No. 1 (February 1982):45–62.

BLAUSTEIN, ALBERT P., and ROBERT L. ZANGRANDO. *Civil Rights and the Black American.* New York: Washington Square Press, 1968.

BLUMER, HERBERT G. "Collective Behavior." In ALFRED MCCLUNG LEE, ed., *Principles of Sociology.* 3rd ed. New York: Barnes & Noble Books, 1969:65–121.

BOBO, LAWRENCE, and VINCENT L. HUTCHINGS. "Perceptions of Racial Group Competition: Extending Blumer's Theory of Group Position to a Multiracial Social Context." *American Sociological Review.* Vol. 61, No. 6 (December 1996):951–72.

BOGARDUS, EMORY S. "Social Distance and Its Origins." *Sociology and Social Research.* Vol. 9 (July/August 1925):216–25.

———. *A Forty-Year Racial Distance Study.* Los Angeles: University of Southern California Press, 1967.

BOHANNAN, CECIL. "The Economic Correlates of Homelessness in Sixty Cities." *Social Science Quarterly.* Vol. 72, No. 4 (December 1991):817–25.

BOHON, STEPHANIE A., and CRAIG R. HUMPHREY. "Courting LULUs: Characteristic of Suitor and Objector Communities." *Rural Sociology.* Vol. 65, No. 3 (September 2000):376–95.

BONANNO, ALESSANDRO, DOUGLAS H. CONSTANCE, and HEATHER LORENZ. "Powers and Limits of Transnational Corporations: The Case of ADM." *Rural Sociology.* Vol. 65, No. 3 (September 2000):440–60.

BONNER, JANE. Research presented in the Public Broadcast System telecast *The Brain #6: The Two Brains.* Videocassette VHS 339. Newark, N.J.: WNET-13 Films, 1984.

BONO, AGOSTINO. "John Jay Study Reveals the Extent of Abuse Problem." [Online] Available September 13, 2006, at http://www.americancatholic.org/news/clergysexabuse/johnjaycns.asp

BOOTH, ALAN, and ANN C. CROUTER, eds. *Just Living Together: Implications of Cohabitation on Families, Children, and Policy.* Mahwah, N.J.: Erlbaum, 2002.

BOOTH, WILLIAM. "By the Sweat of Their Brows: A New Economy." *Washington Post* (July 13, 1998):A1, A10–A11.

BORMANN, F. HERBERT. "The Global Environmental Deficit." *BioScience.* Vol. 40, No. 2 (1990):74.

BOSWELL, TERRY E. "A Split Labor Market Analysis of Discrimination against Chinese Immigrants, 1850–1882." *American Sociological Review.* Vol. 51, No. 3 (June 1986):352–71.

BOSWELL, TERRY E., and WILLIAM J. DIXON. "Marx's Theory of Rebellion: A Cross-National Analysis of Class Exploitation, Economic Development, and Violent Revolt." *American Sociological Review.* Vol. 58, No. 5 (October 1993):681–702.

BOTT, ELIZABETH. *Family and Social Network.* New York: Free Press, 1971; orig. 1957.

BOULDING, ELISE. *The Underside of History.* Boulder, Colo.: Westview Press, 1976.

BOWEN, WILLIAM G., and DEREK K. BOK. *The Shape of the River: Long-Term Consequences of Considering Race in College and University Admissions.* Princeton, N.J.: Princeton University Press, 1999.

BOWLES, SAMUEL, and HERBERT GINTIS. *Schooling in Capitalist America: Educational Reform and the Contradictions of Economic Life.* New York: Basic Books, 1976.

BOYER, DEBRA. "Male Prostitution and Homosexual Identity." *Journal of Homosexuality.* Vol. 17, Nos. 1–2 (1989):151–84.

BOYLE, ELIZABETH HEGER, FORTUNATA SONGORA, and GAIL FOSS. "International Discourse and Local Politics: Anti-Female-Genital-Cutting Laws in Egypt, Tanzania, and the United States." *Social Problems.* Vol. 48, No. 4 (November 2001):524–44.

BRADY CAMPAIGN. "Firearm Facts." April 2008. [Online] Available April 16, 2008, at http://www.bradycampaign.org/issues/gvstats/firearmoverview

BRIANS, CRAIG LEONARD, and BERNARD GROFMAN. "Election Day Registration's Effect on U.S. Voter Turnout." *Social Science Quarterly.* Vol. 82, No. 1 (March 2001):170–83.

BRINES, JULIE, and KARA JOYNER. "The Ties That Bind: Principles of Cohesion in Cohabitation and Marriage." *American Sociological Review.* Vol. 64, No. 3 (June 1999):333–55.

BRINK, SUSAN. "Living on the Edge." *U.S. News & World Report* (October 14, 2002):58–64.

BRINTON, MARY C. "The Social-Institutional Bases of Gender Stratification: Japan as an Illustrative Case." *American Journal of Sociology.* Vol. 94, No. 2 (September 1988): 300–34.

BROCKERHOFF, MARTIN P. "An Urbanizing World." *Population Bulletin.* Vol. 55, No. 3 (September 2000):1–44.

BRODKIN, KAREN B. "How Did Jews Become White Folks?" In JOHN J. MACIONIS and NIJOLE V. BENOKRAITIS, eds. *Seeing Ourselves: Classic, Contemporary, and Cross-Cultural Readings in Sociology.* 7th ed. Upper Saddle River, N.J.: Prentice Hall, 2007.

BROOKS, DAVID. *Bobos in Paradise: The New Upper Class and How They Got There.* New York: Simon & Schuster, 2000.

BROWN, LESTER R. "Reassessing the Earth's Population." *Society.* Vol. 32, No. 4 (May/June 1995):7–10.

BROWN, LESTER R., ET AL., eds. *State of the World 1993: A Worldwatch Institute Report on Progress toward a Sustainable Society.* New York: Norton, 1993.

BUCKLEY, STEPHEN. "A Spare and Separate Way of Life." *Washington Post* (December 18, 1996):A1, A32–A33.

BUCKS, BRIAN K., ARTHUR B. KENNICKELL, and KEVIN B. MOORE. "Recent Change in U.S. Family Finances: Evidence from the 2001 and 2004 Survey of Consumer Finances." *Federal Reserve Bulletin.* 2006. [Online] Available May 11, 2006, at http://www.federalreserve.gov/pubs/bulletin/2006/financesurvey.pdf

BUECHLER, STEVEN M. *Social Movements in Advanced Capitalism: The Political Economy and Cultural Construction of Social Activism.* New York: Oxford University Press, 2000.

BURKETT, ELINOR. "God Created Me to Be a Slave." *New York Times Magazine* (October 12, 1997):56–60.

BUSHAW, WILLIAM J., and ALEC M. GALLUP. "The 40th Annual Phi Delta Kappa/Gallup Poll." September 2008. [Online] Available April 19, 2009, at http://www.pdkmembers.org/members_online/publications/e-GALLUP/kpoll_pdfs/pdkpoll40_2008.pdf

BUSSOLO, MAURIZIO, RAFAEL E. DeHOYOS, DENIS MEDVEDEV, and DOMINIQUE VAN DE MENSBRUGGHE. *Global Growth and Distribution: Are China and India Reshaping the World?* Policy Research Working Paper No. 4392. New York: World Bank, 2007.

BUTLER, ROBERT N. *Why Survive? Being Old in America.* New York: Harper & Row, 1975.

CALIFORNIA NEWSREEL. "Race: The Power of an Illusion: Genetic Diversity Quiz." 2003. [Online] Available February 9, 2006, at http://www.pbs.org/race/000_About/002_04_a-godeeper.htm

CALLAHAN, DANIEL. *Setting Limits: Medical Goals in an Aging Society.* New York: Simon & Schuster, 1987.

CAMARA, EVANDRO. Personal communication, 2000.

CAMERON, WILLIAM BRUCE. *Modern Social Movements: A Sociological Outline.* New York: Random House, 1966.

CAP INDEX, INC. "The Risk of Violent Crime across the United States." 2009. [Online] Available April 29, 2009, at http://www.capindex.com

CARLE, ROBERT. "Islamists in the 'Rainbow' Coalition." *Society.* Vol. 45, No. 2 (March/April 2008):181–90.

CARLSON, ALLAN. "Agrarianism Reborn: The Curious Return of the Small Family Farm." *Intercollegiate Review.* Vol. 43, No. 1 (Spring 2008):13–23.

CARLSON, NORMAN A. "Corrections in the United States Today: A Balance Has Been Struck." *American Criminal Law Review.* Vol. 13, No. 4 (Spring 1976):615–47.

CARMICHAEL, STOKELY, and CHARLES V. HAMILTON. *Black Power: The Politics of Liberation in America.* New York: Vintage Books, 1967.

CASTELLS, MANUEL. *The Urban Question.* Cambridge, Mass.: MIT Press, 1977.

CASTILLA, EMILIO J. "Gender, Race, and Meritocracy in Organizational Careers." *American Journal of Sociology.* Vol. 113, No. 6 (May 2008):1479–1526.

CATALYST. "Research and Knowledge." 2008. [Online] Available December 7, 2008, at http://www.catalyst.org/publication/271/women-ceos-of-the-fortune-1000

CENTER FOR AMERICAN WOMEN AND POLITICS. "Women in Elective Office, 2008." Eagleton Institute of Politics, Rutgers University. November 5, 2008a. [Online] Available December 8, 2008, at http://www.cawp.rutgers.edu/press_room/news/documents/PressRelease_11-5-08updated.pdf

———. "Women in State Legislatures, 2008." Eagleton Institute of Politics, Rutgers University. April 2008b. [Online] Available May 12, 2008, at http://www.cawp.rutgers.edu/Facts/Officeholders/stleg.pdf

———. "Women in State Legislatures, 2009." Eagleton Institute of Politics, Rutgers University. April 2009. [Online] Available April 2, 2009, at http://www.cawp.rutgers.edu/Facts/Officeholders/stleg.pdf

CENTER FOR RESPONSIVE POLITICS. "Banking on Becoming President." 2008a. [Online] Available April 19, 2009, at http://www.opensecrets.org/pres08/index.php

———. "2006 Election Cycle—Big Picture: The Money behind the Elections." 2008b. [Online] Available May 29, 2008, at http://www.opensecrets.org/bigpicture/index.php

———. "Lobbying Database." 2009. [Online] Available June 1, 2009, at http://www.opensecrets.org/lobby/index.php

CENTER FOR THE STUDY OF THE AMERICAN ELECTORATE. "2008 Election Turnout." 2008. [Online] Available January 26, 2009, at http://www.american.edu/ia/cdem/csae/pdfs/2008pdffinaledited.pdf

CENTER FOR WOMEN'S BUSINESS RESEARCH. "Key Facts about Women-Owned Businesses." 2008. [Online] Available December 7, 2008, at http://www.nfwbo/facts/index.php

CENTERS FOR DISEASE CONTROL AND PREVENTION (CDC). "Annual Smoking-Attributable Mortality." *Morbidity and Mortality Weekly Report.* Vol. 54, No. 25 (July 1, 2005): 625–28.

———. *Sexually Transmitted Disease Surveillance, 2005.* Atlanta: U.S. Department of Health and Human Services, 2006.

———. "Tobacco Use among Adults—United States, 2005." *Morbidity and Mortality Weekly Report.* Vol. 55, No. 42 (October 27, 2006):1145–48.

———. "Youth Risk Behavior Surveillance—United States, 2005." *Morbidity and Mortality Weekly Report.* Vol. 55, No. 5 (June 9, 2006).

———. "Smoking and Tobacco Use Fact Sheet: Cigarette Smoking-Related Mortality." September 2006. [Online] Available July 16, 2008, at http://www.cdc.gov/tobacco/data_statistics/Factsheets/cig_smoking_mort.htm

———. "Cigarette Smoking among Adults—United States, 2006." *Morbidity and Mortality Weekly Report.* Vol. 56, No. 44 (November 9, 2007):1157–61.

———. "Health, United States, 2007, with Chartbook on Trends in the Health of Americans." 2007. [Online] Available January 8, 2009, at http://www.cdc.gov/nchs/data/hus/hus07.pdf

———. *HIV/AIDS Surveillance Report, 2005.* Vol. 17, rev. ed. Atlanta: U.S. Department of Health and Human Services, 2007.

———. "Overweight and Obesity: Economic Consequences." May 2007. [Online] Available July 16, 2008, at http://www.cdc.gov/nccdphp/dnpa/obesity/economic_consequences.htm

———. *Sexually Transmitted Disease Surveillance, 2006.* Atlanta: U.S. Department of Health and Human Services, 2007.

———. *HIV/AIDS in the United States.* March 2008. [Online] Available July 16, 2008, at http://www.cdc.gov/hiv/resources/factsheets/PDF/us.pdf

———. *HIV/AIDS Surveillance Report, 2006.* Vol. 18. Atlanta: U.S. Department of Health and Human Services, 2008.

———. *Morbidity and Mortality Weekly Reports.* 2008. [Online] Available February 3, 2009, at http://www.cdc.gov/mmwr/preview/mmwrhtml/mm5745a2.htm

———. "Targeting Tobacco Use: The Nation's Leading Cause of Preventable Death." March 2008. [Online] Available July 16, 2008, at http://www.cdc.gov/NCCDPHP/publications/aag/osh.htm

———. "Trends in the Prevalence of Sexual Behaviors: National Youth Risk Behavior Survey, 1991–2007." 2008. [Online] Available April 19, 2009, at http://www.cdc.gov/HealthyYouth/yrbs/pdf/yrbs07_us_sexual_behaviors_trend.pdf

———. "Chronic Disease Prevention and Health Promotion, Quick Facts." 2009. [Online] Available February 3, 2009, at http://www.cdc.gov/NCCDPHP/press/index.htm

CENTRAL INTELLIGENCE AGENCY. *The 2008 World Factbook.* [Online] Available January 26, 2009, at https://www.cia.gov/library/publications/the-world-factbook/geos/xx.html-Military

CHAGNON, NAPOLEON A. *Yanomamö: The Fierce People.* 4th ed. Austin, Tex.: Holt, Rinehart andWinston, 1992.

CHANDLER, TERTIUS, and GERALD FOX. *3000 Years of Urban History.* New York: Academic Press, 1974.

CHANG, ALICIA. "Study: Cleaner Air Adds 5 Months to U.S. Life Span." *Yahoo News* (January 21, 2009). [Online] Available April 10, 2009, at http://www.newsvine.com/_news/2009/01/21/2339450-study-cleaner-air-adds-5-months-to-us-life-span

CHANG, LESLIE T. *Factory Girls: From Village to City in a Changing China.* New York: Spiegel & Grau, 2008.

CHERLIN, ANDREW J., LINDA M. BURTON, TERA R. HART, and DIANE M. PURVIN. "The Influence of Physical and Sexual Abuse on Marriage and Cohabitation." *American Sociological Review.* Vol. 69, No. 6 (December 2004):768–89.

CHIRICOS, TED, RANEE MCENTIRE, and MARC GERTZ. "Perceived Racial and Ethnic Composition of Neighborhood and Perceived Risk of Crime." *Social Problems.* Vol. 48, No. 3 (August 2001):322–40.

CHODOROW, NANCY. *Femininities, Masculinities, Sexualities: Freud and Beyond.* Lexington: University of Kentucky Press, 1994.

CHOPRA, ANUJ. "Iranian Rap Music Bedevils the Authorities." *U.S. News & World Report* (March 24, 2008):33.

CHRISTLE, CHRISTINE A., KRISTINE JOLIVETTE, and C. MICHAEL NELSON. "School Characteristics Related to High School Dropout Rates." *Remedial and Special Education.* Vol. 28, No. 6 (2007):325–39.

CHUA-EOAN, HOWARD. "Profiles in Outrage." *Time* (September 25, 2000):38–39.

CIMINO, RICHARD, and DON LATTIN. "Choosing My Religion." *American Demographics.* Vol. 21, No. 4 (April 1999):60–65.

CLARK, KIM. "Bankrupt Lives." *U.S. News & World Report* (September 16, 2002):52–54.

CLARK, MARGARET S., ed. *Prosocial Behavior.* Newbury Park, Calif.: Sage, 1991.

CLAWSON, DAN, and MARY ANN CLAWSON. "What Has Happened to the U.S. Labor Movement? Union Decline and Renewal." *Annual Review of Sociology.* Vol. 25 (1999):95–119.

CLOUD, JOHN, and JODIE MORSE. "Home Sweet School." *Time* (August 27, 2001):46–54.

CLOWARD, RICHARD A., and LLOYD E. OHLIN. *Delinquency and Opportunity: A Theory of Delinquent Gangs.* New York: Free Press, 1966.

COHEN, ADAM. "Test-Tube Tug-of-War." *Time* (April 6, 1998):65.

———. "A First Report Card on Vouchers." *Time* (April 26, 1999):36–38.

COHEN, ALBERT K. *Delinquent Boys: The Culture of the Gang.* New York: Free Press, 1971; orig. 1955.

COHEN, ELIAS. "The Complex Nature of Ageism: What Is It? Who Does It? Who Perceives It?" *Gerontologist.* Vol. 41, No. 5 (October 2001):576–78.

COHEN, PHILIP N., and MATT L. HUFFMAN. "Individuals, Jobs, and Labor Markets: The Devaluation of Women's Work." *American Sociological Review.* Vol. 68, No. 3 (June 2003): 443–63.

COHN, D'VERA. "Do Parents Spend Enough Time with Their Children?" Population Reference Bureau. January 2007. [Online] Available July 3, 2008, at http://www.prb.org/Articles/2007/DoParentsSpendEnoughTimeWithTheirChildren.aspx

COLE, GEORGE F., and CHRISTOPHER E. SMITH. *Criminal Justice in America.* 3rd ed. Belmont, Calif.: Wadsworth, 2002.

COLEMAN, JAMES S. "The Design of Organizations and the Right to Act." *Sociological Forum.* Vol. 8, No. 4 (December 1993):527–46.

COLEMAN, JAMES S., and THOMAS HOFFER. *Public and Private High Schools: The Impact of Communities.* New York: Basic Books, 1987.

COLEMAN, JAMES S., THOMAS HOFFER, and SALLY KILGORE. *Public and Private Schools: An Analysis of Public Schools and Beyond.* Washington, D.C.: National Center for Education Statistics, 1981.

COLEMAN, JAMES S., ET AL. *Equality of Educational Opportunity.* Washington, D.C.: U.S. Government Printing Office, 1966.

COLEMAN, RICHARD P., and BERNICE L. NEUGARTEN. *Social Status in the City.* San Francisco: Jossey-Bass, 1971.

COLLEGE BOARD. "Total Group Profile Report." 2009. [Online] Available February 2, 2009, at http://professionals.collegeboard.com/profdownload/Total_Group_Report.pdf

COLLEGE TOBACCO PREVENTION RESOURCE. "College Tobacco Resources, 1990–2005." 2006. [Online] Available July 9, 2007, at http://www.ttac.org/college/pdfs/TTACFINALLitReview.pdf

COLLINS, RANDALL. *The Credential Society: A Historical Sociology of Education and Stratification.* New York: Academic Press, 1979.

COLLYMORE, YVETTE. "Migrant Street Children on the Rise in Central America." *Population Today.* Vol. 30, No. 2 (February/March 2002):1, 4.

COLTON, HELEN. *The Gift of Touch: How Physical Contact Improves Communication, Pleasure, and Health.* New York: Seaview/Putnam, 1983.

COMMISSION FOR RACIAL JUSTICE. *CRJ Reporter.* New York: United Church of Christ, 1994.

COMTE, AUGUSTE. *Auguste Comte and Positivism: The Essential Writings.* GERTRUD LENZER, ed. New York: Harper Torchbooks, 1975, orig. 1851–54.

CONNETT, PAUL H. "The Disposable Society." In F. HERBERT BORMANN and STEPHEN R. KELLERT, eds., *Ecology, Economics, and Ethics: The Broken Circle.* New Haven, Conn.: Yale University Press, 1991:99–122.

COOLEY, CHARLES HORTON. *Social Organization.* New York: Schocken Books, 1962; orig. 1909. ———. *Human Nature and the Social Order.* New York: Schocken Books, 1964; orig. 1902.

CORRELL, SHELLEY J. "Gender and the Career Choice Process: The Role of Biased Self-Assessment." *American Journal of Sociology.* Vol. 106, No. 6 (May 2001):1691–1730.

CORTESE, ANTHONY J. *Provocateur: Images of Women and Minorities in Advertising.* Lanham, Md.: Rowman & Littlefield, 1999.

CORTEZ, MICHELLE FAY. "Memory Loss Grows Less Common among Older Americans, Study Says." *Bloomberg.com.* February 20, 2008. [Online] Available January 8, 2009, at http://www.bloomberg.com/apps/news?pid=20601103&sid=a667F2gzkXoE&refer=us

COWLEY, GEOFFREY. "The Prescription That Kills." *Newsweek* (July 17, 1995):54.

COX, HARVEY. *The Secular City.* Rev. ed. New York: Macmillan, 1971.

CRANE, DIANA. *Fashion and Its Social Agenda: Class, Gender, and Identity in Clothing.* Chicago: University of Chicago Press, 2000.

CROSSETTE, BARBARA. "Female Genital Mutilation by Immigrants Is Becoming Cause for Concern in the U.S." *New York Times International* (December 10, 1995):11.

CROUSE, JAMES, and DALE TRUSHEIM. *The Case against the SAT.* Chicago: University of Chicago Press, 1988.

CSERE, CSABA. "If Drivers Aren't Allowed to Watch TV in Cars, Why Are Texting and E-Mailing Legal?" *Car & Driver* (November 2008):11.

CTIA (THE WIRELESS ASSOCIATION). "Wireless Quick Facts: Midyear Figures for June 2008." 2008. [Online] Available November 3, 2008, at http://www.ctia.org/media/industry_info/index.cfm/AID/10323

CUMMING, ELAINE, and WILLIAM E. HENRY. *Growing Old: The Process of Disengagement.* New York: Basic Books, 1961.

CUMMINGS, SCOTT, and THOMAS LAMBERT. "Anti-Hispanic and Anti-Asian Sentiments among African Americans." *Social Science Quarterly.* Vol. 78, No. 2 (June 1997):338–53.

CURRIE, ELLIOTT. *Confronting Crime: An American Challenge.* New York: Pantheon Books, 1985.

CURRY, ANDREW. "The Gullahs' Last Stand?" *U.S. News & World Report* (June 18, 2001): 40–41.

CURTISS, SUSAN. *Genie: A Psycholinguistic Study of a Modern-Day "Wild Child."* New York: Academic Press, 1977.

CUTCLIFFE, JOHN R. "Hope, Counseling, and Complicated Bereavement Reactions." *Journal of Advanced Nursing.* Vol. 28, No. 4 (October 1998):754–62.

DAHL, ROBERT A. *Who Governs?* New Haven, Conn.: Yale University Press, 1961. ———. *Dilemmas of Pluralist Democracy: Autonomy vs. Control.* New Haven, Conn.: Yale University Press, 1982.

DAHRENDORF, RALF. *Class and Class Conflict in Industrial Society.* Stanford, Calif.: Stanford University Press, 1959.

DALMIA, SHIKHA. "Obama and Big Labor." *Forbes* (October 29, 2008). [Online] Available May 8, 2009, at http://www.forbes.com/2008/10/28/obama-card-check-oped-cx_sd_1029dalmia.html

DANFORTH, MARION M., and J. CONRAD GLASS JR. "Listen to My Words, Give Meaning to My Sorrow: A Study in Cognitive Constructs in Middle-Aged Bereaved Widows." *Death Studies.* Vol. 25, No. 6 (September 2001):413–30.

DANG, ALAIN, and CABRINI VIANNEY. *Living in the Margins: A National Survey of Lesbian, Gay, Bisexual, and Transgender Asian and Pacific Islander Americans.* New York: National Gay and Lesbian Task Force Policy Institute, 2007.

DARROCH, JACQUELINE E., ET AL. "Teenage Sexual and Reproductive Behavior in Developed Countries: Can More Progress Be Made?" 2001. [Online] Available May 30, 2005, at http://www.guttmacher.org/pubs/eurosynth_rpt.pdf

DAVIDSON, JULIA O'CONNELL. *Prostitution, Power, and Freedom.* Ann Arbor: University of Michigan Press, 1998.

DAVIES, CHRISTIE. *Ethnic Humor around the World: A Comparative Analysis.* Bloomington: Indiana University Press, 1990.

DAVIES, JAMES B., SUSANNA SANDSTROM, ANTHONY SHORROCKS, and EDWARD N. WOLFF. *The World Distribution of Household Wealth.* Helsinki: United Nations University/World Institute for Development Economics Research, March 2008.

DAVIES, MARK, and DENISE B. KANDEL. "Parental and Peer Influences on Adolescents' Educational Plans: Some Further Evidence." *American Journal of Sociology.* Vol. 87, No. 2 (September 1981):363–87.

DAVIS, DONALD M., cited in "TV Is a Blonde, Blonde World." *American Demographics,* special issue: *Women Change Places.* 1993.

DAVIS, KINGSLEY. "Extreme Social Isolation of a Child." *American Journal of Sociology.* Vol. 45, No. 4 (January 1940):554–65. ———. "Final Note on a Case of Extreme Isolation." *American Journal of Sociology.* Vol. 52, No. 5 (March 1947):432–37. ———. "Sexual Behavior." In ROBERT K. MERTON and ROBERT NISBET, eds., *Contemporary Social Problems.* 3rd ed. New York: Harcourt Brace Jovanovich, 1971:313–60.

DAVIS, KINGSLEY, and WILBERT MOORE. "Some Principles of Stratification." *American Sociological Review.* Vol. 10, No. 2 (April 1945):242–49.

DEATH PENALTY INFORMATION CENTER. "Innocence and the Death Penalty, 2008." 2008. [Online] Available November 13, 2008, at http://www.deathpenaltyinfo.org/innocence-and-death-penalty-inn-yr-rc

DECARLO, SCOTT, ed. "The World's Biggest Companies." *Forbes* (April 2, 2008). [Online] Available May 28, 2008, at http://www.forbes.com/business/2008/04/02/worlds-largest-companies-biz-2000global08-cx_sd_0402global_land.html

DEDRICK, DENNIS K., and RICHARD E. YINGER. "MAD, SDI, and the Nuclear Arms Race." Unpublished manuscript. Georgetown, Ky.: Georgetown College, 1990.

DEFENSE FINANCE AND ACCOUNTING SERVICE. "Military Pay Tables, 2008." 2008. [Online] Available November 19, 2008, at http://www.dfas.mil/militarypay/militarypaytables.html

DEFINA, ROBERT H., and THOMAS M. ARVANITES. "The Weak Effect of Imprisonment on Crime, 1971–1998." *Social Science Quarterly.* Vol. 83, No. 3 (September 2002):635–53.

DELACROIX, JACQUES, and CHARLES C. RAGIN. "Structural Blockage: A Cross-National Study of Economic Dependency, State Efficacy, and Underdevelopment." *American Journal of Sociology.* Vol. 86, No. 6 (May 1981):1311–47.

DELLA CAVA, MARCO R. "For Dutch, It's as Easy as Asking a Doctor." *USA Today* (January 7, 1997):4A.

DEMUTH, STEPHEN, and DARRELL STEFFENSMEIER. "The Impact of Gender and Race-Ethnicity in the Pretrial Release Process." *Social Problems.* Vol. 51, No. 2 (May 2004):222–42.

DEPARTMENT FOR CHILDREN, SCHOOLS AND FAMILIES. "Pupil Characteristics and Class Sizes in Maintained Schools in England." January 2008. [Online] Available February 1, 2009, at http://www.dcsf.gov.uk/rsgateway/DB/SFR/s000786/index.shtml

DERBER, CHARLES. *The Wilding of America: Money, Mayhem, and the New American Dream.* 3rd ed. New York: Worth, 2004.

DERSHOWITZ, ALAN. *The Vanishing American Jew.* Boston: Little, Brown, 1997.

DEUTSCHER, IRWIN. *Making a Difference: The Practice of Sociology.* New Brunswick, N.J.: Transaction, 1999.

DICKINSON, AMY. "When Dating Is Dangerous." *Time* (August 27, 2001):76.

DICKLER, JESSICA. "Best-Paid Executives: The Gender Gap Exaggerated." October 3, 2007. [Online] Available May 12, 2008, at http://money.cnn.com/2007/10/02/news/news-makers/mpwpay/index.htm

DIXON, WILLIAM J., and TERRY BOSWELL. "Dependency, Disarticulation, and Denominator Effects: Another Look at Foreign Capital Penetration." *American Journal of Sociology.* Vol. 102, No. 2 (September 1996):543–62.

DOBYNS, HENRY F. "An Appraisal of Techniques with a New Hemispheric Estimate." *Current Anthropology.* Vol. 7, No. 4 (October 1966):395–446.

DOLLARD, JOHN, ET AL. *Frustration and Aggression.* New Haven, Conn.: Yale University Press, 1939.

DOMHOFF, G. WILLIAM. *Who Rules America Now? A View of the '80s.* Englewood Cliffs, N.J.: Prentice Hall, 1983.

DONAHUE, JOHN J., III, and STEVEN D. LEAVITT. Research cited in "New Study Claims Abortion Is Behind Decrease in Crime." *Population Today.* Vol. 28, No. 1 (January 2000):1, 4.

DONNELLY, PATRICK G., and THEO J. MAJKA. "Residents' Efforts at Neighborhood Stabilization: Facing the Challenges of Inner-City Neighborhoods." *Sociological Forum.* Vol. 13, No. 2 (June 1998):189–213.

DONOVAN, VIRGINIA K., and RONNIE LITTENBERG. "Psychology of Women: Feminist Therapy." In BARBARA HABER, ed., *The Women's Annual, 1981: The Year in Review.* Boston: Hall, 1982:211–35.

DOWNEY, DOUGLAS B., PAUL T. VON HIPPEL, and BECKETT A. BROH. "Are Schools the Great Equalizer? Cognitive Inequality during the Summer Months and School Year." *American Sociological Review.* Vol. 59, No. 5 (October 2004):613–35.

DOYLE, JAMES A. *The Male Experience.* Dubuque, Iowa: Brown, 1983.

DRORI, GILI S. *Global E-litism: Digital Technology, Social Inequality, and Transnationality.* New York: Worth, 2006.

DU BOIS, W. E. B. "The Souls of Black Folk." In JOHN J. MACIONIS and NIJOLE V. BENOKRAITIS, eds. *Seeing Ourselves: Classic, Contemporary, and Cross-Cultural Readings in Sociology.* 7th ed. Upper Saddle River, N.J.: Prentice Hall, 2007.

DU BOIS, W. E. B. *The Philadelphia Negro: A Social Study.* New York: Schocken Books, 1967; orig. 1899.

DUBOS, RENÉ. *Man Adapting.* Enlarged ed. New Haven, Conn.: Yale University Press, 1980.

DUDLEY, KATHRYN MARIE. *Debt and Dispossession: Farm Loss in America's Heartland.* Chicago: University of Chicago Press, 2000.

DUNCAN, CYNTHIA M. *Worlds Apart: Why Poverty Persists in Rural America.* New Haven, Conn.: Yale University Press, 1999.

DUNCAN, GREG J., W. JEAN YEUNG, JEANNE BROOKS-GUNN, and JUDITH R. SMITH. "How Much Does Childhood Poverty Affect the Life Chances of Children?" *American Sociological Review.* Vol. 63, No. 3 (June 1998):406–23.

DURKHEIM, EMILE. *Moral Education: A Study in the Theory and Application of the Sociology of Education.* New York: Free Press, 1961.

———. *The Division of Labor in Society.* New York: Free Press, 1964a; orig. 1893.

———. *The Rules of Sociological Method.* New York: Free Press, 1964b; orig. 1895.

———. *The Elementary Forms of Religious Life.* New York: Free Press, 1965; orig. 1915.

———. *Suicide.* New York: Free Press, 1966; orig. 1897.

———. *Sociology and Philosophy.* New York: Free Press, 1974; orig. 1924.

DWORKIN, ANDREA. *Intercourse.* New York: Free Press, 1987.

EBAUGH, HELEN ROSE FUCHS. *Becoming an Ex: The Process of Role Exit.* Chicago: University of Chicago Press, 1988.

EBOH, CAMILLUS. "Nigerian Woman Loses Appeal against Stoning Death." 2002. [Online] Available August 19, 2002, at http://dailynews.yahoo.com

ECK, DIANA L. *A New Religious America: How a "Christian Country" Has Become the World's Most Religiously Diverse Nation.* San Francisco: HarperSanFrancisco, 2001.

EDITOR AND PUBLISHER. "Ongoing Tally of Newspaper Endorsements." October 2008. [Online] Available October 27, 2008, at http://www.editorandpublisher.com/eandp/news/article_display.jsp?vnu_content_id=1003875230

EDWARDS, TAMALA M. "Flying Solo." *Time* (August 28, 2000):47–55.

EHRENREICH, BARBARA. *The Hearts of Men: American Dreams and the Flight from Commitment.* Garden City, N.Y.: Anchor Books, 1983.

———. "The Real Truth about the Female Body." *Time* (March 15, 1999):56–65.

———. *Nickel and Dimed: On (Not) Getting By in America.* New York: Holt, 2001.

EICHLER, MARGRIT. *Nonsexist Research Methods: A Practical Guide.* Winchester, Mass.: Unwin Hyman, 1988.

EISENBERG, LEE. "Where Do You Stand on America's Wealth Spectrum?" November 1, 2007. [Online] Available August 10, 2008, at http://finance.yahoo.com/banking-budgeting/article/103815/Where-Do-You-Stand-on-America's-Wealth-Spectrum

EISENSTADT, JILL. "The Maid's Tale." *New York Times* (July 25, 2004). [Online] Available March 22, 2005, at http://www.researchnavigator.com

EISLER, BENITA. *The Lowell Offering: Writings by New England Mill Women, 1840–1845.* Philadelphia: Lippincott, 1977.

EKMAN, PAUL. "Biological and Cultural Contributions to Body and Facial Movements in the Expression of Emotions." In A. RORTY, ed., *Explaining Emotions.* Berkeley: University of California Press, 1980a:73–101.

———. *Face of Man: Universal Expression in a New Guinea Village.* New York: Garland Press, 1980b.

———. *The Expression of Emotions in Man and Animals.* New York: Oxford University Press, 1998.

———. *Emotions Revealed: Recognizing Faces and Feelings to Improve Communication and Emotional Life.* New York: Tribune Books, 2003.

EL-ATTAR, MOHAMED. Personal communication, 1991.

ELIAS, ROBERT. *The Politics of Victimization: Victims, Victimology, and Human Rights.* New York: Oxford University Press, 1986.

ELLIOT, DELBERT S., and SUZANNE S. AGETON. "Reconciling Race and Class Differences in Self-Reported and Official Estimates of Delinquency." *American Sociological Review.* Vol. 45, No. 1 (February 1980):95–110.

ELLISON, CHRISTOPHER G., JOHN P. BARTKOWSKI, and MICHELLE L. SEGAL. "Do Conservative Protestant Parents Spank More Often? Further Evidence from the National Survey of Families and Households." *Social Science Quarterly.* Vol. 77, No. 3 (September 1996): 663–73.

ELLWOOD, ROBERT S. "East Asian Religions in Today's America." In JACOB NEUSNER, ed. *World Religions in America: An Introduction.* Louisville, Ky.: Westminster John Knox Press, 2000:154–71.

ELSON, JEAN. *Am I Still a Woman? Hysterectomy and Gender Identity.* Philadelphia: Temple University Press, 2004.

EMBER, MELVIN, and CAROL R. EMBER. "The Conditions Favoring Matrilocal versus Patrilocal Residence." *American Anthropologist.* Vol. 73, No. 3 (June 1971):571–94.

———. *Anthropology.* 6th ed. Englewood Cliffs, N.J.: Prentice Hall, 1991.

EMERSON, JOAN P. "Behavior in Private Places: Sustaining Definitions of Reality in Gynecological Examinations." In H. P. DREITZEL, ed., *Recent Sociology.* Vol. 2. New York: Collier, 1970:74–97.

EMERSON, MICHAEL O., GEORGE YANCEY, and KAREN J. CHAI. "Does Race Matter in Residential Segregation? Exploring the Preferences of White Americans." *American Sociological Review.* Vol. 66, No. 6 (December 2001):922–35.

ENGELS, FRIEDRICH. *The Origin of the Family.* Chicago: Kerr, 1902; orig. 1884.

ENGLAND, PAULA. "Three Reviews on Marriage." *Contemporary Sociology.* Vol. 30, No. 6 (November 2001):564–65.

ENGLAND, PAULA, JOAN M. HERMSEN, and DAVID A. COTTER. "The Devaluation of Women's Work: A Comment on Tam." *American Journal of Sociology.* Vol. 105, No. 6 (May 2000):1741–60.

ERIKSON, ERIK H. *Childhood and Society.* New York: Norton, 1963; orig. 1950.

———. *Identity and the Life Cycle.* New York: Norton, 1980.

ERIKSON, KAI T. *Everything in Its Path: Destruction of Community in the Buffalo Creek Flood.* New York: Simon & Schuster, 1976.

———. *A New Species of Trouble: Explorations in Disaster, Trauma, and Community.* New York: Norton, 1994.

———. Lecture at Kenyon College, February 7, 2005a.

———. *Wayward Puritans: A Study in the Sociology of Deviance.* New York: Wiley, 2005b; orig. 1966.

ESTES, RICHARD J. "The Commercial Sexual Exploitation of Children in the U.S., Canada, and Mexico." Reported in "Study Explores Sexual Exploitation." [Online] Available September 10, 2001, at http://dailynews.yahoo.com

ETZIONI, AMITAI. *A Comparative Analysis of Complex Organization: On Power, Involvement, and Their Correlates.* Revised and enlarged ed. New York: Free Press, 1975.

———. "How to Make Marriage Matter." *Time* (September 6, 1993):76.

———. "The Responsive Community: A Communitarian Perspective." *American Sociological Review.* Vol. 61, No. 1 (February 1996):1–11.

———. *My Brother's Keeper: A Memoir and a Message.* Lanham, Md.: Rowman & Littlefield, 2003.

EUROPEAN UNION. "Eurostat." 2009. [Online] Available February 3, 2009 at http://epp.eurostat.ec.europa.eu

EVELYN, JAMILAH. "Community Colleges Play Too Small a Role in Teacher Education, Report Concludes." *Chronicle of Higher Education Online* (October 24, 2002). [Online] Available October 24, 2002, at http://chronicle.com/daily/2002/10/2002102403n.htm

EWERS, JUSTIN. "Saving Symbols of Shame." *U.S. News & World Report.* Vol. 144, No. 7 (March 10, 2008):31.

EXECUTIVE LEADERSHIP COUNCIL. "2008 Women and Minorities on *Fortune* 100 Boards." January 22, 2008. [Online] Available January 21, 2009, at http://www.elcinfo.com/reports.php

FALLON, A. E., and P. ROZIN. "Sex Differences in Perception of Desirable Body Shape." *Journal of Abnormal Psychology.* Vol. 94, No. 1 (1985):100–105.

FARRIS, COREEN, TERESA A. TREAT, RICHARD J. VIKEN, and RICHARD M. MCFALL. "Perceptual Mechanisms That Characterize Gender Differences in Decoding Women's Sexual Intent." *Psychological Science.* Vol. 19, No. 4 (2008):348–54.

FATTAH, HASSAN. "A More Diverse Community." *American Demographics.* Vol. 24, No. 7 (July/August 2002):39–43.

FEAGIN, JOE R., and HERNÁN, VERA. *Liberation Sociology.* Boulder, Colo.: Westview Press, 2001.

FEDERAL BUREAU OF INVESTIGATION. "Crime in the United States, 2006." 2007. [Online] Available April 16, 2008, at http://www.fbi.gov/ucr/cius2006/index.html

———. "Crime in the United States, 2007." September 2008. [Online] Available June 15, 2009, at http://www.fbi.gov/ucr/cius2007/data/table_01.html

———. "Crime in the United States, 2008." September 2008a. [Online] Available November 13, 2008, at http://www.fbi.gov/ucr/cius2007/data/table_38.html

———. "Hate Crime Statistics, 2007." October 27, 2008b. [Online] Available November 12, 2008b, at http://www.fbi.gov/ucr/hc2007/victims.htm

FEDERAL ELECTION COMMISSION. "FEC Records Slight Increase in the Number of PACs." January 17, 2008. [Online] Available May 29, 2008, at http://www.fec.gov/press/press2008/20080117paccount.shtml

FEDERAL INTERAGENCY FORUM ON AGING-RELATED STATISTICS. "Older Americans, 2008: Key Indicators of Well-Being." March 2008. [Online] Available January 18, 2009, at http://www.agingstats.gov/agingstatsdotnet/Main_Site/Data/2008_Documents/tables/Tables.aspx

FEDERAL RESERVE BOARD. "2004 Survey of Consumer Finances Survey Results." May 2007. [Online] Available November 21, 2008, at http://www.federalreserve.gov/pubs/oss/oss2/2004/bulletin.tables.int.xls

Fellman, Bruce. "Taking the Measure of Children's TV." *Yale Alumni Magazine* (April 1995):46–51.

"Female Opinion and Defense since September 11th." *Society*. Vol. 39, No. 3 (March/April 2002):2.

Fernandez, Roberto M., and Nancy Weinberg. "Sifting and Sorting: Personal Contacts and Hiring in a Retail Bank." *American Sociological Review*. Vol. 62, No. 6 (December 1997):883–902.

Ferraro, Kenneth F., and Jessica A. Kelley-Moore. "Cumulative Disadvantage and Health: Long-Term Consequences of Obesity?" *American Sociological Review*. Vol. 68, No. 5 (October 2003):707–29.

Ferree, Myra Marx, and Beth B. Hess. *Controversy and Coalition: The New Feminist Movement across Four Decades of Change*. 3rd ed. New York: Routledge, 1995.

Fetto, John. "Drug Money." *American Demographics*. Vol. 25, No. 2 (March 2003a):48.

———. "Me Gusta TV." *American Demographics*. Vol. 24, No. 11 (January 2003b):14–15.

Firebaugh, Glenn. "Growth Effects of Foreign and Domestic Investment." *American Journal of Sociology*. Vol. 98, No. 1 (July 1992):105–30.

———. "Does Foreign Capital Harm Poor Nations? New Estimates Based on Dixon and Boswell's Measures of Capital Penetration." *American Journal of Sociology*. Vol. 102, No. 2 (September 1996):563–75.

———. "Empirics of World Income Inequality." *American Journal of Sociology*. Vol. 104, No. 6 (May 1999):1597–1630.

Firebaugh, Glenn, and Frank D. Beck. "Does Economic Growth Benefit the Masses? Growth, Dependence, and Welfare in the Third World." *American Sociological Review*. Vol. 59, No. 5 (October 1994):631–53.

Firebaugh, Glenn, and Kenneth E. Davis. "Trends in Antiblack Prejudice, 1972–1984: Region and Cohort Effects." *American Journal of Sociology*. Vol. 94, No. 2 (September 1988):251–72.

Firebaugh, Glenn, and Dumitru Sandu. "Who Supports Marketization and Democratization in Post-Communist Romania?" *Sociological Forum*. Vol. 13, No. 3 (September 1998):521–41.

Fischer, Claude W. *The Urban Experience*. 2nd ed. New York: Harcourt Brace Jovanovich, 1984.

Fisher, Elizabeth. *Woman's Creation: Sexual Evolution and the Shaping of Society*. Garden City, N.Y.: Anchor/Doubleday, 1979.

Fisher, Roger, and William Ury. "Getting to Yes." In William M. Evan and Stephen Hilgartner, eds., *The Arms Race and Nuclear War*. Englewood Cliffs, N.J.: Prentice Hall, 1988: 261–68.

Flaherty, Michael G. "A Formal Approach to the Study of Amusement in Social Interaction." *Studies in Symbolic Interaction*. Vol. 5. New York: JAI Press, 1984:71–82.

———. "Two Conceptions of the Social Situation: Some Implications of Humor." *Sociological Quarterly*. Vol. 31, No. 1 (Spring 1990).

Flynn, Kevin. "Colorado Voters Preserve Affirmative Action." *Rocky Mountain News* (November 7, 2008). [Online] Available December 7, 2008, at http://www.rockymountainnews.com/news/2008/nov/06/colorado-voters-preserve-affirmative-action

Foliart, Donne E., and Margaret Clausen. "Bereavement Practices among California Hospices: Results of a Statewide Survey." *Death Studies*. Vol. 25, No. 5 (July 2001): 461–68.

Fonda, Daren. "The Male Minority." *Time* (December 11, 2000):58–60.

Forbes.com. "The Celebrity 100." June 11, 2008. [Online] Available November 18, 2008, at http://www.forbes.com/lists/2008/53/celebrities08_The-Celebrity-100_EarningsPrevYear.html

Ford, Clellan S., and Frank A. Beach. *Patterns of Sexual Behavior*. New York: Harper Bros., 1951.

Forliti, Amy. "R.I. Nightclub Fire Kills at Least 39." [Online] Available February 21, 2003, at http://www.yahoo.com

Foucault, Michel. *The History of Sexuality: An Introduction*. Vol. 1. Robert Hurley, trans. New York: Vintage, 1990; orig. 1978.

Fowler, Bree. "GM 3Q Sales Drop 11 Percent, Trail Toyota." October 29, 2008. [Online] Available April 20, 2009, at http://www.iconocast.com/EB000000000000051/O4/News1.htm

Fox, Justin. "Why Denmark Loves Globalization." *Time* (November 15, 2007). [Online] Available March 15, 2008, at http://www.time.com/time/magazine/article/0,9171,1684528,00.html

———. "Pay Them Less? Hell, Yes." *Time* (March 2, 2009):30.

Frank, André Gunder. *On Capitalist Underdevelopment*. Bombay: Oxford University Press, 1975.

———. *Crisis: In the World Economy*. New York: Holmes & Meier, 1980.

———. *Reflections on the World Economic Crisis*. New York: Monthly Review Press, 1981.

Frank, Robert. "Will the Crisis Hit the Rich Like 1990 or 1929?" November 19, 2008. [Online] Available November 23, 2008, at http://blogs.wsj.com/wealth/2008/11/19/will-the-crisis-hit-the-rich-like-1990-or-1929

Frank, Thomas. "Coal Mine Deaths Spike Upward." *USA Today* (January 1, 2007). [Online] Available March 4, 2007, at http://www.usatoday.com

Franklin, John Hope. *From Slavery to Freedom: A History of Negro Americans*. 3rd ed. New York: Vintage Books, 1967.

Frazier, E. Franklin. *Black Bourgeoisie: The Rise of a New Middle Class*. New York: Free Press, 1965.

Freedman, Estelle B. *No Turning Back: The History of Feminism and the Future of Women*. New York: Ballantine Books, 2002.

Freedom House. *Freedom in the World, 2008*. 2008. [Online] Available May 29, 2008, at http://www.freedomhouse.org

———. "Freedom in the World: Comparative and Historical Data, 2009." 2009. [Online] Available January 23, 2009, at http://www.freedomhouse.org/uploads/fiw09/FIW09_OverviewEssay_Final.pdf

French, Howard W. "Teaching Japan's Salarymen to Be Their Own Men." *New York Times* (November 27, 2002):A4.

French, Marilyn. *Beyond Power: On Women, Men, and Morals*. New York: Summit Books, 1985.

Frias, Sonia M., and Ronald J. Angel. "Stability and Change in the Experience of Partner Violence among Low-Income Women." *Social Science Quarterly*. Vol. 88, No. 5 (2007): 1281–1306.

Friedan, Betty. *The Fountain of Age*. New York: Simon & Schuster, 1993.

Friedman, Meyer, and Ray H. Rosenman. *Type A Behavior and Your Heart*. New York: Fawcett Crest, 1974.

Friedman, Milton, and Rose Friedman. *Free to Choose: A Personal Statement*. New York: Harcourt Brace Jovanovich, 1980.

Fuller, Rex, and Richard Schoenberger. "The Gender Salary Gap: Do Academic Achievement, Intern Experience, and College Major Make a Difference?" *Social Science Quarterly*. Vol. 72, No. 4 (December 1991):715–26.

Furstenberg, Frank F., Jr., and Andrew J. Cherlin. *Divided Families: What Happens to Children When Parents Part*. Cambridge, Mass.: Harvard University Press, 1991.

———. "Children's Adjustment to Divorce." In Bonnie J. Fox, ed. *Family Patterns, Gender Relations*. 2nd ed. New York: Oxford University Press, 2001.

Gagné, Patricia, Richard Tewksbury, and Deanna McGaughey. "Coming Out and Crossing Over: Identity Formation and Proclamation in a Transgender Community." *Gender and Society*. Vol. 11, No. 4 (August 1997):478–508.

Galano, Ana Maria. "Land Hungry in Brazil." August 1998. [Online] Available December 4, 2008, at http://www.unesco.org/courier/1998_08/uk/somm/intro.htm

Gallagher, Charles A. "Miscounting Race: Explaining Whites' Misperceptions of Racial Group Size." *Sociological Perspectives*. Vol. 46, No. 3 (2003):381–96.

Gallagher, Maggie. "Does Bradley Know What Poverty Is?" *New York Post* (October 28, 1999):37.

Gallup Organization. "U.S. Schools: Whole Lotta Cheatin' Going On." May 11, 2004. [Online] Available November 12, 2008, at http://www.gallup.com/poll/171644/US-Schools-Whole-Lotta-Cheatin-Going.aspx

Gans, Herbert J. *People and Plans: Essays on Urban Problems and Solutions*. New York: Basic Books, 1968.

Gardyn, Rebecca. "Retirement Redefined." *American Demographics*. Vol. 22, No. 11 (November 2000):52–57.

———. "The Mating Game." *American Demographics*. Vol. 24, No. 7 (July/August 2002): 33–37.

Garfinkel, Harold. "Conditions of Successful Degradation Ceremonies." *American Journal of Sociology*. Vol. 61, No. 2 (March 1956):420–24.

———. *Studies in Ethnomethodology*. Cambridge, Mass.: Polity Press, 1967.

Garland, Sarah. "Study Backs Results of For-Profit Schools." *New York Sun Online*. April 11, 2007. [Online] Available March 31, 2008, at http://www2.nysun.com/article/52198

Garreau, Joel. *Edge City*. New York: Doubleday, 1991.

Gave, Eleni N. "In the Indigenous Muxe Culture of Mexico's Oaxaca State, Alternative Notions of Sexuality are Not Only Accepted, They're Celebrated." *Travel and Leisure* (November 2005). [Online] Available June 15, 2009, at http://travelandleisure.com/articles/stepping-out/page/2/print

Geertz, Clifford. "Common Sense as a Cultural System." *Antioch Review*. Vol. 33, No. 1 (Spring 1975):5–26.

Gelles, Richard J., and Claire Pedrick Cornell. *Intimate Violence in Families*. 2nd ed. Newbury Park, Calif.: Sage, 1990.

Gerber, Theodore P., and Michael Hout. "More Shock than Therapy: Market Transition, Employment, and Income in Russia, 1991–1995." *American Journal of Sociology*. Vol. 104, No. 1 (July 1998):1–50.

Gerlach, Michael L. *The Social Organization of Japanese Business*. Berkeley: University of California Press, 1992.

Gerth, H. H., and C. Wright Mills, eds. "Marx and Weber." In *From Max Weber: Essays in Sociology*. New York: Oxford University Press, 1946.

Geschwender, James A. *Racial Stratification in America*. Dubuque, Iowa: Brown, 1978.

Gewertz, Deborah. "A Historical Reconsideration of Female Dominance among the Chambri of Papua New Guinea." *American Ethnologist*. Vol. 8, No. 1 (1981): 94–106.

Gibbs, Nancy. "The Pulse of America along the River." *Time* (July 10, 2000):42–46.

———. "What Kids (Really) Need." *Time* (April 30, 2001):48–49.

———. "Darkness Falls." *Time* (April 30, 2007):36–52.

Giddens, Anthony. *The Transformation of Intimacy*. Cambridge: Polity Press, 1992.

Gilbert, Neil. "Family Life: Sold on Work." *Society*. Vol. 42, No, 3 (2005):12–17.

Gilbertson, Greta A., and Douglas T. Gurak. "Broadening the Enclave Debate: The Dual Labor Market Experiences of Dominican and Colombian Men in New York City." *Sociological Forum*. Vol. 8, No. 2 (June 1993):205–20.

Gillespie, Mark. "Trends Show Bathing and Exercise Up, TV Watching Down." January 2000. [Online] Available April 9, 2006, at http://www.gallup.com

Gilligan, Carol. *In a Different Voice: Psychological Theory and Women's Development*. Cambridge, Mass.: Harvard University Press, 1982.

———. *Making Connections: The Relational Worlds of Adolescent Girls at Emma Willard School*. Cambridge, Mass.: Harvard University Press, 1990.

Gillon, Raanan. "Euthanasia in the Netherlands: Down the Slippery Slope?" *Journal of Medical Ethics*. Vol. 25, No. 1 (February 1999):3–4.

GIOVANNINI, MAUREEN. "Female Anthropologist and Male Informant: Gender Conflict in a Sicilian Town." In JOHN J. MACIONIS and NIJOLE V. BENOKRAITIS, eds., *Seeing Ourselves: Classic, Contemporary, and Cross-Cultural Readings in Sociology*. 2nd ed. Englewood Cliffs, N.J.: Prentice Hall, 1992:27–32.

GLEICK, ELIZABETH. "The Marker We've Been Waiting For." *Time* (April 7, 1997):28–42.

GLENMARY RESEARCH CENTER. *Religious Congregations and Membership in the United States, 2000*. Nashville, Tenn.: Glenmary Research Center, 2002.

GLENN, NORVAL D., and BETH ANN SHELTON. "Regional Differences in Divorce in the United States." *Journal of Marriage and the Family*. Vol. 47, No. 3 (August 1985):641–52.

GLOBAL MARCH AGAINST CHILD LABOUR. *Worst Forms of Child Labour Report, 2005*. 2008. [Online] Available May 15, 2008, at http://www.globalmarch.org/worstformsreport/world/index.html

GLUECK, SHELDON, and ELEANOR GLUECK. *Unraveling Juvenile Delinquency*. New York: Commonwealth Fund, 1950.

GOESLING, BRIAN. "Changing Income Inequalities within and between Nations: New Evidence." *American Sociological Review*. Vol. 66, No. 5 (October 2001):745–61.

GOFFMAN, ERVING. *The Presentation of Self in Everyday Life*. Garden City, N.Y.: Anchor Books, 1959.

———. *Asylums: Essays on the Social Situation of Mental Patients and Other Inmates*. Garden City, N.Y.: Anchor Books, 1961.

———. *Stigma: Notes on the Management of Spoiled Identity*. Englewood Cliffs, N.J.: Prentice Hall, 1963.

———. *Interactional Ritual: Essays on Face to Face Behavior*. Garden City, N.Y.: Anchor Books, 1967.

———. *Gender Advertisements*. New York: Harper Colophon, 1979.

GOKHALE, JAGADEESH. "Mandatory Retirement Age Rules: Is It Time to Reevaluate?" Statement before the United States Senate. September 9, 2004. [Online] Available January 1, 2009, at http://www.cato.org/testimony/ct-jg040909.html

GOLDBERG, BERNARD. *Bias: A CBS Insider Exposes How the Media Distort the News*. Washington, D.C.: Regnery, 2002.

GOLDBERG, STEVEN. *The Inevitability of Patriarchy*. New York: Morrow, 1974.

GOLDBERGER, PAUL. Lecture delivered at Kenyon College, Gambier, Ohio, September 22, 2002.

GOLDEN, FREDERIC, and MICHAEL D. LEMONICK. "The Race Is Over." *Time* (July 3, 2000):18–23.

GOLDFIELD, MICHAEL. "Rebounding Unions Target Service Sector." *Population Today*. Vol. 28, No. 7 (October 2000):3, 10.

GOLDSCHEIDER, CALVIN. *Studying the Jewish Future*. Seattle: University of Washington Press, 2004.

GOLDSMITH, H. H. "Genetic Influences on Personality from Infancy." *Child Development*. Vol. 54, No. 2 (April 1983):331–35.

GOLDSTEIN, JOSHUA R., and CATHERINE T. KENNEY. "Marriage Delayed or Marriage Forgone? New Cohort Forecasts of First Marriage for U.S. Women." *American Sociological Review*. Vol. 66, No. 4 (August 2001):506–19.

GOODE, ERICH. "No Need to Panic? A Bumper Crop of Books on Moral Panics." *Sociological Forum*. Vol. 15, No. 3 (September 2000):543–52.

GOODE, WILLIAM J. "The Theoretical Importance of Love." *American Sociological Review*. Vol. 24, No. 1 (February 1959):38–47.

———. "Encroachment, Charlatanism, and the Emerging Profession: Psychology, Sociology, and Medicine." *American Sociological Review*. Vol. 25, No. 6 (December 1960):902–14.

GORDON, JAMES S. "The Paradigm of Holistic Medicine." In ARTHUR C. HASTINGS ET AL., eds., *Health for the Whole Person: The Complete Guide to Holistic Medicine*. Boulder, Colo.: Westview Press, 1980:3–27.

GORDON, RAYMOND G., JR., ed. *Ethnologue: Languages of the World*, 15th ed. Dallas, Tex.: SIL International, 2005. [Online] Available April 20, 2009, at http://www.ethnologue.com/ethno_docs/distribution.asp?by=size-2

GORE, AL. *An Inconvenient Truth: The Crisis of Global Warming*. Emmaus, Pa.: Rodale Books, 2006.

GORMAN, CHRISTINE. "Stressed-Out Kids." *Time* (December 25, 2000):168.

GOTHAM, KEVIN FOX. "Race, Mortgage Lending, and Loan Rejections in a U.S. City." *Sociological Focus*. Vol. 31, No. 4 (October 1998):391–405.

GOTTFREDSON, MICHAEL R., and TRAVIS HIRSCHI. "National Crime Control Policies." *Society*. Vol. 32, No. 2 (January/February 1995):30–36.

GOTTMANN, JEAN. *Megalopolis*. New York: Twentieth Century Fund, 1961.

GOULD, STEPHEN J. "Evolution as Fact and Theory." *Discover* (May 1981):35–37.

———. "Curveball." *New Yorker* (November 28, 1994):139–49.

GRANT, DONALD L. *The Anti-Lynching Movement*. San Francisco: R&E Research Associates, 1975.

GRANT, DON SHERMAN, II, and MICHAEL WALLACE. "Why Do Strikes Turn Violent?" *American Journal of Sociology*. Vol. 96, No. 5 (March 1991):1117–50.

GRAYBOW, MARTHA. "Women Directors Help Boost Corporate's Financial Performance: Study." *International Business Times*. October 2, 2007. [Online] Available December 2, 2008, at http://in.ibtimes.com/articles/20071002/women-directors-help-boost-corporate-financial-performance.htm

GREELEY, ANDREW M. "Symposium: Neo-Darwinism and Its Discontents." *Society*. Vol. 45, No. 2 (2008):162–63.

GREEN, GARY PAUL, LEANN M. TIGGES, and DANIEL DIAZ. "Racial and Ethnic Differences in Job-Search Strategies in Atlanta, Boston, and Los Angeles." *Social Science Quarterly*. Vol. 80, No. 2 (June 1999):263–90.

GREENBERG, DAVID F. *The Construction of Homosexuality*. Chicago: University of Chicago Press, 1988.

GREENE, BOB. "Empty House on the Prairie." *New York Times* (March 2, 2005). [Online] Available May 24, 2005, at http://www.researchnavigator.com

GREENHOUSE, LINDA. "Supreme Court Allows Lethal Injection for Execution." *New York Times* (April 17, 2008). [Online] Available June 15, 2009, at http://www.nytimes.com/2008/04/17/us/16cnd-scotus.html

GREENHOUSE, STEVEN. "Despite Defeat on China Bill, Labor Is on the Rise." *New York Times* (May 20, 2000): A1, A18.

———. "Many Entry-Level Workers Find Pinch of Rough Market." *New York Times* (September 4, 2006).

GREENSPAN, STANLEY I. *The Four-Thirds Solution: Solving the Child-Care Crisis in America*. Cambridge, Mass.: Perseus, 2001.

GRIER, PETER. "How to Slow the Spread of the Bomb." *Christian Science Monitor* (June 5, 2006). [Online] Accessed July 29, 2006, at http://news.yahoo.com/s/csm/20060605

GRIM, BRIAN J., and DAVID MASCI. "The Demographics of Faith." August 19, 2008. [Online] Available February 23, 2009, at http://www.america.gov/st/diversityenglish/2008/August/20080819121858cmretrop0.5310633.html

GROSS, MATT. "It's My (Virtual) World." *New York Times Online*. November 3, 2006. Available November 7, 2006, at http://www.nytimes.com.

GURNETT, KATE. "On the Forefront of Feminism." *Albany Times Union* (July 5, 1998):G-1, G-6.

GUTIERREZ, CARL. "Bear Stearns Announces More Job Cuts." *Forbes* (October 3, 2007). [Online] Available May 28, 2008, at http://www.forbes.com/markets/2007/10/03/bear-stearns-layoffs-markets-equity-cx_cg_1003markets23.html

GWYNNE, S. C., and JOHN F. DICKERSON. "Lost in the E-Mail." *Time* (April 21, 1997):88–90.

HABERMAS, JÜRGEN. *Toward a Rational Society: Student Protest, Science, and Politics*. JEREMY J. SHAPIRO, trans. Boston: Beacon Press, 1970.

HADAWAY, C. KIRK, PENNY LONG MARLER, and MARK CHAVES. "What the Polls Don't Show: A Closer Look at U.S. Church Attendance." *American Sociological Review*. Vol. 58, No. 6 (December 1993):741–52.

HAGAN, JACQUELINE MARIA. "Social Networks, Gender, and Immigrant Incorporation: Resources and Restraints." *American Sociological Review*. Vol. 63, No. 1 (February 1998): 55–67.

HAGOPIAN, ELAINE C. *Civil Rights in Peril: The Targeting of Arabs and Muslims*. London: Photo Press, 2004.

HALBERSTAM, DAVID. *The Reckoning*. New York: Avon Books, 1986.

HALBFINGER, DAVID M., and STEVEN A. HOLMES. "Military Mirrors Working-Class America." *New York Times* (March 20, 2003). [Online] Available May 4, 2009, at http://www.cwalocal4250.org/news/binarydata/Military%20Mirrors%20Working-Class%20America.pdf

HALL, JOHN R., and MARY JO NEITZ. *Culture: Sociological Perspectives*. Englewood Cliffs, N.J.: Prentice Hall, 1993.

HAMER, DEAN, and PETER COPELAND. *The Science of Desire: The Search for the Gay Gene and the Biology of Behavior*. New York: Simon & Schuster, 1994.

HAMILTON, ANITA. "Speeders, Say Cheese." *Time* (September 17, 2001):32.

HAMILTON, BRADLEY E., JOYCE A. MARTIN, and STEPHANIE J. VENTURA. "Births: Preliminary Data for 2007." [Online] Available: April 21, 2009, at http://www.cdc.gov/nchs/data/nvsr/nvsr56/nvsr56_07.pdf

HAMRICK, MICHAEL H., DAVID J. ANSPAUGH, and GENE EZELL. *Health*. Columbus, Ohio: Merrill, 1986.

HANDLIN, OSCAR. *Boston's Immigrants, 1790–1865: A Study in Acculturation*. Cambridge, Mass.: Harvard University Press, 1941.

HANEY, CRAIG, W. CURTIS BANKS, and PHILIP G. ZIMBARDO. "Interpersonal Dynamics in a Simulated Prison." *International Journal of Criminology and Penology*. Vol. 1 (1973): 69–97.

HANEY, LYNNE. "After the Fall: East European Women since the Collapse of State Socialism." *Contexts*. Vol. 1, No. 3 (Fall 2002):27–36.

HARFORD INSTITUTE FOR RELIGION RESEARCH. "Are More or Less Women Entering Seminaries Today?" 2009. [Online] Available January 15, 2009, at http://hirr.hartsem.edu/research/quick_question44.html

HARFORD, TIM. "The Beauty of Everyday Economics." *U.S. News & World Report* (January 28, 2008):14.

HARLOW, HARRY F., and MARGARET KUENNE HARLOW. "Social Deprivation in Monkeys." *Scientific American* (November 1962):137–46.

HARPSTER, PAULA, and ELIZABETH MONK-TURNER. "Why Men Do Housework: A Test of Gender Production and the Relative Resources Model." *Sociological Focus*. Vol. 31, No. 1 (February 1998):45–59.

HARRIES, KEITH D. *Serious Violence: Patterns of Homicide and Assault in America*. Springfield, Ill.: Thomas, 1990.

HARRINGTON, MICHAEL. *The New American Poverty*. New York: Penguin Books, 1984.

HARRIS, CHAUNCY D., and EDWARD L. ULLMAN. "The Nature of Cities." *Annals of the American Academy of Political and Social Sciences*. Vol. 242, No. 1 (November 1945):7–17.

HARRIS, DAVID R., and JEREMIAH JOSEPH SIM. "Who Is Multiracial? Assessing the Complexity of Lived Race." Vol. 67, No. 4 (August 2002):614–27.

HARRIS, MARVIN. *Cultural Anthropology*. 2nd ed. New York: Harper & Row, 1987.

HARRISON, C. KEITH. "Black Athletes at the Millennium." *Society*. Vol. 37, No. 3 (March/April 2000):35–39.

HARTOCOLLIS, ANEMONA. "Man Is Convicted of Attempted Murder as Hate Crime in Village Rampage." *New York Times* (March 2, 2007):B6.

HAUB, CARL. "Tracking Trends in Low Fertility Countries: An Uptick in Europe?" Population Reference Bureau. September 2008. [Online] Available January 8, 2009, at http://www.prb.org/Articles/2008/tfrtrendsept08.aspx

HAWTHORNE, PETER. "South Africa's Makeover." *Time* (July 12, 1999). [Online] Available May 4, 2009, at http://www.time.com/time/magazine/article/0,9171,991487,00.html

HAYDEN, THOMAS. "Losing Our Voices." *U.S. News & World Report* (May 26, 2003):42.

HEATH, JULIA A., and W. DAVID BOURNE. "Husbands and Housework: Parity or Parody?" *Social Science Quarterly.* Vol. 76, No. 1 (March 1995):195–202.

HELGESEN, SALLY. *The Female Advantage: Women's Ways of Leadership.* New York: Doubleday, 1990.

HELIN, DAVID W. "When Slogans Go Wrong." *American Demographics.* Vol. 14, No. 2 (February 1992):14.

HELLMICH, NANCI. "Environment, Economics Partly to Blame." *USA Today* (October 9, 2002):9D.

HENLEY, NANCY, MYKOL HAMILTON, and BARRIE THORNE. "Womanspeak and Manspeak: Sex Differences in Communication, Verbal and Nonverbal." In JOHN J. MACIONIS and NIJOLE V. BENOKRAITIS, eds., *Seeing Ourselves: Classic, Contemporary, and Cross-Cultural Readings in Sociology.* 2nd ed. Englewood Cliffs, N.J.: Prentice Hall, 1992:10–15.

HERDA-RAPP, ANN. "The Power of Informal Leadership: Women Leaders in the Civil Rights Movement." *Sociological Focus.* Vol. 31, No. 4 (October 1998):341–55.

HERMAN, DIANNE. "The Rape Culture." In JOHN J. MACIONIS and NIJOLE V. BENOKRAITIS, eds., *Seeing Ourselves: Classic, Contemporary, and Cross-Cultural Readings in Sociology.* 5th ed. Upper Saddle River, N.J.: Prentice Hall, 2001.

HERON, MELONIE P., ET AL. "Deaths: Preliminary Data for 2006." June 2008. [Online] Available April 21, 2009, at http://www.cdc.gov/nchs/data/nvsr/nvsr56/nvsr56_16.pdf

HERPERTZ, SABINE C., and HENNING SASS. "Emotional Deficiency and Psychopathy." *Behavioral Sciences and the Law.* Vol. 18, No. 5 (September/October 2000):567–80.

HERRING, HUBERT B. "An Aging Nation Is Choosing Younger Bosses." *New York Times* (February 20, 2005). [Online] Available May 4, 2009, at http://query.nytimes.com/gst/fullpage.html?res=9F06E6DC113AF933A15751C0A9639C8B63

HERRNSTEIN, RICHARD J., and CHARLES MURRAY. *The Bell Curve: Intelligence and Class Structure in American Life.* New York: Free Press, 1994.

HERZOG, BRAD. "A Man of His Words." *Cornell Alumni Magazine.* Vol. 106, No. 4 (January/February 2004):58–63.

HESKETH, THERESE, LI LU, and ZHU WEI XING. "The Effects of China's One-Child Family Policy after 25 Years." *New England Journal of Medicine.* Vol. 353, No. 11 (November 2005):1171–76.

HESS, BETH B. "Breaking and Entering the Establishment: Committing Social Change and Confronting the Backlash." *Social Problems.* Vol. 46, No. 1 (February 1999):1–12.

HEWLETT, SYLVIA ANN, and CAROLYN BUCK LUCE. "Off-Ramps and On-Ramps: Keeping Talented Women on the Road to Success." March 2005. [Online] Available December 8, 2008, at http://0-search.ebscohost.com.dewey2.library.denison.edu:80/login.aspx?direct=true&db=buh&AN=16235203&site=ehost-live

HEYMANN, PHILIP B. "Civil Liberties and Human Rights in the Aftermath of September 11." *Harvard Journal of Law and Public Policy.* Vol. 25, No. 2 (Spring 2002):441–57.

HILL, MARK E. "Race of the Interviewer and Perception of Skin Color: Evidence from the Multi-City Study of Urban Inequality." *American Sociological Review.* Vol. 67, No. 1 (February 2002):99–108.

HIRSCHI, TRAVIS. *Causes of Delinquency.* Berkeley: University of California Press, 1969.

HOCHSCHILD, ARLIE RUSSELL. "Emotion Work, Feeling Rules, and Social Structure." *American Journal of Sociology.* Vol. 85, No. 3 (November 1979):551–75.

———. *The Managed Heart.* Berkeley: University of California Press, 1983.

HOLMSTROM, DAVID. "Abuse of Elderly, Even by Adult Children, Gets More Attention and Official Concern." *Christian Science Monitor* (July 28, 1994):1.

HOPE, TRINA L., HAROLD G. GRASMICK, and LAURA J. POINTON. "The Family in Gottfredson and Hirschi's General Theory of Crime: Structure, Parenting, and Self-Control." *Sociological Focus.* Vol. 36, No. 4 (November 2003):291–311.

HORN, WADE F., and DOUGLAS TYNAN. "Revamping Special Education." *Public Interest.* No. 144 (Summer 2001):36–53.

HORTON, HAYWARD DERRICK. "Critical Demography: The Paradigm of the Future?" *Sociological Forum.* Vol. 14, No. 3 (September 1999):363–67.

HORWITZ, JULIANA. "Winds of Political Change Haven't Shifted Public's Ideological Balance." November 25, 2008. [Online] Available January 23, 2009, at http://pewresearch.org/pubs/1042/winds-of-political-change-havent-shifted-publics-ideology-balance

HOSTETLER, JOHN A. *Amish Society.* 3rd ed. Baltimore: Johns Hopkins University Press, 1980.

HOU, FENG, and JOHN F. MYLES. "The Changing Role of Education in the Marriage Market: Assortative Marriage in Canada and the United States since the 1970s." Analytical Studies Branch Research Paper Series. Ottawa: Statistics Canada, 2008.

HOUT, MICHAEL, CLEM BROOKS, and JEFF MANZA. "The Persistence of Classes in Post-Industrial Societies." *International Sociology.* Vol. 8, No. 3 (September 1993):259–77.

HOUT, MICHAEL, and CLAUDE S. FISHER. "Why More Americans Have No Religious Preference: Politics and Generations." *American Sociological Review.* Vol. 67, No. 2 (April 2002):165–90.

HOUT, MICHAEL, ANDREW M. GREELEY, and MELISSA J. WILDE. "The Demographic Imperative in Religious Change in the United States." *American Journal of Sociology.* Vol. 107, No. 2 (September 2001):468–500.

HOWDEN, DANIEL. "Latin America's New Socialist Revolution." *New Zealand Herald* (December 20, 2005). [Online] Available February 13, 2006, at http://www.nzherald.co.nz

HOYT, HOMER. *The Structure and Growth of Residential Neighborhoods in American Cities.* Washington, D.C.: Federal Housing Administration, 1939.

HSU, FRANCIS L. K. *The Challenge of the American Dream: The Chinese in the United States.* Belmont, Calif.: Wadsworth, 1971.

HUCHINGSON, JAMES E. "Science and Religion." *Miami Herald* (December 25, 1994):1M, 6M.

HUFFMAN, KAREN. *Psychology in Action.* New York: Wiley, 2000.

HUMAN RIGHTS WATCH. "Children's Rights: Child Labor." 2006. [Online] Available April 9, 2006, at http://www.hrw.org/children/labor.htm

HUNTER, JAMES DAVISON. *American Evangelicalism: Conservative Religion and the Quandary of Modernity.* New Brunswick, N.J.: Rutgers University Press, 1983.

———. "Conservative Protestantism." In PHILIP E. HAMMOND, ed., *The Sacred in a Secular Age.* Berkeley: University of California Press, 1985:50–66.

———. *Evangelicalism: The Coming Generation.* Chicago: University of Chicago Press, 1987.

HYMOWITZ, CAROL. "World's Poorest Women Advance by Entrepreneurship." *Wall Street Journal* (September 9, 1995):B1.

HYMOWITZ, KAY S. "Kids Today Are Growing Up Way Too Fast." *Wall Street Journal* (October 28, 1998):A22.

IANNACCONE, LAURENCE R. "Why Strict Churches Are Strong." *American Journal of Sociology.* Vol. 99, No. 5 (March 1994):1180–1211.

IDE, THOMAS R., and ARTHUR J. CORDELL. "Automating Work." *Society.* Vol. 31, No. 6 (September/October 1994):65–71.

IGNATIUS, ADI. "A Tsar Is Born." *Time* (December 31, 2007):46–62.

INCIARDI, JAMES A. *Elements of Criminal Justice.* 2nd ed. New York: Oxford University Press, 2000.

INCIARDI, JAMES A., HILARY L. SURRATT, and PAULO R. TELLES. *Sex, Drugs, and HIV/AIDS in Brazil.* Boulder, Colo.: Westview Press, 2000.

INGLEHART, RONALD. *Modernization and Postmodernization: Cultural, Economic, and Political Change in 43 Societies.* Princeton, N.J.: Princeton University Press, 1997.

———. "Inglehart-Welzel Cultural Map of the World." Rev. 2009. [Online] Available June 5, 2009, at http://www.worldvaluessurvey.org

INGLEHART, RONALD, and WAYNE E. BAKER. "Modernization, Cultural Change, and the Persistence of Traditional Values." *American Sociological Review.* Vol. 65, No. 1 (February 2000):19–51.

INGLEHART, RONALD, and CHRISTIAN WELZEL. *Modernization, Culture Change, and Democracy.* New York: Cambridge University Press, 2005.

INGLEHART, RONALD, CHRISTIAN WELZEL, and ROBERTO FOA. "Happiness Trends in 24 Countries, 1946–2006." 2009. [Online] Available February 15, 2009, at http://margaux.grandvinum.se/SebTest/wvs/articles/folder_published/article_base_106

INGLEHART, RONALD, ET AL. *World Values Surveys and European Values Surveys, 1981–1984, 1990–1993, and 1995–1997.* Ann Arbor, Mich.: Interuniversity Consortium for Political and Social Research, 2000.

INSTITUTE FOR WOMEN'S POLICY RESEARCH. "The Economic Security of Older Women and Men in the United States." November 2007. [Online] Available January 3, 2009, at http://www.iwpr.org/pdf/BPD480.pdf

INTERNAL REVENUE SERVICE. "IRS Updates Tax-Gap Estimates." February 14, 2006. [Online] Available January 20, 2009, at http://www.irs.gov/newsroom/article/0,,id=154496,00.html

———. "SOI Tax Stats: Individual Statistical Tables by Tax Rate and Income Percentile." 2008a. [Online] Available December 8, 2008, at http://www.irs.gov/taxstats/article/0,,id=185880,00.html

———. "SOI Tax Stats: Returns of Active Corporations, Table 2." 2008b. [Online] Available May 29, 2008, at http://www.irs.gov/taxstats/article/0,,id=170544,00.html

INTERNATIONAL BUSINESS MACHINES (IBM). "Select a Country/Region and Language." 2008. [Online] Available March 6, 2008, at http://www.ibm.com/planetwide/select/selector.html

INTERNATIONAL LABOUR ORGANIZATION. "Key Indicators of the Labour Market," 6th ed. 2009. [Online] Available June 15, 2009, at http://www.ilo.org/public/english/employment/strat/kilm/index.htm

———. "LABORSTA Internet." 2009. [Online] Available April 21, 2009, at http://laborsta.ilo.org/data_topic_E.html

INTERNATIONAL MONETARY FUND. *World Economic Outlook.* April 2000. [Online] Available June 1, 2001, at http://www.imf.org/external/pubs/ft/weo/2000/01/index.htm

———. *World Economic Outlook.* October 2007. [Online] Available May 2, 2008, at http://www.imf.org/external/pubs/ft/weo/2007/02

INTERNATIONAL PANEL ON CLIMATE CHANGE. *Climate Change, 2007.* New York: United Nations, 2007.

INTERNATIONAL TELECOMMUNICATION UNION. *World Telecommunication Development Report.* Data cited in WORLD BANK, *2006 World Development Indicators.* Washington, D.C.: World Bank, 2006.

———. *World Telecommunication Development Report.* Data cited in WORLD BANK, *2007 World Development Indicators.* Washington, D.C.: World Bank, 2007.

———. *World Telecommunication Development Report.* Data cited in WORLD BANK, *2008 World Development Indicators.* Washington, D.C.: World Bank, 2008.

INTER-PARLIAMENTARY UNION. "Women in National Parliaments." 2008. [Online] Available December 28, 2008, at http://www.ipu.org/wmn-e/classif.htm and at http://www.ipu.org/wmn-e/world.htm

ISRAEL, GLENN D., LIONEL J. BEAULIEU, and GLEN HARTLESS. "The Influence of Family and Community Social Capital on Educational Achievement." *Rural Sociology.* Vol. 66, No. 1 (March 2001):43–68.

ITZKOFF, DAVE. "Television: A Brave New World for TV? Virtually." *New York Times Online.* June 24, 2007. [Online] Available July 7, 2007, at http://www.nytimes.com

JACOBSON, JENNIFER. "Professors Are Finding Better Pay and More Freedom at Community Colleges." *Chronicle of Higher Education Online.* 2003. [Online] Available March 7, 2003, at http://www.chronicle.com

JACOBY, RUSSELL, and NAOMI GLAUBERMAN, eds. *The Bell Curve Debate.* New York: Random House, 1995.

JACQUET, CONSTANT H., and ALICE M. JONES. *Yearbook of American and Canadian Churches, 1991.* Nashville, Tenn.: Abingdon Press, 1991.

JANIS, IRVING L. *Victims of Groupthink.* Boston: Houghton Mifflin, 1972.

———. *Crucial Decisions: Leadership in Policymaking and Crisis Management.* New York: Free Press, 1989.

JASPER, JAMES M. "The Emotions of Protest: Affective and Reactive Emotions in and around Social Movements." *Sociological Forum.* Vol. 13, No. 3 (September 1998):397–424.

JEFFERSON, CORD. "Driving Concerns." *National Geographic* (January 2009):33.

JENKINS, J. CRAIG. *Images of Terror: What We Can and Can't Know about Terrorism.* Hawthorne, N.Y.: Aldine de Gruyter, 2003.

JENKINS, J. CRAIG, DAVID JACOBS, and JON AGONE. "Political Opportunities and African-American Protest, 1948–1997." *American Journal of Sociology.* Vol. 109, No. 2 (September 2003):277–303.

JENKINS, J. CRAIG, and CHARLES PERROW. "Insurgency of the Powerless: Farm Worker Movements, 1946–1972." *American Sociological Review.* Vol. 42, No. 2 (April 1977):249–68.

JENKINS, J. CRAIG, and MICHAEL WALLACE. "The Generalized Action Potential of Protest Movements: The New Class, Social Trends, and Political Exclusion Explanations." *Sociological Forum.* Vol. 11, No. 2 (June 1996):183–207.

JIMÉNEZ, TOMÁS R. "Weighing the Costs and Benefits of Mexican Immigration: The Mexican American Perspective." *Social Science Quarterly.* Vol. 88, No. 3 (2007):599–618.

JOHNSON, BARRY W., and BRIAN G. RAUB. "Personal Wealth, 2001." *Statistics of Income Bulletin* (Winter 2005–06). 2006. [Online] Available September 20, 2006, at http://www.irs.gov/pub/irs-soi/01pwart.pdf

JOHNSON, CATHRYN. "Gender, Legitimate Authority, and Leader-Subordinate Conversations." *American Sociological Review.* Vol. 59, No. 1 (February 1994):122–35.

JOHNSON, DIRK. "Death of a Small Town." *Newsweek* (September 10, 2001):30–31.

JOHNSON, KENNETH M. "The Rural Rebound." *Population Reference Bureau Reports on America.* Vol. 1, No. 3 (September 1999). [Online] Available October 9, 2004, at http://www.prb.org/Content/NavigationMenu/PRB/AboutPRB/Reports_on_America/Reporton-AmericaRuralRebound.pdf

JOHNSON, KENNETH M., and GLENN V. FUGUITT. "Continuity and Change in Rural Migration Patterns, 1950–1995." *Rural Sociology.* Vol. 65, No. 1 (March 2000):27–49.

JOHNSON, PAUL. "The Seven Deadly Sins of Terrorism." In BENJAMIN NETANYAHU, ed., *International Terrorism.* New Brunswick, N.J.: Transaction Books, 1981:12–22.

JOHNSTON, R. J. "Residential Area Characteristics." In D. T. HERBERT and R. J. JOHNSTON, eds., *Social Areas in Cities. Vol. 1: Spatial Processes and Form.* New York: Wiley, 1976:193–235.

JONES, ANDREW E. G., and DAVID WILSON. *The Urban Growth Machine: Critical Perspectives.* Albany: State University of New York Press, 1999.

JONES, CHARISSE. "Upon Release from Prison, Some Can Feel Lost." *USA Today* (December 14, 2007):5A.

JONES, D. GARETH. "Brain Death." *Journal of Medical Ethics.* Vol. 24, No. 4 (August 1998):237–43.

JONES, KATHARINE W. *Accent on Privilege: English Identities and Anglophilia in the U.S.* Philadelphia: Temple University Press, 2001.

JORDAN, ELLEN, and ANGELA COWAN. "Warrior Narratives in the Kindergarten Classroom: Renegotiating the Social Contract?" *Gender and Society.* Vol. 9, No. 6 (December 1995):727–43.

JOSEPHY, ALVIN M., JR. *Now That the Buffalo's Gone: A Study of Today's American Indians.* New York: Knopf, 1982.

KADLEC, DANIEL. "Everyone, Back in the (Labor) Pool." *Time* (July 29, 2002):22–31.

KAIN, EDWARD L. "A Note on the Integration of AIDS into the Sociology of Human Sexuality." *Teaching Sociology.* Vol. 15, No. 4 (July 1987):320–23.

KALLEBERG, ARNE L., BARBARA F. RESKIN, and KEN HUDSON. "Bad Jobs in America: Standard and Nonstandard Employment Relations and Job Quality in the United States." *American Sociological Review.* Vol. 65, No. 2 (April 2000):256–78.

KAMINER, WENDY. "Volunteers: Who Knows What's in It for Them?" *Ms.* (December 1984):93–96, 126–28.

———. "Demasculinizing the Army." *New York Times Review of Books* (June 15, 1997):7.

KANE, EMILY W. "Racial and Ethnic Variations in Gender-Related Attitudes." *Annual Review of Sociology.* Vol. 26 (August 2000):419–39.

KANTER, ROSABETH MOSS. *Men and Women of the Corporation.* New York: Basic Books, 1977.

KANTER, ROSABETH MOSS, and BARRY A. STEIN. "The Gender Pioneers: Women in an Industrial Sales Force." In ROSABETH MOSS KANTER and BARRY A. STEIN, eds., *Life in Organizations.* New York: Basic Books, 1979:134–46.

KANTROWITZ, BARBARA, and PAT WINGERT. "Unmarried with Children." *Newsweek* (May 28, 2001):46–52.

———. "What's at Stake." *Newsweek* (January 27, 2003):30–37.

KAO, GRACE. "Group Images and Possible Selves among Adolescents: Linking Stereotypes to Expectations by Race and Ethnicity." *Sociological Forum.* Vol. 15, No. 3 (September 2000):407–30.

KAPFERER, JEAN-NOEL. "How Rumors Are Born." *Society.* Vol. 29, No. 5 (July/August 1992):53–60.

KAPLAN, DAVID E., and MICHAEL SCHAFFER. "Losing the Psywar." *U.S. News & World Report* (October 8, 2001):46.

KAPSTEIN, ETHAN B. "The New Global Slave Trade." *Foreign Affairs* (November/December 2006). [Online] Available April 21, 2009, at http://www.foreignaffairs.com/articles/62094/ethan-b-kapstein/the-new-global-slave-trade

KAPTCHUK, TED. "The Holistic Logic of Chinese Medicine." In BERKELEY HOLISTIC HEALTH CENTER, *The New Holistic Health Handbook: Living Well in a New Age.* SHEPARD BLISS ET AL., eds. Lexington, Mass.: Greene Press, 1985:41.

KARATNYCKY, ADRIAN. "The 2001–2002 Freedom House Survey of Freedom: The Democracy Gap." In *Freedom in the World: The Annual Survey of Political Rights and Civil Liberties, 2001–2002.* New York: Freedom House, 2002:7–18.

KARJANE, HEATHER M., BONNIE S. FISHER, and FRANCIS T. CULLEN. "Sexual Assault on Campus: What Colleges and Universities Are Doing about It." U.S. Department of Justice. 2005. [Online] Available December 8, 2008, at http://www.ncjrs.gov/pdffiles1/nij/205521.pdf

KARP, DAVID A., and WILLIAM C. YOELS. "The College Classroom: Some Observations on the Meaning of Student Participation." *Sociology and Social Research.* Vol. 60, No. 4 (July 1976):421–39.

KARRFALT, WAYNE. "A Multicultural Mecca." *American Demographics.* Vol. 25, No. 4 (May 2003):54–55.

KAUFMAN, LESLIE. "Surge in Homeless Families Sets Off Debate on Cause." *New York Times* (July 29, 2004). [Online] Available May 4, 2009, at http://www.nytimes.com/2004/06/29/us/surge-in-homeless-families-sets-off-debate-on-cause.html?fta=y

KAUFMAN, ROBERT L. "Assessing Alternative Perspectives on Race and Sex Employment Segregation." *American Sociological Review.* Vol. 67, No. 4 (August 2002):547–72.

KAUFMAN, WALTER. *Religions in Four Dimensions: Existential, Aesthetic, Historical, and Comparative.* New York: Reader's Digest Press, 1976.

KAY, PAUL, and WILLETT KEMPTON. "What Is the Sapir-Whorf Hypothesis?" *American Anthropologist.* Vol. 86, No. 1 (March 1984):65–79.

KEISTER, LISA A. *Wealth in America: Trends in Wealth Inequality.* Cambridge: Cambridge University Press, 2000.

———. "Religion and Wealth: The Role of Religious Affiliation and Participation in Early Adult Asset Accumulation." *Social Forces.* Vol. 82, No. 1 (September 2003):175–207.

KEISTER, LISA A., and STEPHANIE MOLLER. "Wealth Inequality in the United States." *Annual Review of Sociology.* Vol. 26 (August 2000):63–81.

KELLER, HELEN. *The Story of My Life.* New York: Doubleday Page, 1903.

KELLERT, STEPHEN R., and F. HERBERT BORMANN. "Closing the Circle: Weaving Strands among Ecology, Economics, and Ethics." In F. HERBERT BORMANN and STEPHEN R. KELLERT, eds., *Ecology, Economics, and Ethics: The Broken Circle.* New Haven, Conn.: Yale University Press, 1991:205–10.

KENT, MARY M., and MARK MATHER. "What Drives U.S. Population Growth?" *Population Bulletin.* Vol. 57, No. 4 (December 2002):3–40.

KENTOR, JEFFREY. "The Long-Term Effects of Foreign Investment Dependence on Economic Growth, 1940–1990." *American Journal of Sociology.* Vol. 103, No. 4 (January 1998):1024–46.

———. "The Long-Term Effects of Globalization on Income Inequality, Population Growth, and Economic Development." *Social Problems.* Vol. 48, No. 4 (November 2001):435–55.

KERR, RICHARD A. "Climate Models Heat Up." *Science Now* (January 26, 2005):1–3.

KEWALRAMANI, ANGELINA, LAUREN GILBERTSON, MARY ANN FOX, and STEPHEN PROVASNIK. *Status and Trends in the Education of Racial and Ethnic Minorities, 2005.* National Center for Education Statistics. September 2007. [Online] Available May 19, 2008, at http://nces.ed.gov/pubs2007/minoritytrends

KEYS, JENNIFER. "Feeling Rules That Script the Abortion Experience." Paper presented at the annual meeting of the American Sociological Association, Chicago, August 2002.

KILBOURNE, BROCK K. "The Conway and Siegelman Claims against Religious Cults: An Assessment of Their Data." *Journal for the Scientific Study of Religion.* Vol. 22, No. 4 (December 1983):380–85.

KILGORE, SALLY B. "The Organizational Context of Tracking in Schools." *American Sociological Review.* Vol. 56, No. 2 (April 1991):189–203.

KING, KATHLEEN PIKER, and DENNIS E. CLAYSON. "The Differential Perceptions of Male and Female Deviants." *Sociological Focus.* Vol. 21, No. 2 (April 1988):153–64.

KINKEAD, GWEN. *Chinatown: A Portrait of a Closed Society.* New York: HarperCollins, 1992.

KINSEY, ALFRED, WARDELL BAXTER POMEROY, and CLYDE E. MARTIN. *Sexual Behavior in the Human Male.* Philadelphia: Saunders, 1948.

KINSEY, ALFRED, WARDELL BAXTER POMEROY, CLYDE E. MARTIN, and PAUL H. GEBHARD. *Sexual Behavior in the Human Female.* Philadelphia: Saunders, 1953.

KITTRIE, NICHOLAS N. *The Right to Be Different: Deviance and Enforced Therapy.* Baltimore: Johns Hopkins University Press, 1971.

KIVANT, BARBARA. "Reassessing Risk." *Time* (November 17, 2008):Global 1–4.

KLEIN, DANIEL B., and CHARLOTTA STERN. "How Politically Diverse Are the Social Sciences and Humanities? Survey Evidence from Six Fields." National Association of Scholars. 2004. [Online] Available January 13, 2005, at http://www.nas.org/aa/klein_launch.htm

KLUCKHOHN, CLYDE. "As an Anthropologist Views It." In ALBERT DEUTH, ed., *Sex Habits of American Men.* New York: Prentice Hall, 1948.

KOHLBERG, LAWRENCE. *The Psychology of Moral Development: The Nature and Validity of Moral Stages.* New York: Harper & Row, 1981.

KOHLBERG, LAWRENCE, and CAROL GILLIGAN. "The Adolescent as Philosopher: The Discovery of Self in a Postconventional World." *Daedalus.* Vol. 100, No. 4 (Fall 1971):1051–86.

KOHN, MELVIN L. *Class and Conformity: A Study in Values.* 2nd ed. Homewood, Ill.: Dorsey Press, 1977.

———. "*The Bell Curve* from the Perspective of Research on Social Structure and Personality." *Sociological Forum.* Vol. 11, No. 2 (June 1996):395.

KOHUT, ANDREW. "Post-Election Perspectives." November 13, 2008. [Online] Available January 23, 2009, at http://pewresearch.org/pubs/1039/post-election-perspectives

KONO, CLIFFORD, DONALD PALMER, ROGER FRIEDLAND, and MATTHEW ZAFONTE. "Lost in Space: The Geography of Corporate Interlocking Directorates." *American Journal of Sociology.* Vol. 103, No. 4 (January 1998):863–911.

KORNHAUSER, WILLIAM. *The Politics of Mass Society.* New York: Free Press, 1959.

KOSKELA, ROGER. "Life after Work: 'Stage' Your Retirement to Max Your Transition." *Kitsap (Wash.) Sun.* August 17, 2008. [Online] Available January 1, 2009, at http://www.kitsapsun.com/news/2008/aug/17/life-after-work-145stage-your-retirement-to-max

KOZOL, JONATHAN. *Rachel and Her Children: Homeless Families in America.* New York: Crown, 1988.

———. *Savage Inequalities: Children in America's Schools.* New York: Harper Perennial, 1992.

KRAL, BRIGITTA. "The Eyes of Jane Elliott." *Horizon Magazine.* 2000. [Online] Available June 8, 2005, at http://www.horizonmag.com/4/jane-elliott.asp

KRAYBILL, DONALD B. *The Riddle of Amish Culture.* Baltimore: Johns Hopkins University Press, 1989.

———. "The Amish Encounter with Modernity." In DONALD B. KRAYBILL and MARC A. OLSHAN, eds., *The Amish Struggle with Modernity.* Hanover, N.H.: University Press of New England, 1994:21–33.

KRAYBILL, DONALD B., and JAMES P. HURD. *Horse-and-Buggy Mennonites: Hoofbeats of Humility in a Postmodern World.* University Park: Pennsylvania State University Press, 2006.

KRAYBILL, DONALD B., and MARC A. OLSHAN, eds. *The Amish Struggle with Modernity.* Hanover, N.H.: University Press of New England, 1994.

KROLL, LUISA, ed. "Special Report: The World's Billionaires." *Forbes* (March 5, 2008). [Online] Available November 21, 2008, at http://www.forbes.com/2008/03/05/richest-people-billionaires-billionaires08-cx_lk_0305billie_land.html

KROLL, LUISA, MATTHEW MILLER, and TATIANA SERAFIN, eds. "Special Report: The World's Billionaires. *Forbes* (March 11, 2009). [Online] Available June 15, 2009, at http://www.forbes.com/2009/03/11/worlds-richest-people-billionaires-2009-billionaires_land.html

KRUGMAN, PAUL. "For Richer: How the Permissive Capitalism of the Boom Destroyed American Equality." *New York Times Magazine* (September 20, 2002):62–67, 76–77, 141–42.

KRUKS, GABRIEL N. "Gay and Lesbian Homeless/Street Youth: Special Issues and Concerns." *Journal of Adolescent Health.* Special Issue. No. 12 (1991):515–18.

KRYSAN, MARIA. "Community Undesirability in Black and White: Examining Racial Residential Preferences through Community Perceptions." *Social Problems.* Vol. 49, No. 4 (November 2002):521–43.

KÜBLER-ROSS, ELISABETH. *On Death and Dying.* New York: Macmillan, 1969.

KUBRIN, CHARLES E. "Gangstas, Thugs, and Hustlas: Identity and the Code of the Street in Rap Music." *Social Problems.* Vol. 52, No. 3 (August 2005):360–78.

KUNG, HSIANG-CHING, DONNA L. HOYERT, JIAQUAN XU, and SHERRY L. MURPHY. "Deaths: Final Data for 2005." *National Vital Statistics Reports.* Vol. 56, No. 10 (January 2008). Hyattsville, Md.: National Center for Health Statistics, 2008.

KUNKEL, DALE, ET AL. *Sex on TV, 2005.* Menlo Park, Calif.: Henry J. Kaiser Family Foundation, 2005. [Online] Available September 13, 2006, at http://www.kff.org/entmedia/upload/Sex-on-TV-4-Full-Report.pdf

KUUMBA, M. BAHATI. "A Cross-Cultural Race/Class/Gender Critique of Contemporary Population Policy: The Impact of Globalization." *Sociological Forum.* Vol. 14, No. 3 (March 1999): 447–63.

KUZNETS, SIMON. "Economic Growth and Income Inequality." *American Economic Review.* Vol. 14, No. 1 (March 1955):1–28.

———. *Modern Economic Growth: Rate, Structure, and Spread.* New Haven, Conn.: Yale University Press, 1966.

LACAYO, RICHARD. "The Brawl over Sprawl." *Time* (March 22, 1999):44–48.

———. "Blood at the Root." *Time* (April 10, 2000):122–23.

LACEY, MARC. "A Distinct Lifestyle: The Muxe of Mexico." *New York Times* (December 7, 2008), p. 4.

LACH, JENNIFER. "The Color of Money." *American Demographics.* Vol. 21, No. 2 (February 1999):59–60.

LAGORIO, CHRISTINE. "Pepperdine in a Treehouse." *New York Times* (January 7, 2007). [Online] Available January 30, 2007, at http://www.nytimes.com

LAH, KYUNG. "Report: More Elderly Japanese Turn to Petty Crime." CNN.com/Asia. December 24, 2008. [Online] Available April 20, 2009, at http://www.cnn.com/2008/WORLD/asiapcf/12/24/elderly.shoplifters

LAI, H. M. "Chinese." In *Harvard Encyclopedia of American Ethnic Groups.* Cambridge, Mass.: Harvard University Press, 1980:217–33.

LANDSBERG, MITCHELL. "Health Disaster Brings Early Death in Russia." *Washington Times* (March 15, 1998):A8.

LANG, DERRIK J. "Virtual World Keeps Tabs on Election." November 4, 2008. [Online] Available April 21, 2009, at http://www.msnbc.msn.com/id/27535286

LANGBEIN, LAURA I., and ROSEANA BESS. "Sports in School: Source of Amity or Antipathy?" *Social Science Quarterly.* Vol. 83, No. 2 (June 2002):436–54.

LAPCHICK, RICHARD. "The 2006 Racial and Gender Report Cards." Institute for Diversity and Ethics in Sport, University of Central Florida. 2007. [Online] Available February 26, 2008, at http://www.bus.ucf.edu/sport/cgi-bin/site/sitew.cgi?page=/ides/index.htx

LAPCHICK, RICHARD, ERIC LITTLE, and COLLEEN LERNER. "The 2008 Racial and Gender Report Card: National Football League." August 27, 2008. [Online] Available October 7, 2008, at http://www.bus.ucf.edu/sport/public/downloads/2008_NFL_RGRC_PR.pdf

LAPPÉ, FRANCES MOORE, and JOSEPH COLLINS. *World Hunger: Twelve Myths.* New York: Grove Press/Food First Books, 1986.

LAPPÉ, FRANCES MOORE, JOSEPH COLLINS, and PETER ROSSET. *World Hunger: Twelve Myths.* 2nd ed. New York: Grove Press, 1998.

LAREAU, ANNETTE. "Invisible Inequality: Social Class and Childrearing in Black Families and White Families." *American Sociological Review.* Vol. 67, No. 5 (October 2002): 747–76.

LARSON, GERALD JAMES. "Hinduism in India and in America." In JACOB NEUSNER, ed., *World Religions in America: An Introduction.* Louisville, Ky.: Westminster/John Knox, 2000:124–41.

LASLETT, PETER. *The World We Have Lost: England before the Industrial Age.* 3rd ed. New York: Scribner, 1984.

LAUMANN, EDWARD O., JOHN H. GAGNON, ROBERT T. MICHAEL, and STUART MICHAELS. *The Social Organization of Sexuality: Sexual Practices in the United States.* Chicago: University of Chicago Press, 1994.

LAVIN, DANIELLE, and DOUGLAS W. MAYNARD. "Standardization vs. Rapport: Respondent Laughter and Interviewer Reaction during Telephone Surveys." *American Sociological Review.* Vol. 66, No. 3 (June 2001):453–79.

LEACH, COLIN WAYNE. "Democracy's Dilemma: Explaining Racial Inequality in Egalitarian Societies." *Sociological Forum.* Vol. 17, No. 4 (December 2002):681–96.

LEACOCK, ELEANOR. "Women's Status in Egalitarian Societies: Implications for Social Evolution." *Current Anthropology.* Vol. 19, No. 2 (June 1978):247–75.

LEAVITT, JUDITH WALZER. "Women and Health in America: An Overview." In JUDITH WALZER LEAVITT, ed., *Women and Health in America.* Madison: University of Wisconsin Press, 1984:3–7.

LE BON, GUSTAVE. *The Crowd: A Study of the Popular Mind.* New York: Viking Press, 1960; orig. 1895.

LEE, BARRET A., and MATHEW MARLAY. "The Right Side of the Tracks: Affluent Neighborhoods in the Metropolitan United States." *Social Science Quarterly.* Vol. 88, No. 3 (2007): 766–89.

LEE, FELICIA R. "Long Buried, Death Goes Public Again." *New York Times* (November 2, 2002). [Online] Available November 2, 2002, at http://www.nytimes.com/2002/11/02/arts/long-buried-death-goes-public-again.html

LEFEBVRE, HENRI. *The Production of Space.* Oxford: Blackwell, 1991.

LEFF, LISA. "California Gay Marriage Vote Still Undecided." November 5, 2008. [Online] Available November 5, 2008, at http://news.yahoo.com/s/ap/20081105/ap_on_el_ge/ballot_measures

LELAND, JOHN. "Bisexuality." *Newsweek* (July 17, 1995):44–49.

LEMERT, EDWIN M. *Social Pathology.* New York: McGraw-Hill, 1951.

———. *Human Deviance, Social Problems, and Social Control.* 2nd ed. Englewood Cliffs, N.J.: Prentice Hall, 1972.

LEMONICK, MICHAEL D. "The Search for a Murder Gene." *Time* (January 20, 2003):100.

———. "Are We Losing Our Edge?" *Time.* Vol. 167, No. 7 (February 13, 2006):22–33.

LENGERMANN, PATRICIA MADOO, and JILL NIEBRUGGE-BRANTLEY. *The Women Founders: Sociology and Social Theory, 1830–1930.* New York: McGraw-Hill, 1998.

LENGERMANN, PATRICIA MADOO, and RUTH A. WALLACE. *Gender in America: Social Control and Social Change.* Englewood Cliffs, N.J.: Prentice Hall, 1985.

LENSKI, GERHARD E. *Power and Privilege: A Theory of Social Stratification.* New York: McGraw-Hill, 1966.

LENSKI, GERHARD E., PATRICK NOLAN, and JEAN LENSKI. *Human Societies: An Introduction to Macrosociology.* 7th ed. New York: McGraw-Hill, 1995.

LEONARD, CHRISTOPHER. "Six Dead after Kirkwood City Council Shooting." *Missourian* (February 8, 2008). [Online] Available February 9, 2008, at http://www.columbiamissourian.com/stories/2008/02/08/gunman-opens-fire-kirkwood-city-council-meeting

LEONARD, EILEEN B. *Women, Crime, and Society: A Critique of Theoretical Criminology.* White Plains, N.Y.: Longman, 1982.

LEOPOLD, EVELYN. "Sudan's Young Endure 'Unspeakable' Abuse: Report." [Online] Available April 19, 2007, at http://www.news.yahoo.com

LEVAY, SIMON. *The Sexual Brain.* Cambridge, Mass.: MIT Press, 1993.

LEVER, JANET. "Sex Differences in the Complexity of Children's Play and Games." *American Sociological Review.* Vol. 43, No. 4 (August 1978):471–83.

LEVINE, MICHAEL P. *Student Eating Disorders: Anorexia Nervosa and Bulimia.* Washington, D.C.: National Educational Association, 1987.

———. "Reducing Hostility Can Prevent Heart Disease." *Mount Vernon* (Ohio) *News* (August 7, 1990):4A.

LEVINE, SAMANTHA. "The Price of Child Abuse." *U.S. News & World Report* (April 9, 2001): 58.

———. "Playing God in Illinois." *U.S. News & World Report* (January 13, 2003):13.

LEVINSON, F. JAMES, and LUCY BASSETT. "Malnutrition Is Still a Major Contributor to Child Deaths." Population Reference Bureau. 2007. [Online] Available December 4, 2008, at http://www.prb.org/pdf07/Nutrition2007.pdf

LEWIN, TAMAR. "Girls' Gains Have Not Cost Boys, Report Says." *New York Times* (May 20, 2008). [Online] Available December 7, 2008, at http://www.nytimes.com/2008/05/20/education/20girls.html?partner=permalink&exprod=permalink

LEWIS, OSCAR. *The Children of Sanchez.* New York: Random House, 1961.

LIAZOS, ALEXANDER. "The Poverty of the Sociology of Deviance: Nuts, Sluts, and Perverts." *Social Problems.* Vol. 20, No. 1 (Summer 1972):103–20.

———. *People First: An Introduction to Social Problems.* Needham Heights, Mass.: Allyn & Bacon, 1982.

LICHTER, DANIEL T., and MARTHA L. CROWLEY. "Poverty in America: Beyond Welfare Reform." *Population Bulletin.* Vol. 57, No. 2 (June 2002):3–34.

LICHTER, DANIEL T., and RUKMALIE JAYAKODY. "Welfare Reform: How Do We Measure Success?" *Annual Review of Sociology.* Vol. 28 (August 2002):117–41.

LICHTER, S. ROBERT, and DANIEL R. AMUNDSON. "Distorted Reality: Hispanic Characters in TV Entertainment." In CLARA E. RODRIGUEZ, ed., *Latin Looks: Images of Latinas and Latinos in the U.S. Media.* Boulder, Colo.: Westview Press, 1997:57–79.

LIN, GE, and PETER ROGERSON. Research reported in DIANE CRISPELL, "Sons and Daughters Who Keep in Touch." *American Demographics.* Vol. 16, No. 8 (August 1994):15–16.

LIN, NAN, KAREN COOK, and RONALD S. BURT, eds. *Social Capital: Theory and Research.* Hawthorne, N.Y.: Aldine de Gruyter, 2001.

LIN, NAN, and WEN XIE. "Occupational Prestige in Urban China." *American Journal of Sociology.* Vol. 93, No. 4 (January 1988):793–832.

LINDAUER, DAVID L., and AKILA WEERAPANA. "Relief for Poor Nations." *Society.* Vol. 39, No. 3 (March/April 2002):54–58.

LINDLAW, SCOTT. "President Signs Education Bill." 2002. [Online] Available January 8, 2002, at http://news.yahoo.com

LINDSTROM, BONNIE. "Chicago's Post-Industrial Suburbs." *Sociological Focus.* Vol. 28, No. 4 (October 1995):399–412.

LING, PYAU. "Causes of Chinese Emigration." In AMY TACHIKI ET AL., eds., *Roots: An Asian American Reader.* Los Angeles: UCLA Asian American Studies Center, 1971:134–38.

LINO, MARK. *Expenditures on Children by Families, 2006.* U.S. Department of Agriculture, Center for Nutrition Policy and Promotion. Washington, D.C.: U.S. Government Printing Office, 2007.

———. *Expenditures on Children by Families, 2007.* U.S. Department of Agriculture, Center for Nutrition Policy and Promotion. Washington, D.C.: U.S. Government Printing Office, 2008.

LINTON, RALPH. "One Hundred Percent American." *American Mercury.* Vol. 40, No. 160 (April 1937a):427–29.

———. *The Study of Man.* New York: Appleton-Century, 1937b.

LIPSET, SEYMOUR MARTIN. *Political Man: The Social Bases of Politics.* Garden City, N.Y.: Anchor/Doubleday, 1963.

———. "Canada and the United States." CHARLES F. DONAN and JOHN H. SIGLER, eds. Englewood Cliffs, N.J.: Prentice Hall, 1985.

LIPTAK, ADAM. "More than 1 in 100 Adults Are Now in Prison in U.S." *New York Times* (February 29, 2008):A14.

LISKA, ALLEN E., and BARBARA D. WARNER. "Functions of Crime: A Paradoxical Process." *American Journal of Sociology.* Vol. 96, No. 6 (May 1991):1441–63.

LITTLE, CRAIG, and ANDREA RANKIN. "Why Do They Start It? Explaining Reported Early-Teen Sexual Activity." *Sociological Forum.* Vol. 16, No. 4 (December 2001):703–29.

LIU, MELINDA, and DUNCAN HEWITT. "The Rise of the Sea Turtles." *Newsweek* (August 18, 2008):29–31.

LOBO, SUSAN. "Census-Taking and the Invisibility of Urban American Indians." *Population Today.* Vol. 30, No. 4 (May/June 2002):3–4.

LOFLAND, LYN. *A World of Strangers.* New York: Basic Books, 1973.

LOGAN, JOHN R., RICHARD D. ALBA, and WENQUAN ZHANG. "Immigrant Enclaves and Ethnic Communities in New York and Los Angeles." *American Sociological Review.* Vol. 67, No. 2 (April 2002):299–322.

LOGAN, JOHN R., DEIDRE OAKLEY, and JACOB STOWELL. "School Segregation in Metropolitan Regions, 1970–2000: The Impacts of Policy Choices on Public Education." *American Journal of Sociology.* Vol. 113, No. 6 (May 2008):1611–44.

LOHR, STEVE. "In Bailout Furor, Wall Street Salaries Become a Target." *International Herald Tribune* (September 24, 2008). [Online] Available November 6, 2008, at http://www.iht.com/articles/2008/09/24/business/24pay.php

LONG, JASON, and JOSEPH FERRIE. "The Path to Convergence: Intergenerational Occupational Mobility in Britain and the U.S. in Three Eras." *Economic Journal.* Vol. 117, No. 519 (2007):C61–C71.

LONGINO, CHARLES F., JR. "Myths of an Aging America." *American Demographics.* Vol. 16, No. 8 (August 1994):36–42.

LOOMIS, CAROL. "Getting Women to the Highest Levels." *Fortune: 50 Most Powerful Women in Business.* October 4, 2007. [Online] Available May 12, 2008, at http://money.cnn.com/2007/10/04/magazines/fortune/loomis_boards.fortune/index.htm

LORD, MARY. "Good Teachers the Newest Imports." *U.S. News & World Report* (April 9, 2001):54.

LORD, WALTER. *A Night to Remember.* Rev. ed. New York: Holt, Rinehart and Winston, 1976.

LORENZ, FREDERICK O., and BRENT T. BRUTON. "Experiments in Surveys: Linking Mass Class Questionnaires to Introductory Research Methods." *Teaching Sociology.* Vol. 24, No. 3 (July 1996):264–71.

LOVEMAN, MARA. "Is 'Race' Essential?" *American Sociological Review.* Vol. 64, No. 6 (December 1999):890–98.

LOVGREN, STEFEN. "Will All the Blue Men End Up in Timbuktu?" *U.S. News & World Report* (December 7, 1998):40.

LUND, DALE A. "Conclusions about Bereavement in Later Life and Implications for Interventions and Future Research." In DALE A. LUND, ed., *Older Bereaved Spouses: Research with Practical Applications.* London: Taylor-Francis-Hemisphere, 1989:217–31.

———. "Caregiving." *Encyclopedia of Adult Development.* Phoenix, Ariz.: Oryx Press, 1993:57–63.

LUND, DALE A., MICHAEL S. CASERTA, and MARGARET F. DIMOND. "Gender Differences through Two Years of Bereavement among the Elderly." *Gerontologist.* Vol. 26, No. 3 (1986):314–20.

LYND, ROBERT S., and HELEN MERRELL LYND. *Middletown in Transition.* New York: Harcourt, Brace & World, 1937.

MABRY, MARCUS, and TOM MASLAND. "The Man after Mandela." *Newsweek* (June 7, 1999):54–55.

MACE, DAVID, and VERA MACE. *Marriage East and West.* Garden City, N.Y.: Doubleday/Dolphin, 1960.

MACIONIS, JOHN J. "Intimacy: Structure and Process in Interpersonal Relationships." *Alternative Lifestyles.* Vol. 1, No. 1 (February 1978):113–30.

———. "A Sociological Analysis of Humor." Presentation to the Texas Junior College Teachers Association, Houston, 1987.

———. *Social Problems.* 3rd ed. Upper Saddle River, N.J.: Prentice Hall, 2008.

———. *Social Problems.* 4th ed. Upper Saddle River, N.J.: Pearson Prentice Hall, 2010.

MACIONIS, JOHN J., and LINDA GERBER. *Sociology.* 6th Canadian ed. Scarborough, Ontario: Prentice Hall Allyn & Bacon Canada, 2008.

MACIONIS, JOHN J., and VINCENT R. PARRILLO. *Cities and Urban Life.* 5th ed. Upper Saddle River, N.J.: Pearson Prentice Hall, 2010.

MACKAY, JUDITH. *The Penguin Atlas of Human Sexual Behavior.* New York: Penguin, 2000.

MADENSEN, TAMARA D., and JOHN E. ECK. "The Problem of Student Party Riots." Center for Problem-Oriented Policing. 2006. [Online] Available January 25, 2009, at http://www.popcenter.org/problems/student_riots

MADDOX, SETMA. "Organizational Culture and Leadership Style: Factors Affecting Self-Managed Work Team Performance." Paper presented at the annual meeting of the Southwest Social Science Association, Dallas, February 1994.

MALTHUS, THOMAS ROBERT. *First Essay on Population, 1798.* London: Macmillan, 1926; orig. 1798.

Many Voices, One City: The NYCMA Guide to the Ethnic Press of New York. 4th ed. New York: New York Community Media Alliance, 2008.

MANZA, JEFF, and CLEM BROOKS. "The Religious Factor in U.S. Presidential Elections, 1960–1992." *American Journal of Sociology.* Vol. 103, No. 1 (July 1997):38–81.

MARATHONGUIDE.COM. "Marathon Records." 2008. [Online] Available May 12, 2008, at http://www.marathonguide.com/history/records/index.cfm

MARCUSE, HERBERT. *One-Dimensional Man.* Boston: Beacon Press, 1964.

MARÍN, GERARDO, and BARBARA VAN OSS MARÍN. *Research with Hispanic Populations.* Newbury Park, Calif.: Sage, 1991.

MARKOFF, JOHN. "Remember Big Brother? Now He's a Company Man." *New York Times* (March 31, 1991):7.

MARQUAND, ROBERT. "Worship Shift: Americans Seek Feeling of 'Awe.'" *Christian Science Monitor* (May 28, 1997):1, 8.

MARQUAND, ROBERT, and DANIEL B. WOOD. "Rise in Cults as Millennium Approaches." *Christian Science Monitor* (March 28, 1997):1, 18.

MARQUARDT, ELIZABETH, and NORVAL GLENN. *Hooking Up, Hanging Out, and Hoping for Mr. Right.* New York: Institute for American Values, 2001.

MARQUEZ, LAURA. "Nursing Shortage: How It May Affect You." *ABC News.* January 21, 2006. [Online] Available April 1, 2008, at http://abcnews.go.com/WNT/Health/story?id=1529546

MARSHALL, MELISSA J., and ANIRUDH V. S. RUHIL. "The Pomp of Power: Black Mayoralties in Urban America." *Social Science Quarterly.* Vol. 87, No. 4 (2006):828–50.

MARSHALL, SUSAN E. "Ladies against Women: Mobilization Dilemmas of Antifeminist Movements." *Social Problems.* Vol. 32, No. 4 (April 1985):348–62.

MARWELL, GERALD, and N. J. DEMERATH III. "'Secularization' by Any Other Name." *American Sociological Review.* Vol. 68, No. 2 (2003):314–15.

MARTIN, CAROL LYNN, and RICHARD A. FABES. "The Stability and Consequences of Young Children's Same-Sex Peer Interactions." *Developmental Psychology.* Vol. 37, No. 3 (May 2001):431–46.

MARTIN, JOHN M., and ANNE T. ROMANO. *Multinational Crime: Terrorism, Espionage, Drug and Arms Trafficking.* Newbury Park, Calif.: Sage, 1992.

MARTIN, JOYCE A., ET AL. "Births: Final Data for 2006." January 7, 2009. [Online] Available April 21, 2009, at http://www.cdc.gov/nchs/data/nvsr/nvsr57/nvsr57_07.pdf

MARTINEZ, RAMIRO, JR. "Latinos and Lethal Violence: The Impact of Poverty and Inequality." *Social Problems.* Vol. 43, No. 2 (May 1996):131–46.

MARULLO, SAM. "The Functions and Dysfunctions of Preparations for Fighting Nuclear War." *Sociological Focus.* Vol. 20, No. 2 (April 1987):135–53.

MARX, KARL. Excerpt from "A Contribution to the Critique of Political Economy" (1859). In KARL MARX and FRIEDRICH ENGELS, *Marx and Engels: Basic Writings on Politics and Philosophy.* LEWIS S. FEURER, ed. Garden City, N.Y.: Anchor Books, 1959:42–46.

———. *Karl Marx: Early Writings.* T. B. BOTTOMORE, ed. New York: McGraw-Hill, 1964; orig. 1848.

———. *Capital.* FRIEDRICH ENGELS, ed. New York: International Publishers, 1967; orig. 1867.

MARX, KARL, and FRIEDRICH ENGELS. "Manifesto of the Communist Party." In ROBERT C. TUCKER, ed., *The Marx-Engels Reader.* New York: Norton, 1972:331–62; orig. 1848.

———. *The Marx-Engels Reader.* 2nd ed. ROBERT C. TUCKER, ed. New York: Norton, 1978; orig. 1859.

MASON, DAVID S. "Fairness Matters: Equity and the Transition to Democracy." *World Policy Journal.* Vol. 20, No. 4 (Winter 2003). [Online] Available February 21, 2008, at http://www.worldpolicy.org/journal/articles/wpj03-4/mason.html

MASSEY, DOUGLAS S., and NANCY A. DENTON. "Hypersegregation in U.S. Metropolitan Areas: Black and Hispanic Segregation along Five Dimensions." *Demography.* Vol. 26, No. 3 (August 1989):373–91.

MATLOFF, JUDITH. "Nomadic 'Blue Men' of the Desert Try to Go Roam Again." *Christian Science Monitor* (September 9, 1997):7.

MATTHIESSEN, PETER. *Indian Country.* New York: Viking Press, 1984.

MAUER, MARC. *The Crisis of the Young African American Male and the Criminal Justice System.* Report prepared for U.S. Commission on Civil Rights. Washington, D.C., April 15–16, 1999. [Online] Available June 5, 2005, at http://www.sentencingproject.org/pdfs/5022.pdf

MAURO, TONY. "Ruling Likely Will Add Fuel to Already Divisive Debate." *USA Today* (January 7, 1997):1A, 2A.

MAUSS, ARMAND L. *Social Problems of Social Movements.* Philadelphia: Lippincott, 1975.

MAYO, KATHERINE. *Mother India.* New York: Harcourt, Brace, 1927.

MCADAM, DOUG. *Political Process and the Development of Black Insurgency, 1930–1970.* Chicago: University of Chicago Press, 1982.

———. "Tactical Innovation and the Pace of Insurgency." *American Sociological Review.* Vol. 48, No. 6 (December 1983):735–54.

———. *Freedom Summer.* New York: Oxford University Press, 1988.

———. "The Biographical Consequences of Activism." *American Sociological Review.* Vol. 54, No. 5 (October 1989):744–60.

———. "Gender as a Mediator of the Activist Experience: The Case of Freedom Summer." *American Journal of Sociology.* Vol. 97, No. 5 (March 1992):1211–40.

McAdam, Doug, John D. McCarthy, and Mayer N. Zald. "Social Movements." In Neil J. Smelser, ed., *Handbook of Sociology.* Newbury Park, Calif.: Sage, 1988:695–737.

———. "Introduction: Opportunities, Mobilizing Structures, and Framing Processes—Toward a Synthetic, Comparative Perspective on Social Movements." In Doug McAdam, John D. McCarthy, and Mayer N. Zald, eds., *Comparative Perspectives on Social Movements: Political Opportunities, Mobilizing Structures, and Cultural Framings.* New York: Cambridge University Press, 1996:1–19.

McCarthy, John D., and Mayer N. Zald. "Resource Mobilization and Social Movements: A Partial Theory." *American Journal of Sociology.* Vol. 82, No. 6 (May 1977):1212–41.

McCartney, Scott. "U.S. Mulls Raising Pilot Retirement Age." *Baltimore Sun* (February 28, 2005). [Online] Available April 16, 2005, at http://www.Baltimoresun.com

McClay, William M. "Secularism, American Style." *Society.* Vol. 44, No. 6 (2007):160–63.

McConnell, Tristan. "Tuareg Nomads Set to Intensify Rebellion in Niger." *Christian Science Monitor* (October 11, 2007). [Online] Available October 13, 2008, at http://www.csmonitor.com/2007/1011/p12s01-woaf.html

McDonald's Corporation. *2007 Annual Report.* April 2008. [Online] Available November 3, 2008, at http://216.139.227.101/interactive/mcd2007

McDowell, Margaret A., Cheryl D. Fryar, Cynthia L. Ogden, and Katherine M. Flegal. "Anthropomorphic Reference Data for Children and Adults: United States, 2003–2006." *National Health Statistic Reports,* No. 10 (October 22, 2008). [Online] Available April 21, 2009, at http://www.cdc.gov/nchs/data/nhsr/nhsr010.pdf

McGeehan, Patrick. "Adding to Recession's Pain, Thousands to Lose Job Benefits." *New York Times* (January 11, 2009). [Online] Available January 12, 2009, at http://www.nytimes.com/2009/01/12/nyregion/12benefits.html.

McGirk, Tim. "Crossing the Lines." *Time* (February 27, 2006):36–43.

McGuire, Meredith B. *Religion: The Social Context.* 2nd ed. Belmont, Calif.: Wadsworth, 1987.

McKee, Victoria. "Blue Blood and the Color of Money." *New York Times* (June 9, 1996): 49–50.

McKibben, Bill. *Deep Economy: The Wealth of Communities and the Durable Future.* New York: Times Books, 2007.

McLanahan, Sara. "Life without Father: What Happens to the Children?" *Contexts.* Vol. 1, No. 1 (Spring 2002):35–44.

McLeod, Jane D., and Michael J. Shanahan. "Poverty, Parenting, and Children's Mental Health." *American Sociological Review.* Vol. 58, No. 3 (June 1993):351–66.

McLeod, Jay. *Ain't No Makin' It: Aspirations and Attainment in a Low-Income Neighborhood.* Boulder, Colo.: Westview Press, 1995.

McPhail, Clark. *The Myth of the Maddening Crowd.* New York: Aldine, 1991.

McPhail, Clark, and Ronald T. Wohlstein. "Individual and Collective Behaviors within Gatherings, Demonstrations, and Riots." *Annual Review of Sociology.* Vol. 9. Palo Alto, Calif.: Annual Reviews, 1983:579–600.

McRoberts, Omar M. *Streets of Glory: Church and Community in a Black Urban Neighborhood.* Chicago: University of Chicago Press, 2003.

McVeigh, Rory, Michael Welch, and Thoroddur Bjarnason. "Hate Crime Reporting as a Successful Social Movement Outcome." *American Sociological Review.* Vol. 68 (2003): 843–67.

Mead, George Herbert. *Mind, Self, and Society.* Charles W. Morris, ed. Chicago: University of Chicago Press, 1962; orig. 1934.

Mead, Margaret. *Sex and Temperament in Three Primitive Societies.* New York: Morrow, 1963; orig. 1935.

Meadows, Donella H., Dennis L. Meadows, Jorgan Randers, and William W. Behrens III. *The Limits to Growth: A Report on the Club of Rome's Project on the Predicament of Mankind.* New York: Universe, 1972.

Meltzer, Bernard N. "Mead's Social Psychology." In Jerome G. Manis and Bernard N. Meltzer, eds., *Symbolic Interaction: A Reader in Social Psychology.* 3rd ed. Needham Heights, Mass.: Allyn & Bacon, 1978.

Melucci, Alberto. *Nomads of the Present: Social Movements and Individual Needs in Contemporary Society.* Philadelphia: Temple University Press, 1989.

Merton, Robert K. "Social Structure and Anomie." *American Sociological Review.* Vol. 3, No. 6 (October 1938):672–82.

———. *Social Theory and Social Structure.* New York: Free Press, 1968.

Metz, Michael E., and Michael H. Miner. "Psychosexual and Psychosocial Aspects of Male Aging and Sexual Health." *Canadian Journal of Human Sexuality.* Vol. 7, No. 3 (Summer 1998):245–60.

Metzger, Kurt. "Cities and Race." *Society.* Vol. 39, No. 1 (December 2001):2.

Michels, Robert. *Political Parties.* Glencoe, Ill.: Free Press, 1949; orig. 1911.

Milbrath, Lester W. *Envisioning a Sustainable Society: Learning Our Way Out.* Albany: State University of New York Press, 1989.

Milgram, Stanley. "Behavioral Study of Obedience." *Journal of Abnormal and Social Psychology.* Vol. 67, No. 4 (1963):371–78.

———. "Group Pressure and Action against a Person." *Journal of Abnormal and Social Psychology.* Vol. 69, No. 2 (August 1964):137–43.

———. "Some Conditions of Obedience and Disobedience to Authority." *Human Relations.* Vol. 18, No. 1 (February 1965):57–76.

———. "The Small World Problem." *Psychology Today* (May 1967):60–67.

Miller, Alan S., and Rodney Stark. "Gender and Religiousness: Can Socialization Explanations Be Saved?" *American Journal of Sociology.* Vol. 107, No. 6 (May 2002): 1399–1423.

Miller, Arthur G. *The Obedience Experiments: A Case of Controversy in Social Science.* New York: Praeger, 1986.

Miller, David L. *Introduction to Collective Behavior.* Belmont, Calif.: Wadsworth, 1985.

Miller, Frederick D. "The End of SDS and the Emergence of Weatherman: Demise through Success." In Jo Freeman, ed., *Social Movements of the Sixties and Seventies.* White Plains, N.Y.: Longman, 1983:279–97.

Miller, Matthew, and Duncan Greenberg, eds. "The *Forbes* 400." September 17, 2008. [Online] Available December 8, 2008, at http://www.forbes.com/lists/2008/09/16/richest-american-billionaires-lists-400list08-cx_mm_dg_0917richintro.html

Miller, Matthew, and Peter Newcomb, eds. "The *Forbes* 400." *Forbes* (Special issue, October 10, 2005).

Miller, Terry, and Kim Holmes, eds. "15th Annual Index of Economic Freedom." January 15, 2009. [Online] Available January 19, 2009, at http://www.heritage.org/index/Default.aspx

Miller, Walter B. "Lower-Class Culture as a Generating Milieu of Gang Delinquency" (1958). In Marvin E. Wolfgang, Leonard Savitz, and Norman Johnston, eds., *The Sociology of Crime and Delinquency.* 2nd ed. New York: Wiley, 1970:351–63.

Miller, William J., and Rick A. Matthews. "Youth Employment, Differential Association, and Juvenile Delinquency." *Sociological Focus.* Vol. 34, No. 3 (August 2001):251–68.

Mills, C. Wright. *The Power Elite.* New York: Oxford University Press, 1956.

———. *The Sociological Imagination.* New York: Oxford University Press, 1959.

Miniño, Arialdi M., Melonie P. Heron, and Betty L. Smith. "Deaths: Preliminary Data for 2004." *National Vital Statistics Reports.* Vol. 54, No. 19 (June 28, 2006).

Miracle, Tina S., Andrew W. Miracle, and Roy F. Baumeister. *Human Sexuality: Meeting Your Basic Needs.* Upper Saddle River, N.J.: Prentice Hall, 2003.

Miringoff, Marc, and Marque-Luisa Miringoff. "The Social Health of the Nation." *Economist.* Vol. 352, No. 8128 (July 17, 1999):suppl. 6–7.

Mishel, Lawrence, Jared Bernstein, and Sylvia Allegretto. *The State of Working America, 2008.* Ithaca, N.Y.: Cornell University Press, 2009.

Mitchell, Chris. "The Killing of Murder." *New York Magazine* (January 8, 2008). [Online] Available February 9, 2008, at http://nymag.com/news/features/crime/2008/42603

Moen, Phyllis, Donna Dempster-McClain, and Robin M. Williams. "Successful Aging: A Life-Course Perspective on Women's Multiple Roles and Health." *American Journal of Sociology.* Vol. 97, No. 6 (May 1992):1612–38.

Moghadam, Valentine M. "The 'Feminization of Poverty' and Women's Human Rights." July 2005. [Online] Available December 4, 2008, at http://portal.unesco.org/shs/en/files/8282/11313736811Feminization_of_Poverty.pdf/Feminization%2Bof%2BPoverty.pdf

Molotch, Harvey. "The City as a Growth Machine." *American Journal of Sociology.* Vol. 82, No. 2 (September 1976):309–33.

Montaigne, Fen. "Russia Rising." *National Geographic.* Vol. 200, No. 5 (September 2001): 2–31.

Moore, Gwen, et al. "Elite Interlocks in Three U.S. Sectors: Nonprofit, Corporate, and Government." *Social Science Quarterly.* Vol. 83, No. 3 (September 2002):726–44.

Moore, Wilbert E. "Modernization as Rationalization: Processes and Restraints." In Manning Nash, ed., *Essays on Economic Development and Cultural Change in Honor of Bert F. Hoselitz.* Chicago: University of Chicago Press, 1977:29–42.

———. *World Modernization: The Limits of Convergence.* New York: Elsevier, 1979.

Morell, Virginia. "Minds of Their Own: Animals Are Smarter than You Think." *National Geographic.* Vol. 213, No. 3 (March 2008):36–61.

Morris, Aldon. "Black Southern Sit-In Movement: An Analysis of Internal Organization." *American Sociological Review.* Vol. 46, No. 6 (December 1981):744–67.

Morris, Dick and Eileen McGann. *Outrage. How Illegal Immigration, the United Nations, Congressional Ripoffs, Student Loan Overcharges, Tobacco Companies, Trade Protection, and Drug Companies Are Ripping Us Off…And What to Do About It.* New York: Harper-Collins, 2007.

Morrison, Denton E. "Some Notes toward Theory on Relative Deprivation, Social Movements, and Social Change." In Louis E. Genevie, ed., *Collective Behavior and Social Movements.* Itasca, Ill.: Peacock, 1978:202–9.

Morse, Jodie. "A Victory for Vouchers." *Time* (July 8, 2002):32–34.

Mosher, William D., Anjani Chandra, and Jo Jones. "Sexual Behavior and Selected Health Measures: Men and Women, 15–44 Years of Age, United States, 2002." September 15, 2005. [Online] Available November 8, 2008, at http://www.cdc.gov/nchs/data/ad/ad362.pdf

Mouw, Ted. "Job Relocation and the Racial Gap in Unemployment in Detroit and Chicago, 1980 to 1990." *American Sociological Review.* Vol. 65, No. 5 (October 2000):730–53.

"Much Ado about Evolution." *Time* (November 21, 2005):23.

Muller, Chandra, and Christopher G. Ellison. "Religious Involvement, Social Capital, and Adolescents' Academic Progress: Evidence from the National Education Longitudinal Study of 1988." *Sociological Focus.* Vol. 34, No. 2 (May 2001):155–83.

Mumford, Lewis. *The City in History: Its Origins, Its Transformations, and Its Prospects.* New York: Harcourt, Brace & World, 1961.

Munroe, Susan. "Abolition of Capital Punishment in Canada." About.com: Canada Online. July 2007. [Online] Available April 16, 2008, at http://canadaonline.about.com/od/crime/a/abolitioncappun.htm

Murdock, George Peter. "Comparative Data on the Division of Labor by Sex." *Social Forces.* Vol. 15, No. 4 (May 1937):551–53.

———. "The Common Denominator of Cultures." In Ralph Linton, ed., *The Science of Man in World Crisis.* New York: Columbia University Press, 1945:123–42.

———. *Social Structure.* New York: Free Press, 1965; orig. 1949.

Murphy, John. "Some Rise but Most Sink in Soweto's Sea of Slums." *Baltimore Sun* (October 6, 2002). [Online] Available November 15, 2008, at http://www.baltimoresun.com/news/health/balte.soweto06oct06,0,1833961.story

Murray, Stephen O., and Will Roscoe, eds. *Boy-Wives and Female-Husbands: Studies of African Homosexualities.* New York: St. Martin's Press, 1998.

MYERS, DAVID G. *The American Paradox: Spiritual Hunger in an Age of Plenty.* New Haven, Conn.: Yale University Press, 2000.

MYERS, NORMAN. "Humanity's Growth." In SIR EDMUND HILLARY, ed., *Ecology 2000: The Changing Face of the Earth.* New York: Beaufort Books, 1984a:16–35.

———. "The Mega-Extinction of Animals and Plants." In SIR EDMUND HILLARY, ed., *Ecology 2000: The Changing Face of the Earth.* New York: Beaufort Books, 1984b:82–107.

MYERS, SHEILA, and HAROLD G. GRASMICK. "The Social Rights and Responsibilities of Pregnant Women: An Application of Parsons' Sick Role Model." Paper presented to the Southwestern Sociological Association, Little Rock, Ark., March 1989.

MYRDAL, GUNNAR. *An American Dilemma: The Negro Problem and Modern Democracy.* New York: Harper Bros., 1944.

NATIONAL ALLIANCE FOR CAREGIVING and AARP. "Caregiving in the U.S." 2004. [Online] Available January 18, 2009, at http://www.caregiving.org/data/04finalreport.pdf

NATIONAL ASSESSMENT OF EDUCATIONAL PROGRESS. "The Nation's Report Card." 2007. [Online] Available August 11, 2008, at http://nationsreportcard.gov

NATIONAL ATLAS OF THE UNITED STATES. "Map Maker: Per Capita Personal Income, 2003." July 2007. [Online] Available September 14, 2007, at http://www.nationalatlas.gov/natlas/Natlasstart.asp

NATIONAL CENTER FOR EDUCATION STATISTICS. *Digest of Education Statistics.* "2007 Tables." March 2008. [Online] Available May 12, 2008, at http://nces.ed.gov/programs/digest/d07/tables_1.asp

NATIONAL CENTER FOR HEALTH STATISTICS. "Health Data Interactive." 2009. [Online] Available January 8, 2009, at http://www.cdc.gov/nchs/hdi.htm

NATIONAL CENTER ON ELDER ABUSE. *Elder Abuse Prevalence and Incidence.* Washington, D.C.: U.S. Government Printing Office, 2005. [Online] Available August 23, 2007, at http://www.elderabusecenter.org/pdf/publication/FinalStatistics050331.pdf

NATIONAL COALITION FOR THE HOMELESS. "How Many People Experience Homelessness?" NCH Fact Sheet No. 2. August 2007. [Online] Available April 30, 2008, at http://www.nationalhomeless.org/publications/facts/How_Many.pdf

NATIONAL COALITION OF ANTI-VIOLENCE PROGRAMS. *Annual Report, 2007.* 2007. [Online] Available November 12, 2008, at http://www.ncavp.org/common/document_files/Reports/2

NATIONAL COMMISSION ON EXCELLENCE IN EDUCATION. *A Nation at Risk.* Washington, D.C.: U.S. Government Printing Office, 1983.

NATIONAL CONFERENCE OF STATE LEGISLATURES. "Same-Sex Marriage, Civil Unions, and Domestic Partnerships." May 2008a. [Online] Available November 9, 2008, at http://www.ncsl.org/programs/cyf/samesex.htm

———. "State Laws regarding Marriages between First Cousins." 2008b. [Online] Available November 6, 2008, at http://www.ncsl.org/programs/cyf/cousins.htm

———. "State Traffic Safety Legislation." 2008c. [Online] Available November 12, 2008, at http://www.ncsl.org/programs/transportation/trafsafdb.cfm?action=billresults

NATIONAL GOVERNORS ASSOCIATION. "Governors Database." 2008. [Online] Available April 21, 2009, at http://www.nga.org/portal/site/nga/menuitem.216dbea7c618ef3f8a278110501010a0

NATIONAL HIGHWAY TRAFFIC SAFETY ADMINISTRATION. "2007 Traffic Safety Annual Assessment." August 2008. [Online] Available February 15, 2009, at http://www-nrd.nhtsa.dot.gov/Pubs/811016.PDF

NATIONAL VIRTUAL TRANSLATION CENTER. "Languages Spoken in the U.S." 2007. [Online] Available November 20, 2008, at http://www.nvtc.gov/lotw/months/november/USlanguages.html

NAVARRO, MIREYA. "Puerto Rican Presence Wanes in New York." *New York Times* (February 28, 2000):A1, A20.

———. "For Younger Latinas, a Shift to Smaller Families." *New York Times* (December 5, 2004). [Online] Available April 30, 2005, at http://www.researchnavigator.com

NELSON, JOEL I. "Work and Benefits: The Multiple Problems of Service Sector Employment." *Social Problems.* Vol. 42, No. 2 (May 1994):240–55.

NESSMAN, RAVI. "Stampede at Soccer Match Kills 47." [Online]. Available April 11, 2001, at http://www.news.yahoo.com

NEUGARTEN, BERNICE L. "Grow Old with Me. The Best Is Yet to Be." *Psychology Today* (December 1971):45–48, 79, 81.

———. "Personality and Aging." In JAMES E. BIRREN and K. WARNER SCHAIE, eds., *Handbook of the Psychology of Aging.* New York: Van Nostrand Reinhold, 1977:626–49.

NEUHOUSER, KEVIN. "The Radicalization of the Brazilian Catholic Church in Comparative Perspective." *American Sociological Review.* Vol. 54, No. 2 (April 1989):233–44.

NEWMAN, KATHERINE S. *Declining Fortunes: The Withering of the American Dream.* New York: Basic Books, 1993.

NEWMAN, WILLIAM M. *American Pluralism: A Study of Minority Groups and Social Theory.* New York: Harper & Row, 1973.

NEWPORT, FRANK. "Americans Turn More Negative toward Same-Sex Marriage." Gallup News Service, April 2005. [Online] Available July 3, 2008, at http://www.gallup.com/poll/15889/Americans-Turn-More-Negative-Toward-SameSex-Marriage.aspx

NICHOLSON, NIGEL. "Evolved to Chat: The New Word on Gossip." *Psychology Today* (May/June 2001):41–45.

NIELSEN MEDIA RESEARCH. "Nielsen Reports TV, Internet, and Mobile Usage among Americans." July 8, 2008a. [Online] Available October 27, 2008, at http://www.nielsenmedia.com/nc/portal/site/Public/menuitem.55dc65b4a7d5adff3f65936147a062a0/?allRmCB=on&newSearch=yes&vgnextoid=fe63c9769fcfa110VgnVCM100000ac0a260aRCRD&searchBox=website

———. "National Universe Estimates." January 1, 2008b. [Online] Available April 21, 2009, at http://www.nielsenmedia.com/nc/nmr_static/docs/2008_FINAL_National_UEs_Mkt_Brks%20_Pers.xls

NIESSE, MARK. "Some Bars Pan Hawaii's Tough Smoking Ban." [Online] Available February 19, 2007, at http://news.yahoo.com

NISBET, ROBERT A. *The Sociological Tradition.* New York: Basic Books, 1966.

———. *The Quest for Community.* New York: Oxford University Press, 1969.

NOCK, STEVEN L., JAMES D. WRIGHT, and LAURA SANCHEZ. "America's Divorce Problem." *Society.* Vol. 36, No. 4 (May/June 1999):43–52.

NOLAN, PATRICK, and GERHARD E. LENSKI. *Human Societies: An Introduction to Macrosociology.* 10th ed. Boulder, Colo.: Paradigm, 2007.

NORBECK, EDWARD. "Class Structure." In *Kodansha Encyclopedia of Japan.* Tokyo: Kodansha, 1983:322–25.

NORC. *General Social Surveys, 1972–2006: Cumulative Codebook.* Chicago: National Opinion Research Center, 2007.

———. *General Social Surveys, 1972–2007: Cumulative Codebook.* Chicago: National Opinion Research Center, 2008.

NOVAK, VIVECA. "The Cost of Poor Advice." *Time* (July 5, 1999):38.

NULAND, SHERWIN B. "The Hazards of Hospitalization." *Wall Street Journal* (December 2, 1999):A22.

OAKES, JEANNIE. "Classroom Social Relationships: Exploring the Bowles and Gintis Hypothesis." *Sociology of Education.* Vol. 55, No. 4 (October 1982):197–212.

———. *Keeping Track: How High Schools Structure Inequality.* New Haven, Conn.: Yale University Press, 1985.

OBAMA, BARACK. *The Audacity of Hope: Thoughts on Reclaiming the American Dream.* New York: Random House, 2007.

OBERSCHALL, ANTHONY. *Social Conflict and Social Movements.* Englewood Cliffs, N.J.: Prentice Hall, 1973.

OGAWA, NAOHIRO, and ROBERT D. RETHERFORD. "Shifting Costs of Caring for the Elderly back to Families in Japan: Will It Work?" *Population and Development Review.* Vol. 23, No. 1 (March 1997):59–95.

OGBURN, WILLIAM F. *On Culture and Social Change.* Chicago: University of Chicago Press, 1964.

OGDEN, RUSSEL D. "Nonphysician-Assisted Suicide: The Technological Imperative of the Deathing Counterculture." *Death Studies.* Vol. 25, No. 5 (July 2001):387–402.

O'HARE, WILLIAM P., WILLIAM H. FREY, and DAN FOST. "Asians in the Suburbs." *American Demographics.* Vol. 16, No. 9 (May 1994):32–38.

O'HARROW, ROBERT, JR. "ID Theft Scam Hits D.C. Area Residents." [Online] Available February 21, 2005, at http://news.yahoo.com

OHLEMACHER, STEPHEN. "Official Count: 754,000 People Believed Homeless in U.S." *Seattle Times* (February 28, 2007). [Online] Available March 9, 2007, at http://seattletimes.nwsource.com/html/nationworld/2003592874_homeless28.html

———. "Obama's Victory May Show the Way to Win in Future." *USA Today* (November 9, 2008). [Online] Available January 13, 2009, at http://www.usatoday.com/news/politics/2008-11-08-1164297038_x.htm

OLSON, ELIZABETH. "Community Colleges Want You." *New York Times* (October 24, 2006):E2.

OLZAK, SUSAN. "Labor Unrest, Immigration, and Ethnic Conflict in Urban America, 1880–1914." *American Journal of Sociology.* Vol. 94, No. 6 (May 1989):1303–33.

OLZAK, SUSAN, and ELIZABETH WEST. "Ethnic Conflict and the Rise and Fall of Ethnic Newspapers." *American Sociological Review.* Vol. 56, No. 4 (August 1991):458–74.

ONISHI, NORIMITSU. "In a Graying Japan, Lower Shelves and Wider Aisles." *New York Times* (September 4, 2006): A4.

"Online Privacy: It's Time for Rules in Wonderland." *Business Week* (March 20, 2000):82–96.

ORGANISATION FOR ECONOMIC CO-OPERATION AND DEVELOPMENT. *Society at a Glance: OECD Social Indicators.* Paris: OECD, 2007.

———. "Education at a Glance: 2008 OECD Indicators." September 9, 2008a. [Online] Available October 2, 2008, at http://www.oecd.org/document/9/0,3343,en_2649_39263238_41266761_1_1_1_1,00.html

———. "OECD Factbook, 2008: Economic, Environmental, and Social Statistics." 2008b. [Online] Available February 1, 2009, at http://oberon.sourceoecd.org/vl=7054771/cl=25/nw=1/rpsv/factbook/090101.htm

———. "Statistical Extracts: Society at a Glance, 2008." 2008c. [Online] Available January 19, 2009, at http://lysander.sourceoecd.org/vl=1123806/cl=27/nw=1/rpsv/society_glance/eq5-1.htm

ORHANT, MELANIE. "Human Trafficking Exposed." *Population Today.* Vol. 30, No. 1 (January 2002):1, 4.

ORLANSKY, MICHAEL D., and WILLIAM L. HEWARD. *Voices: Interviews with Handicapped People.* Columbus, Ohio: Merrill, 1981.

OSTRANDER, SUSAN A. "Upper-Class Women: The Feminine Side of Privilege." *Qualitative Sociology.* Vol. 3, No. 1 (Spring 1980):23–44.

———. *Women of the Upper Class.* Philadelphia: Temple University Press, 1984.

OUCHI, WILLIAM. *Theory Z: How American Business Can Meet the Japanese Challenge.* Reading, Mass.: Addison-Wesley, 1981.

"Our Cheating Hearts." Editorial. *U.S. News & World Report* (May 6, 2002):4.

OVADIA, SETH. "Race, Class, and Gender Differences in High School Seniors' Values: Applying Intersection Theory in Empirical Analysis." *Social Science Quarterly.* Vol. 82, No. 2 (June 2001):341–56.

OWEN, CAROLYN A., HOWARD C. ELSNER, and THOMAS R. MCFAUL. "A Half-Century of Social Distance Research: National Replication of the Bogardus Studies." *Sociology and Social Research.* Vol. 66, No. 1 (1977):80–98.

PACKARD, MARK. Personal communication (2002).

PACKER, GEORGE. "Smart-Mobbing the War." *New York Times Magazine* (March 9, 2003):46–49.

PAKULSKI, JAN. "Mass Social Movements and Social Class." *International Sociology.* Vol. 8, No. 2 (June 1993):131–58.

PALMORE, ERDMAN. "Predictors of Successful Aging." *Gerontologist*. Vol. 19, No. 5 (October 1979):427–31.

PAMPEL, FRED C. "Socioeconomic Distinction, Cultural Tastes, and Cigarette Smoking." *Social Science Quarterly*. Vol. 87, No. 1 (March 2006):19–35.

PARINI, JAY. "The Meaning of Emeritus." *Dartmouth Alumni Magazine* (July/August 2001): 40–43.

PARIS, PETER J. "The Religious World of African Americans." In JACOB NEUSNER, ed. *World Religions in America: An Introduction*. Revised and expanded ed. Louisville, Ky.: Westminster/ John Knox, 2000:48–65.

PARK, ROBERT E. *Race and Culture*. Glencoe, Ill.: Free Press, 1950.

PARKER-POPE, TARA. "Love, Sex, and the Changing Landscape of Infidelity." *New York Times* (October 27, 2008). [Online]: Available April 22, 2009, at http://www.nytimes.com/2008/ 10/28/health/28well.html?_r=1

PARRILLO, VINCENT N. "Diversity in America: A Sociohistorical Analysis." *Sociological Forum*. Vol. 9, No. 4 (December 1994):42–45.

PARRILLO, VINCENT, and CHRISTOPHER DONOGHUE. "Updating the Bogardus Social Distance Studies: A New National Survey." *Social Science Journal*. Vol. 42, No. 2 (April 2005): 257–71.

PARSONS, TALCOTT. "Age and Sex in the Social Structure of the United States." *American Sociological Review*. Vol. 7, No. 4 (August 1942):604–16.

———. *The Social System*. New York: Free Press, 1951.

———. *Essays in Sociological Theory*. New York: Free Press, 1954.

———. *Societies: Evolutionary and Comparative Perspectives*. Englewood Cliffs, N.J.: Prentice Hall, 1966.

PASSY, FLORENCE, and MARCO GIUGNI. "Social Networks and Individual Perceptions: Explaining Differential Participation in Social Movements." *Sociological Forum*. Vol. 16, No. 1 (March 2001):123–53.

PATTERSON, ELISSA F. "The Philosophy and Physics of Holistic Health Care: Spiritual Healing as a Workable Interpretation." *Journal of Advanced Nursing*. Vol. 27, No. 2 (February 1998):287–93.

PATTILLO, MARY. "Church Culture as a Strategy of Action in the Black Community." *American Sociological Review*. Vol. 63, No. 6 (December 1998):767–84.

———. *Black on the Block: The Politics of Race and Class in the City*. Chicago: University of Chicago Press, 2007.

PAXTON, PAMELA, MELANIE M. HUGHES, and JENNIFER L. GREEN. "The International Women's Movement and Women's Political Participation, 1893–2003." *American Sociological Review*. Vol. 71, No. 6 (December 2006):898–920.

PEAR, ROBERT, and ERIK ECKHOLM. "When Healers Are Entrepreneurs: A Debate over Costs and Ethics." *New York Times* (June 2, 1991):1, 17.

PEARSON, DAVID E. "Post-Mass Culture." *Society*. Vol. 30, No. 5 (July/August 1993):17–22.

———. "Community and Sociology." *Society*. Vol. 32, No. 5 (July/August 1995):44–50.

PEASE, JOHN, and LEE MARTIN. "Want Ads and Jobs for the Poor: A Glaring Mismatch." *Sociological Forum*. Vol. 12, No. 4 (December 1997):545–64.

PEDERSON, DANIEL, VERN E. SMITH, and JERRY ADLER. "Sprawling, Sprawling . . ." *Newsweek* (July 19, 1999):23–27.

PERLMUTTER, PHILIP. "Minority Group Prejudice." *Society*. Vol. 39, No. 3 (March/April 2002):59–65.

PERRUCCI, ROBERT. "Inventing Social Justice: SSSP and the Twenty-First Century." *Social Problems*. Vol. 48, No. 2 (May 2001):159–67.

PERRY, ALEX. "South Africa Looks for a Leader." *Time* (April 27, 2009):38–41.

PESSEN, EDWARD. *Riches, Class, and Power: America before the Civil War*. New Brunswick, N.J.: Transaction, 1990.

Peters Atlas of the World. New York: Harper & Row, 1990.

PETERSEN, TROND, ISHAK SAPORTA, and MARC-DAVID L. SEIDEL. "Offering a Job: Meritocracy and Social Networks." *American Journal of Sociology*. Vol. 106, No. 3 (November 2000): 763–816.

PETERSON, PAUL E., and ELENA LLAUDET. "On the Public-Private School Achievement Debate." Paper prepared for the annual meetings of the American Political Science Association, August 2006. [Online] Available July 15, 2008, at http://www.hks.harvard. edu/pepg/PDF/Papers/PEPG06-02-PetersonLlaudet.pdf

PETERSON, SCOTT. "Women Live on Own Terms behind the Veil." *Christian Science Monitor* (July 31, 1996):1, 10.

PEW FORUM. "A Religious Portrait of African Americans." January 30, 2009. [Online] Available March 8, 2009, at http://pewforum.org/docs/?DocID=389#a

PEW RESEARCH CENTER. "As Marriage and Parenthood Drift Apart, Public Is Concerned about Social Impact." July 1, 2007a. [Online] Available January 31, 2009, at http:// pewsocialtrends.org/pubs/542/modern-marriage

———. "Muslim Americans: Middle Class and Mostly Mainstream." May 22, 2007b. [Online] Available May 19, 2008, at http://pewresearch.org/assets/pdf/muslim-americans.pdf

———. "Social and Demographic Trends: Reports." 2008. [Online] Available July 3, 2008, at http://pewsocialtrends.org/pubs

———. "Independents Take Center Stage in Obama Era: Trends in Political Values and Core Attitudes, 1987–2009." May 21, 2009. [Online] Available June 18, 2009, at http:// people-press.org/report/517/political-values-and-core-attitudes)

PHILADELPHIA, DESA. "Rookie Teacher, Age 50." *Time* (April 9, 2001):66–68.

———. "Tastier, Plusher—and Fast." *Time* (September 30, 2002):57.

PHILLIPS, MELANIE. "What about the Overclass?" *Public Interest* (Fall 2001):38–43.

PICHARDO, NELSON A. "The Power Elite and Elite-Driven Countermovements: The Associated Farmers of California during the 1930s." *Sociological Forum*. Vol. 10, No. 1 (March 1995):21–49.

PICKLER, NEDRA, and LIZ SIDOTI. "Campaigns Unleash Massive Get-Out-Vote Drives." *Yahoo News* (November 2, 2008). [Online] Available November 2, 2008, at http://news.yahoo .com/s/ap/20081102/ap_on_el_pr/campaign_rdp

PINCHOT, GIFFORD, and ELIZABETH PINCHOT. *The End of Bureaucracy and the Rise of the Intelligent Organization*. San Francisco: Berrett-Koehler, 1993.

PINHEY, THOMAS K., DONALD H. RUBINSTEIN, and RICHARD S. COLFAX. "Overweight and Happiness: The Reflected Self-Appraisal Hypothesis Reconsidered." *Social Science Quarterly*. Vol. 78, No. 3 (September 1997):747–55.

PINKER, STEVEN. *The Language Instinct*. New York: Morrow, 1994.

———. "Are Your Genes to Blame?" *Time* (January 20, 2003):98–100.

PIRANDELLO, LUIGI. "The Pleasure of Honesty" (1917). In *To Clothe the Naked and Two Other Plays*. New York: Dutton, 1962:143–98.

PITTS, LEONARD, JR. "When a Win Sparks a Riot." *Philadelphia Inquirer* (June 26, 2000):A11.

PIVEN, FRANCES FOX, and RICHARD A. CLOWARD. *Poor People's Movements: Why They Succeed, How They Fail*. New York: Pantheon Books, 1977.

"Places Where the System Broke Down." *Time* (September 19, 2005):34–41.

PLEIS, JOHN R., and MARGARET LETHBRIDGE-ÇEJKU. *Summary Health Statistics for U.S. Adults: National Health Interview Survey, 2005*. Vital and Health Statistics, Series 10, No. 232. Hyattsville, Md.: National Center for Health Statistics, 2006.

PODOLNY, JOEL M., and JAMES N. BARON. "Resources and Relationships: Social Networks and Mobility in the Workplace." *American Sociological Review*. Vol. 62, No. 5 (October 1997): 673–93.

POLSBY, NELSON W. "Three Problems in the Analysis of Community Power." *American Sociological Review*. Vol. 24, No. 6 (December 1959):796–803.

POPENOE, DAVID. "Family Decline in the Swedish Welfare State." *Public Interest* (Winter 1991): 65–77.

———. "American Family Decline, 1960–1990: A Review and Appraisal." *Journal of Marriage and the Family*. Vol. 55, No. 3 (August 1993a):527–55.

———. "Parental Androgyny." *Society*. Vol. 30, No. 6 (September/October 1993b):5–11.

———. "Scandinavian Welfare." *Society*. Vol. 31, No. 6 (September/October, 1994):78–81.

———. "Can the Nuclear Family Be Revived?" *Society*. Vol. 36, No. 5 (July/August 1999):28–30.

POPENOE, DAVID, and BARBARA DAFOE WHITEHEAD. *Should We Live Together? What Young Adults Need to Know about Cohabitation before Marriage*. New Brunswick, N.J.: National Marriage Project, 1999.

POPULATION ACTION INTERNATIONAL. *People in the Balance: Population and Resources at the Turn of the Millennium*. Washington, D.C.: Population Action International, 2000.

POPULATION REFERENCE BUREAU. *2003 World Population Data Sheet*. Washington, D.C.: Population Reference Bureau, 2003.

———. *2006 World Population Data Sheet*. Washington, D.C.: Population Reference Bureau, 2006.

———. *2007 World Population Data Sheet*. Washington, D.C.: Population Reference Bureau, 2007.

———. *European Demographic Data Sheet, 2008*. Washington, D.C.: Population Reference Bureau, 2008a.

———. *World Population Data Sheet, 2008*. Washington, D.C.: Population Reference Bureau, 2008b.

———. "Datafinder." 2009. [Online] Available February 5, 2009, at http://www.prb.org/ DataFinder.aspx

———. *2009 World Population Data Sheet*. Washington, D.C.: Population Reference Bureau, 2009.

POPULATION REFERENCE BUREAU and AFRICAN POPULATION AND HEALTH RESEARCH CENTER. *Africa Population Data Sheet, 2008*. Washington, D.C., and Nairobi, Kenya: Population Reference Bureau and African Population and Health Research Center, 2008.

PORTER, EDUARDO. "Old, in the Way, and Hard at Work." *New York Times* (August 29, 2004). [Online] Available May 5, 2009, at http://www.nytimes.com/2004/08/29/weekinreview/ the-world-economic-strains-old-in-the-way-and-hard-at-work.html?sec=health&&n= Top%2FReference%2FTimes%20Topics%2FSubjects%2FL%2FLabor

———. "Study Finds Wealth Inequality Is Widening Worldwide." *New York Times* (December 6, 2006). [Online] Available April 22, 2009, at http://query.nytimes.com/gst/fullpage .html?res=9802E5DB1631F935A35751C1A9609C8B63&sec=&spon=&pagewanted=2

PORTES, ALEJANDRO, and LEIF JENSEN. "The Enclave and the Entrants: Patterns of Ethnic Enterprise in Miami before and after Mariel." *American Sociological Review*. Vol. 54, No. 6 (December 1989):929–49.

POTTER, DENA. "Fear of Dem Crackdown Leads to Boom in Gun Sales." November 8, 2008. [Online] Available April 22, 2009, at http://www.dailyamerican.com/articles/2009/04/ 20/business/business091.txt

POWELL, BILL. "Postcard: Dongguan." *Time* (December 15, 2008):4.

POWELL, CHRIS, and GEORGE E. C. PATON, eds. *Humor in Society: Resistance and Control*. New York: St. Martin's Press, 1988.

PRIMEGGIA, SALVATORE, and JOSEPH A. VARACALLI. "Southern Italian Comedy: Old to New World." In JOSEPH V. SCELSA, SALVATORE J. LA GUMINA, and LYDIO TOMASI, eds., *Italian Americans in Transition*. New York: American Italian Historical Association, 1990:241–52.

PROENGLISH. "English in the 50 States." 2009. [Online] Available April 22, 2009, at http:// www.proenglish.org/issues/offeng/states.html

PRYOR, JOHN H., ET AL. *The American Freshman: National Norms for Fall 2005*. Los Angeles: UCLA Higher Education Research Institute, 2005.

———. *The American Freshman: National Norms for Fall 2006*. Los Angeles: UCLA Higher Education Research Institute, 2006.

———. *The American Freshman: National Norms for Fall 2007*. Los Angeles: UCLA Higher Education Research Institute, 2007.

———. *The American Freshman: National Norms for Fall 2008*. Los Angeles: UCLA Higher Education Research Institute, 2008.

PUTKA, GARY. "SAT to Become a Better Gauge." *Wall Street Journal* (November 1, 1990):B1.

Pyle, Ralph E. "Trends in Religious Stratification: Have Religious Group Socioeconomic Distinctions Declined in Recent Decades?" *Sociology of Religion*. Vol. 67, No. 1 (Spring 2006):61–79.

Pyle, Ralph E., and Jerome R. Koch. "The Religious Affiliation of American Elites, 1930s to 1990s: A Note on the Pace of Disestablishment." *Sociological Focus*. Vol. 34, No. 2 (May 2001):125–37.

Quaid, Libby. "Study: Math Teachers One Chapter ahead of Students." *Yahoo News* (November 25, 2008). [Online] Available November 25, 2008, at http://news.yahoo.com/s/ap/20081125/ap_on_re_us/qualified_teachers

Quillian, Lincoln, and Devah Pager. "Black Neighbors, Higher Crime? The Role of Racial Stereotypes in Evaluations of Neighborhood Crime." *American Journal of Sociology*. Vol. 107, No. 3 (November 2001):717–67.

Quinney, Richard. *Class, State and Crime: On the Theory and Practice of Criminal Justice*. New York: McKay, 1977.

Rainforest Foundation. "Rainforest Facts and Figures." 2009. [Online] Available April 22, 2009, at http://www.rainforestfoundationuk.org/Rainforest_facts

Raley, R. Kelly, T. Elizabeth Durden, and Elizabeth Wildsmith. "Understanding Mexican-American Marriage Patterns Using a Life Course Approach." *Social Science Quarterly*. Vol. 85, No. 4 (December 2004):872–90.

Ramirez, Jessica. "Campaign 2008: The Big Picture." *Newsweek* (November 10, 2008). [Online] Available February 15, 2009, at http://www.newsweek.com/id/168269

Raphael, Ray. *The Men from the Boys: Rites of Passage in Male America*. Lincoln: University of Nebraska Press, 1988.

Reckless, Walter C., and Simon Dinitz. "Pioneering with Self-Concept as a Vulnerability Factor in Delinquency." *Journal of Criminal Law, Criminology, and Police Science*. Vol. 58, No. 4 (December 1967):515–23.

Rector, Robert. "America Has the World's Richest Poor People." *Wall Street Journal* (September 24, 1998):A18.

Research and Markets. "Prospects for the Textile and Garment Industry in Bangladesh." September 2008. [Online] Available April 18, 2009, at http://www.researchandmarkets.com/research/d5cd87

Reskin, Barbara F., and Debra Branch McBrier. "Why Not Ascription? Organizations' Employment of Male and Female Managers." *American Sociological Review*. Vol. 65, No. 2 (April 2000):210–33.

Richburg, Keith B. "School Privatization Plan Sputters." *Washington Post* (June 29, 2008). [Online] Available February 3, 2009, at http://www.boston.com/news/education/k_12/articles/2008/06/29/school_privatization_plan_sputters

Rideout, Victoria. "Entertainment Media." June 2007. [Online] Available October 27, 2008, at http://www.kff.org/entmedia/entmedia061907nr.cfm

Rideout, Victoria, Donald F. Roberts, and Ulla G. Foehr. "Generation M: Media in the Lives of 8–18-Year-Olds." March 2005. [Online] Available October 27, 2008, at http://www.kff.org/entmedia/upload/Executive-Summary-Generation-M-Media-in-the-Lives-of-8-18-Year-olds.pdf

Ridgeway, Cecilia L. *The Dynamics of Small Groups*. New York: St. Martin's Press, 1983.

Ridgeway, Cecilia L., and Lynn Smith-Lovin. "The Gender System and Interaction." *Annual Review of Sociology*. Vol. 25 (August 1999):191–216.

Riesman, David. *The Lonely Crowd: A Study of the Changing American Character*. New Haven, Conn.: Yale University Press, 1970; orig. 1950.

Rimer, Sara. "Blacks Carry Load of Care for Their Elderly." *New York Times* (March 15, 1998):1, 22.

Ripley, Amanda. "Can She Save Our Schools?" *Time* (December 8, 2008):36–44.

———. "The Moment." *Time* (February 2, 2009):17.

Ritzer, George. *The McDonaldization of Society: An Investigation into the Changing Character of Contemporary Social Life*. Thousand Oaks, Calif.: Pine Forge Press, 1993.

Ritzer, George, and David Walczak. *Working: Conflict and Change*. 4th ed. Englewood Cliffs, N.J.: Prentice Hall, 1990.

Robinson, Thomas N., et al. "Effects of Reducing Children's Television and Video Game Use on Aggressive Behavior." *Archives of Pediatrics and Adolescent Medicine*. Vol. 155, No. 1 (January 2001):17–23.

Roesch, Roberta. "Violent Families." *Parents*. Vol. 59, No. 9 (September 1984):74–76, 150–52.

Roethlisberger, F. J., and William J. Dickson. *Management and the Worker*. Cambridge, Mass.: Harvard University Press, 1939.

Rogers, Richard G., Rebecca Rosenblatt, Robert A. Hummer, and Patrick M. Krueger. "Black-White Differentials in Adult Homicide Mortality in the United States." *Social Science Quarterly*. Vol. 82, No. 3 (September 2001):435–52.

Romero, Francine Sanders, and Adrian Liserio. "Saving Open Spaces: Determinants of 1998 and 1999 'Antisprawl' Ballot Measures." *Social Science Quarterly*. Vol. 83, No. 1 (March 2002):341–52.

Rose, Fred. "Toward a Class-Cultural Theory of Social Movements: Reinterpreting New Social Movements." *Sociological Forum*. Vol. 12, No. 3 (September 1997):461–94.

Rose, Jerry D. *Outbreaks*. New York: Free Press, 1982.

Rosenbaum, Marc. "Americans' Views on Taxes." Report of an NPR/Kaiser Family Foundation/Kennedy School of Government poll. Lecture delivered at Kenyon College, Gambier, Ohio, April 23, 2003.

Rosenberg, Mica. "Mexican Transvestite Fiesta Rocks Indigenous Town." Reuters, November 23, 2008. [Online] Available June 15, 2009, at http://www.reuters.com/article/lifestyleMolt/idUSTRE4AM1PB20081123

Rosendahl, Mona. *Inside the Revolution: Everyday Life in Socialist Cuba*. Ithaca, N.Y.: Cornell University Press, 1997.

Rosenfeld, Michael J., and Byong-Soo Kim. "The Independence of Young Adults and the Rise of Interracial and Same-Sex Unions." *American Sociological Review*. Vol. 70, No. 4 (August 2005):541–62.

Rosenfeld, Richard. "Crime Decline in Context." *Contexts*. Vol. 1, No. 1 (Spring 2002):20–34.

Rosenthal, Elizabeth. "Canada's National Health Plan Gives Care to All, with Limits." *New York Times* (April 30, 1991):A1, A16.

Rosnow, Ralph L., and Gary Alan Fine. *Rumor and Gossip: The Social Psychology of Hearsay*. New York: Elsevier, 1976.

Rossi, Alice S. "Gender and Parenthood." In Alice S. Rossi, ed., *Gender and the Life Course*. New York: Aldine, 1985:161–91.

Rostow, Walt W. *The Stages of Economic Growth: A Non-Communist Manifesto*. Cambridge: Cambridge University Press, 1960.

———. *The World Economy: History and Prospect*. Austin: University of Texas Press, 1978.

Rothenberg, Paula. *White Privilege*. 3rd ed. New York: Worth, 2008.

Rothman, Stanley, and Amy E. Black. "Who Rules Now? American Elites in the 1990s." *Society*. Vol. 35, No. 6 (September/October 1998):17–20.

Rothman, Stanley, Stephen Powers, and David Rothman. "Feminism in Films." *Society*. Vol. 30, No. 3 (March/April 1993):66–72.

Roudi-Fahimi, Farzaneh, and Mary Mederios Kent. "Challenges and Opportunities: The Population of the Middle East and North Africa." *Population Bulletin*. Vol. 65, No. 2 (June 2007). Washington, D.C.: Population Reference Bureau, 2007.

Rousseau, Caryn. "Unions Rally at Wal-Mart Stores." [Online] Available November 22, 2002, at http://dailynews.yahoo.com

Rozell, Mark J., Clyde Wilcox, and John C. Green. "Religious Constituencies and Support for the Christian Right in the 1990s." *Social Science Quarterly*. Vol. 79, No. 4 (December 1998):815–27.

Rubenstein, Eli A. "The Not So Golden Years." *Newsweek* (October 7, 1991):13.

Rubin, Joel. "E-Mail Too Formal? Try a Text Message." Columbia News Service, March 7, 2003. [Online] Available April 25, 2005, at http://www.jrn.columbia.edu/studentwork/cns/2003-03-07/85.asp

Rubin, Lillian Breslow. *Worlds of Pain: Life in the Working-Class Family*. New York: Basic Books, 1976.

Rudel, Thomas K., and Judith M. Gerson. "Postmodernism, Institutional Change, and Academic Workers: A Sociology of Knowledge." *Social Science Quarterly*. Vol. 80, No. 2 (June 1999):213–28.

Ruggeri, Amanda. "A Quiet Fight over Gay Adoption." *U.S. News & World Report* (November 3, 2008):29.

Rule, James, and Peter Brantley. "Computerized Surveillance in the Workplace: Forms and Delusions." *Sociological Forum*. Vol. 7, No. 3 (September 1992):405–23.

Russell, Cheryl. "Are We in the Dumps?" *American Demographics*. Vol. 17, No. 1 (January 1995a):6.

———. "True Crime." *American Demographics*. Vol. 17, No. 8 (August 1995b):22–31.

Ryan, Patrick J. "The Roots of Muslim Anger." *America* (November 26, 2001):8–16.

Rymer, Russ. *Genie*. New York: HarperPerennial, 1994.

Sachs, Jeffrey D. "The Case for Bigger Government." *Time* (January 19, 2009):34–36.

Saint James, Margo, and Priscilla Alexander. "What Is COYOTE?" 2004. [Online] Available May 28, 2008, at http://www.coyotela.org/what-is.html

Saint Jean, Yanick, and Joe R. Feagin. *Double Burden: Black Women and Everyday Racism*. Armonk, N.Y.: Sharpe, 1998.

Sala-i-Martin, Xavier. "The World Distribution of Income." Working Paper No. 8933. Cambridge, Mass.: National Bureau of Economic Research, 2002.

Sale, Kirkpatrick. *The Conquest of Paradise: Christopher Columbus and the Columbian Legacy*. New York: Knopf, 1990.

Sansom, William. *A Contest of Ladies*. London: Hogarth, 1956.

Sapir, Edward. "The Status of Linguistics as a Science." *Language*. Vol. 5, No. 4 (1929):207–14.

———. *Selected Writings of Edward Sapir in Language, Culture, and Personality*. David G. Mandelbaum, ed. Berkeley: University of California Press, 1949.

Saporito, Bill. "Can Wal-Mart Get Any Bigger?" *Time* (January 13, 2003):38–43.

Savishinsky, Joel S. *Breaking the Watch: The Meanings of Retirement in America*. Ithaca, N.Y.: Cornell University Press, 2000.

Sax, Linda J., et al. *The American Freshman: National Norms for Fall 2003*. Los Angeles: UCLA Higher Education Research Institute, 2003.

Scanlon, Stephan J. "Food Availability and Access in Less Industrialized Societies: A Test and Interpretation of Neo-Malthusian and Technoecological Theories." *Sociological Forum*. Vol. 16, No. 2 (June 2001):231–62.

Schaffer, Michael. "American Dreamers." *U.S. News & World Report* (August 26, 2002):12–16.

Scheff, Thomas J. *Being Mentally Ill: A Sociological Theory*. 2nd ed. New York: Aldine, 1984.

Scherer, Ron. "Could Bailout's Pay Caps Launch Wall Street Trend?" *Yahoo News* (September 30, 2008). [Online] Available September 29, 2008, at http://news.yahoo.com/s/csm/20080930/ts_csm/apaycut&printer=1;_ylt=Al3doZ_4Ps07Lcen.QlvU92Oe8UF

Schlesinger, Arthur M., Jr. "The City in American Civilization." In A. B. Callow Jr., ed., *American Urban History*. New York: Oxford University Press, 1969:25–41.

Schlosser, Eric. *Fast-Food Nation: The Dark Side of the All-American Meal*. New York: Perennial, 2002.

Schmidt, Roger. *Exploring Religion*. Belmont, Calif.: Wadsworth, 1980.

Schmitt, Eric. "Whites in Minority in Largest Cities, the Census Shows." *New York Times* (April 30, 2001):A1, A12.

Schneider, Mark, Melissa Marschall, Paul Teske, and Christine Roch. "School Choice and Culture Wars in the Classroom: What Different Parents Seek from Education." *Social Science Quarterly*. Vol. 79, No. 3 (September 1998):489–501.

Schnittker, Jason, Bernice A. Pescosolido, and Thomas W. Croghan. "Are African Americans Really Less Willing to Use Health Care?" *Social Problems*. Vol. 52, No. 2 (May 2005):255–71.

SCHOEN, ROBERT, and YEN-HSIN ALICE CHENG. "Partner Choice and the Differential Retreat from Marriage." *Journal of Marriage and the Family.* Vol. 68 (2006):1–10.

SCHULTZ, R., and J. HECKHAUSEN. "A Lifespan Model of Successful Aging." *American Psychologist.* Vol. 7, No. 7 (July 1996): 702–14.

SCHUR, LISA A., and DOUGLAS L. KRUSE. "What Determines Voter Turnout? Lessons from Citizens with Disabilities." *Social Science Quarterly.* Vol. 81, No. 2 (June 2000): 571–87.

SCHWARTZ, CHRISTINE R., and ROBERT D. MARE. "Trends in Educational Assortative Marriage from 1940 to 2003." July 2005. [Online] Available April 22, 2009, at http://www.ccpr.ucla.edu/ccprwpseries/ccpr_017_05.pdf

SCOMMEGNA, PAOLA. "Increased Cohabitation Changing Children's Family Settings." *Population Today.* Vol. 30, No. 7 (July 2002):3, 6.

SEAGER, JONI. *The Penguin Atlas of Women in the World.* 3rd ed. New York: Penguin Putnam, 2003.

SEARS, DAVID O., and JOHN B. MCCONAHAY. *The Politics of Violence: The New Urban Blacks and the Watts Riot.* Boston: Houghton Mifflin, 1973.

SEGAL, MADY WECHSLER, and AMANDA FAITH HANSEN. "Value Rationales in Policy Debates on Women in the Military: A Content Analysis of Congressional Testimony, 1941–1985." *Social Science Quarterly.* Vol. 73, No. 2 (June 1992):296–309.

SENNETT, RICHARD, and JONATHAN COBB. *The Hidden Injuries of Class.* New York: Vintage Books, 1973.

SENTENCING PROJECT. "Felony Disenfranchisement Laws in the United States." September 2008. [Online] Available January 25, 2009, at http://www.sentencingproject.org/Admin%5CDocuments%5Cpublications%5Cfd_bs_fdlawsinus.pdf

SHAPIRO, JOSEPH P. "Back to Work, on Mission." *U.S. News & World Report* (June 4, 2001).

SHEA, RACHEL HARTIGAN. "The New Insecurity." *U.S. News & World Report* (March 25, 2002):40.

SHEDDEN, DAVID. "School Shootings (1997–2008)." Poynteronline. April 16, 2008. [Online] Available July 15, 2008, at http://www.poynter.org/column.asp?id=49&aid=1025

SHEEHAN, TOM. "Senior Esteem as a Factor in Socioeconomic Complexity." *Gerontologist.* Vol. 16, No. 5 (October 1976):433–40.

SHELDON, WILLIAM H., EMIL M. HARTL, and EUGENE MCDERMOTT. *Varieties of Delinquent Youth.* New York: Harper Bros., 1949.

SHELER, JEFFREY L. "Faith in America." *U.S. News & World Report* (May 6, 2002):40–44.

SHERKAT, DARREN E., and CHRISTOPHER G. ELLISON. "Recent Developments and Current Controversies in the Sociology of Religion." *Annual Review of Sociology.* Vol. 25 (1999): 363–94.

SHERMAN, LAWRENCE W., and DOUGLAS A. SMITH. "Crime, Punishment, and Stake in Conformity: Legal and Informal Control of Domestic Violence." *American Sociological Review.* Vol. 57, No. 5 (October 1992):680–90.

SHEVKY, ESHREF, and WENDELL BELL. *Social Area Analysis.* Stanford, Calif.: Stanford University Press, 1955.

SHIPLEY, JOSEPH T. *Dictionary of Word Origins.* Totowa, N.J.: Rowman & Allanheld, 1985.

SHIVELY, JOELLEN. "Cowboys and Indians: Perceptions of Western Films among American Indians and Anglos." *American Sociological Review.* Vol. 57, No. 6 (December 1992): 725–34.

SHOVER, NEAL, and ANDREW HOCHSTETLER. *Choosing White-Collar Crime.* New York: Cambridge University Press, 2006.

SHUPE, ANSON. *In the Name of All That's Holy: A Theory of Clergy Malfeasance.* Westport, Conn.: Praeger, 1995.

SHUPE, ANSON, WILLIAM A. STACEY, and LONNIE R. HAZLEWOOD. *Violent Men, Violent Couples: The Dynamics of Domestic Violence.* Lexington, Mass.: Lexington Books, 1987.

SIERRA CLUB. "Clean Water." 2009. [Online] Available February 11, 2009, at http://www.sierraclub.org/cleanwater/overview

SIMMEL, GEORG. *The Sociology of Georg Simmel.* KURT WOLFF, ed. New York: Free Press, 1950; orig. 1902.

———. "Fashion." In DONALD N. LEVINE, ed., *Georg Simmel: On Individuality and Social Forms.* Chicago: University of Chicago Press, 1971; orig. 1904.

SIMON, JULIAN. *The Ultimate Resource.* Princeton, N.J.: Princeton University Press, 1981.

———. "More People, Greater Wealth, More Resources, Healthier Environment." In THEODORE D. GOLDFARB, ed., *Taking Sides: Clashing Views on Controversial Environmental Issues.* 6th ed. Guilford, Conn.: Dushkin, 1995.

SIMON, ROGER, and ANGIE CANNON. "An Amazing Journey." *U.S. News & World Report* (August 6, 2001):10–19.

SIMONS, MARLISE. "The Price of Modernization: The Case of Brazil's Kaiapo Indians." In JOHN J. MACIONIS and NIJOLE V. BENOKRAITIS, eds., *Seeing Ourselves: Classic, Contemporary, and Cross-Cultural Readings in Sociology.* 7th ed. Upper Saddle River, N.J.: Prentice Hall, 2007.

SINGER, S. FRED. "Global Warming: Man-Made or Natural?" *Imprimis.* Vol. 36, No. 8 (2007):1–5.

SIVARD, RUTH LEGER. *World Military and Social Expenditures, 1987–88.* 12th ed. Washington, D.C.: World Priorities, 1988.

SIZER, THEODORE R. *Horace's Compromise: The Dilemma of the American High School.* Boston: Houghton Mifflin, 1984.

———. "Private Profit, Public Good?" *Frontline* interview. July 3, 2003. [Online] Available May 20, 2006, at http://www.pbs.org/wgbh/pages/frontline/shows/edison/etc/private.html

SKOCPOL, THEDA. *States and Social Revolutions: A Comparative Analysis of France, Russia, and China.* Cambridge: Cambridge University Press, 1979.

SMAIL, J. KENNETH. "Let's *Reduce* Global Population!" In JOHN J. MACIONIS and NIJOLE V. BENOKRAITIS, eds., *Seeing Ourselves: Classic, Contemporary, and Cross-Cultural Readings in Sociology.* 7th ed. Upper Saddle River, N.J.: Prentice Hall, 2007.

SMART, TIM. "Not Acting Their Age." *U.S. News & World Report.* (June 4, 2001):54–60.

SMELSER, NEIL J. *Theory of Collective Behavior.* New York: Free Press, 1962.

SMITH, ADAM. *An Inquiry into the Nature and Causes of the Wealth of Nations.* New York: Modern Library, 1937; orig. 1776.

SMITH, DOUGLAS A. "Police Response to Interpersonal Violence: Defining the Parameters of Legal Control." *Social Forces.* Vol. 65, No. 3 (March 1987):767–82.

SMITH, DOUGLAS A., and PATRICK R. GARTIN. "Specifying Specific Deterrence: The Influence of Arrest on Future Criminal Activity." *American Sociological Review.* Vol. 54, No. 1 (February 1989):94–105.

SMITH, DOUGLAS A., and CHRISTY A. VISHER. "Street-Level Justice: Situational Determinants of Police Arrest Decisions." *Social Problems.* Vol. 29, No. 2 (December 1981):167–77.

SMITH, RYAN A. "Race, Gender, and Authority in the Workplace: Theory and Research." *Annual Review of Sociology.* Vol. 28 (2002):509–42.

SMITH, TOM W. "Anti-Semitism Decreases but Persists." *Society.* Vol. 33, No. 3 (March/April 1996):2.

———. "Are We Grown Up Yet? U.S. Study Says Not 'til 26." [Online] Available May 23, 2003, at http://news.yahoo.com

———. "American Social Behavior: Trends, Socio-Demographic Differences, and Behavior." March 2006. [Online] Available January 29, 2009, at http://www.norc.org/NR/rdonlyres/2663F09F-2E74-436E-AC81-6FFBF288E183/0/AmericanSexualBehavior2006.pdf

SMITH-LOVIN, LYNN, and CHARLES BRODY. "Interruptions in Group Discussions: The Effects of Gender and Group Composition." *American Journal of Sociology.* Vol. 54, No. 3 (June 1989): 424–35.

SMOLOWE, JILL. "When Violence Hits Home." *Time* (July 4, 1994):18–25.

SNELL, MARILYN BERLIN. "The Purge of Nurture." *New Perspectives Quarterly.* Vol. 7, No. 1 (Winter 1990):1–2.

SNYDER, HOWARD N. "Sexual Assault of Young Children as Reported to Law Enforcement: Victim, Incident, and Offender Characteristics." 2000. [Online] Available November 9, 2008, at http://www.ojp.usdoj.gov/bjs/pub/pdf/saycrle.pdf

SOBEL, RACHEL K. "Herpes Tests Give Answers You Might Need to Know." *U.S. News & World Report* (June 18, 2001):53.

SOUTH, SCOTT J., and STEVEN F. MESSNER. "Structural Determinants of Intergroup Association: Interracial Marriage and Crime." *American Journal of Sociology.* Vol. 91, No. 6 (May 1986):1409–30.

SOWELL, THOMAS. *Ethnic America.* New York: Basic Books, 1981.

———. *Race and Culture.* New York: Basic Books, 1994.

———. "Ethnicity and IQ." In STEVEN FRASER, ed., *The Bell Curve Wars: Race, Intelligence, and the Future of America.* New York: Basic Books, 1995:70–79.

SPECTER, MICHAEL. "Plunging Life Expectancy Puzzles Russia." *New York Times* (August 2, 1995):A1, A2.

SPEIER, HANS. "Wit and Politics: An Essay on Laughter and Power." ROBERT JACKALL, ed. and trans. *American Journal of Sociology.* Vol. 103, No. 5 (March 1998):1352–1401.

SPITZER, STEVEN. "Toward a Marxian Theory of Deviance." In DELOS H. KELLY, ed., *Criminal Behavior: Readings in Criminology.* New York: St. Martin's Press, 1980:175–91.

STACEY, JUDITH. *Patriarchy and Socialist Revolution in China.* Berkeley: University of California Press, 1983.

———. *Brave New Families: Stories of Domestic Upheaval in Late Twentieth-Century America.* New York: Basic Books, 1990.

———. "Good Riddance to 'the Family': A Response to David Popenoe." *Journal of Marriage and the Family.* Vol. 55, No. 3 (August 1993):545–47.

STACK, STEVEN, IRA WASSERMAN, and ROGER KERN. "Adult Social Bonds and the Use of Internet Pornography." *Social Science Quarterly.* Vol. 85, No. 1 (March 2004):75–88.

STAPINSKI, HELENE. "Let's Talk Dirty." *American Demographics.* Vol. 20, No. 11 (November 1998):50–56.

STARK, RODNEY, and WILLIAM SIMS BAINBRIDGE. "Of Churches, Sects, and Cults: Preliminary Concepts for a Theory of Religious Movements." *Journal for the Scientific Study of Religion.* Vol. 18, No. 2 (June 1979):117–31.

———. "Secularization and Cult Formation in the Jazz Age." *Journal for the Scientific Study of Religion.* Vol. 20, No. 4 (December 1981):360–73.

STATISTICS CANADA. "Ethnic Diversity and Immigration, 2007." 2008. [Online] Available November 13, 2008, at http://www40.statcan.ca/l01/cst01/legal01.htm

STEELE, RANDY. "Awful but Lawful." *Boating* (June 2000):36.

STEELE, SHELBY. *The Content of Our Character: A New Vision of Race in America.* New York: St. Martin's Press, 1990.

STEGER, BRIGITTE. "Sleeping through Class to Success." *Time and Society.* Vol. 15, No. 2–3 (2006):197–214. [Online] Available January 17, 2009, at http://tas.sagepub.com/cgi/content/abstract/15/2-3/197

STEINHAUER, JENNIFER. "Sex Sells, So Legislator Urges State to Tax It." *New York Times* (May 26, 2008). [Online] Available November 9, 2008, at http://www.nytimes.com/2008/05/26/us/26porn.html?_r=1&scp=4&sq=pornography%2industry&st=cse&oref=slogin

STEPHENS, JOHN D. *The Transition from Capitalism to Socialism.* Urbana: University of Illinois Press, 1986.

STEYN, MARK. "Is Canada's Economy a Model for America?" *Imprimis.* Vol. 37, No. 1 (January 2008):1–7.

STIER, HAYA. "Continuity and Change in Women's Occupations following First Childbirth." *Social Science Quarterly.* Vol. 77, No. 1 (March 1996):60–75.

STOBBE, MIKE. "Cancer to Be World's Top Killer by 2010, WHO Says." *Yahoo News* (December 9, 2008). [Online] Available December 10, 2008, at http://news.yahoo.com/s/ap/20081209/ap_on_he_me/med_global_cancer

STOCKHOLM INTERNATIONAL PEACE RESEARCH INSTITUTE. "SIPRI Data on Military Expenditures." [Online] Available June 25, 2007, at http://www.sipri.org/contents/milap/milex/mex_data_index.html

STONE, LAWRENCE. *The Family, Sex, and Marriage in England, 1500–1800.* New York: Harper & Row, 1977.

STORMS, MICHAEL D. "Theories of Sexual Orientation." *Journal of Personality and Social Psychology.* Vol. 38, No. 5 (May 1980):783–92.

STORY, LOUISE. "Top Hedge Fund Managers Do Well in a Down Year." *New York Times* (March 25, 2009):B1. [Online] Available April 27, 2009, at http://www.nytimes.com/2009/03/25/business/25hedge.html?_r2

STOUFFER, SAMUEL A., ET AL. *The American Soldier: Adjustment during Army Life.* Princeton, N.J.: Princeton University Press, 1949.

STOUT, DAVID. "Supreme Court Splits on Diversity Efforts at University of Michigan." [Online] Available June 23, 2003, at http://news.yahoo.com

STRATTON, LESLIE S. "Why Does More Housework Lower Women's Wages? Testing Hypotheses Involving Job Effort and Hours Flexibility." *Social Sciences Quarterly.* Vol. 82, No. 1 (March 2001):67–76.

STREIB, GORDON F. "Are the Aged a Minority Group?" In BERNICE L. NEUGARTEN, ed., *Middle Age and Aging: A Reader in Social Psychology.* Chicago: University of Chicago Press, 1968:35–46.

STUESSY, JOE, and SCOTT LIPSCOMB. *Rock and Roll: Its History and Stylistic Development.* 6th ed. Upper Saddle River, N.J.: Pearson Prentice Hall, 2008.

SULLIVAN, ANDREW. Lecture delivered at Kenyon College, Gambier, Ohio, April 4, 2002.

SULLIVAN, BARBARA. "McDonald's Sees India as Golden Opportunity." *Chicago Tribune* (April 5, 1995):B1.

SULLIVAN, WILL. "Road Warriors." *U.S. News & World Report* (May 7, 2007):42–49.

SUMNER, WILLIAM GRAHAM. *Folkways.* New York: Dover, 1959; orig. 1906.

SUN, LENA H. "WWII's Forgotten Internees Await Apology." *Washington Post* (March 9, 1998): A1, A5, A6.

SUTHERLAND, EDWIN H. "White Collar Criminality." *American Sociological Review.* Vol. 5, No. 1 (February 1940):1–12.

SVEBAK, SVEN. Cited in MARILYN ELIAS, "Study Links Sense of Humor, Survival." [Online] Available March 14, 2007, at http://www.usatoday.com

SWARTZ, STEVE. "Why Michael Milken Stands to Qualify for Guinness Book." *Wall Street Journal* (March 31, 1989):1, 4.

SZASZ, THOMAS S. *The Myth of Mental Illness: Foundations of a Theory of Personal Conduct.* New York: Dell, 1961.

———. *The Manufacturer of Madness: A Comparative Study of the Inquisition and the Mental Health Movement.* New York: Harper & Row, 1970.

———. "Cleansing the Modern Heart." *Society.* Vol. 40, No. 4 (May/June 2003):52–59.

———. "Protecting Patients against Psychiatric Intervention." *Society.* Vol. 41, No. 3 (March/April 2004):7–10.

TAJFEL, HENRI. "Social Psychology of Intergroup Relations." *Annual Review of Psychology.* Palo Alto, Calif.: Annual Reviews, 1982:1–39.

TAKAKI, RONALD. *Strangers from a Different Shore.* Boston: Back Bay Books, 1998.

TALLICHET, SUZANNE E. "Barriers to Women's Advancement in Underground Coal Mining." *Rural Sociology.* Vol. 65, No. 2 (June 2000):234–52.

TANNEN, DEBORAH. *You Just Don't Understand: Women and Men in Conversation.* New York: Morrow, 1990.

———. *Talking from 9 to 5: How Women's and Men's Conversational Styles Affect Who Gets Heard, Who Gets Credit, and What Gets Done at Work.* New York: Morrow, 1994.

TAVRIS, CAROL, and CAROL WADE. *Psychology in Perspective.* 3rd ed. Upper Saddle River, N.J.: Prentice Hall, 2001.

TAYLOR, FREDERICK WINSLOW. *The Principles of Scientific Management.* New York. Harper Bros., 1911.

TEENAGE RESEARCH UNLIMITED. "Survey Reveals Abuse in Teen Relationships." CNN.com. July 8, 2008. [Online] Available November 9, 2008, at http://www.cnn.com/2008/LIVING/personal/07/08/teen.dating.abuse.index.html?iref=newssearch

TEJADA-VERA, BETZAIDA, and PAUL D. SUTTON. "Births, Marriages, Divorces, and Deaths: Provisional Data for 2007." October 15, 2008. [Online] Available February 9, 2009, at http://www.cdc.gov/nchs/data/nvsr/nvsr56_21.htm

TERRY, DON. "In Crackdown on Bias, a New Tool." *New York Times* (June 12, 1993):8.

THERNSTROM, ABIGAIL, and STEPHAN THERNSTROM. "American Apartheid? Don't Believe It." *Wall Street Journal* (March 2, 1998):A18.

THOMAS, EDWARD J. *The Life of Buddha as Legend and History.* London: Routledge & Kegan Paul, 1975.

THOMAS, EVAN, and MARTHA BRANT. "Injection of Reflection." *Newsweek* (November 19, 2007):40–41.

THOMAS, PIRI. *Down These Mean Streets.* New York: Signet, 1967.

THOMAS, W. I. "The Relation of Research to the Social Process." In MORRIS JANOWITZ, ed., *W. I. Thomas on Social Organization and Social Personality.* Chicago: University of Chicago Press, 1966:289–305; orig. 1931.

THOMMA, STEVEN. "Christian Coalition Demands Action from GOP." *Philadelphia Inquirer* (September 14, 1997):A2.

THOMPSON, DICK. "Gene Maverick." *Time* (January 11, 1999):54–55.

THOMPSON, MARK. "Fatal Neglect." *Time* (October 27, 1997):34–38.

———. "Shining a Light on Abuse." *Time* (August 3, 1998):42–43.

THOMPSON, MARK, and DOUGLAS WALLER. "Shield of Dreams." *Time* (May 8, 2001):45–47.

THORNBERRY, TERRANCE, and MARGARET FARNSWORTH. "Social Correlates of Criminal Involvement: Further Evidence on the Relationship between Social Status and Criminal Behavior." *American Sociological Review.* Vol. 47, No. 4 (August 1982):505–18.

THORNBURGH, NATHAN. "Dropout Nation." *Time* (April 17, 2006):30–40.

THORNE, BARRIE, CHERIS KRAMARAE, and NANCY HENLEY, eds. *Language, Gender, and Society.* Rowley, Mass.: Newbury House, 1983.

TILLY, CHARLES. *From Mobilization to Revolution.* Reading, Mass.: Addison-Wesley, 1978.

———. "Does Modernization Breed Revolution?" In JACK A. GOLDSTONE, ed., *Revolutions: Theoretical, Comparative, and Historical Studies.* New York: Harcourt Brace Jovanovich, 1986:47–57.

TINGWALL, ERIC. "Auto Insurance Gets Cheaper but Potentially More Invasive." *Automobile* (December 2008):74.

TITTLE, CHARLES R., WAYNE J. VILLEMEZ, and DOUGLAS A. SMITH. "The Myth of Social Class and Criminality: An Empirical Assessment of the Empirical Evidence." *American Sociological Review.* Vol. 43, No. 5 (October 1978):643–56.

TOCQUEVILLE, ALEXIS DE. *The Old Regime and the French Revolution.* STUART GILBERT, trans. Garden City, N.Y.: Anchor/Doubleday, 1955; orig. 1856.

TÖNNIES, FERDINAND. *Community and Society (Gemeinschaft und Gesellschaft).* New York: Harper & Row, 1963; orig. 1887.

TOOSSI, MITRA. "Labor Force Projections to 2016: More Workers in Their Golden Years." *Monthly Labor Review* (November 2007):33–52. [Online] Available May 28, 2008, at http://www.bls.gov/opub/mlr/2007/11/art3full.pdf

TOPPO, GREG, and ANTHONY DEBARROS. "Reality Weighs Down Dreams of College." *USA Today* (February 2, 2005):A1.

TORRES, LISA, and MATT L. HUFFMAN. "Social Networks and Job Search Outcomes among Male and Female Professional, Technical, and Managerial Workers." *Sociological Focus.* Vol. 35, No. 1 (February 2002):25–42.

TREAS, JUDITH. "Older Americans in the 1990s and Beyond." *Population Bulletin.* Vol. 50, No. 2 (May 1995).

TROELTSCH, ERNST. *The Social Teaching of the Christian Churches.* New York: Macmillan, 1931.

TUCKER, JAMES. "New Age Religion and the Cult of the Self." *Society.* Vol. 39, No. 2 (February 2002):46–51.

TUCKER, MARIA. "How Big Was the Inaugural Crowd? Good Question." *News & Observer* (January 21, 2009). [Online] Available April 28, 2009, at http://www.sacbee.com/inauguration/story/1563105.html

TUMIN, MELVIN M. "Some Principles of Stratification: A Critical Analysis." *American Sociological Review.* Vol. 18, No. 4 (August 1953):387–94.

TUMULTY, KAREN. "Should They Stay or Should They Go?" *Time* (April 10, 2006):30–41.

TURNER, JONATHAN. *On the Origins of Human Emotions: A Sociological Inquiry into the Evolution of Human Emotions.* Stanford, Calif.: Stanford University Press, 2000.

TURNER, RALPH H., and LEWIS M. KILLIAN. *Collective Behavior.* 3rd ed. Englewood Cliffs, N.J.: Prentice Hall, 1987.

TURNER, RALPH H., and LEWIS M. KILLIAN. *Collective Behavior,* 5th ed. Upper Saddle River, NJ: Prentice Hall, 1993.

TYLER, S. LYMAN. *A History of Indian Policy.* Washington, D.C.: U.S. Department of the Interior, Bureau of Indian Affairs, 1973.

UDRY, J. RICHARD. "Biological Limitations of Gender Construction." *American Sociological Review.* Vol. 65, No. 3 (June 2000):443–57.

UGGEN, CHRISTOPHER. "Ex-Offenders and the Conformist Alternative: A Job-Quality Model of Work and Crime." *Social Problems.* Vol. 46, No. 1 (February 1999):127–51.

UGGEN, CHRISTOPHER, and JEFF MANZA. "Democratic Contraction? Political Consequences of Felon Disenfranchisement in the United States." *American Sociological Review.* Vol. 67, No. 6 (December 2002):777–803.

UNAIDS. "2008 Report on the Global AIDS Epidemic." August 2008. [Online] Available February 6, 2009, at http://www.unaids.org/en/KnowledgeCentre/HIVData/GlobalReport/2008/2008_Global_report.asp

UNESCO. Data reported in "Tower of Babel Is Tumbling Down—Slowly." *U.S. News & World Report* (July 2, 2001):9.

———. "Literacy Portal." 2008. [Online] Available November 18, 2008, at http://www.un.org/ga/search/view_doc.asp?symbol=A%2F63%2F172&Submit=Search&Lang=E

———. INSTITUTE OF STATISTICS. "Data Centre." April 2008. [Online] Available February 1, 2009, at http://stats.uis.unesco.org/unesco/TableViewer/document.aspx?ReportId=121&IF_Language=eng&BR_Country=3560&BR_Region=40535

UNICEF. "Child Protection." In *The State of the World's Children, 2008.* December 2007. [Online] Available June 15, 2009, at http://www.unicef.org/sowc08/docs/sowc08_table_9.xls

———. "Female Genital Mutilation/Cutting." Statistical table. Rev. April 2008. [Online] Available May 13, 2008, at http://www.childinfo.org/areas/fgmc/tables.php

———. UNITED NATIONS. *The State of Food Insecurity in the World, 2006.* New York: United Nations, 2006.

———. *2006 Report on the Global AIDS Epidemic.* 2006. [Online] Available September 27, 2006, at http://www.unaids.org/en/HIV_data/2006GlobalReport/default.asp

———. *WHO AIDS Epidemic Update, December 2006.* 2006. [Online] Available July 9, 2007, at http://www.unaids.org/en/HIV_data/epi2006/default.asp

———. *The World's Women, 2005: Progress in Statistics.* New York: United Nations, 2006.

———. *2007 AIDS Epidemic Update.* Joint United Nations Programme on HIV/AIDS (UNAIDS) and World Health Organization (WHO). 2007. [Online] Available July 16, 2008, at http://data.unaids.org/pub/EPISlides/2007/2007_epiupdate_en.pdf

———. "China: Basic Public Services for 1.3 Billion People." November 2008. [Online] Available November 18, 2008, at http://hdr.undp.org/en/reports/nationalreports/asiathepacific/china/China_2008_en.pdf

———. "Executive Summary." *World Urbanization Prospects: The 2007 Revision.* February 2008. [Online] Available July 16, 2008, at http://www.un.org/esa/population/publications/wup2007/2007WUP_ExecSum_web.pdf

———. *2007 UNAIDS Annual Report: Knowing Your Epidemic.* Joint United Nations Programme on HIV/AIDS (UNAIDS). 2008. [Online] Available July 16, 2008, at http://data.unaids.org/pub/Report/2008/jc1535_annual_report07_en.pdf

———. "World Contraceptive Use, 2008." 2008. [Online] Available May 24, 2008, at http://www.un.org/esa/population/publications/contraceptive2005/WCU2005.htm

United Nations Development Programme. *Human Development Report 1990*. New York: Oxford University Press, 1990.

————. *Human Development Report 2000*. New York: Oxford University Press, 2000.

————. *Human Development Report 2005*. New York: Oxford University Press, 2005.

————. *Human Development Report 2006*. New York: Palgrave Macmillan, 2006.

————. *Human Development Report 2007/2008*. New York: Palgrave Macmillan, 2007. [Online] Available February 26, 2008, at http://hdr.undp.org/en

————. "Human Development Indices: A Statistical Update, 2008." December 12, 2008. [Online] Available January 19, 2009, at http://hdrstats.undp.org/2008/countries/country_fact_sheets/cty_fs_KOR.html

————. "The Millennium Development Goals Report, 2008." August 2008. [Online] Available April 28, 2009, at http://www.undp.org/publications/MDG_Report_2008_en.pdf

United Nations Environmental Programme. "Vital Water Graphics: An Overview of the State of the World's Fresh and Marine Waters." 2nd ed. 2008. [Online] Available February 9, 2009, at http://www.unep.org/dewa/vitalwater/article186.html

United Nations Population Reference Division. "World Population Prospects: The 2007 Revision." 2009. [Online] Available February 9, 2009, at http://data.un.org/Data.aspx?d=PopDiv&f=variableID%3a46

United Nations Statistics Division. "Millenium Development Goals Database." 2008. [Online] Available November 5, 2008, at http://data.un.org/Data.aspx?q=internet+users&d=MDG&f=seriesRowID:605 - MDG

————. "UNdata Explorer." [Online] Available April 2, 2008, at http://data.un.org/Browse.aspx?d=CDB

U.S. Bureau of Justice Statistics. "Sentences Imposed in Cases Terminated in U.S. District Courts." *Sourcebook of Criminal Justice Statistics Online*. [Online] Available May 20, 2007, at http://www.albany.edu/sourcebook

U.S. Census Bureau. *The Two or More Races Population, 2000*. Census 2000 Brief, C2KBR/01-6. Washington, D.C.: U.S. Government Printing Office, 2001. [Online] Available August 28, 2007, at http://www.census.gov/population/www/cen2000/briefs.html

————. *The White Population, 2000*. Census 2000 Brief, C2KBR/01-4. Washington, D.C.: U.S. Government Printing Office, 2001. [Online] Available August 28, 2007, at http://www.census.gov/population/www/cen2000/briefs.html

————. *The American Indian and Alaska Native Population, 2000*. Census 2000 Brief, C2KBR/01-15. Washington, D.C.: U.S. Government Printing Office, 2002. [Online] Available August 28, 2007, at http://www.census.gov/population/www/cen2000/briefs.html

————. *The Asian Population, 2000*. Census 2000 Brief, C2KBR/01-16. Washington, D.C.: U.S. Government Printing Office, 2002. [Online] Available August 28, 2007, at http://www.census.gov/population/www/cen2000/briefs.html

————. *The Arab Population, 2000*. Census 2000 Brief, C2KBR-23. Washington, D.C.: U.S. Government Printing Office, 2003.

————. *Language Use and English-Speaking Ability, 2000*. Census 2000 Brief, C2KBR-29. Washington, D.C.: U.S. Government Printing Office, 2003.

————. *Ancestry, 2000*. Census 2000 Brief, C2KBR-35. Washington, D.C.: U.S. Government Printing Office, 2004.

————. *Statistical Abstract of the United States, 2004–2005*. Washington, D.C.: U.S. Government Printing Office, 2004.

————. "Census 2000 Demographic Profile Highlights." [Online] Available September 22, 2006, at http://factfinder.census.gov

————. *We the People: American Indians and Alaska Natives in the United States*. Census 2000 Special Reports, CENSR-28. Washington, D.C.: U.S. Government Printing Office, 2006.

————. *The American Community: Hispanics, 2004*. February 2007. [Online] Available August 22, 2007, at http://www.census.gov/prod/2007pubs/acs-03.pdf

————. *Educational Attainment in the United States, 2006*. Detailed tables. Rev. March 20, 2007. [Online] Available May 27, 2007, at http://www.census.gov/population/www/socdemo/education/cps2006.html

————. *Housing Vacancies and Homeownership*. (CPS/HVS). Annual Statistics, 2006. Table 20. Rev. February 12, 2007. [Online] Available May 27, 2007, at http://www.census.gov/hhes/www/housing/hvs/annual06/ann06ind.html

————. "International Database (IDB): Pyramids." Rev. July 16, 2007. [Online] Available August 28, 2007, at http://www.census.gov/ipc/www/idb/pyramids.html

————. "Annual Estimates of the Population by Sex and Five-Year Age Groups for the United States." 2008 [Online] Available October 17, 2008, at http://www.census.gov/popest/national/asrh/NC-EST2007-sa.html

————. "Current Population Survey, 2008: Annual Social and Economic Supplement." August 26, 2008 [Online] Available October 27, 2008, at http://pubdb3.census.gov/macro/032008/pov/new01_100_01.htm

————. "Detailed Tables." American Community Survey. 2008. [Online] Available October 13, 2008, at http://factfinder.census.gov/servlet/STTable?_bm=y&-geo_id=01000US&-qr_name=ACS_2007_1YR_G00_S0501&-ds_name=ACS_2007_1YR_G00_&-_lang=en&-redoLog=false&-format=&-CONTEXT=st

————. "Housing and Household Economic Statistics." 2008. [Online] Available January 28, 2009, at http://www.census.gov/population/www/socdemo/fertility.html-hist

————. "International Data Base." June 18, 2008. [Online] Available April 28, 2009, at http://www.census.gov/ipc/www/idb/country/japortal.html

————. "Projections of the Population by Age and Sex for the United States: 2010 to 2050." 2008 [Online] Available April 28, 2009, at http://www.census.gov/population/www/projections/summarytables.html

————. "Racial and Ethnic Classification Used in Census 2000 and Beyond." 2008. [Online] Available December 30, 2008, at http://www.census.gov/population/www/socdemo/race/racefactcb.html

————. "Selected Characteristics of the Native and Foreign-Born Populations, 2007." American Community Survey. 2008. [Online] Available February 23, 2009, at http://factfinder.census.gov/servlet/DTTable?_bm=y&-state=dt&-ds_name=ACS_2007_1YR_G00_&-mt_name=ACS_2007_1YR_G2000_B02006&-redoLog=true&-_caller=geoselect&-geo_id=01000US&-geo_id=NBSP&-format=&-_lang=en

————. *Statistical Abstract of the United States, 2008*. 127th ed. Washington, D.C.: Government Printing Office. 2008. [Online] Available November 18, 2008, at http://www.census.gov/compendia/statab/tables/08s1182.pdf

————. "2008 National Population Projections: Tables and Charts." August 14, 2008. [Online] Available April 28, 2009, at http://www.census.gov/population/www/projections/tablesandcharts.html

————. "U.S. Trade in Goods." 2008. [Online] Available December 5, 2008, at http://www.census.gov/foreign-trade/statistics/historical/goods.pdf

————. "Voting and Registration in the Election of November 2004." April 8, 2005. [Online] Available April 28, 2009, at http://www.census.gov/population/www/socdemo/voting/cps2004.html

————. "World Vital Events per Time Unit, 2009." 2009. [Online] Available February 11, 2009, at http://www.census.gov/cgi-bin/ipc/pcwe

U.S. Charter Schools. "Charter School Dashboard." 2008. [Online] Available July 15, 2008, at http://www.uscharterschools.org/cs/r/query/q/1558?x-title=New+Non-Federal+Research+and+Reports

U.S. Conference of Mayors. *Hunger and Homelessness Survey*. December 2007. [Online] Available April 30, 2008, at http://usmayors.org/HHSurvey2007/hhsurvey07.pdf

U.S. Department of Agriculture. "Historical Highlights: 2002 and Earlier Census Years." 2004. [Online] Available April 28, 2009, at http://www.agcensus.usda.gov/Publications/2002/Volume_1,_Chapter_1_US/st99_1_001_001.pdf

U.S. Department of Education. "National Assessment of Adult Literacy." 2003. [Online] Available November 17, 2008, at http://nces.ed.gov/naal/kf_demographics.asp

————. "The Condition of Education, 2008." 2008. [Online] Available February 3, 2009, at http://nces.ed.gov/programs/coe/2008/section1/indicator08.asp-info

————. "U.S. Digest of Education Statistics, 2008." August 2008. [Online] Available December 7, 2008, at http://nces.ed.gov/programs/digest/d07/tables/dt07_275.asp

U.S. Department of Health and Human Services. "The National Family Caregiver Support Program: Compassion in Action." July 22, 2004. [Online] Available January 18, 2009, at http://www.aoa.gov/prof/aoaprog/caregiver/careprof/progguidance/resources/docs/FINAL%20NFCSP%20Report%20July22,%202004.pdf

————. *Child Maltreatment, 2006*. Washington, D.C.: U.S. Government Printing Office, 2008. [Online] Available January 31, 2009, at http://www.acf.hhs.gov/programs/cb/pubs/cm06

————. "National Health Expenditure Data, 2008." 2009. [Online] Available February 6, 2009, at http://www.cms.hhs.gov/NationalHealthExpendData/25_NHE_Fact_Sheet.asp

U.S. Department of Homeland Security. "Estimates of the Unauthorized Immigrant Population Residing in the United States, January 2007." September 4, 2008. [Online] Available April 28, 2009, at http://www.dhs.gov/xlibrary/assets/statistics/publications/ois_ill_pe_2007.pdf

————. *Legal Permanent Residents, 2007*. March 2008. [Online] Available May 20, 2008, at http://www.dhs.gov/xlibrary/assets/statistics/publications/LPR_FR_2007.pdf

————. "Persons Obtaining Legal Permanent Resident Status by Region and Selected Country of Last Residence, Fiscal Years 1820 to 2007." September 4, 2008. [Online] Available April 28, 2009, at http://www.dhs.gov/xlibrary/assets/statistics/yearbook/2007/table02.xls

————. *Yearbook of Immigration Statistics, 2007*. Data tables. 2008. Rev. April 2, 2008. [Online] Available May 21, 2008, at http://www.dhs.gov/ximgtn/statistics/publications/LPR07.shtm

U.S. Department of Housing and Urban Development. *Annual Homeless Assessment Report to Congress*. February 2007. [Online] Available April 30, 2008, at http://www.huduser.org/Publications/pdf/ahar.pdf

U.S. Department of Justice. *The Sexual Victimization of College Women*. December 2000. [Online] Available May 12, 2008, at http://www.ncjrs.gov/pdffiles1/nij/182369.pdf

————. "Recidivism." October 25, 2002. [Online] Available November 13, 2008, at http://www.ojp.usdoj.gov/bjs/reentry/recidivism.htm

————. "Disposition of Criminal Cases." 2005. [Online] Available November 13, 2008, at http://www.ojp.usdoj.gov/bjs/pub/html/fjsst/2005/tables/fjs05st402.htm

————. "Hate Crime Statistics, 2007." October 27, 2008. [Online] Available November 12, 2008, at http://www.fbi.gov/ucr/hc2007/table_01.htm

————. "Criminal Victimization in the United States: Statistical Tables Index." 2008. [Online] Available April 28, 2009, at http://www.ojp.usdoj.gov/bjs/abstract/cvus/rape_sexual_assault304.htm

————. "Crime in the United States, 2007." 2008. [Online] Available November 9, 2008, at http://www.fbi.gov/ucr/cius2007/data/table_01.html

————. "Number of Victimizations, by Type of Crime and Relationship to Offender." 2008. [Online] Available April 28, 2009, at http://www.ojp.usdoj.gov/bjs/pub/pdf/cvus/current/cv0633.pdf

————, Bureau of Justice Statistics. "Corrections Statistics." 2008. [Online] Available April 28, 2009, at http://www.ojp.usdoj.gov/bjs/correct.htm

U.S. Department of Labor. "Civilian Labor Force, 2006–2016." June 18, 2008. [Online] Available January 20, 2009, at http://www.bls.gov/emp/emplab1.htm

————. "Compliance Assistance: Fair Labor Standards Act." 2008. [Online] Available May 19, 2008, at http://www.dol.gov/esa/whd/flsa

————. "Current Employment Statistics." 2008. [Online] Available January 19, 2009, at http://www.bls.gov/webapps/legacy/cesbtab1.htm

————. *Employment and Earnings*. 2008. [Online] Available April 17, 2008, at http://www.bls.gov/cps/#annual

———. "Forced Labor and Human Trafficking." 2008. [Online] Available October 27, 2008, at http://www.dol.gov/ilab/media/factsheets/20080320OCFT.pdf

———. "Labor Force Statistics from the Current Population Survey." 2008. [Online] Available December 7, 2008, at http://www.bls.gov/cps/demographics.htm-women

———. *Occupational Outlook Handbook.* 2008–09 ed. Washington, D.C.: Government Printing Office, 2008. [Online] Available February 6, 2009, at http://www.bls.gov/oco/ocos083.htm-oes_links

———. "Employment Situation." January 9, 2009. [Online] Available January 19, 2009, at http://www.bls.gov/news.release/empsit.t01.htm

U.S. DEPARTMENT OF LABOR, BUREAU OF LABOR STATISTICS. "American Time Use Survey." 2007. [Online] Available June 15, 2009, at http://www.bls.gov/TUS/CHARTS/HOUSEHOLD.HTM

———. "Consumer Expenditure Survey, 2006." October 27, 2007. Washington, D.C.: U.S. Government Printing Office, 2007.

———. "Employment and Earnings." 2007. [Online] Available May 20, 2007, at http://www.bls.gov/cps/#annual

U.S. DEPARTMENT OF LABOR, WOMEN'S BUREAU. "Quick Facts on Registered Nurses (RNs)." 2008. [Online] Available February 6, 2008, at http://www.dol.gov/wb/factsheets/Qf-nursing-07.htm

U.S. DEPARTMENT OF STATE. *Patterns of Global Terrorism, 2002.* 2002. [Online] Available December 26, 2003, at http://www.usis.usemb.se/terror/rpt2002/index.html

———. *Country Reports on Terrorism, 2006.* April 2007. [Online] Available June 25, 2007, at http://www.state.gov/s/ct/rls/crt

———. "Background Notes Archive." 2009. [Online] Available January 23, 2009, at http://www.state.gov/r/pa/ei/bgn

U.S. ENVIRONMENTAL PROTECTION AGENCY. "Basic Information: Municipal Solid Waste." Rev. January 3, 2008. [Online] Available July 16, 2008, at http://www.epa.gov/epaoswer/non-hw/muncpl/facts.htm

———. "Municipal Solid Waste Generation, Recycling, and Disposal in the United States: Facts and Figures for 2007." 2008. [Online] Available February 10, 2009, at http://www.epa.gov/osw/nonhaz/municipal/pubs/msw07-fs.pdf

U.S. EQUAL EMPLOYMENT OPPORTUNITY COMMISSION. "Job Patterns for Minorities and Women in Private Industry." 2006. [Online] Available November 5, 2008, at http://www.eeoc.gov/stats/jobpat/2006/national.html

———. "Occupational Employment in Private Industry by Race/Ethnic Group/Sex and by Industry, United States, 2006." Rev. March 14, 2008. [Online] Available April 3, 2008, at http://www.eeoc.gov/stats/jobpat/2006/national.html

U.S. HOUSE OF REPRESENTATIVES. *1991 Green Book.* Washington, D.C.: U.S. Government Printing Office, 1991.

U.S. OFFICE OF MANAGEMENT AND BUDGET. "The Budget for Fiscal Year 2009." 2008. [Online] Available January 23, 2009, at http://www.gpoaccess.gov/usbudget/fy09/pdf/budget/tables.pdf

U.S. SMALL BUSINESS ADMINISTRATION. *Women in Business: A Demographic Review of Women's Business Ownership,* August 2006. [Online] Available May 30, 2007, at http://www.sba.gov/advo/research/rs280tot.pdf

U.S. SOCIAL SECURITY ADMINISTRATION. *The 2008 Annual Report of the Board of Trustees of the Federal Old-Age and Survivors Insurance and Federal Disability Insurance Trust Funds.* Washington, D.C.: Government Printing Office, March 25, 2008. [Online] Available January 8, 2009, at http://www.ssa.gov/OACT/TR/TR08/V_demographic.html-167717

UPTHEGROVE, TAYNA R., VINCENT J. ROSCIGNO, and CAMILLE ZUBRINSKY CHARLES. "Big Money Collegiate Sports: Racial Concentration, Contradictory Pressures, and Academic Performance." *Social Science Quarterly.* Vol. 80, No. 4 (December 1999):718–37.

VALDEZ, A. "In the Hood: Street Gangs Discover White-Collar Crime." *Police.* Vol. 21, No. 5 (May 1997):49–50, 56.

VALLAS, STEPHEN P., and JOHN P. BECK. "The Transformation of Work Revisited: The Limits of Flexibility in American Manufacturing." *Social Problems.* Vol. 43, No. 3 (August 1996): 339–61.

VAN BIEMA, DAVID. "Buddhism in America." *Time* (October 13, 1997):71–81.

VAN DYKE, NELLA, and SARAH A. SOULE. "Structural Social Change and the Mobilizing Effect of Threat: Explaining Levels of Patriot and Militia Organizing in the United States." *Social Problems.* Vol. 49, No. 4 (November 2002):497–520.

VEBLEN, THORSTEIN. *The Theory of the Leisure Class.* New York: New American Library, 1953; orig. 1899.

VENTURA, STEPHANIE J., JOYCE C. ABMA, WILLIAM D. MOSHER, and STANLEY K. HENSHAW. "Estimated Pregnancy Rates by Outcome for the United States, 1990–2004." April 14, 2008. [Online] Available April 28, 2009, at http://www.cdc.gov/nchs/data/nvsr/nvsr56/nvsr56_15.pdf

VINOVSKIS, MARIS A. "Have Social Historians Lost the Civil War? Some Preliminary Demographic Speculations." *Journal of American History.* Vol. 76, No. 1 (June 1989):34–58.

VISSER, JELLE. "Union Membership Statistics in 24 Countries." *Monthly Labor Review* (January 2006):38–49. [Online] Available June 2, 2006, at http://www.bls.gov/opub/mlr/2006/01/art3full.pdf

VOGEL, EZRA F. *The Four Little Dragons: The Spread of Industrialization in East Asia.* Cambridge, Mass.: Harvard University Press, 1991.

VOGEL, LISE. *Marxism and the Oppression of Women: Toward a Unitary Theory.* New Brunswick, N.J.: Rutgers University Press, 1983.

VOLD, GEORGE B., and THOMAS J. BERNARD. *Theoretical Criminology.* 3rd ed. New York: Oxford University Press, 1986.

VON DREHLE, DAVID. "The Financial Crisis: Who Can Lead Us out of This Mess?" *Time* (October 6, 2008):32–36.

VONNEGUT, KURT, JR. "Harrison Bergeron." In *Welcome to the Monkey House.* New York: Delacorte Press, 1968:7–13.

WAHL, JENNY B. "From Riches to Riches: Intergenerational Transfers and the Evidence from Estate Tax Returns." *Social Science Quarterly.* Vol. 84, No. 2 (June 2003):278–96.

WALDFOGEL, JANE. "The Effect of Children on Women's Wages." *American Sociological Review.* Vol. 62, No. 2 (April 1997):209–17.

WALKER, KAREN. "'Always There for Me': Friendship Patterns and Expectations among Middle- and Working-Class Men and Women." *Sociological Forum.* Vol. 10, No. 2 (June 1995):273–96.

WALL, THOMAS F. *Medical Ethics: Basic Moral Issues.* Washington, D.C.: University Press of America, 1980.

WALLERSTEIN, IMMANUEL. *The Modern World-System: Capitalist Agriculture and the Origins of the European World-Economy in the Sixteenth Century.* New York: Academic Press, 1974.

———. *The Capitalist World-Economy.* New York: Cambridge University Press, 1979.

———. "Crises: The World Economy, the Movements, and the Ideologies." In ALBERT BERGESEN, ed., *Crises in the World-System.* Beverly Hills, Calif.: Sage, 1983:21–36.

———. *The Politics of the World Economy: The States, the Movements, and the Civilizations.* Cambridge: Cambridge University Press, 1984.

WALLERSTEIN, JUDITH S., and SANDRA BLAKESLEE. *Second Chances: Men, Women, and Children a Decade after Divorce.* New York: Ticknor & Fields, 1989.

WALLIS, CLAUDIA. "How to Make Great Teachers." *Time* (February 14, 2008). [Online] Available March 1, 2008, at http://www.time.com/time/nation/article/0,8599,1713174,00.html

WALLIS, CLAUDIA, and SONJA STEPTOE. "How to Fix No Child Left Behind." *Time.* Vol. 169, No. 23 (June 4, 2007): 34–41.

WAL-MART. "Corporate Facts: Wal-Mart by the Numbers." April 2008. [Online] Available January 20, 2009, at http://walmartstores.com/FactsNews/NewsRoom/8784.aspx

WALSH, BRYAN. "How Business Saw the Light." *Time* (January 15, 2007):56–57.

WALSH, MARY WILLIAMS. "No Time to Put Your Feet Up as Retirement Comes in Stages." *New York Times* (April 15, 2001):1, 18.

WARR, MARK, and CHRISTOPHER G. ELLISON. "Rethinking Social Reactions to Crime: Personal and Altruistic Fear in Family Households." *American Journal of Sociology.* Vol. 106, No. 3 (November 2000):551–78.

WATERS, MELISSA S., WILL CARRINGTON HEATH, and JOHN KEITH WATSON. "A Positive Model of the Determination of Religious Affiliation." *Social Science Quarterly.* Vol. 76, No. 1 (March 1995):105–23.

WATTS, DUNCAN J. "Networks, Dynamics, and the Small-World Phenomenon." *American Journal of Sociology.* Vol. 105, No. 2 (September 1999):493–527.

WEBER, ADNA FERRIN. *The Growth of Cities.* New York: Columbia University Press, 1963; orig. 1899.

WEBER, MAX. *The Protestant Ethic and the Spirit of Capitalism.* New York: Scribner, 1958; orig. 1904–05.

———. *Economy and Society: An Outline of Interpretive Sociology.* GUENTHER ROTH and CLAUS WITTICH, eds. Berkeley: University of California Press, 1978; orig. 1921.

WEEKS, JOHN R. "The Demography of Islamic Nations." *Population Bulletin.* Vol. 43, No. 4 (December 1988):5–54.

WEIDENBAUM, MURRAY. "The Evolving Corporate Board." *Society.* Vol. 32, No. 3 (March/April 1995):9–20.

WEINBERG, GEORGE. *Society and the Healthy Homosexual.* Garden City, N.Y.: Anchor Books, 1973.

WEISBERG, D. KELLY. *Children of the Night: A Study of Adolescent Prostitution.* Lexington, Mass.: Heath, 1985.

WEITZMAN, LENORE J. *The Divorce Revolution: The Unexpected Social and Economic Consequences for Women and Children in America.* New York: Free Press, 1985.

———. "The Economic Consequences of Divorce Are Still Unequal: Comment on Peterson." *American Sociological Review.* Vol. 61, No. 3 (June 1996):537–38.

WELCH, SUSAN, and LEE SIGELMAN. "Who's Calling the Shots? Women's Coaches in Division I Women's Sports." *Social Science Quarterly.* Vol. 88 (2007, special issue):1415–34.

WELLER, JACK M., and E. L. QUARANTELLI. "Neglected Characteristics of Collective Behavior." *American Journal of Sociology.* Vol. 79, No. 3 (November 1973):665–85.

WELLS, HODAN FARAH, and JEAN C. BUZBY. *Dietary Assessment of Major Trends in U.S. Food Consumption, 1970–2005.* Economic Information Bulletin No. (EIB 33). Washington, D.C.: U.S. Department of Agriculture, March 2008.

WENDLE, JOHN. "Russia's Millionaires Keep Their Heads Up." *Time* (January 12, 2009):4.

WERTH, CHRISTOPHER. "To Watch the Watchers." *Newsweek* (October 20, 2008):E4.

WERTHEIMER, BARBARA MAYER. "The Factory Bell." In LINDA K. KERBER and JANE DeHART MATHEWS, eds., *Women's America: Refocusing the Past.* New York: Oxford University Press, 1982:130–40.

WESSELMAN, HANK. *Visionseeker: Shared Wisdom from the Place of Refuge.* Carlsbad, Calif.: Hay House, 2001.

WEST, CORNEL. "The Obama Moment." *U.S. News & World Report* (November 17, 2008):29.

WHALEN, JACK, and RICHARD FLACKS. *Beyond the Barricades: The Sixties Generation Grows Up.* Philadelphia: Temple University Press, 1989.

WHEELIS, ALLEN. *The Quest for Identity.* New York: Norton, 1958.

WHITAKER, MARK. "Ten Ways to Fight Terrorism." *Newsweek* (July 1, 1985):26–29.

WHITE, JACK E. "I'm Just Who I Am." *Time* (May 5, 1997):32–36.

WHITE, RALPH, and RONALD LIPPITT. "Leader Behavior and Member Reaction in Three 'Social Climates.'" In DORWIN CARTWRIGHT and ALVIN ZANDER, eds., *Group Dynamics.* Evanston, Ill.: Row & Peterson, 1953:586–611.

WHITE, WALTER. *Rope and Faggot.* New York: Arno Press/New York Times, 1969; orig. 1929.

WHORF, BENJAMIN LEE. "The Relation of Habitual Thought and Behavior to Language." In *Language, Thought, and Reality.* Cambridge, Mass.: Technology Press of MIT; New York: Wiley, 1956:134–59; orig. 1941.

WHYTE, WILLIAM FOOTE. *Street Corner Society.* 3rd ed. Chicago: University of Chicago Press, 1981; orig. 1943.

WILCOX, CLYDE. "Race, Gender, and Support for Women in the Military." *Social Science Quarterly.* Vol. 73, No. 2 (June 1992):310–23.

WILDAVSKY, BEN. "Small World, Isn't It?" *U.S. News & World Report* (April 1, 2002):68.

WILES, P. J. D. *Economic Institutions Compared.* New York: Halsted Press, 1977.

WILKES, RIMA, and JOHN ICELAND. "Hypersegregation in the Twenty-First Century." *Demography.* Vol. 41, No. 1 (February 9, 2004):23–36.

WILLIAMS, JOHNNY E. "Linking Beliefs to Collective Action: Politicized Religious Beliefs and the Civil Rights Movement." *Sociological Forum.* Vol. 17, No. 2 (June 2002):203–22.

WILLIAMS, PETER W. *America's Religions: From Their Origins to the Twenty-First Century.* Urbana: University of Illinois Press, 2002.

WILLIAMS, RHYS H., and N. J. DEMERATH III. "Religion and Political Process in an American City." *American Sociological Review.* Vol. 56, No. 4 (August 1991):417–31.

WILLIAMS, ROBIN M., JR. *American Society: A Sociological Interpretation.* 3rd ed. New York: Knopf, 1970.

WILLIAMSON, JEFFREY G., and PETER H. LINDERT. *American Inequality: A Macroeconomic History.* New York: Academic Press, 1980.

WILLIAMSON, SAMUEL H. "Six Ways to Compute the Relative Value of a U.S. Dollar Amount, 1790 to Present." 2008. [Online] Available November 18, 2008, at http://www.measuringworth.com/calculators/uscompare/result.php

WILSON, BARBARA J. "National Television Violence Study." Reported in JULIA DUIN, "Study Finds Cartoon Heroes Initiate Too Much Violence." *Washington Times* (April 17, 1998):A4.

WILSON, EDWARD O. "Biodiversity, Prosperity, and Value." In F. HERBERT BORMANN and STEPHEN R. KELLERT, eds., *Ecology, Economics, and Ethics: The Broken Circle.* New Haven, Conn.: Yale University Press, 1991:3–10.

WILSON, JAMES Q. "Crime, Race, and Values." *Society.* Vol. 30, No. 1 (November/December 1992):90–93.

WILSON, THOMAS C. "Urbanism and Tolerance: A Test of Some Hypotheses Drawn from Wirth and Stouffer." *American Sociological Review.* Vol. 50, No. 1 (February 1985):117–23.

———. "Urbanism and Unconventionality: The Case of Sexual Behavior." *Social Science Quarterly.* Vol. 76, No. 2 (June 1995):346–63.

WILSON, WILLIAM JULIUS. *The Declining Significance of Race.* Chicago: University of Chicago Press, 1978.

———. *When Work Disappears: The World of the New Urban Poor.* New York: Knopf, 1996a.

———. "Work." *New York Times Magazine* (August 18, 1996b):26 ff.

WINSHIP, CHRISTOPHER, and JENNY BERRIEN. "Boston Cops and Black Churches." *Public Interest* (Summer 1999):52–68.

WINTER, GREG. "Wider Gap Found between Wealthy and Poor Schools." *New York Times* (October 6, 2004). [Online] Available May 7, 2009, at http://www.nytimes.com/2004/10/06/education/06gap.html

WIRTH, LOUIS. "Urbanism as a Way of Life." *American Journal of Sociology.* Vol. 44, No. 1 (July 1938):1–24.

WITKIN, GORDON. "The Crime Bust." *U.S. News & World Report* (May 25, 1998):28–40.

WITT, LOUISE. "Why We're Losing the War against Obesity." *American Demographics.* Vol. 25, No. 10 (January 2004):27–31.

WOLF, NAOMI. *The Beauty Myth: How Images of Beauty Are Used against Women.* New York: Morrow, 1990.

WOLFE, DAVID B. "Targeting the Mature Mind." *American Demographics.* Vol. 16, No. 3 (March 1994):32–36.

WOLFF, EDWARD N. "Changes in Household Wealth in the 1980s and 1990s in the U.S." Working Paper No. 407. Levy Economics Institute of Bard College. May 2004. [Online] Available July 30, 2007, at http://www.levy.org/pubs/wp407.pdf

———. "Recent Trends in Household Wealth in the United States: Rising Debt and the Middle-Class Squeeze." Working Paper No. 502. Levy Economics Institute of Bard College. June 2007. [Online] Available April 28, 2009, at http://www.levy.org/pubs/wp502.pdf

WOLFGANG, MARVIN E., ROBERT M. FIGLIO, and THORSTEN SELLIN. *Delinquency in a Birth Cohort.* Chicago: University of Chicago Press, 1972.

WOLFGANG, MARVIN E., TERRENCE P. THORNBERRY, and ROBERT M. FIGLIO. *From Boy to Man, from Delinquency to Crime.* Chicago: University of Chicago Press, 1987.

WONDERS, NANCY A., and RAYMOND MICHALOWSKI. "Bodies, Borders, and Sex Tourism in a Globalized World: A Tale of Two Cities—Amsterdam and Havana." *Social Problems.* Vol. 48, No. 4 (November 2001):545–71.

WONG, BUCK. "Need for Awareness: An Essay on Chinatown, San Francisco." In AMY TACHIKI ET AL., eds., *Roots: An Asian American Reader.* Los Angeles: UCLA Asian American Studies Center, 1971:265–73.

WOODWARD, KENNETH L. "Feminism and the Churches." *Newsweek* (February 13, 1989):58–61.

WORLD BANK. *World Development Report 1993.* New York: Oxford University Press, 1993.

———. *World Development Report 2000/2001.* Washington, D.C.: World Bank, 2001.

———. *2007 World Development Indicators.* Washington, D.C.: World Bank, 2007.

———. "The Developing World Is Poorer than We Thought but No Less Successful in the Fight against Poverty." August 26, 2008. [Online] Available December 3, 2008, at http://go.worldbank.org/C9GR27WRJ0

———. *2008 World Development Indicators.* Washington, D.C.: World Bank, 2008.

———. "Edstats." 2009. [Online] Available February 1, 2009, at http://ddpext.worldbank.org/ext/DDPQQ/member.do?method=getMembers&userid=1&queryId=189

———. "Health, Nutrition, and Population Stats." 2009. [Online] Available February 5, 2009, at http://ddpext.worldbank.org/ext/DDPQQ/member.do?method=getMembers&userid=1&queryId=225.

WORLD HEALTH ORGANIZATION. "Female Genital Mutilation: New Knowledge Spurs Optimism." *Progress in Sexual and Reproductive Health Research.* No. 72 (2006). [Online] Available May 13, 2008, at http://www.who.int/reproductive-health/hrp/progress/72.pdf

———. "Russian Federation." 2007. [Online] Available July 9, 2007, at http://www.who.int/countries/rus/en

WORLD RESOURCES INSTITUTE. "EarthTrends: Environmental Information." 2007. [Online] Available October 28, 2008, at http://earthtrends.wri.org/searchable_db/index.php?these=4+variable_ID=558&action=select_countries

WORLD VALUES SURVEY. "Online Data Analysis." 2006. [Online] Available July 7, 2008, at http://www.worldvaluessurvey.org

———. "Inglehart-Welzel Cultural Map of the World." 2008. [Online] Available July 22, 2008, at http://www.worldvaluessurvey.org

WORSLEY, PETER. "Models of the World System." In MIKE FEATHERSTONE, ed., *Global Culture: Nationalism, Globalization, and Modernity.* Newbury Park, Calif.: Sage, 1990:83–95.

WREN, CHRISTOPHER S. "In Soweto-by-the-Sea, Misery Lives on as Apartheid Fades." *New York Times* (June 9, 1991):1, 7.

WRIGHT, JAMES D. "Ten Essential Observations on Guns in America." *Society.* Vol. 32, No. 3 (March/April 1995):63–68.

WRIGHT, QUINCY. "Causes of War in the Atomic Age." In WILLIAM M. EVAN and STEPHEN HILGARTNER, eds., *The Arms Race and Nuclear War.* Englewood Cliffs, N.J.: Prentice Hall, 1987:7–10.

WRIGHT, RICHARD A. *In Defense of Prisons.* Westport, Conn.: Greenwood Press, 1994.

WRIGHT, STUART A., and ELIZABETH S. PIPER. "Families and Cults: Familial Factors Related to Youth Leaving or Remaining in Deviant Religious Groups." *Journal of Marriage and the Family.* Vol. 48, No. 1 (February 1986):15–25.

WU, XIAOGANG, and DONALD J. TREIMAN. "Inequality and Equality under Chinese Socialism: The Hukou System and Intergenerational Occupational Mobility." *American Journal of Sociology.* Vol. 113, No. 2 (September 2007):415–45.

WUTHNOW, ROBERT. *All in Synch: How Music and Art Are Revitalizing American Religion.* Berkeley: University of California Press, 2003.

YABROFF, JENNIE. "The Myths of Teen Sex." *Newsweek* (June 9, 2008):55.

YANG, FENGGANG, and HELEN ROSE FUCHS EBAUGH. "Transformations in New Immigrant Religions and Their Global Implications." *American Sociological Review.* Vol. 66, No. 2 (April 2001):269–88.

YARDLEY, JIM. "China Sticking with One-Child Policy." *New York Times* (March 11, 2008). [Online] Available December 23, 2008, at http://www.nytimes.com/2008/03/11/world/asia/11china.html?_r=1

YEATTS, DALE E. "Creating the High-Performance Self-Managed Work Team: A Review of Theoretical Perspectives." Paper presented at the annual meeting of the Southwest Social Science Association, Dallas, February 1994.

YIN, SANDRA. "Wanted: One Million Nurses." *American Demographics.* Vol. 24, No. 8 (September 2002):63–65.

YOELS, WILLIAM C., and JEFFREY MICHAEL CLAIR. "Laughter in the Clinic: Humor in Social Organization." *Symbolic Interaction.* Vol. 18, No. 1 (1995):39–58.

YUDELMAN, MONTAGUE, and LAURA J. M. KEALY. "The Graying of Farmers." *Population Today.* Vol. 28, No. 4 (May/June, 2000):6.

ZAGORSKY, JAY. "Divorce Drops a Person's Wealth by 77 Percent." Press release (January 18, 2006). [Online] Available January 19, 2006, at http://www.eurekalert.org/pub_releases/2006-01/osu-dda011806.php

ZHAO, DINGXIN. "Ecologies of Social Movements: Student Mobilization during the 1989 Prodemocracy Movement in Beijing." *American Journal of Sociology.* Vol. 103, No. 6 (May 1998):1493–1529.

ZIMBARDO, PHILIP G. "Pathology of Imprisonment." *Society.* Vol. 9, No. 1 (April 1972):4–8.

ZUCKERMAN, MORTIMER B. "The Russian Conundrum." *U.S. News & World Report* (March 13, 2006):64.

ZURCHER, LOUIS A., and DAVID A. SNOW. "Collective Behavior and Social Movements." In MORRIS ROSENBERG and RALPH H. TURNER, eds., *Social Psychology: Sociological Perspectives.* New York: Basic Books, 1981:447–82.

Photo Credits

Michael Branscomb/The Lawrenceville School, 536; Redux Pictures/ Suzanne DeChillo/ *The New York Times*, 536; Getty Images/David McNew, 537; AP Wide World Photos/ Obama Transition Office, Callie Shell, 537.

CHAPTER 21: PhotoEdit Inc./Rachael Epstein, 540–541 (*top*); PhototakeNYC/Gary Conner, 540 (*bottom*); iStockphoto International/Royalty Free/Jeffrey Smith/Courtesy of www.istockphoto.com, 541 (*bottom left*);); iStockphoto International/Royalty/ Milanovic/ Courtesy of www.istockphoto.com, 541 (*bottom right*); Magnum Photos, Inc./Martin Parr, 542; Corbis – NY/Steve Prezant. 545; Peter Arnold, Inc./George Mulala, 551; © Tom Nebbia/Corbis, All Rights Reserved, 553; AP Wide World Photos/Sergei Karpukhin, 554; © Phil Schermeister/Corbis, All Rights Reserved, 557; © Lauren Greenfield, 558; Black Star/Steve Murez, 561; Aurora Photos, Inc., 562; AP Wide World Photos/ Xinhua/Wang Song, 563 (*inset*); U.S. Department of Labor/Mine Safety and Health Administration (MSHA), 563.

CHAPTER 22: Shutterstock/Tony Campbell, 566–567 (*top*); Peter Arnold, Inc./Mark Edwards, 566 (*bottom*); The Image Works/James Marshall, 567 (*bottom left*); Stock Connection/Joe Sohm/Chromosohm, 567 (*bottom right*); Getty Images/Nina Raingold, 568; AP Wide World Photos, 573; © David and Peter Turnley/Bettmann/Corbis, All Rights Reserved, 575; © Bohemian Nomad Picturemakers/Corbis, All Rights Reserved, 576; Bloomberg News/Jamie Rector/Bloomberg News, 579; Getty Images/Michael Smith, 580; Pieter Breughel the Elder (c. 1525/30-1569), *Peasant Dance*, c. 1565, Kunsthistorisches Museum, Vienna/Superstock, Inc., 581 (*left*); Lily Furedi (1896-1969) American, *Subway*, ca. 1934. Oil on canvas, 39 in. x 48 1/4 in. (99.1 x 122.6 cm). Transfer from the U.S. Department of the Interior, National Park Service. Smithsonian American Art Museum, Washington, DC, USA, Art Resource, NY, 581 (*right*); AP Wide World Photos/Paul Sancya, 583; Corbis – NY//Wilfried Krecichwost/Zefa, 585; Culver Pictures, Inc., 589; Landov Media/Dave Amit/Reuters, 590; © Remi Benali/Corbis, All Rights Reserved, 591; Getty Images, Inc. – Agence France Presse/Valery Hache, 592; Newscom/Richard B. Levine, 594; © David Cooper/ *Toronto Star*/Zuma/Corbis, All Rights Reserved, 595.

CHAPTER 23: © Les Stone/Zuma/Corbis, All Rights Reserved, 598-599 (*top*); Getty Images/David McNew, 598 (*bottom*); AP Wide World Photos/Gary Friedman/*Los Angeles Times*, 599 (*bottom left*); Getty Images/Mario Tama, 599 (*bottom right*); Bloomberg News/Mario Villafuerte, 600; Landov Media/Lucas Jackson/Reuters, 601; AP Wide World Photos/David Duprey, 603; © Globe Photos, Inc. 2004, 605; Corbis – NY/Rick Wilking/ Reuters, 607 (*left*); Peter Arnold, Inc./Al Grillo, 607 (*middle*); Getty Images, Inc. – Agence France Presse/Salah Omar/AFP, 607 (*right*); Corbis – NY, 608; Getty Images, Inc. – Agence France Presse/Stan Honda, 610; AP Wide World Photos, 611; © Corbis, 612 (*left*); AP Wide World Photos/Huynh Cong "Nick" Ut, 612 (*right*); Everett Collection/Paramount Classics, 616; PhotoEdit Inc./Bob Daemmrich, 620; AP Wide World Photos/Chris Gardner, 620; AP Wide World Photos/Jacquelyn Martin, 621.

CHAPTER 24: PhotoEdit Inc./Bill Bachmann, 624–625 (*top*); PhotoEdit Inc./Jeff Greenberg, 624 (*bottom*); Shutterstock/Mircea Bezergheanu, 625 (*bottom left*); iStockphoto International/ Royalty Free/Dmitriy Shironosov/Courtesy of www.istockphoto.com, 625 (*bottom right*); Culver Pictures, Inc., 626; Paul Gauguin, French, (1848-1903), *Nave Nave Moe (Sacred Spring)*, 1894. Hermitage, St. Petersburg, Russia. Oil on canvas, 73 x 98 cm. © The Bridgeman Art Library International Ltd., 627; Getty Images, Inc. AFP/Mike Clarke/AFP, 628; Pearson Education/PH College, 633; George Tooker (b. 1920), *The Subway*, 1950, egg tempera on gesso panel, 18 1/8 x 36 1/8", Whitney Museum of American Art, New York, purchased with funds from the Juliana Force Purchase Award, 50.23. Photograph courtesy of The Whitney Museum of American Art, 635; © Alison Wright/Corbis, All Rights Reserved, 637; Getty Images Inc. – Stone Allstock/Ed Pritchard, 639 (*left*); AP Wide World Photos/Wally Santana, 639 (*right*); Mauri Rautkari, 640; Kelly-Mooney Photography/Corbis/Bettmann, 641; Getty Images, Inc.- Photodisc./Royalty Free/Buccina Studios, 642; Getty Images Inc. – Stone Allstock/Brad Rickerby, 643; Alamy Images/Jim West, 644; Alamy Images/Paul Prescott, 646; AP Wide World Photos/Efrem Lukatsky, 647 (*inset*); Redux Pictures/Shawn Baldwin/*The New York Times*, 647.

TIMELINE: *1807*: MPI/ Getty Images, Inc. – Hulton Archive Photos; *1829*: Association of American Railroads; *1848*: North Carolina Museum of History; *1876*: AT&T Archives; *1886*: Irene Springer/ Pearson Education/PH College; *1893*: Library of Congress; *1902*: Library of Congress; *1910*: Tim Ridley/Dorling Kindersley Media Library; *1912*: Chris Alan Wilton/ Getty Images, Inc. – Image Bank; *1913*: Library of Congress; *1921*: Getty Images, Inc. – Hulton Archive Photos; *1927*: Corbis/Bettmann; *1931*: Texas State Library and Archives; *1945*: U.S. Air Force; *1946*: Unisys Corporation; 1947: Corbis/Bettmann; *1953*: Corbis/Bettmann; *1964*: CBS Photo/ Getty Images, Inc. – Hulton Archive Photos; *1969*: Robert F. Bukaty/AP Wide World Photos; *1969*: NASA/ Johnson Space Center; *1970*: Jason Laure/Woodfin Camp & Associates; *1980*: Laima Druskis/ Pearson Education/PH College; *1981*: Jan Butchofsky-Houser/ Corbis/Bettmann; *1987*: John Serafin; *1990s*: Gerald Lopez/ Dorling Kindersley Media Library; *2000*: Brady/Pearson Education/ PH College.

Name Index

Subject Index

Argentina, as a high-income country, 6, 302, 303
Arithmetic average, 32
Arithmetic progression, 572–73
Arms race
    nuclear weapons, 453
    rationale for, 452
Arranged marriages, 468–69
Artifacts, 68–69
Ascribed status, 139
Asexuality, 196, 198
Asia
    (*see also* name of country)
    age at death, global median, 308
    agricultural employment, map of global, 416
    family size, 471
    female genital mutilation, 341
    high-income countries in, 6, 303, 304, 307
    HIV/AIDS in, 550
    housework performed by women, 142
    low-income countries in, 7, 303, 305, 307
    middle-income countries in, 6, 303, 305, 307
    political freedom, 439
    population growth, 571
    service-sector employment, 416
    slavery in, 310
    smoking in, 546
    water supply problems, 588
Asian Americans
    (*see also* Race; Racial discrimination; Racial segregation; Racism)
    achievements of, 372
    arrest rates, 233
    Chinese Americans, 372–73
    crime rates, 233
    demographics map, 376
    education and, 372
    fertility and, 569
    Filipinos, 372
    HIV/AIDS and, 551
    income of, 372
    intelligence and racism, 364
    interracial marriages, 474–75
    Japanese Americans, 373–74
    Koreans, 372
    model minority image, 372
    parenting, single, 474, 478
    political party identification and, 444
    poverty and, 289, 372
    self development in adolescents, 127
    sexually transmitted diseases and, 548
    social standing, 372
    statistics on, 372
    stereotypes, 360
    women, as head of household, 474
    women, working, 420–21, 428
    work and, 420–21, 428
Asian American women (*see* Women, Asian American)
Asian Indian Americans, 372, 374
Assemblies of God, 509
Assimilation
    defined, 366–67
    interracial marriages, 474–75
    Native Americans and, 368
Athletes (*see* Sports)
Atomic disaster, 608
Australia
    Aborigines, 89
    comparable worth, 336
    cultural differences, 74
    female genital mutilation, 341
    gross domestic product, 307
    as a high-income country, 6, 303, 304
    homosexual marriages in, 479
    quality of life index, 307
    women, social status of, 330, 331
Authoritarianism, defined, 440

Authoritarian leadership, 164
Authoritarian personality theory, 363–65, 368
Authority
    bureaucracy and, 437
    charismatic, 437
    defined, 436
    patterns, 466
    politics and, 436–37
    rational-legal, 437
    traditional, 436–37
Automobiles, modernization and, 631
Autonomy
    bureaucratic, 437
    charismatic, 437
    creative, 177
    Erikson's stage, 120
    rational-legal, 437
Average middle class, 280

Baby boomers
    as caregivers, 397, 472
    premarital sex and, 195
    sandwich generation, 472
    sexual revolution and, 193
    time span of, 129, 386–87, 571
Baby bust, 571
Bahrain, monarchy in, 438n
Balkans, genocide, 367
Bangladesh
    education in, 517
    garment industry in, 300, 309
    gross domestic product, 307
    as a low-income country, 305, 307
    quality of life, 307
Baptists, 494, 502, 507
    social class and, 502
Barter system, 91
Batek, 89
Bay of Pigs, groupthink and, 165–66
B.C.E. (before common era), use of term, 12n
Beauty
    cultural differences, 59, 69, 189
    eating disorders, 546–47
    myth and advertising, 334
Behavior (*see* Collective behavior; Mass behavior)
Behaviorism, 113
Belarus, 305
Belgium
    affection, display of, 191
    homosexual marriages in, 479
    monarchy in, 438n
Beliefs
    defined, 66
    deviance and, 224
    social control and, 224–25
    values and, 64, 66–67
Bell curve, 266–67, 364
Bell Curve: Intelligence and Class Structure in American Life, The (Herrnstein and Murray), 266–67
Bereavement, 403–5
Bhutan, monarchy in, 438n
Bias
    old age and, 129
    standardized testing and, 522
    television and, 124, 333
Bible, 488, 489
    fundamentalist view, 508
    portrayal of women, 492
Bilateral descent, 466
Bill of Rights, U.S.
    due process, 235
    individualism and, 442
Biodiversity, declining, 591
Biology
    aging and, 389–90
    deviance and, 216–17

emotions and, 150
    human development and, 113
    sex determination, 189–90
    sexual orientation and, 198
Birth control
    map of global use of, 194
    oral contraceptives, 193
    pill, introduction of, 193
    statistics on, 347
Birth rates
    childbearing, globally, 4
    crude, 568, 569
    decline in U.S., 386, 471
Bisexuality
    defined, 196, 198
    HIV/AIDS and, 551
Black Americans
    (*see* African Americans)
Black churches, 503
Black Power, 371
Blame society for poverty, 291
Blame the poor for poverty, 289–91
Blaming the victim
    deviant behavior and, 230
    men for prostitution, 203
    rape/date rape, 203
    victimless crimes, 202–3, 230
Blasé urbanite, 580–81
Blended families, 477
Blue-collar occupations
    defined, 260
    self-employment, 423
Body language, 62, 147–48, 149, 150
Body mass index (BMI), calculating, 547
Bolivia
    as a middle-income country, 305
    socialist economy, 420
Bosnia, genocide, 367
Bourgeoisie, 96, 577
Brazil
    crime in, 234
    economic inequality, 257
    gross domestic product, 307
    income inequality, 265
    Kaiapo, 640–41
    as a middle-income country, 305, 307
    quality of life, 307
    socialist economy, 420
    Yąnomamö, 60, 61, 69, 451
Britain
    class system, 251–53
    colonialism, 316, 317
    comparable worth, 336
    economic inequality, 257, 265
    education in, 517–19
    estate system, 252–53
    gross domestic product, 307
    as a high-income country, 302, 303
    homosexual marriages in, 479
    medicine in, 555
    meritocracy, 250
    modernization theory and, 314
    monarchy in, 438n
    multiculturalism in, 72
    quality of life, 307
    religion in, 493
    slavery issues, 309
    terrorism in, 72
Brown v. Board of Education of Topeka, 365
Brunei, monarchy in, 438n
Buddhism, 499–500
Bulgaria
    gross domestic product, 307
    market reforms, 419, 420
    as a middle-income country, 307
    quality of life, 307
    socialism, decline of, 419
Bulimia, 546–47

Bureaucracy
    (*see also* Formal organizations; Organizations)
    alienation, 173
    authority, 437
    characteristics of, 170–71
    defined, 101, 170
    democracy and, 438
    inefficiency, 173
    inertia, 174
    informality of, 172–73
    organization environment, 171–72
    privacy issues, 180–81
    problems with, 173–74
    ritualism, 173
    in schools, 122–23, 528–29
    social movements and, 617
    Weber's views of, 101
Bureau of Indian Affairs, 368
Burkina Faso, social status of women, 330, 331
Bushmen, 89
Busing, school, 523

Call girls, 201
Calvinism, capitalism and, 100, 491
Cambodia
    genocide, 367
    monarchy in, 438n
Canada
    capital punishment in, 239
    culture in, compared with the U.S., 81
    economic inequality, 257
    female genital mutilation, 341
    gross domestic product, 307
    as a high-income country, 6, 302, 303, 307
    homosexual marriages in, 479
    Kaska Indians, 89
    medicine in, 555
    population growth, 571
    quality of life index, 307
    union membership, decline in, 422
Capitalism
    alienation of workers and, 97
    Calvinism and, 100, 491
    class conflict and, 96–97, 259–61
    compared to socialism, 418–19
    defined, 417
    democracy and freedom and, 439–40, 455
    deviance and, 226
    features of, 417
    gender and, 346
    invisible hand, 417, 428
    Marx, views of, 94–98, 259–60, 633–35
    medicine and, 554–55
    modernization and, 633–35
    Protestantism and, 100, 491
    rationality and, 99–100
    reasons there has been no overthrow, 260–61
    state, 418
    welfare, 418
    unions and, 261
Capitalists
    defined, 94–95
    revolution, 633
Capital punishment
    global map, 234
    pros and cons of, 239–40
Care, access to, 559
Care and responsibility perspective, 118
Career deviance, corporate crime, 227
Careers
    deviant, 223
    in sociology, 9–11
Caregivers, 397, 472
Case studies, 44
Caste system, 249–50
    importance and summary of, 268–71
Category, 162

Corporations
(*see also* Multinational corporations)
competitiveness and, 427
conglomerates, 426–27
crime, 226, 227
defined, 425–26
economic concentration, 426
global, 427–29
Correction systems
community-based, 240–41
death penalty, global map, 234
deterrence, 237
rehabilitation, 237
retribution, 236, 237
societal protections, 237–38
Correlation
defined, 34
spurious, 34
variables, relationships among, 33–34
Counterculture, 70, 72
Courts, role in criminal justice system, 236
Courtship, 468–69
social-exchange analysis, 468
Cousin marriage laws in U.S., first-, 191
Creative autonomy, in the workplace, 177
Credential society, 527
Crime
(*see also* Deviance; Violence)
against people, 230
against property, 230
age and, 232
community-based corrections, 240–41
corporate, 226, 227
cultural differences, 233–35
defined, 216, 217, 230
deterrence, 237
economy and effects on, 241
gender differences, 232
genetics and, 216–17
global perspective, 233–35
hate, 228, 229
importance and summary of, 242–45
organized, 226, 227
prostitution as a victimless, 202–3
race and ethnicity, 232–33
rape, 203–4
social class and, 232
statistics on, 231–32, 238–39
subcultures, 220–21, 222
types of, 230–31
victimless, 230–31
violent, rates down, 241
white-collar, 226–27
Crime in the United States (FBI), 230
Criminal intent, 230
Criminal justice system
courts, 236
defined, 216, 217
due process, 235
plea bargaining, 236
police role of, 235–36
punishment, reasons for, 236–40
Criminal law, focus of, 227
Criminal recidivism, 238
Criminals
profile of, 232–33
voting and, 447
Criminal subcultures, 220
Crisis, social, 5–6
Critical sociology, 36–37
Crowds
defined, 162, 601
explaining behavior of, 603–4
types of, 601–2
Crude birth rate, 568, 569
Crude death rate, 569
Cuba
Bay of Pigs and groupthink, 165–66
meeting with foreigners, banned, 218
social inequality, 264

Cuban Americans
education and, 374
ethnic communities, 375
income of, 374
poverty and, 374
social standing of, 374
Cults, 494–95
Cultural capital
defined, 122
education and, 525
family and, 122
Cultural change
aging society and, 387–88
causes of, 73
cultural lag, 72–73
Cultural differences
affection, showing, 191
aging and, 390–93
beauty and, 59, 69, 189
childbearing, map of, 4
child labor, map, 126
communication and, 62
crime and, 233–35
deviance and, 218
emotions, showing, 150
homosexuality and, 197
humor and, 154
intelligence and, 364
kissing, 191
languages and, 64, 65
male circumcision, 207
modesty and, 191
nonverbal communication and, 148
personal space and, 148
sexual expression and, 191
sexuality and, 191, 207
status and roles and, 140
symbols and, 62–63
U.S. and Canada compared, 81
Cultural integration, 72
Cultural lag, 72–73, 627
Cultural relativism, 73–76
Cultural transmission, 64
Cultural universals, 77
Culture
change, 72–73, 74–75
conflict and, 70
counter-, 72
defined, 58–62
diversity in, 70–77
elements of, 62–69
emotions and influence of, 150
evolution and, 78–80
freedom and, 80
functions of, 77, 80
gender and, 328–32
global, 76–77
high versus popular, 70
ideal versus real, 66
importance and summary of, 82–85
inequality and, 77–78
information technology and, 69
intelligence and, 60–62
language and, 64, 65
material, 59, 60, 68–69
modernization theory, 313
multi-, 71–72
nonmaterial, 59, 60
norms, 67–68
poverty and, 290, 310
reality building and, 64, 145
shock, 60, 61
social change and, 628
social-conflict analysis, 77–78, 80
sociobiology approach, 78–80
structural-functional analysis, 77, 80
sub-, 70–71
symbols, 62–63
technology and, 68–69
theoretical analysis of, 77–81

theory, 12, 616
theory and racism, 365
transmission of, 64
values and beliefs, 64, 66–67
Cyberface, 146–147
Cyber symbols, 62, 63
Czechoslovakia, socialism, decline of, 419
Czech Republic, market reforms, 419–20

Darwin, Charles, 78, 112, 258, 509
Data
qualitative, 36
quantitative, 36
in tables, 44
using existing research, 47–48
Date rape, 203–4, 340
Dating, 468
Muslims in America, 470–71
Davis-Moore thesis, 257–59
Death and dying
(*see also* Mortality rates)
age at death, global median, 308
bereavement, 403–5
defining, 402, 551
ethical issues, 401–3, 551–52
euthanasia, 402, 403, 551–52
historical patterns, 401
hospice movement, 405
leading causes of, in U.S., 543
penalty, 239–40
right-to-die debate, 402–3, 551–52
of spouse, 472
as a stage of life, 129–30
stages of, 129, 403–4
Death instinct, 115
Death rates
of Americans, in wars, 450
crude, 569
Death with Dignity Act (1997), 403
Debt bondage, 310
Deception, spotting, 148
Declaration of Independence, 11, 370
Decline, social movements and, 617–18
Deductive logical thought/reasoning, 49–50
De facto segregation, 367
Degradation ceremony, 223
Dehumanize, 173
De jure segregation, 367
Delinquent subculture, 221
Demeanor, social interaction and, 148
Democracy
bureaucracy and, 438
capitalist versus socialist approaches, 439–40
defined, 438
economic inequality and, 438
freedom and, 439–40, 455
gap, 455
political freedom, map of, 439
U.S. value, 66
Democratic leadership, 164
Democratic party, 444
Democratic Republic of the Congo
as a low-income country, 305
population growth, 574, 575
Demographic divide, 575
Demographic transition theory, 573–74
Demography
(*see also* Population/population growth)
defined, 568
fertility, 568–69
migration, 569–70
mortality, 691
social change and, 628–29
Denmark
equality in, 420
homosexual marriages, 478–79
monarchy in, 438n
Denominations, 493–94
Dependency theory
capitalist world economy, 317–18

colonialism and, 317
compared to modernization theory, 320
defined, 316–17
evaluation of, 319–20
high-income countries and, 318–19
historical, 317
Dependent variables, 33
Deprivation theory, 610–11, 617
Descent patterns, 465–66
Descriptive statistics, 32
Deterrence
of criminals, 237
of war, 454
Development, human (*see* Human development)
Deviance
(*see also* Crime)
biological context, 216–17
capitalism and, 226
control theory, 224–25
cultural differences, 218
defined, 216–17
differential association theory, 224
Durkheim's work, 219–20
functions of, 219–21
gender and, 228–30
Hirschi's control theory, 224–25
importance and summary of, 242–45
inequality and, 225–28
labeling theory, 221–25
medicalization of, 223–24
Merton's strain theory, 220
personality factors, 217–18
power and, 225–26
primary, 222–23
Puritans, example of, 219–20
secondary, 222–23
social change and, 219
social-conflict analysis, 225–28
social control, 216
social foundations of, 218–19
strain theory, 220
structural-functional analysis, 219–21, 228
subcultures, 220–21, 222
Sutherland's differential association theory, 224
symbolic-interaction analysis, 221–25, 228
Deviant career, 223
Dharma, 499
Differential association theory, 224
Diffusion
cultural change and, 73
social change and, 628
Diplomacy, peace and, 454
Direct-fee system, 555
Directorates, interlocking, 427
Disabilities, physical, 140
Disabled
changes in attitudes toward, 140
education for, 533
Disarmament, peace and, 454
Disasters
defined, 607
impact of, 607–9
intentional, 607
natural, 607
technological, 607
Discipline problems, school, 528
Discoveries
cultural change and, 73
social change and, 628
Discrimination
(*see also* Racial discrimination)
age, 386, 397–98
defined, 365
institutional, 365
prejudice and, 365
women and, 337
workplace, 175–76

reality and, 64
reasons for the decline in number of, 62
social interaction and, 152
in the U.S., 72
Laos
gross domestic product, 307
as a low-income country, 307
quality of life, 307
Las colonias, 304
Latchkey kids, 471
Latent functions, 14, 15
Latin America
(*see also* name of country)
age at death, global median, 308
family size, 4, 471
high-income countries in, 6
housework performed by women, 142
income inequality, 264, 265
low-income countries in, 7, 303, 305
middle-income countries in, 6, 303, 305, 307
modernity, 641
political freedom, 439
population growth, 570, 571
prostitution, 202
slavery, 310
street children, 309
Latinos (*see* Hispanic Americans/Latinos)
Latvia, market reforms, 420
Laws
(*see also* Criminal justice system)
to protect workers, 261
Leadership
charismatic, 437
expressive, 164
group, 163–64
instrumental, 164
styles, 164
Learning
cognitive development, 115–16
imitation and, 119
Lenski, society and work of, 88–93
Lesbians (*see* Homosexuality/homosexuals)
Lesotho, monarchy in, 438n
Liberal feminism, 347–48
Liberals, social issues, 444
Liberation theology, 493
Liechtenstein, monarchy in, 438n
Life course
(*see also* Human development)
patterns and variations, 130
sex over the, 196
socialization and, 125–30
Life expectancy
of children in the U.S., 544, 545, 546
defined, 569
gender differences, 329, 386, 472, 569
globally, map, 391
increase in, in the U.S., 129, 386–87
Life instinct, 115
Limits to growth, 586–87
Literacy (*see* Education)
Lithuania, market reforms, 420
Living wills, 403, 551
Lobbyists, 444
Looking-glass self, 118–19
Love, courtship and, 469–70
Loving v. Virginia, 474
Lowell, Massachusetts, mills, 414
Lower class, 280
Lower-middle class, 280
Lower-upper class, 279
Low-income countries
(*see also* name of country)
age at death, global median, 308
childbearing, map on, 4
child labor, 126
countries considered, 7, 303, 305
defined, 6, 7, 301–4
dependency theory, 316–20
economic sectors, 414, 415

education, 517
family size, 4–5, 471
gross domestic product (GDP), 303n, 307
health in, 543
high technology, map on, 99
HIV/AIDS in, 549, 550
housework, map of, 142
Internet users map, 169
map of, 303
modernization theory, 312
population density, 305
poverty in, 543
productivity in, 305
prostitution and, 202
quality of life index, 307
roles and, 140
urbanization in, 583–84
values in, 67, 68
Lutherans, social class and, 502
Luxembourg, monarchy in, 438n
Lynching, 16, 371, 602

Machismo, 473
Macro-level orientation, 17
Magnet schools, 532
Mainstreaming, 533
Malaysia
Batek, 89
as a high-income country, 303, 304
monarchy in, 438n
Semai, 60, 89, 451
women forbidden to wear tight-fitting jeans, 218
Male traits (*see* Men)
Mali
gross domestic product, 307
as a low-income country, 307
quality of life, 307
Tuareg, 88, 90, 99
Malthusian theory, 572–73
Management
impression, 145, 146–47
scientific, 175
Mandatory education, 519
Manifest functions, 14, 15
Manifesto of the Communist Party (Marx and Engels), 96
Manila
crime in, 234
description of, 305–6
Manufacturing
(*see also* Work/workplace)
factories, 413, 414
Industrial Revolution and, 413
social change and, 11
Maoris (New Zealand), 191
Maps
adolescent pregnancy in U.S., 201
age at death, median, 308
agricultural employment, 416
birth control, 194
Buddhism, globally, 500
capital punishment, 234
on childbearing, 4
child labor, 126
Christianity, globally, 497
cultural values, global, 68
demographics of African Americans, Arab Americans, Asian Americans, and Hispanic Americans, 376
economic development, globally, 303
elderly population in the U.S., 389
family size, 4
female genital mutilation, 207, 340, 341, 342
government positions, women in, 338, 339
health patterns across the U.S., 544
Hinduism, globally, 500
HIV/AIDS, 550
housework performed by women, 142

illiteracy, global, 518
income across the U.S., 280
income inequality, 265
Internet users, 169
Islam, globally, 497
job projections to 2020, 429
land controlled by Native Americans, 369
language diversity in the U.S., 72
languages, global, 65
on languages, 65, 72
life expectancy, 391
marital forms, 465
marriage laws in U.S., first-cousin, 191
minorities across the U.S., 359
obesity in U.S., 547
per capita income in U.S., 280
political freedom, 439
population change across U.S., 570
population growth, global, 571
poverty across U.S., 289
presidential election of 2008 popular vote, 445
prostitution, 202
racial diversity in the U.S., 121
religious affiliation across U.S., 503
religious diversity across U.S., 503
residential stability across U.S., 629
service-sector employment, 416
on suicide rates, 14
teachers' salaries across U.S., 523
on technology, high, 99
violent crimes in U.S., 230
virtual march across U.S., 613
women, status of, 330, 331
Marginality, 5–6
Marital rape, 477
Market economy, capitalism and, 418
Marriage
arranged, 468–69
child weddings, 468–69
courtship, 468–69
death of spouse, 472
defined, 462
delay in, 474
descent patterns, 465–66
divorce, 475–76
endogamy, 249, 463
exogamy, 463
extramarital sex, 30, 195–96
global map, 465
health and, 475
homogamy, 470
homosexual, 199–200, 478–79
importance and summary of, 22–25
incest taboo, 191–92
infidelity, 470
interracial, 474–75
laws in U.S., first-cousin, 191
love, romantic, 469–71
mate selection, 468–69
mobility and, 285
monogamy, 463
patterns, 463
polyandry, 463
polygamy, 463
polygyny, 463
reasons for, 2, 22–23
remarriage, 477
residential patterns, 463–64
same-sex, 2, 23, 199–200
servile forms of, 310
sexual satisfaction in, 470
sibling, 191–92, 466
social mobility and, 285
social structure and, 2
violence in, 477
working class, 283
Marxism
capitalism, 94–97, 633–35
class conflict, 94, 96–97, 259–60, 628

class-society theory, 636–37
communism, 96
critical sociology, 36–37
criticism of, 260
ideology and, 257
materialism, 95
modernity and, 633–35
political-economy model, 447, 448–49, 615, 617
religion and, 490, 491
revolution, 97–98
social change and, 628
social conflict, 94–98, 628
socialism, 97, 418
social movements and, 615
social stratification and, 257
society, model of, 96
society and production, 94–95
suffering and law of nature, 573
Marxist revolution, 633
Masai, 63
Masculine traits (*see* Men)
Massage parlors, 201
Mass behavior
(*see also* Collective behavior; Social movements)
defined, 604
disasters, 607–9
fads, 606
fashion, 606
gossip, 604
mass hysteria/moral panic, 606–7
panic, 606–7
propaganda, 606
public opinion, 604–5
rumors, 604, 605
Mass hysteria, 606–7
Mass media (*see* Media)
Mass production, 413
Mass society
class society versus, 611, 638
defined, 611, 635
modernity and, 635–36
Mass-society theory, 611–12, 617
Master status, 139, 140, 359
Mate selection
(*see also* Marriage)
importance and summary of, 22–25
Material culture, 59, 60
Materialism, 68–69
culture and, 68–69
Marx and views on, 95
U.S. value, 66
Matriarchy, 330
Matrilineal descent, 465
Matrilocality, 463–64
Matrimony (*see* Marriage)
Mauritania, slavery in, 310, 311
McDonaldization concept, 178–80
importance and summary of, 182–85
McDonald's, 162
"Me," Mead's self, 119
Mead's social self theory, 118–19
Mean, 32
Meaning, importance of, 36
Measurements
defined, 31, 32
reliability and validity, 33
statistical, 32
Mechanical solidarity, 103, 580, 632
Media
advertising, 333
definition of mass, 123, 124
gender differences, 333
gender socialization and, 333
importance and summary of, 210–13
socialization and, 123–25
television, 123–25
war and role of, 453
Median, 32

Medicaid, 556
Medicalization of deviance, 223–24
Medicare, 556
Medicine and medical care
    access to, 559
    in Britain, 555
    in Canada, 555
    in capitalist countries, 554–55
    in China, 553
    defined, 552, 553
    future for, 560–61
    genetic research, 561
    holistic, 553
    importance and summary of, 562–65
    insurance companies, 556
    in Japan, 555
    new reproduction technology, 479–80
    nursing shortage, 556–57
    oral contraceptives, 193
    paying for, 553–56
    physicians, role of, 557
    politics and, 559–60
    in Russia, 553–54
    scientific, 552–53
    social-conflict analysis, 559–60
    in socialist countries, 553–54
    socialized, 553–554, 555
    structural-functional analysis,
        557, 560
    in Sweden, 554
    symbolic-interaction analysis,
        557–59, 560
    in the U.S., 555–56
Megalopolis, 579
Melanesians, sexuality and, 207
Melting pot, 70–71, 366
Men
    (*see also* Gender differences; Gender
        inequality)
    advertising, portrayed in, 333
    aggressiveness in, 332
    child support, 476, 477
    circumcision, 207
    extramarital sex, 196
    feminism and, 348–49
    homosexual, 198–99
    machismo, 473
    masculine traits a health threat, 545
    patriarchy, 330–32
    patrilineal descent, 465
    patrilocality, 463
    political party identification and, 444
    premarital sex, 195
    rape of, 203
    social mobility and, 285
    Type A personality, 331, 545
    violence against, 341–42
Mens rea, 230
Mental illness as deviant, 223–24
Mercy killing (euthanasia), 402, 403, 552
Meritocracy
    in Britain, 251–53
    defined, 250
Metaphysical stage, 11, 12
Methodists, 496
    social class and, 502
Metropolis, defined, 578
Metropolitan statistical areas (MSAs), 579
Mexican Americans, 374–75
    education and, 374
    income of, 374
    poverty and, 374
    social standing of, 374
Mexico
    age-sex pyramid, 570–72
    economic inequality, 257
    gross domestic product, 307
    as a high-income country, 302, 303, 307
    modernization theory, 314, 641
    political freedom, 439

street children in, 309
    water supply problems, 588
Micro-level orientation, 17
Microsoft Corp., 172
Middle Ages, 11
    absolute monarchs, 438
    children in, 125
    cities in, 577
    crime, as a sin, 236
    estate system, 252–53
    sexuality, control of, 206
Middle class, 279–80, 578
Middle East
    (*see also* under name of country)
    agrarian societies, 90–91
    female genital mutilation, 207
    high-income countries in, 302, 303
    HIV/AIDS in, 550
    income inequality, 265
    marriage in, 435
    middle-income countries in, 307
    personal space, 148
    prostitution, 202
    slavery, 310
    water supply problems, 588
Middle-income countries
    (*see also* name of country)
    age at death, global median, 308
    childbearing, map on, 4
    child labor, 126
    countries considered, 6, 303, 305
    defined, 6, 301, 305
    economic sectors, 414, 415
    gross domestic product (GDP), 303n, 307
    map of, 303
    per capita income, 305
    population figures, 306
    productivity of, 305
    quality of life index, 307
Midlife (*see* Adulthood)
Migration
    defined, 569
    global, 76
    internal, 570
    net, 570
    social change and, 629
    voluntary versus involuntary, 570
Military
    -industrial complex, 452–53
    interest in, on the rise, 12–13
    social class, 451
    women in, 338–39
Minorities
    (*see also* Ethnicity; Race)
    assimilation, 366–67
    characteristics of, 359
    in cities, 582
    defined, 339, 358, 359
    elderly as, 398
    genocide, 367, 607
    HIV/AIDS and, 551
    intersection theory, 339–40
    model minority image, 372
    national map of, 359
    pluralism, 366
    segregation, 367
    stereotypes, 360
    women as, 339–40
    workplace discrimination, 175–76
Miscegenation, 367
Mixed (interracial) marriages, 474–75
Mobility (*see* Social mobility)
Mobs, 602–3
Mode, 32
Model minority image, 372
Modernity
    capitalism, Marx, 633–35, 636–37
    class society, 636–38, 639
    defined, 629
    division of labor, Durkheim, 631–32

effects on society, 103, 105
    future for, 643–45
    globally, 641
    importance and summary of, 646–49
    individualism and, 638–39
    loss of community Tönnies, 630–31
    mass society and, 635–36, 638–39
    post-, 642–43
    progress and, 640–41
    rationalization, Weber, 632–33
    social-conflict analysis, 636–38
    structural-functional analysis, 635–36
    traditional societies versus, 634
Modernization
    characteristics of, 629–30
    defined, 629
    stages of, 313–15
Modernization theory
    compared to dependency theory, 320
    culture and, 313
    defined, 311, 312
    evaluation of, 316
    high-income countries and, 315
    historical, 312
    stages of, 313–15
Modesty, cultural differences, 191
Monaco (monarchy in), 438n
Monarchy (monarchies)
    absolute, 438
    constitutional, 438
    countries that have, 438n
    defined, 437–38
Money (*see* Economy; Income)
Mongoloid, racial type, 357
Monocultural, 70
Monogamy, 463
Monopolies, 427
Monotheism, 496
Moral development
    gender differences, 117–18
    Gilligan's theory, 117–18
    Kohlberg's theory, 117
Moral panic, 606
Moral reasoning, 117
Mores, 67, 68
Mormons, 502, 507
Morocco, 6, 73
    beauty in, 189
    monarchy in, 438n
Mortality rates
    children and, 545, 546, 569
    gender differences, 5
    infant, 544, 545, 546, 569
    measuring, 569
    racial differences, 5
MoveOn.org, 613
Multicentered model, 582–83
Multiculturalism
    assimilation, 366–67
    controversies over, 71–72
    defined, 62, 71–72
    terrorism and, 72
    in the U.S., 58, 62
Multinational corporations
    (*see also* Corporations)
    defined, 311–12
    growth and control by, 415
    neocolonialism and, 311
Multiracial, 32–33, 358, 360–61
Mundugumor, New Guinea, Mead's gender
        studies, 329
Music, cultural change and, 74–75, 78–79
Muslims
    (*see also* Arabs; Islam; Islamic societies)
    courtship, 470–71
    social distance and, 361
Muslim women (*see* Women, Islamic)
Musuo, 330
Mutual assured destruction (MAD), 454
Myanmar (Burma), beauty in, 189

NAACP (National Association for the
    Advancement of Colored People),
    16, 17
Namibia
    gross domestic product, 307
    as a middle-income country, 305, 307
    quality of life, 307
Nation
    defined, 62
    states, 437
Nation at Risk, A (NCEE), 530, 531
National Rifle Association, 444
Native Americans
    animism and, 495
    assimilation, 368
    citizenship for, 368
    cultural revival, 369
    descent patterns, 463
    education of, 368
    family life, 472–73
    gambling, 369
    genocide, 367, 368
    HIV/AIDS and, 551
    incest taboo, 191, 466
    income of, 368, 369
    Indians, use of term, 368
    intersexual people and, 190
    land controlled by, map of, 369
    norms and, 67
    on reservations, 368–69, 473
    residential patterns, 463–64
    sexually transmitted diseases and, 548
    social standing, 369
    use of term, 368
Natural disasters, 607
Natural environment
    (*see also* Environment)
    defined, 584
Natural selection, 78
Nature versus nurture, 112–13
Navajo
    incest taboo, 191, 466
    intersexual people and, 190
Nazis
    Holocaust, 367, 499
    mass-society theory, 611
Ndebele, South Africa, 69
Negroid, racial type, 357, 358
Neocolonialism
    defined, 311
    poverty and, 311
Neolocality, 464
Nepal, child labor in, 76
Netherlands
    euthanasia in, 402, 403, 552
    homosexual marriages in, 479
    monarchy in, 438n
Networks
    defined, 168
    gender differences, 170
    grapevines, 172
    Internet, 168, 169
    social groups ad, 168–70
New Age religion, 506–7
New Guinea
    Mead's gender studies, 329
    Sambia and homosexuality, 198
New social movements theory, 616, 617
New Zealand
    as a high-income country, 304
    Maoris, 191
Nicaragua
    education in, 517
    quality of life, 316
Niger
    family size in, 4
    gross domestic product, 307
    as a low-income country, 307
    quality of life, 307
    women, social status of, 330, 331

population growth, 574
summary of, 94–95
work in, 413–14, 420–25
Positivist sociology
cause and effect, 33
concepts, 31–34
defined, 31, 36
limitations, 35
objectivity and, 34–35
reliability and validity, 33
summary of, 36
variables, 31, 32–34
Postmodernity, 642–43
Poverty
(see also Global poverty)
absolute, 288, 307
age and, 288, 395
causes of, 289–91
children and, 288, 309, 474
culture of, 290
elderly and, 288, 395–97
extent of, 307–9
family, 289
feminization of, 289
health and, 543
homelessness, 292–93
race and, 288–89
relative, 288, 307
severity of, 306–7
shantytowns, 309, 314, 319
single (one)-parent and, 474, 478, 479
in the U.S., 288–93
urban versus rural, 289
welfare dilemma, 292
women and, 309
working poor, 291–92
Power
authority and, 436–37
defined, 436
deviance and, 225–26
-elite model, 447, 448
global relationships and, 311
in-groups and, 167
language and, 152
Marxist political-economy model, 447, 448–49
pluralist model, 447–48
political elites, 419
poverty and, 311
wealth and, 275–76
Powerlessness, modernity and, 639
Practicality, U.S. value, 66
Prayer, in schools, 505, 506
Preconventional level, Kohlberg's moral development theory, 117
Predestination, 100, 491
Pregnancy
abortion, 151, 208–9
adolescents and, 200, 201
Preindustrial societies (see Agricultural societies; Hunting and gathering societies; Pastoral societies)
Prejudice
authoritarian personality theory, 363–65
conflict theory, 365
culture theory, 365
defined, 358, 360
discrimination and, 365–66
ethnocentrism, 73–76
measuring, 360–61
racism and, 361–62
scapegoat theory, 362–63
stereotypes, 360
theories of, 362–65
Premarital sex, 195
Preoperational stage, 116
Presbyterians
Scottish, 369
social class and, 502
Presentation of self, 145

Presidential election of 2008
popular vote by county, map, 445
rural-urban division, 445
Prestige, occupational, 276, 277
Pretesting, 42
Primary deviance, 222–23
Primary economic sectors, 414
Primary groups, 162–63, 164
Primary labor market, 421
Primary sex characteristics, 190
Primates, Rhesus monkeys social isolation experiment, 113–14
Primogeniture, 252
Prisons
community-based corrections versus, 240
increase in inmates, 238–39
justification for, 236–38
resocialization, 130–31
setting, 40
Stanford County prison experiment, 40–41, 49
statistics on number of inmates, 238–39
voting and criminals, 447
Privacy
laws related to, 181
surveillance methods, 181
technology and erosion of, 180–81
Private schools, in the U.S., 523
Probation, 240
Profane, defined, 488
Professions
characteristics of, 422–23
defined, 422
para-, 423
Profit
capitalism and personal, 417
medicine and, 559
schooling for, 532
Progress
modernity/social change and, 640–41
U.S. value, 66
Progressive education, 519
Projective labeling, 223
Proletarians, 94, 95
Promise Keepers, 509, 609
Propaganda, 606
Property crimes, 230–31
Property ownership
capitalism and, 417
collective, 417
estate system, 252–53
inheritance rules, 467
socialism and, 417
Proselytize, religious, 494
Prostitution
defined, 201
global, 201, 202
human trafficking, 310
latent functions, 205–6
legalized, 201
types of, 201
as a victimless crime, 202–3
Protestantism
capitalism and, 100, 491–92
denominations, 493–94
fundamentalism, 507–9
social class and, 502
suicide rates, 5
white Anglo-Saxon, 369–70
women and, 492
work ethic, 369, 492
Protestant Reformation, 100, 491
Psychoanalysis, 115
Psychological changes, aging and, 390
Psychosomatic disorders, 558
Public opinion, 604–5
Public policy, sociology and, 9
Public schools, in the U.S., 523–25
Puerto Ricans
education and, 374
income of, 374

poverty and, 374
revolving door policy, 375
social standing of, 374
Spanish language, use of, 375
Puerto Rico, modernization theory, 314
Punishment, for criminals, 236–40
Puritan Boston and Quaker Philadelphia (Baltzell), 47–48
Puritans, 47–48, 192, 219–20
Pygmies, 89
Pyramids of Giza, Egypt, 91

Qatar
modernity in, 641
monarchy in, 438n
Quakers, 47–48
Qualitative data, 36
Quality circles, work in Japan, 176
Quality of life
elderly and, 393
globally, 307
Quantitative data, 36
Queer theory, 208–9
Questionnaires, research, 41–42
Quid pro quo, sexual harassment and, 343
Qur'an (Koran), 488, 492, 497

Race
(see also Ethnicity)
assimilation, 366–67
categories/types, 357–58
-conflict approach, 15, 16
consciousness, 365
crime and, 232–33
defined, 356–57
diversity map for the U.S., 121
future issues, 378–79
group dynamics and, 168
hate crimes, 228, 229
importance and summary of, 380–83
income inequality and, 276–78
intelligence and, 364
majority/minority patterns of interaction, 366–67
pluralism, 366
poverty and, 288–89
prejudice, 360–66
religion and, 503–4
riots, 602, 610
social class and, 276–78
socialization and, 121–22
socially constructed, 356
social mobility and, 284
stereotypes, 124, 360
U.S. Census Bureau definition of, 32–33
Racial blends (mixture), 358
Racial differences
feminism and, 349
health and, 544–45
physical traits and, 356
political party identification and, 444
suicide rates and, 5
television and, 124, 333
unemployment and, 371, 424, 425
work and, 420–21, 425
Racial discrimination
affirmative action, 378–79
African Americans and, 370–71
anti-Semitism, 499
apartheid, 250, 251
arrests and, 232–33
Asian Americans and, 372–74
civil rights movement, 370, 371, 610
Dred Scott case, 371
Du Bois, work of, 16, 17, 28n, 371
institutional, 365
Japanese Americans and, 373–74
Jim Crow laws, 371, 610
lynching, 371, 602
prejudice, 360–65

sports and, 19–20
successful African Americans and, 43
in the U.S., 370–71
voting rights, 370
in the workplace, 175, 176
Racial segregation
apartheid, 250, 251
Brown v. Board of Education of Topeka, 365
civil rights movement, 370, 371, 610
de jure and de facto, 367
history of, in the U.S., 367
hyper-, 367
Japanese American internment, 373
Native Americans and, 368–69
in schools, 367, 371, 523
in U.S. cities, 367
Racism
defined, 361–62
effects of, 28, 43, 44
environmental, 591–92
future issues, 378–79
hate crimes, 228, 229
intelligence and, 364
lynching, 371, 602
U.S. value, 66–67
Radical feminism, 348
Rain forests, 590
Random sampling, 41
Rape
date, 203–4
defined, 203
marital, 477
of men, 203
pornography and, 201
statistics on, 203, 340
Rationality
alienation and, 101–2
bureaucracy and science and, 101
capitalism and, 99–100
defined, 98
McDonaldization concept, 179–80
modernization and, 632–33
Weber and, 632–33
Rationalization of society, 98–102
Rational-legal authority, 437
Real culture, 68
Reality
language and, 64
social construction of, 141–45
Rebellion, 220
Recidivism, criminal, 238
Recycling, 588, 589
Redemptive social movements, 609
Red tape, bureaucratic, 173
Reference groups, 166
Reflexes, 113
Reformative social movements, 609
Reformatories, 237
Rehabilitation, of criminals, 237
Reincarnation, 499
Relative deprivation, 610
Relative opportunity, 220
Relative poverty, 288, 307
Reliability, 32, 33
Religion
(see also name of)
in agrarian societies, 91, 495
basic concepts, 488–89
capitalism and, 491–92
civil, 505
in colonial America, 369
defined, 488, 489
diversity across U.S., map, 503
East versus West, 501
electronic church, 509
ethnicity and, 502–3
functions of, 489–90
fundamentalism, 507–9
future for, 509
gender issues, 490–91, 492
in history, 495

About the Author

John J. Macionis (pronounced "ma-SHOW-nis") was born and raised in Philadelphia, Pennsylvania. He earned a bachelor's degree from Cornell University and a doctorate in sociology from the University of Pennsylvania.

His publications are wide-ranging, focusing on community life in the United States, interpersonal intimacy in families, effective teaching, humor, new information technology, and the importance of global education. In addition to authoring this bestseller, Macionis has also written *Society: The Basics*, the best-selling paperback text in the field, now in its tenth edition. He collaborates on international editions of the texts: *Sociology: Canadian Edition; Society: The Basics, Canadian Edition*; and *Sociology: A Global Introduction. Sociology* is also available for high school students and in various foreign-language editions.

In addition, Macionis and Nijole V. Benokraitis have edited the best-selling anthology *Seeing Ourselves: Classic, Contemporary, and Cross-Cultural Readings in Sociology*, also available in a Canadian edition. Macionis and Vincent Parrillo have written the leading urban studies text, *Cities and Urban Life* (Pearson Prentice Hall). Macionis's most recent textbook is *Social Problems* (Pearson Prentice Hall), now in its third edition and the leading book in this field. The latest on all the Macionis textbooks, as well as information and dozens of Internet links of interest to students and faculty in sociology, are found at the author's personal Web site: http://www.macionis.com or http://www.TheSociologyPage.com. Additional information, instructor resources, and online student study guides for the texts are found at the Pearson Prentice Hall site: www.pearsonhighered.com

John Macionis is Professor and Distinguished Scholar of Sociology at Kenyon College in Gambier, Ohio, where he has taught for more than thirty years. During that time, he has chaired the Sociology Department, directed the college's multidisciplinary program in humane studies, presided over the campus senate and the college's faculty, and taught sociology to thousands of students.

In 2002, the American Sociological Association presented Macionis with the Award for Distinguished Contributions to Teaching, citing his innovative use of global material as well as the introduction of new teaching technology in his textbooks.

Professor Macionis has been active in academic programs in other countries, having traveled to some fifty nations. He writes, "I am an ambitious traveler, eager to learn and, through the texts, to share much of what I discover with students, many of whom know little about the rest of the world. For me, traveling and writing are all dimensions of teaching. First, and foremost, I am a teacher—a passion for teaching animates everything I do."

At Kenyon, Macionis teaches a number of courses, but his favorite class is Introduction to Sociology, which he offers every semester. He enjoys extensive contact with students and invites everyone enrolled in each of his classes to enjoy a home-cooked meal.

The Macionis family—John, Amy, and children McLean and Whitney—live on a farm in rural Ohio. In his free time, Macionis enjoys tennis, swimming, hiking, and playing oldies rock-and-roll (he recently released his third CD). Macionis is as an environmental activist, focusing on the Lake George region of New York's Adirondack Mountains where he works with a number of organizations, including the Lake George Land Conservancy, where he serves as president of the board of trustees.

Professor Macionis welcomes (and responds to) comments and suggestions about this book from faculty and students. Write to him at the Sociology Department, Palme House, Kenyon College, Gambier, OH 43022, or send e-mail to macionis@kenyon.edu.

Age of dinosaurs

All humans are hunters and gathe

Earth takes form

Earliest life forms

Earliest mammals

Earliest primates

Evolutionary divide, eventually yielding apes and humans with larger brains

Bones in Ethiopia attest to "Stone Age" human ancestors who used tools and fire

Species *homo sapiens* appears

Anatomicall modern hun (*homo sapie sapiens*) roa the Earth

THE EARTH'S ORIGINS

OUR HUMAN ORIGINS

| 5 billion B.P. | 4 billion B.P. | 3 billion B.P. | 2 billion B.P. | 1 billion B.P. | 100 million B.P. | 90 million B.P. | 80 million B.P. | 70 million B.P. | 60 million B.P. | 50 million B.P. | 40 million B.P. | 30 million B.P. | 20 million B.P. | 10 million B.P. | 1 million B.P. | 900,000 B.P | 700,000 B.P. | 500,000 B.P. | 300,000 B.P. | 100,000 B.P. |

Birth rates fall in Europe and U.S.

U.S. life expectancy 47 years

U.S. majority in cities

Immigration to U.S. restricted

Northward migration of African Americans

Great Depression

"Baby boom"

1938 Rise of bluegrass

1935 Swing era begins

1947 Rhythm and blues music gains popularity

1910 Jazz era begins

THE MODERN ERA

1953 Rise Rock 'n Roll First record Elvis Presle

1916 First birth control clinic

1932 First woman cabinet member

1942 Chemist Albert Hoffman takes first LSD "trip"

1948 Armed forces desegregate

1900 20% of U.S. women in labor force

1916 First sanitary landfill

1921 First Miss America pageant

1938 Word "teenager" coined

1909 NAACP founded

1912 Sinking of Titanic

1917 Russian Revolution

1924 Native Americans eligible for citizenship

1931 First woman governor

1938 Minimum wage enacted

1947 Jackie Robinson breaks baseball "color line"

1920 Women win right to vote

1925 First College Board tests

1933 First Major League baseball game under lights

1949 First NASCAR race

1924 First woman senator

World War I 1914–1918

World War II 1938–1945

Korean War 19

1925

1950

1914 First coast-to-coast telephone call

1927 Lindbergh flies across Atlantic

1947 Aerosol spray can invented

1915 Juke box invented

1926 Middle East starts pumping oil

1945 First atomic explosion

1948 Record debuts

1903 Airplane invented

1914 First stop sign (Detroit)

1931 First electric guitar

1902 Air conditioner invented

1920 First commercial radio station

1940 First interstate road (PA Tpke)

1927 Television invented

1946 Computer invented

1913 Ford assembly line

1947 Transistor invented

1945 Leo Fender sells first music amplifier

Decline industr jobs

2 billion

150 mi

1902–1931 Cooley and Mead reflect on the self

1902 Simmel analyzes small groups

1903 Du Bois describes racial consciousness

c.1915 Weber sees expanding bureaucracy

1931 W.I. Thomas discusses defining situations as real

SOCIETY IN HISTORY: TIMELINES

A timeline is a visual device that helps us understand historical change. The timeline at the right represents 5 billion years of the history of the planet Earth. This timeline is divided into three sections, each of which is drawn to a different scale of time. The first section, The Earth's Origins, begins with the planet's origins 5 billion years before the present (B.P.) and indicates that another full billion years passed before the earliest forms of life appeared. The second section, Our Human Origins, shows that plants and animals continued to evolve for billions more years until, approximately 12 million years ago, our earliest human ancestors came onto the scene. In the third section of this timeline, Earliest Civilization, we see that what we call civilization is relatively recent indeed, with the first permanent settlements occurring in the Middle East a scant 12,000 years ago. But the written record

of our species' existence extends back only half this long, to the time humans invented writing and first farmed with animal-driven plows some 5,000 years B.P.

Sociology came into being in the wake of the many changes to society wrought by the Industrial Revolution over the last few centuries—just the blink of an eye in evolutionary perspective. The lower timeline provides a close-up look at the events and trends that have defined The Modern Era, most of which are discussed in this text. Innovations in technology are charted in the panel below the line and provide a useful backdrop for viewing the milestones of social progress highlighted in the panel above the line. Major contributions to the development of sociological thought are traced along the very bottom of this timeline.

SOCIAL MILESTONES

Slave trade underway (began 1619)

Colonization of Latin America/India underway

U.S. is small, agrarian society

Death rates fall in Europe and United States

Opening of U.S. Western frontier

Chinese immigration to U.S. begins

European colonization of Africa

Japanese immigration to U.S. begins

"Great European Immigration"

1890 Rise of blues

1849 Elizabeth Blackwell is first woman to earn M.D. degree

1883 U.S. adopts Standard time zones

1861 First department store (Marshall Field's, Chicago)

1790 First U.S. census

1892 Pledge of Allegiance written

1789 George Washington sworn in as first U.S. president

1821 First women's college (Troy Female Seminary)

1857 Dred Scott decision

1870 First African American elected to U.S. House of Representatives

1886 Statue of Liberty

1776 U.S. Independence from Great Britain

WOMEN bring all VOTERS into the world. Let Women Vote

1848 Women's suffrage movement begins

1859 Charles Darwin's Origin of Species

1872 First woman runs for U.S. president

1890 Massacre at Wounded Knee

1787 Court defines a slave as 3/5 a citizen

Negroes for Sale.

1851 The New York Times founded

1865 U.S. bans slavery

1884 NYC outlaws wifebeating

1892 First sociology department (University of Chicago)

1807 U.S. bans slave trade

Rev. War 1775–1783

U.S. Civil War 1861–1865

TECHNOLOGY

| 1775 | 1800 | 1825 | 1850 | 1875 | 1900 |

1793 Eli Whitney invents the cotton gin

1839 Photography invented

1879 Light bulb invented

1895 Radio invented

1825 Erie Canal opens

1869 Transcontinental railroad completed

1844 Telegraph invented

1850 Rubber condom invented

1885 First 10-story skyscraper (Chicago)

1825 First U.S. textile mills (in New England)

1876 Telephone invented

1893 First car (the Duryea)

1847 Founding of American Medical Association signals rise of scientific medicine

1860 Isaac Singer invents sewing machine and forms first multinational corporation

1880 Home refrigerator invented

1877 Phonograph invented

1829 Steam locomotive invented

1860 Louis Pasteur kills germs in milk by heating (pasteurization)

1886 Coca-Cola invented

1889 Jukebox invented

Industrial Revolution begins to transform Europe

Industrialization underway in U.S.

WORLD POPULATION	1 billion		
U.S. POPULATION	5.3 million	23.2 million	76.0 million

THEORY

1776 Adam Smith applauds capitalism

1798 Malthus warns of perilous population increase

1838 Comte coins term "sociology"

1848 Marx challenges capitalist class conflict

Freud formulates psychoanalysis

1897 Durkheim studies suicide

I did not start out to become a sociologist.

Guided by teachers and counselors who pointed to my good grades in high school mathematics and physics courses, I applied to and entered an engineering college. Although I can't say that I enjoyed the engineering classes, I did what I had to and made it through the first year. But early in my sophomore year, I realized that all was not well. I had lost whatever interest I had in becoming an engineer and, to be honest, the college was quickly losing whatever interest it had in me. My engineering career came to a crashing halt at the end of the fall term when I earned a grade-point average of 1.3, was placed on academic probation, and was told by my academic advisor that I should consider some other line of work.

I left campus for winter break realizing that it was time to take a hard look at other fields of study. The following spring, I enrolled in my first sociology class (and now the story starts getting better). This one course ended up truly changing my life. Sociology helped me make sense of the world, and most important, sociology was *fun*. Forty years later, I am still in the classroom and I can still say the same thing.

The importance of one person's experience lies in the fact that countless people have been turned on to sociology in the introductory course. Across the United States and elsewhere, tens of thousands of students can recall discovering the excitement of sociology, and many have gone on to make this discipline part of their life's work.

If you are a student, I invite you to open this book, to enjoy it, and to discover a new and very useful point of view for looking at the world. **To my colleagues teaching sociology,** let me say that, even after almost forty years of teaching sociology, I am still in the classroom with you, finding the deep satisfaction that comes from making a difference in the lives of our students. There is surely no greater reward for our work than transforming young women and men by sharing with them the power as well as the fun that comes with using the sociological perspective. And there is no better reason for striving for ever-better revisions of *Sociology*, which, along with the brief paperback version, *Society: The Basics*, stands out as the discipline's most popular text. **Thank you for making this book a part of your course!**

Your colleague,

John J. Macionis